THE OXFORD HANDBOOK OF

THE ARCHAEOLOGY
OF THE
CONTEMPORARY
WORLD

THE OXFORD HANDBOOK OF

THE ARCHAEOLOGY OF THE CONTEMPORARY WORLD

Edited by

PAUL GRAVES-BROWN
RODNEY HARRISON
ANGELA PICCINI

OXFORD
UNIVERSITY PRESS

UNIVERSITY PRESS

Great Clarendon Street, Oxford, OX2 6DP,
United Kingdom

Oxford University Press is a department of the University of Oxford.
It furthers the University's objective of excellence in research, scholarship,
and education by publishing worldwide. Oxford is a registered trade mark of
Oxford University Press in the UK and in certain other countries

© Oxford University Press 2013

The moral rights of the authors have been asserted

First Edition published in 2013

Impression: 1

Published in the United States of America by Oxford University Press
198 Madison Avenue, New York, NY 10016, United States of America

British Library Cataloguing in Publication Data
Data available

Library of Congress Control Number: 2013938775

ISBN 978–0–19–960200–1

Printed and bound in Great Britain by
CPI Group (UK) Ltd, Croydon, CR0 4YY

In memory of William L. Rathje,
1 July 1945–24 May 2012

ACKNOWLEDGEMENTS

SINCE its formation in 2003, the Contemporary and Historical Archaeology in Theory (CHAT) Group has provided an important forum for the development of an emerging sub-field concerned with the archaeology of the contemporary world, and this Handbook would have been inconceivable without the support and groundwork laid down by this group through the lively participation of its members in annual conferences and the email discussion list CONTEMP-HIST-ARCH@jiscmail.ac.uk. Similarly, this volume would not have been possible without the support and encouragement of contributors, editors at Oxford University Press, colleagues, friends, and family. The Oxford Handbooks in Archaeology series is an ambitious project that has enabled archaeologists to synthesize innovative and interdisciplinary scholarship that addresses current key concerns and questions, and this present volume joins an impressive community. We particularly wish to thank Hilary O'Shea, Taryn Das Neves, and Cathryn Steele at Oxford University Press for guiding and supporting this process. Specific thanks also go to the Institute of Archaeology, University College London, University of Bristol, Carolyn Graves-Brown, and J. and M. who have all supported the production of the Handbook in different ways. Finally, we dedicate this Handbook to the memory of Bill Rathje, whose pioneering work on the Tucson Garbage Project and innovative thinking in relation to the archaeology of the contemporary world continues to be a source of inspiration to us all.

Contents

PART I CROSS-DISCIPLINARY PERSPECTIVES

PART II RECURRENT THEMES

PART IV MEDIA AND MUTABILITIES

PART V THINGS AND CONNECTIVITIES

LIST OF FIGURES

LIST OF TABLES

LIST OF CONTRIBUTORS

Anna Badcock ArcHeritage

Steven Bond Photographer

Denis Byrne Office of Environment and Heritage NSW; University of Technology Sydney

Tim Cole Department of Historical Studies, University of Bristol

Alan Costall Department of Psychology, University of Portsmouth

Sean Cubitt Professor of Film and Television, Goldsmiths, University of London

Shannon Lee Dawdy Department of Anthropology, University of Chicago

David de Léon Sony Mobile Communications, Sweden

Caitlin DeSilvey Department of Geography, University of Exeter

James R. Dixon PLaCE Bristol

Matt Edgeworth Department of Archaeology and Ancient History, University of Leicester

Kathryn Fewster Independent researcher

James Gordon Finlayson Department of Philosophy, University of Sussex

Christine Finn Visiting Researcher, JB Priestley Library, University of Bradford

Severin Fowles Barnard College, New York

Alfredo González-Ruibal Institute of Heritage Sciences, CSIC (Consejo Superior de Investigaciones Científicas-Spanish National Research Council)

Alice C. Gorman Department of Archaeology, Flinders University; Adjunct Fellow, Research School of Astronomy and Astrophysics, The Australian National University

Richard A. Gould Department of Anthropology, Brown University

Paul Graves-Brown Institute of Archaeology, University College London

Yannis Hamilakis Department of Archaeology, University of Southampton

Rodney Harrison Institute of Archaeology, University College London

Penny Harvey Department of Social Anthropology, University of Manchester

Kaet Heupel Columbia University, New York

Stephen Hodge Wrights & Sites; Department of Drama, University of Exeter

Cornelius Holtorf School of Cultural Sciences, Linnaeus University, Kalmar

Fotis Ifantidis Department of History and Archaeology, Aristotle University of Thessaloniki

Robert Johnston Department of Archaeology, University of Sheffield

Pierre Lemonnier Aix Marseille Université, Marseille, France

Gavin Lucas Department of Archaeology, University of Iceland

Richard Maxwell Media Studies, Queens College of the City University of New York

Sarah May Independent researcher

Laura McAtackney School of Social Justice, University College Dublin

Peter Merriman Institute of Geography and Earth Sciences, University of Aberystwyth

Peter Metelerkamp Department of Drama: Theatre, Film and Television, University of Bristol

Toby Miller Department of Media and Cultural Studies, University of California, Riverside

Gabriel Moshenska Institute of Archaeology, University College London

Paul R. Mullins Department of Anthropology, Indiana University-Purdue University Indianapolis

Jem Noble Artist

Beth Laura O'Leary Department of Anthropology, New Mexico State University

Laurent Olivier Département des Ages du Fer, Musée d'Archéologie nationale, Saint-Germain-en-Laye

Bjørnar Olsen Department of Archaeology and Social Anthropology, University of Tromsø

Sefryn Penrose Atkins Heritage; Institute of Archaeology, University of Oxford

Simon Persighetti Wrights & Sites; School of Media and Performance, Falmouth University

Angela Piccini Department of Drama: Theatre, Film and Television, University of Bristol; Visiting Scholar, Department of Anthropology, University of British Columbia

Natasha Powers Museum of London Archaeology

Joshua Reno Department of Anthropology, Binghamton University

Ann Richards Independent researcher

Uzma Z. Rizvi Social Science & Cultural Studies, Pratt Institute, New York

Michael Brian Schiffer School of Anthropology, University of Arizona

John Schofield Department of Archaeology, University of York

Mimi Sheller Department of Culture and Communications, Drexel University

Nick Shepherd Centre for African Studies, University of Cape Town

Lucy Sibun Archaeology South East, Centre for Applied Archaeology; Institute of Archaeology, University College London

Phil Smith Wrights & Sites; School of Humanities and Performing Arts, Plymouth University

Cathy Turner Wrights & Sites; Department of Drama, University of Exeter

Liz Watkins School of Fine Art, History of Art and Cultural Studies, University of Leeds

Timothy Webmoor Department of Anthropology, University of Colorado

Carolyn L. White Department of Anthropology, University of Nevada, Reno

Helen Wickstead Faculty of Art, Design and Architecture, Kingston University, London

Laurie A. Wilkie Department of Anthropology, University of California, Berkeley

Albena Yaneva Manchester Architecture Research Centre, School of Environment and Development, University of Manchester

Larry J. Zimmerman Department of Anthropology, Indiana University-Purdue University Indianapolis

CHAPTER 1

···

INTRODUCTION

···

PAUL GRAVES-BROWN, RODNEY HARRISON, AND ANGELA PICCINI

1.1 INTRODUCTION

···

ARCHAEOLOGY is, by very definition, the study of 'old' or archaic things. Its etymological origin lies in the ancient Greek ἀρχαιολογία (or archaiologia)—ἀρχαῖος (arkhaios) meaning 'ancient' and—λογία (-logia) meaning '-logy' or 'science of'. But contained within the name itself is an important sleight of hand, for we would argue that it is impossible to study the 'past' as if it were somehow separate and external to the 'present'. While this point was made forcefully by Walter Benjamin in his 'Theses on the Philosophy of History' (Benjamin 1999[1968]), the impossibility of separating the present from the past has only recently been extensively thought through in relation to archaeology (e.g. see Olivier 2011; Olivier, this volume). Nonetheless, it has been clear for many years that the ways in which archaeology is practised have always been a direct product of a particular set of social, cultural, and historical circumstances; archaeology is always undertaken *in* the present (Trigger 1990). More recently, many have begun to consider how archaeological methodologies and techniques might be used to reflect more directly on the contemporary world, how we might undertake archaeologies *of*, as well as *in* the present (Holtorf and Piccini 2009; Harrison 2011). The broad parameters of the development of this archaeological 'subfield' have been covered in detail by others (Fewster, this volume; Harrison and Schofield 2010; Harrison 2011), but it is worth noting that it is generally perceived to have catalyzed around the publication of the co-edited volume *Archaeologies of the Contemporary Past* (Buchli and Lucas 2001a), and it is by this title that much of the work has been distinguished since that time.

   Unlike many of the other Handbooks in this series, we do not survey an established disciplinary field, but rather seek to explore the boundaries of an emerging subdiscipline and to suggest some future lines along which it might develop. It is not our intention in this introduction to reiterate the historical perspective on the emergence of the subfield. Neither will we offer any justification for its topic, since critique of the subfield, or the lack of it, is also covered elsewhere (see Harrison 2011; Horning 2011). Rather, we want to take this opportunity, in the light of the contributions that follow, to look forward: to identify the challenges and pitfalls of an archaeology of the contemporary world and to explore the methodologies for doing it.

Nonetheless, identifying the proper 'subject' of this Handbook has proven difficult within a discipline which, in its modern guise, was developed specifically to create *distance* between the past and present (Graves-Brown 2011). We can begin with the rather cumbersome title of this *Oxford Handbook of the Archaeology of the Contemporary World*. Our aim is to survey an archaeology 'in and of the present' (after Harrison 2011). To call this 'contemporary archaeology' invites confusion, whereas an 'archaeology of the contemporary past', apart from being an oxymoron, tends to overlook the sense that what is of interest to us is what is happening *now*, or is imminent and *about to happen*. Equally, in a globalized world, our approach must attempt to be global. An archaeology of the contemporary world must also be interdisciplinary, if indeed that is possible (see Webmoor, this volume). Unlike the seemingly more distant past, long the exclusive preserve of archaeologists, we have to share this particular academic territory with a wide range of other disciplines. Accordingly we have included contributions from philosophers, psychologists, communications and media scholars, sociologists, anthropologists, historians, film scholars, geographers, and artists, whose chapters are intended to reflect on the ways in which other disciplinary approaches to the contemporary world might be drawn on by archaeologists as the relative newcomers in the study of the present. We hope that readers will appreciate the different nuances of approach that these disciplines bring to the study of material culture. Needless to say, not all contributors agree with one another, particularly on questions of ontology (Harvey, this volume; Webmoor, this volume; see also Alberti et al. 2011; Ingold 2011) and agency (Finlayson, this volume; Olsen, this volume; Webmoor, this volume), where there are disagreements as to what constitutes reality and what really is (or is *not*) an agent. Whilst the term 'Handbook' might imply a kind of authorized manual for doing the archaeology of the contemporary world, that world is in fact far too messy for such authority, and in any case some kind of dialectic must be desirable, if not indeed essential in studying it.

In order to grapple with both this 'mess' (Law 2004) and with the range of disciplinary approaches to understanding archaeology in and of the present, we sought to construct this volume in such a way as to invite readers into an initial conversation with disciplinarity. Direct encounter with the territories that archaeologists share with others is a productive introduction to specific methods and concerns. Hence, we begin this volume with a collection of chapters in which authors from within and outside of archaeology reflect on cross-disciplinary concerns. Students and experienced scholars alike have much to gain in their understandings and practices of archaeology from engaging with its proximities to other disciplines. An historian's use of archives and GIS to discuss the materialities and spatialities of the Hungarian ghetto in the Second World War, for example (Cole, this volume), raises particular questions for the archaeologist about the use of scale by other disciplines. Other core themes begin to emerge from these introductory chapters and the second section of this volume is dedicated to archaeologists' meditations on them. We return to scale directly, for example, in Edgeworth's chapter. Other contributors focus on time (Olivier), absence (Fowles and Heupel), ruins (Lucas), memory (Olsen), authenticity (Graves-Brown), sectarianism (McAtackney), afterlives (Schiffer), waste (Reno), heritage (Harrison), difference (Byrne), modernism (González-Ruibal), protest (Badcock and Johnston), homelessness (Zimmerman), conflict (Moshenska), and disaster (Gould). To extend and complicate the interdisciplinary overviews and archaeological thematics, contributors in the final sections of the book present in-depth case studies on mobilities, space, and place; media and mutabilities; and things and connectivities. These case studies intersect at various places and we have indicated what we consider to be productive cross-references for our readers. Finally, with this volume we were keen to find a way to incorporate a range of archaeology's representational practices, to remind our readers that archaeology produces the subject it names through *visual* as well as *textual* marking practices. Given the important role that photography has played in emerging methodologies within the subfield (Harrison and Schofield 2010: 86, 120–4), we invited three sets of contributors—representing disciplinary interests in archaeology, geography, and photography—to produce photoessays in which they reflect on some of the key themes in an archaeology of the contemporary world. In keeping with the thematic approach of this volume, in this Introduction we do not intend to provide précis of each chapter. Instead, we feel that a more important editorial task lies in our own direct engagement with the entangled themes our contributors bring to life in the book.

1.2 Academic Tribes and the Question of Discipline

We begin with the question of interdisciplinarity. How do archaeologies of the contemporary world inform an understanding of the disciplining of knowledges? How might the encounters of multiple disciplines within a volume such as this one contribute to our understanding of academic boundary-making practices more generally? Where are the frictions and irreconcilable differences? Where are the synergies? Furthermore, how might a collection of interventions *in* the contemporary world, focussed *on* its materialities, shift our understandings of the *practice*, rather than the discipline, of archaeology?

Archaeology, specifically, faces a difficult challenge. Freud (see Thomas 2004, 2009) and Foucault (1970, 1972) ensured that any attempt at close analysis, at the disentangling of micro-histories, could be labelled 'an archaeology of'. Perhaps the most recent example of this has been the emergence of 'media archaeology' (Perriault 1981; Huhtamo and Parikka 2011; Parikka 2012). Having nothing to do with the production and circulation of 'archaeology' across media (see 'Matter, media, and mobilities' below, for further discussion), it instead applies a Foucauldian genealogical approach to contemporary media as a challenge to a perceived ahistoric and uncritical celebration of media as always 'new'. Archaeology therefore travels as discourse across disciplines where it continues to serve a central metaphoric function. Given the number of volumes that use the word 'archaeology' in their titles, archaeology might be said to be how we all do 'history' now. As such, perhaps archaeology becomes a case limit for interdisciplinarity as it is the one discipline that is so freely and exuberantly adopted, complicated, and transformed by other disciplines (see González-Ruibal forthcoming). We can see this at work in the contributions to the first section of this volume, and in case studies such as Maxwell and Miller's, which approach their discussions of disciplinary orientations towards material culture in the light of Foucault's legacy.

The second challenge for archaeology that our volume addresses is the fact that other disciplines often engage with material culture in ways that are recognizable to the archaeologist, whilst not situated within archaeology as an institutional discipline. As Cornelius Holtorf first argued, perhaps 'today we are all archaeologists' (2005: 160; Shanks 2012; see also Harrison and Schofield 2010: 12; Lemonnier, this volume). Beyond epistemological excavations of the Foucauldian kind, many disciplines have witnessed a 'material-cultural turn' since the 1980s or 1990s (see discussion in Preda 1999; Brown 2004; Tilley et al. 2006; Trentmann 2009; Bennett and Joyce 2010; Hicks 2010; Miller 2010). Anthropologists turned to material culture to ask questions about everything from consumption (Miller 1991) to entangled human and non-human worldings (Ingold 2007a). Philosophers and historians of technology and science documented the entanglement of humans and machines and used this to open up the question of the nature/culture divide (Haraway 1991). Sociologists explored the materializing practices of everyday life (De Certeau 1984) and the ways in which knowledges are produced via actor-networks of technicians, equipment, laboratory spaces, and germs (Latour 1993). Quantum physicists concerned themselves with the performative materialities of the intra-activity of particle-apparatus (Barad 2007) and political philosophers trained their attentions to rubbish on the streets as a way in to considering the ethical demands of vibrant matter (Bennett 2010). Whether interrogating agential realism and the 'thingness' of things, or engaging in empirical fieldwork mapping, collecting, and analysing objects, it is clear that other disciplines *do* archaeology in one way or another.

Yet, we know from David Clarke that 'archaeology is what archaeologists do' (1973: 6), which would suggest that others *cannot* do archaeology. Conversely, while borrowing archaeology as metaphor or conceptual framework may be productive in another discipline, the scholar in a film department, for example, would not necessarily desire to claim a specific identity as an archaeologist. As Tony Becher argues (1989), academic tribes are distinct ethnicities that seek to mark themselves out as distinct through 'specific patterns of communication, publication, division of labour, hierarchies and careers' (Huber 1990: 242; see also Bourdieu 1984). Contemporary academic retrenchment appears to be producing increasing calls for disciplinary specialism and 'purity' (see Appadurai 1996; Gill and Flood 2009; Lehtonen 2009: 75, 78), at the same time that institutional discourses appear very much in favour of interdisciplinarity due to the potential cost-centre savings of aggregation and shared teaching, even if such mixing of academic tribes and sharing territory can be seen to threaten the 'natural' order of modern disciplinary rigour (Lehtonen 2009).

While no contribution directly addresses the archaeology of contemporary disciplinarity (but see Webmoor, this volume), we suggest that the volume as a whole might be seen as a gesture in that direction. We neither uncritically celebrate nor reject what Mieke Bal terms 'travelling concepts in the humanities' (2002). Instead, as editors we have often struggled with the question of how and when 'archaeology' emerges from the research practices of those who self-identify as archaeologists and those who do not. It is in this sense that our volume responds to Bal's suggestion that critically open interdisciplinary cultural analysis has 'forced the academy to realize its collusion with an elitist white-male politics of exclusion and its subsequent intellectual closure' (2002: 6). We hope that this is something the contributors and readers of this Handbook may wish to continue to explore critically.

At the same time, there is a productive uneasiness across the contributions in the Handbook. We asked all writers to include clear statements about their methodological approaches to help readers contextualize individual chapters. Many contributors found this challenging, due, perhaps, to the same difficulties of interdisciplinary communication that Bal outlines (2002). Where Bal argues that it is in concepts rather than methods that we may come to understand interdisciplinarity, a methodological focus can helpfully evoke conceptual differences and similarities. In their attempt to interrogate interdisciplinarity, Garrow and Shove (2007) test this idea through their analysis of an exchanged twentieth-century toothbrush and Neolithic hand axe to suggest that the archaeologist requires assemblage while the sociologist focuses on the object as an actor in a set of human relations. Indeed, many disciplines have, until recently, specifically excluded material assemblages from their consideration of networks of actors (see Costall and Richards, this volume; Finlayson, this volume; Joerges 1988; Molotch 2007). This supports Harrison's discussion (2011) of the performative act of assembling as constitutive of archaeological work, which problematizes any neat distinction between method and concept. Our present volume similarly produces a surface upon which evidence is assembled in order to propose unfolding potentialities for archaeologies of the contemporary world, rather than to fix a what-has-been: a present as past. Bal suggests that

> Analysis, in pursuing its goal—which is to articulate the 'best' (most effective, reliable, useful?) way to 'do', perform, the pursuit of knowledge—puts [concepts] together with potential objects that we wish to get to know [and] in the best of situations, this…does not imply a rigid division of people or groups along the lines of disciplines or departments. For such a division deprives all participants of the key to a genuine practice of *cultural analysis: a sensitivity to the provisional nature of concepts.* (2002: 55)

Our editorial production of conceptual and methodological proximities among contributors acknowledges this provisionality, but also suggests that the differences evident in our practices generate new understandings of potential archaeologies of the contemporary world. These questions of academic tribes and the boundary-making practices of disciplinarity raise important issues of ownership, to which we will now turn.

1.3 Who is the 'Us' in the 'Archaeology of Us'? On Ownership and the Politics of the Present

While 'Who owns the past?' has become a perennial question in archaeology and heritage (see review in Harrison 2008), the question of 'Who owns the *present*?' raises its own set of ethical and political concerns for archaeologists working on contemporary material culture and 'sites'. Equally, 'Who has the right to speak of and for the present?' is a related issue which touches on disciplinary boundaries (see above), the politics of academia, and its relationship to laypersons and the contemporary world more generally. Such questions have a sense of urgency when dealing with contemporary material culture, simply because those who have, or continue to produce the objects of analysis are alive and may wish to speak for, and interpret, these materials themselves (albeit sometimes, if not often, within the context of unequal power relations, be they social, political, economic, class, age or gender-based). In the same way in which questions of copyright and intellectual property are raised in relation to archaeological investigations of indigenous pasts (e.g. Hollowell and Nicholas 2008), so too are they raised in relation to the present (see Graves-Brown, this volume), although to date there has been little significant discussion of the issues which arise as a result of this (but see Tarlow 2001; Holtorf 2009; Nicholas 2012). Indeed, many of the issues relating to 'indigenous' and postcolonial archaeology can be seen to apply to the archaeology of the present, given that we are dealing with living communities who often have similar concerns to indigenous or diverse descent communities, even if the politics may be very different.

For this reason, the question of ownership of the 'archaeological materials' which form the subject of analysis arises in a number of chapters in the Handbook. In this context, perhaps we might say that the traditional appeal of ruins to archaeologists (cf. Harrison 2011) has always been that 'abandoned' objects and places can be more or less assumed to be no longer owned. Nonetheless, it is possible to argue (as Fewster, this volume, does), that archaeologies of the present represent a kind of trespass on the lives of others (see also Reno, this volume). Although again, these questions have been perceived to be most salient in indigenous and postcolonial contexts (Byrne, this volume; Shepherd, this volume), clearly they are equally applicable across all archaeologies of the contemporary world. While the ethical issues relating to working with the archaeology of contemporary homeless people (Zimmerman, this volume) might seem particularly acute, similar ethical issues are raised across all of the subjects covered by contributors. This invokes important issues relating to the boundaries between 'public' and 'private' in relation to archaeologies of the present.

1.3.1 Archaeologies of 'Us'?

Who *are* we referring to when we speak about doing the 'archaeology of us'? Clearly, many (but equally importantly, *not all*) archaeologists write from the privileged position of the comfortable, cosmopolitan middle-class 'West'. Graves-Brown (2000, 2011; see also Buchli and Lucas 2001b) suggested that the aim of the archaeology of contemporary material culture was to produce a sense of the uncanny by making that which is familiar 'unfamiliar'. This aim has been set within a broader interest in the role of archaeology in the study of contemporary everyday life, and the need to overcome the very obviousness of the habitual and routine aspects of the quotidian which make it most easily overlooked (cf. Heidegger 1962: 69; Perec 1997: 210; Lefebvre 2000). The estrangement of the present to better observe and understand it is a goal which acknowledges archaeology's role in the production of an 'other' to itself (Hicks 2010; Graves-Brown 2011; cf. Fabian 1983; Thomas 2004). On the other hand, archaeology has been perceived as a forensic tool with the ability to uncover and reveal that which is hidden, abject, or forgotten and hence outside of the realm of the everyday. In the case of forensic (Powers and Sibun, this volume) or disaster archaeology (Gould, this volume), it is literally *forensic* in being made to account directly for the evidence of crime or disaster. Paradoxically, the object of archaeological attention is simultaneously *imminent*, in the sense that anything the archaeological gaze comes to rest upon could be said to exist in the present, and *hidden*, in the sense that we have to work on those materials to generate the archaeological information on which our interpretations rely. Indeed, it could be argued that proximity and depth, as well as present and past, are on the same ontological level (Harrison 2011: 186).

Nonetheless, the question of who 'us' is remains problematic. That which seems 'familiar' might have different meanings along ethnic or class continua, or even in the exchange between 'I' and another (Irigaray 2008). Archaeology has an important potential role here in drawing attention to the ways in which different individuals and communities might perceive the same, 'familiar' things with different eyes. This issue emerges strongly in relation to the archaeology of 'shared', colonial heritage (Byrne, this volume), but might similarly be explored through the question of scale in relation to the human body (Penrose, this volume) and to micro- and nano-technology (Edgeworth, this volume; Finlayson, this volume), age (May, this volume), gender (Rizvi, this volume), race (Mullins, this volume; Shepherd, this volume), and social class and economic standing (Zimmerman, this volume; Fowles and Heupel, this volume). It is perhaps only in relation to the archaeology of space exploration (Gorman and O'Leary, this volume) that the question of who 'us' is becomes clearer, although even in this case, the ways in which that enterprise is understood and what it symbolizes is incredibly diverse (e.g. Gorman 2005 on different perspectives on the Woomera site in South Australia). None of this is to say that contemporary 'Western' middle-class cultures are themselves unworthy of investigation. It could be argued that one of the ways in which archaeology might address itself to many of the negative aspects of its production of 'others' might be to turn its lens on itself (Harrison and Schofield 2010). Indeed, the archaeology of academic disciplines (cf. Foucault; e.g. Metelerkamp, this volume), for example, and other forms of autoarchaeological investigation (May, this volume; Finn, this volume; Lemmonier, this volume; Rizvi, this volume; and White, this volume) have an important role to play in this regard, especially where they produce further heterogeneity within the assumed 'us' of the Western, developed world.

1.4 The Politics of an Archaeology of the Contemporary World

We have already noted that the problems confronting an archaeology '*in* and *of* the present' are those that have confronted the discipline in colonial and postcolonial contexts for many years. Those of us who work in the Old world are simply 'bringing home' the fact that our subject matter is not just the buried remains of past societies, but as often as not the circumstances of living people. Whilst the artefacts of the more remote past can have contemporary significance, be it the Parthenon Marbles or Caernarfon Castle, the lifeworlds of contemporary people, check points in Iraq (Rizvi, this volume) or the pollutant by-products of the mobile phone industry (Maxwell and Miller, this volume), have a more pressing significance. And in a more general sense, our relationship to that which we perceive as the material culture of 'today' is often quite different to that which is considered the 'heritage' of the past; whilst Greece may demand the return of the Parthenon Marbles, it seems unlikely that the USA will seek the repatriation of all the world's Coca Cola bottles or the classic Chevrolets and Fords that are still on the roads of Cuba. While Coca Cola bottles and the Parthenon Marbles are all contemporary objects in the sense in which they are part of the present (e.g. Lucas 2004), they appear qualitatively different because of their perceived age, and the friction (cf. Tsing 2005) caused by the globalizing flows which have brought them to their present locations.

As Tarlow (2001) discusses, statements on archaeological ethics, such as that produced by the World Archaeological Congress, tend, for obvious reasons, to concentrate on indigenous rights and interests, on the questions of land rights and repatriation of human remains that pervade the postcolonial context. But

> the 'indigenous' peoples of Europe, for example, stand in a very different relationship to their local archaeology. In much of Europe and Asia it is not the indigenous but the immigrant populations who are socially and politically disadvantaged, and against whose interests the past may be used...(Tarlow 2001: 252)

Equally, as Tarlow also points out, there is always potential for an 'uncritical elision of past and present "natives"' which can lead to '[a] politically dangerous essentialism or racism... promulgated through this kind of sleight of time' (Tarlow 2001: 252). This is a situation which can apply to both postcolonial and Old world contexts; consider, for example the conflicts surrounding the Babri Mosque in Ayodhya (McGuire 2008) or attitudes to Islamic artefacts on the Acropolis (Hamilakis and Ifantidis, this volume).

If we think specifically in terms of the material culture of the contemporary world, the problems do not evaporate. As Barthes (1993[1957]) points out, contemporary bourgeois society tends to mythologize its material culture, building those myths into interpretations of the politics of artefacts (see Wilkie, this volume). Quite often this process of mythologization involves forgetting rather than remembering, be it the evidence of past atrocities (Moshenska, this volume), those parts of society that the majority would prefer to overlook (Dawdy, this volume; Zimmerman, this volume), or social practices of which most people would rather not be reminded (Schofield, this volume). Equally, our industrialized/post-industrial world generates both by-products (Maxwell and Miller, this volume) and waste (Reno, this volume) of which we would rather not be aware, and in many cases would rather that others did not look at too closely. Finally, in terms of the specifics of material culture itself, the entire concept of 'heritage' in a contemporary context may be questioned (Graves-Brown, this volume; Graves-Brown and Schofield 2011; Harrison 2013, this volume). Whilst it seems obvious to monumentalize the more scarce artefacts of the past, those of the contemporary world are contentious, often mass-produced, and have life histories which challenge archaeology's habitual notions of provenance and authenticity (Finn, this volume; May, this volume; Metelerkamp, this volume; Noble, this volume; Reno, this volume; and White, this volume). In a sense this is often a problem of choice; with respect to the remote past, time has largely made the choice for us. In the contemporary context we are in the situation of someone trying to choose the 100 greatest pop records or films of 'all time'. When will we know?

Ultimately, these problems come down to what we think archaeology is for, and who it is for. Anthropologists have wrestled with these issues for many years, given that their field practices always involve the lifeworlds of others, and archaeologists can learn from their experience. Should we act as advocates, and if so for whom? Debate within anthropology has generated persuasive arguments both against (e.g. Hastrup and Elsass 1990) and in favour of advocacy (e.g. Scheper-Hughes 1995; see discussion in Kellett 2009). And in any case can we speak for the homeless, or the inhabitants of Baghdad or Valetta? Is this simply a naïve attempt at what Alfredo González-Ruibal and colleagues, drawing on Spivak's (1988) famous question ('Can the Subaltern Speak?'), might characterize as a form of 'archaeological ventriloquism' (González-Ruibal et al. 2011; see also Schmidt 2009)? Again, the indigenous context seems to offer a simple dichotomy between the interests of descendants and settlers, but in practice other more pervasive issues of socio-economic status, class, etc. intervene. As McGuire (2008) points out, whilst issues of ethnicity or nationalism have been widely discussed in archaeology, those of class, for example, have not. Here we might choose to see archaeology as a basis upon which to challenge capitalism (Hamilakis and Duke 2007; McGuire 2008), but most of what we study in the contemporary world is the product of capitalist economies, most of us live in capitalist societies, and certainly all humans are enmeshed to some degree within capitalist networks. Not only are we thus unavoidably complicit in them (Banks 1993), but whatever our personal, capital 'P' politics, we have to acknowledge that other positions may equally claim legitimacy. These are issues which have taken the foreground in postcolonial archaeologies (e.g. Lydon and Rizvi 2010), and work in this field has much to offer in terms of the negotiation of individual and collective identities in relation to archaeology and its 'others'.

It is obvious that any claim to objectivity or being 'apolitical' is illegitimate (González-Ruibal 2012), perhaps doubly so when it is our 'own' society which we study, yet as Van Esterik points out, there are at least two ways in which anthropologists *can* be advocates, and would seem to apply equally to archaeologies of the contemporary world. At one level, we are all, of necessity, advocates; in small 'a' advocacy 'anthropologists should be drawn naturally into at least a passive style of advocacy communication, simply by the way we translate field experiences to a broader audience' (Van Esterik 1986: 61). Archaeology also has a role, as the Society of Friends put it, to 'bear witness' to what we have learned. But there is also a level of large 'A' advocacy, of 'getting involved' or campaigning, which might be construed as a more personal choice. At the very least, we might argue that, in the case of the homeless or any community excluded from formal power structures, archaeologists have a duty to become involved in the development of collaborative, collective action, i.e. a responsibility that supervenes any capital 'P' political stance (see De León 2012). However, in this respect, current codes of practice or ethics for national and international bodies offer little guidance. The SAA *Principles of Archaeological Ethics* (Principle No. 2) state an obligation 'to consult actively with affected group(s)'; the EAA Code of Practice (1.5) states that archaeologists should evaluate the 'social implications of their work for local communities', whilst the British IfA code of practice (1.11) states that members should 'take account of the legitimate concerns of groups whose material past may be the subject of archaeological investigation'. But none of these suggest what, if anything, an archaeologist should actually do about such concerns and implications—or suggest how an archaeologist might work with groups and communities in order to identify, discuss, and design practices to enact truly collaborative and ethically grounded archaeologies. Moreover, the good intentions expressed in current codes of practice are always entangled within messier relationships—industry, property development, resource extraction—that continually threaten to undermine archaeologists' lofty aspirations (La Salle 2010; La Salle and Hutchings 2012).

1.5 WHEN WAS THE CONTEMPORARY PAST? ARCHAEOLOGIES IN AND OF THE PRESENT

When Buchli and Lucas (2001a) designated a subfield of 'archaeologies of the contemporary past', they did so, primarily, to distinguish the work of their contributors from a number of other archaeological studies of contemporary material culture which they deemed to be primarily ethnoarchaeological in focus. These studies they characterized as less concerned with the archaeology of contemporary society *in and of itself*, than with the discovery of general principles which might be applied to the more distant past of the archaeological record (Buchli and Lucas 2001b: 4). Invoking the title of Gould and Schiffer's (1981) co-edited volume, they referred to their own and their contributors' work as 'archaeologies of us' (see above). This distinction between archaeological studies of contemporary material culture which are primarily focused on the *present*, as opposed to ethnoarchaeological studies which are primarily focused on the *past*, has been echoed in more recent accounts of the archaeology of the contemporary past (e.g. Harrison and Schofield 2010; but see Fewster, this volume). Hicks (2003; see also Piccini and Holtorf 2009: 9) refers to this as archaeology's 'loss of antiquity', in the dissolution of a clear boundary which was previously held to separate the archaeologist's field of interest (in the past) from the present. However, more recently, Harrison (2011) has queried this designation of the 'contemporary past', arguing that it represents a tendency within archaeology (and within modernity more generally) to historicize even the present itself, reflecting a traditional view of archaeology as concerning only that which is ruined and has ceased to function. Instead, he argues that by speaking of an 'archaeology *in* and *of* the present', we might reorient the discipline away from the study of the ruin, the derelict, and the abandoned to become a discipline which is concerned both with the 'living' and the 'dead', with past, present, *and* future. Such a position reflects a broader understanding that archaeology can only ever be undertaken *in* the present and, as such, is necessarily a product *of* the present (e.g. Pearson and Shanks 2001; Lucas 2004; Shanks, Platt, and Rathje 2004; Witmore 2004; González-Ruibal 2006; Högberg 2007; Olivier 2011; Holtorf 2012).

As we have already mentioned, it is with this in mind that we avoid reference to 'the archaeology of the contemporary past' in the title of this Handbook, seeking instead to emphasize archaeology's potential role in the investigation of 'now', while simultaneously acknowledging archaeology as a creative process of assembling and reworking contemporary and historic materials where they intervene in the present. These concerns are reflected in the chapters in the Handbook in various ways. De León (this volume) argues convincingly that the past does not just exist in the present as relics and ruins, but is incorporated into the very designs and components of contemporary material culture. Similarly Olsen (this volume), drawing on Bergson, refers to the ways in which the past predetermines the present by 'gnawing' into the future (see also Wrights and Sites, this volume). As Bergson notes, '*Practically we perceive only the past*, the pure present being the invisible progress of the past gnawing into the future' (1950: 150; original emphasis). Other chapters reflect on the extent to which the past is appropriated and creatively reimagined in the present, either in relation to the production of 'authenticity' (Graves-Brown, this volume), failed utopias (Fowles and Heupel, this volume; González-Ruibal, this volume), the afterlives of objects (Schiffer, this volume), ongoing political, religious, social, or other forms of sectarian conflict (Dixon, this volume; McAtackney, this volume; Moshenska, this volume; Rizvi, this volume), or the mediation and management of the politics of heritage (Harrison, this volume; Shepherd, this volume). The ruin, as a spectral trace of that which is simultaneously past and present, as well as both absent and in attendance, plays an important role in archaeology's mediation of time (Lucas 2010). The ruin is not only an archetypal leitmotif of modernity's sense of time and its passage (Lucas, this volume; Olsen, this volume), but also provides rich physical and symbolic material for remediating, and hence creating the future

(Wilkie, this volume). The ruin is also both a product of modern capitalism and its associated processes of material production, consumption, and disposal, as well as a producer of the particular forms of nostalgia (May, this volume) and desire which help shape and drive these processes in their late capitalist form. Within this context, archaeology and heritage mediate powerful impulses to salvage and conserve traces of the past (Harrison 2013), but in the process, might also be held to contribute to degenerating it (De Silvey, this volume). Like the monument (Dixon, this volume; Mullins, this volume; Piccini, this volume), another of archaeology's traditional objects of interest and disciplinary self-fashioning, the ruin holds an important place within archaeologies of the present, in spite of its temporal proximity.

The need for 'archaeologies in and of the present' to work across multiple temporalities and with traces of both presences and, their flipside, the haunting spectres of absence, is also reflected, either explicitly (Hamilakis and Ifantidis, this volume) or implicitly, across the chapters of the volume. Several archaeologists (Olivier 2008, 2011; Funari and Vieira de Carvalho 2009; Piccini and Holtorf 2009; Harrison 2011; see also Dawdy 2010) have suggested that Walter Benjamin's notion of *Jetztzeit* or 'now-time' might be helpful in working towards this goal. For Benjamin, 'now' represents the point at which a constellation of images, objects, agencies, ideas, and trajectories coalesce to form a unique image or assemblage (Rosen 2003: 2) which in turn generates a dialectical realization of the past being gathered up in the present (Osborne 1995: 143). This implication of both the 'past' and the 'future' in the present warns us against treating 'archaeology in and of the present' as simply another period study (see also González-Ruibal 2008; Piccini and Holtorf 2009; Harrison and Schofield 2010; Harrison 2011; Holtorf 2012). Archaeologies in and of the present must address themselves not only to the present itself, but also to the spaces in which the past and future intervene within it. The archaeology of the present thus comes to encompass not only the study of contemporary material cultures, but also the pasts and futures which they embody and evoke.

It may appear counter-intuitive for our readers to consider archaeology as a practice of the future. However, a number of philosophers have argued that any study of the past is for the living (Nietzsche 1980) and those yet to come. Bergson focuses his study of perception (1950) on the relationship between past and present, the fact that in order to recognize the chair as something other than a random collection of materials we must have past experiences of chair-ness (see Costall and Richards, this volume). It is in this way that (social) memory is materialized, with the past and future gathered together to make the event of perception possible. Heidegger extends this property through *dasein* (1962). For Heidegger, the 'authentic past' is understood in futural terms, with *dasein* understanding the past as a set of future possibilities. And what emerges out of the future is our having-been, our pastness. This is why archaeology, whether its focus is on Palaeolithic remains or motorway signage (Merriman, this volume) or preserving city parks (Wilkie, this volume), is a form of futurology, in that it imagines a future in which this past has significance (see also Holtorf 2012; Wrights and Sites, this volume). This form of futurology and its accompanying 'salvage paradigm', generated out of a modern perception of vulnerability and threat, was central to the history of the development of heritage conservation (e.g. see Harrison 2013), museum collecting, archaeology, and anthropology more generally. Archaeologies in and of the present have an important role to play in challenging the salvage paradigm by drawing attention to the creative potential of change (Bradley et al. 2004; Penrose 2007) and the ways in which the values of things are not inherent but emerge in dialogue with other actors (be they human or non-human).

1.6 MATTER, MEDIA, AND MOBILITIES

Archaeology's projection of itself into the future, a future in which the past is significant, is a particular concern within archaeologies of the contemporary world. Where Iron Age hillforts or medieval field systems appear already settled into future significance, archaeologies of the contemporary world suggest a future in which urban checkpoints (Rizvi, this volume), aluminium (Sheller, this volume), the remains of space exploration (Gorman and O'Leary, this volume), or an assemblage of institutional ephemera (Metelerkamp, this volume) are materials that will travel in and transform through space and time as mobile media to tell us something of a past *not yet past*. In this way, these archaeologies extend our understanding of the mobility of matter, a mobility that suggests the operation of matter as *media* (see Graves-Brown 2013). As we have already suggested, no volume on archaeology can be written without reference to the material turn across the academic disciplines. Our aim in this introduction is not to decide whether Tim Ingold's critique (2007b) of the tautologous connotations of material cultural studies is useful, although the problem of whether culture can be anything other than material certainly haunts our Introduction. Instead, what strikes us across many of the contributions to this volume is how they extend through practice what Karen Barad terms 'processes of mattering' (2003: 817). Our contributors would also appear to agree with Barad's estimation of matter as *practice*. A significant field of exploration for the writers here is how matter 'on the move' (pace Cresswell 2006) is both a medium, and is produced, expressed, circulated, and repeated via media. That is, our contributors explore matter *as* media and the materiality *of* media.

In this volume, contributors pursue questions of materiality that appear to owe much to another contribution from Walter Benjamin, his unfinished *Arcades Project* (2002), a distinctively spatial exploration of the ruins and debris of the arcades of Paris. Specifically, the focus on the multiplication and spatial-temporal movement of matter is taken up in those discussions highlighted above about modernity's reliance on aluminium (Sheller, this volume) and space travel (Gorman and O'Leary, this volume); in analyses of materials that convey ideas about nation and community, whether focusing on travel in its literal sense with regards to automobility (Lemonnier, this volume; Merriman, this volume) and across Iraqi checkpoints (Rizvi, this volume), or in terms of the metaphysical and ontological transportation from life into death (Dawdy, this volume), from human into animal (Holtorf, this volume), and from infant into desiring subject (May, this volume); and in discussions about the ways in which the movements of materials are themselves contingent and politically implicated in the production of neo-liberal globalization (Maxwell and Miller, this volume) and national myth (Dixon, this volume; Finn, this volume). These contributions productively resist tendencies in archaeologies of the contemporary world to fetishize the ruin (Graves-Brown 2011; Lucas, this volume). For our contributors, the fragments of what remain can be understood and mobilized in terms of multiplicities rather than ruination, so that we move beyond the romantic voice of loss (see also Reynolds 2006; Harrison 2013) to consider matter on the move, as a form of media.

Why should it be useful or even desirable for us to discuss matter in such terms? Conventional media scholarship may be characterized in terms of contrasting media as communication with media as technology. For Raymond Williams, technology produces cultural effects: media communicate; they carry a message of power and ideology. For Marshall McLuhan, media are technological 'extensions of man' [sic] (2001[1964]). Williams critiqued McLuhan's work for apparently attending to the specificity of media, while never addressing media as practice, preferring instead to give media psychic functions that ignored the entangled and specific relationships between humans and non-humans (2003: 130–1). Yet, Williams's cultural approach to media privileged their practices of power at the level of discourse rather than any sense of material discursivity. Beyond a narrow focus on broadcast media, Roger Silverstone has argued that heritage itself is media; that is, heritage constitutes mass-produced material narratives of pastness as mediational processes moving meaning through space and time (1989). The process of media 'involves the work of institutions, groups and technologies' (Silverstone 1999: 15). This is where archaeological practices might find themselves in close proximity to media. Yet, all of these media scholars rely on a rather settled sense of the media as representational, their technologies encoded with meaning. Even Silverstone, who saw media as involving process, conceptualized media as some-thing. What might happen, instead, if media are considered by way of what Mitch Rose terms 'a surplus of meaningfulness gathering and circulating through a number of orbiting practices' (2006: 550)? That is, media as imminent material-discursive practices?

Archaeological approaches to the materiality of movement and the movements of materials flow in to contributors' concerns with archaeological practices themselves as media that transport and transform ideas, ideologies, and inequalities. In Malta, the photographic practices of archaeology produce the subjectivities they seek to describe (Schofield, this volume). At Prestwich Street, Cape Town, archaeological practices as media misfire, reproducing systems of inequalities that are entrapped by the spectres of apartheid (Shepherd, this volume). At a different scale, specific archaeological media can be understood as material-discursive practices. Wickstead (this volume) discusses the mark-making of archaeological drawing as media, to consider its performative production of the archaeological subject, rather than as a static medium transporting archaeological knowledge. Finally, the three photoessay contributions to this volume clearly demonstrate archaeology's relationship to media practices as they open out photography's production of surplus meaning from attempts to convey the unobserved lives of forgotten things (De Silvey, this volume), to the political lives of institutions and the tensions between public disclosures and the lived everyday (Metelerkamp, this volume), to the potential multiplicities in-between that are generated in a World Heritage Site (Hamilakis and Ifantidis, this volume; see also Harrison, this volume).

Contributors to the Handbook also investigate the materialities of conventionally recognized media, and do so by examining media as mark-making. Maxwell and Miller argue that a cultural materialist approach allows us to understand the global, material, and ecological impacts of mobile phone technology production and distribution. Cubitt explores the Internet as a simultaneously physical and virtual network. Noble's VHS-based practice enacts the material-discursive potentialities of magnetic tape by exploring both the multiple movements of a single video from rental shop to home and the disruptions to the magnetic properties of the tape through this transport, which registers as a physical marking of the tape itself. Watkins' discussion of marks on the celluloid of early film not only opens out a fascinating micro-landscape, but disrupts the idea of 'the film' altogether to demonstrate its mutability across different edits, transfers, and restorations (see also Schiffer, this volume, on the afterlives of artefacts). Piccini rescales media to explore the role of the screen itself in producing urban landscapes, in this instance, the ephemeral landscape of the Olympic city. Finn revisits the assemblings and disappearances of the material culture of computing media in Silicon Valley, thus returning the discussion of media to a global scale, in order to argue that our understanding of networked media is fundamentally enacted through practices of collection and display.

Yet, archaeological practices are not confined to working with only the substantive and durational (if multiple) materialities of metals or fibre optics or magnetic tape. If matter is mediational, if it transforms and transports itself to produce specific experiences of space and time, then perhaps the ephemeral event becomes a productive site for extending our understandings of matter, media, and mobility. In this volume, contributors have focused their attentions on spectacular events as sites of material intensity. Protest and riot (Badcock and Johnson, this volume; Dixon, this volume), the sporting mega-event (Piccini, this volume), and the festival (White, this volume) potentially allow readers to see the processes of multiplication that 'emerge in the interplay between event, document and the multiple sites of production and exhibition' (Connolly 2009: 115). Such archaeological approaches to the event as site for thinking through moving assemblies of material as media also present key methodological challenges for our readers (Yaneva, this volume). It is to these challenges that we now turn.

1.7 METHODOLOGIES: WHY? WHAT? AND HOW?

1.7.1 Why...

...is the methodology of an archaeology in and of the contemporary world any different from other archaeologies? In studying the contemporary world we are confronted by what Hakim Bey (1991) calls the 'closure of the map'; 'The last bit of Earth unclaimed by any nation-state was eaten up in 1899. Ours is the first century without terra incognita, without a frontier.' Most archaeological methodologies imply an exploratory trope; the excavation represents a journey into the unknown (Thomas 2004). By contrast, we must deal with a 'death of affect', shared with psychogeography, which 'seeks to overcome the processes of "banalisation" by which the everyday experience of our surroundings becomes one of drab monotony' (Coverley 2010: 13). The contemporary world is also ever changing but '[m]ost superficial change belongs in the context of the word "new"...Real change is largely invisible' (Ballard 1993: 128).

This banality is compounded by the fact that we study the not-yet-discarded (or recently discarded). Material culture that is of interest is still in use, and hence in common with anthropology, we have to balance our desire to encounter the material etically with a purely archaeological sensibility against the need to engage emically with people themselves (see above; Fewster, this volume). Indeed this might be seen to produce a third category of analysis; not *things* or *people*, but the observation of *things in action* (Yaneva, this volume).

Another factor in the banality of the contemporary lies in its sheer scale. There is on the one hand a vast amount of information available about the contemporary world, an information overload, but on the other hand it remains difficult to apprehend what is significant. The accusation of triviality levelled at studies of the contemporary (e.g. 'the Van', Bailey et al. 2009) can be construed as a failure to penetrate the mythologies which information builds around us. Here again study of the contemporary is different, even with respect to historical archaeology, in that there are at least three strands of evidence: material culture, documentation, and verbal/observational accounts.

1.7.2 What…

…are the sources of an archaeology of the contemporary? Clearly material culture is central in several ways. Using fairly traditional methods of archaeological survey and artefact/ material culture studies, we can explore the material aspect of the contemporary in its own right. Although excavation does have a place in such methodologies, particularly in forensic contexts and garbology (Gould, this volume; Powers and Sibun, this volume; Reno, this volume), the active nature of the subject field tends to encourage approaches concentrated on surfaces and assemblages (Harrison 2011). Conversely, from a more ethnoarchaeological perspective, we also have the opportunity to observe how people actually use places and things, and the traces left by that use (Graves-Brown 2007; Noble, this volume; Penrose, this volume; Yaneva, this volume).

The role of written and verbal accounts cannot be underestimated; whilst prehistory and other historical archaeologies are forced to rely entirely or almost entirely on material culture, we would be foolish to ignore such sources. However, this does raise questions as to the relative values placed on evidence of different types; as Olivier (this volume) suggests, there is a qualitative difference in the nature of material and documentary evidence in terms of constructions of history and time. Even Hume (1964), who coined the phrase 'Archaeology: Handmaiden to History', had reservations about historical data: 'written history can deliberately distort and obscure, and…archaeology can sometimes set the record straight' (1964: 217). Equally, Schiffer (2000) cautions against the acceptance of 'indigenous theory' at face value, suggesting that verbal accounts may also incorporate distortions. Yet, all accounts— verbal, historical narrative, legal, regulatory—are always-already contingent and, therefore, 'distorted' (Portelli 1981; Martindale forthcoming). Indeed, this is the central point of Barthes' critique of mythologies—our society tends to build popular accounts around its cultural products which often serve to obscure. To single out 'indigenous theory' in this regard simply reproduces ahistoric and racist hierarchies of knowledge. It may be arguable, then, that whilst taking other sources into account, the archaeology of the contemporary world must always be grounded in the material in the first instance, and seek to situate other evidence in this context (e.g. Gorman and O'Leary, this volume).

1.7.3 How…

…do we research the contemporary world? Whilst the traditional territory of archaeology is always and already the 'other' (Fabian 1983), we necessarily approach the contemporary from within. We begin as participants, rather than excavators. Different participant approaches are possible, including what we might call interventions (Wrights and Sites, this volume), participation in events (White, this volume), and engagement with communities (Fewster, this volume; Fowles and Heupel, this volume; Kiddey and Schofield 2011; Zimmerman, this volume). They can also involve what we might call more peripheral participation in terms of 'bimbling' (Schofield, this volume), 'story-trekking' (Green, Green, and Neves 2003), the field recording of 'landscape biography' (Harrison 2004), and other walking-based observations, as have developed through the history of psychogeography from Baudelaire to Benjamin to Debord (Coverley 2010). At times, the researcher can quite deliberately contrast the tourist gaze with that of the ethnographer (Yaneva, this volume).

In effect we may say that the form of participation is going to reflect the situation under study. Where fixed events are concerned, such as the Burning Man festival (White, this volume) it seems logical for the archaeologist to 'embed' him- or herself in the event. Indeed this is in effect the form of participant-observation that ethnoarchaeologists originally borrowed from anthropology. Where specific groups or communities are involved, it may not be possible for such total participation to take place. In some cases, such as the study of undocumented migrants on the US Mexico border (Drake 2011; De León 2012; Rodriguez 2012), practical and ethical considerations may even preclude the co-presence of archaeologist and participant. Similar, but less stringent issues arise around the archaeology of homelessness (Kiddey and Schofield 2010; Zimmerman, this volume). Equally there are necessarily situations, such as in the context of forensic archaeology, where participation is never in question, per se.

Beyond such instances, a more overtly psychogeographical approach may be particularly suited to contemporary urban contexts. In this instance participation is, by definition, not a function of a fixed place or community but the observation of fluid movements of people in what are often 'non-places' (Augé 1995). In such situations the archaeologist must become an archaeo-flâneur (e.g. see Byrne 2007); accepting the method of *dérive* (drift; see Coverley 2010) as an essential part of comprehending the urban landscape. This might seem a little 'airy-fairy' and postmodern from a more traditional archaeological point of view, but differs little in practical terms from the approach used in rural landscape archaeology (Hoskins 1969). Further, it might be arguable that in terms of the comprehension of scale (Edgeworth, this volume), *dérive* could also include travelling by car, train, or other means of contemporary mobility (Merriman, this volume; Noble, this volume). Needless to say, this would also include virtual travel (Cubitt, this volume; Harrison 2009).

Given that the archaeology of the contemporary is about surfaces and assemblages (Harrison 2011), and moreover a world that is being lived, it follows that photography and other similar forms of recording (film/video, audio) will tend to be the primary media of record. This is not to say that traditional methods of excavation (e.g. Kiddey and Schofield 2010) or field walking (Gorman pers. comm.) are not of value in certain circumstances (see further discussion of these issues in Harrison and Schofield 2010). However, a photographic record is not 'value free', not least because it is itself a form of both intervention and transformation; as Metelerkamp (this volume) observes, 'the camera both underwrites and challenges the "real"'. Indeed, as we know from the world of the paparazzi, the camera can also be transgressive and intrusive. Equally, photography can constitute a form of reification, which can have positive effects in contributing to the scene photographed, but can equally be seen as a negative intrusion which, by fixing the ephemeral and transient, both detracts from and transforms it (De Silvey, this volume). Arguably, photography, just like drawing before it, is performative in that it produces the subjects that it names (Butler 1993; Wickstead, this volume).

1.8 Conclusion

It remains to us to make some concluding remarks which look towards the future of the subfield. While we have argued that archaeology is itself a form of futurology, we must follow Aldiss and Wingrove (1986: 27) in their history of science fiction by suggesting that such 'Frontiers are by tradition ill defined.' Nonetheless, we have, with the help of our contributors, identified a series of themes which represent contemporary and future vectors for an archaeology in and of the present. Because 'the present' or 'now' is not a fixed field, but is constantly shifting and emergent, these themes will necessarily also shift and change. But as archaeologists in and of the present we are not simply hostage to the future's fortune—-indeed, in our discussion of the role of advocacy, we have suggested that archaeologists have a key role to play in *shaping* that future, both as individuals and in taking collective action on issues of contemporary social, political, environmental, and economic concern (see also Dawdy 2009). In this way, archaeologies in and of the present have a relevance in the contemporary world which they study, and archaeology is locked into a dialogue with the future by way of its production of the past in the present.

Clearly, reorienting archaeology to engage with and intervene in the emergent present and its possible futures requires a radical rethinking of both its methods and its tropes (Harrison 2011). As a newly emerging subfield, a key concern is the development of both cross-sectional and longitudinal studies with the potential to act as dialogical thought experiments and experiential proving grounds for the advancement of new methodologies and techniques—studies which take on the challenges of working in the 'now' to go beyond the limits of traditional archaeological practice, but which also provide material for productive synergy with the constellation of disciplines which share archaeology's concerns with the emerging present. It is of critical importance that archaeologists explore dialogically the ways in which they might work both in conjunction with, and independently of, these various adjacent disciplines to develop their own critical insights into the contemporary world and what it means to live and work within it. We hope that this Handbook will provide some helpful signposting to those who are involved in this process.

References

Alberti, Benjamin, Fowles, Severin, Holbraad, Martin, Marshall, Yvonne, and Witmore, Christopher. 2011. 'Worlds Otherwise': Archaeology, Anthropology, and Ontological Difference. *Current Anthropology* 52(6): 896–912.

Aldiss, Brian W. and Wingrove, David. 1986. *Trillion Year Spree: The History of Science Fiction*. London: Gollancz.

Appadurai, Arjun. 1996. Diversity and Disciplinarity as Cultural Artifacts. In *Disciplinarity and Dissent in Cultural Studies*, ed. Cary Nelson and Dilip Parameshwar Gaonkar, pp. 23–36. London and New York: Routledge.

Augé, Marc. 1995. *Non-Places: Introduction to an Anthropology of Supermodernity*. London: Verso.

Bailey, Greg, Newland, Cassie, Nilsson, Anna, and Schofield, John. 2009. Transit, Transition: Excavating J641 VUJ. *Cambridge Archaeological Journal* 19(1): 1–27.

Bal, Mieke. 2002. *Travelling Concepts in the Humanities: A Rough Guide*. Toronto: University of Toronto Press.

Ballard, James G. 1993. *The Atrocity Exhibition*. London: Flamingo.

Banks, Iain. 1993. *Complicity*. London: Little, Brown.

Barad, Karen. 2003. Posthumanist Performativity: Toward an Understanding of How Matter Comes to Matter. *Signs: Journal of Women in Culture and Society* 28(3): 801–31.

—— 2007. *Meeting the Universe Halfway: Quantum Physics and the Entanglement of Matter and Meaning*. Durham, NC: Duke University Press.

Barthes, Roland. 1993[1957]. *Mythologies*. London: Vintage.

Becher, Tony. 1989. *Academic Tribes and Territories: Intellectual Enquiry and the Cultures of Disciplines*. Milton Keynes: Open University Press.

Benjamin, Walter. 1999[1968]. Theses on the Philosophy of History. In *Illuminations,* ed. Hannah Arendt, pp. 245–55. London: Pimlico.

—— 2002. *The Arcades Project*, ed. Rolf Tiedemann, tr. Howard Eiland and Kevin McLaughlin. Cambridge, MA: Belknap Press of Harvard University Press.

Bennett, Jane. 2010. *Vibrant Matter: A Political Ecology of Things*. Durham, NC: Duke University Press.

Bennett, Tony and Joyce, Patrick (eds.). 2010. *Material Powers: Cultural Studies, History and the Material Turn*. Abingdon and New York: Routledge.

Bergson, Henri. 1950. *Matter and Memory*. London: Allen & Unwin.

Bey, Hakim. 1991. *TAZ: Temporary Autonomous Zones*. Available at: <http://hermetic.com/bey/taz_cont.html> (accessed 1 March 2012).

Bourdieu, Pierre. 1984. *Homo Academicus*. Paris: Minuit.

Bradley, Andrea, Buchli, Victor, Fairclough, Graham, Hicks, Dan, Miller, Janet, and Schofield, John. 2004. *Change and Creation: Historic Landscape Character 1950–2000*. London: English Heritage.

Brown, Bill (ed.). 2004. *Things*. Chicago: University of Chicago Press.

Buchli, Victor and Lucas, Gavin (eds.). 2001a. *Archaeologies of the Contemporary Past*. London: Routledge.

—— 2001b. The Absent Present: Archaeologies of the Contemporary Past. In *Archaeologies of the Contemporary Past*, ed. V. Buchli and G. Lucas, pp. 3–18. London: Routledge.

Butler, Judith. 1993. *Bodies that Matter: On the Discursive Limits of 'Sex'*. London: Routledge.

Byrne, Denis. 2007. *Surface Collection: Archaeological Travels in Southeast Asia*. Lanham, MD: Altamira Press.

Cavell, Richard. 2002. *McLuhan in Space: A Cultural Geography*. Toronto: University of Toronto Press.

Clarke, David. 1973. Archaeology: The Loss of Innocence. *Antiquity* 47: 6–18.

Connarty, Jane and Lanyon, Josephine (eds.). 2006. *Ghosting: The Role of the Archive within Contemporary Artists' Film and Video*. Bristol: Picture This.

Connolly, Maeve. 2009. *The Place of Artists' Cinema: Space, Site and Screen*. Bristol: Intellect.

Coverley, Merlin. 2010. *Psychogeography*. Harpenden: Pocket Essentials.

Cresswell, Tim. 2006. *On the Move: Mobility in the Modern Western World*. London: Routledge.

Dawdy, Shannon Lee. 2009. Millennial Archaeology: Locating the Discipline in the Age of Insecurity. *Archaeological Dialogues* 16(2): 131–42.

—— 2010. Clockpunk Anthropology and the Ruins of Modernity. *Current Anthropology* 51(6): 761–93.

De Certeau, Michel. 1984. *The Practice of Everyday Life*. Berkeley: University of California Press.

De León, Jason. 2012. Victor, Archaeology of the Contemporary, and the Politics of Researching Unauthorized Border Crossing: A Brief and Personal History of the Undocumented Migration Project. *Forum Kritische Archäologie* 1: 141–4. Available at: <http://www .kritischearchaeologie.de/repositorium/fka/2012_1_19_DeLeon.pdf> (accessed 17 January 2013).

Drake, Nadia. 2010. Immigration Tracked through Desert Detritus. *Nature News Online*. Available at: <http://www.nature.com/news/2011/110411/full/news.2011.225.html> (accessed 30 May 2012).

Fabian, Johannes. 1983. *Time and the Other: How Anthropology Makes Its Object*. New York: Columbia University Press.

Foucault, Michel. 1970. *The Order of Things: An Archaeology of the Human Sciences*. London: Tavistock Press.

—— 1972. *The Archaeology of Knowledge*. London: Tavistock Press.

Funari, P. P. and Vieira de Carvalho, A. 2009. The Uses of Archaeology: A Plea for Diversity. *Archaeological Dialogues* 16(2): 179–81.

Garrow, Duncan and Shove, Elizabeth. 2007. Artefacts Between Disciplines: The Toothbrush and the Axe. *Archaeological Dialogues* 14(2): 1–15.

Gill, Rosalind and Róisín Ryan-Flood (eds.). 2009. *Secrecy and Silence in the Research Process: Feminist Reflections*. London: Routledge.

González-Ruibal, Alfredo. 2006. The Past is Tomorrow: Towards an Archaeology of the Vanishing Present. *Norwegian Archaeological Review* 39: 110–25.

—— 2008. Time to Destroy: An Archaeology of Supermodernity. *Current Anthropology* 49(2): 247–79.

—— 2012. Against Post-politics: A Critical Archaeology for the 21st Century. *Forum Kritische Archäologie* 1: 157–61. Available at: <http://www.kritischearchaeologie.de/repositorium/ fka/2012_1_21_Gonzalez-Ruibal.pdf> (accessed 17 January 2013).

—— Forthcoming. *Reclaiming Archaeology: Beyond the Tropes of Modernity*. London: Routledge.

González-Ruibal, Alfredo, Sahle, Yonatan, and Vila, Xurxo Ayán. 2011. A Social Archaeology of Colonial War in Ethiopia. *World Archaeology* 43(1): 40–65.

Gorman, Alice C. 2005. The Cultural Landscape of Interplanetary Space. *Journal of Social Archaeology* 5(1): 85–107.

Gould, Richard A. and Schiffer, Michael B. (eds.). 1981. *Modern Material Culture: The Archaeology of Us*. London: Academic Press.

Graves-Brown, Paul. 2000. Introduction. In *Matter, Materiality and Modern Culture*, ed. Paul Graves-Brown, pp. 1–9. London: Routledge.

—— 2007. Concrete Islands. In *Contemporary and Historical Archaeology in Theory*. Papers from the 2003 and 2004 CHAT conferences, ed. Laura McAtackney, Mathew Palus, and Angela Piccini, pp. 75–81. BAR Int Series 1677. Oxford: Archaeopress.

—— 2011. Touching from a Distance: Alienation, Abjection, Estrangement and Archaeology. *Norwegian Archaeological Review* 44(2): 131–44.

——— 2013. Inside is Out: An Epistemology of Surfaces and Substances. In *Reclaiming Archaeology: Beyond the Tropes of Modernity*, ed. Alfredo González-Ruibal, pp. 298–310. London: Taylor and Francis.

Graves-Brown, Paul and Schofield, John. 2011. The Filth and the Fury: 6 Denmark Street, (London) and the Sex Pistols. *Antiquity* 85: 1385–401.

Green, Lesley F., Green, David R., and Neves, Eduardo Góes. 2003. Indigenous Knowledge and Archaeological Science: The Challenges of Public Archaeology in the Reserva Uaçá. *Journal of Social Archaeology* 3(3): 366–98.

Hamilakis Yannis and Duke, Phillip (eds.). 2007. *Archaeology and Capitalism: From Ethics to Politics*. Walnut Creek, CA: Left Coast Press.

Haraway, Donna. 1991. *Simians, Cyborgs and Women: The Reinvention of Nature*. New York: Routledge.

Harrison, Rodney. 2004. *Shared Landscapes: Archaeologies of Attachment and the Pastoral Industry in New South Wales*. Sydney: UNSW Press.

——— 2008. The Politics of the Past: Conflict in the Use of Heritage in the Modern World. In *The Heritage Reader*, ed. Graham Fairclough, Rodney Harrison, John H. Jameson, and John Schofield, pp. 177–90. Abingdon and New York: Routledge.

——— 2009. Excavating Second Life: Cyber-Archaeologies, Heritage and Virtual Communities. *Journal of Material Culture* 14: 75–106.

——— 2011. Surface Assemblages: Towards an Archaeology *in* and *of* the Present. *Archaeological Dialogues* 18(2): 141–96.

——— 2013. *Heritage: Critical Approaches*. Abingdon and New York: Routledge.

Harrison, Rodney and Schofield, John. 2010. *After Modernity: Archaeological Approaches to the Contemporary Past*. Oxford: Oxford University Press.

Hastrup, Kirsten and Elsass, Peter. 1990. Anthropological Advocacy: A Contradiction in Terms? *Current Anthropology* 31(3): 301–11.

Heidegger, Martin. 1962. *Being and Time*, tr. John Macquarie and Edward Robinson. London: HarperCollins.

Hicks, Dan. 2003 Archaeology Unfolding: Diversity and the Loss of Isolation. *Oxford Journal of Archaeology* 22(3): 315–29.

——— 2010. Intimate Distance: Three Kinds of Detachment in the Archaeology of the Modern. Available at: <http://weweremodern.blogspot.com/2010/04/three-kinds-of-detachment-in.html> (accessed 26 April 2012).

Högberg, Anders. 2007. The Past is the Present: Prehistory and Preservation from a Children's Point of View. *Public Archaeology* 6(1): 28–46.

Hollowell, Julie and Nicholas, George. 2008. Intellectual Property Issues in Archaeological Publication: Some Questions to Consider. *Archaeologies* 4(2): 208–17.

Holtorf, Cornelius. 2005. *From Stonehenge to Las Vegas: Archaeology as Popular Culture*. Lanham, MD: Altamira Press.

——— 2009. A European Perspective on Indigenous and Immigrant Archaeologies. *World Archaeology* 41(4): 672–81.

——— 2012. *Search the Past—Find the Present: Qualities of Archaeology and Heritage in Contemporary Society*. Oxford: Archaeopress.

Holtorf, Cornelius and Piccini, Angela. 2009. *Contemporary Archaeologies: Excavating Now*. Frankfurt: Peter Lang.

Horning, Audrey. 2011. Compelling Futures and Ever-Present Pasts: Realigning the Archaeology of Us. *Archaeological Dialogues* 18(2): 161–4.

Hoskins, William G. 1969. *The Making of the English Landscape*. London: Hodder & Stoughton.

Huber, Ludwig. 1990. Disciplinary Cultures and Social Reproduction. *European Journal of Education* 25(3): 241–61.

Huhtamo, Erkki and Parikka, Jussi (eds.). 2011. *Media Archaeology*. Berkeley: University of California Press.

Hume, Ivor Noel. 1964. Archaeology: Handmaiden to History. *North Carolina Historical Review* 41(2): 215–25.

Ingold, Tim. 2007a. *Lines: A Brief History*. London: Routledge.

—— 2007b. Materials Against Materiality. *Archaeological Dialogues* 14(1): 1–16.

—— 2011. *Being Alive: Essays on Movement, Knowledge and Description*. London: Taylor & Francis.

Irigaray, Luce. 2008 *Sharing the World*. London: Continuum.

Joerges, Bernward. 1988. Technology in Everyday Life: Conceptual Queries. *Journal for the Theory of Social Behaviour* 18: 221–37.

Kellett, Peter. 2009. Advocacy in Anthropology: Active Engagement or Passive Scholarship? *Durham Anthropology Journal* 6(1): 22–31.

Kiddey, Rachael and Schofield, John. 2010. Embrace the Margins: Adventures in Archaeology and Homelessness. *Public Archaeology* 10(1): 4–22.

La Salle, Marina. 2010. Community Collaboration and Other Good Intentions. *Archaeologies: The Journal of the World Archaeological Congress* 6(3): 401–22.

La Salle, Marina and Hutchings, Rich. 2012. Commercial Archaeology in British Columbia. *The Midden* 44(2): 8–16.

Latour, Bruno. 1993. *We Have Never Been Modern*. Cambridge, MA: Harvard University Press.

Law, John. 2004. *After Method: Mess in Social Science Research*. London and New York: Routledge.

Lefebvre, Henri. 2000. *Everyday Life in the Modern World*. London and New York: Continuum.

Lehtonen, Mikko. 2009. Spaces and Places of Cultural Studies. *Culture Unbound* 1: 67–81.

Lucas, Gavin. 2004. Modern Disturbances: On the Ambiguities of Archaeology. *Modernism/Modernity* 11(1): 109–20.

—— 2010. Time and the Archaeological Archive. *Rethinking History* 14: 343–59.

Lydon, Jane and Uzma Z. Rizvi (eds.). 2010. *Handbook of Postcolonial Archaeology*. Walnut Creek, CA: Left Coast Press.

McGuire, Randall. 2008. *Archaeology as Political Action*. Berkeley: University of California Press.

McLuhan, Marshall. 2001[1964]. *Understanding Media: The Extensions of Man*. London: Routledge.

Martindale, Andrew. Forthcoming. Archaeology Taken to Court: Unraveling the Epistemology of Cultural Tradition in the Context of Aboriginal Title Cases. In *The Archaeology of the Colonized in Archaeological Theory*, ed. Neal Ferris, Rodney Harrison and Michael V. Wilcox. Oxford: Oxford University Press.

Miller, Daniel. 1991. *Material Culture and Mass Consumption*. Oxford: Blackwell.

—— 2010. *Stuff*. Cambridge and Malden, MA: Polity Press.

Molotch, Harvey. 2007. Display Matters. *Archaeological Dialogues* 14(2): 26–9.

Nicholas, George P. 2012. Intellectual Property Issues. In *The Oxford Companion to Archaeology*, 2nd edn., ed. Neal Asher Silberman, pp. 106–9. Oxford: Oxford University Press.

Nietzsche, Friedrich. 1980. *On the Advantage and Disadvantage of History for Life*. Indianapolis: Hackett Publishing.

Olivier, Laurent. 2004. The Past of the Present: Archaeological Memory and Time. *Archaeological Dialogues* 10(2): 204–13.

—— 2008. *Le sombre abîme du temps. Archéologie et mémoire*. Paris: Seuil.

—— 2011. *The Dark Abyss of Time: Archaeology and Memory*. Lanham, MD: Altamira Press.

Osborne, Peter. 1995. *The Politics of Time: Modernity and the Avant-garde*. London: Verso.

Parikka, Jussi (ed.). 2012. *What is Media Archaeology?* Cambridge and Malden, MA: Polity Press.

Pearson, Michael and Shanks, Michael. 2001. *Theatre/Archaeology*. London and New York: Routledge.

Penrose, Sefryn (ed.). 2007. *Images of Change: An Archaeology of England's Contemporary Landscape*. Swindon: English Heritage.

Perec, Georges. 1997. *Species of Spaces and Other Pieces*. Harmondsworth: Penguin.

Perriault, Jacques. 1981. *Mémoires de l'ombre et du son. Une archéologie de l'audio-visual*. Paris: Flammarion.

Piccini, Angela and Holtorf, Cornelius. 2009. Introduction: Fragments from a Conversation about Contemporary Archaeologies. In *Contemporary Archaeologies: Excavating Now*, ed. Angela Piccini and Cornelius Holtorf, pp. 9–29. Frankfurt: Peter Lang.

Portelli, Allessandro. 1981. The Peculiarities of Oral History. *History Workshop Journal* 12(1): 96–107.

Preda, Alex. 1999. The Turn to Things: Arguments for a Sociological Theory of Things. *The Sociological Quarterly* 40(2): 347–66.

Reynolds, Lucy. 2006. Outside the Archive: The World in Fragments. In *Ghosting: The Role of the Archive within Contemporary Artists' Film and Video*, ed. Jane Connarty and Josephine Lanyon, pp. 14–23. Bristol: Picture This.

Rodriguez, Cindy Y. 2012. The Undocumented Migration Project: University of Michigan Researcher Documents Belongings Left Behind While Crossing the Border. *The Huffington Post*, 24 January. Available at: <http://www.huffingtonpost.com/2012/01/19/migrants-belongings-us-mexico-border_n_1213910.html?1327014301&ref=latino-voices> (accessed 29 May 2012).

Rose, Mitch. 2006 Gathering 'Dreams of Presence': A Project for the Cultural Landscape. *Environment and Planning D: Society and Space* 24: 537–54.

Rosen, Phillip. 2003. Introduction. In *Benjamin Now: Critical Encounters with the Arcades Project*, ed. Kevin McLaughlin and Phillip Rosen, pp. 1–15. Durham, NC: Duke University Press.

Scheper-Hughes, Nancy. 1995. The Primacy of the Ethical: Propositions for a Militant Anthropology. *Current Anthropology* 36(3): 409–40.

Schiffer, Michael B. 2000. Indigenous Theories, Scientific Theories and Product Histories. In *Matter, Materiality and Modern Culture*, ed. Paul Graves-Brown, pp. 72–96. London and New York: Routledge.

Schmidt, Peter. 2009. What is Postcolonial about Archaeologies in Africa? In *Postcolonial Archaeologies in Africa*, ed. Peter Schmidt, pp. 1–20. Santa Fe: SAR Press.

Schofield, John. 2006. Review column: John Schofield on Archaeology, Art and the Contemporary Past. *European Association of Archaeologists Blog*. Available at: <http://e-a-a.org/blog/?p=131> (accessed 17 January 2013).

Shanks, Michael. 2012. *The Archaeological Imagination*. Walnut Creek, CA: Left Coast Press.

Shanks, Michael, Platt, David, and Rathje, William L. 2004. The Perfume of Garbage: Modernity and the Archaeological. *Modernism/modernity* 11(1): 61–83.

Silverstone, Roger. 1989. Heritage as Media: Some Implications for Social Research. In *Heritage Interpretation, Volume 2*, ed. David Uzzell, pp. 138–48. London: Belhaven.

—— 1999. *Why Study the Media?* London: Sage.

Spivak, Gayatri Chakravorty. 1988. Can the Subaltern Speak? In *Marxism and the Interpretation of Culture*, ed. Cary Nelson and Lawrence Grossberg, pp. 271–313. Urbana, IL: University of Illinois Press.

Tarlow, Sarah. 2001. Decoding Ethics. *Public Archaeology* 1(4): 245–59.

Thomas, Julian. 2004. *Archaeology and Modernity*. London: Routledge.

—— 2009. Sigmund Freud's Archaeological Metaphor and Archaeology's Self-understanding. In *Contemporary Archaeologies: Excavating Now*, ed.Cornelius Holtorf and Angela Piccini, pp. 33–46. Frankfurt: Peter Lang.

Tilley, Chris, Keane, Web, Kuechler, Susan, Rowlands, Mike, and Spyer, Patricia (eds.). 2006. *Handbook of Material Culture*. London: Sage.

Trentmann, Frank. 2009. Materiality in the Future of History: Things, Practices, and Politics. *Journal of British Studies* 48(2): 283–307.

Trigger, Bruce. 1990. *A History of Archaeological Thought*. Cambridge: Cambridge University Press.

Van Esterik, Penny. 1986. Confronting Anthropology, Confronting Advocacy. In *Advocacy and Anthropology*, ed. Robert Paine, pp. 59–77. St. John's, Newfoundland: Institute for Social and Economic Research (ISER).

Williams, Raymond. 2003[1974]. *Television: Technology and Cultural Form*. London: Routledge.

Witmore, Christopher L. 2004. On Multiple Fields: Between the Material World and Media. Two Cases from the Peloponnesus, Greece. *Archaeological Dialogues* 11: 133–64.

PART I

CROSS-DISCIPLINARY PERSPECTIVES

CHAPTER 2

··

THE RELATIONSHIP BETWEEN ETHNOARCHAEOLOGY AND ARCHAEOLOGIES OF THE CONTEMPORARY PAST: A HISTORICAL INVESTIGATION

··

KATHRYN FEWSTER

2.1 INTRODUCTION

··

MODERN material culture studies and archaeologies of the contemporary and historical past are relatively new fields within the discipline of archaeology, developing their own possibilities, ontologies, and epistemologies (Graves-Brown 2000a; Buchli and Lucas 2001a; Schofield 2009b; Harrison and Schofield 2010; Holtorf and Piccini 2011). The aim of this chapter is not to attempt a definitive overview of these emerging fields, but rather to make some comment about the possible directions of these studies from within the context of their intellectual history. In particular, I shall examine the relationship of modern material culture studies with regard to what may be considered to be their obvious predecessor, and current sister subdiscipline: ethnoarchaeology. Harrison and Schofield (2010: 30) state that, '. . . the precedents for the archaeology of the contemporary past were developed out of early ethnoarchaeological studies in the US' whereas more recent publications (e.g. Graves-Brown 2000a; Buchli and Lucas 2001a) represent a 'significant shift in orientation away from the ethnoarchaeological focus of most of the earlier work on the archaeology of the contemporary past towards a more specific focus on contemporary life' (Harrison and Schofield 2010: 30). I do not necessarily disagree with either statement, but as an ethnoarchaeologist myself, I think the trajectory is slightly more convoluted, and the two subdisciplines would benefit from a more nuanced understanding of their intellectual roots. Many modern material culture studies read very much like ethnoarchaeologies in terms of their methods (e.g. Zimmerman, this volume; Schofield 2009a, 2009c; Kiddey and Schofield 2011) and they represent informants' voices in the form of oral testimonies, interviews, blogs, etc. Others place greater emphasis on an archaeological methodology that was a facet of early modern material culture studies, and that does not necessarily seek the opinions of living informants (e.g. Leone 1973; Salwen 1973; Rathje 1978, 1981; Buchli and Lucas 2001c; Graves-Brown 2007; Harrison and Schofield 2010). Of this second group I want to make two points: firstly that despite their stated aims to multivocality, some archaeologies of the contemporary past, by their chosen methodology, are in danger of producing the opposite; and second, that archaeologies of the contemporary past, sometimes referred to as 'archaeologies of us' (first cited in Gould and Schiffer 1981, restated in Buchli and Lucas 2001b: 8; Harrison and Schofield 2010: 12), need to pay more attention to defining who 'us' includes and—more to the point—excludes.

I begin with a brief examination of Binfordian ethnoarchaeology. Binford's Middle Range Theory was not synonymous with the New Archaeology, and there were a number of processual archaeologists engaged in other types of what was then termed ethnoarchaeology; including taphonomy (Gifford 1978), experimental archaeology, and indeed what might now, in retrospect, be termed modern material culture studies (Leone 1973; Salwen 1973; Rathje 1978), whose aim was neither law-like generalizations nor indeed analogy. Thus it emerges that in order to find the academic bloodline of archaeologies of the contemporary past it is necessary to make a distinction between Binfordian ethnoarchaeology and other studies which were not necessarily considered mainstream ethnoarchaeology at the time they were produced. Although they lacked a subdisciplinary self-consciousness (until, arguably the publication of Gould and Schiffer 1981), these approaches are the distant predecessors of archaeologies of the historical and contemporary past. They differed from earlier ethnoarchaeology in two important ways. Firstly, processual ethnoarchaeologies involved the observation of present human relationships with material culture such that analogy could be made to reconstruct the dynamics of human behaviour from the statics of material culture of the past (Binford 1967, 1972, 1973, 1978, 1983) while postprocessual ethnoarchaeologies aimed to aid archaeological interpretation (Hodder 1982). Yet many early forms of modern material culture studies (Salwen 1973; Rathje 1978, 1981; Schiffer 1978) claimed no such ontological discipline, expressly stating that their work was an archaeological approach to increase the understanding of the present. Secondly, the majority of ethnoarchaeologies, especially of the post-processual school, used anthropological methodologies to gather information from living people about their own interpretations of meanings and connotations of their material culture (Moore 1986; Tilley 1996; Fewster 2007; Parker-Pearson and Ramilisonina 1998). This in itself was a particularly post-processual concern with the issue of subjectivity, unlike processual ethnoarchaeologies which had been necessarily reductionistic in order to produce the laws needed for analogy. By contrast, many early forms of modern material culture studies and later ones use a specifically archaeological methodology, studying the contemporary period as though it were an archaeological site, devoid of human subject. By doing so the practitioner of modern material culture studies and archaeologies of the historical and contemporary past tends to set him- or herself up as the sole objective observer and commentator, despite the potential presence of other living voices.

2.2 AMERICAN PROCESSUAL ETHNOARCHAEOLOGY 1960S–1980S

The paradigm by which Binford was much influenced was logical positivism. He sought to produce a Middle Range Theory using the hypothetico-deductive method to produce general laws of human behaviour and material culture which could be tested to achieve a quantifiable statement of truth with regard to their accuracy as explanations of the material culture of the past.

> It is argued that as a scientist one does not justifiably employ analogies to ethnographic observations for the 'interpretation' of archaeological data. Instead, analogies should be documented and used as the basis for offering a postulate as to the relationship between archaeological forms and their behavioural context in the past. Such a postulate should then serve as the foundation of a series of deductively drawn hypotheses which, on testing, can refute or tend to confirm the postulate offered. (Binford 1972: 33)

Ethnoarchaeology—the observation and recording of living human behaviour and the material cultural patterning it produces, such that analogy could be made to the past— was the methodological tool central to the first stages of Binford's Middle Range Theory. Binford argued that archaeologists should carry out the ethnographic part of the study for themselves, and not simply rely on other people's written ethnographies. He was convinced that the ethnoarchaeologist should remain an outside observer of human behaviour and its material consequence because as such he or she had an observational advantage in understanding people's relationships with their material world that the people themselves were not able to see, being too embedded in their own lives. Thus for Binford, his ethnoarchaeological studies were deliberately reductionistic. Binford is probably best known for his ethnoarchaeological study of the Nunamiut (Binford 1978) and his use of the ideas generated from that study to make cross-cultural analogy to the Mousterian of France (Binford 1973). Binford himself had carried out what might in retrospect be regarded as an archaeology of the contemporary past, in terms of its methodology, if not its aim. During his fieldwork with the Nunamiut he paid particular attention to the observation and recording of one particular house—Palangana's house—at Tulugak Lake, Alaska (Binford 1983: 176–84) while it was occupied. When Palangana's house was abandoned, as a test of his own theories, Binford excavated it to see if he could accurately reconstruct the gender relationships of the space he had observed using only the archaeological evidence.

Binford had high expectations of ethnoarchaeology and its practitioners. Moreover Binford's methodology required two periods of original fieldwork—one among living people and another of an archaeological database. Thus for all that Lewis Binford is associated with processual ethnoarchaeology, there are few examples of studies that managed to carry through his Middle Range Theory to an effective end (cf. Yellen 1977; Gifford 1978; Schiffer 1978; Gould 1980). Problems with Binfordian ethnoarchaeology were highlighted from within the contemporary archaeological community; firstly, the search for laws of human behaviour and material culture was criticized by the culture historians (Flannery 1973: 51) and secondly, some processual archaeologists signalled their dissent from Middle Range Theory by setting up schema of analogy of their own (see Gould 1980; Yellen 1977; Gould 1980).

2.3 EARLY FORMS OF MODERN MATERIAL
CULTURE STUDIES 1970S–1980S

A third group of processual archaeologists went in a different direction altogether, being more excited by the idea of the observation of human behaviour and its correlating material dimensions in the present. In Redman's edited volume of 1973, *Research and Theory in Current Archeology*, Salwen proposed a modern material culture study of Manhattan Island, New York. His definitive framework was explicitly based on a temporal distinction: 'Once we cross the line from prehistory to history, where should we draw a new temporal boundary?... it might be argued that a site becomes the proper domain of the anthropological archaeologist as soon as the behaviour stops and as soon as the actors leave the scene!' (Salwen 1973: 154). He emphasized the difference between his proposed programme of urban research with those of his ethnoarchaeological colleagues by stating that although the archaeology of urban areas might be of use in law-making for the purpose of analogy to the past, these studies did not need to be 'justified as aids to the prehistorian' (Salwen 1973: 163). In the same volume Leone (1973: 136) argued that,

> archeology is tied to the present. Not only are all of its models derived from the present but, more to the point here, one of archeology's major roles is a function of how it is used in the present. Should not archaeology then study how it is used, how its data (i.e. material culture) are used by the present, and how material culture, when used affects the culture doing the using?

He looked at a Mormon town in Arizona, and went beyond a simple techno-environmentalist explanation for its layout by suggesting that for Mormon pioneers, proximity of dwelling was a means of facilitating the social and religious order. 'It is not just that Mormons and their religion created settlements and spatial subdivisions and made life work; Mormonism could not exist without the spatial representation and technological devices that allowed its population to exist' (Leone 1973: 149).

By 1981 it appears that early versions of modern material culture studies had developed a self-conscious status in the form of Gould and Schiffer's edited book of that year, *Modern Material Culture: The Archeology of Us*. It would appear that the rationale at that time for defining modern material culture studies was a temporal, or chronological one, i.e. that they were studies of the material culture of the present or recent past. There were some typically processual papers in that volume (for example, Gould 1981). However, there were also some papers in the volume that were remarkably forward looking, given the context in which they were produced. For example, Leone (1981) demonstrated that the presentation of the past cannot be separated from the politics of the present, by observing inherent racism in the activities of heritage presentation at the open air museum of Colonial Williamsburg in Virginia. In a similarly non-processual vein, Bath (1981) attempted to map the underlying order of categorization in a modern supermarket using structuralist principles. Finally, Rothschild (1981) introduced to the volume the non-processual concept of human choice, or aesthetic preference being a determinant of coin distribution that overrode functionality (Rothschild 1981: 180). Despite the potential turn in the tide demonstrated by these three studies—all using new concepts in the US processual context—there were other chapters in the volume that demonstrated classically processual methodologies, derived from Binfordian ethnoarchaeologies. Rathje (1981) took the extreme processual position with regard to reductionism. He had this to say about the role of informants' testimonies:

> their [i.e. that of modern material culture studies] contribution to traditional archaeological interests has yet to be demonstrated, perhaps because of the tempting sirens archaeologists find waiting in modern settings to lure them into other pursuits. The first bait that subverts archaeologists is encountering living informants. With the potential to talk to people comes an interest in what peoples say, in 'meanings and values'. (Rathje 1981: 55).

He called the archaeologists' attempt to elucidate belief systems in material culture 'mentalist archaeology', and described it as, '[h]eady stuff…for an archaeologist to attempt' (Rathje 1981: 56) Little did Rathje know that in the following year a book would be published on post-processual theory in ethnoarchaeology in Britain that would positively encourage archaeologists to be tempted by 'meaning' and 'value' in material culture. Moreover, it would lay the foundation for British post-processual ethnoarchaeologists to actively seek out those 'tempting sirens', the living informants that have become central to the subdiscipline today.

2.4 BRITISH POST-PROCESSUAL ETHNOARCHAEOLOGY 1980S–PRESENT DAY (2011)

Post-processual ethnoarchaeologies differed significantly in both methodology and ontology from their processual predecessors. In 1982 Hodder expressed his reservations about Binfordian ethnoarchaeology and offered an alternative, 'softer' approach to the use of ethnographic data in archaeology. He defined ethnoarchaeology as 'the collection of original ethnographic data in order to aid archaeological interpretation' (Hodder 1982: 28). By 1985 the tide against processual ethnoarchaeology was visibly turning (Wylie 1985). Firstly, in terms of method, the concern to prove anything about the past was not an aim, thus few post-processual archaeologies sought to produce general laws of human behaviour and material culture from their studies of the present. Secondly, because of the emphasis in post-processualism as a whole on hermeneutics, as well as subjectivity (Shanks and Tilley 1987a, 1987b) post-processual ethnoarchaeologies rejected the processual method whereby the observer is set up as the sole interpreter of material culture vis-à-vis material culture. Thus informants were now frequently, if not overwhelmingly, consulted with regard to their own interpretations of the intrinsic meaning of their material culture.

But perhaps the greatest influence on post-processual etshnoarchaeology came from anthropological archaeology. In 1986 Henrietta Moore studied the Marakwet of Kenya, who have a strong sexual division of labour in which men keep goats and women are responsible for cereal agriculture. Moore recorded the physical structures of Marakwet compounds and showed that the two houses on them, one for males and the other for females, are interpreted by the Marakwet as symbolic of the binary oppositions between men and women (Moore 1986: 45 (fig. 18)). The physical mapping of social space by the Marakwet extends to the deposition of waste—ash, goat dung, and chaff—whereby each is carefully deposited in areas outside the compound separate from one another but related to the positions of the female and male houses. Moore argued that: 'the most common reason the Endo [Marakwet] give for not mixing ash, animal dung and chaff is the relationship between refuse and burial: "Not good to mix *takataka* [rubbish] because when a woman dies she should be buried where the chaff is, because her work is to dig and remove the chaff... [o]ld men should be buried near the goat dung"' (Moore 1986: 102). Thus Moore argued that material culture was created according to social meaning and this meaning was imbued with issues of gender, power, and time. Moreover the meaning of the material culture of the Marakwet was gleaned, not by herself, as scientist-observer, but rather by consulting the subjects of the study themselves. She actively sought the insider's, or the emic view. Similarly, in 1998, in order to aid his interpretation of Stonehenge, England, Mike Parker Pearson carried out ethnoarchaeological research in Madagascar with Ramilisonina, an archaeologist from the University of Antananarivo. Although their ultimate aim was to make a cross cultural generalization separated by geography and time, law-like statements linking human action and material culture were eschewed and instead Parker Pearson and Ramilisonina (1998) made an analogy of materiality. This was a direct influence from modern material culture studies. Although there are perhaps criticisms that could be made of some of the interpretations (see Barrett and Fewster 1998), the paper is seminal in that it plays out the struggle between the archaeologists' desire to use ethnoarchaeology as an interpretive tool but not to get caught up in processual epistemology.

By 2001 ethnoarchaeology was sufficiently confident that it would survive as a subdiscipline under the new paradigm. This is demonstrated in Nic David and Carol Kramer's (2001) book *Ethnoarchaeology in Action*. The theoretical approaches discussed in the book included both American processualism and the British post-processualism of the 1980s and 1990s and the aim was synthesis. By this time ethnoarchaeologists were also beginning to realize that they could use their methodologies to understand the present, and the possible future, without necessarily having to make ethnoarchaeological fieldwork purely for the purposes of analogy. It was within this intellectual context that one of my own ethnoarchaeological studies (Fewster 2007) was set. Fieldwork was undertaken in Spain to explore why people in the village of Solosancho had differential knowledge of, and regard for, the medieval and Iron Age remains in their locality. During interviews with informants, and the observation of their physical engagement with the artefacts and architectures of their own past, I came to understand that it was linked to the pervasive rural narrative of anxiety about increasing social inequality in the village as a result of mechanization, rural–urban migration, and misguided agricultural policy in Spain. Although this research *looks* like a modern material culture study, and it certainly benefited from developments in modern material culture studies, I call it ethnoarchaeological because I alone would not have been able to interpret the action of people in the present with regard to their material culture without listening to the testimonies of those people themselves. This is a critical difference between the methodology of ethnoarchaeology and the archaeological methodologies of modern material culture studies. It is a methodological difference which has important ethical implications with regard to the means by which the subjects of study are represented. It gives the researcher more *clues* about the significance of modern material culture to people, which act as insights to narrative linking material culture to wider processes of social life and social change, and in that sense it facilitates an archaeology of practice. It does not set the scientist-observer (myself) up as the sole interpreter of modern material culture, as though it were an empty archaeological site, but it acknowledges the various accounts of the users of that material culture. It is a means by which multivocality, as far as is possible, may be achieved. For example, a retired farmer, José Martín Muñoz, showed me his collection of 'old stuff' and spoke while he played with the leather braids on an old ploughing yoke, designed to keep the flies out of the oxen's eyes. He said,

> each farmer braided these tassles for his own plough team, and he decorated them individually using different colours and knots. It was a source of great pride and some competition...farmers cosseted their plough oxen, they loved them, and they loved showing them off. Now the tractor has changed all that. Whoever felt enough love for a tractor to decorate it? It has destroyed so much of what we valued. (José Martín Muñoz recorded in Fewster 2007: 96)

It is at this point of *frisson*, this moment of co-presence, this fingering of braided tassles with thick old farmer's fingers, that I feel closest to an understanding of the concerns of a human being other than myself, and archaeologies of the contemporary past that adhere to a predominantly archaeological methodology (Rathje 1978, 1981; Buchli and Lucas 2001c; Graves-Brown 2007; Harrison and Schofield 2010) could benefit from this methodological privilege (see Harrison 2006).

2.5 Modern Material Culture Studies and Archaeologies of the Recent and Historical Past 1980–2000

Although there was a lot of work done around issues of cultural identity which dealt with the contemporary past (e.g. Shennan 1994; Kohl and Fawcett 1995), between 1980 and 2000 there was a hiatus in formal (university-based) modern material culture studies, whilst there was a growing body of eclectic studies on the margins of the discipline—in art, performance, wreckology, popular and commercial activity—by which people were finding their own ways of engaging with the material culture of the present and recent and historical past. Eventually, it could be argued that it was these various studies that pushed archaeologists into formulating an academic route through which they could channel some of these ideas themselves. For example, as Holtorf (2007) later describes, archaeology was becoming popularized outside of academia in literature, film, computer games, and heritage theme parks to a degree that it became obvious that people's archaeological knowledge and experience of archaeology was dominated by sources other than the university, and that these sources had little desire to engage professional archaeologists in consultation of 'authenticity' or 'truth' (see also Graves-Brown, this volume; Holtorf, this volume). Holtorf realized early on that if archaeologists did not find a way of understanding the ways that people were engaging with the material culture of the present (see also Holtorf 2011) they would become obsolete. At around the same time, artists and performers appeared to be having much more fun with modern material culture than were professional archaeologists; examples of this include Richard Long's (2002) *Walking the Line* and Cliff McLucas's (2000)

'Ten Feet and Three Quarters of an Inch of Theatre', both of which explored the recounting of narrative through movement and performance, materiality and space.

2.6 Modern Material Culture Studies and Archaeologies of the Recent and Historical Past 2000–Present Day (2011)

Thus at the time ethnoarchaeology was going through a major overhaul, both epistemological and ontological, modern material culture studies experienced a hiatus of development of some two decades and were not adopted formally into British universities until the noughties, when they made a fully self-conscious resurgence with the publication of two edited volumes (Graves-Brown 2000a; Buchli and Lucas 2001a). This meant that early forms of modern material culture studies were not subject to the same degree of challenge as when the twenty years of theoretical battles saw processual ethnoarchaeology replaced by post-processual ethnoarchaeologies. The result is that while modern material culture studies in the noughties are situated within eclectic post-processual ontologies (popular culture, embodiment, multivocality, performance, storytelling, etc.) their methodologies (epistemologies) have changed little since the eighties.

There is no doubt that some modern material culture studies have contributed greatly to the discipline despite this. Some of the very best modern material culture studies are guided by the sociology of modern life and appear to be truly pushing the boundaries of sociological theory aiding our understanding of the modern human condition in a way that only a modern material culture study could. Graves-Brown studies the modern phenomenon of the privatization of experience in a series of case studies (2000b, 2009, 2011). Another example of this is Holtorf's (2011) exploration of the 'experience economy' as an aspect of modernity. Others are using material culture studies to explore new ways of telling history. Piccini's (2011) extraordinary micro road movie retells parts of the history of Bristol and links the story to the present by using the materiality of the road itself as a narrative device. It is also clear that modern material culture studies and archaeologies of the contemporary and recent past have added immensely to the archaeologist's understanding of the dualistic nature of human action and material culture with 'an awareness that material culture is not passive and reflective but can act back upon us in unexpected ways' (Buchli and Lucas 2001b: 5; see also Latour 2000; Graves-Brown 2007).

2.7 Multivocality and the Archaeology of Us?

However, there are two interrelated problems that stem from the fact that modern material culture studies and archaeologies of the contemporary and recent past did not go through the same post-processual ring of fire that ethnoarchaeology did. Many modern material culture studies characterize their work as being 'the archaeology of us' (Gould and Schiffer 1981), while at the same time stressing a commitment to multivocality. *Us* is defined variously in socio-economic terms as modernity, post-modernity, after modernity (Harrison and Schofield 2010), Capitalism, Consumerism, or mass consumption—of which it surely cannot be suggested that all people have the same material experience. Harrison and Schofield (2010: 3) qualify the term 'after modernity' as being a deliberate choice because it is a 'non-period' and homogeneity cannot be assumed, but then define themselves in terms of time. They argue that, 'the "contemporary" period cannot be fixed to a precise chronological bracket, and unusually it might be best to see this as a period defined in reverse, from the present day back to a time when the past seems (subjectively) no longer recent (2010–1950, as opposed to the more conventional form of 1950–2010)' (Harrison and Schofield 2010: 5). The problem of definition extends into a problem of methodology. For example, when Harrison and Schofield argued that they were capable of interpreting the material culture of the present...'[b]ecause we have lived and experienced this period [2010–1950]' (Harrison and Schofield 2010: 5) and Buchli and Lucas (2001b) argued that archaeological methods of the studies of contemporary material culture could render 'the familiar unfamiliar' (Buchli and Lucas 2001b: 9), they denied the voices of their subjects by leaving no epistemological mechanism that would allow multivocality to be 'known'. For example, when Buchli and Lucas (2001c) excavated a recently abandoned British council house they made a strong case for adopting an archaeological methodology. 'What characterises this study above all, is the archaeological context in which the work was done; there were no informants—just like an archaeological site, the people had left, leaving only their material culture behind' (Buchli and Lucas 2001c: 159). In the absence of informants, Buchli and Lucas categorized the material culture in the house on 'broad consumption divisions, such as one might find in a department store' (Buchli and Lucas 2001c: 158). This assumes that Buchli and Lucas's experience of a department store is the same as that of the council house tenants, and denies them the voice of their own belongings. This was an opportunity for material culture studies to display its potential for demonstrating, not assuming, the multivocality that is expressed in material goods. Buchli and Lucas are from what is, after all, the specific material cultural background of academe and they cannot simply assume an a priori familiarity with their subjects' material culture simply because of a putative shared experience of 'modernity', 'consumerism', or time line.

If 'us' is to be defined implicitly as a shared experience of material culture, who does 'us' include, and who is excluded? Are only those icons of heteronormativity—white, male, educated adults—to be included? (Dowson 2009). What about blind people, children, mothers with prams, old men? Are certain mental states such as autism and psychosis to be excluded? As Williams and Costall (2000) note: 'the difficulties children with autism have in dealing with and making sense of objects are a significant problem for themselves and their caregivers, not least because their idiosyncratic way of relating to objects sets them apart from other people' (Williams and Costall 2000: 108). This raises serious ethical issues. As Harrison and Schofield argue: 'Clearly, when dealing with recent history, the ethical questions that should be a part of all archaeological practice...become even more urgent' (Harrison and Schofield 2010:15; see also Moshenska 2008).

2.8 CONCLUSION

In the period since the first modern material culture studies were published in the 1970s and 1980s, ethnoarchaeology has undergone major epistemological changes in Britain as a result of the post-processual critique. Over the same time period there was a general absence of developmental work in modern material culture studies in the university context (other than the body of work on cultural identity, mentioned above) until Paul Graves-Brown's (2000a) and Buchli and Lucas's (2001a) books were published. Both claimed vague historical links to the early American school of modern material culture studies (1970–80). Perhaps because of the two-decade gap in its development, at a crucial time in the history of the discipline, modern material culture studies missed out on some of the theoretical developments made in post-processual ethnoarchaeology in Britain. It is this that perhaps explains the current differences in modern material culture studies and post-processual ethnoarchaeology.

Thus it is worth investigating Harrison and Schofield's (2010: 30) statement that

> the precedents for the archaeology of the contemporary past were developed out of early ethnoarchaeological studies in the US in the 1970s and early 1980s' and that the development of the subdiscipline saw simply a 'significant shift in orientation away from the ethnoarchaeological focus of most of the earlier work on the archaeology of the contemporary past towards a more specific focus on contemporary life. (Harrison and Schofield 2010: 30)

A more nuanced history of the intellectual roots of the archaeology of the contemporary past would benefit this emergent field, highlighting perhaps that it embraced ethnoarchaeology at its processual worst, and veered away from it at its post processual best. Thus many archaeologies of the contemporary past adhere to an archaeological methodology of the 1970s–1980s and remain affiliated to a concept, 'the archaeology of us' (first cited in Gould and Schiffer 1981, restated in Buchli and Lucas 2001b: 8; Harrison and Schofield 2010: 12) that perhaps hampers it in its claim to multivocality and ethical representation of subject (although see Zimmerman, this volume; Schofield 2009a, 2009c; Kiddey and Schofield 2011). Notwithstanding, some archaeologies of the contemporary past have undoubtedly pushed the boundaries of social theory and contributed greatly to our understanding of the relationships between human social behaviour and material culture. For these the subdiscipline has contributed not only to archaeology and to ethnoarchaeology, but to the social sciences as a whole.

ACKNOWLEDGEMENTS AND DEDICATION

My heartfelt thanks go to Paul Graves-Brown. The work is dedicated to the memory of Marek Zvelebil. Like everything I do, it is because of Quentin.

REFERENCES

Barrett, John C. and Fewster, Kathryn J. 1998. *Is* the Medium the Message? (Reply to Parker-Pearson and Ramilisonina 'Stonehenge for the Ancestors'). *Antiquity* 72: 847–52.

Bath, Joyce E. 1981. The Raw and the Cooked: The Material Culture of a Modern Supermarket. In *Modern Material Culture: The Archeology of Us*, ed. Richard A. Gould and Michael B. Schiffer, pp. 183–95. New York: Academic Press.

Binford, Lewis R. 1967. Smudge Pits and Hide Smoking: The Use of Analogy in Archeological Reasoning. *American Antiquity* 32: 1–12.

—— 1972. *An Archaeological Perspective*. New York: Seminar Press.

—— 1973. Interassemblage Variability: The Mousterian and the 'Functional' Argument. In *The Explanation of Culture Change: Models in Prehistory*, ed. Colin Renfrew, pp. 227–54. London: Duckworth.

—— 1978. *Nunamiut Ethnoarchaeology*. New York: Academic Press.

—— 1983. *In Pursuit of the Past*. London: Thames and Hudson.

Buchli, Victor and Lucas, Gavin (eds.). 2001a. *Archaeologies of the Contemporary Past*. London: Routledge.

—— 2001b. The Absent Present: Archaeologies of the Contemporary Past. In *Archaeologies of the Contemporary Past*, ed. Victor Buchli and Gavin Lucas, pp. 3–18. London: Routledge.

—— 2001c. The Archaeology of Alienation: A Late Twentieth-Century British Council House. In *Archaeologies of the Contemporary Past*, ed. Victor Buchli and Gavin Lucas, pp. 158–67. London: Routledge.

David, Nicolas and Kramer, Carol. 2001. *Ethnoarchaeology in Action*. Cambridge: Cambridge University Press.

Dowson, Thomas. 2009. 0053 Hrs, 12 October 1998: The Murder of Matthew Wayne Shephard: An Archaeologist's Personal Defining Moment. In *Defining Moments: Dramatic Archaeologies of the Twentieth Century*, ed. John Schofield, pp. 135–45. BAR International Series 2005. British Archaeological Reports, Oxford.

Fewster, Kathryn J. 2007. The Role of Agency and Material Culture in Remembering and Forgetting: An Ethnoarchaeological Case Study from Central Spain. *Journal of Mediterranean Archaeology* 20: 89–114.

Flannery, Kent V. 1973. Archeology with a Capital 'S'. In *Research and Theory in Current Archeology*, ed. C. Redman, pp. 47–58. New York: John Wiley and Sons.

Gifford, Diane P. 1978. Ethnoarchaeological Observations of Natural Processes Affecting Cultural Materials. In *Explorations in Ethnoarchaeology*, ed. Richard A. Gould, pp. 77–102. Albuquerque: University of New Mexico Press.

Gould, Richard A. 1980. *Living Archaeology*. Cambridge: Cambridge University Press.

——1981. Brandon Revisited: A New Look at Old Technology. In *Modern Material Culture: The Archaeology of Us*, ed. Richard A. Gould and Michael B. Schiffer, pp. 269–81. New York: Academic Press.

Gould, Richard A. and Schiffer, Michael B. (eds.). 1981 *Modern Material Culture: The Archeology of Us*. New York: Academic Press.

Graves-Brown, Paul M. (ed.). 2000a. *Matter, Materiality and Modern Culture*. London: Routledge.

—— 2000b. Always Crashing in the Same Car. In *Matter, Materiality and Modern Culture*, ed. Paul M. Graves-Brown, pp. 155–65. London: Routledge.

—— 2000c. Introduction. In *Matter, Materiality and Modern Culture*, ed. Paul M. Graves-Brown, pp. 1–9. London: Routledge.

—— 2007. Concrete Islands. In *Contemporary and Historical Archaeology in Theory*, ed. L. McAtackney, M. Palus, and Angela Piccini, pp. 75–81. BAR International Series 1677. British Archaeological Reports, Oxford.

—— 2009. March 1993: The Library of Babel: Origins of the World Wide Web. In *Defining Moments: Dramatic Archaeologies of the Twentieth Century*, ed. John Schofield, pp. 123–34. BAR International Series 2005. British Archaeological Reports, Oxford.

—— 2011. The Privatisation of Experience and the Archaeology of the Future. In *Contemporary Archaeologies: Excavating Now*, ed. Cornelius Holtorf and Angela Piccini, pp. 201–14. Frankfurt: Peter Lang.

Harrison, Rodney. 2006. An Artefact of Colonial Desire? Kimberly Points and the Technologies of Enchantment. *Current Anthropology* 47(1): 63–88.

Harrison, Rodney and Schofield, John. 2010. *After Modernity: Archaeological Approaches to the Contemporary Past*. Oxford: Oxford University Press.

Hodder, Ian. 1982. *The Present Past: An Introduction to Anthropology for Archaeologists*. New York: Pica Press.

Holtorf, Cornelius. 2007. *Archaeology is a Brand! The Meaning of Archaeology in Contemporary Popular Culture*. Oxford: Archaeopress.

—— 2011. Imagine This: Archaeology in the Experience Economy. In *Contemporary Archaeologies: Excavating Now*, ed. Cornelius Holtorf and Angela Piccini, pp. 47–64. Frankfurt: Peter Lang.

Holtorf, Cornelius and Piccini, Angela (eds.). 2011. *Contemporary Archaeologies: Excavating Now*. Frankfurt: Peter Lang.

Kiddey, Rachael and Schofield, John. 2011. Embrace the Margins: Adventures in Archaeology and Homelessness. *Public Archaeology* 10(1): 4–22.

Kohl, Philip L. and Fawcett, Clare (eds.). 1995. *Nationalism, Politics and the Practice of Archaeology*. Cambridge: Cambridge University Press.

Latour, Bruno. 2000. The Berlin Key or How to do Words with Things. In *Matter, Materiality and Modern Culture*, ed. Paul M. Graves-Brown, pp. 10–21. London: Routledge.

Leone, Mark P. 1973. Archeology as the Science of Technology: Mormon Town Plans and Fences. In *Research and Theory in Current Archeology*, ed. C. L. Redman, pp. 125–50. New York: John Wiley and Sons.

—— 1981. Archeology's Relationship to the Present and the Past. In *Modern Material Culture: The Archeology of Us*, ed. Richard A. Gould and Michael B. Schiffer, pp. 5–14. New York: Academic Press.

Long, Richard. 2002. *Walking the Line*. London: Thames and Hudson.

McLucas, Cliff. 2000. Ten Feet and Three Quarters of an Inch of Theatre. In *Site-Specific Art: Performance, Place and Documentation*, ed. N. Kaye, pp. 125–38. London: Routledge.

Moore, Henrietta. 1986. *Space, Text and Gender: An Anthropological Study of the Marakwet of Kenya*. Cambridge: Cambridge University Press.

Moshenska, Gabriel. 2008. Ethics and Ethical Critique in the Archaeology of Modern Conflict. *Norwegian Archaeological Review* 41(2): 159–75.

Parker Pearson, Michael and Ramilisonina. 1998. Stonehenge for the Ancestors: The Stones Pass on the Message. *Antiquity* 72: 306–26.

Piccini, Angela. 2011. Guttersnipe: A Micro Road Movie. In *Contemporary Archaeologies: Excavating Now*, ed. Cornelius Holtorf and Angela Piccini, pp. 183–200. Frankfurt: Peter Lang.

Rathje, William L. 1978 Archaeological Ethnography … Because Sometimes it is Better to Give than to Receive. In *Explorations in Ethnoarchaeology*, ed. Richard A. Gould, pp. 49–76. Albuquerque: University of New Mexico Press.

—— 1981. A Manifesto for Modern Material Culture Studies. In *Modern Material Culture: The Archeology of Us*, ed. Richard A. Gould and Michael B. Schiffer, pp. 51–6. New York: Academic Press.

Redman, Charles L. (ed.). 1973. *Research and Theory in Current Archeology*. New York: John Wiley and Sons.

Rothschild, Nan A. 1981. Pennies from Denver. In *Modern Material Culture: The Archeology of Us*, ed. Richard A. Gould and Michael B. Schiffer, pp. 161–81. New York: Academic Press.

Salwen, Bert. 1973. Archeology in Megalopolis. In *Research and Theory in Current Archeology*, ed. C. L. Redman, pp. 151–63. New York: John Wiley and Sons.

Schiffer, Michael B. 1978. Methodological Issues in Ethnoarchaeology. In *Explorations in Ethnoarchaeology*, ed. Richard A. Gould, pp. 229–48. Albuquerque: University of New Mexico Press.

Schofield, John. 2009a. *Aftermath: Readings in the Archaeology of Recent Conflict*. New York: Springer.

—— (ed.). 2009b. *Defining Moments: Dramatic Archaeologies of the Twentieth Century*. BAR International Series 2005. British Archaeological Reports, Oxford.

—— 2009c. Peace Site: An Archaeology of Protests at Greenham Common. *British Archaeology* 104: 44–9.

Shanks, Michael and Tilley, Christopher. 1987a. *Re-Constructing Archaeology: Theory and Practice*. Cambridge: Cambridge University Press.

—— 1987b. *Social Theory and Archaeology*. Cambridge: Polity Press.

Shennan, Stephen J. (ed.). 1994. *Archaeological Approaches to Cultural Identity*. London: Routledge.

Tilley, Christopher. 1996. *An Ethnography of the Neolithic: Early Prehistoric Societies in Scandinavia*. Cambridge: Cambridge University Press.

Williams, Emma and Costall, Alan 2000. Taking Things More Seriously: Psychological Theories of Autism and the Material–Social Divide. In *Matter, Materiality and Modern Culture*, ed. Paul M. Graves-Brown, pp. 97–111. London: Routledge.

Wylie, Alison. 1985. The Reaction against Analogy. In *Advances in Archaeological Method and Theory*, ed. Michael B. Schiffer, Volume 8, pp. 63–111. New York: Academic Press.

Yellen, John E. 1977. *Archaeological Approaches to the Present: Models for Reconstructing the Past*. New York: Academic Press.

CHAPTER 3

....

FORENSIC ARCHAEOLOGY

....

NATASHA POWERS AND LUCY SIBUN

3.1 INTRODUCTION: DEFINING FORENSIC ARCHAEOLOGY

....

As the younger sibling of 'traditional' archaeology, in the final decades of the twentieth century forensic archaeology passed through an accelerated process of trial, recognition, development, improvement, and standardization.

Forensic archaeology can be defined as the application of archaeological methods and theories in a criminal framework; integrating those methods and theories (and paradigms such as 'context' (Connor and Scott 2001: 5)) with those of forensic science and criminalistics. Others have defined it as 'the application of mapping and excavation skills...to recent death scenes or places where bodies have been disposed' (Skinner et al. 2003: 83; Skinner et al. 2005: 223). Whilst such cases may form a significant part of the forensic archaeologist's workload, the application of archaeological methods need not be and is not limited to the investigation of suspicious deaths (Scott and Connor 2001: 101). As González-Ruibal (2008: 249) notes, forensic archaeology is simply concerned with the documentation and reconstruction of the events of the recent past.

The term forensic archaeology is much misused and often applied to studies involving the detailed examination of human remains of any date or to the scientific dissection of evidence of past societies. Archaeologists are guilty of perpetuating this incorrect usage, using the term 'forensic' to imply enhanced scientific validity or to refer to studies where techniques which are also used in criminal cases were applied.

The time scales over which the term forensic archaeology applies vary. In England and Wales, the introduction of the Human Tissue Act 2004 effectively defined 'archaeology' as beginning 100 years ago from today, meaning that tomorrow, one more day of the past will fall within this category. This legislation gave the remains of those who died within this time frame a different legal status from those who died before. In practice, a cut-off point of 75 years is usually applied to human remains.

Archaeology is a multidisciplinary subject drawing together the arts and sciences (e.g. geophysics or chemical analyses of bone), adopting and adapting tools and techniques from many areas and, as such, lends itself well to the flexibility required in crime scene investigation. Perhaps more than any other archaeological subdiscipline, the forensic archaeologist creates a tangible link to the living. In fact it could be argued that if they have not done so then they have failed in their task. Whilst their work may not be widely publicized, many high-profile cases have drawn upon the skills of an archaeologist. The skills of archaeologists in interpreting the fluidity of processes and the changes which occur to a site over time have been noted as of particular benefit when excavating mass graves (Skinner et al. 2003: 83; Skinner et al. 2005: 224).

3.2 A SHORT HISTORY OF FORENSIC ARCHAEOLOGY

The development of forensic archaeology as a profession, and its acceptance by law enforcement authorities, has taken different paths in different countries, largely influenced by the academic framework in which the subject sits. In the United States both archaeology and physical anthropology are traditionally seen as subdisciplines of anthropology. In 1972, the American Academy of Forensic Sciences (AAFS) created a Physical Anthropology section, acknowledging the place of anthropologists within the investigative team (Grisbaum and Ubelaker 2001: 3), and today, anthropologists are often approached to provide advice and expertise where decomposed or skeletonized remains are concerned (Schultz and Dupras 2008: 399). Grisbaum and Ubelaker (2001) noted that most practising forensic anthropologists were employed in universities and that the discipline had grown from the need to consult anatomy departments in matters of human skeletal variation. Although archaeological techniques were used during the Second World War to recover the dead from mass graves, it was not until the 1970s that the discipline truly emerged with those who were experts in human remains seeking to acquire archaeological skills (Schultz and Dupras 2008: 401). Body recovery usually fell to the police and concerns were raised that the methods used were compromising evidence and showed little respect to the victim (Morse et al. 1983). One of the earliest cases to be significantly helped by the investigations and careful archaeological excavation of the crime scene by archaeologists was the investigation into the death of a young man in Tennessee in 1977. His well-preserved, decapitated remains, found within a cemetery, proved to be the embalmed body of a soldier from the Civil War (Hunter 1999: 209). General acceptance of the usefulness of archaeology to criminal investigation was accepted by the 1990s (Hunter 1999: 210). However, today the American Academy of Forensic Sciences still does not have a separate section for forensic archaeology (AAFS 2010).

In the United Kingdom, where archaeology and anthropology are traditionally distinct disciplines, the police were more likely to consult with medical practitioners or pathologists when skeletalized remains were found. Although archaeological skills were used in the hunt for victims of the Moors Murderers in 1986 (Hunter et al. 1994: 758), Professor John Hunter's investigation of the death of Stephen Jennings is considered to be the first criminal case in which archaeological techniques were utilized (Davenport and Harrison 2011). Stephen was beaten to death by his father in 1962 and his remains recovered in 1988, found at the base of a partially collapsed dry stone wall. The question of whether there had been deliberate concealment of his body was determined by the careful archaeological excavation and recording of the scene, stratigraphic excavation revealing a clearly placed arrangement of stones directly over the body. The case set a legal precedent for the use of archaeological evidence (Hunter et al. 1994: 758; Hunter et al. 1996: 55–6). However, forensic archaeology did not immediately gain widespread acceptance and when the garden of a property in Cromwell Street, Gloucester, was searched for the remains of a number of young women in 1994, archaeological expertise was notably absent (Hunter et al. 1994: 758; Hunter et al. 1996: 16). In the mid-1990s, Hunter et al. identified the benefits which archaeological science (e.g. geophysics, chemical and taphonomic studies) could bring to the investigation of crime (1994: 765).

The divide between archaeology and anthropology meant that the forensic branches of each developed on somewhat different trajectories and only relatively recently was greater cohesion sought (see Black 1996: 127–8). The young age of the discipline also means that whilst some practitioners will have come through an academic route, many others, including the pioneers of the 1980s and 1990s, developed their skills 'in the field', applying the knowledge of years of archaeological experience in different historic and/or forensic circumstances to criminal investigations.

Not only has forensic archaeology in the US been developing for longer than it has in the UK, but considerably more murders and concealments take place there each year: rates between just 2 and 9 per cent are cited for the proportion of UK murders which involve the burial of the victim (Hunter et al. 1994: 758; Hunter et al. 2001: 173).

Elsewhere in the world, forensic archaeology has been adopted to various degrees and at varied rates. The Netherlands Forensic Institute (NFI) maintains a state-funded forensic archaeological presence (Groen and de Leeuwe 2011). Most European countries have not followed this lead, though law enforcement agencies may work with external specialists (M. Groen pers. comm). Donlon (2008: 102) notes that the development of forensic anthropology and archaeology has been slow in Australia: of 153 anthropological cases in New South Wales from 1992 to 2006, just 5 per cent involved archaeologists (for a history of the development of forensic archaeology in Australia, see Blau 2004). In contrast, following a kidnapping in Costa Rica an anonymous tip-off identified where the victim was buried. Despite archaeologists having been involved in only a few previous cases, the police determined from the outset that an archaeologist would lead the search (in consultation with the Crime Scene Manager (CSM)) (Congram 2008: 793).

Clearly, mass conflict has provided a proving ground for the use of numerous archaeological techniques and methodological development has occurred from necessity (Gould, this volume). The establishment of national and international human rights organizations and legal institutions increased the necessity to employ archaeological specialists within the investigation of atrocities and to facilitate the identification of the victims (Mark 2010). Methodological advances were made as the result of work following the Balkan conflict. Yet excavations of mass graves sometimes lead to neither prosecution nor victim identification (Mark 2010: 277), simply enabling a process of repatriation and reinclusion of the marginalized group, and are therefore somewhat different from the work carried out for 'individual' criminal cases.

3.3 The Role of the Forensic Archaeologist

The majority of forensic work carried out by archaeologists involves rapidly identifying that a potential crime scene is non-suspicious (e.g. Duhig 2003). Construction work may uncover previously unknown (or unknown to the developer) cemetery sites or ancient burials, whilst many stray finds of bone can be rapidly determined to be animal in origin. The determination of the origin of bone and bone fragments should be within the range of skills of the forensic archaeologist. However, some skeletal elements appear morphologically similar to humans, particularly those of primates and bears. The latter presents a greater problem to those working in North America, but archaeological finds of bear bone are not uncommon in Britain (Hammon 2010). Importantly, the archaeologist generally works within a multidisciplinary team that will include experts in human and faunal osteology (as well as artefact specialists) and which will be able to identify when it is appropriate to call upon the expertise of the forensic anthropologist.

When human remains were found encased within concrete on a building site in Southwark in 2002, suspicions were, unsurprisingly, raised. Archaeological attendance at the site quickly established that the remains were of numerous adults and children, mixed with animal bone reflecting domestic waste. Visual examination of the stratigraphic relationships and an understanding of the construction process made it clear that the remains had been placed within the base of a foundation trench sometime in the 1960s and concrete poured directly onto this. Whilst this action indicated an attempt to hide the human remains, they were clearly both skeletalized and disarticulated when they entered the trench and the close proximity of a disused parish cemetery provided a reasonable explanation for their origin.

Forensic archaeologists may assist the criminal investigation without putting a trowel in the ground. Archaeologists are well-versed in the need to undertake historical and background research into an area prior to commencing a search or excavation. In the UK, the planning process specifically introduced a phase of work (often known as the desk-based assessment) whereby historic maps are scrutinized and documentary evidence for landscape change investigated. In a forensic search, the archaeologist must take account of geological and topographic information which may influence the selection of search areas or the survival of deposits and evidence within them. Contemporary and historic maps and aerial photographs may all be consulted to ensure that the forensic archaeologist is aware of archaeologically sensitive areas and historic burial grounds and that they can identify features that have the potential to reduce the visibility of areas of interest.

Archaeologists are trained to recognize areas of disturbance and the presence of cut features within a landscape and archaeological skills ('fieldcraft') can be invaluable in a police search. The forensic archaeologist needs to have a sound understanding of archaeological formation processes; the way in which archaeological deposits are created and subsequently change up to the point of excavation. This requirement includes understanding the way in which the action of geological and environmental forces (wind, water, animal activity, etc.) shapes deposits. Only with this knowledge can the archaeologist determine those processes which result from human intervention and indicate actions relating to any supposed crime. An understanding of taphonomic processes is similarly vital as it can ensure differentiation between damage which has occurred after deposition and changes which indicate processes

FIGURE 3.1 Vegetational changes indicating the presence of long disused flower beds in a municipal park which were otherwise invisible in the turf. The same principle can be used to identify areas of disturbance in criminal cases (photograph: Natasha Powers)

which took place before the concealment of evidence. Visual survey of the ground surface to examine changes in vegetational cover and so forth (Figure 3.1), together with topographical survey consisting of the systematic measurement and location of changes in the ground surface to create a plan or three-dimensional reconstruction of an area of landscape, can identify areas where victims or evidence may have been concealed and by the same token, and given the correct parameters, can enable large areas to be dismissed from further investigation.

Before commencing a search, the forensic archaeologist must assist in the production of a specialist search strategy compatible with the requirements of the CSM. Using the information provided by the investigative team and their own research, the forensic archaeologist should identify areas which are of high priority and those with a lower priority, so that resources can be deployed effectively (Powers and Sibun 2011: 12). Such considerations are of particular importance when there may be only a short time in which to locate vital evidence.

Non-destructive search methods are the ideal in both the hunt for historic remains and the search for clandestine burials, and for many years archaeology has looked to the application of shallow geophysical prospection techniques to assist the search for buried features. In the UK, geophysical methods have been used with some success in criminal cases. In 2007, ground penetrating radar (GPR) was used successfully to identify the location of a grave in the back garden of a house formerly owned by serial killer Peter Tobin. The non-invasive nature of this method meant that once an anomaly had been identified, archaeologists could carefully investigate and excavate the undisturbed grave, having been provided with information on the location, dimensions, and depth of the feature. Geophysical survey has been extensively used in the search for missing victims of the sectarian conflict in Ireland

(C. Graham, pers. comm.) (Figure 3.2). On the back of such success, and because GPR can be relatively easily set up and utilized (though interpretation is difficult), some police forces have sought to bring such skills 'in-house'. Regardless, forensic archaeologists are also instrumental in the academic and research development of this field. Scientific experiments led by archaeologists in the UK and the Netherlands have used the burial of pigs to examine the effects of the method of concealment, temperature, depth of burial, etc. on the ability to locate a clandestine grave (Hunter et al. 2001: 174). Researchers in the US have conducted similar experiments to evaluate the usefulness of GPR (Schultz et al. 2006; Schultz 2008). Experimental work has also shown that geophysical techniques are highly effective in locating other forms of buried evidence such as caches of firearms (Rezos et al. 2011).

Although locating and recovering buried remains forms a significant part of forensic archaeologists' workloads, they may also be called upon to assist in the recovery of surface remains where the body has become partially and naturally buried through time, for example by many seasons of leaf-fall, or when the remains are partially or completely decomposed and have been scattered by animals. Here, an understanding of the taphonomic processes associated with the body may aid the interpretation of the scene and help determine whether a body was dumped, whether concealment was deliberate, and when deposition occurred. To this end, the ability to produce an accurate scale plan of the scene with relative speed—a basic archaeological skill—is extremely useful. Not only can it help with the interpretation of the scene in question but it may also provide data for future cases. As yet there is a scarcity of comparative information available to guide the search team as to how extensive a search area should be in relation to the time scales involved, or because of animal behaviour patterns.

FIGURE 3.2 Ground penetrating radar (GPR) in use in the search for missing persons in Northern Ireland (reproduced with permission from Stratascan)

Excavation in forensic archaeology applies the principles of stratigraphy in microcosm. Whereas traditional archaeological disciplines look at the formation of features and deposits over years, decades, or eras, the forensic archaeologist may be faced with the unpicking of events which took minutes (see Edgeworth, this volume). The interval between the death and burial of an individual, the degree of planning and forethought evident in actions reflected in the archaeological record can mean the difference between an arrest for murder or manslaughter and conviction or acquittal. Extrapolating temporal relationships from physical evidence is vital, and since archaeological excavation is destructive, compiling clear and detailed records which will enable the reconstruction of the processes used during an investigation is of the utmost importance.

Both positive and negative discoveries need to be recorded and the forensic archaeologist must report previously unknown archaeological (non-suspicious) findings to the appropriate monitoring authorities (with the permission of the Senior Investigating officer (SIO)) and advise on the legal requirements pertaining to the discovery of historic human remains.

During a forensic excavation, the archaeologist must constantly evaluate and reconsider the most appropriate methods to apply to the particular set of parameters presented. There has been some discussion of techniques in the academic and professional literature and practitioners may have their preferred working methods, for example excavation in spits is frequently and successfully used (Hunter 1999: 214).

The search for human remains believed to have been concealed in the back garden of a London property some fifty years previously required the full excavation of a significant depth of garden soil within which no cut features could be seen due to repeated reworking. The garden was therefore divided into 1.5 metre grid squares and each square was hand dug in spits. The soil from each square was sieved and retained separately until the area could be established to be free from human remains and other evidence. This enabled the rapid but careful evaluation of the garden and the reduction of the area down to the level at which cut features became visible in the subsoil. A similar method for excavation of discreet features has been described by Ruffell et al. (2009).

In many circumstances, single context recording provides the most robust method for disentangling the events of the recent past: whilst the spit or grid square is in effect an arbitrary division, the archaeological context has intrinsic interpretive value. As Skinner et al. (2003: 84, 86) noted, the contextual information at a scene may provide information on the events directly surrounding a death, and as such the *in situ* recording of physical remains and their relationships is vital as such 'non-material' evidence is destroyed by excavation.

Excavation methods cannot be prescriptive, as the circumstances of excavation and the type and nature of the evidence to be retrieved are so varied. Even within the investigation of one feature it may be necessary to adapt and alter the methodological approach for forensic, archaeological, or practical reasons: the effective retrieval of evidence may require the removal of one side of a clandestine grave or the extension of a feature to create a working platform (Hunter 1996: 50; Ruffell 2009: e13).

The overriding aims of all such work are to excavate and record in such a way that the stratigraphic integrity of the scene can be maintained, the recovery of evidence maximized, and details of the scene reproduced through written, drawn, and photographic records (Powers and Sibun 2011: 16). The archaeologist may also provide advice to the SIO and CSM on taking and retaining samples, when and what to photograph, whether to retain the spoil from an excavated feature, and how recovered materials should be packaged and stored to ensure they do not degrade. Wet or dry-sieving of spoil may be employed to ensure that even the smallest items of evidence are recovered.

In 2001, archaeologists were asked to assist with a case involving a woman who was reportedly killed by her husband and her body subsequently burnt on a bonfire. The archaeological work involved the systematic dry sieving of a large mound of, mostly burnt, material. The lengthy process uncovered, amongst other things, a finger ring and limited quantities of burnt human bone, but enough for an expert to identify the remains as adult and female.

3.4 FORENSIC ARCHAEOLOGY VS. TRADITIONAL ARCHAEOLOGY

Whilst the archaeology of the crime scene falls within the framework of 'supermodernity' (González-Ruibal 2008: 248), working within a legal framework separates forensic archaeology from traditional, theoretical, and political archaeological dialogues. Forensic archaeology has been criticized for transferring archaeological methods to the crime scene without a proper appreciation of the theoretical basis behind them, adhering to inappropriate methods, and unnecessarily excluding others (Connor and Scott 2001: 1).

All archaeologists 'document the remains of the past in the present' (Holtorf 2008: 266), but whilst 'processing a crime scene is a destructive process akin to excavating an archaeological site' (Schultz and Dupras 2008: 403), and forensic archaeology has much in common with the investigation of the more distant past, it is subject to far greater scrutiny and review. Issues which might be desirable in traditional archaeology are vital when applied in the forensic sphere. Equally, whilst archaeology seeks to contextualize the events under excavation (González-Ruibal 2008: 249), the forensic archaeologist must focus objectively on the documentation of the deposits and objects within a search area or crime scene; their role is to provide data and interpretations which can add to the information available to the investigative team. The ethical considerations of working with human remains, much debated in archaeological circles, are increased when working with the recent dead (Davenport and Harrison 2011: 177). Whilst traditional archaeology seeks to identify, engage with, and understand the various debates which this emotive subject raises, when working in the forensic sphere, a level of professional, emotional detachment is required.

The forensic archaeologist must actively maintain their professional expertise, desirable in all professions and a move supported in traditional archaeology by organizations such as the Institute for Archaeologists (IfA), but essential where the archaeologist's level of expertise is open to challenge in court. Keeping up to date with both archaeological and legal developments and maintaining a broad awareness of the work of other related specialisms also ensures that the forensic archaeologist can provide advice to the investigative team and, importantly, that their work will not compromise the recovery of other forms of evidence (Figure 3.3). The forensic archaeologist must also have an understanding of the specific national legal framework within which their work sits.

FIGURE 3.3 A forensic archaeologist excavates a clandestine grave site (reproduced with permission from Sussex Police)

Theorizing from sometimes limited data is encouraged in traditional archaeological excavation, indeed the discipline thrives because of this. In forensic archaeology such speculation is inappropriate (Crist 2001: 46). Steele (2008: 417) noted how, in applying archaeological techniques in the forensic sphere, archaeologists have had to examine archaeological theory and method from a different perspective, whilst Skinner et al. (2005: 224) outlined that the different theoretical frameworks in which anthropologists and archaeologists were positioned led to differing foci when examining mass graves (the body vs. the formation processes). It could be argued that on a practical level, detachment from such discussions is essential in forensic archaeology. The forensic archaeologist has failed if they applied selective collection to political or other ends or varied recording methods based on preconceived ideas of the nature of the crime or guilt of a suspect. Quite simply, it is the duty of the forensic archaeologist to record and recover all possible information from the scene or search area (Steele 2008: 421). Ensuring an apolitical stance is essential, as is objective collection and recording. The sequential deposition of material is a process devoid of imposed meaning and it is only in interpretation of this evidence that a subjective viewpoint should be expected. The forensic archaeologist will interpret based on their own experience and knowledge, their position clearly outlined to the jury by a statement which includes information on their background.

Although methodological discussions do occur, their scope is limited by the absence of published, comparative reports, since the publication of written work is not possible whilst investigations and subsequent court cases are underway, and may not be desirable for professional or ethical reasons. This limits the ability to disseminate information on the techniques employed (Steele 2008: 417, 419). Nonetheless, various authors have recommended techniques for dealing with certain types of clandestine grave (e.g. Hunter et al. 1996). The forensic archaeologist must ensure each interpretation is supported by appropriate evidence and the integrity of that evidence is paramount. To this end, a chain of custody must be documented and followed. It is also essential that all practical measures are taken to avoid cross-contamination between sites. Tools must be cleaned or disposed of, and equipment maintained to recognized standards. In some cases, items of equipment used on the scene may be exhibited (collected as evidence) to enable the elimination of materials such as brush fibres or features such as tool marks from the subsequent enquiry.

Speed of work is vital in criminal cases, both to effectively deploy resources (e.g. write off a non-suspicious scene as quickly as possible) and in instances where a suspect may be being held for a limited time period. The date of finds or features cannot simply be assigned to a vague historic period but needs to be narrowed to the smallest possible range by the use of relative (stratigraphic and contextual) and/or absolute (e.g. radiocarbon) dating techniques. This means that, in a case where remains are discovered accidentally, it is vital that they are left *in situ* for observation so that associations with objects which carry an intrinsic date can be securely established. In the UK, the SIO or CSM has responsibility for ensuring the integrity of the crime scene and must decide on the order of priority for collection of different evidence types (e.g. archaeological and entomological) and problems of role definition and management may appear (see Duhig and Turnbull 2007). Ultimately, the forensic archaeologist is employed as an expert adviser working within the parameters set by the law enforcement agency.

Forensic archaeologists may find themselves dealing with secondary grave sites and with the recovery of evidence from unusual and unpleasant locations such as a sealed septic tank (Schultz and Dupras 2008), farmyard slurry pits (R. Janaway, pers. comm. 2011) or rubbish dumps (Scott and Connor 2001: 102). Such circumstances emphasize the need for flexibility of approach when applying archaeological techniques to crime scenes. In historic archaeology, a grave feature would be considered completely excavated once the contexts had been removed and recorded, but in the forensic sphere a cut must be investigated for toolmarks (e.g. the profile of a spade) or footprints which may themselves have significant evidential value. Projectiles such as bullets might also have penetrated the base of a clandestine grave (Hunter 1996: 51).

Once site work is completed, the resulting report requires a critical conclusions check from a suitable peer and the archaeologist must be aware of, and be prepared to openly acknowledge, their professional limitations. The reporting framework is 'judicial rather than academic' (Hunter 1999: 220), and the forensic archaeologist may appear in court as an expert witness, a potentially arduous and stressful process. In the United Kingdom and elsewhere, unused materials such as rough sketches and notes taken at the scene must be made available to the defence and so there is an increased emphasis on ensuring all field notes are accurate (Crist 2001: 45).

The meticulous archaeological work is a means to an end, ensuring maximum recovery and recording of evidence, which will then be passed on to other forensic scientists. However, the interpretation of a scene can be crucial to the investigation and the outcome of a trial. The archaeologist should be confident in their methods, results, and interpretations, and must be prepared to explain and justify these to a lay audience in an unfamiliar environment. Once in court, effective communication (also the aim of traditional archaeology) is therefore essential. In recent years, expert evidence has come under increasing scrutiny which, whilst necessary, emphasizes the need for the forensic archaeologist to be both competent in the field and confident in court. The psychological effects of carrying out such work and dealing with unpleasant and upsetting situations should not be overlooked. On a more positive note, 'the forensic archaeologist can have his or her interpretation corroborated by confession' (Hunter 1999: 220), a phenomenon otherwise limited to ethnoarchaeological contexts.

3.5 CURRENT AND FUTURE DIRECTIONS

Methods remain in continuous development, with no central text governing how the excavation of a crime scene should be approached, but as with other branches of the forensic sciences, the discipline is moving to produce clear standards, providing law enforcement agencies with a framework against which to measure the appropriateness of the archaeologist's work.

In 1999, the Council for the Regulation of Forensic Practitioners (CRFP) was formed in the United Kingdom and for the first time it was possible for those working in the field to register as archaeologists and/or anthropologists, through a process of peer review which required case-work to be scrutinized. The impetus behind the formation of the CRFP was a number of high-profile miscarriages of justice, but many felt that the scheme was unnecessarily expensive and unworkable. In 2009, the National Policing Improvement Agency stated that they would not be contributing towards the cost of registration, shortly followed by the Metropolitan Police Service. This effectively made the scheme unviable, and at the end of the financial year the Home Office withdrew financial support, leading to the closure of the CRFP. The Forensic Science Regulator (FSR) is now replacing registration with a series of professional standards documents, whilst ISOs are to be adopted in forensic science and crime scene attendance (Rennison 2011). This has led to the recent development of guidance and standards for forensic archaeologists operating in the UK (Powers and Sibun 2011). The document was followed by the formation of a special interest group within the IfA and an expert panel within this, to provide a discussion group to whom practitioners could turn for advice on (non-*sub judice*) cases. It is intended that in the future, all practising forensic archaeologists in the UK will demonstrate competency against these standards. Interestingly, during the creation of the UK standards, the major points of discussion were not methodological but procedural. It was agreed early on that there were 'many ways to skin a cat' and that what was required was a clear definition of when the cat was acceptably skinned, not prescriptive guidance on how to do the skinning.

In the UK, the relatively recent development of the subject, the fact that many practitioners work outside academic spheres, and the problems of publishing details from cases where information may be confidential or *sub judice* have, in the opinion of some authors, hampered the development of theoretical framework which could itself be used to monitor the work of the forensic archaeologist (Davenport and Harrison 2011: 177). However, a field guide for non-archaeologists has existed since 1983 (Morse et al. 1983) and the publication record includes advice on location, recovery, and numerous aspects of taphonomy (Hunter 1999: 210). Despite the increasing number of academic institutions teaching forensic archaeology, there is still little published on subjects other than the recovery of victims of conflict from mass graves (Davenport and Harrison 2011: 176). However, 'the development of forensic archaeology is a two-way exercise' (Hunter 1999: 211). Archaeologists and the police must share information and understand the frameworks in which each work. It is notable that a present trend in the UK sees expertise being taken in-house, with the use of a crime scene or search specialist who may also have archaeological skills or background, due to the financial constraints placed on forces. As recently as 2005, there was still much disagreement about whether a forensic archaeologist should form an integral part of the search and recovery team (Menez 2005).

The discipline of forensic archaeology has undergone relatively rapid development, but now, as never before, we see widespread acceptance that archaeological skills and techniques can be invaluable in the search for and recovery of criminal evidence. Each scene presents unique challenges and questions. Whilst traditional archaeological techniques may be adapted and applied within a forensic framework, there remain crucial differences, most notably in the level of scrutiny which the techniques and interpretations of the forensic archaeologist must withstand. This raises particular challenges for a discipline in which the experiment is rarely repeatable and the interpretation of deposits is often based on previous personal experience, rather than empirical evidence, leaving it open to challenge and reinterpretation. The accurate recording and documentation of both processes and observations is therefore essential to ensure that the evidence presented to a court is robust and can be explained in a clear and convincing manner. At present there are no overarching professional codes of practice for forensic archaeologists (Steele 2008: 420). International collaboration and agreed standards for practitioners will enable the profession as a whole to move forwards, particularly under circumstances which see the numbers of those regularly working in forensic archaeology (and the number of cases which they attend) remaining relatively small.

ACKNOWLEDGEMENTS

The authors wish to thank Sussex Police and Claire Graham of Stratascan for kindly providing photographs used in this chapter, and our colleagues on the IfA Forensic Archaeology Expert Panel whose discussions have helped to shape our thoughts.

REFERENCES

American Academy of Forensic Sciences. 2010. *Policy and Procedure Manual*. Colorado Springs: AAFS.

Black, S. M. 1996. Alas Poor Yorick. *Science & Justice* 36(2): 127–8.

Blau, Soren. 2004. Forensic Archaeology in Australia: Current Situations, Future Possibilities. *Australian Archaeology* 58: 11–14.

Congram, Derek R. 2008. A Clandestine Burial in Costa Rica: Prospection and Excavation. *Journal of Forensic Science* 53(4): 793–6.

Connor, Melissa and Scott, Douglas D. 2001. Paradigms and Perpetrators. *Historical Archaeology* 35(1): 1–6.

Crist, Thomas A. J. 2001. Bad to the Bone? Historical Archaeologists in the Practice of Forensic Science. *Historical Archaeology* 35(1): 39–56.

Davenport, Anna and Harrison, Karl. 2011. Swinging the Blue Lamp: The Forensic Archaeology of Contemporary Child and Animal Burial in the UK. *Mortality* 16(2): 176–90.

Donlon, Denise. 2008. Forensic Anthropology in Australia: A Brief History and Review of Casework. In *Forensic Approaches to Death, Disaster and Abuse*, ed. Marc Oxenham, pp. 97–110. Brisbane: Australian Academic Press.

Duhig, Corinne. 2003. Non-Forensic Remains: The Use of Forensic Archaeology, Anthropology and Burial Taphonomy. *Science & Justice* 43(4): 211–14.

Duhig, Corinne and Turnbull, Ron. 2007. Crime-Scene Management and Forensic Anthropology: Observation and Recommendations from the United Kingdom and International Cases. In *Forensic Archaeology and Human Rights Violations*, ed. Roxanna Ferllini, pp. 76–100. Springfield, IL: Charles C. Thomas.

González-Ruibal, Alfredo. 2008. Time to Destroy: An Archaeology of Supermodernity. *Current Anthropology* 49(2): 247–79.

Grisbaum, Gretchen A. and Ubelaker, Douglas H. 2001. An Analysis of Forensic Anthropology Cases Submitted to the Smithsonian Institution by the Federal Bureau of Investigation from 1962 to 1994. *Smithsonian Contributions to Anthropology* 45: 1–15.

Groen, Mike and de Leeuwe, Roosje. 2011. *Forensic Archaeology in the Netherlands*. The Hague: Netherlands Forensic Institute.

Hammon, Andy. 2010. The Brown Bear. In *Extinctions and Invasions: A Social History of British Fauna*, ed. Terry O'Connor and Naomi Sykes, pp. 95–103. Oxford: Windgather Press.

Holtorf, Cornelius. 2008. Comments. *Current Anthropology* 49(2): 265–6.

Hunter, John. 1999. Excavation of Modern Murder. In *The Loved Body's Corruption: Archaeological Contributions to the Study of Human Mortality*, ed. Jane Downes and Tony Pollard, pp. 209–23. Glasgow: Cruthine Press.

Hunter, John with Heron, Carol, Janaway, Robert C., Martin, Anthony L., Pollard, A. Mark, and Roberts, Charlotte A. 1994. Forensic Archaeology in Britain. *Antiquity* 68: 758–69.

Hunter, John, Roberts, Charlotte, and Martin, Anthony (eds.). 1996. *Studies in Crime: An Introduction to Forensic Archaeology*. London: Batsford.

Hunter, John, Brickley, Megan B., Bourgeois, Jean, Bouts, W., Bourguignon, L., Hubrecht, F., de Winne, J., Van Haaster, H., Hakbijl, T., de Jong, H., Smits, L., Van Wijngaarden, L. H., and Luschen, M. 2001. Forensic Archaeology, Forensic Anthropology and Human Rights in Europe. *Science & Justice* 41(3): 173–8.

Mark, James. 2010. What Remains? Anti-Communism, Forensic Archaeology and the Retelling of the National Past in Lithuania and Romania. *Past and Present* Supplement 5: 276–300.

Menez, Laura L. 2005. The Place of a Forensic Archaeologist at a Crime Scene Involving a Buried Body. *Forensic Science International* 152: 311–15.

Morse, Dan, Duncan, Jack, and Stoutamire, James. (eds.). 1983. *Handbook of Forensic Archaeology and Anthropology*. Tallahasse, FL: D. Morse.

Powers, Natasha and Sibun, Lucy. 2011. *Standards and Guidance for Forensic Archaeologists*. Reading: Institute for Archaeologists.

Rennison, Andrew. 2011 Codes of Practice and Conduct for Forensic Science Providers and Practitioners in the Criminal Justice System, Forensic Science Regulator. Available at: <http://webarchive.nationalarchives.gov.uk/+/http://www.homeoffice.gov.uk/publications/police/forensic-science-regulator1/codes-conduct-practice?view=Binary> (accessed 10 January 2012).

Rezos, Mary M., Schultz, John J., Murdock, Ronald A., and Smith, S. A. 2011. Utilising a Magnetic Locator to Search for Buried Firearms and Miscellaneous Weapons at a Controlled Research Site. *Journal of Forensic Science* 56(5): 1289–95.

Ruffell, Alastair, Donnelly, Colm, Carver, Naomi, Murphy, Eileen, Murray, Emily, and McCambridge, James. 2009. Suspect Burial Excavation Procedure: A Cautionary Tale. *Forensic Science International* 183: e11–e16.

Schultz, John J. 2008. Sequential Monitoring of Burials Containing Small Pig Cadavers Using Ground Penetrating Radar. *Journal of Forensic Science* 53(2): 279–87.

Schultz, John J. and Dupras, Tosha L. 2008. The Contribution of Forensic Archaeology to Homicide Investigations. *Homicide Studies* 12: 399–413.

Schultz, John J., Collins, M. E., and Falsetti, Anthony B. 2006. Sequential Monitoring of Burials Containing Large Pig Cadavers Using Ground Penetrating Radar. *Journal of Forensic Science* 51(3): 607–16.

Scott, Douglas D. and Connor, Melissa. 2001. The Role and Future of Archaeology in Forensic Science. *Historical Archaeology* 35(1): 101–4.

Skinner, Mark and Sterenberg, John. 2005. Turf Wars: Authority and Responsibility for the Investigation of Mass Graves. *Forensic Science International* 151: 221–32.

Skinner, Mark, Alempijevic, Djordje, and Djuric-Srejic, Marija. 2003. Guidelines for International Forensic Bio-archaeology Monitors of Mass Grave Exhumations. *Forensic Science International* 134: 81–92.

Steele, Caroline. 2008. Archaeology and the Forensic Investigation of Recent Mass Graves: Ethical Issues for a New Practice of Archaeology. *Archaeologies: Journal of the World Archaeological Congress* 4(3): 414–28.

CHAPTER 4

ANTHROPOLOGICAL APPROACHES TO CONTEMPORARY MATERIAL WORLDS

PENNY HARVEY

4.1 INTRODUCTION: THE TEMPORALITY OF CONTEMPORARY MATERIAL WORLDS

ANTHROPOLOGICAL studies of human lifeworlds reveal the many ways in which human beings struggle to harness or contain the vitality of materials, not just in their efforts to make things, but also in their attempts to make things go away. Jane Bennett refers to 'the quarantines of matter and life' that 'encourage us to ignore the vitality of matter and the lively powers of material formations' (Bennett 2010: vii). But in recent times the modern capacity to generate waste has also begun to generate concerns about the material future of the planet, taking us rapidly back to an awareness of material life—its shape, its potential, and its limits.

Mary Douglas's seminal discussion of the symbolic value of notions of cleanliness and dirt, or 'matter out of place' (Douglas 1966) has extended in more recent times to a preoccupation with environmental pollution, the global circulation of discarded materials, and the disposal of toxic waste (e.g. Fortun 2001; Redclift 1996; Rathje and Murphy 2001; Sawyer 2004; Fortun and Fortun 2005; Hawkins 2005; Gregson et al. 2010; Reno, this volume). The negotiation of value and divergent understandings of harm and of danger still feature in contemporary analyses of these material relations. However, scholars of what has become known as the 'new materialism' (Coole and Frost 2010) pay particular attention to the vibrancy of matter, to the temporal dimensions and the transformational potential of materials. The notion of 'waste' as the unwanted or unusable by-product of some other activity is, as Douglas taught us, an effect of prior categorization. Such categorizations are destabilized by the diverse modes of recycling through which waste matter is now routinely recovered, its value reconfigured, and its future managed. Contemporary concerns over our planetary ecologies,

combined with the impulse to solve the problem of widespread industrial pollution via technological means, have transformed understandings of waste futures, creating not only new
markets in waste products, but stimulating the production of new materials. At the core of
these concerns is an awareness of the vitality of matter. Indeed it is this vitality that renders
waste an issue of public concern, for so much of the waste of industrialized societies tends
to the toxic.

Archaeologists are no strangers to waste. Discarded materials are routinely recovered
and examined for what they can tell us of the world in which these things were once valued.
In the 1970s the path-breaking 'Garbage Project' grew from an archaeological interest in
discarded things, and established the significance of garbage to the study of contemporary human lifeworlds, revealing habits and patterns that were often reported differently in
interviews and surveys.[1] More recently a research programme on the 'Waste of the World'
extended these interests to anthropologists and geographers interested in the afterlife of
waste, its planetary circulations, its potential for recycling, and its toxic effects.[2] However,
it is those materials that point beyond our known human worlds that interest me, as they
introduce a central concern in contemporary anthropology, namely how to address the possibility of a disturbing alterity or sense of ontological difference. I start with waste in order
to invoke material life that exceeds semiotic analysis. My argument works with the idea that
the disturbing qualities of such materials are somewhat glossed over in current research
(within both anthropology and archaeology) that follows Ingold's call to attend to materials
and to life processes rather than to objects per se (Ingold 2007b). While acknowledging the
significance that he rightly attributes to material life, I want to retain the sense of threat that
certain objects and materials generate. Moving by way of these threatening materials I seek
to recover the focus on affect that characterized previous writing on material agency and
which animates contemporary discussions of ontological politics.

Nowhere is this sense of the threatening vitality of matter more explicit than in those studies of the disposal and circulation of nuclear waste (Gusterson 1996; Petryna 2002; Masco
2006). Here we are facing the dilemma of how to contain matter with enduring toxicity. In a
remarkable documentary, Danish film-maker Michael Madsen (2010) explores the world's
first permanent storage facility for nuclear waste that is being constructed in a place they call
Onkalo, in Finland.[3] In the film, the engineers discuss the multiple temporalities of the materials with which they are engaged, particularly the contrasts between the relative instability of
events at the earth's surface by comparison with the durable configuration of the granite deep
below which holds out the possibility of a secure medium for the storage of the nuclear waste.
Beyond this image of divergent temporalities or speeds of transformation, the film enthralls
through its evocation of a time-scale that exceeds the human imagination. It has taken one
hundred thousand years for our species to evolve; it will take another hundred thousand for
this toxic matter to decompose. Who we might have become, and what the waste material or
what our planet might have become by then, cannot be understood experientially.

This sense of matter out of time and the rescaling of the human shifts our sense of the
anthropological. Those working on climate change talk of the 'anthropocene' (Chakrabarty

[1] See <http://traumwerk.stanford.edu:3455/GarbologyOnline/Home>.
[2] See <http://www.esrc.ac.uk/my-esrc/grants/res-060-23-0007/read>.
[3] I am grateful to Juan Salazar, University of Western Sydney, for introducing me to this film and
pointing out its significance for the study of material affect.

2009; Crutzen and Stoermer 2000), the geological age in which human life came to definitively shape planetary ecosystems. And yet the force and impact of our species on the
planet is hard to grasp, and harder to control for it involves beyond-human temporal scales.
The ways in which we imagine and relate to these beyond-human temporal dimensions is
nevertheless a space of the contemporary human imaginary, particularly in the mediated
world of scientific exploration and technological innovation (Rabinow 1996; Haraway 1997;
Franklin 2007; Helmreich 2009; Edgeworth, this volume). Indeed Madsen suggests that the
preoccupation with non-human scales, materials, and life-forms is perhaps defining of our
contemporary modern human imaginary.[4]

It is thus not so much that the vitality of matter is at issue, as that the boundaries of life
itself are tangibly extending in ways that challenge the modernist distinctions between 'matter' and 'life' that Bennett invokes. Indeed recent developments at the interface of chemistry,
materials science, and electronics have seen dramatic innovations in the design of new,
'smart' materials. Such materials are now routinely produced as technological artefacts with
sensory capacities, extending the possibilities of artificial life from the electronic engineering of environments, to a reconfiguration of materials themselves (Kuchler 2008; Kuchler
and Oakley 2013).

4.2 LIVING WITH MATERIALS

Beyond current anthropological interests in technological innovations and the ways in which
the life sciences now include synthetic chemistry and informatics, we should acknowledge
that anthropologists and archaeologists have always engaged the liveliness of matter via the
preoccupations and interests of people who never assumed a world in which living beings
acted upon a passive material environment. The vibrancy of matter is hardly hot news in
either discipline—which have long held an interest in animate objects, in fetishes, and in the
relational dynamics between humans and the environments in which they live and move.
Mundane productive activities, such as farming, herding, hunting, fishing, and gathering
have always entailed a sophisticated ecological awareness, and always entangled the material,
the vital, and the spiritual in ways that appeared strange to modern ways of thinking. The
understanding of materials and artefacts as forming the very fabric of human life has been the
foundational assumption of studies of 'material culture', exemplified by the work of Miller (e.g.
1997, 2005, 2009) and his many collaborators.[5] So too Appadurai's (1988) specific interest in
the social life of things involved an exploration of how human lives are shaped by the movements of commodities and the ever fluctuating and dynamic formation of value. Both these
broad approaches pay considerable attention to the political conditions and effects of object
movements, attending to how material artefacts mediate human relations to the world.

But some have argued that this focus on artefacts detracts attention from more significant
material relations. Ingold has called on anthropologists to take materials more seriously

[4] See <http://www.intoeternitythemovie.com/synopsis/>.
[5] See Miller's website for further detail: <http://www.ucl.ac.uk/anthropology/people/academic_
staff/d_miller>. See also the *Journal of Material Culture*: <http://intl-mcu.sagepub.com> and the
material world blog: <www.materialworldblog.com> for ongoing debate in this field.

(2007a, 2007b, 2011). For Ingold materials are the stuff of life itself. He argues that human life—and thus human action—is intrinsically material in that it is embodied, and it is sustained through immersion in a material world. Material relations are basic to how we live in the world; they are the medium in and through which we live our lives. Key to this approach is the understanding that materials are themselves instrinsically relational, dynamic open structures that transform over time, with or without human intervention. This approach to the dynamic movement of matter draws on Bergsonian understandings that life is not contained in things, but manifest in movement: 'It is movement itself, wherein every organism emerges as a peculiar disturbance that interrupts the linear flow, binding it into the forms we see. So well does it feign immobility, however, that we are readily deceived into treating each "as a *thing* rather than as a *process*, forgetting that the very permanence of its form is only the outline of a movement" (Bergson 1911: 135).'[6]

In developing his argument Ingold generates an explicit critique of studies of 'material culture'. His objections to this thriving subfield of contemporary anthropology rest on the way in which the feigned immobility of things is left unquestioned. From Ingold's perspective an intellectual acceptance of (or failure to question) the bounded form of things colludes in reproducing a deceptive understanding of life itself. The focus on the circulation of objects or the symbolic value of things, he argues, tends to abstract the 'object' both from the specificity of the materials of which it is composed, and from the wider relational field in and through which both humans and things are enmeshed. Ingold's primary commitment is to express a theory of human culture (human processes of learning, of knowledge, and of skill) that does not have recourse to either an abstract (non-material) theory of mind, or a determinist view of biology. His position draws strongly from Gibson's ecological psychology (Gibson 1979). For Gibson, human perception (and by extension human learning, skill, and knowledge) is intrinsically relational, and should thus be approached via an ecological or situated understanding of human practice. Ingold develops this approach by arguing that all beings, human and non-human alike, live immersed in material worlds, and all beings have substance and engage other substances via their surface interactions. In this respect life is taken as that which is constituted in the constant interplay between media (such as air, water, earth), substances (the more or less stable material entities that constitute a world), and the surfaces through which engagement takes place.

Broadly phenomenological approaches to the study of traditional craft practice that focused on the embodied and attentive skills through which the craft practitioner engaged the material world became central to this particular anthropology of perception. The craft practitioner's attention to the 'affordances' (the material possibilities) and the resistance of matter exemplified a sense of engagement which, for Ingold, offered a counterpoint to modernist production practices reliant on abstraction and planning, and a mechanistic understanding of the relation between active human agency and a passive material world. 'Craft' itself was reconfigured in this approach away from a static notion of traditional practice to an emphasis on the relational dynamics of a practice founded on skilled attention and responsiveness to the emergent properties of materials. It is in this embodied relationship to materials that craft practice became the template or exemplar of all human learning, and ultimately for life itself. For what people learn in their dynamic and embodied engagements with the world is the specificity of their own humanity (Keller and Keller 1996; Bunn 1999,

---

6 Cited in Ingold 2011: 13.

2010; Marchand 2001, 2009; Venkatesan 2002, 2009). The insights of this approach allow for a dynamic yet situated understanding of the formation of cultural worlds. At the same time the generality of the claims suggests that these relational dynamics could and should be extended to those fields of skill and expertise more commonly associated with modern knowledge and learning that Ingold is less interested in. Modern science and craft practice tend to be construed as mutually exclusive by those who take science to exemplify a modern determination either to ignore the liveliness of matter, or to attempt to transform or tame such liveliness from the outside, rather than assuming an engaged participation in the ongoing process of the world's transformation (Ingold 2011: 8).

There are different arguments and tensions here than previously discussed with respect to studies of material culture, although once again it is the distinction between the opening of materials and the closure of objects that comes to the fore. Latourian actor-network-theory comes in for particular criticism with what Ingold sees as a predilection for the tracing of networks of engagement between fixed human and material entities rather than an appreciation of the provisional and contingent meshworks that better describe the relations between media, substance, and surface that characterize Gibsonian ecological thinking. However, those who engage more directly with the practices of science and technology have many interests and understandings in common—not least the recognition of the vitality of materials, and the importance of moving away from assumptions of material passivity.

The ground-breaking studies of historians of science (e.g. Latour 1988, or Shaffer and Shapin 1989) set out to examine precisely how it was that the hard and fast modern world of 'matters of fact' was ever established in a world of movement, process, and intrinsic relationality. Latour was fascinated by the ways in which modern scientific practice enables the abstraction and mobilization of entities such as the microbe (Latour 1988), and the development of the instruments and institutions through which such objects could be both created and replicated has been central to our understandings of the ways in which modern science has come to shape human and planetary environments (Latour 1987; Haraway 1989, 1991; Bensaude and Stengers 1996). The key point that these STS (science and technology studies) scholars draw attention to is the extent to which scientific practice, like any other, involves both sensory perception and practical engagement (see also Webmoor, this volume). Indeed the development of scientific instruments is primarily an attempt to extend rather than to simply replace human sensory capacities—to enable the scientist to make visible the imperceptible (Lynch and Woolgar 1990; Daston 2000, 2007; Galison and Daston 2007; Edwards, Harvey, and Wade 2010), to capture the traces of those physical movements that human beings cannot otherwise detect (Traweek 1988), and to fashion the environments in which specific non-human relations might be coaxed into the realm of human perception. Indeed far from taking objects for granted, the struggle is often primarily to try to arrest the movement of matter sufficiently to understand something of what relation a specific ecology might or might not entail, or to detect basic patternings of material transformations such that something can be made of them. It is in this respect that the craft practice of the weaver or the hunter is not necessarily of a different order from that of the scientist. The skills of effective engagement are still acquired through practice and participation (Grasseni 2007). Neither surgeons nor engineers learnt their craft from books alone (Lave and Wenger 1991; Harvey and Venkatesan 2010; McDonald 2013), and even the skills of the historian or philosopher emerge from an attentive and embodied engagement with books and words as the materials of their craft. Furthermore, what

Latour's ANT is too static and doesn't allow for the enmeshed nature of life.

much of this work on modern knowledge practice brings back into the frame is the central importance of the tensions between engaged connectivity and the need to establish one's distance, to the many ways in which abstraction and engagement are combined in human practice—whether of craftspersons (Jones and Yarrow forthcoming), artists (Leach 2004; Pinney 2005), hunters and shamans (Willerslev 2007), scientists and engineers (Candea 2010).[7]

It thus appears that if we focus on the intrinsic entanglements of materials and persons then we can look at the material relations that compose human worlds without deciding in advance that some material relations are more authentic, engaged, or indeed material than others. But there is perhaps a further step that we might take, one that projects us back to alchemical worlds of hidden properties and substances that do not easily reveal their provenance, or to the histories that mark the terms of our environmental engagement from within. Here I return to the sense of ontological politics with which we began—and the unsettling qualities of materials that threaten to overwhelm human capacity to contain them.

4.3 THE UNSETTLING FORCE OF MATERIALS IN HUMAN LIFE

Material culture studies has itself taken a decidedly material turn in recent years with some calling for a radical move away from those modes of analysis that focus on how humans invest meanings in things, or project agency into things, by allowing things to speak for themselves (Henare, Holbraad, and Wastell 2007).[8] The suggestion is a call to researchers to embrace the radical alterity of matter, and to approach the material world ontologically, asking not how things become meaningful to human beings, but what these things are or might be, on their own terms. The ambition of such a project is perhaps thwarted from the start by our incapacity to interrogate the material world, except via human capacities of perception. Nevertheless the positing of an approach to materials via a sense of ontological disturbance is an interesting one and could perhaps be thought about in relation to another long-standing anthropological interest in the liveliness of inorganic materials and artefacts, which although prior to the current so-called 'ontological turn' (Viveiros de Castro 1998) always did argue for a non-representational approach to life (Wagner 1986; Strathern 2001).

Many readers will have come across the arguments on agency in anthropological accounts which attend to the ways in which things appear, or act, as persons. In Melanesian ethnographies the focus has been primarily on the ways in which objects are seen to gather prior relations, skills, materials, and ideas, and carry these relations with them as they circulate, as in the famous accounts of Melanesian exchange (e.g. Mauss 1954; Munn 1986; Strathern

---

[7] This ongoing tension between engagement and detachment has been explored in a collaborative anthropological project on 'detachment'; see: <http://detachmentcollaboratory.org>.

[8] For interesting exchange between Danny Miller and Martin Holbraad on the core thesis of this book, see Miller's Material World Blog at <http://blogs.nyu.edu/projects/materialworld/2006/12/thinking_through_things.html>.

1988). The anxiety that surrounds ceremonial exchanges derives from the sense that these exchange objects are made and/or put into circulation with transformative intent (Gell 1998). That is they do not simply materialize their own prior context (Pinney 2005), but potentially reconfigure relations between human beings, placing at risk a person's sense of who they are (Strathern 1991).

In a seminal essay Pels (1998) distinguished those theories of animate matter that assumed the presence of spirit in matter (the animate force in this case being external to the material that houses it) and theories of the fetish, where it is the spirit of matter itself that energizes the artefact. For Ingold these distinctions between intrinsic and extrinsic power and the related concerns to classify and tease out the terms of the relationship between humans and inorganic matter miss the point (Ingold 2011: 28–9). He appreciates Pels's description of the intrinsic force of materials, but argues that there is no need to invoke the 'spirit' of matter. There is no mystery here, no need to develop theories of agency or notions of immaterial force. Those who approach the material world as a world of animate force are simply acknowledging the transforming and transformational dynamics of life. And indeed such an attitude is simply common sense to those who have not been steeped in the feigned immobility imposed by the categories of modern thought.

However, skilled attention and responsiveness to the emergent properties of materials can be deeply disturbing, threatening, and undermining to human beings. In many parts of the world what is glossed as resource extraction is experienced as a dangerous confrontation with material forces, often imagined or portrayed as persons. To follow these consequences of human material engagements, engagements which are ultimately the only way that humans can interrogate the vitality of matter, can have profound consequences that are not explored in the worlds of craft practice that Ingold is interested in. One of the most influential ways of approaching this terrain can be found in the work of Taussig, an anthropologist deeply indebted to Walter Benjamin's fascination with the power of the intertextual, the non-explicit, and the concealed. Taussig's approach to materials and animate or lively matter entangles us in quite different relations than those which tend to appear in the pages of Ingoldian analyses. Specifically his work exemplifies what Thoburn (2013), following Pels, refers to as the 'excessive materiality of the fetish' (Pels 1998: 99).

> Gold and cocaine are fetishes, which is to say substances that seem to be a good deal more than mineral or vegetable matter....As fetishes, gold and cocaine play subtle tricks upon human understanding. For it is precisely as mineral or as vegetable matter that they appear to speak for themselves and carry the weight of human history in the guise of natural history. (Taussig 2004: xviii)

The ways in which objects and materials come to carry the weight of human history has been explored from many diverse perspectives that can take us into the psychoanalytic traditions that Freud initiated, through Marxist understandings of commodity fetishism and more recent explorations of the social life of things, and the biographical accretions that material culture studies has traced for all manner of things as they move between persons and across time and space. The significance of human memory looms large in these debates, as does the contemporary interest in the centrality of sensory engagement (Seremetakis 1994; Stoller 1997; Cowan and Navaro-Yashin 2007; Navaro-Yashin 2009).

Taussig's interest in human histories of extraction and of trade differ from many other studies on the circulation of commodities because of the way in which he dwells on the visceral material engagements of human labour. The particularity of Taussig's work comes in the connections he draws between the materials that craftsmen engage through their work, and the labour involved in producing these materials in the first place. Most memorable perhaps is his description of the indigo workers. Taussig describes the ways in which pigments and smells invaded their bodies, the indigo seeping into the pores of the skin, staining their internal organs, becoming integral to their bodies (Taussig 2008). Elsewhere he looks at gold extraction, describing how workers' lung capacities are stretched to the limit as they dive below the water to fix the pumps that drive the gold deposits up into the mesh filters on the shores of Amazonian rivers (Taussig 2004). Taussig's work shows how hard it is to distinguish materials from objects, or to sustain a sense of discrete materiality in circumstances where bodily surfaces are routinely breached. It is not simply that the quite different practices of artist and labourer imply a different relationship between media, substance, and surface. It is about how the categories of objects and material are themselves porous; they lack self-evidence. The histories of materials tend to be hidden. They shock when they emerge.

The capacity of materials to shock in this way is not immediately accessible to a Gibsonian perspective where the material surfaces through which human/material interaction takes place are discrete (they don't seem to seep into each other in the ways that the indigo seeps into the pores of the worker), and while the surface engagements through which we all live in the world are indeed sensory, there is no clear explanation of how our sensory engagements become charged with emotions, desires, or fears. I thus want to retain a way of addressing the tangible presence of the immaterial, and the sense or suspicion that all might not be as it seems, that material relations might be deceptive, devious, or indeed miraculous and enchanting. My concern is that Ingoldian approaches to material life do not take the immaterial seriously enough.

But many people in the world take such things very seriously indeed and one of the peculiarities of the anthropological approach is that we try to take our lead from local concerns and assumptions about life, watching and learning how others work out the implications of living with living matter in worlds where life is precarious, and where other than human forces routinely impinge on daily life. Such preoccupations may take us into spaces of pragmatic accommodation, where the possibility of spiritual forces is respectfully embraced, particularly in moments or spaces of existential uncertainty, such as those confronted by the Siberian hunter in times of scarcity (Willerslev 2007) or the Tlingit traveller forced to negotiate the dangerous ice-floes of the north-west American coastline (Cruikshank 2005). Such precautionary attitudes are characteristic of human responses to uncertainty and they are played out through a widespread awareness of the need to engage the material forces of life in ways that are not simply traditional, but which promise new possibilities for confronting challenging circumstances. Thus, for example, we find the recent change in the Bolivian constitution to recognize the rights of Mother Earth[9] suggests an opening to a new ontological politics, as the material world is recognized as a significant force in combating climate change. However, this recognition is not necessarily ontologically continuous with other modes of ecological thinking. Timothy Mitchell, for example, has recently argued that sustainable approaches to energy consumption should focus on energy as depletable material substance, that is, as coal, oil, gas, rather than as abstract rates of flow (Mitchell

[9] See <http://www.scribd.com/doc/44900268/Ley-de-Derechos-de-la-Madre-Tierra-Estado-Plurinacional-de-Bolivia>.

2011). His approach takes an ecological or relational orientation, but does not posit the personhood of carbon.

Archaeologists typically work from fragments. As archaeologists face the mystery of things in their incompletion and detachment from life processes, the tendency is to look for ways to reconnect and to imaginatively reconstruct their relational dynamics. However, at this time when awareness of the vitality of matter is creating new and unforeseen alliances, and philosophers of science begin to articulate the need for a new accommodation and understanding between modern science and other knowledges (Stengers 2010, 2011) it is perhaps important to bear in mind all that we do *not* know about what materials are and what they might become.

This chapter opened with the extreme example of nuclear waste disposal in order to invoke the specific challenge that our contemporary relational awareness creates for those of us invested in the social consequences of material life. I was struck by the way in which the engineers at Onkalo were looking to foster a sense of ontological doubt in future generations. They wondered if they might propagate a legend that would deter the curious, and that might wrap the site of nuclear disposal with a sense of dread sufficient to deter human intrusion in the future. Their deliberations continue. Meanwhile as other people in other places try to imagine the future of the planet both for and beyond humans we find the acknowledgement of the significance of the vitality of matter returning to centre stage— and along with it perhaps a new curiosity concerning other ways of relating to non-human worlds as central to the survival of our species.

REFERENCES

Appadurai, Arjun. 1988. *The Social Life of Things: Commodities in Cultural Perspective.* Cambridge: Cambridge University Press.

Bennett, Jane. 2010. *Vibrant Matter: A Political Economy of Things.* Durham, NC: Duke University Press.

Bensaude-Vincent, B. and Stengers, I. 1996. *A History of Chemistry.* Cambridge, MA: Harvard University Press.

Bergson, Henri. 1911. *Creative Evolution*, tr. A. Mitchell. London: Macmillan.

Bunn, Stephanie. 1999. The Importance of Materials. *Journal of Museum Ethnography* 11: 15–28.

—— 2010. *Nomadic Felts.* London: British Museum Press.

Candea, Matei. 2010. 'I fell in love with Carlos the Meerkat': Engagement and Detachment in Human–Animal Relations. *American Ethnologist* 37(2): 241–58.

Chakrabarty, Dipesh. 2009. The Climate of History: Four Theses. *Critical Inquiry* 35(2): 197–222.

Coole, Diana and Frost, Samantha (eds.). 2010. *New Materialisms: Ontology, Agency, and Politics.* Durham, NC: Duke University Press.

Cowan, J. and Navaro-Yashin, Yael (eds.). 2007. Phantasmatic Realities, Passionate States. *Anthropological Theory* Special Issue 7(1).

Cruikshank, Julie. 2005. *Do Glaciers Listen? Local Knowledge, Colonial Encounters, & Social Imagination.* Seattle: University of Washington Press.

Crutzen, Paul J. and Stoermer, Eugene. 2000. The Anthropocene. *IGBP [International Geosphere-Biosphere Programme] Newsletter* 41: 17.

Daston, Lorraine (ed.). 2000. *Biographies of Scientific Objects*. Chicago: University of Chicago Press.

—— (ed.). 2007. *Things that Talk: Object Lessons from Art and Science*. Boston, MA: Zone Books.

Douglas, Mary. 1966. *Purity and Danger: An Analysis of the Concepts of Pollution and Taboo*. London: Routledge & Kegan Paul.

Edwards, Jeanette, Harvey, Penny, and Wade, Peter (eds.). 2010. *Technologized Images, Technologized Bodies*. Oxford: Berghahn Books.

Fortun, Kim. 2001. *Advocacy After Bhopal: Environmentalism, Disaster, New Global Orders*. Chicago: University of Chicago Press.

Fortun, Kim and Fortun, Mike. 2005. Scientific Imaginaries and Ethical Plateaus in Contemporary U.S. Toxicology. *American Anthropologist* 107(1): 43–54.

Franklin, Sarah. 2007. *Dolly Mixtures: The Remaking of Genealogy*. Durham, NC: Duke University Press.

Galison, Peter and Daston, Lorraine. 2007. *Objectivity*. Boston, MA: Zone Books.

Gell, Alfred. 1998. *Art and Agency*. Oxford: Oxford University Press.

Gibson, James J. 1979. *The Ecological Approach to Visual Perception*. Boston, MA: Houghton Mifflin.

Grasseni, Cristina. 2007. *Skilled Vision: Between Apprenticeship and Standards*. Oxford: Berghahn Books.

Gregson, Nicky, Watkins, Helen, and Calestani, Melania. 2010. Inextinguishable Fibres: Demolition and the Vital Materialisms of Asbestos, *Environment and Planning A* 42: 1065–83.

Gusterson, Hugh. 1996. *Nuclear Rites: A Weapons Laboratory at the End of the Cold War*. Berkeley, CA: University of California Press.

Haraway, Donna. 1989. *Primate Visions: Gender, Race, and Nature in the World of Modern Science*. New York: Routledge.

—— 1991. *Simians, Cyborgs and Women: The Reinvention of Nature*. New York: Routledge.

—— 1997. *Modest_Witeness@Second_Millennium.FemaleMan© Meets OncoMouse™ Feminism and Technoscience*. New York: Routledge.

Harvey, Penny and Venkatesan, Soumhya. 2010. Faith, Reason and the Ethic of Craftsmanship: Creating Contingently Stable Worlds. In *The Social After Gabriel Tarde: Debates and Assessments*, ed. Matei Candea, pp. 129–42. London: Routledge.

Hawkins, Gay. 2005. *The Ethics of Waste: How We Relate to Rubbish*. Lanham, MD: Rowman & Littlefield.

Helmreich, Stefan. 2009. *Alien Ocean: Anthropological Voyages in Microbial Seas*. Berkeley, CA: University of California Press.

Henare, Amiria, Holbraad, Martin, and Wastell, Sari (eds.). 2007. *Thinking Through Things: Theorising Artefacts Ethnographically*. London: Routledge.

Ingold, Tim. 2007a. *Lines: A Brief History*. London: Routledge.

—— 2007b. Materials Against Materiality. *Archaeological Dialogues* 14(1): 1–16.

—— 2011. *Being Alive: Essays on Movement, Knowledge and Description*. London: Routledge.

Jones, S. and Yarrow, Tom. Forthcoming. Craft as Detached Engagement: An Ethnography of Stone Masonry. *Journal of the Royal Anthropological Institute*.

Keller, Charles and Keller, Janet. 1996. *Cognition and Tool Use: The Blacksmith at Work*. Cambridge: Cambridge University Press.

Kuchler, Susanne. 2008. Technological Materiality: Beyond the Dualist Paradigm. *Theory, Culture & Society* 25(1): 101–20.

Kuchler, Susanne and Oakley, P. 2013. New Materials and Their Impact on the Material World. In *Objects and Materials: A Routledge Companion*, ed. Penny Harvey et al. London: Routledge.

Latour, Bruno. 1987. *Science in Action: How to Follow Scientists and Engineers Through Society*. Cambridge, MA: Harvard University Press.

—— 1988. *The Pasteurization of France*. Cambridge, MA: Harvard University Press.

Lave, Jean and Wenger, Etienne. 1991. *Situated Learning: Legitimate Peripheral Participation*. Cambridge: Cambridge University Press.

Leach, James. 2004. Modes of Creativity. In *Transactions and Creations*, ed. Eric Hirsch and Marilyn Strathern, pp. 151–75. Oxford: Berghahn Books.

Leach, Michael and Woolgar, Steve. 1990. *Representation in Scientific Practice*. Cambridge, MA: MIT Press.

McDonald, Maryon. 2013. The Mutual Articulation of Bodies and Cadavers. In *Objects and Materials: A Routledge Companion*, ed. P. Harvey et al. London: Routledge.

Madsen, Michael. 2010. *Into Eternity*. Magic Hour Films, Denmark. Available at: <http://www.intoeternitythemovie.com/> (accessed 2 December 2012).

Marchand, Trevor. 2001. *Minaret Building and Apprenticeship in Yemen*. Richmond, UK: Curzon Press.

—— 2009. *The Masons of Djenné*. Bloomington, IN: Indiana University Press.

Masco, Joseph. 2006. *The Nuclear Borderlands: The Manhattan Project in Post-Cold War New Mexico*. Princeton: Princeton University Press.

Mauss, Marcel. 1954. *The Gift: Forms and Functions of Exchange in Archaic Society*. Glencoe, IL: The Free Press.

Miller, Daniel. 1997. *Material Culture and Mass Consumption*. Cambridge, MA: Wiley-Blackwell.

—— 2005. *Materiality (Politics, History and Culture)*. Durham, NC: Duke University Press.

—— 2009. *Stuff*. Cambridge: Polity Press.

Mitchell, Timothy. 2011. *Carbon Democracy: Political Power in the Age of Oil*. London: Verso.

Munn, Nancy. 1986. *The Fame of Gawa: A Symbolic Study of Value Transformation in a Massim (Papua New Guinea) Society*. Cambridge: Cambridge University Press.

Navaro-Yashin, Yael. 2009. Affective Spaces, Melancholic Objects: Ruination and the Production of Anthropological Knowledge. *Journal of the Royal Anthropological Institute* 15(1): 1–18.

Pels, Peter. 1998 The Spirit of Matter: On Fetish, Rarity, Fact, and Fancy. In *Border Fetishisms: Material Objects in Ustable Spaces*, ed. Patricia Spyer, pp. 92–121. London: Routledge.

Petryna, Adriana. 2002. *Life Exposed*. Princeton: Princeton University Press.

Pinney, Christopher. 2005. Things Happen: Or, From Which Moment Does That Object Come? In *Materiality*, ed. Daniel Miller, pp. 256–72. Durham, NC: Duke University Press.

Rabinow, Paul. 1996. *Making PCR: A Story of Biotechnology*. Chicago: University of Chicago Press.

Rathje, William and Murphy, Cullen. 2001. *Rubbish!* Tempe, AZ: University of Arizona Press.

Redclift, Michael R. 1996. *Wasted: Counting the Costs of Global Consumption*. London: Earthscan.

Sawyer, Suzana. 2004. *Crude Chronicles: Indians, Multinational Oil, and Neoliberalism in Ecuador*. Durham, NC: Duke University Press.

Seremetakis, C. Nadia. 1994. *The Senses Still: Perception and Memory as Material Culture in Modernity*. Boulder, CO: Westview Press.

Shaffer, Steven and Shapin, Simon. 1989. *Leviathan and the Air-Pump: Hobbes, Boyle, and the Experimental Life*. Princeton: Princeton University Press.

Stengers, Isabelle. 2010. *Cosmopolitics I*. Minneapolis: University of Minnesota Press.

—— 2011. *Cosmopolitics II*. Minneapolis: University of Minnesota Press.

Stoller, Paul. 1997. *Sensuous Scholarship*. Philadelphia: University of Pennsylvania Press.

Strathern, Marilyn. 1988. *The Gender of the Gift: Problems with Women and Problems with Society in Melanesia*. Berkeley, CA: University of California Press.

—— 1991. *Partial Connections*. Lanham, MD: Rowman & Littlefield.

Taussig, Michael. 2004. *My Cocaine Museum*. Chicago: University of Chicago Press.

—— 2008. Redeeming Indigo. *Theory, Culture & Society* 25(3): 1–15.

Thoburn, Nicholas. 2013. Useless Objects. In *Objects and Materials: A Routledge Companion*, ed. P. Harvey et al. London: Routledge.

Traweek, Sharon. 1988. *Beamtimes and Lifetimes: The World of High Energy Physics*. Cambridge, MA: Harvard University Press.

Venkatesan, Soumhya. 2002. *Crafting Culture: Pattamadai Mats from South India*. Cambridge: Cambridge University Museum of Archeology and Anthropology.

—— 2009 *Craft Matters: Artisans, Development and the Indian Nation*. Hyderabad: Orient Blackswan.

Viveiros de Castro, Eduardo. 1998. Cosmological Deixis and Amerindian Perspectivism. *Journal of the Royal Anthropological Institute* 4(3): 469–88.

Wagner, Roy. 1986. *Symbols That Stand For Themselves*. Chicago: University of Chicago Press.

Willerslev, Rane. 2007. *Soul Hunters: Hunting, Animism, and Personhood among the Siberian Yukaghirs*. Berkeley, CA: University of California Press.

CHAPTER 5

....

THE PLACE OF THINGS IN CONTEMPORARY HISTORY

....

TIM COLE

5.1 INTRODUCTION

....

IN the museum at the former concentration camp at Auschwitz I, one of the barracks houses an exhibit entitled 'Material Proofs of Crimes'. Inside visitors pause, silent, before vast cases filled with mounds of suitcases, shoes, toothbrushes, cookware, crutches, prosthetic limbs, and human hair. This stuff was confiscated on arrival and then sorted by prisoners in the so-called *Kanada* section of the camp before being parcelled up for transporting to Germany. However, when the camp was liberated by Soviet troops in January 1945, they found storage barracks filled with objects awaiting shipment. These objects have become a central element of the display at the museum—persisting through the various incarnations of museum display in the shifting politics of post-war Poland—and iconic symbols of the Holocaust. Whenever I have visited Auschwitz, it is this block out of all of those within the museum where visitors pause the longest, take the most photographs, and shed the most tears. For the museum, the tangible presence of these material objects—that in the case of the shoes you can smell as well as see—become 'proofs of crimes'. Not only are they seen to attest to the sheer numbers of victims brought to this place, but also the near-total exploitation of those victims and their belongings by the Nazi state at this factory of death.

These objects have emerged as a must-have item within the Holocaust museum world. At the United States Holocaust Memorial Museum (USHMM) in Washington, DC, a loan agreement with the Auschwitz museum brought thousands of suitcases, toothbrushes, glasses, and shoes across the Atlantic to feature as the centrepiece of the permanent exhibition which takes visitors on the journey of the victims to Auschwitz.[1] The importance of these material objects is in part a reflection of their status within post-war Holocaust iconography. But they also play the same function at USHMM that they are seen to play at

---

[1] While piles of women's hair were also sent, the museum decided—largely on the advice of survivors—to leave this material object in their off-site storage facility and display a large photograph of these bundles of hair instead.

Auschwitz as 'material proofs of crimes'. At USHMM there is an awareness of the persistence of Holocaust denial, and the museum in part self-consciously seeks to combat denial through the display of material objects with their assumption of tangible proof. In this museum, as at Auschwitz, seeing (but not touching) is believing.

However, while material culture is a central—and arguably *the* central—plank of museum display in Holocaust museums both where the event happened and distant from Europe, it plays a far more peripheral role in Holocaust historiography in particular and historical practice more generally. Historians tend to privilege the paperwork in the archives over material objects in their research and analysis. That paperwork is of course, itself, material, and yet the materiality of what historians find in the archives remains relatively underexplored. In this essay, I seek to critically examine the historiography of the Holocaust as a case study for a broader discussion of the place of material culture within historical analysis. Digging beneath the surface, there are glimpses of a material turn within history. As Frank Trentmann puts it: 'things are back' (Trentmann 2009: 283).

5.2 HISTORIES FROM THINGS AND HISTORIES OF THINGS

Broadly speaking, where historians have engaged with material culture in their work they have done so in two main ways. Firstly, historians have used material objects as evidence to generate and answer broader questions of the past. Variously dubbed 'object driven' (Herman 1992) and 'history from things' (Riello 2009), historians approach 'objects as evidence of other complex social relationships' (Herman 1992: 11). Here, 'historians are not much interested in things or their thingness for their own sake, but as routes to past experience' (Harvey 2009: 7). Secondly, and more significantly within historical writing over the last two decades, material cultures of the past have become the focus of analysis. This 'object centred' (Herman 1992) or 'history of things' (Riello 2009) approach has been most influential amongst cultural historians of the eighteenth century who have turned their collective gaze upon the materiality of consumption and everyday life (White 2006).[2] These concerns, as an important edited collection by Amanda Vickery and John Styles attests, have captured the imagination of historians of both sides of the Atlantic (Vickery and Styles 2006). The title of this important volume—*Gender, Taste, and Material Culture in Britain and North America, 1700–1830*—signals the chronological, geographical, and thematic centre of gravity of the dominant strand of historiography of past material cultures. While the range of both chronology and geography of such studies has broadened out, there remains a tendency for the focus to remain broadly speaking fixed in the domestic sphere and on questions of identity (Cohen 2006; Clark 2009). The end result, as Frank Trentmann characterizes the situation, is that

> quilts, handkerchiefs, shoes, chintzes, porcelain cups, wallpaper, and cupboards…are the kinds of objects that crowd the pages of historical inquiries into the material culture of

---

[2] See the influential blog Things C18th at <http:thingsc18th.wordpress.com/>

Georgian Britain and early America…Material culture mainly stops at the domestic door-step, rarely connecting to urban networks, to the office, or to the brutal materiality or iron, steel, or bullets. (2009: 287)

However, within Holocaust historiography, perhaps the most striking, unusual, and controversial example of a material turn centres precisely around bullets.

Over the last decade or so, a French Catholic priest named Patrick Debois has used forensic archaeology to uncover the history of mass shootings in the Ukraine. For Debois, it was not enough simply to interview surviving non-Jewish neighbours who told him where the killings took place. Rather, he took their information about the location of massacre sites to physically uncover evidence of the killings at the sites themselves. His methodology revolves in large part around digging up and counting bullet casings, based on the assumption that each spent cartridge equates with one killing, and so he estimates the numbers of Jews killed in each locale he uncovers (Debois 2008). These deadly objects dug up from the soil in a Ukrainian forest clearing play a similar role to the piles of shoes exhibited at Auschwitz, USHMM, and countless other memorial museums. Their physicality is seen as proof of the crimes in a context where the post-war Soviet Union as well as post-Soviet national governments have sought to erase the history of Jewish murder in their midst (Bartov 2007). Debois's work is not only positivist assertion of the basic facts—what happened, when, where, and specifically how many Jews were killed—but also an act of documenting the scene(s) of the crime.

His work shares much with other approaches that can be broadly dubbed 'archaeological' at former sites of mass killings (Koff 2004) including the sites of former death camps (Gilead et al. 2009). At Bełżec and Sobibór, Kola—controversially given the nature of the site and Orthodox Jewish sentiments against disturbing human remains—extracted core samples to identify the site of mass graves (Kola 2000). Such archaeological work shares with Debois an aim to quite literally uncover the scene of the crime through the methodology of excavation (see also Powers and Sibun, this volume and Gould, this volume)—which for González-Ruibal is both 'the primary trope of archaeology' and a political act of uncovering the work of burying and hiding exercised by genocidal regimes (González-Ruibal 2011). My sense is that Debois would certainly see his own excavation as an ethical uncovering after the double burial of the killings themselves by the Nazis and the memory of the killings by the Soviets and post-Soviet national governments. His work is an act of 'manifestation' akin to that called for by González-Ruibal (2008: 251), which is a theme I want to return to at the close of this essay.

However, in the main, historical writing has concerned itself less with manifestation and more with explanation. As with other traditional historical analysis, the overriding concern within the dominant strand of Holocaust historiography has focused on causation. The questions of how and why the Holocaust was enacted have been most persistently asked from the earliest historiography onwards. The pioneering work of Raul Hilberg in the early 1960s sought to explain how a bureaucratic state defined, robbed, concentrated, and deported Jews (Hilberg 1961). During the 1970s and 1980s, a vigorous international historiographical debate between those dubbed 'Intentionalists' and 'Functionalists' argued over the causation of the Holocaust as primarily ideological, carefully planned and implemented from the top-down (Intentionalist) or as a more chaotic and bottom-up event that developed through 'cumulative radicalization' in the locale as a result of more structural and socio-economic concerns (Functionalist) (Browning 2004; Matthäus 2004). By the 1990s, attention had shifted to explaining the behaviour of 'ordinary' perpetrators with the publishing of Christopher Browning's ground-breaking study of 'Ordinary Men' (1993). His suggestion that the most ordinary of reasons—careerism and peer pressure—explain why the members of a German auxiliary police battalion killed Jews face-to-face in occupied Poland, was later challenged by the controversial and problematic work of Daniel Goldhagen, who asserted the importance of ideology and argued for the widespread influence of 'eliminationist antisemitism' in inter-war Germany (Goldhagen 1996; Eley 2000).

Whatever the differences in explanation, what characterized this varied historiography was that, overwhelmingly, the sources used were textual. The paperwork produced by the perpetrators, and in particular the documents utilized by and created for a series of post-war trials, have been extensively mined in the post-war effort by historians to understand what happened, when, where, and why. In short, the paperwork of a judicial process has been—and continues to be—critical to a historiography focused above all else on motivation and causation (Browning 1992; Bloxham 2001). Here, the specific historiography of the Holocaust reflects a wider preference within traditional historiography more generally to privilege paperwork from state archives. To understand why states did what they did, the first port of call has been to examine state actors' own words in the memoranda, correspondence, and minutes carefully catalogued in national archives.

5.3 EXPANDING THE ARCHIVE

However, even taking these dominant questions of motivation and causation, my own work in part has sought to broaden the potential source base beyond the purely textual to consider writing histories of causation 'from things'. In a study of the implementation of one critical stage of the Holocaust—placing Jews into ghettos—in the Hungarian capital, Budapest, I examined the materiality of the reshaping of the urban landscape as a way to uncover shifting motivations behind ghettoization. In doing this, I was responding to the early call issued to future scholars by two pioneering post-war historians of the Holocaust that, 'a careful examination of the ghetto maps is ... of utmost importance in the study of the trends and objectives of Nazi ghetto planning' (Friedman and Robinson 1960: 74). In seeking to understand ghettoization in Budapest, I examined not simply what the perpetrators said—in memoranda, planning documents, and minutes of meetings—but also what they did on the ground as they reshaped the city along racialized grounds. In particular I suggested that the shifting physicality of the ghetto in Budapest signalled shifting motivations on the part of those urban planners or—adopting a term coined by Henri Lefebvre—'doctors of space' who decided where Jews and non-Jews would live in the city (Cole 2003).

My own work on the materialities of ghettoization in Budapest reflects a broader set of interests within a recent historiography in the materiality of the political (Thompson 2007) and the material expression of power (Joyce 2003). Historians of modern states have examined the ways that power has been materialized in everything from postal systems and engineering projects to water and road networks (Bennett and Joyce 2010). However, the danger in work adopting rather Foucauldian notions of power implemented in and through the material world is that they tend towards the monolithic. But things are less compliant than that. As Frank Trentmann memorably reminds us, 'things are not just friendly companions or instruments of power. Things are also trouble. They break down. They cause us grief, anger, or bewilderment' (Trentmann 2009: 300). There is a need to think not just about the materiality of power, but also the power of materiality.

Within historiography perhaps the greatest engagement with the power of materiality can be seen in the work of environmental historians who, as Ellen Stroud memorably put it, 'pay attention to dirt'. For Stroud, environmental histories' concerns with the materiality of the natural environment offers 'a tool for telling better histories' of power relationships and she invites 'other historians' to 'join us in our attention to the physical, biological, ecological nature of dirt, water, air, trees, and animals (including humans)' in order to uncover 'new questions and new answers about the past' (Stroud 2004: 75–6, 80). For environmental historians, nature is 'real, active presence' and 'material object and intellectual idea [take] an active role' (Steinberg 2002; Asdal 2003: 73; Brady 2005: 2). Here are shared concerns with those developed by Bruno Latour and others under the auspices of actor-network-theory that signal not simply nature but other aspects of non-human worlds as active agents in the past, present, and future (Latour 2005). As Ewa Domanska argues,

> Questions concerning the status of relics from the past, relations between the human and the nonhuman, the organic and the inorganic, between people and things and among things themselves, are of fundamental importance not only for reconceptualizing the study of the past, but also for the future of a world that involves technologies such as cloning, genetic engineering, nanotechnology, biotechnology, and transplantation using animal organs and biotronic implants. (2006: 338)

As my reference to environmental history signals, history has moved dramatically beyond the political (and indeed the human) and in so doing has asked new sets of questions and looked in new places for answers. Most striking here has been the impact of social and cultural history in reshaping the concerns of historians. Asking new questions has quite literally forced historians out of the state archives to consider a far wider range of sources. In part this has been inspired by a concern to access the voices of those who have no voice in official records, but it is also recognition that texts 'miss the wordless experience of all people [and I might add flora and fauna], rich or poor, near or far' (Glassie 1999: 44). The end result is that far greater attention has been paid to a wider range of non-textual sources—in particular the visual and oral—in examining and explaining the past (Burke 1991). The wealth of work on eighteenth-century domestic interiors that I referred to above can be seen as emerging out of the cultural turn which signalled a new interest in consumption over production. Historians interested in exploring a consumer revolution in the eighteenth century have not simply defaulted to the state archives, but have worked with a wider variety of sources including the vast array of material objects found in European and American homes in this period.

As this important body of work shows, there is a tendency within historical methodology to start from the present with a (new) set of questions—such as identities of consumption in the eighteenth century—and then to look to the past for the kinds of sources—textual, visual, material, oral—that provide answers to those questions. Far less common is travel in the other direction—starting with the past and a discrete set of traces and working forwards from these seeing what questions these sources stimulate (Burke 1991; Cole 2011). In reality of course, being a historian is about a bouncing between these two poles of present (historiographical questions) and past (material traces/sources). Going into the archive and examining the sources necessarily reframes the questions we ask. However, my sense is that historians—and perhaps this is particularly the case with historians of the modern or contemporary era which is characterized by an overabundance of sources—go to the archives with at least a hint of the kinds of questions we are interested in. Hence meta-shifts in the kinds of historical questions being asked (such as those seen in, for example, the new social and cultural histories) result in shifts in the kinds of sources being examined. While historians may still see the past as, to take David Lowenthal's term, 'a foreign country' best visited through the archive (Lowenthal 1985), the notion of the archive has expanded considerably. Historians are an eclectic bunch who not only range widely in the types of sources they work with over a single career, but also within a single article or monograph. The result is that new sources, including the material, are fairly readily embraced within the discipline as just one more means of accessing the illusive past. However, as Karen Harvey suggests, 'history is not at heart an "object-centred" discipline' (Harvey 2009: 7). The material is rarely the historian's starting point and while it may be her destination, it is generally not the sole destination and it may take her a long time to get there!

One example of such a journey to the material can be seen in the historian of madness and psychiatry, Bronwyn Labrum, who recalls a eureka moment when she turned from her initial archival exploration of a psychiatric institution, to walking the corridors of the site itself for the very first time. As she reflected back on the experience:

> I realise now, that walking through the extant buildings and spaces of an institution, even one suffering from 'demolition through neglect', provides a different order of evidence and a distinctive engagement with the past. It enables the reconstruction of the world of the asylum in three dimensional and tangible terms, rather than through the words of medical men writing in casebooks and in annual reports or even in photographs, usually posed for an inquiring public. The experience of seeing the grounds, the grouping of different buildings in different areas, starting grandly and then getting progressively utilitarian, the confined exercise yards and then going into the upstairs wards, with their strong doors and peepholes, brought home to me things about the experience and being confined in an asylum that I had previously not paid much attention to. The distinct material and social worlds were interweaved that afternoon. (2010: 805–6)

Although revelatory for Labrum, the site visit came as a belated addition to a thorough analysis of written texts in the archives rather than early field survey. Starting off in the archives, as Labrum did, reveals the persistence of a hierarchy of sources within historiographical methodology. As Simon Schama suggests, historians generally assume that they 'are supposed to reach the past always through texts, occasionally through images; things that are safely caught in the bell jar of academic convention; look but don't touch' (Schama 1995: 24). Yet, influenced by one of his own history teachers who he describes as 'an intellectual hell-raiser and a writer of eccentric courage, [who] had always insisted on directly experiencing "a sense of place", of using "the archive of the feet"', Schama set off to explore the landscapes of the past he was writing (Schama 1995: 24).

He is not alone in this emphasis on the importance of actually going there to look, listen, smell, and touch. An increasing number of historians have joined him in not only visiting the sites they study as part of the research process, but also writing the act of visiting into more self-reflective narratives. In part, this is a result of an increased interest in memory amongst historians who have turned their attention to studying the traces of the past and not only their precedents, as well as the ways that the past is retold in the present. In physically going there, historians tend to be very conscious of visiting multi-layered places with multiple pasts (and presents). Those historical layers have increasingly been uncovered in a growing number of studies of landscapes of memory (Young 1993).

However, the importance of physically going there also reflects the impact on history of the broader so-called 'spatial turn' in the humanities (Ethington 2007). Drawing on the longer tradition of pioneers within historical geography (Hoskins 1955), the landscapes of the past themselves have become sources to be read alongside—and in tension with—the paperwork of the archive. Within Holocaust studies pioneering work has been undertaken here by historical geographer Andrew Charlesworth, who positions reading urban and rural landscapes where the Holocaust was implemented as a central research and pedagogical methodology (Charlesworth 1994, 2004). His work has inspired an international research team bringing together historians, historical geographers, cartographers, and GIS scientists to uncover (and exploratively produce) the materiality and spatiality of the Holocaust, paying particular attention to distance and proximity, visibility and invisibility, and landscapes imagined and real (Beorn et al. 2009; Giordano and Cole 2011; Knowles, Cole, and Giordano forthcoming 2013).

My own experience of working with the interdisciplinary group, drawing on field research, and foregrounding the materiality of the Holocaust has led to a reframing of my own view of ghettoization in Budapest. In earlier work that was dominated by textual sources, I made much of the differences between two lists of ghetto addresses issued in quick succession on 16 June and 22 June 1944, seeing in them a shift in how ghettoization was imagined first as 'Jewish absence' (clearing the Jews from one part of the city) and then as 'Jewish presence' (placing the Jews in another part of the city). I had read all the petitions sent by non-Jews and Jews in this chaotic week in mid-June that I found in the Budapest archives and assumed from this mass of paperwork that things had changed dramatically in that period (Cole 2003). In some ways they had. The number of houses where the city's close to 200,000 Jews were permitted to live dropped dramatically from over 2,600 to just over 1,900. However, in my own earlier mapping of this I had simply placed points on the map to mark individual ghetto houses in one district.

Engaging in more critically interdisciplinary fieldwork, I quickly became aware that mapping these houses as equal sized dots on the map (as their textual undifferentiated listing in state produced ghetto lists suggested) did not do justice to the material architecture of interwar Budapest, which ranged from large multi-storey apartment buildings in the centre of the city through small single-storey family homes in the suburban outskirts (Figure 5.1).

In order to rectify this, Alberto Giordano and I reconstructed the entire city, block by block, in a digital map that draws on census returns to weight properties. Applying a number of GIS analytical methods (mean centre analysis, directional distribution, standard distance, and kernel density[3]) to this mapping was, for me, a eureka moment (Figures 5.2 and 5.3).

---

[3] Mean centre analysis identifies the geographic centre of a distribution, shown as a solid circle on the map. Directional distribution finds the overall directional pattern of the data. Standard distance measures the degree of concentration; the larger the circle, the more dispersed the locational pattern. Unlike the mean centre, standard distance, and deviational ellipse, which return a single value, kernel analysis calculates a density surface around points or areas, returning a set of continuous values. The result is a more detailed representation of the phenomenon under study.

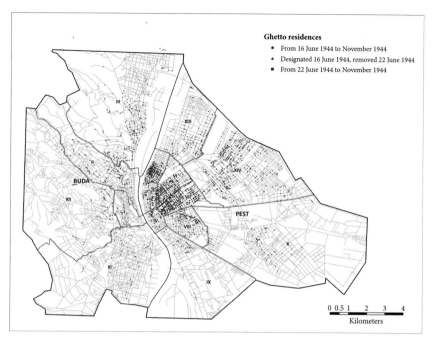

FIGURE 5.1 Ghetto houses designated on 16 and 22 June 1944 (Tim Cole and Alberto Giordano)

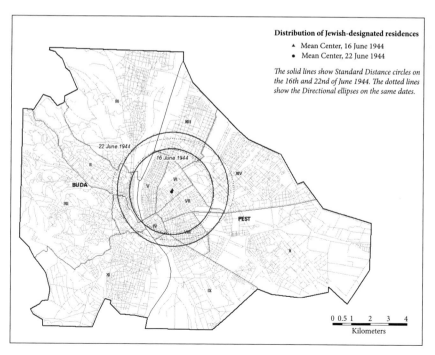

FIGURE 5.2 Mean centre and standard distance of dispersed ghettoization on 16 and 22 June 1944 (Tim Cole and Alberto Giordano)

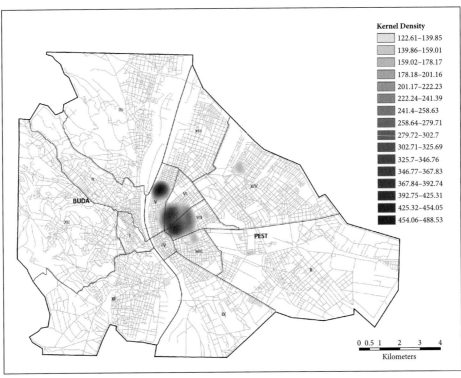

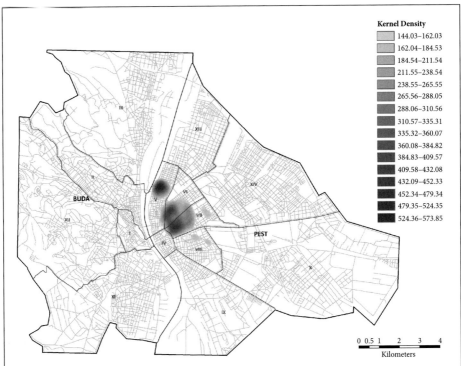

FIGURE 5.3 Kernel density analysis of dispersed ghettoization on 16 and 22 June 1944. Areas of highest residence concentration (Tim Cole and Alberto Giordano)

It suggested that the centre of gravity of ghettoization barely shifted between 16 and 22 June (nor indeed did it change that much between the utopian plans of early May 1944 through the ultimate implementation of two ghettos in the winter of 1944–5). In short, taking the materiality of the ghetto houses seriously suggested that there were greater continuities in ghettoization in Budapest than might be imagined when considering simply the seemingly radically different spatial strategies adopted (7 ghetto areas in May, 2,639 ghetto houses on 16 June, 1,948 ghetto houses on 22 June and 2 ghetto areas in November/ December) in both plans and policy found in the paperwork generated during 1944. Rather than emphasizing changes in ghettoization in terms of shifting concerns with absence and presence, as I did in previous work, weighted mapping points to a dominant story of continuities in ghettoization throughout 1944 that drew upon (and hardened) a longer history of Jewish demographic patterns in Budapest. Jews had historically resided in much greater numbers, and higher proportions, in the central districts than in the rest of the city. The increased concentration of Jewish residences in central Pest was a change in the degree but not in the kind of residential patterns that had prevailed for many years. The dominant idea that remained constant throughout the process of ghettoization in Budapest was taking the ghetto to the Jew, rather than taking the Jew to the ghetto (Cole 2010). While ideology is a part of this story—a notion of the Jew's place in the city—bringing the ghetto to the Jew signalled the persuasiveness of pragmatic concerns that ghettoization avoid displacing non-Jews (Cole and Giordano forthcoming 2013).

5.4 Histories and Things

Two things about my own experience here raise broader issues. Firstly, working with things has the potential to reframe the kinds of questions we ask as historians and the kinds of answers we come up with. Secondly, working with things has the potential to reframe the ways in which we narrate our findings—moving beyond the textual to the visual and beyond. Both conclusions emerge in research undertaken by Leora Auslander into the confiscation and return of furnishings in Jewish apartments in wartime and post-war Paris (Auslander 2005). Her work into the 'history of [French Jewish] things' shares the wider, and dominant, concerns of cultural historians of modern Europe and America with the material culture of domestic interiors, and in this way builds on her own earlier work on French-Jewish interiors (Auslander 1996). Drawing on textual sources, albeit textual sources about material objects, Auslander reconstructs a story of French Jewish petitioning to reclaim confiscated wartime property as a mechanism of 'psychological and emotional healing' where 'Parisian Jews used the forum inadvertently offered them by the provisional government to start to mourn the passing of lost lives and to imagine the future' (Auslander 2005: 1036, 1044).

As Auslander demonstrates, 'expanding the range of our canonical sources' to include material objects such as the furnishings of Jewish Parisian families, not only has the potential to 'provide better answers to familiar questions' but also to 'change the very nature of the questions we are able to pose and the kind of knowledge we are able to acquire about the past' given that 'limiting our evidentiary base to…the linguistic…renders us unable to grasp important dimensions of human experience' (Auslander 2005: 1015). For her, paying attention to the narratives of loss found in these post-war petitions opens up new questions about 'the relationship between Jewish returnees and the French state and society and into the relationship between people and their homes as well as processes of mourning and healing' (Auslander 2005: 1045). In short, working the other way round by starting with the material has the potential of opening up a whole different set of questions, experiences, and subjects to historical analysis.

As Auslander herself is aware, historians taking material culture seriously—or the 'thingliness of things' (González-Ruibal 2008: 251)—not only changes the kinds of questions we ask, but also the ways we communicate our answers. Here, we tend to default to the textual, although she suggests that digital publishing may provide alternative technologies (Auslander 2005: 1045). Historians are aware of the 'thingliness of things' across the range of sources with which they work. This is something that oral historians have been perhaps the most aware of, recognizing the oral history interview as so much more than the production of a textual transcript. Not only is the interview an act of listening as well as speaking (Greenspan 1998) but those speech acts are moments of embodied, performative retelling. Hence historians drawing on oral histories have increasingly paid attention not just to what is said (and not said), but also how it is said as evidence of the past and its retelling (Thomson 1995; Layman 2009).

Of course the same is true of the most traditional of documents that historians use: the paperwork in state archives. In Claude Lanzmann's celebrated film *Shoah* (1985), there is a scene in which the pioneering Holocaust scholar Raul Hilberg talks through a document that he holds sitting at his desk in a wintry Vermont. As he tells Lanzmann, 'when I hold a document in my hand, particularly if it's an original document, then I hold something which is actually something that the original bureaucrat held in his hand. It's an artefact. It's a leftover.' The source as material object is, for Hilberg—and he is far from alone here amongst historians—a physical, tangible connection with the past (and in particular the document's producer) in a manner akin to the museum display of material objects at Auschwitz or USHMM. The end result is a tendency towards a fetishization of the *original* document in the archive as material object (Derrida 1995; Steedman 2002; see Graves-Brown, this volume).

But, as an increasing number of historians have recognized, it is not only the original creator of that document and the contemporary historian who have held this object in their hands. In most cases—and of course this is especially the case with texts found in state archives—many others have had their hands on this material object between then and now. As Ann Stoler has emphasized, archives are not simply fixed things where historians go to get their hands on documents, but archiving is process and archives sites 'of knowledge production…monuments of states…[and] of state ethnography' (Stoler 2002: 90; Stoler 2009). That documents (and their archiving) have their own histories is perhaps most striking in the case of visual sources such as photographs, where a history of various display and captioning leads towards unstable meanings (Struk 2004; see also Noble, this volume, and Watkins, this volume). As Arjun Appadurai has signalled, there is a 'social life of things' and that includes the stuff in the archive (Appadurai 1986).

Here, historians reflect a broader concern with interdisciplinary attempts to tell the story of the reception of the past in their retelling of the past, something advocated by James Young in an important essay that called for Holocaust scholars to self-consciously write how the event has been 'received' into their work (1997). Within Holocaust representation, one pioneering example of such an approach can be seen in Art Spiegelman's celebrated two-part graphic novel, *Maus* (1986) where the commix of image and text allowed him to tell two stories simultaneously. One is the story of his father's wartime experiences in Poland. The other is the story of the (very material) act of retelling (and subsequently authoring and publishing) in contemporary America (Spiegelman 1986, 1991). Here, Spiegelman rejected the sense of linear time of historicism and adopted in its place a more complex sense of time (and space) that moved between the past and present (and Poland and America) and offered a simultaneity of the two.

Spiegelman's co-mixture of text and image provides one potential narrative strategy for conveying more complex and chaotic pasts, as does adopting strategies of multi-vocality (Price 1990; Cole 2011). But what do we do with the material (or the oral), if in rendering them either textually or visually we reduce them to an object described or photographed? Here I return to Alfredo González-Ruibal's notion of the 'manifestation' of the archaeology of supermodernity (or a laying bare of presence) as 'a rhetoric that preserves the "thingliness" of the thing without being trapped in a verbal discourse and does justice to the troubling nature of the record we work with' (González-Ruibal 2008: 251). His words are a challenge to historians—and perhaps particularly historians of the Holocaust. If we have begun to engage with the materiality of this event (and the materiality of other histories) both as a 'history from things' and a 'history of things' we have still not really fully engaged with a third perspective that Giorgio Riello dubs 'history and things'. As he suggests, 'history has been slow to recognize the material world's capacity to challenge the overall concept of the analysis of the past by evoking and shaping new processes or gathering, systematizing and presenting ideas' (Riello 2009: 26). In short, we are still searching for new languages to narrate the 'thingliness of things'. But here, my sense is that we historians are not alone!

5.5 Conclusions (or Thoughts from a Historian Writing for Archaeologists of the Contemporary World)

What then might history (and historians) offer to archaeologists of the contemporary world, aside from a shared sense of angst over the dilemmas of narrating the 'thingliness of things'? One thing that I hope I have conveyed are the ways that historians use an ever-widening range of sources as the basis for the stories that they tell about the past. For me, that is one of the most exciting things about researching and writing history. Literally anything is a potential source for answering—or throwing up—new questions about the past. In a sense then, history is a discipline that is constantly reinventing itself, through asking new questions, seeking new sources, and adopting new methodologies. While state archives are still mined by researchers, historians have moved beyond the state archive and—in the case of Stoler's work in particular—treated the archive as object of study (Stoler 2009). I wonder if something of that eclectic reinvention lies behind Rodney Harrison's plea for contemporary archaeologists to look on the surface and not only to pursue the traditional methodologies of literally digging beneath it (Harrison 2011). Sometimes the most interesting things that you find in the archive are the 'failed proposals, utopian visions and improbable projects...[the] "non-events"' (Stoler 2002: 101). It is not only the stuff that was made which is of interest to the historian, but also the stuff that was never made, the pipe dreams on paper consigned to the archives. As a historian of the Holocaust, I am just as interested in how, for example, ghetto planners in Budapest or the editors of a provincial Hungarian newspaper in Szeged imagined ghettoization in utopian terms, as I am in what they actually ended up building on the ground (Cole 2003, 2011). Moreover, explaining the mismatch between plans imagined and realized is both a critical act of understanding and explaining the past, and also—perhaps—an act of pricking the bubble of a genocidal 'supermodernity' (González-Ruibal 2008).

As well as being eclectic in where we look for sources for our storytelling, there is also a certain eclecticism in the way we tell those stories, recognizing that different stories demand different narrative modes (White 1973, 1987, 1992). I have always been struck by Richard Price's suggestion that

> different historical or ethnographic situations lend themselves to different literary forms (and vice-versa), and that the ethnographer or historians [and perhaps I can add, archaeologist of the contemporary] should...face each society or period—or for that matter each potential book—in a form that does not come pre-selected or ready-made, in order to effectively evoke that particular society, or that particular moment. (Price 2001: 359)

Price's call to—and modelling of—narrative experimentation has the potential for telling more complex stories of the past (and present). As Spiegelman's *Maus* so brilliantly portrays, stories that we tell of the past have multiple temporalities to them (1986, 1991). If archaeologists of the contemporary past are to follow Rodney Harrison's call to 'forgo its search for origins to focus instead on the present and only subsequently on the circumstances in which the past intervenes within it' (Harrison 2011: 144) then telling stories of the simultaneity of past and present is another narrative challenge alongside that of not losing 'the thingliness of things'. While historians are only just beginning to grapple with representing materiality without merely reducing things to textual description, my sense is that for some time we have been grappling with narrating the simultaneity of the present and the past, the becoming and been, us and them, and surface and depth.

REFERENCES

Appadurai, Arjun. 1986. *The Social Life of Things: Commodities in Cultural Perspectives.* Cambridge: Cambridge University Press.

Asdal, Kristin. 2003. The Problematic Nature of Nature: The Post-Constructivist Challenge to Environmental History. *History and Theory* 42(4): 60–74.

Auslander, Leora. 1996. *Taste and Power: Furnishing Modern France.* Berkeley, CA: University of California Press.

—— 2005. Beyond Words. *American Historical Review* 110(4): 1015–45.

Bartov, Omer. 2007. *Erased: Vanishing Traces of Jewish Galicia in Present-Day Ukraine.* Princeton: Princeton University Press.

Bennett, Tony and Joyce, Patrick. 2010. *Material Powers: Cultural Studies, History and the Material Turn.* London: Routledge.

Beorn, Waitman, Cole, Tim, Gigliotti, Simone, Giordano, Alberto, Holian, Anna, Jaskot, Paul B., Knowles, Anne Kelly, Masurovsky, Marc, and Steiner, Erik B. 2009. Geographical Record: Geographies of the Holocaust. *The Geographical Review* 99(4): 563–74.

Bloxham, Donald. 2001. *Genocide on Trial: War Crimes and the Formation of Holocaust History and Memory*. Oxford: Oxford University Press.

Brady, Lisa. 2005. The Wilderness of War: Nature and Strategy in the American Civil War. *Environmental History* 10(3): 421–47.

Browning, Christopher. 1992. German Memory, Judicial Interrogation and Historical Reconstruction: Writing Perpetrator History from Postwar Testimony. In *Probing the Limits of Representation: Nazism and the 'Final Solution'*, ed. Saul Friedlander, pp. 22–36. Cambridge, MA: Harvard University Press.

—— 1993. *Ordinary Men: Reserve Police Battalion 101 and the Final Solution in Poland*. New York: HarperCollins.

—— 2004. The Decision Making Process. In *The Historiography of the Holocaust*, ed. Dan Stone, pp. 173–96. Basingstoke: Palgrave Macmillan.

Burke, Peter. 1991. *Eyewitnessing: The Use of Images in Historical Writing*. London: Reaktion.

Charlesworth, Andrew. 1994. Teaching the Holocaust through Landscape Study. *Immigrants and Minorities* 14(1): 65–76.

—— 2004. The Topography of Genocide. In *The Historiography of the Holocaust*, ed. Dan Stone, pp. 216–52. Basingstoke: Palgrave Macmillan.

Clark, Anna. 2009. Editor's Introduction. *Journal of British Studies* 48(2): 279–82.

Cohen, Deborah. 2006. *Household Gods: The British and Their Possessions*. New Haven, CT: Yale University Press.

Cole, Tim. 2003. *Holocaust City: The Making of a Jewish Ghetto*. New York: Routledge.

—— 2010. Contesting and Compromising Ghettoization: Hungary, 1944. In *Lessons and Legacies IX: History and Responsibility: Reassessments of the Holocaust, Implications for the Future*, ed. Jonathan Petropoulos, Lynn Rapaport, and John Roth, pp. 152–66. Evanston, IL: Northwestern University Press.

—— 2011. *Traces of the Holocaust: Journeying in and out of the Ghettos*. London: Continuum.

Cole, Tim and Giordano, Alberto. Forthcoming 2013. Bringing the Ghetto to the Jew: The Shifting Geography of the Budapest Ghetto. In *Geographies of the Holocaust*, ed. Anne Kelly Knowles, Tim Cole, and Alberto Giordano. Bloomington, IN: Indiana University Press.

Debois, Patrick. 2008. *The Holocaust by Bullets*. Basingstoke: Palgrave Macmillan.

Derrida, Jacques. 1995. *Archive Fever: A Freudian Impression*. Chicago: Chicago University Press.

Domanska, Ewa. 2006. The Material Presence of the Past. *History and Theory* 45(3): 337–48.

Eley, Geoff. 2000. *The Goldhagen Effect: History, Memory, Nazism—Facing the German Past*. Ann Arbor: University of Michigan Press.

Ethington, Philip. 2007. Placing the Past: 'Groundwork' for a Spatial Theory of History. *Rethinking History* 11(4): 465–94.

Friedman, Philip and Robinson, Jacob. 1960. *Guide to Jewish History Under Nazi Impact*. Jerusalem and New York: Yad Vashem and YIVO.

Gilead, Isaac, Haimi, Yoram, and Mazurek, Wojciech. 2009. Excavating Nazi Extermination Centres. *Present Pasts* 1: 10–39.

Giordano, Alberto and Cole, Tim. 2011. On Place and Space: Calculating Social and Spatial Networks in the Budapest Ghetto. *Transactions in GIS* 15(s1): 143–70.

Glassie, Henry. 1999. *Material Culture*. Bloomington, IN: Indiana University Press.

Goldhagen, Daniel. 1996. *Hitler's Willing Executioners: Ordinary Germans and the Holocaust*. New York: Vintage.

González-Ruibal, Alfredo. 2008. Time to Destroy: An Archaeology of Supermodernity. *Current Anthropology* 49(2): 247–79.

—— 2011. In Praise of Depth. *Archaeological Dialogues* 18(2): 164–8.

Greenspan, Hank. 1998. *On Listening to Holocaust Survivors*. Westport, CT: Praeger.

Harrison, Rodney. 2011. Surface Assemblages: Towards an Archaeology *in* and *of* the Present. *Archaeological Dialogues* 18(2): 141–96.

Harvey, Karen. 2009. *History and Material Culture*. London: Routledge.

Herman, Bernard. 1992. *The Stolen House*. Charlottesville: University Press of Virginia.

Hilberg, Raul. 1961. *The Destruction of European Jews*. Chicago: Quadrangle Books.

Hoskins, William. 1955. *The Making of the English Landscape*. Leicester: Leicester University Press.

Joyce, Patrick. 2003. *The Rule of Freedom: Liberalism and the Modern City*. London: Verso.

Knowles, Anne Kelly, Cole, Tim, and Giordano, Alberto (eds.). Forthcoming 2013. *Geographies of the Holocaust*. Bloomington: Indiana University Press.

Koff, Clea. 2004. *The Bone Woman: A Forensic Anthropologist's Search for Truth in the Mass Graves of Rwanda, Bosnia, Croatia and Kosovo*. New York: Random House.

Kola, Andrzej. 2000. *Belzec: The Nazi Camp for Jews in the Light of Archaeological Sources— Excavations 1997–1999*. Washington, DC: USHMM.

Labrum, Bronwyn. 2010. Material Histories in Australia and New Zealand: Interweaving Distinct Material and Social Domains. *History Compass* 8(8): 805–16.

Lanzmann, Claude. 1985. *Shoah: An Oral History of the Holocaust—The Complete Text of the Film*. New York: Pantheon Books.

Latour, Bruno. 2005. *Reassembling the Social: An Introduction to Actor-Network-Theory*. Oxford: Oxford University Press.

Layman, Lenore. 2009. Reticence in Oral History Interviews. *Oral History Review* 36(2): 207–30.

Lowenthal, David. 1985. *The Past is a Foreign Country*. Cambridge: Cambridge University Press.

Matthäus, Jürgen. 2004. Historiography and the Perpetrators of the Holocaust. In *The Historiography of the Holocaust*, ed. Dan Stone, pp. 197–215. Basingstoke: Palgrave Macmillan.

Price, Richard. 1990. *Alabi's World*. Baltimore: Johns Hopkins University Press.

—— 2001. Invitation to Historians: Practices of Historical Narrative. *Rethinking History* 5(3): 357–65.

Riello, Giorgio. 2009. Things that Shape History: Material Culture and Historical Narratives. In *History and Material Culture*, ed. Karen Harvey, pp. 24–47. London: Routledge.

Schama, Simon. 1995. *Landscape and Memory*. New York: Alfred A. Knopf.

Spiegelman, Art. 1986. *Maus: A Survivor's Tale*. New York: Pantheon.

—— 1991. *Maus II: And Here My Troubles Began*. New York: Pantheon.

Steedman, Caroline. 2002. *Dust: The Archive and Cultural History*. New Brunswick: Rutgers University Press.

Steinberg, Ted. 2002. Down to Earth: Nature, Agency and Power in History. *American Historical Review* 107(3): 797–821.

Stoler, Ann Laura. 2002. Colonial Archives and the Art of Governance. *Archival Science* 2: 87–109.

—— 2009. *Along the Archival Grain: Epistemic Anxieties and Colonial Common Sense.* Princeton: Princeton University Press.

Stroud, Ellen. 2004. Does Nature Always Matter? Following Dirt through History. *History and Theory* 42(4): 75–81.

Struk, Janina. 2004. *Photographing the Holocaust: Interpretations of the Evidence.* London: I. B. Tauris.

Thompson, James. 2007. Pictorial Lies? Posters and Politics in Britain, 1880–1914. *Past and Present* 197(1): 177–210.

Thomson, Alistair. 1995. Memory as a Battlefield: Personal and Political Investments in the National Military Past. *Oral History Review* 22(2) 55–73.

Trentmann, Frank. 2009. Materiality in the Future of History: Things, Practices, and Politics. *Journal of British Studies* 48(2): 283–307.

Vickery, Amanda and Styles, John. 2006. *Gender, Taste, and Material Culture in Britain and North America, 1700–1830.* New Haven, CT: Yale University Press.

White, Hayden. 1973. *Metahistory: The Historical Imagination in Nineteenth-Century Europe.* Baltimore: Johns Hopkins University Press.

—— 1987. *The Content of the Form: Narrative Discourse and Historical Representation.* Baltimore: Johns Hopkins University Press.

—— 1992. Historical Emplotment and the Problem of Truth. In *Probing the Limits of Representation: Nazism and the 'Final Solution'*, ed. Saul Friedlander, pp. 37–53. Cambridge, MA: Harvard University Press.

White, Jonathan. 2006. A World of Goods? The 'Consumption Turn' and Eighteenth-Century British History. *Cultural and Social History* 3: 93–104.

Young, James. 1993. *The Texture of Memory: Holocaust Memorials and Meaning.* New Haven: Yale University Press.

—— 1997. Toward a Received History of the Holocaust. *History and Theory* 36(4): 21–43.

CHAPTER 6

CANONICAL AFFORDANCES: THE PSYCHOLOGY OF EVERYDAY THINGS

ALAN COSTALL AND ANN RICHARDS

…subject and object antithetically defined can have logically no transactions with each other.

(Dewey 1958 [1925]: 239)

…things are objects to be treated, used, acted upon and with, enjoyed and endured, even more than things to be known. They are things *had* before they are things cognized.

(Dewey 1958 [1925]: 21)

6.1 INTRODUCTION

PSYCHOLOGISTS have a 'thing' about things. If anything, they would prefer, for reasons we will explain, to have nothing to do with them. However, in 1989, the cognitive psychologist Donald Norman published a book with the eye-catching title, *The Psychology of Everyday Things*. For him, the whole point of the title was to make clear that 'inanimate objects had a psychology' (Norman 1998: vii). The book sold well and to a readership well beyond psychologists—so much so, that a second edition appeared. But the new edition had the much less eye-catching title—*The Design of Everyday Things* (1998). Norman's new publishers, and his own inquiries among potential readers, convinced him that the original title would only cause confusion.

The idea that 'inanimate objects' do *not* have a psychology is prevalent within psychology. This cannot be put down entirely to the unworldliness of psychologists. The division of people and things is institutionalized within the structure of modern academic disciplines. The natural sciences have, as Joerges nicely put it, constructed a 'material world' independent of human concerns, and the human sciences, in turn, created 'a world of actors devoid of things' (Joerges 1988: 220).

Scientists, and especially psychologists, usually put the blame for this dualism of the objective and subjective upon a single *philosopher*, René Descartes, and then proceed as though it has nothing to do with themselves as clear-headed, no-nonsense *scientists*. (In fact, Descartes himself made important contributions to science, not least, the system of Cartesian coordinates.) But, ever since the time of Galileo and Kepler, mind–body dualism had been fundamental to the project of physical science.

> The dualistic idea of matter was designed explicitly as a pure Object to balance the pure Subject. It was incapable of life because, for dualism, life, along with subjectivity, was an alien extra, something spiritual which God infused only into human beings, *leaving the rest of the natural world as inanimate machinery.* Yet now, when theorists dropped the idea of spirit, this thin, inert kind of matter was supposed to be the only reality left in the world and thus, of course, the only possible subject-matter for science. *Life and subjectivity were either mere surface phenomena or some kind of illusion.* (Midgley 2006: 10; emphases added)

Of course, the Darwinian revolution, and also developments within physics (such as quantum theory and special relativity) challenged the dualist ontology of mechanistic physics (on Darwin, see Dewey 1910; on physics, see Whitehead 1926; Burtt 1954 [1923]; Koyré 1965; Toulmin 1982; Bohm 1988). The radical implications of these scientific developments were widely acknowledged around the turn of the twentieth century. As the philosopher Arthur Bentley neatly put it:

> Since the 'mental' as we have known it in the past was a squeeze-out from Newtonian space, the physicist may be asked to ponder how it can still remain a squeeze-out when the space out of which it was squeezed is no longer there to squeeze it out. (Bentley 1938: 165)

Yet scientific dualism has somehow remained remarkably entrenched, and, in relation to 'the psychology of inanimate things', there have been two consequences:

1. Things have mainly failed to figure on the scientific agenda of psychologists, or even other social scientists.
2. To the limited extent that things *have* figured within psychological discourse, their *meaning* has been radically subjectivized.

This chapter is about 'what things are for' and will draw upon James Gibson's concept of 'affordances' to rematerialize—but also problematize—*the* meaning of things.

6.2 MEANING AS REPRESENTATION

The standard line within traditional physical science has been that *meaning* (along with sensory qualities such as colour and warmth, the so-called 'secondary qualities') does not exist in the real world but in our minds *instead*. (Descartes, of all people, was a notable exception; he regarded sensations as *both* mental and physical; see Cottingham 1985.)

That meaning is subjective, *not* objective, is now widely regarded as proven scientific fact, along the lines of the following curious argument:

> it used to be thought that perceptions, by vision and touch and so on, can give direct knowledge of objective reality....*But, largely through the physiological study of the senses over the*

last two hundred years, this has become ever more difficult to defend.... ultimately we cannot know directly what is illusion, any more than truth—for we cannot step outside perception to compare experience with objective reality. (Gregory 1989: 94; emphasis added)

That this line of argument has, from the time of Galileo, seemed so compelling to otherwise highly intelligent scientists is truly astonishing. For the argument presupposes what it claims to deny: that people—*well, scientists, at least!*—can, indeed, come to know what things are like in the world, in this case, the nature of the physiology of the senses.

This dualism of objects and subjects is the basis of 'the representationalist theory of mind': the world as we experience it does not correspond to the real world, but as it is *re*-presented within our minds. Long before representationalism became a central dogma within psychology in the 1950s, it had been essential to the 'metaphysics' of physical science, and already subject to fundamental criticism by, for example, the philosophers David Hume, E. B. Holt, and George Herbert Mead:

> In general, the connections between the experiencing individual and the things experienced—conceived in their physical reality—were reduced to a passive conditioning of states of consciousness by a mechanical nature. Into such a mind was carried... whatever in nature could not be stated in terms of matter in motion.... The result of this was to force upon the mind the presentation of the world of actual experience with all its characters, except, perhaps, the so-called primary characters of things. Mind had, therefore, a representational world that was supposed to answer to the physical world, and *the connection between this world and the physical world remained a mystery.* (Mead 1938: 359, emphasis added; on Hume, see Palmer 1987; on Holt, see Costall 2011)

Fundamental problems with representationalism have long been recognized within psychology itself (see, for example, Bickhard and Richie 1983; Costall and Still 1987; Harnad 1990; Button et al. 1995; Shaw 2003). Yet, somehow, representationalism continues to create the impression that it not only is, but *has* to be 'the only game in town' (to use Jerry Fodor's smug expression). So, according to representationalist theory, the meaning of *things* could not inhere in the things themselves but must, *instead*, be projected onto them on the basis of how we happen to represent them subjectively or 'cognitively':

> Representation is a fundamental process of all human life; it underlies the development of mind, self, societies and cultures.... The reality of the human world is in its *entirety* made of representation; in fact there is no sense of reality for our human world without the work of representation. (Jovchelovitch 2006: 10; emphasis added).

This representationalist view of the meanings of things is not restricted to psychology. It is prevalent within the study of so-called 'material culture', and became influential when archaeologists came to draw not only upon hard-core cognitivist theory, but also structuralism and post-structuralism (see Thomas 1999; Jones 2004; see also Marcoulatus 2003). To the extent there are differences between disciplines, it concerns the 'location' of the meaning of things—as either in individual, private minds, or else in collective representations or 'discourse':

> Things don't mean: we construct meaning, using representational systems—concepts and signs.... According to [the social constructionist] approach, we must not confuse the *material* world, where things and people exist, and the symbolic practices and processes through which representation, meaning and language operate. Constructivists do not deny the

existence of the material world. *However, it is not the material world which conveys meaning: it is the language system or whatever system we are using to represent our concepts.* (Hall 1997: 25; emphasis added; cf. Danziger 2003, on 'discourse reductionism'!)

So, according to representationalism, the meanings of things are, one way or another, in 'us' and *not* in things. They are either in our individual minds or our 'group minds'. The mistake of representationalism—a direct consequence of its dualistic foundation—is to suppose that there is no skill or intelligence in action outside of representation. Yet, the *intelligent* use of rules and representations depends upon an intelligence that is not itself embodied in explicit rules and representations. Skilful action and judgement precede reflective knowing (Ryle 1949; Merleau-Ponty 1962; Dewey 1983 [1922]; Schön 1991; Burkitt 2002).

6.3 GIBSON'S CONCEPT OF AFFORDANCES

One influential argument *for* the representationalist approach to the meaning of things has been that any thing could, in principle, mean *anything*. Thus, an apple can be eaten, but it can also be used as a missile, to make cider, a target for archery practice, as a brand image, etc., etc., etc. The deeply ambiguous nature of things has also been deployed as an influential argument *against* James Gibson's theory of affordances.

The fundamental point of Gibson's concept of affordances is that we need to take *things* themselves much more seriously in our account of *their* meaning precisely because, although we can do many different things with *any* thing, we cannot do *anything* with anything. Objects can *object* to certain ways of being used:

> I have coined this word [affordances] as a substitute for values, a term which carries an old burden of philosophical meaning. I mean simply what things furnish, for good or ill. *What they afford…*[1] *after all, depends on their properties.* (Gibson 1966: 285; emphasis added; see also Hutchby 2001)

In our view, the theory of affordances was the only serious attempt within modern psychology to *reconcile* subjects and objects—agents and their resources for action. (For an excellent account of Gibson's 'ecological approach', see Heft 2001; for discussion of Gibson from the perspective of archaeology and anthropology, see Ingold 2000; Knappett 2004.)

According to Gibson, the affordances of things are real, but they come into being in relation to particular agents and their activities and capacities. Gibson defined an 'affordance' as 'a combination of physical properties of the environment that is uniquely suited to a given animal—to his nutritive system or his action system or his locomotor system' (Gibson 1977: 79). Gibson's purpose was to undermine the dualism of subjectivity and objectivity that keeps trapping us into locating the meaning of things *exclusively* within ourselves. The meaning of things is a *relation*:

> An affordance is not what we call a 'subjective' quality of a thing. But neither is it what we call an 'objective' property of a thing if by that we mean that a physical object has no

---

[1] We have deleted Gibson's own term here, 'observer', here. Gibson's later work shifted from his earlier focus on perception or observation to the resources for *agency*: information and affordances (see Costall 2003).

reference to any animal. An affordance cuts across the dichotomy of subjective-objective and helps us to understand its inadequacy. The affordances of the environment are facts of the environment, not appearances. But they are not, on the other hand, facts at the level of physics concerned only with matter and energy *with animals left out*. (Gibson 1977: 69–70; emphasis added)

For example, food really is *there* in the world—indeed it is an essential biological resource—but only in relation to those animals with the capacities to access and digest it. So the fundamental point is that affordances 'have *unity* relative to the posture and behavior of the animal being considered' (Gibson 1979: 127–8; emphasis added). Thus grass constitutes food for cows but not for humans, and it only *became* food—and indeed evolved, as it were, to take this into account (Bateson 1973: 128)—with the advent of grazing animals. Essentially the same point had been made by the philosopher, Maurice Merleau-Ponty:

> Already the mere presence of a living being transforms the physical world, bringing to view here 'food', there a 'hiding place', and giving to 'stimuli' a sense which they have not hitherto possessed. *A fortiori* does this apply to the presence of man in the animal world. Behaviour creates meanings which are transcendent in relation to the anatomical apparatus, and yet immanent to the behaviour as such. (Merleau-Ponty 1962: 189)

The theory of affordances is an account of meaning that can exist *prior to* the development of language, symbolization, and categorization. For this reason, the concept of affordances has long been dismissed as both universalist and reductionist. For example, George Lakoff, although generally sympathetic to the thrust of Gibson's ecological approach, complained that 'the Gibsonian environment is monolithic and self-consistent and the same for all people', and that his approach 'cannot make sense of experiential or cultural categories' (Lakoff 1987: 216).

In fact, the theory of affordances is a challenge to the non-developmental, ahistorical, and unworldly foundation of modern cognitive theory. Cognitive theory is non-developmental and ahistorical precisely because it takes the specific human practices of representation, rule-following, and categorization for granted as *universal*, and as *the starting point* rather than as *a problem* for psychological theory, not only in relation to human activity in general but to other animals as well (see Brooks 1991 for an important critique). The theory of affordances, far from being reductionist, is an attempt to define the *conditions of possibility* for the evolution and development of language and representational systems (see Reed 1991).

One real limitation of Gibson's concept of affordances is that although it is relational, the relation is restricted to the agent–object dyad. Yet the affordance of any artefact is not confined to that object in isolation, but depends on a 'constellation' (Keller and Keller 1996) or 'utensil-totality' (Gurwitsch 1979: 82–3) of not only other objects but also events. A group of archaeology students at Copenhagen University excavating the camp area attached to the annual rock music festival at Roskilde were reported to be finding plenty of used condoms and beer cans, a few food wrappers, and a single hash-pipe. The students, however, were mainly impressed by what their excavation was *failing* to reveal—the event that was *holding* these different artefacts together. 'We cannot see the music in the festival's soil' (*'man ikke kan se musikken i festivalens muld'*) (Skyum-Nielsen 2007: 25). We think Gibson's 'dyadic' approach is a serious limitation, but not an issue that, as far as we are aware, has been previously raised by psychologists.

However, we want to focus upon a related criticism: that Gibson seems to be presenting an entirely *static* account of affordances, of meanings *inhering* in objects just waiting to be 'discovered'. In many of our spontaneous interactions with things, as John Shotter has emphasized, their meanings come into being within the flow of activity:

> the beings in Gibson's world are depicted merely as observers, not as actors, i.e. not as beings able to provide for themselves, by their own actions, conditions appropriate to support their action's continuation. They may move about, but they do not act; thus rather than 'makers', they are presented merely as 'finders' of what already exists. Such a view, I would argue, fails to recognize the peculiar form-producing character of activity in a biological and social world; it fails to assign a proper role to time and to processes of growth and development. (Shotter 1983: 20)

So, according to Shotter, it seems that *everything* must be in flux. We can never 'step' into the same flow of affordances twice.

6.4 CANONICAL AFFORDANCES

In fact, Gibson himself was blatantly inconsistent in his account of affordances, at times acknowledging their fundamentally 'open', relational status, and, at other times, 'lodging' affordances in an 'objectivated world' (Noble 1991: 204). This confusion derives from Gibson's insistence upon the continuity between human artefacts and 'natural' objects in general:

> It is a mistake to separate the natural from the artificial as if there were two environments; artifacts have to be manufactured from natural substances. It is also a mistake to separate the cultural environment from the natural environment, as if there were a world of mental products distinct from the world of material products. There is only one world, however diverse, and all animals live in it, although we human animals have altered it to suit ourselves. (Gibson 1979: 130)

Although Gibson was right to stress the materiality of the artificial and the cultural, it does not follow that artefacts do not also have a special psychological status. Gibson's treatment of the affordances of artefacts in much the same terms as 'natural' objects has led to two important problems. The first is the one identified by Shotter and Noble: the objectification of affordances *in general—by unwittingly generalizing from the special case of artefacts.* The second problem is the failure of Gibson (and, indeed, Shotter and Noble) to recognize that the meanings of things *can become objectified*. Artefacts *already* embody human intentions.

A chair is *for*-sitting-on whether or not anyone happens to be using it for that purpose. And it remains a chair even when someone is standing on it to change a light-bulb. Its 'canonical affordance'—the *thing* it is *for* (Costall 1995)—is objective, or better, *impersonal* (Morss 1985): '*one* sits on chairs'. Nevertheless, canonical affordances still imply *us*, but in the plurality rather than the singular. As is the case for other 'social facts', the impersonality of canonical affordances is 'an ongoing accomplishment of the concerted activities of daily life' (Garfinkel 1967: vii).

Contrary to Shotter's *general* claim, therefore, artefacts—humanly constructed objects—would seem to be an exception. Their users do not *normally* relate to these kinds of objects as 'makers' but mainly (although, as we shall argue, *not exclusively*) as *partakers*. In relation to the things they are for, and the routine practices into which they enter, objectification is not a fallacy but a fact of life.

6.5 THE PLAY OF THINGS

> There is no problem, however complicated, which, when looked at in the right way, does not become ever more complicated. (After Poul Andersen)

So far we have drawn a distinction between the 'canonical affordances' of artefacts, and the affordances of other kinds of things. But things are more complicated than that. First of all, 'natural' objects, and not just artefacts, can become incorporated into standard practices and attain a conventional or normative significance. Furthermore, any object with a canonical affordance still also affords, in principle, limitless other uses and meanings.

The classic research by Karl Düncker on 'functional fixedness' suggests that once we come to understand the 'real' or 'proper' function of something we can become 'blinded' to its other possible uses (Düncker 1945: 85ff.). Experiments on 'functional fixedness' present people with a choice of objects which they can use to solve a problem set to them, but where some of the objects will need to be used in a non-standard way, e.g. using a box not as a container but turned upside down as a supporting surface, or pliers not as a tool but a pendulum bob. German and Defeyter (2000) have shown that the onset of 'functional fixedness' occurs relatively early. Children of school age already face difficulties on such creative problem-solving tasks, in contrast to younger children.

Functional fixedness is, however, difficult to reconcile with the everyday fact that people improvise in their use of conventional objects. Düncker (1945: 88) himself considered whether it might arise from a 'bias in the subjects' rather than 'in the objects', but dismissed as rationalization the claims of some of the participants in his study that they thought that they were not *allowed* to use the box in which the other objects had been presented. It is important to note that the school-age children, in the study by German and Defeyter, and related research, have been tested at school, and therefore under the somewhat repressive 'regimes' of such places. When, for example, children are asked to solve a multiplication problem, they are not supposed to use a calculator or phone a friend.

It is certainly the case that, *out of school*, even school-age children are seriously into the business of 'misusing' things. An obvious example is symbolic or pretend play, where objects with a conventional meaning are used in amusingly different ways, such as wearing a colander as a helmet, or kneading a pillow as though it were bread dough. According to Alan Leslie, all this playing about with the meanings of things is paradoxical given that it is occurring at just the time children are also supposed to be discovering the 'real' meaning of things:

> The perceiving, thinking organism ought, as far as possible, to get things right. Yet pretense flies in the face of this fundamental principle. In pretense we deliberately distort reality. (Leslie 1987: 412)

Much of the recent research on play has adopted a remarkably unworldly cognitive approach and almost completely disregarded the nature of the play objects themselves. In contrast, Ágnes Szokolsky (2006), adopting an affordance approach, has found that young children's pretend play is, in fact, nicely tuned to the affordances of the available play objects, even if the affordances are not immediately obvious to anyone else. Her own son once announced, unpromisingly, that his discarded sock was a gun, but then, to her surprise, he stretched it taut between his hands and 'aimed' it at her (see Costall and Dreier 2006: 4). Contrary to Leslie's cognitivist view of play, she concludes:

> Pretend play is imaginative, *but not by turning away from the real world*. Children perceive and use affordances while they play and this is surely part of the developmental process. (Szokolsky 2006: 83; emphasis added)

Furthermore, even as adults, we routinely 'misuse' things, appropriating them into the flow of our activity in non-standard ways. Paper clips are hardly ever used for their intended function, but used instead, among many other things, as toothpicks, nail and ear cleaners, makeshift fasteners for blouses, nylons, and bras, and decorative chains (Petrovski 1993: 51). Sometimes, these improvised uses 'take on' the status of an additional canonical affordance. Opened-out paper clips became the approved way to remove computer discs stuck in disc drives. The now defunct, alkaline 'blue bags', used in laundry for whitening clothes, also served as a widely recognized, ready to hand remedy for bee stings. Aspirin, initially 'designed' for pain relief, is now also used to enhance blood circulation.

Sometimes, these alternative affordances require adopting a quite different 'angle' towards the object, or attending to characteristics that are incidental to its main function. As we discovered as students, the so-called 'mini-computers' of the 1970s (in fact, power-hungry giants) could serve as highly effective heaters when the university central heating system was switched off at the weekends. Using an upturned glass as a pastry cutter requires disregarding its 'contain-ability', and attending instead to the cutting ability of its edge. In some parts of rural China, the baskets used to transport pigs to market are also used as a standard part of the local looms. It is the *outer* surface of the baskets in these 'pig-basket' (or 'pig-cage') looms that is then functional, where it serves to support and maintain the sequence of pattern sticks (Ågren 1992).

There is a psychological test of creativity that requires people to think of as many different possible uses they can of a commonplace object, such as a brick. The problem, of course, in this particular context, is to forget that the thing *is* a brick. Indeed, according to Susanne Langer, it is only when we *stop* looking at things with 'the economy of practical vision' that 'their suppressed forms and their unusual meanings emerge for us' (Langer 1951: 239). However, in everyday life, our creativity usually occurs in practice, when, within the flow of activity, we appropriate things, often unthinkingly, in novel ways to achieve our current goals. We do not work backwards from the possible uses of objects, as in a creativity test, but *forwards* from what it is *we* are trying to do.

Such improvisation can lead to an interesting interplay between designers and producers, on the one hand, and users. Here is Donald Schön's account of the 'career' of Scotch Tape:

> Shortly after World War II, to take one rather celebrated example, the 3M Corporation put on the market a clear cellulose acetate tape, coated on one side with pressure-sensitive adhesive, which they called Scotch Tape. They had intended it for use as a book-mending material, a way of preserving things that would otherwise have to be thrown away; hence

the name Scotch. But in consumers' hands, the product came to be used in many different ways, most of which had nothing to do with mending books. It was used to wrap packages, to fasten pictures to the wall, to make labels, to decorate surfaces, even to curl hair. 3M's managers did not regard these surprising uses as a failure of their initial marketing plan, nor did they merely accept them as a happy accident. They *noticed* them and tried to make sense of them as a set of messages about potential markets. The company began to market types of Scotch Tape specially designed for use in such applications as packaging, decorating, and hair curling.

> 3M's marketing managers treated their product as a projection test for consumers.... Their marketing process was a reflective conversation with consumers. (Schön 1991: 245; see du Gay et al. 1997, on the similar fate of the Sony Walkman)

The extent to which any object is used in more than just one way depends on many factors, including its personal and monetary value, and its vulnerability to damage if used in the non-standard way. When, for example, we use a chisel as a screwdriver, we can impair its future use as a chisel, even though, in this case, we 'handle' the object in more or less the same way. There are also cultural differences. Visiting English kitchen shops, we are struck by the absurd degree of specificity of the various utensils, especially given the small size of most English kitchens. In contrast, within Zapotek communities in Mexico, for example, objects are used in many different conventional ways. The gourds, baskets, and stools are routinely 'inverted' to cover food, constrain the movement of chickens, or to serve as pot-holders. Given their multiple uses, there is no single canonical orientation for these objects, and this is reflected in Zapotek children's performance on spatial imitation tasks (Jensen de López 2006).

6.6 CONCLUSION

In their classic text, *The Social Construction of Reality*, Berger and Luckman presented the following wonderfully reassuring account of the archaeological interpretation of *the* meaning of things:

> I am constantly surrounded by objects that 'proclaim' the subjective intentions of my fellow-men, although I may sometimes have difficulty being quite sure just what it is that a particular object is 'proclaiming', especially if it was produced by men whom I have not known well or at all in face-to-face situations. Every ethnologist or archaeologist will readily testify to such difficulties, but the very fact that he can overcome them and reconstruct from an artifact the subjective intentions of men whose society may have been extinct for millennia is eloquent proof of the enduring power of human objectivations. (Berger and Luckman 1971: 50)

Unfortunately, as we have been arguing, 'the enduring power of human objectivations' would not seem to provide a sufficient warrant for the interpretation of 'subjective intentions' from artefacts, even artefacts belonging to modern industrial societies, where the trend has certainly been towards a greater specialization of function.

First of all, the affordance of an object is not neatly self-contained within the agent–object dyad, but implicates a 'constellation' of other objects and events (Keller and Keller 1996). Secondly, even commonplace objects can end up being *for* more than one thing.

Thirdly, as Shotter and Noble rightly emphasized, there can also be a good deal of 'play' in the flow of everyday use: 'the *Spiel* of usability' (Keller 2005). And this is where new possibilities are realized:

> an affordance is only completely specified as the affordance it is when the activity it affords is complete. (Shotter 1983: 27)

In such cases, affordances are not simply *dis*covered, but nor are they mentally projected upon inherently meaningless things. They are negotiated. In such cases, the verb, 'affording' rather than the noun, 'affordance', is, therefore, by far the more appropriate term. But then, of course, from a wider historical and archaeological perspective, this is true of canonical affordances as well (see de Léon, this volume, and also 2006). Over successive 'generations' of production, the things themselves are in flux, as they, in turn, newly resource, and thereby reconstruct, human agency.

References

Ågren, K. 1992. Kinesisk vävkonst. *Hemslöjden* 5: 26–7.

Bateson, Gregory. 1973. *Steps to an Ecology of Mind*. London: Paladin.

Bentley, Arthur F. 1938. Physicists and Fairies. *Philosophy of Science* 5: 132–65.

Berger, Peter L. and Luckman, Thomas. 1971. *The Social Construction of Reality*. Harmondsworth: Penguin.

Bickhard, Mark H. and Richie, D. Michael. 1983. *On the Nature of Representation*. New York: Praeger.

Bohm, David. 1988. Postmodern Science and a Postmodern World. In *The Reenchantment of Science*, ed. D. R. Griffin, pp. 57–78. Albany, NY: State University of New York.

Brooks, Rodney A. 1991. Intelligence without Representation. *Artificial Intelligence* 47: 139–59.

Burkitt, Ian. 2002. Technologies of the Self: Habitus and Capacities. *Journal for the Theory of Social Behaviour* 32: 220–37.

Burtt, Edwin A. 1954. *The Metaphysical Foundations of Modern Physical Science*. London: Kegan Paul, Trench, Trubner [first published in 1923].

Button, Graham, Coulter, John, Lee, John, and Sharrock, Wes. 1995. *Computers, Minds and Conduct*. Oxford: Polity Press.

Costall, Alan. 1995. Socializing Affordances. *Theory and Psychology* 5: 467–81.

—— 2003. From Direct Perception to the Primacy of Action: A Closer Look at James Gibson's Ecological Approach to Psychology. In *Theories of Infant Development*, ed. G. J. Bremner and A. M. Slater, pp. 70–89. Oxford: Blackwell.

—— 2011. Against Representationalism: James Gibson's Secret Debt to E. B. Holt. In *A New Look at New Realism: The Psychology and Philosophy of E. B. Holt*, ed. E. P. Charles, pp. 243–62. New Brunswick: Transaction Publishers.

Costall, Alan and Dreier, Ole. 2006. Introduction. In *Doing Things with Things: The Design and Use of Everyday Objects,* ed. Alan Costall and Ole Dreier, pp. 1–12. Aldershot: Ashgate.

Costall, Alan and Still, Arthur (eds.). 1987. *Cognitive Psychology in Question*. Brighton: Harvester.

Cottingham, John. 1985. Cartesian Trialism. *Mind*, NS 94: 218–30.

Danziger, Kurt. 2003. Where History, Theory, and Philosophy Meet: The Biography of Psychological Objects. In *About Psychology: Essays at the Crossroads of History, Theory, and*

Philosophy, ed. Darryl B. Hill and Michael J. Kral, pp. 19–33. New York: State University of New York Press.

de Léon, David. 2006. The Cognitive Biography of Things. In *Doing Things with Things: The Design and Use of Everyday Objects,* ed. Alan Costall and Ole Dreier, pp. 113–30. Aldershot: Ashgate.

Dewey, John. 1910. The Influence of Darwin on Philosophy. In Dewey, *The Influence of Darwin on Philosophy and Other Essays,* pp. 1–19. New York: Henry Holt & Co. [first published in *Popular Science Monthly,* July 1909].

—— 1922 *Human Nature and Conduct.* New York: Henry Holt & Co.

—— 1958 [1925]. *Experience and Nature.* New York: Dover [Based on the Paul Carus lectures of 1925].

du Gay, Paul, Hall, Stuart, Janes, Linda, MacKay, Hugh, and Negus, Keith. 1997. *Doing Cultural Studies: The Story of the Sony Walkman.* London: Sage Publications in association with the Open University.

Düncker, Karl. 1945. On Problem Solving. *Psychological Monographs* 58 (5, Whole No. 270).

Garfinkel, Harold. 1967. *Studies in Ethnomethodology.* Englewood Cliffs, NJ: Prentice-Hall.

German, Tim P. and Defeyter, Margaret A. 2000. Immunity to Functional Fixedness in Young Children. *Psychonomic Bulletin and Review* 7: 707–12.

Gibson, James J. 1966. *The Senses Considered as Perceptual Systems.* Boston: Houghton Mifflin.

—— 1977. The Theory of Affordances. In *Perceiving, Acting and Knowing: Toward an Ecological Psychology,* ed. Robert Shaw and John Bransford, pp. 67–82. Hillsdale, NJ: Erlbaum.

—— 1979. *The Ecological Approach to Visual Perception.* Boston: Houghton-Mifflin.

Gregory, Richard L. 1989. Dismantling Reality. In *Dismantling Truth: Reality in the Post-Modern World,* ed. Hilary Lawson and Lisa Appignanesi, pp. 93–100. London: Weidenfeld & Nicolson.

Gurwitsch, Aron. 1979. *Human Encounters in the Social World,* ed. A. Métrauz, tr. F. Kersten. Pittsburgh: Duquesne University Press.

Hall, Stuart. 1997. The Work of Representation. In *Representation: Cultural Representations and Signifying Practices,* ed. Stuart Hall, pp. 13–64. London: Sage.

Harnad, Steven. 1990. The Symbol Grounding Problem. *Physica D* 42: 335–46.

Heft, Harry. 2001. *Ecological Psychology in Context: James Gibson, Roger Barker, and the Legacy of William James's Radical Empiricism.* Mahwah, NJ: Erlbaum.

Hutchby, Ian. 2001. Technologies, Texts and Affordances. *Sociology* 35: 441–56.

Ingold, Tim. 2000. *The Perception of the Environment: Essays in Livelihood, Dwelling and Skill.* London: Routledge.

Jensen de López, Kristine. 2006. Culture, Language and Canonicality: Differences in the Use of Containers between Zapotek (Mexican indigenous), and Danish Children. In *Doing Things with Things: The Design and Use of Everyday Objects,* ed. Alan Costall and Ole Dreier, pp. 87–109. Aldershot: Ashgate.

Joerges, Bernward. 1988. Technology in Everyday Life: Conceptual Queries. *Journal for the Theory of Social Behaviour* 18: 221–37.

Jones, Andrew. 2004. Archaeometry and Materiality: Materials-Based Analysis in Theory and Practice. *Archaeometry* 3: 327–38.

Jovchelovitch, Sandra. 2006. *Knowledge in Context: Representations, Community and Culture.* Hove, UK: Routledge.

Keller, Charles M. and Keller, Janet D. 1996. *Cognition and Tool Use: The Blacksmith at Work.* Cambridge: Cambridge University Press.

Keller, Kurt D. 2005. The Corporeal Order of Things: The *Spiel* of Usability. *Human Studies* 28: 173–204.

Knappett, Carl. 2004. The Affordances of Things: A Post-Gibsonian Perspective on the Relationality of Mind and Matter. In *Rethinking Materiality: The Engagement of Mind with the Material World*, ed. Elizabeth DeMarrais, Chris Gosden, and Colin Renfrew, pp. 43–51. Cambridge: McDonald Institute Monographs.

Koyré, Alexandre. 1965. *Newtonian Studies*. London: Chapman & Hall.

Lakoff, George. 1987. *Women, Fire, and Dangerous Things: What Categories Reveal about the Mind*. Chicago: University of Chicago Press.

Langer, Susanne. 1951. *Philosophy in a New Key*, 2nd edn. New York: New American Library.

Leslie, Alan M. 1987. Pretense and Representation: The Origins of 'Theory of Mind'. *Psychological Review* 94: 412–26.

Marcoulatus, Iordanis. 2003. The Secret Life of Things: Rethinking Social Ontology. *Journal for the Theory of Social Behaviour* 33: 245–78.

Mead, George Herbert. 1938. *The Philosophy of the Act*. Chicago: University of Chicago Press.

Merleau-Ponty, Maurice. 1962. *The Phenomenology of Perception*, tr. C. Smith. London: Routledge & Kegan Paul.

Midgley, Mary. 2006. Editorial Introduction. *Journal of Consciousness Studies* 13: 8–16.

Morss, John R. 1985. Old Mead in New Bottles: The Impersonal and the Interpersonal in Infant Knowledge. *New Ideas in Psychology* 3: 165–76.

Noble, William. 1991. Ecological Realism and the Fallacy of 'Objectification'. In *Against Cognitivism*, ed. Arthur Still and Alan Costall, pp. 199–223. New York: Harvester Wheatsheaf.

Norman, Donald A. 1989. *The Psychology of Everyday Things*. New York: Basic Books.

—— 1998. *The Design of Everyday Things*. Cambridge, MA: MIT Press.

Palmer, Anthony. 1987, Cognitivism and Computer Simulation. In *Cognitive Psychology in Question*, ed. Alan Costall and Arthur Still, pp. 55–69. Brighton: Harvester.

Petrovski, Henry. 1993. *The Evolution of Useful Things*. London: Pavilion.

Reed, Edward S. 1991. James Gibson's Ecological Approach to Cognition. In *Against Cognitivism*, ed. Arthur Still and Alan Costall, pp. 171–97. New York: Harvester Wheatsheaf.

Ryle, Gilbert. 1949. *The Concept of Mind*. London: Hutchinson.

Schön, Donald A. 1991. *The Reflective Practitioner: How Professionals Think in Action*. Aldershot: Avebury.

Shaw, Robert E. 2003. The Agent–Environment Interface: Simon's Indirect or Gibson's Direct Coupling. *Ecological Psychology* 15: 37–106.

Shotter, John. 1983. 'Duality of Structure' and 'Intentionality' in an Ecological Psychology. *Journal for the Theory of Social Behavior* 13: 19–43.

Skyum-Nielsen, R. 2007. I Roskilde Vejer Provokationen Tungere end Musikken. *Nyhedsavisen* 5 July: 24–5.

Szokolsky, Ágnes. 2006. Object Use in Pretend Play: Symbolic or Functional? In *Doing Things with Things: The Design and Use of Everyday Objects*, ed. Alan Costall and Ole Dreier, pp. 67–85. Aldershot: Ashgate.

Thomas, Julian. 1999. Some Problems with the Notion of External Symbolic Storage, and the Case of Neolithic Material Culture in Britain. In *Cognition and Material Culture*, ed. C. Renfrew and C. Scarre, pp. 149–56. Cambridge: McDonald Institute Monographs.

Toulmin, Stephen. 1982. The Construal of Reality: Criticism in Modern and Postmodern Science. *Critical Inquiry* 9(1): 93–111.

Whitehead, Alfred N. 1926. *Science and the Modern World*. Cambridge: Cambridge University Press.

CHAPTER 7

TO THE THINGS THEMSELVES AGAIN: OBSERVATIONS ON WHAT THINGS ARE AND WHY THEY MATTER

JAMES GORDON FINLAYSON

7.1 INTRODUCTION

I was a clumsy child. I used to break and lose things. As a consequence I had a keen sense of their fragility, and of the badness or wrongness of breaking or losing them. I never stopped to ask: Why does it matter if I break this thing? After all, the things I broke—cups, plates, bowls, vases—were mass-produced goods of relatively low value. If they could not be replaced by a replica, an adequate substitute could be found. The wrong that I sensed on such occasions was not merely due to the fact that I was depriving someone *else* of their possession. Whether they belonged to me or to someone else, it was still wrong, though breaking someone else's things was bad in another way too.

Though, I am not the only one not to have asked that question, it is the case that philosophers have paid scant attention to it. One might think that surprising, given that philosophers have always spent their lives inquiring into the question of being, the question of what the world is like—whether the natural or social world—and what truly is. On one influential view—Cicero's—'Philosophy begins with Socrates, and it actually gets going when he turns his back on speculation about the natural world and turns to ethics' (Cicero, *Tuscular Disputations*, cited in Geuss 2009: 16). In spite of its inquiries into nature (physics and metaphysics) and morality (ethics) Western philosophy has yielded little insight into the question of why things matter.

Perhaps that is because philosophy has tended to hold material things in small regard. In the metaphysical tradition stemming from Plato and Aristotle there is a hierarchy of substances at the apex of which are gods, who are most fundamentally real, then human beings, then animals, plants, and at the foot of which are inanimate and inorganic beings (Lovejoy 1933: 59). A certain axiology accompanies this metaphysical hierarchy of being. Gods and man stand at the apex, while artefacts and other inanimate and inorganic entities lie at the bottom. These last are of low value and accordingly merit little philosophical interest (*Republic* VI 510a [Plato 1989a: 745]).

Deeply ingrained in Greek philosophy, particularly in Plato, Cynicism, and Stoicism, is also the view that material possessions are only of earthly value and that attachment to them detracts from what is truly good and important. Medieval Christian thought also teaches of the dangers of attachment to earthly things and worldly possessions.

Finally, since the time of Roman law, ownership is conceived as the right of disposal. If I borrow something, or lease it, I have a duty to look after it, whereas if I own something it is mine to do as I please with. The belief that the owner disposes over her possessions and that she may use them or abuse them at will is still prevalent and enshrined in law (Proudhon 1969: 64).

What these three examples suggest is that there are certain tendencies within Western philosophical thinking about metaphysics, ethics, and law, which combine to encourage the disregard of the question of things. Martin Heidegger (1980a: 1), one of few philosophers to consider this question, is right in his judgement that the question of the thing still more than ever needs to be asked. This essay will do just that. Drawing from the history of philosophy, phenomenology, ordinary language philosophy, and conceptual analysis, as well as the sociology and anthropology of material culture, I attempt to recover a notion of 'thing' that is distinct from and not to be conflated with that of 'object' and 'entity', and which can help throw light on the neglected question of why things matter.

7.2 THE CURRENT STATE OF THINGS
IN PHILOSOPHY

The same tendency exists within current academic philosophy (and other academic disciplines). The Harvard moral philosopher Christine Korsgaard is one of few contemporary philosophers even to have considered these questions, albeit in a footnote in an essay on another topic (2005: 106, n.69). Her discussion is so rare and illuminating that it is worth citing at length:

> Why shouldn't we think that implicit in our endorsement of our self-concern is a concern for the good of anything that has a good?...[C]ould it even be that we have duties not only to our fellow creatures, but to our fellow entities? Granted it sounds absurd to suggest that we might have duties to machines, yet still there is something in the far reaches of our normative thought and feeling that corresponds even to this. A general discomfort in the face of wanton destructiveness, a tendency to wince when objects are broken, an objection to the neglect or abuse of precision tools, that isn't rooted completely in the idea of economic waste...Perhaps we *should* treat every kind of thing in accordance with...the kinds of goods and bads to which it is subject.

Korsgaard addresses the question of why things matter. Her answer is that things matter (i.e. so far as she is concerned, they have 'moral standing') because of their fellowship with humans. However, her observation that the 'wanton destructiveness' of things is wrong clouds the issue. Wanton destruction is usually deemed wrong because it is anti-social, that is, because it expresses an underlying attitude that presages harm to humans. 'Brutality towards things is potentially brutality towards people' as Adorno (1997: 232) observed. This may or may not be true, but it sheds no light on the question of why things matter in themselves. The focus here has switched from our question to the different one of the moral reprehensiveness of a certain subjective attitude.

Moreover, the usual answer given to this different question is that things matter ultimately because people matter and people for whom things don't matter may show the same indifference towards people. This is similar to what Kant says about animals. A human being, according to Kant (1996: 192–3), has a duty to himself to refrain from 'violent and cruel treatment of animals'. Kant's argument is inadequate in the same way as the previous thought was: if it is wrong to maltreat animals this ought to be because of the kind of being they are, rather than a matter of the kind of beings we are. (Note, by the way, that the special value of animals and their fellowship with humans is obscured from view if we divide up the world into humans and non-humans.) Analogously, insofar as things matter, this fact should be explained by their nature, by what things are, rather than by the nature or value of human beings.

What is it in the nature of things that makes them matter? Korsgaard comes close to answering this question when she claims that the fellowship between things and people stems from the fact that both are subject to goods and bads, and that in virtue of this similarity they have 'moral standing'.

7.3 THINGS, OBJECTS, AND ENTITIES

I want to answer the question of why things matter by looking more closely at the question of what a thing is. It is a deceptively simple question, and along with the question of why things matter, another that has been neglected. Philosophers and academics have tended to ignore the specificity of things and of the concept 'thing', and to treat 'thing' as equivalent 'object' and 'entity'.

The reasons for this are broadly as follows. The several traditions of modern philosophy divide roughly into two: the philosophy of consciousness, and naturalism or scientism. In the philosophy of consciousness, the world and our relation to it are conceived according to the categories of subject and object. The object has both epistemological and ontological significance; it is both what is known, and what exists. However, an object is always the correlate to a subject; right up to the time of Descartes, the terms 'objective' and 'subjective' had almost the opposite meaning to that which they have today (Daston and Galison 2007: 31). What was 'objective' was what was presented in consciousness to the subject; whereas what was 'subjective' was the underlying substrate or substance of things. But under the influence of Kant, 'objective' came to mean having to do with an external (subject-independent) object, while 'subjective' meant 'personal, inner, inhering in us, in opposition to objective'.

In a strict sense, which is central to the philosophy of consciousness, an object has an inbuilt relation to a subject. This is even true of objects considered in themselves, that is, in their independence from the contributions of the subject, for it is the subject that achieves objectivity by abstracting away from what it contributes to the object, leaving only the subject-independent object. Objectivity is therefore defined in relation to a subject (albeit one that has been eliminated from the picture), so that it is still the relation to the subject that distinguishes 'object' from 'entity'. This inbuilt relation to a subject can take different forms. It can be a relation of knowledge or intentionality. What is known by a subject counts as an object in the epistemological sense. There are a vast number of these. There are even more intentional objects.

Intentional objects need not really exist. They can be the objects of hallucinations, or fictional objects like unicorns. Less controversially we can think of abstract objects, such as numbers, and other kinds of entities that exist, but not as bodily presences, such as subatomic particles. Philosophers of science disagree about whether not one should be realist about such objects. Yet all such entities can quite properly deemed objects in the strict sense, since we can think of them, refer to them, know them, and so forth, even though none of these count as things.

If we turn now to the other broad tendency within modern philosophy, naturalism, we observe a similar tendency to equate things and entities, the concept 'thing' with the concept 'entity'. The concept of an entity as opposed to an object is not that of something presented to a subject, but rather of something that just *is*. But not any old entity is an object. Absent any conscious subject, there would exist all kinds of entities none of which would be actual objects (though they would be potential objects). Or again, there might exist all kinds of entities, but if subjects were incapable of performing the cognitive operations by which alone they can be received, perceived, thought of, referred to (and arguably constituted), no objects.

Nor, for different reasons, are any old objects entities. One cannot uncontroversially maintain that numbers, colours, or Higgs boson are entities, since it is a matter of dispute whether they really exist, and if so in what sense; yet there is no such problem with their being objects in the strict sense. An object does not have to exist to be an object, whereas an entity has to exist in some sense, to be an entity.

The conflation of things with objects and entities is not specific to philosophy: sociologists, anthropologists, even 'thing theorists' are prone to it. For example Bruno Latour and Bill Brown are guilty of the same conflations (Latour 2000: 10–22; Brown 2001: 1–22; Latour 2007: 63–87). Latour comes close to making such a distinction, when he claims that, as distinct from objects, things are matters of concern (Latour 2004, 2005). There is some truth in this, since—as we will see—things are indeed essentially material and of concern to humans, but their being matters of concern does not distinguish them adequately from objects and entities. After all, objects in the strict sense are of some concern to human subjects. Yet they are not things by dint of that alone.

I maintain that these different theoretical and academic ways of looking at and speaking about the world deflect attention away from the specificity of thinghood, by taking them to be equivalent with objects and or entities. And this is a mistake, since it unduly narrows our repertoire of ontological concepts, and in turn atrophies our experience of the world, and blinds us to its peculiar texture, and our place in it. Against this, I want to excavate a notion of 'thing' that is distinct from that of 'object' and 'entity', and has some specific and determinate features of its own. Understanding what these peculiar features are will help us to understand why things matter.

7.4 ON WHAT THINGS ARE NOT

Let me start by making some observations about what things are not. To begin with a thing is not a human being. They are not persons, however this be conceived. For example:

(a) Things do not have souls.
(b) Things do not have wills.
(c) Things are not selves.
(d) Things are not subjects, in the sense that they do not think or cognize or reason and they are not rational.
(e) Things do not speak in the same sense that human beings speak.

It is equally true that whoever is a 'person' is not a mere thing. Kant seems to think that this is necessarily true, and that it has moral implications about how we must treat ourselves and other people.

A thing is not an animal. Things lack the specific characteristics of animals. For example, they do not have the capacity for voluntary movement. Generally speaking, things do not move on their own. Relative to human beings and animals, they stay where they are unless moved by someone or something else. Things are not spry. If they moved around all the time, or if they constantly dematerialized and rematerialized in different locations, our world would be much more chaotic than it is. The fact that most things normally stay put is central to the relative stability and permanence of the world, and to our everyday experience of it.

This insight is lost on Latour and actor-network-theorists, who employ a simple binary distinction between human and non-human, a distinction that arguably goes back to Descartes, who thought of animals as *res extensa*, material substance, as opposed to *res cogitans*, thinking substance. In his mind animals were exquisite mechanisms, capable of sense perception but not of thought and intentional action. It follows that things are not agents: that they lack agency. Latour (2000: 19) likes to deny this. He claims that some things have agency, such as the Berlin keys; 'the steel key assumes all the dignity of a mediator, a social actor, an agent, an active being'. But Latour overstates the case. Keys do not lock doors. Human beings with keys do (although see Webmoor, this volume). The fact that some keys oblige one to perform certain actions is neither here nor there. Doors oblige people to open them when leaving or entering buildings. They do not on that account have agency; they merely articulate human actions.

Things do not perceive or experience their environment in the same way that animals and human animals do, Descartes notwithstanding. Kant also maintains that animals are things (Kant 1996: 34 (AA 4: 428)). He makes this claim in order to distinguish things from persons, who in virtue of their specific dignity (which he equates with their rationality) may not be treated as mere means. Animals, by contrast, may be treated as mere means, even though human beings should not treat them with cruelty, or inflict needless suffering upon them. Because things are not sentient in the same way that animals and human beings are, they cannot suffer in the same way, as sentient beings. That said, most things can be damaged and destroyed, and this is not an insignificant fact about them.

Finally, things are not living beings. They are inanimate. If a being is a thing, it is not alive, and if a being is alive, it is not a thing. Things do not grow. Some minerals such as volcanic rock formations, crystals, and stalactites get bigger. But they do not require nutrition and grow and mature as part of their life-cycle. They are not organisms. Though they can be destroyed, they cannot die.

7.5 ON WHAT THINGS ARE

So far I have tried to demarcate a kind of being, and a mode of being, that differs from that of human, animal, and living being. I have not said anything positive about what things are. In order to grasp thinghood, we need to say more about the physical existence and physical properties of things. For all things have a physical existence.

This means, for example, that they have a certain size and shape, and a location in space. They are what Husserl calls 'bodily presences'. We can be more specific on the notion of size. Things qua things cannot be just any size. No thing is as large as a planet or as small as an electron. Things are of such a size that they are readily apprehensible by humans in perception.

Things present themselves to us in another way too, because they are normally in reach. Things are near to us; they are to hand (Heidegger 1980c: 167). This also means that they must be of a certain size. Things are proportionate to the human form. They are manipulable. Perhaps this is one of the more straightforward implications of the saying of Protagoras of Abdera, that 'human beings are the measure of all things'. It is also implied by the description of material things as 'medium-sized dry goods' in the corruption of J. L. Austin's phrase that has now become part of the lingua franca of analytic philosophy.

To say that things are medium-sized is vague. Yet it is determinate enough to imply that some constructions like buildings, large aircraft, ocean liners, space stations, etc. do not readily count as things. Of course one might object that these are just very large things, just as the constructs of nano-engineering are just very small things (see Edgeworth, this volume). It is true that human beings are capable of making stuff that is extremely large and very small. Yet it also seems true that the bigger something is, the more gargantuan its proportions, or the more microscopic it is, the more its thinghood recedes.

As bodily presences things occupy space in a particular way. They are solid and indivisible. They not like air or water, gaseous or liquid. The indivisibility and solidity of things, properties they have no matter how fragile or light they are, is as essential and important to their identity as is their size and shape. A table or chair, once cut in half, is no longer what it is. True, some materials, like string or ribbon or timber can be cut to size. But there is normally a point at which a thing cannot be further divided, without its being altered or spoiled. A shoe, a pen, a jug, these things are not like an amount of water, or a knob of butter, or a bowl of soup. Water, soup, and butter, being divisible, remain the substances that they are, even if their quantity is altered.

As bodily presences, things have a position in space, and a duration in time. Things persist, and remain. They perdure relative to a human life-span. This is why it is odd to say that food or any kind of consumable is a thing. If things had a very fleeting existence they would lose their capacity to belong to the world, a capacity which presupposes a certain duration and persistence. They would be more like events or occurrences.

Something Husserl (1973 [1907]: 6–7) writes in his early work, 'Thing and Space', suggests that the fellowship between human beings and things rests on their both being bodily presences. 'They [both things with minds] have colour and shape, a position in space, permanence through time…etc.' There is a lot to consider here. However, I think it is too slender a connection to explain the fellowship between things and people that I am talking about, one that would capture what they are and explain why they matter.

All these features of things, their being medium-sized, their being near and not remote, their being bodily presences occupying space and perduring through time, contribute to our familiarity with things and the way they are.

Things are generally something. Though the word 'thing' is nondescript, things are present to us as individuals. This means, firstly, that they have an integrity and unity. They are one thing. It also means that they are particular things: not just a pen, a paperweight, or a chair, but *this* particular pen, *this* paperweight, and *this* chair. Heidegger talks of a thing as a '*je dieses*', an 'in each case "this"'. He takes the expression to mean that things are proximate; ultimately he rejects this way of speaking as not apt to reveal the thing in its true way of being, but only a 'merely subjective addition on our part'. There is more to Heidegger's idea than he admits. It means that things have an identity. They are what Aristotle calls a '*tode ti*' or 'this *something*' (see the discussion of this phrase in Lear 1988: 273–93). The vulnerability of things to damage and breakage is the vulnerability of individuals. This point is lost if one thinks of a thing as an instance of a form, idea, or kind. If I break this pen, I do not break pens in general or the pen form. True, nowadays, being mass-produced, most things are easily substitutable with something similar. But there is still a sense in which this pen and each pen is unique (see Graves-Brown, this volume). It is unique not just in the sense that it is numerically identical, and occupies a certain determinate point in space and time. Nor is it merely unique only in that it is the one that belongs to me and with which I write. It is unique also in virtue of other properties of which I may or may not be able to give an account. It feels a particular way in the hand. The nib is set at a certain angle, etc.

Things are individuals in a second sense because they have completeness and integrity. They are not parts or bits, but wholes, and this is crucial to their identity. A pen without a nib and a table without a top is not just incomplete, but not a pen and table proper. One can also call this feature of things their finality. Something is final when it is complete and has an end. And the end of something, or to use the Greek word, its '*telos*', is its fulfilment and purpose—what it is for. The finality of things is bound up with their function.

Many things are artefacts. They have been made for a purpose. They have functions. They are for something. A pen is for writing and a cup is for drinking. Here I am talking about a thing's proper function, namely what it is supposed to do, and what it, like its ancestors, were made in order to do (see De Léon, this volume). A thing can have several functions (Preston 2000: 24–34): a book is for reading but can be used as a paperweight. A chair can have a symbolic function, e.g. when it is a throne, and an aesthetic function, in virtue of its design. Moreover a thing's proper function can change; pipe cleaners are now made mostly for craft purposes, rather than for cleaning pipes. And of course many things are designedly multifunctional. However, these complications do not detract from the point that most things have functions. Their function is part of what gives them value. Things that work well are good, and those that work poorly are bad. Though things are not only valuable in virtue of their working well. They may be valuable for all kinds of other reasons too, for the sources of value are many.

Because things have functions, and because their being and their value are closely tied to function, they are peculiarly vulnerable to damage. If things break, they lose capacity. A shell on the beach may be broken in the sense that it is chipped and incomplete. A pen with a broken nib is broken in the sense that it cannot write or writes badly. It no longer does what it is supposed to do. While all entities are susceptible to damage, and to the goods and bads that befall their existence as bodily presences, things are prone in addition to loss of function. When they lose their proper function, they also lose their customary place in the context of human action. Of course they may take up another function. Jewellery too precious or fragile to wear may become an investment or museum piece, and there may be a corresponding re-uptake into a different context of human action.

Made things have a particular value, besides that of their usefulness, due to the labour, skill, thought, and imagination that have gone into their construction. Most things are artefacts, and most artefacts are goods. This is another reason why the phrase analytic philosophers use to describe material objects, 'medium-sized dry goods', is so apposite and enduring. That things are goods means that they are good for someone, and as such they have their place in human life and in the human good.

As a good, a thing also has a use value. This does not mean that it is a commodity. Strictly speaking a good becomes a commodity only when it is traded and has an exchange value, and when it is made in order to be exchanged (Marx 1984: 49). Nowadays most goods are also commodities, though the commodity-form of a thing is incidental to its thinghood, and overlaid upon it (see Graves-Brown, this volume).

Things are generally made (or found and put to use) by human beings, and human beings are social animals. Hence things are *for us* in the sense that they have their proper place in human society. This is not true of natural entities and objects, most of which (apart from those we have cultivated and interfered with) are not intrinsically social and do not participate in human association. Heidegger (1980c) reminds us of the etymological origins of the word 'thing' (*dinc*) in the Old High German which means 'a gathering to deliberate on a matter under discussion, a contested matter'. It is true that human beings gather around things, and gather things around them. It is also true, as we have seen, that things articulate human actions in the sense that doors need to be opened and closed, and some keys have to be rotated through 270 degrees before they can be retracted.

This brings us to Protagoras's saying: 'Human beings are the measure of all things, of the things that are, that they are, and of the things that are not, that they are not' (*Theaetetus* 152a [Plato 1989b: 856]). Heidegger's interpretation of the fragment brings out its significance to this debate. 'Of all things (that man has in customary use, and therefore constantly around him, χρήματα, χρῆσθαι) the (individual) man is the measure of those that are present, that they are present as they are present, and also of those who are prohibited from being present, that they are not present' (Heidegger 1980b: 103). Heidegger's reading is supported by the Greek scholar Laszlo Versenyi (1962). The word that Protagoras uses for things—'χρήματα'—is apposite, for 'χρήματα' does not mean 'things, beings or objects in general, but things with a special relation to our involvement in them: things one uses or needs; goods, property etc.; when generalized, it can mean affairs, events, matters we are concerned with. χρῆμα is derived from χρῆσθαι, χράομαι: to use, to have dealing with, to live with something…' (Versenyi 1962: 182). It would be hubristic to claim that human beings are the measure of all entities, or even of all objects of perception which is how Plato interprets the saying in the *Theaetetus*. However, the claim that man is the measure of all χρήματα is more modest and justifiable. Human beings are inherently concerned with things, namely with the goods and artefacts around them, for these are in turn calibrated to their lives and concerns. Things are part of the world of human affairs, the social world, and as such they share in its intelligibility and transparency. Nature is not like that. Much of nature is obscure, unknown, indifferent, and resistant to human inquiry and endeavour.

7.6 To the Things Themselves Again

These reflections do not begin to provide a definition of a thing. Something as multifarious and nebulous as thinghood is not apt to be defined. They are the first steps in the recovery of a notion of things that respects the nuances of the concept and avoids the obfuscations of the philosophical tradition.

Let us recapitulate. A thing is a single, complete, individual, inanimate, material being. It is a bodily presence, occupying space and time. It is visible under normal conditions. It has a determinate shape, is solid, indivisible, and of medium size relative to human beings. Generally things are to hand, though they are not always capable of being moved by a person or persons. Things are normally at rest. They remain in place. They perdure and maintain their identity throughout their term, which is long enough relative to a human life for them to belong to the world. Things are for the most part artefacts. They have a proper function. They are for something. As such they belong to the world of human affairs, and articulate human actions and association. Things are goods and contribute to the good of human life. Generally we can tell what they are for, and thus know what they are. They are familiar, and their meaning is transparent, and intelligible.

No doubt the conception of the thing I offer is more refined than ordinary usage, and there is a danger that I am being too prescriptive about the application of the term. But my refined conception is closer to our everyday experience of things and throws some light on what things are and why they matter.

How does this conception of the thing compare with that of Heidegger, the only philosopher to have devoted serious philosophical inquiry into the thing? Consider the following passage from the lecture, 'The Thing'.

> Ring is the thing; the jug and the bench; the bridge and the plough. Also, however, each in its own way, the tree and the pond, the stream and the mountain, is a thing. Things are, always thinging in their own way, heron and deer, horse and ox. (Heidegger 1980c: 183–4)

Heidegger, in his lecture, aims to rescue the notion of the thing from the object ontology of the philosophy of consciousness, and to reveal the thinghood of the thing as a manifestation of what he calls 'the fourfold': earth, sky, gods, and mortals. As a consequence, he ends up ignoring the specificity and individuality of the thing that emerges from his illuminating phenomenological analysis. Heidegger loses sight of what things are because he conflates them with natural entities. According to him, the things thinging in the world include trees, ponds, streams, mountains, herons, deer, etc. In my view, none of these are things, although jug, bench, bridge, plough, mirror, etc., are.

Now let us return to the passage from Austin (1962: 7–8):

> We are given, as examples 'familiar objects'—chairs, tables, pictures, books, flowers, pens, cigarettes; the expression 'material thing' is not here (or anywhere else in Ayer's text) further defined. But *does* the ordinary man believe that what he perceives is (always) something like furniture, or like these other 'familiar objects'—moderate-sized specimens of dry goods? We may think, for instance, of people, people's voices, mountains, flames, rainbows, shadows, pictures on the screen at the cinema, pictures in books or hung on the walls, vapours, gases— all of which people say that they see (or in some cases) hear or smell, i.e., 'perceive'. Are these all 'material things'?

Austin complains that Ayer offers no account of what he means by 'material things', but neither does he. But he poses a good question: why do 'people, people's voices, mountains, flames, rainbows, shadows…vapours, gases' not count as 'material things'? I have an explanation. People are not inanimate inorganic entities. Mountains are not artificial, but natural. Voices, flames, rainbows, and screen images are not bodily presences and lack the spatio-temporal characteristics of things. Vapours and gases are not solid and indivisible. However, 'chairs, tables, pictures, books, pens, cigarettes, and furniture'—these are all things according to my conception.

Can my conception of thing explain why things matter? Korsgaard suggests that it is in the nature of things that they are subject to goods and bads, and that they should be treated accordingly. Bicycles call to be looked after: it is good to keep the chain oiled, because it functions better if the chain runs freely. And we humans cannot help but treat things as if they experience their own good, even though they do not.

I think the answer lies at a more general level: things belong to our world. Our fellowship with them is a complex matter. It has to do with their proper function. It is also to do with their physical properties, their size and shape and duration. Things are such that we live among and alongside them. They reticulate the human domestic and social world. This is the insight which guides Latour and actor-network-theory. But beyond that, things belong because they have their place in the world, they articulate human actions and thus shape individual and social life. This helps to explain our familiarity with and attachment to them, which in turn help explain why the appropriate relation to things is one of solicitude. Things matter because there is no world properly speaking without them. It seems wrong to claim, as Kant does, that our concern for things flows from a deeper underlying moral concern for persons. The wrongness or badness inherent in the destruction, damage, neglect, and abuse of things, whether intentional or not, is of a different colour, the colour of desuetude: the cessation of an attachment to something that one has reason to value, and the desolation of something that no longer belongs.

ACKNOWLEDGEMENTS

Many thanks to John David Rhodes, Jane Elliot, Bill Brown, and especially David (A. D.) Smith, Lorna Finlayson, Henry W. Pickford, and Paul Graves-Brown.

REFERENCES

Adorno, Theodor W. 1997. *Aesthetic Theory*, tr. R. Hullot-Kentor. London: Athlone Press.
Austin, John L. 1962. *Sense and Sensibilia*. Oxford: Oxford University Press.
Brown, Bill. 2001. Thing Theory. *Critical Inquiry* 28(1), Things: 1–22.
Daston, Lorraine and Galison, Peter. 2007. *Objectivity*. Boston: Zone Books.
Geuss, Raymond. 2009. Goals, Origins, Disciplines. *Arion* 17(2): 1–24.
Heidegger, Martin. 1980a [1935/1936]. *Die Frage nach dem Ding. Heidegger Gesamtausgabe*, vol. 41, pp. 1–247. Frankfurt am Main: Vittorio Klostermann.
—— 1980b [1950]. Die Zeit des Weltbildes. In *Holzwege. Heidegger Gesamtausgabe*, vol. 5, ed. Petra Jaeger, pp. 75–115. Frankfurt am Main: Vittorio Klostermann.
—— 1980c [1954]. Das Ding (1950). *Vorträge und Aufsätze. Heidegger Gesamtausgabe*, vol. 7, ed. F. W. von Herrmann, pp. 165–89. Frankfurt am Main: Vittorio Klostermann.
Husserl, Edmund. 1973 [1907]. Ding und Raum. In *Husserliana*, vol. XVI, ed. Ulrich Claesges, pp. 3–337. The Hague: Martin Nijhoff.
Kant, Immanuel. 1996. *The Metaphysics of Morals*, tr. and ed. Mary Gregor. Cambridge: Cambridge University Press.
Korsgaard, Christine. 2005. Fellow Creatures: Kantian Ethics and Our Duties to Animals. In *The Tanner Lectures on Human Values, vol. 25*, ed. Grethe B. Peterson, pp. 78–110. Salt Lake City: Utah University Press.
Latour, Bruno. 2000. The Berlin Key or How to do Words with Things. In *Matter, Materiality and Modern Culture*, ed. Paul M. Graves-Brown, pp. 10–21. London: Routledge.
—— 2004. Why Has Critique Run out of Steam? From Matters of Fact to Matters of Concern. *Critical Inquiry* 30: 225–48.
—— 2005. From Realpolitik to Dingpolitik—or How to Make Things Public. In *Making Things Public: Atmospheres of Democracy*, ed. Bruno Latour and Peter Weibel, pp. 14–43. Cambridge, MA: MIT Press.
—— 2007. *Reassembling the Social: An Introduction to Actor-Network-Theory*. Oxford: Oxford University Press.
Lear, Jonathan. 1988. *Aristotle: The Desire to Understand*. Cambridge: Cambridge University Press.
Lovejoy, A. Owen. 1933. *The Great Chain of Being*. Cambridge, MA: Harvard University Press.
Marx, Karl. 1984 [1867]. *Capital, vol. 1*. In *Marx Engels Werke*, vol. 23. Berlin: Dietz Verlag.
Plato. 1989a [1961]. *Republic. The Collected Dialogues of Plato*, ed. Edith Hamilton and Huntingdon Cairns. Princeton, NJ: Princeton University Press (Bollingen Series), pp. 575–844.
—— 1989b [1961]. *Theaetetus.The Collected Dialogues of Plato*, ed. Edith Hamilton and Huntingdon Cairns. Princeton, NJ: Princeton University Press (Bollingen Series), pp. 845–920.
Preston, Beth. 2000. The Function of Things: A Philosophical Perspective on Material Culture. In *Matter, Materiality and Modern Culture*, ed. Paul M. Graves-Brown, pp. 22–49. London: Routledge.
Proudhon, Pierre-Joseph. 1969. *What is Property? An Inquiry into the Principle of Right and of Government*, tr. B. R. Tucker. London: William Reeves.
Versenyi, Laszlo. 1962. Protagoras/Man-Measure Fragment. *The American Journal of Philology* 83(2): 178–84.

CHAPTER 8

STS, SYMMETRY,
ARCHAEOLOGY

TIMOTHY WEBMOOR

8.1 INTRODUCTION

IN the world of knot making, there is a particular arrangement of two ropes that doubles the reach of either singly. It is not an especially complex knot, but it is incredibly useful, even lifesaving, when it is relied upon in circumstances such as Alpine mountaineering. Rope work is an ancient craft and the origins of particular knots are obscure (Hoste 2005). As a matter of course they derive, however, from mundane and practical pursuits. Only later did they re-emerge as integral to the success of rather more lofty pursuits. Though humbly deployed and, when capably acting, receding from immediate attention, we may nonetheless acknowledge their integral, if inconspicuous, role in a multitude of mundane activities and adrenaline-charged courses of action. There is all the same a remarkable sophistication to knot theory and an irreducible elegance in the performance of a finely made knot (Figure 8.1).

In sketching the cross-disciplinary setting involving Science and Technology Studies (STS) and archaeology, two fields in which I have held posts, practise as a 'boundary scholar', and serve (however loosely) as a knot, I am going to suggest that knots themselves offer a rich heuristic for understanding their relations. I do not want to push the knot metaphor so far that it slips from rhetorical purchase. Yet I am sympathetic with Ingold's (2000, 2007, 2010) 'organic scholarship' with its attempt to forefront craft metaphors and everyday tools for thought. More importantly, these (sometimes) literal conceptual tools such as knots draw together our focus on ontological relations as opposed to the predominance of episte-mological metaphors that figure prominently as guides for modernist thought (e.g. Peirce 1955; Rorty 1979; Putnam 1981). Contrary to these, knots urge actualism (Harman 2005, 2009b: 127–30); they focus knowing upon the effect, outcome, or action accomplished by objects, humans, and non-humans. Most importantly, I find that the topology of a knot aptly describes cross-disciplinary collaboration. Especially as the topology of knots urges our attention along the lines of engagement to discern the crucial distinctions that make a difference: when knots are actually unknots.

FIGURE 8.1 Double Fisherman's knot (photograph: Timothy Webmoor)

The Fisherman's knot is a symmetrical knot that is itself composed of a series of overhand knots. Symmetry is critical for the overall knot-strength of the Fisherman's, and hence for its reliability in critical situations. To hold, the strands must enfold themselves in such a manner that they 'strangle' one another. That way, an increase in the load weight lends greater friction between the ropes—pull harder, add more weight (to a point of course!), and the symmetry of the Fisherman's folds only tighten together.

Tracing the topology of STS and archaeology under 'load', when they grapple with intellectual problems, it becomes apparent that they are entangled. However, when the weave of these intellectual fields is detailed we find asymmetric tension, but little friction. While the two lines of empirical investigation both contribute object-oriented inquiries and seem capable, in concert, to expand our understanding of how we are ourselves knotted in the material world, their engagement with one another is passing and not binding in a productive sense. The weave is not a knot.

In this contribution I will first briefly consider the collegial ideal of disciplinary cooperation which frames the premise of this section of the volume. I then move to the points of contact between STS and archaeology, exploring whether there is friction or slippage between the two disciplines. Here symmetry, not just as metaphor of parity but in the specific analytic form of generalized or 'radical symmetry' is unpacked as one point of contact between the fields. After the currents of thought in the fields are followed, I conclude by suggesting waypoints for orienting around what I feel to be eddies in the disciplines' respective radical currents, to offer a knot in the future of object-oriented inquiries.

8.2 THE MEREOLOGY OF INTERDISCIPLINARY DOGMA

Before moving on to describe the disciplines' literary networks, I want to push a bit on the academic politics of interdisciplinarity (see Jensen and Rödje 2009; Garrow and Yarrow 2010). Equally, I feel provocation may be beneficial, especially when it comes in the form of questioning assumptions and operating principles. I am going to make the perhaps unpopular suggestion that discussions of collaboration across fields of practice are overly saccharine (see also Barry et al. 2009).

This is because such ideals of partnering across differences of background knowledge, working assumptions, practical skill, research goals, and so forth predominantly operate according to mereological reasoning; this is, following Strathern, the guiding framework for scholarship that believes that partial perspectives sum up to a more complete understanding of a whole (1991, 2010: 175). Mereology suffuses modernist thought. To be sure, there is debate within STS over how prevalent the modernist mode of being actually is (compare Latour 1993; Law 1994), and whether there are properly two competing sets of sensibilities or logics in operation through modernity (on the 'baroque' and the 'romantic', see Kwa 2002; Mol and Law 2002: 20).

Mereology, nonetheless, stands out as a materializing logic of modernity when contrasted with metaphysics that place emphasis upon differing modes of existence, such as alterity, complexity, contingency, or incomprehensibility. While these metaphysical systems have been exhibited within Euro-American logic, with some in STS urging complexity and irreducible mess as the norm of modern socio-technical systems (Law 2004a), mereology seems to best stand in relief when contrasted with non-Western examples (Viveiros de Castro 1992, 1996). Nature stands monolithic behind the vagaries of perspective upon a singular reality. However, other metaphysics do not experience contradiction in, or the impossibility of, allowing multiple cultures and multiple natures, questioning our more familiar scenario of multi-culturalism set against mono-naturalism. Such symmetry between epistemic and ontological pluralism opens vast venues to be negotiated. In considering collaboration, however, the significance of mereology is how it justifies the possibility of complete knowledge through a unified ontology (Nature) which serves to arbitrate the many partial, incomplete, situated, or even erroneous 'voices'.

Stengers (2010, 2011: 368) draws our attention to the manifestation of mereology in myriad scientific procedures. This is especially so in the correlative species of mereology: reductionism (see Latour 1998). Mol and Law (2002: 3–8) argue that the 'power of reductionism in the modern world' forms part of an oscillation between simplicity and complexity. It is an urge to simplify going back to the Enlightenment that they suggest may be expressive of dynamics of the human psyche. Reducing and simplifying are integral gestures of mereological thought.

For if parts may be added to understand a singular whole, then the reliability of knowledge acquisition begins with breaking complex wholes into assimilable constituents. Let us consider, on the material register, the manner in which archaeologists routinely split 'wholes' apart in excavation so that artefacts, features, soil samples, and various media may be reassembled as a whole, as an archive of a (transformed) site (see Lucas 2001a, 2001b, 2012; Olsen et al. 2012). Or consider the assembly of outputs of investigations in archaeology or STS, whether textual, laboratory analyses, or visual media (in archaeology, see Witmore 2004, Shanks and Webmoor 2012; in STS, see Woolgar 1988, Ashmore 1989).

Reaching far beyond mereological reasoning, these operational procedures and organizational devices partially fix how collaborative research is performed. While the earliest premodern experimental laboratories operated with a division of labour along class lines (Shapin and Schaffer 1985; Shapin 1988: 395, 1989: 557), separated tasks led to collective work of ostensibly more equal scholars. We might also look to the disciplining of antiquarian practice into what was to emerge as archaeology (Schnapp 1996; Schlanger and Nordbladh 2008; Olsen et al. 2012: chapter 3). Both reflexive archaeologists (e.g. Berggren and Hodder 2003) and STS ethnographers (e.g. Latour and Woolgar 1986; Mol 2002, 2008; Mol et al. 2010) draw attention to the organizational practices, hierarchies, and relations of accountability that federate individual efforts. 'Audit culture' and 'audit society' in the contemporary academy bureaucratize the socio-material arrangement of interdisciplinary collaboration (Power 1997; Strathern 2000). But it is constraining, even counterproductive, to require collaboration in terms of measurable outputs and 'impact factors'. Moreover, I would add that it further normalizes mereology by dissimulating its peculiar rationale behind everyday operations.

We might also ask, aside from requirements to do so, what really motivates researchers to form partnerships? Is this how the process of thinking and working together really happens? To the contrary, studies of interdisciplinary practices from the history of science and STS suggest that the notion of piecing partial contributions together is both more complex and more contentious than is suggested by the mereology of interdisciplinary partnerships. Such undertakings often work only by constituting a new hybrid output. Rather than intercalating research products into a predetermined deliverable, the process and temporary outcomes are both more uncertain and risky. Mol (2002, 2008) presents, in detail, how socio-material 'coordination work' may stabilize 'boundary objects' (Star and Griesemer 1989) in order that knowledge may be attached to them through shared 'language' and exchangeable media (also Galison 1997).

Against mereology, Strathern argues that 'disparate viewpoints can never add up' (2010: 175). Social multiplicity is not vouchsafed by the singular ontology of a 'Nature' and partial descriptions of an object or socio-material process do not add up to a complete description. Nor could they ever. We can only describe what is always partially in flux. A consequence is that, with Stengers (2011), we may spend more effort 'wondering about materiality' than explaining it. Such a position of humility resonates with recent calls within archaeology and anthropology to (re)affirm radical, unknowable alterity (Alberti and Bray 2009; Holbraad 2009; Garrow and Yarrow 2010), while STS scholars remind us that such a non-mereological mode of being opens up alterity within our own socio-material processes and collective selves. 'Bad' matter, unruly ruins, awkward or abject things have too readily been excised from the 'us' of humanity (Webmoor and Witmore 2008).

The consequences, then, of mereological reasoning extend to material practices of the scientific endeavour, the possibilities of knowing, and to our ontological make-up. We must question the starting assumption of interdisciplinary collaboration as a concept and goal and unpack how it prefigures relations between practitioners.

Let's return to the topology of the knot. If partnering through disciplines works, then we ought to look to the boundary objects, the mongrel materials that are composed to do work. A knot requires the type of coordination work that Mol (2002; also Mol et al. 2010) has sketched in complex medical settings. As a boundary object, a knot exemplifies non-mereological symmetry in partnerships. Under load, it moves attention to how it performs, rather than to its static composition. When working properly, the knot is a mixture, 'more than one and less than many' (Mol and Law 2002: 11; also Harman 2009b: 156, 2011: 79). To continue with the suggestion that ontological composition is a paradox, too fluid to be rendered satisfactorily in mereological reasoning, I would urge letting go the interdisciplinary goal in the manner of a Zen kōan: loosen hold of the goal in order to attain it. It is to affirm that we can be collegial without being interdisciplinary.

8.3 Knot Knowing

Shed of the idea(l) of synergy, how do we describe the relations between STS and archaeology? Like our climber on the cliff setting up a rescue abseil, ensuring that what is in the hands is not an unknot requires understanding whether the topology will 'bind' when under load. I look at two primary sets of literature where disciplinary interests connect: ethnographies of practice and discussions of descriptive work. Sketching these literary networks I identify four points of slippage between archaeology and STS: temporality; representationalism/performativity; scale; and symmetry.

8.3.1 Temporality

The ethnographic examination of archaeological practice has become an established subdomain (Yarrow 2003; Edgeworth 2006, 2010), although this reflexive platform has not developed in explicit contact with STS ethnographies of science (Knorr-Cetina and Mulkay 1983; Lynch 1985; Latour and Woolgar 1986). The characterization of scientific activity as craft work (Revetz 1971; Amann and Knorr-Cetina 1990; Shanks and McGuire 1996) has been influential; affirming the skill and material integument bound together in practical activities brings the acknowledgement that archaeologists do not discover the past. Similar to STS accounts that follow the collective effort of rendering textual and media outputs from scientific settings, it is a position that undercuts the romantic idea of a neutral 'discovery' of (a past) reality.

Such ethnographic and craft oriented appraisals of archaeology merge with more focused studies of the representational forms of the discipline (Shanks 1997; Webmoor 2005; Shanks and Webmoor 2012). Refracting STS lessons through archaeological examples offers a radical break with the inherited view of representing the past in the present.

Archaeology, through unpacking its practices and descriptive work, has bound itself to STS lines of research. This is a point of contact where archaeology's unique temporality places friction on this line of STS inquiry. And there is much to be gained from knotting these insights. For instance, the descriptions of coordination work in scientific and other settings are often a retroactive activity. Consider, for instance, Latour's (1988) unfolding of how Pasteur successfully mobilized a vast network in order to establish, through trials of strength, the reality of microbes. Or Law's (1986) discussion of the feat of heterogeneous engineering that allowed Portuguese sailing vessels to tread vast oceanic distances to trade. We are not presented with the microbes or Portuguese sailing vessels per se. An odd swapping of disciplinary expectations occurs. STS becomes archaeological in the conventional sense. These socio-material assemblages leave distributed traces that STSers must gather with their descriptive narratives and recording instruments to offer an account that registers a definite presence of what was otherwise too ephemeral, far flung, or unapparent to connect together. It takes keen observation, a willingness to look beyond the apparent, good recording devices and reliable media. Textual records, photographs of configurations of materials, architectures (laboratories or equipment), accepted entities (like microbes), or skeumorphs are critical points of these STS exhibitions. The activity is not dissimilar to long-established archaeological practice.

However, unlike most STS descriptive accounts, archaeological mobilizations of the past are simultaneously retroactive and proactive. This is 'the isotopy of the past(s)' (Webmoor 2012). Like unstable, isotopic elements, archaeological materials may be obdurate, but their former networks, their relations with other objects, tend towards 'radioactive' dispersion. So archaeologists stabilize certain configurations of materials in the present in designing for the future. Even in a more representationalist register, most archaeologists would not disavow the basic premise of the conservation ethic (Lipe 1974). There may be no claim to objectively represent the 'past as it was'. Yet in its most elemental form, whether contemporary archaeology or prehistory, the endeavour attempts to say: 'this happened here'.

There is more. Merging the recognition that archaeological work, like STS descriptions, actively stabilizes certain configurations of socio-material in the present, archaeologists nonetheless design for future engagement with an interested public (see Olsen et al. 2012: chapters 6, 8; Webmoor 2012). There is a temporal continuity or flow through the archaeological process: retroactive descriptions that forecast future engagements. In the practical arrangement and stabilization of materials of the past within the present there is a temporal pleat that makes all archaeology 'archaeology of the contemporary past' (Olsen et al. 2012: chapter 7; also Olivier, this volume).

In stark contrast to this applied design of archaeology, there is worry of wider relevance amongst STS practitioners (Collins and Evans 2002; Woolgar 2004; Lynch and Cole 2005; Woolgar et al. 2009). I would argue that it is an absence of an extended temporality passing from past events and objects to future configurations that in the first place reduces relevance of STS accounts. While most archaeologists are aware of the temporality of their activities, creating productive tension in the lines of object inquiries, STSers have yet to grapple empirically with these temporal issues. In part this detracts from its direct engagement with public concerns that are future oriented. As a result we often encounter a temporal swapping between the descriptive work of archaeology and STS. There is discussion of the crossover between academic STS and the private industry, especially with respect to user-centred or user-generated design. Yet these 'applied' examples do not deploy the full armature of STS practice and theorization, but rather focus upon ethnographic inquiry. A result is that published examples of this type of work more closely resemble commercial socio-cultural anthropology than STS (e.g. Wilkie and Michael 2009; though see Marres 2009).

More recent ethnographies of archaeology draw explicitly upon the work of STSers (Garrow and Yarrow 2010; Harrison 2011; Harrison et al. 2013). While many of these archaeologists offer archaeological expertise as reciprocal contribution (e.g. Edgeworth 2010: 58; Gosden 2010: 115), there is scant friction along these ethnographic lines of investigation. A point of contact is anthropologist Charles Goodwin's (1984) influential description of the disciplining of skill in particular fields. He detailed the archaeological excavations at Arroyo Secco, and his example of 'professional vision' is widely deployed both in archaeology and STS. The study, as Edgeworth (2010: 62) notes, contributes reflexive insight into archaeology's material practices and development of Goodwin's anthropological theory of language and visualization (see also Gero 1996). Notwithstanding the apparent richness and potential of archaeological examples of practice, it has remained by and large archaeologists themselves who have developed them.

Even the few examples of direct referencing or engagement (Lynch 1985; Lemonnier 1993; Latour and Lemonnier 1994; Latour 1996) spend little effort in illuminating issues by working through archaeological case studies (though see Watts 2005; Ratto 2006). It is as if the unalloyed insights of STS can illuminate archaeological problems without archaeologists or archaeological materials. Consequently the situation is redolent of the philosophical importation debates of the 1970s in archaeology (Schiffer 1981; Flannery 1982). For STS, some practitioners are beginning to worry that without renewed radicalism the importation of its concepts and sensibilities into other fields of practice actually dissipates its provocative influence (Woolgar et al. 2009: 18).

8.3.2 Representationalism/Performativity

I would argue that engagement with archaeological case studies might usefully disrupt what is somewhat of a stale standstill in STS amongst what may be glossed 'representationalism' and 'performativity' orientations (see Law and Singleton 2000; Madsen 2012: 53–6). These orientations place different emphasis upon the role of the STSer when she or he documents practices. Some STSers insist that there is no neutral, external vantage point from which to make descriptions, that we are always already inside the 'belly of the machine' (Haraway 1999: 176). Our own descriptions are not only situated and local, but additionally are caught up in the very socio-material network or sets of relations that they (partially) describe. As material-semiotic inscriptions, they also perform action and have consequences. This camp of STSers (e.g. Star 1991; Haraway 1999; Law and Singleton 2000) argue that politics is built into our work as scholars. Indeed, that STS work is 'ontological politics' (Mol and Law 2002; Law 2004b, 2009: 11). Situated, political, and performative, many such scholars attempt to *intervene* with their own descriptions in particular gendered, class-based, military, or governmental materializing agendas.

While the representationalism camp cannot be grafted onto actor-network-theory (ANT), it is most directly associated with early studies undertaken by the developers of ANT (e.g. Callon 1986; Law 1986; Latour 1987, 1993). This camp does not disavow such connections between STS descriptions and phenomena under study—the performativity angle. To be sure, ANT typically presents rich empirical examples to demonstrate the extensiveness of networks and the ontological proximity amongst entities. Yet, as other STS scholars have pointed out, ANT lacks an explicit politics (Star 1991; Law 2009). John Law himself provides an interesting exception (Mol and Law 2002; and see Law and Singleton 2000, Law 2009). Furthermore, the role of description, the work of the scholar her/himself does not figure prominently in representationalism accounts. Without an apparent rear-view mirror, accounts offered by this camp of STSers may come off as objective, authoritative, and further from the objects than they appear: as if they perform Haraway's (1999: 176) 'god-trick' and remove themselves from local settings where they undertake description.

8.3.3 Scale

The ambivalence within STS over the effects of and goals for representational work relates to another slippage between STS and archaeological descriptions. It is a scalar issue. A good STS description must make apparent what is beyond the scale of immediate recognition. Consider again the example of Portuguese sailing vessels; assembling good descriptions of these 'objects' is not to present boats, but to make evident the vast ocean of mobilized ingredients behind and beyond these more readily discernible things. If objects are more readily recognized, then the onus upon STS description is to make apparent the linkages, the relations that bind together these things. Yet this leads to an overemphasis upon relations, so that in focusing upon the network that things take part in, objects themselves drop out of view and descriptions pass quickly to a 'higher order' scale.

Is it intellectually blasé or even disreputable to describe objects themselves? Does this scale seem too inconsequential? As archaeologists such as Gosden (2010: 113) and Olsen (2010) remind us, the discipline is good at thick descriptions of things. That part of the care for things is an obligation to attend to the mundane and minute details of humble objects (Olsen et al. 2012; Webmoor 2012). Yet this tendency to scale-down does not inhibit archaeologists from producing scenarios of tidal movements at the scale of regions and world history. Scalar effects seem to be well handled by archaeologists (e.g. Dolwick 2009; see Edgeworth, this volume). There is a demonstrated capacity to integrate object-intensive materials science descriptions within larger scale socio-material networks. The shifting of analytic scale from objects *qua* objects to objects in association with other humans, non-humans, life-fellows and materials as networks is anchored in the principle of symmetry.

8.3.4 Symmetry

More recently, there has been sustained focus upon the principle of symmetry, as developed by ANT, and its archaeological implications (Webmoor and Witmore 2005, 2008; Shanks 2007; Webmoor 2007; Witmore 2007; Knappett and Malafouris 2008; Gonzalez-Ruibal et al. 2011; Olsen et al. 2012; Olsen, this volume). This 'radical symmetry', or the type of symmetry that has merged with archaeological thinking to amalgamate into the discipline's so-called ontological turn, was, however, first formulated by sociologists and amphibious philosophers of science (Callon 1986; Latour 1986, 1987; Callon and Law 1997). A symmetrical orientation advocates an analytic agnosticism with respect to who or what the 'players' are in any socio-technical account. Developed from a 'sociology of translations' (Callon and Latour 1981) and a 'sociology of associations' (Latour 1986), it has become recognized as the analytic attitude of ANT (Law and Hassard 1999; Latour 2005; Yaneva, this volume). It has proven to be both influential and controversial, particularly in granting the real possibility of non-anthropocentric agency in socio-material accomplishments (see Callon and Latour 1992; Collins and Yearley 1992; Finlayson, this volume).

If calling out humanity's vanity has raised the ire of some in STS and archaeology (see Webmoor and Witmore 2008 on 'social' archaeology), then this issue is a ripple on the pond of metaphysics (see Harman 2009b; Webmoor 2012). With symmetry follows the issue of essentialism. If all action is fundamentally collective, with humans only some act-ants working with other materials and life-fellows as networks, then where do we ascribe qualities such as agency, identity, intentionality, causality? As we considered with scalar issues, ANT places emphasis upon the larger network. Indeed, single and isolated humans, objects, and other entities are incapable of much effect on their own. So in terms of quali-ties, the glue or relations holding the network together becomes paramount. For without these relations holding, however provisionally, a network together, then little action could be accomplished. There would be no microbes and 'Pasteur', no Portuguese sailing vessels. It seems with actualism that the capacity to act eclipses any notion of non-relational, non-contextual identity. Is there any abiding solidity or substance to things-themselves? Or, to put it differently, what is the object that has been symmetrized?

For Graham Harman (2011: 7–19) these two tendencies amount to age-old philosophi-cal predilections to see things-themselves as too unimportant to be invested with inherent qualities, or too profound for their real qualities to be known. In spite of, or rather because of, ANT's success in 'following the actors', they and many of their colleagues in STS have 'left the objects' (see Costall and Richards, this volume). Instead, it is primarily archaeologists and rogue philosophers who are tackling these matters of concern (Harman 2005, 2009a, 2009b, 2011; Olsen et al. 2012). While a phenomenological penchant urges this questioning for many of the emerging group of speculative realists, archaeologists perform double vision in exhaustively describing objects themselves, manifesting them in their accounts, while considering the larger sweep of events that they are enrolled in. Perhaps more importantly, the simultaneity of scales involved in archaeological accounts discourages any lapse back into the fetishization of objects; to simply retreat from relations into stand-alone objects. The paradox of symmetry is that it must be continually performed. Otherwise, archaeology may assume objects to be the locus where qualities of interest inhere. Symmetry is attained in descriptive work through letting it go.

8.4 Disciplinary Agency and Load Failure

While there is the perpetual risk of performative contradiction with the symmetrical atti-tude, it has been an ambassador of sorts for ANT and STS more generally. Yet to discuss archaeology and STS in terms of disciplinary agency, or impact upon theoretical precepts, research practices, and overall intellectual currents, STS would overshadow 'the discipline of things'. As it is, if we looked to established metrics for impact, archaeology would seem to be in the shadows of interdisciplinary research; conspicuously absent in citation practices and literature connected to the academy's ontological turn. For instance, if we examine a recent overview (Trentmann 2009; and see Olsen et al. 2012: 2), we have an inventory pre-sented that inscribes anthropology, STS, material culture studies, human geography, even literary studies as the progenitors of object-oriented approaches. From STS practitioners themselves we have voluminous attempts at *Making Things Public*, enlisting the efforts of just about every discipline in the social sciences and humanities, from art history to political theorists, but not archaeology. Not a single archaeologist is asked about objects! How can this be for a discipline which boasts a panoply of sophisticated approaches to documenting

FIGURE 8.2 'Critical failure' of Double Fisherman's knot (photograph: Timothy Webmoor)

the entanglements and mixtures of people and things over the long-term (see Hodder 2011 for a review; Olsen et al. 2012)?

While STS has certainly been influential in shifting academic concerns to the ontological register, the slippages in the seeming knot of STS and archaeology's engagement endanger both to load failure. For STS there slips away a set of empirics and unique practices that offer the potential to rekindle its intellectual radicality through pushing the issues of temporality, representationalism/performativity, scale, and symmetry. For archaeology, without symmetrical binding of the Fisherman's knot, it's liable to slip free and miss contributing to the timely considerations of things that transverse the disciplines (Figure 8.2).

8.5 CONCLUSION: METROLOGY MATTERS

So how to knot the insights of archaeology and STS? Let us return to the knot as a useful heuristic tool. If we place ourselves in those moments when knots are doing work, we are not concerned with the usual preoccupations of modernist thought—with mereological pursuits of parsing out ontological parts, reducing out irrelevant entities and qualities, adding up the resultant components to make a supposed whole explanation. Instead, grappling with gravity shocks us out of such disinterested and passive intellectual tendencies to oscillate between simplifying and complexifying. Discernment of ontological distinctions and categorization into human, materials, and other non-humans is less important. These are, of course, all blended in the activity at hand. But there is no value given to knowing these in the moment. Metrology rather than mereology suggests itself when we approach the bewilderingly rich variety of mixtures of the world through engagement and wonder. At the end of our (Double Fisherman's knotted) rope, woven concerns such as elemental stability, extension, weightiness, and compositional durability come to the fore. Either everything is holding, fulfilling the activity, or it is not. These are the matters of concern when engaged with knots.

As a waypoint to begin knotting STS and archaeology I would propose a statement: practice does not exhaust a thing. Archaeologists ought to ask with STSers: what are the archaeological practices that enable objects to enter relations? This has been a valuable insight of STS. To reciprocate, however, we refract the focus upon practice in STS through archaeology's object-orientation: what does the resistance of objects and their 'thingliness' tell us about the presumptive centrality and presumptive agency of practice in STS accounts? As a habit of mereological thought, we should remind ourselves to avoid a redux of social constructivism in the guise of 'practice'.

In the collegial mode we can look at the interrelatedness of objects, relations, and practices. What are the ratios of agency and causality? Or the ratios of qualities to relations in the ontology of things? Do we, for instance, ascribe too much to practices in STS accounts of phenomena? What about things themselves? What stake do they have in entering into relations and stabilizing certain constellations of reality? It is too tempting to fall back upon the middling position of affordances (compare Costall and Richards, this volume). Instead, I suggest archaeology, through its practical engagement with temporality, 'performative representation', scale, and symmetry, has a more nuanced metrology for appreciating why and how certain realities of the past endure. It is a knot knowing.

ACKNOWLEDGEMENTS

I want to thank the camaraderie of Alison Wylie in being, as she would say, a fellow 'amphibious scholar'. Also I am most appreciative for the strands of my intellectual knot: Steve Woolgar and the vibrant STS group at Oxford University—Torben Elgaard Jensen, Helene Ratner, and Malte Ziewitz offered sage insights on practice; and the collegiality of archaeologists Ian Hodder, Bjørnar Olsen, Michael Shanks, and Chris Witmore. Great thanks go to the editors of this collection, Paul Graves-Brown, Rodney Harrison, and Angela Piccini. Finally, my gratitude goes to the life-saving rope work of Raimund Rapf. Any slippage in this chapter is, however, due to my own (knot) work.

REFERENCES

Alberti, Benjamin and Tamara L. Bray (eds.). 2009. Animating Archaeology: Of Subjects, Objects and Alternative Ontologies, a special section for *Cambridge Archaeological Journal* 19(3): 337–441.

Amann, K. and Knorr-Cetina, Karen. 1990. The Fixation of (Visual) Evidence. In *Representation in Scientific Practice*, ed. Michael Lynch and Steve Woolgar, pp. 85–122. Cambridge, MA: MIT Press.

Ashmore, Malcolm. 1989. *The Reflexive Thesis: Wrighting Sociology of Scientific Knowledge*. Chicago: University of Chicago Press.

Barry, Andrew, Born, Georgina, and Weszkalnys, Gisa. 2009. Logics of Interdisciplinarity. *Economy and Society* 37(1): 20–49.

Berggren, Åsa and Hodder, Ian. 2003. Social Practice, Method and Some Problems of Field Archaeology. *American Antiquity* 68: 421–34.

Callon, Michel. 1986. Some Elements of a Sociology of Translation: Domestication of the Scallops and the Fishermen of St. Brieuc Bay. In *Power, Action and Belief: A New Sociology of Knowledge?* ed. John Law, pp. 196–233. London: Routledge.

Callon, Michel and Latour, Bruno. 1981. Unscrewing the Big Leviathan: How Actors Macrostructure Reality and How Sociologists Help Them to Do So. In *Advances in Social Theory and Methodology: Toward an Integration of Micro and Macro Sociologies,* ed. Karen Knorr-Cetina and Aaron Victor Cicourel, pp. 277–303. London: Routledge.

—— 1992. Don't Throw the Baby Out With the Bath School! A Reply to Collins and Yearley. In *Science as Practice and Culture,* ed. Andrew Pickering, pp. 343–63. Chicago: University of Chicago Press.

Callon, Michel and Law, John. 1997. After the Individual in Society: Lessons on Collectivity from Science, Technology and Society. *Canadian Journal of Sociology* 22(2): 165–82.

Collins, Harry M. and Evans, Robert. 2002. The Third Wave of Science Studies: Studies of Expertise and Experience. *Social Studies of Science* 32(2): 235–96.

Collins, Harry M. and Yearley, Steven. 1992. Epistemological Chicken. In *Science as Practice and Culture,* ed. Andrew Pickering, pp. 321–6. Chicago: University of Chicago Press.

Dolwick, Jim S. 2009. 'The Social' and Beyond: Introducing Actor-Network Theory. *Journal of Maritime Archaeology* 4: 21–49.

Edgeworth, Matt (ed.). 2006. *Ethnographies of Archaeological Practice: Cultural Encounters, Material Transformations.* Lanham, MD: Alta Mira Press.

—— 2010. On the Boundary: New Perspectives from Ethnography of Archaeology. In *Archaeology and Anthropology: Understanding Similarity, Exploring Difference,* ed. Duncan Garrow and Thomas Yarrow, pp. 53–68. *Oxford:* Oxbow.

Flannery, Kent V. 1982. The Golden Marshalltown: A Parable for the Archaeology of the 1980s. *American Anthropologist* 84(2): 265–78.

Galison, Peter. 1997. *Image and Logic: A Material Culture of Microphysics.* Chicago: University of Chicago Press.

Garrow, Duncan and Yarrow, Thomas (eds.). 2010. *Archaeology and Anthropology: Understanding Similarity, Exploring Difference.* Oxford: Oxbow.

Gero, Joan. 1996. Archaeological Practice and Gendered Encounters with Field Data. In *Gender and Archaeology,* ed. R. Wright, pp. 126–39. Philadelphia: University of Pennsylvania Press.

González-Ruibal, Alfredo, Hernando, Almudena, and Politis, Gustavo. 2011. Ontology of the Self and Material Culture: Arrow-Making among the Awá Hunter-Gatherers (Brazil). *Journal of Anthropological Archaeology* 30: 1–16.

Goodwin, Charles. 1984. Professional Vision. *American Anthropologist* 96(3): 606–33.

Gosden, Chris. 2010. Words and Things: Thick Description in Archaeology and Anthropology. In *Archaeology and Anthropology: Understanding Similarity, Exploring Difference,* ed. Duncan Garrow and Thomas Yarrow, pp. 110–16. Oxford: Oxbow.

Haraway, Donna. 1999. Situated Knowledges: The Science Question in Feminism and the Privilege of Partial Perspective. In *The Science Studies Reader,* ed. Mario Biagioli, pp. 172–88. New York: Routledge.

Harman, Graham. 2005. *Guerrilla Metaphysics: Phenomenology and the Carpentry of Things.* Chicago: Open Court.

—— 2009a. Dwelling with the Fourfold. *Space and Culture* 12(3): 292–302.

—— 2009b. *Prince of Networks: Bruno Latour and Metaphysics.* Melbourne: Re.Press.

—— 2011. *The Quadruple Object.* Alresford, UK: Zero Books.

Harrison, Rodney. 2011. Surface Assemblages. Towards an Archaeology *in* and *of* the Present. *Archaeological Dialogues* 18(2):141–61.

Harrison, Rodney, Byrne, Sarah, and Clarke, Anne. (eds.). 2013. *Reassembling the Collection: Ethnographic Museums and Indigenous Agency*. Santa Fe: SAR Press.

Hodder, Ian. 2011. Human–Thing Entanglement: Towards an Integrated Archaeological Perspective. *Journal of the Royal Anthropological Institute* 17: 154–77.

Holbraad, Martin. 2009. Ontology, Ethnography, Archaeology: An Afterword on the Ontology of Things. *Cambridge Archaeological Journal* 19(3): 431–41.

Hoste, Jim. 2005. The Enumeration and Classification of Knots and Links. In *Handbook of Knot Theory*, ed. W. Menasco and M. Thistlethwaite, pp. 209–32. Amsterdam: Elsevier.

Ingold, Tim. 2000. *The Perception of the Environment: Essays on Livelihood, Dwelling and Skill.* London: Routledge.

—— 2007. *Lines: A Brief History*. London: Routledge.

—— 2010. The Textility of Making. *Cambridge Journal of Economics* 34: 91–102.

Jensen, Casper Bruun and Rödje, Kjetil (eds.). 2009. *Deleuzian Intersections: Science, Technology, Anthropology*. Oxford: Berghahn Books.

Knappett, Carl and Malafouris, Lambros (eds.). 2008. *Material Agency: Towards a Non-anthropocentric Approach*. New York: Springer.

Knorr-Cetina, Karen and Mulkay, Michael (eds.). 1983. *Science Observed: Perspectives on the Social Study of Science.* London: Sage.

Kwa, Chunglin. 2002. Romantic and Baroque Conceptions of Complex Wholes in the Sciences. In *Complexities: Social Studies of Knowledge Practices,* ed. John Law and Annemarie Mol, pp. 23–52. Durham, NC: Duke University Press.

Latour, Bruno. 1986. Visualization and Cognition: Thinking with Eyes and Hands. In *Knowledge and Society: Studies in the Sociology of Culture Past and Present*, volume 6, ed. H. Kuklick and E. Long, pp. 1–40. Greenwich, CT: Jai Press.

—— 1987. *Science in Action: How to Follow Scientists and Engineers Through Society*. Cambridge, MA: Harvard University Press.

—— 1988. *The Pasteurization of France*, tr. Alan Sheridan and John Law. Cambridge, MA: Harvard University Press.

—— 1993. *We Have Never Been Modern*, tr. Catherine Porter. Cambridge, MA: Harvard University Press.

—— 1996. *Aramis, Or the Love of Technology,* tr. Catherine Porter. Cambridge, MA: Harvard University Press.

—— 2005. *Reassembling the Social: An Introduction to Actor-Network-Theory.* Oxford: Oxford University Press.

—— 2010. An Attempt at Writing a 'Compositionist Manifesto'. *New Literary History* 41: 471–90.

Latour, Bruno and Lemonnier, Pierre. 1994. *De la préhistoire aux missiles balistiques*. Paris: La Découverte.

Latour, Bruno and Woolgar, Steve. 1986. *Laboratory Life: The Construction of Scientific Facts,* 2nd edn. Princeton, NJ: Princeton University Press.

Law, John. 1986. On the Methods of Long Distance Control: Vessels, Navigation, and the Portuguese Route to India. In *Power, Action and Belief: A New Sociology of Knowledge?* Sociological Review Monograph 32, ed. John Law, pp. 234–63. London: Routledge.

—— 1994. *Organizing Modernity*. Oxford: Blackwell.

—— 2004a. *After Method: Mess in Social Science Research.* London: Routledge.

—— 2004b. Matter-ing: Or How Might STS Contribute? Electronic document. Available at: <http://www.comp.lancs.ac.uk/sociology/staff/law/law.htm> (accessed 15 May 2011).

—— 2009. The Greer-Bush Test: On Politics in STS. Electronic document. Available at: <http://www.heterogeneities.net/publications/Law2009TheGreer- BushTest.pdf> (accessed 1 April 2011).

Law, John and Hassard, John (eds.). 1999. *Actor Network Theory and After*. Oxford: Blackwell.

Law, John and Mol, Annemarie (eds.). 2002. *Complexities: Social Studies of Knowledge Practices*. Durham, NC: Duke University Press.

Law, John and Singleton, Vicky. 2000. Performing Technology's Stories: On Social Constructivism, Performance, and Performativity. *Technology and Culture* 41(4): 765–75.

Lemonnier, Pierre (ed.). 1993. *Technological Choices: Transformation in Material Cultures Since the Neolithic*. London: Routledge.

Lipe, William. 1974. A Conservation Model for American Archaeology. *The Kiva* 39(3–4): 213–45.

Lucas, Gavin. 2001a. *Critical Approaches to Fieldwork: Contemporary and Historical Archaeological Practice*. London: Routledge.

—— 2001b. Destruction and the Rhetoric of Excavation. *Norwegian Archaeology Review* 34(1): 35–46.

—— 2012. *Understanding the Archaeological Record*. Cambridge: Cambridge University Press.

Lynch, Michael. 1985. *Art and Artifact in Laboratory Science: A Study of Shop Work and Shop Talk in a Research Laboratory*. London: Routledge.

Lynch, Michael and Cole, Simon. 2005. Science and Technology Studies on Trial: Dilemmas of Expertise. *Social Studies of Science* 35(2): 269–311.

Madsen, Anders Koed. 2012. Web-visions as Controversy-lenses. In *Computational Picturing*, ed. Annamaria Carusi, Aud Sissel Hoel, and Timothy Webmoor, a special section for *Interdisciplinary Science Reviews* 37(1): 51–68.

Marres, Noortje. 2009. Testing Powers of Engagement: Green Living Experiments, the Ontological Turn and the Undoability of Involvement. *European Journal of Social Theory* 12(1): 117–33.

Mol, Annemarie. 2002. *The Body Multiple: Ontology in Medical Practice*. Durham, NC: Duke University Press.

—— 2008. *The Logic of Care*. London: Routledge.

Mol, Annemarie and Law, John. 2002. Complexities: An Introduction. In *Complexities: Social Studies of Knowledge Practices*, ed. John Law and Annemarie Mol, pp. 1–22. Durham, NC: Duke University Press.

Mol, Annemarie, Moser, Ingunn, and Pols, Jeannette (eds.). 2010. *Care in Practice: On Tinkering in Clinics, Homes and Farms*. Bielefeld: Transcript Verlag.

Olsen, Bjørnar. 2010. *In Defense of Things: Archaeology and the Ontology of Objects*. Lanham, MD: Alta Mira Press.

Olsen, Bjørnar, Shanks, Michael, Webmoor, Timothy, and Witmore, Christopher. 2012. *Archaeology: The Discipline of Things*. Berkeley, CA: University of California Press.

Peirce, Charles Sanders. 1955. *The Philosophical Writings of Peirce*. New York: Dover Publications.

Power, Mike. 1997. *Audit Society: Rituals of Verification*. Oxford: Oxford University Press.

Putnam, Hilary. 1981. *Reason, Truth and History*. Cambridge: Cambridge University Press.

Ratto, Matt. 2006. Epistemic Commitments and Representation in Archaeology. Paper presented at the Society for the Social Study of Science (4S), Vancouver.

Ravetz, Jerome. 1971. *Scientific Knowledge and Its Social Problems*. Oxford: Clarendon Press.

Rorty, Richard. 1979. *Philosophy and the Mirror of Nature*. Princeton, NJ: Princeton University Press.

Schiffer, Michael Brian. 1981. Some Issues in the Philosophy of Archaeology. *American Antiquity* 46(4): 899–908.

Schlanger, Nathan and Nordbladh, Jarl (eds.). 2008. *Archives, Ancestors, Practices: Archaeology in the Light of Its History*. Oxford: Berghahn Books.

Schnapp, Alain. 1996. *The Discovery of the Past: The Origins of Archaeology*, tr. I. K. a. G. Varndell. London: British Museum Press.

Shanks, Michael. 1997. Photography and Archaeology. In *The Cultural Life of Images: Visual Representation in Archaeology*, ed. Brian Molyneaux, pp. 73–107. London: Routledge.

—— 2007. Symmetrical Archaeology. *World Archaeology* 39(4): 589–98.

Shanks, Michael and McGuire, Randall. 1996. The Craft of Archaeology. *American Antiquity* 61: 75–88.

Shanks, Michael and Webmoor, Timothy. 2012. A Political Economy of Visual Media in Archaeology. In *Re-Presenting the Past: Archaeology Through Image and Text*, ed. Sheila Bonde and Stephen Houston, pp. 87–110. Oxford: Oxbow.

Shapin, Steven. 1988. The House of Experiment in 17th Century England. *Isis* 79(3): 373–404.

—— 1989. The Invisible Technician. *American Scientist* 77: 554–63.

Shapin, Steven and Schaffer, Simon. 1985. *Leviathan and the Air-Pump*. Princeton, NJ: Princeton University Press.

Star, Susan Leigh. 1991. Power, Technologies and the Phenomenology of Conventions: On Being Allergic to Onions. In *A Sociology of Monsters: Essays on Power, Technology and Domination*, ed. John Law, pp. 26–56. London: Routledge.

Star, Susan Leigh and Griesemer, James. 1989. Institutional Ecology, 'Translations' and Boundary Objects. *Social Studies of Science* 19: 387–420.

Stengers, Isabelle. 2010. *Cosmopolitics I*. Minneapolis: University of Minnesota Press.

—— 2011. Wondering About Materialism. In *The Speculative Turn: Continental Materialism and Realism,* ed. Levi Bryant, Nick Srnicek, and Graham Harman, pp. 368–80. Melbourne: Re.Press.

Strathern, Marilyn. 1991. *Partial Connections*. New York: Rowman & Littlefield Publishers.

—— 2000. Introduction: New Accountabilities. In *Audit Cultures: Anthropological Studies in Accountability, Ethics, and the Academy,* ed. Marilyn Strathern, pp. 1–18. London: Routledge.

—— 2010. Commentary: Boundary Objects and Asymmetries. In *Anthropology and Archaeology: Understanding Similarity, Exploring Difference,* ed. Duncan Garrow and Thomas Yarrow, pp. 171–8. Oxford: Oxbow Books.

Trentmann, Frank. 2009. Materiality in the Future of History: Things, Practices, and Politics. *Journal of British Studies* 48(2): 283–307.

Viveiros de Castro, Eduardo. 1992. *From the Enemy's Point of View: Humanity and Divinity in an Amazonian Society*, tr. C. Howard. Chicago: University of Chicago Press.

—— 1996. Os pronomes cosmológicos e o perspectivismo amerindio. *Mana* 2(2): 115–44.

Watts, Laura. 2005. Towards an Archaeology of the Future. Paper presented at the Society for the Social Study of Science (4S), Pasadena.

Webmoor, Timothy. 2005. Mediational Techniques and Conceptual Frameworks in Archaeology: A Model in 'Mapwork' at Teotihuacan, Mexico. *Journal of Social Archaeology* 5(1): 52–84.

—— 2007. What About 'One More Turn After the Social' in Archaeological Reasoning? Taking Things Seriously. *World Archaeology* 39(4): 563–78.

—— 2012. An Archaeological Metaphysics of Care. On Heritage Ecologies, Epistemography and the Isotopy of the Past(s). In *Contemporary and Historical Archaeology in Theory,* ed. Brent Fortenberry and Laura McAtackney, pp. 13–23. Oxford: British Archaeological Reports, Oxbow.

Webmoor, Timothy and Witmore, Christopher L. 2005. Symmetrical Archaeology Collaboratory. Electronic document. Available at: <http://humanitieslab.stanford.edu/ Symmetry> (accessed 1 October 2011).

—— 2008. Things Are Us! A Commentary on Human/Things Relations Under the Banner of a 'Social' Archaeology. *Norwegian Archaeology Review* 41(1): 53–70.

Wilkie, Alex and Michaels, Mike. 2009. Expectation and Mobilisation: Enacting Future Users. *Science, Technology and Human Values* 34(4): 502–22.

Witmore, Christopher L. 2004. On Multiple Fields. Between the Material World and Media: Two Cases from the Peloponnesus, Greece. *Archaeological Dialogues* 11: 133–64.

—— 2007. Symmetrical Archaeology: Excerpts from a Manifesto. *World Archaeology* 39(4): 546–62.

Woolgar, Steve. 1988. *Knowledge and Reflexivity: New Frontiers in the Sociology of Knowledge.* London: Sage Publications.

—— 2004. What Happened to Provocation in Science and Technology Studies? *History and Technology* 20(4): 339–439.

Woolgar, Steve, Coopmans, Catelijne, and Neyland, Daniel. 2009. Does STS Mean Business? *Organization* 16(1): 5–30.

Yarrow, Thomas. 2003. Artefactual Persons: The Relational Capacities of Persons and Things in the Practice of Excavation. *Norwegian Archaeological Review* 36(1): 65–73.

....

CHAPTER 9

ACTOR-NETWORK-THEORY APPROACHES TO THE ARCHAEOLOGY OF CONTEMPORARY ARCHITECTURE

....

ALBENA YANEVA

9.1 INTRODUCTION

....

BY advocating a need to focus on the recent past rather than engaging in historical recollection of the distant past, Victor Buchli and Gavin Lucas (2001) redirected the subject matter of archaeological inquiry to contemporary material culture. Drawing upon cross-disciplinary perspectives on contemporary material culture studies, the methods of archaeology were brought close to the exploration of contemporary social phenomena to outline a new agenda for the study of the materiality of late modern societies (Harrison and Schofield 2010); the familiar became 'unfamiliar', engaged in deciphering layers of meaning and materiality (Graves-Brown 2000: 2) and relying on 'the archaeology of places and events that relate to the period of recent or living memory' (Harrison and Schofield 2009). Showcasing how archaeology can inform the study of our own society through detailed case studies triggered novel forms of anthropological analysis.

Yet, 'archaeology of the contemporary past' is hindered by the continuation of a modernist trope that construes archaeology-as-excavation, which alienates and distances the subject from the present. Rodney Harrison argued recently that to move the issue forward required dispensing with a trope that is reliant on the idea of a past that is buried and hidden. Rather than an archaeology conceived as the pursuit of origins or focused on particular time periods, it should be understood as 'a process of working from the present and its surface assemblages longitudinally across all of the pasts and potential futures which it contains' (Harrison 2011: 158). To capture this, an alternative trope of archaeology-as-surface-survey and as a process of assembling/reassembling was defined by Harrison. This recent conceptual shift from the idea of an 'archaeology of the contemporary past' to speak instead of an archaeology of emergent processes, an archaeology 'in and of the present', needs a closer dialogue with methods of inquiry that bring a better understanding of emergent processes and practices. One such method of enquiry that engages with the present is actor-network-theory (ANT). This chapter will outline the possible contributions of ANT to archaeology and how it can assist in devising this new trope of surface as an allegory for a creative experiential engagement with the present and the spaces in which the past intervenes within it. It can contribute to enriching the repertoire of programmes of inquiry that can capture the 'concrescence' of the emergent present.

The suggestion of bringing the ANT approach to the field of archaeology of the contemporary past is not new (Harrison and Schofield 2010). Yet, ANT-inspired studies of archaeology remain scarce. For me, the questions are: how can we make ANT *transportable* to the field of contemporary archaeology? Is ANT transportable to *all* sorts of material practices? How long can we multiply the physicality and multiple materialities of things without tracing out the network-stabilizing regularities? Can the abstention or engagement in archaeology of the recent past play a productive role in deciphering the deployment of the actual present? By addressing these questions, the chapter will contribute to unravelling how ANT as a method of inquiry can inform the archaeological understanding of the contemporary world (see also Webmoor, this volume).

First, I discuss some recent developments in the field of architecture studies, a field to which I have 'transported' ANT methods and insights. It is also a field where the use of these methods has resulted in a series of detailed, longitudinal studies of the emergent processes of design and invention; the introduction of such methods has nurtured further interest in ethnography of architectural practices. To illustrate the potentials of ANT-inspired studies of architecture concisely, I construct and compare the epistemological positions of the *hasty sightseer* and the *slow ethnographer* of architecture. The first demonstrates an understanding of architectural objects as static surfaces where meaning can be projected; the second refers to a more dynamic understanding of the processes that make buildings possible not by asking what a building means, but what *it does* and how it *works*. Second, I demonstrate ANT's potential to contribute to archaeology of the present that goes beyond the early-developed, laboratory studies-inspired approach to archaeological practices.

9.2 ANT IN ARCHAEOLOGY

The field of archaeology has already benefited from the influence of science and technology studies approaches generally, and by laboratory studies in particular (Latour and Woolgar 1979; Latour 1987, 1993; Woolgar 1988). This influence has led to ethnographies of archaeological practice that explored archaeology and its relationship with other modern scientific fields (Edgeworth 2003, 2006; Yarrow 2003). The archaeological interest in science and technology studies happened during a moment of ANT methods expanding to different material practices (Law and Hassard 1999). Originally developed by scholars tackling science, technology, and engineering practices, ANT was taken outside of its privileged domains of action. Subsequently, it is used as a method to look at other fields as varied as music (Hennion 1993), drug addiction (Gomart and Hennion 1999), markets (Muniesa 2009), accounting

(Lépinay 2011), contemporary art (Yaneva 2003), and architectural design (Yaneva 2005, 2009b; Houdart 2006; Latour and Yaneva 2008; Houdart and Minato 2009).

As an anthropologist trained by Bruno Latour, my research consists in studying the activities and beliefs of the tribe of architects and designers; their strange obsession with time, novelty, and innovation; their enigmatic attachments to models, sketches, and drawing software; and the extraordinary inconsistency in how they define themselves and their practices. I have spent the last ten years studying architects, their cultures, their enigmas, and their exoticism (specifically in the practices of Rem Koolhaas, Mosche Safdie, and Alejandro Zaera-Polo among others). Questioning *what matters to* architects and designers and *what truly defines their practices,* I have developed an anthropology of architecture practices with the help of ANT (Yaneva 2009a, 2009b) which contributes to a different— pragmatist, realist—understanding of architecture and design practices. It relies on symmetrical understanding of nature and culture taken in their multiplicity; a perspective where no prioritization of a *privileged* point of view is taken.

ANT is not a theory. It is a different method of social inquiry (Latour 2005). It is impossible to describe ANT in the abstract because it is grounded on empirical case studies; we can only understand the approach if we have a sense of those case studies (Law 2007). There was a lot of confusion among ANT scholars regarding ANT's status as theory. John Law argued that ANT is not a Theory because it is descriptive rather than foundational in explanatory terms. He claimed: 'it is a toolkit for telling interesting stories...about how relations assemble' (Law 2007). Instead, by following and accounting the networks in these empirical cases, new implicit theories (with a small 't') emerge: new theories about the nature of markets (MacKenzie et al. 2007); about the nature of the human body (Mol 2002; Pasveer and Akrich 1996), about scientific facts and truth (Latour and Woolgar 1979), about the nature of design (Law 1987, 2002). As those 'interesting stories' unfold, we find implicit theories that come right from the actors' worlds and are told with their native words. So, the use of an ANT methodology does not lead to the generation of one foundational Theory, but inevitably generates many new implicit theories that are better suited to explain the actors' world-building activities.

ANT reconfigures the relation between meaning and materiality. Traditionally, material culture studies considered the diversity of the material world (including architecture and design) as being significant in its own right without reducing it to models of the social world (Miller 1998). It focused on the materiality of modern culture by trying to decipher objects' embodied meanings and societal expectations. Drawing on interdisciplinary perspectives, archaeologists of the contemporary past have moved towards a more immanent, performative understanding of objects as actors rather than symbols (Hicks 2010). Yet, both material culture studies and archaeology of the contemporary past paradoxically eluded fully tackling the physicality and varying materiality of the objective world (Buchli 2007). Grasping the multiple materiality and the unpredictable agency of things is precisely what ANT can bring to the field of the archaeology of the contemporary past.

ANT-informed researchers followed various ongoing practices. Practices, as we all know, produce multiplicities. Only by following 'the making of...', 'the practice of...' can we describe the variable ontology of entities that are shaped in an intermediary, non-stabilized state of the world. Only then can we witness moments in which the network has neither the complete status of an object, nor that of a subject, and where new and different forms of objectivity and subjectivity emerge. ANT aims at accounting the unstable state of the social, the technical, the natural, the aesthetic, in order to be able to describe what *happens* in these extreme situations of volatility; situations that are so rarely investigated. The social sciences mostly tackle stabilized entities—technical, scientific, aesthetic. Their major task is to identify and characterize the different formulas of relationship between technology, science, art, and nature on the one hand, and 'society', on the other, presuming that they are all fixed, defined, and determined. Instead, ANT is interested in analysing what is normally an exception for sociological theory and is more often tackled by anthropologists: non-stabilized series of technical/social, natural/social, scientific/social. ANT traces these heterogeneous entities by following their gradient of stabilization. That is probably the common denominator of all the empirical case studies, of all the stories told with ANT methods. They *all* tell a story of the making of the social. However, they tell it in different ways: by recalling different orderings of reality; by tracing different circuits of elements that are glued together to make the social; by following different types of associations. I will now tell you one such ANT-inspired story of architecture, narrated by my two epistemological figures: the *hasty sightseer* and the *slow ethnographer*.

9.3 IN THE STEPS OF GUATTARI

In the 1980s Félix Guattari met the Japanese architect, Shin Takamatsu, then visited Japan and engaged in dialogue with him. A short and somehow forgotten piece—*Les Machines de Shin Takamatsu*—published in the journal *Chimères* in 1994 bears witness to his fascination with the concept of machine in Takamatsu's architecture. Recollecting Guattari's encounter with Japanese architecture, I have become equally fascinated by the architect who inspired his thinking. I was eager to witness and empirically recount different ways of exploring machinic architecture. Following Guattari, I visit Takamatsu's office in Kyoto. I stroll the streets of different Japanese cities to find his buildings and engage in an exploration of the ontology of presence of architectural machines.

Osaka. A hot day in the summer of 2010. Wandering around downtown Osaka to find the iconic Kirin Plaza building of Takamatsu, a strange machinic building catches my attention. The air conditioners look tempting, and here I begin strolling through the building with a different pace of speed; I experience it. Later, I discover, I had actually experienced a Takamatsu building. This is the recently built namBa HIPS building—an entertainment complex poised to become Osaka's newest landmark (Figure 9.1). At 280 feet tall, the building houses a variety of entertainment facilities with separate floors for golf, beauty salons, and restaurants. Integrated into an exterior wall of the building is the Yabafo—Japan's first building-mounted free-fall amusement ride. It is seen as the building's main attraction. From 240 feet up, the ride provides passengers with a panoramic view of the city before dropping them down the side of the building at a top speed of 50 miles per hour.

There are two ways of exploring this building, which correspond to two epistemological positions. The first one is the quick one, the one of the *hasty sightseer* whose perception of a building will not be better than that of a racing car driver travelling across the fields and seeing only the flitting landscapes. She will visit the building once, will take pictures and produce a quick theory by connecting it with meanings, memories, and stories related to the building's design; these stories will then be connected to key concepts in architectural theory and history. Or she will visit the office of Takamatsu for a day, yes only a day! She will

FIGURE 9.1 The namBa HIPS building, Osaka (photograph: Albena Yaneva)

FIGURE 9.2 Shin Takamatsu with his collaborators and the author in his office in Takeda (photograph: Albena Yaneva)

undertake an interview with the star architect from the 1980s (Figure 9.2), she will take pictures of the models in his office and enjoy a chat with the younger designers. She will then go back home and reconnect the materials from the quick visits with the contextual materials on machinic architecture, and the 1980s in Japanese design and architectural theory.

The second epistemological position is a painstaking one. The *slow ethnographer* visits the building every day, trying to understand its ontology by experiencing it, keeping her diary carefully, trying to recognize words and movements in a strange environment. The *slow ethnographer* will be able to see and experience a building differently. She will move about, within and without, and through repeated visits she will let the building gradually yield itself to her in various lights, speeds, and intensities, and in connection with changing moods, crowds of people, and flows of things. Or another type of slow ethnography will consist in visiting the office of Takamatsu and witnessing the daily process of design through interviews and ethnographic conversations with all designers; following the process slowly as it unfolds, trying to witness and make sense of the agency of scale models and drawings, and the networks of humans and non-humans deployed in design venture.

9.4 QUICK, QUICKER...

An instantaneous experience of this building is impossible. The *hasty sightseer* will flee through the building, take a picture, and hope that the image will provide her with the possibility of coming back and slowly discovering all those features that the short moment of perception hampered her from seeing. But she never comes back. She believes that she has seen the building all at once, and this belief relies on the assumption that buildings occupy space, and reach us from various points in space as a single simultaneous perception. When she takes a picture of it, she believes that the building is *on* the picture, trapped there, solid, motionless, *in* there (see DeSilvey, this volume). Passing quickly by the building, she can have an impression of it, but hardly an experience of it. When she takes a picture, the building becomes an aesthetic object—and it becomes a flat image, a static one.

She has some knowledge about Takamatsu, having earlier read different accounts of his architecture, and newspapers from the 1980s. She conducts the interview mobilizing this knowledge. She makes specific assumptions when setting the questions. She strolls around the office and takes pictures. She sets up the tape recorder: chats in English; silence; chats in Japanese; silence. Her expectations are met. She gets what she expected; but isn't that already said in other writings or recent archives? Yes. The answers of Takamatsu are predictable. They do not add anything new to the writings of Guattari. In the formal setting of a dark conference room, bordered by solemnly displayed scale models and waiting to be photographed, Takamatsu rather stubbornly repeats the existing discourse. Nothing new; nothing unexpected. Our *hasty sightseer* is now a hasty visitor of an architectural practice in the Takeda suburb of Kyoto. Going home she will become a hasty writer and will produce a quick account of this visit that relies on causalities and symbolic interpretations of static models and confirmed discursive expectations.

Embracing the position of a *hasty sightseer*, she goes back home with an image of a part of the building totality; and an interview that confirmed all expectations. Such a swift and partial perception will inevitably limit any theory of it as well. Its interpretation will be analytical and one-sided. Her aesthetic theory will rely on rigid conceptualizations based on principles and ideas (of styles, the architect's specific language, functions, typologies, etc.) that are framed outside of direct aesthetic experience. It will be expressed in strict categories of symbols and meanings. The classifications will set limits to perception. The experience of the *hasty sightseer* is reminiscent of that of an archaeologist who will quickly disentangle the multiple and intricate structures of Takamatsu's design philosophy, of Japanese architecture from the 1980s, of Guattari's concept of architectural machines and will swiftly recollect them through operations of exhumation, identification, classification—rather than slowly excavating intricate meaning from materiality. The *hasty sightseer* never allows herself the time to become a slow ethnographer. That is why she will begin to replace the missing experience of the building with unrelated notions coming from other worlds—the world of theory, the background of the architect, the society, the period. Her interpretations will arbitrarily define the random equivalent relationships between the building, on one side, and the interpretations produced after it was built, on the other. This will situate the building in much larger circuits of meta-symbols, societies, and cultures.

9.5 SLOWING DOWN

A slow exploration of the architectural presence of the namBa HIPS building in Osaka makes me experience accidentally its machinic effects. Accounting the namBa HIPS building ethnographically leads me to engage in a cartography of architectural presence, relying on the trajectories, the events, and the happenings in this building. Here am I, a *slow ethnographer*. When I engage in a day-to-day ethnography of the building, keeping my precious diary to hand, I engage in a continuously unfolding process of cumulative interactions; instead of discovering a part of it 'at once', I gradually witness the building growing in front of me and with me (see Schofield, this volume, for a similar process). Experiencing the building is complex; its qualities are rich and form a spectrum that can hardly be put into rigid categories. I account for the play of light on a building with the constant change of shadows, intensities and colours, and shifting reflections. A building is never immobile or still in perception. It can be perceived only in a cumulative series of interactions. There is a continuous building up of the architectural object. I visit the namBa HIPS building many times and I describe what I see. I interact with it and with the users and keep a diary of these interactions. I practice a form of 'site-writing'—a term coined by Jane Rendell. That is, a form of writing that happens between words and things, between writing and speaking, between one place and another; 'it is a two-way inscription, dreamed and remembered, of sites written and writings sited' (Rendell 2010: 151). Inspired by Rendell, and taking the concept outside the field of art criticism, this form of writing involves a double movement to and fro between inside and outside, between the researcher and the work of architecture and suspends what might be a purely subjective judgement. The building cannot make an instantaneous impression on me. It is through a continuous process of interactions that it becomes possible to introduce enriching and defining elements of the machinic nature of namBa HIPS.

As an ethnographer who strolls in the building and wanders around it, I *extract* speeds from the building. Not meanings. These speeds are not given once and forever. They could not happen on their own. Hidden in steel and glass, wood and concrete, slick and bold surfaces, they conceal in the thresholds, they spy from the corners, they sleep in the shadows of darker and lighter colours. The contrast of materials, colours and textures can awaken them and activate their energies. Diverse means are employed to sense the building gaining rhythm: ruptures of symmetry, discontinuous segments, decentred forms fitted together, a vertical slit where the Yabafo structure is placed as part of the façade, the steeply inclined back part of the building as opposed to a flat and open façade. An abyss-like void opens to the sky when Yabafo has moved down, thus inviting the blue Osaka sky to enter the building. I stroll again. If it is all steel, then aluminium would be the material that will make the dark and light grey steel vibrate and produce intensities. In order to obtain this effect of rupture, crossed by diverse transversal elements, the symmetries are systematically derived from the two circles of the façade slot, which become semi-circles when the movement of the Yabafo traverses the building. I feel the pulsations of the façade machine, the vibrations; the subsequent openings of the sky destabilizing the dimensions and forms anticipated by ordinary perception. The slit remains the focus, the attractor of subjectivity. 'The becoming machine' can only be obtained, as Guattari argued, through the crossing of a threshold, in the course of which an effect of faciality [visagéite] will seize the building in order to make it live, in an animal-animist, vegetal-cosmic manner (Guattari 1994: 136). The faciality is expressed through the many repetitions of the Yabafo—as a pulsating, virulent machinic core—and different intensities are produced. What matters is the constant succession of slow and fast, fast and slow; that is what makes the building dynamic. What runs with a great speed, then gradually slows down; what runs with a slow cadence, then suddenly speeds up.

Experiencing this Takamatsu building and its 'becoming machine', I stroll in the building and I follow the people who walk around every day. I do not ask the questions: What does this big machine-like structure stand for? What does it mean? I just stroll; I follow the circuits; I lend myself to the different intensities of the building rhythms. Nothing is really neutral or passive. There is something vital, and powerful. The colours, the materials do not say anything either. I witness only speeds; slow and fast, fast and slow. I do not question the meaning. Taken by the fine circuits of this machinic entity, making me immerse into different intensities of flows, speeding up and slowing down, slowing down and speeding up, I just ask: 'How does this building work?' 'What does it do?' 'How and where?' 'Who sets it in motion?' 'In what cases?' 'What are its modalities of action?'

If the *hasty sightseer* relies on existing past or recent *archives* of the building she can quickly connect to a history of events and meanings, as a *slow ethnographer* I rely on *the diagram of the building* as a configuration of forces and fields of energies that shape the way that I experience it. The machine-like building does not symbolize anything. The movement does not mean anything. The setting in which I am strolling while writing these lines does not say anything. It *works*. What makes it work is the network of light grey metal modules that set disjunctions, outline colour contrasts and speeds, and the reversible game of transformations, of reactions, of inversions, of inductions, of slowing down, and speeding up; the moving core of Yabafo includes the disjunctions and distributes the connections. That is, a strange life circulating in the building, a vital force. Speeds. Not meanings. That is what we get from the building. Races of pace, speeds, accelerations, intensities, a twinge of new velocity, turns, degrees of swiftness. Speeds flow from all the materials used by Takamatsu: metal, aluminium, decorative tubes and steel brooches, parallel bars, metallic adornments, and glass. Takamatsu extracts the speeds from the contrast of materials, from their different surfaces and colour shades.

Back to the practice of Takamatsu, we know what questions to pose. Asking an architect 'why do you do this?' has no meaning, no importance. We should rather ask: how do you do this? How does this building work? His discourses might turn around issues of meaning and symbols, as they did in the hasty visit of the office, but while designing he will be experiencing different speeds and moves (Figures 9.3, 9.4). When projecting and sketching a movement, Takamatsu speeds up and slows down and he wants this to happen in the different successions of dark grey and light grey metal surfaces of the building-to-be. Just like the visitors strolling in the building and wandering around it, the architect is *to extract* those speeds from the building in the process of drawing and designing it (Yaneva 2005). They are not given once and forever. They could not happen on their own. While working with the speeds, he does not express or symbolize anything; he simply immerses into the tempo of design, and adjusts its different rhythms with engineers, contractors, users, commercial agents, and neighbours.

The slow ethnographer can gain an experience of the building that will be the product of her continuous and cumulative interactions with its world. It is this rich experience of the vast range of the building qualities that will form the core of her interpretations; this should be the only foundation for architectural theory. A building experience should be expressed slowly in adjectives that will narrate the physical conditions of its perception; the large spectrum of building qualities cannot be recounted in a rigid repertoire of categories and fast concepts. Historical and cultural information will throw light on the building, but will not substitute the understanding of the architectural object in its own qualities and relations. Its

FIGURE 9.3 Architects at work in the office of Shin Takamatsu (photograph: Albena Yaneva)

FIGURE 9.4 Architects at work in the office of Shin Takamatsu (photograph: Albena Yaneva)

interpretation will derive from the world of a building that 'opens to interpretation' because of its own activities, from its immediate presence.

Exploring the namBa HIPS architectural presence as a *slow ethnographer* I find out different spatial and temporal parameters that are able to generate properties and inform differently about the intensities produced. Experiencing slowly the building would mean following series of events, internal resonances and movements. We can find in its organization different spatio-temporal dynamisms, confrontations of spaces, flights of time, syntheses of speeds, directions, and rhythms. The namBa HIPS building appears as a field composed of differential relationships that define each other reciprocally in a network; there is a distribution of singularities, of differences, of intensities, of trajectories. The building is not immobile. It does not express anything. *It works*, and its meanings vary according to the distribution of properties manifested in its process of working.

9.6 ANT for Archaeologists

Judging a complex object like the namBa HIPS building as an aesthetic and static object would require the *hasty sightseer* to embrace an authoritative way of speaking on behalf of established principles and reference to the works of other leading architects, of other buildings of this style or period, of architectural Theory. Such a way of interpreting the building relies on quick images taken by the *hasty sightseer* and fast interviews, archives and accounts. It will treat it in its rigid aesthetic form and will have a limiting direct response in perception. When we say a building expresses Japanese culture, we rather think about a stable form that would reify subjective meanings.

The *slow ethnographer* engages instead in an inquiry into the architectural presence of the building that can only be understood in meticulous studies of the specific works of architecture. The object of the ethnographer is far from stable; it appears rather as a dynamic map of all the trajectories and events it triggers; and it changes according to different speeds. The notion of presence and immediacy leads us to explore the concept of surface that Harrison (2011) referred to as being the new trope for understanding archaeological practices. We need epistemological practices that will rely on the posture of the *slow ethnographer* to engage in archaeology-as-a-dynamic-deployment-of-flat-networks, i.e. of surfaces (not as excavation). That is, a process of creative and immediate engagement with the present that will make us immerse in assembling and reassembling all human and non-human ingredients that an object (in our case a building) is made of.

This type of archaeology will lead us towards a better understanding of the architectural work we engage with, its qualities, forces, and events, its different materials and textures, the noises, the accidents, the runners traversing it, the dramas in its premises. As witnessed here in the short story of the ethnographer, the apprehension of the machinic nature of the namBa HIPS building grows from the architectural object as it enters into the experience of slow observation by interaction with her own knowledge and sensitivity. Thus, experiencing and describing an object does not derive from objective standards nor is it the outcome of purely subjective impressions and feelings. When conducted in an architectural practice, slow ethnography helps us to witness the difficulties and the unpredictable turns in the process of its design and invention (Yaneva 2009b). It opens the inquiry to situations where subjective and objective are again not stable but multiple and changing; a situation where all distributions are possible.

With ANT in hand, we do not unravel meanings. We rather show how things become knowable and new realities are obtained. Following ANT's methodological ambition, a new agenda for archaeology of the contemporary world can be brought to the fore. Archaeologists should be able to witness and describe the modes of existence of various objects and account for numerous connections that flow out of these streams of experience. They should focus their efforts on gradually accounting and understanding (like a *slow ethnographer*), not replacing these objects, institutions, and different cultures with the quick concepts of society and culture (like a *hasty sightseer*). Such an approach consists in investigating *the making of*, not the *made* objects, institutions, rituals, cultures, and groupings in contemporary societies.

Yet, such an approach does not consist in the simple description of practices, nor is it enough to discuss and analyse the relevant theories. It rather aims at making explicit the performative or pragmatic dimension that connects objects with the practices of their making, with the streams of experiences, with their makers and users. Following the particular connections, ways and actions, individual moves and collective groupings in practice, a new and richer repertoire of descriptions of objects, practices, institutions, and connections can be generated. Made in a situationist, pluralist, associationist, morphologic, and psychotopographic fashion these accounts can better seize the erratic behaviour of an object (just like we have seen with the namBa HIPS building). Only by generating such ethnographic accounts, tracing pluralities of concrete entities in the specific spaces and times of their coexistence, will archaeology be better prepared to grasp the changing contemporary realities.

What ANT will do to complement the existing tradition of archaeological ethnography (Hamilakis and Anagnostopoulos 2009; Edgeworth 2010; Hamilakis 2011) can be summarized in the following three observations:

First, such an approach assumes that the divide between the 'subjective' and 'objective' is abandoned. Objects are often grasped in archaeological accounts in two different ways: either through their intrinsic materiality (something that would define them as material, real, objective, and factual) or through their more 'symbolic' aspects (that would define them as social, subjective, and lived). ANT helps us escape this modernist division. Suggesting that matter is absorbed into meaning, that it is *in the world*, archaeology could engage in analysis of how materiality from one side, and morality, ethics, and politics from the other are to coalesce.

Second, drawing on ANT, we could do justice to the many material dimensions of things (without limiting them in advance to pure material properties or to social symbols). Matter is much too multidimensional, much too active, complex, surprising, and counter-intuitive to be represented in stabilized artefacts and static institutions. A second advantage of an ANT perspective is that it offers us a fuller view of these dimensions and makes us embrace a complex conglomerate of many surprising agencies that are rarely taken into account. Such accounts reveal the unpredictable attachments to non-humans both in the processes of making and experiencing; and that is what makes them so materially interesting.

Third, instead of looking for explanations outside the particular field, by following an ANT perspective we should consider context as a variable; that is, as something moving, evolving, and changing along with the various objects and practices. Context is made of the many dimensions that impinge at every stage on the development of a project, at every stage of experience. And this is the third advantage of an ANT perspective to archaeology. Instead of analysing the impact of external factors (market forces, class divisions, economic constraints, social conventions, cultural climate, marketing games, or politics) on contemporary material culture and the processes that produce them, we should attempt to grasp the erratic behaviour of different types of matters, of objects, technological settings, and institutions. ANT gives us one more tool with which to follow the painstaking ways humans interact with objects and environments, and shape dynamic contemporary cultures at different scales.

I have shown here how ANT can help archaeology become a study of the surface, of assemblages of humans and non-humans jumbled together in the present. Drawing on two epistemological figures—the *hasty sightseer* and the *slow ethnographer*—I demonstrated two different approaches to contemporary architecture. I argued that ANT methodologies can help to create a space in which the past, present, and future are combined and are still in the process of *becoming*. Equipped with ANT-inspired methods, contemporary archaeologists will not focus on the recent and contemporary past in its own right. They will rather engage in explorations of the vibrant contemporary world, i.e. of emergent processes, of world-building activities of various actors, of the fascinating epistemological techniques of engaging with, and making the present last.

References

Buchli, Victor. 2007. Immateriality and Things. Lecture presented at the Manchester Architecture Research Centre, The University of Manchester, 7 June. Electronic document. Available at: <http://www.sed.manchester.ac.uk/research/marc/documents/victor-buchli.pdf> (accessed 31 May 2012).

Buchli, Victor and Lucas, Gavin (eds.). 2001. *Archaeologies of the Contemporary Past.* London: Routledge.

Edgeworth, Matt. 2003. *Acts of Discovery: An Ethnography of Archaeological Practice.* BAR International Series, 1131. Oxford: Archaeopress.

—— (ed.). 2006. *Ethnographies of Archaeological Practice: Cultural Encounters, Material Transformations Worlds of Archaeology.* Lanham, MD: Altamira Press.

—— 2010. On the Boundary: New Perspectives from Ethnography of Archaeology. In *Archaeology and Anthropology: Understanding Differences, Exploring Similarities*, ed. Duncan Garrow and Thomas Yarrow, pp. 53–68. Oxford: Oxbow.

Gomart, E. and Hennion, Antoine. 1999. A Sociology of Attachment: Music Amateurs, Drug Users. In *Actor Network Theory and After*, ed. John Law and John Hassard, pp. 220–48. Oxford: Blackwell.

Graves-Brown, Paul (ed.). 2000. *Matter, Materiality and Modern Culture.* London and New York: Routledge.

Guattari, Félix. 1994. Les machines architecturales de Shin Takamatsu. *Chimères* 21: 127–41.

Hamilakis, Yannis. 2011. Archaeological Ethnography: A Multi-Temporal Meeting Ground for Archaeology and Anthropology. *Annual Review of Anthropology* 40: 399–414.

Hamilakis, Yannis and Anagnostopoulos, Aris. 2009. What is Archaeological Ethnography? *Public Archaeology* 8(2–3): 65–87.

Harrison, Rodney. 2011. Surface Assemblages: Towards an Archaeology *in* and *of* the Present. *Archaeological Dialogues* 18(2): 141–61.

Harrison, Rodney and Schofield, John. 2009. Archaeo-Ethnography, Auto-Archaeology: Introducing Archaeologies of the Contemporary Past. *Archaeologies: Journal of the World Archaeological Congress* 5(2): 185–209.

—— 2010. *After Modernity: Archaeological Approaches to the Contemporary Past.* Oxford and New York: Oxford University Press.

Hennion, Antoine. 1993. *La passion musicale. Une sociologie de la médiation.* Paris: Métailié.

Houdart, Sophie. 2006. Des multiples manières d'être reel—Les représentations en perspective dans le projet d'architecture. *Terrain* 46: 107–22.

Houdart, Sophie and Minato, Chihiro. 2009. *Kuma Kengo: An Unconventional Monograph.* Paris: Editions Donner Lieu.

Hicks, Dan. 2010. The Material-Cultural Turn: Event and Effect. In *The Oxford Handbook of Material Culture Studies*, ed. Dan Hicks and Mary C. Beaudry, pp. 25–98. Oxford: Oxford University Press.

Latour, Bruno. 1987. *Science in Action: How to Follow Scientists and Engineers through Society.* Cambridge, MA: Harvard University Press.

—— 1993. *We Have Never Been Modern.* Cambridge, MA: Harvard University Press.

—— 2005. *Reassembling the Social: An Introduction to Actor-Network-Theory.* Oxford: Oxford University Press.

Latour, Bruno and Woolgar, Steve. 1979 *Laboratory Life: The Construction of Scientific Facts.* Beverly Hills and London: Sage.

Latour, Bruno and Yaneva, Albena. 2008. Give me a Gun and I will Make All Buildings Move: An ANT's View of Architecture. In *Explorations in Architecture: Teaching, Design, Research*, ed. Reto Geiser. Basel: Birkhäuser.

Law, John. 1987. Technology and Heterogeneous Engineering: The Case of the Portuguese Expansion. In *The Social Construction of Technical Systems: New Directions in the Sociology and History of Technology*, ed. Wiebe E. Bijker, Thomas P. Hughes, and Trevor Pinch, pp. 111–34. Cambridge, MA, and London: MIT Press.

Law, John. 2002. *Aircraft Stories: Decentering the Object in Technoscience*. Durham, NC: Duke University Press.

—— 2007. Actor Network Theory and Material Semiotics. Version of 25 April 2007. Available at: <http://www.heterogeneities.net/publications/Law-ANTandMaterialSemiotics.pdf> (accessed 18 May 2007).

Law, John and Hassard, John. 1999. *Actor Network Theory and After*. Oxford: Blackwell.

Lépinay, Vincent A. 2011. *Codes of Finance: Engineering Derivatives in a Global Bank*. Princeton, NJ: Princeton University Press.

MacKenzie, Donald, Muniesa, Fabian, and Siu, Lucia (eds.). 2007. *Do Economists Make Markets? On the Performativity of Economics*. Princeton, NJ: Princeton University Press.

Miller, Daniel (ed.). 1998. *Material Cultures: Why Some Things Matter*. London and New York: Routledge.

Mol, Annemarie. 2002. *The Body Multiple: Ontology in Medical Practice*. Durham, NC: Duke University Press.

Muniesa, Fabian. 2009. The Description of Financial Objects. *Anthropology Today* 25(2): 26–7.

Pasveer, Bernike and Akrich, Madeline. 1996. *Comment la naissance vient aux femmes*. Paris: Les Empêcheurs de Penser en Rond.

Rendell, Jane. 2010. *Site-Writing: The Architecture of Art Criticism*. London: I. B. Tauris.

Woolgar, Stephen. 1988. *Science: The Very Idea*. London: Ellis Horwood.

Yaneva, Albena. 2003. Chalk Steps on the Museum Floor: The 'Pulses' of Objects in Art Installation. *Journal of Material Culture* 8(2): 169–88.

—— 2005. Scaling up and Down: Extraction Trials in Architectural Design. *Social Studies of Science* 35: 867–94.

—— 2009a. *The Making of a Building: A Pragmatist Approach to Architecture*. Oxford: Peter Lang.

—— 2009b. *Made by the Office for Metropolitan Architecture: An Ethnography of Design*. Rotterdam: 010 Publishers.

Yarrow, Thomas. 2003. Artefactual Persons. The Relational Capacities of Persons and Things in the Practice of Excavation. *Norwegian Archaeological Review* 36(1): 65–73.

CHAPTER 10

GLOBAL MEDIA AND ARCHAEOLOGIES OF NETWORK TECHNOLOGIES

SEAN CUBITT

10.1 INTRODUCTION

AMONG the alien artefacts discovered on a distant moon in Frederick Pohl's *Gateway* (Pohl 1977) are elaborately formed objects that the humans, quite ignorant of their use, refer to as 'prayer fans'. Eventually, when someone accidentally turns one on, it becomes apparent that they are information storage and retrieval devices left behind by a fleeing race of extra-terrestrials. If future archaeologists came upon the physical remains of the Internet without the electric current and batteries on which it depends, would they too find the whole mighty artifice a silent, inexplicable Stonehenge of wire and plastic?

Internet archaeology must first analyze the material it is made of, and secondly respect the fact that these objects constitute a system. Given the planetary nature of network communications, interpretation will have to incorporate global systems of political economy and ecology, so grounding cultural interpretation in the physical and systemic infrastructure (see Edgeworth, this volume). This is the method employed here. Archaeology is perhaps the only science that confronts symbols in the absence of a system. Without a system, symbols are merely artefacts whose function and purpose are opaque: are the cave paintings immersive training for hunters, proto-scientific star maps, or temples for drug-induced communion with the gods? Where we have only the symbols, not the structural relationships or grammar, we cannot ascertain the meanings. In the case of the Internet as archaeological remainder, the symbolic functions of code will not persist in the absence of electric power. There will be no operating systems, protocols, mark-up languages, codecs, instruction sets. The principle that things connect with one another will be as clear as it is in a woven cloth, but no more so. Even if, say, the principles of routing were decipherable from the physical properties of routers, the nature of what was routed will be lost. Optical and magnetic storage media are notoriously short-lived: there will be no records other than those saved on paper. The era when finally we do 'read the f***ing manual' will arrive when the machines they were designed for can no longer respond to the commands written there.

The second reason for imagining a dead Internet is that the thought experiment counters the belief that Internet communication is friction-free, light-speed, or weightless. That is the core message of this chapter: the thesis that digital media are immaterial, as propounded by thinkers as different as Virno (2008) and Virilio (2009) is premised on ignorance of how things work, carefully calculated in the guiltless consumerism of which digital media have become both vehicles and examples—the trip being very short from permanent revolution to built-in obsolescence. Older material networks left traces of their construction: the evidence of abandoned quarries and stone-cutting tools, sources of wood for transport, and some traces of human dwelling. Today resource extraction, design, manufacture, transport and their human and non-human agents are invariably scattered, isolated from one another, and only visible as a network assemblage from the vantage point of a metropolitan manager of a corporation looking down a supply chain connected by contracts and arbitrage, subcontracts and offshore suppliers, and, in a descending hierarchy which the imaginary executive no longer wishes to know about, feasibly deniable relations to sweatshops whose relation to the retail brand has become almost wholly invisible.

10.2 INTERNET AS PHYSICAL ENVIRONMENT

If the analogy with Stonehenge is valid, then we face the problem that any ordinary networked device—a handheld or a laptop say—will contain lithium from the high Andes, conflict sapphires from Madagascar, and will connect places—like Cupertino and Ciudad Juárez—which are far more distant from one another than mere mileage would suggest. Manufacture of chips in unregulated or lightly regulated offshore plants uses substantial amounts of toxic materials: the arsenic used to dope silicon wafers appears in minute quantities in any one chip, but the plants host regular deliveries of kilograms of such dangerous materials, and spills are far from uncommon. Meanwhile, massive population increases in free trade zones without attendant improvements in sanitation have led to major environmental degradation along the US–Mexican border and elsewhere in the Pacific Rim.

Motherboards, memory, drives, screens, and batteries, once manufactured, often employing subassemblies from subcontractors, are freighted as parts and finished goods by container, via the worldwide maritime container industry, itself a major user of digital control systems. They will be connected to the global telecommunications cable, satellite, and cellnet networks, with their server farms (Cubitt et al. 2011) and energy requirements: local solar, wind and tide generation, privately owned hydro or oil generators, and the now highly interconnected spot market for real-time electrical energy. As demonstrated by the blackout on the north-eastern seaboard of Canada and the US in 2006, tripped by untrimmed trees growing into the path of overhead supply lines, the articulation of these planetary hardwired installations with the local and global ecology is extremely material. Thus, even though Microsoft's rumoured Siberian servers (Fiveash 2007) need less power because of the natural cooling effect of the local environment, the heat remains in the planetary heat budget as it warms the local environment.

When the server industry alone is estimated to consume more power than the airline industry (Global Action Plan 2007), while personal computer use requires almost double that used in the server industry, one influential report suggests ICTs (information and communications technologies) will account for 3 per cent of global emissions by 2020 (Boccaletti et al. 2008), a figure which may well be underestimated, given that they account for over 4 per cent already in the USA and the UK. Now, although energy itself does not leave any major archaeological trace, its use can leave clear indicators, as on Easter Island and around Chernobyl. Moreover, the archaeology of middens, which reveals the source of organic energy, is comparable to that which might take as site the high-tech dumping grounds of Southern China, Nigeria, and Ghana: toxic dumps whose effects on people and their environments have been extensively documented by the Basel Action Network (2002, 2005), and which leave indefinitely long-lasting chemical traces in the local ecology. The scale is perhaps best observed in the negative: the European Parliament, already bound in international law to stop all exports of WEEE (waste electrical and electronic equipment), legislated in February 2011 to recycle within the Union a target of 85 per cent of WEEE by 2016: an admission that the effort to stop illegal dumping of toxic electronic waste has been, to date, unsuccessful (TechEye 2011). Some strategic materials, such as indium, are so rare that there is more available from recycling than from mining, and since easily minable seams are already exhausted or, in the case of China's resources, strictly controlled, prices are rising steadily. This begins to make both recycling and mining tougher extractions economically feasible but leaves them energy-intensive in a period of rising energy costs, which is unlikely to come to an end in the foreseeable future (US Geological Survey 2013). Cheap labour and uncontrolled recycling processes in third-world conditions are still the most economically viable way of recuperating the materials from which such rare minerals can be obtained. Quite apart from the human costs, the leaching of by-products of burning plastics to retrieve metal parts will likely leave a powerful trace for future archaeologists to decipher.

In resource extraction, manufacture, business-to-business and business-to-consumer distribution, in use and in product end-of-life management, the supposed transition from atoms to bits has not done away with the weight of human commerce. The Internet is a physical presence. An alternative view, paralleling not only the *Wired* techno-utopianism of Nicholas Negroponte (1995) and Bill Gates (2000) but the critical immaterialization evoked by post-autonomist political economists like Hardt and Negri (2009), is captured in a jokey item in *Discover* magazine, which calculated in 2007 that, with about 40 petabytes of information multiplied by the mass of individual electrons, 'The weight of the Internet adds up to just about 0.2 millionths of an ounce' (Cass 2007; citing another calculation by Russell Seitz from 2007 giving a weight of 2 ounces). There is a traditional humanities approach to support this: the works of Shakespeare are not bindings, paper, and ink but words, and the music of words. A friendly, fuzzy consensus between entrepreneurs, engineers, economists, and English professors that thought is weightless promotes a belief that externalities need not be accounted. An archaeological approach demands that they should.

10.3 PROTOCOL AND CODEC

However, the HeeChee prayer fans should alert us to the necessity of dealing with technically massless formations on which the Internet depends. Binary computing (indeed any imaginable form of discrete computation) is based on switching, the familiar binary off

and on, which itself is constrained by the laws of physics, and demands physical apparatus. But a different approach argues that the essence of digital media is not necessarily
binary but code (see Fuller 2003; Chun 2011), the formal logic structures which convert
data from any input—keyboard, camera, scientific instrument, traffic flows—into manipulable information.

Among the myriad operating systems and software platforms used in computers, games
consoles, and mobiles, the Internet adds a series of key protocols, rule sets used to control
data transmission, the first of which was implemented in 1968 with the earliest experiments
in computer networking at ARPA (Abbate 1999). At its heart lies the TCP/IP (Transmission
Control Protocol/Internet Protocol) suite, the founding layer that allows different computers to share data streams. On top of this layer lie more specific protocols, among them
FTP (File Transfer Protocol) and SMTP (Standard Mail Transfer Protocol). Another layer
is constituted by HTML (Hypertext Mark-up Language), the basic code of the World Wide
Web, which in turn hosts a number of file formats for images, sound, and audiovisual content transported through codecs (compression-decompression algorithms). Though these
tools are almost universal, there exist other ways to network, notably FidoNet, the system
used for pre-Web BBS (Bulletin Board Services), and still widely used by old-school hackers
and in parts of the former Soviet Union. The proviso is important because it is easy to slip
into the belief that there can only ever be one Internet. As a network of networks, allowing
local nets to interconnect, the Internet also partitions off password-protected, secure, and
other 'dark Internet' and 'deep Web' networks. It is also, and this is of crucial importance for
any media archaeology, a hybrid of physical and symbolic structures. This has a number of
consequences, the first of which is governmental.

Books in libraries, the previous apogee of organized knowledge, are linked firstly through
their mutual reference to one another, explicit or implicit, and secondly through the catalogue, a connection without physical links to the books, but with coded addresses to allow
users to find the subject matter, author, size, and location of the book and other features.
What links the library's 'parts' (readers, books, shelves, catalogue) is not only the architecture but the shared knowledge of users concerning the locative and semantic functions of
the cataloguing system. The Internet adds a layer of machine-readable automation, operating on the principle of packet switching, in which whole messages—e-mails, attachments,
websites—are split into discrete packages for sending. Each package of data is placed in a
data-envelope with crucial information at the beginning and end: how big is the packet,
who sent it, where is it going, how does it fit back with the other parts of the message, how
long has it been travelling? Each packet is sent to find its own way through the maze of
connections, only reassembling at its destination. The beauty of this system is that all packets are equal: the system has no knowledge of what is inside the 'envelope' (because in the
early days that required more machinery than was available; and now because anonymity
makes surveillance difficult). An elaborated system of interconnecting providers of different services, from address management to international call routing, ensures the codes are
able to transmit swiftly, efficiently, and democratically—given the equal anonymity of packages carriers cannot privilege one message over another—with very close to 100 per cent
reliability.

This remarkable system, cobbled together by brilliant engineers more or less in their
spare time, reflects the problem-solving, results-oriented, and collegial style of electronic
engineering in the pioneering years. It is thus entirely fitting that the 'killer app' that turned

the Internet into a mass medium in 1993, the World Wide Web, was originally a document management system in the most arcane of all scientific enquiries: quantum physics at the European Centre for Nuclear Research (CERN). Reliant on telecommunication infrastructures which are variously intensely competitive or regulated by authoritarian state governments, politically and ethically supercharged by its extremely rapid public take-off in the first 20 years of its life, and now inseparable from the operations of the global economy (as proven by the dotcom crash of 2001) the Internet can look like a Heath Robinson machine made of thin air and wish-fulfilment, whose continued operation is miraculous not only as technical achievement but as political fact: a quasi-autonomous field of communication over which corporations and governments struggle to gain and maintain control. 'We don't believe in presidents, kings, or voting; we believe in rough consensus and running code': the slogan of the Internet Engineering Task Force (IETF) suggests an ideal Habermasian public sphere of common and goal-oriented rational communication (Froomkin 2003). Allowing for a slow but meaningful progress towards internationalization and gender balance (see deNardis 2009), Internet governance has been largely in the hands of the people who made it. This consensual expert administration has, however, become increasingly politicized since the turn of the century, and the stakes are important to understanding the arguments over otherwise obscure technical details in the infrastructure of network communication.

10.4 Nation, Commerce, and Network in Internet Governance

Three major trends can be identified: the failure of traditional international bodies to take control of the nascent Internet; the unpopularity of attempts in the early 1990s to commercialize Internet governance; and the development of network-native modes of governance. Internet governance is very different in form and practice from the central cluster of global instruments: the United Nations system, including the World Bank and the International Monetary Fund, and the World Trade Organization, all founded or descended from institutions founded in the wake of the Second World War. In these instances, the most significant achievements, from the Universal Declaration of Human Rights to the General Agreement on Trade and Tariffs, have been inter-national agreements, agreements between states as to how they are to conduct their internal polities and their external commerce. With the exception of those aspects of global trade that escape national contract law (Sassen 2006), global governance in almost all areas is handled through agencies formed by national signatories to appropriate treaties. Such is the International Telecommunications Union (ITU). Among its tasks, the ITU is responsible for ensuring that fees for international communications are distributed appropriately, and for allocating broadcast-frequency electromagnetic ('radio') spectrum to national governments. Even in the age of Internet, the broadcast spectrum is a vital and finite resource needed for any over-the-air communications: military, navigational, emergency services, and scientific networks, as well as information, communication, trade, and—one of the smallest though most debated uses—entertainment. Competition between these users, and between broadcast and cellnet industries, spill over into international relations, especially where countries share borders and signals interfere with one another.

Common regulation on standards—allowing first telegrams, then voice calls and data transmissions to be passed from country to country—became part of the ITU's remit over time. However, for a number of reasons (O'Siochru and Constanza-Chock 2003) the ITU was in no position to undertake management of the nascent Internet, which grew from its two- and three- machine beginnings in 1969 to a significant professional network by the end of the 1980s without a unified UN or other international body with sole authority over it.

Even in the boom years of the 1990s and 2000s, when SMS, Web, and e-mail became mass media, the ITU was unable to exert authority. In its place, an initially ad hoc arrangement of bodies formed, simply to make the system work. In addition to the IETF and its Habermasian slogan, the Internet Corporation for Assigned Names and Numbers (ICANN) is a characteristic body with dominion over a resource as strategic as spectrum. 'Address space' comprises a numerical address of 12 or 32 digits for every computer on the Internet, plus the human-readable universal resource locators (URLs). URLs operate a hierarchy of TLDs and ccTLDs (Top Level Domains such as .net and .org; and country-code Top Level Domains such as .uk, the contentious .tw given to Taiwan against Chinese opposition, and the re-marketed .tv domain granted to Tuvalu). A system of registries authorizes lawful (but also sometimes 'carpetbagging' unlawful) users of domain names like 'harrypotter' or 'wallmart'. URLs are strategic resources because the original numerical address space is now close to exhaustion, due to the explosion in Internet-connected devices, including many which have no human operator, but report automatically on their status to central computers. In the early days, TLDs fell under the jurisdiction of US Defense Department, a result of their early investment in the nascent Internet. Passed on to the NSF (National Science Foundation), the role was commercialized in 1992, and rights to all but .mil (military) domains passed to a registrar service provided by NSI (Network Solutions Inc.), a subsidiary of defence contractor SAIC (Science Applications International Corporation) until March 1998. The company charged for registration of domains, arguing that costs rose with the boom in requests. By the time they had administered 1.5 million domains, the scale of potential profit—and the possible brake on development of an open and equal, rationalist model of the engineers—became clear, as did the company's limited ability to handle the volume of demand. In addition, NSI began to suffer from trademark and related legal disputes because it failed to develop a conflict resolution process; and finally, a crash in the company's root server in July of 1997 led to a catastrophic crash of the entire Internet (Mathiason and Kuhlman 1998; Mathiason 2009).

At this juncture, however, the ITU was in a particularly parlous state. During the 1980s and early 1990s, widespread deregulation of telecom industries pushed the nation-based regulatory function of the ITU to the margins. Over the following years, the ITU would open its doors increasingly to corporate participation (MacLean 2003), but in the interim control over address space passed from NSI to a new company, formed under California law and contracted to the US government: ICANN. Both the corporate nature of ICANN, and its ties to the US government, along with internal political issues and issues concerning membership of its boards, were major political issues in the Internet community throughout the 1990s and 2000s, among them the controversial Uniform Dispute Resolution Policy, the failure to develop a promised membership system, and consequent restriction of elections to the board (Mueller 2004, see also ICANNwatch <http://www.icannwatch.org/>).

Largely due to the influence of the BRICK (Brazil, Russia, India, China, Korea) block of countries seeking ways to lessen perceived US dominance over the Internet, especially the 'critical Internet resource' of address space, the ITU gained traction during this period, representing a resurgent demand for nations to participate in control of the Internet. The UN called a World Summit on the Information Society (WSIS) for 2007. The event was overshadowed by disputes over the regulation of name-space, so much so that other efforts to achieve security for e-commerce, protection from data-theft, and closing the information divide were tangibly marginalized. As the BRICK group pushed for the ITU to take control of the Internet, the powerful US IT industry lobby pushed for a liberalization of ICANN's status as a US corporation in order to preserve commercial and ideological freedoms from what they perceived as surveillant and censorious national interests. After much diplomatic activity, the Obama legislature finally amended the Memorandum of Understanding binding ICANN to the US government, leaving it

> a private not for profit organization....ICANN is independent and is not controlled by any one entity. It commits ICANN to reviews performed BY THE COMMUNITY—a further recognition that the multi-stakeholder model is robust enough to review itself. (ICANN 2009; capitalization in original)

The struggle over control of addressing and name-space has left a mass of documentation for future analysts. At present it is unclear whether the expert consensus model of the IETF, the inter-governmental model of the ITU, or the increasing commercial pressures to deregulate the domain-name market will triumph; what forms of more or less agonistic equilibrium they may agree to; and which alternative economic and socio-political structures may result. The uncertainty is exacerbated by the exhaustion of the existing address space, the consequent necessity to provide a new one (IPv6 or Internet Protocol version 6), the challenge posed by the fact that the new system is not backwardly compatible with its predecessor, and the possibility that this situation might lead to a split between the old and new Internets, akin to the coexistence of Internet and Fidonet.

Future archaeologists seeking clear demarcations between strata of historical change will find instead multiple network systems and protocols coexisting. Moreover, US institutions have a large reserve of spare addresses for the old system, acquired when addresses were not reckoned scarce, and therefore have less need to undertake the expensive transition to IPv6; whereas newly networking nations like China have a scarcity of old addresses and therefore the motivation to move. As with other early-adopter technologies, older systems retain the older technology while the newer migrate to the new. Traditional archaeology has been site-specific: Internet archaeology, and perhaps all archaeologies of the present, will be faced with the challenge of locating a planetary (and in certain features such as satellite transmission extra-terrestrial) artefact. At the same time however, the mixed adoption of IPv6 indicates that geographical distinctions will continue to operate. The re-emergence of geography into what was once rated an immaterial and de-territorialized universe, set apart from geopolitics (see for example Barlow 2001 [1996]), is one of the stranger artefacts of the brief history of the Internet.

The case of ICANN is one of several indicating the continuing fragility of Internet governance by a network of interrelated bodies, many of them membership bodies or bodies which, like the IETF, are run through open discussion of publicly circulated 'requests for comment'. Prominent think-tank, the Internet Governance Project (<http://www.internetgovernance .org/>), lists fifteen organizations with direct governance roles, with jurisdictions including human rights, intellectual property, economic relations, enforcement of order, and operational policies. The Tunis world summit on the Information Society restricted the number of NGOs attending to 6,000, including churches, charities, political, and moral groups as well as a variety of business interests. Thus network governance is itself a network, one in which contradiction and conflict still arise. Ironically however, Internet archaelogists may have less access to documents, because so much Internet documentation is in fragile digital form.

10.5 Intellectual Property Rights and the State

Two important factors in this fragility are corporate demands for increased intellectual property rights, and governmental control over censorship and surveillance. Together with the history traced in the previous paragraphs of the emergence of the network paradigm in Internet engineering and governance, these cases help us understand the three agencies operating to define the shape and operation of network communications—that is, all electronically mediated communications—in the twenty-first century. The contemporary formation of the Internet can be read as a struggle or counterpoint of three agencies: the nation-state, the market, and the network. In an earlier phase of the network, it was possible to regard interconnectivity itself as a worthwhile political, economic, and social goal, as either a new stage in the history of democracy (Mulgan 1997) or the basis for the chaotic emergence of permanent invention (Kelly 1994). However, in the contemporary formation, the network is no longer the goal of development but at once the terrain of struggle for dominance, and the prize. Control over the operational principles of the network delivers political power to the state and wealth to corporate capital (Castells 2009). In the conclusion to this chapter, we will see what network-native motivations and goals might be.

The market's position in Internet communications is nowhere more visible than in attempts to build intellectual property rights (IPRs) into its code infrastructure. The introduction of IPv6 allows new options to be added to the root code governing packet-switching and TCP/IP. Among those options, particularly controversial has been the attempt, at this fundamental level of traffic control, to assert legal rights over intangible and non-rivalrous goods, that is goods which can be enjoyed by more than one person without the common stock being diminished: I have an idea, and you can share it, without my use of the idea diminished. The Statute of Anne of 1710, commonly regarded as the founding document of copyright legislation, was designed to protect authors of written works from pirate printers. It introduced both the concept of the author as owner of a work and the idea of a fixed term during which the author had the monopoly right to profit from it. The 1886 Berne Convention internationalized the idea of copyright, extending these rights to cover all nations signatory to the Convention (notably not the United States, which only signed in 1989), on the basis that a limited monopoly term would encourage the generation of new works, thus contributing to the common good, while works in which copyright expired would become part of the common stock of knowledge.

During the nineteenth and early twentieth centuries, the USA had a reputation for playing fast and loose with copyright. Weak legislation and lax enforcement were excused by the expense of importing intellectual goods from abroad, versus the huge demand produced by unusually high literacy rates and a culture of innovation and invention (Starr 2004). Something of this maverick attitude to intellectual property (including designs, trademarks, and most significantly patents) remains in two features of twenty-first-century digital culture: the principle that patent law should not extend to mathematical expressions, including software, and the ease and ubiquity of copying using digital devices. However, in the digital era, intellectual property has become a major driver of the US economy, in the key sectors of military technology, software, and entertainment, to the extent that the US government, on behalf of well-organized industry lobbies, has become one of the most aggressive players in the assertion of longer and longer terms of copyright, and looser and looser requirements of patent applications. In theory, patents must undergo tests of both originality and usefulness; but the practice of pre-emptive patenting (for example patenting a family of molecules whose members have not yet been synthesized and whose properties are unknown) is now commonplace. The 1998 US Copyright Term Extension Act extended copyright for authored works to the life of the author plus 70 years, and for corporately authored works to 120 years after creation (or 95 years after publication, whichever is longer) (US Copyright Office 2010: 5). Widely nicknamed the Mickey Mouse Act because of its application to Disney's brand, this extension to the duration of copyright was predated by the European Union, which fixed the 70 year *post mortem* term in 1993, having established its first pan-European harmonization of copyright in the matter of computer programs in 1991, an early indication of the importance of digital media to copyright law, and vice versa.

Legal instruments, however, proved inadequate to stem file-sharing, especially through peer-to-peer networks like Napster and BitTorrent, connections sitting on top of the TCP/IP suite which allow each computer attached to a network to act as a server, so that packets can be distributed without needing to use central file storage. Millions of music and film fans opened their hard-drives to peers, and in return shared the contents of others' drives. This technology, which would later be legitimated as the spine of Skype's Voice-Over-Internet Protocol (VOIP) telephony, was hotly disputed by Hollywood. Film and record companies frequently alter the software properties of recording, and latterly of the Internet as a whole, in order to protect copyright. Promoting this family of technologies, known as digital rights management (DRM), the news and entertainment industries have secured optional 'layers'—segments of a software platform—that can be used to control copying of digital files, in particular in the MPEG-4 codec, used in DVD, Blu-Ray, HDTV, and increasingly for Internet Protocol TV (IPTV), especially on IPv6. This threatens to change the nature of the Internet, struggling to wrest it back from the anarchic open-sharing culture of its early days. It reflects a changing balance between the rights of owners and purchasers. In older times, the purchaser of a book could quote from it, lend it, sell it, or give it away: the purchaser of software or MP3 files has only the rights of a licensee, and cannot copy, lend, sell on, or gift. In the phrase made famous by Lawrence Lessig (2006), 'Code is Law': the operation of software, especially of basic protocols like TCP/IP, does not simply discipline citizens: it makes it nearly impossible to break the law (Galloway 2004). This drift from legal discipline to software protocol would appear to mirror a feature of liberalism and neo-liberalism identified by Michel Foucault in his late lectures on biopolitics (2007): that the supposedly free market rests on a strong state capable of making and upholding a rigid legal apparatus on the back of which commerce can go on.

While the introduction of IPv6 indicates that the network of networks is capable of splintering into more than one Internet, the struggle over IPRs suggests that the market is capable of controlling the operation of root code, and therefore influencing at the most profound level the structure and working of the Internet. Recent attempts to patent software—as mathematical expression traditionally excluded from intellectual property rights in most jurisdictions—suggest a conflict between monetization and open invention. Internet governance obscures its traces and goes largely uncommented in public media and scholarship. Such changes do leave other tracks: the official IPv6 book store on Amazon lists over a hundred books, while the literature on IPRs in legal journals and popular books as well as national and international legal and contractual documents is immense. At the same time, future archaelologists will have difficulty rescuing evidence of the content of sites like library.nu, a vast online repository of academic and scientific texts which was closed on the orders of a Munich court (Kelty 2012); or of the files exchanged through sharing site Megaupload, like library.nu closed in 2012. Only certain forms of action will be preserved: accurate assessment of the activities of quasi-legal and illegal networks is likely to disappear leaving little trace other than the fact of their illegality.

The policing of national interests has become an increasingly significant aspect of the contemporary Internet (Collins 2010; Goldsmith and Wu 2008; Nuechterlein and Weiser 2007), the most famous case being that of the Chinese Golden Shield, or Great Firewall of China. Meanwhile the 'walled garden' approach of mobile phone operators is mimicked by app stores for tablet computing, and by the 'black box' approach to new product design (Zittrain 2008). Surveillance technologies are employed busily by both corporate and government agencies (Elmer 2004). A third player is, however, emerging alongside states and the market: peer-to-peer (Bauwens 2005; <http://p2pfoundation.net/>). Among its most significant achievements are the Linux operating system, Wikipedia, and Creative Commons. The concept of a commons (Hardt and Negri 2009) connects the ethos of the open Internet to socially oriented movements in the real world (Juris 2008; Kelty 2008). It remains to be seen whether the ecological struggles articulated by many of the actors in the P2P movement, and the ecological metaphors employed in it, will be turned towards managing the environmental impact of the Internet and digital media. From electricity grids to popular political movements, the Internet is intimately entwined in the physical world, on which it draws, but to which it also contributes. For example, dependent as it is on electrical supply, Internet control over generation, transmission, billing, and the spot market in deregulated electricity industries makes electrical supply dependent on the Internet. Such closed circuits create vulnerabilities, such as that evinced in the 2006 blackouts. On the other hand, social movements like the Arab Spring mixed mass demonstrations with digital networks, and have demonstrated their ability to survive the closure of Internet channels by opposing governments (see Elseewi 2011). Where nation and commerce come into the Internet from outside, peer-to-peer and other network-native groupings come to the real world from the network. This *Aufhebung* of the digital infrastructure on mass movements suggests a new relationship to communications emerging in the network era.

10.6 BITROT

We can trace a deep history of the Internet in older global structures of communication. The trans-Asian Silk Road, travelling from oasis to oasis, was followed by the steam-trains that also needed water, then by the telegraph. Internet cabling followed. Transoceanic cable-laying follows the seasonal winds and currents exploited by the Polynesian navigators and by the Vikings. The material geometry of the Internet follows ancient routes, and serves many of the same ancient purposes: exchange of songs, recipes, and sexual favours; inmixing of religions; trade, and cultural congress which, through wars and pogroms, provided a spine of civilization throughout the heart of the Old World. Current struggles over the meaning and purpose of the Internet reflect both these ancient structures and the more modern displacement of politics from the social to the media sphere. It has been suggested (Dean 2009) that the 'obligation to communicate' has substituted for the clash of opinions in democratic fora; but this view misses the ongoing struggle to determine the future shape of the Internet, between three competing value-systems of power, wealth, and connectivity. Future archaeologists of the Internet may never know what the outcome of that struggle was, but its traces will be writ large over the remains that they unearth. The problem will be that both in quantity and in its decay, it will be increasingly difficult to distinguish the historical signal from the noise.

The last great challenge to network archaeology will be the physical ephemerality of electronic media. While much of the Internet's architecture is physical, much exists only as code, a form of writing that is 'performative', in the sense that it performs quasi-linguistic statements that enact what they describe (Mackenzie 2006). But code is only performative if it has the correct machinery to run on, and a key problem already for digital archivists is that not only software but hardware disintegrates with age, and even before then the pace of obsolescence renders hardware platforms obsolete, spares difficult to find, and code therefore inoperable. Without the match of hard and software, neither operates. And since so much Internet documentation is stored digitally, the documentation itself is vulnerable not only to 'bitrot' (the decay of digital files) but to being excluded from new iterations of file types, operating systems, storage media, and chips. Forensic engineers can retrieve data even from damaged hard-drives, or from encrypted files, but the disintegration of data over longer periods is a harsh fact of digital archiving. As mass storage moves to remote 'cloud' servers, transmission errors and minor fluctuations in the electrical and magnetic environment accumulate to the point when the files can no longer be recuperated. The sheer scale of information produced in the twenty-first century (Bohn and Short 2009), and the limits to the materials and energy that can be devoted to storing it, are massively increased by the IPR regime that insists that each user have a discrete copy of a file or application. One research project holds that the amount of information being produced has already outstripped the quantity of storage media available to house it (Gantz 2011). In the field of media arts history, works and documentation are disappearing in a matter of years after their creation (<http://www.mediaarthistory.org/>). Many digital artefacts—photographs, X-rays, text messages, and e-mails among them—are only intended for specific occasions, and their loss is 'only' that of the quotidian. This, however, is a quality of history that has been a specific preserve of archaeology, and its loss signals a concentration of historiography on the grander scale of major events like the introduction of IPv6. At another level, one standard definition of information is 'structured data', which implies that in the absence of the structuring properties of databases, spreadsheets, geographical information systems, and other orderings, data descend into entropy. When we combine this tendency to randomness with the loss of other system-specific modes of organization such as file-sharing, increasingly threatened by both legal and protocological assaults, we begin to sense the transitory nature of so much of the operating system for our increasingly networked planet, and the difficulties it will present to archaeologists of the future.

References

Abbate, Janet. 1999. *Inventing the Internet*. Cambridge, MA: MIT Press.

Barlow, John Perry. 2001 [1996]. A Declaration of the Independence of Cyberspace. In *Crypto Anarchy, Cyberstates and Pirate Utopias*, ed. Peter Ludlow, pp. 27–30. Cambridge, MA: MIT Press.

Basel Action Network. 2002. Exporting Harm: The High-Tech Trashing of Asia. Available at: <http://www.ban.org/E-waste/technotrashfinalcomp.pdf> (accessed 17 March 2009).

—— 2005. The Digital Dump: Exporting High-Tech Re-use and Abuse to Africa. Available at: <http://www.ban.org/BANreports/10-24-05/index.htm> (accessed 17 March 2009).

Bauwens, Michel. 2005. The Political Economy of Peer Production. *C-Theory*. Available at: <http://www.ctheory.net/articles.aspx?id=499) (accessed 30 April 2012).

Boccaletti, Giulio, Löffler, Markus, and Oppenheim, Jeremy M. 2008. How IT Can Cut Carbon Emissions. *McKinsey Quarterly*, October. Avalable at: <http://www.mckinseyquarterly .com/How_IT_can_cut_carbon_emissions_2221> (accessed 7 February 2013).

Bohn, Roger E. and Short, James E. 2009. How Much Information? 2009 Report on American Consumers. San Diego: Global Information Industry Center, University of California, updated January 2010.

Cass, Stephen. 2007. How Much Does the Internet Weigh? *Discover*. Available at: <http:// discovermagazine.com/2007/jun/how-much-does-the-internet-weigh/article_view?b_ start:int=0&-C=> (accessed 26 March 2011).

Castells, Manuel. 2009. *Communication Power*. Oxford: Oxford University Press.

Chun, Wendy Hui Kyong. 2011. *Programmed Visions: Software and Memory*. Cambridge, MA: MIT Press.

Collins, Richard. 2010. *Three Myths of Internet Governance*. Bristol: Intellect.

Cubitt, Sean, Hassan, Robert, and Volkmer, Ingrid. 2011. Does Cloud Computing Have a Silver Lining? *Media, Culture and Society* 33(1) 149–58.

Dean, Jodi. 2009. *Democracy and Other Neoliberal Fantasies: Communicative Capitalism and Left Politics*. Durham, NC: Duke University Press.

deNardis, Laura. 2009. *Protocol Politics: The Globalization of Internet Governance*. Cambridge, MA: MIT Press.

Elmer, Greg. 2004. *Profiling Machines: Mapping the Personal Information Economy*. Cambridge, MA: MIT Press.

Elseewi, Tarik Ahmed (ed.). 2011. Special Section: The Arab Spring & the Role of ICTs. *International Journal of Communication*. Available at: <http://ijoc.org/ojs/index.php/ijoc/ issue/view/6> (accessed 30 April 2012).

Fiveash, Kevin. 2007. Microsoft signs MOU with Siberia. *The Register*. Available at: <http:// www.theregister.co.uk/2007/11/27/microsoft_siberia_data_centre/> (accessed 30 April 2012).

Foucault, Michel. 2007. *Security, Population, Territory: Lectures at the Collège de France 1977– 1978*, ed. Michel Senellart, tr. Graham Burchell. Basingstoke: Palgrave Macmillan.

Froomkin, A. Michael. 2003. Habermas@Discourse.net: Toward a Critical Theory of Cyberspace. *Harvard Law Review* 116: 751–873.

Fuller, Matthew. 2003. *Behind the Blip: Essays on Software Culture*. New York: Autonomedia.

Galloway, Alexander R. 2004. *Protocol: How Control Exists After Decentralization*. Cambridge, MA: MIT Press.

Gantz, John. 2011. *The Diverse and Exploding Digital Universe*. IDC White Paper, March. Framingham MA: IDC. Available at: <http://uk.emc.com/leadership/programs/digital-universe.htm> (accessed 7 February 2013).

Gates, Bill. 2000. *Business @ the Speed of Thought: Succeeding in the Digital Economy*. New York: Business Plus.

Goldsmith, Jack and Wu, Tim. 2008. *Who Controls the Internet? Illusions of a Borderless World*. Oxford: Oxford University Press.

Hardt, Michael and Negri, Antonio. 2009. *Commonwealth*. Cambridge, MA: Harvard University Press.

ICANN (Internet Corporation for Assigned Names and Numbers). 2009. The Affirmation of Commitments—What it Means. Available at: <http://www.icann.org/en/announcements/announcement-30sep09-en.htm> (accessed 28 March 2011).

Juris, Jeffrey S. 2008. *Networking Futures: The Movements against Corporate Globalization*. Durham, NC: Duke University Press.

Kelly, Kevin. 1994. *Out of Control: The New Biology of Machines*. London: 4th Estate.

Kelty, Christopher M. 2008. *Two Bits: The Cultural Significance of Free Software*. Durham, NC: Duke University Press.

—— 2012. The Disappearing Virtual Library. *Al-Jazeera*, 1 March. Available at: <http://www.aljazeera.com/indepth/opinion/2012/02/2012227143813304790.html> (accessed 7 February 2013).

Lessig, Lawrence. 2006. *Code v.2: Code and Other Laws of Cyberspace*. New York: Basic Books. Available at: <http://codev2.cc/> (accessed 7 February 2013).

Mackenzie, Adrian. 2006. *Cutting Code: Software and Sociality*. New York: Peter Lang.

MacLean, Don. 2003. The Quest for Inclusive Governance of Global ICTs: Lessons from the ITU in the Limits of National Sovereignty. *Information Technologies and International Development* 1(1): 1–18.

Mathiason, John. 2009. *Internet Governance: The New Frontier of Global Institutions*. London: Routledge.

Mathiason, John and Kuhlman, Charles C. 1998. International Public Regulation of the Internet: Who Will Give You Your Domain Name? *International Studies Association*, 21 March. Available at: <http://www.intlmgt.com/domain.html> (accessed 28 March 2011).

Mueller, Milton L. 2004. *Ruling the Root: Internet Governance and the Taming of Cyberspace*. Cambridge, MA: MIT Press.

Mulgan, Geoff. 1997. *Connexity: How to Live in a Connected World*. London: Chatto & Windus.

Negroponte, Nicholas. 1995. *Being Digital*. London: Coronet.

Nuechterlein, Jonathan E. and Weiser, Philip J. 2007. *Digital Crossroads: American Telecommunications Policy in the Internet Age*. Cambridge, MA: MIT Press.

O'Siochru, Sean and Constanza-Chock, Sasha. 2003. *Global Governance of Information and Communication Technologies: Implications for Transnational Civil Society Networking*. New York: Social Science Research Council. Available at: <http://sd-cite.iisd.org/cgi-bin/koha/opac-detail.pl?biblionumber=26047> (accessed 7 February 2013).

Pohl, Frederick. 1977. *Gateway*. New York: Galaxy.

Sassen, Sakia. 2006. *Territory, Authority, Rights: From Medieval to Global Assemblages*. Princeton, NJ: Princeton University Press.

Starr, Paul. 2004. *The Creation of the Media: Political Origins of Modern Communications*. New York: Basic Books.

TechEye. 2011. European Parliament gets tough on WEEE directive. *TechEye*, 7 February. Available at: <http://www.techeye.net/business/european-parliament-gets-tough-on-weee-directive> (accessed 26 March 2011).

US Copyright Office. 2010. *Circular 1: Copyright Basics*. Washington, DC: US Copyright Office.

US Geological Survey. 2013. Indium. *Mineral Commodity Summaries 2013*. Washington, DC: US Geological Survey/US Department of the Interior: 74–5.

Virilio, Paul. 2009. *Futurism of the Instant: Stop-Eject*, tr. Julie Rose. Cambridge: Polity Press.

Virno, Paolo. 2008. *Multitude: Between Innovation and Negation*, tr. Isabella Bertoletti, James Cascaito, and Andrew Casson. New York: Semiotext(e).

Zittrain, Jonathan. 2008. *The Future of the Internet and How to Stop it*. London: Allen Lane.

....

CHAPTER 11

PERFORMANCE AND THE STRATIGRAPHY OF PLACE: EVERYTHING YOU NEED TO BUILD A TOWN IS HERE

....

WRIGHTS & SITES
(STEPHEN HODGE, SIMON PERSIGHETTI, PHIL SMITH, AND CATHY TURNER)

11.1 INTRODUCTION

....

DESPITE turning our attention away from the theatre after our first major project (*The Quay Thing*, 1998) and moving increasingly towards peripatetic practices, we have continued to draw on our performance backgrounds; this turn began as we explored the quotidian world as if searching for new performance sites. Then and now we employ disrupted walking strategies as tools for playful debate, collaboration, intervention, and spatial meaning-making. Our work, like walking, is intended to be porous; for others to read into it and connect from it and for the specificities and temporalities of sites to fracture, erode, and distress it. We have sought to pass on our dramaturgical strategies to others: to audiences, readers, visitors, and passers-by. The outcomes of our work vary from project to project, but frequently include site-specific performance, Mis-Guided Tours or published Mis-Guides (for example, *A Mis-Guide To Anywhere*, 2006), 'drifts', mythogeographic mapping, public art or installations, and public presentations and articles. We have assisted explorations of the Wienfluss, excavated subterranean library stacks, and recently installed a network of plaques across an English seaside resort (*Everything you need to build a town is here*, 2010). In every case our outcomes are incomplete, intended to provoke and invite acts that go beyond spectatorship. Today, walking and exploring the everyday is at the heart of all we do and what we make seeks to facilitate walker-artists, walker-makers, and everyday pedestrians to become partners in ascribing significance to place.

We invite you to treat the following chapter as a site rather than as a treatise.

We have structured the text in four layers. Some materials drop through from one layer to another. Elements are introduced at one level and imitated or digested at another. There is massive faulting at page and line endings. The layers are variously unfinished and indiscrete, subject to influences and interferences, partly reconciled and partly not. While each of the layers has been written *towards* something, they were all attenuated at approximately the same time. There are coincidences.

We suggest that you can 'get most out of' the chapter if you approach it with a strategy for excavation. The layout allows your eye to move up and down the page for a kind of fuzzy geofizz, but you can also go one stratum at a time, apparently peeling back the layers…the excavation metaphor will stop making sense sooner or later.

We are happy for you to tell stories about this terrain as a means to extracting its parts, to sample it, or to process it analytically by separation and categorization. You may, of course, loot.

'IMAGINE A TOWN AS A PIECE OF MUSIC. THIS OPEN SPACE IS A CRESCENDO THAT…

In this stratum I will attempt to recover fragments of a seam of work partly realized…

This stratum sifts through the contrapuntal layers of 'The Great Architect' and 'The…

The signs in the stratum we labelled 'Time', rather than indicating traces of the…

…ECHOES FROM WALLS THE SHAPE OF A TOWN. SING A SONG OF WESTON.'

…by a falling away of some things and partly by an excavation of others: my 'Foundations' layer of plaques at Weston-super-Mare (UK), where I made a working somewhere in the midst of erosion and structural reconstruction.

…Amateur Builder', and highlights the function of walking as both a research tool and a potential outcome within the work of Wrights & Sites.

…past, point towards gaps, erasures, missed opportunities and loss. In one of our *Mis-Guides*, Phil Smith suggested doing 'reverse archaeology': 'look for ruins on which the future can be built' (Wrights & Sites 2003: 14). As I mentally re-trace my steps around Weston, thinking of how ideas were gathered for the 'Time' layer, it strikes me that I too was doing a kind of archaeology in reverse. Rather than imagining or positing what was once present, I was, perhaps, more cognisant of what is forgotten, and the impermanence and irretrievability of presence itself.

'Archaeology' is the term Foucault used during the 1960s to describe his approach to writing history. Archaeology is about examining the discursive traces and orders left by the past in order to write a 'history of the present'. In other words archaeology is about looking at history as a way of understanding the processes that have led to what we are today (O'Farrell 2007).

Each plaque is a thing, a textual representation of other things and a memorial of itself; traces of a journey from prop to relic. Like pavement slabs, the plaques are political things subject to permissions. Some are absent, subject to refusals. Some, literally, have a beach beneath them.

'"the whole town is built on sand"... The sand dunes once came halfway up Meadow Street.' In order to make sense of the plaques I will barely refer to them, but work my way around and beneath them.

Walking became central to our practice in the late 1990s after a large-scale site-specific pro-gramme of work made for Exeter's quay and canal (UK). The impulse to walk came from a desire to circumnavigate issues of space management and access that had begun to sap our energy. Leaving our theatre baggage behind us, we became more interested in journeying, in displace-ment and disruption, in the porosity of the city, and the acts of walking and talking with each other and those we invited to join us or chanced across en route. Paying little attention to existing signage, our post-Situationist walking methods offered us new way-finding opportuni-ties. *Everything you need to build a town is here* (commissioned by Situations for Wonders of Weston) emerged from ten months of reconnaissance walking in Weston-super-Mare.

As we drifted, we kept encountering stories of shifting foundations, subsidence, holes in walls, bomb damage to jerry-built housing, roofless churches, sand-castles. The speed with which time passes is vertiginous, sweeping us towards the cliff's edge. Even to remember that we have forgotten can be a struggle.

'IMAGINE A TOWN AS A PIECE OF MUSIC...'
This text, written for a 'Panoptic' layer of the town, borrows from the work and writing of twentieth-century architect Eliel Saarinen who considers cities as places of trade and exchange that develop slowly and organically with expansion as a result of cause and effect rather than structured design. He also based his theory about the structure of a medieval city in relation to landscape, organic forms, and musical composition.

This, I recovered from a file titled description of signage, *added in blue: 'part of (a) wider set of signs across the town that identify the presence of meaningful layers... grasp the connectedness of the signs... "sliding" along the different planes of the town.' This, in black text: 'We remain interested in ideas of the "anti-sign" or "mis-sign" (ours are deliberately over-loaded).'*

Lying in an Exeter hospital bed in April 2010, the tendons in my right thumb severed, I wonder what effect it'll have on my Weston research. I mention it to Geoffrey in the bed opposite, and he starts to talk about his childhood. Turns out he grew up on a farm in Sand Bay, less than a mile to the north of Weston. He talks of Auntie Nellie's beard, of fashioning Davy Crockett hats from grey squirrels up in the woods, and of steering a pleasure boat for a man called Juicy Payne. I drift into a drug-induced sleep, and when I awake he's gone.

I was thinking of architectural form and function, architecture's apparent, yet shifting solidity, and its participation in the performance of a city. Performance brings the dimen-sion of time to a consideration of architecture. I was thinking of the time-lapse photog-raphy of Reggio's 1982 film, Koyaanisqatsi, where city life passes at a frenetic pace, set against shots of housing projects in the process of demolition, and moments of slow motion.

As musical impressions are received through a certain rhythm and cadence of tune and time, so are architectural impressions received through a certain proportion and rhythm of material, color,

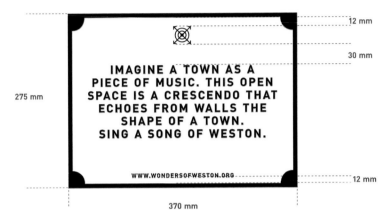

Format: 370 x 275 mm

Font: Flat Faced Gothic

Body text size: 5/8inch/15.9mm

Web address size: 1/4inch/6.35mm

Symbol:

Line thickness: 1.5 mm

Size: 28 x 28 mm

Frame:

Border thickness: about 7–8mm

Round corner size: 25 mm

IMAGINE A TOWN AS A PIECE OF MUSIC. THIS OPEN SPACE IS A CRESCENDO THAT ECHOES FROM WALLS THE SHAPE OF A TOWN. SING A SONG OF WESTON.

WWW.WONDERSOFWESTON.ORG

12 mm

30 mm

275 mm

12 mm

370 mm

FIGURE 11.1 Sign design ('The Panoptic' stratum) (reproduced with permission from Polimekanos)

and space. The fundamental laws are the same in both cases. The reactions are related, yet different. Generally speaking, we may say that musical reactions are 'conscious', whereas architectural reactions are primarily 'subconscious' (Saarinen 1943: 64).

In Lubimov's 1971 production of Hamlet *at the Taganka Theatre (Moscow), a curtain was dragged around the performance space, defining the bounds of the action. Late in the show, it suddenly seemed to move on its own, embodying the thing-life of the production itself. 'I realized that the capacity of these (nonhuman) bodies was not restricted to a passive "intractability" but also included the ability to make things happen, to produce effects' (Bennett 2010: 4–5).*

Trailblaze westwards from the town library at one end of Boulevard to the newspaper offices at the other end and the Old Town Quarry up on Worlebury Hill pops in and out of sight as you walk. Much of Boulevard and the surrounding town architecture were fashioned of limestone from this quarry.

Then I crossed a road and saw a blue flower, an iris, that seemed to stand outside architecture's gestures towards permanence ('at least five years' was the definition of 'permanence' for our commission). Lasting a short season, the iris seemed too ephemeral to count as form, too small a gesture to count as function, despite the fact that its colour struck me like a blue hammer and its shape reminded me of the stonework on church ceilings. It marked the way a moment can bloom and disappear.

Saarinen was also acutely aware of the historical factors of land ownership and the guilds of the medieval towns and cities he describes, where an aesthetic related to notions of transcendental architecture were built into the fabric and philosophy of castle and cathedral builders.

The Weston-super-Mare plaques are anachronistic in design, modelled after cast iron plaques of the late industrial period. But too accurately cast to be nostalgically artisanal. Their quasi-veracity does not sit still in an assumption; it irritates the heritage landscape. Their tough alloy will survive the walls on which they are fixed. They are premonitions of their own floating free. The 'Foundations' plaques reference dunes far inland, an olfactory theatre, two private geologies, an elegant construction built under warlike conditions, and a subsiding former temple.

The muse for 'The Great Architect' layer was Hans Fowler Price (1835–1912), responsible for many of the key municipal buildings in Weston's rapid Victorian expansion, including the town hall, sanatorium, gaslight company buildings, and the Masonic Lodge of St Kew.

Most of our signs desired the reader to take some action, whether mentally or physically; the iris seemed to require the opposite, a kind of quiet. Presence is the experience of limit. As Giannachi and Kaye put it, 'presence is the ecology… that inexorably ties the "I am" with its past and future, and that forces "I am" to confront itself with what is other from "it"' (Giannachi and Kaye 2011: 5). Presence is characterized by silence, propelled by 'what might have been and what has been', and caught between 'time past and time future' (Eliot 1989: 190).

The notion of a city having all its facets as relational echoes of the hierarchical and monumental keystone buildings of Church and State has been replicated in more recent times when at the peak of the industrial revolution workers' housing also bore signs of ornamentation that might previously have been the preserve of the powerful and the wealthy.

In the 1993 production The Murder of Sherlock Holmes *(TNT, Munich), the head and limbs of a murder victim are hidden in suitcases. The body is 'reconstructed' when the characters arrange these containers into a recognizably human relation. 'Constitution(al) Club swallowed a Masonic temple. An Iron Age burial mound… swallowed by the Milton Road Cemetery. The Dorville Hotel… swallowed Dorville House—the original bay windows are still visible.'*

Upstairs in the public library at the eastern end of Boulevard lie numerous master plans for the town. You are free to visit these unrealized Westons, or imagine the town afresh. Price's striking red brick library is now somewhat overshadowed by the concrete BT exchange next door. Post-war visions of 'a garden city by the sea' drowned by waves of digital audio, texts, and email attachments.

In the cemetery, I placed a sign that proposed an 'architecture of forgetting'. This is Mark Sandberg's phrase. Writing about Ibsen's plays, he suggests that various characters within them try to use architecture to forget or to build over the past (Sandberg 2007). Ibsen, Sandberg says, mistrusted the lies monuments tell. His Mrs Alving spends her life trying to build a complex of orphanage buildings to eradicate the corrupt legacy of her

FIGURE 11.2 Found sign (Milton Road Cemetery) (photograph: Wrights & Sites)

dead husband, only to have the buildings burn and to discover her son's genetic inherit-ance of syphilis. In *John Gabriel Borkman*, Gunhild suggests a different kind of monument: 'It will be as if a living fence, a woven hedge of trees and bushes was planted thick, thick around your buried life. All the dark past will be screened away...' (Ibsen cited in Sandberg 2007: 16).

During the late nineteenth to early twentieth centuries mass-produced classical plaster mouldings and ornate wrought iron embellishments became common affectations in the lowliest ranks of ter-raced housing INCOMPLETE FRAGMENT: ARCHITECTURAL EMBELLISHMENT.XXXXXXXXXXXXXX XXXXXXXXXXXXXXXXXXXXXXXXXXXXXXXXXXXXXXXXXXXXXXXXXXXXXXXXXXXXXXXXXXXXXXXXXX XXXXXXXXXXXXXXXXXXXXXXXXXXXXXXXXXXXXXXXXXXXXXXXXXXXXXXXXXXXXXXXXXXXXXXXXXX XXXXXXXXXXXXXXXXXXXXXXXXXXXXXXXXXXXXXXXXXXX

Theatricality is that part of things that we do not see, but imagine as happening between their parts, generated not by a unique labour necessary for its production, but by the work we do (consumption) to render it absent. Theatricality dissolves one thing so that something else can be invisible. The hollowness of containers (like a studio or theatre) conjures objects that become imbued with something other than thing-ness: the autonomous capacity to reduce bodies to the idea of one.

Price's eclectic, even proto-postmodernist approach is visible in the Weston Mercury office at the seaward end of Boulevard. 'That sacred seer, whose comprehensive view, / The past, the present and the future knew' (Homeric reference in Price's *Weston Mercury* obituary, November 1912).

The gravestones in Weston intend to be truthful. They aim at preserving a trace, or at least a memory, to transcend death. Yet they cannot tell the full story, or preserve memory. So they are misleading, at least, with their hopeful, yet clearly questionable, statement 'PURCHASED IN PERPETUITY'.

These observations may be useful in considering the psychic and psychological impact of the physical environment upon its inhabitants but also to think about the building of towns as a symbiotic loop mechanism, as a call and response by its builders to the ever-changing built and being-built environment. Here it is tempting to think about the 'archaeology of knowledge' [as well as the habitat where the makers and carriers of knowledge exist] (Foucault 1972).

The Royal Albert Memorial Museum (Exeter, UK) displays, equivalent with fire brigade regalia and stuffed bison, gifts to a magical child the mystic Joanna Southcott, aged 64, promised she would bear. Dying in the 'birth bed', Southcott achieved an amputated afterlife in unsuccessful campaigns for bishops to open her sealed box of prophesies. New Southcott boxes appeared, opened with ceremony and disappointment. A dwindling sect hid the original in Morecombe. No longer vibrant or exoteric correlatives, the boxes (both unrevealed and spurious) became occult theatrical properties, enabling something else to become invisible: British Israelism, an influence on the Christian Identity movement.

Price, architect to the Somerset County Council Board of Education, designed a number of Weston schools. One of our signs can be found outside Walliscote Primary School, and wonders 'WHAT KIND OF ARCHITECTURE THE CHILDREN WHO ARE NOW FOUR YEARS OLD WILL BUILD'.

I thought maybe we could invent an architecture that allowed us to remember forgetting—that is, to remember that we forget. If, as Huyssens puts it, 'every act of memory carries with it a dimension of betrayal, forgetting and absence' (2003: 4), how might we mark such a betrayal, acknowledge it? This could be an architecture that marks the repressed, like Gunhild's, or it might be a less ominous architecture, one that marks the transient moment and the unrecognized effect. Like hers, it might also be to do with growing things—letting seeds blow on the wind, so that flowers blossom in places we have never visited, or have not remembered.

INCOMPLETE FRAGMENT: Daniel Libeskind SHARD, Imperial War Museum, Manchester. A building the shape of the world torn asunder. IWMIWMIWMIWMIWMIWMIWMIWMIWMIWMIWW MNNNNNNNNNNNNNNNNNNNNNNNNNNNNNNNNNNNNNNNNNNNNNNNNNNN NNNNNNNNNNNNNN
The IWM (Imperial War Museum) is fundamentally based on this world; the contemporary world shattered into fragments and reassembled as fundamental emblem of conflict. These fragments, shards or traces of history are in turn assembled on this site and projected beyond it. (Libeskind 2001: 63)
NNNNNNNNNNNNNNNNNNNNNNNNNNNNNNNNNNNNNNNNNNNNNNNNNNNN NNNNNNNNNNNNNNNNNNNNNNNNNNNNNNNNNNNNNNNNNNNNNNNNNNNN NNNNNNNNNNNNNNNNNNNNNNNNNNNNN

At the height of the 'industrial revolution', Western theatre developed an enduring strategy for suppressing such materiality. It overthrew the common, generic, and symbolic properties of the

*travelling theatre in the name of a radical naturalism of appearances and a positivist, psychologi-
cal interiority, ushering in the dominance of décor and private property.*

Aside from architecture, Price's passion was chess. He co-founded the town's chess club and
once arranged a visit from the World Champion, Emmanuel Lasker, who impressed with his
simultaneous match-play. Today the Weston-super-Mare Chess Club meets at the ramshackle
Football Club buildings on Winterstoke Road. This drive-by eyesore is well off the checkerboard
where Price planned his opening gambit for the town.

It might seem that the sign in the Carlton Street car park is more directly archaeological,
asking us to conjecture the spaces that were once rooms. However, here, the archaeological imagination prompts a gesture towards the future, the possibility of claiming a space
in an unexpected way. I was shamelessly borrowing an idea from French company, Ici-Même,
whose *Chronoclub* (1994) presents a spoof housing scheme, with homes designed for
parking spaces and rentable by the hour. This is performance positing a new architecture,
asking questions about urban planning, speculating about what makes a home a home.

Archaeology, writes Colin Renfew is, 'Primarily about knowledge, information, and it depends
mainly on stratigraphic excavation giving particular attention to the precise context from which
each find comes' (Coles and Dion 1999: 15).

In 1979, I was present as the curtain rose on a performance of All My Sons *at the Bristol Old Vic
(Bristol, UK), revealing a shining white house; the well-heeled audience roared its appreciation of
the set as real estate as much as its exemplification of 'the real Belasco'.*

Back in the library L71.0642 struggles for attention. 'Most of our coastal resorts indeed are
the dismal cemeteries of dead chances dubiously awaiting a distant resurrection that nothing short of a drastic re-development could possibly assure' (Williams-Ellis and Brett 1947: 1).
The introduction to another shelved 'master plan', this time from the 'architect errant' behind
Portmeirion (North West Wales).

At the launch of our project, we stood in the rain in the car park and ate fondant fancies,
accompanied by a few theatrical props, under a roof of umbrellas. In the dampness and
dark of the present, it was not easy to imagine a house, past or future.

Whilst the materiality of a city is very much the evidence sought after by the agents of archaeology it is rare to think of sound as a plausible factor in evidencing the 'Time Stamps' of history.
Obviously it is in the realms of ethnomusicology to ascertain cultural transmissions via songs or
scores or even to reconstruct lost musical instruments and sound makers, but to think of the structure
of a whole town as a musical score or a place where sound resonates and generates invisible
architectures in the spaces between floors and ceilings, pavements and rooftops might not be commonly considered in the archaeological sphere.

During a 1973 performance of Bequest to the Nation *at the Belgrade Theatre (Coventry, UK),
I witnessed Lady Hamilton hurl her tiara to the ground. Made of a springy, non-metallic substance, it bounced into the ninth row.*

During our first official visit, a thin layer of snow covers Weston. 'If you've ever stood, in the early hours of the morning, and watched a city fill with snow, you will know that the first walker changes everything' (Wrights & Sites 2006: 61, fold-out central insert). Under the snow, the beach.

The station sign is about the body's lost minutes. I am always early. What I most often do is walk very slowly from one end of the platform to the other and this made me think about the way that time and space are entwined—and to all practical intents and purposes the same thing. My brothers live about five hours away. My Mum, less than an hour. My friend, a day.

INCOMPLETE FRAGMENT: . . . *to Acoustic Archaeology and Neolithic Monuments* (Maes Howe, Camster, Easter Aquorthies, Newgrange).XXXXXXXXX Devereux, P. and Jahn, R. G. (1996) 'Preliminary investigations and cognitive considerations of the acoustical resonances of selected archaeological sites', *Antiquity* 70, pp. 665–6.XXXXXXXXXXXXXXXXXXXX Also Ref. John Cage and *Silence* XXXXXXXXXXXXXXXXXXXXXXXXXXXXXXXXXXXXXXXXXXXXXXXXX

Encouraged by memories of such accidents and by exemplary postdramatic theatres, I came (late) to challenge the inevitable authority of the actor over the prop, of representation over material vibrancy.

Throughout 2010, as we reconnoitre the edgelands of Weston on foot, urban developers decorate the seafront parades.

Simon Persighetti has suggested that secret choreographies can be carried out on the platforms of railway stations. I was also thinking of that. When the body is neither here nor there, doing its private dances in the non-place of a journey (see Penrose, this volume).

Mike Pearson refers to text in a site-specific performance not primarily as a way of imparting information or narrative but as a means of allowing 'the grain of the voices' (in Kaye 1998: 220) to be part of a musical patterning in a site. To that extent, in an everyday setting we might consider human exchanges in a park, a restaurant, or on a railway platform not as conversations or functional communications but as choral collages that provide other kinds of information about the place. For example, the sonic quality of human voices might be considered as utterances that help us understand the surfaces and architecture of a space.

Equality between props and actors liberates theatricality from mimesis and the scriptural restrictions of the copy, opening the way for the entrance of the speechless thing into our engagement with being. Such equality releases all things from the burden to represent, setting them free to play a 'progressive' role in performative acts through their fragmentation and decay: this is the relic. '(P)rogressive' because the ideas of, and plans for, utopia, collapsed in fragments, were re-articulated by Ernst Bloch as 'hope', an alternative future skulking in the ruins of past experiments and the margins of classical, popular and trashy narratives: 'a utopian residue or surplus that can be used for social critique and to advance political emancipation' (Brereton 2005: 22).

'At the other end of the scale to The Great Architect lies The Amateur Builder. A layer of naivety, of playfulness, of naughtiness and of function over form. Of unconventional and unapproved building extensions. Of DIY and cobbledtogetherness' (Wrights & Sites in Doherty and Bergne 2010: 47).

In the Indian restaurant, I eavesdropped on a conversation which marked gaps in spaces and time between the two diners and the waiter who chatted with them. He seemed to struggle with what they said about cookery, that spices went off before they were used up. They, for their part, talked about an India they had only seen on the television. I ended the sign that marks the restaurant by suggesting that the reader should 'take time'— time to see what is otherwise missed.

Perhaps when we think of a clearing in a forest we might find that in our mind's eye we are not just evoking the visual elements of a place but our visualization of such a location might also trigger memories of odours and sonic phenomena.

'We do not know where life begins, if it has a beginning. There may be and probably is no ulti-mate distinction between the living and the dead' (Heaviside 1951: 386). There are many books about actors. One of the very few about the things they use, Andrew Sofer's The Stage Life of Props (2003), traces this imbalance to Aristotle, as if it might have its origins in philosophy rather than the material of the prop itself.

Inspiration for 'The Amateur Builder' layer came from a most unlikely sort of fellow—Alfred William (aka 'Juicy') Payne, Weston lifeboatman for 51 years. There's a sand sled, built by Juicy, in the North Somerset Museum. If you look closely, you'll see it's fashioned from dismantled doors. The processes of walking and talking with Westoners offer us unlikely ways-in sometimes—the caretaker of the Theatre In The Hut gives us an impromptu backstage tour—the doormen at the strictly male-only Constitutional Club escort us past gleaming portraits of former Tory leaders to the inner sanctum of the former lodge.

But time is what they (and we) don't have.

In the case of the location where the 'CRESCENDO' plaque was placed, a number of elements of the site are exploited so that the 'Panoptic' or viewpoints of the site are excavated, amplified, or suggested with a degree of simultaneity. At its most superficial, the musical motif refers to the octagonal bandstand that acts as a focal point to this place (Grove Park) but also echoes the idea of the central observation tower in the panoptic model of the nineteenth century prison or mental hospital.

In Relics and Processions (a project with Simon Persighetti) we were diggers and gatherers 'grub-bing around in decayed garbage, recovering traces of things and processes which go largely unno-ticed today—what happens to broken bits of pot, to things that get lost, abandoned buildings, rotted fences, microbial action…' (Pearson and Shanks 2001: 10). From one street, over three years, we accumulated objects, stories, events, patterns.

In a café at the far north-west corner of the town, a ship's wheel is attached to the wall. To its left, from the antler of a tatty stag's head a sack of potatoes dangles in the face of Winston

FIGURE 11.3 Sign *in situ* ('The Amateur Builder' stratum, Weston Woods) (reproduced with permission from Jamie Woodley)

Churchill—a century's worth of deposits cling to this place. Out the back, a series of huts and gardens cling to the edge of the cliffs. Here we invite you to take a break and to 'play with your food' architecturally, to explore erosion, appetite, and taste.

In each of those people, chatting, lived different spaces and times. I suppose their conversation allowed a glimpse of those expanses. 'I like history', said one of the women, before correcting herself: 'I am history'.

Each of the plaques bore some kind of instruction, provocation, or action to be carried out at any level by its readers. At its simplest it could be described as a thought exercise but we also hope that consciously or unconsciously some readers might carry out a physical or realized response to the suggestion.

From the beginning of Relics and Processions *we introduced objects and props. These included alchemical containers and 'sardine sticks'. In the containers our found objects were transformed into relics and (or perhaps as a result of their being) displayed in their extraordinariness, their non-inevitability, their destroying of alternative possibilities. The sticks drew uncollected things into a focus, highlighted or stirred. Apparently a pointer, the sardine stick draws in things, relinquishing a phallic, searching, targeting quality; it is sexual but not aroused, attractive for not yet being driven. Like the theatrical object's invisibility—not an arrow of narrative, but an inviting conduit.*

In the 'Valley of the Pylons' just off Hutton Moor Road, the population of a shanty suburb potter around—digging and sifting; arranging and rearranging sheds, urban jetsam, and vegetables—offering hope to even the most provisional architect or fieldworker.

Performance builds with people, space, and time. So does architecture. The Weston project was part of a plan for architectural regeneration of this seaside resort. In my notes, I've written:

In the case of the 'CRESCENDO' plaque the idea of a place as a song might lead someone to consider what the elements of the place might add up to as a poetic and musical representation of a town. It might be claimed that the song of a place is capable of transmitting or sustaining memory of place. As such the folk song is seen as an evocative device of belonging.

TNT used a sardine stick-like object in their manifesto production Harlequin: *a small tassel tied to the sleeve of Pierrot/Stanislavsky, rooting this character in realism and self-interest, a vector from him into the 'earth', indicating that he is not an exception from the world, but systematic of it.*

Just off the Royal Parade we walk past a newspaper billboard—'Human head and bones found on beach' (*Weston & Somerset Mercury*, 30 September 2010). If you mind your footsteps, you will find that the untrained architectures of animals take precedence. A new town on the sand constructed from the exoskeletons of crabs and the tunnels of sandworms.

'To me, the *difference* between our work and poetry found embossed on the pavement and coal hole covers etc is in the way that it asks something of the reader' (Coal hole covers? I was thinking of Maria Vlotides' 2005 project in Notting Hill). I continue, 'But also part of *regeneration* prog—proposes a democratic investigation towards what regeneration might mean.'

INCOMPLETE FRAGMENT: (REF. SONG and IDENTITY OF PLACE.) VVVVVVVVVVVVVVVV VVVVVVVVVVVVVVVVVVVVVVVVVVVVVVVVVVVVVVVVVVVVVVV . . . it is perhaps surprising that music and its relation to place has been a rather neglected topic in human geography. (Hudson 2006: 626)
NNNNNNNNNNNNNNNNNNNNNNNNNNNNNNNNNNNNNNNNNNNNNNNNNNNNNNNNNNNNN
NNNNNNNNNNNNNNNNNNNNNNNNNNNNNNNNNNNNNNNNNNNNNNNNNNNNNNNNNNNNN
NNNNNNNNNNN

I have often used a caricature of a ranging rod; a bent, knobbly stick painted with long uneven red and white stripes. Some things should be assessed by uneven measures. On the day before the demolition of the central shopping area in Exeter began, I placed eight détourned ranging rods in one of its flowerbeds. They remained there for some weeks, then disappeared, then reappeared, carefully returned to their original positions.

If you walk up into Weston Woods, you are encouraged to rediscover the lost den-making skills of your childhood. 'EVERYTHING YOU NEED TO BUILD A TOWN IS HERE.'

This project, then, was a kind of performance event and directed towards the future. The signs depend on the dynamics of presence. They point to the passer-by, with the proposition offered in our title: 'everything you need to build a town is here'. Here, inside you, inside us, and in our hands. However, this rebuilding is founded on an acknowledgement both of what we know and what we don't know of the past and those who lived there—as

FIGURE 11.4 Sign *in situ* ('Ands' stratum, Royal Parade) (photograph: Wrights & Sites)

Tim Etchells, another performance maker, has written in neon on Weston's pavilion with admirable succinctness: 'The things you can't remember' as well as 'The things you can't forget'.

Whilst I do not envisage a folkloric opera to be the outcome of this 'sing a song of' instruction, I am interested in the notion of a place as a series of interlinked phrases that suggest the mental architecture of a particular location. In a song of place can the phrase be the place and the place be the phrase? This may echo with Walter Benjamin's notions of writing the city or Robin Moore's description of walking beyond the functional when he says, 'To wander through a diverse terrain is to feel the surroundings pass through one's body as the body passes through the surroundings...' (Moore 1986: 57).

The 'Foundations' plaques are some version of the sardine sticks—pointers but also symbol-carriers; compromised, accommodated, and vibrant things. The 'Foundations' plaques are some version of the alchemical containers—dressed in nostalgia as the boxes are sealed with ropes. They behave very differently from a thing-to-hand; they are bodies of text and matter that prise apart being and identity, tiny suicide pacts made with the things around them.

From the Iron Age 'old British encampment' on the edge of the woods you can look back down on Weston. You can cross it mentally, map it, plan it. You can see the Old Town Quarry—the hole where the buildings of Boulevard once were, and where Williams-Ellis imagined a new town Rugby Club the size of Wembley. Our layers of architectural way-markers, interwoven across the town's surface, echo the effects of folding and faulting visible in the exposed geology.

In the quarry, I noticed that roads began here in a literal sense. And I suggested a kind of mapping of past and future.

The notion of porosity in which the body makes the city and the city is a body, invites Walter Benjamin's dream image of 'a book that is a city street cut through the body of the author by his lover' (Burgin 1996: 141). XXXXXXXXXXXXXXXXXXXXXXXXXXXXXXXXXXXXXXXXXXXXXXXXXXXXXXXXXXX

Old before the plaques' time, their materials will not allow them to decay—they have solved the 'problem' of conserving decay, by simulating and preserving it in modern, long-lasting materials. Their friction with the decaying world around them is our attempt to generate a surplus of redundancy forcing itself upon public attention, a torque upon contemporaneousness, opening up its gaps and voids, a museum of a museum set free from the museum container; abject in their pretence, fakery, and half-baked historicism, but unable to disappear—an attempt to bring a corrupted artwork from behind the veil and hang its frame around a seaside resort. The trick is...

Everything you need to build a town is here marks a departure for Wrights & Sites. A work that on one foot resists the monumental nature of most public art works (each small-scale piece of viral signage is smaller than a piece of A3 paper), but on the other foot is enormous (it covers the whole town). It is our first 'permanent' municipal work, which sits at odds with our itinerant practice. But how permanent is permanent? Contingency budgets, held by North Somerset Council, will, in theory, cover the cost of short-term damage and replacement, where necessary. We have discussed these issues, but are somewhat ambivalent as to the pros and cons of...

Looking back on it, though, the signs in this layer suggest a map that has many blank spaces, many parts marked 'Here be dragons', or noted as unexplored territory. This is not about giving up the attempt to understand, becoming defeated by the impossibility of certain knowledge. However, it is about noticing how very blurry and unformed a view we can have of the town and its people as past event. Time has washed over the past like the sea, taking memory with it. In this watery present, we are building on the ruins of...

...XXXXXXXXXXXXXXXXXXXXXXXXXXXX.

...to allow the materials to do most of the work.

...maintenance and natural decay.

...sand-castles.

REFERENCES

Bennett, Jane. 2010. *Vibrant Matter*. Durham, NC, and London: Duke University Press.
Brereton, Pat. 2005. *Hollywood Utopia*. Bristol: Intellect.
Burgin, Victor. 1996. *In/Different Spaces: Place and Memory in Visual Culture*. Berkeley, CA, and London: University of California Press.

Coles, Alex and Dion, Mark. 1999. *Mark Dion/ARCHAEOLOGY*. London: Black Dog Publishing.

Doherty, Claire and Bergne, Theresa. 2010. *Wonders of Weston: Guide*. Bristol: Situations.

Eliot, Thomas S. 1989. *Collected Poems, 1909–1962*. London: Faber & Faber.

Foucault, Michel. 1972. *The Archaeology of Knowledge and the Discourse on Language*, tr. Alan M. Sheridan Smith. New York: Pantheon.

Giannachi, Gabriella and Kaye, Nick. 2011. *Performing Presence: Between the Live and the Simulated*. Manchester and New York: Manchester University Press.

Heaviside, Oliver. 1951 [1912]. *Electromagnetic Theory*. London: E. & F. N. Spon.

Hudson, Ray. 2006. Religion and Place: Music, Identity and Place. *Progress in Human Geography* 30(5): 626–34.

Huyssen, Andreas. 2003. *Present Pasts: Urban Palimpsests and the Politics of Memory (Cultural Memory in the Present)*. Palo Alto, CA: Stanford University Press.

Kaye, Nick. 1998. *Art into Theatre: Performance Interviews and Documents*. Amsterdam: Harwood Academic.

Libeskind, Daniel. 2001. *The Space of Encounter*. London: Thames & Hudson.

Moore, Robin C. 1986. *Childhood's Domain: Play and Place in Child Development*. Dover, NH: Croom Helm.

O'Farrell, Clare (ed.). 2007. *Michel Foucault: Key Concepts*. Available at: <http://www.michel-foucault.com/concepts/index.html> (accessed 14 July 2011).

Pearson, Mike and Shanks, Michael. 2001. *Theatre/Archaeology*. London and New York: Routledge.

Saarinen, Eliel. 1943. *The City: Its Growth, Its Decay, Its Future*. New York: Reinhold Publishing.

Sandberg, Mark. 2007. The Architecture of Forgetting. *Ibsen Studies* 7(1): 4–21.

Sofer, Andrew. 2003. *The Stage Life of Props*. Ann Arbor: University of Michigan Press.

Williams-Ellis, Clough and Brett, Lionel. 1947. *Weston-super-Mare: Post-War Development*. mimeo, unpublished.

Wonders of Weston, <http://www.wondersofweston.org/> (accessed 3 May 2013).

Wrights & Sites. 2003. *An Exeter Mis-Guide*. Exeter: Local Heritage Initiative/Arts Council England.

—— 2006. *A Mis-Guide to Anywhere*. Exeter: Arts Council England/CCEP.

PART II

RECURRENT THEMES

CHAPTER 12

··

TIME

··

LAURENT OLIVIER

12.1 INTRODUCTION: MIGHT ARCHAEOLOGY BE NOTHING MORE THAN A TALENT FOR COLLECTING STUFF/ARTEFACTS?

··

IN the Western tradition, the idea of archaeology proceeds from the Greek notion of *archaiologia*. *Archaiologia*, or knowledge of ancient things: for the Greeks, archaeology is defined first of all as the discovery of origins. Whereas the ambition of history is to tell what happened in the past, the purpose of archaeology is to show what the past was made of. These are two very different perspectives, although both have the same object: to know the past. Thus it is not so much in their objectives as in their materials that history and archaeology diverge. Unlike history, which begins with the stories, archaeology begins with the objects, or the material remains, from which it must construct knowledge. The Romans were right in speaking of antiquities (*antiquitates*) instead of archaeology. Since its beginnings, archaeology has proceeded from *collecting* and *collection*.

What type of specialized knowledge, then, may claim to be archaeology? Long before there was any question of an 'archaeological discipline', Plato gives us a very precise idea in his *Hippias Major*, the dialogue in which Socrates, the wily philosopher, confronts Hippias, whose profession is the trade in knowledge. Hippias has just returned from Sparta, where the Lacedaemonians have engaged him so as to benefit from his teaching.

'About what did you speak to them', Socrates then asks him: 'about astronomy or mathematics?'

'Not at all', answers Hippias; 'these people hardly know how to count. In fact, I harangued them about archaeology; that is to say, about the genealogy of heroes and of great men, about the origin of cities and how they were founded in the earliest times, and in general about everything that has to do with the knowledge of the past [*archaiologia*].'

'What labour!'/'What a pain!', Socrates says to him. 'If one had to do that for Athens, one would have to cite the whole list of the men who have ruled the city from the time of Solon.'

'You forget', answers Hippias proudly, 'that I can remember a list of fifty names after reading it only once!'

Swollen with self-importance, Hippias does not see that Socrates is touching on a great weakness of archaeology, *accumulation*. As a fundamentally descriptive discipline, archaeology can only amass details about the past, scraps of information that are self-sufficient insofar as, being all that remains of the past, they are all that one can know of it. Under these conditions, archaeology has no point of view on the past and takes from it no particular knowledge. It is perfectly suited to Hippias, for whom knowledge is a matter of accountancy. Even as he flatters him, Socrates says to him slyly: 'I see then that the Lacedaemonians are quite right to be pleased with your speeches—since you know so many things—and to come to you, as children come to old women, to hear entertaining stories.'

Here Socrates exposes the social function of archaeology, which is to keep the conscience of men/people asleep by telling them old wives' tales. From this point the matter is settled: Hippias sells a knowledge that he does not possess, or rather offers, with this pseudo-science of the past called archaeology, an appearance of knowledge that is nothing more than a heaping up of factual data. Hippias mistakes his opinions for knowledge, or rather is guided only by his prejudices in addressing this distant past of origins. Under the accumulation of the apparently 'objective' data/evidence of archaeology, accepted ideas about the past are sure to prosper, since archaeology has no role but constituting the *illustration* of a history already known from other sources.

In these terms, everything had already been said, even before the extraordinary expansion of archaeology in the nineteenth and twentieth centuries. It is striking to realize how much the discipline of archaeology developed along the Graeco-Roman lines laid down by this focus on antiquities. Archaeology was established on the basis of an accumulation of objects. Yet the discovery of new remains of the past, not hitherto identified as such, necessitated new regions in the history of origins. The irruption of these new objects from the past accelerated in the nineteenth century, reaching a tremendous pace in the years 1850–60, when the foundations of present-day archaeology were laid. First came the discovery of a humanity 'before history', which required the recognition of a 'Stone Age' that far preceded classical antiquity. Very quickly the proliferation of finds revealed the existence of a 'proto-history' located between prehistory and Roman civilization; while in the Mediterranean world the succession of the great pre-classical civilizations was constructed. In the second half of the twentieth century, the extension of archaeology to new chronological periods was effected in the same way: it is because excavations uncovered a new mass of medieval and modern materials that the archaeology of those eras could be established. The last dozen years have seen an analogous process under way for the archaeology of the contemporary period, even of the very recent past of the twentieth century.

Nonetheless, as the dialogue of Socrates and Hippias reminds us, stones and potsherds do not make history. Is this to say that archaeology is forever condemned to inconsistency? Yes, if we persist in wishing to make it the para-historical discipline that it has no calling to be. But no, if we consider that the object of archaeology eludes history by its very nature, that it resists all inclusion in history. For it is not the events of the past, or even the things of the past as it once was, that constitute the material of archaeology; it is the *memory of material things*.

12.2 THE PAST DOES NOT DIE: IT LASTS

In every age, human societies have confronted the permanence of the manifestations of their past, which have always constituted the framework of their own present. From the earliest times, it has been monuments and objects, but also landscapes and places, that have been already there, produced by earlier cultures or civilizations. They have been the material from which societies have constructed their identity. Therefore, present modifications of the remains of the past—whether in the form of reconstructions, reworkings, or even of destructions—bear directly on the work of remodelling the collective memory that nourishes societies' identity. As the British prehistorian Richard Bradley (2002) has brilliantly demonstrated, this particular relation with the material remains of the past is not the prerogative of historical societies alone, for it is completely at home in the prehistoric European societies of the Neolithic, whose monumental constructions tend to occur in particular places and forms, which they reproduce through the whole of a lengthy occupation, on the scale of a series of generations.

The relation with the past is thus an essential element in the construction of collective identities (Hobsbawm and Ranger 1983; Lowenthal 1985; Gosden 1994). It nourishes the construction of a *collective memory*, whose functional mechanisms the sociologist Maurice Halbwachs (1980 [1949]) has been among the first to describe. Nevertheless, these are questions that at bottom concern anthropology more than archaeology. On the other hand, archaeology is directly concerned with the question of the status of material remains that persist into periods after their creation, insofar as these physical remnants call into question the identity of the past from which they have emerged and, in that very way, the possible approach to them. Currently, something is changing in our vision of the past, which we now perceive as more variable, less monolithic—something that affects our way of conceiving of history, or more exactly the way in which we think of the transformation of past societies over time. What is the nature of this change? In the first place, it is becoming more and more clear today that the material environment of human societies has always been *composite*, in the sense that it has always been principally composed of elements coming from their past while still continuing to exist in their present.

Every day we directly experience this situation, which is not as banal as one might think. Our material universe, at the beginning of this third millennium, is not the one predicted by the naïve images of twentieth-century science fiction. We still live in cities whose urban infrastructure dates overwhelmingly from the nineteenth century; for the most part, our houses are at least one hundred years old; not all of our furniture is new—far from it; as for our automobiles, few of us can have a new one every year. Thus from the viewpoint of archaeology, the materiality of the 'current' present seems essentially composed of things from the past—a past more or less recent—while the creations of the present moment—those of this very day—have only a tiny place in a material present really saturated with the past(s). The present has always been *multi-temporal*, and above all it has never been young, *never completely current*.

In regard to material things (which constitute all the material of archaeology), the present is nothing but the joining of all the pasts that coexist physically in the present moment.

After all, though prehistoric cut-stone tools were originally produced some tens of thousands of years ago, the fact remains that it is *in the present* that we find them: *here, in our present, now*. Indeed, it is because of their condition of being *covered over* in this present (Are they *in situ*? Or are they displaced, complete, or fragmentary?) that we will be able to say anything about them. Material productions—of which archaeological remains are a part—possess an essential quality of their own, which they do not share with the events of history: they remain, they last as long as the material of which they are made. They insinuate themselves into all the presents that come after them; long after they have ceased to be used, they continue to *be*. Thus although the Roman Empire may have definitively collapsed in long-bygone times, its material remains continue to occupy our present, as they will do for the generations that come after us.

12.3 WE (ALSO) CONSTRUCT TIME

Nevertheless, the recognition of the existence of *ancient* or *other* remains in our material universe is not self-evident, insofar as it involves our representation of time. As the American prehistorian Lewis Binford has very justly said,

> *The archaeological record is here with us in the present.* . . . it is very much part of our contemporary world and the observations we make about it are in the here and now, contemporary with ourselves. (Binford 1983: 19)

This means, he goes on to say, that

> archaeology is not a field that can study the past *directly*. . . . On the contrary, it is a field wholly dependent upon inference to the past from things found in the contemporary world. (Binford 1983: 23)

Binford here reminds us that the perception of the past depends on the interpretation of things recognized as ancient, which are observed in the material environment of the present. But how do we recognize a thing as ancient, as belonging to a humanity different from our own?

Archaeology, or more generally the procedure of collecting and identifying the material remains of the past, is possible only under certain conditions, which have not occurred together except at very specific moments in history: during Graeco-Roman antiquity, at the time of the great Chinese empires, in ancient Japan, and in Europe since the Renaissance. In these different cases, these conditions are connected to the idea of a *human history*, that is, to the awareness that people have not always lived and thought as we ourselves do. The development of archaeology is therefore fundamentally linked with that of the discovery of *otherness*, of the recognition of one's difference from one's fellows. Thus, in Europe, archaeology receives its impulse as a discipline from the moment when it is recognized that the remains of the past are *different* and *distinctive*, and that this *foreignness* is the mark of their antiquity (although see Graves-Brown 2011; Harrison 2011). In demonstrating that the 'thunderstones' found by peasants in their fields had not fallen from the sky, but that they come from very ancient stone axes, the researchers of the Enlightenment provided not only the proof of their antiquity: they showed at the same time that we ourselves have been preceded by 'savage' populations analogous to the 'cannibals' of the New World, who still used stone tools similar to those buried in the soil of Europe.

Why hadn't this presence of the ancient past been discovered sooner? Because the recognition of the existence of ancient things is part of a larger movement, in Europe, that from the sixteenth century involved voyages of discovery and the astronomical exploration of the heavens. This movement concerns the representation of the world. In order to recognize the difference and the singularity expressed by ancient remains, we must ourselves be ready to accept the world as *open*, that is to say, largely unknown, unexplored, heterogeneous. Willingly or not, we must have accepted the element of *strangeness* and *unsettledness* implicit in a world of which we are no longer the centre and sole point of reference. Above all, time itself must have lost its apparent familiarity, to appear henceforth, as Buffon says, as a 'dark abyss', a bottomless gulf capable of having swallowed whole worlds, whole series of civilizations whose memory was later completely lost.

In the *closed world* of the medieval tradition, on the other hand, time is collapsed upon itself. It is completely filled with a history in which everything has been said, where everything that will happen has been foretold. Nonetheless, the remains of the past still continue to persist in the ground, but they are seen as alien bodies in the premodern material universe. In the countryside, one often sees megaliths and tumuli; everywhere one encounters Roman ruins, some of them still standing. They cannot be explained except as *prodigies*; fifteenth-century representations, such as those of the magnificent *Livre des propriétés des choses* of Barthélémy de Glanville (Schnapp 1993: 144, figure), show us ceramic vessels that emerge spontaneously from the earth, as wild animals emerge at night from their dens or burrows, or as fish secretly populate the depths of the water. In the flat time inherited from the Middle Ages, there is no place for imagining that the pots sometimes coming to the surface of the earth could have been made by other men, in other times. At least until the beginning of the eighteenth century, fossils posed exactly the same sort of problem (Rossi 1984). For most authors, the remains of seashells found in rock could not be the manifestation of anything but an extraordinary property of the stone—a *virus lapidifera*, a *vis plastica*—that produced petrified animal forms within it, as the sea spontaneously produced live molluscs or fish.

In a world that was ignorant of the notion of deep time introduced in the nineteenth century by Lyell and Darwin, prodigy was the only plausible explanation for the absolute singularity of the remains of the past. Megaliths must be the tables of giants, tumuli the tombs of fairies, ancient ruins castles of the Sleeping Beauty. To discover the past is, fundamentally, to become aware of the heterogeneity of the present. In this sense, we may say that trying to reconstruct the past, the project of archaeology, comes back basically to studying the present. Time constructs us (it is time that ages us and transforms the world around us), but on the other hand *we also construct time*; we make it, because the past has definitively vanished and because what remains of it—that which constitutes the past—is only a *memory in the present* (see Chouquer 2007). This material memory of the present constitutes the only object of archaeological study.

12.4 THE ARCHAEOLOGY OF THE PRESENT: A DISRUPTION OF TIME

The recognition of the '*past in the present*' is part of a more general disruption of traditional conceptions about the identity of the past and the nature of time. This disruption, which is still in its infancy, belongs especially to the extension of the conceptual revolution begun just before the Second World War by the observations of the German philosopher Walter Benjamin (1999 [1968]) on time and history. Long misunderstood, these reflections find their direct application in archaeology—that is, as we have just seen, in the study of the material remains that constitute the depth of the present. The first consequence of this 'archaeology of the present' is to explode the conventional time of history, that unilinear time on which are based *all* the approaches to the archaeological past, including those that now seem the most critical.

Indeed, in our conventional representation of historical times, we are in some sense removed from time, like spectators who watch a passing procession of human history. As we watch them unfold from our imaginary viewpoint of historian or archaeologist, each of these periods has its own colours and is distinguished from the others by a particular temporal identity, a specific *temporality*. In this sense, as the philosopher Henri Bergson (1911 [1907]) stresses, our representation of time is fundamentally *cinematographic*: for us, historical time goes in only one direction at once, and each evolution in time (like each movement of the image) can be broken down into a series of successive moments (like the succession of twenty-four frames per second that allows for the reconstitution of reality in cinematographic projection). In other words, it is because (historical) time can be decomposed into a precise series of instants (or of homogeneous sequences) that the processes can become visible to us. More precisely, it is because the series of sequences is subordinated to an order of strict succession that we can read the phenomena taking place in time.

For us, historical time—the time that runs through the evolution of past societies—is at once both fundamentally *unilinear* and intrinsically *cumulative*. But it is nothing else than that: in reality, time is emptied of its substance, or more precisely of its capacity to act, by this folkloric perception of the past, which assimilates history to a series of *pictures/scenes* and *contexts*. This idea of time is found at the heart of the *historicist* approach to the past, which is really an anti-historical conception of history. As Benjamin (1999 [1968]: 254) emphasizes, this conventional approach to the past 'proceeds by *addition*: it mobilizes the mass of facts *to fill up homogenous and empty time*'. But time cannot so easily be shut away. As in dreams where a situation progressively takes on a different meaning as more and more unexpected details are discovered, the figures of the conventional procession of history seem to move with elements that do not belong to them: on close observation, the procession of human history shows signs of survivals or, conversely, characteristics of anticipation (see Focillon 1943; Kubler 1962). The recognition of the 'past in the past' destroys the preconceived idea by which the moments of time carry particular temporalities because they are situated in individual—and hence unique—moments of time.

To say that the fragments of the past are inscribed in the materiality of the present is to open the possibility of a radical re-evaluation of the notion of history and, more precisely, to question fundamentally our understanding of the mechanisms of historical evolution. For if historical time is no longer what links, step by step, events strictly succeeding each other—in short, if time is now *loosened*—then we may place in relation events located far from each other. If the past remains inscribed in the present, we may reawaken and reactivate *in the present* processes believed to have been definitely ended because they belonged to a completely bygone past. We must never forget that archaeology is not an ordinary historical discipline: it deals with the *memory* recorded in material and not with events or moments of the past. The research of the British prehistorian Geoff Bailey allows us to show that in Epirus, in Greece, phenomena of current soil degradation are connected to the reactivation by intensified agriculture of environmental problems originally set in motion in the Palaeolithic, more than 20,000 years ago (Bailey 2007). If the past returns, it is because it has never really left; it was hidden motionless in the folds of the present, forgotten but in fact ready to spring forth. This lightning encounter of the past with the present is, according to Benjamin's (1999 [1968]: 253) famous expression, 'the leap of the tiger into the past', which can cover millennia in a single bound. As Benjamin (1999 [1968]: 255) writes in his 'Theses on the Philosophy of History':

> Historicism contents itself with establishing a *causal connection* between different moments of history. But no factual reality becomes a historical fact by virtue only of its quality of cause. It becomes one, posthumously, *under the influence of events that can be separated from it by millennia*. The historian who begins from this premise ceases to tell the sequence of events like a rosary. He grasps the constellation that his own epoch forms with a previous epoch. Thus he establishes a concept of the present as the 'now', in which are catalogued the fragments of messianic time.

12.5 THE PRESENT IN THE PAST

This notion of the present embedded in the past has the deepest implications for understanding archaeological materials, implications that can only be sketched here. In particular, it means that the present, the now, is not what is happening in this moment alone, but rather *what has always been repeated*: it is the ageing of matter, the wearing down of places, the growth and movements of bodies in space. In short, it is the effect of time expressed by the life of beings and of things that expresses the present of today, like all the other presents, past and future. As a consequence, the present, instead of bearing the mark of incessant change—as we see it—bears much more that of the *eternal return* of Schopenhauer and Nietzsche, an uninterrupted rebirth of the world, always like itself in its diversity and uniqueness. Like memory, archaeological material bears the mark of *repetition*, as shown by the specifically archaeological forms that are palimpsests. In the superimpositions of archaeological occupations found particularly in cemeteries and cities, it is essentially the same site that is reproduced, each time similar and different, because unique at each moment of time. In the same way, each time a new object is manufactured, it is either the same form or the same type that is reproduced, but an absolutely unique artefact that is created (see Finlayson, this volume).

Nevertheless, if the present, as Benjamin (1999 [1968]: 254) writes, is this 'now' that keeps itself '*immobile on the threshold of time*',[1] something is continually being changed by the effect of time. This is what archaeological materials systematically show us. Each time a material thing is reproduced (such as an object, a structure, a landscape...), there is the opportunity for a small difference—Darwin would say a small *variation*—to be introduced. As is well known, it is the accumulation of these small differences over time that creates chronological trajectories, or what we call *evolutionary trends*. But what is less understood

---

[1] More often translated into English as 'in which time stands still and has come to a stop'.

is that this type of change, known henceforth by the name of evolution, is the specific effect of processes of *repetition*. Why? Because in this case repetition does not function as a simple reproduction of what already exists: it is also, in some sense, its *putting back into play* each time something is created in the now. As Freud demonstrated, this particular mechanism is that of memory. Thus it is not, properly speaking, a *history* that is created by the effect of the phenomena of repetition, or of reproduction, manifested by archaeological materials; it is a *memory* recorded in the material. This distinction is essential, since the time of memory functions in a wholly different way from historical time.

12.6 'They don't Know that we are Bringing them the Plague'

'They don't know that we are bringing them the plague', Freud is supposed to have said on the ship that carried him from Europe to the United States, where he was to attend a series of conferences. This 'plague' of which Freud spoke was, of course, nothing other than psychoanalysis, the new discipline that he had founded and that studied specifically the psychic memory. To understand the mechanisms by which memory functions is, in effect, to assimilate a seemingly abnormal functioning of time and, consequently, to expose oneself to exclusion from the community of those who perceive the past in a conventional, 'normal' way. For them, the past occupies a defined place in time and possesses a specific identity that it carries within itself. Therefore the past cannot 'come back' in the present, and the present, conversely, cannot modify the content of the past. Those who conceive of time differently, in the eyes of these traditional historians or archaeologists, are using a deviant, not to say heretical, approach to the past.

And yet we have no choice but to conceive of the functioning of the material memory precisely in these terms that are unacceptable to the traditional perception of the past. Here the question of the present, in whatever form one takes it, occupies an absolutely essential place. The present as a moment in time does not have the same sense for conventional history (or archaeology) as it does for archaeology as the study of material memory. In the first place, the present as 'now' has no meaning for the memory of matter, since, for archaeological materials, the present has no temporal significance except insofar as something is recorded in it. If nothing is registered in matter—in the form of transformations or of archaeological constructions—the present does not exist as a moment in time. As Binford noted, the archaeological record of the past is fundamentally *discontinuous*, essentially *aleatoric* (Binford 1981). Hence if archaeological time—the time recorded in archaeological materials—is interrupted, how can it function like the 'true' time of conventional history, which on the contrary is perfectly continuous? And if it does not function like conventional historical time, how then can it be articulated?

Archaeological time does not unfold like conventional time, because its future is not constructed in unilinear fashion from pure innovation introduced at each successive moment of the present, as in the historicist understanding of the past, which subordinates the trajectory of historical time to the action of *progress*. Things do not happen in that way, if only because the present is *filled with the past*. In any case, the construction of the future is conditioned by the past of the present. It makes little difference, in reality, that this past embedded in the present is or is not recognized as such; what matters is that it exists. It is not important that we do or do not know that the line of a certain street was originally that of the ancient city's Roman *decumanus*; what matters is rather that the ancient urban plan still functions, though faint and mutilated, in the contemporary urban plan.

This particular configuration of material memory has two principal consequences. The first is that, since each period of time is highly heterogeneous (i.e. filled with fragments of different pasts), it brings into relation material archaeological moments that may be far separated from each other. The history recorded in archaeological materials is neither unilinear nor unidirectional. The second consequence is that the memory of the past is systematically *masked* in its functioning, since, in slipping into the current moment, it takes the form of the present: in the contemporary city, the Roman *decumanus* survives as a memory of the ancient urban plan, in the guise of a street with no a priori difference from others.

The urgent question raised by consideration of the 'past in the past' is that of determining the implications of this particular situation of material memory for our approach to the past. Once we have recognized this phenomenon, the unilinear history of events no longer has any meaning: the work of the historian or archaeologist becomes the revealing of these correspondences across time. It is there that the specific sense of the archaeological approach resides, the approach that studies not the history of material things, but their *memory*. As Benjamin insists, the traditional historicist approach works by addition: it accumulates 'facts' or descriptive details in order to fill with *narration* the void opened by the yawning of deep time. Since the middle of the nineteenth century, this task has been specifically assigned to prehistory. Conversely, the approach attentive to the material memory constituted by archaeological materials must function by *construction*: putting material facts themselves, and not what they are thought to represent, into relation with each other. Therefore archaeological remains are no long the necessary links in a great chain of events, but instead become (again) the site of all possibilities. Thus they offer to archaeologists, as Benjamin (1999 [1968]: 254) writes, 'this chance to make a defined epoch emerge by housebreaking from the homogenous course of history'.

12.7 NATURE LOVES TO HIDE HERSELF

'Nature loves to hide herself', says Heraclitus, adding, still mysteriously: 'if one does not expect the unexpected, one will not find it, for it is difficult to find'. Indeed, the past is hidden in archaeological remains, which as a consequence do not necessarily say what their formal appearance suggests. We must seek those signs that constitute, par excellence, the material of archaeology. An indication, a sign: in the language of medicine, we call this a *symptom*. A symptom is not only a signal, but is above all a manifestation that stands visibly for something that acts invisibly, such as an illness or a pathology. From this it must be understood that archaeological remains are not evidence of the history of the past, but are instead evidence of the existence of an active memory of the past.

Archaeology must be rethought as a discipline specifically attuned to these symptoms of material memory that we call archaeological remains (Olivier 2011). In this connection, it is not out of place to observe that, in the field of the psychic memory, it is from the study of the symptoms of memory—as they are manifested especially in dreams—that Freud was able to construct the particular approach called psychoanalysis. More precisely, once Freud grasped the functioning of these symptoms of memory, he could deduce from them his theory of the psychic unconscious. The task of archaeologists is, at bottom, very similar: to explore the *unconscious of time* by means of archaeological remains themselves.

The crux in understanding the construction of this fugitive or hidden memory is to be found in the grasping of the mechanisms of repetition or reiteration. Each time a form is created in matter, it is in fact reproduced. Repetition in itself introduces transformation, insofar as the act of creation is fundamentally an act of negotiation: that which is coming must find its proper place among everything that surrounds it and that has been created before it. This is why forms evolve: their morphology gradually changes, while the transformation of their structure may sometimes display spectacular changes in detail. This fundamental structure of forms is what we may call the typological or iconological structure of material creations or representations. The study of the transformations of objects produced over the course of time consists in elaborating this *palaeontology of forms*.

Is this to say that under these conditions we must abandon the historical perspective that is the foundation of archaeology, which seeks to restore the material reality of the past? Certainly not. In fact, the fundamental misconception of the functioning of the 'memory objects' constituted by archaeological remains pushes the discipline of archaeology towards a form of archaic history. Paradoxically, it is the historicist dimension of archaeology that has always prevented it from establishing itself as a truly historical discipline. It cannot do so because, as it assimilates the vestiges of the past to explicit evidences of the reality of ancient times, it finds itself deprived of the possibility of making them into objects of history as such—that is to say, objects that question history or, more precisely, challenge it.

The answer to this problem is theoretical: *archaeology must find its true object.* This object is not the past, but what we may call the subjects of the past: if history seeks to reconstruct what happened, archaeology tells what happened to the 'entities'/'bodies' of the past. By 'entities'/'bodies' we must understand the beings and things that constitute the material universe of human collectives. Archaeology examines, in the various scales of time and space, how these entities/'bodies' have 'taken' the events of the past, that is, how, according to the different states and legacies from which they proceed, they have received/incorporated these evolutions, and how, conversely, they have contributed to their construction. In this configuration, archaeology is no longer the simple material illustration of history. It becomes instead a privileged field of observation of the world, enriching history with all the diversity of the individual trajectories followed by the subjects of the material universe. It is the neglected nymph with the power to re-enchant time.

Translation by Jay Kardan

REFERENCES

Bailey, Geoff. 2007. Time Perspectives, Palimpsests and the Archaeology of Time. *Journal of Anthropological Archaeology* 26(2): 198–223.

Benjamin, Walter. 1999 [1968]. Theses on the Philosophy of History. In *Illuminations*, ed. Hannah Arendt. London: Pimlico, pp. 427–43.

Bergson, Henri. 1911 [1907]. *Creative Evolution*, tr. Arthur Mitchell. London: Henry Holt.

Binford, Lewis. 1981. Behavioral Archaeology and the 'Pompeii Premise'. *Journal of Anthropological Research* 37: 195–208.

—— 1983. *In Pursuit of the Past: Decoding the Archaeological Record*. London: Thames and Hudson.

Bradley, Richard. 2002. *The Past in Prehistoric Societies*. London: Routledge.

Chouquer, Gérard. 2007. *Quels scénarios pour l'histoire du paysage? Orientations de recherche pour l'archéogéographie*. Coimbra e Porto: Centro de estudos Arqueologicos das Universidades de Coimbra e Porto.

Focillon, Henri. 1943. *Vie des formes*. Paris: Presses Universitaires de France.

Gosden, Christopher. 1994. *Social Being and Time*. Oxford: Blackwell.

Graves-Brown, Paul. 2011. Touching from a Distance: Alienation, Abjection, Estrangement and Archaeology. *Norwegian Archaeological Review* 44(2): 131–44.

Halbwachs, Maurice. 1980 [1949]. *The Collective Memory*. New York: Harper & Row Colophon Books.

Harrison, Rodney. 2011. Surface Assemblages: Towards an Archaeology *in* and *of* the Present. *Archaeological Dialogues* 182: 141–61.

Hobsbawm Eric and Ranger, Terrence. 1983. *The Invention of Tradition*. Cambridge: Cambridge University Press.

Kubler, George. 1962. *The Shape of Time: Remarks on the History of Things*. New Haven: Yale University Press.

Lowenthal, David. 1985. *The Past is a Foreign Country*. Cambridge: Cambridge University Press.

Olivier, Laurent. 2011. *The Dark Abyss of Time: Archaeology and Memory*. Walnut Creek, CA: Altamira Press.

Rossi, Paolo. 1984. *The Dark Abyss of Time: The History of the Earth and the History of Nations from Hooke to Vico*. Chicago: University of Chicago Press.

Schnapp, Alain. 1993. *La conquète du passé. Aux origines de l'archéologie*. Paris: Editions Carréfig.

CHAPTER 13

···

ABSENCE

···

SEVERIN FOWLES AND KAET HEUPEL

13.1 INTRODUCTION

···

INCREASINGLY, one encounters two quite different images of the modern world and its material condition. The more common presents modernity as a quantum proliferation of things, the implication being that the world is heavier now than ever before, stuffed cheek-to-jowl with an ever-expanding clutter of toasters, iPhones, baseball caps, skyscrapers, Styrofoam cups, and so on. 'Humans are no longer by themselves,' writes Bruno Latour (1999: 190), by which he means that modern society has come to be defined by the radical interdependence and intimacy of people and artefacts. To be modern is to participate in material collectives of unprecedented scale, to delegate one's actions to non-humans like never before, to build one's self through a continuously unfolding web of alliances with things (Knorr Cetina 1997; Dant 2006: 290; Olsen 2010: 9–10; Olsen, this volume). 'The history of goods', writes Smail et al. (2011: 220), 'cannot help being a history of more and more stuff.' There is nothing particularly new about this claim. For centuries, dominant Western scholarship has portrayed social evolution as a great amassing of material possessions in which primitive things do not so much disappear as become relics and ruins, buried beneath the inexorable avalanche of new creations. From this perspective, industrialization and advanced global capitalism simply intensify a process of accumulation that began in the Neolithic (Hodder 2012).

But there is a second image of modernity in which industrialization and the mass production of things—rather than signifying material fullness—instead signify the profound emptiness and poverty of our current condition. Here, the logic is subtractive, and the focus is on how much has been lost in the course of modernization. There are many variants. Certain theologians and philosophers mourn the spiritual vacuum at the heart of the modern subject in the wake of secularism, the Bomb, and the rise of unbridled consumerism. Environmentalists decry the vanishing forests, shrinking ice caps, and the loss of 'nature' itself. Art historians and literary critics, for their part, entertain lengthy discussions of the alleged 'dematerialization of the world' as images replace objects and as signs eclipse their referents. And social commentators of many different stripes accuse capitalism of alienating us from the sensuous world of things. For them, modernity seems less a progressive accumulation of things than a tragic proliferation of losses.

Can we resolve these two opposed images? Is modernity any more or any less material than premodernity? Are we moderns really entangled with things more intimately than ever before? Conversely, are we really more alienated from the sensuous world than our predecessors?

The archaeology of the contemporary past is one of the few disciplines that might be interested in these sorts of questions. Archaeologists, of course, have already devoted a great deal of effort to tallying up and typologizing the material artefacts of the premodern world, and work by Rathje and Murphy (2001) and others (see Harrison and Schofield 2010) has demonstrated the great promise of applying archaeological methods to the study of the modern world as well. In this sense, a critical analysis of the relative 'materiality' of human history up to the contemporary moment would seem in reach. But even if archaeology were to take up this project, it would still be deficient in one key respect: whatever abilities we, as archaeologists, may have in the documentation of present things, we have yet to develop comparable techniques for the enumeration of the many absent things that also fill up the world around us. Archaeologists, not surprisingly, have little taste for absence. Most ignore it altogether. Indeed, those archaeologists who do express an interest in the subject inevitably talk about absences as mournful and alienated from the start, like silent subalterns waiting to be 'presenced' through the gift of archaeology's material evidence (e.g. Buchli and Lucas 2001; Harrison and Schofield 2010: 285; Olivier 2011). It goes without saying that there is no comparable enthusiasm within archaeology for absencing presence. Absence is inevitably treated as a problem to be solved.

In privileging presence, archaeology has plenty of company, of course, but there is something distinctive about the discipline's methodological materialism that makes rigorous engagement with the problem of absence seem especially difficult (see Fowles 2008, 2010a). Evidential claims within archaeology traditionally depend on the mobilization of tangible objects or traces. Archaeology is the 'discipline of things' (Olsen et al. 2012); it is a mode of inquiry that stands 'in defense of things' (Olsen 2010), we are told. Missing things, that which is conspicuously not found, the non-occurrence of sites or shellfish or suntan lotion—absences such as these often possess at least as much cultural significance as the solid objects that get photographed and written up in reports. Most, however, would regard it as absurd to attempt an inventory of the crowds of things *not* encountered while in the field.

13.2 THE NEW BUFFALO COMMUNE

Here, we seek both to redress this methodological omission and to offer preliminary thoughts on the special relationship between absence and modernity through a brief consideration of the case of the New Buffalo Commune in New Mexico (Figure 13.1), which since 2008 has been the site of archaeological and oral historical research. New Buffalo was established in 1967 by a small group of young idealistic expatriates from urban America, who fled to the sage-covered mesas of the Southwest in an effort to rebuild American society without the violence, inequality, and perceived artificiality of modern industrial life. 'Old way, good way' is how Robbie Gordon, one the New Buffalo's early members, sums up the simple philosophy that guided the commune's early years. Such themes were common among 1960s hippies, of course, but New Buffalo was distinctive in that its version of the 'old way' was explicitly modelled on the nearby indigenous community at Taos Pueblo, which by the

FIGURE 13.1 New Buffalo in 1967 (reproduced with permission from Lisa Law)

mid-twentieth century had come to be regarded by many Euro-American outsiders as a spiritual centre and a bastion of native non-modern ways. In fact, Taos Pueblo already had a venerable countercultural pedigree by the time long-haired drop-outs drove their painted school buses into town and dubbed the pueblo 'America's original commune'. Since the early 1920s, scores of bohemian artists and intellectuals had relocated to Taos, most hoping to find spiritual reinvigoration in the pueblo's 'ancient' ritual traditions and 'primitive' lifeways (Rudnick 1996). New Buffalo participated in this neo-primitivist tradition, but in a far more proletarian manner: most were there to retrain themselves in the lost arts of sustainable agricultural production, peaceful cohabitation, political equality, and spiritual exploration. They were, in their own words, 'a lost tribe who had forgotten how to live—to plant, dance, sing, raise children—and how to die' (as quoted in Houriet 1971: 140).

There are plenty of reasons to be interested in New Buffalo as an archaeological site. For those who lived through the revolutions of the 1960s, New Buffalo represents a quintessential locus of American counterculture, a place where a rural back-to-the-land strategy was pursued as an alternative to the violence and aggression of urban protest movements. Visited by the likes of Dennis Hopper, Timothy Leary, and Alan Ginsberg, and popularized in the film *Easy Rider*, New Buffalo has become a beloved icon of the hippie generation and an increasingly memorialized heritage site (for tributes, see Law 1987; Keltz 2000; Kopecky 2004). But it also provides a remarkable setting in which to investigate the politics of absence in the modern age. How did anti-capitalism, anti-materialism, and voluntary simplicity—central themes in the 1960s back-to-the-land movement—unfold in the material practices of day-to-day life? How might we undertake an archaeology that gave full analytical weight to all those things that the commune aggressively sought to do without?

The available evidence comes in three forms: archival materials (photographs, film clips, newspaper articles, personal journals), oral histories, and the material remains of the site itself, which continues to be run as an intentional farming and artistic community but also contains a number of ruins of the late 1960s and 1970s occupation. Among the latter are the crumbling remains of a large pit house, numerous tipi clearings, and a trash dump, all of which were excavated as part of our research, resulting in an assemblage of artefacts now being used to structure object-oriented interviews with former commune residents.

Needless to say, much can be learned about the practices and aspirations of the commune by attending, in a traditionally archaeological mode, to what is materially present. One is immediately struck, for instance, by the obvious use of architecture to signal the community's desired solidarity with American Indians. New Buffalo drew heavily on native symbolism, in name (as the buffalo sustained the Plains tribes, so was 'New Buffalo' supposed to sustain the hippies) and in form (the main compound was explicitly designed in the shape of the sacred sun symbol of Zia Pueblo) (Figure 13.2). Adobes were made on site, Ponderosa trees were gathered in the mountains, roofs were made of dirt, and elders from nearby Taos Pueblo were consulted for architectural guidance. Summer visitors typically resided in Plains-style tipis, or in the commune's Navajo-style hogan, or the Pueblo-style pit house. Rituals took place in peyote lodges, sweat lodges, and a large circular commons area alternately referred to as the Buffalo Room or the Kiva. Following Deloria (1998), all of this can be read within a long-standing Euro-American tradition of 'playing Indian'; however, at New Buffalo this project was undertaken with unusual gravity and purpose.

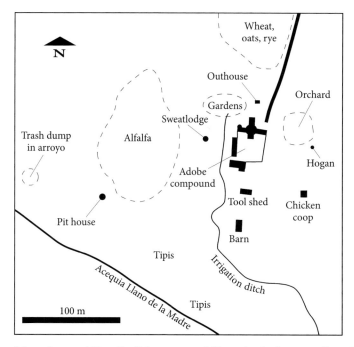

FIGURE 13.2 Map of central New Buffalo, as it would have looked in 1973 (based on a drawing of the site by Tony Sommers in Kopecky 2004: xviii)

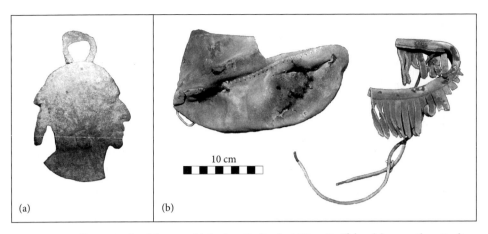

FIGURE 13.3 Excavated evidence of 'playing Indian' at New Buffalo: (a) = a silver Indian head pendant (approx. 3 cm tall); (b) = a leather moccasin (photograph: Severin Fowles and Kaet Heupel)

Our archaeological research has added intimate detail to this picture. Certain personal effects pulled from the ground, for instance, reveal that hippie bodies were regularly decorated with Indian signifiers: moccasins, beads, an Indian head pendant (Figure 13.3). Excavation of the New Buffalo pit house proved especially revealing (Figure 13.4). Mentioned only in passing in the surviving documents on the commune, the pit house nevertheless marked the commune's most concerted effort to align modern Euro-American domestic life with precolonial native practice. Architecturally, it was very much like the pit houses produced in the region a thousand years ago: the floor was composed of packed earth with a central basin hearth as the only evident feature; the walls were finished with a thin coat of simple clay plaster applied directly to the native soil; and a ventilator extended from the structure's eastern wall towards the rising sun. To dwell within this subterranean space, as members of the commune did for over a decade, was to commit to the flickering firelight, to the insects, and to an unmediated contact with the ground that had been part of Native American daily life for hundreds of years.

Many of the other artefacts recovered during our excavations complicate the image of New Buffalo as a back-to-the-land, neo-primitivist enterprise, however. Sustainable agriculture and, later, on-site dairy production figure prominently in the journals and oral histories of many former occupants, but actual consumption patterns—as evidenced in the trash left behind—point to a complex relationship with industrial, mass-produced commodities. Should it be at all surprising to discover that an early 1970s trash deposit in the United States includes packaging debris for Hormel Vienna sausages, Minute Maid frozen limeade, Johnston's low-fat yogurt, and Bel-air unsweetened frozen blueberries? Only, perhaps, if those who discarded the trash expressly built their identities on an assertive non-engagement with such mainstream commodities. Indeed, a strange dissonance arises when one attempts to resolve the back-to-nature ethos of the community with deteriorating plastic fragments of a Holsum Enriched plain white sandwich bread bag (Figure 13.5a). (Holsum, not wholesome.)

FIGURE 13.4 The pit house at New Buffalo, after excavation. Note the ventilator in shadow at upper right, the central basin hearth, and the two large rocks, apparently used as primitive furniture (photograph: Severin Fowles and Kaet Heupel)

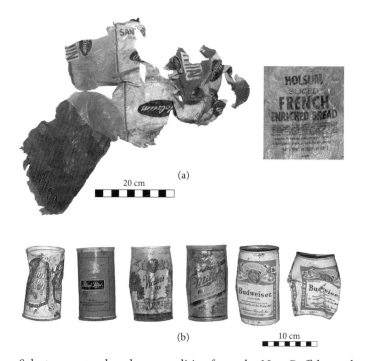

FIGURE 13.5 Select mass-produced commodities from the New Buffalo trash dump: (a) = 'Holsum' white sandwich and French bread bags; (b) = beer cans (photograph: Severin Fowles and Kaet Heupel)

That said, our informants regularly stress that New Buffalo's broadly anti-capitalist stance was of the waste-not-want-not variety that never looked a gift horse in the mouth. If someone brought industrial mass-produced commodities into the commune, they would surely be consumed. It is significant, in this respect, that our evidence reveals almost no commitment to particular brands, which would have been expected had the occupants been regular supermarket shoppers. Instead, an almost random pattern prevails with, for instance, eleven different brands represented in the group of seventy-nine rusted beer cans recovered from the trash deposit (Figure 13.5b). Such high variability signals a community that was quick to accept gifts, and readily partook of whatever came its way, but that never sought to define itself through stable brand commitments. As non-participants in the wage labour economy, most lacked the monetary resources to be regular shoppers anyway.

Much more could be said about the present material things of New Buffalo, but let us turn to the many absent things that also clutter the site. The commune, as we have noted, was built on a countercultural discourse of absence. Indeed, while there is no question that some residents sought to appropriate Native American traditions by wearing moccasins, living in tipis, taking peyote, and building with mud, others did not. Buddhism, acid, music, guns, subsistence farming—any of these might have served as the cornerstone for one's personal identity. The common thread that drew so many young people to the commune, then, was not the act of 'playing Indian' per se, so much as it was their unified rejection of certain restrictive or offensive aspects of mainstream American society. Like other countercultural experiments of the time, New Buffalo was characterized by its assertive absence of middle-class commitments to private ownership and rampant consumerism and by its elimination of conventional rules governing health, sex, spirituality, family structure, and drug use.

This resulted in a variety of conspicuous absences. The early construction of the commune's buildings, for instance, was nothing less than an anti-modern collective ritual, focused on doing without industrial products, tools, and conveniences; adobes were fashioned by hand and logs were laboriously stripped without the use of heavy machinery. Wood was chopped for heating and cooking, a daily labour that rehearsed non-reliance on coal, gas, or oil and the industries that supply them. The original buildings were purposely not wired for electricity. In time, the central kitchen and Buffalo Room were electrified, but individual sleeping areas and structures like the pit house were always off the grid during the commune years. 'No electric lights here', wrote one occupant in 1973:

> only candles and kerosene lanterns illuminate dim figures in this great house lit by the night. We are people living in the earth—to be stumbled upon—in the great desert. This is the picture of being close to the earth. My window is right at ground level. I am actually underground…(Kopecky 2004: 112)

The commune's ambivalent relationship with electricity paralleled—consciously, most likely—a similar ambivalence at nearby Taos Pueblo. After much debate regarding the balance between native tradition and Western conveniences, Taos finally accepted electricity during the 1970s with the proviso that no electricity be permitted in the sacred eastern half of the pueblo. It is the assertive absence of electricity (and plumbing and cars) in this sacred precinct that was of greatest cultural importance to the tribe. The same might be said of New Buffalo: that some spaces came to be electrified was probably less important than the fact that other spaces, like the commune's pit house and tipis, were not.

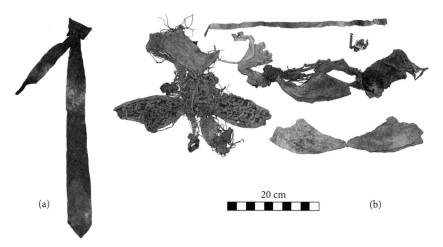

(a)

20 cm

(b)

FIGURE 13.6 Unlikely artefacts from New Buffalo: (a) = men's clip-on tie; (b) = bra fragments (photograph: Severin Fowles and Kaet Heupel)

Most things at the commune simultaneously marked a presence and an absence in this way. Consider another of New Buffalo's iconic structures: its communal outhouse, built in the late 1960s with an infamous row of eight cheek-to-cheek toilet seats. Beyond contributing to an unfortunate outbreak of hepatitis, the outhouse materialized the residents' desire (1) to foreground, rather than hide, 'natural' processes, (2) to literally dismantle the walls separating female and male activities, and (3) to do so in a collectivist setting. At the same time, however, one must acknowledge that it was less the presence of the communal outhouse than the intentional absence of private bathroom facilities that would have been especially jarring to ex-suburbanites who joined the sixties revolution at New Buffalo. Again, 'doing without' was a conscious and creative act of self-fashioning.

This simple observation also helps us interpret the more unexpected artefacts uncovered during our excavations. What, for instance, is one to do with a men's black clip-on necktie (Figure 13.6a) or a women's high-heel shoe, both of which were among the remains in the trash dump? Such objects are wildly at odds with the aesthetics and, indeed, the politics of those who lived at the site, as conventionally understood. The tie that constrains the neck making it hard to breathe, the high-heel shoe that imprisons the foot making it difficult to walk—these were precisely the tools of middle-class bodily discipline that had supposedly been so roundly rejected. Were some hippies at New Buffalo really wearing ties and high heels?

The problem with the last question is that it is phrased entirely from a presentist perspective. Certainly the high-heel shoe in the trash dump has many potential meanings. But so too does the absence of the shoe on the foot of the woman who has thrown it away. In fact, the most plausible explanation for such an artefact is not that it was regularly worn on-site, but rather that it was discarded by one of the many women who were seeking escape from the confines of middle-class America. Identities are remade in the New Mexican desert every day, and in the sixties, the act of throwing away the trappings of one's former life was regarded in many circles as a productive act of voluntary non-consumption. This was as true for neckties and high-heel shoes as for toiletries and televisions.

And it was especially true for another politicized category of objects that emerged from our trash dump excavations: bras. Here too, it would be wrong to focus solely on the presence of bras and bra fragments in the trash and not also on the absence of bras on the bodies of the women who discarded them. Photographs and oral histories suggest that women at New Buffalo generally did not wear bras; bralessness appears to have been both a matter of personal freedom and a statement of solidarity with broader feminist critiques of the bra as an instrument of oppression. We are again led to imagine the situation of a recent arrival to New Buffalo who soon decided that bras did not have a place in her new life. The objects ended up in the trash, only to be indiscreetly extracted by archaeologists four decades later (Figure 13.6b).

Similar events, needless to say, were taking place across the United State during the late 1960s. An organization known as the New York Radical Women (NYRW), for instance, famously coordinated a protest of the 1968 Miss America Beauty Pageant in Atlantic City in which the theatrical trashing of bras, high-heel shoes, hair curlers, and make-up was intended not just as a critique of the objectification of women but also as an indictment of the pageant organization itself, which, among other things, used women as instruments of consumerism to promote product lines. In concert with the protest, the NYRW organized a boycott of the pageant's sponsors. This critical stance became even more central to the group's identity when it reorganized in 1969 as the 'Women's International Terrorist Conspiracy from Hell' (WITCH) and started performing anti-capitalist hexes on Wall Street (Brownmiller 2000).

13.3 THE GODS MUST BE CRAZY

The case of New Buffalo underscores the observation that an archaeology defined solely as 'the discipline of (present, material) things' is always bound to be blind in one eye. This is true whether we are talking about an archaeology of ancient remains or the study of the contemporary past. All species, needless to say, dwell in a world that is seamlessly filled with present things. Fish may not reflect upon the water they swim in, nor worms the dirt they dig in, but the water and the dirt, as material presences, are there all the same. With humans, it is a bit different. Our worlds are seamlessly material as well, but we always find ingenious ways to squeeze more in by surrounding ourselves with a proliferation of absent things that only exist and hold power as a consequence of human perception. There were plenty of female coyotes in northern New Mexico during the 1960s who went about braless, but it is safe to say that, for them, bralessness was nothing at all. Women on communes like New Buffalo, however, experienced bralessness as an absence that was strongly marked and influential in the same way that the cardboard and ink of a protest sign can be influential. Humans occupy worlds filled with present *and* absent things, and they build their lives using both. For those who grow up wearing bras, bralessness becomes a thing to contend with. In a society inundated by cars, computers, and cell phones, doing without such technologies becomes an act of rejection that one must constantly defend. Absences, no less than presences, can be expensive.

Absences frequently also require substantial construction projects. We have seen this in the countercultural rejection of industrial lifeways at New Buffalo, but the tradition of consciously labouring to 'do without' has a far deeper heritage. Indeed, counterculture is surely as old as culture itself (Fowles 2010b). Anthropology in the late 1960s was, in its own way, awakening to this idea just as protests were taking place outside classrooms and students were dropping out to join communes in rural New Mexico. Perhaps the most potent anthropological commentary produced during this period was by Marshall Sahlins (1972) who offered a re-reading of the ethnography of 'simple' hunter-gatherer societies that is now a common reference point for many anarcho-primitivist writers. For Sahlins, it is entirely misleading to interpret the hunter-gatherer's lack of agriculture, land ownership, surplus, fixed residences, technologies, and the like—in short, the hunter-gatherer's lack of property—as an inherently undesirable state of primitive poverty. On the contrary, argued Sahlins, such absences were actively protected precisely because they afforded a 'richer' life with greater freedoms and larger amounts of leisure time. Sahlins famously portrayed this as a Zen road to affluence in which material satisfaction is attained by wanting less rather than consuming more. In contrast, the capitalist's road to affluence—the quest for ever more things to sate a limitless desire—only began to spread during the early modern period, firstly through what Graeber (2011) refers to as the 'privatization of desire' and secondly as a consequence of the expansion of capitalist markets.

Sahlins' key contribution was to flip our understanding of 'primitive' societies from negative to positive. Shortly afterwards, Pierre Clastres (1989) published *Society Against the State*, which radicalized Sahlins' inversion by petitioning for the complete elimination of any image of primitivity as a 'pre-state' condition. All societies are haunted by the spectre of the 'state', he suggested; all societies imagine and defend against worlds of domination in which the few control the many. Consequently, there can be no meaningful anthropology of 'pre-state societies', nor even of 'non-state societies', but only an anthropology of state and *anti-state* societies, the latter defined by their assiduously preserved absence of political domination and wealth inequities to the same extent that the former are defined by their aggressively institutionalized presence of political domination and their insatiable hoarding logics.

For the general public, the most iconic, quasi-anthropological image of a 'primitive' society defined by its rejection of the state came in 1980 with the wildly popular film, *The Gods Must Be Crazy* (dir. Jamie Uys). Drawing upon documentary-style voiceovers in staged ethnographic scenes of daily life among the Ju/'hoansi tribe of the Kalahari Desert, *The Gods Must Be Crazy* was a comedic, anti-modern parable informed by both Sahlins' depiction of the 'original affluent society' as well as the neo-tribal, back-to-the-land movements at communes like New Buffalo. The film's premise was memorable: while flying over the Kalahari, an airplane pilot tosses away a Coca-Cola bottle, which falls from the sky and into the lives of Xi and his fellow foragers who live in blissful innocence, entirely naïve to the modern industrial world. The Coca-Cola bottle—the quintessential mass-produced commodity— ironically creates havoc precisely because it is singular; it can be neither duplicated nor easily shared and so becomes the object of competition as well as the source of strange new desires to possess things. The social fabric begins to tear, and Xi is forced to undertake an epic journey to the ends of the earth where, in the final scene, he finally succeeds in eliminating personal property once again through the picturesque act of throwing the Coca-Cola bottle off a cliff.

These days, most anthropologists recoil at the slightest whiff of neo-primitivism. And anti-consumerist arguments are considered, at best, acts of overly simplistic, non-scholarly activism and at worst, an elitist romanticization of poverty. Neo-primitivist experiments of the 1960s and 1970s as well as popular films like *The Gods Must Be Crazy* did much to solidify this disciplinary cynicism. Both used anthropological knowledge in ways that made anthropologists very uncomfortable. A fair number of the hippies at New Buffalo, for instance, had books by Carlos Castaneda and Margaret Mead in their back pocket, and they knew enough about Native American ethnography to engage in what most academics would stigmatize as the disrespectful appropriation of indigenous culture. *The Gods Must Be Crazy* went even further in claiming a kind of anthropological knowledge base, yet it did so in the service of what anthropologists roundly regarded as thinly veiled racism—not just because it perpetuated dehumanized images of child-like primitives but also because these images were paired with absurd portrayals of black politicians and guerrillas that came straight out of the insidious logic of apartheid (Volkman 1985).

There are two issues to consider here. First, the fact that anthropologists may not want to personally endorse the statements or actions of neo-primitivist and anti-consumerist movements in no way means that such movements aren't themselves worth studying. Communes like New Buffalo have always been especially awkward objects of inquiry for anthropologists, of course, precisely because their residents are so uncannily similar to anthropologists themselves. Again, a fair number of the hippies in the New Buffalo scene had taken anthropology courses in college. One, in fact, had originally come to New Mexico as a Ph.D. student, with intentions of writing an ethnography of a neighbouring commune. He eventually dropped out of graduate school, 'went native', and joined the hippies. In his case, 'going native' operated on two registers, insofar as it involved adopting the lifestyle of hippies who were busily adopting the lifestyle of American Indians (very loosely conceived). Hippie communes of the 1960s and 1970s, then, were peopled by rogue anthropologists, and this heightens their inauthenticity in the eyes of many scholars.

Second, scholarly cynicism about popular anti-consumerism has resulted in a reactionary embrace of popular consumerism, and this has left a strong mark on the material culture studies of both anthropologists and archaeologists. Daniel Miller has been quite explicit in this respect, attacking what he considers to be the dominant 'myth of the past, or of the primitive' in which an original lack of possessions is valorized as a form of 'true unmediated sociality' (1995: 21). A haughty disdain for consumer goods has gone hand-in-hand with this position, he suggests, perverting our anthropological understanding of the modern world. 'Not having things is no evidence that you don't want them,' writes Miller in response. 'An Amazonian Indian may be much more desirous of possessions than we are, but simply be unable to obtain them' (Miller 2010: 5). 'The very concept of poverty,' he emphasizes, 'rests upon the...assumption...that many people who don't have goods desire them' (Miller 1995: 20).

Surely this is unacceptable. Poverty is firstly an accusation, and only secondarily an internalized set of culturally constructed desires on the part of the accused. We should not forget that the remaining hunter-gatherers in sub-Saharan Africa had to be tricked and forced, against their will, into land ownership and participation in a capitalist economy; nor should we forget that the indigenous communities of the American Southwest only came to be labelled 'impoverished' once the Spanish conquistadors, seeking gold, invaded and realized the natives had none.

13.4 CONCLUSION

We are led, then, to three main conclusions. (1) Poverty is founded upon the cultural production of desire; desire is not a natural or originary state that the discourse of 'poverty' simply names, after the fact. (2) Primitivity is an ideological creation of civilization; civilization is not an evolutionary product of primitivity. (3) And absences—as artefacts of perception—always stand at the end of a history of human entanglement with present things. Some absences certainly may be regrettable or even painful in the sense of being desired things in one's mind but not in one's grasp. As often as not, however, absences come to be the objects of desire themselves, and as ongoing construction projects, these absences become productive spaces of non-consumption or non-possession that are as much a part of the architecture of modernity as sports cars and skyscrapers (see Lemonnier, this volume).

What does this mean for an archaeology of the modern world, for our excavations of the contemporary past? Minimally, we might seek the inclusion of 'non-production' and 'non-consumption' as critical keywords alongside 'production' and 'consumption' in the next round of Oxford Handbooks. More ambitiously, we might aim for a reorientation of archaeological theory that would move us beyond presentist preoccupations altogether, beyond our traditional portrayals of history either as a great accumulation of durable things or as a tragic piling up of ruin upon ruin. Is the world more material than in the past? Has modernization filled our lives with unprecedented quantities of stuff? Are our actions today more deeply mediated by tangible objects than in hoary antiquity? Absolutely not. Industrialism has obviously increased the net quantity of *industrial* things, but the world of the Ju/'hoansi forager is just as materially dense and present as the world of the Wall Street banker. Indeed, one cannot even say that what we are really talking about is the successive transformation of natural things into a proliferation of cultural or man-made things—and not just because the nature/culture divide turns out to be philosophically impossible. Tribal ethnographies repeatedly document the impressive degree to which pre-industrial societies *already* regarded their surroundings as fully constructed and maintained through human labour. The material worlds of humans, in other words, are never not manufactured.

If the net sum of present things hasn't changed, however, this is not to say that the net sum of absent things has been similarly stable. Absences are effects of perception, and it is precisely because they take up no space at all that one can pack an ever-increasing number of them into one's closet. Perhaps, then, John Zerzan (1994: 144) and his fellow anarcho-primitivists are correct in thinking about modernity as a vast, unfolding 'landscape of absence'. Capitalism depends on bottomless desire; it depends on the mass production of absent things in the lives of those who are then compelled to engage in the (ultimately futile) effort to eliminate their absences through marketplace purchases. In this sense, one might say that modernization has always been, first and foremost, a growing awareness of everything society lacks. Anti-moderns, for their part, also aspire towards a proliferation of absences, though their end goals obviously differ. Boycotts, strikes, voluntary simplicity, assertive non-consumption—these are among the many strategies they deploy to build meaningful and politically potent non-presences. The lesson is ultimately the same: any archaeology of the contemporary past that restricts itself to the analysis of material things will be missing much of what makes the contemporary world what it is. Here we have advocated a negative methodology as an alternative.

References

Brownmiller, Susan. 2000. *In Our Time: Memoir of a Revolution*. New York: Dial Press.

Buchli, Victor and Lucas, Gavin. 2001 Models of Production and Consumption. In *Archaeologies of the Contemporary Past*, ed. Victor Buchil and Gavin Lucas, pp. 21–5. London: Routledge.

Clastres, Pierre. 1989. *Society Against the State*. New York: Zone Books.

Dant, Tim. 2006. Material Civilization: Things and Society. *The British Journal of Sociology* 57(2): 289–308.

Deloria, Philip. 1998. *Playing Indian*. New Haven: Yale University Press.

Fowles, Severin. 2008. Steps Toward an Archaeology of Taboo. In *Religion, Archaeology, and the Material World*, ed. Lars Fogelin, pp. 15–37. Center for Archaeological Investigations, Occasional Paper No. 36. Carbondale, IL: Southern Illinois University Press.

—— 2010a. People Without Things. In *The Anthropology of Absence: Materialisations of Transcendence and Loss*, ed. Mikkel Bille, Frida Hastrup, and Tim Flohr Sørensen, pp. 23–41. New York: Springer.

—— 2010b. A People's History of the American Southwest. In *Ancient Complexities: New Perspectives in Pre-Columbian North America*, ed. Susan Alt, pp. 183–204. Provo: University of Utah Press.

Graeber, David. 2011. Consumption. *Current Anthropology* 52(4): 489–511.

Harrison, Rodney and Schofield, John. 2010. *After Modernity: Archaeological Approaches to the Contemporary Past*. Oxford: Oxford University Press.

Hodder, Ian. 2012. *Entangled: An Archaeology of the Relationships Between Humans and Things*. New York: Wiley-Blackwell.

Houriet, Robert. 1971. *Getting Back Together*. New York: Coward, McCann, and Geohegan.

Keltz, Iris. 2000. *Scrapbook of a Taos Hippie*. El Paso, TX: Cinco Puntos Press.

Knorr Cetina, Karin. 1997. Sociality with Objects: Social Relations in Postsocial Knowledge Societies. *Theory, Culture & Society* 14(4): 1–30.

Kopecky, Arthur. 2004. *New Buffalo: Journals from a Taos Commune*. Albuquerque: University of New Mexico Press.

Latour, Bruno. 1999. *Pandora's Hope: Essays on the Reality of Science Studies*. Cambridge, MA: Harvard University Press.

Law, Lisa. 1987. *Flashing on the Sixties*. Santa Rosa, CA: Squarebooks.

Miller, Daniel. 1995. Consumption as the Vanguard of History. In *Acknowledging Consumption*, ed. Daniel Miller, pp. 1–52. London: Routledge.

—— 2010. *Stuff*. Cambridge: Polity Press.

Olsen, Bjørnar. 2010. *In Defense of Things: Archaeology and the Ontology of Objects*. New York: Altamira Press.

Olsen, Bjørnar, Shanks, Michael, Webmoor, Timothy, and Witmore, Christopher L. 2012. *Archaeology: The Discipline of Things*. Berkeley, CA: University of California Press.

Rathje, William J. and Murphy, Cullen. 2001 [1992]. *Rubbish! The Archaeology of Garbage*. New York: HarperCollins.

Rudnick, Lois Palken. 1996. *Utopian Vistas: The Mabel Dodge Luhan House and the American Counterculture*. Albuquerque: University of New Mexico Press.

Sahlins, Marshall. 1972. *Stone Age Economics*. Hawthorne, NY: Aldine de Gruyter.

Smail, Daniel Lord, Stiner, Mary C., and Earl, Timothy. 2011. Goods. In *Deep History: The Architecture of Past and Present*, ed. Andrew Shryock and Daniel Lord Smail, pp. 219–41. Berkeley: University of California Press.

Volkman, Toby Alice. 1985. Review of *The Gods Must Be Crazy*. *American Anthropologist* 87(2): 482–4.

Zerzan, John. 1994. Feral. In Zerzan, *Future Primitive and Other Essays*, pp. 144–6. New York: Autonomedia.

CHAPTER 14

....

RUINS

....

GAVIN LUCAS

14.1 INTRODUCTION

....

RECENT ruins, like contemporary garbage (Rathje and Murphy 2001; Reno, this volume), provide one of the more familiar contexts for those archaeologists studying the contemporary past. They may be recent, but at least they still possess much of the same properties as the conventional archaeological record. An abandoned factory can be compared to a classical temple, a landfill to a Bronze Age midden, and much the same methods and approaches can be used on all of them. They constitute, or at least *appear* to constitute a static, archaeological context in contrast to the dynamic, systemic contexts of occupied buildings and spaces. But as I hope this chapter will demonstrate, such oppositions break down when we examine a space like the recent ruin and actually challenge ourselves to rethink some of our more fundamental methodological concepts. Indeed, the danger lies precisely in treating the recent ruin as if it were a classical one, in domesticating it and, concomitantly, domesticating the present as just another archaeological period—the contemporary past (Harrison 2011). The challenge is rather to reverse this process and instead of making the recent ruin comparable to the classical one, to use the recent ruin to rethink the way we conceive of all ruins, and indeed of the archaeological record itself.

Ruins have arguably formed a key site for self-reflection in the West since at least the Renaissance (Macauley 1964; Woodward 2001). Literature and the visual arts abound with citations to and representations of ruins, especially from the eighteenth century as ruins became part of a new aesthetic. Throughout the period and up to today, a common and recurring ambivalence pervades such reflections (Ginsberg 2004: 315–34). On the one hand, ruins acted as *memento mori*, testaments to the mortality of all things; medieval and Renaissance ideology explicitly drew on analogies between human and architectural decay (Woodward 2001: 93), and just as a human skeleton or rotting corpse signalled the death of the human body, so a ruined building signalled the end of a society or culture. On the other hand, ruins also acted as monuments, hinting at the possibility of immortality through material persistence—reminders of a civilization or way of life. Indeed, ruins are as much about the future as they are about the past, insofar as they act as media for reflection on history and the trope of progress. This is most clearly evident in the genre of futuristic views, artworks which depicted a contemporary building or city as if it was a ruin and which have a long pedigree from the late eighteenth century up to the present, from Hubert Robert's painting of the *Louvre in ruins* (1796) and Joseph Gandy's similar work on the *Bank of England* (1798) to Albert Speer's 'Theory of Ruin Value' which would make Hitler's Berlin appear glorious even centuries after the end of the Third Reich (Woodward 2001: 155, 161; Yablon 2009: 263–79). The same, yet more dystopic visions are a stock feature of many contemporary science fiction films, from *Planet of the Apes* (dir. Franklin J. Schaffner 1968) to *Terminator* (dir. James Cameron 1984). For Walter Benjamin, it was this allegorical aspect of ruins as futuristic visions and material testaments to the impossibility of unending progress that was central, and underlay his sense of history and critique of modernity (Benjamin 1985: 177–82).

Parallel with this ambivalence, however, is also another tension between viewing ruins aesthetically and archaeologically; if the aesthetic of ruins revolves around allegories of decay versus memory, archaeological reflection is caught between the desire to reconstitute the past and the limitations posed by the fragmentary nature of remains. Cornelia Vismann (2001) has argued that over the course of the nineteenth century, reflection on ruins increasingly became tied to scientific discourse (linked to the rise of professional history and archaeology). Indeed, many ancient ruins have been transformed in the wake of archaeological work and heritage management practices since the late nineteenth century, dramatically altering their aesthetic effect, a point to which I will return. Yet, it is questionable how far one can actually separate the aesthetics of decay and memory from a science of ruins and, in fact, recent archaeological work is precisely drawing on the concepts of decay and memory to rethink the nature of archaeology as a science of the past. As Michael Shanks and Mike Pearson put it: 'Decay and morbidity are the condition of archaeological enquiry' (Shanks and Pearson 2001: 156; also see Olsen 2010; Shanks et al. 2004). Moreover, it is particularly in the case of recent ruins that such linkages can be explored, precisely because such ruins have been least affected by these heritage practices (e.g. see Andreasson et al. 2010). Indeed, recent ruins tend to contradict many of the defining criteria of classical ruins as articulated by Georg Simmel over a century ago in his classic short paper on *The Ruin* (Simmel 1959 [1911]).

For Simmel, the ruin in particular embodied the balanced tension between two forces: Nature and the human Spirit. Unlike other fragmentary and decaying remains which often merely exhibited some form of attrition or entropy (e.g. a broken statue, a flaking painting), the ruin incorporated new forces and energies which actively reshaped a structure. For Simmel, this was more than a reversal, of nature reclaiming what human spirit had transformed from natural raw materials, but nature transforming human labour into something *new again*. We may dislike Simmel's terminology here of Nature and Spirit but the underlying point remains highly relevant: the ruin is the very mirror image of material culture. If material culture or an artefact embodies the human transformation of nature, the ruin is its opposite; the natural transformation of the human. However, one of the consequences of this view of the ruin is that, for Simmel, many places we would call ruins actually lack the specific fascination of the ruin insofar as the ruin is the product not of nature but of human destruction. For Simmel, such destruction could be articulated either actively through intentional acts of violence or passively through letting a site decay. Either way, they contrasted to authentic abandonment where human presence has altogether disappeared and nature is

FIGURE 14.1 Inside of an abandoned farmhouse in the countryside of Iceland (photograph: Gavin Lucas)

ascendant. Simmel suggested many Roman ruins had this character of human destruction, though perhaps the most obvious examples would be found decades after Simmel wrote his paper, in the bombed-out cities of Europe (Vidler 2010) or derelict industrial sites in towns and cities (Edensor 2005). Indeed, modern ruins in general would appear to be excluded from Simmel's category of an authentic ruin.

At a superficial level, modern ruins (think of a derelict factory) can indeed be seen to stand almost diametrically opposed to the classical ruin (think of an abandoned medieval abbey), incorporating a series of connected dichotomies with respective positive and negative valuations (Table 14.1). Where classical ruins evoke an aesthetic of attraction, the modern ruin might elicit disgust and revulsion; if the classical ruin is a form of art, the modern ruin is simply garbage (Figure 14.1). Indeed, while the classical ruin seems to exhibit graceful decay through natural processes, the modern ruin is like a fresh carcass spilling out its guts, where intentional human abandonment or destruction is often as prevalent as Nature reclaiming its own.

While such oppositions may operate within contemporary culture, they are not necessarily the most productive way to start thinking about an archaeology of recent ruins. Indeed, as Tim Edensor has shown, ruins such as derelict factories and other abandoned industrial sites offer a much richer, more complex and varied aesthetic than these simple negative valuations suggest. Edensor's study of industrial ruins reminds us of the multiple contemporary uses of such spaces: for reclamation of materials and spare parts, as living spaces for travellers or the homeless, as arenas of play whether for children or urban exploration, and as sites for contemporary art. Such practices reveal the potential of modern ruins to contest the over-regulated nature of conventional urban order and the experience of urban space; visiting such sites, Edensor suggests, is a form of anti-tourism (Edensor 2005: 95). Moreover, these kinds of ruins not only contest our conventional views of urban space,

Table 14.1 Contrived dichotomies between the modern and classical ruin

Classical	Modern
Romantic	Gothic
Pleasure	Disgust
Art	Waste
Natural decay	Human destruction

they also help us question our normative perception of the material world; whether it is the objects littering such sites as matter out of place or the exposure of the inner workings of a building, our material world is suddenly defamiliarized yet at the same time made more visible. What we took for granted or was hidden is now laid bare (Edensor 2005: 109–10).

In many ways, the recent ruin thus offers a much richer and more positive field for thinking though issues of materiality, time, and space than the classical ruin and part of this is because recent ruins are so *fresh*. The classical ruin is an aged ruin, one that has settled almost into stasis where the actual process of ruination and decay has either *already happened* or has slowed down so much as to be imperceptible. In contrast, the recent ruin is new, is still decaying. Indeed, it may be this distinction which makes recent ruins more problematic for heritage management; for the paradox of preserving a ruin is only apparent when one realizes that what defines a ruin is, fundamentally, the very *process of decay* or ruination. Preservation arrests or even reverses this process, and thus the notion of preserving ruins is surely an oxymoron. Examples of such sites where decay is ongoing might include the Cold War atomic research station at Orford Ness on the east coast of England (Davis 2008) or the former Soviet mining town of Pyramiden in Svalbard, Norway (Andreasson et al. 2010)—both of which are also set within nature reserves.

But if this paradox is not so apparent with classical ruins today, it was not always thus. In the eighteenth century, the interest in classical ruins lay precisely in foregrounding the notion of decay and erosion, something which most old ruins now conceal as they have been sanitized, preserved, or restored; today their value lies elsewhere (Huyssen 2010: 19). For example, English botanist Richard Deakin wrote a whole monograph about the flora colonizing the ruins of the Coliseum in Rome in 1855. Yet less than a quarter of a century later, after archaeologists had moved in, the Coliseum was cleaned up and ceased to become a source of inspiration to artists and writers thereafter (Woodwood 2001: 25–7). Such sanitation is not about human destruction—active or passive—but rather the denial of the very thing that constitutes a ruin: abandonment.

Andreas Huyssen has argued that ruins are central to the identity of modernity (Huyssen 2010). The ruin challenges the belief in unending progress, it represents the fear of future apocalypse—of a time when the modern is no longer modern, but superseded by another era. At the same time, ruins—ancient ones at least—are what help to define modernity's sense of identity as *modern*. For that reason, the classical ruin is easily assimilated into modernity's project as part of a past to be reconstituted through practices of archaeology, history, and heritage. Through such practices, the ruin becomes sanitized and its sting (as a metaphor for the future state of modernity itself) removed. By contrast, the recent ruin is much less easy to domesticate—its very proximity to the present means that rather than simply a metaphor for the end of modernity, it literally materializes the earliest stages of such an end. The recent ruin haunts modernity in a way that no ancient ruin can. Yet, are such anxieties and identifications really so new? One of the problems with evoking a distinction between modern and classical ruins or indeed a distinctly modern ruin imaginary is that it perpetuates the exceptionalism of modernity: to paraphrase Latour, have we ever really been modern? (Latour 1993; Dawdy 2010). This is one of the reasons why I have usually preferred to use the term 'recent' as opposed to 'modern' ruin in this chapter; recent is unambiguously relative to our present, whereas modern is too laden with its association to modernity as a period. In the rest of this chapter, I want to explore in more detail some of the themes which have already been raised in this introduction and elaborate on them through three concepts: agency, speed, and memory.

14.2 RUIN AGENCY

If Simmel's characterization of the ruin as the tension between the forces of nature and culture rings true, it is perhaps because it rests on a deep dichotomy within contemporary thought which creates strong boundaries between the natural and the cultural (Latour 1993). One of the problems with this characterization though, is that it would exclude many sites from the category of ruin; bombed-out buildings in Dresden in 1945 or the World Trade Center in 2001. Under Simmel's scheme and modernist dichotomies, these classify as human acts of destruction—there is no nature involved in their ruination. But if these are not authentic ruins, perhaps then neither are sites such as Pompeii and Herculaneum or even the more recent so-called 'Pompeii of the North', a modern town on Heimaey, Iceland which was half buried under lava and pumice in a 1973 eruption and has recently been partially re-exposed (Figure 14.2). Although abandoned due to a natural catastrophe (a volcanic eruption), such sites could hardly be defined as ruins insofar as they were buried completely under volcanic tephra. It is only through human intervention (i.e. excavation) that they emerged as visible and tangible ruins; their status *as ruins* is only made possible through human agency. In what sense then, can these sites really be called ruins if Simmel is correct? Perhaps only if, once exposed, such sites are then left to naturally decay and thus undergo, in effect, a *double* ruination.

The issue here is about circumscribing agency in the formation of ruins to *either* natural *or* cultural/human forces. But if we follow Latour's suggestion that agencies have always been hybrid (Latour 1993), then Simmel's characterization is no longer relevant. Edensor (2011) provides an insightful example of how a building is always a volatile mix of hybrid forces; in his example of St Ann's Church in Manchester, he reveals the entanglement of human and non-human agencies involved in creating and maintaining a structure first erected in 1709 and still standing today. In particular, Edensor focuses on how the material properties of sandstone used in the church both define it and also the nature of erosion to which it is susceptible; from air pollution to biofilms, from sandblasting to rendering, a historical and material study of the church reveals an assemblage which is in flux, involving a multiplicity of agents to keep it going as a viable entity. In a sense, ruination is always ongoing and if hybrid forces are at work in creating and maintaining a standing building, then

FIGURE 14.2 Pompeii of the North; half-exposed houses buried under volcanic pumice from a 1973 eruption on the island of Heimaey, Iceland (photograph: Gavin Lucas)

the same is no less true of a ruined one (DeSilvey 2006). From this perspective, the distinction between a standing building and a ruin is somewhat blurred and, in fact, highly partial or contingent. Indeed, few ruins are completely abandoned in the sense that no human presence ever affects them. Whether it is people reclaiming objects or building parts, graffiti artists, or homeless people bedding down, ruins continue to be shaped and defined by a mixture of agencies.

Thus, there should be no issue with seeing the rubble and remains of buildings destroyed by war and terrorist acts as ruins. But equally, an inhabited house in a bad state of disrepair could also be seen as a ruin. What is at stake then, is not any essentialist definition or ontology of the ruin per se, but rather the agencies bound up with buildings. If anything defines the contemporary sensibility to ruins (as opposed to a classical one that emerged in the eighteenth century), it is not that human agencies have replaced natural agencies as the cause of ruin, but that the very distinction between human and natural agencies has become unstable. The recent ruin unsettles one of the fundamental boundaries of modernity: between nature and culture. In the next section, I explore another unsettling aspect of such ruins: time.

14.3 RUIN SPEED

One of the features of recent ruins, as opposed to the classical ruin, is their obvious status *as* recent or new; for some writers in the nineteenth century, this very quality seemed to unsettle the aesthetic of the ruin as developed in the preceding century. Alexis de Tocqueville on a grand tour of the Americas in the 1830s encountered such ruins in the wilderness exclaiming 'What! Ruins so soon!' (from *Democracy in America*, quoted in Yablon 2009: 20; also see Dawdy 2010: 761). Such day-old ruins (*ces ruines d'un jour*) formed part of a broader, emerging discourse in the Americas about ruins, which Yablon argues revolved around their *untimeliness*. Over the nineteenth and early twentieth centuries, the North American landscape was replete with all kinds of examples of such untimely ruins, from Tocqueville's abandoned farmstead to initially unsuccessful cities like Cairo, Illinois; from the havoc caused by the San Francisco earthquake to the short life-span of urban buildings. In all these cases, their untimeliness comes from being ruined too soon—before their 'natural' end (Yablon 2009: 11). Yablon argues that the untimely ruin *is* the modern ruin and it is this that distinguishes it from the classical ruin.

For Yablon, the modern ruin's untimeliness is especially linked in to the temporary nature of modern architecture: buildings are not intended to last. More to the point, in many cases, they are not allowed to become ruins, but are pulled down and a new structure rebuilt on the same site. Such processes are well exemplified in the life expectancy of urban office buildings, and for Henry James indicated the impossibility of ruins within the modern urban landscape (Yablon 2009: 257–63). Of course this is not so—modern cities are full of abandoned and ruined buildings, some of which are indeed so untimely that they have been ruined before they have even been finished (Figure 14.3). Abandoned construction sites and half-finished apartment blocks are a common feature of the urban landscape, especially after financial collapses, and are what Yablon calls 'ruins-in-reverse' (Yablon 2009). Yet James's notion of the impossibility of ruins should not be read too literally, but rather as a reflection on the modernist trope of hyperconsumption: the constant desire for the new, planned obsolescence. However, this same trope also conceals an anxiety about endings. What better way to defer the death of a city, a civilization even, than to never let buildings decay or fall into ruin in the first place. This is clearly underlined in the wake of post-war urban reconstruction in European cities devastated by bombing raids, where architects were planning not just in expectation of a new future but also for the fear of future loss (Vidler 2010). Such fears might even be extended further back, to Hausmann's rebuilding of Paris, whose signature boulevards materialized the fear of future civil war (Benjamin 2002). There is thus a paradox at the heart of modern urban architecture which the ruin exposes: a utopian vision of the modern, manifest by rebuilding, and an apocalyptic or dystopic vision of the end of modernity, manifest by designs which take account of future catastrophes—natural or human caused. Modernity's hyperconsumption fuels its own demise; for Walter Benjamin, the Paris arcades were thus ruins even before they had crumbled (Benjamin 2002; also see Dawdy 2010).

Such ruins bring out another aspect to ruin temporality: speed. The untimeliness of recent ruins might be seen to be not only about a premature end, but also about the velocity of ruination. Instead of the gradual and slow decay of classical ruins which takes place over centuries, many contemporary buildings are reduced to rubble in minutes. Such fast ruins can be found exemplified not only in bombed-out sites but also modern demolition projects; indeed, many such ruins are not only fast, they are also ephemeral, their existence as ruins lasting only as long as it takes to clear the rubble and prepare the plot for reconstruction. Yet again, such ruin speed is not exclusive to recent ruins or even to intentional destruction; natural catastrophes such as earthquakes, floods, and eruptions are equally swift and often more extensive in their destruction than human acts of demolition and can be found throughout human history. Shannon Lee Dawdy's work on the ruin effects of

FIGURE 14.3 Abandoned building project in Reykjavík, Iceland in the wake of the 2008 financial collapse (photograph: Gavin Lucas)

Hurricane Katrina on New Orleans reveals a very different type of modern ruin landscape and one which, again, refutes any exceptionalism one might wish to grant to modernity: disaster archaeology can occur any place, any time (Dawdy 2010). Indeed, whether fast or slow (for modern ruins of all speeds are distributed through contemporary urban and rural landscapes), such sites mix up the temporal boundaries of modernity, collapsing past, present, and future. In the next section, I want to explore how memory—and forgetting—is articulated in the context of such ruins.

14.4 RUIN MEMORY

One of Walter Benjamin's fundamental observations on the ruin was that it stripped away ideology and mythology and exposed a hidden truth content (Benjamin 2002). Benjamin was of course closely connected with the Marxist Frankfurt School and his articulation of the ruin as a material manifestation of ideology critique is not surprising. The idea of the ruin as exposure (in Benjamin's case, of the inner workings of capitalism) has been rendered more literal by Edensor who talks about how ruins expose the inner workings of build-ings or indeed, matter itself (Edensor 2005: 109). The redemptive power of ruins which Benjamin identified thus connects to a more positive reading of recent ruins, especially in their fresh state of decay, which usually elicits revulsion through association with the abject, with waste matter. This aspect has been brought out most forcefully by Caitlin DeSilvey's work on a Montana homestead where ruination is linked not to forgetting, but the recovery of memory (DeSilvey 2006, 2007; also see Olsen 2010: 166–72). DeSilvey's work emerged out of an uncertainty around what to keep and what to discard during her curatorial task of sifting through a recently abandoned homestead in the Rocky Mountains; the paradox was that such a task was simultaneously destructive as well as preservative. Moreover, she found that focusing on the very processes of decay—many of which were too far advanced or irreversible to retrieve objects—elicited questions about history, memory, and materiality that would not otherwise have been raised.

What DeSilvey's work brings to light (see also DeSilvey, this volume) is the link between ruination and memory; rather than purely foster forgetting, the very process of ruination and decay can actually bring to the surface submerged or forgotten histories. Another example reveals a similar complexity between ruins and memory: Alfredo González-Ruibal's work on Galician houses. Between the late nineteenth century and the 1960s, hundreds of thousands of people emigrated from Galicia to America and when many started to return in the 1970s, they were confronted with a past they wanted to forget (González-Ruibal 2005). This past was the poverty and peasant lifestyle of their ancestors (or themselves), expressed most strongly in the vernacular architecture. The returnees built grand new homes in new styles and materials which deliberately contrasted with the vernacular; on the other hand, the old buildings were not destroyed or pulled down, but simply left to rot and ruin. What is interesting in the Galician case is that leaving the houses as ruins (rather than demolishing them) engenders forgetfulness, but at the same time their very persistence is a reminder of that past. Indeed, many people, although ashamed of their past poverty, still retained an attachment to its material forms. Letting go is not always that easy. González-Ruibal calls these ruins counter-monuments: instead of serving to commemorate, they materialize oblivion. More than that, though, they embody the dilemma of a people seeking to be 'modern'.

What emerges from these examples—and has cropped up throughout this chapter—is the importance of ruins *as* ruins; that is, not as carefully managed or preserved sites as part of conventional heritage strategies, but sites where decay and entropy are in full swing, with little or no attempt at intervention. As a corollary of this, this is also about foregrounding the archaeology of a ruin *as* a ruin; that is, not exclusively focusing on what the ruin once was, i.e. an occupied building in use, but on its post-abandonment phase, which, as discussed earlier, is never really abandoned but remains in use, just in different ways (Dawdy 2010). This aspect of recent ruins can be linked to Paul Connerton's discussion of memory and modernity. To understand how modernity forgets, we need to understand how it remembers. Closely linking memory to place, he identified two forms of place memory: the memorial and the locus (Connerton 2009: 10). He argues that while the memorial explicitly attempts to sustain memory, it actually performs worse than the locus, which is a place linked to quotidian routines, like the home. The reason relates to the dynamic and productive nature of loci as opposed to the relatively passive and inert character of memorials. Time stands still in memorials, unlike loci. By extension, ruins as dynamic, entropic places as opposed to managed and quarantined sites, are surely far more productive sites for exploring the processes of memory and forgetting (also see Nora 1989). Gabriel Moshenska's comparison of the London memorial to those killed in the Blitz with a rebuilt church, bombed during the same, provides a perfect illustration of this distinction (Moshenska 2010). Even though St James's church has been repaired, its bombing partly forgotten and fragmented, it still remains for Moshenska a more successful memory of the Blitz. Unlike the memorial, a diminutive and drab object outside St Paul's which calls attention to itself as a monument and actually sanitizes the bombing of London, St James's church demands an active memory work, where the bombing remains foregrounded (also see Schofield 2002). The same, more powerful responses emerged during recent archaeological excavations of London homes bombed during the Blitz (Moshenska 2009).

14.5 Concluding Remarks

The link between bombed ruins and memory has perhaps been most eloquently explored in W. G. Sebald's *A Natural History of Destruction*, part of which addressed the collective amnesia in Germany about its own bombed cities from the Second World War (Sebald 2003). Indeed, in many ways the paradigmatic 'modern' ruin is arguably a site reduced to rubble in the context of conflict—the very kind of ruin Simmel would have excluded from his categorization. González-Ruibal has argued that sites of destruction—indeed destruction itself—characterizes contemporary modernity, or supermodernity (González-Ruibal 2008). Although destruction comes in many forms, most of the sites González-Ruibal discusses are sites of conflict and it is the destructive forces of modernity that he seeks to promote over the conventional focus on consumption. Yet, the concept of destruction can of course be extended beyond the obvious war-torn ruin to industrial extraction plants which devastate environments (LeCain 2009) and to usable buildings torn down to make way for the new—or simply abandoned because it is 'cheaper' to build elsewhere than re-use. In fact, Yablon's untimely ruins arguably are equivalent to ruins created through destruction in the sense that a site destroyed is a site which has come to an end before its time. Destruction in all its forms has certainly been a prominent feature of human history for the last one hundred years, although as pointed out before, it is not exclusive to this contemporary past. Yet at the same time, such destruction is often invisible—either concealed or simply forgotten.

For Sebald, the amnesia of Germany's war ruins was linked to shame about the war; but forgetting is arguably a more widespread feature of supermodernity. One of the recurrent characteristics in reflections on modern forms of memory is how short it is (Connerton 2009); whether it is historical events or academic ideas, modernity's memory is like that of the proverbial goldfish. Connerton links this short memory span to the disconnection between the scale of social processes and the scale of human, lived experience tied to locales (2009: 5). In particular, he highlights three processes which foster the cultural amnesia so characteristic of modernity: the speed at which people, objects, and ideas move through what Harvey has called time-space compression (Harvey 1990; also see Virilio 2005) leading to the emergence of non-places (Augé 1995); the size of human settlements, exemplified by the megacity or post-metropolis (Soja 2000); and the intentional destruction of the built environment to make way for new buildings. We might indeed question whether these constitute an exceptional period in human history, i.e. modernity; but the implications they carry for memory are important to consider and thus remain relevant to any discussion of recent ruins.

Throughout this chapter, I have tried to draw out some key themes with regard to ruins and in particular to highlight what is distinctive about both recent ruins and the modern imaginary about the ruin. But there is one final point that needs to be made here and that is the importance of the recent ruin to an archaeology of the contemporary past—or indeed any archaeology. I opened this chapter by referencing the fact that ruins comprise a familiar context for archaeologists because they appear to be already of the past. Yet as my discussion of the issues of agency, speed, and memory has, I hope, indicated, such an assumption is deeply problematic. Ruins remain active, not inert, and challenge the dichotomies of past/present or static/dynamic. In short, they destabilize the separation of archaeological and systemic (or ethnographic) contexts. Indeed, occupying as it does an interstitial position between conventional buried archaeological remains and standing, inhabited buildings, it is only fitting that the ambivalent status of the ruin is deployed to question such separations. However, in directing our attention to one set of dichotomies, we need to be equally aware of the dangers of another: namely giving the recent ruin some kind of exceptional status. We may wish to avoid subsuming the modern ruin into the aesthetic of the classical ruin, but not at the cost of sustaining a separation between the modern and premodern. One of the features of the recent ruin is its untimeliness, but this might present us with a skewed image of (super)modernity—an over-heightened awareness of the role of destruction, of even living in exceptional times. But it may also be one of the most important ways to stay grounded. As González-Ruibal suggests, our focus as archaeologists on ruins and sites of waste and decay is a vital reminder that—despite the dominating notion that we are living in an increasingly virtual world—our reality is very much material (González-Ruibal 2008: 254).

ACKNOWLEDGEMENTS

This chapter would not have been possible without the inspiration and knowledge acquired through working with my colleagues in the Ruin Memories team. I would like to offer them a collective acknowledgement—even if the views expressed here do not always coincide with their own.

REFERENCES

Andreasson, Elin Hein Bjerck and Olsen, Bjørnar. 2010. *Persistent Memories: Pyramiden—A Soviet Mining Town in the High Arctic*. Trondheim: Tapir Academic Press.

Augé, Marc. 1995. *Non-Places: An Introduction to Supermodernity*. London: Verso.

Benjamin, Walter. 1985. *The Origin of German Tragic Drama*. London: Verso.

—— 2002 [1935]. Paris—Capital of the Nineteenth Century. In *The Arcades Project*, ed. Rolf Tiedeman, pp. 77–88. Cambridge, MA: Harvard University Press.

Connerton, Paul. 2009. *How Modernity Forgets*. Cambridge: Cambridge University Press.

Davis, Sophia. 2008. Cultural Geographies in Practice: Military Landscapes and Secret Science: The Case of Orford Ness. *Cultural Geographies* 15: 143–9.

Dawdy, Shannon L. 2010. Clockpunk Anthropology and the Ruins of Modernity. *Current Anthropology* 51(6): 761–93.

DeSilvey, Caitlin. 2006. Observed Decay: Telling Stories with Mutable Things. *Journal of Material Culture* 11(3): 318–38.

—— 2007. Art and Archive: Memory-Work on a Montana Homestead. *Journal of Historical Geography* 33: 878–900.

Edensor, Tim. 2005. *Industrial Ruins: Space, Aesthetics and Materiality*. Oxford: Berg.

—— 2011. Entangled Agencies, Material Networks and Repair in a Building Assemblage: The Mutable Stone of St Ann's Church, Manchester. *Transactions of the Institute of British Geographers* 36(2): 238–52.

Ginsberg, Robert. 2004. *The Aesthetics of Ruins*. Amsterdam: Rodopi.

González-Ruibal, Alfredo. 2005. The Need for a Decaying Past: An Archaeology of Oblivion in Contemporary Galicia (NW Spain). *Home Cultures* 2(2): 129–52.

—— 2008. Time to Destroy: An Archaeology of Supermodernity. *Current Anthropology* 49(2): 247–79.

Harrison, Rodney. 2011. Surface Assemblages: Towards an Archaeology *in* and *of* the Present. *Archaeological Dialogues* 18(2): 141–61.

Harvey, David. 1990. *The Condition of Postmodernity*. Oxford: Blackwell.

Huyssen, Andreas. 2010. Authentic Ruins: Products of Modernity. In *Ruins of Modernity*, ed. Julia Hell and Andreas Schönle, pp. 17–28. Durham, NC: Duke University Press.

Latour, Bruno. 1993. *We Have Never Been Modern*. Cambridge, MA: Harvard University Press.

LeCain, Timothy. 2009. *Mass Destruction: The Men and Giant Mines that Wired America and Scarred the Planet*. Piscataway: Rutgers University Press.

Macauley, Rose. 1964. *The Pleasure of Ruins*. London: Thames & Hudson.

Moshenska, Gabriel. 2009. Resonant Materiality and Violent Remembering: Archaeology, Memory and Bombing. *International Journal of Heritage Studies* 15(1): 44–56.

—— 2010. Charred Churches or Iron Harvests? Counter-Monumentality and the Commemoration of the London Blitz. *Journal of Social Archaeology* 10(1): 5–27.

Nora, Pierre. 1989. Between Memory and History: Les Lieux de Mémoire. *Representations* 26: 7–24.

Olsen, Bjørnar. 2010. *In Defense of Things: Archaeology and the Ontology of Objects*. Lanham, MD: Altamira Press.

Rathje, William and Murphy, Cullen. 2001. *Rubbish! The Archaeology of Garbage*. Tuscon: University of Arizona Press.

Schofield, John. 2002. Monuments and the Memories of War: Motivations for Preserving Military Sites in England. In *Matériel Culture: The Archaeology of Twentieth Century Conflict*, ed. John Schofield, William Gray Johnson, and Colleen M. Beck, pp. 143–58. London: Routledge.

Sebald, Winfried Georg. 2003. *On the Natural History of Destruction*. New York: Random House.

Shanks, Michael and Pearson, Mike. 2001. *Theatre/Archaeology*. London: Routledge.

Shanks, Michael, Platt, David, and Rathje, William. 2004. The Perfume of Garbage: Modernity and the Archaeological. *Modernism/modernity* 11(1): 61–84.

Simmel, Georg. 1959 [1911]. The Ruin. In *Georg Simmel, 1858–1918: A Collection of Essays, with Translations and a Bibliography*, ed. Kurt H. Wolff, pp. 259–66. Columbus: Ohio State University Press.

Soja, Edward. 2000. *Postmetropolis: Critical Studies of Cities and Regions*. Oxford: Blackwell.

Vidler, Anthony. 2010. Air War and Architecture. In *Ruins of Modernity*, ed. Julia Hell and Andreas Schönle, pp. 29–40. Durham, NC: Duke University Press.

Virilio, Paul. 2005. *Negative Horizon: An Essay in Dromoscopy*. London: Continuum.

Vismann, Cornelia. 2001. The Love of Ruins. *Perspectives on Science* 9(2): 196–209.

Woodward, Christopher. 2001. *In Ruins*. London: Chatto & Windus.

Yablon, Nick. 2009. *Untimely Ruins: An Archaeology of American Urban Modernity 1819–1919*. Chicago: University of Chicago Press.

CHAPTER 15

....

MEMORY

....

BJØRNAR OLSEN

15.1 INTRODUCTION

....

MODERNITY is often said to be characterized by its detachment from the past. Contrary to previous and 'traditional' societies where the past is supposed to have lived on in what Pierre Nora (1984) has termed 'real environments of memory', the accelerated history of the modern is claimed to have left the past behind. However, as number of theorists, ranging from Marx, Bergson, and Benjamin to Serres and Latour, have argued, this modernist leitmotif is hard to sustain. Rather, it may be claimed that the past proliferates more and more, that each new generation actually is receiving an increasingly greater share of it—or, as Walter Benjamin would have said, nothing is less ended than the past.

This piling up of the past has not so much to do with our deliberate practices of recollection in terms of archives, museums, and disciplinary knowledges, the consciously developed aide-mémoires for storing and transmitting information about the past (cf. Huyssen 2003). Quite the contrary, such distinct past-restoring practices may be seen as the explicit outcome of what Friedrich Nietzsche once denounced as the 'illness of historicism', the modern idea that the past is slipping away and dying and thus has to be rescued and restored with such great eagerness.

The accumulation of the past is not driven by some agendas of restoring, selecting, or editing the past; in fact, it happens mostly according to material trajectories that are beyond human control and intervention. And most crucial, most fundamental, in this respect are the solid and durable qualities of things; given these qualities we are destined to live in environments increasingly conditioned by the assemblages and formations of the past. In different shapes, and in various conditions, these assemblages gather and thus sediment into potentially new environments of memory. Most obvious, of course, is the ongoing layering of all working and useful matters, such as roads, streets, bridges, buildings, monuments, etc., that constitute such an effective and taken for granted part of our 'contemporary' lifeworld. However, contributing to this gathering and temporal hybridization are also the debris of the stranded, the redundant and outdated. And paramount among them are the ruins of the recent past: derelict factories, vacant shopping malls, overgrown bunkers, and abandoned mining towns; a ghostly world of decaying modern debris utterly marginalized in the current political economy of the past.

In this chapter I shall explore how the conception of a gathering past allows—and impels—us to rethink the way we conceive of memory and the archaeological exposition of the past. An issue to be particularly scrutinized is the role of the material past that persists despite being discarded, ignored, and made superfluous, most conspicuously manifested in the leftover and stranded of our own time. Caught up somewhere between disposal and history, waste and heritage, these discarded things give face to a past too recent, too grim or repulsive to be embraced as heritage (González-Ruibal 2008). But precisely by being marginal and thus gathering in suspense to the functional and ideologically useful, these spoils of history carry the potential to trigger critical and involuntary memories—memories that illuminate what conventional cultural history has left behind. The case I will be using is the abandoned mining town of Pyramiden, a stranded Soviet enterprise in the High Arctic (Andreassen, Bjerck, and Olsen 2010). My take on these issues is informed by what more or less aptly has been called 'symmetrical archaeology' and I shall start by giving a brief introduction to this archaeology.

15.2 WHAT IS SYMMETRICAL ARCHAEOLOGY?

Looking back over the last fifty years of archaeological reasoning we have witnessed the emergence of a rich vocabulary of adjectival prefixes supposed to grasp and announce an increasing disciplinary diversity, ranging from the 'new', 'processual', and 'analytical' to the 'contextual', 'feminist', and 'social'. As we all know, concepts are not used only as handy analytical and discursive tools; they also act as strategic and rhetoric devices in scientific and public combating: they confront and challenge previous concepts, emblematically proclaiming identities, differences, commitments, and new attitudes.

Although far from sharing the fame and influence of the aforementioned approaches, 'symmetrical archaeology' can be seen as yet another and late addition to this inventory. It actually started quite innocently, even perhaps accidentally, as a proposition or suggestion that conveniently mobilized the familiar rhetoric of oppositional semantics (Olsen 2003: 88). However, it soon became 'connected', started to circulate and assembled allies (and critics), and thus acquired a certain strength, mass, and visibility (e.g. Witmore 2004, 2006, 2007; Olsen 2006, 2007, 2010, 2012; González-Ruibal 2007; Shanks 2007; Webmoor 2007; Kenderdine 2008; Perry 2009; Johnson 2010; Jervis 2011; Olsen et al. 2012). A main reason for this receptiveness, I guess, was that the concept and its early propositions apparently appealed to, and even named, a growing concern among a number of archaeologists with the fate of things in an interpretive environment increasingly dominated by relativist and anti-materialist theories. An environment where things rarely were allowed to perform in their primary mode of being *qua* things, but increasingly were disguised as symbol, text, language, or whatever the prevailing intellectual fashion required of them (cf. Brown 2003: 82).

This worry with the fate of things was a concern shared in what has become known as science (and technology) studies. Here various 'principles of symmetry' had been proposed since the 1970s (cf. Bloor 1976) but by far the most relevant and directly decisive for their archaeological manifestation were the principles of symmetry proposed by Bruno Latour in his manifesto *We Have Never Been Modern* (1993). In its original French edition this work even carried the subtitle 'essays in symmetrical anthropology' (Latour 1991), which for some

reason never found its way to the English edition. Here Latour argued that modernity institutionalized a 'Great Divide', two completely distinct ontological zones that became constitutive of the social and philosophical conducts of this regime. Humans and non-humans
were delegated to different ontological and disciplinary zones, one concerned with humans,
the other with the inanimate object world. This divide also brought about a second divide
by separating 'us' (the moderns), who mastered the skill of purifying and splitting, from
'them' (the premoderns), who lacked it and thus mixed everything together.

Latour's cardinal point is of course that this split image reflects nothing but the modern 'discrepancy between self-representation and practice' (Latour 2003: 38). The modern
condition is more than anything a meshwork of hybrid (and symmetrical) relations and
translations between humans and non-humans; actually the mess has never been greater!
Acknowledging the 'symmetry' implied by all societies being mixtures of natures–cultures,
humans and non-humans, also discloses another principle of symmetry: that there is no a
priori ontological distinction between the constitution of our worlds and those of the 'others' (Latour 1993: 103–6). In other words—and this is the very paradox of this trope—we
have never been modern.

At the outset the use of the concept symmetrical archaeology was clearly an allusion to
Latour's 'symmetrical anthropology' (Olsen 2003). It came to embrace the growing concern
among some archaeologists with how things largely had ended up as epiphenomenal or residual
to the 'social' and 'cultural', and rarely were allowed the right to be the source of their own signification (see Webmoor, this volume). Those who adhered to it were of course never claiming
any symmetry between humans and non-humans (cf. Latour 2005: 76), or even more absurd,
that they are equal. It started out, naively perhaps, as an egalitarian plea for paying more attention to how societies consist of far more entities than those usually given precedence, not for
an undifferentiated world (Witmore 2007: 547). The entities of the world are of course different, in fact they exhibit—between and among themselves—extremely varied forms of beings.
What was claimed was that this difference should not be conceptualized in compliance with
the ruling ontological regime of dualities and negativities; it is a non-oppositional or relative
difference that facilitates collaboration, delegation, and exchange (Olsen 2003, 2010).

What has been called symmetrical archaeology may in my view be stripped down to four
programmatic propositions: Firstly, that humans have always been cyborgs and that the
human condition is characterized by its inextricable enmeshment with things and other
non-human entities (Olsen 2003; Witmore 2007). In other words, humans are not naked
hominids that *enter into* relationships with things and non-humans; they rather emerge *from*
such mixtures. Secondly, these non-human entities which we are immersed amidst are not
passive or meaningless entities sitting in silence waiting to be embodied with socially constituted meanings. Places, animals, and things possess their own unique qualities and competences, both in their individuality and through their own material bonding and internship,
which they bring to our cohabitation with them (Olsen 2010). Thirdly, a symmetrical archaeology is an urge for a new realism in archaeology and material culture studies, and holds the
view that the world, reality, things, and places, are something far more, independent, and
complex than a correlate of human cognition (Olsen 2003, 2010; cf. Bryant, Srnicek, and
Harman 2011; Harman 2011). And finally, a symmetrical archaeology is first of all archaeology, not philosophy, sociology, or science studies. It is an urge for disciplinary confidence
that rather than proposing something radically new seeks to realize the great potential of
the archaeological project. Our persistent concern with things, with materials, constitutes
an intellectual skill that is more than ever relevant to current debates and discourses. What

is needed today is an archaeology that doesn't look at its own past and its own practices with embarrassment but seeks to work for its branding as a distinct and content-filled undertaking: the discipline of things. In other words, and to rephrase some of our most famous ancestors, to show that archaeology is archaeology or its nothing (Olsen et al. 2012).

15.3 The Past that Gathers

In what way, then, does a symmetrical archaeology also challenge the way we conceive the past and its remembering? In compliance with the modernist doctrine of living in a new time that radically breaks with the past, a central trope of historicism and historical narratives is the recalling and sequencing of a past gone. As the narratives proceed and progress the past is inevitably left behind. Stone ages are replaced by metal ages, medieval by modern, feudalism by capitalism, industrialization by post-industrialization. This conception of the closure and finitude of the past is of course related to the persistent conception of time and history as something that passes as irreversible series of discrete moments, as a line of instants (cf. Lucas 2005; Olivier 2001, 2011, and this volume).

Less frequently talked about is how this finitude and loss also came to ground the historical inquiry. It was precisely due to the feeling that the past was lost or vanishing, 'the simple fact that man found himself emptied of history' (Foucault 1989: 369), that the historical urge to recover it became so imperative and compelling. The past became a challenging problem, a mystery to be solved because it was hidden to us in the present; it was made *past* and replaced—the very condition for recalling and remembering it. In other words, and paradoxically, historical remembering became possible only as a certain mode of forgetting; an oblivion which erases the past that lives on and constantly folds into, and thus forms, the present (Heidegger 1962: 388–9).

Maybe more than any other discipline archaeology has the potential to cure this 'illness of historicism'. And we should start in the simplest way possible by showing how things, the material ingredients and residues of all these claimed replacements, object to the finitude and pace of history. Although ageing and transforming, they stubbornly linger on. Megaliths, rock art, Roman roads and walls, medieval farms and townscapes, the myriad used and discarded materials of the increasingly more recent past, are all gathering around us. The new and radically different presents we claim to live in turn out to be little but palimpsestal collections of a past supposedly gone. Inspired by Henri Bergson's concept of duration (2004 [1896]), Laurent Olivier has nicely portrayed things' obstinacy to the instantness of linear and historical time (Olivier 2001). Reflecting on the moment of time when his writing takes place (1999), he notes the 'invisibility' of the 1990s in what he sees from the window in his study. What he sees are houses and constructions dating back to the seventeenth, eighteenth, and nineteenth centuries. The late twentieth century seems reduced to details in the material surroundings. Thus, the present is not comprised of things belonging to the same age, but takes the form of a multitemporal field in which the past through the palimpsest of its durations has accumulated itself (Olivier 2001: 66–7).

Our archaeological interventions into presumed past moments reveal no less hybridized presents. What the excavating archaeologist encounters is always a manifestation of coextensive and gathered conditions: overlapping and compressed layers, superimposed structures, artefacts and debris mixed together—in short, sites that object to modernity and historicism's wished-for ideal of completeness, order, and purified time. The archaeo-logical site is truly mixed, it makes manifest not a linear history or narrative but discloses a 'flattened' and coexistent past, 'consisting of a palimpsest of structures and rubbish pits, constructed and deposited at different periods' (Renfrew 1989: 36). However, rather than actively using this material record to challenge historicism, the opted-for solutions have nearly always been to purify this entangled mess, and to reassemble the entities to conform to the expectation of linear time and narrative cultural history. Time is not allowed to be mixed, paused or reversible, but has to be cleansed and sequenced, in short, 'unlocked'. Through ever more fine-grained dating methods and advanced stratigraphical and typolog-ical sequencing, archaeological sites are cut into increasingly thinner slices of time, disen-tangling and purifying them from the historical conditions that grounded these presents.

The claimed rationale for this chronological (and stratigraphical) purification is that it provides a necessary rewinding of the destructive transformational process that the archae-ological record has undergone. Thus, what we have left is the distorted impression of 'com-pressed' time caused by decay and non-human disturbances; that beyond and prior to the entangled mess we excavate, there is a historical order to be restored, a pure temporal spe-cificity (cf. Schiffer 1976). However convincing this argument may sound how would such instantial slicing work if applied to a presumed modern and contemporary site? To which age does Rome belong? How do we identify the contemporary New York, its present? By excluding all entities that are more than ten, fifty, or one hundred years old? What would be left of Cairo, in fact any site, if we applied such a rigorous chronological approach? In any case, what we would have lost is that which makes these sites what they are: the outcome of a gathering past constantly conditioning the conduct of the present.

The past endures, it accumulates in every becoming 'now', making these presents chrono-logical hybrids by definition and thus objecting to the common conception of time (and the past) as the succession of instants. Each archaeological present is a compressed and coextensive past formed by myriads of mixed and accumulating deposits of stranded and useful things. These diverse palimpsestal gatherings, at the same time reflecting processes uniformitarian and dynamic, urge us to conceive the past very different from the way it has been presented and ontologized in the historical narratives. An archaeological past more akin to the one envisaged by Walter Benjamin, a past decomposing into images and objects, not into narratives. In this past, things are not reflections or illustrations of a plot defined in advance or of meanings produced elsewhere, but are blasted out of continuous history and gathers and sediments as moments of 'nowness' to be disclosed and actualized (Benjamin 1999: 473–6, cf. Harrison 2011: 182–3).

The immediate conclusion to be draw from this is that an archaeology of the past neces-sarily is different from a history of the past (see also Olivier 2011: 86–100). Though this may seem a radical suggestion it is in fact an urge to be more true to the archaeological material we work on. Its apparent radicalness primarily stems from its departure from a dominant disciplinary imperative of producing cultural history: to narrate regional, national, and glo-bal trajectories, to fill in gaps, in short to heal the material past as history. This departure does not imply a rejection of issues such as chronology, pace, and change—only a sym-metrical realization that these concepts may take on very different meanings when things are given a say.

Laurent Olivier has argued that archaeology is in essence not a form of history but more in line with memory, and thus has both the urge and potential to overcome the historicist inclination (Olivier 2011: 93–5 and this volume). The realization of this potential, however, requires that things themselves must be emancipated from their synchronous imprisonment to which also archaeology has most effectively contributed. The division of the past into clear-cut periods and phases was perpetuated by disciplining things into clients and servants of spatial and linear time, effectively visualized through typological alignments of artefact and monument types in museum displays, books, and papers from the mid-nineteenth century onward. This ordering of things in a hierarchical and efficiently visible spatial organization of typological continuities and discontinuities gave reality to the serial image of time as moving between discrete immobile states (Olsen and Svestad 1994).

However, as Olivier has remarked, 'things do not work like that' (2001: 64). In their own being, things are viscous, 'polychronic, multi-temporal, and [reveal] a time that is gathered together, with multiple pleats' (Serres with Latour 1995: 60). Not only does this fit well with their conventional and much alluded to etymology (Old Norse, Old English þing/Old High German Thing), meaning 'gathering' or 'assembly'. A less widely known and possibly older etymological root (tenku) discloses an even more suggestive temporal dimension: 'duration', or, literally, 'extended' or 'stretched time' (Falk and Torp 1906: 903; Bjorvand and Lindeman 2000: 939ff.).

15.4 THE MEMORIES THAT THINGS HOLD

Our everyday perception of things is intimately related to the potential of actions—and reactions—created by the contacts, interfaces, and spaces between bodies and things. As noted by Henri Bergson, things act on us, they 'indicate at each moment, like a compass that is being moved about, the position of a certain image, my body, in relation to the surrounding images' (Bergson 2004: 10). This symmetrical acquaintance produces material habitual competence and spatial knowledge for 'how to go on' in a landscape, a city, a university campus, or a house. Our active cohabitation with things regulates and routinizes our behaviour, making it repetitive and recognizable; we repeat certain actions by habits, by bodily skills instructed and impelled by the things themselves. Through this interchange actions become standardized and predicable, producing what we like to think of as (social) structures and institutions (Durkheim 1951: 313–14; Arendt 1958: 137).

As Bergson also asserted, herein lies the potential for a different kind of memory, a habit memory not related to mental representations and conscious recalling but which emerges as an outcome of habitual schemes of bodily practices. In contrast to cognitive or 'recollective' memory, which involves a conscious gaze at a particular past, habit memory is a lived or acted memory preserved by repetitious practice. In this memory the past continues by being relived in our routines and ways of dealing with things so that 'it no longer *represents* our past to us, it *acts* it' (Bergson 2004: 93, emphasis original). The past is made manifest, 'stored up', through presences and practices.

Being a matrix of habitual action the body is clearly decisive for habit memory. However, it cannot be reduced to a human corporal capacity. Habitual action would generally be very difficult or even impossible without things and their facilitating capacities and arrangements. Just try the experiment of remembering how to bike without a bicycle—or to remember your bodily skill as a pianist without a piano. Things are fundamentally involved, not only as a means for the action to be completed, but also in making the action and material experience familiar, repetitious, and predictable. By their very design, physiognomy, and operational affordances things assign or 'instruct' bodily behaviour; they require certain formalized skills to actualize *their* competences.

Crucial to things' mnemonic capacity is their persistency. Contrary to actions, performances, and speech which only occur as temporary or situational presences, things *last*. There are of course enormous differences in their duration, but the conception of a past still present and even accumulating cannot be accounted for without the lasting quality of so many things. Despite temporary discontinuities in human involvement and use, things *are* even in their dormant state and can be approached again and again to be constitutive of new actions and memories. Due to this persistency and duration, the (past) material world is always directed ahead of itself; it presses against the present, 'gnaws into the future and...swells as it advances' (Bergson 1998: 4).

As mentioned at the outset of this chapter it is important to acknowledge that this gathering of the past mostly happens according to material trajectories that are beyond or unrelated to human control and intervention. Contrary to what is often asserted in critical studies of memory, where emphasis is placed on how the past is used and staged, this material formation of the past is for a large part unpredictable and not subjected to some suspicious plan, censorship, or ideological script. The promising symmetrical outcome is thus that it allows for less edited or censored memories than is often assumed and, as we shall see, enables alternative modes of remembering unfolding at the interface between recollective and habitual memory.

Crucial for the triggering of these alternative memories is the survival and gathering also of the ruined and redundant. Things are after all mostly democratic beings and despite the fact that they do age differently and that their expected life lengths also vary greatly there is a certain egalitarianism and care associated with their ageing. This means that in addition to those functional and 'unbroken' things that facilitate continuous and smooth practices there is a survival also of the outdated and stranded. This is the material past that persists despite being discarded, ignored, and made superfluous—in short, the surviving material redundancy of the past. Thus, in the notion of a past that sediments and swells in our midst, there is also and always a component of the neglected, the unwanted.

The ruins of modernity itself, of our own marginalized pasts, provide perhaps the most conspicuous manifestation of this. Since the nineteenth century, mass production, consumerism, and thus cycles of material replacement have accelerated; increasingly larger amounts of things are, with increasing rapidity, victimized and made redundant. These ruined things were once useful, and thus embedded in repetitious practice and infused with habit memory. When outmoded and discarded, their lived and habitual significance is lost while their physical presence, albeit ruined, continues: the abandoned farmhouse, the one-eyed doll in the garbage pit, the wrecked Skoda in the overgrown field. As such these broken things survive and gather as the material antonyms to the habitually useful, creating a tension-filled constellation that carries the potential of triggering a particular kind of involuntary memory or what Benjamin (1999) called 'dialectical images'. Contrary to the harmonious past–present fusion associated with the effective history of habit memory, these unreconciled interfaces create moments of disturbance and disruption, a charged force field. Embedded in them are also the temporal tensions between their own pre-history (of uses, success, hopes, and wishes) and their after-history, their fate as stranded rubble in the present (Benjamin 1999: 473–6; Buck-Morss 1999: 110ff., 219–21).

Just by stubbornly being (t)here the derelict fur farm or the abandoned whaling station openly rebuke the conception of history as sequenced, biographical, and progressive; they bring forth the abject memories that mostly seem lost in conventional history. In their very own positivistic manner they show that history is not a projected stream leaving the past behind, but that it bends and twists in a disorderly manner, interrupting the expectations of the *have been* and the *becoming*. And precisely by being modern ruins, and thus somehow closer or at least more familiar, they enact this resistance more effectively than their ancient fellow beings.

By often being negative features within the contemporary geopolitical order, the ruins of the modern also hold on and make manifest alternative geographies and other cultural or economical landscapes, displaying past presences in strange places: derelict Norwegian whaling stations at South Georgia, a stranded English train engine in an Icelandic harbour, a frozen German weather station in east Greenland, a ruined Soviet missile hangar in Cuba (cf. Burström, Gustafsson, and Karlsson 2011; Jensen and Krause 2012). The abandoned mining town of Pyramiden in the Arctic archipelago of Svalbard (Andreassen, Bjerck, and Olsen 2010),[1] provides yet another example of what is discussed above.

15.5 REMEMBERING PYRAMIDEN

In 1998 the Russian Arctic Coal Company (Trust Artikugol) decided to end its activity in Pyramiden. A remarkably abrupt abandonment left behind a site devoid of humans but still filled with all stuff constituting a modern city. Rapid development during the 1960s and 1970s had transformed Pyramiden into a modern Soviet town hosting 1,100 inhabitants and equipped with most urban facilities (such as a library, studios for music, dance, and fine arts, theatre/cinema, basketball court, swimming hall, football stadium, ice hockey range, hospital, school, kindergarten, canteen/mess hall, hotel, bars, pubs/lounges, post office, hair parlours, museum, radio station). Stocks of cows, pigs, and poultries were kept at 79°N for local supplies of milk, meat, and eggs, and a greenhouse provided fresh vegetables, herbs, and ornamental plants (Andreassen, Bjerck, and Olsen 2010: 33–52, 173–8). As stated by general director Gnilorybov at the 30th anniversary of Pyramiden in 1976, 'The Soviet people's hands have transformed it into a modern society, where all that is needed for work and rest under harsh Arctic conditions are found' (Andreassen, Bjerck, and Olsen 2010: 173). These forming hands had—with some help—also imbued it with the familiar signatures of *Sovietness*: concrete architecture, iron installations, and socialist iconology, all framed

---

[1] Although Norway holds 'the full and absolute sovereignty' over Svalbard (Spitsbergen) according to the adopted Svalbard Treaty (1920), it also assigns the 39 signature states equal rights to residence and trade and to Svalbard's natural resources. After the Second World War only one of these states, the USSR, and now Russia, has made significant use of these rights by exploiting the huge coal reserves found at Svalbard. This means that throughout the entire Cold War, Svalbard hosted both Norwegian and Soviet societies creating a rather unique geopolitical situation, not the least considering Norway's status as a member of NATO since 1949.

FIGURE 15.1 Approaching the abandoned mining town of Pyramiden, July 2006 (photograph: Bjørnar Olsen)

within a strict spatial grammar that overruled topography and the other attributes of the nature of place. Increasingly alienated from its natural surroundings, Pyramiden was turned into the peculiar Soviet version of the 'non-place', a place at the same time everywhere and nowhere; conspicuous in its own geopolitical setting, but literally indistinguishable from the thousands of other Soviet towns dotting the vast northern Eurasian landscape.

Despite its human abandonment Pyramiden did not end in 1998. In its alluded ghost town state it survived, and still survives, as a petrified image of Soviet ambitions in the High Arctic. When arriving at the town to conduct fieldwork in 2006 little seemed changed (Figure 15.1). Buildings, streets, gangways, monuments, piers, and various mining facilities gave face to a dormant town stubbornly clinging to the barren ground. In the Cultural Palace most of the 60,000 books were still on shelves in the library, solitary musical instruments awaited their players in the music studio, and the grand swimming hall, basketball court, and movie theatre all lay ready-equipped. It all seemed an almost too perfect scripting of Benjamin's maxim of the 'Messianic power' of history, in other words, that 'our coming was expected' (Benjamin 2003: 390).

Things' abundant presence triggered a feeling of something postponed rather than deserted; in fact, they perpetuate the tension of a 'double' postponement. Despite the seven years of post-communist existence prior to its abandonment, little of the Soviet era seemed ended in Pyramiden (Figure 15.2). The façade of the town was still imbued with the regime's iconic affordances; in the director's office in the administration building Lenin's collected works were still on the shelf. Thus, already before its abandonment Pyramiden was postponed and out of time with conventional historical chronology, surviving as a Soviet town in a post-Soviet era (Andreassen, Bjerck, and Olsen 2010: 152–5).

What other and alternative memories does Pyramiden hold? Not being a prehistoric site, at least in conventional terms (cf. Lucas 2004), written accounts are of course abundant but

FIGURE 15.2 Still ready for celebration. Soviet stand for banners and flags in the town square of Pyramiden (photograph: Bjørnar Olsen)

mostly narrowly concerned with issues such as production rates, cargo and shipment details, geomorphological data, and logistic challenges. Beyond political rhetoric hardly anything is said about everyday life and social struggles. However, and despite the strictly casted dominant materiality, its immensely rich archaeology reveals a wealth of material memories that testify to a far more diverse and contested Pyramiden; memories that seem sharpened in its abandoned state or perhaps only are possible to grasp at second hand when no longer immersed in their withdrawn reality of habitual remembering. One striking feature was the immense affluence of creative bricolage, individuality, and political irony which characterized the material expressions of the workers' apartments (Andreassen, Bjerck, and Olsen 2010: 111–35). Despite their spatial uniformity, no two of the flats looked alike. Creative use of wallpaper, floor coverings, paint, self-produced furniture, mixed with the sublime bricolage of using whatever was at hand for decoration and difference—cigarette boxes, beer bottle labels, advertisements, pin-ups, and air cargo package tape—made these interiors not only different among themselves but also created an astonishing contrast to the purity and disciplined utterances dominating the materiality of public spaces.

The semantic of this opposition is undoubtedly layered, e.g. reflecting strategies of material resistance, individual skills, and the creation of homes in a potentially alienating materiality. For example, the materials used for decorating the interiors were not chosen arbitrarily; what the imagery display and offer is very much what public space and Soviet ideology is *not* about: glamour pictures and advertisements for capitalist consumer goods (Figure 15.3); in other words, a kind of inverse expression of official living and ideology. Thus, if Pyramiden was to comply with Boym's somewhat sarcastic characteristic of the ruined post-communist east as a 'theme park of lost illusions' (2001: xiii), the utopias it contains are obviously diverse. Petrified in these 'residues of a dream world' (Benjamin 2003: 13) are not only the prehistoric wish images of socialism, the already outdated dreams inscribed

FIGURE 15.3 'The last thing you ever need ...' Seiko wish-images decorating worker apartment in block 38, Pyramiden (photograph: Bjørnar Olsen)

into its monuments, kitsch, and town planning. Made manifest also are the 'too early' *ur*-phenomena of a utopian consumer society, of which the glossy images were mostly what were ready for the miners to consume. In short, Pyramiden reveals to us the 'pre-history' of socialism and capitalist consumerism, both of which are dormant in its after-history, in its fate as stranded and discarded in the present. By upholding a forgotten past, making it present and tangible, Pyramiden continues to seize the ambiguous dialectics between the 'too early' and the 'already gone', so constitutive of its own historical destiny.

This account calls for some comments on fieldwork, interpretation, and archaeological sensibility. An important issue here is the immediacy in the archaeological experience which makes it comparable to—if not isomorphic with—our everyday being with things. As briefly discussed above, this being is mostly routinized, habitual, or 'lived' but when interrupted or disturbed involuntary memories and reflections may be triggered. This thing lesson became most imperative during our fieldwork in Pyramiden, an educational enterprise which encouraged and enforced a naïve but essential attitude of 'tuning in' and being attentive to what things themselves make manifest. Surely, we arrived with questions, strategies, contexts, and preconceptions which by no means should be dismissed or made insignificant. However, it soon became evident that Pyramiden itself wanted a strong say by constantly 'talking' to us through its physiognomic rhetoric and the 'presence effects' (Gumbrecht 2004) evoked.

Being left in an isolated Arctic town devoid of other humans probably made these articulations more immediate and imperative than in other contexts; at least it provoked reflections and memories that hardly can be voluntarily triggered. Not only did things become more present, more manifest, but in some ways they also become more pestering and disquieting. In their outmoded and stranded fate things suddenly 'appeared' to us in ways never noticed, exposing some of their own unruly 'thingness' and becoming their own source of signification. This also explains why photos became so essential in our dissemination of Pyramiden since such wealth of ineffable sensations is hard to express or mediate through ordinary narrative accounts (Andreassen, Bjerck, and Olsen 2010). Apart from that, and the other basic modes of documentation applied, there is no method to be prescribed for a fieldwork such as this other than being there, being attentive; in short, recalling the best of both archaeological empiricism and phenomenology.

15.6 CONCLUSION: ARCHAEOLOGY AND MEMORY

The example of Pyramiden reveals different and not necessarily harmonizing aspects of material memory, and also helps to make manifest how archaeology as a project differs from the historical. One crucial issue is the viscosity of solid matter. Even before its abandonment Pyramiden was postponed and out of time with conventional historical chronology. The regime's effective and distributed extensions and constituents were, to borrow Bergson's term, 'gnawing' into its future. As witnessed in current settlements all over the vast Eurasian landscape, this effective historical memory ranges from the gauge of railways, Stalin and Khrushchev era apartment houses to power grids and city planning; what Riegel (1982) might have called the 'unintentional monuments' of the Soviet empire but which actually constitutes its tenacious limbs and guts. Thus, the past not only weighs like a nightmare on the *brains* of the living (pace Marx), the viscous Soviet deposits impact on all attempts for 'how to go on' in what is thought of as a radically new time. When did the Soviet Union end— and has it ended? What is the date of Pyramiden? Asking these questions against the backdrop of the material sedimentation of the past, highlights some of the differences between the archaeological and the historical project, including their basic diverging chronologies.

Due to their durable qualities solid things last, they convey the past to us, make it gather. Without this persistency the past would be gone, memories lost, archaeology made impossible. As discussed in this chapter, a particular feature of this persistency is its 'democratic' nature, affording the survival also of the outdated and stranded; a material care for the past which also extends to the victimized, superfluous, neglected, and ignored. Acting as material antonyms to the habitually useful, ideologically correct, and aesthetically pleasing, discarded and abandoned things, sites such as Pyramiden, become agents of disturbance and disruption. Through their 'petrified unrest', these othered things give face to forgotten or neglected pasts, to the trivial, the outdated, or embarrassing, to the failed or never completed undertakings. They bring forth, remember, what conventional history has left behind (Figure 15.4).

Embedded in this mnemonics is also another dialectics, contained in Benjamin's allegorical phrase of the 'at once scattered and preserved', in other words, of ruins and discarded things as at the same time restless and petrified, conveying both destruction and recovery (Benjamin 1985: 162–79, 2003: 169). Because beyond the immediate impression of standstill, sites such as Pyramiden also age, wrinkle, fragment, and wither. Walls and concrete decompose; paint and wallpaper surrender to gravity; doors and windows become broken. Such processes of decay and ruination are often understood negatively through the tropes of loss and deprivation whereby also the memories that things hold become lost along the way. However, as we have seen ruination and abandonment can also be regarded as an act of disclosure—as a recovery of memory (DeSilvey 2006).

FIGURE 15.4 'Freed from the drudgery of being useful' (after Benjamin): shoes left outside worker apartment in Pyramiden (photograph: Bjørnar Olsen)

Experiencing a working, populated city, or an inhabited and well-kept building, may not reveal much about the way it actually works, the diversity of materials and technologies that are mobilized to construct and operate it. And if not cunningly hidden by design and architectural styles these materials and implements themselves are often absorbed by their tasks, they disappear into usefulness, enslaved in their chains of relations. Decay, ruination, abandonment, and disposal disturb the routinized and ready-to-hand and produce a defamiliarized landscape of released objects, buildings with open walls, exposed interiors, new ecologies, and strange companionships (Edensor 2005: 109). In the destruction process new meanings may be revealed, meanings that perhaps are only possible to grasp at second hand when things are no longer immersed in their withdrawn and useful reality. Thus as Benjamin noted, the ruin may be more telling—more memory revealing—than the complete building.

References

Andreassen, Elin, Bjerck, Hein, and Olsen, Bjørnar. 2010. *Persistent Memories: Piramida—a Soviet Mining Town in the High Arctic*. Trondheim: Tapir.

Arendt, Hannah. 1958. *The Human Condition*. Chicago: University of Chicago Press.

Benjamin, Walter. 1985. *The Origin of the German Tragic Drama*. London: Verso.

—— 1999. *The Arcades Project*. Cambridge, MA: The Belknap Press of Harvard University Press.

—— 2003. *Selected Writings, Volume 4: 1938–1940*. Cambridge, MA: The Belknap Press of Harvard University Press.

Bergson, Henri. 1998. *Creative Evolution*. Mineola, NY: Dover Publications.

—— 2004 [1896]. *Matter and Memory*. Mineola, NY: Dover Publications.

Bjorvand, Harald and Lindeman, Fredrik. 2000. *Våre arveord. Etymologisk ordbok*. Oslo: Novus Forlag.

Bloor, David. 1976. *Knowledge and Social Imagery*. Chicago: University of Chicago Press.

Boym, Svetlana. 2001. *The Future of Nostalgia*. New York: Basic Books.

Brown, Bill. 2003. *A Sense of Things: The Object Matter of American Literature*. Chicago: University of Chicago Press.

Bryant, Levi, Srnicek, Nick, and Harman, Graham. 2011. Towards a Speculative Philosophy. In *The Speculative Turn: Continental Materialism and Realism*, ed. Levi Bryant, Nick Srnicek, and Graham Harman, pp. 1–18. Melbourne: Re.Press.

Buck-Morss, Susan. 1999. *The Dialectics of Seeing: Walter Benjamin and the Arcades Project*. Cambridge, MA: MIT Press.

Burström, Mats, Gustafsson, Anders, and Karlsson, Håkan. 2011. *World Crisis in Ruin: The Archaeology of the Former Soviet Nuclear Missile Sites in Cuba*. Gothenburg: Bricoleur Press.

DeSilvey, Caitlin. 2006. Observed Decay: Telling Stories with Mutable Things. *Journal of Material Culture* 11(3): 318–38.

Durkheim, Émile. 1951. *The Suicide: A Study in Sociology*. New York: Free Press.

Edensor, Timothy. 2005. *Industrial Ruins: Space, Aesthetics and Materiality*. Oxford: Berg.

Falk, Hjalmar and Torp, Alf. 1994 [1906]. *Etymologisk ordbog over det norske og det danske sprog*. Oslo: Bjørn Ringstrøms antikvariat.

Foucault, Michel, 1989. *The Order of Things: An Archaeology of the Human Sciences*, tr. Alan Sheridan. London: Tavistock Publications.

González-Ruibal, Alfredo. 2007. Arqueología simétrica: Un giro teórico sin revolución para-digmática. *Complutum* 18: 283–6.

—— 2008. Time to Destroy: An Archaeology of Supermodernity. *Current Anthropology* 49(2): 247–79.

Gumbrecht, Hans U. 2004. *Production of Presence: What Meaning Cannot Convey*. Stanford: Stanford University Press.

Harman, Graham. 2011. On the Undermining of Objects: Grant, Bruno, and Radical Philosophy. In *The Speculative Turn: Continental Materialism and Realism*, ed. Levi Bryant, Nick Srnicek, and Graham Harman, pp. 21–40. Melbourne: Re.Press.

Harrison, Rodney. 2011. Surface Assemblages: Towards an Archaeology *in* and *of* the Present. *Archaeological Dialogues* 18(2): 141–61.

Heidegger, Martin. 1962. *Being and Time*. New York: Harper & Row.

Huyssen, Andreas. 2003. *Present Pasts: Urban Palimpsests and the Politics of Memory*. Stanford: Stanford University Press.

Jensen, Jens F. and Krause, Tilo. 2012. Wehrmacht Occupations in the New World: Archaeological and Historical Investigations in Northeast Greenland. *Polar Record* 48(3): 269–79.

Jervis, Ben. 2011. A Patchwork of People, Pots and Places: Material Engagements and the Construction of 'the Social' in Hamwic (Anglo-Saxon Southampton), UK. *Journal of Social Archaeology* 11(3): 239–65.

Johnson, Matthew. 2010. *Archaeological Theory: An Introduction*. Oxford: Blackwell.

Kenderdine, Sarah. 2008. The Irreducible Ensemble: Place-Hampi. *The International Journal of Digital Cultural Heritage and E-Tourism (IJDCE)* 1 (2–3): 139–56.

Latour, Bruno. 1991. *Nous n'avons jamais été modernes. Essai d'anthropologie symétrique*. Paris: La Découverte.

—— 1993. *We Have Never Been Modern*. Cambridge, MA: Harvard University Press.

—— 2003. Is Re-modernization Occurring? *Theory, Culture & Society* 20(2): 35–48.

—— 2005. *Reassembling the Social: An Introduction to Actor-Network-Theory*. Oxford: Oxford University Press.

Lucas, Gavin. 2004. Modern Disturbances: On the Ambiguities of Archaeology. *Modernism/ Modernity* 11: 109–20.

—— 2005. *The Archaeology of Time*. London: Routledge.

Nora, Pierre. 1984. Entre mémoire et histoire. La problématique des lieux. In *Les lieux de mémoire*, volume 1: *La République*, ed. Pierre Nora, pp. xv–xlii. Paris: Gallimard.

Olivier, Laurent. 2001. Duration, Memory and the Nature of the Archaeological Record. In *It's About Time: The Concept of Time in Archaeology*, ed. Håkan Karlsson, pp. 61–70. Gothenburg: Bricoleur Press.

—— 2011. *The Dark Abyss of Time: Archaeology and Memory*. Lanham, MD: Altamira Press.

Olsen, Bjørnar. 2003. Material Culture After Text: Remembering Things. *Norwegian Archaeological Review* 36(2): 87–104.

—— 2006 Ting-mennesker-samfunn: Introduksjon til en symmetrisk arkeologi. *Arkæologisk Forum* 14: 13–18.

—— 2007. Keeping Things at Arm's Length: A Genealogy of Asymmetry. *World Archaeology* 39(4): 579–88.

—— 2010. *In Defense of Things: Archaeology and the Ontology of Objects*. Lanham, MD: Altamira Press.

—— 2012. Symmetrical Archacology. In *Archaeological Theory Today*, 2nd edn., ed. Ian Hodder, pp. 208–28. Cambridge: Polity Press.

Olsen, Bjørnar and Svestad, Asgeir. 1994. Creating Prehistory: Archaeology, Museums and the Discourse of Modernism. *Nordisk Museologi* 1: 3–20.

Olsen, Bjørnar, Shanks, Michael, Webmoor, Timothy, and Witmore, Christopher. 2012. *Archaeology: The Discipline of Things*. Berkeley: University of California Press.

Perry, Sara. 2009. Fractured Media: Challenging the Dimensions of Archaeology's Typical Visual Modes of Engagement. *Archaeologies* 5(3): 389–415.

Renfrew, Colin. 1989. Comments. *Norwegian Archaeological Review* 22(1): 33–41.

Riegl, Alois. 1982 [1903]. The Modern Cult of Monuments, tr. K. W. Forster and D. Ghirardo. *Oppositions* 25 (Fall): 21–50.

Schiffer, Michael B. 1976. *Behavioural Archaeology*. New York: Academic Press.

Serres, Michel with Latour, Bruno. 1995. *Conversation on Science, Culture and Time*. Ann Arbor: University of Michigan Press.

Shanks, Michael. 2007. Symmetrical Archaeology. *World Archaeology* 39(4): 589–96.

Webmoor, Timothy. 2007. What about 'One More Turn after the Social' in Archaeological Reasoning? Taking Things Seriously. *World Archaeology* 39(4): 563–78.

Witmore, Christopher. 2004. Four Archaeological Engagements with Place: Mediating Bodily Experience through Peripatetic Video. *Visual Anthropology Review* 20(2): 57–72.

—— 2006. Vision, Media, Noise and the Percolation of Time: Symmetrical Approaches to the Mediation of the Material World. *Journal of Material Culture* 11(3): 267–92.

—— 2007. Symmetrical Archaeology: Excerpts of a Manifesto. *World Archaeology* 39(4): 546–62.

CHAPTER 16

....

AUTHENTICITY

....

PAUL GRAVES-BROWN

16.1 INTRODUCTION

....

IN the summer of 1993, I visited the cave of Lascaux. At the time I had visited many
Perigordian cave sites, but none evoked the visceral reaction I felt in the Hall of Bulls.
A frisson that I still attribute to the fact that this was the real Lascaux, and not the copy.
Nonetheless, in this chapter, I want to argue that the concept of authenticity, which pervades archaeology and heritage, is problematic given the paradoxes it generates. And that
the ways in which this concept is entrained in the contemporary world make these paradoxes particularly salient. As Gilmore and Pine (2007) argue, authenticity is one of the
primary drivers of our 'experience economy', but is pursued in a world that is almost
entirely 'fake'.

Authenticity involves at least three tropes: (i) pragmatic—what things do; (ii) natural—
what things are; and (iii) historical—where or from whom things originate. These can
apply both singly and collectively, to both things and persons, and yet can also contradict one another. At different times these tropes have varied in their apparent importance.
Archaeology is obliged to deal with authenticity; fakes or false attributions necessarily
constitute misinformation. Most archaeological research concerns historical authenticity;
the relationship of material culture to tradition; the biography of individual objects and
sites; and provenance or verification of origin (Jones 2010). However, archaeologies of the
contemporary world confront industrialization, mass production, lived experience, and in
particular the re-evaluation of material culture brought about by the Modernist movement.
Archaeology is the product of modernity (Thomas 2004), but crucially, Modernism is not
just modernity, carrying with it a rejection of the past and tradition in favour of a more
pragmatic stance on authenticity. This rejection of the past might then seem problematic for
archaeology, but as I shall try to demonstrate, it can actually give us a more robust grasp of
authenticity that is, in turn, applicable to archaeology more generally.

FIGURE 16.1 Lead cross from the 'tomb' of King Arthur, Glastonbury Abbey (Paul Graves-Brown, redrawn from Camden 1586)

16.2 THE ROOTS OF AUTHENTICITY

In 1191, the monks of Glastonbury Abbey discovered a log coffin containing two bodies. Above it was a stone slab, on the underside of which was a lead cross (Figure 16.1). This 'discovery' was a forgery motivated by the need to attract pilgrims to the abbey, whose church had burned down in 1184. But what does forgery mean in this context? 'The idea of forgery is a serious need in a belief system predicated upon a clear-cut distinction between what is factually true and what is not; in the middle ages it was no so important' (Pearsall 2003: 12). The tomb of Arthur offered a prestige underwritten by the all-pervasive power of the church, requiring nothing more than faith. The charters of abbeys and monasteries were often 'forged' because whilst they either did not exist, or had been lost, there was a need for them to exist. Similarly, many of the holy relics that circulated around Europe were not 'genuine', but if they displayed some miraculous efficacy, this did not matter (Geary 1986); their authenticity was underwritten by their empirical effect.

The Reformation compromised the power of the church, much as the end of the feudal system challenged temporal power. The centuries of the Renaissance and the Enlightenment marked the emergence of modernity which required different epistemes of value and truth. Where a person's sincerity was no longer guaranteed by family, heredity, or religious status, new ways of establishing trustworthiness were required (Trilling 1972). In the mid-fourteenth century, authentic came to mean 'entitled to acceptance as factual' and 'authoritative'. The usage 'authenticity' does not appear until *ca.* 1650 and seems gradually to have replaced 'sincerity', which had once held a similar meaning (Trilling 1972).

One principal distinction in this 'modern' notion of authenticity is that of individuality in opposition to commonality or, in another sense, commodity (Kopytoff 1986). In mercantile and capitalist societies, a person acts on one's own authority, whilst the social and use value of things is subsumed by their exchange value. Commodities are characterized by sameness, but their authenticity is measured by their purity; it is in their nature and their empirical properties. They are 'unadulterated'. Conversely, individualism implies uniqueness. This is well illustrated in the arts; by the eighteenth century, systems of art dealership involved 'the producer's relative freedom not only from the demands of employers but also from the audience' (Lurie 1993: 22). The artist achieves total individuality, but the work of art became a commodity, although its commodity value depends upon personified provenance in a way that bulk commodities do not.

In the Enlightenment of the eighteenth century, the relationship between the individual and society is further stretched. Rousseau (1992 [1755]: 22) placed the individual in opposition to the corrupt society of eighteenth-century Paris: 'Most of our ills are of our own making, we could have avoided nearly all of them by preserving the simple, regular and solitary lifestyle prescribed to us by nature.' These ideas can be followed through the philosophies of the nineteenth and twentieth centuries. Hegel argued that 'Individual consciousness looks on the power of the state as a chain, as something suppressing its separate, autonomous existence' (Trilling 1972: 35). Nietzsche expressed similar views stating 'become what you are', whilst Heidegger develops another variant of the theme in his emphasis on the finitude of life, a 'narrative account' (Guignon 2004: 134) of authenticity where 'what really matters in the historical situation in which you find yourself and take a resolute stand on pursuing those ends'. How, then, does this individualistic notion of personal authenticity relate to that of material culture?

16.3 Persons and Things

Kopytoff's (1986) analysis of the biography of things draws a series of parallel oppositions. As commodity is opposed to individuality, so things are opposed to persons, the common to the singular, the profane to the sacred. However, as we have already seen, these distinctions do not always hold; a work of art can become a commodity even if it is singular, unique. Similarly, the authenticity of a bulk commodity, such as coffee or tea, can be tied to a specific provenance. The European Union's Protected Designation of Origin covers such things as Champagne, Cheddar cheese, Melton Mowbray pork pies, and Columbian coffee. As Kopytoff himself discusses, persons can be treated as commodities. Equally, whilst the Rousseauian model of the authentic self stresses individuality, authentic persons are judged by tradition and identity. It has at times been seriously argued that white people lack the necessary ethnic baggage to sing the blues (Rudinow 1994). In order to deal with these entanglements, I think the first step is to try to distinguish the different senses in which authenticity applies to persons and things.

It is now a common practice, which we owe in great part to Kopytoff, to talk of things in terms of their biographies. In this context the authenticity of an artefact can be viewed in terms of the continuum of its biography (see Schiffer, this volume). Traditionally, origin is stressed; in fine art the authenticity of a work is established by its firm provenance with a specific artist. In archaeology provenance is established by a physical, spatial findspot, such that the value of 'unprovenanced' finds is compromised. In both cases, things can be subjected to a range of physical and chemical tests to establish dating and origin, emphasizing, as Jones (2010) points out, that the authenticity of an artefact is somehow a natural/intrinsic attribute. At the opposite end of the continuum, whatever their past, artefacts exist in the present; they are still 'about becoming' (see Holtorf 2005). In this context, it may be argued that the authenticity of things is essentially about the construction we place upon them;

the Venetian (hotel and casino) in Las Vegas might seem as authentic, if not more so, than the 'real' Venice (Gilmore and Pine 2007). And why not, given that the 'original' medieval Venice has and continues to undergo change as its biography unfolds?

Following Jones (2010) I see problems with both these extremes. On the one hand, those who believe that things can and should be preserved in a pristine state ignore the fact that change is inevitable and that, ironically, the value or authenticity of things is often in large part a product of the patina they acquire during their life histories (see Ruskin 1920 [1849]). Conversely, the constructivist approach espoused by Holtorf and many others (e.g. Grint and Woolgar 1997; Woolgar 1991; see also Hutchby 2001), ignores the fact that things do have intrinsic properties; their value cannot simply be 'read into' them. 'In the theory of affordances, Gibson challenged the long-standing assumption that quality, meaning and value are unreal, residing solely in the mind of the beholder' (Costall 1995: 468; see also Bruner 1994; Handler and Linnekin 1984). Whilst, in a sense, many affordances have the commodity property of being 'natural'; flat surfaces afford walking, small boulders afford sitting; much of our world consists in the socially constructed; 'Objects have been shaped... through the intentional activities of others; they have a "place" in relation to definite cultural practices and "represent" various human purposes' (Costall 1995: 477). George Herbert Mead (1934; see also Richardson 1989) called artefacts 'collapsed acts', perhaps prefiguring the concept of artefact biography. But more than this, artefacts are made in order to embody action (see de Léon, this volume). Effectively, then, every artefact has a dual biography; its actual life history from the time it was made, and the life history of experience, design, and thought that went into creating that which it affords. In the case of works of art, which are perhaps an exceptional but none the less salient case, their authenticity lies not just in proof of provenance, but also in the vision and skill of the particular artist, which can in part be 'carried over' into reproductions.

> The animals painted on the walls of Lascaux are not there in the same way as the fissures and limestone formations...I would be at great pains to say where is the painting I am looking at....I do not fix it in its place...It is more accurate to say that I *see according to it*, or with it, than that I see it. (Merleau-Ponty 1964: 164, my emphasis)

By contrast, in the contemporary world 'we are not in the position of an archaeologist trying to determine the meaning of a "defunct" object. We experience objects in relation to the community within which they have meaning' (Costall 1995: 471–2). The authenticity of things can only be understood in the context of their pragmatic use in constructing (authentic) persons. A key point here is that people, like artefacts, are 'collapsed acts'. It is just that many if not most of those acts are their own. In the Rousseauian model of the authentic self, truth resides in nature; rock musician Kurt Cobain blamed his suicide on his inability to remain faithful to his true nature under the pressures of the music business (Barker and Taylor 2007). But as in the case of artefacts, this essentialist appeal to nature ignores the fact that people have biographies, or more precisely, autobiographies. It is, perhaps, telling that the written autobiography first appears at the end of the sixteenth century when the individual was first coming to the fore.

The problem with persons is that they have a kind of triple biography: a physical organism that is the product of heredity; the culture they are brought into; and the physically/socially constructed self which changes over time. In this nature/nurture duality lies the essential paradox of Rousseauian authenticity; a person's true nature is only expressed through the actions that develop the self. And in as much as persons are collapsed acts, they are the products of the acts of others as well as their own; as both G. H. Mead and the Russian social constructivists argued, the self is a social product, a result of joint action between the individual and others, such that nature and nurture are indivisible. Here we might wish to argue perversely that the authenticity of the individual can only exist as a social product. In his essay 'Kafka and his Precursors' Borges recounts:

> 'At first I had considered [Kafka] to be as singular as the phoenix of rhetoric praise ... [but] ... I came to think I could recognise his voice ... in texts from diverse literatures and periods.'

After discussing these he concludes:

> 'In each of these texts we find Kafka's idiosyncrasy to a greater or lesser degree, but if Kafka had never written a line, we would not perceive this quality ... The fact is that every writer *creates* his own precursors. His work modifies our conception of the past, as it will modify the future' (Borges 1970 [1964]: 234–6).

Kafka is effectively the historical node which defines what is authentically Kafkaesque.

16.4 Modernity and Modernism

The paradox of both persons and things is that their 'nature' is subject to change, and that they could not be authentically themselves without change. This paradox comes to the fore at the end of the nineteenth century with the emergence of Modernism, in its various forms. As Thomas (2004: 2) writes: 'Modern societies are unusual in recognising their own material and social conditions as being unlike those of the past.' Yet until the late nineteenth century, modernity still measured itself against tradition. Architectural neo-Classicism drew its authority from Greek and Roman architecture. Similarly the neo-Gothic looked to medieval tradition for its values. The architect Louis B. Sullivan was perhaps the first to break with this sense of tradition with his Chicago Stock Exchange building (1894) and the iconic Prudential building in Buffalo. Although new materials such as concrete and steel were widely used in late nineteenth-century architecture, most buildings (e.g. London's Tower Bridge) clothed themselves in a façade of traditional style. Sullivan (1896) rejected the styles of the past in favour of a 'truth' to the new materials, believing that 'form follows function'. The subsequent history of architecture in the twentieth century can then be seen as a struggle between this formalism, later expressed in works by the Bauhaus and Mies van der Rohe, and styles which either softened the Modernist message (Art Deco) or rejected it in favour of new extremes of classicism, as in the work of Albert Speer or Soviet era Stalinist Gothic.

A similar questioning or rejection of tradition can be traced in the visual arts. Since authentic representation was rendered largely obsolete by photography (again, the effect of new materials) the art of Picasso or Modigliani no longer needed to offer a 'true' likeness. Modernism's break with traditional notions of authenticity is perhaps best exemplified in the work of Marcel Duchamp. It seems unclear whether Duchamp ever intended that his ready-mades should be considered as 'works of art' as opposed to simply being objects chosen because they were interesting. The 'Fountain' of 1917; a porcelain urinal signed 'R. Mutt', was probably submitted for exhibition as a joke (Cros 2006). Rejected for exhibition, it became a cause célèbre through the magazine *The Blind Man* (Roche et al. 1917); shortly afterwards the actual artefact disappeared, possibly discarded as were most of the original 'ready-mades'. None the less you can now visit the Tate Modern in London, the Museums of Modern Art in New York, San Francisco, and Paris, and various other locations and see 'Duchamp's Fountain' in all of them. Or rather one or other of twelve officially sanctioned replicas. Most of the other ready-mades currently on display are also replicas. In a sense these resemble medieval 'fakes', created because they ought to exist. Yet the Modernism of Duchamp is a revolt against authenticity, both in terms of the artefact and the self. 'Duchamp adamantly asserted that he wanted to "de-deify" the artist' (Saltz 2006).

Finally, in the case of the written word, Modernism also signals a rejection both of tradition and the self. The written word was not originally attributed to an author (Barthes 1967); the author-ity of sacred texts, etc. came from God in the same way as the authority of sacred relics and the tomb of King Arthur. Conversely, author-ity emerges in literature in reference to classical sources (much as this chapter has references) and, as Foucault (1977) argues, in the ascription of responsibility to an author; a named author could be punished for subversion. As with the development of art as a commodity in the eighteenth century, so writers also became a commodity both through journalism and in the emergence of the novel. Yet, as Barthes (1967) suggests, Modernist writers such as Mallarmé and Valéry sought to subvert the author function, whilst Thomas Mann used the 'fallible narrator' to question the author-ity of the author.

In scientific writing, this death of the author can be traced back to the empiricism of Roger Bacon; the rejection of traditional validation of fact in favour of experiment (see Thomas 2004). As Foucault (1977) argues, the attribution of scientific principle, be it Euclid's geometry or Heisenberg's uncertainty principle, becomes almost entirely formal, since the validation of science lies in praxis. In science, as in art, architecture, and literature, Modernist values stress what things empirically are, rather than their place in a tradition or even their authorship. On the one hand this might be construed in terms of the intrinsic 'nature' mentioned above; that science assumed that the authenticity of things lies within them. Yet in point of fact both science and the arts entertain an ambiguity; quantum physics necessitates the involvement of the observer in the observed, whilst in art, be it Duchamp's ready-mades or the use of sampling in music, creativity becomes about choice and discrimination, rather than origination (see Reynolds 2011). In effect, Modernism is not about the realist representation of nature, it is about things being experientially real in themselves (Orvill 1989).

16.5 The Dreams All Made Real

Marinetti and the Futurists represent the most extreme rejection of the past as a locus for the authentic (Banham 1960; Marinetti 1909). Calling for the destruction of museums and libraries, Marinetti specifically mocked John Ruskin and 'his nostalgia for Homeric cheeses and legendary wool-winders' (Marinetti 2005 [1910/1915]). In their embrace of the excitement of new technologies, the Futurists embody the sense in which the twentieth and twenty-first centuries have abandoned the validation of the past in favour of a faith in experience and novelty (see Sheller, this volume). Indeed this goes beyond the reference to either tradition or nature as a measure of the authentic, in that, as Eco (1998 [1986]: 44) says of the 'hyperreal', 'Disneyland tells us that technology can give us more reality than nature can.'

The future we have arrived at is characterized by a sense in which the real is unreal and the unreal real. The airports and shopping centres of the contemporary world as 'non-places' (Augé 1995; see also Relph 1987), and much of the 'experience economy' described by

FIGURE 16.2 Ripley's Believe It or Not, Fisherman's Wharf, San Francisco (photograph: Paul Graves-Brown)

Eco (1998 [1986]: 31) share this sense of unreality: 'the Absolute fake is offspring of the unhappy awareness of a present without depth'. The places of Modernism do not just incorporate the rejection of the past, they have no past: 'The authenticity that Ripley's museums advertise is not historical, but visual. Everything looks real and therefore it is real' (Eco 1998 [1986]: 31; Figure 16.2). This ambiguity is complemented by Baudrillard's (1995) hyperreality of simulation; where so much of life is conducted through electronic media, we experience what Giddens (1991) calls 'reality inversion' where remote 'content' appears more real than embodied experience. Or, as in the case of Eco's absolute fakes, the simulation of reality becomes more real to us than reality itself.

The Sherlock Holmes Museum in Baker Street, London, is a case in point of the permeability of reality (Figure 16.3). Opened in 1990, the museum has its own, self-created, blue plaque claiming the location of 221b Baker Street, and may well be the first museum housing artefacts 'belonging' to a fictional character. In point of fact, 221 Baker Street did not exist in the 1890s when Conan Doyle was writing for the *Strand Magazine*, and the museum is actually between numbers 237 and 241 of an extended Baker Street that came into existence after the Second World War. Until 2002 the actual street number was part of the headquarters of the Abbey National Building Society, which had, for many years, received letters addressed to the consulting detective. Holmes, then, represents a character from Baudrillard's domain of simulation, the subject of numerous films, TV shows, and even computer games, who has been given a real world locus, stocked with memorabilia of his fictional life.

In effect, the Sherlock Holmes Museum is a modern equivalent of the tomb of King Arthur, much as Eco sees many of the hyperreal sites he visited as the equivalent of

FIGURE 16.3 The Sherlock Holmes Museum, Baker Street, London (photograph: Paul Graves-Brown)

medieval cabinets of curiosities. He suggests that, with respect to the modern examples 'the difference lies in the more casual attitude to the problem of authenticity' (1998 [1986]: 16). Rather, I suggest, it is a question of changing criteria for the basis of authenticity. Medieval authenticity depended upon faith; medieval texts were not authored but came from God. In what we might call pre-Modernist modernity, authenticity derived from sincerity, either through reference back to tradition or through a claim to a natural purity. In late modernity, authenticity is an experiential function; what seems to be real, uncorrupted, or unmediated appears to be genuine (Bolter and Grusin 1998). Whilst in one sense this might be seen as the constructivism discussed above, it is perhaps better equated with the empiricist logic of science; reality and authenticity are not judged against standards sacred or profane, but are empirically tested.

16.6 DIFFERENT AND ORIGINAL LIKE EVERYBODY ELSE

Where modern, pragmatic authenticity differs from that of the Middle Ages is in its emphasis on novelty. According to Oscar Wilde (1891), 'The first duty in life is to be as artificial as possible' and also that 'Lying, the telling of beautiful untrue things, is the proper aim of Art.' In the context of the experience economy 'Businesses can render their inauthentic offerings as authentic. Doing so requires embracing this essential paradox: all human enterprise is ontologically fake—that is, in its very being it is inauthentic—and yet, output from that enterprise can be phenomenologically real' (Gilmore and Pine 2007: 89). The term 'original' is paradoxical; for Wilde, art had to be judged by its originality, and yet original also implies an ontology of tradition.

The answer to the paradox lies in the power of persons to *originate*, to create, as Borges says, their own precursors, such that novelty cannot be traced to a particular locus and hence its authenticity is difficult, if not impossible to evaluate. This problem is clear in the *Nara Document on Authenticity* which supplements the *UNESCO Charter of Venice*. 'It is . . . not possible to base judgements of values and authenticity within fixed criteria. On the contrary, the respect due to all cultures requires that heritage properties must considered and judged within the cultural contexts to which they belong' (UNESCO 1994). This formulation derives from the need to accommodate non-Western cultures which do not reify fixed monuments, but can equally apply to 'modern' societies.

Indeed, in contemporary society, the desire for novelty and originality leads to a rejection of authenticity based on tradition. Post-Second World War consumers became dissatisfied with the plenitude of standardized commodities; they needed the sense of 'added value' contributed by experiences that were different (Southgate 2003), a means of establishing their individuality in a world of mass production. This has most clearly manifested in anti-establishment and counter-cultural movements including Rock and Roll, 1960s Hippies, Punk, Hip-Hop, and electronic dance music. Each arose as an opposition to social norms, but at the same time came to assert its own canon of authenticity. In more general terms, this counter-cultural disdain for mainstream society is summed up by the term 'cool', which has its origins in Afro-American reactions to racism and segregation (Frank 1997; Pountain and Robins 2000).

The problem is, as we have seen in the case of fine art, that the original can itself become a commodity. Since the late 1990s (if not indeed the 1920s, see Riesman 1950: 158), this has manifested in the phenomenon of 'coolhunting': the deliberate search for novelty conducted by big-business and market researchers in the effort to attach coolness to corporate brands (Frank 1997; Gladwell 1997; Southgate 2003; McGuigan 2012). The paradox as ever is that once that which is cool has been commoditized, it rapidly ceases to be cool, and the search must begin again (Nuttall 1968; Melly 1989). Whilst in the early modern era, people struggled to establish their sincerity in terms of belonging to society, it has now become difficult to establish that you do not belong.

16.7 ACCENTUATE THE POSITIVE

Archaeology's traditional concern with ruins means that we unthinkingly seek them out in the contemporary world (see Harrison 2011). Our concepts of authenticity accentuate this, stressing tradition and the past as the locus of value, and making the modern and the novel intrinsically inferior. But as I have sought to demonstrate, these ideas are fraught with contradiction and paradox. It is ironic that both Adolf Loos, the prophet of Modernism, and John Ruskin, the champion of Gothic, could conceive of the past as offering corruption, stagnation, and sterility. Ruskin, whilst praising the virility of medieval architecture, saw the neo-Classical as a dead end and even equated it with the industrialization he hated (Ruskin

1981 [1851–3]). The copying of Classical models made 'plagiarists of its architects, slaves of its workmen', and hence they were no better than the factories turning out mass-produced goods. For Loos (2002 [1908]: 32), by contrast, the elaboration and decoration that characterized the neo-Gothic, and other late nineteenth-century styles, was degenerate, primitive, and backward looking; 'Those who measure everything by the past impede the cultural development of nations and of humanity itself.' Rather than freeing the creativity of the worker, elaborate work was wasted effort, for the 'Modern man... His own inventions are concentrated on other things'.

Both Ruskin and Loos are moderns. As Jones (2010) points out, Ruskin, although one of the founders of the conservation movement, believed that ageing, 'The Lamp of Memory', was an essential part of 'voicefullness... walls that have been long washed by the passing waves of humanity' (Ruskin 1920 [1849]: 195). But here is the danger in eliding modernity and Modernism; whilst Ruskin embraced creativity inspired by the past, the likes of Loos and Sullivan rejected the past out of hand. Yet the Modernist project remains unrealized; the 'modern' world is still composed of and depends upon the past (Edgerton 2006). Rather than a Modernist, or perhaps more precisely Futurist world, we inhabit what Eco (perhaps with his tongue in his cheek) calls a new Middle Ages, an eclectic, multi-vocal culture in which attitudes to authenticity resemble those of the monks of Glastonbury.

It might be countered that the work of art possesses a unique 'aura' (Benjamin 1999 [1968]); a view which echoes Ruskin's hatred of mechanical reproduction. But in fact it can be argued that the products of mass manufacture have an aura all of their own. Frank Lloyd Wright and Walter Gropius saw no contradiction between the aims of art and craft and mechanization. Indeed Wright (1901) anticipates Marinetti in his celebration of the machine, pointing out among other things that printing was not the death, but the rebirth of the written word. Modernists saw mechanization as the democratization of aesthetics, a process that came to fruition in the 'popular Modernism' (Pountain and Robins 2000) of the post-Second World War era; '[a] Coke is a Coke and no amount of money can get you a better Coke than the one the bum on the corner is drinking' (Warhol 2007 [1975]: 100–1).

Pop art, pop music, and pop culture are a machine aesthetic. The 'aura' of every CD recording is identical to the original (Graves-Brown 2009). The argument that modernity aims to eliminate heterogeneity and hybridity (Latour 1993) assumes that homogeneity lacks life and creativity. Yet as we have seen, commodities can still be considered 'authentic', in the sense of being pure or unadulterated. And by contrast the heterogeneous can be equally sterile. The passing fashion for the post-modern, which was perhaps neither post nor modern, saw an embrace in architecture and the arts of the eclecticism which Eco discusses. But in a very real sense this period represented the kind of sterility that Ruskin perceived in the neo-Classical; an 'End of History', not the beginning of anything genuinely novel.

Where does this leave me with Lascaux? In one sense I would have to accept that as an exact copy, Lascaux II has the same 'aura' as the original. In Merleau-Ponty's (1964) terms, looking at the copy it is still possible to 'see according to' the vision of the prehistoric 'artists'. But on the other hand there is a nagging sense that the 'real' cave paintings offer a visceral connection with their creators. It can be argued that the proliferation of holy relics in the Middle Ages was a consequence of the inaccessibility of the Holy Land, that relics offered a physical link to Jerusalem. Perhaps this sense of 'magical contagion' applies to all constructions of authenticity (Evans et al. 2002). The essential problem for students of the contemporary past is that mass production turns authenticity into a property of commodities;

one Coke bottle or can is as authentic as any other. In this context, magical contagion is experienced pragmatically; it can be constructed or invented, as in the case of the Sherlock Holmes Museum. Conversely, the limits of Modernism are that we can neither escape the past nor indeed live in it. The life histories of the material culture around us embed us in the past (see Olivier, this volume) and the extent to which we can construct the past is defined by the materials that it provides us with: 'every writer creates his own precursors'. But none the less the new can emerge from the bricolage of the past, because persons are not simply, as artefacts are, the collapsed acts of the past, but are actors in their own right.

REFERENCES

Augé, Marc. 1995. *Non-Places: Introduction to an Anthropology of Supermodernity.* London: Verso.

Banham, Reyner. 1960. *Theory and Design in the First Machine Age.* London: Architectural Press.

Barker, Hugh and Taylor, Yuval. 2007. *Faking It: The Quest for Authenticity in Popular Music.* London: Faber and Faber.

Barthes, Roland. 1967. The Death of the Author. In *Aspen*, vols. 5–6, ed. Brian O'Doherty. New York: Roaring Fork Press. Available at: <http://www.ubu.com/aspen/aspen5and6/three Essays.html#barthes> (accessed 17 January 2013).

Baudrillard, Jean. 1995. *Simulacra and Simulation.* Ann Arbor: University of Michigan Press.

Benjamin, Walter. 1999 [1968]. *Illuminations*, ed. and introd. Hannah Arendt. London: Pimlico.

Bolter, J. David and Grusin, Richard. 1998. *Remediation: Understanding New Media.* Cambridge, MA: MIT Press.

Borges, Jorge L. 1970. *Labyrinths.* Harmondsworth: Penguin.

Bruner, Edward M. 1994. Abraham Lincoln as Authentic Reproduction: A Critique of Postmodernism. *American Anthropologist* 962: 397–415.

Costall, Alan. 1995. Socializing Affordances. *Theory and Psychology* 54: 467–81.

Cros, Caroline. 2006. *Marcel Duchamp.* London: Reaktion Books.

Eco, Umberto. 1998 [1986]. *Faith in Fakes: Travels in Hyperreality.* London: Vintage.

Edgerton, David. 2006. *The Shock of the Old: Technology and Global History since 1900.* London: Profile Books.

Evans, E. Margaret, Mull, Melinda S., and Poling, Devereaux A. 2002. The Authentic Object? A Child's-Eye View. In *Perspectives on Object-Centred Learning in Museums*, ed. S. G. Paris, pp. 55–77. London: Lawrence Erlbaum Associates.

Foucault, Michel. 1977. What is an Author? tr. Donald F. Bouchard and Sherry Simon. In *Language, Counter-Memory, Practice*, pp. 124–7. Ithaca, NY: Cornell University Press.

Frank, Thomas. 1997. *The Conquest of Cool.* Chicago: University of Chicago Press.

Geary, Patrick. 1986. Sacred Commodities: The Circulation of Medieval Relics. In *The Social Life of Things: Commodities in Cultural Perspective*, ed. Arjun Appadurai, pp. 169–94. Cambridge: Cambridge University Press.

Giddens, Anthony. 1991. *Modernity and Self-Identity: Self and Society in the Late Modern Age.* Stanford: Stanford University Press.

Gilmore, James and Pine, Joseph. 2007. *Authenticity. What Consumers Really Want.* Boston, MA: Harvard Business School Press.

Gladwell, Malcolm. 1997. The Coolhunt. *The New Yorker*, 17 March. Available at: <http://www.gladwell.com/1997/1997_03_17_a_cool.htm> (accessed 17 January 2013).

Graves-Brown, Paul. 2009. Nowhere Man: Urban Life and the Virtualisation of Popular Music. *Popular Music History* 4(2): 220–41.

Grint, Keith and Woolgar, Steve. 1997. *The Machine at Work*. Cambridge: Polity Press.

Guignon, Charles. 2004. *On Being Authentic*. London: Routledge.

Handler, Richard and Linnekin, Jocelyn. 1984. Tradition, Genuine or Spurious. *Journal of American Folklore* 97(385): 273–90.

Harrison, Rodney. 2011. Surface Assemblages: Towards an Archaeology *in* and *of* the Present. *Archaeological Dialogues* 182: 141–61.

Holtorf, Cornelius. 2005. *From Stonehenge to Las Vegas: Archaeology as Popular Culture*. Oxford: Altamira.

Hutchby, Ian. 2001. Technologies, Texts and Affordances. *Sociology* 352: 441–56.

Jones, Sîan. 2010. Negotiating Authentic Objects and Authentic Selves: Beyond the Deconstruction of Authenticity. *Journal of Material Culture* 152: 181–203.

Kopytoff, Igor. 1986. The Cultural Biography of Things: Commoditization as Process. In *The Social Life of Things: Commodities in Cultural Perspective*, ed. Arjun Appadurai, pp. 64–94. Cambridge: Cambridge University Press.

Latour, Bruno. 1993 *We Have Never Been Modern*. London: Prentice-Hall.

Loos, Adolf. 2002 [1908]. Ornament and Crime. In *Crime and Ornament: The Arts and Popular Culture in the Shadow of Adolf Loos*, ed. Bernie Miller and Melony Ward, pp. 29–36. Toronto: XYZ Books.

Lurie, Celia. 1993. *Cultural Rights: Technology, Legality and Personality*. London: Routledge.

McGuigan, Jim. 2012. The Coolness of Capitalism Today. *TripleC* 10(2): 425–38. Available at: <http://www.triple-c.at> (accessed 13 June 2012).

Marinetti, Filippo T. 1909. The Founding and the Manifesto of Futurism. *Gazzetta dell'Emilia Bologna*, 5 February, pp. 1–2.

—— 2005 [1910/1915]. Futurist speech to the English. In *Modernism: An Anthology*, ed. L. Rainey, pp. 6–9. Oxford: Oxford University Press.

Mead, George H. 1934. *Mind, Self and Society*. Chicago: University of Chicago Press.

Melly, George. 1989. *Revolt into Style: Pop Arts in the 50s and 60s*. Oxford: Oxford University Press.

Merleau-Ponty, Maurice. 1964. *The Primacy of Perception*, tr. Carleton Dallery. Seattle: Northwestern University Press.

Nuttall, Jeff. 1968. *Bomb Culture*. London: MacGibbon & Kee.

Orvill, Miles. 1989. *The Real Thing: Imitation and Authenticity in American Culture 1880–1940*. London: University of North Carolina Press.

Pearsall, Derek. 2003. Forging Truth in Medieval England. In *Cultures of Forgery: Making Nations, Making Selves*, ed. Judith Ryan and Alfred Thomas, pp. 3–24. London: Routledge.

Pountain, Dick and Robins, David. 2000. *Cool Rules: Anatomy of an Attitude*. London: Reaktion Books.

Relph, Edward. 1987. *The Modern Urban Landscape: 1880 to the Present*. Baltimore: Johns Hopkins University Press.

Reynolds, Simon. 2011. *Retromania: Pop Culture's Addiction to its Own Past*. London: Faber and Faber.

Richardson, Miles. 1989. The Artefact as Abbreviated Act: A Social Interpretation of Material Culture. In *The Meaning of Things*, ed. Ian Hodder, pp. 172–7. London: HarperCollins.

Riesman, David, Glazer, Nathan, and Denney, Reuel. 1950. *The Lonely Crowd*. London: Yale University Press.

Roche, Henri-Pierre, Wood, Beatrie, and Duchamp, Marcel (eds.). 1917. *The Blind Man* 2. Available at: <http://sdrc.lib.uiowa.edu/dada/blindman/index.htm> (accessed 3 January 2012).

Rousseau, Jean-Jacques. 1992 [1755]. *Discourse on the Origin of Inequality*, tr. Donald A. Cress. Indianapolis: Hackett Publishing.

Rudinow, Joel. 1994. Race, Ethnicity, Expressive Authenticity: Can White People Sing the Blues? *The Journal of Aesthetics and Art Criticism* 521 (The Philosophy of Music): 127–37.

Ruskin, John. 1920 [1849]. *The Seven Lamps of Architecture*. London: Dent.

—— 1981 [1851–3]. *The Stones of Venice*, ed. Jan Morris. London: Faber and Faber.

Saltz, Jerry. 2006. Idol Thoughts: The Glory of Fountain, Marcel Duchamp's Ground-Breaking 'moneybags piss pot'. *Village Voice*, 21 February. Available at: <http://www.villagevoice.com/2006-02-21/art/idol-thoughts/> (accessed 17 January 2013).

Southgate, Nicholas. 2003. Coolhunting with Aristotle. *International Journal of Market Research* 45(2): 167–89.

Sullivan, Louis B. 1896. The Tall Office Building Artistically Considered. *Lippincott's Magazine* 57 (March): 403–9.

Thomas, Julian. 2004. *Archaeology and Modernity*. London: Routledge.

Trilling, Lionel. 1972. *Sincerity and Authenticity*. London: Oxford University Press.

UNESCO. 1994. *Nara Document on Authenticity*. Available at: <http://whc.unesco.org/archive/nara94.htm> (accessed 17 January 2013).

Warhol, Andy. 2007 [1975]. *The Philosophy of Andy Warhol*. Harmondsworth: Penguin.

Wilde, Oscar. 1891. The Decay of Lying. In *Intentions*. London: Dodd Mead.

Woolgar, Steve. 1991. Configuring the User: The Case of Usability Trials. In *A Sociology of Monsters: Essays on Power, Technology and Domination*, ed. John Law, pp. 57–102. London: Routledge.

Wright, Frank L. 1901. The Art and Craft of the Machine. An address by Frank Lloyd Wright to the Chicago Arts and Crafts Society, at Hull House, 6 March.

CHAPTER 17

....

SECTARIANISM

....

LAURA MCATACKNEY

17.1 INTRODUCTION

....

THE internecine conflict in Northern Ireland, colloquially known as 'the Troubles', is broadly agreed to have begun in the late 1960s and ended with the signing and ratifying of the Belfast Agreement (hereafter 'the Agreement') in 1998. A low-level guerrilla war, it was one of the longest running conflicts in post-Second World War Western Europe with over 3,600 people killed (McKitterick et al. 1999), over 40,000 injured. Estimates suggest that almost half of the province's population personally knew a casualty of the conflict (Fitzduff and O'Hagan 2000). Over 25,000 people (predominantly men) were imprisoned due to paramilitary offences, an extraordinary figure compared to the pre-Troubles prison population of less than 700 (Purbrick 2004: 91). The societal turmoil that such an extended period of civil unrest created is difficult to overestimate, but it has been suggested that it caused 'nothing less than the political fracturing of Northern Ireland' (Fraser 2000: 47). Whilst the Northern Irish conflict and peace process is important in a European context, it has wider resonance as a global case study in understanding long-standing, intra-state conflict due to its form and longevity (see Moshenska, this volume). As Eric Hobsbawm has argued, the proliferation of this form of conflict—sectarian and small group insurgencies—is rewriting our understandings of contemporary warfare beyond traditional distinctions between 'war' and 'peace' as mobilized by nation states (2007).

Defining an 'abnormal' society such as evidenced by the Northern Irish Troubles can take a distinctly material approach. Militarized landscapes, government buildings, commercial zones, and even residential housing are frequently used as indicators of the existence of conflict. My conception of an archaeological approach to exploring the period of transition from conflict to peace in Northern Ireland is to dissect the changing appearance, function, and role of materializations of conflict in the immediate post-conflict context. Such research can have broader resonance, through actively engaging with the artefacts of war that become *de facto* 'normal' in a conflict situation and exploring how they are used and conceptualized in a transitional society. A central aspect of this research is to explore whether materializations of conflict are ignored, actively engaged with, and/or conform to political rhetoric about 'peace dividends'.

17.2 SITUATING THE NORTHERN IRISH TROUBLES

The Troubles are often presented as fundamentally about the incompatible desires of opposed nationalisms and their associated identities: Catholic versus Protestant, Nationalist versus Unionist, and Republican versus Loyalist. However, the conflict was more complex and any attempt to understand it needs to move beyond the 'two community thesis' (Vaughan-Williams 2006). In particular, the intermixing of religion with politics, the roles of class and gender within paramilitary groupings—as well as their wider communities— should be considered alongside the degrees of complicity of the general public in explaining the longevity of the conflict.

In 1998 the major political parties in Northern Ireland, with high-profile inputs from the governments of Great Britain, the Republic of Ireland, and the United States of America, agreed to a new political consensus for the province, which was ratified by referendum in Northern Ireland and the Republic of Ireland. However, the centrality of compromise was not necessarily a sign of change as much as pragmatism: 'events made it clear that first preferences were unattainable, at least in the short term' (McGarry 2001: 118). Now, over a decade later, the chance to critically assess how this political compromise has materially impacted on the lived experiences of 'peace' can be attempted.

Unsurprisingly, urban working-class areas were most severely impacted by the conflict, particularly the most vulnerable in society—working-class women and children (Muldoon 2004: 454). As Fay, Morrissey, and Smyth have stated: 'There has not been one uniform conflict in Northern Ireland, rather the Troubles are a mosaic of different types of conflict. Accordingly, the "reality" of the Troubles is different for people in different locations and in different occupations' (1999: 136). This chapter examines the material realities and lived experience of the places most impacted by the Troubles in the post-conflict context as a critique of high-level political agreements and the ascendancy of 'working-class' parties (with the DUP eclipsing the UUP for Unionists and Sinn Féin overtaking the SDLP for Nationalists) since the Agreement.

17.3 POST-CONFLICT NORTHERN IRELAND AND CONTEMPORARY ARCHAEOLOGY

Whilst oral and written communications of local and national government as well as paramilitary and community leaders have been studied widely by commentators and academics, the material realities of ordinary, lived experience in Northern Ireland have largely been ignored. Of course there are exceptions, with the work of Neil Jarman (1993, 1997, 1998; Jarman and O'Halloran 2001), Frederick Boal (1994, 2002), Brian Graham (Ashworth and Graham 2005), Sara McDowell (2008a, 2008b; Graham and McDowell 2007), and Elizabeth Crooke (2005) being particularly important explorations of material aspects of conflict and post-conflict Northern Ireland. These analyses and perspectives have been valuable in highlighting the public displays and memory of the Troubles; however, there has been no overt attempt to articulate a material critique of the ongoing peace process.

Archaeological approaches to studying the transition from 'war' to (relative) 'peace' has the potential to reveal a complexity that is frequently ignored by the media and politicians. Contemporary archaeology has undergone a notable shift in recent years from embracing laissez-faire 'archaeologies of us' to more engaged and politically sensitive contemporary subject areas (see Fewster, this volume). Whether in archaeologies of labour relations (Beaudry and Mrozowski 2001), homelessness (Zimmerman et al. 2010; Zimmerman, this volume), council house living (Buchli and Lucas 2001; Harrison 2009), or anti-nuclear protests (Schofield and Anderton 2000), it has been demonstrated that we are not simply limited to dig, record, and describe. As James Symonds (2010) has argued,

> we need to challenge taken-for-granted assumptions about modern life head on, and through community engagement, and with a focus on high-profile contemporary concerns such as the nature of conflict, consumerism, poverty, and environmental sustainability.

Contemporary archaeology holds appropriate methodologies and theories to allow understanding of how post-conflict Northern Ireland, as lived by many of its inhabitants, contradicts the political promises of the peace process.

17.4 MATERIAL APPROACHES TO A PEACE PROCESS

In contrast to the traditional archaeological presumption that we are dealing with events that are completed, finished, and even forgotten, this material exploration, focusing on 'the present and its surfaces' (Harrison 2011: 153), aims to explore artefacts, structures, and landscapes that remain overtly present and active in social life. In exploring the negotiations of the present we can encounter messiness, erratic changes in meaning, intention, and action that remind us that the past that feeds into this present is similarly multiple, unfinished, and uncertain. Often, our conclusions will be at best tentative and at worst quickly redundant, but these material explorations can highlight ongoing inequalities and ignored lived realities that may be in the process of resolving but can often remain overlooked.

In order to archaeologically explore whether the peace process is reflected in the material reality of society, we must first present its underlying political rhetoric. The 'Declaration of Support' states that: '...we firmly dedicate ourselves to the achievement of reconciliation, tolerance, and mutual trust...' (the Agreement 1998: 1). To test such an aspiration archaeologically, the first step is to highlight a number of material signifiers of the violence and abnormal social relations associated with the conflict and then investigate any transformations in form, context, and/or meaning following in the wake of the Agreement.

Once material manifestations of conflict and abnormal societal relationships were identified, field walking was undertaken to explore the sites and their wider landscape settings over an extended period of time. Material changes to the structures, sites, and environments—both lasting and ephemeral—were located, noted, and photographically recorded over a number of years to create a constantly updated record of post-conflict landscapes of the Troubles. Such an approach provides a spatial and temporal depth to facilitate understanding of how the predominantly urban environment has been shaped as a result of the official cessation of conflict and initiation of a peace process.

The chapter headings of the Agreement highlight potential inclusions: 'Decommissioning', 'Security', 'Policing and Justice', and 'Prisoners' alongside the 'removal of security installations' (2008: 25). Security installations include prominent civic and military buildings such as police stations, courthouses, army barracks, and prisons, but also less tangible elements such as semi-permanent vehicle and pedestrian barriers and checkpoints. The exclusion of 'peace lines' from the Agreement—the euphemism used to describe the semi-permanent walls placed between antagonistic working-class, urban communities that appeared during the conflict—is telling in the lack of high-level political engagement with the more subtle and less overtly militaristic materialities of conflict. This examination highlights examples of security installations, prisons, and peace lines so as to include two elements explicitly referenced in the Agreement and one that is unmentioned.

17.5 SECURITY INSTALLATIONS

Security infrastructure associated with the conflict in Northern Ireland has been a prominent feature in both rural and urban landscapes since the late 1960s. Despite ebbs and flows in the ferocity of the violence, temporary constructions became increasingly permanent with the progression of the conflict. It is not hyperbolic to suggest that the conflict has had 'a profound effect on cultural landscapes' (McDowell 2008b: 406), most noticeable through the creation of militarized zones, murals, and memorials that not only create but maintain so-called 'sectarian geographies' (Reid 2004: 103). Increasingly 'place identity' (Reid 2004) in Northern Ireland has involved overtly political forms that are not only used to display (or claim) identity and loyalty to internal communities but also act as marks of defiance and warning to external audiences. Whilst this relationship between place and identity has been used to explore localized, unofficial use and meaning of place (see Reid 2004 and McDowell 2008a), this section will act as a counterpoint by examining official interactions.

During the course of the Troubles, police stations became extensive fortresses, prominent army bases were implanted in strategic locations and even police vehicles evolved to heavily fortified 'Saracens'—armoured personnel carriers (APCs)—patrolling the streets. Where new security installations were imposed in communities that were fundamentally opposed to their presence, they were often implanted overnight. They were inserted into strategic locations with little care for the reception of their new neighbours or the extreme levels of overt surveillance that they facilitated. Some districts, such as working-class Nationalist areas of West Belfast, were under constant surveillance and any public buildings—including libraries and leisure centres—were heavily fortified with access tightly monitored. Those who lived in public housing tower blocks found their roofs closed to the inhabitants and covered with lights and cameras to survey the surroundings areas. This high level of security and surveillance could fluctuate over time, but with multiple elements often simultaneously in place they heightened the sense of particular landscapes being war-zones. Those who lived in affluent, residential middle class areas—regardless of perceived religious or political perspective—were largely untroubled by these presences.

The immediate post-conflict context saw a significant reduction in the form, scale, and number of these security installations. Barriers and checkpoints that had created a 'ring of steel' around commercial districts of towns and cities in the province since the 1970s

(McKitterick 1992) quickly disappeared. Not until the mid-2000s were heavily fortified security structures in Nationalist areas removed. In 'flashpoint' areas, on the interfaces between opposing communities, secured zones were usually pared down but continued to exist, with some being replaced by less overtly militaristic models as the years extended post-Agreement. However short or protracted the period between the Agreement and removal, disposal often mirrored the original processes of erection: the majority were closed, remodelled or demolished with little consultation with their immediate neighbours or facilitated access to the sites. Whilst the authorities have often stressed that the complete demolition of security installations was a health and safety issue, relating to decontamination of sites (see Maze Consultation Panel 2005), they have exhibited little concern for recording, preserving, or more importantly allowing public interaction with these remnants of conflict.

A number of high-profile sites connected to the conflict were officially and very publicly transferred from the United Kingdom government to the Office of First Minister and Deputy First Minister (OFMDFM) in May 2002. Although presented as a peace dividend, the material transformation of these sites became increasingly important to the media and general public, as pressure was placed on the newly installed devolved government to decide how they would be used. Recording at these sites has evidenced how few of them have actually been truly materially transformed. With the exception of those located in commercial locations—such as an army base on the affluent Malone Road—most have not been helped by their marginal location. More typically, after the security infrastructure has been removed, the cleared site would be fenced with signage proclaiming its status as a 'Regeneration Zone' being the only standing structure. These Regeneration Zones effectively create physical voids that materially represent the cessation of overt violent conflict, rather than a movement towards peace, reconciliation, and reconnections amongst the broader population.

However, the lack of official regeneration does not mean that such places always remain static entities. A Regeneration Zone located on Lanark Way, in the working-class Loyalist Shankill Road area close to the interface with the Nationalist Springfield Road, shows repeated evidence of interventions since its clearance and recategorization. The unofficial reuse of this Regeneration Zone is not a coincidence: place identity is important in Northern Ireland and central to the desire of both communities to maintain what is conceived as 'a natural and indisputable belonging in place' (Reid 2004: 103). Friction and violence—as well as performances of identity—between and within communities frequently take place at these interfaces. This particular Regeneration Zone cyclically becomes the home of the annual '11th night' bonfire—a climatic event in the Loyalist calendar that commemorates a perceived 'Protestant' victory at the Battle of the Boyne in 1690. The importance of this event is difficult to define precisely, but it remains popular, being simultaneously 'political, religious and carnivalesque' (Bryan 1994: 41). In preparation for the bonfire the Regeneration Zone becomes openly active: the site is filled with bonfire materials, its official signage is despoiled, and the sheet-metal fencing becomes a notice-board. Alongside graffiti detailing bonfire-related directions anti-immigrant sentiments appear: 'C[ombat]-18 rules' and 'No trampy imigrants [sic]' (Figure 17.1) and are actively contested through graffiti sabotage. Such interactions identify the site as a cyclically active community place where conceptions of historic identity and contemporary meanings are continually negotiated.

The removal of security installations in the immediate aftermath of the Agreement was heralded as a 'move to normalisation' (*Irish News*, 28 August 2005). However, their swift disposal has not resulted in the expected eradication of difficult public memory. Instead, derelict

FIGURE 17.1 Anti-immigrant graffiti, Lanark Way, Belfast, July 2011 (photograph: Laura McAtackney)

lots pepper urban working-class areas, highlighting the past conflict through absences—not transformations—that allow communities to utilize the space—or not—in haphazard and often counterproductive ways. The disposal of security installations without consideration as to their roles and links to the conflict ignores those who, often without choice, lived amongst them. Liam Clarke has suggested that this official control of disposal has ensured that 'some of Ulster's vanishing fortresses are now regarded with something approaching nostalgia' (Clarke 2005: 2). Perhaps 'nostalgia' is overstating the emotional connections, but there has been a palpable public unease about their swift removal without public interaction and a clear plan of what they are to become. The mass disposal of sites so intrinsically linked to the conflict, without transparency and openness, has followed a noticeable trajectory of the post-Troubles political context that prefers official forgetting of the past rather than attempts to engage with painful truths and responsibilities. This tendency is as a result of the unresolved issues bypassed by the Agreement—including 'how the past should be remembered and explained' (McGrattan 2009: 164)—and can be further exemplified in the fortunes of the most iconic remnant of the conflict: Long Kesh/Maze prison.

17.6 Long Kesh/Maze Prison

It is difficult to overstate the importance of Long Kesh/Maze due to the longevity and intricacies of its connections to the conflict in Northern Ireland. Its biography as a place of political imprisonment can be traced to the early stages of the conflict and its functional life as a prison ended just two years after the signing of the Agreement. Long Kesh/Maze opened (on the site of a disused Second World War base) in August 1971, as a direct result of the introduction of the controversial policy of internment without trial. By November 1972 it began to hold other Troubles-related prisoners within its 'Compounds' of Nissen huts in self-selecting 'green or orange hive[s]' (Snodden 1996: 26), until the burning of the majority of the camp by Republican prisoners in October 1974. The recommendations of the resultant Gardiner Report (1975) highlighted the 'thoroughly unsatisfactory' Compound prison form and also criticized the introduction of special category status in 1972 as 'a serious mistake' (NIO/12/160A 1980 PRONI). To rectify both the physical form and prisoner regime, the building of a new cellular structure was initiated alongside the ending of special category status. HMP Maze opened on 1 September 1976. This new prison structure was conceived as a tool for enforcing prison authority, control, and prisoner compliance, but was beset by fluctuating mass prisoner protests. Republicans were the most numerous, steadfast, and effective at maintaining ongoing protests with the initiation of the 'Blanket Protest' in 1976, which evolved to the 'Dirty Protests' and finally to the Hunger Strikes of 1980 and 1981. The latter protest resulted in the deaths of ten prisoners.

Although the Hunger Strikes initially ended with defeat for the prisoners, such was the negative publicity that most of the original 'five demands' were granted by the mid-1980s. From this time the control of the prison began to move perceivably in favour of the prisoners, with an escape in September 1983 displaying the ability of Republican prisoners to abscond en masse, through to the negotiation of a Loyalist paramilitary ceasefire in 1994. Effectively, the prison reverted back to the type of regime associated with the Compounds (which had eventually closed in 1989) whereby the prisoners had almost complete freedom of their wings. HMP Maze officially closed in September 2000 when the last prisoners, not eligible for release under the Agreement, were transferred elsewhere.

There is little need to justify the inclusion of this site; as Louise Purbrick has stated, 'The architecture of the Maze contains a history of the conflict' (2004: 92). Since its closure this 'icon' of the Troubles has occupied the majority of political, media, and public attention as to the role of the remnants of conflict in the transition to 'peace'. Whilst the site effectively remained in limbo until its transferral to the Northern Ireland government, its prominence rose with the creation of the cross-community, cross-bench Maze Consultation Panel (MCP) in May 2003. Media attention quickly focused on the seemingly irreconcilable desires of the two communities to either retain or remove the prison. Local newspapers have promoted such oppositional preferences as a 'victory' for one community and resultant 'defeat' for the other.

In contrast to these popular oppositions, the deliberately balanced make-up of the panel ensured that compromise would be the inevitable conclusion and the publication of the first report—A New Future for Maze/Long Kesh (2005)—confirmed this presumption. The proposals centred on the retention of a small representative sample of the site with the vast majority being demolished and replaced with various functional 'zones' (MCP 2005: 9). The report emphasized the need to transform the meaning of the site to 'an internationally recognizable physical expression of the ongoing transformation from conflict to peace' (MCP 2005: 14). Tellingly, after a negative reception by Unionists this report was surpassed by the Maze/Long Kesh: Masterplan and Implementation Strategy (Masterplan Consortium 2006), which forwarded the same proposals couched in more subtle language. The second report introduced concepts such as sustainability and environmentally friendly outputs, and the removal of most overt references to the prison history of the site. Regardless of the vocabulary chosen to express the proposals, the fundamental decision to (partially) retain the prison remained. Such a decision was important. For a contemporary prison to be selected to be partially preserved, thereby elevating its status from functional to cultural, indicates the tacit acceptance of its continuing relevance and significance. For the conventional tendency to assess archaeological heritage value on the basis of precedent means that preservation of unlikely and unusual structures and sites reveals their contemporary importance (Carver 1996: 50).

In the latest proposals a 'Peace Building and Conflict Resolution Centre', to encompass 32 acres of the 360 acre site, is to be the only area retaining current structures (Figure 17.2). Despite the limited nature of this retention, fears were expressed that it would constitute a 'Museum of the Troubles' and a place of pilgrimage for Republican ex-prisoners. The Unionist pressure group FAIR (Families Acting for Innocent Relatives) has strongly condemned the potential for the prison to become a shrine to the 1981 hunger strikers: 'Yes there will be no physical shrine such as a statue, but actually retaining the hospital itself would be there [sic] shrine' (FAIR Press Release, 26 July 2007). Whilst apprehension remains, it is clear that the government aims to regenerate not only the physical site, but also its meaning, whilst retaining enough of the original structures to satisfy Republicans. Unfortunately, despite the initial activity and hard-fought compromises, the site has been slowly demolished since 2006 without regeneration and only the proposed representative sample remains. The site remains closed to the public.

By mid-2011 foundations from previously demolished structures were being extracted, a reversion to controlled wilderness for much of the site is actively encouraged and the

FIGURE 17.2 Front of H Block, which stands *in situ* on the Maze regeneration site, November 2007 (photograph: Laura McAtackney)

existing structures are accessed only on official tours of the site. The demolished concrete buildings have been turned into aggregate to create a car park, which remains unused, and the original aims to create new housing, enterprise parks, and the highly publicized national stadium have receded. Without the political will, financial support, and public interest in creating a diverse, multi-functional 'symbol of confidence and hope for the people of Northern Ireland' (MCP 2005: 31), the productive, commercial, and forward-looking elements of the two reports have been quietly sidelined. In the post-conflict context, it has become increasingly clear that identification of the site with Republicans has deepened. Far from being forgotten, imprisonment continues to be a 'badge of honour' (McKeown 2001: xiii) signified through the medium of wall murals and community memorials. If the meaning of the site has transformed at all it has only shifted to being more polarizing and singular than when the prison closed. Long Kesh/Maze acts as a cautionary tale: attempts to use regeneration to alter the meaning of place do not necessarily ensure official interpretations are accepted without unofficial subversion (Ashworth and Graham 2005: 4)

17.7 BELFAST'S 'PEACE LINES'

It could be argued that 'peace lines' were excluded from the Agreement as they have been placed over extended periods by civic authorities at the request of the communities that they separate and, as such, are not military 'security installations'. However, so-called 'peace lines' are significant, physical obstacles. They have been erected at the interfaces of working-class areas to prevent conflict—and effectively perpetuate sectarian and religious differences— and this section will examine how their form, presence, and role have developed over the course of, and in reaction to, the peace process.

The number of peace lines has grown dramatically since they first took material form in the years of the Troubles. Ceasefires and peace processes have had little impact on their continued erection. The creation of the first peace lines in Belfast was as a direct result of the notorious violent, arson attacks between near neighbours along the Falls/Shankill interface in West Belfast in August 1969, resulting in the erection of 'walls of corrugated sheets of iron bolted to metal posts sunk in concrete' (Mulholland, 2001: 73). They have insidiously proliferated since this time and continue to exist in the present day. Recent figures from the Community Relations Council (CRC) show that whilst there were 18 barriers recorded in Belfast in the early 1990s, this figure had reached 88 by 2009 (c.2009: 3). However, this number has been disputed as it is often difficult to define what a 'peace line' actually is.

As temporary constructions, peace lines do not appear on official maps and are often extended—as can be seen in the variations of form and style in adjacent panels—as continuations of existing structures. Their form varies from solid concrete or brick constructions and planes of metal sheeting to metal fencing or transparent grilles. Peace lines have been created for a number of reasons and this diversity has resulted in the medium of segregation varying in form, style, and visibility (Jarman and O'Halloran 2001: 4). This variety results not only from the different bodies responsible for erecting the structures— including the Northern Ireland Housing Executive, Belfast City Council, and Department of the Environment (NI)—but also the different roles they are intended to perform. For whilst they are associated with preventing violent interactions—e.g. between the Catholic Short Strand and its Protestant neighbours in East Belfast—they have also been erected to prevent demographic changes caused by population movement and depopulation—such as encroachment by Catholics into now depopulated, traditional Protestant areas in North Belfast. Furthermore, their effectiveness as barriers can also be questioned as the majority of peace lines have crossing points, which have 'not so much ended inter-community tension as changed its form' (CRC *c.*2009: 4). Of fundamental importance to this study, they remain the only infrastructure associated with the Troubles that has continued to grow in the post-conflict period (Jarman 2002: 287).

Walking amongst the various peace lines that litter the backstreets and alleyways of Belfast, a patchwork of structures reveals differences in erection, landscaping, subsequent interactions and meaning to those who live amongst them. The Belfast City Council project to cover swathes of peace lines on the Protestant Shankill Road from Lanark Way to Northumberland Road with the work of international graffiti artists (Figure 17.3) visually contrasts to the 'other side' of the wall in the Clonard area of the Falls Road. Here houses are packed tightly against the barrier and the only spaces are landscaped with lawns contained behind wire fencing or unofficial memorials to the Troubles prominently located alongside them, referencing and maintaining their permanence (Figure 17.4). Cluan Place, a one-street Protestant enclave that intrudes into the Catholic Short Strand in East Belfast, has towering structures solely enclosing this street with internal wall murals detailing their experiences of segregation: '5 people shot/Houses Burnt/House Bombed', but defiantly proclaiming 'Still Loyalist', 'Always British', and 'No Surrender'. For such residents the dividends of the peace process are yet to be experienced.

FIGURE 17.3 Graffiti sponsored by Belfast City Council at Cupar Way, Belfast, July 2011 (photograph: Laura McAtackney)

FIGURE 17.4 Houses backing on to the peace line at Bombay Street, Belfast, July 2011 (photograph: Laura McAtackney)

It is not surprising that 'peace lines' were not referenced in the Agreement as their continued presence—and indeed growth—materially contradicts the promises of the peace process. Politicians allowing their creation and acquiescing in their continued extension facilitate the hidden, acceptable face of segregation. Peace lines are a phenomenon of working-class areas that predominantly contain ghettos of social housing in locales of economic deprivation. They do not scar commercial zones or act as backdrops to city centres newly landscaped with public art, nor do they separate affluent, middle-class areas. They sit alongside abandoned 'Regeneration Zones' and liminal, semi-derelict housing estates. They present physical proof that segregation and associated conflict is ongoing, that the authorities are prepared to facilitate it, and highlight the deprivation that this causes in the areas in which they are situated. One must ask why have working-class areas been allowed to self-segregate and formalize their antagonistic relationships during a period of supposed reintegration?

Whilst sectarian conflict—often resulting in spontaneous or orchestrated clashes and rioting—has a long history in the province, the responses of the authorities have changed since the peace process. Short-term, financial expediency and an unofficial policy of responding 'to a divided community by giving way to its preferences' (Hepburn 2001: 95) have the added pressures of international interest and financial support of the peace process to encourage their continuation. Cal Muckley has estimated that the incremental costs of one contemporary terrorism-related fatality would be 'equivalent to £3.69 million sterling in 2009 prices' to the Northern Irish economy (Muckley 2010: 9). Therefore there is vested interest in maintaining 'peaceful' segregation alongside low-expenditure, cyclically funded community projects that facilitate piecemeal interactions across the divides, rather than swiftly, and perhaps prematurely, tearing down walls.

In a post-conflict context it is clear that, by continuing to permit segregated working-class urban areas, the authorities are choosing to allow a small number of violent clashes alongside piecemeal community-group initiatives, rather than attempt to actively resolve long-standing and deeply felt social divisions that predate the Troubles. I suggest that peace lines are an ugly manifestation of continuing, officially sanctioned societal segregation. They exist because they can effectively contain potentially deeper societal fractures and allow communities to feel secure in places with long histories of abortive paramilitary ceasefires and civil unrest. More than poverty or conflict, the continuing presence of peace lines materializes insecurity: of a reluctance to accept that the peace process is permanent and an official acquiescence to this fear.

17.8 Conclusions

Exploring the ongoing transitions of post-Troubles Northern Ireland through an archaeological perspective highlights that there is no singular, stable experience of the peace process. It is difficult to draw lasting or broad conclusions, except to say that the political promises of the Agreement are often contradicted by current material realities. Whilst the majority of security installations referenced by the Agreement no longer physically exist, a lack of insight into the variety of relationships that exist between past, present, and future at specific places allows negative associations with the past to remain unchallenged. The empty spaces of the newly created Regeneration Zones do not always facilitate new, positive 'place identity' (Reid 2004), but instead can allow unsavoury contemporary concerns to intermix with old understandings. Attempts to create a new meaning for Long Kesh/Maze have continued to falter and in the meantime identification with place does not stagnate: polarizations widen, myths propagate and a 'sum zero heritage site' (Graham and McDowell 2007: 363) is created in spite of incomplete official interventions. Peace lines reveal at best apathy—at worst collaboration—in facilitating social segregation through their continued creation and maintenance throughout the peace process. Their existence belies the superficial rhetoric and promises of an Agreement that retains caution and ambivalence at its centre. Perhaps these structures more than any other are a fitting material representation of the continued societal antagonisms that the peace process has chosen to ignore.

In a broader sense, these case studies add a contemporary material dimension to the vast quantities of political, sociological, and historical analyses of the conflict and violence in Northern Ireland. By concentrating on the material entanglements of peace and conflict in the context of the peace process, a physicality is added to our understanding of how conflict can be experienced differently over time and place. Equally, the interplay between the past, present, and future at specific times and places adds a time dimension that goes some way towards explaining the messiness of the present day. For contemporary archaeologies, particularly those that take an overtly political stance, this study allows the dimensions of class to be overtly considered alongside religious and political sectarianism in understanding Northern Ireland as a transitional society. In exploring spatial contexts and social demographics of conflict, we can add nuance to our understandings of those who suffer the consequences of long-term, low-level wars and how these consequences can continue in various forms after 'peace' is declared.

REFERENCES

Ashworth, Gregory J. and Graham, Brian. 2005. Introduction. In *Senses of Place: Senses of Time*, ed. Gregory J. Ashworth and Brian Graham, pp. 3–15. Aldershot: Ashgate.

Beaudry, Mary C. and Mrozowski, Stephen A. 2001. Cultural Space and Worker Identity in the Company City: 19th Century Lowell, Massachusetts. In *The Archaeology of Urban Landscapes: Explorations in Slumland*, ed. Alan Mayne and Tim Murray, pp. 118–32. Cambridge: Cambridge University Press.

Boal, Frederick W. 1994. Encapsulation: Urban Dimensions of National Conflict. In *Managing Divided Cities*, ed. Seamus Dunn, pp. 30–41. Keele: Ryburn Publishing in association with the Fulbright Commission.

—— 2002 Belfast: Walls Within. *Political Geography* 21: 687–94

Bryan, Dominic. 1994. Interpreting the Twelfth. *History Ireland* 2(2): 37–41.

Buchli, Victor and Lucas, Gavin. 2001. The Archaeology of Alienation: A Late Twentieth-Century British Council House. In *Archaeologies of the Contemporary Past*, ed. Victor Buchli and Gavin Lucas, pp. 158–67. London: Routledge.

Carver, Martin. 1996. On Archaeological Value. *Antiquity* 70: 45–56.

Clarke, Liam. 2005. Introduction. In Jonathan Olley, *Castles of the North*, pp. 2–3. Available at: <http://www.coldtype.net/castles/Castles.LR.pdf > (accessed 12 December 2010).

Community Relations Council. c.2009. *Towards Sustainable Security: Interface Barriers and the Legacy of Segregation in Belfast*. Belfast: Community Relations Council.

Crooke, Elizabeth. 2005. The Construction of Community through Heritage in Northern Ireland. In *Ireland's Heritages: Critical Perspectives on Memory and Identity*, ed. Mark McCarthy, pp. 223–35. Aldershot: Ashgate.

Fay, Marie-Therese, Morrissey, Mike, and Smyth, Marie. 1999. *The Northern Ireland Troubles: The Human Costs*. London: Pluto Press.

Fitzduff, Mary and O'Hagan, Liam. 2000. The Cost of the Conflict. *The Northern Ireland Troubles: INCORE Background Paper*. Available at: <http://cain.ulst.ac.uk/othelem/incore-paper.htm> (accessed February 2012).

Fraser, T. G. 2000. *Ireland in Conflict 1922–1998*. London: Routledge.

Government records held at the Public Record Office of Northern Ireland (PRONI), Belfast: NIO/12/160A. 1979–81. Protest Action: Protest Action Arising from Claim to Special Category Status—Hunger Strike, October 1979–January 1981 (PRONI).

Graham, Brian and McDowell, Sara. 2007. Meaning in the Maze: The Heritage of Long Kesh. *Cultural Geographies* 14(3): 343–68.

Harrison, Rodney. 2009. Towards an Archaeology of the Welfare State in Britain. *Archaeologies* 5(2): 238–62.

—— 2011. Surface Assemblages: Towards an Archaeology *in* and *of* the Present. *Archaeological Dialogues* 18(2): 141–61.

Hepburn, Anthony C. 2001. Long Division and Ethnic Conflict: The Experience of Belfast. In *Managing Divided Cities*, ed. Seamus Dunn, pp. 88–105. Keele: Keele University Press.

Her Majesty's Stationery Office. 1998. *The Agreement*. Belfast: HMSO.

Hobsbawm, Eric. 2007. *Globalisation, Democracy and Terrorism*. London: Abacus.

Irish News [Belfast, Northern Ireland]. 2005. News report 'The Road to Normalisation', 28 August.

Jarman, Neil. 1993. Intersecting Belfast. In *Landscape: Perspective and Politics*, ed. Barbara Bender, pp. 107–39. London: Berg.

—— 1997. *Material Conflicts: Parades and Visual Displays in Northern Ireland*. Oxford: Berg.

—— 1998. Painting Landscapes: The Place of Murals in the Symbolic Construction of Urban Space. In *Symbols in Northern Ireland*, ed. Anthony D. Buckley, pp. 121–47. Belfast: Institute of Irish Studies.

—— 2002. Troubling Remnants: Dealing with the Remains of Conflict in Northern Ireland. In *Matériel Culture: The Archaeology of Twentieth Century Conflict*, ed. John Schofield, William G. Johnson, and Colleen M. Beck, pp. 281–95. London: Routledge.

Jarman, Neil and O'Halloran, Chris. 2001. Recreational Rioting: Young People, Interface Areas and Violence. *Childcare in Practice* 7(1): 2–16.

McDowell, Sara. 2008a. Commemorating Dead 'Men': Gendering the Past and Present in Post-Conflict Northern Ireland. *Gender, Place & Culture: A Journal of Feminist Geography* 15(4): 335–54.

—— 2008b. Selling Conflict Heritage through Tourism in Peacetime Northern Ireland: Transforming Conflict or Exacerbating Difference? *International Journal of Heritage Studies* 14(5): 405–21.

McGarry, John. 2001. Northern Ireland, Civic Nationalism, and the Good Friday Agreement. In *Northern Ireland and the Divided World: Post-Agreement Northern Ireland in Comparative Perspective*, ed. John McGarry, pp 109–37. Oxford: Oxford University Press.

McGrattan, Cillian. 2009. 'Order Out of Chaos': The Politics of Transitional Justice. *Politics* 29(3): 164–72.

McKeown, Liam. 2001. *Irish Republican Prisoners, 1971–2000*. Dublin: Beyond the Pale Publications.

McKitterick, David. 1992. Belfast Security Measures Accepted as Normal: People in Belfast have become accustomed to police checks and the 'ring of steel' which protects the city's commercial heart. *The Independent*, 7 December. Available at: <http://www.independent.co.uk/news/uk/belfast-security-measures-accepted-as-normal-people-in-belfast-have-become-accustomed-to-police-checks-and-the-ring-of-steel-which-protects-the-citys-commercial-heart-david-mckittrick-reports-1562036.html> (accessed January 2012).

McKitterick, David, Kelters, Seamus, Feeney, Brian, and Thornton, Chris. 1999. *Lost Lives: The Stories of the Men, Women and Children Who Died as a Result of the Northern Ireland Troubles*. Edinburgh: Mainstream Publishing.

Masterplanning Consortium. 2006. *Maze/Long Kesh: Masterplan and Implementation Strategy. Executive Summary, Final Report*. Belfast: HMSO.

Maze Consultation Panel (MCP). 2005. *A New Future for Maze/Long Kesh*. Belfast: HMSO.

Muckley, Cal B. 2010. Terrorism, Tourism and FDI: Estimating a Lower Bound on the Peace Dividend in Northern Ireland. Available at: <http://ssrn.com/abstract=1689510> or doi:10.2139/ssrn.1689510 (accessed 8 January 2012).

Muldoon, Orla T. 2004. Children of the Troubles: The Impact of Political Violence in Northern Ireland. *Journal of Social Issues* 60(3): 453–68.

Mulholland, Marc. 2001. *The Longest War: Northern Ireland's Troubled History*. Oxford: Oxford University Press.

Purbrick, Louise. 2004. The Architecture of Containment. In *The Maze*, ed. Donovan Wylie, pp. 91–110. London: Granta.

—— 2006. Long Kesh/Maze, Northern Ireland: Public Debate as Historical Interpretation. In *Re-mapping the Field: New Approaches in Conflict Archaeology*, ed. John Schofield, Axel Klausmeier, and Louise Purbrick, pp. 81–7. Berlin: Westkreuz-Druckerei Ahrens JG.

Reid, Bryonie. 2004. Labouring Towards the Space to Belong: Place and Identity in Northern Ireland. *Irish Geography* 37(1): 103–13.

Schofield, John and Anderton, Michael. 2000. The Queer Archaeology of Green Gate: Interpreting Contested Space at Greenham Common Airbase. *World Archaeology* 32(2): 236–51.

Snodden, Mark. 1996 Culture Behind the Wire. *Journal of Prisoners on Prison* 7(2): 25–56.

Symonds, James. 2010. Yes We Can! But So What? Some Observations on Contemporary Archaeology. Available at: <http://traumwerk.stanford.edu/archaeolog/2010/01> (accessed 12 January 2012).

Vaughan-Williams, Nick. 2006. Towards a Problematisation of the Problematisations that Reduce Northern Ireland to a 'Problem'. *Critical Review of International Social and Political Philosophy* 9(4): 513–26.

Zimmerman, Larry, Singleton, Courtney, and Welch, Jessica. 2010. Activism and Creating a Translational Archaeology of Homelessness. *World Archaeology* 42(3): 443–54.

CHAPTER 18

....

AFTERLIVES

....

MICHAEL BRIAN SCHIFFER

18.1 INTRODUCTION

....

THE term 'afterlife' commonly refers to a person's participation after death in a *supernatural* world. Archaeologists dutifully infer a group's beliefs about this non-material world by analysing mortuary assemblages. However, researchers taking a different tack have developed new meanings of afterlife—*material* meanings—that apply to varied entities. Walker (1999, 2008) notes that living people relate to witches and animal remains in depositional context, and such ritual interactions comprise the afterlives of these symbolically animated objects. For Harrison (2010: 528), a stone tool's afterlife begins when it 'ceases to be functionally useful'. Scholars in sundry disciplines have further expanded the meaning of afterlife to include the fate of entities such as a disbanded East German film company (Heiduschke 2006) and an Atari video game that flopped (Guins 2009). In general, then, any entity—person, artefact, organization, or place—that has undergone a change from some sort of 'life' to some sort of 'death' may have an afterlife.

An *afterlife artefact* is one made during the afterlife that represents, mimics, commemorates, alludes to, or incorporates part of the original entity. Afterlife artefacts are a material means by which 'memories' of people from Jesus to Elvis as well as of artefacts and other entities are created and perpetuated.

There are many interpretations of afterlife, depending on how one defines an entity's 'death'. If death is the loss of one or more utilitarian or symbolic functions, then an afterlife may equate to secondary use. By this interpretation afterlives include an old trolley car converted into a restaurant, an heirloom platter hung permanently on a wall, and an old mining town such as Silverton, Colorado, that became a tourist attraction. Examples of afterlife artefacts include a drawing of the trolley-restaurant, a photograph of the platter on the wall, and a visitor's brochure for Silverton. Artefacts like the foregoing that endured largely intact, despite a loss of some functions, may have an afterlife replete with facsimiles, forgeries, replicas, reproductions, caricatures, and the like (see Graves-Brown, this volume).

An entity's death may also be defined as the utter loss of integrity through deterioration or destruction, which precludes the performance of *any* function. Some long-gone artefacts have a rich afterlife, such as the Lighthouse of Alexandria. Built in the third century BCE, it succumbed to earthquakes, lack of maintenance, and later construction. Although no person today has seen this lighthouse, its afterlife is marked by varied images in books and articles; on postcards, postage stamps, and models; and in the monumental George Washington Masonic Memorial in Alexandria, Virginia. Artefacts that survive only as relics or remnants, such as a house foundation or a pot fragment, may give rise to afterlife artefacts such as reconstructions, restorations, or museum displays.

This chapter focuses on the afterlife artefacts of artefacts that suffered a total loss of integrity, which tend to be weak evidence for building inferences about the original artefact's life. However, afterlife artefacts made and used in recent times have considerable research potential as *modern material culture* for studying present-day human behaviour (Reid, Schiffer, and Rathje 1975). Research on afterlife artefacts may lead to inferences about: (1) how and why they are produced, (2) post-manufacture activities, and (3) their societal contexts.

18.2 THE *GREAT EASTERN* STEAMSHIP

To illustrate the research potential of afterlife artefacts as modern material culture, I engage a celebrated dead artefact, the enormous steamship known as the *Great Eastern*. This ship had an interesting life (Dugan 1953; Beaver 1969; Emmerson 1981), and is having an equally interesting afterlife.

The *Great Eastern* was conceived by Isambard Kingdom Brunel, famed British civil engineer of the mid-nineteenth century, who built 25 railroads, 130 bridges, and eight harbour systems; he also designed three steamships, of which the *Great Eastern* was the last and largest.

In the early 1850s, Brunel envisioned the *Great Eastern* as a solution to the 'coaling problem'. In voyages from England to Australia or India, steamships refuelled periodically by detouring to coaling stations where coal was pricey. Brunel believed that a huge ship could solve the problem by carrying all the coal needed to make a direct round trip. With two big ships already on his résumé, Brunel was able to convince the Eastern Steam Navigation Company to bankroll his vision. Stock was issued and subscribed, and Brunel set to work.

The iron ship he designed was five times larger than any previous vessel. She would be 692 feet long, able to carry 4,000 passengers, 12,000 tons of coal, and cargo. Launched in 1858, the *Great Eastern* remained, tonnage-wise, the largest ship in the world until 1899—but by then she no longer existed.

In order to reach the target speed of 14–15 knots, she had both a screw propeller and side paddle wheels, which required two enormous engines. The four pistons of the paddle engine had a diameter of 74 inches and a stroke of 14 feet (Figure 18.1a). The screw engine also had four pistons with a diameter of 84 inches and a stroke of 4 feet (Figure 18.1b). The engine designs differed because of the unequal heights of the screw and paddle shafts and because they revolved at different speeds (ca. 10 rpm for the paddle and 33 rpm for the screw).

To ensure that the ship was safe, Brunel contrived a modular design consisting of watertight longitudinal and transverse bulkheads, and a double hull below the waterline. Thus, any breach would be localized, leaving the ship afloat. The *Great Eastern* would be a formidable vessel, built largely of wrought iron plates held together by 3 million rivets. It also had six masts and 6,500 yards of sails.

John Scott Russell, a respected shipbuilder, received the construction contract for a bid of £275,000. Construction began in his shipyard on the River Thames in greater London

(a)

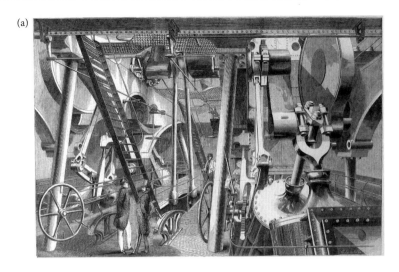

(b)

FIGURE 18.1 The *Great Eastern's* engines: (a) the paddle engine; (b) the screw engine (reproduced with permission from *The Illustrated London News*)

in 1853, and went fairly smoothly until the money ran out. The original stockholders lost much of their investments as the project was reorganized. A new company—The Great Ship Company—raised capital to continue by selling 330,000 shares at £1 each. In the end, the ship cost more than £800,000—about $100 million in 2010 dollars.

In late 1857, the ship was finally ready for a sideways launch into the river. An oft-reproduced photograph shows Brunel standing before a giant chain coiled on an immense drum—one of two restraints to prevent the ship from moving too quickly down the launchway. But the restraints weren't needed because the great ship barely budged. In the following months, she was nudged inches at a time by the largest hydraulic rams in England, that is, by the ones that didn't explode. The launch killed several workers and cost around £100,000, putting the new company in dire financial straits.

During the ship's first sea trial, a steam explosion scalded five workers to death and did significant damage. Repairs were made, and the Great Ship Company put the *Great Eastern* on the shorter and less expensive transatlantic route, already amply covered by steamships. The directors believed this move would yield cash in the short run, but it didn't, as passengers were exceedingly scarce. On its maiden voyage to New York, in June of 1860, only 35 tickets were sold. Owing to the company's continuing financial woes, the *Great Eastern* was never put on the long routes for which Brunel had designed her.

The Great Ship Company hung on until 1864, when it entered bankruptcy. The white elephant of the sea was put up for auction, but fetched just £25,000. The buyer was Daniel Gooch, who believed she could be used to lay a new Atlantic cable.

The *Great Eastern*'s first cable-laying attempt, in 1865, failed owing to machinery problems but in 1866 she succeeded. The cable worked well and was immediately profitable. During the next several years, the *Great Eastern* helped to create great wealth and tied together the continents by laying several long submarine cables, including one from Aden to Bombay (now Mumbai). These halcyon years lasted until 1874, when she was replaced by the *Faraday*, a special-purpose cable ship.

The rest of the *Great Eastern*'s life was a pitiful decline. Docked at Milford Haven for a dozen years, she never again ventured across the high seas. The ship was auctioned several more times, and for a while served as a floating amusement park on the Mersey, representing Lewis's department store. In this incarnation the cable tanks became a vast music hall, and the decks hosted a variety of sideshows and stalls. After this indignity she was put briefly on display in Dublin. Finally, in 1888 she was auctioned for scrap, fetching £16,000. Although the Liverpool ship-breaker sold many of the *Great Eastern*'s parts at auction, in the end he made a loss because it took twice as long to dismantle her than the original estimate.

18.3 AFTERLIFE ARTEFACTS OF
THE *GREAT EASTERN*

Information about the *Great Eastern* includes many primary sources. Documents and images about Brunel's involvement are present in several archives in England, including the vast Brunel Collection at Bristol University. In addition, hundreds of newspaper and magazine articles in British, French, German, and American periodicals contemporaneously chronicled the ship's construction, vicissitudes, and cable work; *The London Illustrated News* is an especially rich source of articles and images.

Other artefacts used on the ship or associated with it also survive as primary sources (cf. Harvey 2009), such as the credenza, meat dish, coffee pot, and saloon lamp in the Liverpool Maritime Museum. The National Maritime Museum, at Greenwich, holds a collection of tokens sold when the *Great Eastern* visited ports such as New York and Dublin. Also extant are genuine relics that have been incorporated into afterlife artefacts. At Anfield, home to the Liverpool Football Club, there stands a flagpole made from the *Great Eastern*'s topmast. The National Museum of American History, Smithsonian Institution, has a wooden cane given originally to Cyrus Field, the Atlantic cable's promoter. On the cane's silver knob is an inscription, bearing the date 1890, noting that the wood came from the *Great Eastern*.

Secondary sources created during the twentieth century—most of them afterlife artefacts— are also plentiful. There are three books about the *Great Eastern* (cited above), several on

Brunel's ships (e.g. Dumpleton and Miller 1984; Griffiths, Lambert, and Walker 1999), and dozens about ships and the Atlantic cable project that discuss the *Great Eastern* at length (e.g. Dibner 1959; Hearn 2004)—as do biographies of Brunel (e.g. Vaughan 1991; Buchanan 2002) and Russell (Emmerson 1977). The many primary and secondary sources can be used as evidence, subject to source criticism, about activities that took place during the ship's life.

On the Internet we encounter many *Great Eastern* afterlife artefacts made in recent decades. These objects are neither produced by serious scholarship nor targeted at scholars, and should not be confused with primary or secondary sources. They include paintings, posters, and postcards of the ship or its engines, a $20 coin from Liberia, mugs, mouse pad, refrigerator magnet, Meissen porcelain plate, and model kits made by Mercator, Entex, and Revell. This potpourri of objects indicates that the *Great Eastern*'s afterlife artefacts play varied roles in today's commercial world. To explore the commercial connections further, I now turn to trading cards and postage stamps. These afterlife artefacts show how commercial activities incorporate images of the *Great Eastern* in products aimed at collectors.

18.3.1 Trading Cards

A trading card is a small piece of cardboard, ca. 3–6 cm × 5–10 cm, which is packaged as a premium along with a product such as cigarettes or tea. As one way to remain competitive, dozens of tobacco and tea companies embraced trading cards, issuing them in numbered sets such as 50 or 75 different flowers or sports figures or ships. Some companies produced several sets annually, and a few even sold inexpensive albums to encourage collecting.

In the United States, baseball cards began as tobacco trading cards in the late nineteenth century, but in the mid-twentieth century were premiums in gum and candy packages. Probably the best-known brand of the post-Second World War period was Topps, which made a variety of sports cards as well as other series that originally accompanied large pieces of gum. A brilliant marketing move, the adoption of trading cards provided two-fold incentives for children, the principal collectors, to buy or otherwise acquire the products. And manufacturers encouraged a relationship with two consumer groups: those who wanted the product and those who wanted the trading card. Indeed, children no doubt nagged their parents to buy the brand of tea or cigarettes that yielded particular cards.

On the back of a trading card is a description of the pictured object. I have tallied the factoids—'sound-bite history'—on my sample of eight *Great Eastern* cards from several countries. The most common factoids state that the ship was: (1) designed by Brunel, (2) the largest vessel, (3) propelled by paddle wheels and screw, (4) not a commercial success, and (5) responsible for laying the Atlantic telegraph cable. Each card has a unique mix of factoids, most of which are essentially correct, but there is one anomalous card. Made by Topps in 1955 as part of the 'Rails and Sails' series (Figure 18.2, middle row, middle), it is the only American card in my sample, and the only one containing blatant errors. Curiously, two factoids that occur often in secondary sources did not make the above list but might have: (1) the ship's double hull and many bulkheads enhanced safety, and (2) Brunel and Russell showed that an enormous iron ship could be built and would be seaworthy.

Images of the ship itself vary greatly, and some are misleading or erroneous. A few (Figure 18.2, upper row, left and right) show her under steam with all sails unfurled—an

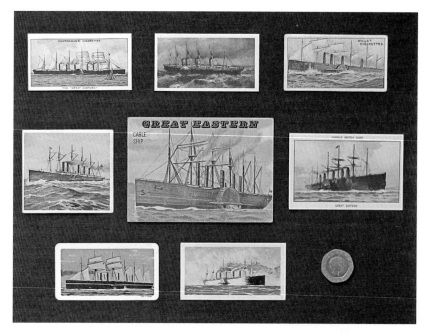

FIGURE 18.2 An assemblage of trading cards with images of the *Great Eastern* (photograph: Michael Brian Schiffer)

unlikely configuration. Two cards (Figure 18.2, upper row, left; middle row, left) depict the ship with a gentle convexity in the hull found on many ships but not the *Great Eastern*. The ships are also immersed to varying degrees; the extreme immersion in two images (Figure 18.2, upper row, left; middle row, left) is unrealistic because paddle wheels cannot work efficiently at that depth. The rigging also varies and in some cases is fanciful (Figure 18.2, various). The reader is invited to inspect the images for other inconsistencies.

Clearly, many designers of trading cards, who probably exploited secondary sources or worse, selected among the more dramatic and widely known factoids, knew little about ship technology of this era, and exercised considerable artistic licence. Because the target audience was children, not scholars poised to pounce on errors, designers apparently got by with superficial research.

18.3.2 Postage Stamps

The collecting of postage stamps—philately—began shortly after the first stamps were issued in the 1840s (Bryant 1981). Serious collectors conduct research on specific stamps and postal history, publishing their findings in specialized newsletters, journals, and books (Bryant 1981). In recent decades, scholars in many disciplines have discovered that postage stamps are a source of data that can be mined for nuggets of meaning. The prevailing theme is that stamps are political technologies, whose images reflect a nation's political priorities and ideologies (e.g. Altman 1991; Scott 1995; Skaggs 1978), such as promoting heritage awareness or creating a common identity for its citizens (Covington and Brunn 2006).

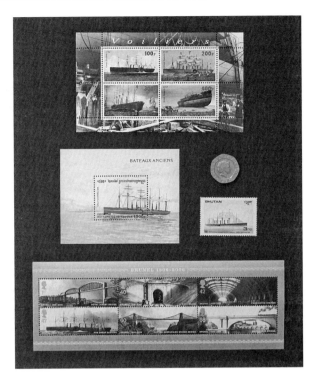

FIGURE 18.3 Several postage stamps with images of the *Great Eastern* (photograph: Michael Brian Schiffer)

Reid (1984: 223) suggested that 'stamps are excellent primary sources for the symbolic messages which governments seek to convey to their citizens and to the world'. He later added that 'Around the world, stamps are a form of propaganda through which governments project selected images, and they are too illuminating to be left only to the philatelist' (Reid 1993: 77; see also Stoetzer 1953; Cusack 2005: 591; Deans and Dobson 2005: 3). Case studies have focused on countries such as Japan (Dobson 2002; Frewer 2002), Finland (Raento and Brunn 2005), Indonesia (Leclerc and Scott 1993), Iraq (Reid 1993), Portugal (Cusack 2005), and regions such as Latin America (Child 2005) and East Asia (Deans and Dobson 2005). Some analyses have been comparative yet narrowly focused. Jones (2001), for example, studied the celebration of science on stamps from Germany, France, and Britain; and Brunn (2000) compared the first issues of 19 newly independent nations of Europe and Central Asia.

Images of the *Great Eastern* on 20-plus stamps from 13 countries call into question the assumption that postage stamps are simply icons of nationalist ideology and purveyors of propaganda.[1] Although the UK has issued several stamps picturing the *Great Eastern*, including one on a souvenir sheet commemorating, on the bicentennial of Brunel's birth, some of his most enduring designs (Figure 18.3, lower), others come from Bhutan (Figure 18.3, middle

---

[1] Bhutan, Burundi, Cambodia, Congo People's Republic, Great Britain, Grenada Grenadines, Guinea, Monaco, Niger, Paraguay, Portugal, Tanzania, and Virgin Islands (British).

row, right) and Burundi (Figure 18.3, upper row), land-locked nations that have no maritime heritage to celebrate. Likewise, it is doubtful that Congo, Tanzania, Paraguay, and Cambodia (Figure 18.3, middle row, left) had any relationship with Brunel or the *Great Eastern*, yet all have issued stamps featuring the ship. And what about stamps from many countries containing images of Disney characters, Einstein, JFK, and space exploration? Evidently, these subjects are unrelated to the issuing country, and so apparently cannot express a country-specific political ideology. As I show below, this is a widespread and relatively recent pattern that complicates the interpretation of stamp images as political technology.

In explaining how such stamps come about, I turn to the activities of philatelists, stamp dealers, postal institutions, and entrepreneurs. Philatelists usually begin as generalists, but soon realize the impossibility of collecting everything. Eventually, most focus on one or just a few countries or regions, early time periods, varieties of particular stamps, or subjects such as ships, musicians, or mushrooms; the latter collecting subjects are called 'topicals'. There are at least 49 groups that cater to topical collectors, including the Watercraft Philately Study Unit, Medical Subjects Study Unit, and the Old World Archaeological Study Unit, all of which are divisions of the American Topical Association (Kloetzel 2010, vol. 2, p. 10A). Some stamp dealers specialize in topicals, offering hundreds of kinds, and any collector can conjure up a new kind. Many topicals are afterlife artefacts, abundantly representing dead people and, in much smaller numbers, defunct ships, airplanes, automobiles, locomotives, spacecraft, and structures. Some images stand for an artefact class such as the Model T Ford or DC-3 airliner whose surviving examples—most no longer exist—have reduced functions.

Postal institutions have an economic incentive to issue stamps depicting subjects that appeal to topical collectors because it is profitable: a sheet costing pennies to produce may have a face value equivalent to tens of dollars or pounds. In a few cases, such as Pitcairn Island, stamp sales yield 'a substantial portion of the country's revenue' (Steinberg and McDowell 2003: 62). Several tiny polities in Europe—Liechtenstein, Luxembourg, Monaco, and San Marino—also depend greatly on stamp revenue, and virtually all other countries cultivate the collector market (despite declining ranks of young collectors).

As an archaeologist, I wondered how developing countries, micro-states, territories, and semi-autonomous islands with few residents, manage to issue dozens of topicals annually. Not surprisingly, entrepreneurs have been at work. Beginning in 1957 with newly independent Ghana, the Inter-Governmental Philatelic Corporation (IGPC), based in New York City, has supplied these services to stamp-issuing entities (SIEs). In late 2010, this corporation had 80 customers, ranging from Aitutaki to Zambia.[2] The IGPC designs a range of *all-purpose* topicals such as Disney characters, media celebrities, and space hardware that recur on many stamps from many places, as well as *customized* topicals, including native flora and fauna, craft items, archaeological sites, and notable citizens and historical events. So that they qualify as real postage stamps, samples are purportedly made available in local post offices. SIEs that do not require the services of the IGPC, including the United States, also issue a plethora of all-purpose and customized topicals.

Through this convergence of interests, images of long-dead artefacts such as the *Great Eastern* appear on stamps from many places, including countries having neither a maritime heritage nor the ability to produce and distribute their own stamps.

---

[2] <http://www.igpc.net/> (accessed 29 November 2010).

18.3.3 Stamp Pandering

In a paper about ways that countries commercialize their sovereignty, Slemrod (2008) recently asked, 'Why is Elvis on Burkina Faso Postage Stamps?' To qualify as a 'stamp panderer' according to Slemrod, an SIE had to issue one or more stamps depicting Elvis, Princess Diana (or one of her children), or a Disney character (2008: 694). These criteria generated a list of 42 stamp panderers (697), which is only half of IGPC customers. Slemrod—who mentions neither topicals nor the IGPC—missed the majority of SIEs that obviously cater to collectors.

I asserted above that virtually all SIEs today *are* stamp panderers and that widespread stamp pandering is a relatively recent phenomenon. To furnish evidence in support of both claims and to provide additional insights into the creation of afterlife artefacts, I now turn to a simple analysis of the prevalence of, and temporal trends in, stamp pandering.

To serve the ostensible function of postage stamps—indicating on a piece of mail that the proper postage has been paid—an SIE requires no more than a few dozen regular-issue (so-called 'definitive') stamps at any given time. These have a range of face values, combinations and multiples of which can denote any postage. Thus, the most robust indicator of stamp pandering should be an SIE's *rate* of new issues that exceed basic postage requirements. Even in an era before stamp pandering, however, an SIE might refresh its stamps by occasionally issuing a new series in response, for example, to inflation, currency devaluation, changes in postal rates, new fashions in commercial art, or to commemorate important events. But, except in extreme cases, such factors should not have required more than several dozen new stamps per *decade*.

There are about 200 SIEs worldwide today. Adding Slemrod's 42 SIEs to the IGPC's 80 customers and subtracting the 30 SIEs on both lists yields 92 identified stamp panderers, which leaves more than 100 SIEs on neither list. From the *latter* group I chose a sample of 10, drawing data from *Scott's Standard Postage Stamp Catalogue* (Kloetzel 2010, vols. 1 and 2).[3] To provide time depth, I selected only SIEs that began issuing stamps before 1880. New issues were tabulated for three periods: (1) 1880–1900, (2) 1900–62, and (3) 1962–2008 (2008 is the last year when data were consistently available).

The mean *annual* rate of new stamps issued is as follows:

Period	Mean	Range
1880–1900	3.1	0.4–6.8
1900–62	7.4	2.0–14.3
1962–2008	33.7	17.8–88.0

The trends are pronounced: (1) there is little evidence of stamp pandering in the nineteenth century, (2) during the first half of the twentieth century, modest stamp pandering

---

[3] The sample of SIEs: Afghanistan, Argentina, Cuba, Denmark, Dominican Republic, Egypt, Ecuador, Falkland Islands, Finland, and France. I counted only regular issues, excluding semi-postal, airmail, postage due, and revenue stamps.

begins but not all SIEs participate, (3) after 1962, stamp pandering at a high level is essentially universal.

The global predominance of stamp pandering and the consequent explosion of topicals since about 1960 suggest that we reconsider whether images on these stamps exclusively reflect political ideology. How are we to interpret, for example, images of the *Great Eastern* on stamps of Guinea, Grenada Grenadines, Bhutan, and Burundi—all current customers of the IGPC? I suggest that these images were used because officials in these countries trusted the IGPC to design stamps having collector appeal. Thus, whether a stamp's subject is related to an SIE's history or political ideology matters only for customized topicals. The many SIEs that are not IGPC customers doubtless also choose designs that appeal to collectors. In short, the political-ideological content of all postage stamps, particularly topicals, cannot be assumed a priori: some carry political messages but others do not. The researcher who would interpret the images is advised to assess, on a stamp-by-stamp basis, any political content and to make explicit the assessment criteria.

Mingo (1997) claimed that all-purpose topicals, like Mickey Mouse and JFK, are instruments of Western—especially American—cultural imperialism. However, most ordinary people in developing countries never see or use the stamps. Far more potent vehicles of cultural imperialism are music, movies, television programmes, and icons of American consumerism such as Coca Cola and McDonald's. In addition, the commercial arrangement between the IGPC and various polities seems to benefit all parties, except for naïve collectors who believe that common topicals are a sound investment.

18.3.4 Topical Stamps as Investments

Collectors learn rapidly that there are catalogues for nearly every interest, and these teach some basic principles of the marketplace, especially in capitalist countries (Gelber 1992). Stamp catalogues, for example, have been published since the mid-nineteenth century. Authoritative catalogues contain complete inventories and assign each stamp a 'value'. Schnitzel (1979) estimated that about 80 per cent of the catalogue values for mint US commemorative stamps, issued between 1893 and 1938, are explained by two variables: age and number issued. However, his sample period preceded the flood of topicals, and he failed to note that, in calculating values, catalogue publishers work hand in glove with stamp dealers to promote growth in the number of philatelists and to reinforce the notion that stamps are investments. Shortly after a stamp is issued, the catalogue price is set above face value, implying an immediate but phoney gain. Over the decades, appreciation of common topicals continues but is glacially slow, a tacit acknowledgement that they have scant resale value. US commemorative stamps issued in the 1950s and 1960s are a telling example. Having a face value of 3 and 4 cents, respectively, these stamps have a 2010 catalogue value (mint or used) of 20 cents (Kloetzel 2010, vol. 1). This apparently sizeable gain is illusory because it lags inflation during the past half century, and actual resale value hovers at or below face value. Topical stamps of other SIEs exhibit similar patterns. Clearly, catalogue values of topicals are akin to 'suggested retail price', not resale value. So-called 'investment-grade' stamps, which are generally old and rare *non*-topicals, do appreciate significantly over the long term, but not at a steady rate (Dimson and Spaenjers 2011).

Some unusual topicals are issued in small numbers so as to create artificial scarcity, such as stamps printed on gold foil or silk, rendered as a hologram, or having a very high face value; there is even a 'scratch and sniff' stamp from Switzerland that smells like chocolate. Such oddities may have a slight investment appeal.

Collectors who learn that buying *common* new topicals is a poor investment may become more discerning or abandon the hobby. However, some people continue to buy new issues because they may yield an emotional benefit, and collections afford—in stamp clubs, for example—opportunities to socialize, trade duplicates, compete for prestige in stamp shows, and exhibit specialized expertise. Also, some collectors focus on topicals related to their professions such as dentistry, nursing, and archaeology. And, lest we forget, most topicals are rather pleasing miniature works of art.

18.4 DISCUSSION AND CONCLUSION

Trading cards and postage stamps are two collecting hobbies that illuminate the intersection of artefact afterlife, commercial activities, and the behaviour of consumers. Anticipating a consumer base of passionate collectors, companies and governments seek entities whose images can be profitably exploited. One result is families of artefacts that portray some long-gone artefacts, such as the *Great Eastern*. Brunel's cult status and the *Great Eastern*'s high profile in secondary sources make the big ship an ideal subject for afterlife artefacts.

Archaeologists and historians contribute—deliberately and inadvertently—to the making of afterlife artefacts. Archaeologists, for example, recover the remains of artefacts, structures, and settlements that have utterly lost their integrity, and historians study documents about dead people, artefacts, and places. Through our scholarly products, these deceased entities may provoke the making of new things. In books and magazines, movies and TV shows, museums, souvenir shops, heritage sites, and tourist traps, for example, our finds and publications are the basis of new drawings, movie sets, murals and dioramas, sometimes full-scale reconstructions and replicas, and trinkets (cf. Kirshenblatt-Gimblett 1998). Because the originals no longer exist, the designers of afterlife artefacts have much latitude in creating representations. Thus, personal preferences, stereotypes, and contemporary ideologies may influence the product. Like trading cards and stamps, the afterlife artefacts of ancient entities also serve commercial interests, including those of authors, publishers, production companies, television networks, manufacturers, museums, and the proprietors of heritage sites. Because our scholarly products lead to afterlife artefacts, we are enmeshed in the commercial world, though not as deeply as Topps and the IGPC.

Whether or not stimulated by scholarly works, afterlife artefacts—broadly defined—are abundant today, calling the attention of knowledgeable people to, and informing others about, the past life of some entity. In addition to grave markers, there are monuments celebrating the lives and deeds of noteworthy people, and in many places we encounter plaques that mark the site 'where once stood...' There are also replicas and reproductions of famous structures, trains, and ships no longer extant, such as Francis Drake's *Golden Hind*. Commercial leisure activities create faint replicas of past structures such as Disneyland's Sleeping Beauty Castle and Main Street, movie sets such as 'Old Tucson', and the pyramids and sphinxes in many US miniature golf courses. The Luxor Hotel in Las Vegas is itself an enormous modernist pyramid with a sphinx and lion phalanx in front. In Washington, DC the two- and three-story façades of nineteenth-century buildings are incorporated into twenty-first century office towers. Another class of afterlife artefacts is revival styles, such as Federalist architecture that alludes to structures of Classical Greece and Rome, as well as modern ethnic goods, such as pottery made by the Hopi of Northern Arizona that uses design elements from prehistoric sherds. In their training, aspiring artists copy great works that no longer decorate the original owner's house, and some modern sculptors use pieces of 'found objects' in their creations. Any class of afterlife artefact invites study as modern material culture. By asking archaeological questions of afterlife artefacts, we may gain insights into little-explored domains of human behaviour.

The archaeological study of modern material culture began in the United States during the 1970s, but—despite William L. Rathje's famous and long-lasting *Projet du Garbage* (e.g. Rathje and Murphy 1992; see also Reno, this volume) and a handful of other studies— did not achieve its full potential there (see Fewster, this volume). Rather, coupled to heritage studies and other present-day interests, a 'contemporary archaeology' in the spirit of modern material culture has prospered recently in England and several countries on the continent, as documented by Harrison and Schofield's *After Modernity* (2010). Although historians, sociologists, and practitioners of other disciplines have also discovered that the study of contemporary material culture has much to teach us about ourselves, the archaeological perspective remains unique, for only we are trained to study all aspects of material culture—technological, social, ideological, etc.—from both scientific and humanistic perspectives. Perhaps the next generation of archaeological studies will realize more fully the field's rich potential to shed light on contemporary societies.

ACKNOWLEDGEMENTS

Much of this research was carried out while I held a Fellowship at the Dibner Library of the National Museum of American History, Smithsonian Institution, in summer 2010. For many kindnesses, I thank Smithsonian curators Deborah Warner, Paul Johnston, Harold Wallace, Peggy Kidwell, and Helena Wright. I also thank Myron Molnau for help in finding stamps depicting the *Great Eastern*. William H. Walker's seminal contributions on afterlife phenomena stimulated my interest. Michael J. O'Brien, Deborah Warner, and the editors furnished comments on a draft.

REFERENCES

Altman, Dennis. 1991. *Paper Ambassadors: The Politics of Stamps*. North Ryde, New South Wales: Angus & Robertson.
Beaver, Patrick. 1969. *The Big Ship: Brunel's Great Eastern—A Pictorial History*. London: Hugh Evelyn.
Brunn, Stanley D. 2000. Stamps as Iconography: Celebrating the Independence of New European and Central Asian States. *GeoJournal* 52: 315–23.
Bryant, John. 1981. Stamp and Coin Collecting. In *Handbook of American Popular Culture, Volume 3*, ed. M. Thomas Inge, pp. 1329–65. Westport, CT: Greenwood Press.

Buchanan, R. Angus. 2002. *Brunel: The Life and Times of Isambard Kingdom Brunel*. London: Hambledon.

Child, Jack. 2005. The Politics and Semiotics of the Smallest Icons of Popular Culture: Latin American Postage Stamps. *Latin American Research Review* 40: 108–37.

Covington, Kate and Stanley D. Brunn. 2006. Celebrating a Nation's Heritage on Music Stamps: Constructing an International Community. *GeoJournal* 65: 125–35.

Cusack, Igor. 2005. Tiny Transmitters of Nationalist and Colonial Ideology: The Postage Stamps of Portugal and its Empire. *Nations and Nationalism* 11: 591–612.

Deans, Phil and Dobson, Hugo. 2005. Introduction: East Asian Postage Stamps as Socio-Political Artefacts. *East Asian* 22: 3–7.

Dibner, Bern. 1959. *The Atlantic Cable*. Burndy Library Publication 16.

Dimson, Elroy and Spaenjers, Christophe. 2011. Ex Post: The Investment Performance of Collectible Stamps. *Journal of Financial Economics* 100: 443–58.

Dobson, Hugo. 2002. Japanese Postage Stamps: Propaganda and Decision Making. *Japan Forum* 14: 21–39.

Dugan, James. 1953. *The Great Iron Ship*. New York: Harper & Brothers.

Dumpleton, Bernard and Miller, Muriel. 1984. *Brunel's Three Ships*. Melksham, UK: Colin Venton.

Emmerson, George S. 1977. *John Scott Russell: A Great Victorian Engineer and Naval Architect*. London: John Murray.

—— 1981. *The Greatest Iron Ship: S.S. Great Eastern*. Newton Abbot: David & Charles.

Frewer, Douglas. 2002. Japanese Postage Stamps as Social Agents: Some Anthropological Perspectives. *Japan Forum* 14: 1–19.

Gelber, Steven M. 1992. Free Market Metaphor: The Historical Dynamics of Stamp Collecting. *Comparative Studies in Society and History* 34: 742–69.

Griffiths, Denis, Lambert, Andrew, and Walker, Fred. 1999. *Brunel's Ships*. London: Chatham Publishing.

Guins, Raiford. 2009. Concrete and Clay: The Life and Afterlife of E.T. The Extra-Terrestrial for the Atari 2600. *Design and Culture* 1: 345–64.

Harrison, Rodney. 2010. Stone Tools. In *The Oxford Handbook of Material Culture Studies*, ed. Dan Hicks and Mary C. Beaudry, pp. 521–42. Oxford: Oxford University Press.

Harrison, Rodney and Schofield, John. 2010. *After Modernity: Archaeological Approaches to the Contemporary Past*. Oxford: Oxford University Press.

Harvey, Karen (ed.). 2009. *History and Material Culture: A Student's Guide to Approaching Alternative Sources*. London: Routledge.

Hearn, Chester G. 2004. *Circuits in the Sea: The Men, the Ships, and the Atlantic Cable*. Westport, CT: Praeger.

Heiduschke, Sebastian. 2006. The Afterlife of DEFA in Post-Unification Germany: Characteristics, Traditions and Cultural Legacy. Ph.D. dissertation, University of Texas at Austin.

Jones, Robert A. 2001. Heroes of the Nation? The Celebration of Scientists on the Postage Stamps of Great Britain, France and West Germany. *Journal of Contemporary History* 36: 403–22.

Kirshenblatt-Gimblett, Barbara. 1998. *Destination Culture: Tourism, Museums, and Heritage*. Berkeley: University of California Press.

Kloetzel, James E. (ed.). 2010. *Scott 2010 Standard Postage Stamp Catalogue*. 6 vols. Sidney, OH: Scott Publishing Company.

Leclerc, Jacques and Scott, Nora. 1993. The Political Iconology of the Indonesian Postage Stamp (1950–1970). *Indonesia* 57: 15–18.

Mingo, Jack. 1997. Postal Imperialism. *The New York Times Magazine*, 16 February.

Raento, Pauliina and Brunn, Stanley D. 2005. Visualizing Finland: Postage Stamps as Political Messengers. *Geografiska Annaler: Series B, Human Geography* 87: 145–64.

Rathje, William L. and Murphy, Cullen. 1992. *Rubbish! The Archaeology of Garbage*. New York: HarperCollins.

Reid, Donald M. 1984. The Symbolism of Postage Stamps: A Source for the Historian. *Journal of Contemporary History* 19: 223–49.

—— 1993. The Postage Stamp: A Window on Saddam Hussein's Iraq. *Middle East Journal* 47: 77–89.

Reid, J. Jefferson, Schiffer, Michael B., and Rathje, William L. 1975. Behavioral Archaeology: Four Strategies. *American Anthropologist* 77: 864–9.

Schnitzel, Paul. 1979. A Note on the Philatelic Demand for Postage Stamps. *Southern Economic Journal* 45: 1261–5.

Scott, David. 1995. *European Stamp Design: A Semiotic Approach to Designing Messages*. London: Academy Editions.

Skaggs, David C. 1978. Postage Stamps as Icons. In *Icons of America*, ed. Ray B. Browne and Marshall Fishwick, pp. 198–208. Bowling Green, KY: Popular Press.

Slemrod, Joel. 2008. Why is Elvis on Burkina Faso Postage Stamps? Cross-Country Evidence on the Commercialization of State Sovereignty. *Journal of Empirical Legal Studies* 5: 683–712.

Steinberg, Philip E. and McDowell, Stephen D. 2003. Mutiny on the Bandwidth: The Semiotics of Statehood in the Internet Domain Registries of Pitcairn Island and Niue. *New Media Society* 5: 47–67.

Stoetzer, Carlos. 1953. *Postage Stamps as Propaganda*. Washington, DC: Public Affairs Press.

Vaughan, Adrian. 1991. *Isambard Kingdom Brunel: Engineering Knight-Errant*. London: John Murray.

Walker, William H. 1999. Ritual, Life Histories, and the Afterlives of People and Things. *Journal of the Southwest* 41: 383–405.

—— 2008. Practice and Nonhuman Social Actors: The Afterlife Histories of Witches and Dogs in the American Southwest. In *Memory Work: Archaeologies of Material Practice*, ed. Barbara J. Mills and William H. Walker, pp. 137–57. Santa Fe: School for Advanced Research Press.

CHAPTER 19

....

WASTE

....

JOSHUA RENO

19.1 INTRODUCTION

....

IN this chapter I will discuss the potential for an archaeology of the contemporary world that comes from interpretations of recently discarded wastes. Transforming the waste of contemporary societies from a problem into empirical evidence provides one of the clearest means of fostering a publicly engaged and politically relevant archaeology. This was the insight of William Rathje and his pioneering 'Garbage Project'. Begun in Tucson in 1973 and ending with Rathje's retirement over two decades later (Randall McGuire, personal communication), it was one of the longest running social science research initiatives in history. Maintained by Rathje, his students, and colleagues at the University of Arizona, the Project offered fledgling archaeologists an opportunity to train themselves in archaeological methods and learn about their society through its rubbish, which they excavated, sifted, and sorted like the material remains of any civilization. Initially, this involved processing waste materials left for roadside pickup, and by 1984 over a million items had been recovered in this fashion. The Garbage Project went on to excavate the landfills and dumps of fifteen different cities (see Rathje 2011: 176).

I will review the origins of the Garbage Project in archaeological theory, as well as the 'stranger society' of Cold War America, to which it owes its epistemological and material roots. I will then move on to consider the folk-archaeological activities of some waste workers, whose interactions with their society's rubbish parallel those of professional archaeologists in interesting ways. In particular, I will examine landfill labourers at a large dump in south-eastern Michigan, where I conducted fieldwork as an employee from 2005 to 2006. Using these case studies, I will argue that what Rathje terms the 'garbology' of the modern world introduces distinct ethical and political complications into archaeological practice. This stems from the lingering association between things and persons that persists even when the two are radically separated, as they are by forms of modern waste management, and upon which both the opportunities and dilemmas of garbology are predicated. It is generally accepted that the distribution of waste affects how and what we experience (see Douglas 1966), but the more radical proposal from Rathje's project is that the production and circulation of mass waste also mediates our capacities for reflexivity, that is, how and what we can know about one another and ourselves. But embracing this idea means getting closer to garbage.

19.2 THE GARBAGE PROJECT AS 'BEHAVIORAL ARCHEOLOGY'

The Garbage Project can be understood as a development in the 'New Archaeology' that emerged in the 1960s (Buchli and Lucas 2001; Harrison and Schofield 2010; see also Fewster, this volume). It is in many ways a logical counterpart to the methodological and theoretical approach known as 'behavioral archeology', identified most closely with the work of Michael Schiffer (1976, 1985), a graduate student at the University of Arizona when the project was founded.[1] Indeed, in one of the first essays to use the term 'behavioral archeology', co-written by J. Jefferson Reid, Schiffer, and Rathje (1975), the newly developed Garbage Project is depicted as the last of four strategies, each representing a different way of using material culture to describe and explain human behaviour (see Figure 19.1).

If strategies 1 and 2 represent traditional archaeological approaches, with a shared focus on interpreting past behaviour through material culture, the latter two suggest that archaeological methods might offer insights into contemporary life as well. Rather than imagine archaeology as merely derivative of ethnology, as if the discipline were nothing more than an imperfect means of documenting a culture that one cannot experience directly (i.e. observation without the possibility of being a participant) Reid, Schiffer, and Rathje suggest that archaeological techniques can provide unique insights even when applied to present-day Tucson. This is so because archaeological methods challenge social scientists to concentrate their focus on matters of empirical detail and keep in check their tendencies to ascribe their own interpretations to observed phenomena.

It is helpful to understand the roots of behavioral archeology, which can be partly traced to Schiffer's arguments concerning the formation processes of the archaeological record, first published in 1972. Schiffer's central methodological insight is that cultural deposits must undergo a transition between the 'systemic context' within which they first became meaningful, and the 'archaeological context' within which they are later recognized as the artefacts of a particular cultural tradition. Furthermore, he argued that developing accurate archaeological interpretations required more than an understanding of the objects themselves, but familiarity with the processes by which they come to be preserved and found. This was not an entirely novel approach. As Lewis Binford (1981) pointed out in his critique of behavioral archeology, Robert Ascher had made similar claims in the early 1960s:

> Every living community is in the process of continuous change with respect to the materials which it utilizes. At any point in its existence some proportion of materials are falling into disuse and decomposing, while new materials are being added as replacements. In a certain sense, a part of every community is becoming, but is not yet, archaeological data. (Ascher 1961: 324)

[1] Throughout this chapter, 'behavioral archeology' is rendered in its American spelling in order to signal the historical and social context from which this perspective emerged. Where 'archaeology' and 'behaviour' are employed as general terms, however, the British spelling is preferred.

Material Objects

		Past	Present
Human Behavior	Past	1	2
	Present	3	4

FIGURE 19.1 Strategies of a behavioral archeology (Josh Reno, redrawn from Reid, Schiffer, and Rathje 1975)

According to Ascher, no data that a living community leaves behind can do justice to this continuous material becoming. He described the fallacious view that archaeological evidence can be taken for granted as a snapshot of a past culture, frozen in time for observation, as the 'Pompeii premise' (1961: 324), in reference to the ideal state of preservation of that historic Italian city after a sudden volcanic eruption in the first century AD. In his later account of Ellis Island Immigration Station in New York City (Ascher 1974), Ascher would show that such a premise was invalid even for an archaeology of the recent past. Decaying and abandoned, the cultural deposit of Ellis Island represents the inverse of Pompeii, a place that, despite its spatio temporal proximity, has moved on from the past in a way that resists straightforward archaeological interpretation.

At Binford's provocation, Schiffer (1985) agreed with Ascher that a 'Pompeii premise' lurked behind a great deal of archaeological interpretation. His distinct response was that this could be countered by focusing more attention to the formation processes that assemble archaeological sites, placing them on a continuum closer to or more distant from the Pompeii extreme. Ascher's more cybernetic argument portrayed the process of archaeological site formation as if different forms of entropic 'noise' were hopelessly distorting cultural messages from the past; without the corroboration of collateral evidence, any archaeological interpretations would be highly spurious. Ascher's answer to this quandary was to pioneer forms of experimental archaeology, the uses of modern techniques and materials to learn about past behaviour, or the second behavioral archeological strategy outlined by Reid, Schiffer, and Rathje (1975). But they were more optimistic than Binford would have them be. Unlike Ascher they argued that there is hope for archaeological interpretation, because formation processes, though distorting, are regular and predictable. They were perhaps emboldened in their assessment by the rise of ecological and environmental sciences in the 1960s and 1970s, which promised to clarify the influence of non-human variables in the journey of objects towards the status of archaeological artefact. But their views also reveal a novel reflection on the human tendency towards object discard and abandonment. These waste practices were not merely incidental to past and living communities, but rather represented a key to revealing habits obscured by too much distance or, alternatively, too much familiarity.

Indeed, the patterns of human discard might themselves be subject to laws, ones that those who get close to waste—whether by choice or circumstance—are in the best position to deduce. From this perspective, a landfill becomes an ideal archaeological setting. For one thing, it offers a means to understand that aspect of humanity so central to archaeological interpretations in a 'behavioral' vein. Through observation, one could deduce laws about practices of human discard, thereby assisting in the ability to decipher the formation processes leading from systemic to archaeological context. Indeed, the additional benefit of studying landfills is that, arguably, they seem to represent an almost entirely 'cultural' formation process, one that does not allow non-cultural variables to play a leading role. The movement of wastes from bins to garbage collection facilities to dumps is entirely regularized in modern industrial societies. That is where objects (and sometimes people) go when someone wishes to be rid of them or, more precisely, rid of the relationship they share. When something is disposed of, it is not necessarily that the person discarding does not want the discarded object to be reused, but that they wish to be morally and physically detached from its further existence, in Ascher's terms, its becoming. The choice to place the object in the bin reflects a decisive behavioural outcome, one that can be discerned from the discovery of that item in a landfill, in the same way that the removal of discard leaves a trace or 'absent presence' behind (Hetherington 2004; see also Fowles and Heupel, this volume). This is possible because the moment of object detachment can be isolated from the formation processes that led that item to be buried in that site. Because waste management practices are so regularized and systematic, in other words, their contribution to the artefact can be held constant as a variable, and recovered discards can be directly linked to the behavioural habits of those to whom they were formerly 'attached'.

With Rathje, I argue that much can be learned about the contemporary world through its waste, even beyond the isolation of consumer behaviours. I will make this claim with reference to the history of garbology as a technique of journalism and police investigation, as well as to my anthropological fieldwork at a landfill in Michigan, which I call 'Four Corners'. If waste sites provide good 'archaeological contexts' to scientific garbologists, as with all archaeological sites, they attract their share of amateurs as well, suggesting a possible fifth behavioural strategy, encompassing the folk-archaeological interpretations of those who live and work with waste.

19.3 THE GARBAGE PROJECT

'In the three or so million years of humankind', Rathje writes, 'we have never had more reason than we have today to try to understand our relation to our artifacts—what we manufacture, use, and discard—and how our artifacts both mirror and *shape* our actions and attitudes' (1984: 9). The implication of this statement, and much of Rathje's popular writing on the subject of the Garbage Project, is that there are not only scientific, but also moral and political reasons why modern people ought to examine themselves more closely through their rubbish. Environmental concerns, for example, played a decisive role in the evolution of the Garbage Project and the motivations behind it (see Rathje 2011). When Rathje and his students began excavating landfills in 1987, they were not only interested in categorizing the contents of these waste sites, but also in assessing the rate at which household waste materials break down, their contribution to pollution, and the impact of recycling, composting, and other methods of diverting waste from landfill (see Rathje 1996).

The timing of their studies was not arbitrary; it was around this time that new environmental regulations were coming into effect regarding sanitary landfills. As old dumps were rendered obsolete, new sites appeared like Four Corners, the site of my fieldwork in south-eastern Michigan. These new landfills attempted to prevent the leakage of toxicants into groundwater and emissions into the air and were strictly monitored for their environmental impacts.

In a sense, the Garbage Project's move towards exploring the insides of landfills mirrored the evolution of waste management and its regulation in Euro-American contexts.

Even before the rise of new waste regulations, the Garbage Project was invested in contemporary social issues surrounding resource use and, more centrally, deciphering the sometimes-beguiling behaviour of consumers. The first method of waste recovery, the 'Regular Sort', employed specific categories to facilitate the deduction of rules behind the seemingly arbitrary decisions of household waste producers. One of the first patterns often cited by Rathje is the truism that self-reports are an unreliable way of gathering evidence of people's discard practices. As an example, Rathje and his students demonstrate a substantial difference between reported levels of alcohol consumption and actual consumption, as indicated by the average number of beverage containers disposed of per household (see, for example, Rathje 1996). This discrepancy is important, not only because it offers evidence of a general behavioural regularity, but because it provides justification for the Garbage Project as a whole.

Precisely because of the Garbage Project's comparatively objective method of assessing patterns of material use and discard, Rathje was called to testify before dozens of government committees, congressional, legislative, and local, on the waste industry, resource use, and American waste habits. In 1980, the United States Department of Agriculture (USDA) began working with the Garbage Project in order to address a discrepancy in their data. In the 1977–8 USDA survey, it was found that as much as 35 per cent of total food energy was 'lost' somewhere between purchase and consumption and could not be accounted for (Ritenbaugh and Harrison 1984: 52). Overall, the 'Food Loss Project' did not find that edible food was being discarded at high rates, as was proposed to explain the discrepancy, but became a means of pointing out the limitations of various methods of refuse analysis (see Rathje 1984). In this way, the Garbage Project remains true to behavioral archeology; cultivating better understanding of material formation processes is paramount to understanding behaviour.

If the results of the Garbage Project are meant to complement a search for socio-culturally invariant behaviours, in conjunction with the other three behavioral strategies outlined above, the timely social concerns associated with each study during the 1970s and 1980s (food waste, meat shortages, and alcohol abuse) illustrate that behavioral archeology was intended as a means of improving the governance of household conduct through better social science (see Rathje 2011: 178). In this sense, the methods of archaeologists of modern garbage cannot be separated from larger political and moral questions of their time, not only concerning which particular social behaviours are of interest, but also how experts relate to their surveillance and control (see also Buchli and Lucas 2001: 6).

19.4 THE ORIGINS OF GARBOLOGY

The study of modern garbage, what Rathje also terms 'garbology', has always been subject to political and moral concerns, which are evident in the development of the practice in the twentieth-century US. The concern that people might either intentionally or inadvertently obscure what they really do 'behind closed doors' was a guiding motivation for innovations in the social sciences, policing, and journalism leading up to the Second World War and throughout the Cold War era.

The first self-described 'garbologist' was the radical American journalist A. J. Weberman, who began by recovering the household waste of celebrities as a means of writing and speculating about their lives and secrets: including Bob Dylan, Norman Mailer, and Richard Nixon (Weberman 1980). Garbology presumes that one of the best ways to know someone is to know what they throw away, which is based on a modern fascination with the difference between the 'real person' and the public front they present to others. The idea of unveiling the 'real person' concealed behind closed doors had already been a prevailing concern of modern states, increasingly paranoid about political subversives and radical movements, leading ultimately to the pre-war creation of secret police and intelligence agencies. Intelligence and security operations boomed with the start of the Cold War. In the US, law enforcement agencies performed surveillance by manipulating and violating the ideological public/private boundary, as well as rerouting the transfer of materials and messages across it. Along with wire-tapping, 'mail cover', and break-ins, so-called 'trash cover' was a frequently used surveillance technique of J. Edgar Hoover's Federal Bureau of Investigation (FBI) during the 1950s and early 1960s (Powers 2004: 271). The FBI routinely used trash cover against those deemed to be real or potential enemies of the state, including leftists, organized crime, and the Ku Klux Klan. Around the same time, a cultural fascination around subversive and abject lives conducted in private inspired everything from the sex studies conducted by the Kinseys at Indiana University to the popular literature about serial killers and the dramaturgical sociology of Erving Goffman. Weberman's journalistic garbology was only the most recent incarnation of a broader cultural and political trend.

If waste has become a resource for revelations about the private individual and household in the twentieth-century US, so too has it helped to bring about the very divisions that these revelatory practices are predicated upon. The hidden self is partly a product of a waste management system that allows households to conceal their activities from observation. Waste is not only a sign of behaviour behind closed doors, in other words, but is precisely one of the modern elements that has allowed for such concealment. Just as waste practices define culture and society, they introduce the possibility of garbology as a meaningful enterprise.

If garbology became meaningful as a folk-archaeological practice in the context of the twentieth-century US, it is evident in many of the modern assumptions behind the practice. Firstly, that it is meaningful to distinguish between that which is open to the public and that which is concealed in 'private', the most foundational of which is the 'true' self. Secondly, and following on from this, there is seemingly greater objectivity, not just in material remains in general, but in those remains made available through the impersonal formation processes associated with landfilling. The conditions of modern waste removal and disposal reinforce these assumptions by separating households from their discards, thereby creating anonymous, aggregate waste streams that belong to no individual.

Landfilling is but one very common means of disposal within contemporary waste regimes. Zsuzsa Gille (2007) coined the term 'waste regime' in order to situate waste disposal within the encompassing modes of material production and imagination that characterize particular places and times. Landfilling disposes of the majority of wastes in Anglophone countries, but even where other methods predominate the prevailing waste regime tends to include the separation of the world's relatively affluent populations, and hence those most 'rich' in material culture, from sites of disposal. Professional and informal garbologists exploit the conditions of contemporary waste regimes to different ends: whether they peek into dumpsters or explore the contents of landfills they rely on the importance other people place on being separate from waste matter (see Douglas 1966; Hawkins 2004).

Mass wasting of this sort is particularly suitable to the purposes of a discipline like archaeology (see Shanks, Platt, and Rathje 2004: 66), which is primarily based on recovering other people's excess material in order to feed 'an unceasing demand for more facts' (Shanks 1992: 56). But the archaeology of recent wastes introduces at least two significant complications. Firstly, as is oftentimes the case for other artefacts, the ownership of waste and control of access to waste sites can be highly contested. This is mediated by a second complication, which is the contemporaneity of the archaeologist and those who provide them with excess 'evidence'. Both of these dilemmas shape the possibilities of folk-archaeological interactions with wastes at dumping sites.

19.5 THE DILEMMAS OF GARBOLOGY

'Landfill sites are modernity's ruins'. (Shanks, Platt, and Rathje 2004: 67)

If garbology is older than the Garbage Project, it is also more commonplace. And, the exploits of journalists and policeman aside, none have more access to the wealth of rubbish produced by industrial societies than those who deal with it on behalf of others. Informal recycling is a particularly important economic activity for poor and marginalized populations the world over (Medina 2007). The fact that those who sort through waste are marginalized does not prevent them from making the most out of their proximity to trash (Hill 2001; Millar 2008; Reno 2009; Alexander and Reno 2012). We should not presume that in an ideal world everyone would be further from their wastes, especially when more proximity make some wealthier or more socially reflexive. At the landfill I call Four Corners, where I was employed as a common labourer for nine months, one is constantly reminded that rubbish has an origin, including other people to whom it relates, and about whom it might tell a story.

In Schiffer's terms, landfilled wastes are technically artefacts in an 'archaeological context', since they are bits of refuse removed from their original 'systemic context' wherein they had a social meaning and function (see also Schiffer, this volume, on 'afterlives'). However, in the case of landfills both contexts co-occur: items in the landfill are always potentially reactivated as systemically meaningful. Rathje (1984) and Ritenbaugh and Harrison (1984) both refer to the 'reactivity' of waste studies, their ability to impact upon those who released them into the hands of archaeological students. They indicate what this means for garbology as a form of data collection, but not its status as an ethical and political act.

The benefit of collapsing the distance between archaeological and systemic context is that without concern for the original meaning of artefacts, the garbologist can reinvent and reimagine material. One can engage in random acts of play and enjoyment (see Reno 2009), but also in theory speculate on formation processes and eschew meaning altogether. Due to the closeness of the systemic and archaeological context in the folk-archaeology of the contemporary, however, there remains the possibility that material remains will carry trace evidence that can be linked to particular people.

After I had worked at Four Corners for a few months I learned this first-hand when Zack, the youngest mechanic, offered me a desktop computer. Zack had retrieved the computer some time ago from the small tool shed at the top of the landfill, left behind by a machine operator who had recovered it from one of the garbage loads. He cleaned it out but had never used it, now he was eager to part with the find in order to make room in his house for his new wife's things, as well as to have an excuse to lend me some of his video games, which he had been interested in doing for some time. I gladly accepted the gift. Given the rapid rate at which computers become obsolescent, in terms of fashion and functionality, my existing 1998 model was practically a dinosaur and receiving a replacement at no cost was too good a deal to turn down. But this was not a new computer, I would soon discover. When I first turned the machine on, traces of the former owner were suddenly everywhere. Pictures, documents, and applications still existed in abundance on the hard drive along with the full name of their former owner. I cleared the machine of all its contents, burdened with an ethical responsibility inadvertently foisted upon me by a person I could readily identify, perhaps even locate. For a time I considered trying to find the person, to create an interview opportunity to learn about the movement of waste out of an accidental garbological find, but I quickly decided against it.

At the landfill, it was not necessary to make such ethical decisions on one's own. Sometimes collective will would overrule someone's attempt to cling to a found object. In one instance, groups of us spent the week 'picking paper' that had blown down the northern face of the landfill from where they were tipping waste haulers up top. On the first day, I and two other young labourers stumbled across a large number of Polaroid photographs of a woman in various states of undress. They excitedly began to collect the photos and gather them under a large rock. I was deeply distressed by this, but was still new to the landfill and did not feel comfortable asserting control over garbological activities with which I had little experience. To my relief, on another day I found myself again in that area of the landfill with two of the senior labourers, who asked me about the collection when they found it. After I explained, they promptly uttered their disapproval and threw all of the photos into the garbage bags with the rest of the stray paper, to be buried in the landfill.

When Rathje states, in one of the more widely cited findings of the Garbage Project, that paper constitutes more than half of the discards that he and his students have documented, he does not point out that these documents might be credit card statements, cheques, diaries, homework, or personal photographs. The everyday encounters that landfills make possible between labourers and waste regularly provide access to the people and lives they were once intimately connected to. Whether or not landfill workers wish to consider themselves scientists of human behaviour, they are forced to recognize that waste can speak volumes about others and I have often been impressed by their commitment to honouring the wishes of people they don't know and disposing of what they find. This may be done out of courtesy, or it may be a consequence of the fact that the relationships that concern landfill workers most are those they maintain with their co-workers and managers on a day-to-day basis, not the virtual connections that arise, linking them to absent people whose waste ended up at their feet. This, I believe, they share with archaeologists on the Garbage Project, where student–teacher relationships or those between academic colleagues exert more influence in shaping everyday ethical practice, in many ways, than relations to waste makers themselves.

It is in this regard, arguably, that professional garbologists, of the archaeological sort, have the most to learn from the comportments to waste that landfill work can foster. Because of their employment working with waste, landfill labourers form different interpretations of waste that can reveal interesting characteristics, perhaps even amounting to a fifth behavioral strategy, the folk-archaeological interpretation of modern waste to interpret modern society and behaviours. Through the perspective of waste workers, the regularities that Rathje and his colleagues derive from the behaviour of individuals and households can take on other forms. For people working at Four Corners, for example, there were similar pseudo-archaeological laws that people shared. I will describe four.

The first concerns a general realization that comes from repeatedly witnessing the arrival of fresh waste loads and the complementary growth of the landfill itself: no matter what happens, waste keeps coming. That waste cannot be connected to individual places or groups, except of the most general sort (e.g. 'Canadian', 'municipal', 'construction and demolition'). It may adopt the appearance of a collectively produced entity but, in its most generalized manifestation as part of the mass waste stream, industrial discards become nothing more than brute matter. Assessed in terms of weight and volume, waste streams appear discultural or postcultural, and regardless of changing consumer tastes and habits they never stop flowing.

A second insight comes from regular encounters with other people's waste. No matter how personal, people will throw anything away without a thought, as is evidenced by my computer and the photographs. Regular scavenging reveals that people will also throw things away that are 'perfectly good' and can be remade with the right skill and commitment (see Reno 2009). Once again, these encounters have more to do with relationships at the landfill than they do connections between landfill workers and households.

A third insight arises from the conflicts that occur on occasion between landfill scavengers and the landfill company or the government operatives who sometimes appear to ensure materials are properly disposed of rather than reclaimed, for example spoiled alcohol. There is a general sense that whatever people throw away on an individual basis, corporate profiteering and government regulations are even more wasteful than the public. They may block access to scavenging, for example, or they may just commit profligate acts of wasting that defy explanation. On one occasion I stood atop the landfill and watched with a fellow labourer as someone's former home, a double wide trailer, was dragged to the dumping area, carved up by a bulldozer, and pushed into the sludge pit. This was frequently done when homes were vacated and not considered worth the cost of clearing out and reselling. Sometimes landfill workers would be allowed—without management's knowledge—to grab anything of value before they were destroyed, but not this time. We watched as the accumulated memories of a household spilled out of the structure, furniture and photos and clothing, and all were shoved into the liquid muck below. The tragedy of Hurricane Katrina had recently been in the news (see also Dawdy, this volume), and the instant reaction of my associate was disgust that people were homeless in the gulf region and we were destroying homes here.

This leads to a fourth and final insight. Landfills do not only alter landscapes, but environmental and social consciousness as well. By making so much waste disappear so efficiently, they can also make it harder to grasp mass wasting at greater scales, which is perhaps why the image of waste production so often falls back on the more familiar image of household bins and individual consumers. Only those garbologists who peer into the contents of bins and landfills have access to alternative images of waste production; an abandoned trailer full of possessions torn to pieces, for example. I would submit that it is not only householder behaviour that can be analysed and about which regularities can be deduced, but—due to the familiar systemic context that garbologists share with those who make garbage—other social collectives as well. It is arguably the activities of corporations and other aggregate social actors that are most responsible for the waste regimes, and hence formation processes of modern societies (see Graeber 2012: 281–2). Indeed, without the waste industry itself garbology would not be possible at all. Landfill labourers and other waste workers offer valuable reminders about the untapped possibilities of garbological study.

The question remains: might alternatives to landfill disposal, including incinerators, anaerobic digestors, pyrolizers, plasma arcs, gasifiers, and composting operations, involve potentially very different forms of social consciousness in turn? One can characterize these as more future-oriented technologies, because they rely on the transformation of materials into something entirely new, eliminating the possibility of reflection on their past relationships and meanings. The benefit of this is that it ideally unfetters mass waste from its association with pollution and impurity, allowing its commodification as a source of biofuel, fertilizer, and green credits. In Europe, for example, this has meant an increasing push—on the part of the waste industry—to rebrand their activities as centrally concerned with managing 'resources'. But this future-orientation also potentially obscures their conditions of possibility, the waste regime of which they are only the most recent manifestation. While providing the image of sustainable loops of matter and energy, landfill alternatives threaten to maintain a similar detachment between waste producers and waste products, with the main difference being that no garbologist can ever reconnect them.

But this is only the case if waste is separated so thoroughly from those who produce it that it travels many miles, crossing social and geographical boundaries, before coming to rest. To the extent that waste settles 'locally' and its producers are required to tend to it in some way, for example by sorting their food waste for separate collection (Reno 2011), there are possibilities that such new practices could encourage more reflection concerning collective and individual waste production. In this sense, alternatives to landfill could do more than turn wastes into new resources, but make garbologists of us all.

19.6 CONCLUSION

If changes to the waste industry are to popularize garbological consciousness, to make of it something more than a tool of surveillance, this would require more opportunities for waste producers to meditate on their outputs. This would require not only disciplining waste disposal habits, for example training households and industries to separate their biodegradable wastes for collection, but also providing them opportunities to think about where their waste goes, who is affected by it, and what it says about the way in which they live. Zap Rowsdower writes in a similar manner about the availability of industrial ruins to non-archaeological actors, those who are 'explicitly or implicitly enculturated to identify ... the implications of these discards of development and progress' (2011: 3; see also Lucas, this volume). He writes about lay urban explorers and professional archaeologists cultivating a nostalgic appreciation for the meaning of decay and loss, but one could just as easily refer to this as a cultivated comportment towards material possibility or, following Ascher, the continual becoming of places and things.

Garbology is older and more widespread than the Garbage Project or the sanitary landfill. Waste workers become amateur archaeologists when they peruse the wastes of capitalist modernity, and they too can draw on their encounters with material detritus to make broader claims about their present moment and human formation processes in general. They also highlight the ethical and political complications that challenge and inspire any archaeology of the contemporary world, complications which follow from the lack of distance between, in Schiffer's terminology, the archeological context and the systemic one.

Rather than dismiss the efforts of folk-garbologists as irrelevant or quaint, I would argue that their insights can contribute new ways of understanding the material patterns that constitute everyday life in capitalist modernity and the formation processes of the record they leave behind. For one thing, as compared with the more practised analytical methods of archaeologists like Rathje and his students, their perspectives open up an appreciation for the 'behaviours' of collectives beyond the modern individual, such as the state and the corporation, and the formation processes they take a hand in shaping. Taken together, different groups of garbologists offer unique contributions to a future-oriented archaeology (see Dawdy 2009), as well as opportunities to reflect on the role of archaeological practice in shaping and living in that world.

REFERENCES

Alexander, Catherine and Reno, Joshua (eds.). 2012. *Economies of Recycling: Global Transformations of Materials, Values and Social Relations*. London: Zed Books.

Ascher, Robert. 1961. Analogy in Archaeological Interpretation. *Southwestern Journal of Anthropology* 17: 317–25.

—— 1974. Tin Can Archaeology. *Historical Archaeology* 8: 7–16.

Binford, Lewis. 1981. Behavioral Archaeology and the 'Pompeii Premise'. *Journal of Anthropological Research* 37(3): 195–208.

Buchli, Victor and Lucas, Gavin. 2001. The Absent Present: Archaeologies of the Contemporary Past. In *Archaeology of the Contemporary Past*, ed. Victor Buchli and Gavin Lucas, pp. 3–18. London: Routledge.

Dawdy, Shannon Lee. 2009. Millennial Archaeology: Locating the Discipline in the Age of Insecurity. *Archaeological Dialogues* 16: 131–42.

Douglas, Mary. 1966. *Purity and Danger: An Analysis of Concepts of Pollution and Taboo*. New York and London: Routledge.

Gille, Zsuzsa. 2007. *From the Cult of Waste to the Trash Heap of History: The Politics of Waste in Socialist and Post-socialist Hungary*. Bloomington: Indiana University Press.

Graeber, David. 2012. Afterword: The Apocalypse of Objects—Degradation, Redemption and Transcendence in the World of Consumer Goods. In *Economies of Recycling: The Global Transformation of Materials, Values and Social Relations*, ed. Catherine Alexander and Joshua Reno, pp. 277–90. London: Zed Books.

Harrison, Rodney and Schofield, John. 2010. *After Modernity: Archaeological Approaches to the Contemporary Past*. Oxford: Oxford University Press.

Hawkins, Gay. 2004. *The Ethics of Waste: How We Relate to Waste*. Boulder, CO: Rowman & Littlefield.

Hetherington, Kevin. 2004. Secondhandedness: Consumption, Disposal, and Absent Presence. *Environment and Planning D: Society and Space* 22: 157–73.

Hill, Sarah. 2001. The Environmental Divide: Neoliberal Incommensurability at the U.S.–Mexico Border. *Urban Anthropology and Studies of Cultural Systems and World Economic Development* 30(2/3): 157–87.

Medina, Martin. 2007. *The World's Scavengers: Salvaging for Sustainable Consumption and Production*. Lanham, MD and New York: Altamira Press.

Millar, Kathleen. 2008. Making Trash into Treasure: Struggles for Autonomy on a Brazilian Garbage Dump. *Anthropology of Work Review* 29(2): 25–34.

Powers, Richard. 2004. *Broken: The Troubled Past and Uncertain Future of the FBI*. New York: Free Press.

Rathje, William. 1984. The Garbáge Decade. *American Behavioral Scientist* 28(1): 9–29.

—— 1996. The Archaeology of Us. In *Encyclopaedia Britannica's Yearbook of Science and the Future—1997*, ed. David Calhoun, pp. 158–77. New York: Encyclopaedia Britannica.

—— 2011. Archaeological Intervention in the Past, Present and Future Tense. *Archaeological Dialogues* 18(2): 176–80.

Reid, J. Jefferson, Schiffer, Michael, and Rathje, William. 1975. Behavioral Archaeology: Four Strategies. *American Anthropologist* 77(4): 864–9.

Reno, Joshua. 2009. Your Trash is Someone's Treasure: The Politics of Value at a Michigan Landfill. *Journal of Material Culture* 14(1): 29–46.

—— 2011. Managing the Experience of Evidence: England's Experimental Waste Technologies and their Immodest Witnesses. *Science, Technology and Human Values* 36(6): 842–63.

Ritenbaugh, Cheryl and Harrison, Gail. 1984. Reactivity of Garbage Analysis. *American Behavioral Scientist* 28(1): 51–70.

Rowsdower, Zap. 2011. Fresh Rot: Urban Exploration and the Preservation of Decay. *Journal of the University of Manitoba Archaeology* 29: 1–15.

Schiffer, Michael. 1972. Archaeological Context and Systemic Context. *American Antiquity* 37: 156–65.

—— 1976. *Behavioral Archeology*. New York: Academic Press.

—— 1985. Is there a 'Pompeii Premise' in Archaeology? *Journal of Anthropological Research* 41(1): 18–41.

Shanks, Michael. 1992. *Experiencing the Past: On the Character of Archaeology*. London and New York: Routledge.

Shanks, Michael, Platt, David, and Rathje, William. 2004. The Perfume of Garbage: Modernity and the Archaeological. *Modernism/Modernity* 11(1): 61–83.

Weberman, Alan J. 1980. *My Life in Garbology*. New York: Stonehill.

CHAPTER 20

....

HERITAGE

....

RODNEY HARRISON

20.1 INTRODUCTION

THIS chapter has two related concerns. The first is to consider archaeology and heritage as two of a series of connected ideas about the relationship between the past and the present in late modern societies. I argue that archaeology is one of a number of historical sciences concerned with the production of heritage as part of a modern conception of time, in which the past is made to appear distant and the present appears as a 'contemporary past'. As such, heritage can be viewed as a manifestation of a society in which the past is perceived to be both immanent (contained within) and imminent (impending) in the present, or as Marc Augé puts it, always 'on our heels, following us like shadows' (1995: 26). The second concern is to explore the role of archaeological methods in investigating heritage as a contemporary social phenomenon. Drawing on two brief examples, this chapter considers the production of heritage 'experiences' as a key manifestation of the nature of heritage in late modern experience societies. Each heritage site is understood to represent an assemblage (or *agencement*) composed of a number of different ancient and modern devices, technologies, and apparatuses (*dispositifs*) (see further discussion in Harrison 2013b) which might be subject to archaeological investigation. In this way, the chapter is both an exploration of contemporary archaeology *and* heritage, and a contemporary archaeology *of* heritage in late modern societies.

20.2 THE PRESENCE OF THE PAST IN LATE MODERN SOCIETIES

We live in an age in which heritage might appear to be both universal and ever-present. In speaking of heritage, I refer to objects, places, and practices which are officially recognized through formal listing on some type of heritage register or list and which are actively

managed, conserved, and/or presented as heritage ('official' as opposed to 'unofficial' heritage; see Harrison 2010b and Wilkie, this volume). Despite its designation as something
which is rare, endangered, and 'at risk' (Cleere 1989; Harrison 2013a), a non-renewable
resource to be 'treasured' (Carman 1996), valued (Mason 2002), and appropriately 'managed' (Lipe 1984), heritage is ubiquitous in contemporary post-industrial societies (and in
many developing and industrialized ones) and is a fundamental part of our contemporary
material world (see discussion in Holtorf 2002). But why should this be so? In an age which
emphasizes its all-pervasive modernity, even 'postmodernity', why should the past continue
to have such a powerful hold on our imagination and to so thoroughly permeate our material worlds?

It might seem counterintuitive to suggest that heritage is a distinctively *modern* notion
(e.g. Smith 2006; Harrison 2013b). By using this term 'modern', I mean not only that the
professional governmental practices of the conservation and management of objects, places,
and practices from the past developed relatively recently (predominately over the past 200
years in Western Europe and in North America), but that the 'idea' of heritage emerged
within the context of a series of distinctive philosophies and social and political movements
which we would associate with the experience of modernity. There is now a well-rehearsed
argument which suggests that it is the very way in which modernity contrasts itself in relation to its past which makes heritage such an important factor in determining how modern societies conceptualize themselves (e.g. Jameson 1991; Harvey 2001). Putting aside the
problems of treating modernity as a single unified project (instead of the form taken by a
heterogeneous set of interests which draw on a similar underlying philosophical justification for the exercising of certain modes of power/knowledge), as Osborne (1995: 13–14)
notes, the 'time' of modernity is not straightforward, as it involves a complex doubling in
which it defines itself simultaneously as both 'contemporary' and 'new'. In doing so, it constantly creates the present as 'contemporary past' whilst it anticipates the future as embodied
within its present. In other words, modernity creates for itself a past which is perceived to
be both immanent (contained within) and imminent (impending) in the present (Harrison
2011). This simultaneity of the past in the present is part of the way in which modernity is
experienced as a state of rapid progress and technological and social change (e.g. Berman
1983; Virilio 2000).

In a consideration of the relationship between archaeology and modernity, Julian Thomas
has tracked the connection between archaeology and the foundation stories of modern
nation-states, arguing that they are connected by a series of preoccupations, including
the ordering of time, the idea of a normative with which to contrast a non-normative (or
'Other'), with ideas of human development, the relationship between historical change
and human reason, and analytical and comparative perspectives (2004: 224–6; see also
Fabian 1983; Olsen and Svestad 1994; Lucas 2004, 2005, 2006; Shanks, Platt, and Rathje
2004). While sociologists, political historians, and art historians have tended to define the
modern differently, it is generally associated with a set of ideas and social and economic
conditions which emerged in the course of the Enlightenment and is linked historically
with the rise of modern nation-states and political forms based on liberal government
(Giddens 1998).

This cluster of philosophies and their underlying social, political, and economic movements both facilitated and underpinned the development of a particular set of relationships
with the past which were necessary prerequisites to the development of modern ideas of

heritage, including an increased emphasis on empiricism and reason as the primary source of knowledge and authority (e.g. Smith 2004, 2006), and a way of defining the present in opposition to the past (Lucas 2004, 2006, 2010; Harrison 2011). Importantly, the discipline of archaeology has been an integral instrument in the production of the 'time' of modernity through its emphasis on the correlation of depth with chronological distance and decay and hence in generating the sense of threat which makes the conservation and management of objects, places, and practices from the past (as heritage) necessary.

Acknowledging heritage as a concept with deep historical and philosophical roots, I argue that new approaches to heritage developed in North America, the UK, and Europe following the Second World War, and accelerated in response to a series of changes that occurred in post-industrial societies after 1970 (see also Harrison 2010b: 21–2). These changes are perhaps most clearly articulated in the 1972 UNESCO World Heritage Convention and its aftermath. Andreas Huyssen (2003) has suggested this period saw a shift from modernity's focus on 'present futures' to a late modern focus on 'present pasts' and suggests this shift is connected with a series of globalizing processes which have worked together to transform the late modern experience of time and space (see also Appadurai 1996, 2001). These changes have been partially driven by an overwhelming sense of risk and threat which also forms an integral aspect of the experience of modernity. Indeed, Ulrich Beck (1992; see also Giddens 1990; Douglas 1992) argues that the concept of risk is generated by a perception that 'threat' and 'vulnerability' are integral components of modernity itself.

This sense of risk is integral to the cultural logics of conservation and the application of various scientific techniques (such as archaeology and other conservation sciences) and modes of ordering (for example by way of the museum and other forms of heritage collection or registers) to the assemblage, classification, preservation, exhibition, and consumption of heritage (see Harrison 2013a). Elsewhere, drawing particularly on the work of Harvey (1990), Augé (1995, 2002, 2004), and Appadurai (1996), Virilio (2000), I have summarized this set of late modern shifts to highlight the way in which they have influenced our engagement with the past (see Harrison and Schofield 2010: 128). These changes might be said to include:

- processes of deindustrialization;
- the growth of new communicative technologies and electronic media;
- the globalization of technology, and its association with altered patterns of production and consumption;
- the widespread experience of mass migration and the associated rise of transnationalism (in terms of capital, technology, labour, and corporations);
- new modes of capitalism involving more flexible forms of capital accumulation and distribution; and
- changes in the experience of time and space associated with a perception of accelerated change and 'speed'.

The discipline of archaeology has been integral to the production of the sense of simultaneous intimacy and distance of the past which defines the experience of the (late modern) present, and the subfield referred to as the 'archaeology of the contemporary past' can be seen to have been particularly implicated in this process (Harrison and Schofield 2010; Graves-Brown 2011; Harrison 2011).

20.3 EXPERIENCING THE PAST: HERITAGE IN THE EXPERIENCE ECONOMY

One of the most distinctive aspects of late modern societies is the shift from a service-based economy to an experience-based one (this section draws closely on Harrison and Schofield 2010: 266ff.; see also Holtorf 2009 and this volume). In *The Experience Economy*, Pine and Gilmore (1999) argue for a shift to an economic model in which goods and services have come to be valued not so much for their function, but in terms of their engagement of the senses and the experiences which surround their purchase and use. They see the origins of the experience economy in the opening of Disneyland in 1955, and urge their readers in business to consider the experiences they create as an integral part of the goods and services they provide (see also Sundbo and Darmer 2008). Similarly, Jensen (1999) has argued that the late twentieth century saw the emergence of a 'Dream Society' characterized by the commercialization of emotion and the opening of new markets with which to exploit the economic potential of human emotions (see also González-Ruibal, this volume, on the connection between late modernity, fantasy, and utopianism).

Some authors have related this shift in the nature of consumption with other conditions of late modernity, in particular with new modes of capitalism involving more flexible forms of capital accumulation and distribution (e.g. Harvey 1990; Jameson 1991). The manifestations of the experience economy—casinos, museums, entertainment spaces—have formed important subjects for archaeologists of the present. For example, archaeologist Martin Hall and anthropologist Pia Bombardella have written on the entertainment spaces of the new South Africa (Hall 2005, 2006a; Hall and Bombardella 2005, 2007), and Cornelius Holtorf (2005, 2007, 2009) has undertaken research on contemporary entertainment spaces such as archaeological theme parks and resorts in the US, UK, continental Europe, and South Africa.

While it is possible to argue that 'theming' has reconfigured almost all aspects of contemporary economies in late modern societies, theme parks are generally considered to represent the most fundamental manifestation of the experience economy (Clavé 2007: 155), and are central to the discussion of the emergence of 'experience' as a commodity. Although there was a long tradition of amusement and trolley parks, which provided picnic areas, mechanical rides, and other forms of entertainment (themselves evolving from a tradition of travelling fairs and expositions), the opening of Disneyland is considered to represent one of the world's first fully themed amusement parks, which has subsequently acted as a model for the development of not only other theme parks, but themed attractions such as shopping malls, casinos, hotels, and restaurants (e.g. see papers in Sorkin 1992; Mitrašinović 2006). Bryman refers to this process as the 'Disneyization' of society, and notes that this process has several dimensions (2004: 2). The first dimension he refers to as 'theming'—where institutions or objects are given an overall narrative unrelated to its history or function. The second he describes in terms of hybrid consumption—'a general trend whereby the forms of consumption associated with different institutional spheres become interlocked with each other and increasingly difficult to distinguish' (2004: 2). The third relates to the area of merchandising, where goods and services are produced which bear images and logos for sale. The fourth dimension relates to performative labour, where frontline service work is increasingly viewed as a form of performance and a certain display of mood is linked to the performance of that service. This draws on a much longer tradition of the association of labour and its management with the language of performance (e.g. Schön 1983; Csikszentmihalyi 1990). Mitrašinović (2006: 35) argues that homogenization is a necessary prerequisite for 'theming' to work, by creating a blank template prior to the requisite fusing of what had previously existed as separate domains of human culture and experience into a single themed whole. These are all processes which are based in material culture and are hence able to be studied archaeologically.

Elsewhere I have demonstrated the potential for an archaeological study of these processes in relation to both abandoned and functioning theme parks, and to airports and their associated shopping malls (Harrison and Schofield 2010), but theming and an emphasis on 'experience' have also had an important influence on the idea of heritage in the later part of the twentieth century and the early twenty-first (see also Baxter 2010; Holtorf 2010a, 2010b; Silberman 2010). 'Experience' has emerged as an important focus for heritage in two key ways. The shift from processes of collecting and mobilizing cultural relics (for example, in the form of museums and collections of antiquities) to one of *in situ* conservation of heritage objects, places, and practices had an important influence on the changing nature of heritage during the latter part of the twentieth century. Because heritage was perceived as best conserved 'in place', it became caught up in changing patterns of travel and tourism (see Urry 1990). As Bella Dicks notes, heritage was no longer simply about conserving the past, but about staging it as a 'visitable experience' (2003: 119):

> Modernity allows tradition to be disembedded from the constraints of situated and localized interaction, and to be 're-moored' in new and diverse contexts within the multiple forms of mediated spectacle...What this means is that heritage is produced within the cultural economy of visitability in which the object is to attract as many visitors as practicable to the intended site, and to communicate with them in meaningful terms. (Dicks 2003: 132–4)

Heritage sites thus became places to which members of the public travelled to gain an 'experience' of the past (e.g. Handler and Gable 1997). The second is through the increasing emphasis on 'intangible' heritage, either staged as an aspect of traditional culture (for example in the form of traditional dances, songs, food, and various other cultural 'performances' which are enacted 'in place'), or heritage re-enactments of various kinds involving actors and/or audience members in some aspect of fantasy role play.

I would suggest that there is a close connection between the 'rise' of the experience economy and the 1990s and 2000s venture capital, dotcom, and real estate bubbles. While 'experience' has persisted as an important element in the marketing and consumption of heritage into the period following the late 2000s global financial crisis, there has also been a notable re-emergence of the question of authenticity (e.g. Hall 2006b; see also Graves-Brown, this volume), an increasing focus on the really 'real'. In some ways, such an emphasis would seem inconsistent with the growing importance of 'virtual' forms of heritage and the increased emphasis on intangible heritage as a result of the 2003 UNESCO Convention for the Safeguarding of the Intangible Cultural Heritage. Gilmore and Pine (2007) refer to this focus on authenticity as part of the 'consumer sensibility' of developed experience economies, but I think in the case of heritage, we might also see this as a reaction to the apparent decadence of certain forms of marketed experience in the wake of the financial crisis and an accompanying increasing focus on value. However, the form that this expectation of authenticity takes in relation to heritage is perhaps counterintuitive. As Holtorf (2005,

2009) points out, themed heritage experiences are very much a part of lived reality, and far from being 'duped' by heritage theme parks, people visit them to gain an 'authentic' affective and emotional connection with the past. Indeed, gaining emotional satisfaction from a themed heritage experience may not rely on the accurate presentation of factual material, even where the gaps between fact and fantasy are made clear to the consumer (Gable and Handler 1996; Holtorf 2009). What seems more important is that the various apparatuses and techniques by which heritage experiences are created are made apparent so that the consumer feels empowered to make a judgement about the factuality (or otherwise) of the experience and information presented to them. The focus is on sincerity, rather than facts.

Various forms of theming and a range of physical apparatuses are generally involved in knitting 'experiences' together and determining the ways in which the visitor interacts with the heritage site during their visit. As Timothy Webmoor notes in his study of the UNESCO World Heritage Site of Teotihuacan in Mexico (2007a, 2007b, 2008), the heritage site is not simply a material backdrop for the interactions of archaeologists, locals, tourists, and 'new age' visitors, but structures and forms a part of these interactions in many different ways.

> Tracing the associations formed through an 'Aztec bailador' or dancer reveals the active quality of things, or a swapping of properties between things and humans. The stepped causeways of tezontle, or volcanic rock, surrounding the plaza of the Pyramid of the Sun determine now (as they did in the prehispanic period) where such performances are carried out. As elevated boundaries, these things also provide seating for tourists seeking a spectacle. But the movement of tourists to the dance spectacle is equally guided by the modern system of fences and gates of the Instituto Nacional de Antropología e Historia (INAH) which arrest ambulation at the plaza before the performative spectacle. Instead of nationalist identity politics or valorization of Teotihuacan as constitutive of a mythic and unifying past, things, both past and present, equally enervate the spiritual spectacle... The 'archaeological engine' drives all these associations at Teotihuacan, mixing humans and things in inter-connected networks that extend well beyond any ideational or meaning privileging notion of 'heritage'. (Webmoor 2007b: 573)

As Webmoor demonstrates, symmetrical approaches to archaeology (see also Olsen, this volume; Webmoor, this volume) are full of potential for the study of heritage. An examination of the various modern and historic physical infrastructural interventions—conservation devices, crowd controlling apparatuses, infrastructure associated with movement around a site, and the various interpretive devices which have been introduced alongside the material which forms the heritage site itself—constitutes one approach to a contemporary archaeology of heritage in the late modern experience society. I will briefly illustrate this with reference to two short examples.

20.4 ARCHAEOLOGIES OF HERITAGE IN THE LATE MODERN EXPERIENCE SOCIETY

Here I present two short, impressionistic accounts of visits to two different World Heritage Sites, paying particular attention to the ways in which the contemporary physical infrastructure of heritage site management interacts with the 'historic' or 'natural' features of the heritage site to structure visitor experience. I want to suggest that it is not helpful to distinguish between the 'historic' materials or 'natural' aspects of a site and the 'modern' infrastructure of heritage site management in terms of their influences on visitors and their experiences of heritage, despite the fact that it is conventional to draw a very clear distinction between them in archaeological accounts and in the discourse of heritage management. From the point of view of the visitor, all of these physical aspects of the heritage site are mixed and work together to structure the heritage experience. These necessarily brief accounts are not intended to represent detailed archaeological case studies, but instead point to the potential for an archaeology of the present to investigate questions which arise from a consideration of the role of heritage in the late modern experience society, and to the ways in which such archaeological work might contribute to a more general rethinking of concepts of authenticity and the value of the material remains of the past in the present.

My approach is archaeological in the sense in which it is concerned with recording and describing the physical infrastructure of heritage as a socio-technical and/or biopolitical assemblage (*agencement*), its affective qualities, and the affordances generated by this assemblage in terms of the circulation of objects, people, and ideas. In doing so, I make reference to archaeology as the study of surfaces and assemblages and a process of assembling and reassembling which I have outlined in more detail elsewhere (see Harrison 2011), drawing on the assemblage theory of Deleuze and Guattari (1988) and de Landa (2006). This approach also seeks to expose the relationships between distinct groupings of various entities—including texts, objects, people, and machinery—which in Foucault's work (e.g. 1980; see also Rabinow 2003) appear as different devices or apparatuses (*dispositifs*) by which particular administrative, institutional, and/or technological mechanisms and knowledge structures are produced, in relation to heritage (see also Bennett and Healy 2009; Macdonald 2009; Harrison 2013b). Drawing on these ideas, I make some general observations around which a more detailed archaeology of contemporary heritage sites might be built as part of a future research agenda for an archaeology of late modern heritage.

20.4.1 Experiencing the Simultaneous Past and Present at Angkor Archaeological Park World Heritage Site, Cambodia

Angkor Archaeological Park covers an area of some 400 square kilometres containing a series of monuments and archaeological remains associated with the former Khmer capitals dating from the ninth to fifteenth centuries CE and is located approximately eight kilometres north of the city of Siem Reap in central Cambodia. It was gazetted as a World Heritage Site in 1992, and a recent estimate suggested the site would receive in excess of three million visitors in 2010 (Sharp 2008). The site is currently managed by the Authority for the Protection and Management of Angkor and the Region of Siem Reap (APSARA).

Having negotiated transport from Siem Reap to the Archaeological Park, I am whisked efficiently along the highway to the ticket office, where staff attend to the thousands of tourists who have arrived by bus, car, motorbike, remorque moto, and bicycle. The system of roads, car parks, signs, ticket checkpoints, ramps and walkways around the site constitute a circulation system around which these thousands of tourists flow (as I do over the course of my three days), facilitating and constraining movement around the heritage site and establishing an initial system of perambulation across the landscape. Within this system at each of the individual temples or 'sites', further constraints on movement are produced by

FIGURE 20.1 Visitors at Ta Prom, Angkor Archaeological Park World Heritage Site. Note the various elements of scaffolding and piles of stone relating to contemporary heritage conservation work, and the well-worn pathway within the temple site (photograph: Rodney Harrison)

another series of ticket checkpoints, signs, walkways, benches, rubbish bins, food vendors, scaffolding, and barriers erected to stop passage across parts of the site unsafe for visitors or undergoing conservation works (see Figure 20.1). Piles of stone which have fallen from the temples and have been bundled together for future conservation efforts create further barriers to movement. Dozens, if not hundreds of mobile and stationary souvenir, soft drink, and book sellers ply their trade amongst the pathways around the ruins, while APSARA staff sweep the pathways and drive across the site collecting rubbish and pruned branches. Once the temples themselves have been reached, the visitor experiences a palimpsest of ancient and modern sculpture, a pastiche of conservation works dating back over 100 years from the first involvement of the École Française d'Extrême-Orient (EFEO) in the conservation of the site to the present and comprising metal, concrete, and wooden scaffolding, and modern sandstone and concrete carved panels set in amongst the historic architecture. Fallen stonework provides informal seating for the hundreds wishing to climb Angkor Wat's central tower (see Figure 20.2), their ascent facilitated by further scaffolding and wooden steps behind a ticket checkpoint surrounded by bollards.

While conventional archaeological representations such as maps and plans are often reproduced on signage at heritage sites to provide a way of visualizing the site in the *absence* of the contemporary infrastructure of cultural heritage management, the visitor actually experiences all of these physical aspects of the site simultaneously. Those parts of the site which would be considered to be the 'authentic' historic remains—the temples themselves and their physical setting—are actually indistinguishable from the contemporary infrastructure of cultural heritage management. Therefore, an archaeology of the contemporary heritage experience must concern itself with surveying, mapping, and documenting all of the materials which exist on the site in the present. Indeed, in many cases this contemporary

FIGURE 20.2 Visitors climbing the staircase to the top of the central tower, Angkor Wat. Uniformed staff check tickets in the foreground (photograph: Rodney Harrison)

infrastructure may leave a far more lasting impression on visitors and determine the nature of their experience of the site more strongly than the historic materials themselves. Perhaps the visitor will best remember the drive out to the site along the modern highway, or the elephant ride she had in the grounds of the temple? But the point of my observation is not to draw a distinction between the ancient and modern (Dawdy 2010) but to see all aspects of the site as part of its contemporary archaeology. Taking as its framework the present and its material traces, 'Angkor Archaeological Park' becomes not only its historic remains, but also its entire contemporary infrastructure relating to tourism and site management. Thus the experience of Angkor Archaeological Park emerges as one shaped by a technological network that displays archaeologically informed narratives and produces its own archaeological traces, rather than an archaeological experience shaped by a technological network devoted to crowd management (see also Piccini, this volume). This material has a clear stratigraphy which could also be mapped, but this would miss the point of exploring the materials which determine the contemporary experience of the place as a heritage destination concurrently, as an assemblage which occurs as part of a single surface. This relates to an argument I have developed in more detail elsewhere, that the aim of an archaeology of the present is to consider contemporary material culture and only the traces of the past where they intervene within it (see also Harrison 2010a, 2011; Harrison and Schofield 2010). All of these physical traces and their affective qualities must be mapped and recorded in documenting the contemporary archaeology of the site (an issue which itself raises the dilemma of mapping in the fixing and representation of whole by part). Indeed, one could go further in suggesting that the site's contemporary archaeology involves not only the material things which are *in situ* on the site, but also the various documents (both virtual and real) which determine its management, alongside the many virtual representations which prepare the visitor in advance for their visit and structure their gaze once they are there.

FIGURE 20.3 Floating hotels designed to look like 'Chinese Junks' at Ha Long Bay, Vietnam (photograph: Rodney Harrison)

20.4.2 Theming and the Experience of Natural Heritage at Ha Long Bay World Heritage Site, Vietnam

The framing of the tourist gaze and the staging of the tourist experience is even more of an issue in relation to 'natural' heritage sites, particularly those which have physical constraints relating to their 'visitability'. One such site is Ha Long Bay World Heritage Site in the Gulf of Tonkin in northern Vietnam, which was listed as a natural World Heritage Site in 1994 (with the boundary extended in 2000) and received over 1.4 million visitors in 2005 (UNESCO 2007). The site covers an area of over 1,500 square kilometres comprising the bay itself and a series of almost two thousand limestone islands and islets and is listed for its scenic, biogeographic, and geological heritage values.

Tourists typically access the bay in one of the many tourist boats, of which there are approximately 500, in addition to almost 100 'bed and breakfast' boats, which operate to accommodate the thousands of tourists visiting the bay every day (see UNESCO 2007). These 'bed and breakfast' boats offer collection from hotels in Hanoi, a four-hour minibus trip to the port on the bay, then one or two nights' accommodation and meals on board. The majority of the boats are designed to look like 'Traditional Chinese junks' (the phrase occurring often on promotional websites and other materials) and are effectively floating hotels (see Figure 20.3). The tours may offer additional activities such as kayaking, visits to one of the three floating fishing villages which are located within the World Heritage Area, or trips to one of the many limestone caves which occur in its islands and islets (Figure 20.4). As in the case of Angkor Wat, the roads, minibuses, and boats constitute a vast infrastructure for the circulation and distribution of visitors across the heritage site, a gigantic networked machine concerned with governing the visitation, exhibition, and experience of the natural heritage of the bay. The 'Chinese junk' motif and its resonance with what appear to be the

FIGURE 20.4 Tourists being ferried to one of the three floating fishing villages in Ha Long Bay, Vietnam (photograph: Rodney Harrison)

more 'traditional' presence of humans in floating fishing villages in the bay allows an opportunity for the construction of a themed natural heritage 'experience' which legitimizes the intrusion of hundreds of floating hotels and other tourist boats into an area which is valued for its remote 'wilderness' values. So here we see a range of 'technologies', devices, and apparatuses which work together in the construction of the heritage experience to frame the tourist gaze while making themselves appear to be a 'natural' part of the heritage of the place itself. A contemporary archaeology of this heritage experience must include the road and port infrastructure, the boats and their design, the various methods by which food and drink is circulated to the boats for consumption and waste is removed, the floating fishing villages, and the islands and islets of Ha Long Bay themselves. Similarly, it must include the images of the Bay which circulate on tourist websites, the World Heritage Listing and its framing of the site as 'visitable' heritage experience, and the various administrative systems for its management. All work together as part of a colossal late modern heritage experience generating assemblage or *agencement*.

20.5 DISCUSSION AND CONCLUSION

The chapter raises a number of questions for future investigation in relation to the contemporary archaeology of late modern heritage. In what ways are the varied apparatuses of World Heritage assembled and reassembled at different sites? What are the collisions and collusions between and amongst such global heritage sites in terms of the varied technologies and materials with which they are assembled? And what creative friction (cf. Tsing 2005) is generated in the intersection of the various global and local processes in which these heritage sites, the people who live with, work in and visit them, and their heterogeneous ancient and modern equipment are caught up and redeployed?

What becomes immediately obvious in taking an archaeological approach to contemporary heritage sites is just how much physical infrastructure the contemporary process of cultural heritage management has generated. There are not only the remains of the heritage sites themselves which are conserved, but also enormous quantities of material culture relating to conservation and visitor management and the production of the heritage 'experience' which work together to 'create' it as a heritage site (as opposed to being viewed simply as an abandoned building, defunct piece of material culture, or vacant 'natural' landscape). We might think of these as the 'technologies' of heritage—the various mechanisms and apparatuses by which the heritage experience is created. At the same time as this increasing mechanization of the technologies of heritage, we are seeing a vast global increase in the number of places which are classified and managed as heritage sites (Harrison 2010b, 2013b). Even in the case of natural and so-called 'intangible' heritage, these landscapes and cultural practices are increasingly being linked to sites of consumption (and their associated technologies of heritage experience) where they are staged and reframed for exhibition and consumption. Once a place is defined as heritage and listed on one of the various international, national, regional, or local planning instruments, there seems to be little inclination to remove it. The implication of this is a rapid piling up of heterogeneous traces of the past in the present (see Harrison 2013b), alongside the contemporary infrastructures or apparatuses which frame each of them as heritage, which has occurred over the course of the late twentieth and early twenty-first centuries. This constitutes an important and widespread material record of changes in the ways in which we relate to time and space in post-industrial societies in the late modern period.

Archaeology has played a major role in fuelling this rapid accumulation of the past, through its contribution to modern understandings of time and the underlying sense of risk and threat of loss which are integral preconditions for the ways of relating to the material traces of the past which drive our late modern conception of heritage. But in addition to its role in helping produce the modern conception of the past as both imminent and immanent in the present, it also provides an invaluable tool for the study of heritage as a cultural phenomenon. A contemporary archaeology of heritage has an important role to play not only in helping us to understand the material affects of the various changes which have occurred in relation to the development of late modern experience societies, but also their implications for our changing relationship with the past, present, and future.

References

Appadurai, Arjun. 1996. *Modernity at Large*. Minneapolis: University of Minnesota Press.
—— 2001. The Globalisation of Archaeology and Heritage: A Discussion with Arjun Appadurai. *Journal of Social Archaeology* 1(1): 35–49.
Augé, Marc. 1995. *Non-Places: Introduction to an Anthropology of Supermodernity*. London: Verso.
—— 2002. *In the Metro*. Minneapolis: University of Minnesota Press.
—— 2004. *Oblivion*. Minneapolis: University of Minnesota Press.

Baxter, Ian. 2010. Global Heritage Tourism: The Value of Experiencing the Past. In *Heritage Values in Contemporary Society*, ed. George S. Smith, Phyllis Mauch Messenger, and Hilary A. Soderland, pp. 241–54. Walnut Creek, CA: Left Coast Press.

Beck, Ulrich. 1992. *Risk Society: Towards a New Modernity*. London: Sage Publications.

Bennett, Tony and Healy, Chris. 2009. Introduction: Assembling Culture. *Journal of Cultural Economy* 3(1–2): 3–10.

Berman, Marshall. 1983 *All that is Solid Melts into Air: The Experience of Modernity*. London: Verso.

Bryman, Alan. 2004. *The Disneyization of Society*. London, Thousand Oaks, and New Delhi: Sage Publications.

Carman, John. 1996. *Valuing Ancient Things: Archaeology and Law*. Leicester: Leicester University Press.

Clavé, Salvador Anton. 2007. *The Global Theme Park Industry*. Wallingford: CABI Publishing.

Cleere, Henry. 1989. Introduction: The Rational of Archaeological Heritage Management. In *Archaeological Heritage Management in the Modern World*, ed. Henry Cleere, pp. 1–19. London: Allen & Unwin.

Csikszentmihalyi, Mihaly. 1990. Society, Culture and Person: A Systems View of Creativity. In *The Nature of Creativity: Contemporary Psychological Perspectives*, ed. Robert J. Sternberg, pp. 325–39. Cambridge: Cambridge University Press.

Dawdy, Shannon L. 2010. Clockpunk Anthropology and the Ruins of Modernity. *Current Anthropology* 51(6): 761–93.

de Landa, Manuel. 2006. *A New Philosophy of Society: Assemblage Theory and Social Complexity*. London and New York: Continuum.

Deleuze, Gilles and Guattari, Félix. 1988. *A Thousand Plateaus: Capitalism and Schizophrenia*. London: Athlone Press.

Dicks, Bella. 2003. *Culture on Display: The Production of Contemporary Visitability*. Milton Keynes: Open University Press.

Douglas, Mary. 1992. *Risk and Blame: Essays in Cultural Theory*. London: Routledge.

Fabian, Johannes. 1983. *Time and the Other: How Anthropology makes its Object*. New York: Columbia University Press.

Foucault, Michel. 1980. *Power/Knowledge: Selected Interviews and Other Writings, 1972–1977*. New York: Pantheon.

Gable, Eric and Handler, Richard. 1996. After Authenticity at an American Heritage Site. *American Anthropologist* 98(3): 568–78.

Giddens, Anthony. 1998. *Conversations with Anthony Giddens: Making Sense of Modernity*. Stanford: Stanford University Press.

—— 1990. *The Consequences of Modernity*. Cambridge: Polity Press.

Gilmore, James H. and Pine II, B. Joseph. 2007. *Authenticity: What Consumers Really Want*. Boston: Harvard Business School Press.

Graves-Brown, Paul. 2011. Touching from a Distance: Alienation, Abjection, Estrangement and Archaeology. *Norwegian Archaeological Review* 44(2): 131–44.

Hall, Martin. 2005. The Industrial Archaeology of Entertainment. In *Industrial Archaeology: Future Directions*, ed. Eleanor Conlin Casella and James Symonds, pp. 261–78. New York: Kluwer/Plenum.

—— 2006a. Identity, Memory, and Countermemory: The Archaeology of an Urban Landscape. *Journal of Material Culture* 11: 189–209.

—— 2006b. The Reappearance of the Authentic. In *Museum Frictions: Public Cultures/ Global Transformations*, ed. Ivan Karp, Corinne A. Krantz, Lynn Szwaja, and Tomás Ybarra-Frausto, pp. 70–101. Durham, NC, and London: Duke University Press.

Hall, Martin and Bombardella, Pia. 2005. Las Vegas in Africa, *Journal of Social Archaeology* 5(1): 5–24.

—— 2007. Paths of Nostalgia and Desire through Heritage Destinations at the Cape of Good Hope. In *Desire Lines: Space, Memory and Identity in the Post-Apartheid City*, ed. Noeleen Murray, Nick Shepherd, and Martin Hall, pp. 245–58. London: Routledge.

Handler, Richard and Gable, Eric. 1997. *The New History in an Old Museum: Creating the Past at Colonial Williamsburg*. Durham, NC, and London: Duke University Press.

Harrison, Rodney. 2010a. Exorcising the 'Plague of Fantasies': Mass Media and Archaeology's Role in the Present; or, Why We Need an Archaeology of 'Now'. *World Archaeology* 42(3): 328–40.

—— 2010b. What is Heritage? In *Understanding the Politics of Heritage*, ed. Rodney Harrison, pp. 5–42. Manchester and Milton Keynes: Manchester University Press and The Open University.

—— 2011. Surface Assemblages: Towards an Archaeology *in* and *of* the Present. *Archaeological Dialogues* 18(2): 141–96.

—— 2013a. Assembling and Governing Cultures 'At Risk': Centers of Collection and Calculation, from the Museum to World Heritage Lists. In *Reassembling the Collection: Ethnographic Museums and Indigenous Agency*, ed. Rodney Harrison, Sarah Byrne, and Anne Clarke, pp. 89–115. Santa Fe: SAR Press.

—— 2013b. *Heritage: Critical Approaches*. Abingdon and New York: Routledge.

Harrison, Rodney and Schofield, John. 2010. *After Modernity: Archaeological Approaches to the Contemporary Past*. Oxford: Oxford University Press.

Harvey, David. 1990. *The Condition of Postmodernity: An Enquiry into the Origins of Cultural Change*. Oxford: Blackwell.

Harvey, David C. 2001. Heritage Pasts and Heritage Presents: Temporality, Meaning and the Scope of Heritage Studies. *International Journal of Heritage Studies* 7(4): 319–38.

Holtorf, Cornelius. 2002. Is the Past a Non-Renewable Resource? In *The Destruction and Conservation of Cultural Property*, ed. Robert Layton, Peter Stone and Julian Thomas, pp. 286–97. London and New York: Routledge.

—— 2005. *From Stonehenge to Las Vegas: Archaeology as Popular Culture*. Lanham, MD: Altamira Press.

—— 2007. *Archaeology is a Brand! The Meaning of Archaeology in Contemporary Popular Culture*. Oxford: Archaeopress.

—— 2009. Imagine This: Archaeology in the Experience Society. In *Contemporary Archaeologies: Excavating Now*, ed. Cornelius Holtorf and Angela Piccini, pp. 47–64. Frankfurt: Peter Lang.

—— 2010a. Heritage Values in Contemporary Popular Culture. In *Heritage Values in Contemporary Society*, ed. George S. Smith, Phyllis Mauch Messenger, and Hilary A. Soderland, pp. 43–54. Walnut Creek, CA: Left Coast Press.

—— 2010b. Meta-stories of Archaeology. *World Archaeology* 42(3): 381–93.

Huyssen, Andreas. 2003. *Present Pasts: Urban Palimpsests and the Politics of Memory*. Stanford: Stanford University Press.

Jameson, Fredric. 1991. *Postmodernism: Or, the Cultural Logic of Late Capitalism*. London and Durham, NC: Duke University Press.

Jensen, Rolf. 1999. *The Dream Society: How the Coming Shift from Information to Imagination Will Transform Your Business*. Maidenhead: McGraw-Hill.

Lipe, William D. 1984. Value and Meaning in Cultural Resources. In *Approaches to the Archaeological Heritage: A Comparative Study of World Cultural Resource Management Systems*, ed. Henry Cleere, pp. 1–11. Cambridge: Cambridge University Press.

Lucas, Gavin. 2004. Modern Disturbances: On the Ambiguities of Archaeology, *Modernism/modernity* 11(1): 109–20.

—— 2005. *The Archaeology of Time*. London and New York: Routledge.

—— 2006. Historical Archaeology and Time. In *The Cambridge Companion to Historical Archaeology*, ed. Dan Hicks and Mary C. Beaudry, pp. 34–47. Cambridge: Cambridge University Press.

—— 2010 Time and the Archaeological Archive. *Rethinking History* 14: 343–59.

Macdonald, Sharon. 2009. Reassembling Nuremberg, Reassembling Heritage. *Journal of Cultural Economy* 2(1–2): 117–34.

Mason, Randall. 2002. Assessing Values in Conservation Planning: Methodological Choices and Issues. In *Assessing the Values of Cultural Heritage*, ed. Maria de la Torre, pp. 5–30. Los Angeles: The Getty Conservation Institute.

Mitrašinović, Miodrag. 2006. *Total Landscape, Theme Parks, Public Space*. Aldershot: Ashgate.

Olsen, Bjørnar and Svestad, Asgeir. 1994. Creating Prehistory: Archaeology Museums and the Discourse of Modernism. *Nordisk Museologi* 1: 3–20.

Osborne, Peter. 1995. *The Politics of Time: Modernity and the Avant-Garde*. London: Verso.

Pine, B. Joseph and Gilmore, James H. 1999. *The Experience Economy: Work is Theatre and Every Business a Stage*. Boston: Harvard Business School Press.

Rabinow, Paul. 2003. *Anthropos Today: Reflections on Modern Equipment*. Princeton, NJ: Princeton University Press.

Schön, Donald A. 1983. *The Reflective Practitioner: How Professionals Think in Action*. London: Temple Smith.

Shanks, Michael, Platt, David, and Rathje, William L. 2004. The Perfume of Garbage: Modernity and the Archaeological. *Modernism/Modernity* 11(1): 61–83.

Sharp, Rob. 2008. Heritage Site in Peril: Angkor Wat is Falling Down. *The Independent*, 14 March. Available at: <http://www.independent.co.uk/news/world/asia/heritage-site-in-peril-angkor-wat-is-falling-down-795747.html> (accessed 8 September 2011).

Silberman, Neil Asher. 2010. Technology, Heritage Values, and Interpretation. In *Heritage Values in Contemporary Society*, ed. George S. Smith, Phyllis Mauch Messenger, and Hilary A. Soderland, pp. 63–74. Walnut Creek, CA: Left Coast Press.

Smith, Laurajane. 2004. *Archaeological Theory and the Politics of Cultural Heritage*. Abingdon and New York: Routledge.

—— 2006. *Uses of Heritage*. Abingdon and New York: Routledge.

Sorkin, Michael (ed.). 1992. *Variations on a Theme Park: The New American City and the End of Public Space*. New York: Hill & Wang.

Sundbo, Jon and Darmer, Per. 2008. *Creating Experiences in the Experience Economy*. Cheltenham: Edward Elgar.

Thomas, Julian. 2004. *Archaeology and Modernity*. London: Routledge.

Tsing, Anna Lowenhaupt. 2005. *Friction: An Ethnography of Global Connection*. Princeton, NJ: Princeton University Press.

UNESCO. 2007. State of Conservation of World Heritage Properties Inscribed on the World Heritage List. Available at: <http://whc.unesco.org/archive/2007/whc07-31com-7be.pdf> (accessed 8 September 2011).

Urry, John. 1990. *The Tourist Gaze*. Thousand Oaks, London, and New Delhi: Sage Publications.

Virilio, Paul. 2000. *A Landscape of Events*. Cambridge, MA: MIT Press.

Webmoor, Timothy. 2007a. Reconfiguring the Archaeological Sensibility: Mediating Heritage at Teotihuacan, Mexico. Ph.D. Dissertation, Department of Anthropology, Stanford

University. Electronic document from the Metamedia Lab, Stanford Archaeology Center. Available at: <metamedia.stanford.edu> (accessed 6 September 2011).

—— 2007b. What About 'One More Turn after the Social' in Archaeological Reasoning? Taking Things Seriously. *World Archaeology* 39(4): 547–62.

—— 2008 From Silicon Valley to the Valley of Teotihuacan: The 'Yahoo!s' of New Media and Digital Heritage. *Visual Anthropology Review* 24(2): 183–200.

CHAPTER 21

....

DIFFERENCE

....

DENIS BYRNE

21.1 INTRODUCTION: IN THE FOREST

....

I spent much of 1981 in the eucalypt forests of the far south coast of New South Wales, Australia, looking for flaked stone artefacts. These forests cover a band of ridges which are the foothills of the Great Dividing Range and which along this part of the coast reach eastward to within a few kilometres of the Pacific Ocean. The stone artefacts were almost all found along the top of ridgelines in surface concentrations that I took to represent 'moments' in the precolonial past when Aboriginal people had stopped to camp or perform activities associated with hunting and gathering forays they had made into this steeply dissected country from base camps on the coast or in the big coastal valleys. On many of my own archaeological forays I was accompanied, or should I say led, by Uncle Ted Thomas (1909–2002),[1] an Aboriginal man who was in his early seventies at the time but who had the vitality of a much younger man.

Uncle Ted lived in the Aboriginal settlement situated on a spur overlooking Wallaga Lake which itself was immediately adjacent to the ocean. The settlement had been established by the Aborigines Protection Board in 1891 and had been home to people drawn from this part of the coast as well as further afield.[2] During the early and mid-twentieth century these people had fished for a living as well as working for local farmers clearing bush and building fences. They frequently walked through the forested hills to get to local towns or to visit other Aboriginal settlements and many of them also worked in the local timber industry, cutting railway sleepers and mine props. Uncle Ted had done that kind of work when he was younger. He had also worked on road gangs, been employed in commercial fishing, and had harvested vegetables during the picking season.

---

[1] He had recently adopted the name Guboo but since I called him Uncle Ted I will use that name here. In Aboriginal English in south-east Australia, 'Uncle' is used as a respectful term of address for older men regardless of their relationship to you.

[2] For a history of this Aboriginal community see: <http://www.daa.nsw.gov.au/publications/ BGfinalreport05.pdf> (accessed June 2011).

It was peaceful up on the ridges, in the forests. We walked along looking at the ground, alert for the angular shapes of small stone flakes and cores exposed between the dead leaves and fallen bark. If our eyes weren't on the ground we were looking through the trees at the view of a neighbouring ridge or perhaps the more distant vista down to the farmed coastal flats and the sea beyond. When it was nearly time to sit down to drink milky tea from our Thermoses we naturally sought out a spot with a view and quite often the view then inspired Uncle Ted to tell stories about the Koori side of the history of the area we were looking at (the term Koori is widely used by Aboriginal people in that part of south-east Australia as a collective term for themselves). In the 1830s white pastoralists had arrived in the area with their cattle, this representing the furthest extension of the white invasion of Aboriginal land which had begun with the establishment of a British penal colony in 1788 at Sydney, 370 kilometres to the north. Uncle Ted's stories ranged from the time he was a schoolboy at Wallaga Lake in the 1910s through the 1920s when, among other things, he was a member of the local Aboriginal gum leaf band, to the late 1970s when he began campaigning to protect Aboriginal sacred sites from commercial logging operations. On the lower slopes of Mumbulla Mountain, a topographic landmark that had been a male initiation site last used in the late nineteenth century, he had stood his ground in front of a forestry bulldozer, a deed he was intensely proud of. 'If looks could kill', he would say, laughing, 'I'd have been a dead man.'

Up on the forest ridges I walked along with a topographic survey map and stone artefact recording sheets in hand (see Figure 21.1). For me, each new day meant a few more artefact scatters to add to the pattern of sites which I was beginning to propound into a model suggesting that Aboriginal people in the past had moved through the forests by following the ridgelines, carrying out their activities—those at least that resulted in the discard of flaked stone artefacts—mostly on the flat saddles and summits of the ridges (Byrne 1983). I assumed Uncle Ted was engaged in this same project of archaeology. He was certainly an avid searcher for stone artefacts and had developed an astonishingly sharp eye for them.

'Another one!' he would call out. 'So they were here too!', referring to his ancestors, as I plotted one more location onto the map. But I realize now that he and I were really not engaged in quite the same project. For him, it seems clear in retrospect, these stone artefacts were important partly because they were material proof that his ancestors had been all over this landscape in the past. Why this had assumed such importance to him now was because generations of non-Indigenous settlers had gotten used to thinking of Aborigines as people who lived in generally poor quality housing in country towns and city suburbs or in former Aboriginal Reserves, like the one overlooking Wallaga Lake. In the 150 years since Aboriginal people in this part of New South Wales had been dispossessed, the settled landscape had been filled up with white people and their projects—even the eucalypt forests were populated by the conflicting visions of loggers and conservationists whose natural habitat it had, in a sense, become.

And yet, for someone like Uncle Ted, it was critical to somehow be able to show that his people had been there first. Why archaeological remains like stone artefacts were perfect for this purpose was that they had physical presence on and in the land and that presence had an insistence that text in a history book could never quite match. The Aboriginal people of New South Wales had been dispossessed of their land, and yet to be Indigenous means to be *of* the land. Landlessness cuts the ground out from under Aboriginal people's status as Indigenous. It is partly in this context that stone artefacts and other 'archaeological' traces have taken on such importance for Aborigines: they act as quasi land deeds, or land titles

FIGURE 21.1 Site of stone artefact scatter in the South Coast forests, 1981 (photograph: Denis Byrne)

(Byrne 2003a: 74). By the early 1980s tens of thousands of Aboriginal archaeological sites had already been recorded all across New South Wales. For people like Uncle Ted this vast dispersion proclaimed that 'we' had once been everywhere.

21.2 RENDERING DEEP PASTS CONTEMPORARY

So up in the forests Uncle Ted and I were not quite on the same team. In a sense we were actually in competition. With my graph paper and my artefact recording sheets I was engaged in rendering stone artefacts as the archaeological heritage of the colonial nation. Via the discourse of archaeology, I was identifying these bits of stone as things belonging to a precolonial Aboriginal past while, at the same time, via the discourse of heritage, I was making them over as Australia's patrimony. Courtesy of these discursive moves, the artefacts came to belong as much to me as to Uncle Ted.

Looking back, I think that for Uncle Ted the ancientness of the stone artefacts was neither here nor there. He always spoke of them as being personally connected to him; it was never a matter of these things belonging to his precolonial forebears. He collapsed duration whereas my fieldwork seemed intent on emphasizing it. For him, this was an archaeology of the contemporary past.

It seems safe to assume that Uncle Ted's ancestors never spoke or thought of these artefacts (which, after all, they had thrown away) in the way he did. Even in the 1950s, as far as

I know, Aboriginal people were not referring to these objects as their 'heritage'. The heritage discourse was emerging in Australia around that time—filtering down from the north Atlantic—but Aboriginal people did not begin hijacking it until the 1970s (Byrne 1996: 103). At that time they began deploying heritage discourse in the struggle for land rights, often asserting the spiritual significance of particular areas of land where archaeological assessments failed to demonstrate heritage significance (Byrne 1993: 220–5).

Heritage discourse was born of nationalism: it functioned to convert old things into a form of cultural capital for the national state. The use of heritage discourse by contemporary Aboriginal people to lay claim to pieces of land—fragments of the national 'geobody' (Thongchai 1994)—and to bolster their claim to a separate cultural identity, effectively turned heritage discourse back on the nation-state. If nation-states seek to finesse an abiding and almost religious affinity with the national soil, a move that Jean-Pierre Warnier (2011) has referred to as 'territorialization', this is a territorialization that often seems to entail removal of certain minority or local groups from the soil. Michael Herzfeld documents instances of this in the Monti district of Rome (2009) and the Pom Mahakan residential enclave in Bangkok (2006). In the case of the Pom Mahakan enclave, residents have boned up on heritage discourse and used it 'back at' the Thai heritage authorities who are trying to orchestrate their eviction. Such counter-deployments would seem akin to the subaltern practice of writing back to the centre using the colonizer's own language (Ashcroft et al. 2002).

Heritage professionals appear reluctant to credit Aboriginal people in places like New South Wales with a creative remaking of heritage discourse (Byrne 2003a; Harrison 2010). A raft of professional 'best practice' guidelines as well as national and international protocols and charters serve to lend a sense of stability to heritage discourse. There are widely accepted conventions, for instance, guiding the way stone tools are spoken about in Australia by archaeologists and heritage practitioners and also by environmental regulators, the media, and others who look to archaeology and heritage discourse for their cues. But if the 'authorised discourse' (Smith 2006) on stone tools can be learned, equally it can be creatively reworked and redeployed; it cannot easily be policed. I suggest that the heritage discourse of colonizers can be reworked by the colonized much the way the latter have reworked the former's material culture.

Rodney Harrison's (2002a) analysis of early to mid-twentieth-century archaeological assemblages from Aboriginal camp sites on a pastoral property in north-western Australia led him to an appreciation of how a range of European objects had taken on different forms and functions in Aboriginal hands: fencing wire was used for pressure-flaking stone and for making fishhooks, toy cars were made from tobacco tins, drinking vessels and oil lamps were made from food tins (2002a: 71–3). Such objects 'are not what they were made to be, but what they become in the process of creative recontextualisation' (Harrison 2002a: 74). Working with Native American archaeological assemblages from the colonial period, Stephen Silliman (2005, 2010) similarly critiques archaeology's failure to engage with the materiality of cross-cultural entanglement.

Both Harrison and Silliman are alert to the extent to which most of us are, as it were, overcome by the 'original' identity of the objects; it is what jumps out at us; it is what seems to constitute the inherent identity of objects. Our minds hasten to say 'tobacco tin' when we see the rusted tin pierced by a piece of wire lying on the ground, even though we see it has been reinvented as a toy car. This 'privileging of material origins' (Silliman 2010: 36) is related to the history of 'origins research' (Silliman 2010: 35) in archaeological practice which has been exposed to critique by archaeologists alert to the way this discourse can negate or underplay agency and creativity on the part of those who use objects others have 'originally' created. It privileges *makers* over *users*.

In the south coast forests in 1981, I was overwhelmed by the precolonial origins of the stone artefacts I was measuring and was oblivious to the way Uncle Ted was recontextualizing them; the way he was incorporating them into contemporary Aboriginal culture to serve a very contemporary political role (see Byrne 2003a for a general discussion of this role; also Harrison 2010: 538–40). I now want to reflect more closely on Uncle Ted's field methods in the forests.

21.3 CLASSIFICATORY SLIPPAGE

Many of the precolonial artefacts we found in the forests were small quartz flakes. A particular aspect of Uncle Ted's archaeology was his special interest in quartz crystals. He had an extraordinarily sharp eye for stone artefacts in general but his facility in finding quartz crystals bordered on the uncanny. I think he himself believed this facility said something about who he was as an Aboriginal elder, someone spiritually attuned to his country. These crystals were uncommon—we couldn't expect to find one every day up on the ridgelines— and while some of them showed signs of percussion flaking most did not. I regarded the unflaked ones as 'non-artefactual'. Uncle Ted, though, believed they might have been associated with the activities of Aboriginal 'clever men' and, indeed, there is ethnographic evidence for this in the late nineteenth century in this part of the south coast of New South Wales. The amateur anthropologist A. W. Howitt (1904: 357–8) recorded that quartz crystals for sorcery were carried by the 'medicine men' of the Yuin tribe in bags made from the hair of deceased relatives. Surely, though, such 'clever' crystals would be vastly outnumbered by naturally occurring ones, especially in the ridge country. My view that the crystals were a natural occurrence in this geological region, and that they were non-artefactual, was never a matter of contention between Uncle Ted and I—he would show them to me and then quietly pocket them. I have no idea what happened to them later, but it seemed clear from the way he handled them that he regarded them with a degree of reverence.

Looking back, though, I am struck by my failure to engage with the cultural dimension of what Uncle Ted was doing. I still believe the unflaked crystals had almost certainly not been artefacts in the precolonial past but I can now see that they were very much a part of Uncle Ted's contemporary Aboriginal material culture. He appeared to see them as continuous with his own cultural being. They held what Harrison (2010: 536) refers to as an 'intense poignancy' for him. Luke Godwin and James Weiner (2006) have criticized the constraints imposed by a heritage regime which dichotomizes the material and 'metaphysical' dimensions of culture. In Queensland, New South Wales, and Victoria, material traces such as flaked stone artefacts are dealt with by archaeologists while the metaphysical 'traces'—such as sacred Dreaming sites (typically consisting of natural landscape features without archaeological traces)—are dealt with by anthropologists (Godwin and Weiner 2006: 129).

The problem with this approach is that contemporary Aboriginal people, in practice, are liable to interpret archaeological remains metaphysically. For them, in the words of Godwin and Weiner (2006: 135), such traces 'are a physical demonstration that their "old people" have been there, and continue to be there: in this sense, the sites are their footprints'. In Lynn Meskell's words, these things have 'residual afterlives in living communities' (2010: 448; see also Schiffer, this volume). By any conventional measure, contemporary Aboriginal people on the far south coast of New South Wales possess less traditional knowledge than their central and northern Queensland counterparts and have been exposed to a much more intensive history of colonization, but I cannot see how Uncle Ted's situation differs in essence from what these authors describe. Godwin and Weiner (2006: 128) maintain that Aboriginal people, 'are free to interpret and re-interpret their prehistorical record in line with the changing conditions of the present'. Insofar as I simply ignored Uncle Ted's engagement with the crystals, this was not a freedom my 1981 self was ready to extend to him.

Harrison (2004: 199–201, 2010: 536) refers to contemporary Aboriginal people in western New South Wales treating precolonial flaked stone artefacts, as well as artefacts at archaeological sites from the recent past, as extensions of, and as links to, the persons of the ancestors who were associated with them. In this context, he sees how the objects have 'material agency' (2010: 529). He cites the account of a Muruwari woman who described the feeling of the ancestor's spirits coming into your body when you rubbed stone artefacts on your skin (Harrison 2004: 199). This very graphic dissolution of the classificatory boundary between the secular and sacred, as well as between the artefactual and the corporeal, provides a depiction of past materiality being 'updated' as it is folded into the affective present of contemporary people. Similarly, Shelley Greer (2009: 40–3, 2010: 53) has shown that Cape York shell middens which archaeologists have classified as secular rather than sacred, are approached by their Aboriginal custodians as 'portals' or 'gateways' not just to the spirits of past occupants which are still present there but to the past of the Dreaming (or *bifortaim*). She shows how this spiritual framing of the middens is not one that excludes archaeology; it is open to an archaeology willing to be 'interactive' with local values, a far cry from those situations in which communities can only respond in a 'reactive' way to an 'expert-driven agenda' (Greer 2010: 46).

As Jane Lydon (2006, 2008) has shown, European visuality contributed significantly to the way Aboriginal people were apprehended and 'managed' in colonial Australia. The primacy enjoyed by visuality in Western modernity, described by Jay (1993) as 'ocularcentrism', can be said also to have profoundly shaped the way archaeology has represented the Aboriginal material past and contemporary Aboriginal engagements with that materiality. The archaeological eye has been privileged as providing access to the objective, universal truth of what objects 'are'—they are, in other words, what they are *seen* to be (Moser 2001). It seems clear, now, that Uncle Ted was responding to affective and spiritual qualities in the stone artefacts and crystals found lying on the forest floor, qualities that I had passed over.

21.4 ON NOT SEEING THE ARCHAEOLOGY OF THE ABORIGINAL CONTEMPORARY PAST

One day in 1981 I was driving down the Princes Highway from Sydney to the south coast forests in the company of a young Aboriginal man who lived down there. He mentioned there had 'always' been a lot of movement of Aboriginal people up and down this coast and, looking at the cars approaching us on the other side of the road, he assured me he could tell a 'Koori car' (Aboriginal car) from a couple of hundred metres away just by the look of it. Over the next hour or so he did exactly that, which mystified me because I could see nothing peculiar about them. Sure, they tended to be family-sized cars and generally not new, but that applied to half the cars on the road. Yet as the ones he indicated passed us by, sure enough I saw Aboriginal faces in the front and back seats.

There must, I realized, be 'Aboriginal cars' moving along other roads in the landscape, on the way to visit relatives, attend meetings and football games, weddings and funerals. They would be moving between nodes of rural Aboriginal settlement and between these and the suburbs of Sydney, like Redfern and Mount Druitt where Aboriginal Sydneysiders were concentrated (Figure 21.2). I had a vision of a whole alternative traffic moving on a web of routes criss-crossing the state of New South Wales and beyond; an alternative road map invisible to people like myself but common knowledge to my Aboriginal fellow citizens.

The momentary window onto this traffic closed and did not open again until, much later, I was working on a heritage study of historic-period Aboriginal cemeteries. It was then that I read of the dispersal of Aboriginal population that occurred in the second half of the twentieth century when many people moved from the old, often remote, settlements to larger towns and cities. The same roads that took people away were then used to bring them back to visit those who had stayed behind. The road network became instrumental in maintaining contact between the dispersed kin groups. Jeremy Beckett (1988: 119) used the term 'beats' to describe these networks of movement (and see Birdsall 1988 for a comparable situation in south-western Western Australia). My own particular interest was in the way this road network brought relatives and friends back to attend funerals at the old

FIGURE 21.2 Wallaga Lake Aboriginal settlement, 1977 (reproduced with permission from National Archives of Australia)

settlements and sometimes also to return the bodies of those who had died in towns and cities back to be buried with their relatives in their own Country (Byrne 2004). The 'white road' had morphed into an Aboriginal 'kinship object' (Ahmed 2010: 248), as had cars, despite their origin in settler transportation history.

I turn now to consider the situation of contemporary Aboriginal culture in Sydney. In doing so I am mindful of Stephen Silliman's argument, mentioned earlier, that an archaeological focus on the cultural origin of objects can lead 'Indigenous people to disappear from past colonial spaces that they otherwise occupied...' (Silliman 2010: 33). He urges us to remember that material culture and space in the colonial setting has an ambiguous status—we must look to the dimension of *use* rather than *origin*. We should look to Indigenous labour relations, for instance, if we hope to reinstate the colonized in colonial space (Silliman 2010; see also Harrison 2002a, 2004). If this is true of colonial times, how much more so is it of the contemporary past? Aboriginal people living in contemporary Sydney are entangled via their labour relations, their welfare dependency, their sporting pursuits, and so many other spheres of life, not only with the cultural world of white Australians but with those of the members of a myriad of other cultures who, particularly since the 1950s, have made the city their home.

The western and south-western suburbs of Sydney in 2006 were home to 28,065 Aboriginal people though this represented only 1.5 per cent of the area's total population (Department of Aboriginal Affairs 2011). These people mostly live in the same housing (much of it public housing) as non-Indigenous people and they wear much the same clothes and eat much the same food as their Anglo-Australian neighbours. The anthropologist Gillian Cowlishaw (2009), who in the 1990s carried out ethnographic fieldwork among Aboriginal residents of one of these suburbs, Mount Druitt, found that by outward appearances there was less obvious distinction between Aboriginal people and their non-Indigenous fellow-residents of this suburb than between both these groups and someone like herself who came from the wealthier inner-city parts of Sydney. She describes how Aboriginal cultural difference is masked by superficial similarity:

> In Mt Druitt, cultural difference is masked by superficial similarity. There is no other language, public ceremonial life, or radically different epistemology among the Aboriginal population. Cultural specificity is more elusive, a matter of subtle attributes and orientations. (Cowlishaw 2009: 63)

On the track of these elusive 'different differences' Cowlishaw (2009: 64) documents culturally distinct 'manners' and speech habits of the Aboriginal people she spends time with in Mt Druitt. Though the language is English, she finds that 'local rhythms and expressions lay traps for... [her own] usual speech habits' (2009: 155).

For much of the twentieth century, up until the 1970s, the 'assimilation' of Aboriginal people into white society was official government policy in Australia, only abandoned when cultural diversity came to be valued. Cowlishaw notes that assimilation is now equated with 'reprehensible social destructiveness' (2009: 158) and yet she finds that in Mt Druitt 'an assimilative process is ubiquitous, inevitable and to some extent necessary if a colonised minority people is to survive with some sense of its (different) self' (2009: 158-9).

Cowlishaw helps us see assimilation as a creative as well as destructive process. Arguably in response to state multiculturalism's call upon Indigenous subjects 'to perform an authentic difference in exchange for the good feeling of the nation' (Povinelli 2007: 6), some Aboriginal people in Mt Druitt produce carved 'traditional' artefacts, paintings featuring distinctively Aboriginal motifs, and take part in modern renditions of 'traditional' dances. Cowlishaw acknowledges the validity of this performative aspect of contemporary Aboriginality but she juxtaposes the self-conscious performance of difference against what could almost be seen as a striving for sameness evident in much of Aboriginal history since 1788. This is not to be seen as an Aboriginal aspiration to whiteness but rather an aspiration for 'the good life' under colonial conditions.

Heather Goodall (1990, 1996) documents the eagerness of many Aboriginal people in New South Wales in the early and mid-nineteenth century to adopt elements of the white settler farming economy, an eagerness that saw them seeking to reacquire portions of land (their former country) and clear it for agriculture. In a counter-narrative which sits uncomfortably with the accepted vision of fringe camp lethargy and degeneracy she writes of Aboriginal people building houses, planting gardens, and spending farm profits on curtains, pianos, and most particularly on horses. We have to remember that by this time colonialism had almost completely redefined the possibilities of Aboriginal life in most of the area of New South Wales. Aboriginal people were powerless to prevent the colonial remaking of the environment that rendered hunting and gathering virtually impossible and the continuance of customary ritual practices impracticable. By the mid-nineteenth century many formerly secluded ritual sites were exposed in open paddocks grazed by cattle and sheep, with fences blocking access to sacred sites that had formerly anchored the traditional belief system. But we should not take this occlusion to mean Aboriginal people were blind to the attractions of farms and horses or that they did not see their culture as capable of 'forging ahead' (Silliman 2005: 66) under radically new conditions.

One of the tragedies of Australian history is that white society and the colonial state did so much to stifle this creativity, this reaching for the new. Stepping forward in time to the mid-twentieth century, a distinctive Aboriginal rural lifestyle comes into view. Most of the land Aboriginal people farmed had by now been taken off them (Goodall 1996). People are living in huts on government reserves or in fringe camps around country towns. In reminiscing about these days, contemporary Aboriginal people remember going hungry to bed, playing with home-made toys and wearing second-hand clothes.[3] It is a lifestyle which resonates with that which many white Australians were reduced to living in the Great Depression (1929 till the late 1940s), which was particularly severe in Australia (unemployment peaked at 30 per cent in 1932, a rate exceeded in the industrial world of the time only by Germany). During the Depression, thousands of urban white Australians, having defaulted on their mortgages or being unable to pay rent, set up squatter camps on the edges of cities. Some of these were in close proximity to Aboriginal reserve settlements, as was the case with the Happy Valley camp at La Perouse, Sydney, where Aboriginal and poor white people who had previously had no contact across the racial boundary found themselves mixing socially (Kensy 2008). Lydon (2009: 198) mentions a similar situation in north-western Victoria. There were also instances of poor white people living in sandstone rock shelters in the ocean cliffs on the southern side of Sydney, the kind of rock shelters that frequently contain archaeological evidence of Aboriginal occupation in precolonial times (see Figures 21.3 and 21.4).

[3] Autobiographies by, and biographies of New South Wales Aboriginal people which reference the mid-twentieth century include Langford (1988), Crawford (1993), Beckett (2000), Meehan (2000), and Flick and Goodall (2004)

FIGURE 21.3 Non-Indigenous residents in their rock shelter home at Kurnell, Sydney, during the 1930s Depression (reproduced with permission from National Library of Australia)

FIGURE 21.4 Non-Indigenous residents outside their cliff-top rock shelter home at Kurnell, Sydney, during the 1930s Depression (reproduced with permission from National Library of Australia)

In New South Wales the 1930s were perhaps the low-point of Aboriginal impoverishment in the post-invasion, post-frontier era. Aboriginal people suffered from loss of employment, as did whites, but most were ineligible for the dole. The origins of Aboriginal poverty, however, were grounded in colonial dispossession, racism, and government policies far more than they were in the 1929 Wall Street crash, and while white society returned to affluence in the 1950s Aboriginal impoverishment, especially in rural areas, continued. When 'observing' Depression-era white poverty in Australia via photographs and historical accounts one is drawn to question whether the materiality of Aboriginal culture in the recent past might not simply be the materiality of poverty. Certainly the use of cast-off artefacts and materials—the use of flattened-out kerosene tins for cladding and roofing huts, for instance, and the lining of interior walls with newspaper—were common to both Aboriginal camps and white Depression camps. But poverty is a reality that can be lived in many different ways.

Many older Aboriginal women whose reminiscences of the mid-twentieth century were recorded for a project on Aboriginal women's heritage in New South Wales recall living as children in dirt-floored huts on Aboriginal reserves and in fringe camps.[4] They often make particular note of how their mothers went to great efforts to keep these floors clean. Many also reminisce nostalgically about time spent with their mothers on the edges of creeks and rivers while the laundry was done. Clothes and bed linen were washed in buckets of river water or boiled in 'coppers' over open fires and bleached with Reckitt's Blue whitener. White women also, of course, made comparable efforts to keep clothes clean and keep the whites white but Aboriginal women were doing this, I suggest, in a context of exposure to a critical white gaze in which their pride in cleanliness seems partly a refutation of racist stereotyping. This goes back to Cowlishaw's point about the inevitability of a certain assimilative effort by contemporary Aboriginal people. In a situation where the only way they could get respect from whites was by being as like them as possible (e.g. laundering their clothes white) it would be understandable if many Aboriginal people made efforts in that direction. This may have been especially so if their identity as Aboriginal was grounded more in a distinctive sociality, including a distinctive array of 'manners' (Cowlishaw 2009: 155–9), than in a distinctive materiality. In such circumstances, strategically emulating—might one say 'counterfeiting'?—white culture may not have cost them greatly. Can strategic sameness then be considered a matter of cultural distinction?

21.5 THE SOUTH COAST WHISTLE AND THE ARCHAEOLOGY OF ENTANGLEMENT

One afternoon in the early 1980s I was in George Street in the Sydney Central Business District when I ran into Uncle Ted waiting to cross at an intersection. I think we were both disoriented for a moment, accustomed as we were to seeing each other only on the south coast. We walked up the street exchanging news and at a certain point I noticed he was looking past me, across the lanes of traffic to the opposite pavement.

[4] A series of illustrated booklets present the results of this project. See <http://www.environment.nsw.gov.au/nswcultureheritage/AboriginalWomensHeritage.htm>.

'That looks like a Koori over there', he said.

Following his gaze I saw what could have been an Aboriginal man of about 30 over on the other side of the busy street, heading in the same direction and a little ahead of us. This part of George Street, going north to the Town Hall, is quite steep and with Uncle Ted at my side it was a bit like walking up one of those ridgelines in the south coast forests, looking for stone artefacts among the fallen leaves and bark. It was just as if he had paused to point out some feature of interest through the trees, over on an adjacent ridge.

'Do you know about the south coast whistle?' he asked. 'We've got a special whistle so we can get each other's attention.'

So saying, he put his fingers to his lips and whistled loudly and quite melodiously. Though I can't recall now quite what it sounded like, it worked, however. Everyone else of the other side of the street kept walking but that particular man paused and turned around.

'You see, you see!' Uncle Ted said, laughing in that delighted-by-the-world way of his.

We watched while for a couple of moments the man over there scanned the street, and then he saw Uncle Ted and raised his arm and waved. Uncle Ted waved back and the man continued on his way up the street.

'Who was he?' I asked.

'No idea', said Uncle Ted absently, as if he'd already forgotten the incident.

Whoever he was, the south coast whistle had stopped him in his tracks. Moments later the flow of life on the street closed back over this rupture which had, anyway, only existed in the consciousness of three people. In retrospect, this incident seems a metaphor for the invisibility of contemporary Aboriginal culture in mainstream Australian society.

From about the mid-nineteenth century in Australia, Aboriginal people were widely held to be biologically different to Europeans and to be innately deficient racially and culturally in their capacity to compete with or survive alongside Europeans—they were considered to be a dying race (McGregor 1997; Anderson 2007: 145). Eventual extinction of the 'full-blood' Aboriginal 'race' was anticipated and it was expected that those of 'mixed-blood' would, through continued interbreeding, be biologically assimilated into white Australia. The passing of traditional Aboriginal artefacts into European hands (e.g. into museum collections) seemed to consolidate white identity-in-superiority. The corresponding flow of European products into Aboriginal hands was, by contrast, seen by whites as indexing Aboriginal cultural impoverishment (Byrne 1996). Rodney Harrison (2002b: 368) points to the way 'blood' and artefacts were commensurate in settler thought: the movement of European objects into Aboriginal society meant Aboriginal technologies were being 'bred out'. 'The process of incorporation of settler material culture into indigenous technologies was considered to mirror the biological processes that were occurring within the bodies of Aboriginal people themselves' (Harrison 2002b: 368). I suggest that this way of thinking, or a version of it, is still current in Australia: a lack of obvious distinctiveness, especially at the level of materiality and except in 'performative' registers such as craft, art, dance, and eco-tourism, confirms for mainstream Australian that 'authentic' culture in Aboriginal New South Wales has been 'bred out'.

To what extent might an archaeology of the Aboriginal contemporary past offer potential to counter this perception? Heidi Norman (2006, 2009) has shown how something as seemingly emblematic of white Australia as Rugby League has taken on distinctive characteristics in New South Wales Aboriginal society, one manifestation of which is the annual 'knockout' competition which she likens to a corroboree (a term used to describe Aboriginal ceremonial gatherings often featuring song and dance performances). It is reasonable to think the

Aboriginal culture of football also has a distinctive materiality, one that surely would extend into Mt Druitt Aboriginal households. Nor need we think that a microscopic archaeological vision is required for such distinction to come into view. It can, after all, be argued that in some ways Aboriginal culture is *more* distinctive in New South Wales today than it was in the nineteenth century. Ben Highmore (2011) has recently drawn attention to Gregory Bateson's 1930s writings on 'schismogenesis', a term Bateson developed to denote the way cultural distinction was often intensified as a result of culture contact. Bateson agued that this applied not just to cultures but also to gender and class—class differentiation may, for instance, 'intensify at moments of close proximity' (Highmore 2011: 127).

Cowlishaw (2009) points to the distinctiveness of Aboriginality in Mt Druitt as stemming partly from the weight of a certain history of engagement with white culture. The Aboriginal experience of the Protection system[5] (*c*.1883–1940) was layered onto the prior frontier experience of dispossession and the experience of Assimilation and the Stolen Generations[6] (*c*.1909–69) was layered over that, and this is to mention only a few of the accumulated traumas and grievances that have resulted in what today might be described as the standoff between Aboriginal and white society. Cowlishaw comments on the hope of many presumably well-meaning Australians that this history can be reversed: 'We aspire to be post-colonial, hoping to reverse or neutralize colonialism's consequences, yet *we are* those consequences' (2009: 188). For Aboriginal people the sedimentation of this shared history forms part of their distinctive identity. The task for an archaeology of the contemporary past is not to excavate that history but to excavate its present.

21.6 CONCLUSIONS

It may be that non-Indigenous Australians with an interest in the archaeology of the Aboriginal contemporary past should concentrate on what we know best—ourselves. I mean by this that we might focus on our side of the 'contact' situation, bearing in mind, though, that the historical 'entanglement' (Thomas 1991) of the Aboriginal and non-Indigenous cultures means the archaeology and heritage of a place like Australia is always a 'shared' one (Harrison 2004). Some years after the incident on the Princes Highway, mentioned earlier, in which my eyes were opened to the existence of a whole web of 'Aboriginal roads' stretching across the state, I became interested in the cadastre (the division of the landscape into surveyed allotments) as an instrument of colonialism in New South Wales but also as a white artefact implicated in the 'nervous landscape' of racial segregation (Byrne 2003b). The cadastral grid had numerous implications for Aboriginal movement through the colonized landscape and it provoked a 'tactical' (De Certeau 1984) culture of subversion.

The cadastral grid was a 'hybrid' artefact and the millions of kilometres of wire fences that sprang up along the lines of that grid ended up entangling Aboriginal and white people

[5] During this period a large proportion of the Aboriginal population of New South Wales lived on reserves under the control and surveillance of the Aborigines Protection Board.

[6] The 'Stolen Generations' refers to the phenomenon of the government-sponsored removal of children from Aboriginal families. The children were institutionalized, fostered by, or adopted by white people. See the Human Rights and Equal Opportunity Commission (1997).

alike. The fences provoked an Aboriginal fence-jumping culture as people endeavoured to move cross-country and as Aboriginal kids took the risk of taking a summertime dip in a farmer's dam or raiding his orchard (Byrne 2003b; Byrne and Nugent 2004). The fences often kept Aborigines out of white properties and they thus helped construct those peculiarly monocultural rural landscapes in which Aboriginal people were rendered almost invisible. Or, as was sometimes the case, the fences failed to keep Aborigines out and then they became a focus of white anxiety. Either way, the fences and the cadastral grid came to be elements in a hybrid heritage and we cannot now understand white cadastral history without also seeking to understand its Aboriginal implications.

Theoretically, the fences helped keep Aboriginal and white people spatially separate and they were thus entailed in the project of segregation. Racial segregation always strove to create two hyper-distinct life worlds but, as Ann Stoler (2002) shows, in many ways it just heightened and complicated their mutual entanglement. That entanglement was and is highly spatialized and materialized and would seem to be an eminent subject for archaeological unravelling.

I offer the cadastral grid as an example of a materiality that exists in shared Aboriginal–white space and would seem to invite investigation by either side. Colonialism's legacy of cross-cultural tension may, however, mean that there are spaces where white archaeologists are unlikely to be welcome. During the bad old days of the Protection era, government officers regularly 'inspected' Aboriginal households. The intrusiveness of these inspections, deeply resented by Aboriginal householders, extended to the officers peering into the cupboards in people's kitchens (Byrne 2003b: 176–7). Archaeology, for its part, is a notoriously nosey profession—who else except the police goes poking around in people's garbage?—but given the history of the Aboriginal recent past, I suspect that few contemporary Aboriginal people would tolerate white archaeologists entering even abandoned Aboriginal houses to enact an archaeology of the contemporary past. Such investigations might seem like some kind of re-enactment of Protection era prying and surveillance.

Notwithstanding such obvious limitations, I suggest that, regardless of who it is undertaken by, the importance of an archaeology of the recent and contemporary Indigenous past in settler colonies such as Australia, the United States, or New Zealand, will always lie in what it might offer in the way of cross-cultural understanding leading in however small a way to alternative futures. The obsessive focus on Indigenous *difference* and the fetishization of difference in the archaeology of colonial others has always been to do with a denial of 'coevalness' (Fabian 1983). In positioning the colonized other in another time—past time—it withholds recognition of them as people who can 'invent local futures' (Clifford 1988: 284). It is that kind of future-making that Uncle Ted seemed to have been engaged in when we walked the south coast ridgelines in the early 1960s and I regret the lost opportunity to have been part of that.

ACKNOWLEDGEMENTS

I wish to acknowledge Guboo Ted Thomas (1909–2002) for his companionship on the south coast in the early 1980s and for sowing the seeds for much of this chapter, unintentionally I assume. I thank my colleagues Caroline Ford and Steve Brown for their intellectual companionship during the writing of it and also thank Rodney Harrison for his valuable editorial comments.

References

Ahmed, Sara. 2010. Orientations Matter. In *New Materialities: Ontology, Agency, and Politics*, ed. Diana Coole and Samantha Frost, pp. 234–57. Durham, NC: Duke University Press.

Anderson, Kay. 2007. *Race and the Crisis of Humanism*. London: Routledge.

Ashcroft, Bill, Griffiths, Gareth, and Tiffin, Helen. 2002. *The Empire Writes Back: Theory and Practice in Post-Colonial Literatures*. London: Routledge.

Beckett, Jeremy. 1988. Kinship, Mobility and Community in Rural New South Wales. In *Being Black*, ed. Ian Keen, pp. 117–36. Canberra: Aboriginal Studies Press.

—— 2000. *Wherever I Go: Myles Lalor's 'Oral History'*. Melbourne: Melbourne University Press.

Birdsall, Chris. 1988. All One Family. In *Being Black*, ed. Ian Keen, pp. 137–58. Canberra: Aboriginal Studies Press.

Byrne, Denis. 1983. Survey Strategy for a Coastal Forest. In *Site Surveys and Significance Assessment in Australian Archaeology*, ed. Sharon Sullivan and Sandra Bowdler, pp. 61–70. Canberra: Research School of Pacific Studies, Australian National University.

—— 1993. The Past of Others: Archaeological Heritage Management in Thailand and Australia. Ph.D. dissertation, Department of Prehistory and Anthropology, Australian National University, Canberra.

—— 1996. Deep Nation: Australia's Acquisition of an Indigenous Past. *Aboriginal History* 20: 82–107.

—— 2003a. The Ethos of Return: Erasure and Reinstatement of Aboriginal Visibility in the Australian Historical Landscape. *Historical Archaeology* 37(1): 73–86.

—— 2003b. Nervous Landscapes: Race and Space in Australia. *Journal of Social Archaeology* 3(2): 169–93.

—— 2004. Archaeology in Reverse: The Flow of Aboriginal People and their Remains through the Space of New South Wales. In *Public Archaeology*, ed. Nick Merriman, pp. 240–54. London: Routledge.

Byrne, Denis and Nugent, Maria. 2004. *Mapping Attachment: A Spatial Approach to Aboriginal Post-contact Heritage*. Department of Environment and Conservation, New South Wales.

Clifford, James. 1988. *The Predicament of Culture: Twentieth-century Ethnography, Literature, and Art*. Cambridge, MA: Harvard University Press.

Cowlishaw, Gillian. 2009. *The City's Outback*. Sydney: University of New South Wales Press.

Crawford, Evelyn. 1993. *Over My Tracks: A Remarkable Life*. Ringwood, Victoria: Penguin.

De Certeau, Michel. 1984. *The Practice of Everyday Life*, trans. Steven F. Rendall. Berkeley, CA: University of California Press.

Department of Aboriginal Affairs, NSW. 2011. *Demographic Profile of the Aboriginal Population of NSW*. Available at: <http://www.daa.nsw.gov.au/publications/2ways_indicators_pdf/Chapter_Three_240408.pdf> (accessed July 2011).

Fabian, Johannes. 1983. *Time and the Other: How Anthropology Makes its Object*. New York: Columbia University Press.

Flick, Isabel and Goodall, Heather. 2004. *Isabel Flick: The Many Lives of an Extraordinary Aboriginal Woman*. Sydney: Allen & Unwin.

Godwin, Luke and Weiner, James F. 2006. Footprints of the Ancestors: The Convergence of Anthropological and Archaeological Perspectives in Contemporary Aboriginal Heritage Studies. In *The Social Archaeology of Australian Indigenous Societies*, ed. Bruno David, Bryce Barker, and Ian J. McNiven, pp. 124–38. Canberra: Aboriginal Studies Press.

Goodall, Heather. 1990. Land in Our Own Country: The Aboriginal Land Rights Movement in South-Eastern Australia, 1860–1914. *Aboriginal History* 14(1): 1–24.

Goodall, Heather. 1996. *Invasion to Embassy: Land in Aboriginal Politics in New South Wales, 1770–1972*. Sydney: Allen & Unwin.

Greer, Shelley. 2009. Portals in a Watery Realm: Cultural Landscapes in Northern Cape York. *Historic Environment* 22(1): 38–43.

—— 2010. Heritage and Empowerment: Community-Based Indigenous Cultural Heritage in Northern Australia. *International Journal of Heritage Studies* 16(1–2): 45–58.

Harrison, Rodney. 2002a. Australia's Iron Age: Aboriginal Post-Contact Metal Artefacts from Old Lampoo Station, Southeast Kimberley, Western Australia. *Australasian Historical Archaeology* 20: 67–76.

—— 2002b. Archaeology and the Colonial Encounter: Kimberley Spearpoints, Cultural Identity and Masculinity in the North of Australia. *Journal of Social Archaeology* 2(3): 352–77.

—— 2004. *Shared Landscapes: Archaeologies of Attachment and the Pastoral Industry in New South Wales*. Sydney: Department of Environment and Conservation NSW and the University of NSW Press.

—— 2010 Stone Tools. In *The Oxford Handbook of Material Culture Studies*, ed. Dan Hicks and Mary C. Beaudry, pp. 221–42. Oxford: Oxford University Press.

Herzfeld, Michael. 2006. Spatial Cleansing: Monumental Vacuity and the Idea of the West. *Journal of Material Culture* 11: 127–49.

—— 2009. *Evicted from Eternity: The Restructuring of Modern Rome*. Chicago: University of Chicago Press.

Highmore, Ben. 2011. Bitter After Taste: Affect, Food, and Social Aesthetics. In *The Affect Theory Reader*, ed. Melissa Gregg and Gregory J. Seigworth, pp. 118–37. Durham, NC: Duke University Press.

Howitt, Alfred William. 1904. *The Native Tribes of South-East Australia*. Edinburgh: Macmillan.

Human Rights and Equal Opportunity Commission. 1997. *Bringing Them Home: National Inquiry into the Separation of Aboriginal and Torres Strait Islander Children from Their Families*. Canberra: Commonwealth of Australia.

Jay, Martin. 1993. *Downcast Eyes: The Denigration of Vision in Twentieth-Century French Thought*. Berkeley, CA: University of California Press.

Kensy, Julia. 2008. La Perouse. In *Dictionary of Sydney*. Available at: <http://www.dictionary ofsydney.org/item/412> (accessed July 2011).

Langford, Ruby. 1988. *Don't Take Your Love to Town*. Ringwood, Victoria: Penguin.

Lydon, Jane. 2006. *Eye Contact: Photographing Indigenous Australians*. Durham, NC: Duke University Press.

—— 2008. Contested Landscapes: Rights to History, Rights to Place: Who Controls Archaeological Places? In *Handbook of Landscape Archaeology*, ed. Bruno David and Julian Thomas, pp. 654–9. Walnut Creek, CA: Left Coast Press.

—— 2009. *Fantastic Dreaming: The Archaeology of an Aboriginal Mission*. Lanham, MD: Altamira Press.

McGregor, Russell. 1997. *Imagined Destinies: Aboriginal Australians and the Doomed Race Theory, 1880–1939*. Melbourne: Melbourne University Press.

Meehan, Donna. 2000. *It Is No Secret: The Story of a Stolen Child*. Sydney: Random House.

Meskell, Lynn. 2010. Ethnographic Interventions. In *Handbook of Postcolonial Archaeology*, ed. Jane Lydon and Uzma Z. Rizvi, pp. 445–57. Walnut Creek, CA: Left Coast Press.

Moser, Stephanie. 2001. Archaeological Representation: The Visual Conventions for Constructing Knowledge about the Past. In *Archaeological Theory Today*, ed. Ian Hodder, pp. 262–83. Cambridge: Polity Press.

Norman, Heidi. 2006. A Modern Day Cooroboree: Towards a History of the New South Wales Rugby League Knockout. *Aboriginal History* 30: 169–86.

—— 2009. An Unwanted Corroboree: The Politics of the New South Wales Aboriginal Rugby League Knockout. *Australian Aboriginal Studies* 2: 112–22.

Povinelli, Elizabeth A. 2007. *The Cunning of Recognition: Indigenous Alterities and the Making of Australian Multiculturalism*. Durham, NC: Duke University Press.

Silliman, Stephen W. 2005. Culture Contact or Colonialism? Challenges in the Archaeology of Native North America. *American Antiquity* 70(1): 55–74.

—— 2010. Indigenous Traces in Colonial Spaces: Archaeologies of Ambiguity, Origin, and Practice. *Journal of Social Archaeology* 10(1): 28–58.

Smith, Laurajane. 2006. *The Uses of Heritage*. London: Routledge.

Stoler, Ann Laura. 2002. *Carnal Knowledge and Imperial Power: Race and the Intimate in Colonial Rule*. Berkeley, CA: University of California Press.

Thomas, Nicholas. 1991. *Entangled Objects: Exchange, Material Culture, and Colonialism in the Pacific*. Cambridge, MA: Harvard University Press.

Thongchai, Winichakul. 1994. *Siam Mapped: A History of the Geobody of Siam*. Honolulu: University of Hawai'i Press.

Warnier, Jean-Pierre. 2011. Territialization and the Politics of Autochthony. In *Heritage, Memory and Identity*, ed. Helmut Anheier and Yudhishthir Raj Isar, pp. 95–105. London: Sage Publications.

CHAPTER 22

....

MODERNISM

....

ALFREDO GONZÁLEZ-RUIBAL

22.1 INTRODUCTION: FANTASY AND UTOPIA

....

UTOPIANISM is a characteristically modern phenomenon that has called the attention of philosophers, political scientists, historians, and, more recently, archaeologists (Levitas 2010). The latter have mostly focused on the utopias of the eighteenth and nineteenth centuries, often using archaeology as a method to complement textual information (e.g. Tarlow 2002; Van Bueren and Tarlow 2006). Archaeologists have paid little attention, however, to those failed social dreams of the contemporary world, probably because small-scale, well-bounded utopian projects are less frequent or less famous than their predecessors or because archaeologists, as other scholars, prefer to study 'the small and friendly, rather than the large, unwieldy and ambiguous' (Levitas 2010: 181). The fantasies of supermodernity have been of another kind, much more transforming and destructive of people and landscape than anything that existed before. Maybe it is precisely because of the ubiquity and massiveness of modernist projects that they often pass unnoticed: it could be argued that the transformation of the world during the twentieth century was mostly driven by utopianism of one kind or the other (liberal and totalitarian, left-wing and right-wing). This transformation has not been only of mentalities and social mores, but also, perhaps basically, of the material environment, from the intimacy of the home to the entire landscape. With the collapse of the communist regimes, the defeat of fascism, and the repeated crises of liberal dreams, it is the sheer material foundations of these systems that have turned out to be the more durable aspect of those fantasies. It is for this reason, also, that the phenomenon of recent utopianism deserves close archaeological examination.

In this chapter, I would like to approach the issue from a conventional archaeological point of view. With conventional archaeology I refer to a discipline that focuses on tangible materiality and, more particularly, on abandoned things and places (the archaeological record). Since the archaeology of supermodern utopianism is yet to be done, the aim of this chapter is not as much to summarize the extant work (although I will refer to the different archaeological projects conducted to date), as to point out some promising areas for research and show the relevance of the topic. I will revise some of the most important failed utopias of the recent past, which have been studied by historians, architectural historians, and political scientists among others, and suggest ways in which archaeology may contribute to the wider debate.

If we are to understand modernist utopias, there is a concept that has to be taken into account: fantasy. A fantasy is a consciously or unconsciously imagined situation that emerges from unsatisfied wishes. Individual fantasies usually have to do with erotic or ambitious wishes—power (Freud 1959: 146–7). Fantasies are not necessarily negative; they can be a defence mechanism against the harshness of reality and they can even be a creative stimulus. However, when they become an obsession and are an increasing part of one's psychic life, they may evince a pathological disorder known as narcissistic personality, which is characterized by megalomaniac desires, a need for unlimited success, and the substitution of relatedness (to other people) by ruthless power (Ledermann 1982: 320). A particular kind of fantasy, and the one that interests us here, is what can be called 'ideological fantasy'. Unlike daydreaming, ideological fantasies are not individual, but shared by a collective. In fact, they are fundamental for the existence of such a collective. According to Slavoj Žižek (1989: 32–3), we all live immersed in ideological fantasies, because they unconsciously structure the totality of the real.

However, there are moments in which unconscious fantasies are rendered conscious. An objectified ideological fantasy is a utopia: a form of fantasy that is neither aimed (or not just) at fulfilling individual desires (daydreaming) nor at organizing reality (ideological fantasy), but at consciously improving the world. From this point of view, we can say that, unlike daydreaming, utopias are inherently political and, unlike ideological fantasies, they are not geared towards sustaining reality, but towards transforming it. Despite their differences, utopias and daydreaming have at least two things in common: they are based on desire and their pathological deviation is characterized by delusions of grandeur and a relentless search for power. Although there are a few examples of non-religious utopias before the fifteenth century (Plato's is the most famous one), the phenomenon seems to be tightly bound with the development of modernity and the process of secularization that it entails. There are other reasons that explain why utopian thinking develops with modernity:

1. *Modernity's self-awareness.* This is especially true from the time of Hegel onwards. Jürgen Habermas (1990: 7) notes that 'Modernity can and will no longer borrow the criteria by which it takes its orientation from the models supplied by another epoch; it has to create its own normativity out of itself. Modernity sees itself cast back upon itself without any possibility of escape.' Modern utopian thinking extracts its ideas from itself and is always forward looking, although it often manipulates elements from the past.

2. *Changes in the conception of time.* The idea that the future can be radically different from the present and the past is typical (though not exclusive) of modern thinking and it allows to conceive a thorough transformation of society. Christian and Muslim thinking also imply a radical reordering of time, with a future different from the present, but this future lies in a different ontological level. Instead, modern utopianism locates the promise of the future in the same existential space of the present.

3. *Individualization.* According to Giddens (1991: 91), in modernity, the self is seen as a reflexive project, for which the individual is responsible: 'We are not what we are, but what we make ourselves.' This idea that individuals can be agents of transformation is also behind the spread of utopias. In addition, with a more individuated self, it is

more likely that individuals feel that the prevailing social order oppresses them and prevents the fulfilment of their aspirations.

4. *Science and technology*. Modernity implies a faith in the human ability to transform the world through theoretical and applied knowledge. All utopias take into consideration the role of technology in making the dream come true: 'Industry, boundless like the river that runs to its destiny, bring us new tools, adapted to this new epoch enlivened by a new spirit' (Le Corbusier 1977 [1920]: xxxii).

22.2 SUCH STUFF AS DREAMS ARE MADE ON

If technology is society made durable, as Latour (1991) has it, then it is understandable that all those regimes and communities that have tried to change society have relied heavily on material culture: they did not simply want to construct a new society; they wanted it to last and contrary to actions or speech, things last (Olsen 2010: 121 and this volume). It is this desire to stabilize networks (using again the Latourian language), that may explain the similarity of many of the materializations of totalitarian regimes in the twentieth and twenty-first centuries—massive, solid, grandiose structures. There is, of course, something else: a modernist spirit that pervades the plans of both left- and right-wing utopias (Scott 1998). This modernism sings the praises of technology as progress and sees in it the cure to all ills: an opportunity to start anew and shape the world of the future at will. This is clear in the poetical vision of futurist artists (Marinetti 2005 [1909]) and in the more practical implementation of Fordism, a great influence in all totalitarian regimes (communist and fascist), from a practical and theoretical point of view (Clarke 1990: 141).

Opposed to this line of thought, there are thinkers that alerted against the dangers of modernist dreams based on technology. Prominent among those is Lewis Mumford, for whom 'the machine, by failing as yet...to allow sufficient play in social existence to the organic, has opened the way for its return in the narrow and inimical form of the primitive. Western society is relapsing at critical points into precivilized modes of thought, feeling and action' (Mumford 2010 [1934]: 302). Herbert Marcuse (1982 [1941]), in turn, criticized the same technological rationality that enthralled other leftist thinkers, such as Gramsci: he saw in the 'ingenious manipulation of the power inherent in technology' one of the pillars of the Nazi regime (1982 [1941]: 139). Interestingly, both Marcuse's critique and Gramsci's praise of technology were based on the same grounds: its capability to force adjustment and compliance, to produce 'new, more complex, rigid norms and habits of order' (Clarke 1990: 144). Note that most critics did not regard technology as inherently evil: it is only so when reason is reduced to instrumental reason and technology becomes a means to absolute power. The same can be said of the conservative critique of technology: Heidegger (1977 [1938]: 152) bemoaned that with the 'planetary imperialism of technologically organized man, the subjectivism of man attains its acme, from which point it will descend to the level of organized uniformity and there firmly establish itself. This uniformity becomes the surest instrument of total, i.e., technological, rule over the earth.' Yet technological rule over the earth is not unavoidable: strangely enough, Heidegger thought, until 1935, that Nazism could be the place of encounter between 'global technology and modern man' (Habermas 1990: 159).

There is one thing that unifies modernist technological utopias and critiques and that is their paradoxical immaterial character. They tend to speak about things in a rather abstract way and understand technology as applied scientific knowledge in which real objects are mostly absent—the futurists are an exception. The stuff modernist dreams are made on has still a dreamy quality, no matter how much they trust technical marvels with the fulfilment of utopia. Thus, Le Corbusier (1977: 161) conceives architecture as 'the pure creation of spirit'. The notions of 'soul' and 'spirit' are equally fundamental in Nazi discourses: Alfred Rosenberg predicted that the Third Reich would be the reign of the spirit, which would 'take over from the kingdom of the Father and the Son' (Michaud 2004: 27). Likewise, Italian fascist architecture strove for transcendence in its 'metaphysical cities' (Pizzi 2005), which, in their intended purity and order, were a disavowal of raw materiality. This stance is not a prerogative of the utopian-totalitarian materialities of the twentieth century. In fact, most modernist material culture from the nineteenth century onwards undergoes the mechanisms of purification that characterize modernity. As Latour (1993: 66) criticizes, 'The moderns indeed declare that technology is nothing but pure instrumental mastery...Purity everywhere! They claim this, but we must be careful not to take them at their word, since what they are asserting is only half of the modern world, the work of purification that distils what the work of hybridization supplies.'

The stuff modernist utopias are made on is not just the kind that theoreticians present us with: technical wonders, such as airplanes or automated factories, grandiose buildings and mathematical urban layouts. Other things have been fundamental in shaping modernist dreams: prisoners' barracks and barbed wire (Myers and Moshenska 2011), razed neighbourhoods (Hall 2000: 156–76; Mullins 2006), farmhouses (Samuels 2010), mass graves (Haglund et al. 2001), concrete and steel (Buchli 1999: 44; Andreassen et al. 2010: 63). The crude fabric of reality contrasts with the clean images of modernist dreams (cf. Levitas 2010). This is one of the areas where archaeology can make a relevant contribution: the crucial role of materiality at large and materials in particular (Ingold 2007) in creating, sustaining, or challenging modern utopias.

22.3 TOTALITARIAN FANTASIES

Totalitarian fantasies are more similar than they might look from an ideological perspective. Their materiality, in fact, shows that their will to control and organize society is homologous, as it is their penchant for the grandiose, the excessive, and the regimented. In what follows, I would suggest four avenues of archaeological research on totalitarian utopias of the recent past: the study of domesticity as an arena of compliance and resistance; a critique of the totalitarian sublime; the exposure of material strategies of elimination; and the deconstruction of totalitarian temporalities.

As opposed to the prevailing focus on monumental architecture and urbanism typical of art history and cultural studies (e.g. MacDonald 2006), archaeology can explore other, more intimate realms, which are equally fundamental for understanding totalitarianism. After all, one of the defining features of totalitarian dictatorships is their desire to regulate every aspect of society. It is in everyday life where the insidiousness of totalitarianism is better grasped. Everyday language has been shown to be fundamental in naturalizing a

FIGURE 22.1 A decorated bedroom in the Soviet mining town of Pyramiden, abandoned in 1998. Although private bedrooms show a degree of personal creativity, there is an overall compliance with rules, which is also reflected in the material record (photograph: Elin Andreassen)

totalitarian regime (Klemperer 2006); the role of things is similar to that of words, but they have not yet been studied in a similar way. However, the private sphere is also where dreams of a total society are more easily disrupted (cf. Buchli 1999; Andreassen et al. 2010). Thus, an archaeological exploration of domestic life under totalitarianism should be a quest for material traces that subvert order (Andreassen et al. 2010: 111–37) (Figure 22.1). These material traces can be considered tactics of resistance, in the sense of De Certeau (1984: 37): an art of the weak, which takes the shape of 'practices that are foreign to the "geometrical" or "geographical" space of visual, panoptic, or theoretical constructions' (De Certeau 1984: 93; see also Harrison and Schofield 2010: 147–8). These daily acts of defiance can provoke, in some cases, the failure of utopian projects, as happened with the rural colonization of Italy during the fascist period (Samuels 2010). The artificial villages (*borghi*) created by the regime were unable to foster a new kind of sociability and ended up abandoned or reused in non-anticipated ways, such as 'country homes' or storage spaces (Samuels 2010: 75).

I have argued elsewhere that one of the objectives of the archaeology of the contemporary past should be to turn the sublime constructs of modern ideology (race, nation, progress, capital) into the abject materiality they actually are (González-Ruibal 2008: 260). Totalitarian regimes lend themselves well to the task. Consider fascist architecture: even today, the materiality of Italian fascism is strongly associated with the fine rationalist buildings that some of its best architects designed. Posters, films, and the buildings themselves offer a powerful imagery of a modern, progressive regime. The other side of the coin can be glimpsed in *Bicycle Thieves* (1948), the film by Vittorio di Sica, set in post-war Rome. The protagonists live in a low-class housing development of the fascist period (Quartiere Flaminio), which was left unfinished. Despite being unfinished and relatively new, the buildings are already a squalid ruin. They are isolated in the middle of a wasteland. They are dirty and have no running water. Even the monuments of fascism, such as Duca d'Aosta Bridge, look desolate and dismal under the gaze of Vittorio di Sica. *Bicycle Thieves* represents perfectly what the task of the archaeologist can be in dealing with failed modernist fantasies: we have to look at the unstable zones of totalitarian power, excavate (metaphorically and literally) under its façade and at its margins. We have to examine the crack in the walls of the fascist monument or the hidden shantytowns where the fascist subaltern dwells: the shabbiness of ideologies that are obsessed with order and cleanliness.

Totalitarian fantasies cannot be carried out without exercising ruthless power. This implies exterminating a large part of the population: dissidents and all those who are deemed incompatible with the totalitarian dream (ethnic, religious, political groups). In turn, large-scale eliminationist policies cannot be undertaken without proper technologies. The ruins and debris produced by such technologies can be studied archaeologically. So far, archaeologists have been working on remains of concentration camps (Gilead et al. 2009), torture centres (Bernbeck and Pollock 2007), prisons (Cocroft and Schofield 2010), and mass graves (Gassiot and Steadman 2008). We have to take entire topographies of terror into account (González-Ruibal 2012). For the first time in history, modern technology and the will to power allowed to effect a deep and large-scale material transformation of society and landscape. In that process, landscape became inscribed with signs of fear and trauma. An appraisal of landscape, therefore, is the necessary counterpoise to the first line of research mentioned—domesticity. An examination of totalitarian dreams demands a continuous change of scale, from the micro to the macro, from banality to terror.

A fourth issue that archaeologists can explore is the temporality of totalitarian regimes. Modernism in general, and totalitarianism in particular, abhor the past and the time of tradition. They emphasize youth, speed, change, and the future. To be true, totalitarian modernists do not negate the past wholesale. Only some do, such as the Italian futurist artists, who crave the destruction of museums and libraries (Marinetti 2005 [1909]: 5). Most prefer to pick up from the past what suits their dreams and destroy (or ignore) the rest. This is what happened with the neo-imperial utopia of Spanish fascism in the 1930s and 1940s, when architecture combined rationalism and sixteenth-century elements, or with Mussolini's fantasy of reawakening the Roman Empire, both politically and materially (through archaeological excavations). An interesting line of research would be to explore not only how the past is utilized in a future-oriented present (Galaty and Watkinson 2004), but also how the past haunts utopia and refuses to go away, emerging in a fantasmatic way amidst the purified world of totalitarianism. The material past is a good example of the Real as that which resists symbolization (Žižek 1989: 69): the void left by the burnt down synagogue, the slum that grows in the outskirts of the modernist city, or the yoke and plough of the Ethiopian peasant. Ruins and things from the past are agents of disruption (Olsen 2010: 169). They destabilize totalitarian fantasies.

22.4 LIBERAL FANTASIES

Totalitarian dreams usually have spectacular collapses, which have rendered them particularly attractive. However, liberal regimes can also be utopian and their fantasies, like those of totalitarianism, are similarly prone to failure. This is because both democratic and totalitarian regimes share what James C. Scott (1998: 4) has called a 'high modernist ideology', which he defines as a strong version of 'the self-confidence about scientific and technical progress, the expansion of production, the growing satisfaction of human needs, the mastery of nature (including human nature), and, above all, the rational design of social order commensurate with the scientific understanding of natural laws'. I will consider here four kinds of failures: urban programmes, development projects, suburbia, and mechanisms of immunity of liberal regimes. Each of them is related to a particular modernist dream: creating the ideal city (and therefore the ideal citizenry); ending poverty and fostering ever-growing economies; living in an ideal environment that fulfils one's individual wishes; and being infinitely secure.

Ambitious plans to (re)construct cities or parts of cities along modernist lines go back to the beginnings of modernity itself. Colonial settlements in the Americas were designed according to regular plans in the sixteenth century. In the nineteenth, Hausmann's Paris set the example for the refurbished, rational metropolis. Still, most towns remained socially liveable, albeit part of the population, such as in Paris, had to be expelled to its margins. Things would drastically change during the twentieth century. Cities became inhuman, regimented spaces: factories or machines for living. Le Corbusier saw this modernist urban revolution as utopian: 'It is necessary to create the state of mind of mass-production. The state of mind of mass-producing houses. The state of mind of living in mass-produced houses. The state of mind of conceiving mass-produced houses' (Le Corbusier 1977: 187). It is a dream of cleanliness, speed, and order. Those cities that have been built according to high modernist plans have been an utter failure: Brasilia is the best-known example (Scott 1998: 117–30). Founded in 1960, it was planned to become the new capital of Brazil. As many utopias, it symbolized a radical break with the past and the materialization of a better future. The abolition of the past and the absence of landmarks (all housing blocks and commercial quarters look the same) make Brasilia a perfect example of the anti-social, post-mnemonic city (Connerton 2009: 99). The new metropolis, with its regimented layout and immense, empty spaces, soon proved to be unliveable and, by 1980, 75 per cent of the population was residing outside the planned areas (Scott 1998: 129). An archaeology of modernist urban utopias should explore simultaneously the way materiality makes the city inhospitable and the way people struggle to redress the modernist dream and reappropriate the city—turning it social again. As in the case of totalitarianism, this kind of research consists in looking at the subtle material cracks of the modernist façade: signs of creative subversion and nonconformity. An archaeological critique of modernist planning should also look at unruly places, derelict and ruined, and at the alternative practices that take place in them (Edensor 2005; Andreassen et al. 2010; Dawdy 2010: 776–7).

One of the most prominent liberal dreams, at least since 1945, is ending poverty, both in the West and in the rest of the world. Liberal efforts are epitomized in development projects, which have often been geared towards strategic political-economic interests (especially during the Cold War period) rather than to improve the situation of the countries in question. There is already an important amount of anthropological literature on the subject (Ferguson 1990; Escobar 1995), but archaeology can contribute significantly to it. After all, material culture crucially informs the political imaginary of developmentalism. Developing communities usually implies providing technology and artefacts (roads, factories, electricity), as if there was an unproblematic relationship between modern material culture and progress—whatever the latter concept might mean. The injection of technology in the Third World has often been carried out with utmost disregard for local contexts and often with disastrous results. I have had the occasion to study the ruins of the Tana-Beles development project in the lowlands of north-western Ethiopia, a multimillion undertaking of the Italian cooperation during the late 1980s (González-Ruibal 2006: 193–5). The project, which implied the construction of factories, the introduction of new industrial crops, and the resettlement of thousands of people in one of the harshest areas of the country, failed even before it was completed. One of the things that surprises of the Tana-Beles project is its material excess, but redundancy and excess is precisely what characterizes late capitalism and is one of the reasons of its eventual demise. Excess is something that cannot be expressed in numbers or words alone: there is something ineffable in the hundreds of containers spread in the forest, the tractors and other expensive machinery rusting under the sun, thousands of square metres of office buildings, factories, storehouses, concrete, bricks, metal sheet, glass, pipes, tarmac roads, electric lighting, gas pumps, derelict gardens (Figure 22.2). An entire city with its airport turned into a ruin. In Tana-Beles, one realizes that failed modernities are about materiality in the first place. Andreassen et al. (2010) prove the point powerfully through the disturbing images of material excess in the Soviet town of Pyramiden.

Not all failed liberal dreams have the dismal look of derelict development projects or regimented cities. The failures of modernity can look bright and colourful. This is the case of Western suburbia, an original American invention spread through all continents (Knox 2005; MacLeod and Ward 2002). Some geographers see gated communities as bourgeois utopias, *privatopias*—a symbol of collective politics gone awry (Harvey 2000: 239). As

FIGURE 22.2 Abandoned containers from the failed development project of Tana-Beles (Ethiopia). The liberal dream of modernization and ending poverty coincided here with the communist dream of social justice and progress with disastrous results (photograph: Alfredo González-Ruibal)

a testimony of increasing economic inequalities, the destruction of traditional forms of socialization, the imposition of social segregation, and the triumph of the banal, privatopias can be considered a failed modernist dream (Figure 22.3). As such, they can be studied archaeologically in different ways: firstly, archaeologists can explore the ruins they leave behind. The expansion of suburbia goes hand in hand with the degrading and abandonment of historic downtowns (Vergara 1999). Secondly, many suburbs originate in previous villages or neighbourhoods, which are often completely demolished. A critical archaeological research consists in locating, above or below the surface, the remains of the world destroyed by new housing developments. It would show other forms of sociality that have been crushed by the lifestyle fantasies of capitalism: this is what Paul Mullins (2006) has done in an African American neighbourhood in Indiana, which was razed to ground in the 1960s—in this case to build a university campus. Thirdly, suburban sprawls are interesting in themselves from a material point of view (Harrison and Schofield 2010: 224–5). Geographers have criticized the social implications of gated communities, malls, and other developments, but they rarely go into analytic detail on the material reality of these suburban utopias. Archaeology could bring their tools to examine the materiality of suburbia and how they shape 'the political person as well as the ways in which the personal is and can be political' (Harvey 2000: 241). A good example of archaeological analysis of suburban life is Graves-Brown's (2007) study of a commercial centre in Wales.

There is a fourth kind of utopia that characterizes modern liberal regimes: the fantasy of total immunity—against external aggression, disease, natural catastrophes, technical

FIGURE 22.3 A materialized modernist fantasy: a luxurious house of a returned emigrant in Galicia (Spain). Individual success of emigrants is not inconsistent with social failure, as the region continues to be one of the least economically developed in Europe (photograph: Alfredo González-Ruibal)

accidents, and so forth—which is part of the supermodern biopolitics. Italian philosopher Roberto Esposito (2006: 43) notes, in the wake of Foucault, that 'to the degree that liberalism isn't limited to the simple enunciation of the imperative of liberty but implicates the organization of conditions that make this effectively possible liberalism contradicts its own premises…liberalism continually risks destroying what it says it wants to create'. Guantanamo Bay detention camp is probably the most representative example of this paradox of liberalism. Using satellite imagery, Adrian Myers (2010) has been able to retrace the evolution and continuous expansion of the camp, in keeping with the growing immunity concerns of the United States. In this way, he has proved that archaeology can be useful in exploring (and exposing) Western biopolitics.

22.5 VERNACULAR MODERNITIES

When we think about the ruins of modernity, we invariably consider those of the West, or those produced by Western ideologies. However, non-Western nations and groups have developed their own forms of modernism, which do not always easily fit Western political-economic categories. These modernisms, however, often have the same aspirations and have been plagued by the same problems as Western modernisms. Their aspirations have to do with economic growth, industrialization and the modernization of economy, secularization, social change, breaking with a traditional past, constructing a strong and homogeneous nation-state, and cutting colonial ties. The archaeology of the contemporary past is too often centred on Western nations. By looking at vernacular modernities, we can take into account other historical experiences and other societies.

Outside the West, the area of the world that perhaps best exemplifies the failure of modernist dreams is sub-Saharan Africa. The African nations that emerged from colonialism in the mid-twentieth century were a dream of reason full of promise, but, by the 1970s, most of them had degenerated into horrifying nightmares, in which material culture played a prominent role: machetes, automatic weapons, traditional revivals, and totalitarian kitsch. Achille Mbembe (2000) has argued that instead of looking at discourses, we have to tackle material excess and sensuousness in order to understand the nature of power in postcolonial dictatorships. Despite their similarities, modernist regimes in sub-Saharan Africa show a great diversity. Some postcolonial nations developed policies and material practices that were deeply influenced by socialism or communism. Others, such as Mobutu's Congo, gave free rein to predatory capitalism, although this later category of nation-states can hardly be considered a modernist dream. A third group is more difficult to classify in terms of Western ideology. They are a hotchpotch of foreign ideologies and vernacular beliefs and practices. This hybrid character is also visible in its material practices, which draw upon a diversity of sources, both African and Western. An instance of this category is the regime of Francisco Macías Nguema in Equatorial Guinea, a former Spanish colony (Liniger-Goumaz 1989). I will describe this case in some detail, because of my first-hand experience of the area and because I think that it is paradigmatic of the excesses, paradoxes, and failures of African modernist utopias.

After obtaining independence in 1968, Francisco Macías Nguema was elected to the presidency of the country. Scarcely a year had passed when a coup was attempted against the president. Macías used the chance to take total power and start a ruthless persecution

FIGURE 22.4 Ruins of an unfinished house in Corisco (Equatorial Guinea). The wrong-headed developmentalist policies of the present dictator have killed the dreams of many islanders, who hoped for the improvement of their life conditions after the end of colonialism (photograph: Alfredo González-Ruibal)

of political dissent, which became progressively deranged and far-reaching. Until he was deposed in another coup in 1979, up to 15 per cent of the country's population might have been assassinated and a third went into exile. The dream of independence and modernization cherished by many Equatoguineans under the despotic colonial rule was annihilated during independence. The Macías regime was a mixture of badly digested socialist ideas, nationalism, and a return to roots: this was expressed, among other things, in the local currency, which was called *ekwele* after the name of the iron items employed in traditional marriage exchanges. The regime, in any case, is archaeologically interesting not for what it built, which was little, but for what it destroyed: hundreds of villages were abandoned after people were assassinated or took refuge abroad. Their ruins still litter the country. The process did not really stop after the toppling of Macías. A different modernizing utopia is taking hold of the country with the new dictator, Teodoro Obiang, which closely resembles that of other petroleum-driven economies, such as Angola. Equatorial Guinea is being razed to the ground and ostentatious buildings and infrastructures emerge from the ruins of the forest, traditional villages, and colonial towns. Again, the construction of utopia is indissolubly linked here with the destruction of the old world.

Since 2009, I have been conducting research in the Island of Corisco. Archaeology permits to delineate with precision the history of the place for the last century and a half. During the nineteenth century, the population was large and thriving and the material record looks astonishingly rich and diverse: it shows an African bourgeoisie in the rising. By the end of that century, the consolidation of colonial power coincides with a progressive decline in the living standard of Coriscans, characterized by an abrupt disappearance of quality imports and a steady increase in alcoholic containers. The independence period is not marked by socio-economic recovery, but by growing impoverishment and a radical interruption: we recorded dozens of settlements abandoned in the 1970s all over the island. The gradual return of exiles, still a fraction of the original population, is not changing the panorama as it should: the dumps that I have had the occasion to examine were made up basically of containers of cheap alcoholic beverages. A few attempts at making bungalows for tourists lie in ruins, due to the refusal of the present dictatorship to give visas for visitors (Figure 22.4). With the hindsight provided by archaeology, it is possible to envisage another modernity for Corisco, one that was strangled first by colonialism and then by a postcolonial dystopia: a vernacular modernity killed two or three times leaves little room for hope.

22.6 CONCLUSIONS

In this chapter, I have argued that an archaeology of failed modernities has six main objectives, irrespective of the political nature and geographical location of the modernist fantasy in question. First, archaeology has to explore the darkest side of high modernist fantasies—both authoritarian and liberal—and their ability to infiltrate and transform society: this should be carried out at the micro and macro scale (domesticity and landscape). Secondly, archaeology is traditionally concerned with materiality and technology. In the case of supermodern utopias, it can unravel the entanglement of technical knowledge, objects and modernist ideologies, paying close attention to abject materialities, such as those related to strategies of repression (concentration camps, mass graves) and mechanisms of social engineering (resettlement projects, ghettos). Thirdly, archaeology has to look for dissonances, subversive practices, and nonconformity, either as the product of resistance or as the natural outcome of modernism's impossible aspirations to perfect closure. In relation to this point, the discipline is well suited to study 'interstitial places' (Harrison and Schofield 2010: 228–9) at the margins of modernist utopias or shattered by those utopias (slums, semi-abandoned sites, ruins). While manifesting supermodern atrocities and failures is an important archaeological task, we should not stop at that. A fifth aim that has to be taken into account is the production of alternative narratives of modern utopias, based on material remains—ruins and rubbish. Finally, if material culture is one of the elements that define archaeology, the other one is time: the discipline has to denounce the impossible temporality of modernist fantasies—a future-oriented time that intends to abolish the past—and, likewise, to show how the ruins of the past disrupt and haunt the modernist present.

These six objectives mostly focus on the oppressiveness of modernism. However, archaeology can also be a way of retrieving hope. With its long-term perspective, archaeology can relativize modernism, by looking at what happened before and afterwards. It is possible to retrace alternative pathways and show that the road to modernist disaster is not the only option: thus, the archaeology of modernism should not focus only on its failures, but also on the processes that were thwarted by misled utopianism and that could have made the world a different, and probably better, place. An alternative trajectory is suggested, as we have seen, in the precolonial sites of Corisco, in Equatorial Guinea. On the other hand, failures also evince that even the most powerful utopias of high modernity can be defeated: the abandoned fascist farms of Sicily or the ruins of development projects in Africa are a powerful proof that ill-devised utopias are doomed to fail. There is an ethics and aesthetics of failure, which archaeologists should explore: 'Failure works. Which is to say that although ostensibly it signals the breakdown of an aspiration or an agreed demand, breakdown indexes an alternative route or way of doing or making', writes Sara Jane Bailes (2011: 2), who adds that a failed objective establishes an aperture. It is this aperture, and not only the catastrophic closures of modernist fantasies, that archaeologists should explore in the ruins of supermodernity. It is perhaps in the paths not taken, where the true utopia lies.

References

Andreassen, Elin, Bjerck, Hein B. and Olsen, Bjørnar. 2010. *Persistent Memories: Pyramiden—A Soviet Mining Town in the High Arctic*. Trondheim: Tapir Academic Press.

Bailes, Sara J. 2011. *Performance Theatre and the Poetics of Failure: Forced Entertainment, Goat Island, Elevator Repair Service*. London: Routledge.

Bernbeck, Reinhard and Pollock, Susan. 2007. Grabe, wo du stehts! An Archaeology of Perpetrators. In *Archaeology and Capitalism: From Ethics to Politics*, ed. Yannis Hamilakis and Philip Duke, pp. 217–34. Walnut Creek, CA: Left Coast Press.

Buchli, Victor. 1999. *An Archaeology of Socialism*. Oxford: Berg.

Clarke, Simon. 1990. New Utopias for Old: Fordist Dreams and Post-Fordist Fantasies. *Capital & Class* 14: 131–55.

Cocroft, Wayne and Schofield, John. 2010. Hohenschönhausen, Berlin: Explorations in Stasiland. *Landscapes* 11(1): 67–83.

Connerton, Paul. 2009. *How Modernity Forgets*. Cambridge: Cambridge University Press.

Dawdy, Shannon Lee. 2010. Clockpunk Anthropology and the Ruins of Modernity. *Current Anthropology* 51(6): 761–93.

De Certeau, Michel. 1984. *The Practice of Everyday Life*. Berkeley, CA: University of California Press.

Edensor, Tim. 2005. *Industrial Ruins: Spaces, Aesthetics and Materiality*. Oxford: Berg.

Escobar, Arturo. 1995. *Encountering Development: The Making and Unmaking of the Third World*. Princeton, NJ: Princeton University Press.

Esposito, Roberto. 2006. The Immunization Paradigm. *Diacritics* 36(2): 23–48.

Ferguson, James. 1990. *The Anti-Politics Machine: 'Development', Depoliticization and Bureaucratic Power in Lesotho*. Cambridge: Cambridge University Press.

Freud, Sigmund. 1959 [1908]. Creative Writers and Day-Dreaming. In *The Standard Edition of the Complete Psychological Works of Sigmund Freud, Volume 9 (1906–1908): Jensen's 'Gradiva' and Other Works*, ed. James Strachey, pp. 141–54. London: Hogarth Press.

Galaty, Michael L. and Watkinson, Charles. 2004. *Archaeology Under Dictatorship*. New York: Kluwer/Plenum.

Gassiot, Ermengol and Steadman, Dawnie Wolfe. 2008. The Political, Social and Scientific Contexts of Archaeological Investigations of Mass Graves in Spain. *Archaeologies* 4(3): 429–44.

Giddens, A. 1991. *Modernity and Self-Identity: Self and Society in the Late Modern Age*. Stanford: Stanford University Press.

Gilead, Isaac, Haimi, Yoram, and Mazurek, Wojciech. 2009. Excavating Nazi Extermination Centres. *Present Pasts* 1: 10–39.

González-Ruibal, Alfredo. 2006. The Dream of Reason: An Archaeology of the Failures of Modernity in Ethiopia. *Journal of Social Archaeology* 6(2): 175–201.

——— 2008. Time to Destroy: An Archaeology of Supermodernity. *Current Anthropology* 49(2): 247–79.

——— 2012. From the Battlefield to the Labour Camp: Archaeology of the Civil War and Dictatorship in Spain. *Antiquity* 86(332): 456–73.

Graves-Brown, Paul. 2007. Concrete Islands. In *Contemporary and Historical Archaeology in Theory: Papers from the 2003 and 2004 CHAT Conferences*, ed. Laura McAtackney, Matthew Palus, and Angela Picini, pp. 75–82. BAR International Series 1677. Oxford: Archaeopress.

Habermas, Jürgen. 1990. *The Philosophical Discourse of Modernity: Twelve Lectures.* Cambridge, MA: MIT Press.

Haglund, William D., Connor, Melissa, and Scott, Douglas D. 2001. The Archaeology of Contemporary Mass Graves. *Historical Archaeology* 35(1): 57–69.

Hall, Martin. 2000. *Archaeology and the Modern World: Colonial Transcripts in South Africa and the Chesapeake.* London: Routledge.

Harrison, Rodney and Schofield, John. 2010. *After Modernity: Archaeological Approaches to the Contemporary Past.* Oxford: Oxford University Press.

Harvey, David. 2000. *Spaces of Hope.* Edinburgh: Edinburgh University Press.

Heidegger, Martin. 1977 [1938]. *The Age of the World Picture: The Question Concerning Technology and Other Essays*, ed. and tr. William Lovitt, pp. 115–54. New York: Harper & Row.

Ingold, Tim. 2007. Materials Against Materiality. *Archaeological Dialogues* 14(1): 1–16.

Klemperer, Victor. 2006. *The Language of the Third Reich: LTI, Lingua Tertii Imperii: A Philologist's Notebook*, tr. Martin Brady. London: Continuum.

Knox, Paul. 2005. Vulgaria: The Re-enchantment of Suburbia. *Opolis* 1(2): 33–46.

Latour, Bruno. 1991. Technology is Society Made Durable. In *A Sociology of Monsters: Essays on Power, Technology and Domination*, ed. John Law, pp. 103–31. London: Routledge.

——— 1993. *We Have Never Been Modern.* Cambridge, MA: Harvard University Press.

Le Corbusier. 1977 [1920]. *Hacia una arquitectura.* Barcelona: Apóstrofe.

Ledermann, Rushi. 1982. Narcissistic Disorder and its Treatment. *Journal of Analytical Psychology* 27(4): 303–21.

Levitas, Ruth. 2010. *The Concept of Utopia*, 2nd edn. Bern: Peter Lang.

Liniger-Goumaz, Max. 1989. *Small is Not Always Beautiful: The Story of Equatorial Guinea.* London: C. Hurst.

MacDonald, Sharon. 2006. Words in Stone? Agency and Identity in a Nazi Landscape. *Journal of Material Culture* 11(1–2): 105–26.

MacLeod, Gordon and Ward, Kevin. 2002. Spaces of Utopia and Dystopia: Landscaping the Contemporary City. *Geografiska Annaler* 84(3–4): 153–70.

Marcuse, Herbert. 1982 [1941]. Some Social Implications of Modern Technology. In *The Essential Frankfurt School Reader*, ed. Andrew Arato and Eike Gebhardt, pp. 138–62. New York: Continuum.

Marinetti, Filippo Tomasso. 2005 [1909]. The Founding and the Manifesto of Futurism (February 1909). In *Modernism: An Anthology*, ed. Lawrence S. Rainy, pp. 3–6. Oxford: Blackwell.

Mbembe, A. 2000. *De la postcolonie. Essai sur l'imagination politique dans l'Afrique contemporaine.* Paris: Karthala.

Michaud, Eric. 2004. *The Cult of Art in Nazi Germany*, tr. Janet Lloyd. Stanford, CA: Stanford University Press.

Mullins, Paul R. 2006. Racializing the Commonplace Landscape: An Archaeology of Urban Renewal along the Color Line. *World Archaeology* 38(1): 60–71.

Mumford, Lewis. 2010. *Technics and Civilization.* Chicago: University of Chicago Press.

Myers, Adrian. 2010. Camp Delta, Google Earth and the Ethics of Remote Sensing in Archaeology. *World Archaeology* 4(3): 455–67.

Myers, Adrian and Moshenska, Gabriel (eds.). 2011. *Archaeologies of Internment.* New York: Springer.

Olsen, Bjørnar. 2010. *In Defense of Things: Archaeology and the Ontology of Objects.* Lanham, MD: Altamira.

Pizzi, Donata. 2005. *Città metafisiche. Città di fondazione dall'Italia all'oltremare, 1920–1945.* Milan: Skira.

Samuels, Joshua. 2010. Of Other Scapes: Archaeology, Landscape and Heterotopia in Fascist Sicily. *Archaeologies* 6(1): 62–81.

Scott, James C. 1998. *Seeing Like a State: How Certain Schemes to Improve the Human Condition Have Failed.* New Haven: Yale University Press.

Tarlow, Sarah. 2002. Excavating Utopia: Why Archaeologists Should Study 'Ideal' Communities of the Nineteenth Century. *International Journal of Historical Archaeology* 6(4): 299–323.

Van Bueren, Tad and Tarlow, Sarah. 2006. The Interpretive Potential of Utopian Settlements. *Historical Archaeology* 40(1): 1–5.

Vergara, Camilo José. 1999. *American Ruins.* New York: Monacelli.

Žižek, Slavoj. 1989. *The Sublime Object of Ideology.* London: Verso.

CHAPTER 23

....

PROTEST

....

ANNA BADCOCK AND ROBERT JOHNSTON

23.1 INTRODUCTION: THE PLACE OF PROTEST

FOR ten years, a quiet woodland near the village of Stanton Lees, Derbyshire, UK, was home for hundreds of environmental activists. The protesters created a community amongst the trees, using recycled materials to build their dwellings. They populated the woodland with new place names, constructed a communal space, tended vegetable plots, and signposted their occupation with a caravan decorated with slogans and suspended in the trees. The object of their campaign was a proposal to reopen and extend the long-abandoned stone quarries in the woodland. The quarrying could not begin while the protest camp remained, and so the activists used ingenious tactics to resist eviction. The principle underpinning these tactics was to contrive means of putting protesters in vulnerable positions, making it difficult and time-consuming for the bailiffs to clear the camp without causing harm. Under the threat of eviction, the protesters escaped into tree-houses high in the canopy, which they could move between using precarious aerial ropeways. Life in the trees was in some ways a mirror of life on the ground, with the placement of tree-houses and ropeways echoing the distribution of bender tents and paths. The inversion of the everyday world, lifting it into the tree canopy, was both a defence against eviction and a demonstration of intents and beliefs. The threatened eviction of the protest camp at Stanton Lees was never enacted and, by 2009, following the success of the campaign to oppose the quarry, the protesters began dismantling the camp.

It is now only a few years since the protest ended, yet there are few physical traces left of the camp aside from rope scars on the trees. Our knowledge of the camp results from a survey we undertook during the last year it was occupied (Badcock and Johnston 2009). The survey employed conventional archaeological methods to provide an interpretive record of the structures the protesters built and the places they made in the woodland. It also led us to reflect on what an archaeological perspective might contribute to academic research about activism, and to question our standpoint in relation to the anti-quarry campaign and the views the protesters held about the legitimacy of archaeological practice and knowledge.

A key contribution of an archaeological approach seemed, for us, to be its attentiveness to the spaces and materiality of protest (see Dixon, this volume; Moshenska, this volume on archaeologies of conflict). While there is extensive academic and biographical writing about protest, particularly in the social and political sciences, there is relatively little consideration of material culture and landscape (with some exceptions, e.g. Anderson 2004; Nicholls 2007). Considerable potential remains within this research area for archaeology to offer new ways to think about activism, radical social movements, and counter-cultures. This is ably demonstrated by the few examples of archaeologies of twentieth- and twenty-first century protest and activism that have been completed. These have illustrated, for example, the distinctive materiality and spatial grammar of protest culture (Beck et al. 2007), the power of things and places to affirm and unsettle memories and identities (Marshall et al. 2009), and the use of archaeological excavation as a pedagogical process that addresses contemporary political inequalities (McGuire 2008).

Our aim in this chapter is to sketch out some ways in which the study of material culture offers new perspectives on and understandings of protest and activism in the contemporary world. The chapter focuses on peace and environmental protests in Britain during the last thirty years, although we have drawn upon a small number of examples from other times and places. It is organized into five themes, each of which builds upon the description of the Stanton Lees protest camp that opened this introduction: the use of the body in the performance of protest; the creation of novel networks of humans and things through activism; demonstrations as acts of bearing witness to power and letting issues 'speak for themselves'; the histories and technologies that provide the foundations and legitimacy for protest; and finally the politics of researching activism. We begin with the performance of protest: 'The greatest force for change is when individuals stand up to be counted and are prepared to put themselves and their bodies in the way' (Earth First! quoted in Purkis 1996: 199).

23.2 BODIES AND DIRECT ACTION

The body will always be involved in 'direct action' (whether violent or non-violent), but using the human body as the instrument of protest may be the only option available to someone stripped of liberty and material goods. It may also demonstrate a total commitment to a cause. It is a means of renegotiating unbalanced power relations between protesters and what is being protested against, which are often actions or decisions taken by institutions of authority: 'To engage in direct action you have to feel enough passion to put your values into practice; it is literally embodying your feelings, performing your politics… Direct action makes visible the devastation of industrial culture's machinery and returns the body to the centre of politics, of cultural practice' (Jordan 1998: 134; see also Penrose, this volume, on the body as post-industrial artefact).

The campaign for women's suffrage in Britain during the early twentieth century offers a modern example of protests that used the body as the locus for action. As the campaign turned from 'polite' debate to confrontation, the women actively sought physical restraint from the state: heckling at political meetings and assaulting police officers brought prison sentences—and publicity (Rosen 1974). In other instances, suffragettes padlocked themselves to the railings of 10 Downing Street or to trees and used mass demonstrations to

confront and force arrests by the police. Once in prison, some women chose to refuse
food as a form of passive resistance and as a means of retaking control of their bodies.
Their subsequent force-feeding further exposed the authoritarian and gendered relations
of power that existed in British society, although at huge physical and psychological cost
to the women. Further extremes were reached by Constance Lytton who, serving a prison
term in Holloway Gaol in 1908, carved the words 'Votes for Women' into her chest and face
using a piece of sharpened enamel: '[a] literal attempt to write the body as a political act that
turned protest and protestor into one' (Mulvey-Roberts 2000: 165). The body is both material culture—a canvas for slogans—and the self. Critically, biological sex as defined by the
body was the rationale for the repression of women's rights and the means through which
they achieved emancipation.

Moving forward seven decades from women's suffrage campaigns to anti-nuclear peace
protests in the late twentieth century, activists from the Plowshares groups have repeatedly used their own blood in actions against nuclear weapons facilities. In their first protest in 1980, at a General Electric facility for manufacturing Minuteman missiles at King
of Prussia, Pennsylvania, protesters used hammers to break equipment and spilled their
blood over blueprints, tools and aircraft (Meyer 1990: 198, 202). During protests against
the construction of Trident submarines in Groton, Connecticut, the Trident Nein group
poured their own blood down the missile hatches, while others broke into the offices of the
company making the Trident guidance systems, pouring their blood on the prototype computers and breaking them with hammers (Meyer 1990: 204). By using blood as the means
to beat 'swords [the missiles] into plowshares', the activists chose tactics that were shocking,
a metaphor for the human violence that the weapons are intended to inflict, and an expression of their radical Catholic beliefs (Nepstad 2004).

In Britain from the late 1980s, environmental activism took new forms as people became
vehemently opposed to a massive new road construction programme announced by the
government. Robert Lamb (1996) called one of these actions, at Twyford Down in 1991,
one of the 'most radical and active protests ever mounted in Britain in defence of natural
places', which produced 'virtually a new breed of protestor' (Lamb 1996: 1). Twyford also
witnessed the first UK intervention from Earth First!, a loose network which originated in
the United States. Earth First! tactics diverged from the established protest techniques of
organizations such as Friends of the Earth and Greenpeace, introducing a more 'emotional
and spontaneous' approach which at the time generated huge media interest and placed a
large financial burden on the road scheme (Lamb 1996: 6).

A prominent tactic at these protests involved the activists deliberately placing themselves
into carefully crafted positions of potential danger, and creating what Brian Doherty (2000)
has termed 'manufactured vulnerability'. Intervention or forced removal of protesters might
cause injury or even death; in the rebalancing of power relations, the decision to harm, or
not, then rests with the institutions and their agents against whom the protest is directed.
In 1995–6, anti-road protesters inhabited land along the route of the proposed Newbury
Bypass in the UK. The protesters lived in temporary dwellings on the ground and also in
the trees. Forced eviction of the protest camps became a reality as the campaign failed to
prevent the road construction. The conflict to retain occupied ground was manifest in many
ways, from non-violent direct actions to physical and violent clashes. At both the Twyford
Down and Newbury Bypass protests tall tripods created from scaffold poles created effective and quick barricades, and a mechanism for manufacturing vulnerability; a protester

harnessed to the top of the tripod was secure, but if an attempt was made to move the tripod, it would become unstable and collapse (e.g. Merrick 1996).

Forced evictions were threatened at the Stanton Lees protest camp on several occasions but never actually took place, thus many of the defensive features were still visible when the site became the focus for an archaeological survey (Badcock and Johnston 2009). The survey recorded a range of evidence for manufactured vulnerability tactics, including cargo nets slung high on sheer quarry faces, hidden tunnels, and part-buried structures containing clips set into concrete onto which protesters could lock themselves—referred to as a 'lock-on' in contemporary protest literature (Fisher 2007). The most extreme example was the 'skyraft', a two-tier platform suspended from multiple polypropylene ropes above a deep quarry floor. Once protesters were in place on the raft, the ropes could not be cut without endangering life. The boulder-strewn quarry floor prohibited vehicle access from below. The only safe response was to effect a siege and wait for the protesters to run out of food. There was restricted space on the skyraft, and within the other defensive devices such as the tunnels, limiting who could take the risks of occupying the structures. The social configuration of the camp changed, therefore, during an eviction, as distinctions between groups emerged based on the relative exclusivity of the positions of manufactured vulnerability that people adopted.

23.3 NOVEL NETWORKS

The examples offered in the previous section reveal the protesting body identified in its relationship to materials and places, whether chained to a wrought iron fence or suspended by polypropylene ropes from a quarry face. These networks of people and things define the practices as protests, set apart from the flow of ordinary lives. The networks need not be particularly inventive—although on occasions they are—but there is often novelty in the specific arrangements of humans and non-humans (Featherstone 2004). The novelty may lie in the creation of extraordinary or inverted relationships: the hunt saboteurs laying a fox's scent to mislead the hounds, and so the humans become the quarry not the animal. The disruption and inversion of the commonplace and the ordinary challenges the identities with which we are familiar and helps us to see ourselves differently (Szerszynski 2002: 51). Protesters frequently lived in trees during the environmental campaigns, with the treescape of houses, platforms, defences, and suspended walkways mirroring the layout of the camp on the ground. This was both an effective means of making it difficult for the bailiffs and police to evict the protesters, and defined a relationship between people and nature that was important to the environmental ethics of the protesters and at odds with the capitalist doctrine that they opposed (see Griffin 2008).

The networks of social relations that define activist communities may also be structured in alternative ways that counter societal norms and orders. Amongst road protests, there was an explicit counter-culture that was non-hierarchical, made up of rhizomatic networks (Griffin 2008: 92). There was also an emphasis on informal organizational structures or even 'dis-organizations', in McKay's (1996) words. For example, 'The Land is Ours' campaign, which began with the construction of eco-villages on disused land in Surrey and London, was a friendship network more than a structured organization. Yet, there are

FIGURE 23.1 (a) Traces of habitation at Greenham Common, and (b) a circle of stones at the Nevada peace camp (reproduced with permission from John Schofield)

paradoxes within these counter-networks. While environmental protests mark a 'defence of place against the flow of the network society' (Reed 2008: 210), they also exploit communication technologies, such as Internet social networking, that enable normative cultures to function (Lievrouw 2011).

The tension between fragmentation and cohesion that is present in protest networks is reflected in their ideological structures. There are many instances where protest organizations express specific sets of beliefs and agendas for action, as, for instance, with the Earth First! campaign (Wall 1999). Yet protests more commonly draw together diverse communities constituted by people who hold widely differing beliefs and are from diverse backgrounds. Sociological studies of environmental protests and peace camps have highlighted the degrees to which they accommodate a spectrum of perspectives, which may be united by nothing more than a 'common belief in the necessity of direct action' (Barry 1999: 82). Beverley Butler's (1996) interviews with protesters who occupied camps dispersed along the line of the M11 link road in north-east London—a road scheme that affected 350 homes and three green spaces—revealed the varied ways in which they were radicalized. Some of the protesters were residents of the area, middle class with professional careers. Others were working class, some unemployed, and others travellers. They expressed a mix of philosophies, from paganism, New Age mysticism, and Romanticism to more nationalistic agendas (Butler 1996: 351).

During the Greenham Common protests, the different camps located at the gates around the base's perimeter provided one means through which differences could be managed (Figure 23.1). The camps had originally been named to reflect different sectors of the 'alternative scene' but were soon renamed after the colours of the rainbow, representing peace

FIGURE 23.2 Instructions for building a treehouse from *Copse: The Cartoon Book of Tree Protesting* (reproduced with permission from Kate Evans)

as the focus of protest (Roseneil 1995: 75). These distinctions were not necessarily explicit, with the exception of the vegan-only Turquoise Gate. However, the camps did develop distinctive characteristics, with different names, layouts, and philosophies (Fiorato 2007: 144; see also White, this volume), and the names seem to have played an important, if subconscious, role in the constitution and politics of camp life (Roseneil 1995: 82). Archaeological recording has shown that at least some of the distinctions portrayed in oral histories were more complex in practice: an abundance of milk bottles were found around the vegan camp at Turquoise Gate (Reynolds and Schofield 2010: 47). More broadly, the women did not have a single objective: it broadened out to challenge 'all forms of domination, from international militarism and environmental degradation to the everyday patriarchy of the family' (Marshall et al. 2009: 229).

The material expressions of beliefs form physical traces of these networks. The Nevada Peace Camp attracted activists with diverse agendas: anti-war, anti-nuclear, environmentalism, and indigenous land rights (Beck et al. 2007: 299). The signs dotted across the desert landscape are testimony to this eclecticism. In their survey of the camp, Colleen Beck and her colleagues noted hundreds of structures, sculptures, and symbols: stone circles with ceramic and metal masks, sculptures of children and flowers, spirals and peace symbols fashioned from stones. Pagoda Hill, a prominent landmark on the south-western edge of the camp, was an important focus for the deposition of offerings. Amongst the objects placed in and on the three cairns on the hilltop were white quartz stones, a Jamaican dollar, tarot cards, a Zia Pueblo sign, and a tortoise shell. Other symbols and sculptures were placed close to the cairns, including a clay female figure and white rocks arranged as a compass (Beck et al. 2007: 308). The archaeological survey recorded graffiti on the walls of the highway underpasses on the north side of the camp. The symbols of peace and healing that were pervasive elsewhere in the landscape were also present in the graffiti. However, in the covered space of an underground tunnel, out of general view, polemical texts reflected emotions of anger and frustration that were not expressed in more public settings (Beck et al. 2007: 316).

Tensions and contradictions are also present in the scales over which protests operate. The national is made local, the local becomes international. This may be critical to understanding how agency is realized and how identity is contested. At Stanton Lees, materials were recycled between camps, and the protesters were themselves a fluid group, with activists moving from one camp to another throughout the country. At the anti-quarry campaign at Ashton Court, Bristol, the protesters were part of a wider network of environmental direct action groups nationally and internationally, while the protest camp provided a space for new ideas, tactics, and philosophies to be cross-fertilized and disseminated (Anderson 2004: 110–11). Books, pamphlets, newsletters, and websites play a key part in this (Figure 23.2), yet the space of the protest is itself important as it is here that the ideas, tactics, and philosophies of protest can be learnt. At the Blackwood Roads protest in 2004, the camp brought together local residents, mostly teenagers, with more experienced campaigners (Plows 2006: 464), with the latter passing on knowledge of the technologies and the legislation of occupation and direct action. Tracing these networks is therefore an important means through which we can understand how the knowledge and technology of activism are dispersed.

23.4 DEMONSTRATION

Protest draws attention to people, places, and issues, and it makes these political through the act of witnessing. In these terms 'demonstration' takes on two meanings: a demonstration or demonstrator as a 'political actor', and demonstration in the context of scientific education as 'a matter of *witnessing* a technical practice' (Barry 1999: 76). The 'logic of bearing witness' (della Porta and Diani 1999: 178) becomes a means of re-siting politics into the places where power is enacted on people and the environment. Put another way, new social movements were characterized by a desire to 'render power visible' (Purkis 1996: 201) and so to 'demonstrate through their actions a different truth' (Barry 1999: 81). It is a matter of observation—seeing it happen and showing it is happening is enough: 'the issues simply speak for themselves—merely in pointing things out you are being political' (George

Monbiot quoted in Barry 1999: 82). A similar point was made by the last protester to be evicted from the 'Tower', marking the end of the opposition on Claremont Road, London, during the M11 campaign: 'however hard we fought we knew that everything would end in rubble... An elaborate game, one which we had carefully prepared, a game to unveil power and to make visible real issues' (Phil McLeish quoted by Butler 1996: 348).

The tactics of demonstrating, as an act of making power visible—making issues, places, and actions visible—can take varied forms, from the mundane to the dramatic and the spectacular. The drawn-out occupations of peace and environmental camps or the city-centre occupations that catalysed the Arab Spring showed that other ways of living and other political beliefs are possible. In her study of the M11 road protests in London, Beverley Butler describes the occupation of a street of houses on Claremont Road as 'an urban shrine to the culture of protest' (1996: 338). The protest critiques the world around it by declaring that things can be otherwise. At Stanton Lees, the activists used a caravan sited on the main public path through the woodland as a venue to publicize and explain the protest and the beliefs on which it was founded—a quotation painted neatly at the top of one internal wall of the caravan read 'when we dig precious things from the land, we invite disaster'.

Yet showing that there are other possibilities may not be sufficient. Protest, particularly direct action, frequently relies upon spectacular performances to 'destabilize the space of politics' (Barry 1999: 78). During the campaign against the M77 motorway on the south side of Glasgow in the 1990s, a convoy of activists drove from Oxford to the protest camp in Pollok; a 'carhenge' was constructed from their vehicles and ceremonially burned, symbolizing the road protest movement's broader challenge to car culture (Undercurrents 1995; Anon. 1996; Seel 2006: 119). During the campaign against the M65, protesters from Friends of the Earth and Greenpeace planted a garden of saplings in the Cuerden Valley, Lancashire, along the path of the motorway (Wall 1999: 90). As a consequence, the security guards, whose usual job was to protect the road-builders' machinery from sabotage, found themselves trying to stop the protesters' diggers (Figure 23.3).

The boundaries between some of the more spectacular actions and artistic practice are necessarily blurred. The inventiveness and originality of the images and performances provide a means of establishing publicity for protests and for asserting activist identities. During the M11 campaign, the art offered an important means of expressing the beliefs that underpinned the campaign in ways that were novel and challenging: 'whole rooms, domestic interiors, were recreated in the middle of the street. I think it was about breaking down the barriers between private and communal space and the break-down of our society due to car culture' (Roger Geffen quoted in Butler 1996: 354). The potency of the art at Claremont Road stemmed from its incorporation into direct action and being created by the protesters. By contrast, the Art Bypass event organized by Friends of the Earth as part of the Newbury Bypass campaign in August 1996 took place once contractors had cleared the line of the road. The event brought together work by well-known artists, including Christo and Jeanne-Claude's wrapped Volvo, and it did not involve the activists who had occupied the camps opposing the bypass. Perhaps because of this, although there were also political tensions between the activists and Friends of the Earth, Art Bypass was criticized for being no more than a 'publicity stunt': 'it failed as socially engaged art practice. The tree houses and numerous direct actions against the bypass were where true art and radical creativity lay' (Jordan 1998: 284).

Arguably protests became iconic and achieved the most cogent demonstration of their values as a consequence of direct conflicts between activists and the institutions they

FIGURE 23.3 Greenpeace diggers, with decorative artwork (photograph: Tod Hanson; reproduced with permission from Greenpeace)

challenged. For the environmental protests of the 1990s in Britain, these came in the confrontations with private security firms, bailiffs, and police during the protesters' attempts to disrupt the construction teams or when the protest camps were forcibly evicted. There was undoubtedly a playfulness to these actions, as protesters made fun at the expense of the security personnel and made the commonplace seem ridiculous (Jordan 1998). Yet these confrontations were also deeply serious, passionate, terrifying, and dangerous. The evictions that took place at the environmental and peace camps proved to be the focus for most of the press attention, although they also marked the point at which the campaigns failed in their immediate objectives. From another perspective, the publicity generated by these evictions and by the more spectacular or violent actions provided the means to draw attention to the issues. For the anti-road activists, there was some sense of success in saving small numbers of trees from felling (e.g. Mary Hare Camp, Newbury Bypass Protest: Merrick 1996), and a much greater achievement in raising a wider national consciousness to the impact of roads and road building.

23.5 HISTORIES, HERITAGE

Histories, or 'ancestries', of activism and protest are frequently drawn upon to give identity to and legitimate contemporary protests. Connections with the past, in both the short and long term, are also constituted through the practices of activists: the architecture of protest camps, the tactics and tools of direct action. There is, as with all cultural practice, a heritage that people construct and engage with varying formality, and within these engagements there is arguably a place for archaeological practice.

The rural and labour protests in Britain, from the sixteenth century onwards, formed part of the heritage of the late twentieth-century environmental protests: 'Tree houses adorn the branches at Lyminge…167 years earlier, labourers burned ricks and smashed machines at Lyminge in one of the first Swing riots' (Anon. quoted by Griffin 2008: 92). Ancestries of activism were explicitly drawn upon by the camp established by activists from the 'The Land is Ours' campaign on St George's Hill, Weybridge, Surrey, in 1999. Their action celebrated 350 years since the Diggers, a radical egalitarian group, occupied and cultivated common land on the same hill (Featherstone 2005: 251). Also appealing to the seventeenth century, the road protests at Newbury were acclaimed as the 'Third battle of Newbury', their activism situated in relation to two previous Civil War battles: 'a historical narrative of popular conflict against an authoritarian state' (Barry 1999: 80). The explicit connections that activists made with histories of radicalism were, in these and many other examples, rooted in the landscape. There was a sense that the same class and ideological struggles were being fought over the same ground.

While the historic roots of protests are constructed in more or less explicit terms, there are also traditions to be found within the technologies of protest—within the genealogies of materials and tactics. The bender, a shelter constructed with bent greenwood stakes and ubiquitous at the 1980s and 1990s environmental and peace protest camps and a feature of the recent Occupy protests, is an easy-to-build, low-impact structure. Yet it is of equal interest that benders were a traditional dwelling amongst traveller and Gypsy communities. Its adoption by radical social movements in the 1980s can be seen in the light of this, here described at the Stonehenge Free Festival in 1984: 'your first sight is the decrepit twig and polythene benders lining the entry path selling all kinds of drugs' (McKay 1996: 19). The symbolism of the bender tent was evidenced at the Stanton Lees protest camp, where the wooden frame of the 'first bender' was preserved long after the protesters had built more substantial dwellings (Badcock and Johnston 2009).

The 'first bender' at Stanton Lees was dismantled with the rest of the camp in 2009, so it only served as a temporary memorial to the early years of the campaign (Figure 23.4). The tangible heritage of activism is rarely preserved at protest sites. In the case of unsuccessful environmental protests, their physical legacy was destroyed along with the countryside they fought to protect. Where campaigns succeeded, the activists usually removed most traces of their occupation. Returning to Stanton Lees, there is little to mark the protest except for the cleared platforms where benders and other dwellings had stood and the scars in the bark of trees left by the rope from aerial walkways and tree-houses. At Twyford, there are no traces of the camps, but anti-road slogans were still visible on the footbridge across the extended motorway in 2004 and, adjacent to the bridge, a chalk monolith inscribed with the names of officials and politicians who 'ravaged' the land stands as a monument to the campaign (Schofield 2005).

By comparison, there are protest sites where material remains survive and provide a cue for memories and conflicts over heritage. The examples of Greenham Common and Ludlow will be discussed in the next section. At the Long Kesh/Maze prison, Northern Ireland, the setting of the 1980–1 hunger strikes in which ten republican inmates starved to death

FIGURE 23.4 (a) The remains of the first bender, and (b) one of the more obvious archaeological traces of a bender platform at Stanton Lees protest camp (photographs: Anna Badcock and Robert Johnston)

while protesting for recognition as political prisoners, some of the buildings (the H-blocks) are listed and therefore officially protected by law. Three decades later the now-unused buildings are the embodiment of complex heritage values and conflicting ideas about the appropriate future of the site (McAtackney 2007 and this volume). An important part of the buildings' significance rests in the fact that they must now symbolize people and events that have long since disappeared. Through her study of Long Kesh, Laura McAtackney (2007) examined the now-sparse material culture of the prison. Her interviews with site staff revealed the ongoing, intimate relationship that people still have with the place and with the hunger strikes in particular. Poignantly, individual springs from the bed on which Bobby Sands, the most widely known hunger striker, died have been removed over time by some visitors. Although replaced several times, the bedsprings continue to be removed, perhaps as tokens from a significant place, perhaps as a gesture of solidarity—a subtle means by which the essence of the protest is maintained and dispersed, physically, into the wider community.

23.6 ARCHAEOLOGY AS POLITICAL PRACTICE

Randall McGuire (2008) argues that archaeologists, and the knowledge produced by our inquiries, are necessarily a part of political struggles about the past: 'What we choose to remember, what we choose to study, what questions we ask, and how we frame the answers all have political importance for identity, heritage, social agency and fast capitalism...we should make these decisions in a conscious praxis of archaeology' (McGuire 2008: 235; see also Shepherd, this volume). We must not make the simple mistake of conflating the archaeological study of political/protest actions with a politicized archaeological approach, but there is no doubt that a heightened and critical self-awareness of archaeologists' views and political frames of reference emerges from many of the archaeological writings about protest.

The socio-political nature of their inquiry was felt keenly by the Common Ground Group who found they needed to employ different approaches to the work of recording protest at Greenham Common Airbase: the project was an important opportunity to research 'the material cultural legacy of an explicitly feminist space' (Marshall et al. 2009: 226). The Greenham camps were not just about opposition to the Cold War, but a test ground for new forms of gender protest: 'in form, practice and rhetoric the women resisted and challenged all forms of domination, from international militarism and environmental degradation to the everyday patriarchy of the family' (Marshall et al. 2009: 229). In developing their project design, the study of the female-only protest camps necessarily became a feminist (but not all-female) project for some of the group members. They adopted an 'autoethnographic' approach, recognizing their personal investment or standpoints in the work, and becoming subjects of the research (Marshall et al. 2009: 227). Differences of opinion and approach within the team shaped the project, and are explicitly discussed in the resulting publications (Marshall et al. 2009; Schofield and Anderton 2000). Far from being able to approach the project from a politically neutral standpoint, as the original project design proposed, some of the team felt that a strong political focus was essential. During the pilot excavation of the Turquoise Gate they were struck by the 'intimate, personal nature of the archaeological record' and following discussions with the group and some former peace women the excavation methodology was abandoned in favour of mapping surface artefacts over a wider area and leaving objects *in situ*; this was felt to be more appropriate to the legacy of the Greenham women (Marshall et al. 2009: 233).

An archaeological study of activism within the Colorado Coalfield War 1913–14 is a fine example of explicit political awareness shaping archaeological practice (McGuire 2008). In September 1913, a strike organized by the United Mine Workers of America began in the southern Colorado coalfields. Tent encampments on the plains below the mines housed the thousands of workers who had been evicted from their company properties; with some 1,200 residents, Ludlow was the largest of these. Violent clashes ensued over the following months, culminating in a battle between the strikers and the National Guard Officers in which 24 people died, including 13 women and children. A programme of archaeological fieldwork was established at Ludlow with the goal to 'exhume the class struggle of the site' and raise awareness of the contemporary struggles of working families (McGuire 2008: 189). The project was designed to serve different communities, to escape what McGuire terms the 'colonial practice' of archaeology in the United States and to move away from the tendency of archaeology to serve mainly middle-class interests. Integrating the archaeological project into the local community was essential. Equally importantly, the project used the practice of archaeology to teach students the importance of labour rights and class relations, and their own rights as workers (McGuire 2008: 217).

Much has been written about the Colorado Coalfield War, but the archaeological project was able to provide a fresh perspective on mundane, everyday life, very different from the documentary focus upon events, politics, and the organization of labour and unionization (McGuire 2008: 202). Examination of material culture from the Berwind company town showed how women's roles changed as a result of the strike. After the strike, miners' families were forbidden to take in boarders to supplement their income, and this was reflected in the artefacts retrieved from the rubbish pits, where large cooking pots and serving vessels were replaced by smaller vessels and evidence for preserving (McGuire 2008: 208). Documentary research and excavations at the Ludlow tent colony also helped to demonstrate that several long-held beliefs of the unionized community (that the National Guard had used explosive bullets during the massacre, desecrated bodies, and dug mass graves) could not be founded (McGuire 2008: 214–16).

23.7 CONCLUSION: MATERIALIZING ACTIVISM

Time magazine's person of the year in 2011 was 'The Protestor'. This recognized the extraordinary resurgence of popular protest in North Africa and the Middle East, and the global network of protest camps under the banner of the Occupy movement. The magazine hailed the return of protest as 'the natural continuation of politics by other means', 'the protestor once again [becoming] a maker of history' (Andersen 2011: 46). The events that *Time* honoured resonate with the themes reviewed in this chapter. The touchpaper for the protests in Tunisia was Mohamed Bouazizi's act of self-immolation; agency over his body was the only means of protest against a bullying and repressive state. Elsewhere, the Occupy protests took over spaces at the heart of the capitalist project—such as Wall Street and the City of London—from where they could bear witness to the deep, systemic inequalities in Western society.

Recent protests have played a central role in mainstream politics, but many acts of resistance are unacknowledged by conventional histories and their material traces are often fragile and fleeting. This mutability makes their history no less valuable, and so archaeologists may wish to acknowledge a responsibility to balance the dominant constituencies represented by national heritage with narratives of counter-culture and activism (Schofield and Anderton 2000: 236). This is not a straightforward corrective. Histories of protest are complex, conflicting, and potentially difficult. Yet archaeologies of protest may force established authorities to recognize hidden and repressed voices. Equally, they can challenge some of the myths and ideologies of activism. Either way, archaeology can be a process of revealing power as it was, is, and can be—an act of demonstration. Engaging with these pasts is critical. Working in the present, as fast-moving as protests are, is a different and no less important challenge.

REFERENCES

Andersen, Kurt. 2011. The Protestor. *Time* 178(25): 42–81.

Anderson, Jon. 2004. Spatial Politics in Practice: The Style and Substance of Environmental Direct Action. *Antipode* 36: 106–25.

Anon. 1996. Pollok Free State Lives On! *Do or Die* 5: 7–10.

Badcock, Anna and Johnston, Robert. 2009. Placemaking through Protest: An Archaeology of the Lees Cross and Endcliffe Protest Camp, Derbyshire, England. *Archaeologies* 2(2): 306–22.

Barry, Andrew. 1999. Demonstrations: Sites and Sights of Direct Action. *Economy and Society* 28(1): 75–94.

Beck, Colleen M., Drollinger, Harold, and Schofield, John. 2007. Archaeology of Dissent: Landscape and Symbolism at the Nevada Peace Camp. In *A Fearsome Heritage: Diverse Legacies of the Cold War*, ed. John Schofield and Wayne Cocroft, pp. 297–320. Walnut Creek, CA: Left Coast Press.

Butler, Beverley. 1996. The Tree, the Tower and the Shaman: The Material Culture of Resistance of the M11 Link Roads Protest of Wanstead and Leytonstone, London. *Journal of Material Culture* 1(3): 337–63.

della Porta, Donatella and Diani, Mario. 1999. *Social Movements: An Introduction*. Oxford: Blackwell.

Doherty, Brian. 2000. Manufactured Vulnerability: Protest Camp Tactics. In *Direct Action in British Environmentalism*, ed. Benjamin Seel, Matthew Paterson, and Brian Doherty, pp. 62–78. London: Routledge.

Featherstone, David. 2004. Spatial Relations and the Materialities of Political Conflict: The Construction of Entangled Political Identities in the London and Newcastle Port Strikes of 1768. *Geoforum* 35: 701–11.

—— 2005. Towards the Relational Construction of Militant Particularisms: Or Why the Geographies of Past Struggles Matter for Resistance to Neoliberal Globalization. *Antipode* 37: 250–72.

Fiorato, Veronica. 2007. Greenham Common: The Conservation and Management of a Cold War Archetype. In *A Fearsome Heritage: Diverse Legacies of the Cold War*, ed. John Schofield and Wayne Cocroft, pp. 129–54. Walnut Creek, CA: Left Coast Press.

Fisher, Tom. 2007. Objects for Peaceful Disordering: Indigenous Designs and Practices of Protest. *Journal of Conflict Archaeology* 3(1): 95–109.

Griffin, Carl J. 2008. Protest Practice and (Tree) Cultures of Conflict: Understanding the Spaces of 'Tree Maiming' in Eighteenth- and Early Nineteenth-Century England. *Transactions of the Institute of British Geographers* New Series 33: 91–108.

Jordan, John. 1998. The Art of Necessity: The Subversive Imagination of Anti-Road Protest and Reclaim the Streets. In *DiY Culture: Party and Protest in Nineties Britain*, ed. George McKay, pp. 129–51. London: Verso.

Lamb, Robert. 1996. *Promising the Earth*. London: Routledge.

Lievrouw, Leah. 2011. *Alternative and Activist New Media*. Cambridge: Polity Press.

McAtackney, Laura. 2007. The Contemporary Politics of Landscape at the Long Kesh/Maze Prison Site, Northern Ireland. In *Envisioning Landscapes: Situations and Standpoints in Archaeology and Heritage*, ed. Dan Hicks, Laura McAtackney, and Graham Fairclough, pp. 30–54. Walnut Creek, CA: Left Coast Press.

McGuire, Randall H. 2008. *Archaeology as Political Action*. Berkeley, CA: University of California Press.

McKay, George. 1996. *Senseless Acts of Beauty: Cultures of Resistance since the Sixties*. London: Verso.

Marshall, Yvonne, Roseneil, Sasha, and Armstrong, Kayt. 2009. Situating the Greenham Archaeology: An Autoethnography of a Feminist Project. *Public Archaeology* 8(2–3): 225–45.

Merrick. 1996. *Battle for the Trees*. Leeds: Godhaven Ink.

Meyer, David. 1990. *A Winter of Discontent: The Nuclear Freeze and American Politics*. New York: Praeger.

Mulvey-Roberts, Marie. 2000. Militancy, Masochism or Martyrdom? The Public and Private Prisons of Constance Lytton. In *Votes for Women*, ed. June Purvis and Sandra S. Holton, pp. 159–80. London: Routledge.

Nepstad, Sharon E. 2004. Disciples and Dissenters: Tactical Choice and Consequences in the Plowshares Movement. In *Authority in Contention*, ed. Daniel J. Myers and Daniel M. Cress, pp. 139–59. Leeds: Emerald Group.

Nicholls, Walter J. 2007. The Geographies of Social Movements. *Geography Compass* 1(3): 607–22.

Plows, Alexandra. 2006. Blackwoods Roads Protest 2004: An Emerging (Re)cycle of UK Eco-action? *Environmental Politics* 15(3): 462–72.

Purkis, Jonathan. 1996. Daring to Dream: Idealism in the Philosophy, Organization and Campaigning Strategies of Earth First! In *To Make Another World: Studies in Protest and Collective Action*, ed. Colin Barker and Paul Kennedy, pp. 197–217. Aldershot: Avebury.

Reed, Matt. 2008. The Rural Arena: The Diversity of Protest in Rural England. *Journal of Rural Studies* 24: 209–18.

Reynolds, Lucy and Schofield, John. 2010. Silo Walk: Exploring Power Relations on an English Common. *Radical History Review* 108: 154–60.

Rosen, Andrew. 1974. *Rise Up, Women! The Militant Campaigns of the Women's Social and Political Union 1903–1914*. London: Routledge & Kegan Paul.

Roseneil, Sasha. 1995. *Disarming Patriarchy: Feminism and Political Action at Greenham*. Buckingham: Open University Press.

Schofield, John. 2005. Discordant Landscapes: Managing Modern Heritage at Twyford Down, Hampshire (England). *International Journal of Heritage Studies* 11(2): 143–59.

Schofield, John and Anderton, Mike. 2000. The Queer Archaeology of Green Gate: Interpreting Contested Space at Greenham Common Airbase. *World Archaeology* 32(2): 236–51.

Seel, Ben. 2006. Strategies of Resistance at the Pollok Free State Road Protest Camp. In *Contemporary Environmental Politics: From Margins to Mainstream*, ed. Piers H. G. Stephens, John Barry, and Andrew Dobson, pp. 114–42. London: Routledge.

Szerszynski, Bronislaw. 2002. Ecological Rites: Ritual Action in Environmental Protest Events. *Theory, Culture & Society* 19(3): 51–69.

Undercurrents. 1995. *To Pollok with Love*. Available at: <http://www.youtube.com/watch?v=Vueb1vF4C18> (accessed 15 February 2012).

Wall, Derek. 1999. *Earth First! and the Anti-Road Movement: Radical Environmentalism and Comparative Social Movements*. London: Routledge.

CHAPTER 24

···

HOMELESSNESS

···

LARRY J. ZIMMERMAN

24.1 INTRODUCTION

···

AMONG the most important contributions archaeology can make to the study of contemporary culture may be its unique abilities to analyse and interpret material remains, to create grounded, believable narratives from those remains, and to use those narratives to define a heritage that a society may wish to understand more thoroughly and protect (cf. Harrison and Schofield 2010: 283). When applied to matters that society defines as concerns or problems, archaeological approaches can provide accurate, fact-based information instead of conjecture, stereotype, and received wisdom. Such information may be used to suggest simple changes that may better someone's daily life but may even prompt substantive alterations in social policy. While to some people archaeology just seems esoteric, impractical, and expensive, others certainly are fascinated by learning about the 'oldest', 'earliest', or 'first'. People with both views usually express surprise, however, to learn that archaeology can be used to study contemporary homelessness. Almost everyone who knows something about archaeology thinks of it as a discipline that usually studies a more distant past. After all, the 'archae' part of the word means 'ancient'. The reality, however, is that archaeology has always been more about studying 'stuff' than about studying the past.

Whether the past is a millennium ago or just ten minutes, the tools archaeologists use are mostly the same and answer the same fundamental questions: What things did people use? How did they get or make them or where did they get them? How and in what situations did they use them? What did the things mean to the people? How did they dispose of things when they were done using them? What happened to the things after people got rid of them? These basic questions are powerful, and answering them can provide useful information about people's lives. Objects that archaeologists find need to be interpreted, certainly, but they either are or are not present, and when present, they provide a physical reality that demands explanation. Objects allow archaeologists to create a more complete and accurate narrative—to tell a better story—and if done well, they can help a society recognize and preserve a more 'honest' heritage that may actually be useful in recognizing, framing, and alleviating social concerns.

24.2 A Social Concern that Won't Go Away

Homelessness may be one of those social concerns where archaeology can help, and in the past few years archaeologists in the United Kingdom, the United States, and Australia have been applying archaeological methods to a wide range of questions about the lives of homeless people. Because archaeological studies on homelessness are so recent, there is a genuine paucity of archaeological literature on the topic in core journals. Much of what is available is to be found on the Web, in news reports, and in other media aimed at general audiences. Yet from what has been reported, archaeologists have realized that the homeless have a distinctive material culture that can be analysed archaeologically. What they have discovered reflects a pattern of life that has been present in urban cultures since the development of cities. For example, as indicated by graffiti, homelessness was a concern documented in dynastic Egypt (Dixon 1989: 197), and archaeologists have also examined the connection of homelessness to eighteenth-century New York City almshouses (Baugher 2001), the Old World precedence for Dutch and English almshouses in colonial North America (Hughey 2001), and ideological perspectives on Victorian period homelessness (Spencer-Wood 2001). Such research seems to suggest that as a social concern, homelessness won't really go away, no matter how much people might wish or try. Societal efforts to eliminate or reduce homelessness have come and gone. Bad economic conditions might raise homelessness to the level of social crisis, but the worries tend to abate not when the problem is solved, but when a society 'defines away' the problem (Marcus 2006: 2). When that happens, homeless people tend to become barely visible on street corners where they beg for money or when they sleep in parks or other public places. Whatever the case, homelessness seems to be a nearly intractable social problem, and it truly is complex, beyond the scope of this essay to discuss in any thorough way (readers should examine more general volumes such as those by Bogard 2003, Levinson 2004, or Ravenhill 2008 for more detailed information about homelessness, but several of the observations following derive from these sources and others to provide context for the application of archaeological investigation to homelessness).

Even defining homelessness can prove to be difficult. Do people who live in their car count as homeless, or do they have to live on the street? If they stay in a shelter or are squatters in an abandoned house, are they actually homeless? Is someone who chooses to leave their permanent residence in search of a better job as homeless as a family forced into a refugee camp due to natural disaster, civil strife, or warfare? What if they completely reject the notion of being homeless and declare themselves 'home free' as one Vancouver man did, adding that he had no mortgage, no rules to follow, and only worried about a warm place to sleep and finding food (Zimmerman, Singleton, and Welch 2010: 453)? Definitions abound, but a useful one comes from the United Nations Economic and Social Council (2009: 3) which defines two types. *Primary homelessness* (or rooflessness) 'includes persons living in the streets without a shelter that would fall within the scope of living quarters'; the *secondary homeless* 'include persons with no place of usual residence who move frequently between various types of accommodations (including dwellings, shelters and institutions for the homeless or other living quarters)'.

Even though countries count the homeless in varying ways, by the most general definition, millions live homeless every night, and even in some of the wealthiest countries, hundreds of thousands may be in the primary homeless category. In the United States, for example, the count for both types was more than 750,000 in 2005, with almost 340,000 counted as primary homeless (HUD 2007: 23), while in England the primary, rough-sleeping homeless numbered about 1,800 in 2010 (CLG 2010: 1). In both countries, however, many sources challenge the numbers as low.

24.3 COMMONLY ACCEPTED NARRATIVES ABOUT HOMELESSNESS

Whatever the actual count, the common narrative is that even though the problem may be exacerbated by economic conditions, homelessness is mostly centred in the individual and whatever failings they may have. Homeless people are lazy, drug-addicted, or mentally ill, usually responsible for their own fate, and a public nuisance.

A less common, yet powerful, narrative is that homeless people are an indicator of society's failures in its responsibilities to citizens, a condition evolving within industrial societies related to specific economic and social conditions of class, race, immigration, and gender. Both narratives seek to end homelessness by supporting a homeless industry that gets people off the streets. The individual-centred narrative wants to provide mechanisms for self-help to remove or at least reduce the nuisance; the social failure narrative sees providing help as a matter of societal obligation and human compassion. Whatever the narrative basis, both are part of a broader sheltering narrative that seeks, at very least, to reduce the number of primary homeless people by moving them into and maintaining them in the secondary homeless category, which happens to be where most homeless industry effort and funding is targeted.

The homeless industry is a vast network of charities, both religious and non-governmental, as well as numerous governmental agencies with mostly honourable goals. There is, however, pointed criticism from the high costs of administration to the homeless industry's self-serving nature in which it constantly seeks funds to perpetuate its existence. For example, nearly $30 billion a year is spent on homelessness in the USA by one federal agency, the Department of Housing and Urban Development, with several other agencies spending lesser, but substantial amounts. Another common complaint is that the homeless industry even controls the definition of homelessness as part of a powerful narrative aimed at self-sufficiency, providing employment and shelter for all homeless people, when that is clearly impossible and often unwanted by some homeless people. The sheltering narrative is a strong one, and seems compassionate, but often to the neglect of providing essentials to those living rough, in order to force the roofless to come to shelters to get help. If they can be brought to shelters, so the narrative goes, their lives can be changed. Many 'home free' homeless people actually despise shelters, especially faith-based shelters that provide essentials in exchange for subjecting themselves to religious proselytizing. Some see life in shelters as rule-bound and dangerous, with employees who steal from them.

Many primary homeless people feel that the industry narrative emphasizes the most negative of the stereotypes about homeless people as irresponsible, mentally ill, or addictive in order to seek funding.

24.4 USING ARCHAEOLOGY TO PRODUCE A COUNTER-NARRATIVE

Archaeology's potential to affect social policy is that it can offer a different narrative, one that has no agenda related to solving the problem of homelessness and places no particular emphasis on the personal characteristics of homeless people themselves as contributing to their own situation. At the same time, it challenges a segment of the industry narrative that sees bringing homeless people to shelters as a first priority. Rather, the archaeological narrative suggests that people's basic physical needs ought to be met first, without prerequisites or demands, and that archaeological investigation can make solid suggestions as to how this can be done more effectively.

24.4.1 Beginnings: The St. Paul, Minnesota Project

That archaeology could be used to analyse material culture of homeless people had a start in 2003 during an historic archaeological project in St. Paul, Minnesota (Zimmerman 2004: 136). The Minnesota Historical Society sought to reconstruct and interpret the long-abandoned gardens of a nineteenth-century mansion overlooking the city and the Mississippi River valley and carried out archaeological excavations to learn construction information about the collapsing garden walls and to recover any period artefacts. After the original owners left the property, the gardens were abandoned for almost 90 years, becoming overgrown with trees and brush. During that time, homeless people had taken over the gardens, as evidenced by fire circles made from stones from the walls, trash such as clothing, sleeping bags, drug paraphernalia, and food and beverage remnants scattered over the gardens, and even people found sleeping in a partly collapsed mushroom cave built into one garden wall as excavators came to the site each day.

The archaeologists viewed most of the items collected during surface survey or excavated as debris discarded by homeless people, not archaeological artefacts. They were just trash, and following the usual narrative about homelessness, homeless people were barely visible to the archaeologists, more a nuisance than anything else, especially when they would show their displeasure at the intrusion by disturbing and otherwise fouling the excavations. One day, listening to a radio interview with a homeless mother and daughter brought an epiphany of sorts that homeless people actually acquired, used, and disposed of 'stuff' just like everyone else. Eventually trash became artefacts, and the excavators began to recognize that there was patterning in the homeless campsites. Mostly, however, any assessment of the nature of homeless material culture was impressionistic, not systematic.

24.4.2 Systematic Surveys of Homeless Sites: the Indianapolis Project

Beginning in 2005, Zimmerman and Welch (2011) began a systematic survey for homeless sites covering an area of ten by ten city blocks just east of the Indianapolis, Indiana, city centre. The area is divided on a north–south axis by interstate highways and crosscut by rail lines that run roughly east–west. The latter provide easy access to the resource-rich downtown area, including one major homeless shelter, numerous restaurants, and the many convention-goers who can be 'targets' for begging. The survey located 61 sites, 37 of them near the rail lines. They fell into three categories designated as route sites, short-term sites, and campsites. The five route sites contained evidence only of very limited usage, with almost no evidence of camping or sleeping. Most contained little more than a few items such as clothing, human waste, and minor evidence of food consumption indicated by such items as fast food containers, disposable coffee cups, and snack food wrappers. As the name implies, route sites tended to be in outlying areas, usually between short-term and campsites and areas of known resources, often near permanent structures that provided at least a modicum of privacy. These sites sometimes were difficult to distinguish from 'background' trash, but usually were distant enough from areas where permanent residents or local children would litter. The smell of urine was a common enough indicator. Graffiti were found near all the site types, but most commonly near route sites. The 40 short-term sites were evidenced by sleeping and food usage (Figure 24.1), but rarely any cooking of food. Shelters were usually impromptu, using plastic sheets as ground cloths, or more often, pieces of cardboard. Even clumps of tall weeds pulled together at the top and the ground cleared beneath them could be used to provide shelter and privacy. Sixteen campsites were areas of more intensive usage, sometimes in permanent structures such as under bridges, but just as often, in a copse of trees (Figure 24.2). There were probably other campsites in abandoned structures, but for reasons of safety, they were not investigated. Most outdoor campsites had indications of permanence, often housing multiple occupants; many of them had relatively sophisticated living arrangements including such devices as wattle windbreaks and five-gallon, plastic bucket latrines with trash bag liners. Campsites outside abandoned buildings or structures sometimes had cardboard or more durable fabricated shelters, cardboard and even mattresses and pillows on which to sleep, and evidence of food preparation and consumption including well-made fire pits for cooking and providing warmth (Figure 24.3).

Cached materials, usually protected from the elements within plastic trash bags, were often present in or near the sites, usually slightly out of easy reach. Although investigators opened no caches, homeless people report them as containing everything from favourite items of clothing to personal items from their earlier lives, such as photographs or treasured objects, but also important documents related to military service or personal medical history, and importantly, their medications. Items are cached because people don't usually wish to carry them around, but smaller items may be carried in small plastic bags. Although stories differ, most will not touch or take anything from caches owned by others, but a few have said that if people don't return to claim caches after about ten days, they become fair game to open and take out useful items. More mobile or less trusting individuals may move relatively large quantities of items with them in shopping carts of varying types and

FIGURE 24.1 A sleeping bag in a short-term camp in a secluded copse, Indianapolis (photograph: Courtney Singleton)

FIGURE 24.2 A well-developed sleeping area in a campsite under a bridge, Indianapolis (photograph: Courtney Singleton)

FIGURE 24.3 Comfortable sleeping area in an open, short-term camp near busy highway, Indianapolis (photograph: Larry J. Zimmerman)

sizes for which there are apparently preferences and distinct disposal patterns (Montague 2006). The cached materials and shopping carts have in themselves become a legal matter, especially when they have been removed or confiscated by city authorities in cleanup efforts to remove homeless people. In 2008, a federal judge approved a $2.5 million settlement in a class-action suit against the city of Fresno, California, and the California Department of Transportation for destroying the property of hundreds of homeless people. This is part of a long trend. Starting in 1997, the mayor of San Francisco, California, ordered city sanitation workers to confiscate shopping carts and other property of homeless people, but in 2006 ten homeless people filed legal action to stop these sweeps. The shopping cart of one individual, James B., was typical of caches and contained rain gear, a sleeping bag, clothing, and his HIV medication (Zimmerman and Welch 2011: 81).

Cached items were likely to be retained longer than many other items used by homeless people, but some items were disposed of without much or any use. In both the St. Paul and Indianapolis projects unused clothing of all types was ubiquitous in campsites, mostly because access to clothing was relatively easy. In St. Paul, the Hill house gardens were within a few blocks of the Dorothy Day Center, a Catholic Church charity, where clothing and sleeping bags were readily available, and in Indianapolis, clothing was distributed at Wheeler Mission, a shelter on the western edge of the survey area. If clothing was ill-fitting or got dirty, it was thrown away because it was so easily replaced. Trash in or near short-term sites and campsites often included small, hotel or sample bottles of shampoo or hair conditioner, almost always unused, though sample sizes of toothpaste or underarm deodorant were usually empty. Shampoo and conditioner require relatively large amounts of water, which is unavailable in most homeless sites, so were just thrown away, but brushing teeth requires little liquid. As investigators discovered, several churches asked parishioners to collect such items from their hotel stays, which could then be distributed to homeless people in campsites. There was also evidence of reading materials, ranging from bibles to novels and pornography. Foodstuffs or food remains also were present in short-term sites and campsites. Food cans sometimes showed evidence of being exploded in fires or being bashed open with rocks or cut open with knives. Apparently can openers were not distributed along with the canned food, or at least were unavailable. Cans with pull-tabs, however, appeared in several sites, and should have been easier to use. Generally, canned and other less perishable foods seemed to be readily available but as often as not went unused, people not eating what they didn't like or couldn't open. While doing surveys near homeless campsites, archaeologists observed generous individuals who delivered freshly cooked food, but included no serving or eating utensils, or bags of fresh vegetables, with little consideration of how they might be processed or cooked. Most of these were thrown away.

Sometimes surprising items were present in sites. In one instance, several baseball-style caps had been put in what appeared to be a decorative pattern on the branches of a bush. In another, there was a paper bag filled with stuffed animal toys. A large, colourful, stuffed toy cat was placed in the branches of a bush so that people could see it as they occupied a carefully made bed, with a mattress, bedspread, pillows, and a rug. The reason for these items was unclear, but perhaps the idea was to provide a semblance of home. As one might expect, there was also plenty of evidence of cigarette smoking, drinking beer, wine, and liquor, as well as less frequent, but obvious evidence of drug use. Most campsites had at least one area for human waste, segregated from the living areas, usually where some privacy could be found along a wall or where there was adequate brush or tree cover.

Investigators for the Indianapolis project made a determined effort to avoid face-to-face contact with homeless people. Their desire was to keep material culture at the core of the survey. They used photography and drawings to document sites, and rarely even talked with homeless people or service providers so as not to bias a more strictly archaeological, materially focused analysis and interpretation. Their conclusions based on analysis of sites and artefacts were that many homeless people were adept at dealing with their lives in campsites, but also that many of those who provide materials and services to the roofless have little real idea of what is needed on a day-to-day basis.

24.4.3 Virtual Cultural Landscapes? The Blogs Project

Applying archaeological methods to the contemporary requires a shift in viewpoint away from an emphasis on time or the past, and with such a shift, archaeologists must recognize that there may be new kinds of data. This certainly has been the situation with studying homelessness. Inevitably, the result of the field surveys generated questions that could not be answered directly from the material culture in the spatial contexts archaeologists observed. Just as historical archaeology employs a range of documents in support of analyses, investigations of contemporary sites—literally an archaeology of ten minutes ago—in which sites change from almost moment-to-moment led to online sources in search of answers about some objects, as well as factors relating to selection of locations for campsites and other uses of space, such as routes and places just to 'hang out'. Zimmerman and Singleton

(Zimmerman, Singleton, and Welch 2010: 450–1) discovered that blogs written by homeless people were surprisingly numerous and proved useful as a source for archaeological data. They also presented another challenge to the common narrative's assessment of roofless people as unintelligent or uneducated. Homeless people actually demonstrated relatively sophisticated computer skills, personalizing their blog sites and adding photographs, often taken using their mobile phones. Most were very well written, documenting the authors' daily experiences, opinions, and expressions of street living. How homeless bloggers accomplished this was quickly explained. Many blog sites were hosted on free web accounts using open source blog software and computers available in public libraries. A few bloggers apparently had their own laptops and used free Wi-Fi hotspots in coffee shops and other places.

The analysis included 21 blogs written by roofless men, women, and families living in urban environments from Hawai'i to Washington, DC. Any references to material culture and use of or comments about places were recorded. They proved to be enlightening. The blogs represent a virtual place where authors who have little or no private space in real life can have a level of control, yet they are not isolated from each other. Information, experiences, and opinions are shared, connected to a larger virtual landscape of homelessness that reference, depict, and describe real world material culture, places, and events (cf. Harrison and Schofield 2010: 258–66). In other words, they contain a wealth of virtual data that identify real resources accessible in various real places in a city. They often explain how such resources are acquired, modified, used, and disposed of. One was so specific as to list by type and brand name the best ten items to have in your campsite. As important as the discussions of objects were the detailed references to urban landscapes in which bloggers use text, photos, video, and maps to describe the conditions that make one park or space safer or even just more appealing than others.

The blogs show that their lives are spatially marginalized. Local laws sometimes ban feeding homeless people in public parks, but also prohibit sitting, begging, and sleeping there. Bloggers note that such laws are rarely enforced uniformly in cities. However, enforcement is more consistently applied in public areas where there are lots of 'homed' people and in business districts. Generally the homeless get forced into marginalized places where there is little access to public transportation, often industrial areas that tend to be more environmentally unsafe. These observations completely meshed with on-the-ground site surveys. In Indianapolis, for example, many of the short-term sites and campsites were on land around railroads, as well as along river edges and floodplains. Many were in abandoned warehouses or empty manufacturing facilities or under bridges or highway and railroad overpasses. Even along the railroads, enforcement of Homeland Security laws has severely limited the areas in which people can camp. All of this supports Valado's (2006: 10) conclusions based on ethnographic research in Tucson, Arizona, that homeless people 'constantly strategize to find or make private, safe, functional, comfortable, and supportive places for themselves in a landscape designed to exclude them' and transform barren spaces into liveable, meaningful personal spaces.

Some archaeologists have suggested that blogs are ethnographic data, not archaeological material culture (but see Harrison 2009), but at very least they are ethnoarchaeological, information-dense virtual landscapes that reflect the real and perceived landscapes in which homeless people live. Blogs are tools that can communicate useful information to other homeless people, and for archaeologists willing to extend their definitions of material culture into the virtual, they can be as informative as any other kind of archaeological data.

24.4.4 Collaborative Approaches: Stokes Croft, Bristol, and York, UK

Rachael Kiddey and John Schofield (2011) have used collaborative methods to examine homelessness in the UK, working with homeless people as partners to map, excavate, document, and record homeless sites initially in Bristol and now in York. The first project was in Stokes Croft in central Bristol (see Dixon, this volume), an area well known for homelessness by locals for at least the past 40 years, but perhaps longer. On the main route north of the city, records show that the area was used to exclude from the city drunks, social misfits, the mentally ill, and others with whom the city couldn't cope. Today Stokes Croft supports a wide range of support services for the homeless, but also sales of alcohol and drugs. Because the area is being redeveloped rapidly, Kiddey and Schofield began work in 2009 to document places of significance to homeless people. Rather than do 'archaeology of homeless people', the approach was to see if homeless people would be interested in doing 'archaeology of their own culture'.

After identifying a small triangle of land, Turbo Island, which both homeless and non-homeless labelled 'a homeless place', Kiddey arranged for a three-day excavation that included homeless people, archaeology students, and local police officers. The homeless people chose the places to dig, and when it came to odd items they found in the trenches, the homeless archaeologists provided valuable interpretation of remains. A good example was a lighter with a rubber band around it, with the band identified as holding handy a straw or ballpoint pen tube through which to smoke crack. The project was featured on television, and a piece on the project was co-authored by both homeless and non-homeless authors for *The Big Issue*, a magazine sold by homeless people, as well as in the general audience magazine *British Archaeology* (Kiddey and Schofield 2010). Homeless people worked in the laboratory to process the artefacts and one even lectured on the project at Cambridge. Kiddey approached MShed, Bristol's new public museum, to see if they would allow an exhibition about the Turbo Island excavation, but were not allowed to do so, supposedly for lack of space. On squatted land a short distance from Turbo Island, her team put up a small interactive exhibition for five days. For Kiddey, this has reinforced her views of how contemporary society sees homeless people and lifeways, largely following the mostly negative, common contemporary narrative of homelessness.

24.4.5 Indigenous Archaeologies: Darwin's People of the Long Grass

Kellie Pollard has recently started dissertation research on 'contact period' Aboriginal fringe campsites or sites in the urban hinterland around Darwin, documenting the so-called 'People of the Long Grass', people who are essentially homeless. The contact period sites date from the mid-1800s to the present day. Her interest is in understanding the adaptive strategies of Aboriginal people as they were integrated into the European wage-labour system. As they were relocated into the Darwin region and met people of different language groups, mixed language Aboriginal residential groups emerged. People needed to negotiate new social relationships with each other, the people of the Larrakia Nation on whose land they lived, and Europeans. Pollard hopes to trace the material evidence of the changes in social interaction and settlement patterns. The study is intended to inform policy decisions of the Larrakia Nation Aboriginal Corporation related to creating interpretive materials for planned tourism enterprises.

One interest Pollard will consider is the common comparison of homeless people to hunter-gatherers/foragers, for which the People of the Long Grass might provide a unique perspective. When does hunter-gatherer lifestyle make a transition into homeless lifestyle? She recognizes that most of the archaeological work in Australia has been about past colonial impact and not about what is happening now. Her study will consider both past and present use of the Darwin hinterlands. As planned, she will use a mix of methodologies, using archaeological survey and detailed site recording, ethnohistorical and historical documentary evidence, and oral interviews of elders, individuals, and families. Similar to Kiddey's approach, she also hopes to increase the Larrakia Nation's research capacities by involving Larrakia people in the investigations. Doing so, she argues, should reposition Larrakia contributions from the fringe to the centre of knowledge generation, a collaboration involving the Larrakia in the preservation of Larrakia heritage.

24.5 THE NEXT STAGES OF RESEARCH

Archaeological studies of homelessness are really little more than nascent, with scholars only now gaining a feel for methodologies that may prove useful. The epistemological—how we know what we know—problems have barely been considered, and mostly centre on heritage (see below). Methodologically, for the St. Paul and Indianapolis studies, Zimmerman and Welch (2011) attempted to limit the project to *material culture study* just to determine whether archaeological approaches could provide useful insights to homelessness by focusing on camp life. Kiddey and Schofield's (2010, 2011) Bristol and York projects almost immediately moved towards *collaborative* methods by directly engaging homeless people as partners whose research agendas were as important as those of the archaeologists. Zimmerman and Singleton's (Zimmerman, Singleton, and Welch 2010) use of material culture accounts and spatial data from blogs written by homeless bloggers was a sort of *virtual ethnoarchaeology* in which the bloggers' description and opinions provided answers to the archaeologists' questions and insights into how homeless people use and perceive their cultural landscapes. Pollard's People of the Long Grass project uses material culture study, locational information, ethnoarchaeology, documentary evidence, and oral tradition in service to specific policy and planning needs of the Larrakia Nation for the Darwin hinterlands. In one sense her methods are more like *traditional historic archaeology*, and with a time depth of about 150 years, she is adding a temporal dimension the USA and UK projects don't have. At the same time, with research questions that are part of the agenda of an Indigenous group, her project is also a form of *Indigenous archaeology*. Zimmerman and Singleton have recently shifted towards methods that are more collaborative and ethnoarchaeological by adding more strictly *ethnographic* methods to the Indianapolis project. They are concentrating efforts on one site, working closely with the more permanent occupants of the campsite. These include life histories, informant documentation of daily rounds of activities, and informant-drawn site and route maps. In addition, Singleton is experimenting with a number of techniques to document the surface of a campsite that changes every day, if not every hour (cf. Harrison 2011: 152–7). For example, she is taking daily, detailed panoramic photographs of key areas and piece plotting of 1 × 1 metre units in communal and sleeping areas of the site. With the latter she has tried plotting the distribution patterns of cigarette butts flicked from the sleeping areas to the communal area. Following the lead of the Bristol project, with the help of camp occupants, excavations of several areas within the site are being planned, as are two small exhibitions co-curated by homeless people.

The Indianapolis, Bristol/York, and Darwin projects integrate information from interaction with homeless people they encounter or work with on sites or during surveys. They range from casual comments about daily activities to informally offered life histories, and to paraphrase Harrison and Schofield (2010: 75), 'have the clear benefit of giving colour' to what might seem to be dreary, mundane lives. All of this supports Dawdy's (2010: 778) call to 'collapse the line between archaeology and ethnography...'to show that we can learn something about contemporary societies by investigating their material practices' (see also Harrison 2011).

24.6 THE IMPORTANCE OF RECOGNIZING A HERITAGE OF HOMELESSNESS

What has become clear to researchers is that the societies encompassing homeless populations mostly wish to reject homelessness as part of postmodern heritage. Narratives of success in capitalism celebrate individual skill and initiative, so those who fail must at some level be inept and lazy, attributes often assigned to homeless people. Some who buy into such a narrative tend to see the homeless as failures who merit only contempt. Others recognize capitalism's flaws and sometimes seize on the homeless as symbols of capitalism's failure to support the subaltern. The former make the homeless invisible while the latter seek to get them off the streets and into homes. Both ignore the range of reasons for homelessness and often fail to see the realities of day-to-day homeless life. Seeing homelessness as a heritage issue may help change the narratives and provide substance for developing more useful social policy.

Laurajane Smith (Smith and Waterton 2009: 44) believes that heritage is not a thing or place, but an 'intangible process in which social and cultural values are identified, negotiated, rejected, or affirmed'; 'it is something with which people actively, often self-consciously, and critically engage in' (Smith 2006: 83). Although definitions of heritage are debatable, material culture lies at its core, and '[h]eritage is imagined as something old, beautiful, tangible, and of relevance to the nation, selected by experts and made to matter' (Smith and Waterton 2009: 29). In thinking about the common narrative of homelessness, most would never consider homelessness to be old, beautiful, tangible, or of relevance, and more likely the opposite. Zimmerman learned this lesson while he was Head of Archaeology for the Minnesota Historical Society (MHS) and charged with overseeing the archaeology of all of the state's heritage sites. When the MHS determined to build the Mill City Museum, his task was to consider the impact on the archaeology of the site. The Washburn flour mill in Minneapolis, once the world's largest flour mill, was closed in 1965 and gutted by fire in 1991. As the ruins sat empty, the homeless began a decade-long occupation until construction began on the new museum in early 2000. They left behind numerous graffiti, and Zimmerman urged that at least some of the graffiti be left in place as evidence of the homeless occupation. The MHS administration rejected the idea, but allowed a graffito to remain in a tower, out of the view of the general public. They considered the graffiti to be vandalism, not worthy of interpretation, and removed it in spite of the fact that local and national graffiti artists voiced their outrage on an Internet bulletin board.

The rejection of Kiddey's request to have the MShed museum in Bristol include a small exhibition on the Turbo Island excavations reflects the same attitudes. Certainly homelessness was old, perhaps established early in Bristol's history, but even though tangible, rarely is homelessness beautiful, and as a social problem, many citizens, including heritage professionals, might consider it to be irrelevant to the central direction of a country or city or as a societal failure they prefer to marginalize.

What has been intriguing, however, is that the public has been keenly interested in the application of archaeology to homelessness in both the USA and the UK, with numerous inquiries about the projects, requests for lectures, and media coverage. In Indianapolis, the Central Public Library, which daily hosts many homeless people, has now hosted a photo exhibition—'What does homelessness look like?'—about the project and a well-attended public forum featuring the US and UK archaeology projects, in essence being willing to sponsor self-conscious, critical engagement about homelessness that moved beyond the usual narratives (Brown 2011).

24.7 Can Archaeology Actually Influence Social Policy about Homelessness?

The greatest impediment to archaeology's ability to influence social policy stems from commonly held views—including those of many archaeologists—that archaeology only deals with the more distant past. Archaeology can matter (Sabloff 2008), but only if archaeologists find ways to translate their findings into information that helps solve contemporary problems. Some of the public interest in current archaeological studies of homeless life seems to stem from the simplest observations about what is or isn't useful in campsites, but interest actually goes beyond that. The reality is that almost no study of living rough, especially in terms of material culture, has been done outside ethnography and archaeology. Most knowledge is anecdotal, bolstered by dominant narratives about homeless people and their lives.

That archaeology might be able to change the narrative on homelessness remains to be seen. Given the recent nature of investigations, such an assessment is premature. At the very least, what the archaeological studies have already done is to show that existing, shelter-based studies of homelessness provide only a limited picture of homeless lives, a view that tends to support the shelter-first narrative of the homeless industry. The studies also show—and in no uncertain terms—that homeless people can be capable of adapting to profoundly difficult situations, many of them not necessarily of their own making. Archaeology's material culture analysis provides evidence that even simple change in service delivery can improve the lives of the roofless.

These projects allow some different voices to be heard regarding homelessness, voices that are rarely a part of debates about heritage. The problem is that marginalized groups usually have almost no power, and even when there is a recognizable community structure, they have difficulty exercising it. What it may take is a determined effort on the part of archaeologists, as heritage professionals, working in collaboration with communities of homeless people, to translate archaeological findings into activism (Zimmerman, Singleton, and Welch 2010: 444–6).

REFERENCES

Baugher, Sherene. 2001. Visible Charity: The Archaeology, Material Culture, and Landscape Design of New York City's Municipal Almshouse Complex, 1736–1797. *International Journal of Historical Archaeology* 5(2): 175–202.

Bogard, Cynthia J. 2003. *Seasons Such as These: How Homelessness Took Shape in America*. Hawthorne, NY: Aldyne de Gruyter.

Brown, Nathan. 2011. Archaeology of Homelessness (Slideshow). Available at: <http://www.nuvo.net/indianapolis/slideshow-archeology-of-homelessness/Content?oid=2390087> (accessed 14 December 2011).

CLG. 2010. Rough Sleeping Statistics England—Autumn 2010 Experimental Statistics. *Housing Statistical Release*. Department of Communities and Local Government. Available at: <http://www.communities.gov.uk/documents/statistics/pdf/1845810> (accessed 16 September 2011).

Dawdy, Shannon L. 2010. Clockpunk Anthropology and the Ruins of Modernity. *Current Anthropology* 51(6): 761–93.

Dixon, David M. 1989. A Note on Some Scavengers of Ancient Egypt. *World Archaeology* 21(2): 193–7.

Harrison, Rodney. 2009. Excavating Second Life: Cyber-Archaeologies, Heritage and Virtual Settlements. *Journal of Material Culture* 14(1): 75–106.

—— 2011. Surface Assemblages: Towards an Archaeology *in* and *of* the Present. *Archaeological Dialogues* 18(2): 141–96.

Harrison, Rodney and Schofield, John. 2010. *After Modernity: Archaeological Approaches to the Contemporary Past*. Oxford: Oxford University Press.

HUD. 2007. *The Annual Homeless Assessment Report to Congress*. U.S. Department of Housing and Urban Development. Available at: <http://www.huduser.org/Publications/pdf/ahar.pdf> (accessed 16 September 2011).

Huey, Paul R. 2001. The Almshouse in Dutch and English Colonial North America and its Precedent in the Old World: Historical and Archaeological Evidence. *International Journal of Historical Archaeology* 5(2): 123–54.

Kiddey, Rachael. 2011. *Homeless Heritage: Social Inclusive Heritage and Homelessness*. Available at: <http://homelessheritage.wordpress.com> (accessed 16 September 2011).

Kiddey, Rachael and Schofield, John. 2010. Digging for Invisible People. *British Archaeology* 113: 18–24.

—— 2011. Embrace the Margins: Adventures in Archaeology and Homelessness. *Public Archaeology* 10(1): 4–22.

Levinson, David (ed.). 2004. *Encyclopedia of Homelessness*. Thousand Oaks, CA: Sage Publications.

Marcus, Anthony. 2006. *Where Have All the Homeless Gone? The Making and Unmaking of a Crisis*. New York: Berghahn Books.

Montague, Julian. 2006. *The Stray Shopping Carts of Eastern North American: A Guide to Field Identification*. New York: Abrams Image.

Ravenhill, Megan. 2008. *The Culture of Homelessness*. Burlington, VT: Ashgate Publishing.

Sabloff, Jeremy A. 2008. *Archaeology Matters: Action Archaeology in the Modern World*. Walnut Creek, CA: Left Coast Press.

Smith, Laurajane. 2006. *The Uses of Heritage*. London: Routledge.

Smith, Laurajane and Waterton, Emma. 2009. *Heritage, Communities, and Archaeology*. London: Duckworth.

Spencer-Wood, Suzanne M. 2001. Views and Commentaries: What Difference Does Feminist Theory Make? *International Journal of Historical Archaeology* 5(1): 97–114.

United Nations Economic and Social Council. 2009. *Enumeration of Homeless People*. Available at: <http://unstats.un.org/unsd/censuskb20/Attachments/2009MPHASIS_ECE_Homeless-GUID25ae612721cc4c2c87b536892e1ed1e1.pdf> (accessed 16 September 2011).

Valado, Martha T. 2006. Factors Influencing Homeless People's Perception and Use of Urban Space. Ph.D. dissertation, University of Arizona, Tucson.

Zimmerman, Larry J. 2004. Archaeological Explorations of the James J. Hill House Gardens. *Minnesota Archaeologist* 63: 118–36.

Zimmerman, Larry J. and Welch, Jessica. 2011. Displaced and Barely Visible: Archaeology and the Material Culture of Homelessness. *Historical Archaeology* 45(1): 67–85.

Zimmerman, Larry J., Singleton, Courtney, and Welch, Jessica. 2010. Activism and Creating a Translational Archaeology of Homelessness. *World Archaeology* 42(3): 443–54.

CHAPTER 25

··

CONFLICT

··

GABRIEL MOSHENSKA

25.1 INTRODUCTION

··

THE archaeology of twentieth-century conflict is an intellectually challenging, politically loaded, and socially engaged field of practice raising questions of ethics and methodology that resonate across the study of the modern material world. It involves the application of archaeological and allied techniques to the study of the innumerable episodes of violence and repression that punctuated the twentieth century and continue into the present: not just the major conflicts such as the world wars but also less well-known episodes such as civil wars and episodes of violent political oppression.

This chapter presents an overview of some of the principal themes and trends in the archaeology of twentieth-century conflict (see Badcock and Johnston, this volume; Dixon, this volume; McAtackney, this volume). It begins with an overview of some of the key challenges that twentieth-century conflict archaeologists face, a brief discussion of the emergence and development of the field, and a series of case studies illustrating its geographical, temporal, methodological, and thematic diversity. Following this it examines the much-debated value and significance of applying archaeological techniques to twentieth-century conflict, again illustrated by a series of short case studies. Two of these are considered in more depth: the role of archaeology in locating and identifying the bodies of people killed in conflicts; and the role of conflict archaeology as a form of commemoration. The final section considers the future directions of archaeological approaches to conflicts in the twentieth and twenty-first centuries.

In contrast with battlefield archaeology, a well-established and more narrowly defined field of study focusing on sites of combat or violent confrontation, the archaeology of twentieth-century conflict encompasses a wide range of practices, processes, and historical events. The greatest quantity of work focuses on the impacts of the First and Second World Wars, but increasing attention has been given to small wars and insurgencies, class warfare, and other marginal and marginalized processes. From a practical perspective the archaeological study of twentieth-century conflicts presents a number of new and unique challenges: the application of new technologies of remote sensing and underwater exploration are amongst a number of factors that have revolutionized our understanding of the titanic conflicts of the twentieth century and their enduring legacies.

The political implications of this work, as well as the findings, have often proved highly controversial, sometimes to a degree unimaginable in any other field of study. French and Belgian collectors digging for souvenirs on First World War battlefields have been vilified as grave-robbers in the British media; efforts to locate the graves of Republican sympathizers murdered by Francoist militias during and after the Spanish Civil War have been condemned for reopening historical wounds (Elkin 2006; Saunders 2007: 13–15). In the popular imagination digging and unearthing are inextricably linked to ideas of remembering and commemorating, just as burying is associated with forgetting (Moshenska 2009).

The political impacts of modern conflict archaeology evoke the more personal issue of emotion. Excavations of conflict sites can be immensely emotional experiences for survivors, ex-combatants and their descendants, as well as for the archaeologists (Crossland 2000; Brown 2007). Exhumations of human remains and the recovery of personal objects can have significant impacts, both positive and negative, on processes of mourning and grief. The opening of buried sites and the associated sights, smells, and sounds can have strongly negative effects on people suffering from post-traumatic stress and related conditions. For individuals and communities associated with the perpetration of violence and human-rights violations, the response to archaeological interventions such as exhumations can range from guilt and sadness to anger and violence.

Hovering above these political and emotional dimensions is the more general question of archaeological ethics and the unique ethical problems that conflict archaeology presents (Schofield 2005; González-Ruibal 2008; Moshenska 2008; Crossland 2009). A considerable number of these relate to working with the remains of people who have died relatively recently, often violently, and whose names and wishes for their remains are reasonably likely to be known or surmised. While in many cases the human remains are those of victims of violence, archaeologists also encounter the remains of perpetrators of violence; and most commonly the bodies of those, such as combatants, who fall between these often over-simplified categories. Alongside the 'problematic dead' there is the issue of working with the living: as informants, stakeholder communities, and as an interested public with divergent interests, needs, and demands. Conflict archaeologists must juggle their duties or perceived responsibilities towards the dead, the living, and their own professional standards and codes. While the ethics of conflict archaeology remain largely unresolved and widely contested, much has been learned from related fields such as medical ethics.

25.2 THE DEVELOPMENT OF MODERN CONFLICT ARCHAEOLOGY

The establishment of modern conflict archaeology as a recognized subdiscipline is a relatively recent phenomenon, and in many areas it remains marginal, as with the archaeology of the modern world in general. Some of the earliest work in modern conflict archaeology was carried out by amateur archaeologists, and this has remained a strong theme within the discipline, even as the inputs from cultural resource management, and later academic archaeology, have grown. Modern conflict archaeology as a hobby emerged in several fields including souvenir hunting on historic battlefields, metal detecting, recreational diving, and aviation archaeology or 'wreckology' (de la Bédoyère 2000). The latter came to prominence in the 1970s and '80s and led to legislation in the UK and elsewhere restricting excavation of military crash sites where human remains might be found (Holyoak 2002). One of the earliest publications on the material remains of modern conflict is John Laffin's *Battlefield Archaeology* (1987), little more than a handbook for treasure hunters and looters on the fields of the Western Front. In the US the archaeological study of recent conflicts emerged during the same period, including a pioneering study of the site of the Battle of Little Bighorn that contributed to a reinterpretation of Custer's famous 'Last Stand' (Scott and Fox 1987). More recently the field of American Civil War archaeology has also grown considerably, offering archaeological insights into what many regard as the first 'modern' conflict (Geier and Winter 1994; Geier and Potter 2001).

As interest in the history of twentieth-century conflicts has grown and remained strong, the sites and monuments associated with them have begun to be preserved and protected as cultural heritage. This has fuelled a growth in cultural resource management (CRM) archaeology around the world: given the scale of the resource this undoubtedly constitutes the largest body of work in this field. Through the 1990s and early 2000s, English Heritage commissioned and carried out a number of studies to characterize and assess remains relating to twentieth-century conflicts. These sites ranged in date from before the First World War to after the Cold War, and included coastal defences, airfields, command centres, civil defence sites, and supply and communication infrastructure (Schofield 2004). In a number of cases this has formed the basis for further work including community heritage projects, art installations, and exhibitions (Boulton 2006). The value and necessity of a wide-ranging approach to the history and archaeology incorporating oral testimony, local history, and various forms of community engagement are increasingly recognized (Moshenska 2007).

The ever-broadening scope of critical heritage studies is one of several points of contact between CRM, social history, and social archaeology, including material culture studies. It is from the latter that another key strand in modern conflict archaeology has emerged from the late 1990s onward, bringing together anthropological, archaeological, and museological approaches to portable material culture and landscapes (Saunders 2004, 2007). This work offers a new perspective on things as diverse as war memorials, artworks, bodies, souvenirs, and medals as they shape and are shaped by social dynamics from times of conflict into the present (e.g. Joy 2002; Schofield 2005). Such creative reimaginings of the material cultures of conflict have in turn transformed archaeological approaches to new and forgotten sites (e.g. Myers 2010). The emphasis on social relations in the past and heritage issues in the present has made the archaeology of modern conflict a critical, political, problematic, and exciting field to work in.

25.3 Forms of Modern Conflict Archaeology

The techniques and methodologies employed in modern conflict archaeology range across the full spectrum of archaeological field practices, technologies, methods of analysis, and means of recovery. The following case studies illustrate some of the wide variety of site-types and environments encountered within conflict archaeology, emphasizing the global scope of the discipline and its close connections to other specialist fields such as underwater archaeology and the archaeology of caves.

25.3.1 The Cave of Zeret

A recent survey of a cave in Ethiopia examined the site as a refuge used by Ethiopian guerrillas in 1939, during their war with the Italian colonial forces, in which the latter employed poison gas and aerial bombing (González-Ruibal et al. 2011). The cave of Zeret, a refuge and ultimately the site of a massacre using gas, shells and machine guns, was studied using methods and approaches typical to settlement archaeology of any period, including the use of historical and ethnographic data to identify activity areas for food storage and preparation. The archaeologists also found considerable evidence of the siege that ended the occupation of the site, including the deliberate destruction of materials inside the cave by the Italian troops. Amongst the fragmented remains were the bodies of eighteen people, included several children, many of them damaged by scavenging animals (González-Ruibal et al. 2011).

The archaeological survey of the massacre site illuminated the lives and deaths of the guerrilla force: a number of distinctive assemblages were found that were traditionally associated with women's work. These were analysed in light of feminist archaeological concepts of 'maintenance activities' that argue for the relevance and significance of quotidian practices relating to the reproduction of everyday life. The archaeology of the cave of Zeret epitomizes many of the features of modern conflict archaeology as it has developed, including the application of formal archaeological techniques for survey and recording; a critical and constructive engagement with research ethics; a focus on the fine-grained detail of the human experience of conflict; and an awareness of the social and political significance of studying the events in question.

25.3.2 U-869

A rather different form of modern conflict archaeology is described in the book *Shadow Divers* (Kurson 2005), which chronicles the discovery and investigation of a Second World War U-boat off the coast of New Jersey in 1991. This mystery vessel was found hundreds of miles from any reported U-boat contact, presenting a historical conundrum. Due to its remote location and depth, the wreck was difficult and dangerous for divers to explore. Like the cave of Zeret the U-boat wreck contained human remains: in this case more than fifty individuals. Kurson describes the complex historical and archaeological detective work that led to the vessel's ultimate identification as U-869, captained by Hellmut Neuerburg. One of the first portable objects recovered was a knife handle marked 'Horenburg'; this was initially dismissed as evidence, as it was thought that U-869 on which Martin Horenburg served was sunk off the coast of Gibraltar. Further artefacts were recovered from the wreck, ultimately identifying it as U-869. This work forced a review of the historical records of U-boat sinkings.

There are a number of ethical concerns around recreational diving on wrecks such as this that also serve as war graves, including the questionable practice of taking souvenirs, particularly human bones (Iregren 2004). Dives to identify the wreck and thereby the names of the dead can be defended on the grounds of respectful commemoration and the desire to locate the bodies of the missing, and several dives on U-869 have left wreaths on the wreck. Up to the present the debates around recreational diving on conflict sites have been largely distinct from related discourses in conflict archaeology, although the key questions and problems are near-identical, including the issue of health and safety: conflict archaeology often presents hazards of unexploded ordnance, while the wreck of U-869 has to date claimed the lives of three recreational divers.

25.3.3 Trenches of the Western Front

In Flanders you don't have to dig deep to find the archaeological remains of the First World War. Shell fragments, bullets, and other debris reappear and disappear each year as ploughs turn the topsoil over. Each year farmers die when their tractors detonate one of the hundreds of thousands of shells that still litter the battlefields of the First World War. The Plugstreet Archaeological Project works on the site of the 1917 Battle of Messines: cratered fields that hide the remains of trench system and the men who fought and lived in them. While trenches have become a symbol of the war on the Western Front, relatively little is known about them as a military technology (Brown and Osgood 2009). For this reason the project team have excavated the practice trenches that were used for infantry training in Britain, as well as the actual front line trenches: by comparing the real with the simulated versions the archaeologists have been able to see how training was put into practice. The excavators found the front line trenches well preserved, in some cases with sandbags and corrugated iron reinforcements, and with military equipment and personal items still in place.

The Battle of Messines opened with the detonation of nineteen huge mines that had been dug under the German front line. The excavated debris included tiny flecks of human bone, a testament to the power of explosives to annihilate the human body. Amongst these remains the team found the body of an infantryman, lying face-down and buried in full kit. Careful excavation and conservation of the body and associated objects showed that he was an Australian; further historical, forensic, and scientific analyses enabled the team to identify him, restoring humanity and individuality to one body amongst thousands (Brown and Osgood 2009). A great deal of archaeological work takes place on the battlefields of the First World War. Some are rescue excavations in advance of development; others are aimed at souvenir hunting. A number of excavations are aimed specifically at recovering and identifying human bodies, often for repatriation. A small number, like the Plugstreet Archaeological Project, have a clear research agenda and an awareness of the ethics and dangers of working on modern battlefields.

These case studies illustrate a few of the many characteristics that distinguish twentieth-century conflict and its archaeology. Global conflicts, small wars, insurgencies, rebellions, and riots leave distinctive material traces, while advances in transport and weapons technology and the globalization of the arms trade have created a distinctive material culture of modern violence. Some of these technologies such as the Kalashnikov, the gas mask, and the Toyota pickup have recurred in conflicts across the world (e.g. Graves-Brown 2007; Moshenska 2010a). In many respects the archaeology of modern conflict is an industrial archaeology: the mass-production and standardization of war material played a central role in the interpretive elements of these case studies (González-Ruibal 2006, 2008).

25.4 WHAT USE IS TWENTIETH-CENTURY CONFLICT ARCHAEOLOGY?

The most common question asked of twentieth-century conflict archaeology is what it can add to the already rich and detailed histories of warfare derived from documentary sources, film, oral histories, and other media. The archaeology of the modern world often drifts towards what Johnson called 'social-history-plus-artefacts' (1999: 20), in which the material remains of conflict serve as illustrations for an established historical narrative or as static, mute memorials in commemorative processes. One obvious response is to point to the substantial portion of rescue archaeological work on conflict sites that aims to assess, record, and preserve the decaying traces of infrastructure, from individual structures to vast military bases and industrial sites (e.g. Cocroft and Thomas 2003; de Meyer and Pype 2004). Archaeology in the service of conflict heritage resource management needs no justification, not least due to the vast quantity, global distribution, and historical significance of the resource in question.

Conflict heritage sites can also present some unique problems of conservation and management. For example, the wreck of the *USS Arizona*, a battleship sunk in the attack on Pearl Harbor, sits in shallow water overlooked by a viewing platform that attracts more than a million visitors each year (Kelly 1991). Due to natural erosion the wreck is degrading and leaking increasing amounts of oil into the sea, presenting the US National Park Service which manages the site with a serious and expensive conservation problem.

Beyond the vital task of resource management and heritage stewardship there are a number of ways in which archaeological studies of sites of modern conflict can offer unique and substantial contributions to our knowledge and understanding. In some cases, such as the study of the Battle of Little Bighorn mentioned earlier, archaeological studies of conflict sites have strongly challenged accepted historical accounts. In addition, aspects of many conflicts are carried out covertly, and many others are deliberately hidden or erased after the fact. Where there have been attempts to bury the remains—literally or metaphorically— there is a role for archaeologists in uncovering them and telling their story.

25.4.1 Sobibor

The archaeological study of the Sobibor extermination camp demonstrates the validity of this argument. Sobibor was one of the so-called Operation Reinhardt camps, designed by the Nazis for the sole purpose of mass killing. From May 1942 more than 200,000 people were murdered by gassing at Sobibor, the majority of them European Jews, before the camp was closed in late 1943 following a prisoner revolt that allowed 600 to escape. Following closure the camp was demolished, the gas chambers destroyed and buried, and trees planted across the site to conceal it. The only surviving plans of the site are memory maps drawn by former inmates, and the precise layout of the camp and the location of key structures remain unclear. A team of Israeli and Polish archaeologists conducted a programme of surveys and excavations aimed at locating key features of the camp and tying them to the aerial photographs and memory maps (Gilead et al. 2009). A number of features have been identified for the first time, and several assumptions about the layout of the camp have been overturned. Where the historical record had been deliberately erased and most of the eye-witnesses murdered, the unique value of an archaeological approach becomes clear.

25.4.2 The Ludlow Massacre

It is not necessary for a site to be deliberately erased for it to fall from view. The Archaeology of the Colorado Coalfield War Project worked for several years at the site of the Ludlow Massacre, where the families and makeshift homes of striking coal miners were machine-gunned and burnt by the Colorado National Guard in 1914 killing eighteen people, the majority of them children (Ludlow Collective 2001; McGuire and Larkin 2009). Today the United Mine Workers union owns the site and has erected a memorial to the victims of the massacre, but the killings and the much wider context of class warfare in American history remain largely unrecognized. The excavations of the massacre site were designed, in part, to raise awareness of the events in the surrounding community, as well as within the modern-day labour movement. In this sense excavation of a modern conflict site can serve as a highlighter pen on the pages of history, drawing attention to a place, person, or episode. However, the aims of the archaeologists extended beyond mere explication, using the findings from the excavations to address questions of women's roles and issues of ethnicity in the strike, emphasizing a commonality of experience in the strike and in the working-class movement in general (Duke and Saitta 2009). The archaeologists contributed to the annual events held at the memorial, and engaged with the commemoration of the massacre in a number of ways. During the period of the project, the memorial was deliberately and violently vandalized, with the heads being smashed off the statues. While the archaeology of the Ludlow Massacre revealed aspects of the conflict not usually included in any narrative, the vandalism showed that the representation of this conflict—or of any conflict—is a problematic and often highly contested issue.

25.4.3 The Club Atlético

Alongside its ability to reveal what is hidden from history, an archaeological approach to conflict sites offers a high-resolution snapshot of the minutiae of humanity in extraordinary circumstances. The 'Club Atlético' was a clandestine detention and torture site in Buenos Aires operated for several months in 1977 by the Argentinian Junta. During this time approximately 1,500 prisoners passed through the site, most of whom were later murdered. Following its demolition, a road bridge was built over the site: as at Sobibor there was a desire to erase it materially as well as mnemonically. From 2002 an archaeological project on the site aimed to uncover the remains of the prison and trace the lives of the people imprisoned there (Zarankin and Funari 2008). Alongside spatial analysis of the prison, the archaeologists recovered a number of artefacts, including a ping-pong ball. According to former prisoners, the torturers used to play ping-pong in between torture sessions: the prisoners learned to associate the sounds of ping-pong with relief, as it meant that no one was being tortured for a time. The recovery of this apparently innocuous object, and the story associated with it, highlights the important interconnections between memory and materiality in the archaeology of modern conflict, as well as the capacity of contemporary archaeology to find a depth of meaning in quotidian material remains.

25.4.4 London Bombsite

Another archaeological glimpse into everyday life amidst conflict arose during a Museum of London community archaeology project in Shoreditch Park, East London (Simpson and Williams 2008). The site used for the project was a public park, consisting of a thin topsoil covering the ruins of hundreds of slum houses destroyed by bombing during the Second World War, or demolished shortly afterwards. The large, open area excavation revealed the floor-plans of several houses, and a considerable quantity of domestic objects and refuse, ranging in date from the mid-nineteenth century to the mid-twentieth. As with many modern conflict excavations, there were living witnesses to the bombings and other events that destroyed the homes, but more unusually in this case many of them still lived close to the site and visited the excavation repeatedly. Several of these visitors agreed to record their memories and testimonies: the unique circumstances of the excavation meant that many of the interviews took place in the ruins of the homes or walking around the site, and artefacts recovered in the excavation were used as talking points or to stimulate recollections (Moshenska 2007). Only a few of the artefacts were directly related to the war, including two military badges and a broken toy aircraft, but the emphasis on wartime childhoods and domesticity wove the artefacts and the spaces of the ruined homes into a detailed and interconnected web of narratives from the various informants (Moshenska 2007).

25.5 FORENSICS AND FINDING THE FALLEN

Amongst all the material culture of modern conflict the most universal, and one of the most abundant, is the dead body. Some, like the Australian infantryman excavated at Plugstreet, are identifiable and individual; others, like the 200,000 murdered at Sobibor are lost amidst an undifferentiated mass of ash and bone fragments. In the fields around Volgograd the bones of the German Sixth Army lie like a crop in the ground and on the surface; the wreck of the USS Arizona in Pearl Harbor is a war grave, holding the remains of 1,177 servicemen killed in the sinking (Kelly 1991). Casualties of wars, genocides, and other conflicts in the twentieth century numbered in the tens of millions; only a tiny proportion of their bodies lie in individual, accurately marked graves. The few bodies that are identified each year are to a large extent the result of painstaking work by forensic anthropologists and archaeologists.

Throughout the twentieth century the practice of secretly killing or 'disappearing' people has been a common feature of civil conflicts and totalitarian regimes (Crossland 2000).

Following the end of the conflict, or a regime change, it has become increasingly common for the remains of the murdered to be recovered, either as part of a truth and reconciliation process or to aid the prosecution of the perpetrators (Doretti and Fondebrider 2001). In these recovery operations forensic archaeologists and anthropologists work within teams which, depending on circumstances, might include explosive ordnance disposal specialists, translators, bodyguards, local labourers, police, or military personnel. The task of these teams is to locate, recover, and identify the bodies of the disappeared, and to collect evidence relating to their deaths.

The legal, organizational, and political identities of the recovery organizations depend on their contexts. In the former Yugoslavia and Rwanda, the missions took place under the auspices of the United Nations International Criminal Tribunals. In contrast to this, the Committee on Missing Persons in Cyprus, while also sponsored by the United Nations, aims to locate and identify the missing, but does not collect evidence for the prosecution of the killers. One of the earliest recovery groups was the Equipo Argentino de Antropología Forense (EAAF), a non-governmental organization formed by Argentine human rights groups, together with the American anthropologist Clyde Snow. The work of the EAAF focuses on finding the bodies of left-wing activists and sympathizers murdered during Argentina's 'Dirty War' from 1976 to 1983: as recognized pioneers in this field they have also worked in former warzones around the world including East Timor, Angola, and Iraqi Kurdistan (Doretti and Fondebrider 2001).

The exhumation of Republican sympathizers murdered during and after the Spanish Civil War is perhaps the most prominent exhumation campaign of the twenty-first century. The Asociación para la Recuperación de la Memoria Histórica (ARMH) was founded in 2000, with the aim of breaking the 'pact of silence' around the mass murders that had endured throughout the Francoist dictatorship and into the present (Congram and Wolfe Steadman 2008). The volunteer excavators, archaeologists, and physical anthropologists of the ARMH trace and excavate the mass graves, generally located on the outskirts of villages and towns. Their work has proven politically controversial: in many places the relatives of the disappeared have lived for decades alongside the murderers and their families. Exhumation teams have faced violence, threats, and vandalism to sites. The excavations of the mass graves have led to a reappraisal of the legacy of the Spanish Civil War in Spain, with an emerging national discourse including a Law of Historical Memory passed in 2007 that recognizes all the victims of the conflict. This law and the continuing development of local and national historical narratives are tangible outcomes of the archaeological work (Renshaw 2010).

25.6 Digging to Commemorate

A common strand in several of the projects described above is the idea that excavating a site can be an act of commemoration. In Spain, at Sobibor, and at the Ludlow Massacre site, the more conventional roles of conflict archaeology such as research and cultural resource management are joined—and arguably superseded—by the powerful memorial role that excavation can play. The most striking example of digging to commemorate took place in Berlin in 1985, where an unofficial, unsanctioned excavation took place on the site of the former Gestapo headquarters at Prinz-Albrecht-Strasse (Baker 1988). Following political resistance to a proposed memorial by the Christian Democrat Mayor of West Berlin, two grassroots history groups planned an excavation as a protest on the ruins. The team included several people who had been imprisoned and tortured by the Gestapo. The project, entitled 'Lets Dig!', was promoted as a 'commemorative operation'. The slogans of the project revealed the extent to which excavation was regarded as a commemorative process in contrast to burial, associated with forgetting: 'grass must never be allowed to grow over it'; 'the wound must stay open' (Moshenska 2010b). Today the site at Prinz-Albrecht-Strasse is open to the public as the 'Topography of Terror'.

The notion that excavation, conservation, or recording are linked to remembering can extend beyond famous or infamous sites—such as massacre sites and concentration camps—to raise awareness of forgotten or marginalized aspects of past conflicts, as demonstrated by the survey of the cave of Zeret and the excavation of the Club Atlético outlined above. Other categories of conflict sites that have been highlighted by recent archaeological attention are anti-war, anti-nuclear, and peace protest camps. The Green Gate peace camp at Greenham Common Airbase became famous in the 1980s as part of an all-women permanent protest against the presence of nuclear weapons at the base. The protest camp was destroyed and rebuilt several times over the years of its occupation before its final abandonment. Surveys of the site by archaeologists working with former residents of the camp have attempted to place the material remains within their wider context of the peace movement, feminism, and political dissent (Marshall et al. 2009). A similar project in Nevada examined the remains of settlement, art, and other traces of protest at the Peace Camp adjoining the Nevada Test Site, where from 1951 to 1992 the US government conducted most of its nuclear weapons tests (Beck et al. 2007). The inclusion of the archaeology of peace protests within the wider framework of conflict archaeology, alongside battlefield surveys and the conservation of sites of civil repression, demonstrates the breadth and inclusivity of the field.

25.7 THE FUTURE OF MODERN CONFLICT ARCHAEOLOGY

Modern conflict archaeology remains a relatively young discipline with enormous scope for growth and development into new topics and different parts of the world. The maturing of the discipline is evident in the emphasis on ethics, social theory, and social responsibility, alongside activism and advocacy that harness the political and cultural capital that conflict archaeology so often generates.

Trends within recent work offer clues to future directions. The work carried out in Ethiopia by González-Ruibal and others demonstrates the potential for conflict archaeology to shed light on the innumerable colonial wars, massacres, acts of repression, and 'police actions' that characterized European colonialism in Africa, Asia, the Pacific, and elsewhere, as well as the acts of resistance to colonization that ultimately contributed to its decline. This work may not be welcomed by either the former colonial nations or the emergent postcolonial states: the small scale, high resolution historical narratives of colonial conflicts that archaeology can offer are rarely conducive to the simplistic Manichean narratives favoured by both colonial and postcolonial nationalist histories. But as these studies have shown, such work can also broaden the historical narratives by adding dimensions such as women's and children's lives and contributions to the struggle.

Postcolonial nations are just one area where conflict archaeology can reveal inconvenient truths. War and violence in the twentieth and twenty-first centuries have produced an ever-growing number of iconic images of individual suffering that have transcended the increasingly thin rhetoric of 'just war' and become symbols of the inhuman cruelty of state-sanctioned violence. Archaeologies of conflict can rarely contribute to big-picture, strategic histories of warfare: the view from the bottom of the trench, like the view from the front line, is of individual bodies and homes shattered and annihilated. The political impact of conflict archaeology gives its practitioners a potentially powerful voice, as well as a commensurately strong ethical responsibility.

One sign of the maturing of modern conflict archaeology will be found not in what is studied, but in what archaeologists choose to leave alone. There are undoubtedly potential sites that many or most people would regard as too raw, too iconic, too dangerous, or too politically problematic to excavate or survey, even if it was technically possible. The uncovering of some mass graves might reignite ethnic violence in unstable regions; in other places excavations might be regarded as intrusive or culturally insensitive by survivors and descendants of the victims. At Messines one of the enormous ten ton mines remains buried beneath the site: even a small risk of detonating such a vast charge might be considered reason not to excavate. The exercise of instinctive sensitivity, caution, and restraint in these cases must be balanced with a critical assessment of the risks, the benefits, and the ideological or political interests that might seek to exploit the situation.

Whatever the larger trends in the forms and functions of modern conflict archaeology one feature that is certain to endure is the constant stream of discoveries: a few of them terrifying, some of them astonishing, many of them throwing light onto forgotten or neglected episodes in world history. In recent years receding alpine glaciers have revealed the bodies of First World War soldiers and their equipment preserved in the ice, while remote controlled submarines have explored the wreckage of the *Bismarck*, one of the most feared battleships of the Second World War. These discoveries and the insights they provide into past conflicts and the people caught up in them attest to the ever growing relevance, dynamism, and significance of the archaeological study of modern conflicts.

REFERENCES

Baker, Frederick. 1988. History that Hurts: Excavating 1933–1945. *Archaeological Review from Cambridge* 7(1): 93–109.

Beck, Colleen M., Drollinger, Harold, and Schofield, John. 2007. Archaeology of Dissent: Landscape and Symbolism at the Nevada Peace Camp. In *A Fearsome Heritage: Diverse Legacies of the Cold War*, ed. John Schofield and Wayne Cocroft, pp. 297–320. Walnut Creek, CA: Left Coast Press.

Boulton, Angus. 2006. Film Making and Photography as Record and Interpretation. In *Re-Mapping the Field: New Approaches in Conflict Archaeology*, ed. John Schofield, Axel Klausmeier, and Louise Purbrick, pp. 35–8. Berlin: Westkreuz-Verlag.

Brown, Martin. 2007. The Fallen, the Front and the Finding: Archaeology, Human Remains and the Great War. *Archaeological Review from Cambridge* 22(2): 53–68.

Brown, Martin and Osgood, Richard. 2009. *Digging up Plugstreet: The Western Front Unearthed*. Sparkford, UK: Haynes.

Cocroft, Wayne and Thomas, Roger J. C. 2003. *Cold War: Building for Nuclear Confrontation 1946–1989*. London: English Heritage.

Congram, Derek and Wolfe Steadman, Dawnie. 2008. Distinguished Guests or Agents of Ingerence: Foreign Participation in Spanish Civil War Grave Excavations. *Complutum* 19(2): 161–73.

Crossland, Zoe. 2000. Buried Lives: Forensic Archaeology and the Disappeared in Argentina. *Archaeological Dialogues* 3: 146–59.

—— 2009. Of Clues and Signs: The Dead Body and its Evidential Traces. *American Anthropologist* 111(1): 69–80.

de la Bédoyère, Guy. 2000. *Battles over Britain: The Archaeology of the Air War*. Stroud: Tempus.

de Meyer, Mathieu and Pype, Pedro. 2004. *The A19 Project: Archaeological Research at Cross Roads*. Zarren, Belgium: Association for World War Archaeology.

Doretti, Mercedes and Fondebrider, Luis. 2001. Science and Human Rights: Truth, Justice, Reparation and Reconciliation, a Long Way in Third World Countries. In *Archaeologies of the Contemporary Past*, ed. Victor Buchli and Gavin Lucas, pp. 138–44. London: Routledge.

Duke, Philip and Saitta, Dean. 2009. Why We Dig: Archaeology, Ludlow and the Public. In *The Archaeology of Class War: the Colorado Coalfield Strike of 1913–1914*, ed. Karin Larkin and Randall H. McGuire, pp. 351–61. Boulder, CO: University Press of Colorado.

Elkin, Mike. 2006. Opening Franco's Graves: The Victims of Spain's Fascist Past are Beginning to Tell their Stories. *Archaeology* 59(5): 38–43.

Geier, Clarence R. and Potter, Stephen R. 2001. *Archaeological Perspectives on the American Civil War*. Gainesville, FL: University Press of Florida.

Geier, Clarence R. and Winter, Susan E. 1994. *Look to the Earth: Historical Archaeology and the American Civil War*. Knoxville, TN: University of Tennessee Press.

Gilead, Isaac, Haimi, Yoram, and Mazurek, Wojciech. 2009. Excavating Nazi Extermination Centres. *Present Pasts* 1: 10–39.

González-Ruibal, Alfredo. 2006 The Past is Tomorrow: Towards an Archaeology of the Vanishing Present. *Norwegian Archaeological Review* 39(2): 110–25.

—— 2008. Time to Destroy: An Archaeology of Supermodernity. *Current Anthropology* 49(2): 247–79.

González-Ruibal, Alfredo, Sahle, Yonatan, and Vila, Xurxo Ayán. 2011. A Social Archaeology of Colonial War in Ethiopia. *World Archaeology* 43(1): 40–65.

Graves-Brown, Paul. 2007. Avtomat Kalashnikova. *Journal of Material Culture* 12(3): 285–307.

Holyoak, Vince. 2002. Out of the Blue: Assessing Military Aircraft Crash Sites in England, 1912–45. *Antiquity* 76(3): 657–63.

Iregren, Elisabeth. 2004. Humans in Wrecks: An Ethical Discussion on Marine Archaeology, Exhibitions and Scuba Diving. In *Swedish Archaeologists on Ethics*, ed. Håkan Karlsson, pp. 265–86. Lindome: Bricoleur.

Johnson, Matthew. 1999. The New Post-Medieval Archaeology. In *Old and New Worlds*, ed. Geoff Egan and R. L. Michael, pp. 17–22. Oxford: Oxbow.

Joy, Jody. 2002. Biography of a Medal: People and the Things they Value. In *Matériel Culture: The Archaeology of Twentieth Century Conflict*, ed. John Schofield, William G. Johnson, and Colleen M. Beck, pp. 132–42. London: Routledge.

Kelly, Roger E. 1991. The Archaeology of an Icon: The *USS Arizona*. In *Archaeological Studies of World War II*, ed. W. Raymond Wood, pp. 3–12. Columbia, MO: University of Missouri-Columbia Museum of Anthropology Monograph Number 10.

Kurson, Robert. 2005. *Shadow Divers: How Two Men Discovered Hitler's Lost Sub and Solved One of the Last Mysteries of World War II*. New York: Random House.

Laffin, John. 1987. *Battlefield Archaeology*. London: Ian Allan.

Ludlow Collective. 2001. Archaeology of the Colorado Coalfield War 1913–1914. In *Archaeologies of the Contemporary Past*, ed. Victor Buchli and Gavin Lucas, pp. 94–107. London: Routledge.

McGuire, Randall H. and Larkin, Karin. 2009. Unearthing Class War. In *The Archaeology of Class War: The Colorado Coalfield Strike of 1913–1914*, ed. Karin Larkin and Randall H. McGuire, pp. 1–28. Boulder, CO: University Press of Colorado.

Marshall, Yvonne, Roseneil, Sasha, and Armstrong, Kayt. 2009. Situating the Greenham Archaeology: An Autoethnography of a Feminist Project. *Public Archaeology* 8(2–3): 225–45.

Moshenska, Gabriel. 2007. Oral History in Historical Archaeology: Excavating Sites of Memory. *Oral History* 35(1): 91–7.

—— 2008. Ethics and Ethical Critique in the Archaeology of Modern Conflict. *Norwegian Archaeological Review* 41(2): 159–75.

—— 2009. Resonant Materiality and Violent Remembering: Archaeology, Memory and Bombing. *International Journal of Heritage Studies* 15(1): 44–56.

—— 2010a. Gas Masks: Material Culture, Memory and the Senses. *Journal of the Royal Anthropological Institute* 16(3): 609–28.

—— 2010b. Working with Memory in the Archaeology of Modern Conflicts. *Cambridge Archaeological Journal* 20(1): 33–48.

Myers, Adrian. 2010. Camp Delta, Google Earth and the Ethics of Remote Sensing in Archaeology. *World Archaeology* 42(3): 455–67.

Renshaw, Layla. 2010. The Scientific and Affective Identification of Republican Civilian Victims from the Spanish Civil War. *Journal of Material Culture* 15(4): 449–63.

Saunders, Nicholas J. (ed.). 2004. *Matters of Conflict: Material Culture, Memory and the First World War*. London: Routledge.

—— 2007. *Killing Time: Archaeology and the First World War*. Stroud: Sutton.

Schofield, John (ed.). 2004. *Modern Military Matters: Studying and Managing the Twentieth-Century Defence Heritage in Britain—A Discussion Document*. York: Council for British Archaeology.

—— 2005. *Combat Archaeology: Material Culture and Modern Conflict*. London: Duckworth.

Scott, Douglas D. and Fox, Richard A. 1987. *Archaeological Insights into the Custer Battle: An Assessment of the 1984 Field Season*. Norman, OK: University of Oklahoma Press.

Simpson, Faye and Williams, Howard. 2008 Evaluating Community Archaeology in the UK. *Public Archaeology* 7(2): 69–90.

Zarankin, Andrés and Funari, Pedro Paulo A. 2008. Eternal Sunshine of the Spotless Mind: Archaeology and Construction of Memory of Military Repression in South America (1960–1980). *Archaeologies* 4(2): 310–27.

CHAPTER 26

....

DISASTER

....

RICHARD A. GOULD

26.1 INTRODUCTION: WHAT IS DISASTER ARCHAEOLOGY?

....

DISASTER archaeology defies conventional definition as an academic specialty. It can, however, be characterized operationally as the application of scientific skills in field archaeology following mass-fatality disasters to record and recover physical evidence, including human remains, to assist with victim identification and repatriation and to determine what happened at the disaster scene. Disaster archaeologists work under the oversight of the controlling authorities at each scene and according to the medical-legal standards of contemporary forensic science (see Powers and Sibun, this volume). Their results are combined with those of forensic anthropologists, odontologists, pathologists, DNA and fingerprint specialists, radiologists, and other expert practitioners as part of a team effort. The evidence assembled can and often does become part of court proceedings later to determine accountability, compensate victims and their families, establish (or rule out) criminality, and other legal issues arising from the disaster. These efforts place disaster archaeology within the domain of forensic as well as historical science.

26.2 CHARACTERIZING DISASTER ARCHAEOLOGY

....

Scholarly interest in ancient disasters is one of the oldest themes in archaeology, extending back to studies at Herculaneum and Pompeii beginning in the early eighteenth century (McConnell 1996). It continues today in the archaeological examination of battlefields, shipwrecks, and a variety of other human-made and natural disasters. Ancient disaster scenes, however, are not the primary subject of disaster archaeology, which has to do with modem disasters, especially those involving mass fatalities. How can the skills and theoretical approaches of archaeological scholarship as it has been traditionally practised be applied effectively to immediate and specific human needs following a mass-fatality disaster?

Disaster archaeology arises from a combination of humanitarian impulses and the rigorous application of the principles of forensic and historical science to find out 'what happened' at present-day disaster scenes. It is a practical, problem-solving approach to the recording, recovery, and analysis of physical remains and materials in the aftermath of the disaster. Many police and firefighters as well as investigative agencies like the FBI, the Joint POW/MIA Accounting Command (JPAC) of the US Army, and the National Transportation Safety Board (NTSB) already use archaeological methods in their work and are eager to develop and expand their skills. If performed up to current standards, disaster archaeology can aid in the process of victim identification and can provide reliable information about the physical circumstances surrounding the disaster and its aftermath. For the families of disaster victims it offers an element of emotional 'closure' as well as providing critical evidence in relation to post-disaster medical and legal issues during victim identification, property inheritance, and liability.

Disaster archaeology, like most traditional archaeology, is a team effort involving different specialists and a variety of skills. Unlike conventional archaeology, however, disaster archaeologists work under the direction and oversight of the controlling authorities at the scene, following uniform and widely accepted procedures such as the recovery process which can be prolonged and complex after a major, mass-fatality event. Emergency services agencies often tend to emphasize first responses over recovery in their periodic training, so disaster archaeologists can find themselves marginalized when such training occurs. Proactive efforts by archaeologists to organize and train on their own or in combination with agencies like the NTSB who recognize the importance of post-disaster recovery efforts is often required. This means that anyone planning to do this kind of work will need to identify and connect with community and state agencies that are already engaged in disaster planning. Police and firefighters are an obvious place to start this process of communication, but there are also local groups such as Community Emergency Response Teams (CERTs), Urban Search and Rescue Teams (USARs), and groups found under Volunteer Organizations for Assistance in Disasters (VOADs). Acronyms abound in all emergency-services and disaster-response activities, and disaster archaeology is no exception.

26.3 THE 'COURT OF LAW' VERSUS THE 'COURT OF HISTORY'

The term 'forensic' has Greek origins having to do with debate. This might seem odd, but it captures the reality of all forensic activities, which bear on the ability of the evidence to withstand challenges when presented in court or before a tribunal. That is where the actual debate occurs, and every piece of forensic evidence must be gathered and recorded in a manner that anticipates such challenges in the courtroom. Academics are already familiar with the peer-review process that applies to grant proposals and to many publications, where such challenges can also arise. In a court of law, however, lives, reputations, and fortunes are at stake, so the evidentiary standards are high and apply procedures that may be new or unfamiliar to most academically trained archaeologists. A succinct review of the relationship between forensic science and the law appears in Nordby (2005).

Important among these procedures is the *chain of custody* (aka chain of evidence) that must be maintained continuously from the point of evidence collection and recording to the courtroom (Melbye and Jimenez 1997). Any break in the chain can sow doubts in the minds of the jury. The evidence itself may be sound in every respect, but a failure in procedure along the custodial chain is sometimes all it takes to upset the verdict. Courtroom lawyers are trained to find and exploit anything that could create doubts and confuse the jury or judge, no matter how convincing the case might seem.

A typical chain-of-custody will include detailed notes, including sketches and photographs of the physical evidence and the scene where it was collected, to accompany the physical evidence. In many ways this part of the process is similar to good archaeological methods. What follows, however, is different. Each item of evidence is placed in a container or tagged—nowadays electronically—and its passage from hand to hand or into a facility like a police evidence room is recorded and signed off at every step to demonstrate who had control until the evidence appears in court. Trials often move slowly, so it may be years before the evidence is actually presented to a jury. While eyewitnesses may forget, die, or disappear during the lengthy process leading up to and during trial, the physical evidence (including documentation) will be preserved intact if custody was continuously maintained. Normal archaeological scholarship also requires care in the curation and handling of physical evidence, but rarely to this degree.

A related concern for disaster archaeologists and forensic scientists generally is the problem of *contamination* of evidence. In archaeological scholarship taphonomic issues may arise during the post-depositional history of a site, and similar issues occur at crime and disaster scenes. Many post-depositional factors can obliterate or obscure the physical associations in the archaeological record, leading to misleading or even false conclusions. Identifying and controlling for these factors is an area of expertise in which archaeology, along with other related historical sciences like geology and palaeontology, can contribute to the forensic integrity of a disaster scene. Examples of contributions from these historical sciences to forensic problem-solving are presented in Haglund and Sorg (1997, 2002), who address this issue as the 'postmortem fate of human remains'.

For other forensic sciences, especially DNA analysis and fingerprinting, *exclusionary evidence* is collected at the scene to control for contamination. Crime scenes (and disaster scenes) are always cordoned off with tape, and everyone who enters and leaves is logged in and out. Usually a path into the scene is flagged and followed by investigators to avoid trampling on undisturbed deposits and surfaces. Fieldworkers normally wear protective Tyvek suits and latex or nitrile gloves. These routine precautions, however, may be supplemented by the collection of DNA and/or fingerprints from each person who is logged into the scene during the investigation. Similar procedures apply to disaster archaeologists who work inside the demarcated scene in order to exclude their DNA and fingerprints from the total array of this kind of evidence collected there and to ensure that these can be separated from DNA or fingerprints left by people who were present and directly involved with the events at the scene.

Some forensic anthropologists and archaeologists have argued that conventional or academic archaeology lacks the scientific rigour needed to meet courtroom challenges, especially when the stakes are high. Interpretations that may be consistent with the physical evidence but do not necessarily follow from it are generally not acceptable in court, since they can be challenged by alternative (and equally convincing) interpretations, which weakens their credibility in front of a jury. Postmodernist or interpretive approaches are not well suited to the court of law, which is the domain in which disaster archaeology operates.

As a historical science, however, archaeology can—and often does—rise to the same level of credibility as other forensic sciences. An example of this can be seen in the archaeological studies of the Little Bighorn Battlefield in Montana following a grass fire in 1983 that exposed human remains, cartridges, and other battle-related items (Scott et al. 1989). Similar field methods and analysis were later applied in 1992 to sites at Koreme, where Iraqi Kurds were executed during the *Anfal* campaign of 1987–8 (Middle East Watch and Physicians for Human Rights 1993; Scott and Connor 1997) and similar investigations of a mass grave at the village of El Mozote resulting from the civil war in El Salvador in 1980–91 (Scott 2001). These cases offer a guide to connections between archaeology for research purposes and the application of archaeological methods to modem-day disaster scenes—both involving issues of human rights and genocide.

The requirements for credibility in the court of history and in the court of law are really the same if the results are to be taken seriously. Archaeologists are free to interpret their evidence as they wish and to embrace multiple interpretations as equally valid, but their credibility may suffer as a result. Multiple explanations are acceptable only if they follow directly from the evidence with the fewest possible assumptions and can be tested. The goal of the testing process is to find the hypothesis that best accounts for the available evidence. The implication is that, as alternative hypotheses are progressively ruled out, one will emerge as the best—at least until new evidence appears—meaning that disaster archaeology is *evidence driven*. There is no place for *ideologically driven* hypotheses or interpretations based on prior assumptions in disaster archaeology, no matter how logical or internally consistent they are. Disaster archaeologists engage in problem-solving in which there is only one correct (or best) answer to the problem.

With all historical science, the passage of time will degrade the evidence and produce varying degrees of uncertainty or incompleteness which must be recognized. A disaster scene can degrade quickly, for example, due to the movement of first responders and machinery across the site along with the activities of scavengers such as rats or carrion-eating birds. These realities accelerate the pace at which taphonomic factors operate compared with archaeology at more ancient sites. The process of generating and testing hypotheses about 'what happened' may take place within a shorter time frame than traditional archaeology, and methods that speed the work are important in disaster archaeology. The authorities at a disaster scene will always want to know how long it will take to accomplish the recording and recovery tasks. The only correct answer is, 'As long as it takes to get it right', but at the same time disaster archaeologists need to make use of remote sensing and mapping technologies that can speed the process while providing high levels of accuracy. Magnetometry and resistivity surveys have proved useful for locating buried sites, while GPS and the Total Station are now widely accepted as tools for rapid and reliable positioning during surveys and site mapping. GIS is a valuable tool for the post-processing of mapping data. Disaster archaeology is often 'archaeology at warp speed' compared to the more leisurely pace of scholarly research.

26.4 PROTOCOLS AND STANDARD PROCEDURES

The medical-legal requirements of forensic science place a special burden on disaster archaeologists and call for high levels of empirical scepticism in even the most mundane details of fieldwork and subsequent processing of physical evidence. At 'the Station' Nightclub fire scene in West Warwick, Rhode Island, in 2003, the first question our volunteer team, Forensic Archaeology Recovery (FAR), was asked by the Incident Commander was, 'What kind of protocol do you have?' Fortunately FAR had hammered out a protocol and a set of standard operating procedures (SOPs) a few months earlier and had them at the ready for inspection by the authorities. Operating protocols and SOPs require constant attention and updating in the light of new experience and advice, and FAR's have undergone many changes since then. These are living documents that evolve. Much of this evolution involves reviewing and adopting protocols used by other agencies, something which would be regarded as plagiarism in an academic setting.

Heading the list of issues in the protocol and SOP are the health and safety of the fieldworkers. Mainstream archaeologists today are generally more aware of health and safety issues than ever before and are more proactive in dealing with these issues (Poirier and Feder 2001), but the demands of disaster archaeology can be extreme. The safety clothing worn by fieldworkers at disaster scenes not only protects against contamination of physical evidence like DNA but, at the same time, protects the worker from contact with blood-borne pathogens (Hepatatis A and B and HIV/AIDS in particular) and other contaminants. Dust masks and respirators are important, too, with full-face, positive pressure respirators required in heavily contaminated atmospheres. Special measures may be needed to decontaminate fieldworkers' clothing as they leave the crime or disaster scene, and these vary according to the severity and nature of the contamination.

During its deployment to New Orleans and to St. Bernard and adjacent parishes in 2005 following Hurricane 'Katrina', for example, federal Disaster Mortuary Operational Recovery Team (DMORT) workers were fully covered with Tyvek suits and hoods, latex or nitrile gloves, high-topped rubber boots, and dust masks whenever they ventured into areas of standing water and mud. Each DMORT strike team was accompanied by a dedicated decontamination team that followed procedures ensuring that every fieldworker stepped through a cleaning pool and was washed down with a diluted Clorox solution before any outer clothing was removed. This was necessary because the water and mud throughout the area had become a 'toxic soup' of hydrocarbons, sewage, and decomposing remains. As the mud dried in certain places, it turned into contaminated dust. Even more extreme protective measures may be needed in situations involving biological or chemical agents and possibly even radiation, and the Federal Emergency Management Agency (FEMA) provides advanced training programmes at their centre in Anniston, Alabama, for emergency responders wishing to acquire these skills. Emergency-services protocols generally will not allow a fieldworker to enter such contaminated environments without this kind of training and certification along with the necessary protective clothing and equipment.

Any disaster archaeology team should plan to have a trained, full-time Safety Officer on scene at all times with the authority to stop work in hazardous situations when necessary. A dedicated Medical Officer should also be on scene along with ready access to emotional counselling. Responsibility for health and safety, however, cannot be delegated to these officers. While on scene, each fieldworker is expected to watch over other members of the task group to make sure than no one works alone and to be alert for any signs of distress.

Protocols and SOPs are a valuable safeguard in disasters where confusion and stress can be extreme. They are designed to ensure the safe, orderly, and controlled collection of evidence at the scene. This is a huge and complex subject that is better left to manuals and

FIGURE 26.1 Mass-fatality disasters always attract media attention and speculation. This *Providence Journal* article about 'the Station' Nightclub fire recovery contained elements of both. FAR, however, did not give interviews or speak to the press while the recovery was in progress and left that up to the West Warwick Police (photograph: Richard A. Gould)

training programmes. I recommend *The Scientific Investigation of Mass Graves: Towards Protocols and Standard Operating Procedures* (Cox et al. 2008) as an up-to-date guide to procedures that should govern disaster archaeologists as they collect, record, and process evidence under field conditions involving *human-rights archaeology* that closely resemble post-disaster recoveries.

Another domain that calls for protocols and SOPs is communication with the victims' families as well as with the press and media (Figure 26.1). Any team of disaster archaeologists will need to have or to work with a Public Information Officer (PIO) who is in constant contact with the authorities and can speak authoritatively and truthfully about the progress of the recovery operation. Misinformation is to be avoided at all costs. Unauthorized and inaccurate disclosure can damage the credibility of the entire recovery. There are also limitations on publication while post-disaster trials are proceeding through the courts—a process that can take years. During a field operation involving multiple agencies, 'speaking with one voice' is essential to avoid any misinformation. 'The Station' Nightclub fire in Rhode Island occurred in February 2003, and the last criminal and civil cases were not settled until January 2011. For academically trained archaeologists this can be frustrating, since open and timely publication is an important part of scholarship.

There are times, too, when field conditions may call for some departures from standard protocols, so field supervisors need to be flexible and adaptable to the ever-changing circumstances at a disaster scene. Not every contingency can be covered by existing protocols. Who, for example, realized that so many human remains would occur *outside* Ground Zero, the designated crime scene at the World Trade Center in New York? Special efforts were needed to recognize this problem and to persuade the authorities to think 'outside the box' about this issue (Gould 2007: 7–49). Or that the recovery and identification of skeletonized human remains washed out from shallow or above-ground cemeteries would become part of an 'expanded mission' by DMORT during the post-Katrina recovery effort (Gould 2007: 209)?

26.5 Victim Identification Following a Mass-Fatality Disaster

As noted earlier, disaster archaeologists coordinate their activities with other specialists to solve post-disaster problems, and foremost among these problems is victim identification. Disaster archaeologists are encouraged to have a good background in human skeletal biology as part of their overall training. Archaeology's role in the victim identification process relies upon established procedures followed by forensic anthropologists and other specialists (forensic pathologists, radiologists, fingerprint experts, DNA specialists, and dental experts [odontologists]) at their field morgue and in family assistance centres dispersed throughout the affected community. Victim identification following a disaster can be difficult in situations where human remains are fragmented or commingled and where medical and dental records may be unavailable.

In a typical post-disaster deployment, families and friends of victims are systematically interviewed at *family assistance centres* to collect data on the physical characteristics of each victim (age at death, biological sex, stature, ancestry, pathology, tattoos, body-piercing, etc.) as well as information about personal effects and clothing worn at the time of the disaster. Families are encouraged to bring in recent photographs of the victim if they have them. The data for each victim are entered into an electronic database (currently using the WIN-ID format) and in a paper file along with any medical or dental imaging and personal photographs to form an *ante-mortem file*.

Simultaneously, the forensic specialists at the field morgue record and enter similar data for a *post-mortem file* based on direct examination of the physical remains of each victim. Forensic anthropology profiling is important in cases where remains have become skeletonized, but these data comprise only *class-identification criteria*—that is, characteristics that can narrow down or rule out the identification of a victim but do not provide the information needed for an *individual identification*. DNA analysis, odontology, and fingerprinting can provide individual identifications, but only if sufficient evidence can be obtained from the victim's remains and if there are examples for comparison in existing DNA databases, fingerprint files, or dental records and images. Post-mortem data are entered electronically using WIN-ID and on paper forms along with information about clothing and personal effects recovered at the scene.

Finally, the ante-mortem and post-mortem files are systematically compared until positive matches are found, first using WIN-ID and then by visual inspection. Matching is a painstaking process, since the goal is not to declare an identification or release the remains until the results are certain. There can be only one right answer to solving this problem, and this is where 'getting it right' really matters. Much of the data being compared relies on archaeological recording at the scene and assumptions about the physical associations of human remains, personal effects, and other materials present there. Disaster- and crime-scene investigations are increasingly seeing the rigorous application of the principle of association along with a level of empirical scepticism that is a hallmark of good archaeological science.

26.6 RELEVANT THEORY IN DISASTER ARCHAEOLOGY

Many contemporary theories in archaeology address the issue of meaning in a variety of contexts and offer interpretations based on archaeological findings, usually based on anthropological concepts including the use of *critical theory* (Leone and Matthews 1996). As suggested earlier, these theories are often driven by ideological concerns. There is value generally in having archaeologists examine their dominant assumptions critically, especially when matters of politics and social control are involved, and disaster archaeology and human-rights archaeology are no exception. For example, archaeologists contracted by the US Army Corps of Engineers to investigate and record mass graves of Kurds executed by the Iraqi regime of Saddam Hussein (Drew and Mabile 2005) did an exemplary job of recording and recovering remains that provided evidence leading to the conviction of Hussein and his associates by the tribunal convened after his capture.

Lost in the rhetoric of outrage and injustice over the killings, however, was the fact that two of the original American rationales for the invasion of Iraq, which were to find unambiguous evidence of Iraqi weapons of mass destruction and links to al-Qaeda, had proved inconclusive (Keegan 2004: 99, 212–13). One could argue that the search for mass graves and findings of other genocidal acts by the Hussein regime then became an ex post facto case for the post-9/11 invasion of Iraq. Could it be that that the humanitarian efforts of human-rights archaeologists were used for political purposes by the American government to revive support for intervention in Iraq after it became clear that the original aims of the invasion had apparently fizzled out? Archaeologists always need to reflect critically upon the hidden agendas that may be present in situations like this, and this is true whether one formally espouses critical theory or not. Political and ideological issues often surround human-rights archaeology and other kinds of disaster archaeology and must be identified and taken into account, preferably before the investigation begins.

Disaster archaeology and human-rights archaeology share many of the same protocols and procedures as well as the same medical-legal expectations. Both kinds of archaeology arose in response to major, mass-fatality events coupled with a growing awareness of humanitarian needs surrounding such events. The concept of genocide is problematic and has been contested by scholars and diplomats. The reality of genocide, however, is evident in the occurrence of mass graves where victims have been categorized as a group, executed (often in large numbers), and then deposited *en masse*, often in unmarked locations. Sometimes these activities involve 'ethnic cleansing' (as occurred in the Former Yugoslavia), mass killings of prisoners of war (such as the Soviet massacre of Polish Army officers in the Katyn Forest near Smolensk in 1940 [Cienciala, Lebedeva, and Materski 2007]), or the politically motivated 'killing fields' of the Khmer Rouge in Cambodia. Human-rights archaeology was pioneered by Dr Clyde Snow in 1984 when he organized the Argentine Forensic

Anthropology Team (EAAF) to unearth and identify remains of people who 'disappeared' during the military junta of the 1970s. This work eventually led to further efforts of this kind in Rwanda and in the Former Yugoslavia in the mid-1990s by Boston-based Physicians for Human Rights under the auspices of the United Nations. Human-rights archaeologists continue to apply their special skills to the physical consequences of the practice of genocide, which has rightly been termed 'A Problem from Hell' (Power 2002).

Disaster archaeologists, like other forensic specialists, are expected to be careful not to confuse critical interpretations with conclusions based on factual evidence. Any attempt to introduce politically or ideologically driven interpretations as testimony in medical-legal proceedings can damage one's credibility and could taint the evidence with the appearance of prejudice. The practice of disaster archaeology requires theory that is grounded in the historical sciences. Taphonomy and general concerns with post-depositional effects on the physical characteristics and associations at disaster scenes are directly relevant to disaster archaeology along with both the basic and finer principles of association and superposition and the ways these processes can be affected under complex, real-world conditions. The aim is to find out what happened in the past, usually in the context of recent events. Disaster archaeology is not an experimental science, although it is often supported by laboratory methods in the physical, biological, and chemical sciences. One cannot simply re-run the past like a movie or a video. In this case, critical theory of a different kind applies. Forensic scientists and especially disaster archaeologists need to be rigorously empirical in the ways they collect and evaluate their evidence and, as empirical critics, are in a position to challenge assumptions about the use of that evidence when they construct bridging arguments that connect the past with the present.

In the courtroom eyewitness testimony and written documents are admissible, even though they may differ radically in their versions about what was observed. These can be viewed as alternative theories about what happened in a manner similar to alternative hypotheses in science. Forensic evidence can be used to test each version of events to see which one fits best. Following this approach, which is widely accepted in science and in the courts, the jury or judge is expected to choose the one version that follows most convincingly from the evidence. That choice could change if new evidence is introduced, and there are situations where none of the alternative versions of events presented by eyewitnesses or documents may fit the facts in evidence. Such cases have sometimes been decided based on a version of events derived entirely from the forensic evidence. In every case, however, and some archaeological theorists notwithstanding, the evidence does speak for itself if allowed to. Rather than try to construct a general theory of disaster archaeology here, we can turn briefly to a case study that reveals the interplay of historical science, the medical-legal issues in forensic science, and the kinds of critical awareness needed in disaster situations.

26.7 'The Station' Nightclub Fire, West Warwick, Rhode Island, 20 February 2003

At the time of writing, it has been over ten years since 'the Station' fire. All three of the criminal indictments, trials, and convictions are over, and the individuals involved have completed their jail terms. There were a further 46 civil suits arising from the fire, and these have recently been adjudicated or settled. The way is open now for a detailed archaeological report on the post-disaster work at the fire scene, preferably in a peer-reviewed journal. Meanwhile, a preliminary account of the disaster archaeology performed there can be found in Gould (2007: 50–68).

The humanitarian impulses and field experience in archaeology that led to the recovery work at 'the Station' were already evident in the response by FAR when they were invited by the Office of the Chief Medical Examiner (OCME) in New York City to perform a trial excavation outside Ground Zero following the events of 9/11. By then, FAR included members of the Providence Police, who participated fully in these excavations, along with students from Brown University and CUNY-Brooklyn College. The importance for FAR's work at 'the Station' a year later was that this initial foray provided training and visibility in the practice of disaster archaeology which led to further training, contacts with Providence firefighters and other emergency-services personnel, and recruitment, along with the development of a protocol and SOP. So when 'the Station' fire occurred there was a small but credible team in place that was known to the state and local authorities.

The fast-moving fire resulted from a pyrotechnic display by the rock band Great White, within a low-ceilinged and highly combustible space crowded with fans and partygoers. The exact number of people present has never been firmly established, but estimates suggest that it was well above the legal limit for that space. One hundred people died in the fire, and over 200 were horribly burned. First responders at the scene stated that if someone did not escape from the club within the first two minutes they did not survive. Except for the 1938 hurricane, this was the worst mass-fatality disaster in the history of Rhode Island.

The fire and the events surrounding it were recorded in graphic detail in a video produced for television Channel 12, a CBS affiliate in Providence, ironically to illustrate safety issues at crowded venues like nightclubs. The videotape became a primary piece of forensic evidence along with eyewitness accounts by survivors and first responders obtained at the scene or in interviews soon afterwards. DMORT was called in by the state almost immediately. Ante-mortem evidence was collected at the Family Assistance Center set up at the Crowne Plaza Hotel in Warwick, RI, while forensic specialists worked around the clock at the RI State Medical Examiner's Laboratory to collect post-mortem data and to match the two datasets. All of the victims were positively identified and the families were notified within three days.

Meanwhile, as first responders continued working at the scene, new issues emerged that called for a further post-disaster recovery effort there. The State Fire Marshal was tasked by the Governor's Office to perform a full archaeological recovery, and FAR was invited to do this under the Fire Marshal's oversight. I was still at work with the DMORT team at the State Medical Examiner's Laboratory when I received the call on my cell phone to activate FAR and proceed to the site immediately. We loaded our equipment in the middle of the night, and I went to the scene early the next morning to meet with the Fire Marshal (Irving Owens), the Incident Commander (Captain Catherine Ochs of the West Warwick Police), and other agencies. FAR's presence was clearly going to be a 'hard sell' in front of this experienced and sceptical group, although I knew they were aware of FAR's work at the World Trade Center in New York a year earlier. Captain Ochs had already asked for and seen our protocol and SOP. I told the assembled group that they should not just take our word for it that we would do a forensically acceptable job, but that they were welcome to observe the conduct of our activities and look closely at our results before making up their minds.

FIGURE 26.2 A FAR team recovers materials from 'the Station' Nightclub fire scene. The team included both Brown University archaeology students and Providence Police detectives. The paper bag being used here indicates that biological evidence is being collected (photograph: Richard A. Gould)

Officially FAR's mission was to recover personal effects (Figure 26.2) and transmit them via chain of custody to the evidence room at the Medical Examiner's Laboratory. This was true, but it was not the entire story. The Fire Marshal took me aside out at the site and told me that after major fires the general public swarms over the scene once the fences and crime-scene tapes are taken down. They collect almost anything they can find, including human remains, as personal souvenirs or for sale. Given the emotional and highly publicized nature of this tragedy within our tiny state, he was determined not to let that happen. Both of us had lived in Rhode Island for many years, and we appreciated the unique role of FAR to locate, record, and recover everything of a personal nature, essentially to pre-empt this kind of activity. For example, we both dreaded the thought of personal effects and human remains appearing later on eBay for sale or auction, and we agreed that this archaeological cleanup would be FAR's primary mission at the site.

Due to the intense heat of the fire and the physical damage caused by the panic and rush to the exits, burned and fragmented human remains were found at the scene in large amounts (Figure 26.3). They were recorded and entered as evidence, even though by then the victims had all been identified. Personal effects were located and recorded in the same way. Some items, like guitars and jewellery, were specifically sought by the victims' families, and most of these were found and restored to them. As the work progressed, FAR's mission expanded to include evidence that could bear on the origins of the fire and the patterning of remains in and around the escape routes. This evidence included such items as cell phones (some were still working when they arrived at the Medical Examiner's Laboratory) and bar-coded 'loyalty cards' (from supermarkets, for example) that could be swiped for the name of the cardholder.

FIGURE 26.3 FAR sieving teams at 'the Station' Nightclub fire scene, attended by both Brown University students and Providence Police detectives. Due to temperatures close to zero degrees F, wet sieving methods were not used (photograph: Richard A. Gould)

As suggested earlier, these kinds of evidence require a kind of empirical scepticism that is essential to good archaeological science. Cell phones sometimes rang inside the body bags at the ME's Laboratory and could be answered. It was easy to jump to the conclusion that such phones could identify the owners, but it was better to be cautious about making this assumption. Before suggesting a positive ID, it was necessary to establish the physical association of the phone with the victim—for example, if it was found inside a pocket or attached to a belt. Sometime cell phones were found by first responders in the loose fill near a victim's body and were scooped into the body bag, which was a weaker kind of association. It was also important to remember that people often borrow cell phones. Like clothing and other items, this evidence was entered into the post-mortem file to be compared with the ante-mortem data without making any prior assumptions. Similar strictures applied to loyalty cards.

Another issue arose during the archaeological mapping of the site. An experienced Providence policeman on our team asked me how our map related to the one done earlier by the West Warwick Police. He pointed out that in court these two maps of the scene would be compared for differences, which could be presented to the jury as discrepancies that would undermine the credibility of *both* maps and raise doubts in the minds of the jurors. My response was to label FAR's plan explicitly as an archaeological map and to include notes on how such a map serves different functions from a first-responder's plan of the site. This approach seems to have worked, since I was deposed but never called to testify about such supposed discrepancies. The intent here was to anticipate this kind of challenge so it would not become an issue during either the criminal or civil trials.

FIGURE 26.4 The aftermath of a mass-fatality disaster can be long and painful. Here relatives and friends of 'the Station' Nightclub fire victims gather at the site for the first anniversary of the event. Some of the impromptu memorial displays there are visible. These and other memorials are still present, over eight years afterwards, and they are tended regularly and visited often (photograph: Richard A. Gould)

As the work progressed, FAR's mission expanded to include evidence that the Fire Marshal thought might bear on the legal and medical issues surrounding the fire, such as remains of pyrotechnic devices as well as the locations of possible exits and the crowding that took place near them. This was a unique opportunity to systematically compare the videotape, eyewitness testimony, and physical evidence obtained archaeologically, and the resulting comparisons have produced a powerful account of what happened immediately before, during, and after the fire (Figure 26.4).

Without going into too much detail here, it should be clear that 'the Station' Nightclub fire recovery operation, which lasted from 27 February until the crime scene was closed on 9 March 2003, achieved credible results in a short time and under difficult winter conditions. The experiences there suggest that disaster archaeology will always involve tradeoffs between the time, personnel, and resources available as well as the operating conditions as opposed to the goal of absolute precision and detail. It may also involve high levels of physical and emotional stress, but the service it provides to the community is already evident.

26.8 THE DIRECTION OF DISASTER ARCHAEOLOGY

It would be a mistake to over-intellectualize an activity like disaster archaeology. While this work, and the comparable efforts of human-rights archaeologists, depends on scientific skills and academic expertise, the primary impulse for doing it arises from a humanitarian recognition of the urgent needs of victims' families and others affected in the aftermath of a mass-fatality disaster. Archaeological responses to mass-fatality events evolve as they adapt to each new situation. Established forensic procedures, emergency-services training, and skills grounded in good archaeological science will guide these efforts as we encounter new and unexpected events in the future. Archaeologists are trained to treat each site as unique, with the potential for unexpected findings, and to adapt their skills accordingly. This same philosophy of 'expecting the unexpected' permeates the outlook of other emergency responders of all kinds. The experiences so far with disaster archaeology have shown that it is possible to apply medical-legal protocols to achieve a degree of justice for the victims while, at the same time, providing a scientifically grounded basis for emotional 'closure' for their families. In short, disaster archaeology is already 'making a difference' in situations where it is needed and can be expected to continue to do this effectively.

References

Cienciala, Anna M., Lebedeva, Natalia S., and Materski, Wojciech (eds.). 2007. *Katyn: A Crime without Punishment*. New Haven: Yale University Press.

Cox, Margaret, Flavel, Ambika, Hanson, Ian, Laver, Joanna, and Wessling, Roland (eds.). 2008. *The Scientific Investigation of Mass Graves: Towards Protocols and Standard Operating Procedures*. Cambridge: Cambridge University Press.

Drew, Christopher and Mabile, Tresha. 2005. Desert Graves Yield Evidence to Try Hussein. *New York Times*, 7 June.

Gould, Richard A. 2007. *Disaster Archaeology*. Salt Lake City: University of Utah Press.

Haglund, William D. and Sorg, Marcella H. (eds.). 1997. *Forensic Taphonomy: The Postmortem Fate of Human Remains*. Boca Raton: CRC Press.

—— (eds.). 2002. *Advances in Forensic Taphonomy: Method, Theory, and Archaeological Perspectives*. Boca Raton: CRC Press.

Keegan, John. 2004. *The Iraq War*. New York: Alfred A. Knopf.

Leone, Mark P. and Matthews, Christopher. 1996. Critical Theory. In *The Oxford Companion to Archaeology*, ed. Brian M. Fagan, pp. 152–4. New York: Oxford University Press.

McConnell, Brian E. 1996. Herculaneum and Pompeii. In *The Oxford Companion to Archaeology*, ed. Brian M. Fagan, pp. 274–5. New York: Oxford University Press.

Melbye, Jerry and Jimenez, Susan B. 1997. Chain of Custody from the Field to the Courtroom. In *Forensic Taphonomy: The Postmortem Fate of Human Remains*, ed. William D. Haglund and Marcella H. Sorg, pp. 65–75. Boca Raton: CRC Press.

Middle East Watch and Physicians for Human Rights. 1993. *The Anfal Campaign in Iraqi Kurdistan*. New York: Human Rights Publication.

Nordby, Jon J. 2005. Countering Chaos: Logic, Ethics, and the Criminal Justice System. In *Forensic Science*, ed. Stuart H. James and Jon J. Nordby, pp. 637–47. Boca Raton: CRC Press.

Poirier, David A. and Feder, Kenneth L. (eds.). 2001. *Dangerous Places: Health, Safety, and Archaeology*. Westport, CT: Bergin and Garvey.

Power, Samantha. 2002. *'A Problem from Hell': America and the Age of Genocide*. New York: Basic Books.

Scott, Douglas D. 2001. Firearms Identification in Support of Identifying a Mass Execution at El Mozote, El Salvador. In *Archaeologists as Forensic Investigators: Defining a Role*, ed. Melissa A. Conner and Douglas D. Scott, pp. 79–86. Tucson: Society for Historical Archaeology.

Scott, Douglas D. and Connor, Melissa A. 1997. Context Delicti: Archaeological Context in Forensic Work. In *Forensic Taphonomy: The Postmortem Fate of Human Remains*, ed. William D. Haglund and Marcella H. Sorg, pp. 27–38. Boca Raton: CRC Press.

Scott, Douglas D., Fox Jr., Richard Allan, Connor, Melissa A., and Harmon, D. 1989. *Archaeological Perspectives on the Battle of the Little Bighorn*. Norman: University of Oklahoma Press.

CHAPTER 27

....

SCALE

....

MATT EDGEWORTH

27.1 INTRODUCTION

....

IT is all too easy for anyone in the contemporary world to lose their sense of scale. Not just spatial scales but timescales too. In Will Self's vertiginous short story, 'Scale' (1995), an opiate-addicted scholar researching a thesis on the subject of motorway service stations loses his, while exiting from the M40, in the interstices between inaccurately spaced countdown markers indicating the approaching slip road. The resulting merging of road networks with blood-vessel networks, normal-sized buildings with model villages, landscape with body, and so on, ends with an archaeological vision of the English countryside as viewed from the distant future, with timescales collapsed and motorways interpreted as key to understanding seven thousand years of landscape change, from the Mesolithic to the present day.

One way for archaeologists to avoid this scale-slippage and the vertigo entailed is to work securely within the traditional scale-range of the discipline. Safest of all would be to restrict study to hand-held artefacts, hand-excavated features, or buildings/layouts that can be comfortably inhabited or traversed by the body—on what might be called an embodied or body-sized scale of experience. It has been stated that 'As humans in the lived-in world, we are middle-sized objects and develop our knowledge up and down through the cosmos from this position' (Lock and Molyneaux 2006, xi; see also Finlayson, this volume). Being embodied human agents, it is not at all surprising that we feel most at home with artefacts such as pottery vessels that can be grasped and carried in two hands, or features like pits and ditches that we have to jump into in order to dig them out (Lucas 2004). Going outwards from there it would be best not to venture further than the study of landscapes or cityscapes in the upwards direction of scale or microscopic analysis of use-wear patterns in the downwards direction, for these effectively define the limits of archaeology as we know it. An added precaution would be to adhere to time-scales that do not stray too far from those of everyday tasks, human lifespans, or the 'longue durée' of historical change, for to go beyond these into the realms of the very slow (geological time) or the very fast (the speed at which computer processors operate, for example) would also be to overstep the traditional boundaries of the discipline.

But for us as archaeologists to suppose we can simply extend the perspectives developed in the study of ancient cultures onto the study of the more recent and the contemporary, and to imagine that it is business as usual, would be to make a serious mistake. Many of our most taken-for-granted tropes, assumptions, and methods can be questioned and rethought in the light of an archaeology in and of the present (Harrison 2011). As this chapter will show, it is almost impossible to practise archaeology of contemporary material culture without troubling settled notions of scale, and in doing so shifting the boundaries of archaeological inquiry. Disciplines are defined more by their scales of description and analysis than almost any other measure, and archaeology is no exception. Look at any archaeological photo or plan—of landscapes, sites, features, artefacts—and it will probably have a neatly drawn scale as an integral part of the depiction. It is not just that we scale objects or excavated phenomena: they also scale us, and predispose us to perceive and interpret them in particular ways according to that scale. It will be argued here that even the most innocuous modern artefacts have encapsulated within them multiple levels or scales of artefactuality, while at the same time being part of networks ordered through multiple levels of artefactuality on ascending and diminishing scales. Material culture today extends into the realms of the very large and the very small. It can be found in the form of artificial caverns scoured out from under the seabed to serve as stores for natural gas, configurations of satellites and space-junk in orbit around the Earth, invisible patterns of radio-waves that pass through walls and into outer space, and global networks of communication and exchange. Material traces of human handiwork—or at least the unintentional footprint left behind by human activities—can be found in climate patterns, cloud formations, the tides of the sea, and the flow of large rivers. It can also be found in the micro-engineered 'landscapes' of biological and physical systems at hitherto unimaginably small sizes, from artificially modified genetic materials and synthetic chemicals to nano-artefacts and nano-features hardly more than a single atom thick. It is therefore inevitable that scales of analysis will have to change to take account of modern materials and artefacts.

This chapter argues that archaeologists should follow material culture wherever it goes—on whatever scale archaeological patterning manifests itself—even if it entails breaking down or dissolving conventional boundaries between disciplines. Can there be archaeological study of the very large and the very small, the mega and the nano? Can archaeological excavation take place, at least as a thought experiment, on mega-quarries as large as cities or, at the other end of the scale, under the vibrating cantilever tip of an atomic force microscope? That depends on whether archaeologists are prepared to meet the challenges presented by contemporary materials and the multi-scalar realities enfolded and encapsulated within.

27.2 Transforming Archaeological Scales from the Outside-In

Spatial scales. In the last 50 years world population has expanded exponentially from three billion to seven billion. Computer processors have got smaller (and faster), and the invention of the Internet has opened up new digital and virtual spaces. Humans have travelled into space, sent modules with cameras to distant planets in our solar system, and set up networks of orbiting satellites around the Earth (see Cubitt, this volume; Gorman and O'Leary, this volume). Use of remotely controlled equipment extends the reach of human agency onto the surface of other planets and far below the surface of the Earth. The growth of supermarkets has rescaled even everyday activities like shopping. Meanwhile, development of electron microscopes and atomic force microscopes facilitates work on materials at nano-scales of operation, using nano-tools to create nano-artefacts and nano-features. The upshot of all this for archaeologists of the contemporary and recent past is that they are faced with a much wider array of interlocking and colliding scales (on which material culture is manifested and in terms of which it might be understood) than would be the case if studying the more ancient past. Computers have not only transformed scale but also our notion of what scale is. It is ultimately the sheer speed at which computers process information that has facilitated developments in space and nano-technology, for example.

Time scales. The archaeological record encompasses multi-temporalities (Lucas 2005: 48) and archaeologists operate within a multiplicity of time-scales, with 'nested durations' of different lengths (Gosden and Kirsanow 2006). Thus a discovered artefact can be interpreted in terms of inferred micro-events of manufacture or use, perhaps lasting no longer than a few seconds or minutes, and at the same time can be thought of in terms of much longer processes of technological development hundreds or thousands of years long. An important factor is the length of time that separates the archaeologist from the period when the artefact was thought to have been made or used. Archaeologists of the ancient past deal with long time-scales almost by definition, precisely because of the temporal gap between them and the pasts that are the objects of inference and investigation. But what happens when the focus is shifted onto material culture of the contemporary or recent past? Are archaeological time-scales foreshortened, flattened, multiplied, or lengthened as a result?

Spatial and time scales interlinked. Distance between signs on the motorway is as much to do with speed of traffic as it is to do with abstract spatial scale (see Tomlinson 2007). In his short story Will Self (1995) takes up the perspective of just one of millions of motorists moving along the paths of the motorway network. But of course it is the sum total of the actions of all those individual motorists that gives rise to the much greater phenomenon of traffic flow. This gives a clue as to how different scales are connected to each other. It is the countless repetitive actions and interactions of entities at smaller levels of analysis (movements of particles around a nucleus, or cars on a motorway) that give rise to structure and order at greater levels of analysis. In many cases connections between the very large and the very small can only be understood in terms of the very fast or the very slow. The Cern LHC or large hadron collider straddling the border of Switzerland and France is a case in point. With a total circumference of over 26 km, the particle accelerator is truly a megastructure. Yet the whole rationale of the subterranean building is to facilitate the passage of trillions of protons at almost the speed of light, with contrived particle collisions taking place 600,000 times a second when the collider is switched on at full power. The LHC produces 15 petabytes (a petabyte is a million gigabytes) of data annually. These are stored and analysed on a distributed computing infrastructure called the Worldwide LHC Computing Grid, which links tens of thousands of individual computers throughout the world. To understand what is going on, we have to think on very large and very small scales simultaneously.

27.3 TRANSFORMING ARCHAEOLOGICAL SCALES FROM THE INSIDE-OUT

While archaeology faces the challenge of how to deal with the increasing range of scales that it encounters in the material world 'out there', as it extends its scope of study forwards in time to cover ever more recent pasts, it also has to deal with the changing nature of its own technology and the increasing number of scales embodied therein. Being a constituent part of the contemporary world and a product of the recent past, it has itself been transformed by the very technological developments that might now be part of the subject/object of study.

Archaeologists have been quick to embrace multi-scalar technology. Out on site, dumpy levels and theodolites are increasingly being replaced by total stations and GPS global positioning devices. Remote sensing equipment in the form of magnetometers, resistivity meters, and ground penetrating radar systems enable them to investigate and envisage evidence far beyond the practical space immediately in front of the body. Mobile phones are as ubiquitous on archaeological sites as in any other workplace setting. But it is in the office where research, post-excavation analysis, and other indoor tasks take place that the greatest transformation has occurred. Offsite, archaeologists spend most of their time at the computer, to the extent that screenwork could be said to rival spadework as the principal activity of archaeology today. Computer apparatus brings with it new scales which have been speedily integrated into disciplinary ways of seeing and doing.

The introduction and rapid take-up of computer technology—and in particular the extensive use of geographical information systems (GIS)—has transformed material culture and working practices of archaeology over the last three decades or so. Look over the shoulder of a typical archaeologist at work today, in the place where they feel most at home, and you will see someone adept at shifting between scales at the touch of a button or click of a mouse, flitting at speed between radically different viewpoints on computer representations of landscapes and sites, perhaps with several screens open at the same time. A characteristic scenario might take the form of searching for sites on Google Earth, taking advantage of the easy access that geographical information systems provide to aerial photos and satellite mapping data, or building virtual reconstructions of landscape change at different temporal scales on ArcGIS or other geoprocessing software. Multi-scalar computer visualization is on the ascendancy in archaeology. A major trend in universities today is redirection of funds and resources away from excavation towards computer visualization projects—thereby signifying a shift in the material practices of the discipline and the scales of analysis that are embedded in respective technologies (Harris 2006). But this increasing emphasis on visual aspects of scale, if not counterbalanced by other kinds of work away from the computer, may lead to neglect or flattening out of tactile and textural dimensions of archaeological evidence. It might seem odd to think of scale as having any kind of texture to it, but multiple scales can gives rise to textural depth if similar patterns repeat themselves at different scales, indicating an underlying structure, and this is an aspect of contemporary material culture which will be explored in the rest of this chapter.

27.4 Unpacking Networks

Recently I went into a shop in London to buy a box of green tea, as a reward to myself for giving up smoking. I paid £10 for an impressive box of the best quality tea from China, but when I got home and opened it up I got something of a surprise. Instead of containing the expected tea it actually contained eight separate packets, each containing 20 cigarettes. The supposed box of tea was actually a box of smuggled cigarettes. I felt defrauded at first, and was about to take the box back. As I unpacked the contents, however, the realization dawned that I had inadvertently purchased something much more valuable than either green tea or cigarettes. The box contained a network—a multi-scalar network packed and encapsulated in material form!

In unpacking the contents something of the extent of the network unpacked itself too. Like a medium-sized Russian doll, the network seemed to extend in directions of smaller and larger scale on a series of ascending or descending levels. Each scale or level was represented by material objects which were also containers for further objects. Thus in the direction of descending scale the single box was actually a container for eight smaller packets, which exactly fitted the inside of the box. These packets in turn each formed perfectly sized containers for the neatly stacked cigarettes, which in turn formed cylindrical containers for tobacco, filter, and chemical additives (Figure 27.1).

Between each level was a layer of labelling and wrapping which conveyed (often false) information about what the contents were. For example, the golden box that had enticed me with elaborate Chinese letters and designs had a green cellophane seal with the now clearly false statement 'FRESH EVERYDAY TEA'. Likewise the cigarette packets were wrapped in transparent cellophane and a further envelope of golden paper, on which the brand name and the words 'KING SIZE FILTER TIPPED CIGARETTES' were printed (though in actuality they were probably counterfeit; the production of counterfeit cigarettes is closely tied in with the multi-million dollar industry of tobacco smuggling).

The logical progression of scales implies a continuation in the other direction of ascending scales too. In the unpacking of the contents of my box, it was obvious that it was once just one of many similar boxes, most of which contained cigarettes, though the ones on top probably contained tea in order to fool customs inspectors. While in transit these would have been neatly stacked inside similarly disguised larger crates, which in turn would have been stacked inside yet larger shipping containers (with appropriate labelling at each level to enable the deception to be carried out), which in turn were stacked on transporter ships, planes or trucks. Each scale of container implies different scales of operation with regard to the manufacture, distribution, selling, and consumption of the items—from individuals smoking cigarettes in particular times and places, to transactions between two or three people, to the more sustained effort put into the expert forging of brand packaging, to the industrial scale of illegal cigarette production, to the vast global organization of the smuggling operation and its many manifestations over multiple spatial and temporal scales.

Glimmerings of all this were revealed in the unpacking of the box. But it is not just that the opening up of the material object tells us something about the network of which it is a part. Something of the network was literally *packed into* the object, and the person who

(a)

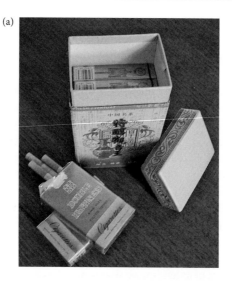

(b)

FIGURE 27.1 Multi-scalar network-in-a-box: (a) smuggled carton of 'tea' containing packets of cigarettes (photograph: Matt Edgeworth), (b) shipping containers, within one or several of which—it is inferred—trunk-loads of such packets may have been illegally transported (photograph: Jim Bahn 2006, CC by 2.0)

opens it, if not already a participant, inevitably becomes part of the network too, able to perceive some of its interrelationships. The 'network-in-a-box' could actually be demonstrated with almost any article purchased from a supermarket, but seems more visible here through the very fact of the network trying to hide itself, with false information and impressions generated at every level of wrapping and labelling. Such multi-level deception renders the ultimate discovery of the true nature of the contents all the more illuminating and revealing.

Now it might be pointed out that ancient artefacts such as Roman amphorae or Middle Palaeolithic hand axes were as much part of trading and communication networks as my box of 'tea', and also need to be understood on multiple scales of analysis. Archaeologists of ancient material culture do undoubtedly shift along a great spectrum of scales of analysis, from the examination of use-wear patterns on artefacts under electron microscopes to the study of whole landscapes (see Lock and Molyneaux 2006). But there is nevertheless an important sense in which contemporary material culture presents a much greater challenge to our use of scale, and that is because networks today extend so much further into the realms of the very large and the very small. Consider a mobile phone. The phone is usually encountered on an embodied scale of interaction just like a pottery vessel or a hand axe. It has been scaled to fit the size and capabilities of the human body, especially the hand and the fingers (and distance between the mouth and the ear). But it cannot be fully grasped on an embodied scale alone. The mobile phone is an intrinsic component of systems and networks that extend far beyond personal and even global limits, with messages routinely routed to and from orbiting satellites. On the other hand the phone is partly made up of micro-components that extend beyond the bounds of the visible into realms of the unimaginably small and incredibly fast. The simple act of making a phone call brings into play multiple spatial and temporal scales simultaneously.

The point is that all people alive today and all contemporary material culture items are caught up in networks which simultaneously exist on the scales of very large and very small. Such multi-scalar networks are 'packed in' to even the most simple and most innocuous objects and containers; these are part and parcel of what needs to be 'unpacked' if their archaeological significance is to be fully understood. That is just one essential reason why contemporary material culture is different from more ancient material culture, and why it raises new challenges for archaeologists.

27.5 THE FRACTAL DIMENSION OF ARCHAEOLOGICAL PATTERNING

The instance of the smuggled goods described above leads us on to a consideration of whether fractal patterns can be observed in contemporary material culture. Fractals can bridge the chasm between scales. It would open up a new form of analysis for archaeologists (not to mention police detectives and forensic scientists) if material patterning characteristic of a particular group or type of activity was manifested at multiple levels or scales. In the case of smuggling networks and counterfeiting gangs, for example, can patterns observable at the large scale of crates and shipping containers be recognized at the smaller level of cigarette packets and 'tea' cartons, and vice versa? It is well known that fractals can be observed in archaeological evidence (Eglash 1999; Brown et al. 2005). The question I want to examine here is whether archaeological features—with their associated cuts and fills—themselves have a fractal dimension to them. Features like pits and postholes are usually encountered (and were originally created) on an embodied scale of perception and action. My question is, given that human action now extends into hitherto unimagined realms of the very large and the very small, might we not expect to find similar patterns on those levels too? Can we use the fractality of archaeological features themselves to explore connections between vastly different scales of contemporary material culture—to span the chasm between the familiar scale of everyday experience and the less familiar scales of the mega and the nano? To take a simple example, subterranean undersea salt caverns utilized as storage containers for natural gas (Edgeworth 2010a) are similar, in form as well as function, to pits for storing grain often found on Iron Age settlement sites. The principal difference, of course, is that Iron Age pits are encountered by archaeologists and were created by people in the past on an embodied scale, using hand-held tools to dig them out. The salt caverns, on the other hand, are created through the use of drilling and pumping equipment operated remotely from the surface. They exist on a mega scale which dwarfs the embodied scale of human beings and their everyday world.

But these features are relatively small compared to some aggregate quarries. A new open-cast limestone quarry proposed for south-western Ontario may cover up to 2,300 acres and be over 200 feet deep—as large as a medium-sized city in lateral extent and somewhat deeper than Niagara Falls. Yet for all their vast size such features have clearly identifiable 'cuts' and 'fills' just like ordinary pits do. Were future archaeologists (equipped with the necessary machinery) to put a section through clay pits associated with brick-works in Bedfordshire, for example, they would find a sequence of different layers of 'landfill' not dissimilar from the sequences of stratigraphy encountered in the excava-tion of prehistoric, Roman, medieval, or post-medieval rubbish pits. The various layers of landfill could be dated and traced to particular cities from which they originated, and the sequence of dumping reconstructed into a series of events, using recording and analytical techniques familiar to archaeologists today (indeed, the innovative Tucson Garbage Project has been carrying out archaeological analyses of landfill deposits since the 1980s—see Rathje 1992; see Reno, this volume). In excavating out landfills, a skilled machine operator could use a dragline excavator to follow down the cut of the quarry rather as an archaeologist might follow down the cut of an ordinary-sized pit with his or her trowel. The only essential difference—and it is an immense one—would be one of scale (Figure 27.2).

Moving to a different scale, now consider the recent 'excavation' of a computer chip, carried out by software engineer Greg James. The chip in question was the MOS Technology 6502, manufactured in the 1970s and used in early Apple and Commodore computers. Although tens of millions were sold, the technology is now obsolete and the details of its design lost. Excavation of a chip bought for a few dollars from a car boot sale involved removing successive layers through application of acids and other chemicals (the excavation 'site' in this instance measuring only 4 × 3.5 mm). After first removing the plastic casing, the top layer of thick metal wiring was taken away to reveal the maze of thin polysilicon wires forming circuits and transistors. This act of revelation and dis-covery was compared to 'the moment when, in a real-world excavation, archaeologists can observe a landscape of artifacts, like canals or foundations of homes'. After careful mapping and recording, this layer was also removed to reveal the silicon wafer 'substrate'. Following usual practices of archaeological recording, photographs were taken of each successive layer uncovered. These were subsequently enlarged during post-excavation analysis and used to reconstruct the paths of logic flow through the circuitry—enabling virtual working models of the chip to be made based on the information uncovered (Swaminathan 2011).

At a microscopic level too, human artefacts and artificial features proliferate. When Michael Lynch carried out his ethnographic study of a neuroscience lab (Lynch 1985), he

(a)

(b)

(c)

FIGURE 27.2 Archaeological features at different scales: (a) mega quarry at Bingham Canyon, Utah—an open-pit copper mine (photograph: Tim Jarrett 2005, CC by 3.0), (b) rubbish pit encountered and re-excavated during archaeological dig at Jewry Street, Winchester (photograph: Wessex Archaeology 2005, CC by 2.0), (c) holes etched into carbon nanowires with a high energy electron beam. The scale in the picture is about 7 nanometres in length (reproduced with permission from Alexey Bezryadin, Physics, UIUC)

noted that scientists spent much time dealing with complex material phenomena they call 'artefacts'—traces of their own agency on objective material evidence. There is an imperative for lab scientists to distinguish between these artefacts of scientific practice and other non-artefactual patterns which were the main object of their activity. The problem encountered is that the artefactual and the real are often completely entangled (a difficulty not specific to scientists in the lab, but to all investigators of materials, including archaeologists). I was intrigued not only by Lynch's findings but also by the way he employed a range of archaeological concepts and metaphors to make sense of his data. Accordingly, I followed up Lynch's study with a short and speculative paper that dealt with the question of whether an archaeological study of scientific discovery would be possible, on a wholly different scale from that on which excavation is usually carried out (Edgeworth 2009). Looking at some of many archaeological features photographed on a thin section of human muscle through the medium of an electron beam microscope, I concluded that these were no different in principle—only in scale—from the kind of archaeological features we are more accustomed to dealing with on an embodied level of experience (also partly artefacts of our own creation).

It is important for us to traverse scales in this way if we are to begin to grasp the immense textural depth of artefactuality in the contemporary world, extending both upwards in the direction of the very large and downwards in the direction of the very small. We start from the embodied level of our own everyday world, which can be described as a complex mix of human and non-human, cultural and natural. Let us say that it has deep artefactuality to it, without implying that it is wholly constructed or manufactured. I suggest that in the same way the material world is also deeply structured artefactually at megascopic and microscopic levels, not only by the implements used to investigate that world (as in the above example), but also by manipulations of the world made possible through wider developments in computer technology, genetics, bio-engineering, synthetic chemistry, and other fields. Thus the muscle tissue examined in a neuroscience lab today may have already have been bio-engineered before being thin-sectioned—in the sense of being grown artificially, treated with hormone, genetically modified, or subject to any number of other types of intervention. That is, its microscopic structure bears multiple material traces of human agency even prior to the act of investigation.

Much the same is increasingly true at a nanoscopic level—many times smaller than the microscopic, so small that normal rules of physics do not necessarily apply—for here too archaeological features and patterning are to be found. Indeed, the observation of phenomena at this scale is inseparable from the cutting and creation of features, or the active intervention into the structure of the material under investigation. In Edgeworth (2012) I described the world's smallest transistor, barely ten atoms across and one atom in thickness. It was carved using an electron beam microscope to fire a beam of electrons across the surface of a sheet of graphene—a membrane so thin it has to be supported by other nano-materials in order for an array of nano-instruments to manipulate them (Westervelt 2008). For a similar account of etching holes in carbon nanotubes and metallic nanowires using a highly focused electron beam, see Aref et al. (2008). Despite vast differences in scale between this level of reality and that of normal archaeological sites, there is also much in common. At both levels there are artefacts that have been made which can be used to shape other things, features that have been cut, architectures that have been designed, structures that have been assembled, layouts that bear the imprints of human thought and action upon them. The boundaries of nature and culture are being redefined on scales of the very small and the very fast. Even the genome of humans and other species can now be directly manipulated using latest DNA technology. Ongoing developments in fields of nanotechnology, genetic engineering, synthetic chemistry, and computer processing are reconstituting material culture on a fundamental level, with resonances and repercussions that reach through to every other scale too, and have massive impact on global systems. Archaeologists need to track these changes, and must be willing to move onto hitherto unfamiliar scales of analysis in order to do so.

27.6 ARCHAEOLOGY AND THE ANTHROPOCENE

Until recently we thought we were living in the Holocene epoch—a warm and stable part of the Quaternary period. But now some biochemists and geologists are suggesting that we may have moved into an entirely different geological epoch, characterized by human impact on Earth systems (Williams et al. 2011). Though not yet formally accepted into standard geological time-frames, the Anthropocene has become one of the hottest topics of interdisciplinary debate, with relevance to some of the most difficult and pressing problems facing human beings today.

The concept of the Anthropocene is not without its problems, including the difficulty of dating its beginning. The very name 'Anthropocene' accords too much primacy to human over non-human agencies, lacking inherent 'symmetry' (Latour 1993: 136; Webmoor and Witmore 2008; Olsen, this volume; Webmoor, this volume). But while acknowledging that its name embodies some possibly mistaken assumptions, it is nevertheless a potentially useful way of framing the contemporary world across disciplines. I have argued elsewhere (Edgeworth 2010b, 2011) that archaeologists have a part to play in this interdisciplinary debate, and a necessary role in the formulation of the very concept of the Anthropocene, but archaeologists are somewhat constrained by the established spatial and temporal scale-range of their discipline. Geologists and other natural scientists are likewise constrained by their own respective disciplinary scales, although geologists have started to make use of archaeological stratigraphy (which they call 'artificial ground') as a marker for the Anthropocene.

Yet if scales of analysis would allow, greater creative contact between the two disciplines would surely lead to important insights concerning the structure of the Anthropocene as manifested across different scales. Proponents of the new geological epoch place so much emphasis upon the intentional and unintentional effects of human agency at a global scale, or potential effects of vast geo-engineering projects, it sometimes seems as though the Earth in the Anthropocene is being characterized as a giant artefact, and that an implicit theory of material culture is being applied to it. But while the proposed new geological epoch tends to be envisaged by geologists in terms of processes which are very large and relatively slow, it actually exists simultaneously on much smaller and faster levels too. Evidence reviewed in this chapter leads to the view that the Anthropocene (or whatever we choose to call the present phase of human–material interaction on a global scale) is fractally structured and has textural depth: that is, apparent artefactuality observed at the global scale is a manifestation and indication of deeper underlying artefactual structures at multiple scales, none of which have primacy over others. To properly understand what is happening to Earth systems, then, we would have to explore processes at all these multiple interconnecting scales, going right the way down beyond the embodied and microscopic levels to the scale of the nano, and right up beyond the global to the interplanetary scale (see Gorman 2005, 2009). Archaeologists can play a key role in this.

If we follow Zalasiewicz's (2008) thought experiment and imagine the material traces of a large city as it would be encountered in outcrops of stratigraphy 100 million years from now, a range of archaeological features and artefacts would be found at every size and scale from the nanoscopic to the megascopic, as well as in the medium or body-scaled material culture with which we are more familiar. But why wait 100 million years—when the human race will presumably be extinct, and the evidence for its civilizations fossilized—to study material culture patterning at all scales of its manifestation? Why not study it now?

REFERENCES

Aref, Thomas, Remeika, Mikas, and Bezryadin, Alexey. 2008. High-Resolution Nanofabrication Using a Highly Focused Electron Beam. *Journal of Applied Physics* 104: 1–6.

Brown, Clifford T., Witschey, Walter R. T., and Liebovitch, Larry S. 2005. The Broken Past: Fractals in Archaeology. *Journal of Archaeological Method and Theory* 12(1): 37–78.

Edgeworth, Matt. 2010a. Beyond Human Proportions: Archaeology of the Mega and the Nano. *Archaeologies* 6(1): 138–49.

—— 2010b. Archaeologists Should Grapple with the Anthropocene too. University of Stanford, Archaeolog website. Available at: <http://traumwerk.stanford.edu/archaeolog/2010/06/archaeologists_should_grapple.html> (accessed 7 July 2011).

—— 2011. Archaeology and Current Debate on the Anthropocene. *Norwegian Archaeological Review* 44(1): 59–62.

—— 2012. Fields of Artefacts: Archaeologies of Contemporary Scientific Discovery. In *Modern Materials*, ed. Brent Fortenberry and Laura McAtackney, pp. 7–12. British Archaeological Reports 2363. New York: Archaeopress.

Eglash, Ron. 1999. *African Fractals: Modern Computing and Indigenous Design*. New Brunswick: Rutgers University Press.

European Organisation for Nuclear Research. Website on Cern large hadron collider. Available at <http://public.web.cern.ch/public/en/lhc/Facts-en.html> (accessed 22 July 2011).

Gorman, Alice C. 2005. The Cultural Landscape of Interplanetary Space. *Journal of Social Archaeology* 5: 85–107.

—— 2009. The Gravity of Archaeology. *Archaeologies* 5(2): 344–59.

Gosden, Chris and Kirsanow, Karola. 2006. Timescales. In *Confronting Scale in Archaeology: Issues of Theory and Practice*, ed. Gary Lock and Brian Molyneaux, pp. 27–37. New York: Springer.

Harris, Trevor M. 2006. Scale as Artifact: GIS, Archaeological Analysis, and Ecological Fallacy. In *Confronting Scale in Archaeology: Issues of Theory and Practice*, ed. Gary Lock and Brian Molyneaux, pp. 39–53. New York: Springer.

Harrison, Rodney. 2011. Surface Assemblages: Towards an Archaeology *in* and *of* the Present. *Archaeological Dialogues* 18(2): 141–61.

Latour, Bruno. 1993. *We Have Never Been Modern*, tr. C. Porter. Cambridge: Cambridge University Press.

Lock, Gary and Molyneaux, Brian (eds.). 2006. *Confronting Scale in Archaeology: Issues of Theory and Practice*. New York: Springer.

Lucas, Gavin. 2004. Modern Disturbances: On the Ambiguities of Archaeology. *Modernism/modernity* 11(1): 109–20.

—— 2005. *The Archaeology of Time*. London: Routledge.

Lynch, Michael. 1985. *Art and Artifact in Laboratory Science: A Study of Shop Work and Shop Talk in a Research Laboratory*. London: Routledge & Kegan Paul.

Rathje, William. 1992. *Rubbish! The Archaeology of Garbage*. New York: HarperCollins.

Self, Will. 1995. *Scale*. London: Penguin Books.

Swaminathan, Nikhil. 2011. Digging into Technology's Past. *Archaeology* 64(4). Available at: <http://www.archaeology.org/1107/features/mos_technology_6502_computer_chip_cpu. html> (accessed 27 July 2011).

Tomlinson, John. 2007. *The Culture of Speed: The Coming of Immediacy*. London: Sage Publications.

Webmoor, Tim and Witmore, Chris. 2008. Things Are Us! A Commentary on Human/Things Relations under the Banner of a 'Social' Archaeology. *Norwegian Archaeology Review* 41(1): 53–70.

Westervelt, Robert. 2008. Graphene Nanoelectronics. *Science* 320(5874): 324–5.

Williams, Mark, Zalasiewicz, Jan, Haywood, Alan, and Ellis, Michael. 2011. The Anthropocene: A New Epoch of Geological Time? *Philosophical Transactions of the Royal Society* 369: 1938.

Zalasiewicz, Jan. 2008. *The Earth After Us: What Legacy Will Humans Leave in the Rocks?* Oxford: Oxford University Press.

PART III

MOBILITIES, SPACE, PLACE

CHAPTER 28

....

ALUMINOLOGY:
AN ARCHAEOLOGY OF
MOBILE MODERNITY

....

MIMI SHELLER

> For the day of lightness is here. The swan song of needless weight is being sung.
> Aluminum has become the *speed metal* of a new and faster age.
>
> ALCOA's Fiftieth Anniversary Message, *Fortune*, 1936

28.1 INTRODUCTION

....

IN the social sciences there has been growing interest in the study of the material and infra-structural systems that support various mobilities of people, objects, and information, including the immobilities of borders, walls, and gates (Urry 2000, 2007; Hannam et al. 2006; Sheller and Urry 2006). This has been accompanied by research on histories of mobility, whether as spatial relations, constructed meanings, or lived experiences of various kinds of (im)mobility (Cresswell 2006). This mobilities turn has significant implications for archaeologies of the contemporary world. On the one hand, it introduces new perspectives on the physical traces of mobility that have shaped various landscapes (e.g. Nesbitt and Tolia-Kelly 2009; Witcher et al. 2010). On the other hand, as pursued in this chapter, mobilities research enables a critical purchase on contemporary material cultures as evidence of particular practices of mobility that have shaped social relations and human–natural relations on a global scale (see Edgeworth, this volume). Although this work is not grounded in the discipline of archaeology, the study of 'metallic modernity' opens up a space for thinking about the material remains that contemporary cultures of mobility have left on the Earth, and beyond, in outer space.

Aluminium is deeply implicated in modern material cultures, practices, and ideologies of speed and mobility that are definitive of the twentieth century and its remnant traces of the future. The physical qualities of aluminium led to the modern dream of frictionless, high-speed travel and gravity-defying flight. This light metal became crucial to the twentieth century not simply as a new material out of which to make particular objects, but because it contributed to an entire shift in the style of 'stuff'. Over the course of around fifty years, from 1910 to the

1960s, aluminium came to play a crucial part in the transportation, electrical, construction, aeronautics, and ship-building industries, as well as in domestic design, architecture, technical equipment, and all kinds of banal aspects of everyday life (from packaging and fasteners, to antiperspirants and makeup, frying pans and Christmas trees). Once you start looking for it, it is everywhere, entering into the design and manufacture of so many artefacts that it fundamentally changed the affordances of the built environment and the motilities of the human body.

Walter Benjamin wrote eloquently about the cultural impact of cast iron, which contributed new materials and visions for the transformation of Paris in the 1820s–1850s into a glittering city of arcades, grand boulevards, and exciting railways. In his seminal *Arcades Project* he spins out a web of cultural connections from the cast iron structures of the gas-lit arcades, to the new department stores, and the cavernous railway stations, into an entire world of capitalist spectacle and new modern attitudes. This was the beginning of a movement towards modernity, and a fascination with the speed of the galloping stagecoach, and soon the steaming locomotive thundering on its iron rails, with the instantaneity of daily newspapers and the fascination with kinetoscopes and moving pictures. But the electrochemical smelting of aluminium (discovered simultaneously by two twenty-year-old inventors in France and the USA in 1886), would open whole new vistas in the quest for speed and lightness. It would bring the apotheosis of speed, new architectures of luminosity, and the conquest of aerial space that nineteenth-century writers like Jules Verne dreamed of, thrilled at, and feared (see Figure 28.1).

FIGURE 28.1 Alcoa Aluminum Advertisement, *Fortune Magazine*, 'Peer Into the Future', 1930s (public domain image original copyright Alcoa)

The combination of electricity and electrochemical production of metals has been called the second industrialization, replacing the classic canals, water-power, coal, iron, and steam power of the first industrial revolution. We might think of this as a shift from heavy to light modernity. Aluminium initiated this shift, and was later joined by other light substances such as plastics, fibreglass, and nylon, all spun off from the petrochemicals industry. Thus an archaeology of modernity requires an excavation of aluminium, an unravelling of its infusion into the materialities and spatialities of the twentieth century as integument, prosthesis, and infrastructure for mobility (see Merriman, this volume). It also remains with us in the twenty-first century as a renaissance material for the 'green' design of a lighter, recyclable set of transition technologies that claim to reduce our carbon footprint.

28.2 THE AGE OF ALUMINIUM

In the mid-twentieth century the aluminium industry pioneered a modernist design aesthetic around its products through an entire culture of product research, cutting-edge design, and technological development. Just as cast iron shaped the city of Paris in the age of the railways and the flâneur, aluminium transformed states of mind as much as states of matter. Marketing departments promoted its ideological attraction, as much as its physical properties, to generate the affective resonance of a light modern material suitable for remaking the world of the future (Hachez-Leroy 1999). All that is shiny, new, and aerodynamic is brushed with the gleam of aluminium, attracting our attention like children marvelling at the bullet-shaped Airstream trailer, a beautiful Eames chair, or the perfect planetary sphere of the Russian Sputnik satellite.

Aluminium made its way into so many places and products in part because it has special qualities as compared to other metals, both in pure form and in alloys. The weight of aluminium is about one-third of an equivalent volume of steel (with a specific gravity of 2.70 versus steel's 7.85), making it especially attractive in the aviation and transport industries, lightweight packaging and fasteners. Aluminium also has a natural oxide layer on its surface that protects it from various types of corrosion, so it is far more durable than other metals. It will not rust like iron, or turn green like copper. It can be painted, plated, or anodized to produce various surface finishes. Because it is non-ferrous, it does not cause sparks, so can be safely used in electronics and in the oil and gas industries. It is also incombustible, weldable, and has good electrical and thermal conductivity, making it an ideal building material that can replace copper in many applications (Wilquin 2001: 10, 12–13).

In the form of cables it moves our electricity, without which many other things would not be able to move. A 1929 advertisement by the Aluminum Company of America declared 'This is the Age of Aluminum':

> Aluminum is acting as the vehicle for the transmission of that most intangible of all travelers—electricity. Hundreds of thousands of miles of Aluminum Cable of every conceivable size—from the great 220,000 volt high tension lines to the small telephone wire—weaves its web of civilization across the countryside . . . bringing light and sound communication and power.
> (Records of Alcoa, 1857–1992, Heinz History Center, Pittsburgh, PA [HHC], MSO 282, 'Aluminum Company of America', *Business Week*, 25 December 1929)

Without 'aluminum cable steel reinforced' national energy grids would not exist because 'ACSR permits the use of longer spans, fewer poles' ('The A-B-C's of Aluminum', Reynolds Metals Company [Louisville, Kentucky, 1950], p. 26). Heavier copper transmission cables are expensive, require almost 50 per cent more pylons per mile, being heavier and harder to erect. Thus aluminium shapes infrastructures and remakes the 'spatio-temporal fixes' (Jessop 2006) that stabilize certain kinds of spatial patterns and their associated mobilities.

Aluminium is also very malleable and versatile compared to other metals, thus it moves around the world, changing shape as it moves. Its myriad fluid forms change the places in which we dwell and the infrastructures that enable our movements. It can be machined, shaped, extruded, and recycled. It can be turned into sheets, wire, castings, alloys, and forgings, thus creating innumerable useful products. Aluminium quickly revolutionized packaging, starting with foil cigarette wrappers and chocolate wraps, and extending into all kinds of foil, lids, linings, and above all the lightweight aluminium can. In terms of the wider food system, from farm to fork, the lightness of aluminium helps farmers more easily move water into their fields, feed and fence their animals, process and store their crops. Aluminium vats serve in canteens, food-processing plants, breweries, and bottling plants, helping to industrialize modern food systems. Aluminium foil perhaps sums up best what is miraculous and beautiful about aluminium. It is part of many people's everyday home life as food cover, pan liner, cooking device, arts and crafts material; always useful, fun, decorative, and hard to live without (see Figure 28.2).

It also revolutionized the capacity of the human body for prosthetic mobility. Around the house it brought us far lighter and more portable equipment: ladders, folding chairs, window frames, screens, outdoor furniture, and canoes. It enables those with limited mobility to

FIGURE 28.2 Alcoa Aluminum Advertisement, *Saturday Evening Post*, 'Christmas Creations of Light, Lasting, Lustrous Aluminum', 3 December 1955 (public domain image original copyright Alcoa)

move again with the assistance of prostheses such as crutches. A seemingly mundane even ugly piece of technology, the walker (or 'Zimmer frame') allows millions of elderly people to continue to live active lives. Aluminium has just the right combination of strength, lightness, and flex to enhance the natural capabilities of the human body to move. It especially contributed to the emergence of lightweight mobile devices, from the revolutionary Sony Walkman in the 1970s to the iconic Apple MacBook laptop computer machined out of a sharp-edged slab of aluminium.

Lightness combined with strength associated aluminium with speed and a 'new and faster age', as Alcoa's fiftieth anniversary message printed in *Fortune* magazine in May 1936 described it. The incorporation of aluminium into road vehicles began with the aluminium crankcase of the 1897 three-wheeled Clark, then the stunning Rolls Royce 'Silver Ghost', in which the entire body, as well as many engine parts, were aluminium; and the much-coveted 1930 Duesenburg boasted a hand-fashioned aluminium body ('Uses of Aluminum', The Aluminum Association, New York [1965], p. 9). Today a new aluminium alloy graces the inner structure of the Audi A8 where it contributes to 'enhanced performance, quicker handling and better fuel consumption'.

The use of aluminium in the design of streamlined aerodynamic forms grew out of the aviation industry and its associations of the metal with speed and lightness. The appeal was as much aesthetic and as practical or pragmatic. For example, pilot and inventor William Hawley Bowlus, who supervised the construction of Charles Lindbergh's *Spirit of Saint Louis* in 1927, pioneered the use of Duraluminium in trailer design in the early 1930s. Travel trailers, pulled behind cars, transferred the materials, feel, and aerodynamic form of airplanes back down to ground-based transportation vehicles. When salesman Wally Byam purchased the Bowlus travel-trailer company in a bankruptcy auction in 1936, its light egg-shaped vehicles became the basis for Airstream Inc. The Airstream epitomizes the aesthetic appeal of aluminium, beckoning to us even today through what sociologist Harvey Molotch refers to as its 'semiotic handle' (Molotch 2005: 82), its aesthetic or material feel, which catches our attention and desire through what it signifies as much as what is does.

The Airstream suggests mobility, lightness, aerodynamic speed, durability, and with these qualities implies American values such as the freedom of the road, liberation from a fixed abode, casual easy living, and maybe even the innocent optimism of modern technology. It allowed for the dynamic domesticity of the mobile home, symbol of American road culture and American ideals.

28.3 AIR POWER

Aluminium's most significant quality is its gravity-defying capacity to make human flight possible. Is it possible to have an archaeology of the air? And what if the material culture of aeriality is deeply implicated in the destructive forces of warfare? Perhaps no one would be surprised to learn that over 30 per cent of global aluminium production goes into the automobile and aviation industries, but few people realize that another 30 per cent goes into military applications. Early military uses were crucial to the development of new markets for the metal, military and later civilian aviation became the most important industry in the widespread use of aluminium, beginning with frames, instruments, and propellers, and extending to many other parts of the aircraft.

During the First and Second World Wars about 90 per cent of US aluminium production went into military uses. In many ways what Eisenhower called the 'military-industrial complex' was (and remains) very much a 'military-aluminium complex'. During the First World War US military requirements for 1917 and 1918 totalled 128,867 tons of aluminium, while in the Second World War, some 304,000 airplanes were produced by the US alone using 1,537,590 tons of metal (Davis 1989: 49–50). Western governments have therefore vociferously protected aluminium as an essential 'strategic industry'. States made huge investments in scientific and commercial development of their air industries (Whitehead 2009). But aerial 'readiness' was not simply about new industries and technologies; it also generated new forms of 'aerial life' (Adey 2010) in which activities related to aviation were promoted to reinforce national security.

In Europe, the 1930s are described as a golden age for aluminium in the domains of transportation, household products, furniture, and architecture (Schnapp 2001: 255). In Italy, for example, this coincided with the rise of Mussolini's fascist government, which embraced the potentials of the light metal. In 1932 the government founded an industry review, *Alluminio*, which carried this quote on its cover: 'Italy has abundant raw materials, abundant enough to forge the new productive Civilization that is already shining on the horizon: a Civilization principally based upon the ubiquity of light metals and their alloys in everything including the national defense' (cited in Schnapp 2001: 255–6, note 17). Another industrial review described aluminium as 'not only the *metal* of the Fatherland; it is also the metal of progress, the real material of unreal velocities [*la materia reale dell'irreale velocita*]' (Schnapp 2001: note 18). The Italian Futurists especially embraced the aesthetics of mobility and dynamism, and initiated an art movement that combined the worship of speed with a fascist politics of national power. Aluminium and the development of an aircraft industry were the realization of such aesthetic and political projects of modernization, and for the rest of the century to have a national airline would become the marker of a modern nation-state.

The aerial superiority of aluminium over all previous metals has made possible what cultural theorist Caren Kaplan calls 'the cosmic view' of militarized air power. 'Mobility is at the heart of modern warfare', writes Kaplan, and 'modern war engages the theories and practices of mobility to a great extent' (Kaplan 2006: 395). Kaplan tracks the emergence of the first phase of the weaponization of the air through Major Alexander De Seversky's famous book *Victory Through Air Power* (1942), which was also made into a Walt Disney animated feature film of the same name. In the aftermath of Pearl Harbor the widely distributed book and film are said to have influenced both Winston Churchill and Franklin Roosevelt, and to have changed national military strategy forever.

In May 1940 President Franklin Delano Roosevelt announced that the government planned to construct 50,000 airplanes over the next two years, as part of a massive war effort; this was extended to 60,000 in 1942, and an astounding 125,000 in 1943 (Brennan 2004: 58). While steel production doubled, US government investment drove aluminium production to grow by more than 600 per cent between 1939 and 1943, outpacing the increase in all other crucial metals (Doordan 1993: 46). 'World War II demonstrated to the world the capacity and power of American industrial production and its ability to expand exponentially to meet wartime needs' (Brennan 2004: 60). This was mainly driven by the frantic fabrication of warplanes, in which 'Ninety percent of the wings and fuselage, 60% of the engine, and all of the propeller was comprised of aluminum' (Brennan 2004: 60).

Aluminium not only mobilizes the technologies of warfare in the form of planes, missiles, and satellites, but also immobilizes enemies in the form of explosives. The 1901 invention of thermite unlocked the power pent up in the very atoms of the molecule:

> While smelters require huge supplies of electricity in order to split aluminum from its bonding with oxygen in molecules of aluminum oxide, thermite reverses this process: a bomb is packed with iron oxide and aluminum powder. [...] This was the basis of the first world war hand grenades, second world war incendiary bombs and napalm, and the 'daisy cutters' used by American planes for 'carpet bombing' from the Korean and Vietnam wars to Iraq. (Padel and Das 2007: 15)

From hand grenades to nuclear missiles, warfare across the world rests on aluminium-based technology. Another surprising use of aluminium during the Second World War was as a radar countermeasure in the form of 'chaff'. Britain's Royal Air Force first used this secret new device, code-named WINDOW, in its bombing of Hamburg in 1943. It consisted of bundles of over 2,000 strips of coarse black paper with aluminium foil stuck on one side. Seven thousand bundles were dropped from a stream of 740 Lancaster and Halifax bombers and they were so highly successful in jamming Hamburg's defensive radar, that the entire warning system was blinded. Hamburg was infamously reduced to ashes, and only twelve British bombers were lost. Aluminium empowers humanity in many ways, but in many cases that power has been used for purposes of massive destruction, including the collapsed towers of the World Trade Center in Manhattan, whose aluminium walls spectacularly folded on 9/11 when struck by the speeding projectiles of aluminium airplanes.

Although aluminium's first association is with the vehicles of the roads and the skies, it also played a crucial part as the material that enabled buildings to rise with new speed and lightness. The light metal enabled the largest man-made structures to soar heavenward with an unfathomable delicacy. Aluminium instigated the emergence of Modernism as an architectural style, not only because it allowed for the streamlining of building forms by the removal of heavy support structures and the incorporation of more glass into external walls, but equally because its machine-age surfaces matched the desire for a lighter, airier, modern kind of styling. Aesthetically it became the material of the moment for the new urbanism of the twentieth century, or as architect Walter Gropius called it, 'the material of the future' (Wilquin 2001: 26).

Skyscrapers as we know them would not have been possible without aluminium. Architectural anodized aluminium was first used on a large scale in the spandrels of the Empire State Building, built in 1935 as the then tallest building in the world. It was also used for the mast at the top, which was originally designed as a mooring for air ships, which were themselves braced with aluminium support structures. This architectural wonder was extolled for the speed with which it was erected, with a stream of materials being delivered with precision timing. 'At one point the "velocity" of this automatic architecture reaches 14½ stories in ten days [...] Empire State seemed almost to float, like an enchanted fairy tower, over New York. An edifice so lofty, so serene, so marvelously simple, so luminously beautiful, had never before been imagined' (Koolhaas 1994: 141, 143). Velocity and luminosity would become the hallmarks of the emerging new architecture using aluminium.

FIGURE 28.3 Alcoa Aluminum Advertisement, *Saturday Evening Post*, '31 Stories of Aluminum Make News', 1953 (public domain image original copyright Alcoa)

The true demonstration of the potentials of architectural use of aluminium came in 1952–3 when Alcoa completed a new company headquarters in Pittsburgh (see Figure 28.3). The 31-storey Alcoa Building was the first multi-storey building to employ aluminium curtain walls. Sheathing these walls progressed at the then remarkable speed of one floor a day. The building also demonstrated how thin, self-supporting, inner walls could increase usable floor space (bringing greater returns on investment). Other features included aluminium ceiling systems of radiant heat and cooling, which also added more floor space; pivoting aluminium windows that could be cleaned from inside; an all-aluminium electrical system; and aluminium plumbing on a scale never before attempted ('Aluminum by Alcoa', Aluminum Company of America, 1969, p. 47).

As Stuart Leslie argues, the 1953 Alcoa Building exemplifies '"architecture parlante", literally buildings that speak of their function and meaning'. Corporations like Alcoa 'intended their signature buildings as larger than life advertisements for their signature products…creating a distinctly modern image' as part of an extreme corporate makeover (Leslie 2011). The company proudly advertised its achievements:

> Efficiency through light weight was the purpose of its builders…and innovation their method. […] *Light-walled*, this building used hundreds of tons less structural steel framing than a conventional building of the same size… *Thin-walled*, it yields thousands of feet of extra floor space.

Architect I. M. Pei was hired to design all of Alcoa's New York corporate properties in high modernist style and he 'looked forwarded to a day when aluminum would be permitted to do "a total functional job in the construction of a building"' ('Aluminum by Alcoa', p. 49). The use of prefabricated aluminium panels had the potential to transform the building industry.

By 1972 'Alcoa aluminum had been used to sheath such architectural landmarks as the Vehicle Assembly Building at Cape Canaveral, Pittsburgh's Hilton Hotel, Chicago's John Hancock Center, and the World Trade Center in New York, where aluminum also adorned the headquarters of Chase Manhattan Bank and Time, Inc.' (Smith 1988: 338). In other words, it was used on some of the biggest buildings in the world, built for the most powerful organizations and corporations, achieving iconic status at the heart of the global metropolis. Any archaeology of this world must include the study of aluminium, or what I call aluminology, understood as both an excavation of the material culture of light metal and an explanation of its cultural impacts, both productive and destructive, on the age of aluminium.

28.4 FORECASTING THE FUTURE

The aluminium-based technologies for waging aerial war were not simply a background or underbelly of modernity, but were constitutive of both power relations and representational practices that spanned art, design, and technology and shaped 'the ground of everyday life' (Kaplan forthcoming). After the war, companies like the Bohn Aluminum and Brass Corporation offered their services in design and technical advice on incorporating aluminium alloys into production processes, helping to kick-start a take-off in new uses. As an 1944 Bohn ad states,

> Mechanized warfare has had a tremendous effect on the development of internal combustion engines. [...] new engine designs will furnish greatly increased horsepower per pound of engine weight. Engines will be smaller and by the greater use of aluminum alloys, will be considerably lighter.

Other advertisements depict a futuristic city with a kind of levitating monorail train, and multi-level expressways snaking through a forest of tall modernist buildings: 'Today America's manufacturing processes are concentrated solidly on war materials for Victory. From this gigantic effort will spring many new developments of vast economic consequence to the entire universe. The City of the Future will be born—startling new architectural designs will be an every day occurrence!' (see Figure 28.4). And others point towards growth in air travel: 'Tremendous increases are foreseen in travel by air in the post-war era. Airports that can handle 25,000 passengers a day may be needed. Aluminium and magnesium will play a vital part in postwar aircraft and other products.'

By tracing the infiltration of this metal into the material cultures of modernity we can uncover a layer of modern artefacts that expressed a certain moment in human existence, and also expressed that period's hopes for the future of humanity. In 1952 Alcoa hired the advertising agency Ketchum, Macleod, and Grove who produced a marketing campaign that they called FORECAST. They announced that the campaign's 'principal objective is not to increase the amount of aluminum used today for specific applications, but to inspire

FIGURE 28.4 BOHN Aluminum and Brass Corporation Advertisement, 'Forecasting by Bohn', *c.*1945 (public domain image original copyright Bohn)

and stimulate the mind of men' (cited in Brennan 2004: 71–2). They devised a multi-faceted marketing campaign with weekly magazine advertisements, the publication of a periodical called *Design Forecast*, and the creation of a new kind of showroom. Most importantly, they commissioned twenty-two well-known designers to create products using Alcoa aluminium. The practice of forecasting and scenario building employed in this advertising campaign built on the practices of the RAND corporation, a major player in research and development for the military-industrial complex.

Airplanes, rockets, satellites, and new architectural forms served not just as applications of aluminium, but as advertisements and exemplars of the achievements of modernity and the benefits that modernization would bring to the entire world. As the Victoria and Albert Museum's 2008 exhibition *Cold War Modern: Design 1945–1970* amply demonstrated,

> Not only signs of military strength and power, but also glittering products, high-tech electronics, skyscrapers and their images were deployed by each side to demonstrate its superior command of modernity. By planting a flag on the Moon, by constructing the world's tallest building or quite simply by ensuring the supply of shining white refrigerators for ordinary homes, the superpowers sought to demonstrate the pre-eminence of their science, their industry, their organization and their design. (Crowley and Pavitt 2008: 13)

When the Soviet Union launched its first Sputnik satellite in October 1957, the shining aluminium orb that was the first man-made object to orbit the Earth captured people's imaginations around the world. The United States and the Soviet Union entered into a 'space race' competing to launch the first rockets, satellites, and humans into outer space. The USSR capitalized on its success by exhibiting Sputnik prototypes around the world. It inspired many designers to embrace sleek curvilinear shapes, fashioned out of aluminium, plastic, fibreglass, and other Space Age materials. Chairs became space-ship pods, radios and televisions looked like spy equipment, and domestic objects went high-tech, with automated push-button operation echoing the technologies of the Cold War.

At the American National Exhibition held in Moscow in 1959, during the USSR's post-Stalin thaw period, American vice-president Richard Nixon and Soviet premier Nikita Khrushchev held a famous discussion of the merits of US consumer culture while standing in front of a model American kitchen display. Arguing over the relative achievements of their political and economic systems while contemplating the Frigidaire refrigerators, General Electric dishwashers, and automatic mixers, Nixon asked Khrushchev, 'Would it not be better to compete in the relative merits of washing machines than in the strength of rockets? Is this the kind of competition you want?' (Crowley and Pavitt 2008: 12). During the Cold War a battle was waged not just with atomic weaponry and missiles (made of aluminium), but also with kitchenware and consumer goods (many also made of aluminium). Aluminium, in other words, was the weapon of choice whether in a war of bombing and destruction or a war of winning hearts and minds in 'the Kitchen Wars', and it is no coincidence that we can find echoes of similar shapes and surfaces in the artefacts produced in each kind of war.

Aluminium stands at every frontier where humankind has pushed the limits of our material existence to the extreme. Wherever we have challenged the constraints of gravity, of heat, of size, and of human survival in the most adverse conditions, aluminium has been there. The USSR also succeeded in launching the first man into space, the cosmonaut Yuri Gagarin, who orbited the earth on 12 April 1961 aboard the Vostok 3KA-2. But the US was not far behind, and prided itself on its lighter more sophisticated rockets. NASA's famous Vehicle Assembly Building, built to house the moon-bound Saturn V rocket, was the world's largest building when completed in 1965, covering ten acres, enclosing 130 million cubic feet of space, and with double doors that are 45 storeys high. Its construction called for more than 3 million pounds of Alcoa aluminium.

And of course, aluminium also made possible the first human landing on the moon on 20 July 1969, when Neil Armstrong and Buzz Aldrin stepped out of their aluminium landing craft onto the Sea of Tranquillity, while the mother ship Columbia orbited the moon. Aluminium has remained central to space exploration. The fuel used in the solid rocket boosters on the US space shuttles contained aluminium powder, the fuel pumps incorporated a highly cored aluminium sand casting, and the shuttles' external fuel tanks were made of an aluminium alloy. The problematic heat panels that faultily protected the exterior were made from a new kind of aluminium foam. In short, the now retired shuttle would not have existed without aluminium, which composed 90 per cent of its materials. Meanwhile, far up in outer space, a ring of aluminium satellites and space debris circles the Earth like a metallic halo, though one that portends disaster due to collisions (see Gorman and O'Leary, this volume). With the Shuttle returning to Earth for the last time in July 2011, NASA turned to its next mission, the launch of the spacecraft Juno on a five-year-long journey to Jupiter. Juno is carrying 'three aluminum

Lego figures: of Galileo, Juno [wife of Jupiter] and Jupiter carrying his thunderbolts', further extending the reach of aluminium into interplanetary realms (Chang 2011: A12).

28.5 CONCLUSION

In 1965 Alcoa launched the 'FORECAST Jet', a kind of 'flying showcase' that displayed the company's products and services. Described as 'an aeronautical ambassador of aluminum', the DC-7CF was flown by a three-man crew and could be expanded on the ground into a 'blue-vinyl-carpeted' reception area formed by 'a semi-circular screen of aluminum beads', with aluminium spiral stairs rising up to an interior conference lounge furnished with woven-aluminium panels, aluminium-fabric upholstery, aluminium sand-casted lighting fixtures, and artworks in aluminium (Brennan 2004: 86–7). The jet 'functioned both as a sign and signifier of its product as well as a metaphor for the new postwar corporation', argues Brennan; the 'corporate jet—the ultimate symbol of corporate achievement—referenced the heyday of Alcoa's production of military aircraft during the war. Here the aluminium airplane—*the* war machine of World War II—transformed into a sleek communication machine in the Cold War marketplace' (Brennan 2004: 88–9).

The notion of forecasting the future was an essential part of the identity of aluminium, gazed into like a kind of crystal ball. Technological optimists envisioned a future made possible by the new human capabilities that might sprout from aluminium, and the new social and cultural practices it would enable. Philosopher, inventor, architect, and designer R. Buckminster Fuller is a key exemplar of the forecaster of the future. In 1933, he designed the Dymaxion Car, a three-wheeled streamlined pod that could carry up to ten passengers, covered in aluminium. His initial idea was to create a vehicle that was part aircraft and part automobile, with wings that would inflate as the car lifted off the ground at higher speeds (Patton 2008). His other visionary schemes included the automated, lightweight, and mobile Dymaxion house, designed in 1927 to be mass-produced, affordable, easily transportable inside a metal tube, and environmentally efficient. He also invented the Dymaxion map, a flat projection that shows the entire world on one surface without the distortions found on usual maps; and the geodesic dome, formed by the 14-sided polyhedron projected out into a spherical system of triangles to form a very strong and economical structure, for which he received a patent in 1954. His geodesic domes led to new experimental building forms that were adopted by the US military as light, strong structures that could be air-lifted into place on difficult terrains. His work was used to promote US industrial design around the world, while also inspiring the environmental movement in the 1960s (see Fowles and Heupel, this volume).

Fuller's book *Operating Manual for Spaceship Earth* (1963) first popularized the idea of the Earth as a spaceship, and the vision of using technology to 'do more with less'. He is one of the first thinkers to argue that we as a species need to draw on energy 'income'—sunlight, water power, wind power, geothermal energy—and stop drawing from our energy 'savings account'—fossil fuels. He himself recognized his role as one of 'prognostication', or forecasting of the future, based on the 'anticipatory design science' that he had learned in the United States Naval Academy. He understood the future as a transition from technologies of warfare and weaponry to technologies of life for an emerging world society, or what he called 'completely tooled-up and organized comprehensive, anticipatory livingry [sic] systems'. In the oracular style of his 1963 book *Ideas and Integrities*, he wrote: 'In a manner similar to the past evolution of weaponry systems the new, architect-designed, world-around, livingry systems will be realized in progressive, economic-industrial-plan increments predicated upon pyramidal reinvestments of the forward years' regeneratively amplifying and progressive techno-economic advantages' (Fuller 1963, cited in Schnapp 2009: 283). Yet he never resolved the contradictions of the material-technical system of modernity, and not least the conundrum of aluminium: would it continue to be an energy-hungry technology of weaponry or would it become a recycled green technology for 'anticipatory livingry'? It is a question that remains unanswered.

REFERENCES

Adey, Peter. 2010 *Aerial Life: Spaces, Mobilities, Affects*. Oxford: Wiley-Blackwell.

Brennan, Annmarie. 2004. Forecast. In *Cold War Hothouses: Inventing Postwar Culture, from Cockpit to Playboy*, ed. Beatriz Colomina, Annmarie Brennan, and Jeannie Kim, pp. 55–90. New York: Princeton Architectural Press.

Chang, Kenneth. 2011. For NASA, Return Trip to Jupiter in Search of Clues to Solar System's Origins. *New York Times*, 5 August: A12.

Cresswell, Tim. 2006. *On The Move: Mobility in the Modern Western World*. London: Routledge.

Crowley, David and Pavitt, Jane (eds.). 2008. *Cold War Modern: Design 1945–1970*. London: V&A Publishing.

Davis, Carlton E. 1989. *Jamaica in the World Aluminium Industry, 1838–1973*, Vol. I. Kingston and London: Jamaica Bauxite Institute.

Doordan, Dennis. 1993. Promoting Aluminum: Designers and the American Aluminum Industry. *Design Issues* 9(2): 44–50.

Fuller, R. Buckminster. 1963. The Future. Excerpt from *Ideas and Integrities: A Spontaneous Autobiographical Disclosure*. Englewood Cliffs, NJ: Prentice-Hall.

Hachez-Leroy, Florence. 1999. *L'aluminium français. L'invention d'un marché 1911–1983*. Paris: CNRS Editions, avec le concours de l'Institut pour l'histoire de l'aluminium.

Hannam, Kevin, Sheller, Mimi, and Urry, John. 2006. Mobilities, Immobilities and Moorings. Editorial Introduction to *Mobilities* 1(1): 1–22.

Jessop, Bob. 2006. Spatial Fixes, Temporal Fixes and Spatio-Temporal Fixes. In *David Harvey: A Critical Reader*, ed. Noel Castree and Derek Gregory, pp. 142–66. New York: Blackwell.

Kaplan, Caren. 2006. Mobility and War: The Cosmic View of US 'Air Power'. *Environment and Planning A* 38(2): 395–407.

—— forthcoming. The Balloon Prospect: Aerostatic Observation and the Emergence of Militarized Aeromobility. In *Aerial Vision*, ed. Peter Adey.

Koolhaas, Rem. 1994. *Delirious New York: A Retroactive Manifesto for Manhattan*. New York: Monacelli Press.

Leslie, Stuart W. 2011. The Strategy of Structure: Architectural and Managerial Style at Alcoa and Owens-Corning. *Enterprise & Society* 12(4): 863–902.

Molotch, Harvey. 2005. *Where Stuff Comes From: How Toasters, Toilets, Cars, Computers, and Many Other Things Come to Be As They Are*. New York and London: Routledge.

Nesbitt, Claire and Tolia-Kelly, Divya. 2009. Hadrian's Wall: Embodied Archaeologies of the Linear Monument. *Journal of Social Archaeology* 9: 368–90.

Padel, Felix and Das, Samarendra. 2007. Double Death: Aluminum's Link With Genocide. *Voices of the Wilderness*, published by Saving Iceland, July 2007: 10–17. Available at: <http://www.savingiceland.org/2007/08/double-death/> (accessed 31 December 2012).

Patton, Phil. 2008. A 3-Wheel Dream that Died at Takeoff. *New York Times*, 15 June.

Schnapp, Jeffrey T. 2001. The Romance of Caffeine and Aluminum. *Critical Inquiry* 28(1): 244–69.

—— (ed.). 2009. *Speed Limits*. Montreal: Canadian Centre for Architecture.

Seversky, Alexander P. de. 1942. *Victory Through Air Power*. New York: Simon & Schuster.

Sheller, Mimi and Urry, John. 2006. The New Mobilities Paradigm. *Environment and Planning A*, Special Issue: Materialities and Mobilities 38: 207–26.

Smith, George David. 1988. *From Monopoly to Competition: The Transformation of Alcoa, 1888–1986* Cambridge: Cambridge University Press.

Urry, John. 2000. *Sociology beyond Societies: Mobilities for the Twenty-First Century*. London: Routledge.

—— 2007. *Mobilities*. Cambridge: Polity Press.

Whitehead, Mark. 2009. *State, Science and the Skies: Governmentalities of the British Atmosphere*. Oxford: Wiley-Blackwell.

Wilquin, Hugues. 2001. *Aluminium Architecture: Construction and Details*. Basel, Berlin, and Boston: Birkhäuser.

Witcher, Robert, Tolia-Kelly, Divya P., and Hingley, Richard. 2010. Archaeologies of Landscape: Excavating the Materialities of Hadrian's Wall. *Journal of Material Culture* 15(1): 105–28.

CHAPTER 29

....

THE ARCHAEOLOGY OF SPACE EXPLORATION

....

ALICE C. GORMAN AND BETH LAURA O'LEARY

29.1 INTRODUCTION

....

SPACE archaeology is the study of 'the material culture relevant to space exploration that is found on earth and in outer space (i.e. exoatmospheric material) and that is clearly the result of human behaviour' (Darrin and O'Leary 2009: 5; O'Leary 2009c; see also Staski 2009: 19). The aims of space archaeology are to illuminate the interaction of technology and human behaviour with a view to understanding a particular technical assemblage on and off Earth, and to promote the inclusion of heritage planning in future space missions, such as orbital debris removal and planetary exploration, both of which may cause damage to culturally significant sites and spacecraft.

The methods and theories of space archaeology are shaped by the unique locations and relationships between places in space and on Earth. In this chapter, we begin by mapping the cultural landscape of space, describing material remains from the Earth's surface to the far reaches of the solar system. The methods used to study the archaeological traces of space exploration draw on those of historical archaeology and include the application of remote sensing to observe orbital and planetary features (Figures 29.2 and 29.3). From its origins in the work of Rathje, who coined the term exoarchaeology as 'the study of artefacts in outer space' (1999: 108), space archaeology has developed from a marginal field to one demanding attention in a world increasingly reliant on space-based services. The predominant underlying framework is behavioural archaeology, focusing on multi-scalar interactions between people and artefacts in all times and places. The main narrative of space exploration is the tangible technology of things, or a story of how objects construct the subject in the contemporary world (Olsen 2003: 100). Lastly, we include a discussion of the complexities—legal, political, and economic—of preserving this recent important heritage for future generations.

The exploration of outer space relied on the descendants of the V2 rocket developed in 1930s Germany, and the growth of associated technologies such as electronics and computing. The historic context of space archaeology is most strongly linked to the Cold War period (1946–89), when the political and social manoeuvres of the western and eastern blocs were played out in space as well as on the Earth's surface (Gorman and O'Leary 2007: 73). However, while missile and rocket technology were developed in tandem, space archaeology in general does not encompass the military applications of missiles in terrestrial arenas, focusing instead on the geopolitical role of space in structuring the nature of these hot and cold conflicts.

Space archaeology can be regarded as a distinct field because it deals with the recent (i.e. last 50 years) exploitation of a previously remote region, taking place in a period of extremely rapid and accelerating technological change facilitated by social and political structures that did not exist before the Second World War. In particular, military and civil development of space technologies required massive state-sponsored complexes for research and development. Numerous scholars have argued that the Space Age—a particular time and level of technological development—is qualitatively different from preceding periods, and that the launch of the first Earth satellite, Sputnik 1, in 1957, was an historical catalyst which altered the 'very proportions of human power in relation to the natural world' (McDougall 1982: 1010; see also Fewer 2009).

29.2 CULTURAL LANDSCAPE: THE DISTRIBUTION AND NATURE OF SPACE MATERIAL CULTURE

The material culture relating to human engagement with space is distributed across the land surface of the Earth (and, in the case of some re-entered spacecraft, in submarine locations), in orbit around the Earth, and in and around numerous other celestial bodies in the solar system. The most distant extent of material evidence is represented by four spacecraft (Pioneer 9, Pioneer 10, Voyager 1, and Voyager 2) which are currently venturing into the interstellar medium.

Facilities on Earth are inexorably linked to those that exist in space or on the surface of other celestial bodies. The concept of a cultural landscape has been extended by Gorman (2005a) to include the Earth and outer space. Objects and sites in space can be viewed as being part of a much larger assemblage that, until the Space Age, were confined to the Earth, but that afterwards could enter the archaeological record elsewhere (Staski 2009: 23)

On Earth, there are places related to the development, manufacture, launch, tracking, and administration of spacecraft. Launch sites tend to be confined to former Cold War 'superpowers' and populous nations such as India, China, and Brazil. Tracking, surveillance, and downlink facilities, with antennas of varying kinds, have a far wider distribution. Every space mission has an associated ground segment that supports its function. Launch sites and ground stations are frequently associated with residential compounds and towns, and with support industries. Where they are built in remote locations, launch sites can have long-lasting impacts on the landscape and nature of human occupation, as they may involve the construction of roads and other infrastructure that enables settlement.

Space material culture can be divided into (usually) stationary ground facilities, and mobile spacecraft and artefacts. Spacecraft include rockets, buses, satellites, probes, landing modules, and return vehicles. Some rockets, such as sounding rockets or missiles developed for warhead delivery, are not intended to enter orbit although they may pass through regions of the atmosphere technically defined as space. Rockets intended to deliver spacecraft or crews to orbit are frequently constructed in stages. Generally the early stages fall back to Earth before orbit is attained, while the final stage ascends to orbit and remains there after releasing its payload; thus there may be components spanning both Earth and space.

In Earth Orbit, satellites generally occupy one of three regions defined by altitude and inclination. Low Earth Orbit, from about 200–1,200 km, is where most Earth observation takes place. Space stations, such as the International Space Station and the now-lost Mir, also use this orbit. Above 700 km, spacecraft must contend with the dangerous radiation field of the Van Allen Belts. The Medium Earth Orbit area is, nevertheless, where the constellations of global navigation satellite systems (GNSS), such as GPS, Galileo, and GLONASS, orbit. Between 350,000 km and 37,000 km are the geosynchronous and geostationary (GEO) orbits, used by telecommunications satellites. The so-called 'graveyard orbit', a few hundred kilometres above GEO, is where satellites in that orbit may be boosted at the end of their operational life. In Low Earth Orbit, most objects will eventually be dragged back into the Earth's atmosphere; however, depending on altitude, orbital configuration, and solar weather, this may take hundreds of years to occur. In higher orbits, such as GEO, re-entry will never occur.

A critical problem is the proliferation of orbital debris or space junk, caused by accumulation of non-functioning spacecraft such as satellites and rocket bodies, and their degradation and break-up through exposure to the space environment and collisions with other debris. Over 19,000 pieces > 10 cm are tracked in Earth Orbit, and many millions of smaller fragments, travelling at velocities in excess of 27,000 km/hr (Emhoff 2009: 78). Damage caused by collision with space junk can result in the loss of the satellite services on which the contemporary world depends, and create risk for human space missions. Proposals to use lasers and other methods to 'clean up' the junk in Low Earth Orbit depend on the international community reaching agreement, a fraught area as the same methods may be used to deliberately destroy the space assets of rival nations.

Currently, Vanguard 1—launched in 1958 by the USA and the oldest human object in orbit—is circling the Earth every two hours and is predicted by NASA to remain in orbit for the next 600 years (Figure 29.1). In orbit it essentially remains preserved and accessible to future generations of space tourists (Gorman 2005b).

Spacecraft, probes, and delivery vehicles are in orbit around the Moon, Mars, Venus, the Sun, and others. Several celestial bodies also have landing sites of robotic or uncrewed missions: these include the Moon, Mars, Venus, Titan (a moon of Saturn), the asteroids Eros and Itokawa, and the comet Tempel 1 (Gold 2009). These missions, particularly in the case of Mars rovers, often include robotic (i.e. the materials and traces created by robots in the exercise of their artificial intelligence) as well as mechanical components. With the retreat from a human physical presence in space, the increasing sophistication of robots with decision-making capacities is likely to add another unique strand of evidence to the archaeological record (see Spennemann 2007).

The Moon currently has over 100 metric tons of material culture on its surface from the Apollo missions and robotic missions (USSR, USA, and various nations), concentrated mostly around its equator, with some exceptions, like the recent Lunar Crater Observation Sensing Satellite (LCROSS) mission which crash-landed on the South Pole on 9 October 2009. The Moon is also the only place where humans have landed.

FIGURE 29.1 Vanguard 1 satellite (reproduced with permission from NASA)

Tranquility Base, the first lunar archaeological site with human activity, is unique in many ways, besides its location (O'Leary 2006). It was created by two humans landing and working at the site in a highly scripted way for approximately 21 hours. As such it is the ultimate single component site, where much of the behaviour of the site's participants was documented in print and can be watched on film. The archaeological study of these hours is worthy of pursuit for its own sake. Applying methods used to study more distant periods calls for more conscious analysis which reflects what Fairclough refers to as the 'apparent obviousness of the material remains that seem to need no interpretation' (2007: 20). For example, how do these human bodies encased in suits and constantly monitored, dependent on machines for their survival, move around in, and negotiate, an alien landscape? Their tracks are as evocative as the line of ancient footprints created by ancestral hominids in the volcanic ash of Laetoli 3.6 million years ago. Archaeological study has the ability to focus on the relationships between material culture, documents, and living memory and to accommodate complexities and conflicting perspectives instead of a single knowable past (Fairclough 2007: 21).

29.3 METHODS

Methodologically, space archaeology uses historical archaeological techniques in combining the study of the documentary record and oral histories with survey, excavation, and artefact analysis. Some space sites and objects are among the most thoroughly documented of the contemporary era. Nevertheless, secrecy is prevalent and rapidly changing technologies mean document attrition with each new plan so there are substantial lacunae. At present, only the terrestrial components can be examined directly; sites on other celestial bodies must be studied from records, satellite imagery, and telemetry, while orbital objects frequently have prototypes and occasional re-entered fragments which can be directly examined (see Szczepanowska 2009).

Reliance on remote sensing technology, such as aerial and satellite imagery, has increased in all fields of archaeology as the data have become more refined, and this is the case for space as well. The images generated by the Lunar Reconnaissance Orbiter (LRO) of the archaeological sites on the Moon in 2009 and 2011 allowed a remote re-visit to many of the Apollo sites. This mission provided data to help locate sites like the Lunakhod 2 and through digital imaging revisited the Apollo 12 site (Figure 29.2).

This remote sensing technique provides a data-gathering strategy that can be used to understand the nature and extent of use on the lunar surface and the archaeological record, without affecting its physical integrity. Although its original intent was not archaeological, the current scale and resolution of the LRO provides a tool for archaeologists to remotely examine significant sites on the Moon and promises to be even more refined in the future. Patterns of use of the Moon can be seen on a larger scale as current maps can be viewed to see where and when sites and artefacts are located. This kind of remote sensing data is critical to any preservation strategy for significant artefacts which will be revisited by future missions.

For the study of Earth Orbit, optical images taken by surveillance networks provide evidence of the materials present. Orbital configuration and tracking data can be studied in conjunction with technical manuals, engineering prototypes and back-up spacecraft, blueprints and photographs, to interrogate the space object as an artefact. NASA tracks orbital debris greater than 10 cm and archaeologists can look at discard patterns in the trails that they leave while in space, much as archaeologists can investigate historic trails on Earth (O'Leary 2009a: 33).

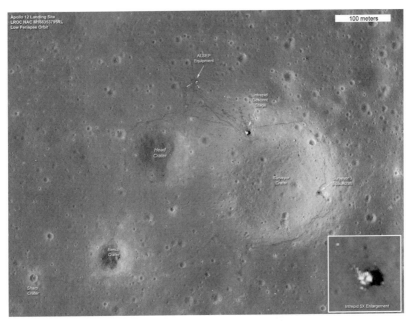

FIGURE 29.2 Apollo 12 taken from the LRO 2011 (reproduced with permission from NASA)

At the core of space archaeology methodology is the contention that the material culture can tell stories inaccessible from the documentary records, reflecting their function and role within the ideology of the era. It is in the difference between what something *is* and what it was *supposed* to be that we can find new perspectives on 'the archaeology of us' (Harrison and Schofield 2010).

29.4 THE DEVELOPMENT OF SPACE ARCHAEOLOGY

The antecedents of space archaeology are almost as old as space exploration itself. A kind of space 'archaeological' investigation may actually have been done on the Moon in 1969. As part of the Apollo 12 mission, the two astronauts Conrad and Bean landed on the lunar surface on 19 November and observed and recorded information about *Surveyor 3*, an unmanned probe that had soft landed on the Moon's surface almost three years earlier (Figure 29.3).

As their NASA mandate was to look at the general effects of the space and lunar environment on the robotic spacecraft, they documented the site photographically, noted the condition of the vehicle, and collected several artefacts from the previous spacecraft for later analyses on Earth, much as a terrestrial archaeologist would do (O'Leary 2009a: 30). Capelotti (2004: 49) writes that this was the first example of

> extraterrestrial archaeology and—perhaps more significant for the history of the discipline—
> formational archaeology, the study of environmental and cultural forces upon the life history
> of human artefacts in space.

FIGURE 29.3 Apollo 12 astronaut Alan Bean with Surveyor 3 on the lunar surface (reproduced with permission from NASA)

Archaeologist Ben Finney (1992) first suggested that it might be worthwhile to look at space sites created by both the USA and USSR. Rathje (1999: 108), who pioneered the study of contemporary garbage from an archaeological perspective in his famous 'garbology' project (see also Reno, this volume), also identified orbital debris as an appropriate area of investigation for archaeologists.

In what is the earliest instance of funded space archaeological research, in 1999, through the New Mexico Space Grant Consortium, NASA funded the *Lunar Legacy Project* to document the artefacts on the lunar surface left at Tranquility Base by the Apollo 11 crew and to investigate the relevant US federal preservation laws and regulations (New Mexico Space Grant Consortium/Lunar Legacy Website 2000). Tranquility Base was selected as the lunar site most iconic and worthy of preservation. The project looked at the site solely as an historical archaeological site. The investigation necessitated retrieving all records, photographs, films, and maps of the location. That inventory of the entire lunar assemblage at Tranquility Base is probably not yet complete, because the actual site has never been visited by archaeologists since it was created (O'Leary 2009b: 763).

Gorman (2005b, 2007a, 2009a) focused on orbital debris. Orbital debris has been defined as 'any human manufactured object in orbit that does not currently serve a useful purpose and is not anticipated to in the foreseeable future' (Gorman 2009a: 382). Gorman (2005a) perceives orbital space as an organically evolved landscape, as defined by the World Heritage Convention. She argues for a significance assessment framework derived from the Burra Charter (1999), including 'social, historical, aesthetic, and scientific significance' for various nations, people, and organizations that have an interest in orbital materials (Gorman 2009a: 382). It is not just the threat of collision and destruction that needs to be managed, but the cultural values of this landscape of space.

From the study of iconic sites like Tranquility Base and Vanguard 1, which could be considered to have outstanding universal value in the terms of the World Heritage Convention, space archaeology has moved to consider the impacts of space on everyday life and towards becoming more integrated into mainstream archaeology, as well as science and technology studies.

29.5 THEORETICAL APPROACHES

By its nature, space archaeology crosses a number of fields such as historical, industrial, and contemporary archaeology, and science and technology studies (STS). Historical archaeology is a diverse field linked to available written, photographic, and oral documentation of the period. Modern historical archaeology defines itself as the study of the post-medieval colonial world, the growth of industrial, capitalist societies, and social inequality (e.g. Lightfoot and Martinez 1995; Orser 1996; Hall and Silliman 2006). Its strength lies in the ability, through archaeological as opposed to historical techniques, to investigate groups or sectors of society frequently absent or poorly represented in the documentary record, such as Indigenous people, women, children, working classes, prisoners, etc. As these groups are also frequently marginalized in the space industry, this kind of research can open windows into material behaviour that is rarely mentioned in space histories. The impacts of space technology on Indigenous people have been explored by Gorman (2005a, 2007b, 2009b, 2009c) at the launch sites of Woomera (Australia), Kourou (French Guiana), and Colomb-Béchar (Algeria).

If historical archaeology deals with the development of global capitalism within the framework of colonialism, then space exploration and industry represent the next phase of inquiry, as capitalist enterprise and colonization extend into a new 'frontier'. The ideological construction and material negotiation of this high frontier can also be approached from a postcolonial perspective. Redfield (2002: 791), for example, has argued that space lies at the intersection of postcolonial and science studies, being the last bastion of unapologetic colonialism.

The predominant framework underlying space archaeology is behavioural archaeology, which focuses on the interactions between artefacts and people irrespective of time frame or location (e.g. Schiffer 1976; Binford 1978; Rathje and Schiffer 1982; see also Fewster, this volume). Behavioural archaeological theory links systems of meaning in relationship to material culture. In this framework technology is seen as socially constructed and material culture as evidence of how humans interact with and understand their world. Humans create artefacts, use them, and, in turn, are influenced by that interaction. Schiffer has opined that most social scientists have 'ignored what might be the most distinctive and significant about our species: human life consists of ceaseless and varied interaction among people and myriad kinds of things' (1999: 2). One approach is through the framework of life history (Schiffer 1976), which follows the artefact from its procurement to its discard, and beyond to post-deposition processes. A life history approach to space artefacts and materials can be used to look at the evolution of technology over time, and frame questions about technological and socio-cultural change.

Behavioural archaeology therefore has much in common with STS. Major research questions in STS include the social construction of technology, and the nature and pace of technological change. Debates include the degree to which technology can have a determining or autonomous impact on human behaviour, irrespective of the motivations or desires of those who create and use it, as opposed to technology being solely the embodiment of specific social groups and aspirations (Ferguson 1974; Schiffer 2001; Winner 1977). However, while STS considers 'things' to be an essential category of inquiry, the field has rarely engaged with archaeological theories, and has used archaeological data in only a limited way (Gerselewitz 1993; see also Webmoor, this volume). Space archaeology's emphasis on material culture, combined with deep time perspectives on innovation and technology transfer, can contribute to understanding how the space industry has influenced late modern human behaviour.

29.6 RESEARCH DIRECTIONS

Here we highlight some of the research possibilities of space archaeology.

29.6.1 Inventories and Recording

Some have argued (e.g. Rausenbach and Sokolsky 1998) that the history of astronautics and rocketry has barely progressed beyond the stage of collating information, with little critical analysis. Much space archaeology to date has focused on the documentary record and describing the material culture while stressing its technological, physical, and locational complexity within a cultural landscape. However, as O'Leary's Lunar Legacy Project demonstrates, there is a role for understanding what it is that constitutes space material culture (O'Leary 2009b). O'Leary (2009b: 764–5) has inventoried over 106 artefacts, structures, and features remaining at the Apollo 11 Tranquility Base. Capelotti (2009, 2010) provides descriptions of material remains at other Apollo and other planetary landing sites. There has, as yet, been no comprehensive characterization of the archaeological record in orbit. Clemens (2009) provides an overview of objects in Earth Orbit, and Gorman (2007a) has evaluated extant satellites in Earth Orbit in the period between the launch of Sputnik 1 in 1957 and the launch of the first geostationary satellite in 1963.

Terrestrial space sites may appear sporadically on national, regional, or state heritage registers, but few heritage organizations have undertaken systematic documentation of space sites. In historical research, Rausenbach and Sokolsky identify a bias towards spacecraft and engines, to the detriment of areas such as control systems, instruments, and ground support equipment (1998: 38). Useful research can be undertaken in identifying what survives in different spatial regimes, for example, Earth, Low Earth Orbit, cis-lunar space, and Mars, along thematic lines which may include nationality, mission type, power source, design influences, and technological lineages. Drawing conclusions about what it means must rest on the foundation of understanding what and where it is.

29.6.2 National and Global Technologies

The human exploration of space is deeply entangled with the maintenance of the late industrial nation state. The Space Age takes place at the same time as a decolonizing process, which saw the proliferation of new nations after the Second World War (Gorman 2009c). Because of the financial and organizational requirements of space technology, space programmes tend to be run at a national level, making nation-states the agents of technological change (McDougall 1982: 1022). Until the fall of the USSR in 1991, national prestige was the principal motivating factor in the development of civil space programmes (Hays and Lutes 2007). Particularly in the case of the USA and the former USSR, missions were designed with the explicit aim of demonstrating ideological superiority through technological achievement, and are frequently associated with the use of nationalist emblems such as flags, medallions, etc.

Within the technical requirements of launch, tracking, and data transmission, the construction and operation of space installations of all kinds is stamped with cultural differences and threads of continuity. The space programmes of the USA, USSR, France, and Britain were all seeded by the forced post-war diaspora of German rockets and rocket scientists; from this common origin, each location co-opted local science, landscapes, and visions of the spatial and organizational role of people within industrial complexes to produce distinct traditions of space design. The study of local expressions of this global technology can illuminate the technological and social choices made during and after the Cold War in participating in the appropriation of space.

29.6.3 Embodied Interactions with Space Technology

Human–machine interfaces are common in space technology: the space suit, the spacecraft, the control room, the interpretation and dissemination of signals transmitted to and from space. The way we perceive the world is moving away from direct experience towards a reliance on 'physical worlds available to human consciousness only through technological prostheses' (Fischer 1999: 468) including Google Earth, navigation devices, and television. Many of these inventions begin in the Space Age and are its direct and indirect descendants. Space archaeology can investigate how the existence of space above our heads, and technologies that interface between humans and space, structure human actions and human embodiment on Earth. Mindell has argued that the Apollo programmes 'exemplified broad changes in human–machine relationships' (2008: 15), perhaps most specifically seen in the boundary lines drawn between what was seen as appropriate for computers and software to do, and what was appropriate for direct human action: boundaries that were negotiated continually between gender and nationality in the US and USSR space programmes.

29.6.4 Impacts of Space on the Material Culture of Everyday Life and Popular Culture

Globalization is the social and economic correlate of the space technologies enabling telecommunications and navigation. Studies of globalization often overlook the technologies on which it increasingly depends in the late modern world (Hays and Lutes 2007: 208). Access to space-based Earth observation data and telecommunications has changed patterns of resource extraction, production, trade, and consumption, which can be studied archaeologically. We can also consider objects and technologies such as televisions, telephones, satellite dishes, navigation devices (such as handheld GNSS receivers), and automatic teller machines as related material culture that depend upon satellite data to function. Hence there are wide-reaching cultural impacts of access to satellite data that can also be considered within the purview of space archaeology.

The Space Age has been translated by commercial entities from the inaccessibility of high technology into vernacular and popular design, manifesting in architecture, furniture, souvenirs, toys, clothes, utensils, food, and even music. The human desire to explore was exploited by vendors to consumers as a vicarious way of being in space themselves. If I eat 'astronaut ice cream' it is as if I am an astronaut. The powdered drink product 'Tang' was advertised to consumers on Earth as being what the astronauts took to space. As with the grand nationalist enterprises, the ideologies of space were consumed and created at a popular level which reflected everyday aspirations of space and expectations of the future. The 'type fossils' of this process might well be astronaut ice cream, or space food sticks (Figure 29.4). The astronaut became the iconic hero of the Space Age in the same tradition as the cowboy on the US western frontier.

Popular cultural expressions of space technology could be argued to demonstrate processes of acculturation and accommodation between state-sponsored technological complexes and the everyday world, outside scientific elites (e.g. Gorman 2010). Public support for monumentally expensive human spaceflight programmes was purchased by the domestication of outer space—creating products that promised participation through their consumption. The echoes of space design in fabrics, foods, shapes, and replicas in the height of the Space Age were explicit; more contemporary manifestations are domestic satellite dishes and GPS units, demonstrating a different kind of consumption.

FIGURE 29.4 Space food sticks, manufactured in Australia (photograph: Alice C. Gorman)

The directions of space archaeology are multiple. The first is the acceptance of the sub-discipline into mainstream archaeology, to move forward into a new period of industrial archaeology where analysis reflects its unique technological characteristics and to pay attention to what Olsen has called 'the other half of the story: how objects construct the subject' (2003: 100). The story of space exploration is visible and tangible in material remains—rocket parts, etc.—and the surprisingly incomplete bricolage of records for this human endeavour. In many ways these artefacts have missed our archaeological gaze. The transmission of knowledge and the skills necessary to get to outer space and other celestial bodies take place in a web that links place, people, and artefacts together. Not just two humans stood on the Moon at the Tranquility Base site; thousands of artefacts and other humans supported them in that endeavour. The very scale of space exploration invites an archaeology of large scale, taking the entire solar system and beyond as its landscape (see Edgeworth, this volume).

29.7 HERITAGE MANAGEMENT ISSUES

Threats to space heritage include neglect, deliberate destruction, salvage, or recycling, and future space missions and industries including resource extraction and space tourism. The potential adverse impacts of souveniring on human material in space have been recognized for some time (e.g. Fewer 2002: 112; O'Leary 2003; NASA 2011). At present, however, the remoteness and cost of accessing material culture in space provides some protection from human impacts.

Activity in space is governed by a system of international conventions and treaties, of which the most important is the 1967 Treaty on Principles Governing the Activities of States in the Exploration and Use of Outer Space, including the Moon and Other Celestial Bodies (UN Outer Space Treaty or OTS). The OTS specifies that space is a global commons and cannot be subject to territorial claim. It also specifies that material in space remains the property and responsibility of the launching state.

Space sites and artefacts on Earth are reliant on national, state, or regional heritage legislation for protection. Numerous nations have no heritage legislation; many more have legislation that does not cover the recent past. Even where appropriate national heritage legislation exists, it usually cannot yet be extended into space without the risk of it being interpreted as a territorial claim in contravention of the OTS. The World Heritage Convention (WHC) explicitly does not cover movable objects, nor is space directly addressed. It is possible that the WHC could be extended to cover sites on other celestial bodies, but this is the subject of contention. Nevertheless, it is possible to argue that several space sites, such as Tranquility Base, meet World Heritage criteria. Fewer has proposed that a new heritage convention would be required to apply to planetary landing sites, starting with the compilation of an 'internationally-funded and publicly-accessible' record of all sites on the Moon and Mars (2002: 119).

Several archaeologists have worked together to address the protection of space heritage, for example on the World Archaeological Congress's Space Heritage Task Force (O'Leary et al. 2001; Gorman and Campbell 2003). In the case of Tranquility Base, this protection has occurred at the state level by listing the objects and structures on the California and New Mexico State Registers of Cultural Properties (O'Leary et al. 2010; Westwood et al. 2010), at the national level by proposing it as a US National Historic Landmark, and at the international level by working with ICOMOS (O'Leary 2009c). NASA (2011) itself has begun to address the issue of the protection of the historic and scientific value of US artefacts on the lunar surface (NASA 20 July 2011). NASA recognizes the increased technical abilities of spacefaring commercial groups and other nations that will go back to the Moon in the near future and now provides interim recommendations for lunar design and mission planning teams (NASA 20 July 2011)

In the absence of encompassing legal instruments or international conventions that can be used for the protection or management of the cultural values of space sites, the internationally recognized Burra Charter (Australia ICOMOS 1999) can be applicable to space. In terms of management, the principle of 'do as much as is necessary but as little as possible' can be used to argue against the deliberate retrieval and return to Earth of significant spacecraft or items on other celestial bodies. The Burra Charter process of significance assessment has also been successfully applied to satellites in Earth Orbit such as Vanguard 1 (Gorman 2005b).

29.8 SIGNIFICANCE OF THE FIELD

Extending the archaeological gaze into space forces us to look back on the Earth from a new perspective and perceive the material culture of the late industrial age as part of a system that reaches into the solar system. We need to understand what is taking place on the surface of the Earth by reference to the material culture of space: the information, images, data, and communications that spacecraft disseminate with a rapidity that has changed the meanings of local and global. Increasingly, we are implicated in our own constant surveillance from space and into space, becoming accustomed to using satellites to situate and navigate ourselves on Earth. As outer space alters the nature of our subjectivity, new paradigms are needed to investigate how material culture is used in mediating human engagement with the exoatmospheric realm.

Space archaeology also has practical applications, such as providing input to mission designs to avoid damaging existing significant heritage sites (e.g. on the Moon), and ensuring that proposals for orbital debris removal take cultural significance into account. In particular, archaeological approaches to technology adoption between technologically dominant colonial groups (i.e. spacefaring nations) and hunter-gatherers, pastoralists and non-industrial groups, who are nonetheless impacted by and contribute to the space age in various ways, can promote the inclusivity that is urged by the United Nations in the use of space. At this time space heritage properties in space remain without preservation protection. But perhaps their principal significance is in the ability to tell stories about the Space Age that are beyond the capacity of purely historical approaches.

By the archaeological study of the material record of space, there is an opportunity to look at a system which falls outside the normal spatial and temporal boundaries for humanity. The trails on the Moon and in space can offer insights into how humans carry their behaviour into space (Capelotti 2010: 5). Humanity has placed its artefacts into space and into the archaeological realm. These data are relevant to the migration of human ancestors out of Africa; they are part of human evolution. By its complexity, space archaeology invites all archaeologists to consider the fallacy of a simple, single past. Artefacts in space are the product of many separate minds and large-scale international cooperation in tracking and telemetry to allow, for example, humans to stand on another celestial body for the first time in 1969. It demonstrates humanity's technological intelligence at a particular historic era of exploration embedded in the Cold War. Some historians argue that we would never have gone into the arena of space without the political destabilization after the Second World War. Space became a military and technological frontier and the Moon a place that was won. This time and place is not well studied. Space is no longer empty as it was before the Cold War: it is now imbued with values encapsulated in memories, histories, objects, and places. As archaeologists, how can we refuse the challenge?

References

Australia ICOMOS. 1999. *The Burra Charter. The Australia ICOMOS Charter for Places of Cultural Significance*.

Binford, Lewis R. 1978. *Nunamiut Ethnoarchaeology*. New York: Academic Press.

Capelotti, Peter J. 2004. Space: The Final (Archaeological) Frontier. *Archaeology* 57(6): 48–55.

—— 2009. Culture of Apollo: A Catalogue of Manned Exploration of the Moon. In *Handbook of Space Engineering, Archaeology and Heritage*, ed. Ann G. Darrin and Beth L. O'Leary, pp. 421–41. Boca Raton: CRC Taylor & Francis.

—— 2010. *The Human Archaeology of Space: Lunar, Planetary and Interstellar Relics of Exploration*. Jefferson, NC: McFarland & Company Inc.

Clemens, Daniel E. 2009. Orbital Artefacts in Space. In *Handbook of Space Engineering, Archaeology and Heritage*, ed. Ann G. Darrin and Beth L. O'Leary, pp. 347–62. Boca Raton: CRC Taylor & Francis.

Darrin, Ann G. and O'Leary, Beth L. 2009. Introduction. In *Handbook of Space Engineering, Archaeology and Heritage*, ed. Ann G. Darrin and Beth L. O'Leary, pp. 3–15. Boca Raton: CRC Taylor & Francis.

Emhoff, Jerold. 2009. Space Basics: Orbital Mechanics. In *Handbook of Space Engineering, Archaeology and Heritage*, ed. Ann G. Darrin and Beth L. O'Leary, pp. 69–81. Boca Raton: CRC Taylor & Francis.

Fairclough, Graham. 2007. The Cold War in Context. In *A Fearsome Heritage: Diverse Legacies of The Cold War*, ed. John Schofield and Wayne Cocroft, pp. 19–32. Walnut Creek, CA: Left Coast Press.

Fewer, Greg. 2002. Toward an LSMR and MSMR (Lunar and Martian Sites & Monuments Records): Recording Planetary Spacecraft Landing Sites as Archaeological Monuments of the Future. In *Digging Holes in Popular Culture: Archaeology and Science Fiction*, ed. Miles Russell, pp. 112–20. Oxford: Oxbow Books.

—— 2009. 2228.34 hrs (Moscow Time), 4 October 1957. The Space Age Begins: The Launch of *Sputnik 1*, Earth's First Artificial Satellite. In *Defining Moments: Dramatic Archaeologies of the Twentieth-Century*, ed. John Schofield. BAR International Series 2005: Studies in Contemporary and Historical Archaeology 5, pp. 105–13. Oxford: Archaeopress.

Finney, Ben R. 1992. *From Sea to Space*. Palmerston North, New Zealand: Massey University.

Fischer, Michael M. J. 1999. Emergent Forms of Life: Anthropologies of Late or Postmodernities. *Annual Review of Anthropology* 28: 455–78.

Ferguson, Eugene S. 1974. Toward a Discipline of the History of Technology. *Technology and Culture* 15(1): 20–1.

Gerselewitz, Michael N. 1993. Archaeology and the Social Study of Technological Innovation. *Science, Technology and Human Values* 18(2): 231–46.

Gold, Robert. 2009. Spacecraft and Objects Left on Planetary Surfaces. In *Handbook of Space Engineering, Archaeology and Heritage*, ed. Ann G. Darrin and Beth L. O'Leary, pp. 399–419. Boca Raton: CRC Taylor & Francis.

Gorman, Alice C. 2005a. The Cultural Landscape of Interplanetary Space. *Journal of Social Archaeology* 5(1): 85–107.

—— 2005b. The Archaeology of Orbital Space. In *Australian Space Science Conference 2005*, pp. 338–57. Melbourne: RMIT University.

—— 2007a. Leaving the Cradle of Earth: The Heritage of Low Earth Orbit, 1957–1963. Paper presented at Extreme Heritage: Australia ICOMOS Annual Conference, James Cook University. Available at: <http://flinders.academia.edu/AliceGorman/Talks/3862/Leaving_the_cradle_of_Earth_the_heritage_of_Low_Earth_Orbit_1957–1963> (accessed 1 June 2012).

—— 2007b. La Terre et l'Espace: Rockets, Prisons, Protests and Heritage in Australia and French Guiana. *Archaeologies: Journal of the World Archaeological Congress* 3(2): 153–68.

—— 2009a. Heritage of Earth Orbit: Orbital Debris—Its Mitigation and Cultural Heritage. In *Handbook of Space Engineering, Archaeology and Heritage*, ed. Ann G. Darrin and Beth L. O'Leary, pp. 381–97. Boca Raton: CRC Taylor & Francis.

—— 2009b. The Archaeology of Space Exploration. In *Space Travel and Culture: From Apollo to Space Tourism*, ed. David Bell and Martin Parker, pp. 129–42. Sociological Review Monographs. Oxford: Wiley-Blackwell.

——2009c. Beyond the Space Race: The Significance of Space Sites in a New Global Context. In *Contemporary Archaeologies: Excavating Now*, ed. Angela Piccini and Cornelius Holtorf, pp. 161–80. Frankfurt: Peter Lang.

——2010. Consuming the Space Age: The Cuisine of Sputnik. Available at: <http://zoharesque. blogspot.com/2011/01/consuming-space-age-cuisine-of-sputnik.html> (accessed 31 August 2011).

Gorman, Alice C. and Campbell, John B. 2003. Terms of Reference for the Space Heritage Task Force. Available at: <http://www.worldarchaeologicalcongress.org/site/active_spac. php> (accessed 12 August 2011).

Gorman, Alice C. and O'Leary, Beth L. 2007. An Ideological Vacuum: The Cold War in Outer Space. In *A Fearsome Heritage: Diverse Legacies of the Cold War*, ed. John Schofield and Wayne Cocroft, pp. 73–92. Walnut Creek, CA: Left Coast Press.

Hall, Martin and Silliman, Stephen W. (eds.). 2006. *Historical Archaeology*. Malden, MA: Blackwell.

Harrison, Rodney and Schofield, John. 2010. *After Modernity: Archaeological Approaches to the Contemporary Past*. Oxford: Oxford University Press.

Hays, Peter L. and Lutes, Charles D. 2007. Towards a Theory of Spacepower. *Space Policy* 23: 206–9.

Lightfoot, Kent and Martinez, Antoinette. 1995. Frontiers and Boundaries in Archaeological Perspective. *Annual Review of Anthropology* 24: 471–92.

McDougall, Walter A. 1982. Technocracy and Statecraft in the Space Age—Toward the History of a Saltation. *The American Historical Review* 87(4): 1010–40.

Mindell, David A. 2008. *Digital Apollo: Human and Machine in Spaceflight*. Cambridge, MA: MIT Press.

NASA. 2011. *NASA's Recommendations to Space-Faring Entities: How to Protect and Preserve the Historic and Scientific Value of U.S. Government Lunar Artefacts*, 20 July.

New Mexico Space Grant Consortium/Lunar Legacy Project. 2000. <http://spacegrant.nmsu. edu/lunarlegacies> (accessed 12 June 2011).

O'Leary, Beth L. 2003. Lunar Archaeology: A View of Federal Historic Preservation Law on the Moon. Paper presented at the Fifth World Archaeological Congress, Washington DC.

——2006. The Cultural Heritage of Space, the Moon and other Celestial Bodies. *Antiquity* 80(307). Available at: <http://antiquity.ac.uk/ProjGall/oleary/index.html> (accessed 1 June 2012).

——2009a. The Evolution of Space Archaeology and Heritage. In *Handbook of Space Engineering, Archaeology and Heritage*, ed. Ann G. Darrin and Beth L. O'Leary, pp. 29–48. Boca Raton: CRC Taylor & Francis.

——2009b. One Giant Leap: Preserving Cultural Resources on the Moon. In *Handbook of Space Engineering, Archaeology and Heritage*, ed. Ann G. Darrin and Beth L. O'Leary, pp. 757–80. Boca Raton: CRC Taylor & Francis.

——2009c. Historic Preservation at the Edge: Archaeology on the Moon, in Space and on Other Celestial Bodies. *Historic Environment* 22(1): 13–18.

O'Leary, Beth L., Gibson, Ralph, Versluis, John, and Brown, Leslie. 2001. Preserving a Lunar Legacy. Poster presented at the joint meetings of the American Astronomical Society and the American Association of Physics Teachers, San Diego, CA.

O'Leary, Beth L., Bliss, Sahrah, DeBry, Robert, Gibson, Ralph, Punke, Matthew, Sam, Deneve, Slocum, Reagyn, Vela, Jaime, Versluis, John, and Westwood, Lisa. 2010. The Artefacts and Structures at Tranquility Base Nomination to the New Mexico State Register of Cultural

Properties. Accepted by unanimous vote by the New Mexico Cultural Properties Review Committee on 10 April 2010.

Olsen, Bjørnar. 2003. Material Culture After Text, Re-Membering Things. *The Norwegian Archaeological Review* 36(2): 77–104.

Orser, Charles. 1996. *A Historical Archaeology of the Modern World*. New York: Plenum Press.

Rathje, William. 1999. An Archaeology of Space Garbage. *Discovering Archaeology* (October): 108–12.

Rathje William L. and Schiffer, Michael B. 1982. *Archaeology*. New York: Harcourt Brace Jovanovich.

Rausenbach, Boris V. and Sokolsky, Viktor N. 1998. Main Fields on the Current Studies on the History of Astronautics and Aeronautics. *Acta Astronautica* 43(1–2): 37–42.

Redfield, Peter. 2002. The Half-life of Empire in Outer Space. *Social Studies of Science* 32(5–6): 791–825.

Schiffer, Michael. 1976. *Behavioral Archeology*. New York: Academic Press.

——1999. *The Material Life of Human Beings: Artefacts, Behavior, and Communication*. London and New York: Routledge.

—— (ed.). 2001. *Anthropological Perspectives on Technology*. Tucson: University of Arizona Press.

Spennemann, Dirk. 2007. On the Cultural Heritage of Robots. *International Journal of Heritage Studies* 13(1): 4–21.

Staski, Edward. 2009. Archaeology: The Basics. In *Handbook of Space Engineering, Archaeology and Heritage*, ed. Ann G. Darrin and Beth L. O'Leary, pp. 17–28. Boca Raton: CRC Taylor & Francis.

Szczepanowska, Hanna. 2009. CORONA KH-4B Museum Preservation of Reconnaissance Space Artefacts: A Case Study. In *Handbook of Space Engineering, Archaeology and Heritage*, ed. Ann G. Darrin and Beth L. O'Leary, pp. 657–77. Boca Raton: CRC Taylor & Francis.

United Nations Office of Outer Space Affairs. 1967. 2222 (XXI). Treaty on Principles Governing the Activities of States in the Exploration and Use of Outer Space, including the Moon and Other Celestial Bodies. Available at: <http://www.oosa.unvienna.org/oosa/en/SpaceLaw/gares/html/gares_21_2222.html> (accessed 1 June 2012).

Westwood, Lisa, Gibson, Ralph, O'Leary, Beth, and Versluis, John. 2010. Nomination of Objects Associated with Tranquility Base to the California State Historical Resources Commission. Accepted by unanimous vote to the California State Register of Historical Resources on 10 April 2010

Winner, Langdon. 1977. *Autonomous Technology: Technics-Out-of-Control as a Theme in Political Thought*. Cambridge, MA: MIT Press.

CHAPTER 30

....

CONTEMPORARY ARCHAEOLOGY IN THE POSTCOLONY: DISCIPLINARY ENTRAPMENTS, SUBALTERN EPISTEMOLOGIES

....

NICK SHEPHERD

30.1 INTRODUCTION

....

RATHER than write about archaeological understandings *of* the contemporary world, I want to use this chapter to pose a set of questions around the meanings and implications of doing archaeology *in* and *on* the contemporary world, so that my point of focus becomes the discipline itself. On the one hand, I want to think about the manner in which the discipline is constituted as a set of guiding ideas and forms of practice, and what it means to be an archaeologist and to be doing archaeology in a particular time and place. On the other hand, I want to think about contemporary contexts of practice and the complex, sometimes spectacular, collision between disciplinary method, the politics of memory and identity, and the interests of local and global elites. Specifically, I want to consider such contexts from the perspective of the Global South, and a set of subaltern struggles framed as a challenge to disciplinary thinking and a discourse on heritage. In other words, using the shorthand of my title, I want to think about forms of disciplinary entrapments, and about the subaltern epistemologies which offer fresh openings and ways out of a certain kind of uncreative assertion of discipline. This chapter situates itself in relation to two bodies of work: a growing literature on archaeology and postcolonialism (Liebmann and Rizvi 2008; Schmidt 2009; Lydon and Rizvi 2010), and a literature on apartheid memory and on the politics of memory and identity in postapartheid society (Murray et al. 2007; Gqola 2010; Coombes 2011).

30.2 TIME-LINE PRESTWICH STREET

To do this I need a way in. I shall use as case study and illustrative example a set of events about which I have written before (Shepherd 2006, 2007), but which remains instructive for present purposes. The exhumation of an early colonial burial site in Prestwich Street, Cape Town, between 2003 and 2005 remains the most contested instance of archaeological work in the post-1994 period. Ten years after the fall of apartheid it brought groups of citizens onto the streets of the city, engaged in forms of public protest, this time against a version of archaeology as science. The story of Prestwich Street begins in the period of Dutch occupation when the area to the north and west of the growing town was the site of a number of formal and informal burial grounds, including the notorious 'White Sands'. Those interred in the informal burial grounds included a cross-section of the underclass of colonial Cape Town: slaves, free-blacks, artisans, fishermen, sailors, maids, washerwomen and their children, as well as executed criminals, suicide deaths, paupers, and unidentified victims of shipwrecks (Hart 2003). In the 1820s this area, the historical District One, was divided up for real estate and renamed Green Point. Later still, light industry moved into the area, and it fell into disrepair. In the late 1960s and early 1970s, black and Coloured residents of the inner-city, working-class neighbourhood of Green Point were forcibly removed in terms of the notorious Group Areas Act, a form of ethnic cleansing. In the property boom of 2000–8 Green Point was reborn as 'De Waterkant', part of the city's glitzy international zone and a centre of 'pink Cape Town'. It is to this latter conjunction that we can attribute the events around Prestwich Street exhumation, and their melancholy aftermath.

In May 2003, in the course of construction activities at a city block in Prestwich Street, Cape Town, human bones were discovered. The developer, Styleprops Ltd., notified the South African Heritage Resources Agency in accordance with the newly passed National Heritage Resources Act, and construction was halted. An archaeological contractor was appointed to handle the management of the site, and to run a public consultation process. At this point, the state heritage agency, the South African Heritage Resources Agency (SAHRA), made the first of a number of questionable decisions. The new heritage legislation, the National Heritage Resources Act, provides for a 60-day notification period during which work on site would normally be halted. It also provides for the possibility of non-exhumation as one of the outcomes of the public consultation process. SAHRA issued a permit for a 'rescue exhumation of human remains' to run concurrently with the notification period (SAHRA 2003b). By the time the first public meeting was held, seven weeks into the 60-day period, 500 individuals had been exhumed from the Prestwich Street site. The public response was angry. The minutes of the first public meeting record '[a] general feeling of dissatisfaction, disquiet and disrespect' (Malan 2003). Opposition to the exhumations came from several quarters: community activists, many of whom had been active in the struggle against apartheid; victims of forced removals; slave-descended persons; Christian and Muslim faith leaders; community-connected academics; and Khoisan representatives. The minutes of the meeting record comments by a number of unnamed individuals:

> Woman at back: On what basis does SAHRA decide on exhumation? Issues of African morality and African rights... (Malan 2003: 4)

Man in green shirt: Developer contacted SAHRA and did marketing strategy for this evening. I don't buy these ideas...Archaeologists can go elsewhere to dig...(Malan 2003: 5)

Rob of the Haven Shelter (a night shelter for homeless people): Many questions come from black people who hang around the site. Why are white people, and white women, scratching in our bones? This is sacrilege...(Malan 2003: 6)

Zenzile Khoisan said: '... these archaeologists, all they want to do is to dust off the bones and check them out with their scientific tests and to put them in the cupboard!' Storming out of the hall he shouted: 'Stop robbing graves! Stop robbing graves!' (Malan 2003: 6). On 1 August 2003 SAHRA announced an 'interim cessation' of archaeological activity on the site until 18 August, to allow for a wider process of public consultation. This was later extended to 31 August. Over a hundred submissions were collected as part of the process of public consultation. Mavis Smallberg from Robben Island Museum said 'my strong suggestion is to cover up the graves...Apart [from] the recently renamed Slave Lodge, there is no other public space that respectfully marks or memorialises the presence of slaves and the poor in Cape Town society...Only scientists are going to benefit from picking over these bones—of what purpose and use is it to the various communities to which the dead belong to know what they ate 150 years ago or where they came from?' (Smallberg 2003). The developer wrote to say that many of the luxury apartments comprising the proposed development on the site had been pre-sold. R21-million worth of sale contracts had been concluded and were at risk due to the delay. He expressed hope for a 'sensible solution' (Van der Merwe 2003).

On 9 August the synod of the Cape Town diocese of the Anglican Church, under the leadership of Archbishop Njongonkulu Ndungane, the successor to Desmond Tutu, unanimously passed a resolution condemning the exhumations and calling for '[our] government, though its heritage agency...to maintain the integrity of the site as that of a cemetery' (Wheeder 2003). On 16 August a second public meeting was convened, and on 29 August SAHRA convened a third public meeting at St Andrew's Church in Green Point 'to wind up the public participation process' (SAHRA 2003a). The verbatim transcript from the meeting records a number of comments from the floor. An unnamed respondent said 'there are multiple implications for this burial ground and its naked openness in the centre of the city...in this city there's never been a willingness to take up [the issue of genocide and the] destruction of human communities that were brought from across the globe...This is an opportunity to get to the bottom of that and time means different things to different people, institutions, stakeholders. Time for the dead—we need to consider what that means' (SAHRA 2003a: 17–18). Michael Wheeder, who was later to play a central role in the Hands Off Prestwich Street Ad Hoc Committee, said:

Many of us of slave descent cannot say 'here's my birth certificate'. We are part of the great unwashed of Cape Town...The black people, we rush into town on the taxis and we need to rush out of town. At a time many decades ago we lived and loved and laboured here. Nothing [reminds us of that history]...and so leave [the site] as a memorial to Mr. Gonzalez that lived there, Mrs. de Smidt that lived there. The poor of the area—the fishermen, the domestic workers, the people that swept the streets here. Memorialise that. Leave the bones there...That is a site they have owned for the first time in their lives *het hulle stukkie grond* (they have a little piece of ground). Leave them in that ground. Why find now in the gentility of this new dispensation a place with which they have no connection? (SAHRA 2003a: 18–19)

On 1 September, despite a clear weight of public opinion opposed to the exhumations, Pumla Madiba, the CEO of SAHRA, announced a resumption of archaeological work at the site. In a statement to the press she said 'Many of the people who objected were highly emotional and did not give real reasons why the skeletons should not be relocated [sic]' (Kassiem 2003: 1). On 4 September the Hands Off Prestwich Street Committee (HOC) was launched. At this point opposition to the exhumations shifted outside the officially mandated process of public consultation, to civil society and the politics of mass action. On 12 September the Hands Off Committee lodged an appeal with SAHRA calling for a halt to the exhumations and 'a full and extended process of community consultation' (HOC 2003). The appeal document notes that '[the] needs of archaeology as a science seem to have been given precedence over other needs: the needs of community socio-cultural history, of collective remembering and of acknowledging the pain and trauma related to the site and this history that gave rise to its existence'. In opposing the exhumations it argues that '[exhumation] makes impossible a whole range of people's identifications with that specific physical space in the city. Such a removal echoes, albeit unintentionally, the apartheid regime's forced removals from the same area' (HOC 2003: 8).

In the run up to the hearing the Hands Off Committee organized regular candle-light vigils at the Prestwich Street site on Sunday evenings. A billboard was erected outside St George's Cathedral, a symbolic site of anti-apartheid protest, with the slogan: 'Stop the exhumations! Stop the humiliation!' Lunchtime pickets were held in the city centre. On 19 November the SAHRA-convened Appeals Committee handed down a written ruling. The excavation permit awarded to the ACO was revalidated and the rights of the developer upheld. The Hands Off Committee reconvened as the Prestwich Place Project Committee (PPPC) to launch an appeal directly to the Minister of Arts and Culture. A letter of appeal was lodged with the Ministry on 12 January 2004. Supporting documents call upon the Minister to expropriate the site and 'to conserve Prestwich Place as a National Heritage Site' and a site of conscience (PPPC 2003). The vision of the PPPC was to preserve the Prestwich Street site as a *vrijplaats*, an open space for memory and identity. The term is Christian Ernsten's, a graduate student in the Centre for African Studies at the University of Cape Town who followed events closely. He writes: 'The Dutch word means something in between the English "shelter" and "free zone", a space of security and creativity at the same time' (Ernsten 2006: 13). At this point, all of the human remains on the original site had been exhumed and were in temporary storage in a warehouse on the adjacent block. During the SAHRA appeal process the developer had applied for, and been granted, permits to disinter human remains on the adjacent block. This was expected to result in the exposure of a further 800–1,000 bodies. On 21 April 2004—Freedom Day in South Africa—the remains were ceremonially transferred from Green Point to the mortuary of Woodstock Day Hospital, on the other side of the city. Some of the remains were carried in procession through the city centre in eleven flag-draped boxes, one for each of the official language groups in the country. On 22 July the developer was informed that the appeal to the Minister had been dismissed and that construction activities on the site could continue.

With the failure of the appeal, the focus of attention shifted to questions of memorialization and access to the remains. Alan Morris, a University of Cape Town-based physical anthropologist, emerged as the most outspoken proponent of a 'pro-science, pro-exhumation' position in the public transcript around Prestwich Street. In his submission to SAHRA as part of the public participation process he fulminated against 'prominent academics' and 'pseudo-politicians' from the historically black University of the Western Cape who were standing in the way of 'development'. In April 2005 two of Morris's graduate students, Jacqui Friedling and Thabang Manyaapelo, applied to SAHRA to conduct basic anatomical research on the Prestwich Street remains. Their application was turned down, largely on the basis of a negative response from the PPPC. An activist in the PPPC described this to me as a 'rearguard action': having failed in their initial objective of halting the exhumations and preserving the integrity of the site with its remains, their concern was to protect the remains against further invasive procedures. In response, Friedling said: 'SAHRA has denied all South Africans the right to know about their heritage...The information we can get from these bones will make these people come alive again' (Gosling 2005). Around this time, the City of Cape Town initiated discussions with SAHRA and the PPPC around a permanent holding place or 'ossuary' for the Prestwich Street human remains, still in temporary storage in the Woodstock Day Hospital. The proposed site was a triangular piece of land owned by the city on the corner of Buitengracht and Somerset Roads, a busy traffic intersection three blocks from the Prestwich Street site. This project went ahead, and construction of the New Prestwich Memorial Building was completed in 2007. With the construction of the Cape Town Stadium in Green Point as part of the preparations for the 2010 FIFA World Cup, this unpromising site was reconfigured through its adjacency to a 'fan walk', laid out from the centre of the city to the new stadium. The dead of Prestwich Street, in their restless transit of the postapartheid city, would be brought into a new set of relationships: this time with the tens of thousands of football fans who walked in mass procession to watch the big games. A number of participants would comment that the last time they had taken to the streets of the city in this way was in the mass marches of the late 1980s, to protest against apartheid.

30.3 A Point of Fracture

Clearly, Prestwich Street constitutes a point of fracture in postapartheid society. At stake were issues of history, memory, and heritage, but also questions of citizenship, restitution, and the possibilities and limitations of a postapartheid public sphere. A number of cleavages emerged, as it were, at the sharp edge of the trowel at Prestwich Street. One of these was the difference in disciplinary responses to the exhumations. Most archaeologists and physical anthropologist were emphatically pro-exhumation. Scholarly opposition to the exhumations was led by a group of historians at the historically black University of the Western Cape. My own position, as an archaeologist based at the University of Cape Town who was opposed to the exhumations and sympathetic to the position of the HOC, was unusual. Additional tensions emerged between national and regional heritage priorities around Prestwich Street. These are instructive to the extent that they cut to the heart of issues of race and class at play in these events (see also Mullins, this volume). It has been suggested that one of the reasons why the PPPC failed in its appeal to the Minister was that this was seen as a 'Cape' issue, tied to Coloured identity politics and Coloured histories. In a South African context the notion of Colouredness denotes a complex amalgamation of creole or mestizo identities, with the descendants of Khoisan groups and persons imported to the Cape as slaves. Enslaved persons were transported from East and West Africa, Madagascar, the Dutch possessions in Batavia, and from as far afield as China and Japan. The creolized nature of identity politics at the Cape, much like the hybrid nature of the Prestwich Street site, with its hotchpotch of the urban poor, is in tension with national heritage priorities articulated in terms of 'Africanization', and accounts of essentialized African cultural histories. Thus it is relevant that most of the archaeological contractors and students who worked on the site are white, and that many of the activists of the HOC are Coloured, just as it is relevant that the CEO of SAHRA at the time and the Minster of Arts and Culture are black and that the developer is white. However, rather than finding in the events a simple fable of racial antagonism, they arguably represent a more complex convergence between new (black) and historical (white) elites, and the continued marginalization of black and Coloured urban working-class histories and imaginaries. Part of the value of Prestwich Street—a value whose loss we may only see clearly in the years to come—was in reminding us of the essential nature of Cape Town as a creolized and cosmopolitan place, an entrepôt and incipient world city in the globalism of colonialism. It was this conception of Cape Town that was replaced by the apartheid conception of the *moederstad* (mother city), a little bit of Europe on the dark tip of Africa. The practice of forced removals, like the forced removals that affected the black former residents of Green Point, gave physical form to this conception, writing apartheid into the landscape (Murray et al. 2007).

30.4 RIVAL DISCOURSES

One of the most instructive identifications made by the Hands Off Committee was an explicit connection between deep histories of slavery at the Cape, and recent histories of forced removal. This conception of transhistorical time and empathetic identification stands in sharp contrast to the linearity of disciplinary time and heritage legislation, where forms of contemporary interest have to be argued in terms of notions of direct descent. At an early stage in the events around Prestwich Street, two distinct discourses emerged and were deployed in public contestations. The first, and more familiar of these, was a disciplinary discourse articulated in terms of notions of the rights of access of science, the value of the remains as a source of 'hidden histories', and the ability of archaeology to deliver 'the truth of the past'. At the first public meeting, the archaeologists of a Special Focus Reference Group established by SAHRA presented a proposal in which they stated: 'These skeletons are also—literally—our history, the ordinary people of Cape Town, whose lives are not written in the official documents of the time…If we want to recover their history, then one of the most powerful ways to do so is through the study of their skeletons' (Sealy 2003: 1). In this case the semantic slide from 'our history' to 'their history' is instructive. A number of tropes emerged and were recycled by archaeologists throughout the process. At the second public meeting Belinda Mutti, an archaeologist, argued in favour of exhumation 'to give history back to the people' (Malan 2003: 12). Liesbet Schiettecatte argued that '[leaving] bones leaves information unknown. Studying them brings them back to life …' (Malan 2003: 13). Mary Patrick argued to '[continue the] exhumation—otherwise half a story is being told' (Malan 2003: 13). As a set of representative responses these reference both local histories of practice and global debates in archaeology. One source is the significant impact of the New Archaeology on South African archaeology in the late 1960s and early 1970s. Coming during a period of increased state repression and increased funding for the sciences, sometimes referred to as 'high apartheid', the resultant turn away from contemporary society, critical theory, and 'politics' provided a crucial orientation for the discipline and remains a deeply entrenched legacy (Shepherd 2003). A second source is the local influence of debates in North American Historical Archaeology in the late 1980s and early 1990s, premised on notions of material culture as a more 'democratic' source able to deliver hidden histories. Important, and even admirable, as such intentions might be, at Prestwich Street they resulted in the considerable irony of removing the remains from a self-identified and passionately articulate group of persons (the activists of the HOC), in the name of returning them as 'history' to a gener-alized conception of 'the people'. It also raises the question of the nature of the narratives returned as history as the result of such disciplinary interventions. In practice, these have tended to be severely curtailed, essentially archaeological data relating to the provenance of the burials, and physical, chemical, and anthropometric measurements of the remains. It was this conception of history that was widely rejected by anti-exhumation campaigners, in favour of more embracing notions of learning, knowledge, and the meaning of the past in the present.

However, the most instructive convergence at Prestwich Street was between a notion of archaeology as science and a discourse of cultural resource management (CRM). Like debates in Historical Archaeology, CRM discourse was an entrant on the South African scene in the late 1980s. Its local significance lay in the manner in which it coincided with a period of political transition. CRM discourse had two notable effects: it gave archaeolo-gists a language through which to speak, or conceptualize, the political events of the period 1990–4, and it substantially reconfigured accountabilities in the discipline. This was not in the direction of popular accountability and narrowing the gap between archaeology and society, as we might have expected in the first flush of democracy, but rather in the direc-tion of corporate accountability, a managerialist ethos, and a notion of professionalization (Shepherd 2008). At Prestwich Street, a notion of the rights of access of science coincided with the interests of the developer, and both were framed and facilitated by the discourse of cultural resource management, with its carefully scripted theatres of consultation, notions of value, and conceptions of what constitutes 'sensible' outcomes and 'reasonable' decisions. The effect of CRM discourse was to reframe archaeology as an instrumentalized practice in the service of development. Archaeologists at Prestwich Street were frequently heard to resent the intrusion of 'politics', and to argue that they were there as technicians, performing a service paid for by the developer. The regime of care that accompanies this conception of discipline might be described as a form of spatial and temporal boxing. Indeed, the image of the cardboard box of human remains haunts the transcript around Prestwich Street. The dead of Prestwich Street were exposed, photographed, exhumed, numbered, bagged, boxed, and transported. Their final apotheosis was in the stacked and numbered boxes on the shelves of the New Prestwich Memorial Building.

30.5 Time for the Dead

The most noteworthy aspect of the events around Prestwich Street was the manner in which the activists of the Hands Off Committee articulated and mobilized a counter-discourse, both as a way of conceptualizing their own relationship to the remains and as a way of mounting a public and legal challenge to the exhumations. In public statements, submissions, and appeals they emphasized the language of memory, experience, and empathetic identification. They sought to articulate an alternative set of values, and alternative notions of space and time. This included notions of the site as a site of memory and conscience (rather than an archaeological site), and in one memorable intervention, the notion of 'time for the dead'. Most of all, they contested the notion of a distanced and objectified past, whose relationship with the present is mediated by expert knowledge. In their more complexly imagined version of this relationship, the re-emergence of the Prestwich Street dead in the world of the living is not described through the trope of discovery (as it is in disciplinary accounts), but rather as a 'learning moment'. As such, it represents both a challenge and an opportunity to reflect on neglected and disavowed pasts, and on the unfinished business of social transformation. Achille Mbembe writes of archives and memorials as spaces of consignment, whose work is to sequester the past and isolate it in space and time (Mbembe 2002). In reviewing the thought and practice of the Hands Off Committee one finds the opposite intention: an attempt to proliferate a set of connections, and to give form to the multiple ties that bind communities of the living and the dead. One expression of this was the kind of ontology of respect that described the Prestwich Street dead as dead persons and named individuals, rather than as 'skeletons' or 'bones' as was prevalent in disciplinary and media accounts. Significantly, the counter-discourse of the HOC was framed as a challenge to conceptions of knowledge in archaeology. They were critical of what they described as the 'archaeologization' of the research process, by which they meant the foregrounding of archaeological methods at the expense of other approaches: oral history, social history, and archival research. In rejecting the 'hidden histories' that archaeologists purported to unearth, they were rejecting a narrowed and restricted conception of history as archaeometric measurement and statements of probability linked to diet and point of origin. In their account, the 'learning' to be derived from Prestwich Street is not confined to a catalogue of facts about the past, but includes the status and meaning of the past in its relation to the present. Disavowed histories of slavery at the Cape have their counterpart in a contemporary set of disavowed debates, around the unfinished agenda of social and economic transformation, and the lack of material restitution for apartheid.

30.6 SPECTRES OF APARTHEID

In *Spectres of Marx*, Jacques Derrida describes 'spectres' as that which history has repressed (Derrida 1994). It would be fair to describe postapartheid Cape Town—a city which remains predominantly racially segregated, where the rich live a fantasy of a kind of displaced Côte d'Azur while the poor struggle to survive in shacks made of cardboard boxes and plastic bags—as a city haunted by the spectres of the past. In this context, the struggle around memory is much more than a struggle to fill the gaps and write inclusive histories. It becomes a struggle around the meaning of the present and the possibilities of the future. Dominant discourses of globalization and development work to conceal local histories and struggles and replace them with a timeless, placeless cosmopolitanism, the everywhere and nowhere of the global postmodern. In doing so they foreclose on other—more interesting, creative, and open—futures in quite particular ways: by presenting us with a world that just *is*, severed from a logic of place and human struggle. For the beneficiaries of violent histories this translates into a world without guilt; for the victims, mute submission before the inevitability of the present. Prestwich Street was that rarest of things, a public and visible surfacing of the spectres of the past, a moment when the ghosts walk in the light. The lost opportunity of Prestwich Street exists at several levels. It was a lost opportunity to rethink and reimagine forms of disciplinary practice in archaeology in the wake of apartheid. It was a lost opportunity to rethink heritage practice, and to mould the new legislation in the direction of a more inclusive set of protocols. It was a lost opportunity to reimagine modes of citizenship in postapartheid society, and to revivify and reinhabit the public sphere. In immediate ways, it was a lost opportunity to reflect on the meaning of histories of racial slavery in the city, and the afterlife of apartheid forced removals. As part of a counter-discourse around Prestwich Street, I saw some powerful proposals around forms of memorialization. These envisaged leaving the site of interment with its remains in the ground as an open space for reflection in an increasingly densely constructed cityscape. In my own work I wrote in favour of the notion of an 'archaeology of silence'. This is premised on the idea that our generation—the first generation after apartheid—stands to learn more by leaving the remains in the ground and starting a conversation around the implications of their 'naked openness in the city', than by exhuming them and subjecting them to disciplinary procedures. For us, the 'learning opportunity' is not about imagined pasts sequestered in deep time, but about the far more urgent and difficult matter of how it is that we meet one another as South Africans who stand on opposite sides of a divided history.

30.7 AT THE TRUTH CAFÉ

That feels like an ending, but wait: we are not done with Prestwich Street yet. I have in front of me a glossy brochure for 'The Rockwell: luxury De Waterkant living' (Dogon and Gavrill 2005). The Rockwell, which was constructed on the Prestwich Street site, consists of 103 'New York-style' apartments, plus parking bays, a private gym, a restaurant, a deli, and a swimming pool. The historical point of reference for the development is the Harlem Renaissance, or as the brochure has it, New York's 'Jazz Age'. According to the brochure: 'Inspired by the early 1900 buildings of downtown Manhattan, The Rockwell displays an inherent richness and warmth.' This is because 'At the turn of the previous century, they did design right. Not only because it was classical in form and function... But because they did it with soul' (Dogon and Gavrill 2005: 1). Doing it 'with soul' becomes a refrain, and the rest of the brochure makes reference to 'Rock and Soul', 'Pure Soul', 'Rich Soul', 'Style and Soul', and 'Rhythm and Soul'. By way of summary, it declares in bold type: 'The craftsmanship must have character. The design must have heart. The Rockwell has it all' (Dogon and Gavrill 2005: 1). The accompanying images show clean, depopulated interiors, dusted free of history, unwelcome associations, and the stain of the earth below. Other photographs illustrate the notion of 'luxury De Waterkant living': caviar perched on a wedge of toast, a bowl of ripe figs, rounds of sushi on a plate. How do we interpret this, other than the annihilation of history? The full force of the phrase 'forced removals' strikes home. It is as though history, memory, every rooted association between a group of people and a site on the landscape, has been evacuated, pulled up at the roots, to make way for a copy-writer's whimsy. At Prestwich

Street we see the instantiation of a new kind of postapartheid historical imaginary, in which history is imagined by the victors and beneficiaries, and in which victims have no place outside the borders of memorial parks and heritage precincts. If The Rockwell suggests a loosening of the forms of historical representation and the bonds of obligation that bind the present and the past, or the living and the dead, then subsequent events confirm this. Faced with the challenge of making the New Prestwich Memorial Building economically sustainable, the City Council turned over most of the public space of the memorial for the establishment of a coffee shop. The website Bizcommunity.com reports: 'Charismatic leader and coffee evangelist David Donde launched his new coffee brand and café, Truth Coffeecult, on Wednesday 24 March 2010, at the Prestwich Memorial'. Truth Coffeecult's own website invites you 'to experience the simple elegance of micro-lots of artisanal roasted relationship coffees prepared by geek baristas'. It continues: 'Not all coffees are created equal. At Truth, the bitter horror of the over-roasted bean is avoided...Experience Truth. Coffee as religion'. Baristas at the Truth Café wear T-shirts with the legend 'Truth'. At the cash register one is invited to give 'Tips for Truth'. A recent promotion invited you to: 'Get a free cup of Truth'. In a more direct set of references, coffee grinders at the Truth Café bear the image of a human skull crossed by the letter 'T', and stacked cardboard boxes of coffee reference the stacked boxes of human remains in the vault next door. Visit the Truth Café on an average day and you will find city-centre yuppies, tourists, and members of Green Point's boho elite sipping coffee, taking advantage of the free Wi-Fi, and enjoying Cape Town's fickle weather.

30.8 Conclusions: Entrapment

There are many kinds of entrapment. We can be entrapped by the energies of unrequited pasts. Or we can be entrapped by the present, and our inability to imagine a different relationship between self, society, and history. The truth of Prestwich Street is not a cup of coffee. Rather, it is the difficult and uncomfortable recognition that forms of historical oppression and atrocity live on in forms of contemporary social injustice. The past is not behind us. My interest in the events around Prestwich Street has been in tracking a kind of discursive entrapment which affected archaeologists close to these events. That is, the sense in which, as archaeologists, we were interpolated by an idea of discipline and a weight of inherited practice, so that we lost a certain freedom and facility in responding to events, crises, and challenges. This becomes especially debilitating in contemporary contexts of practice, in what I would call the postcolonial postmodern. In such contexts, I want to suggest, we move well beyond a familiar thematic of heritage and a simple relationship between remembering and forgetting, or between authenticity and restitution, or between truth and representation. As a way out of this entrapment, the case that I have been making here is for a set of encounters, or conversations, between disciplinary knowledges and the kind of subaltern epistemologies mobilized by groups like the Hands Off Committee. It should be clear that this is an encounter which takes place not as a meeting of science and culture (or tradition), as in the disciplinary scripting of this encounter, but on explicitly epistemological grounds. A set of questions follows: In what ways do local, subaltern, and fugitive knowledges and regimes of care cause us to rethink and reimagine key disciplinary ideas and practices? In what ways do they challenge us to think about the forms of epistemic violence that lie at the heart of disciplinary regimes of care in archaeology? How, in a spirit of humility, openness, and listening, as non-disciplinarians and as disciplinarians of a particular kind, do we begin a conversation about the things that I know and the things that you know (see also Webmoor, this volume)? And what sort of archaeology might be the result?

A salient feature of contemporary contexts of practice is that disciplinary archaeology no longer holds a monopoly on driving intellectual agendas and on the formation of theory. New and challenging forms of theorization are emerging among social movements mobilized around archaeological/sacred sites, material cultures, and human remains. At the same time, disciplinary archaeology has increasingly moved in the direction of cultural resource management, an instrumentalized form of practice framed by a set of largely unquestioned protocols and procedures. Discussions that take place under the heading of archaeological theory frequently take the form of a game of words, substantially delinked from contemporary contexts of practice and communities of concern. Two comments follow. The first is that this might be characterized as a crisis of ideas in contemporary archaeology. The second is that the extent to which archaeology is able to constitute itself as a discipline that is critically engaged and responsive to contemporary contexts will depend, in large part, on the willingness and ability of archaeologists to cross epistemological boundaries to engage with local, subalternized, non-hegemonic, non-disciplinary bodies of knowledge and practice.

REFERENCES

Coombes, Annie E. 2011. Witnessing History/Embodying Testimony: Gender and Memory in Postapartheid South Africa. *Journal of the Royal Anthropological Institute* 17: 92–112.

Derrida Jacques. 1994. *Spectres of Marx: The State of Debt, the Work of Mourning, and the New International.* New York and London: Routledge.

Dogon, D. and Gavrill, G. 2005. *The Rockwell: Luxury de Waterkant Living.* Cape Town: Dogon Gavrill Properties.

Ernsten, Christian. 2006. *Stylizing Cape Town: Problematizing the Heritage Management of Prestwich Street.* University of Cape Town, Cape Town.

Gosling, Melanie. 2005. UCT Students Exasperated as Sahra Blocks Bones Study. *Cape Times,* 22 November: 7.

Gqola, Pumla D. 2010. *What is Slavery to Me? Postcolonial/Slave Memory in Postapartheid South Africa.* Johannesburg: Wits University Press.

Hart, Tim. 2003. Heritage Impact Assessment of West Street and Erf 4721 Green Point, Cape Town. Prepared for Styleprops 120 (Pty) Ltd, December. University of Cape Town, Cape Town.

HOC. 2003. Substantiation of Appeal Submitted by the Hands Off Prestwich Street Ad Hoc Committee. Hands Off Prestwich Street Ad Hoc Committee, Cape Town.

Kassiem, A'Eysha. 2003. Public Given Time to Appeal Against Moving Graves. *Cape Times,* 3 September: 6.

Liebmann, Matthew and Rizvi, Uzma (eds.). 2008. *Archaeology and the Postcolonial Critique.* Lanham, MD: Altamira Press.

Lydon, Jane and Rizvi, Uzma (eds.). 2010. *Handbook of Postcolonial Archaeology.* Walnut Creek, CA: Left Coast Press.

Malan, Antonia. 2003. Prestwich Place: Exhumation of Accidentally Discovered Burial Ground in Green Point, Cape Town [Permit no. 80/03/06/001/51]: Public Consultation Process

9 June to 18 August 2003. Prepared by Dr Antonia Malan, Cultural Sites and Resources Forum for the South African Heritage Resources Agency and the Developer. Cultural Sites and Resources Forum, Cape Town.

Mbembe, Achille. 2002. The Power of the Archive and its Limits. In *Refiguring the Archive*, ed. Caroline Hamilton, Verne Harris, Jane Taylor, Michele Pickover, Graeme Reid, and Razia Saleh, pp. 19–26. Cape Town: David Philip.

Murray, Noëleen, Shepherd, Nick, and Hall, Martin (eds.). 2007. *Desire Lines: Space, Memory and Identity in the Post-Apartheid City*. Abingdon: Routledge.

PPPC. 2003. Submission to DAC Tribunal, Prestwich Place Project Committee, Cape Town.

SAHRA. 2003a. Minutes of South African Heritage Resources Agency Public Consultation Meeting held on 29 August 2003 at St Andrew's Presbyterian Church, Somerset Rd, Green Point. South African Heritage Resources Agency, Cape Town.

—— 2003b. Permit No. 80/03/06/001/51 issued by the South African Heritage Resources Agency (SAHRA) Archaeology, Palaeontology, Meteorites and Heritage Objects Permit Committee to T. J. G. Hart, Archaeology Contracts Office. University of Cape Town, Cape Town.

Schmidt, Peter R. (ed.). 2009. *Postcolonial Archaeologies in Africa*. Santa Fe: School for Advanced Research.

Sealy Judith. 2003. A Proposal for the Future of the Prestwich Street Remains. University of Cape Town, Cape Town.

Shepherd, Nick. 2003. State of the Discipline: Science, Culture and Identity in South African Archaeology. *Journal of Southern African Studies* 29: 823–44.

—— 2006. What Does it Mean to Give the Past Back to the People? Archaeology and Ethics in the Post-Colony. In *Archaeology and Capitalism: From Ethics to Politics*, ed. Y Hamilakis and P. Duke, pp. 99–114. London: UCL Press.

—— 2007. Archaeology Dreaming: Postapartheid Urban Imaginaries and the Bones of the Prestwich Street Dead. *Journal of Social Archaeology* 7: 3–28.

—— 2008. Heritage. In *New South African Keywords*, ed. N. Shepherd and S. Robins, pp. 116–28. Cape Town and Athens, OH: Jacana Media and Ohio University Press.

Smallberg, Mavis. 2003. Email from Mavis Smallberg to Antonia Malan. Cape Town.

Van der Merwe, A. 2003. Report Submitted as Part of the Public Submission Process, August. Cape Town.

Wheeder, Michael. 2003. Email from Michael Wheeder to Mogamat Kamedien. Cape Town.

CHAPTER 31

··

ARCHAEOLOGIES OF
AUTOMOBILITY

··

PETER MERRIMAN

31.1 INTRODUCTION

··

IN Will Self's 1994 short story 'Scale', the main character loses his sense of scale while driving along the M40 motorway in Buckinghamshire, England. The motorway landscape leads him to reflect upon the damage his abuse of kaolin-morphine is doing to his body, depositing kaolin or clay along his veins and arteries with a result not unlike the clay-lined embankments or cuttings lining the nation's transport arteries. One night, in a drug-induced dream or delirium, he envisions the M40 as it will appear 20,000 years in the future, 'when the second neolithic age has dawned over Europe' (Self 1994: 96). The motorway is covered in grass, the signs are horizontal, providing tombs for 'motorway chieftains', and the 'simple' tribes which live on the motorway have adopted specific items of 'prehistoric road furniture' as 'totem[s]' (Self 1994: 96, 97). The primary character's academic thesis, 'No services: reflex ritualism and modern motorway signs (with special reference to the M40)', is now revered as an 'ancient text' which the motorway tribesmen can no longer read, but whose wise words have been transmitted orally through generations, underpinning their new religion and motorway culture (Self 1994: 98). Self's story provides a striking collision of the fictional and surreal with observations of contemporary life and minor fragments of Self's autobiography. Self was a heroin user from age seventeen to his mid-twenties, while he has positioned his interest in motorways as a reaction to his own father's intense dislike of them during his childhood (Self 1993; Shone 1993). For Self, 'the motorways of today are our pyramids, our ziggurats, our great collective earthworks' which he suggests will be studied in detail by archaeologists of the future (Self 1993: 1; see Edgeworth, this volume), and his prophecies do not appear that far-fetched at a time when archaeologists of contemporary life are suggesting that we turn our attention to such spaces (Penrose 2007), and heritage bodies and architectural historians have expressed a concern with the preservation of important examples of motorway architecture and engineering (Calladine and Morrison 1998; Glancey 1992). In Will Self's surreal future, archaeologists may read and fetishize motorways as exotic markers of contemporary Western societies, but for today's archaeologists the material cultures of mobility and automobility are significant as much for their ubiquity and banality as for their former exoticism, and they have become of interest to academics working across a number of disciplines in the humanities and social sciences.

In my own research I have approached the topics of automobility, driving, and the spaces of the road through the disciplinary lenses of geography, history, and sociology; undertaking research in public archives, company archives, and personal archives, as well as in second-hand bookshops and by collecting motorway ephemera through Internet auction sites. As DeLyser et al. (2004) have argued, Internet auction sites such as eBay have led to a significant transformation in cultures of collecting and archiving, becoming important spaces for academic research, and despite the persistence of disciplinary specialisms and methods, one can start to see a convergence of the methods being utilized in fields such as anthropology, geography, cultural studies, history, and archaeology. Different techniques of 'data' collection—from archival research, oral history, and field excavation techniques, to performative and participative methods, ethnography, and the collection of cultural artefacts—may still predominate in *particular* disciplines, but an increasing number of scholars are working with multiple methods, writing between or across these different disciplines.

31.2 ARCHAEOLOGIES OF THE MODERN ROAD

Archaeologists are no strangers to the spaces and materialities of roads. Modern road construction has long been seen as a valuable opportunity to excavate geological specimens and archaeological remains which might either be destroyed or become inaccessible (Carver 2009; Geological Survey 1959), while recent road widening schemes have provided opportunities for archaeologists to investigate sites, as was demonstrated in work by Atkins Heritage on the widening of the M1 in Hertfordshire (Bradley and Walter 2007). Of course, roads and tracks have a much longer history which has been explored by archaeologists. The material culture of prehistoric and Roman roads has provided an important focus for archaeological investigations (Bagshawe 1979; Bryant 1996; Davies 2008), but Roman roads have also exerted a material presence which has shaped later geographies of road construction, as can be seen in the modern incarnations of such roads as Watling Street, Ermine Street, and Fosse Way in Britain. Many routes taken by lanes, streets, and roads have been in use for centuries, being traversed by people of varying status, and it is therefore somewhat surprising that there have not been more archaeological studies of life on the road.

Alongside the massive growth in car ownership that has occurred in the vast majority of nations throughout the twentieth century, there has been a re-engineering of tracks, streets, and roads to cater for the new types and quantities of traffic that are emerging. Older roads have been paved, tarred, and sometimes realigned, widened, or bypassed, new construction techniques and materials have emerged, and roads have been furnished with painted lines, reflector studs, signs, lights, and drainage systems, as well as lay-bys, service areas, and petrol stations. In addition, there have emerged extensive infrastructures that facilitate automobility, including sites for parking/garaging, maintenance, refuelling, vehicle production, and retailing. The material infrastructure and economic networks underpinning automobility spread far and wide, occupying extensive areas of our cities and suburbs (Horvath 1974), requiring oil refineries, fuel distribution centres, and large car manufacturing plants. Over the past decade or so, the material cultures and practices surrounding the motor car have been receiving widespread attention, and alongside the increasing number of sociological, anthropological, historical, and geographical studies of automobility, roads, and driving which have been published in the past decade or so (for example, O'Connell 1998; Miller 2001; Featherstone et al. 2005; Böhm et al. 2006; Merriman 2007, 2012; Dalakoglou and Harvey 2012), archaeologists have started to pay greater attention to the material cultures of modern mobility and automobility (see Jones 1998; Graves-Brown 2000, 2007; Jones 2002; Minnis 2007; Newland et al. 2007; Penrose 2007; Bailey et al. 2009; Harrison and Schofield 2010). One example is the work of design historian Helen Jones. Writing in *British Archaeology* in October 1998, Jones explained how the material culture of British petrol stations had received little academic attention, despite their dramatic evolution throughout the twentieth century, and the existence of one Grade II listed petrol station—the unusual 1929 mock-Tudor, pagoda-roofed Park Langley garage in suburban Beckenham, Kent (Jones 1998). Indeed, I would argue that contemporary and historical archaeologists could usefully turn their attention to the nation's lay-bys, petrol stations, car parks, transport cafés, motorway service areas, and scrap yards, building upon the research already undertaken by scholars such as Sefryn Penrose, members of the 'van' project, and a number of historians and cultural geographers (Jeremiah 1995; O'Connell 1998; Lawrence 1999; Merriman 2007; Newland et al. 2007; Penrose 2007; Bailey et al. 2009).

What kind of studies do I envisage archaeologists undertaking? Well, traversing Britain's main A-roads such as the A1, A2, A4, A5, A6, and A40 one cannot help but notice the distinctive lay-bys, petrol stations, and transport cafés which line their sides (some of them disused and run-down), and I believe there is a great opportunity to undertake archaeological investigations of these sites to complement the already-existing photographic studies by Paul Graham and others (Graham 1983). One could envisage a contemporary archaeology of lay-bys that utilizes field excavation techniques, photography, studies of the material culture of these spaces (the litter, street furniture, botany, etc.), as well as studies using archival, oral history, ethnographic, and other social science and humanities methods. Lay-bys are typical examples of the kinds of mundane spaces which have largely unwritten histories. They are numerous but vary enormously in their appearance and use, from simple parking bays immediately adjacent to the carriageway, to extensive sections of old road (or former bends) that are sometimes screened off with vegetation, or on a different level. Lay-bys may not appear to be under threat, but widening schemes can erase these more-or-less innocuous landscape features in which the majority of motorists only dwell temporarily. Perhaps we do not inhabit lay-bys with much thought. Perhaps we do not inhabit them as we used to, now that many long-distance journeys are undertaken on motorways and dual carriageways with purpose-built service areas. Nevertheless, lay-bys do enter the discourses of official bodies, including governmental and non-governmental organizations, and groups such as the Campaign to Protect Rural England continue to express concern about the amount of rubbish and signs littering lay-bys, just as they did in the 1920s and 1930s (Williams-Ellis 1928, 1938; Peach and Carrington 1930; CPRE 1996).

31.3 MATERIAL CULTURE OF BRITAIN'S MOTORWAYS

Motorways are relatively recent arrivals in the British landscape, the first schemes having been proposed as early as 1902, but with construction only beginning in the late 1950s

(Drake et al. 1969; Charlesworth 1984; Merriman 2007). Contemporary archaeologists have already undertaken some important work in this area. In her English Heritage book *Images of Change: An Archaeology of England's Contemporary Landscape*, Sefryn Penrose includes sections on motorways and motorway service areas, as well as roads and car parks, while photographs of the M1 by Matthew Walter appear on its front cover, title page, and in a number of other sections (Penrose 2007: 27, 50–1, 58–9). Walter's photographs were commissioned by Atkins Heritage to form a 'photographic study of the changing M1 landscape during…widening between junctions 6a and 10', and the photographs capture the processual nature of the construction landscape, where 'temporary landscapes and spaces spring up' (Bradley and Walter 2007: 13). In the broader sphere of heritage and architecture, English Heritage and the Royal Commission on Historic Monuments in England have undertaken surveys of Britain's motorway architecture (Calladine and Morrison 1998), while amateur and professional historians are becoming increasingly interested in the history of these spaces (Bridle and Porter 2002; Baldwin and Baldwin 2004; Merriman 2005, 2006, 2007, 2011; McCoubrey 2008). While today's cultural commentators, artists, and academics frequently portray Britain's motorways as somewhat banal, grey, and characterless 'non-places' devoid of any distinctiveness, specificity, architectural importance, or social relations (Augé 1995; cf. Bracewell 2002; Merriman 2004), they were constructed and experienced as very different kinds of spaces in the late 1950s and 1960s.

Despite the emergence of numerous plans and proposals for motorways by lobby groups before the Second World War, the first phase of Britain's motorway network was very much a product of post-war reconstruction, having been outlined as part of the Labour government's proposals to reconstruct the main national routes in May 1946 (Figure 31.1) (Parliamentary Debates 1946). Engineering and construction companies were proud to align themselves with these pioneering national construction projects, publishing advertisements in national newspapers which informed readers of their role in helping to build 'tomorrow's brave new world' (Blackwood Hodge 1959: 8). In an advertisement placed in *The Times* on the opening day of the M1, 2 November 1959, Caterpillar highlighted their involvement in the physical, social, and economic reconstruction of Britain, 'helping to build a better Britain':

> This is the beginning of a new era. But only the beginning. Our highways will reflect the Nation's prosperity, save the Nation more than they cost to build, benefit each and every one of us—and we need them Now. Caterpillar has contributed much to these new avenues of progress and opportunity—and will contribute more. For Caterpillar earth-moving equipment is as reliable and sure as progress itself. (Caterpillar 1959: 5)

As these adverts attest, it was the completion of motorways which often received the most attention, marked by special sections in newspapers and motoring magazines, and opening ceremonies presided over by senior politicians and dignitaries such as Prime Minister Harold Macmillan and successive Ministers of Transport. Nevertheless, these advertisements and the photographic studies of Matthew Walter also affirm that road construction is a process of engaging with and shaping the landscape, a process whose practices and materialities exceed the finished forms of the motorway structure.

Motorway construction sites present enormous challenges for contracting engineers, due to their linearity, the large number of barriers such as rivers and railway lines that lie along their routes, and the detours necessary to survey a route by road. In the case of rural motorway construction sites, accommodation for labourers often proved an issue, and with

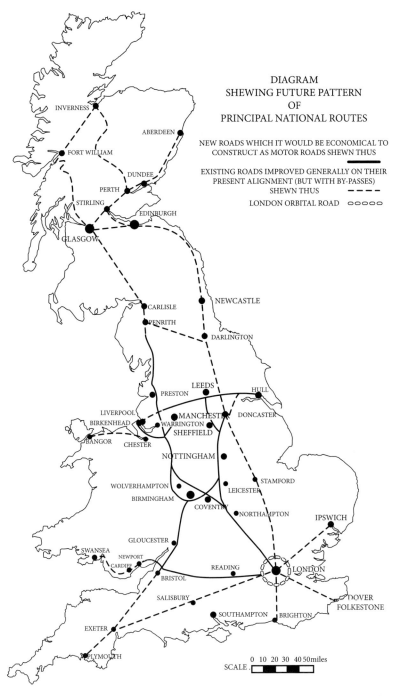

DIAGRAM
SHEWING FUTURE PATTERN
OF
PRINCIPAL NATIONAL ROUTES

NEW ROADS WHICH IT WOULD BE ECONOMICAL TO
CONSTRUCT AS MOTOR ROADS SHEWN THUS

EXISTING ROADS IMPROVED GENERALLY ON THEIR
PRESENT ALIGNMENT (BUT WITH BY-PASSES)
SHEWN THUS
LONDON ORBITAL ROAD

SCALE 0 10 20 30 40 50 miles

FIGURE 31.1 The Ministry of Transport's 1946 plan for reconstructing Britain's national routes (redrawn, from a photograph by Peter Merriman)

the M1 Laing set up caravan sites at Hanslope, Farley Green, Long Buckby, Sherington, and Husborne Crawley for its skilled staff and their families, they rented houses for senior engineers, and arranged hostel accommodation in towns such as Leighton Buzzard, Aylesbury, and Rugby for the casual labour force (*Team Spirit* 1958; Rolt 1959). While it would be easy to conceive the archaeology of the M1 as limited by its embankments and fences, the effects of motorway construction spread far and wide, as gravel and materials were excavated from nearby quarries, construction machines travelled along narrow country lanes, workers lived in nearby communities, and stories of the construction project were not only transmitted to local and national communities through newspapers, newsreels, and television reports, but to Laing employees throughout the world in its company newsletter *Team Spirit* (Merriman 2005). What is more, Laing proudly celebrated the multicultural and multinational nature of its workforce, which was made up of Canadian, South African, Jamaican, Polish, Indian, Hungarian, Australian, Scottish, and Welsh labourers, as well as large numbers of Irish and English workers (Rolt 1959). As the left-wing folk-song composers Ewan MacColl, Charles Parker, and Peggy Seeger revealed in their 1959 BBC Radio ballad about the construction of the M1 motorway, entitled *Song of a Road*, these workers brought folk songs, stories, and memories of home to the construction site, and we can also presume that they carried stories of the project away with them, to their next project or their families back home (MacColl et al. 1999; Merriman 2007: 124–40). Archaeologists of the motorway should pay close attention to these different aspects of motorway construction, and one can envisage archaeologies of the motorway that combine historical research, interviews, and oral histories, with archaeological fieldwork on the ground—investigating the sites where transitory caravan sites, hostels, quarries, and offices were located, as well as the finished structures of motorways themselves.

The designs proposed for the material structures or infrastructures of the M1 generated a large amount of discussion amongst civil servants, engineers, landscape architects, architects, and modern designers. The routing and design of the Luton to Rugby section of the M1 was undertaken by Sir Owen Williams and Partners, a distinguished firm of consulting engineers, but while Sir Owen was a modernist architect-engineer whose structures designed in the 1920s and 1930s were widely praised by architects and architectural critics, his post-war designs for the M1 motorway received widespread criticism from an array of eminent critics (Merriman 2007). Nikolaus Pevsner, John Betjeman, Ian Nairn, and Reyner Banham criticized the mass and bulk of the heavy reinforced concrete bridges spanning the main carriageways, and eminent landscape architects such as Brenda Colvin and Sylvia Crowe asserted similar views, while also criticizing the way the motorway structures were fitted into the surrounding landscape (Colvin 1959; Crowe 1959, 1960; Banham 1960, 1962; Betjeman 1960; Pevsner 1960, 1961; Nairn 1963). While today's heritage bodies and architectural historians focus their attention on the history of motorway structures—from viaducts and bridges to motorway service areas—the landscape architecture and broader design of the motorway is also a key part of its material culture and its architectural, geographical, historical, and archaeological significance. Historical geographers, anthropologists, landscape archaeologists, and landscape architects have all developed a keen interest in the materialities and practices associated with the production and consumption of different landscapes. In the case of the M1, the motorway's landscapes were designed by forestry and landscape consultants engaged by Sir Owen Williams and Partners, but the schemes underwent significant modification following extensive criticisms by the government's Advisory Committee on the Landscape Treatment of Trunk Roads (Sir OWP 1957; Merriman 2006, 2007). The Landscape Advisory Committee deemed the original planting proposals to be too ornamental, urban/suburban, exotic, fussy, and colourful for a rural English motorway (Merriman 2007: 89). Distinctive landscaping and planting ideologies were impressed upon the landscape of the motorway, emphasizing planting which was harmonious with the surrounding rural landscape, creating a sense of visual flow, and was comprised of species which would not excite or distract passing motorists (ACLTTR 1958; Colvin 1959). Archaeologists may find it difficult to trace the design history of the motorway landscapes and vegetation, for while planting proposals, reports, and government committee minutes tell us much about the concerns of various actors, they tell us nothing about how the landscape has evolved and grown since its planting, whether through human intervention—subsequent landscaping, planting, and verge management—or by the colonization of plants—brought in by wind, tyres, animals, or insects. A botanical survey by Nature Conservancy in 1970 revealed how the entire length of M1 between London and Leeds was populated with 384 species of vegetation, including many unusual plants which were not planted by highway agencies, such as yellow vetchling, purging flax, pepper saxifrage, and coriander (Way 1970; Mabey 1974; de Hamel 1976). The materialities of the motorway have been shaped by botanical processes, animal and bird movements, the weather, and other physical processes, while such technologies as crash barriers, signs, cat's eyes, warning signs, and emergency telephones have arrived in these spaces as the result of sometimes protracted discussions between government scientists and committees, engineers, the police, and designers in an attempt to create a transport system and environment that is safe, efficient, and aesthetically pleasing.

Humanities and social science scholars are starting to develop an interest in the embodied performances and more-than-representational practices which enliven and animate motorway environments of the past and present (Edensor 2003; Merriman 2007). The materialities of motorways were not simply different in the 1960s to the early twenty-first century, but the material cultures and practices surrounding these spaces were markedly different, and archaeologists of automobility and motorway culture should be as concerned with tracing these more-or-less transitory practices as they are with examining the material forms of these structures and landscapes. In the late 1950s and 1960s motorways really caught the public's imagination. On the opening day of the M1 motorists queued up to test out this new speed-limitless road, with the queue at the northern terminus of the motorway being three-quarters of a mile long (*Birmingham Mail* 1959). These pioneering motorists included journalists and sports-car drivers, but also ordinary families in ordinary family saloons, keen for an exciting day out. Motor magazines and motoring organizations published special maps and guides to help motorway drivers find and negotiate these spaces safely, but for many other motorists and non-motorists, the excitement of the M1 was consumed through sensational stories in national newspapers, children's books and games, pop songs, postcards, and a range of other popular representations and ephemera which took the spectacle, excitement, and modernity of the M1 into people's everyday lives (Merriman 2011). For today's archaeologists, anthropologists, geographers, and cultural historians interpreting the material cultures of such modern spaces, traditional archives provide only one valuable resource. Indeed, one is more likely to encounter motorway ephemera in charity shops, car boot sales, or second-hand book shops than in formal archives, and these places form important research sites for contemporary and historical archaeologists of popular culture. Many scholars already use eBay as a tool for tracking down materials, engaging in novel practices of digital excavation, and building their own private collections of research materials (DeLyser et al. 2004). In my research on the history of the M1 and other motorways, I have built up my own collection of ephemera, including a glass ash-tray commemorating the opening of the M1 (Figure 31.2), children's toy sets, and a silver-enamel charm (Figure 31.3). Such popular products were purchased or acquired by an unknown population, consumed for varying periods of time, discarded or stored away, and in some cases sold on.

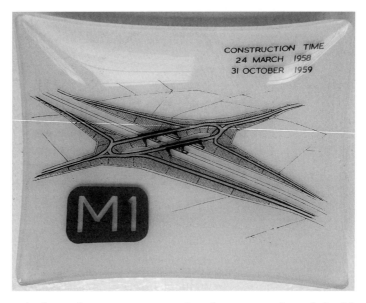

FIGURE 31.2 A glass ash-tray commemorating the construction of the M1 motorway (photograph: Peter Merriman)

FIGURE 31.3 A silver and blue enamel M1 charm to be worn on a charm bracelet (photograph: Peter Merriman)

31.4 ROAD SIGNS AND THE MATERIAL CULTURE OF LANGUAGE POLITICS

Road signs, like motorway carriageways, have a fairly ubiquitous, mundane, and functional material presence in our contemporary landscapes (see Wrights & Sites, this volume), but they have also been targeted as symbols of authority by protest groups. In a recent project undertaken with my colleague Rhys Jones, we have attempted to unpick the cultural history and contemporary archaeology of the campaign for bilingual road signs in Wales (Jones and Merriman 2009, 2012; Merriman and Jones 2009). Drawing upon archival research and oral history interviews, we have traced the history of the bilingual Welsh/English road signs campaign, which started with requests for translation advice from councils in Welsh-speaking areas during 1966 and 1967, was quickly followed with lobbying by Plaid Cymru (the Welsh Nationalist Party) and Cymdeithas yr Iaith Gymraeg (the Welsh Language Society), and eventually escalated into widespread direct action by the Welsh Language Society due to the perceived intransigence of the British government (Cwmni Gwasg Rydd Caerdydd 1972b). In January 1969 the Welsh Language Society started its widespread and very public campaign of destroying English language-only road signs across Wales, which were ritually painted and often removed, smashed up, and dumped outside police stations and other public buildings. Protesters confessed their actions, resulting in high-profile court cases, and between January 1969 and December 1972 over 200 activists were arrested, and a significant number of protesters imprisoned when they refused to cooperate with the authorities or pay court fines (Cwmni Gwasg Rydd Caerdydd 1972a, 1972b; Cymdeithas yr Iaith Gymraeg 1971, 1974). The materiality of road signs was central to the motivations behind, and effectiveness of, the protesters' campaigns. Firstly, road signs were seen as one of the most prominent and ubiquitous 'representatives' of the British government in the Welsh landscape, serving as anglicized technologies of government which were received by Welsh-speakers as 'symbols of injustice' (Cwmni Gwasg Rydd Caerdydd 1972b: 1), 'symbols of oppression' (*The Times* 1971: 2), constituting a form of violence 'towards the Welsh language, on Welsh soil' (Iwan 1969). While first-language English speakers might see English-language road signs as mundane, banal, or functional symbols of official instruction, for first-language Welsh-speakers these signs constituted violent reminders of their subjugation, providing a very public demonstration of British government attitudes to the Welsh language and the perceived severance of the bonds between land and language (Jones 1966; Gruffudd 2000). In addition, it was the ubiquity and mundane functionality of road signs which made this a highly effective campaign, for while earlier protests by language campaigners had had little impact on the wider population, the painting and removal of road signs affected everyone who travelled by road in Wales, whether they were aware of the reasons for the campaign, spoke Welsh, or not.

A key aspect of our study has been to trace the historical archaeology and historical geography of the evolving campaign, but we are also undertaking a contemporary archaeology in which we are examining the present-day material manifestations of the road-signs campaign, discovering the whereabouts of English-only signs which were removed, locating older signs which remain on the road sides, and photographing English-only signs which were modified by council authorities. Firstly, road signs were only removed where place-names were either anglicized misspellings of Welsh names (e.g. Llanelly rather than

FIGURE 31.4 A road sign in Aberystwyth, Wales, which has been modified using a metal panel with the Welsh and English names for the town of Aberteifi/Cardigan (photograph: Peter Merriman)

Llanelli) or English versions of Welsh place-names (e.g. Swansea rather than Abertawe), so many road signs remained in place where only a single Welsh name was in use.[1] What's more, Cymdeithas yr Iaith Gymraeg was a fairly youthful organization—centred round Wales's university colleges, with its 3,780 members in 1972 purported to have an average age of 24—and hence the focus of much of their attention was in the vicinity of the university towns, along the main trunk roads and A-roads of Wales, and in the Welsh-language heartlands of north-west, south-west and mid-west Wales (Owen-Davies 1972). Road signs in other areas sometimes remained untouched, particularly where the local population were largely English speakers, and the impetus for more widespread replacement of monolingual signs only occurred with the government's increasing support for bilingual road signs in the late 1970s and 1980s (*Western Mail* 1978; Jones 1980). Secondly, in largely Welsh-speaking counties such as Cardiganshire and Gwynedd, where the councils supported the erection of bilingual road signs, the councils were quick to erect bilingual road signs once the government empowered them to do so, and in order to reduce the cost of erecting new signs, some councils—such as Cardiganshire—appear to have opted to modify existing signs with the placing of bilingual panels over monolingual sections of signs, as is evidenced in one present-day sign in Aberystwyth—in which a panel reading Aberteifi/Cardigan has been riveted over the original panel reading Cardigan (Figure 31.4). Our contemporary archaeology of

[1] A large number of the signs which were removed from main roads were themselves fairly new, as the government's Traffic Signs Committee (the Worboys Committee) had redesigned Britain's entire system of non-motorway road signs in 1963, and many older signs had already been replaced with the newly designed signs in the late 1960s (see Traffic Signs Committee 1963).

Welsh road signs has revealed a number of such examples of signs which have either evaded destruction or been modified 'economically'. Finally, in an ongoing phase of our research, we are collecting stories from a range of people about what happened to the discarded road signs which were smashed-up, dumped at public buildings, or discarded on verges and in roadside ditches. In one account, we have heard of a farmer who used discarded road signs as a crude foundation for a farm track, but years later he dug them up, and they now assume pride of place on the wall of his bed and breakfast. Much-hated symbols of 'English oppression' and British government control are now consumed as items of protest heritage, aesthetically pleasing reminders of a bygone landscape and political struggle in Wales.

31.5 CONCLUSIONS

Roads, motor cars, and related infrastructures, technologies, and ephemera form an important, if often banal and unthought, place in our everyday lives. Their material presence and cultural significance is wide-ranging, and even though automobiles are regularly bought and sold, reworked and modified, scrapped and preserved, they continue to collectively territorialize our cities and rural landscapes, just as roads appear to have a more persistent material presence over years, decades, and even centuries. Throughout this chapter I have traced how the material cultures of automobility have emerged at the centre of modernist imaginaries, popular practices, and as a focus of political protest, and while sociologists, cultural historians, and cultural geographers have started to make notable contributions to the field, contemporary archaeologists and anthropologists are also bringing invaluable insights to academic debates. Indeed, the spaces, technologies, and practices associated with the road, car, and automotive infrastructures can be studied using a diverse array of disciplinary and interdisciplinary approaches, and a broad-based series of research methods and field techniques, ranging from archival research, oral histories, textual analysis, and excavation techniques, to performative and participative methods, ethnography, and the 'salvage' of cultural artefacts, 'ephemera', and what some may consider to be 'junk' (Lorimer 2010: 257, 259). While we may still be 'disciplined' to research and communicate our findings in particular kinds of ways, scholars are increasingly challenging such disciplinary conventions and boundaries, writing contemporary archaeologies, cultural geographies, and anthropologies which have more in common than they have differences. In my own work I have started to draw insights from work in contemporary archaeology, anthropology, and material culture studies, as well as writings on the geography, history, and sociology of mobility (see Sheller, this volume), and I would encourage archaeologists of automobility to take a multi-methods approach, tracing the cultural practices and materialities associated with distinctive ways of moving in different cultural contexts.

REFERENCES

ACLTTR [Advisory Committee on the Landscape Treatment of Trunk Roads]. 1958. Note of a meeting of sub-committee on 28 January 1958, LT/61. The National Archives of the UK, MT 123/59.
Augé, Marc. 1995. *Non-Places: Introduction to an Anthropology of Supermodernity*. London: Verso.

Bagshawe, Richard W. 1979. *Roman Roads*. Aylesbury: Shire Publications.

Bailey, Greg, Newland, Cassie, Nilsson, Anna, and Schofield, John. 2009. Transit, Transition: Excavating J641 VUJ. *Cambridge Archaeological Journal* 19(1): 1–27.

Baldwin, Peter and Baldwin, Robert (eds.) 2004. *The Motorway Achievement Volume 1: The British Motorway System—Visualisation, Policy and Administration*. London: Thomas Telford.

Banham, Reyner. 1960. The Road to Ubiquopolis. *New Statesman* 59: 784 and 786.

——1962. *Guide to Modern Architecture*. London: Architectural Press.

Betjeman, John. 1960. Men and Buildings: Style on Road and Rail. *Daily Telegraph and Morning Post* [London], 27 June: 15.

Birmingham Mail. 1959. Breakdown rush on M1. 2 November [copy held in press cutting file in Birmingham Central Library].

Blackwood Hodge 1959 Advertisement. *The Times* [London], 2 November: 8.

Böhm, Steffen, Jones, Campbell, Land, Chris, and Paterson, Matthew (eds.). 2006. *Against Automobility*. Oxford: Blackwell Publishing/Sociological Review.

Bracewell, Michael. 2002. *The Nineties: When Surface Was Depth*. London: Flamingo.

Bradley, Andrea and Walter, Matthew. 2007. The M1. *Conservation Bulletin (English Heritage)* 56: 13.

Bridle, Ron and Porter, John (eds.). 2002. *The Motorway Achievement Volume 2: Frontiers of Knowledge and Practice*. London: Thomas Telford.

Bryant, Barbara. 1996. *Twyford Down*. London: E. & F. N. Spon.

Calladine, Tony and Morrison, Katherine. 1998. *Road Transport Buildings: A Report by RCHME for the English Heritage Post-1939 Listing Programme*. Cambridge: Royal Commission on Historic Monuments in England.

Carver, Jay. 2009. Recent Publications in Roads Archaeology. *Antiquity* 83: 218–22.

Caterpillar 1959 Advertisement. *The Times* [London], 2 November: 5.

Charlesworth, George. 1984. *A History of British Motorways*. London: Thomas Telford.

Colvin, Brenda. 1959. The London–Birmingham Motorway: A New Look at the English Landscape. *The Geographical Magazine* 32: 239–46.

CPRE [Council for the Protection of Rural England]. 1996. *The Cluttered Countryside*. London: CPRE.

Crowe, Sylvia. 1959. The London/York Motorway: A Landscape Architect's View. *The Architects' Journal* 130 (10 September): 156–61.

——1960. *The Landscape of Roads*. London: Architectural Press.

Cwmni Gwasg Rydd Caerdydd [Cardiff Free Press]. 1972a. *Achos y Naw*. Cardiff: Cwmni Gwasg Rydd Caerdydd.

——1972b. *Symbols of Justice: Bilingual Signs in Wales. Complete History of the Campaign for Bilingual Road Signs*. Cardiff: Cwmni Gwasg Rydd Caerdydd.

Cymdeithas yr Iaith Gymraeg. 1971. *Achos yr Arwyddion Ffyrdd/The Road Signs Trial*. Aberystwyth: Cymdeithas yr Iaith Gymraeg.

——1974. *Bywyd I'r Iaith/Welsh Must Live*. Aberystwyth: Cymdeithas yr Iaith Gymraeg.

Dalakoglou, Dimitris and Harvey, Penny (eds.). 2012. Roads and anthropology (special issue). *Mobilities* 7(4): 459–586.

Davies, Hugh. 2008. *Roman Roads in Britain*. Oxford: Shire Publications.

de Hamel, Bruno [Department of the Environment]. 1976. *Roads and the Environment*. London: HMSO.

DeLyser, Dydia, Sheehan, Rebecca, and Curtis, Andrew. 2004. eBay and Research in Historical Geography. *Journal of Historical Geography* 30(4): 764–82.

Drake, James, Yeadon, Harry L., and Evans, D. I. 1969. *Motorways*. London: Faber and Faber.

Edensor, Tim. 2003. M6, Junction 19–16: Refamiliarizing the Mundane Roadscape. *Space and Culture* 6(2): 151–68.

Featherstone, Mike, Thrift, Nigel, and Urry, John (eds.). 2005. *Automobilities*. London: Sage.

Geological Survey of Great Britain [DSIR]. 1959. *Summary of Progress of the Geological Survey of Great Britain and the Museum of Practical Geology for the Year 1958*. London: HMSO.

Glancey, Jonathan. 1992. A Bridge too Far? *The Independent Magazine*, 18 July: 24–31.

Graham, Paul. 1983. *A1: The Great North Road*. Bristol: Grey Editions.

Graves-Brown, Paul. 2000. Always Crashing in the Same Car. In *Matter, Materiality and Modern Culture*, ed. Paul Graves-Brown, pp. 155–65. London and New York: Routledge.

—— 2007. Concrete Islands. In *Contemporary and Historical Archaeology in Theory*, ed. Laura McAttackney, Matthew Palus, and Angela Piccini, pp. 75–81. Oxford: Archaeopress.

Gruffudd, Pyrs. 2000. The Welsh Language and the Geographical Imagination 1918–1950. In *'Let's Do Our Best for the Ancient Tongue': The Welsh Language in the Twentieth Century*, ed. G. H. Jenkins and M. A. Williams, pp. 109–35. Cardiff: University of Wales Press.

Harrison, Rodney and Schofield, John. 2010. *After Modernity: Archaeological Approaches to the Contemporary Past*. Oxford: Oxford University Press.

Horvath, Ronald J. 1974. Machine Space. *The Geographical Review* 64(2): 167–88.

Iwan, Dafydd. 1969. An article in *Barn*, March 1969, by Dafydd Iwan. Around your feet (from the January edition of "The Dragon's Tongue"). Translated article in The National Archives of the UK, Kew, file BD 43/139.

Jeremiah, David. 1995. Filling Up: The British Experience, 1896–1940. *Journal of Design History* 8(2): 97–116.

Jones, David S. (ed.). 2002. *20th Century Heritage: Our Recent Cultural Legacy. Proceedings of the Australia ICOMOS National Conference 2001*. Adelaide: School of Architecture, Landscape Architecture & Urban Design, the University of Adelaide & Australia ICOMOS Secretariat.

Jones, Helen. 1998. Buildings Designed to Advertise Fuel. *British Archaeology* 38 (October): 6–7.

Jones, John R. 1966. *Prydeindod* [Britishness]. Llandybïe: Llyfrau'r Dryw.

Jones, Rhys and Merriman, Peter. 2009. Hot, Banal and Everyday Nationalism: Bilingual Road Signs in Wales. *Political Geography* 28(3): 164–73.

—— 2012. Network Nation. *Environment and Planning A* 44: 937–53.

Jones, Tim. 1980. Government to Spend £1m in Support of Welsh Language. *The Times* [London], 16 April: 5.

Lawrence, David. 1999. *Always a Welcome: The Glove Compartment History of the Motorway Service Area*. Twickenham: Between Books.

Lorimer, Hayden. 2010. Caught in the Nick of Time: Archives and Fieldwork. In *The Sage Handbook of Qualitative Geography*, ed. Dydia DeLyser, Steve Herbert, Stuart Aitken, Mike Crang, and Linda McDowell, pp. 248–73. London: Sage Publications.

Mabey, Richard. 1974. *The Roadside Wildlife Book*. Newton Abbot: Readers Union.

MacColl, Ewan, Parker, Charles, and Seeger, Peggy. 1999. *Song of a Road*. Topic Records CD, TSCD802.

McCoubrey, William J. (ed.). 2008. *The Motorway Achievement Volume 3: Building the Network*. London: Thomas Telford.

Merriman, Peter. 2004. Driving Places: Marc Augé, Non-places and the Geographies of England's M1 Motorway. *Theory, Culture & Society* 21(4–5): 145–67.

—— 2005. 'Operation Motorway': Landscapes of Construction on England's M1 Motorway. *Journal of Historical Geography* 31(1): 113–33.

—— 2006. 'A New Look at the English Landscape': Landscape Architecture. *Cultural Geographies* 13: 78–105.

Merriman, Peter. 2007. *Driving Spaces: A Cultural-Historical Geography of England's M1 Motorway*. Oxford: Blackwell.

—— 2009. Automobility and the Geographies of the Car. *Geography Compass* 3(2): 586–99.

—— 2011. Enfolding and Gathering the Landscape: The Geographies of England's M1 Motorway Corridor. In *Routes, Roads and Landscapes*, ed. Mari Hvattum, Britta Brenna, Beate Elvebakk, and Janike Kampevold Larsen, pp. 213–26. Farnham: Ashgate.

—— 2012. *Mobility, Space and Culture*. London: Routledge.

Merriman, Peter and Jones, Rhys. 2009. 'Symbols of Justice': The Welsh Language Society's Campaign for Bilingual Road Signs in Wales, 1967–1980. *Journal of Historical Geography* 35(2): 350–75.

Miller, Daniel. 2001. *Car Cultures*. Oxford: Berg.

Minnis, John. 2007. The Car: An Agent of Transformation. *Conservation Bulletin (English Heritage)* 56: 11–13.

Nairn, Ian. 1963. Look Out. *The Architectural Review* 133: 425–6.

Newland, Cassie, Bailey, Greg, Schofield, John, and Nilsson, Anna. 2007. Sic Transit Gloria Mundi. *British Archaeology* 92: 16–21.

O'Connell, Sean. 1998. *The Car and British Society: Class, Gender and Motoring, 1896–1939*. Manchester: Manchester University Press.

Owen-Davies, John. 1972. Inside the Welsh Language Society: Pop Image Threat to Movement's Future. *Western Mail*, 24 November. Unpaginated press cutting.

Parliamentary Debates, House of Commons. 1946. Highway Development (Government programme) 422 (6 May): 590–5.

Peach, Harry H. and Carrington, Noel C. 1930. *The Face of the Land*. London: George Allen & Unwin.

Penrose, Sefryn. 2007. *Images of Change: An Archaeology of England's Contemporary Landscape*. Swindon: English Heritage.

Pevsner, Nikolaus. 1960. *Buckinghamshire*. Harmondsworth: Penguin.

—— 1961. *Northamptonshire*. Harmondsworth: Penguin.

Rolt, Lionel T. C. 1959. *The London–Birmingham Motorway*. London: John Laing and Son Limited.

Self, Will. 1993. Mad About Motorways. *The Times (Weekend section)*, 25 September: 1.

—— 1994. Scale. In *Grey Area and Other Stories*, pp. 89–123. London: Bloomsbury.

Shone, Tom. 1993. The Complete, Unexpurgated Self. *The Sunday Times Magazine*, 5 September: 39–42.

Sir Owen Williams and Partners [Sir OWP]. 1957. *London–Yorkshire Motorway (South of Luton-Watford Gap-Dunchurch Special Road). Landscape Report and Model*. Unpublished report prepared by A. P. Long for the Ministry of Transport and Civil Aviation. A copy is held in the offices of Owen Williams in Birmingham.

Team Spirit: The Monthly News Sheet Issued by John Laing and Son Limited. 1958. Homes on wheels. 145: 5.

The Times [London]. 1971. English Road Signs 'Symbol of Oppression', 13 May: 2.

Traffic Signs Committee [Ministry of Transport]. 1963. *Report of the Traffic Signs Committee 18th April 1963*. London: HMSO.

Way, John M. 1970. Wildlife on the Motorway. *New Scientist* 47 (10 September): 536–7.

Western Mail [Cardiff, Wales]. 1978. Three Counties Out of Step on Bilingual Road Signs Policy, 18 January: 4.

Williams-Ellis, Clough. 1928. *England and the Octopus*. London: Geoffrey Bles.

—— (ed.). 1938. *Britain and the Beast*. London: Readers Union.

CHAPTER 32

....

ARCHAEOLOGY OF MODERN AMERICAN DEATH: GRAVE GOODS AND BLITHE MEMENTOES

....

SHANNON LEE DAWDY

32.1 INTRODUCTION

....

THIS chapter describes a series of emerging new or revived object-centred death practices in the contemporary United States, including votive offerings, object memorials, and coffin grave-goods. My aims are to describe these phenomena, identify historical genealogies, and explore anthropological implications. My methodological approach is archaeological in the sense that I begin with a description of material objects and the behavioural contexts that account for their deposition in certain spaces. My assumption that these material traces can inform us about both conscious beliefs and deep (though changing) structures of social life is an archaeological one. But my approach is also interdisciplinary, drawing on sources in history and journalism. A future, expanded iteration of the project will include ethnographic interviews. I begin with a description of Holt Cemetery, in New Orleans, a pauper cemetery where some of these practices (such as votive offerings and DIY markers) have roots in vernacular mourning traditions, particularly among African Americans. But at Holt, as elsewhere in the United States, newer and revived practices are also appearing. Brief descriptions of observational visits (made between 2009 and 2012) to a rural California cemetery and an evolving Chicago cemetery flesh out the picture. The selection of these sites by the author was governed by factors both personal and pragmatic, being a long-standing fieldwork site in one case (New Orleans, Louisiana), the city of current residence (Chicago, Illinois), and the author's hometown in the case of the third (Guerneville, California). That said, as I discuss below, these three sites correlate to three quite different American settings and cemetery types. Other sources that help place these examples in a national context are journalistic reviews of the American death scene and professional publications for funeral directors and allied fields. One structural factor in national trends is an exponential growth in cremation which was 38 per cent in 2009 and projected to reach more than 50 per cent by 2025, with some significant regional variation across the country (National Funeral Directors Association 2012). But ideas are also changing. I argue that with these phenomena we are witnessing a movement simultaneously towards more personalized and more consumer-oriented death and mourning practices. Contemporary conditions that could account for these trends are mass-mediated public mourning as well as the extension of consumer individualism into the afterlife.

32.2 HOLT CEMETERY, NEW ORLEANS, LOUISIANA

Holt Cemetery lies on one edge of New Orleans' largest cemetery district, adjacent to Delgado Community College and City Park. It is not visible from the main street (City Park Boulevard), although its perimeter is porous, with a discontinuous chain link fence along the front and a broken ironwork fence along the side and rear that leave it open to the residential neighbourhood that borders it. Dog walkers frequently enter the cemetery to relieve their dogs. Large old oak trees line the back boundary of the cemetery and cluster in a few places in the centre. Large drainage ditches cut across the site. Human bone, bits of cloth, and artefacts jut out from the loose churned soil all across the cemetery which is bumpy with fresh mounds and sunken grave shafts. On a warm day with a mild breeze, the scent of death is undeniably present. Approximately one-half of the visible graves have markers, or remnants of markers of some kind. Approximately half of these are a simple professional stonemason type, such as those provided for war veterans, or others paid for and installed by families. The rest are a mixture of hand-made markers, such as wooden planks with hand-painted or hand-carved text or, more durable and therefore in the present-day more common, cement forms with scratched text. Another common type of grave furniture at Holt are hand-built frames made out of wood, cement, or movable pieces such as concrete blocks, paving bricks, or plumbing pipe (both metal and PVC) that outline the dimensions of the grave. Some of the framed graves have their area filled in with more materials, such as ornamental rocks or artificial turf. On many graves, both framed and unframed, visitors have left various types of artefacts, from the predictable vases with plastic flowers to children's toys, pottery, lawn ornaments, bottles, and photos (Figures 32.1 and 32.2). Some are water- and sun-faded. Some are fresh and have been tended recently.

The maintenance of graves is driven by a combination of local tradition, poverty, and regulation. At Holt as at other New Orleans cemeteries the originally Catholic All Saints' Day (November 1) observances are continued by many as a now broader local practice, regardless of denomination. It is a day when families visit graves of loved ones to perform maintenance of the grave and to remember those missing, adding fresh paint, leaving votive artefacts, etc. As an indigent cemetery where those in need can bury their loved ones without a plot fee, however, the only 'rights' to a plot are essentially usufruct rights (the right to use a property that in title belongs to another, usually with a requirement of improvement or maintenance). If a grave goes unmarked for 101 days, it may be reused. And if a once-marked grave goes many years without maintenance, it will be recycled by city workers. It is estimated that most of the plot sites at Holt have been reused about three times (Bobbi-Ann Lewis, June 2011, personal communication). Some individuals clearly do not limit themselves to All Saints' Day in their grave-tending. They observe birthdays, death days, and other holidays. At Mardi Gras season, some graves are decorated with beads and other parade throws. The same practice is observed at Christmas.

FIGURE 32.1 Holt Cemetery view, with 'Homeless Grave' (photograph: Shannon Lee Dawdy)

FIGURE 32.2 Holt Cemetery detail (photograph: Shannon Lee Dawdy)

One of the most spectacular graves, called 'the homeless grave' (Figure 32.1) by locals who frequent the cemetery, until recently hosted a dense tangle of lawn chairs, colourful plastic tarp, and everyday objects that seemed to provide useful items to the dead. It largely and miraculously survived Katrina, when the site was inundated with 4–6 feet of water, but it succumbed to a sweep by city employees who viewed the artefactual deposits as 'trash' a few years later. The majority of the graves bearing wooden markers and frames, as well as votive artefacts, were badly damaged by Katrina's waters, and in some cases nearly erased. To those familiar with the cemetery, the levee breaches wiped much of the colour away from a unique local landmark.

Depending on the season or day that one visits the cemetery, one can find it nearly overgrown with three-foot tall weeds, or stripped bare of both greenery and artefacts by indiscriminate and unpredictable maintenance efforts. The ground is constantly shifting. On most weekends, and many weekdays, one can observe a freshly dug grave with a new flower arrangement awaiting the funeral procession, or a freshly mounded grave. After a funeral, a stand with a photo of the deceased is often left as a temporary marker, as well as whatever flowers or personal mementoes were placed on the grave by attendees. Other artefacts noted after recent funerals are memorial T-shirts with silk-screened photo portraits of the deceased, set up on flower stands. Presumably many of the funeral attendees now possess the same T-shirts and wear them to remember the deceased and publicly mark their loss.

In two areas near old oak trees in the centre-rear of the cemetery one finds many artefact deposits that do not have obvious associations with a tended grave. On a site visit in June 2011, a chicken carcass hung from a tree limb, wine and rum bottles were stuck in spaces in the trunk, and candles were scattered around the ground. This is evidence of contemporary magico-religious practices reproducing 'voodoo' rituals by unknown actors (whether native New Orleanians, New Age newcomers, or pseudo-voodoo street punks is at present unclear). Such associations with the site have also reputedly contributed to regular vandalism of the vulnerable site since human bones (especially skulls) are valued in these practices (as they are on certain markets). While this peculiarity of local culture might account for some of the votive artefacts and idiosyncratic observances at the site, other practices are more generalized in African American and Catholic burial practices. Goody and Poppi (1994) also note that regionally the South seems more tolerant of a range of memorial practices as well as more conservative in maintaining Victorian death cult practices. Others, which will be the focus of the rest of this essay, appear to be part of a growing horizon of new object-centred death practices.

Holt Cemetery was opened in 1879, one of a series of indigent cemeteries established in the wake of the city's nineteenth-century population explosion (Huber et al. 1997; Florence and Florence 2005; see also Upton 1997). In a city known for its raised, white-washed tombs comprising 'The City of the Dead', almost all of the burials at Holt are below ground. When it was established, the cemetery was the site of mass graves of yellow fever victims and periodic unmarked burials of indigent patients from Charity Hospital. While poverty was the only common marker of the interred in the first generations, by the height of the Jim Crow era around the First World War, the cemetery became almost exclusively African American. It is the known resting place for many of New Orleans' renowned musicians, including jazz pioneer Buddy Bolden (in an unknown, unmarked grave) and several greats of the rhythm and blues era. From time to time the site is a scene of controversy, with its unkempt appearance and unregulated death practices seen alternately as a sign of city incompetence and neglect, or as a site of unbridled sentiment and folkloric beauty.

The personalization of grave-markers, as well as visitation, maintenance, and the deposition of votive artefacts are death practices that were once commonplace in American life, peaking in the Victorian period, but which declined precipitously in the wake of a movement towards standardization that began around the turn of the last century (Mitford 1998; Farrell 1980; Laderman 2003). The 'sanitation' of cemetery space undoubtedly reflected regulatory, denominational, and class undercurrents. However, this national movement did not entirely erase personal artefactual observances among certain populations, such as the African American poor, some Catholic laity, and immigrants. Holt therefore represents a continuation of older American death observances and, at the same time, a resource for revived practices that are becoming widespread across the class spectrum of American cemeteries. What these object-centred practices are and why they seem to be reversing the twentieth-century movement towards cemetery sanitation are the questions this chapter begins to address.

32.3 Votive Offerings and Object Memorials

Jessica Mitford's (orig. 1963, revised 1998) exposé of the American death industry remains one of the most important sources on the rapid changes and peculiarities of American death in the twentieth century. Mitford revealed how quickly the field became professionalized and standardized after the 1880s through a combination of scientific, cultural, and legal factors. But most importantly, she shows how professionalization and corporatization invented and even enforced new 'traditions', leading to an exponential increase in embalming, for example, so it became not only standard, but misunderstood (and misrepresented) as a health or safety requirement rather than as a temporary preservation to augment an ever-more expensive funeral ritual centred around an open casket. In terms of object-centred practices, she notes the movement towards uniform, manicured lawn cemeteries such as Forest Lawn and its corporately owned affiliates in Southern California, where individualized monuments and tombstones became prohibited in lieu of uniform, identical rows of flush-to-the-ground bronze or granite plaques. Rather than aesthetics or regulation, it turns out that this major material transformation of the American cemetery landscape was due to the cost savings incurred by being able to use efficient tractor mowers over the large tracts of suburban cemeteries instead of paying a maintenance crew to weave in and out of individually designed plots with their impeding stone markers. Similarly, the predominantly private cemeteries in the US introduced rules about the types of objects that could be left on graves by family members (which could also chew up the mower blades), sometimes dictating that only plastic flowers be allowed, or arrangements and vases from designated local florists, which would be removed after one week. Mitford explains these restrictions also as a factor of reduced maintenance costs, and a kickback system involving the for-profit management companies that actually operate the large modern cemeteries (and adjacent florists) as a service to ghostly non-profit landholding entities that nominally own the cemetery, making the operations tax-free.

Cost-cutting and profit-taking certainly contribute to the face of American cemeteries, but that is only part of the story. A degree of aesthetic restraint in American mortuary
expression has historical roots in the colonial era that began to distinguish Anglo-American
cemeteries from their English antecedents. Goody and Poppi (1994) in their historical and
anthropological comparison of Anglo-American and Italian cemetery practices note that
Puritan and other Protestant sects frowned upon distinctions after death through mortuary
art and cultic practices such as All Saints' Day and All Souls' Day (see also Laderman 1996).
They argue that this negative view of making too much of a fuss over the dead has had a lasting influence in the United States, becoming an aesthetic rationale that can surpass denominational affiliation, such that Catholic burial practices in New England resemble those of
their Protestant neighbours more closely than they do those of European Catholics. Thus, it
is probably fairer to say that a generalized Protestant aesthetic (as well as a possible modernist and minimalist aesthetic in mid-century landscape design) merged with a Fordist rationalism to produce the flat sea of markers seen in today's suburban American cemetery. But
all that is, once again, changing.

In a very different corner of the country from Holt, serving a very different population,
a small rural cemetery in Northern California sits atop a densely wooded hill overlooking
a town of 5,000. Grave-markers date back to the town's founding in the 1850s and offer a
record of the waves of immigrants the town has received, from Swiss-Italian sheep ranch-
ers in the nineteenth century to white Russians in the early twentieth, to AIDs victims from
the San Francisco area who ended up in the town's vacation-turned-hospice resorts in the
1980s and 1990s. It being the only designated burial ground for the community, it is de facto
non-denominational. The site presents a hotchpotch of grave-markers, from U-shaped
limestone markers to wooden Russian orthodox crosses, to contemporary granite designs
interspersed with a similarly diverse set of plantings, from 200-year old redwood trees to
dogwood and old rose vines. Many of the Russian-language markers contain a painted
cameo or photo-portrait of the deceased, a practice that appeared briefly in late Victorian
America and is now coming back into vogue in the general population through pho-
to-etched granite portraiture and even 3D death masks made possible by NASA-designed
holographic technology (Obit-Mag 2011b).

A pedestrian survey of Guerneville cemetery records a perhaps surprising variety of artefacts, particularly on the more contemporary graves, including music CDs, teddy bears,
beverage bottles, letters to the deceased, and deliberately placed mementoes such as rocks,
shells, crystals, and coins (Figure 32.3). Some of these items are placed on the graves of those
who died 10 years ago or more. Others are more recent. The largest number of votive artefacts have been left for those who died prematurely, such as teenagers and youths in their
twenties, although not necessarily recently. Evidence of recent visitation on perhaps a birthday or death anniversary is clear.

Bohemian National Cemetery, established by Catholic Czech immigrants in 1877 on
Chicago's north-west side presents a third type of cemetery landscape (Hucke and Bielski
1997). From the street, it looks like a typical urban American cemetery, with broad swaths
of manicured lawn and flat markers; however, a central area of older upright monuments
and society tombs set in a lightly wooded landscape anchor the site. And closer inspection
reveals that there is not as much rigid uniformity to the more contemporary graves as one
would find at the highly regulated golf-course cemeteries that Jessica Mitford describes.
Many graves host rose bushes or other ornamentals apparently planted by family members

FIGURE 32.3 Votive artefacts at Guerneville Community Cemetery (photograph: Shannon Lee Dawdy)

and cared for regularly. Markers from across the time spectrum feature porcelain cameo photographs of the deceased. And although not as common as at Holt or the Guerneville cemeteries, votive artefacts such as toys, balloons, candles, sports souvenirs, Christmas wreaths, and flower vases can be observed and are apparently left for a duration by an otherwise meticulous grounds crew.

Architecturally, Bohemian cemetery is known for its columbarium, a neo-classical structure housing hundreds of small glass-fronted niches that each contain the ashes and usually photo-portraits of the deceased, along with flowers, awards, jewellery, books, or other mementoes of their lives in a satin-lined setting resembling a reliquary case. Families may freshen or add to the niches as desired. The original columbarium was erected in 1913. In 2009, with the backing of a local man named Dennis Mascari, a new columbarium called 'Beyond the Vines' was constructed and its 288 receptacles made available for purchase (Drehs 2009). Since the columbarium is designed as a miniature replica of the ivy-covered wall at Wrigley Field (complete with a scoreboard, transplanted sod, and some original Wrigley seats for contemplative visitors), a niche market of former Cubs baseball fans is targeted (Figure 32.4). Mr Mascari was himself the eleventh fan to be interred there, two years after the opening ceremonies (Obit Patrol 2011). While Mr Mascari's die-hard loyalty was undoubtedly the first impulse behind this unique addition to the funerary landscape, he was generously assisted by a company called Eternal Images, which specializes in licensed Major League Baseball 'memorial products' (they also carry trademarked lines of Star Trek and KISS band theme products such as urns and caskets).

Throughout its history, Bohemian cemetery has been tolerant of the votive practices of immigrant Catholics. On the one hand, this preserved old world traditions that did not survive Protestant Americanization in other communities. On the other, it made the staff receptive to one of the most remarkable examples of a new wave of American death practices that simultaneously individualizes memorialization and intersects with the ever-creative entrepreneurialism of mass consumption.

FIGURE 32.4 'Beyond the Vines' Columbarium, Bohemian National Cemetery, Chicago (photograph: Shannon Lee Dawdy)

32.4 BURIAL GOODS

While an upsurge in the practice of leaving votive artefacts on graves can be noted at a wide intersection of American cemeteries, another object-centred death practice is also enjoying a revival. However, it is one only visible during the visitation and funeral periods, and sometimes only by the family and funeral staff. Burial goods are back. Once frowned upon by strict Protestants as a form of idolatry, the practice declined further with the corporate sanitation and professionalization of the American funeral industry in the first half of the twentieth century (Mitford 1998; Laderman 2003; Green 2008). It can be argued that embalming and body dressing transformed and 'cleansed' the body, making it appear untouchable to the living. In fact, the heavy cosmetics used can easily wipe off and many burial clothes lie on top of the corpse like an apron, facts that might become too apparent with close interaction. The body and casket presentation were otherworldly creations of the funeral director which family members became increasingly removed from, though urged to view. Placing burial goods within this pristine environment, even when emotions ran high during a funeral or visitation, may have felt like a violation of unspoken etiquette. However, these days funeral directors have been forced to become more flexible with more assertive families and a range of requests.

Since the 1990s, the placement of jewellery, letters, and photographs inside the casket has become a common step in the American funeral ritual. A growing range of the objects being placed in the coffins veer from this list of typical affective mementoes. In the Los Angeles area, for example, one funeral director reports that cell phones are the most popular items (Jensen 2010), variously explained as being a highly personalized object always carried on the person of the deceased, as a record of that person's relations with the living through their contact list, or even as a device to be used as an amulet against taphophobia (the fear of being buried alive). In Philadelphia, on the other hand, as of 2010 one funeral director reported that TV remotes were 'the hottest thing'. Other commonly reported coffin deposits are favourite foods, liquors, cigars, sports equipment, and CDs or MP3 players with the person's favourite songs loaded, or songs expressing the bereaved's feelings. More unusual deposits include a shotgun, a cheque written out for $1 million (so the friend could die a millionaire), a motorcycle helmet, favourite glow-in-the-dark underwear, a clarinet, and a tool belt (Cullen 2006; Jensen 2010). One enterprising casket company has capitalized on this trend by designing a coffin with a built-in drawer called a 'Memory Safe' (Cullen 2006: 1905). While according to orthodox Jewish and Muslim belief, the dead are not supposed to be buried with goods, the practice has never been an outright prohibition in Christianity and among a growing secular sector of the population it is not quite 'anything goes', but more and more does.

In her journalistic review of contemporary American death practices that follows, in a different key, Jessica Mitford's classic, Lisa Takeuchi Cullen (2006) argues that the primary factor driving these changes are the ageing baby boomers and their habit of being accustomed to personalized consumption—they 'want what they want' and the funeral industry is being forced to change. She would place the rise of burial goods in the category of 'personalization' in consumer choice. There are market responses that support this explanation such as the line of caskets by the same company that makes the Memory Safes called 'LifeSymbols' in which a ready-made fish or golf-club curio can be affixed to a corner of the coffin like a piece of cell phone jewellery. Also available are embroidered thematic scenes of favourite activities such as gardening, or affiliations such as a veteran's unit; these are positioned on the cloth interior of the lid, over the head or upper body. This personalization of the dead, as the profit margin of these companies demonstrates, does not oppose consumer capitalism. It simply departs from an earlier phase of limited, and thus standardized, production that masqueraded in the sales room as 'tradition'. These monogramming touches that identify the hobby enthusiast or other club member suggest an intra-national propagation of what Richard Wilk (1995) calls on the global scale, 'structures of common difference', in which markets thrive by producing items fulfilling a perceived need for differentiation of groups and localities.

Objects have become a key way in which to personalize what for most of the twentieth century had become a very uniform and standardized event. This is particularly evident in the striking arrangements of artefacts now offered in designer, middle-class funerals. These dioramic settings for open caskets and visitations present a peculiar tableau mourant of the deceased's hobby, career, or social connections as seen in examples from a funeral home website, including equestrian, golf, and outdoors themes (Shaw-Davis Funeral Home). On the one hand, these practices can be seen as part of a longer post-Victorian trend towards displaying wealth (or aspirations of wealth) through the event and accoutrements of the funeral ritual. On the other hand, there is far from a 'one-size-fits-all' object language of what constitutes wealth, status, or (good) taste. Individualization of the dead person remains a sought-after effect of the tout ensemble. Whereas Mitford argues that it was the push of the for-profit death industry that created homogenizing standardization in the early-to-mid twentieth century, Cullen argues that it is the pull of consumers that is driving change in the new millennium. However, there is still much to be answered as to *why* the boomers (if they are in fact the prime movers) want the particular things they want.

Given that the new wave of burial goods is most prevalent among non-orthodox or secular families, it is unlikely that their inclusion represents an emerging reconception of the afterlife akin to what the Egyptians practised, despite the functional utility of items such as cell phones or tool belts. Cullen (2006) is undoubtedly right that one major impulse is that of personalization. This drive, however, is reflected not only in increased commercialization and proliferation of object-centred practices, but in a rapidly expanded suite of practices that resists commercialization such as green burials, DIY burials (which are legal in most states, from building your own coffin to preparing the body), cremation and creative ash scattering, and the now quite common use of video montages of the deceased during the memorial event in lieu of an open casket with the embalmed body. Thus, I would argue it is not so much that personalization is a result of niche consumer demand as that market specialization is a response to a broader movement away from standardized 'tradition' and towards personalization.

Contemporary object-centred death practices suggest that the ideological tension between 'mass consumer' and the 'individual person', with the first often understood pejoratively and generically, is the result of a weak dichotomy in populist thought. Perhaps nothing points this out better than yet another trend, in which the matter of the individual person is transformed into an object that resembles, in all other aspects, a commodity. The ashes (called cremains in the industry) of the deceased are now being made into objects such as diamond jewellery, cement garden ornaments, paintings, bullets, and pressed vinyl records (Cullen 2006; Gemperlein 2010; Obit-Mag 2011a). This movement underscores the fast US trend towards cremation (already predominant in the UK [estimated at 70 per cent] and much of Western Europe), but also, and more importantly for my argument, the trend away from commemorating the dead person through treatment of the body in favour of commemoration via individualizing objects. Until recently, even if the deceased was destined to be cremated, families were still expected (or, according to Mitford [1998], pressured) to purchase a casket and schedule a visitation or viewing period as part of the funeral rite. This practice seems to be in rapid decline, not just for economic reasons, but because many Americans now express emotional discomfort with a practice once packaged to them as 'tradition' (Cullen 2006).

Instead of a 'memory picture' provided by the final viewing of the embalmed body made up to look undead and peaceful, many Americans seem to be reaching for 'memory objects'. Some of these are 'sacrificed' as grave-goods, or put to use temporarily as part of the funeral ritual. Others, like the diamond rings and bird baths made from a loved one's remains, are instead a form of living memento or souvenir. This transformation in how the body is conceived of in relation to the deceased person could perhaps not be more radical—from the twentieth-century obsession with 'freezing' and even rolling back the clock on the deceased's body as a sacred symbolic vessel of the person's individual essence, to burning and grinding up the body and transforming it into not just special memento objects like jewellery, that might be safeguarded, but everyday objects like vinyl records, that might be mistaken for common, disposable commodities.

One possible conclusion is that more secular beliefs around death and the afterlife are contributing, somewhat counterintuitively, to a desacralization of the body. But I suggest that in many cases, there may be a quite different mode of logic going on, which is that the molecular essence of the body retains a property that corresponds to the irreplaceable uniqueness of each individual which *cannot* be destroyed, only transformed and shared. Perhaps not yet operating at the level of exegesis, it is tempting to speculate that the knowledge of DNA and genetics is filtering into popular beliefs and mingling with consumer individualism, as embodied in these objects. Thus the LP is doubly an encoded record of the person.

32.5 Conclusion and Discussion: Personalization and the Post-Life Consumer

The hand-made markers and quirky votive memorials at Holt Cemetery might have exotic appeal to some viewers due to their highly personalized expression and folkloric sidestep of commercialization. Despite the tendency to veil many phenomena in New Orleans with an aesthetic of romantic patina (Dawdy in preparation), these continuing practices cannot be explained away simply as 'tradition'; they are the result of a nexus of economic, historical, and contemporary cultural factors. Poverty means that indigent families may have no choice but to create their own markers from a bricolage of materials. The local tradition of observing All Saints' Day with cemetery maintenance and votive activities establishes a habitus of regular visits to graves by family. And the fact that so many of the interred in recent decades have died prematurely, many from gunshot wounds, heightens the impulse towards regular visitation, as seen in the pattern at Guerneville Cemetery with the greater number of memorial observances at the graves of the young. Undoubtedly another structural factor is one identified by Goody and Poppi (1994) in their observation that regular post-burial votive activities are more common in southern Mediterranean communities than elsewhere in Europe. They site the specific land-tenure arrangement of tombs and burial lots as a major influence. According to Goody and Poppi, whereas in northern Europe and the US many families purchase and own their lots in perpetuity, in the southern Mediterranean the more common arrangement is a lease-hold, with family rights renewable only with regular maintenance of the tomb or plot. Leaving fresh flowers, besides undoubtedly serving religious and memorial purposes, also has the effect of maintaining rights to the space. Without these renewing acts, neglected bones can be moved to a mass burial or a charnel house. At Holt, a similar usufruct rule affects the use and reuse of the cemetery, though with a much shorter timeframe of 101 days. There are no reliable maps or public records to identify where even the recently deceased are buried, so if the objects marking the plot are not regularly maintained (or quickly re-established after an event like Katrina), the family not only loses a space for remembering their lost ones, they may not be able to physically locate the grave again. And the dead themselves are recycled into the backfill for the next burial, their identity quickly becoming so much dust. The poor die faster.

While cemetery rights can partially explain the continuation of object memorials at Holt throughout the sanitizing twentieth century, they cannot explain why object memorials are on the rise at more typical American cemeteries with perpetual ownership, such as Guerneville and Bohemian National cemeteries. One possible explanation is that these practices represent an extension of public mourning memorials into private cemetery plots. While public object memorials are not an entirely new phenomenon (particularly in the case of celebrities or war dead), the large scale and mass publicity of votive memorials such as the flowers, cards, and candles left at the site of Princess Diana's death in Paris in 1997, as well as outside Kensington Palace for months, have likely helped create a more widespread phenomenon. Perhaps it is significant, however, that whereas Princess Diana's memorials primarily consisted of flowers, in the dramatic and no-less-televised American case of memorials for the victims of 9/11, a proliferation of objects such as hats, shoes, T-shirts, musical instruments, and toys were used to mark the uniqueness of the individual lost in a mass death event. The rapidly growing new tradition of object votives in the US, then, may be a factor of both mass mediation and an impulse to personalize. In the UK, anthropologists and others have generally been more attentive to changing contemporary death practices. For example, Miller and Parrott (2009: 503) note that cremation in particular has led to a proliferation of 'ad hoc' rituals and commemorative practices in private London homes.

This simultaneity parallels what I argue can be seen in burial goods and in the larger trends towards individualizing burials and memorials in which the journalistic opposition posed between mass consumption and personalization breaks down. These cultural forces intersect, but one does not drive the other in any simple way. In fact, it may be that the American death industry is just a very late bloomer into full-blown cultural capitalism in which 'Something is provided for all so that none may escape; the distinctions are emphasised and extended' (Horkheimer and Adorno 1993 [1944]: 123). The allied businesses such as Eternal Images (among what Cullen calls 'End-trepreneurs') are creatively capitalizing on consumer desires for individualizing touches in funeral and burial practices. Still, some mourners *do* attempt to escape what they themselves articulate as the crassness and homogenizing depersonalization of the market, as seen in DIY and green burials. For many, 'tradition' has become negatively associated with franchise-like uniformity in funeral presentations. In a survey of members of the American Association of Retired Persons, 70 per cent said they would prefer a 'non-traditional' funeral (Cullen 2006: 835). In addition, the popularity of cremation is increasing exponentially in the US, an option that circumvents the main money-makers of the death industry altogether—embalming, caskets, and cemetery plots.

I propose that in the US today, the main vehicle for memorialization of the dead is rapidly moving from the body and its deposition to objects associated with personhood. There are contributing structural and economic reasons for this, from increasing burial costs to the dispersal of American families away from hometown cemeteries. But the more interesting contributory factor emerges precisely at that intersection between the person and the commodity (see Graves-Brown, this volume).

Over the last generation, archaeologists and historians have used the evidence of death practices—from the treatment of the body, to burial goods and memorial activities—to better understand the concept not only of the afterlife, but of personhood among the living, with excellent studies from a range of cultures, from the ancient Egyptians to Iron Age Europeans and Victorian Englishmen (e.g., Ariès 1974; Tarlow 1999; Parker Pearson 1999; Nash 2000; Robben 2004). In a study of collecting and memorialization in contemporary England, Fiona Parrott argues that personhood is constructed out of a 'mnemonic connection between things and people' (2011). In the contemporary American case, although object-centred death practices are a rapidly emerging target, the evidence suggests that the

local cultural concept of the person is indistinguishable from the consumer. The uniqueness of the individual and their station in society is defined by the self-extending accoutrements of purchased objects. It is a phenomenon that demonstrates Miller's (1991) theory
of subject–object dialectics under late consumer modernism with particular clarity. It is
not simply that consumer taste marks a social class or station—the older assemblages of
caskets and monuments reflecting a range of Bourdieusian distinctions could function in
this regard for the family of the deceased. Rather, preferred or associated objects are the
medium through which subjects build social networks through hobbies and leisure—a
kind of re-animation via consumption that occurs after the alienation of production. By
acquiring unique assemblages in their lifetime, consumers develop distinction as *individuals*. Thus it would be to miss a major development of American personhood to think of
these object-centred death practices simply in terms of aspirational or emulative desire.
The fact that these objects stand in for the person—perhaps even better than their physical body—shows that actors think of one another through the mediation of objects. While
secular ideas of the afterlife are often unspecified, one non-denominational element to
point to would be hyper-individualism extended into death. To memorialize a deceased
person—to honour them—in this cultural context means to mark their uniqueness and
irreplaceability. While some of us may harbour some left-over romantic resistance to the
idea that identical, mass-produced objects can be one of the prime vehicles through which
individuals not only express themselves, but constitute themselves, a growing literature in
the anthropology of globalization and consumption challenges this split, while an archaeology of the contemporary demonstrates its collapse with concrete force (Harrison and
Schofield 2010). 'Cremain' jewellery and bird baths take Miller's (1991) sublation of Hegel's
object–subject split one step beyond, merging commodity and person. Reappropriating as
they do the DNA and carbon essence of a person, the producers of such objects make no
error of hypostatization, rather they press an utterly unique blend of spirit–matter into a
replicable mould.

ACKNOWLEDGEMENTS

I am grateful for the suggestions and gentle chides of Paul Graves-Brown, Rodney Harrison
and William Mazzarella that helped tame a rather reckless step into a new project.

REFERENCES

Ariès, Philippe. 1974. *Western Attitudes toward Death: From the Middle Ages to the Present*,
    tr. Patricia M. Ranum. Baltimore: Johns Hopkins University Press.
Cullen, Lisa Takeuchi. 2006. *Remember Me: A Lively Tour of the American Way of Death*. New
    York: HarperCollins.
Dawdy, Shannon Lee. In preparation. *Patina: A Profane Archaeology of Romantic Things* [to be
    submitted to Princeton University Press].
Drehs, Wayne. 2009. For Some Fans, Cubs are an Undying Love. ESPN Chicago. 23 April.
    Available at: <http://sports.espn.go.com/chicago/columns/story?columnist=drehs_wayne
    &id=4090319> (accessed 2 January 2013).

Farrell, James J. 1980. *Inventing the American Way of Death*. Philadelphia: Temple University Press.

Florence, Robert P. and Florence, J. Mason. 2005. *New Orleans Cemeteries: Life in the Cities of the Dead*. New Orleans, LA: Batture Press.

Gemperlein, Joyce. 2010. Play Me, Honey, One More Time. *Obit-Mag*, 23 November. Available at: <http://obit-mag.com/articles/ashes-to-vinyl-play-me-honey-one-more-time> (accessed 26 December 2011).

Goody, Jack and Poppi, Cesare. 1994. Flowers and Bones: Approaches to the Dead in Anglo-American and Italian Cemeteries. *Comparative Studies in Society and History* 36(1): 146–75.

Green, James W. 2008. *Beyond the Good Death: The Anthropology of Modern Dying*. Philadelphia: University of Pennsylvania Press.

Harrison, Rodney and Schofield, John. 2010 *After Modernity: Archaeological Approaches to the Contemporary Past*. Oxford: Oxford University Press.

Horkheimer, Max and Adorno, Theodor W. 1993 [1944]. *Dialectic of Enlightenment*, tr. John Cumming. New York: Continuum.

Huber, Leonard V., McDowell, Peggy, and Christovich, Mary Louise. 1997. *New Orleans Architecture*, Volume III: *The Cemeteries*. Gretna, LA: Pelican Publishing.

Hucke, Matt and Bielski, Ursula. 1997. *Graveyards of Chicago: Their People, History, Art and Lore*. Chicago: Lake Claremont Press.

Jensen, Mike. 2010. The Crowded Casket. *Obit-Mag*, 15 March. Available at: <http://obit-mag.com/articles/the-crowded-casket> (accessed 26 December 2011).

Laderman, Gary. 1996. *The Sacred Remains: American Attitudes Toward Death, 1799–1883*. New Haven, CT: Yale University Press.

—— 2003. *Rest in Peace: A Cultural History of Death and the Funeral Home in Twentieth Century America*. Oxford: Oxford University Press.

Miller, Daniel. 1991. *Material Culture and Mass Consumption*. London: Blackwell.

Miller, Daniel and Parrott, Fiona R. 2009. Loss and Material Culture in South London. *Journal of the Royal Anthropological Institute* 15: 502–19.

Mitford, Jessica. 1998. *The American Way of Death Revisited*. New York: Knopf.

Nash, George H. 2000. Pomp and Circumstance: Archaeology, Modernity and the Corporatisation of Death: Early Social and Political Victorian Attitudes Towards Burial Practice. In *Matter, Materiality and Modern Culture*, ed. Paul Graves-Brown, pp. 112–30. New York: Routledge.

National Funeral Directors Association. 2012. Website, Media Center: Statistics. Available at: <http://www.nfda.org/media-center/statisti.csreports.html> (accessed 20 February 2012).

Obit-Mag. 2011a. Ashes into Bullets, A Legacy in Gunpowder, 3 August. Available at: <http://obit-mag.com/articles/ashes-into-bullets-a-legacy-in-gunpowder> (accessed 26 December 2011).

—— 2011b. LookLikes Brings NASA Engineering to Tombstone Decoration, 5 August. Available at: <http://obit-mag.com/articles/looklikes-brings-nasa-engineering-talent-to-tombstone-decoration> (accessed 26 December 2011).

Parker Pearson, Mike. 1999. *The Archaeology of Death and Burial*. College Station, TX: Texas A&M University Press.

Parrott, Fiona. 2011. Death, Memory and Collecting: Creating the Conditions for Ancestralisation in South London Households. In *Unpacking the Collection: Networks of Material and Social Agency in the Museum*, ed. Sarah Byrne, Anne Clarke, Rodney Harrison, and Robin Torrence, pp. 289–305. New York: Springer.

Robben, Antonius C. G. M. 2004. *Death, Mourning, and Burial: A Cross-Cultural Reader*. Malden, MA: Blackwell.

Shaw-Davis Funeral Home. 2011. Personalization Theme Picture Gallery. Available at: <http://www.shaw-davis.com/gallery2.htm> (accessed 26 December 2011).

Tarlow, Sarah. 1999. *Bereavement and Commemoration: An Archaeology of Mortality*. Oxford: Blackwell.

The Obit Patrol. 2011. Dennis Mascari. Available at: <http://obitpatrol.blogspot.com/2011/06/dennis-mascari.html> (accessed 26 December 2011).

Upton, Dell. 1997. The Urban Cemetery and the Urban Community: The Origin of the New Orleans Cemetery. *Perspectives in Vernacular Architecture* 7: 131–45.

Wilk, Richard. 1995. Learning to be Local in Belize: Global Structures of Common Difference. In *Worlds Apart*, ed. Daniel Miller, pp. 110–33. New York: Routledge.

CHAPTER 33

'A DIRTIER REALITY?' ARCHAEOLOGICAL METHODS AND THE URBAN PROJECT

JOHN SCHOFIELD

33.1 INTRODUCTION

ARCHAEOLOGY: the study of ancient things, and a suite of techniques which promotes understanding of times and lives long past? Well, not exactly, not any more. In this chapter I argue that, for the contemporary past, archaeology can have an additional and very different role, one that still retains focus on 'studying' and 'understanding', but which also recognizes merit in participation, as a way of facilitating engagement with the unfamiliar world around us. By doing archaeology in and of the contemporary past, we encounter place and material culture in ways that can bring social benefit and reward for participants. This is what I mean by 'reality'; not as in authenticity or accuracy, but more in a sense of democracy and multi-vocality, which is fast becoming a twenty-first century reality. In short, archaeology has the potential to reach places (and people) other disciplines cannot reach. And for that reason, archaeology of the contemporary past can be as much (if not more) about opportunity and involvement, about the *process*, as it is about the results, something that relates closely to recent discussions of a more future-oriented archaeology (e.g. González-Ruibal 2006; Dawdy 2009, 2010; Harrison and Schofield 2010; Harrison 2011). This may also be true for earlier periods. This chapter will comprise a close examination of these points, using the case study of recent fieldwork in Valletta (Malta). The emphasis here is on the methodology developed for investigating one of the city's back streets, a methodology that emerged through experience to combine elements of field archaeology, ethnography, creative practice, and psychogeography. For more detail on the project and its results see Schofield and Morrissey (2007, 2013).

33.2 ARCHAEOLOGISTS AND 'THE GUT'

Archaeology as an approach can often be inclusive—demonstrating a willingness to involve, represent, and recall the diversity of humankind in its many forms, principally through the material traces ordinary people leave behind. The Strait Street project was largely about those material traces, presenting an archaeological perspective on the artefacts and places that characterize one particular and extraordinary street in Malta's capital city, Valletta. Many archaeological traces encourage conventional descriptions of how lives are led, and how people adapt and survive to environmental and social circumstances. Some descriptions, however, are distinctly subaltern in their outlook and ambition. It is these 'counter-narratives' that interest me more, and this study provides an extreme example of why there can be fascination in the alternative heritage of the city.

Strait Street (and especially that portion at the lower end known as 'The Gut', Figure 33.1) has a colourful history of occupation and counter-culture from the time of Valletta's foundation. The city was designed and built by the Knights of St John in the sixteenth century with specific zones dedicated to particular types of activity: merchants and public office at the top and central areas of town; residential areas for those who supported these activities at the lower end, in the poorer neighbourhoods of Due Balli and L-Arkipierku. Strait Street runs the length of the town, from the more prosperous upper (western) end near City Gate, to the poorer lower (eastern) end, near the garrison at Fort St Elmo. Evidence gathered by, for example, Bonello (2002a, 2002b, 2002c, 2008) illustrates the range of activities characteristic of Due Balli, especially those dating back to the time of the knights, and during British rule and beyond (1800 onwards), leading up to the final withdrawal of the British in 1979. For this later period, oral historical evidence confirms that this was undoubtedly a street that existed largely, if not entirely, to support service personnel, mostly of the Royal Navy, but also merchant navies, army garrisons, and—from the mid-twentieth century—the Royal Air Force. The street was lined with bars, hotels, lodging houses, and music halls. Some were small, intimate spaces, perhaps opportunistic ventures on the part of their owners, simply opening up a front room to create a bar for profit; others were carefully designed or purpose-built, for the entertainment of larger audiences. This appears true especially for the music halls. There was also prostitution.

FIGURE 33.1 The Gut in 2005 (photograph: John Schofield)

But the character of Strait Street is perhaps best conveyed through two personal accounts. The first of these was offered in response to a call for stories and memories through an advert placed in *Navy News*. The second is from Thomas Pynchon's (2000 [1961]) novel *V*.

In the first account Roger Bigden describes his time in Strait Street during what he refers to as the 'high noon' period, in the first half of the 1960s. Roger was a young aircraft armourer in 807 Squadron HMS *Ark Royal*, progressing during the summer of 1963 to a helicopter aircrewman/diver in HMS *Hermes*' ship's flight. His account introduces a number of themes, places, and characters that are central to the Strait Street story:

> All the bars, dance halls, and cafes were doing a roaring trade. 'Bobby' was playing his piano, 'Tiny', the big, friendly, Maltese policeman was usually in position on the left of the cross-roads halfway down. The 'Sparrow' had long gone from the Egyptian Queen, where she was a legend, amazing and delighting the sailors. Mythology had her marrying an Australian Stoker and emigrating back to Aussie with him. The likely truth is that a drunken matelot threw her down the stairs of the Gyppo [Egyptian] Queen....
>
> I remember noting [in *c*.1961] that a couple of more salubrious pubs had opened up in Birzebuggia, one of which was run by a Maltese man, with an English wife. The seeds of the tourist trade were being sown. The Gut was a concept beyond the comprehension of the average British tourist (like Bugis Street in Singapore) and the end was in sight. It dated back to *Pax Britannica*. Certainly before foreign travel was widely available to ordinary people and more particularly before British public moral standards were generally expected abroad in holiday areas. Oddly, I can remember reflecting on all this back then. (Roger Bigden. Email correspondence, 5 December 2005)

Bigden's comments raise a number of issues that became central to this project. The first is that of mythology. His is not the only story of Sparrow, and what happened to her. And what unites many of these stories is their inaccuracy (challenging the notion of a 'familiar world' around us). Second is the issue of change. Bigden was a perceptive young man. As he says, the world was changing and ultimately The Gut would change too. A third issue (not referred to in this quotation) refers to the way people's circumstances influenced their encounter with Strait Street. One's rank and status (e.g. single or married), and one's service (RAF, Army, Navy) will have shaped one's experience of The Gut: which places were acceptable to visit and which were off-limits. Things were different in wartime no doubt, with heightened tension and more unaccompanied men in Malta, but in peacetime these other considerations are directly relevant. RAF and Army personnel are more likely to have been in Malta with their families than would naval personnel, for instance, as would be the case for officers of all three armed forces.

Thomas Pynchon's 1956 visit to Malta informed his novel *V* (2000 [1961]). His accounts of Valletta are widely considered to be accurate and authentic, his colourful descriptions of Strait Street most likely the result of his own experiences. In one passage he describes one of his leading characters approaching the street thus:

> Here were the borders of this city's Disreputable Quarter; Stencil looked around without much curiosity. It was all the same. What a warped idea of cities one got in this occupation! If no record of this century should survive except the personal logs of F[oreign] O[ffice] operatives, the historians of the future must reconstruct a curious language indeed.
>
> Massive public buildings with characterless facades; networks of streets from which the civilian populace seem mysteriously absent. An aseptic administrative world, surrounded by

an outlying vandal-country of twisting lanes, houses of prostitution, taverns, ill-lit except for rendezvous points, which stand out like sequins on an old and misused ball-gown....

Strada Stretta; Strait Street. A passage meant, one felt, to be choked with mobs. Such was nearly the case: early evening had brought to it sailors ashore from HMS *Egmont* and smaller men-o-war; seamen from Greek, Italian, and North African merchantmen; and a supporting cast of shoeshine boys, pimps, hawkers of trinkets, confections, dirty pictures. Such were the topological deformities of this street that one seemed to walk through a succession of music-hall stages, each demarcated by a curve or slope, each with a different set and acting company but all for the same low entertainment. (Pynchon 2000 [1961]: 468)

Thus Pynchon captures a particular element of the character of Strait Street, of what it felt like at this particular time in its history. Pynchon's descriptions of Strait Street are eloquently expressed in a way that neatly accompanies the (more-or-less) contemporary photographs of Tony Armstrong Jones in the mid-1950s (Sitwell and Armstrong Jones 1958). Some of these photographs convey the 'rendezvous points, standing out like sequins on an old and misused ball-gown'. Any one of the sailors captured in these images could be Stencil, encountering this 'vandal-country', 'the Disreputable Quarter' of Valletta.

33.3 FIELD ARCHAEOLOGY AND THE URBAN PROJECT

The role of archaeology has traditionally been to uncover stories using only archaeological (and ethnoarchaeological—see Fewster, this volume) evidence and approaches, and a criticism levelled at archaeology of the contemporary past is sometimes: 'Why bother? We know all this from other sources.' The Strait Street project challenged that presumption. Why should archaeology not contribute something new? How can one assess the accuracy of those other sources (assuming they exist) without testing the ground, so to speak? And does archaeology not have the potential to engage wider audiences than other forms of historical inquiry? There was a further angle to this: that Strait Street appeared taboo in Malta. Fieldwork felt a little like trying to uncover a secret, one deeply buried in the collective memory. Strait Street was rarely mentioned in the media or in conversation. Few people would talk about it and little was written down. In this case, archaeology provided an entrée that might not otherwise have existed.

Relevant here was the status of the fieldwork team as outsiders (*barranin*), something Mitchell (2002: 63–4) also felt when conducting research for his book *Ambivalent Europeans*. The difference is that Mitchell learnt Maltese and lived with a local family, factors that contributed to him becoming more of an insider, more accepted, and privy therefore to the knowledge and conversations amongst other insiders. That said, there are different contexts within which people are considered 'outsiders', which include nationality, but also village, community, parish, and household. Even if one came from a rural village in Malta, and spoke Maltese, one would still be an outsider to Valletta. Yet as Mitchell explains, language—*Malti*—is nevertheless an essential marker of inclusion and exclusion in Malta. While most Maltese are multi-lingual, speaking English and Italian, they also speak Maltese, which in some places (such as Due Balli) is the main language used in everyday conversations.

Of course it is impossible to know what more would have been learnt, being *Malti* speakers. But there appeared some distinct advantages to being *barranin*; notably a safe distance was created, geographical and cultural, which made it acceptable for some to talk to us freely and at times frankly about the history of Strait Street. As one person explained: 'A Maltese person could not have conducted this study. It is much too *close*. It would have been impossible.'

As *barranin*, how then were the hidden histories of Strait Street and Due Balli investigated? By what methods did we achieve a comparatively in-depth investigation under what appeared difficult circumstances? The first point is that an archaeological approach seemed important. This meant starting the process of investigation not through documentary sources or ethnography, but through the places themselves, the very fabric of Strait Street. It meant studying the buildings and the spaces within and around them, documenting and recording them, and the traces encountered within. It meant—in this case—filming and photographing what we saw, and making notes on the things we encountered; sketches for examples of interior spaces and the artefacts still present or which have accumulated since the building was abandoned (for the afterlife of buildings is important too); and sketching and recording the locations of signage and graffiti in the street. Only then, with the traces documented for each place would we embark on documentary and ethnographic research. This 'staged' process was not always possible of course. At times a first visit was accompanied by the very people we needed to interview (and could therefore interview 'in place'), who often brought original documentation with them. Nonetheless, our archaeological approach to Strait Street always started with its material remains.

33.4 PREPARING FOR FIELDWORK

Before arriving in Malta to begin research, we wrote a letter to the *Times of Malta* asking for information. There was a limited response, but one letter was a clear warning not to pursue our study. The letter directed us, with a map, to the area of coastline below Fort St Elmo on the end of the peninsula where, we were later told, tourists had been attacked and robbed. But this response was an isolated case. Another letter was more positive. This came from Joseph Piccinino who asked us to visit him on our arrival. This meeting shaped our experience of Valletta and of our seven-year (and ongoing) association with Strait Street. It also helped us to realize how much personal connections and introductions matter in a close-knit community like this. From Joseph's enthusiastic support and his initial emails, he clearly understood our interest in Strait Street. We were not voyeurs or trouble-makers, or out to insult Malta or the city (*Beltin*) in any way. He understood our commitment to presenting what he considered 'the reality' of Strait Street, recognizing in this the entrepreneurs, the artistes, the musicians and performers, and those who plied their various trades and professions to make a living. We wanted our research to reflect the character of Strait Street: the buzz, the noise, the smell and chaos—the brouhaha, the lives and loves of those who lived and worked there, and those who visited the place. Strait Street represents a heady mix, and it divides opinion. But we felt sure that no one could deny the fascination of Strait Street. To this end he introduced us to Victor Scerri, and while Joseph faded into the background once these connections were established, Victor did anything but. Without Victor's assistance and generosity this project would never have progressed to the extent that it has, and many doors would have remained firmly bolted. It is because of Victor's kindness to us and his standing in the community that people felt able to talk to us. As we have seen, contacts and connections are everything. If a trusted local resident vouches for you, then access can be assured. Victor was the biggest 'skeleton key' we could have hoped for, giving access to a whole host of other contacts not to mention the many bars and other buildings to which he arranged access.

Let us return to the suspicion with which this project was first received. The aim was to tell a story of Strait Street in as accurate and respectful a way as possible. We feel drawn to the place and the people we have met there. We have been taken into people's confidence and have received generous hospitality from the start. Many of the people we met have become friends. The reputation of Strait Street as 'shameful' is barely evident in the studies we have undertaken. What is apparent is a pride and enthusiasm for a place that shaped the lives of many people and their families over generations, from at least 1800 and arguably earlier. That is not of course to deny elements of an unquestionably troubled past. But it is these different emphases that beg the question: what is it precisely that shapes the perception of Strait Street as a somehow shameful place, and why, when much talk is of regeneration, is the street still avoided? Is Strait Street merely disliked for being unconventional? Either way, Strait Street remains largely empty and unloved, awaiting a change of fortune.

Finally, by way of preparation we had to explore how our thoughts on heritage applied in this unconventional setting. I find the old-fashioned view that heritage must be exclusive, special, and necessarily outstanding to be deeply problematic (see also Smith 2006; Council of Europe 2008), preferring to define it in terms of collective cultural property, material, and other legacies of the past that persist into the present and will be passed on to the future. As such, heritage *can* be special and outstanding, but it can also be 'everyday': the quotidian, the ordinary, and the commonplace.

Denis Byrne (2008: 170) refers to heritage as 'social action'; the relationship between a community and its neighbourhood that is dialectical or 'two-way'. A local community may live in a landscape that is scattered with places where physical traces of past occupation are present. Yet this does not in itself create an association between those traces and the community. That association comes through activities which might include participation in a research project, telling one's story, or rifling through tins of old photographs to re-connect with the past. In Strait Street the connection between place and people appears strong. This project sought to reaffirm and legitimize this bond and re-emphasize the heritage-ness of Strait Street. The cultural legacy of Strait Street is as rich as it is significant for those who live there still, and those who might wish to do so again. Documenting the archaeology of Strait Street, and presenting it explicitly in these terms, as cultural heritage and as archaeology, is one of the main objectives of this study.

33.5 Field Methods

The Strait Street project is what some might call a 'pyschogeography', generating a 'mental map' of the place and the people who inhabit it. Psychogeography is an approach that is increasingly used in archaeological fieldwork, especially with regard to archaeological heritage, and archaeologies of the contemporary past. Depending on emphasis, the labels may vary, but the essentials remain consistent: mapping attachment and stories onto a landscape. Byrne and Nugent refer to this as 'geo-biography' (2004), Harrison (2010) calls it 'landscape biography', while Green et al. (2003) describe the collection process as 'story trekking'. But following Byrne's comment on social action (2008), we might also describe our psychogeography as a concern for 'the specific effects of the geographic environment, consciously organized or not, on the emotions and behaviour of individuals'; or put another way, exploring the behavioural impact of urban space (Debord 1981: 5; see Yaneva, this volume). This approach seems particularly relevant here. And to use another not entirely unconnected parallel, Thomas De Quincey is considered by some (e.g. Coverley 2006: 17) a prototype psychogeographer. His drug-fuelled ramblings through London gave him access to the invisible community of the marginalized and the dispossessed. For De Quincey, the city became a riddle, a puzzle that still perplexes writers and walkers to this day, a dream-scape where nothing was what it seemed, and a place which could only be navigated by those possessing secret knowledge. A predominant characteristic of such an approach is walking, with its promotion of swift circulation and the street-level gaze, enabling the official representation of the city to be challenged by cutting across established routes and exploring those marginal and forgotten areas often overlooked by the city's inhabitants.

With this in mind, we summarize our field methods as comprising three stages:

- being seen in and around the street;
- seeing and recording as many of the places and objects we encountered as possible; and
- the conduct of informal interviews *in situ* combined with information gathered online.

33.5.1 Being Seen

Being seen was an essential first step. We needed to build trust and confidence amongst those living, working, or just frequenting this part of Valletta. We also needed to be careful. There have been instances in the past of students conducting research being seen as intrusive and were therefore intimidated. Initially, therefore, our approach was a cautious one. We wanted to become a familiar sight in Strait Street before we started asking too many questions. We walked up and down Strait Street many times, spending hours during the course of each day doing so. We met people this way and the contacts we made gradually produced a valuable network of informants including owners and occupiers.

33.5.2 Recording Traces and Places

Archaeological recording usually involves meticulous and often forensic attention to detail—the close investigation of even the subtlest traces: small artefacts and the patterns they exhibit—a footprint in the dust, wall markings and graffiti. And these were indeed the types of archaeological evidence we gathered. However, the method of retrieval had to be adapted to a situation where access to bars was either unsafe or where the owner was impatient and access was allowed for a limited time. We had (rather optimistically) intended to compile detailed sketches and survey drawings (see Buchli and Lucas 2001), but this proved impossible in almost every case, as visits were invariably brief and hurried affairs. Instead we made rough, quick sketches which were refined and redrawn after the event, in addition to extensive coverage of the space through high resolution digital photography and digital video. This had the additional benefit of capturing the dialogue that typically accompanied our visits, either our own conversations or those with the owner or tenant.

Harder to capture is the acute sense that something interesting happened in these buildings, and something that remains with the place, in the stones almost. It is not so much enchantment and exoticization, as the place's mystery as a subject of research, raising ethical questions about our own perceptions alongside those of residents and former participants, especially given issues of criminality and—for the Roman Catholic Church—morality. But it was a sense of the exotic that drew us to Strait Street and it is a sense that has remained throughout the study. Tim Edensor captures the mood in his (2005) *Industrial Ruins*, describing the 'limitless possibilities for encounters with the weird, with inscrutable legends inscribed on notice boards and signs, and with peculiar things and curious spaces which allow wide scope for imaginative interpretation' (2005: 4). Edensor's study contests the notion that ruins are spaces of waste, that contain nothing, or nothing of value, arguing rather that they are 'endowed with meaning and function' (2005: 6). This is precisely how we felt, entering old bars, or just peering through cracks or keyholes, recording what we saw, that these were meaningful places with an interesting past.

Any building associated with Strait Street's historic role was examined, even where the space has now been converted for a new use: the annexe to Marks and Spencer, for instance (52–54 Strait Street), and the legal office at Mamo TCV (89–90 Strait Street). Strait Street is changing, albeit slowly. The fact that our visits to Strait Street took place in 2004, 2005, and 2009 meant that we could observe and document some of the incremental changes taking place over that time. The processes that can transform a place and change its character, and in some cases also its fortunes, are often slow. The bombing of Valletta in the Second World War is an example of sudden and rapid transformative change, but typically change happens more slowly. Currently that is what we see in Strait Street: small changes, hopefully for the better, but in a way that incorporates the character of Strait Street's colourful past. The gradual erosion of graffiti, such as that marking the Cambridge Music and Dancing Hall (104–105 Strait Street, Figure 33.2), the removal or tidying up of cables and wires, the removal of bar signs, and the repaving of sections of the street, are all small-scale changes which collectively can transform the place and undermine its historic character. Undertaking this survey over time has allowed us to observe and record this process, and to document details others might miss.

33.5.3 Informal Interviews

Much of the information gathered here stems from the third stage of our investigation, oral historical research, either in the form of informal interviews or conversations conducted in or close to Strait Street or through letters, emails, and telephone conversations. Our interviews followed the advice of social anthropologists such as Anderson (2004) who adopted 'bimbling' as a methodology for investigating sites of environmental protest. For Anderson, 'bimbling' amounts to walking or wandering as a means to providing the ideological space necessary to re-experience people's connections with landscape. Given the people we were

FIGURE 33.2 Faded lettering marks the former location of the Cambridge Dancing Hall, photographed in 2004 (photograph: John Schofield)

meeting (one-time barmaids, cross-dressers, cabaret artistes, and—potentially at least—former petty criminals and prostitutes), we sensed that structured and formalized interviews—including questionnaires—were to be avoided. Through bimbling, we were told stories of Strait Street, the details of which mirrored and enhanced those gathered by Victor Scerri, whose own interviews are published periodically in the left-wing Maltese-language newspaper *IT-TORĊA*. But, most significantly, bimbling—combined with Victor's knowledge and influence—quite literally opened doors, and we gained access to 20 of the 80 or so bars that originally lined the lower end and parts of the upper end of Strait Street. As we had been told we would never get into any of them, this degree of access seemed a successful outcome.

Contacting former service personnel and especially sailors has taken the form of letters, messages strategically placed on Internet message/bulletin boards, or placed in veterans' societies' newsletters. One observation is the different rates of response from British and US navies. Every call for information elicited a response from British former naval personnel; yet similar posts to US Navy websites produced not one single response. One explanation for this might be the closer connection between the British and Malta than for the Americans. Perhaps, for the Americans, Malta and Strait Street were nothing special; just a stop en route to Vietnam.

Another reason for conducting our ethnographic research was a concern to explore the history of social groups excluded from what Mitchell (2002: 40) terms the 'grand historical narratives of political and military history' (and there is significant overlap here with Indigenous archaeologies and the use of oral accounts from non-literate and subaltern peoples). Alternative, subversive histories (such as women's history, black, or gay and lesbian history, e.g. Chetcuti 2009) provide an avenue for emancipation. The approach described here, which combines oral history with archaeological analyses, can focus on the 'authenticity of people's daily lives, and the generalizations made by official elite history' (Mitchell 2002: 41).

It is worth emphasizing also here that many of the stories and memories recounted represent a 'collective memory' (Mitchell 2002: 42), where autobiographical experiences are shared

FIGURE 33.3 Bobby in characteristic pose (photographer unknown)

by a number of people. Many people recall some of the characters of Strait Street, and three in particular: 'Tiny', the policeman; Sparrow the barmaid and 'Empress of the Gut'; and Bobby, the hugely talented artiste and pianist (Figure 33.3). These are people recalled by most of our correspondents, whether naval personnel or local Maltese. And not only that, but many of the same stories are recalled. Perhaps these people had catch-phrases or actions whose repetition was part of their star attraction. Or perhaps it is more a reflection of the large numbers of people they performed to, or whose lives they influenced in some way. There are also examples of 'social memory' where autobiographical memories are carried across generations. This usually applies only for local Maltese and families, where successive generations served in the Royal Navy and in which legends and stories are passed on. We should also not forget or trivialize the sensitivity of some of the subject matter: Strait Street memories can be painful, awkward, embarrassing, shameful, and often hard to handle for those left behind.

33.6 ARCHAEOLOGY, HERITAGE, AND THE FUTURE

In a landmark publication, and in the context of the 2005 Faro Convention on the Value of Heritage for Society, the Director of Culture and Cultural and Natural Heritage of the Council of Europe said that 'in certain communities, heritage consciousness is still dominated by elites and expert concerns. Looked after by professionals and academics, what is the role of the public, except as passive spectators and witnesses to the decisions of others?' (Palmer 2008: 8). He also stressed that 'heritage is not simply about the past; it is vitally about the present and the future. A heritage that is disjointed from ongoing life has limited value. Heritage involves continual creation and transformation. We can make heritage by adding new ideas to old ideas. Heritage is never merely something to be conserved or protected, but rather to be modified and enhanced.'

By any conventional or authorized view, the heritage value of Strait Street would be at best minimal, at worst non-existent. With notable exceptions, the buildings are not spectacular. The decrepit bar signs and other traces of The Gut, the graffiti on the walls and paving all add to a very particular 'down at heel' atmosphere, one that can be discomforting and challenging to town planners and visitors alike. Some visitors see a landscape in need of improvement, or regeneration; others see a place of real character and interest. But beyond visitors' experiences and the street's physical appearance is another layer: people live in the flats above the former bars and music halls, people who are integral to the Strait Street story. All of this forms part of Valletta's rich cultural heritage: the place *and* the people; the memories *and* the traces.

Some might consider this Strait Street story an unnecessary subversion of the official and glorious history of Valletta. They may even dislike the decision to tell this story and to publish it. But this is not alternative history. This is part of the living history of Valletta and arguably one of the more intriguing and entertaining histories the city has on offer. Whoever said history must always be comfortable, easy, and nice?

Archaeology and heritage are no longer only about the past, but about the present and the future. This story of the contemporary past should have the potential to influence thoughts and ideas of what present and future generations of Vallettans think about this episode, along with those who take an interest in how Valletta has become the wonderful city it is today. One might go so far as to suggest that Sparrow, Bobby, Tiny, and others, a few of whom remain resident in Strait Street, form part of the greater historical narrative, alongside de Valette, Falzon, etc., just as New Life and the Egyptian Queen (Figure 33.4) should

FIGURE 33.4 The Egyptian Queen, World Heritage? (photograph: John Schofield)

take their places as historic landmarks alongside the auberges, the fortifications, and other grand and protected buildings of Valletta.

Strait Street and especially The Gut were always marginal places. But archaeology is a subject that can embrace marginality and marginalized communities. This chapter promotes the acceptance of Strait Street as heritage as well as illustrating a methodology for exploring other places like this—'the vandal country'; the 'disreputable quarters' of cities. The hope here must be that one day The Gut will live again as a marginal environment, vital and sustainable, as a lively, chaotic, and colourful place—Valletta's beating heart, for the benefit of all.

ACKNOWLEDGEMENTS

The research described here was conducted jointly with Emily Morrissey. We are grateful to the British Academy and the Farsons Foundation (Malta) for funding the fieldwork, and many others for supporting us during our time in Malta. A full list of acknowledgements appears in Schofield and Morrissey (2013).

REFERENCES

Anderson, Jon. 2004. Talking Whilst Walking: A Geographical Archaeology of Knowledge. *Area* 36(3): 254–61.

Bonello, Giovanni. 2002a. Knights and Courtesans. In *Histories of Malta*. Vol. III: *Versions and Diversions*, ed. Giovanni Bonello, pp. 20–41. Malta: Fondazzjoni Patrimonju Malti.

—— 2002b. Humour and Satire in Old Malta Cards. In *Histories of Malta*. Vol. III: *Versions and Diversions*, ed. Giovanni Bonello, pp. 221–8. Malta: Fondazzjoni Patrimonju Malti.

—— 2002c. Duelling in Malta. In *Histories of Malta*. Vol. III: *Versions and Diversions*, ed. Giovanni Bonello, pp. 69–87. Malta: Fondazzjoni Patrimonju Malti.

—— 2008. Malta, the 'Great Tavern' of Europe. *The Sunday Times of Malta*, 28 September.

Buchli, Victor and Lucas, Gavin. 2001. The Archaeology of Alienation: A Late Twentieth-Century British Council House. In *Archaeologies of the Contemporary Past*, ed. Victor Buchli and Gavin Lucas, pp. 158–68. London and New York: Routledge.

Byrne, Dennis. 2008. 'Heritage as Social Action'. In *The Heritage Reader*, ed. Graham Fairclough, Rodney Harrison, John Jameson, Jr., and John Schofield, pp. 149–73. London: Routledge.

Byrne, Dennis and Nugent, Maria. 2004. *Mapping Attachment: A Spatial Approach to Aboriginal Post-Contact Heritage*. Hurstville, NSW: Department of Environment and Conservation.

Chetcuti, Joseph C. 2009. *Queer Mediterranean Memories: Penetrating the Secret History and Silence of Gay and Lesbian Disguise in the Maltese Archipelago*. Carlton, Victoria: Lygon Street Legal Services.

Council of Europe. 2008. *Heritage and Beyond*. Strasbourg: Council of Europe.

Coverley, Martin. 2006. *Psychogeography*. Ebbw Vale: Pocket Essentials.

Dawdy, Shannon L. 2009. Millennial Archaeology: Locating the Discipline in the Age of Insecurity. *Archaeological Dialogues* 16(2): 131–42.

—— 2010. Clockpunk Anthropology and the Ruins of Modernity. *Current Anthropology* 51(6): 761–93.

Debord, Guy. 1981. 'Introduction to a Critique of Urban Geography'. In *Situationist International Anthology*, ed. K. Knabb, pp. 5–8. Berkeley, CA: Bureau of Public Secrets.

Edensor, Tim. 2005. *Industrial Ruins: Space, Aesthetics and Materiality*. Oxford and New York: Berg.

González-Ruibal, Alfredo. 2006. The Past is Tomorrow: Towards an Archaeology of the Vanishing Present. *Norwegian Archaeological Review* 39: 110–25.

Green, Lesley, Green, David, and Neves, Eduardo G. 2003. Indigenous Knowledge and Archaeological Science. *Journal of Social Archaeology* 3(3): 366–98.

Harrison, Rodney. 2011. Surface Assemblages: Towards an Archaeology *in* and *of* the Present. *Archaeological Dialogues* 18(2): 141–96.

Harrison, Rodney and Schofield, John. 2010. *After Modernity: Archaeological Approaches to the Contemporary Past*. Oxford: Oxford University Press.

Mitchell, Jon P. 2002. *Ambivalent Europeans: Ritual, Memory and the Public Sphere in Malta*. London and New York: Routledge.

Palmer, Robert. 2008. 'Preface'. In Council of Europe, *Heritage and Beyond*, pp. 7–8. Strasbourg: Council of Europe.

Pynchon, Thomas. 2000 [1961]. *V*. London: Random House.

Schofield, John and Morrissey, Emily. 2007. *Titbits* Revisited: Towards a Respectable Archaeology of Strait Street, Valletta (Malta). In *Contemporary and Historical Archaeology in Theory*, ed. Laura McAtackney, Matthew Palus, and Angela Piccini, pp. 89–99. Oxford: British Archaeological Reports.

—— 2013. *Strait Street: Malta's 'Red-Light District' Revealed*. Malta: Midsea Press.

Sitwell, Sacheverell and Armstrong Jones, Tony. 1958. *Malta*. London: Batsford.

Smith, Laurajane. 2006. *The Uses of Heritage*. London and New York: Routledge.

CHAPTER 34

HERITAGE AND MODERNISM IN NEW YORK

LAURIE A. WILKIE

34.1 INTRODUCTION

THE interpretive and analytical practices of archaeology, which make it such a powerful tool for understanding social lives and human experience in the remote past, are equally capable of revealing and illuminating aspects of the contemporary world that are rendered invisible to us as we hurry unreflectively through the familiarity of our everyday lives. Archaeology, as a discipline, has contributed greatly to the development of heritage both as an organized 'official' set of bureaucratic structures and practices, as well as an 'unofficial' set of awarenesses and attitudes about the value of past things and material legacies that exist in Western societies (e.g. see Harrison 2010, 2013).

Archaeology also proves itself, as I will discuss here, a powerful tool for understanding how heritage, through discourses of modernity, has been scripted into a binary relationship that places it as opposing notions of progress, change, and development. This has been particularly true in the recent past in debates regarding quality of life issues for urban dwellers, with preservationists and developers representing diametrically opposed visions. My intent in this chapter is to blur the boundaries between the categories of development and heritage, not only to bring complexity to the histories that are told about the heritage movement, but also to encourage a different perception of the ways that heritage contributes to the quality of life in contemporary cities.

I focus on two cases studies: one showcasing the historical narratives of the preservation movement that focus on the struggle to save Washington Square Park, in New York City; the second, a consideration of the development and use of High Line Park, also in New York. My methodological approach for this work is what might best be labelled a documentary contemporary archaeology, not unlike the documentary archaeology approaches I have employed to study sites created in the more remote past (Wilkie 2006). Archives in New York, particularly collections of the New York Historical Society, New York University, and the New York Public Library, were utilized to interrogate urban myths about the heritage movement in New York. Along with my collaborator, Dan Hicks (Hicks and Wilkie 2009; Wilkie and Hicks 2009), we conducted surveys of Washington Square Park and the High Line, photographing and documenting contemporary uses of spaces and archaeological traces of past land use.

34.2 HERITAGE FOLKLORE

New York City is birthplace to many urban myths. Some, like the rumoured alligators and dog-sized rats reputed to roam the sewers, are laughed at, while others, like 'mole people' or 9/11 conspiracies, are more carefully considered and debated as possible. The folklore of the New York preservation movement includes its own collection of urban myths, many of which have come to surround one particular man—Robert Moses. Moses held a variety of government appointments in New York City, including the position of City Planner, which allowed him to effectively control many aspects of the redevelopment of the city's landscape from 1930 to 1950 (Caro 1975; Krieg 1988).

A convergence of federal funding, the ability to create and manipulate the New York political machine, and simple force of will, allowed Moses to impose his vision of New York's future on the five boroughs and Long Island (Caro 1975; Ballon and Jackson 2007). While some have described Moses as 'a bogey man of urban studies', or the 'Count Dracula of City Planning' (cited in Joerges 1999), I see the Moses character who appears in the folklore of New York's heritage movement as what I will call a 'Trickster of Modernity'. Like Brer Rabbit, Coyote, or Anansi, Moses is portrayed as clever and devious, with his victories earning grudging admiration and his defeats inspiring a satisfied chuckle. Biographies of Moses, like Robert Caro's *The Power Broker* (1975) have committed some of these urban legends to paper in a way that seems to give them veracity. My intent in this chapter is neither to defend nor to vilify Moses, but to discuss why a character such as the Moses Trickster exists and how this character reveals much about the relationship between heritage and modernity in and beyond New York City.

34.3 URBAN MYTH 1: THE BRIDGES OF NEW YORK, OR 'HOW MOSES RUINED THE FUTURE OF NEW YORK CITY'

'Moses the Trickster' has received attention as a trope in a series of discussions about the agency and politics of technology. Langdon Winner (1980) used a story that has circulated around New York in different guises and was committed to paper in Frank Caro's biography of Moses. While the intellectual debate surrounding the 'politics of artefacts' and the 'artefacts of politics' has a bearing on this chapter (see Winner 1980; Joerges 1999), I will first refer to the actual myth that these articles centred on.

The story states that Moses had the bridges and overpasses on the parkways from New York leading to Long Island's beaches built so low that buses could not pass under them, thus preventing those of lower socio-economic circumstances from reaching the beaches. The story goes on to relate that Moses also helped block an extension of the railroad line to

Jones Beach, with similar effect. In short, Moses the Trickster had found a way to ensure that only wealthier (and therefore mostly white) car owners could access Jones Beach and other such places on Long Island. People of colour, perceived as most likely to require public transportation to access the beach, were permanently denied access. Moses, so goes the story, cleverly discovered a means through which to keep his beloved project, the Jones Beach park complex, a racially and economically segregated space. As told by Winner (1980), the parable proved to be an effective means of advocating that 'things have politics'. Joerges (1999) provided a counter-argument showing that the myth was just that—a powerfully illustrative myth with no basis in fact: automotive parkways were by law closed to truck and bus traffic, therefore, there was *no reason* to design the parkways for these vehicles, suggesting that people endowed things with politics they may not have originally had.

While this particular urban myth was told to illustrate the power of things to structure social order, it is also a story that illustrates one of the worries of modernity—the future-shaping power of the present. We will return to this point shortly, but first, let us present a second Moses urban myth.

34.4 Urban Myth 2: Robert Moses and Jane Jacobs; or 'How Moses was Kept from Ruining Washington Square Park's Past'

In Washington Square Park, at the Terminus of 5th Avenue in New York City, there is a lovely fountain. While there has long been a fountain in Washington Square Park, this particular fountain is a twentieth-century incarnation. The fountain is large, and built with deep ledges for sitting, and stepped so that one can easily climb over the ledge if one desires to enter the fountain. On a hot day, numerous children and child-hearted adults can be seen frolicking in the water. On a nice evening, couples can be seen sitting along the fountain's edge, listening to one of the numerous street musicians that come to perform at the park. On a week-end, brides and grooms pose for cameras, the fountain's water framing their nuptial bliss (Figure 34.1).

If you had no prior knowledge of the park, you would look upon the fountain and think, how lovely, what a beautifully designed public space. You would never guess that for certain people, the fountain has been ruined by a recent park renovation—a renovation that dared to move the fountain nine feet from its 'original' position. The reposition has aligned the fountain with the Washington Arch, so that the fountain can be seen through the arch, creating a lovely vista. But for a certain generation, the moving of the fountain is unforgivable, another travesty against a beloved landmark by an uncaring city parks department (Washington Square Redevelopment Collection [WSRD] 1952–66; Washington Square Association Papers [WSAP], meeting minutes, 1933, 1939–44). Never mind that the recent redesign tried to curry favour with preservationists by attempting to bring back elements of the 1890s appearance of the park, introducing replica light fixtures and park benches; never

FIGURE 34.1 A couple poses for wedding pictures in Washington Square Park, the park fountain visible behind them (photograph: Laurie A. Wilkie)

mind that in 1983, it was the wish of the local neighbourhood society that the park be renovated to its pre-1900 design. Which past is most desirable to save is defined generationally.

The fight to 'save' Washington Square Park is an old one, dating back to at least the 1890s (WSAP, 1934 promotional pamphlet). But local mythology places the struggle to 'save' the park as dating to the 1950s, when Robert Moses attempted to renovate the park, in opposition to the desires of the local community (Page and Mason 2004). While the outcry against the particular redevelopment of the park was a grassroots effort led by a Greenwich Village housewife, Shirley Hayes, public intellectuals like Jane Jacobs and Lewis Mumford quickly entered the fray. In the contemporary popular telling of the story, Moses wanted to 'ruin' the park by allowing traffic to run through it, and by eliminating a playground. The populist movement to save the park thwarted Moses and became a turning point in the preservationists' battle against the commissioner (Wood 2008).

This myth, like that of the bridges, demands further excavation. The anti-development crowd shared the battle cry that the park was to be 'preserved', but what preservation meant varied from interest group to interest group. In a radio address in support of closing Washington Square Park to traffic, local activist and mother Shirley Hayes argued 'In any sound, honest and constructive city plans, for large cities and well as small towns, cognizance must be taken and first consideration given to the needs of the people who live there. It's especially important for the great city of New York to preserve its few remaining communities and all that is part of giving them their distinctive qualities, including livability' (Shirley Hayes Papers, undated press release). Meanwhile, in her much-lauded classic, *The Death and Life of the Modern City* (1962), Jane Jacobs touted the notion of how diversity enriched city landscapes, and refers to Washington Square Park and surrounding Greenwich Village as a case study. While a close reading of the work reveals what would now be considered a condescending neo-liberal streak in Jacobs's text, she can be pointed to as the champion of broken windows and run-down buildings, things she identified as parts of a healthy, living city.

We see yet a slightly different view in Lewis Mumford's position: 'Washington Square, one of the few remaining squares from the original plan of 1811 has a claim to our historic respect: a respect that Mr. Moses seems chronically unable to accord any human handiwork except his own' (WSRC, Joint Emergency Committee Meeting, March 1958). Mumford speaks not of liveability, or improvement, or ideas about a better future. He instead invokes the tired and cookie-cutter notions of preservation for the sake of preservation combined with a personal jab against an increasingly unpopular city commissioner. Yet, it is Mumford and Jacobs whose ideas are preserved on bookshelves in preservationist offices.

In this myth about modern New York City, Moses and Jacobs are paired, with one wearing a white hat, the other a black one. The two are comfortably embraced stereotypes of 'the planner' versus 'the preservationist' (see Page and Mason 2004: 3–16). The most important omission from the 'save Washington Square Park' myth, however, is that the park had been perceived to be threatened in earlier periods as well. Left out of the story of Washington Square Park is the appearance of the 1935 plan that Moses had prepared for the park (Shirley Hayes Papers, 1935 Robert Moses park plan). That plan imagined a park that allowed traffic flow around, not through the park, as had been the case in the 1940s and 1950s. A large reflecting pool, with two large adjoining semi-circlular lawn areas would have served as the visual centre of the park. Graceful radiating pathways, lined with trees would fill the rest of the park.

The plan is beautifully rendered, but was rejected by the Washington Square Association (WSA), a neighbourhood group founded in 1906 to serve as a watchdog organization for neighbourhood standards. The fault with the plan? It did not include playgrounds. The WSA were not interested in the city beautiful aesthetic embodied in the 1935 Moses plan. Instead, they rained a storm of complaining letters on the Park Commissioner, asking for repairs to cracks in concrete, bald patches in lawns, and for additional flower plantings (WSAP 1938, 1939, 1940, 1941, 1942, 1944, 1947, meeting minutes). Moses responded with typical diplomacy, raging that they (the WSA) had rejected his beautiful plans for the park, and now the money for park improvements had dried up (WSAP 1939, read into meeting minutes). He proposed his 1935 plan again in 1940, again to have it rejected by the community (WSAP 1940, meeting minutes). When a new plan was designed for the park in 1951, Moses proposed the now infamous street widening and highway through the park. Traffic was already cutting through the park, and given that the community used part of the park as a parking lot, this probably did not seem as vengeful as it has been portrayed. It is at this spot in the history where most of the preservationist stories begin their narrative.

So what of the preservationists, who wrote lovingly of the wonderful park that needed to be saved? A review of aerial photographs—the same sources that Moses used to develop his projects—demonstrates one enduring and remarkable feature about the park: it was a run-down, traffic filled, unattractive urban space. Yet, celebrities of the time—like Jane Jacobs, Lewis Mumford, Margaret Mead, and even Eleanor Roosevelt—came to lend their voices to the cause championed by a confederation of squabbling neighbourhood organizations and action groups brought together by community members like park-mom Shirley Hayes (Shirley Hayes Papers, WSAP, WSRC).

So here are the contradictions: Moses hoped to make Washington Square into a beautiful park in 1935, and again in 1940. He even attempted to preserve those features of the ugly park that community members wanted in the 1950s designs, only to find his attempts met with angry community organizations. How infuriating it must have been for Moses to receive updates from the WSA about the number of cracks in the sidewalks, worries about bald patches in the lawn, and nagging requests for new flowerbeds and shrubs. From his perspective, he was rebuilding the city and these horrible people could not stop obsessing about their horrible little urban park. Yet embedded in this conflict is the same discursive relationship between the past and future that marks modern thought—something of the past, that something that was desirable—needed to be preserved for the future.

An archaeological consideration of the park demonstrates that its design history is more complicated than indicated by the conventional 'heritage' narrative. A survey of the pathways through the park reveals multiple types of paving having different degrees of wear and preservation. An abandoned skate-boarding area in the park has attracted drug dealing and other activities that keep families out of that spot. A variety of different lamp post styles are found throughout the park, testimony to multiple attempts at reimagining the park's aesthetic, and cut-off bench mounts and other abandoned features are visible throughout, despite an ongoing 'restoration' project that seeks to make the park look more like it did during the time of author and Washington Square resident, Henry James.

Robert Moses often used aerial photography in his planning, and a review of his project plans reveal the breathtaking beauty and order of his proposed rewriting of the New York City landscape (Figure 34.2). The beautiful Jones Beach is best considered obliquely from above, the lovely white beach, the water tower disguised as an obelisk, the bathhouses reminiscent of Caribbean forts. But in real life, the pristine perfection of Moses' plans always had a shortcoming: they became dirtied with the bodies of people, who poured themselves across the landscapes Moses designed in ways he had not intended.

Jacobs (1962) also looked at the city from a grand level, looking at the integration of parks, neighbourhoods, building ages, and block size. Her analysis of how to create liveability in the city through preservation and diversity may appear superficially more attentive to the

FIGURE 34.2 A Robert Moses housing development as seen from the Empire State building. From a height, one can immediately identify the modernist influence of Moses on the city landscape (photograph: Laurie A. Wilkie)

needs of the day-to-day living than Moses, but ultimately, her ideas are about maintaining a particular kind of bourgeois charm for a particular set of neighbourhood residents. The lived realities of the day-to-day, the aesthetic of the mundane, fail to materialize in Jacobs's vision, a vision which is as future oriented as any of Robert Moses' projects. Both visions were explicitly political.

And there is the rub. Although portrayed as opposing figures, the simplistically drawn sides characterized by icons like Moses and Jacobs are not really so opposed, they are merely two different manifestations of modernist thinking. Living in the contemporary world, it is easy to forget how ideas of the modern and the counter-modern permeate so much of our thinking. The ideas of modernism are not the reality of the world, but merely a set of spectacles that Westerners use to see the world. So accustomed are we to seeing the world through a modernist lens that we no longer see the frames of the glasses that shape our view. What is necessary is to remove the glasses altogether and to gaze at Jacobs-the-saviour and Moses-the-destroyer intently, to see them for what they are: parts of our creation mythologies, part of our folklore.

Jacobs and Moses were each swept up into grand narratives of progress and improvement—both envisioned a particular future for urban living and likewise had identified a set of pathways that could be followed to those ends. What neither realized was that they were both small blips in the historical narratives of Washington Square, that a different kind of politics, a politics of sidewalks and flowerbeds, of playgrounds and grassy lawns, a politics that was enacted from day to day, since the founding of Washington Square Park, was actually shaping the course of events they had become entangled in. The park had a deep history, a history etched in the fabrics and landscapes of the park. These histories are the inheritance of the Washington Square community; they endure in the physical place, to be enacted by multiple generations of parkgoers.

34.5 PAST FUTURES

To embrace modernity is to internalize the idea that the present is 'better' or 'more advanced' than the past, and that the future will be 'better' or 'more advanced' than the present. Yet, inherent in that ideology is also the notion that it is the obligation of individuals in the present to 'build a better future'. Each generation, then, lives with the spectre of being the people who have failed to ensure continued progress of society (see also Gonzalez-Ruibal, this volume). Moses-the-bridge-builder becomes a metaphor for someone who failed to build bridges to a better future, choosing instead to extend social, racial, and economic inequalities into succeeding generations. It is probably not surprising that stories portraying Moses as racist gained traction during the Civil Rights movement and beyond, when race and racism began to receive serious analysis as social ills that needed to be cured to ensure a healthier society in the future.

It is revealing that Moses is simultaneously presented as someone, who in addition to 'ruining' the future with his projects, also threatened to 'ruin' the past in redesigning Washington Square Park. This is why it is best to see Moses as a Trickster of Modernity, someone positioned in the present that has come to symbolize all of the anxieties of modernity. This simultaneous past-peeking and forward-looking nature of modernity must be considered in discussions of 'heritage' and 'preservation'—particularly now—as the sites of these preservation battles become, themselves, 'historic'. The modernist influenced projects of Robert Moses are now over 50 years old, and are now established components of New York City's landscape. It is a problem not confined to New York, but exists in all contemporary cities, and it is a problem that has not been adequately considered in our academic thinking about heritage and preservation.

Anglophone discussions of urban built heritage have traditionally employed one of two dominant narrative tropes. Most commonly, the historic environment has been presented as constantly under threat from modern development (see also Harrison, this volume). Here, a canon of architectural and archaeological inheritance has been defined, and depicted as antithetical to modern development and urban change. Destruction and loss are used to illustrate a much broader long-standing narrative of modernity as disenchanting (e.g. Kunstler 1993; Diehl 1996; Page and Mason 2004; Wright 2009a; see also Bennett 2003).

Alternatively, the celebratory, nostalgic nature of the British 'heritage industry' and the American historic preservation movement has been critiqued in approaches that emphasize the cultural contingencies of the definition and value of heritage (Brett 1996; Longstreth 2008). Here, a constructivist approach has been adopted, emphasizing the 'intangibility' of cultural heritage (e.g Smith 2006; Smith and Akagawa 2009). Such work calls for conventional concerns with architectural and archaeological preservation to see heritage as a social and political construct (Smith and Akagawa 2009).

On both sides of the Atlantic, literature in urban heritage studies has been caught between evangelizing against loss and 'sneering at theme parks' (Wright 2009b: 238–56). Recently, two processes have started to unravel this distinction. First, the distinction between modern change and the preservation of earlier cultural heritage has been eroded by the gradual recognition in architectural history and historical archaeology of the significance of twentieth-century material, leading to questioning of the utility of conventional approaches to designation and preservation due to the sheer quantities of modern material culture. The potential status of the very recent past as heritage—the remains of processes previously defined as destroying the heritage as themselves understood as part of the historic environment—raises philosophical issues that go to the heart of the opposing conceptions of heritage: as the everyday or the exceptional, as the human or the material.

Secondly, a growing awareness of the need for new critical histories of the historic preservation movement has developed in both the USA and the UK. A range of studies have started critically to assess the idea of a canon of historic sites and buildings, and to question the dematerialization of built heritage in the constructivist idea of 'intangible' or 'immaterial' heritage (Wilkie 2001). The first sustained historical accounts of architectural preservation in the USA (Page and Mason 2004) and the conservation movement in Britain have also emerged. These new studies have moved beyond celebratory accounts, and begin to situate the distinction between future-oriented modernity and backward-looking preservation as distinct historical phenomena; questioning the idea that preservationism was a counter-modern phenomenon (cf. Ballon and Jackson 2007; Menell et al. 2007). While some modernist thinking sought to distance itself from the past (e.g. Gold 2007: 33), even Le Corbusier's characterization of 1930s New York as comparable to medieval Europe—'when the cathedrals were white'—hinted at the modern ambivalences towards the historic built environment (Le Corbusier 1947). Taken together, these developments make possible new writing about modern urbanism and its legacies, which moves beyond the two dominant, opposing tropes outlined above: modernist preservationism and postmodern constructivism.

The importance of the twentieth-century urban spaces like Washington Square Park, or Jones Beach and the Parkways, has been strongly embedded in the everyday experience of these places by those who used them or viewed them. These examples reveal several key points that we who study the contemporary world should keep in mind about modern landscapes and their preservation. First, that we simply cannot escape the past-peeking/future-making dialectic that shapes all modernist thought related to preservation and development. The second, perhaps more subtle lesson, is that there is another binary through which to think about 'preservation'. Preservation can be seen as something that is regulated through policy, at one scale, but also as something that is enacted through lived experience. This returns us to the concepts of 'official' and 'unofficial' forms of heritage (Harrison 2010). Each of the cases above illustrates these contrasting notions. The two are interwoven in complicated ways, but preservation as policy—Preservation with a capital 'P', if you will, or 'official' heritage—receives most of our scholarly attention. Preservation with a capital 'P'—the battles, both successful and unsuccessful to protect buildings form the cannon of preservation history—these are the saved Washington Square Parks, and the lost Penn Stations. Yet, these battles that led to the passing of preservation policy emerged from preservation with a little 'p', or 'unofficial heritage'. Preservation with a little 'p' is enacted in the everyday: it is messy, it is mundane, and it is part of lived experience. Those who experience preservation as an embodied experience may not find official heritage movements speak to them or represent their best interests. This is clearly illustrated in the contrast between the goals of the Washington Square Park Association and the city beautiful movement aesthetic pushed by Moses. Preservation with a little 'p' is the preservation that is part of the everyday politics that people engage in as they move through their material world. It is about concerns with the most seemingly trivial complaints. And importantly, this form of preservation is best explored through archaeologies of the contemporary. When we recognize these forces are at play, we are able to better understand sites of preservation that may at first seem contradictory or 'inauthentic'. Let us now turn our attention towards a case study that cannot be properly understood as either a 'modern' development or a 'preservation project'. This is the recent 'development' of the High Line in New York as 'modern ruins'.

34.6 MODERN RUINS

The High Line opened in 2009 as a new city park in New York. The raised park runs along the former elevated track of the New York Central Railroad (NYCR). The NYCR, first built in 1847, was a vital transportation corridor through New York City's west side. In 1929, the tracks were elevated so that they did not interfere with traffic flow on the streets below. The railroad continued to be important through the 1960s, but eventually fell into disuse and the tracks became overgrown with plants, creating a feral space within the city (Cardwell 2009). For one who climbed up onto and travelled along the tracks, this space was a stark contrast to the busy traffic below; one was transported into a land that was alien, wild, and a bit dangerous. As an off-the-grid area, the overgrown tracks attracted any number of people and activities that demanded secrecy and isolation. Teenagers experimenting with drugs, alcohol, and sex, chronic drug abusers and alcoholics, prostitutes and the homeless were among the denizens of this space which led Mayor Giuliani's administration to identify the tracks as a site for demolition in the late 1990s.

The abandoned tracks had also attracted other users, those desiring an escape from the noise and concrete of the city, those desiring the adventure of discovery and exploration, and yes, possibly even flirtations with danger. To travel along the feral High Line was to experience the thrill of discovering a lost civilization that left behind rotting hulks of track and debris. The traveller confronted modernity and its debris. The viewer could contemplate the cycles of development and decay, and see how progress abandoned the old. The High Line for those visitors was the experience of nostalgia and romance of things and times past. When the High Line was proposed for demolition, it was a group of these latter users of the resource who came forward. In response to a discussion at the community governance meeting, Joshua David and Robert Hammond founded the 'Friends of the High Line' in 1999, with the intent of converting the 'wild space' into a park. The organization rallied supporters and funding, and commissioned economic feasibility studies demonstrating that conversion of the area into a park would increase the tax base for the city at levels greater than the investment necessary to create the park. In 2002, the efforts were rewarded when the city adopted the preservation and reuse of the High Line as official city policy (Friends of the Highline 2008).

David and Hammond explained their motivations behind the preservation drive as follows, 'We had both fallen in love with the landscape that had reclaimed the monumental structure. We hoped to save this self-sown wilderness...' (Friends of the Highline 2008: 2). Eventually, an arrangement unique in New York's history was arranged, where the city paid for the development of the first two segments of the park while the Friends of the High Line took on the task of paying operation costs and raising money for the final four-block segment of the park. A fund-raising campaign, which I will discuss further in a moment, is currently underway, with $85 million of the estimated $150 million need for construction and long-term operating costs being raised. Construction on the final segment is expected to be underway by late 2012 (Foderara 2011).

In 2005, when design plans for the first two segments of the park were released, the past-peeking, future-seeking nature of the project was clearly articulated by designers. The following description was published in the *New York Times*: 'Much of the designer's work has been devoted to seeking a balance between preserving what one called "the romance of the ruin"—wild grasses growing up through the metal skeleton of rails and rivets—and creating a fresh green corridor for pedestrians' (Pogrebin 2005). Particularly intriguing was the call of the architects for new buildings being erected along the stretch of the park to accommodate the High Line by allowing it to pass through structures. The proposed fifteen-storey André Balazs hotel on the project site was redesigned to allow the railroad line to continue uninterrupted through the building (Pogrebin 2005). Here we see reconstituted heritage dictating the form that 'progress' will take.

New Yorkers were thrilled when the High Line first opened in June 2009 (Figure 34.3). Over 300,000 visitors made their way along the High Line's length during the first month, with 3,000–15,000 visiting on weekdays, and 18,000 to 20,000 visitors climbing up to the park on weekends. This turnout was remarkable given the park had a legal maximum limit of 1,700 visitors at any one time. A *New York Times* writer gushed about the impact of the setting on its residents, reporting: 'It even inspires crusty New Yorkers to behave as if

FIGURE 34.3 People exploring the High Line shortly after its opening, July 2009 (photograph: Laurie A. Wilkie)

they were strolling down Main Street in a small town rather than striding the walkway of a hyper-urban park—routinely smiling and nodding, even striking up conversations with strangers' (Cardwell 2009).

As part of a project on the preservation movement in New York, I visited the High Line shortly after it opened in the summer of 2009 with my collaborator, Dan Hicks. Although still under construction, with immature plantings, and an extension planned, the park was already a heavily used public space. There was evidence of international tourists, New Yorkers investigating the new park, and a large number of families and individuals who were clearly already accustomed to using the space as part of everyday habit. The place and the community have become the one and the same. For the young people who now purchase converted lofts along the park, and the men who fought to 'preserve' the wild landscape, their sense of the place was formed after the halting of the railroad as a railroad. To walk the High Line then would have been the kind of subversive act of daring engaged in by children and teenagers, portions of society who escaped the surveillance of their elders to climb through abandoned buildings, spray paint graffiti, drink, screw, and encounter whatever other marginal elements of society used the abandoned railway to move through the city.

The broken windows and faded graffiti along the railway remain, evoking this sense of a subversive past. For those behind the development of the High Line, to restore the area to its historic function, as a rail line, would have been contrary to their memories and perception of the space, yet, here is the irony that confounds the clear lines between preservation and development: to create the park, they destroyed the very landscape that had inspired their efforts to preserve the railway line in the first place. The natural feral landscape that David and Hammond had fallen in love with was torn apart, ripped out, and replaced with professionally designed, carefully laid out nursery-raised plants in landscapes intended to evoke the very plants they replaced.

Is this a development project or a preservation project? In the words of the green move-ment, we could call this a 'repurposing' of the train tracks rather than the preservation of the tracks; but such a label ignores the fact that the tracks themselves have stayed *in situ* and have been interpreted to a particular time in their history. Despite the destruction of the historic feature (the feral landscape) that resulted from the project, this cannot be called a traditional development project either. Instead, it is best to understand this project as the embodiment of a past-peeking, future-bettering mindset that is inherent in modernist thought. The High Line serves to evoke a sense of New York's progress in an aesthetically pleasing way that may promote thoughtful consideration of the relationship between the city's past and present. New Yorkers can escape the bustle of the street below, elevated above traffic to a beauti-ful natural retreat—a retreat that is free of the over-brush, broken glass, human defecation and urine scents, tossed-out needles and syringes, passed-out bums and lurking criminal elements that were also very likely attracted to the reclaimed natural retreat of David's and Hammond's childhood. Yet, it is a retreat that was only made possible by the original con-struction and abandonment of the raised rail line. The park is an inheritance from the past to be enjoyed by future generations. The park very literally celebrates progress in the mate-rial form of abandoned ruins, doing so in a way that highlights contemporary standards of architectural design and environmental consciousness.

For my purpose here, the High Line is the perfect example of the coexistence of the past-peeking, forward-looking state of mind that is modernity. In the design of the High Line, it is no longer the plants covering the abandoned structure, but the ruined structure that seems to emerge from the park—railroads tracks growing out of gardens of wild-like plant-ings (Figure 34.4). It is the legacy of the railroad that has made possible this new and unique, and warmly embraced as progressive, park.

FIGURE 34.4 Which came first? The flowers or the railroad? A reset railroad track at the High Line rewrites the archaeological history of the site (photograph: Laurie A. Wilkie)

This preserved site is not about authenticity or historic integrity (see also Graves-Brown, this volume), words used in historic evaluation processes (or policy heritage), but about liveability and modernity's preservation needs (lived heritage). The development of this space is about making the past a pleasant place to visit while creating a safe and beautiful environment to be carried forward in the city's future. In many ways, this space is the 'natural' inheritance of the Moses–Jacobs argument, yet, perhaps, neither of those protagonists would be completely happy with the High Line. And what would the Washington Square Park Association think of this park, with its beautifully planted flowers side by side with intentionally exposed railroad beams and lovingly preserved cracked window panes in abandoned buildings? More interestingly, what kind of future awaits a space like the High Line? Will the Friends of the High Line argue over future uses and developments of this new urban space? Will a time come when the 'ruined' state of the High Line is no longer cherished? Or perhaps will the ruins need to be updated or improved? And how will the efforts of people like David and Hammond be remembered? Already the two men have become the visible faces for a much larger movement to preserve and create this space. Are we seeing the beginning of a new urban myth about preservation in New York? These are things for archaeologists to follow and consider as we go forth in our contemplations of heritage and preservation—as part of a history of debates and discourses about living in, preserving, and developing a modern world.

34.7 Conclusions: Contemporary Modern

In closing, I started this chapter with a consideration of Robert Moses and the myths that surround him in New York City's preservation movement history. Moses is important not only for what he achieved in forming the modern landscape of New York City, but also for how he has come to be represented in discourses about modernity and preservation. He has come to be what I have termed a 'trickster of modernity', someone who shaped the past, future, and past futures of the city. Moses embodied all the tensions and anxieties of modernity with his past-wrecking and future-destroying abilities. The historical narratives written about the history of the preservation movement tend to pit the future against the past, with the emphasis being on how the future (development) destroys the past (heritage).

The brief examples provided above demonstrate that such narratives are overly simplistic and fail to recognize the way that modernity itself has given rise to the preservation movement (see also Harrison 2013). More importantly, these narratives establish a situation in which the 'modern'—development projects like Jones Beach or contemporary incarnations of Washington Square Park—is naturalized as unworthy of preservation. Yet, when we look at the history of spaces like Washington Square Park or the High Line, we see that it is *liveability* that shapes a community's engagement with 'historic' and 'modern' spaces alike. The High Line is a project that has successfully combined the preservation of a modern landscape with liveability, while also appealing to modernity's desire to demonstrate 'progress' in tangible ways. Ironically, this has been accomplished through the preservation of the railroad in a 'ruined' state. It may be tempting to see such a preservation move as 'postmodern', but in reality, the project is perfectly in keeping with modernity's sensibilities. As archaeologists, we are in a unique position to disentangle narratives about the preservation movement, through excavation of documents and through observation of places and things as they exist in the modern landscape. We can provide an alternative and more complex narrative than those offered by historians of the preservation movement: our narratives do not seek villains or heroes, but seek to account for the material world that shaped the experiences of everyday life. As such, we are also uniquely positioned to enter into conversations about urban liveability. As participants in modernity ourselves, we can use our past-peeking abilities to help imagine better futures.

REFERENCES

Archive collections

Shirley Hayes Papers. New York Historical Society.
Washington Square Association Papers. New York University Archives, Elmer Holmes Bobst Library.
Washington Square Redevelopment Collection. New York Historical Society.

Secondary sources

Ballon, Hilary and Jackson, Kenneth T. (eds.). 2007. *Robert Moses and the Modern City: The Transformation of New York*. New York: Norton.
Bennett, Jane. 2003. *The Enchantment of Modern Life*. Princeton, NJ: Princeton University Press.
Brett, David. 1996. *The Construction of Heritage*. Cork: Cork University Press.
Cardwell, Diane. 2009. For High Line Visitors, Park is a Railway out of Manhattan. *New York Times*, 21 July. Available at: <http://www.nytimes.com/2009/07/22/nyregion/22highline.html?ref=highlinenyc> (accessed 28 January 2012).
Caro, Robert. 1975. *The Power Broker: Robert Moses and the Fall of New York*. New York: Vintage Books.
Diehl, Lorraine. 1996. *The Late Great Pennsylvania Station*. New York: Four Walls, Eight Windows.
Foderara, Lisa W. 2011. Record $20 Million Gift to help finish High Line Park. *New York Times*, 26 October.
Friends of the Highline. 2008. *Designing the Highline: Gansevoort Street to 30th Street*. New York: Friends of the Highline.
Gold, John. 2007. *The Practice of Modernism: Modern Architects and Urban Transformation, 1954–1972*. New York: Routledge.
Harrison, Rodney. 2010. What is Heritage? In *Understanding the Politics of Heritage*, ed. Rodney Harrison, pp. 5–42. Manchester: Manchester University Press.
—— 2013. *Heritage: Critical Approaches*. New York: Routledge.
Hicks, Dan and Wilkie, Laurie A. 2009. Things as Events, Things as Effects. Paper Presented at Contemporary and Historical Archaeology in Theory Conference, Keeble College, Oxford University, October 16-18, 2009.
Jacobs, Jane. 1962. *The Death and Life of Great American Cities*. New York: Vintage Books.
Joerges, Bernward. 1999. 'Do Politics Have Artefacts?' *Social Studies of Science* 29(3): 411–31.
Krieg, Joann (ed.). 1988. *Robert Moses: Single-Minded Genius*. Interlaken, NY: Heart of the Lakes Publications.

Kunstler, James H. 1993. *The Geography of Nowhere: The Rise and Decline of America's Man-made Landscape*. New York: Simon & Schuster.

Le Corbusier. 1947. *When the Cathedrals were White*. New York: Reynal and Hitchcock.

Longstreth, Richard (ed.). 2008. *Cultural Landscapes: Balancing Nature and Heritage in Preservation Practice*. Minneapolis: University of Minnesota Press.

Menell, Timothy, Steffens, Jo, and Klemek, Chistopher (eds.). 2007. *Block by Block: Jane Jacobs and the Future of New York*. Princeton, NJ: Princeton Architectural Press.

Page, Max and Mason, Randall (eds.). 2004. *Giving Preservation a History: Histories of Historic Preservation in the United States*. New York: Routledge.

Pogrebin, Robin. 2005. Designers Detail an Urban Oasis 30 Feet Up. *New York Times*, 18 April. Available at: <http://www.nytimes.com/2005/04/19/arts/design/19high.html?ref=highlinenyc> (accessed 25 January 2012).

Smith, Laurajane. 2006. *Uses of Heritage*. London: Routledge.

—— and Akagawa, Natsuko (eds.). 2009. *Intangible Heritage*. Abingdon: Routledge, Taylor & Francis.

Wilkie, Laurie. 2001. Black Sharecroppers and White Frat Boys: Living Communities and the Construction of their Archaeological Pasts. In *The Archaeology of the Contemporary Past*, ed. V. Buchli and G. Lucas, pp. 108–18. New York: Routledge2006. Documentary Archaeology. In *The Cambridge Companion to Historical Archaeology*, ed. Dan Hicks and Mary C. Beaudry, pp. 13–33. Cambridge: Cambridge University Press.

—— and Hicks, Dan. 2009. Going about Things: A Perspective from Manhattan. Paper presented at Contemporary and Historical Archaeology in Theory Conference, Keeble College, Oxford University, 16–18 October.

Winner, Langdon. 1980. Do Artifacts have Politics? *Daedelus* 109(1): 121–36.

Wood, Anthony. 2008. *Preserving New York: Winning the Right to Protect a City's Landmarks*. New York: Routledge.

Wright, Peter. 2009a. *A Journey Through Ruins: The Last Days of London*. Oxford: Oxford University Press.

—— 2009b. *On Living in an Old Country*. Oxford: Oxford University Press.

....

CHAPTER 35

CHECKPOINTS AS GENDERED SPACES: AN AUTOARCHAEOLOGY OF WAR, HERITAGE, AND THE CITY

....

UZMA Z. RIZVI

PREFACE

....

19 March 2003: President of the United States, George W. Bush announces the beginning of combat with the nation of Iraq. As I write this chapter, combat continues in Iraq with a death toll of nearly 112,000 civilians (<www.iraqbodycount.org/>, accessed 1 November 2011). This chapter cannot articulate the deep trauma that the violence of this war will have on the Iraqi people, nor does it pretend to encapsulate all senses of violence that war produces.

35.1 INTRODUCTION

....

> The US war logs show that there were 13,963 incidents linked to convoys or at checkpoints across Iraq from 2004 to 2009. Most of them ended harmlessly, but when things went wrong it was civilians, more often than not, that got killed. (Slater and Ball 2011)

The landscape of war is a constantly changing stratigraphy of human events. The documentation of such micro-depositional histories is short, rapid, and often ephemeral. This chapter presents such a document through an autoarchaeology of specific urban checkpoints in Iraq, January 2009 (see also Lemonnier, this volume; May, this volume; White, this volume). The crux of the project is the contemporary materiality/immateriality of war and the manner in which its existence and resulting traces affect human beings and cityscapes by highlighting the fluctuating meaning of safety, a shift to an uncanny landscape, and the effects of violence on notions of subjectivity. This chapter focuses on both the tangible and intangible aspects of those issues by locating the analysis on city checkpoints as urban gendered spaces and the manner in which such locales *fracture heritage by unsettling city-spaces.*

Checkpoints are generally thought of as unsafe locales of simmering volatility. It is the place where an aspect of *bare life* is determined by the state—does a body contain the rights to pass or is it to be separated from the rest of the citizenry (Agamben 1998)? There is a heightened sense of urgency, anxiety, and fear in the very air that occupies that space, often making it difficult to breathe. This chapter emerges from experiences at checkpoints in Iraq in the cities of Baghdad, Kauzmain, Najaf, Karbala, and Samarra (Figure 35.1). These checkpoints were woven into and out of the urban fabric. These checkpoints were segregated, presumably by sex, but in fact by gender (marked by clothing). And ironically, the female checkpoints became 'safe spaces' creating a distinct public space and location of discourse. As pedestrian checkpoints, not used for vehicles or convoys, they had the ability to be mobile and were, in fact, moved across the landscape.

These women's checkpoints were camp-like structures, tents held up by poles on city roads (dirt and paved). Older checkpoints could be traced at intersections based on the discoloration of the pavement or dirt from the kerosene heaters used inside the tents (in January it was near 4°C/39°F), and postholes left by the poles holding up the tents. As mentioned previously, the checkpoints located within the cities were generally segregated by gender (assessed by the wearing of gender-marked clothing) with the tent-like stations being gendered female and the open-air checkpoints being gendered male. All the women I encountered in public space during my time there were covered in either an *abbaya* or a *chador* of

FIGURE 35.1 Map of contemporary Iraq with key sites mentioned in the text (map: Leonardo Arias)

some kind. This form of clothing loosely covers the body shape and image, thus making any assessment of sex based on physicality vague. Such ambiguity creates and structures overreliance on heteronormative assumptions of possible genders resulting in the adoption of only two forms of gendered checkpoints in the city: male or female (see Ritchie 2010 for a discussion on queer identity and checkpoints).

The structural violence that checkpoints impose upon the cityscape is intricately linked to some assumed protection of corporeal violence, and yet there is a deeper violence enacted upon the subjectivity of those living in war zones each time one walks through a checkpoint (see Starzmann 2010). This alteration of self happens as the discourse of violence seeps into the everyday. Such structural and self alterations mediate and constantly reconstruct shattered realities of monuments and emotions linked to them. Directly hit by war, the cityscape is fractured; a condition that continues to be structurally enforced by the constant moving of checkpoints across the landscape. This constant shattering of the everyday leads to fragments of reality strung together to create a sense of self and place. A fractured heritage becomes a reality of war.

Efforts to regain some sense of accountability in such a context prompted numerous responses in public discourse, beginning primarily with the listing of antiquities as casualties of war and issues surrounding looting (Bahrani 2003a, 2003b). Looting became a very serious point of discussion with calls for the protection of Iraq's cultural heritage which was explicitly linked to material artefacts (Bogdanos 2005; Brodie and Renfrew 2005; Stone 2005; Warren 2005; Rothfield 2008). Some anthropologists and archaeologists, although sympathetic to the concern about artefacts, raised questions related to the ethical stance of utilizing cultural knowledge extracted from scholars for the 'war on terror' (González 2007), and how discussions with the United States government demonstrated an implicit compliance with the neo-colonial and imperial aspirations of the US in Iraq (Hamilakis 2003, 2009).

Unlike these previous efforts, this chapter is based on corporeal experience within a war-zone. As such, it has created its own methodology, its own data set, and its own trauma.

35.2 WOMAN/ARCHAEOLOGIST/OTHER: A NOTE ON METHODOLOGY

The context is war.

The context is one of life or death.

The context is dictating methodology.

The context is irreproducible in text or image.

The context is segregated based on gender performed.

In *Stranger and Friend*, Hortense Powdermaker elucidates what it meant to be a woman in the field, to pass as black, and the ramifications of 'going native'. Standing in line at a checkpoint in Najaf, I found myself recalling Powdermaker's work, particularly the quote, 'When I inadvertently "passed" for Negro, I would return to the boarding house and look in the mirror, wondering if the color of my skin had changed. There was always some tension in the situation for me' (1966: 196). When there are checkpoints in society that manage the corporeality of assigning identity, there will always be the complications of 'passing' (Ritchie 2010). In the time of war, every *body* is constantly being read, interpreted, and contextualized as a body/subject while traversing the cityscape. As a female academic from an immigrant community from the East/Global South living in a diaspora in the West/global North, the materiality and corporeality of all visual cues on my body were constantly in question, shifting and transmutable (Rizvi 2008; cf. Minh-ha 1989). Inside the (gendered female) checkpoints, the (female) security guards were ready with their own questions as they ran their hands over my chest, and down my arms, '*Ayna Inti?*' '*Ahaal kuja hastid?*' '*Kahan say?*' in various languages (Arabic, Persian, and Urdu, respectively). I would be asked where I was from, based on what they thought I could understand. I would reply in Arabic, '*Ana -amreeki*' (I am American)—at which point they would laugh, pinch their fingers in front of their faces and while moving their hands back and forth would say '*Asli asli*'—what is my origin, my essence. As the guards checked my notebook, one of them would ask about what I was writing and my profession. Unless there was a large group of women waiting, upon hearing that I was an archaeologist, discussions would ensue that focused on where I had done archaeological work, what my level of education was, and what I thought about Iraq's antiquity. My identity as an archaeologist trumped any discussion of my essential origin and triggered a form of archaeological public discourse in the most unlikely areas—the interior spaces of a checkpoint. This identity allowed me to create the context within which discursive data were generated, although in that moment, it was performed to keep me safe, out of suspicion, and most importantly, to help me pass through the checkpoint.

The methodology related to collection strategy was unstable, unexpected, and unplanned. I had not entered into these spaces looking for anything; I had entered these spaces to survive. In those moments, this was not a project, it had not yet started; it was in the process of becoming. The data for this project come from the few scribbled notes I had made with pencils in the back of prayer books, on napkins, and in notebooks. At checkpoints cell phones, pens, cameras, lipstick/chap stick, anything that could potentially be seen or regarded as threatening was confiscated. I travelled only with a handkerchief, a small unsharpened pencil, and a prayer book or notebook. Most of the notes were filled in upon returning to my hotel, and further elaborated back in the United States. As I compulsively wrote these notes, particularly upon my return, I recognized this act as being one of trying to contend with the reality of war, the trauma of war, and the desire for that experience to be recognized and studied—an impulse of an academic trying to make sense of a world in which war was an everyday occurrence. This became an act of transformation from a witness to an historian (cf. Garton-Ash 1990).

Disciplined into my subjectivity as an archaeologist, one of the key absences in this project became transferable data beyond memory and experience of place. What sort of methodology does one employ when disallowed to take photographs, measure things, or document in any way that archaeologists are trained? I have no photographs of the streets, the walls, the buildings. In a space of war, unless permission was granted by the state, there was little to no room for the average citizen or visitor to document public experience, becoming a subtle yet violent stripping of individual rights to document/witness the trauma of war. In some capacity, such a condition suggests that perhaps there exist sites or events that resist archaeological study (Piccini, personal communication). Or it may be that memory and experience become documents in states of emergency (cf. Sebald 2003).

35.3 Documenting the Contemporary: the Space and Place of Memory

> Language has unmistakably made plain that memory is not an instrument for exploring the past, but rather a medium. It is the medium of that which is experienced, just as earth is the medium in which ancient cities lie buried. (Benjamin 1932: 576)

Archaeological data, most traditionally, are studied as emerging from a certain provenance, in a certain matrix, and in association with other forms of data. Within that same discourse, these forms of data are based on both behavioural and transformational processes that are both human and natural (Ashmore and Sharer 2000: 60–7). These data are recovered from a medium and provide information for and about the material and immaterial within a place. Contemplating the medium of memory as context in a time of war, the data extracted follow similar forms of expression. Utilizing memory as a medium that holds the information rather than as information itself allows for a recalibration of remembrance, recognition, and recollection. Whereas individual memory must be able to intertwine and interact with social and collective memory in order to provide a certain degree of authenticity (Olick and Robbins 1998), memory as a medium provides an alternative perspective to the collection of data. In documenting the contemporary, the stratigraphic record of memory is ineluctably contestable thus inherently self-reflexive. It may, in fact, be best documented then as what appears on the surface, rather than hidden deep below (cf. Harrison 2011).

Modernity's anxiety with memory and the super-desire to collect material traces pushes the researcher to both text and image to create the archive (Freud 1968a [1929]; Derrida 1998). Although Freud (2006 [1925]) may argue that the archive is born out of the distrust of memory and the need to write something down in the event of possible forgetfulness, there is something about the archive that, as Jacques Derrida (1998) argues, has its own logic as a thing unto itself and within itself, as well as its own death and undoing. We look to the archive as a repository of national memory. Insofar as that is the case, it is inherently hegemonic in its epistemology, in its formulation. And yet, we assume factual legitimacy of the materials collected within the archive, as if their buriedness, their inaccessibility, renders them truthful. Notes on a napkin and sketches do not often suffice as data for the modern collector of information—but in spaces of war, those ephemera provide additional context to the medium of memory. The idea of the archive, particularly in relation to trauma and violence, is something that most Freudian analysts would argue is contingently unrepresentable. However, in allowing the medium of memory to be surveyed, an archaeology of now has the possibility to resist grand narratives and their associated images.

Photographs are used to bear witness to the atrocities of war, becoming the official gaze and image (Zelizer 1998). And yet, when one looks at the actual images of the war and compares them to the internal images from memory, there is a disjuncture: a moment seeped in the unfamiliar and uncanny. There is a distance that the image forces upon memory—until the memory is only made up of the image that dictates it. Upon returning from Iraq in 2009, I attempted to reconstruct the cityscape through images that I researched—until I realized that those images were replacing my memory. I could not recognize the streets of the every day because in the every day, one moves through spaces not through images of those spaces. In obsessively documenting these spaces through experiences, the 'normal processes that people go through often as a matter of course' (Harrison and Schofield 2010: 70), recently scholars dealing with issues of cultural memory, architectural spaces, and heritage have attempted to radicalize the hierarchies of text and image (Andreassen et al. 2010) and contend with the destruction of architecture as collective memory (Bevan 2006; Herscher 2010). However, in a time of war, space itself is constantly altered.

In order to keep checkpoints effective and safe, military strategy dictates that these points constantly shift and change. Thus, as the cityscape continues to be altered by bombs, it utilizes the one possible web of stability and makes that unstable as well—every few days, while I was in Kauzmain and Najaf, the checkpoint locations changed. The city is left in constant flux—the everydayness of walking through and encountering a city (cf. de Certeau 1984), knowing a city, is disturbed. Each change reminds one of why there is flux; there is a base level of traumatic understanding and reliving of violence in each new checkpoint location that is encountered. There is an everydayness to the distancing, detachment, and disillusionment that the individual feels walking through similarly detached buildings. Buildings that might have had meanings and memories embodied within them no longer exist as those very same buildings. Thus in the recollection of memories, one reconstructs not only the event but the physicality of that event. The building has effectively withdrawn and detached from its everyday guise, only to serve as an index of its own past. In fact, thinkers such as Jalal Toufic (2009) would argue that even if there were no visible marks of violence on the buildings, in the aftermath of a surpassing disaster, even the immaterial, such as tradition and heritage itself, withdraws.

35.4 THE MATERIALITY AND IMMATERIALITY OF WAR: EXPERIENCING CHECKPOINTS AS ARCHITECTURE AND SPACE

Checkpoints generally don the state-sanctioned and instantiated guise of 'security' and the façade of maintaining non-violence. Indexing cartographic aggression, checkpoints mark enforced borders by dominant states or oppressive regimes in order to control access and order the public. They act as in-between spaces through which each body must traverse in order to move between larger places. As compared to most checkpoints in the world and the ways in which they articulate the separation between spaces, such as between nations, along borders, or even security at airports, the checkpoints in the cities in Iraq were, in early 2009, unique. This was partly because of the state of emergency and warfare in the cities themselves and partly due to, what seemed to be, mixed military strategies employed by American and Iraqi forces that had to do with the movement of checkpoints. These Iraqi checkpoints served to fragment the urban terrain in a systematic web of controlled locales, subjugating bodies. In an interesting turn and one that may be read as a form of resistance, many Iraqis utilized Google Earth to locate the shifted locations of these checkpoints so as to by-pass the possible violence, delay, and humiliation of having to go through checkpoints on the way to work or school (Hussein 2009).

Each major intersection in the main cities in Iraq, such as Baghdad, Najaf, Samarra, etc., had a checkpoint, every major monument or building had numerous such points in the surrounding area, even though the building itself was pockmarked with bullet holes, or half of it lay in rubble. These checkpoints structurally enforce new borders and separations in an already war-torn urban landscape. Their multitude became undisclosed potential locales of violence, which allowed them to occupy the same ambiguous space of war—the possibility and impossibility of security.

Albeit contexualized within that uncertainty, the only spaces in which the city had some semblance of order in both the visceral and real (arguably hyperreal) were the spaces within the checkpoints. It was within those uncanny spaces that I became human again, where, although my identity was being questioned and negotiated by my possible answers, there was an ability for human interaction that involved recognition of our lives prior to the trauma of war—the life that I had been living before visiting Iraq, the life before the experience of war—and those normalizing discourses and spaces were where public interaction took place. The emergent reality was culturally context specific (Iraqi culture), with a cosmopolitan mix of women from different nations, and the feeling of 'safety', as tenuous as it was, within the checkpoint allowed for discussion with people one does not usually see or know—an oddly public and urban feel for an enclosed private space.

Checkpoints are situated aesthetic experiences that are simultaneously infused with potential and kinetic violence; an experience that requires constantly negotiated performances of identity, in some cases choosing to reinstate static notions of self and subject. The roads between checkpoints were occupied by the 'public' that included both men and women—upon reaching a checkpoint visually gendered women were separated into tents. Generally, there were two types of checkpoints, one that involved a line outside the tent, in which only one or two women would be allowed at a time, and the second in which a larger tent was used, which easily fit over 20 women.

With the first, that is, the smaller tent, women were ushered into a line, on one or both sides of that line would be a male Iraqi police officer or army personnel with highly visible markers of ammunition, wearing heavy boots. Each woman in line would go in on one side of the tent and come out the other. In each tent, there were two or three female security guards who would physically search body and bags, engage in a brief dialogue, and then let you exit the other side, where there was another male with heavy ammunition and heavy boots. These smaller checkpoints were neither as interactive nor as discussion friendly.

In contrast, in the larger tents, where some six to eight women would be placed as security guards, there were more conversations, and a general buzz would greet us as we walked inside. At the checkpoint there were metal railings that separated each of us as we walked into it, so as to create four or five lines. These railings were attached to a platform, elevating us slightly off the ground in order to make it easier for the guards to search our bodies. In observing this, I realized that it usually placed most women roughly at eye level because they had to take off their shoes (generally black heels) for security. It was in these larger tents that all sorts of discussions would take place between women allowing for more flexibility and textured conversation about everything from the price of tomatoes, to their children, to arguing about who was cutting in line, to asking each other to pray for the other. The normalcy of the inside chatter was in stark contrast to the general silence while walking outside—perhaps it was because there were no visible guns, perhaps it was the number of women in the tent; whatever it was, it allowed a momentary respite from being in a space of war.

It was, in fact, at one of these checkpoints early in my trip, while in Kauzmain, that I first encountered public archaeological discourse. While being searched, a few of the security guards and I discussed the antiquity of Iraq in comparison to what they knew of India. In the background, we could hear men screaming orders and the clamping of boots, indicating movement of soldiers. There was something oddly comforting about the discussion, one in which the stomping of the boots outside and the hands running down my legs checking for weapons were made commonplace by the tone used in the discussion by the guards—and through that first interaction, they normalized the space of war by placing me into a familiar discursive space of archaeology.

In another such encounter, while waiting in line at a checkpoint in Kauzmain, a young woman standing in front of me asked me my name and profession as she pointed to my notebook. Upon hearing that I worked in India as an archaeologist, she remarked upon how I would understand and appreciate the antiquity of Iraq as India also came from an ancient past. She was not the only person to remark upon this parallel relationship of antiquity and how the power of the antiquity of the land was the source of strength in such times. The woman standing in the line next to us nodded her head in solemn agreement, with the woman behind her adding that knowing history was, in fact, the way forward. The internalization of national rhetoric is not surprising (Haider 2001); however, which 'history' they were referring to was very significant. In a post-Saddam era, these women were speaking of a new national history that included a *Shia* history, a history previously silenced. This became apparent as, within the next few minutes, over ten women in line were talking about how significant it was that the historic monuments important to the *Shia* community were now made accessible to the public. As the conversation began to pick up momentum (and volume) within the tent, it was quieted down by the guards. The shushing from the guards brought about many lowered glances and giggles between the women indexing a form of familiarity and shared experience. Within those five or so minutes of discussion, women who did not know each other were brought together to discuss their own interactions with historic monuments, their ideas of what it meant to live in an ancient land, and their formulations of what might constitute a new national heritage.

Inside the checkpoints, publics formed around issues of national heritage and architecture of collective history. That same checkpoints' exteriority partitioned public space. The materiality of these checkpoints ripped the urban plan apart and created a new and constantly shifting ephemeral architecture of the city. This constant parcelling of the city spaces, the destruction of the urban plan, and the construction of violence due to the unfolding war infused the cityscape with a thick, palpable feeling of exhaustion due to constancy of war. There was a simultaneity to the trauma and any attempt to move past that as the post-trauma; a cyclical treachery that led to distancing and detachment, not only in human behaviour, but in the materiality of the buildings and the urban space itself.

35.5 THE TRAUMA OF WAR, THE SUBJECTIVE CITY, AND THE WITHDRAWAL OF HERITAGE

Driving in Beirut's streets, the carcasses of abandoned buildings encrusted between functional buildings and receded to invisibility—in spite of their bulky concrete brownish grey stockiness—often seemed like a tenacious and surly reminder of that street or neighbourhood's previous life. (Salti 2009)

The constant of war, the detachment, withdrawal, and excessive vigilance of space, material, and humans in a contemporary moment provides indicators of the post-traumatic—
and in this case, the manner in which that form of trauma infuses city spaces. The cities,
which are built to function on ordered principles, are completely disordered. In very real
ways, wars affect all civic functions, water and sewage, electricity, phone lines collapse under
the weight. Being unable to perform daily routines drastically alters any human condition
within that context. That inability for the city to enact cityness imbues a certain feeling of
hopelessness, helplessness, and inefficacy within the spaces of the city.

To live through the destructive moments directly affects the subjectivities of the individuals living in those spaces as well as the spaces within which they live. Documenting the
civil war in Beirut, an artists' project/publication entitled *Beirut Bereft: The Architecture of
the Forsaken and Map of the Derelict* (2009) provides an autoethnographic journey through
photographs of the architectural landscape of Beirut by Ziad Antar and an evocative and
mournful account of growing up during the civil war and what happens after, by Rasha Salti.
The haunting account by Salti illustrates the realities of war that go beyond fear of bodily
harm, the moment of a transforming subjectivity:

> To be driven to exhaustion with one's life, out of breath and to the edge of despair, were not
> only sentiments commonplace to all in Beirut, they were sentiments I felt intensely, discerned
> fully, often. So were abrupt and seemingly irreversible departures. Overnight, people packed
> their bags and left their neighborhood, their city, their country, for good. In addition to
> attending wakes, I became accustomed to farewell bidding get-togethers. Departures seemed
> then just as radically irreversible as 'good-byes' and 'so longs' terminal. With postal service
> entirely defunct and phone lines operational on whim, there was no hope of maintaining
> contact. Farewells were more poignant than wakes. I, we, those left behind, were being aban-
> doned by those who chose to leave. The blinding pain of enduring (and accepting) being
> abandoned was only assuaged with the passage of time. Just as with mourning death. Soon
> enough farewell parties and wakes became confused. I remember being scared of being left
> amongst those left behind. (Salti and Antar 2009: 11–15)

The realities of war and separation leave indelible marks on our subjectivity. This fear,
not always of one's own death, but a constant fear of loss infuses every interaction. The
loss of individuals and the loss of normalcy: a simple task of buying fruit or honey from
the local market can never be experienced as an everyday event during a time of war. It
is not only the human factor that creates the uncanny city, but rather, the city itself is
disempowered because it is disordered. In encountering the trauma of an unrecogniz-
able and withdrawn city, in this case, Samarra, Iraq, I experienced what Freud called a
feeling of derealization (*Entfremdungsgefühl*) in his open letter, *A Disturbance of Memory
on the Acropolis*: 'What I see here is not real' (1968b [1936]: 110). The city was not real to
me—although I had *heard* that it had undergone this transformation through war—I had
learnt about it—but the reality of its existence could not compare to the distance I felt
due to the detachedness of the city I was standing in. I knew I was in Samarra, I could see
the wide expanse of the *maidan* (open dusty field) that led up to the Malwiya Tower, and
yet the gates, the walls, the tower all eluded me and any form of documentation. As an
archaeologist who has visited many historical monuments and felt buildings as subjective material forms, it was disconcerting to feel emptiness as I stood next to the Tower.
The transformation of these city spaces seemed beyond what I could understand as real
(cf. Vidler 1994).

In truth, I am willing to accept that perhaps these architectural forms withdrew from my understanding of them as I was nothing more than a visitor, incapable of experiencing the trauma of a city not my own. It was only after my experience in Iraq that the beginning sequence in the film *Hiroshima Mon Amour* (1959) resonated. The inability to experience trauma and memory of trauma as a visitor is best articulated in the beginning of the film in which the emic and etic experiences of trauma determine how memory may or may not be able to form authentic recollection. For individuals whose homes, neighbourhoods, and cities have been affected by violence, the images of the past insist and resist erasure even if the physical elements have been removed for reconstructive purposes. In an ethnography of post-war Beirut, Yasmeen Arif discusses the reconstruction of a neighbourhood with its inhabitants:

> **Mrs. Nabti:** After they (SOLIDERE) finished the demolition we went down to look around and I stood there in front of the past and all I could see was the image even though it was empty. You know how one can be shocked? I was shocked. (2002: 121)

These aspects of architectural and spatial imagination in moments of trauma evoke new formulations of tradition and heritage: some as forms of nostalgia, and others as forms of healing.

35.6 FRACTURED HERITAGE: SOME CONCLUDING THOUGHTS

It was clear during my time in Iraq that although war was taking a heavy toll on the population of people I interacted with, it was not erasing their sense of national heritage. If anything, the discourse around archaeology and the nation was flourishing, in part due to the ability of previously silenced communities to have a say in what that history may include and having more direct access to the past. In one particularly enlightening conversation, a young man who managed a store in Karbala asked me if all archaeologists knew the value of a vessel the moment they saw it and if not, how one put a price tag on the vessel. He provided examples of other forms of value creation such as how jewellers measure out gold, adding in wastage and craftsmanship when establishing the price of a necklace. I responded, as I have been disciplined by my practice to say, that archaeologists could not and should not put price tags on the past and that the inherent value of archaeological objects is the intangible, etc. and that if they saw such artefacts floating around they should make sure to send them back to the museum since it did more good in the public realm. This response was met with an interesting discussion by most of the people in the small group that had formed: they had never been to the museums, not because of lack of interest but because in over 20 years of war (starting with the Iran–Iraq war), the museums were often closed. The concept of cultural and national heritage in connection to artefacts was, I realized, on shaky ground. Many of them knew about the sites, knew about the antiquity of the land, but had not visited the sites because they were either soldiers in the war, or fearful of their safety.

Interestingly enough, in every, if not all conversations about the past, people would articulate very specific relationships that they had with ancient Iraq. For example, in a checkpoint in Kauzmain, the security guard who was patting me down simultaneously provided a commentary about how 'the land was of their ancestors and it is that tie that gave them strength in the face of adversity'. The destruction of ancient monuments and museums was placed in the discursive realm of national heritage. It was something that was being dismantled or fractured, but could not be destroyed. This was because, I was told, of its antiquity, linking in a very direct and continuous manner the nation to a premodern and ancient past in an unchanging form.

Given the war context, I recognized some of the problematic statements linking the past and the present as reinstating national identity, linking a body to a land in a way that excludes all others; particularly not reflective of the many immigrant populations that have settled over the past few millennia. I chose not to engage in that debate at that time. It is also important to note that not all conversations dealt with heritage in this manner. During the time I was in Iraq, reports of a contemporary art exhibition taking place in Baghdad were circulating (see Meyers 2009). In the checkpoints in Karbala, embedded in the discussions of heritage as being linked to antiquity, were a few moments in which the women discussed how such shows of contemporary art might also be considered within national heritage.

Also in these discussions of heritage, the metaphor of roots '*jazwar/gazwar*' was often used. There was a form of resilience in which it seemed to be a given that an Iraqi heritage would grow back as an organic process. National heritage was a form a natural heritage. Whether or not this can be read as a problematic assertion is somewhat irrelevant for this study. The publics which formed around the discourses of the past demonstrate a certain fracturing but not erasure of national heritage in a time of war. In some sense, that fracturing is necessary to allow for a new plurality of histories to find space in national narratives. Although difficult, an archaeology of the present in an ongoing war may provide a mode of witnessing and documenting the trauma of a fractured heritage thereby creating space for new discourses to emerge that may allow for some form of healing in a post-war moment. It is within this context then that such a project simultaneously becomes an archaeology of supermodernity, 'an archaeology of us who are alive ... but more than any other, an archaeology of trauma, emotion, and intimate involvement' (González-Ruibal 2008: 248 and this volume). In this contemporary moment an archaeology of ongoing war, as ephemeral and shifting as it may be, provides nuance to the narratives of war and allows us to encounter an otherwise withdrawn and resistant landscape—not to insist on manifestations of data, but rather, to acknowledge the existence and effects of violence on subjectivities, cityscapes, and heritage.

35.7 POSTSCRIPT

It is important to note that not every interaction with war and the state was so easy and tinged with romantic nostalgia. I am sure I have, during the experience itself and in my recollection of it, chosen specific narratives that provided solace in an otherwise extremely dangerous and hostile environment. It allows me to reconcile the fact that I did not have body armour, nor was I escorted by any military police or security force. I had a black *chador*, with jeans and a sweater on underneath. Uncharacteristically for my usual 'archaeological attire', I had no cell phone, no camera, no GPS, no map. However, I could not step out of my anthropological upbringing and thus continued to document to control my fear. The discussions about national and cultural heritage, a semi-public discourse, became just as much about archaeology as much as they were a way to hold on to some aspect of normality—a memory of life before the context of war. This dual functionality categorizes this project as autoethnographic as well, if for no other reason than to contend with post-traumatic stress combined with culture shock that emerged upon returning to the United States (cf. Behar 1996).

ACKNOWLEDGEMENTS

I would like to thank the editors for their invitation to contribute to this volume. This chapter has benefited from their suggestions, as well as my colleagues at Pratt Institute, Ann Holder and Lisabeth During. A version of this chapter was first presented in the spring of 2010 at the Aesthetics and Politics series and a revised version was presented the following summer (2011) at the workshop Trauma, Memory, Oblivion: On Responsibilities to the Past (III Research Workshop on Identity, Memory and Experience) at Pratt Institute. Discussions from both versions have left a mark on this chapter, and for those insightful and thought-provoking discussions, I thank the participants of both, in particular, Gregg Horowitz, José Medina, Antonio Gomez Ramos, Tracie Morris, and Ira Livingston. Throughout this process I have been indebted to my sounding-board, Murtaza Vali. And finally, I am grateful for the help of D'Angleo Rosario, Leonardo Arias, and Janette Carolina Martinez for the completion of this manuscript.

REFERENCES

Agamben, Giorgio. 1998. *Homo Sacer: Sovereign Power and Bare Life*, tr. Daniel Heller-Roazen. Palo Alto, CA: Stanford University Press.

Andreassen, Elin, Bjerck, Hein, and Olsen, Bjørnar. 2010 *Persistent Memories: Pyramiden—a Soviet Mining Town in the High Arctic*. Trondheim: Tapir Academic Press.

Arif, Yasmeen. 2002. Past Places/Future Spaces: Reconstructing Post-War Beirut. *The Cities of Everyday Life*, Sarai Reader 2: 117–25. Delhi: Sarai Media Lab.

Ashmore, Wendy and Sharer, Robert. 2000. *Discovering our Past: A Brief Introduction to Archaeology*, 3rd edn. Mountain View, CA: Mayfield Publishing Company.

Bahrani, Zainab. 2003a. Iraq's Cultural Heritage: Monuments, History, and Loss. *Art Journal* 62 (4): 11–17.

—— 2003b. Looting and Conquest. *The Nation*, 26 May. Available at: <http://www.thenation.com/article/looting-and-conquest> (accessed 24 October 2011).

Behar, Ruth. 1996. *The Vulnerable Observer: Anthropology That Breaks Your Heart*. Boston, MA: Beacon Press.

Benjamin, Walter. 1932. Excavation and Memory. In *Walter Benjamin: Selected Writings Volume 2, Part 2 1931–1934*, tr. Rodney Livingstone and others, ed. Michael W. Jennings, Howard Eiland, and Gary Smith, p. 576. Cambridge, MA: The Belknap Press of Harvard University Press.

Bevan, Robert. 2006. *The Destruction of Memory: Architecture at War*. London: Reaktion Books.

Bogdanos, Michael. 2005. Casualties of War: Truth and the Iraq Museum. *American Journal of Archaeology* 190: 477–526.

Brodie, Neil and Renfrew, Colin. 2005. Looting and the World's Archaeological Heritage: The Inadequate Response. *Annual Review of Anthropology* 34: 343–61.

de Certeau, Michel. 1984. *The Practice of Everyday Life*, tr. Steven Rendall. Berkeley, CA: University of California Press.

Derrida, Jacques. 1998. *Archive Fever: A Freudian Impression*. Chicago: University of Chicago Press.

Freud, Sigmund. 1968a [1929]. Civilization and its Discontents. In *Civilization, War and Death*, ed. J. Rickman, pp. 26–81. Psycho-Analytical Epitomes No. 4. London: Hogarth Press and the Institute of Psycho-Analysis.

——1968b [1936]. A Disturbance of Memory on the Acropolis. In *Civilization, War and Death*, ed. J. Rickman, pp. 103–15. Psycho-Analytical Epitomes No. 4. London: Hogarth Press and the Institute of Psycho-Analysis.

—— 2006 [1925]. A Note upon the Mystic Writing- Pad. In *The Archive*, ed. C. Merewether, pp. 20–4. Boston, MA: MIT Press.

Garton-Ash, Timothy. 1990. *The Magic Lantern: The Revolution of 1989 Witnessed in Warsaw, Budapest, Berlin, and Prague*. New York: Vintage Books.

González, Roberto J. 2007. Towards Mercenary Anthropology? The New US Army Counterinsurgency Manual FM 3–24 and the Military–Anthropology Complex. *Anthropology Today* 23(3):14–19.

González-Ruibal, Alfredo. 2008. Time to Destroy: An Archaeology of Supermodernity. *Current Anthropology* 49(2): 247–79.

Haider, Hind. 2001. Nationalism, Archaeology, and Ideology in Iraq from 1921 to the Present. Master's Thesis, Institute of Islamic Studies, McGill University, Montreal, Canada.

Hamilakis, Yannis. 2003. Iraq, Stewardship and 'The Record': An Ethical Crisis for Archaeology. *Public Archaeology* 3: 104–11.

—— 2009. The 'War on Terror' and the Military–Archaeology Complex: Iraq, Ethics, and Neo-Colonialism. *Archaeologies: Journal of the World Archaeological Congress* 5: 39–65.

Harrison, Rodney. 2011. Surface Assemblages. Towards an Archaeology *in* and *of* the Present. *Archaeological Dialogues* 18(2): 141–61.

Harrison, Rodney and Schofield, John. 2010. *After Modernity: Archaeological Approaches to the Contemporary Past*. Oxford: Oxford University Press.

Herscher, Andrew. 2010. *Violence Taking Place: The Architecture of the Kosovo Conflict*. Palo Alto, CA: Stanford University Press.

Hussein, Aqeel. 2009. Google Earth, the Survival Tool of War-Torn Iraq. *The Telegraph*, 15 February. Available at: <http://www.telegraph.co.uk/news/worldnews/1542775/Google-Ea rth-the-survival-tool-of-war-torn-Iraq.html> (accessed 1 November 2011).

Meyers, Steven Lee. 2009. A New Role for Iraqi Militants: Patron of the Arts. *The New York Times*, 13 February. Available at: <http://www.nytimes.com/2009/02/14/world/ middleeast/14baghdad.html> (accessed 24 October 2011).

Minh-ha, Trinh. 1989. *Woman, Native, Other: Writing Postcoloniality and Feminism*. Bloomington, IN: Indiana University Press.

Olick, Jeffery and Robbins, Joyce.1998. Social Memory Studies: From 'Collective Memory' to the Historical Sociology of Mnemonic Practices. *Annual Review of Sociology* 24: 105–40.

Powdermaker, Hortense. 1966. *Stranger and Friend: The Way of an Anthropologist*. New York: W. W. Norton.

Ritchie, Jason. 2010. Queer Checkpoints: Sexuality, Survival, and the Paradoxes of Sovereignty in Israel-Palestine. Unpublished PhD Dissertation, Department of Anthropology, Graduate College of the University of Illinois at Urbana-Champaign.

Rizvi, Uzma Z. 2008. Decolonizing Methodologies as Strategies of Practice: Operationalizing the Postcolonial Critique in the Archaeology of Rajasthan. In *Archaeology and the Postcolonial Critique*, ed. Matthew Liebmann and Uzma Rizvi, pp. 109–27. Archaeology and Society Series. Walnut Creek, CA: Altamira Press.

Rothfield, Lawrence (ed.). 2008. *Antiquities Under Siege: Cultural Heritage Protection after the Iraq War*. Lanham, MD: Altamira Press.

Salti, Rasha and Antar, Ziad. 2009. *The Architecture of the Forsaken and Map of the Derelict*. Sharjah: Sharjah Art Foundation.

Sebald, Winfried Georg. 2003. *On the Natural History of Destruction*, tr. Anthea Bell. New York: Random House.

Slater, Emma and Ball, James. 2011. Hundreds of Civilians Gunned Down at Checkpoints. *Iraq War Logs*, 22 October. Available at: <http://www.iraqwarlogs.com/2010/10/22/more-than-600-civilians-killed-in-error-by-coalition-forces-in-iraq/> (accessed 13 October 2011).

Starzmann, Maria T. 2010. Structural Violence as Political Experience in Palestine: An Archaeology of the Past in the Present. *Present Pasts* 2(1): 126–41.

Stone, Peter. 2005. The Identification and Protection of Cultural Heritage During the Iraq Conflict: A Peculiarly English Tale. *Antiquity* 79: 1–11.

Toufic, Jalal. 2009. *The Withdrawal of Tradition Past a Surpassing Disaster*. Los Angeles: California Institute of the Arts/REDCAT/Forthcoming Books.

Vidler, Anthony. 1994. *The Architectural Uncanny: Essays in the Modern Unhomely*. Boston, MA: MIT Press.

Warren, John. 2005. War and the Cultural Heritage of Iraq: A Sadly Mismanaged Affair. *Third World Quarterly* 26(4–5): 815–30.

Zelizer, Barbie. 1998. *Remembering to Forget: Holocaust Memory Through the Camera's Eye*. Chicago: University of Chicago Press.

CHAPTER 36

....

RACE AND PROSAIC MATERIALITY: THE ARCHAEOLOGY OF CONTEMPORARY URBAN SPACE AND THE INVISIBLE COLOUR LINE

....

PAUL R. MULLINS

36.1 INTRODUCTION

....

RACE has long been rendered invisible in everyday materiality or remade to mask the relationship between material things and the colour line. This chapter focuses on a public sculpture project in Indianapolis, Indiana that aspired to reinterpret a little-recognized 1890s statue of an Emancipated captive. The case reveals how racist privileges and African American heritage are at the heart of American experience even as the racial dimensions of seemingly mundane materiality are unseen or concealed, even in the case of a monumental public statue. The Indianapolis experience reflects the ways many communities struggle to simultaneously remember, displace, and memorialize African American heritage and race in cities where there appear to be no contemporary material traces of the colour line.

36.2 'THE EQUALITY OF MAN': MATERIALITY AND THE COLOUR LINE

....

On 15 May 1902 the towering 284-foot tall Soldiers and Sailors Monument was dedicated on Indianapolis, Indiana's central circle. Like many communities in the wake of the Civil War,

Indianapolis aspired to erect a permanent memorial commemorating its wartime experience and defining the meaning of the national conflict. Proposals were solicited in 1887 for an 'American Monument' that would resist classical iconography, and German architect Bruno Schmitz won with a design for a towering shaft with statuary and fountains at its base. The cornerstone for the monument was laid in the centre of the city's 'Mile Square' grid in August 1889. When the monument was finally officially unveiled in 1902 the *Indianapolis News* (1902: 4) waxed that it was testimony that 'this country stands, as it did not and could not during the slave days, for the equality of man' (Figure 36.1).

That ideological 'equality of man' has often rendered the colour line invisible, aspiring to preserve white privilege even as it inelegantly masks or conceals the profound impression of race and racism on materiality (see also Shepherd, this volume). Few of the thousands of people in the 1902 crowd likely inspected the frieze of 'Peace' that occupied the monument's western side, yet it materialized the colour line in rather typical ways that rendered racial privilege invisible (Figure 36.2). In 1897 German sculptor Rudolfo Schwarz was commissioned to complete 'War' and 'Peace' statuary groupings that had been modelled by Hermann Matzen for placement on the eastern and western sides of the monument respectively. Nestled rather unobtrusively at the base of the Peace side is the figure of an emancipated African American, reclining and holding up broken chains towards the female figure of Liberty, who resides at the centre of the sculptural group. The motif of the emancipated captive was quite common in post-war statues, which intended to be permanent commemorations of the Civil War—and define black freedom—even as the meaning of the

FIGURE 36.1 The Soldiers and Sailors Monument western face with the Peace grouping at its base (photograph: Paul R. Mullins)

FIGURE 36.2 The Peace grouping with the emancipated captive figure in the lower right (photograph: Paul R. Mullins)

war and Emancipation were being actively constructed (Savage 1997: 74). In the 1860s and 1870s, the placement of an unchained and kneeling captive in relation to Abraham Lincoln was the most common mechanism sculptors used to imagine Reconstruction and black freedom, a manoeuvre that cast Emancipation as an act of white agency (Savage 1997: 65). Yet as Reconstruction collapsed in the 1870s even those public representations of African Americans disappeared. By the time the Soldiers and Sailors Monument was unveiled, the relative optimism of post-Emancipation motifs had been replaced with new signifiers that rarely depicted black bodies.

Nestled within a dense statuary group, the emancipated captive was simultaneously monumental and invisible, and for more than a century he passed mostly unnoticed by the scores of people who walked by it. However, in 2007 artist Fred Wilson noted the black figure paradoxically hidden in Indianapolis's most public space, and he conceived a statue that would draw attention to that image and colour line heritage. Wilson had been commissioned to produce an artwork for the Indianapolis Cultural Trail, a downtown bike and pedestrian path linking five urban historic districts punctuated with public artworks. Wilson spied the kneeling captive on the Soldiers and Sailors Monument and contemplated how recontextualizing that concealed black motif could produce dialogue about the colour line that apparently had never been triggered from its placement in the monument itself. He proposed to recast the freed captive in a more upright position and situate him grasping a flag of Wilson's design that represents the African Diaspora. The proposed work was intended to be placed along the Trail at the City-County Building, which is home to Indianapolis's city government and just a few blocks from Monument Circle. Wilson dubbed the work *E Pluribus Unum* (Out of Many, One), and Trail planners optimistically celebrated that such a work 'speaks to diverse audiences and…is long overdue' (fredwilsonindy.org 2011).

Wilson's implication that race remains largely unrecognized in Indianapolis's cityscape holds true for virtually all of urban America, and we might conclude that it is typical of nearly all contemporary materiality. Race is paradoxically an essential dimension of all public materiality even as it has been simultaneously rendered largely invisible in concrete material terms; that is, race is invisible in the sense that colour line privilege is rarely acknowledged in everyday materiality, and race is only 'seen' in its most stereotypical ideological aesthetics. As the Emancipated Monument captive passed largely unseen for more than a century, its hollow dominant narrative of white altruism likewise passed unexamined, even though it was among the most prominent material representations of African America in the city. Yet its nineteenth-century racial aesthetics conflict with most contemporary perceptions of black subjectivity, and some audiences have resisted immortalizing those conventions for fear they will reproduce the racist privileges the monument had effectively condoned for a century.

Wilson's proposed statue and its reception raise the question of how the colour line can be made materially visible in the contemporary world and how archaeology can illuminate racial privilege. On the surface the discourse over Wilson's proposal is simply an assessment of an aesthetic work that aspires to redefine stale ideological motifs, and stakeholders intent to craft certain pictures of African America disagree over whether such symbols can frame productive conversation about African American heritage. The reception also reflects the lines of power that materially represent African America, especially how culture brokers in Indianapolis's arts community have partnered with (and potentially misunderstood) African American constituencies.

Yet perhaps the most critical dimension of this discussion is how materially illuminating race reveals a vast network of unquestioned privileges and deep-seated sentiments about racial subjectivity. Like the long-ignored freedman who has ignited a discussion of Indianapolis's colour line, the city's broader landscape is a material testament to racial privilege: broad swaths of state offices, a university campus, and prosaic apartment complexes inhabit what were predominately African American neighbourhoods for more than a century. Nevertheless, these mundane or unexamined spaces pass without critical reflection and little or no acknowledgement that they are products of racial ideology. In an early twenty-first century society that often transparently bills itself as 'post-racial', African American heritage is often more thoroughly masked than it was just a half-century ago. Black materiality was overwhelmingly effaced from American cityscapes in the wake of the Second World War, when urban renewal projects took aim on predominantly black neighbourhoods and razed massive tracts of historically African American communities in the heart of cities like Indianapolis. The remaining public spaces including places like Monument Circle are inelegantly cast as being 'race-less' or simply assumed to have been outside African American experience. Urban renewal projects aspired to remove nearly all material traces of African American heritage that revealed the impression of white racial privilege, which extended the Soldiers and Sailors Monument's sanitized history that completely ignores African American agency. Black materiality has been nearly completely erased from public spaces, sequestered in newly marginalized areas, and submerged in ideologically distorted histories.

Consequently, much of historically African American cities are today either literally erased or ideologically effaced.

The neighbourhoods transformed by urban renewal have rarely been viewed as products of systematic racism directly linked to the original freedman statue or his contemporary recasting. Most public space has simply been assumed to have no connection to the colour line, and material forms like the Monument and the cityscape cleared by urban renewal have rarely been approached in ways that examine how such materiality is experienced along and across the colour line. Racial privilege persists because it is embedded in material culture yet its impact on material symbolism remains largely unspoken or unacknowledged. From the most quotidian commodities to the most monumental spatial materiality, racial privilege is silently reproduced, masked, and accented by materiality that appears to have no tangible connection to the colour line. The freed captive on the Soldiers and Sailors Monument and the largely erased landscape of African American Indianapolis reflect how race has often been ideologically rendered invisible, and the reception to the freedman's recasting underscores the complicated ways such representations are contested in the contemporary world.

36.3 MATERIALIZING BLACK HERITAGE: URBAN RENEWAL AND AFRICAN AMERICAN LANDSCAPES

Since almost the moment Europeans settled the city in the 1820s, Indianapolis's near-Westside had African American residents. While they were often settled in pockets, they had white and European immigrant neighbours alike throughout the nineteenth century; white and black children went to the same secondary schools until 1927; African Americans were much less densely settled and more often in single-family homes than in other northern cities; and African Americans who left the South found much less suffocating racist codes and violence than they escaped in the South. Much of this changed at the dawn of the twentieth century, though, when the city became starkly segregated as both European and African American immigration alarmed city administrators (Crocker 1992: 44). A typical 1910 study of neighbourhoods just south of the African American near-Westside found that 'Twenty-five percent of them are foreigners, either Irish, German, Italian or Hungarian...Of the remainder of the people of the district 14% are negroes....Consider this mass of people—foreigners of different nationalities, negroes, Americans from a dozen different states, and a handful of native citizens of Indianapolis. Could they be expected to mix well in any sort of social organization, or to have many common interests or aims?' (Campbell Adams 1913: 122). The nadir perhaps came after the First World War, when the Ku Klux Klan mobilized widespread nativism to fashion itself into Indianapolis's single largest social organization between 1921 and 1928 (Moore 1991: 59). The Klan gathered sufficient backing by 1924 to win the election of a Klan-endorsed slate of state officials including the Governor and a Klan-supported majority in the state legislature (Moore 1991: 152). The Klan has often been caricatured as a racist vigilante organization, but in Indiana the hooded order was a truly mainstream political and social force with historically deep-seated racist sentiments that did not disappear after their 1920s zenith in power.

One of the most significant material effects of such racism was colour line spatial segregation and neighbourhood material decline, a commonplace pattern in twentieth-century American cities (cf. Lands 2009). African Americans became increasingly spatially segregated in twentieth-century Indianapolis by *de facto* segregation by white realtors and neighbourhood associations, and this fuelled a significant black housing shortage as many African Americans were forced to secure housing in the near-Westside (Pierce 2005: 59–60). That housing shortage was intensified by the growth of the African American community by 175 per cent between 1900 and 1930 (Pierce 2005: 60). As the population swelled, landlords seized upon desperate tenants and much of the near-Westside housing declined. Alarmed city administrators launched one of the city's first 'slum reform' projects in 1933 with the planning for a New Deal public housing settlement that came to be known as Lockefield Gardens (Barrows 2007). When it opened in 1937 Lockefield Gardens' 748 units provided stylish and spacious housing for working black families, but it could not remotely address African American housing problems in Indianapolis.

In the wake of the Second World War, federally funded slum clearance programmes were boosted by urban blight rhetoric. In 1947, for instance, a *Saturday Evening Post* article on Indianapolis snidely suggested that 'the people of Indianapolis are considerably more attractive than much of the town they live in', concluding that 'some of the most hideous slums in the United States are in the "Mile Square"' (Ellen and Murphy 1947: 113–14). That same year, John Gunther (1947: 387) indicated that 'Indianapolis is an unkempt city, unswept, raw' and added a dig at the Soldiers and Sailors Monument when he suggested that 'in it you may see the second ugliest monument in the world'. In 1953, an *Indianapolis Star* study reported that 'Twenty per cent of the city today is under the scrutiny of the Indianapolis Redevelopment Commission and needing possible slum clearance', concluding that '900 buildings should be razed immediately…and another 1000 ramshackle buildings run the 900 a close second in disrepair and other substandard conditions' (Connor 1953a: 1). The newspaper reported that 959 homes had no indoor toilets, another 20,649 households had neither bathtubs nor showers, and 140 miles of the city's 923 miles of streets had no water mains at all (Connor 1953b: 1, 3). Many of these conditions may have intensified before and after the Second World War, but they had been present for much of the twentieth century and not at all restricted to African American neighbourhoods. For instance, Nelda Weathers's (1924) survey of 137 houses in the predominantly African American near-Westside identified only six with 'inside toilets' and 16 others using outhouses connected to the city sewers, but the remainder was using enclosed privy vault outhouses that in many cases remained until the homes were razed in the 1960s (cf. Bureau of Municipal Research 1917: 326). These conditions were tolerated by the city and hastened by racist housing practices until urban renewal funds gave the city the concrete financial capacity to remove such overwhelmingly black neighbourhoods, which took aim on material decline but also targeted areas that wielded significant political power.

Indiana University was one of the most prominent players in the post-war transformation of the near-Westside. Universities became especially active in urban renewal when the Federal Housing Act was amended in 1959 to expressly direct federal aid for 'urban renewal areas involving colleges and universities' (Hechinger 1961: E7). In 1958, the Indianapolis Redevelopment Commission's master design for the near-Westside proposed an undergraduate campus of Indiana University that would adjoin the Indiana University Medical Center, where students had been trained since the early twentieth century. The planners indicated that around 'the present medical center is a large area of blighted dwellings and scattered commercial and industrial buildings. The Department proposes that this area be redeveloped for housing to primarily serve the university campus' (Metropolitan Planning Department 1958: 14). Yet in the early 1960s, Indianapolis's city government shocked the University by rejecting federal urban renewal funds in favour of locally financed projects. The University was compelled to expand into the densely settled neighbourhoods around the Medical Center by purchasing single lots, spending most of the 1960s purchasing between 10 and 20 properties each month and continuing that growth through the 1970s and into the 1980s. A rush of landlords eager to sell descended on the University when its expansion designs became public, and by 1974 the University lamented that a 'substantial backlog of property owners wanting to sell endangers the University's commitment to the immediate campus neighborhood' (IUPUI 1974: 65).

Today that African American neighbourhood has been completely materially displaced, uprooted for parking lots and a scatter of brutal modernist buildings that make up the campus of Indiana University-Purdue University, Indianapolis (IUPUI). The black material heritage that escaped the wrecking ball in post-Second World War Indianapolis generally conformed to ideological visions of community history. A few historic churches survived, for instance, structures that institutionally situate African Americans in deeply held Midwestern faith traditions that are ideologically cast as unifying people across the colour line. However, churches are actually among the most segregated of community spaces, and these African American congregations had very distinctive anti-racist politics. In the city's near-Westside, for example, the Bethel AME Church built in 1867 replaced a structure that was burnt in 1862, almost certainly by slavery supporters who opposed the congregation's public abolitionist leanings. Likewise, the 1929 landmark Madame C. J. Walker Theatre commemorates one of the city's most prominent entrepreneurs, celebrating an African American woman whose hard work, ingenuity, and good fortune built one of the twentieth century's most affluent cosmetics firms. Yet that transparent public accounting of Madam Walker routinely ignores her anti-racist activism. It also conveniently sidesteps her own flight from Indianapolis to live in Harlem and escape Indianapolis's persistent racist codes imposed on even its wealthiest black citizen. The central thoroughfare in the neighbourhood, Indiana Avenue, was almost entirely depopulated in the 1960s and 1970s as businesses and music clubs lost their customers; the city's African American high school, Crispus Attucks, was legally desegregated in 1949 (though *de facto* segregation continued through the 1970s) (Gonis 1965); and all but seven of the original 24 buildings in Lockefield Gardens were razed in 1983.

36.4 ART, MEMORY, AND THE MONUMENTAL AESTHETICS OF RACE

The Soldiers and Sailors Monument was typical of later nineteenth-century statuary that aspired to celebrate the everyday soldier, the mostly anonymous men who were cast as typical citizens preserving the Union. When President Benjamin Harrison spoke at the laying of the monument's cornerstone in 1889, he saw the future statue as a memorial to those unknown soldiers, indicating that he had long hoped that 'there might be built a noble shaft, not to any man, not to bear on any of its majestic faces the name of a man, but a monument about which the sons of veterans, the mothers of our dead, the widows that are yet with us, might gather, and, pointing to the stately shaft, say: "there is his monument"' (*The Ohio Democrat* 1889: 3). At the monument's dedication in 1902, the *Indianapolis News* underscored that this selfless if anonymous service to the state was the central lesson of the monument, which demonstrated that 'Private and general are entitled to the same measure of our love and gratitude if they do what they are bidden to do without thought of self. There is now no man so humble but he can greatly serve the country.' The 1902 speeches and newspaper articles on the Monument apparently said nothing about the relationship between the war and black freedom, but in his 1889 speech Harrison called the end of bondage one of the war's greatest victories, arguing that 'I do seriously believe that if we can measure among the States the benefits resulting from the preservation of the Union, the rebellious States have the larger share. It destroyed an institution that was their destruction' (Hedges 1916: 215). Yet presaging the ideological turn towards celebrating the common soldier and ignoring African America, Harrison also underscored that 'This is a monument by Indiana to Indiana soldiers.'

The kneeling, freed captive on the Soldiers and Sailors Monument memorialized the black experience of the war as the gift of freedom won by countless white citizen-soldiers. Hidden in the recesses of the monument, the freed captive was whites' self-congratulatory mechanism that applauded their ability to secure freedom, forgave themselves for the patriarchal racism that followed Emancipation, and materially and ideologically submerged race and the colour line within a broad ideological narrative. In 1916, Freeman Henry Morris Murray (1916: 124) noted how the statue's design buried its single captive amongst a cacophony of wartime symbols, observing that the monument aspired 'to represent so much of the tumult and carnage as well as the glory of war, on a large scale; and brings into action so many arms of the service in so many stages of the fray; and, moreover, introduces such an over-load of the symbolical and the figurative—and finally, in the lower part, a glimpse of the aftermath of the struggle—that one is at first bewildered, and after a time wearied in the effort to disentangle, to correlate, and to interpret'. Murray (1916: 125) criticized the placement of the freed captive in the monument's 'Peace' grouping rather than the 'War' side of the monument, where 'we see no black man, though here, if anywhere—here, where there is powder smoke—he would seem most fittingly to have a place, both for his honor's sake and the truth's sake'.

Fred Wilson recognized the effacement of black material heritage and the paradoxical invisibility of the emancipated captive in Indianapolis's most public space. His work commonly 're-purposes' symbols and goods to compel audiences to rethink or simply acknowledge their meanings, so the unshackled monument captive provided a potentially productive motif to trigger a discussion about freedom, privilege, and the colour line. The Cultural Trail has many artworks installed along it or planned, but Wilson's is separated by its conscious ambition to trigger discourses about culture, heritage, and materiality. In 2009 and 2010 the Cultural Trail planners in the Central Indiana Community Foundation shared their vision of this and other works in a series of public meetings. Blogger Tyler Green (2010b) argues that the planners 'held a series of meetings to try to introduce Wilson and *E Pluribus Unum* to the community. Art students showed up and maybe a few other folks did too. The groups that Wilson and the ICT most wanted to engage—the quarter of Indianapolis

residents who are African-American—were mostly disinterested.' Green certainly mis-
interprets those absences as 'disinterest', but he was probably correct in his depiction of
conventional 'community meetings' that gathered together people who saw themselves as
part of an 'art community'. Such a conception of community misunderstands black grassroots organization—which occurs in very different institutional channels than public art
meetings—and risks underestimating the profoundly deep African American commitment
to heritage and its public representation. Deep-seated mistrust of the state and a sober realism
about the limits of black community voices likely kept all but the most committed stakeholders from initial public meetings, particularly in an arts community that has not often included
voices of colour. The Trail's artistic curator and public art coordinator acknowledged their difficulty reaching African American stakeholders in October, 2010, saying that 'Honestly, it had
been a little bit difficult to get a lot of people from the community involved' (Green 2010b).

This effort to 'locate' the African American community risks misunderstanding
Indianapolis's distinctive heritage of colour line civility, which continues to shape the ways
race is discussed in the city today. As Richard Pierce (2005) has thoughtfully argued, African
Americans were an integral part of the city long before twentieth-century wartime migra-
tions that swelled the populations of many other Midwestern cities. Those cities, however,
did not share Indianapolis's heritage of generations of black and white residents living alongside each other or the long-term relationships between the city's white and black elite. Even
in the face of rising separatism from the 1920s onward, African Americans in Indianapolis
tended to contest civil inequalities through patient negotiation across the colour line within
existing power structures and through community representatives. This yielded a distinctive twentieth-century colour line politics that avoided radical public protest and overt racist hostility.

Nevertheless, a range of people became part of the discussion about the Wilson project
in autumn 2010. One of the first volleys came in a September 2010 letter to the *Indianapolis
Recorder* from an African American high school teacher who complained that when he
'saw the picture of the sculpture that was created (or recreated) by artist Fred Wilson, I was
appalled, embarrassed, disappointed, and outright mad. My initial thought was that the features around the shoulders, neck, head and face looked "ape-ish" to say the least' (Robinson
2010). That uneasiness focused on the material aesthetics of black representation, arguing
that 'this is not the 19th century and the African-American community in Indianapolis does
not need another "image" in downtown Indianapolis to remind us of how downtrodden,
beat down, hapless, and submissive we once may have been. We don't need any more images
of lawn jockeys, caricatures . . . no more buffoonery, no more shuckin' and jiven', and no more
ape-ish looking monuments.'

That discord was a somewhat narrow critique of racist aesthetics and the apprehension
that their visibility would fortify or resurrect racist stereotypes. It did not address the thorny
community politics of representing racialized symbols in a public, permanent, and monumental piece of material culture. A public monument is a distinctive material object in its
ambition to represent something with timeless permanence, so much of the debate over the
project revolved around how the motif was selected and how the statue's meaning and interpretation could be subsequently managed. Wilson himself recognized the folly of aspiring
to control such meanings, arguing that 'Public art is . . . in public and people can interpret
it in the way they will and often without any mediation, which is really great' (Green 2011).
Yet the critics of the project soon orchestrated a group calling itself the Citizens Against

Slave Image that rejected the suggestion that the nineteenth-century aesthetics of captivity could frame a productive discourse on race. The dispute was fundamentally over control of public, permanent material representations of African America, not simply one statue. The letter to the *Indianapolis Recorder*, for instance, concluded with a criticism that exposed the politics of materiality and representation across the colour line, asking 'whose culture is this image along the Indianapolis Cultural Trail attempting to represent, the oppressor or the oppressed?' Wilson appeared on a local African American radio show soon after, and a caller against the statue again intoned 'Who decides what is appropriate and what is not appropriate?' (Green 2010a).

In 1996 a statue of tennis star and AIDS activist Arthur Ashe was dedicated on Richmond, Virginia's Monument Avenue, and that project was also dogged by a complicated community review process that inelegantly manoeuvred around deep-seated sentiments over race and heritage. Between 1890 and 1929, Monument Avenue was lined with five bronze and marble monumental statues that memorialized five iconic figures of the rebelling Confederacy's 'Lost Cause' (i.e. Confederate Generals Robert E. Lee, Thomas 'Stonewall' Jackson, and J. E. B. Stuart; Confederate President Jefferson Davis; and Confederate Navy Commander Matthew Fontaine Maury) (Edwards and Howard 1997). When the 60-foot tall Robert E. Lee monument was dedicated on what was then Richmond's unpopulated western edges in 1890, an estimated 100,000 people gathered for its unveiling (Leib 2002: 286). Influenced by the City Beautiful movement, late nineteenth- and early twentieth-century planners soon placed a central grass median along Monument Avenue's grand straight boulevard, which was rapidly lined with stately Colonial Revival homes. Kathy Edwards and Esme Howard (1997: 93) argue that the community's exceptional architectural homogeneity was a 30-year-long process that informally but strategically reflected the post-Reconstruction politics of Richmond's white elite. Public statuary and the materiality of Monument Avenue invoked pre-war heritage even as it was funded by—and rationalized the new influence of—newly wealthy post-war elite professionals who replaced the Old South planter class (Edwards and Howard 1997: 95; Savage 1997: 148). Veterans' reunions and Southern cultural events became commonplace along Monument Avenue and won the exclusively white neighbourhood the transparent status of 'sacred ground'. When it was proposed that an Ashe statue join this landscape, the Richmond discussion most explicitly focused on physical placement of the statue within a landscape that ideologically heralded Southern chivalry, the defence of home and honour, and new, post-Civil War Southern affluence. A majority of whites and African Americans alike opposed the placement of the Ashe statue alongside the fathers of the Confederacy; some of the former questioned the statue's aesthetic worthiness and whether Ashe deserved the status accorded the likes of Lee and Jackson, while the latter often cast those same figures as traitors whose monuments commemorate the defence of enslavement (Leib 2002: 299–301). Ultimately the statue was erected in 1996, effectively accepting the heroic status of the Confederate icons while elevating Ashe to a position that conceded the multicultural dimensions of Southern heritage and questioned the unchallenged heroism of those icons and the cause they defended (Leib 2002: 307).

The very absence of African American images on Monument Avenue and in Indianapolis alike somewhat counterintuitively underscores the profound power of the colour line (cf. Savage 1997: 154). Fred Wilson's Indianapolis sculpture raises the issue of exactly how we see race in materiality, and historically Americans have chosen not to see it at all. Wilson's design intentionally appropriated an ideologically charged racialized symbol, but, as Wilson recognized, the precise discussion it hoped to foster when installed—beyond simply illuminating race and racism—is not mediated by the state, socially powerful collectives in the city, an arts community, or any other social group. A reflective public discussion of race and privilege has historically failed Americans for half a millennium, but discussions about racial representation occur constantly in African America in secluded discursive spaces that rarely find their way across the colour line into white public space. Tyler Green's prescient analysis of the Wilson sculpture and its public reception concludes that reception to the proposal 'is the kind of artist-public discourse wherein art can play an important role as a community protagonist'. However, these discussions about racist representations and African American heritage have always been at the heart of African American culture and discourse, so the 'arts community' has awkwardly found its way into that discussion and risks appearing self-congratulatory about initiating it.

In a city that has often sought contrived racial consensus, some people saw the disputed Indianapolis statue as an unacceptably inflammatory if not racist illumination of the colour line. Tyler Green lamented that simply eliminating the statue from the Cultural Trail would yield 'a false unanimity' that ignores all the complications of racism. Despite such fears, in July 2011 the Central Indiana Community Foundation (CICF) announced that it no longer supported placing the statue in front of the City-County Building. Their inelegant retreat focused on the sculpture's siting at the City-County Building, which is home to the city jail as well as the Mayor's Office, a space Wilson chose in part because it was within sight of the Soldiers and Sailors Monument. In December 2011 the CICF finally reached the conclusion that the project could not be salvaged anywhere in Indianapolis, and they withdrew their support, so it somewhat curiously has been a powerful material thing without actually having any genuine material presence.

36.5 'Our Own Peculiar Viewpoint': Finding the Racialized Landscape

Fred Wilson's intentions were in many ways much the same as Freeman Henry Morris Murray's had been in his 1916 study of the representation of African Americans in public statuary. Murray (1916: xix) underscored that 'when we look at a work of art, especially when "we" look at one in which Black Folk appear—or do not appear when they should,—we should ask: What does it mean? What does it suggest? What impression is it likely to make on those who view it? What will be the effect on present-day problems, of its obvious and also of its insidious teachings? In short, we should endeavor to "interpret" it; and should try to interpret it from our own peculiar viewpoint.' Facing the Soldiers and Sailors Monument, Murray (1916: 125–6) saw the well-concealed captive as a fundamental misrepresentation of the war and African American agency, finding that in 'the Peace group—wherein a black man appears, seemingly as an afterthought or a sort of supernumerary—there is, artistically viewed, as much confusion and incoherence as in the other [i.e. War group], and there is more over-loading; and in it the symbolical and the figurative are heedlessly and hopelessly mixed with the realistic and commonplace.... I feel an impulse to seize this "super" by his dangling foot and slide him gently off into oblivion—or else say to him, as sternly as I can: "Awake, awake, put on thy strength…shake thyself from the dust; arise. You deserve a place at Liberty's side, not at her feet. Assist her soberly to uphold the Flag, while others rejoice; for, but for your strong right arm the Flag would even now perhaps be trailing in the dust!'"

Wilson aspired to do much as Murray hoped by illuminating an otherwise invisible racial symbol, a symbol that like most racialized modern materiality was hidden in plain view. Potentially the recast freedman might cast doubt on the hollow white beneficence posed by the Soldiers and Sailors Monument a century ago. Wilson's intentions were to recontextualize the freedman's agency simply by drawing attention to him and posing the question of why legions of visitors to the Circle had mostly ignored that captive over more than a hundred years. Wilson's reimagination of that symbol will not become a concrete material reality on Indianapolis's Cultural Trail, but the captive, the Wilson statue, and the public contestation of representation reveal the ways in which race is invested in material landscapes in a vast range of forms. Contemporary archaeology provides exceptionally powerful tools to interrogate these historically deep-seated discourses on race as they intrude into the present-day world, marshalling ethnographic rigour and material insights into the ways race is impressed into contemporary life in profoundly clear and unseen ways alike. Myriad landscapes bear the symbolism of race and racism, and nearly all public space in a city like Indianapolis is invested with unacknowledged colour lines experiences.

Disassociating the landscapes of urban renewal from the narrow racialized materiality of the Monument freedman risks underestimating the genuine power of racial ideology. Yet the contestation of the freedman's representation of race and African Diasporan heritage demonstrates the genuine power of—and challenges confronting—materialities of the colour line. The arts community that commissioned this project certainly understood the power of public materiality and the productive discourses a thoughtful piece could trigger, but they ultimately failed to grapple ethnographically with African American receptions of blackness or the ways some African American constituencies contested precisely who had the power to publicly represent African Diaspora. Much of the mission of contemporary archaeology is to reveal how race is invested in mundane and monumental materiality alike, and it does that by assessing the material forms themselves as well as the breadth of constituencies who encounter and give meaning to things. Admitting racialized symbolism and acknowledging white privilege challenges communities along and across colour lines, and material culture—even the mere spectre of material representations of African America like Fred Wilson's sculpture—can foster productive conversations about the sway of race and racism.

ACKNOWLEDGEMENTS

Modupe Labode discussed many of her ideas about the Wilson discourse in particular and race and representation more broadly and strengthened my arguments significantly. Thanks to Glenn White, Liz Kryder-Reid, and Richard McCoy for discussing various factors surrounding the Wilson project and its reception in the African American community. Thanks to Rodney Harrison for inviting me to make the contribution. All the misinterpretations in the chapter are mine alone.

REFERENCES

Barrows, Robert G. 2007. The Local Origins of a New Deal Housing Project: The Case of Lockefield Gardens in Indianapolis. *Indiana Magazine of History* 103: 125–51.

Bureau of Municipal Research. 1917. Report on a Survey of the City Government of Indianapolis, Indiana. William B. Burford, Indianapolis, Indiana.

Campbell Adams, L. M. 1913. An Investigation of Housing and Living Conditions in Three Districts of Indianapolis. *Indiana University Studies* 1(10): 111–41.

Connor, Lawrence. 1953a. Slums Blight 20 Pct. of City. *Indianapolis Star*, 17 August, pp. 1, 14.

—— 1953b. Bad Sanitation, Water in Slums Take Heavy Toil of Infants. *Indianapolis Star*, 19 August, pp. 1, 3.

Crocker, Ruth. 1992. *Social Work and Social Order: The Settlement Movement in Two Industrial Cities, 1889–1930*. Urbana: University of Illinois Press.

Edwards, Kathy and Howard, Esmé. 1997. Monument Avenue: The Architecture of Consensus in the New South, 1890–1930. *Perspectives in Vernacular Architecture* 6: 92–110.

Ellen, Mary and Murphy, Mark. 1947. Indianapolis. *Saturday Evening Post* 221(6): 16–17, 115–17.

Fredwilsonindy.org. 2011. About the Project. Available at: <http://www.fredwilsonindy.org/aboutproject.html> (accessed 9 August 2011).

Gonis, Sophia N. 1965. An Analysis of Desegregation Trends in the Indianapolis Public Schools. Graduate Thesis Collection Paper 33. Available at: <http://digitalcommons.butler.edu/grtheses/33> (accessed 21 August 2011).

Green, Tyler. 2010a. The Very Public Debate over Fred Wilson's Indy Sculpture. *Modern Art Notes*. Available at: <http://blogs.artinfo.com/modernartnotes/2010/10/fred-wilsons-indy-sculpture-and/> (accessed 11 August 2011).

—— 2010b. Introducing Fred Wilson's Indy Project—and the Backlash. *Modern Art Notes*. Available at: <http://blogs.artinfo.com/modernartnotes/2010/10/introducing-fred-wilsons-indianapolis-project-and-the-backlash/ > (acessed 29 August 2011).

—— 2011. 'Anti-slave rally' to Oppose Fred Wilson Project. *Modern Art Notes*. Available at: <http://blogs.artinfo.com/modernartnotes/2011/07/anti-slave-rally-to-oppose-fred-wilson-project/> (accessed 29 August 2011).

Gunther, John. 1947. *Inside U.S.A.* New York: Harper and Brothers.

Hechinger, Fred M. 1961. Campus vs. Slums: Urban Universities Join Battle for Neighborhood Renewal. *The New York Times*, 1 October, p. E7.

Hedges, Charles (ed.). 1916. *The Speeches of Benjamin Harrison*. New York: John W. Lovell Company.

IUPUI. 1974. IUPUI Master Plan. Unpublished manuscript on file, Indiana University-Purdue University, Indianapolis Archives, Indianapolis, Indiana.

Lands, LeeAnn. 2009. *The Culture of Property: Race, Class, and Housing Landscapes in Atlanta, 1880–1950*. Athens, GA: University of Georgia Press.

Leib, Jonathan I. 2002. Separate Times, Shared Spaces: Arthur Ashe, Monument Avenue and the Politics of Richmond, Virginia's Symbolic Landscape. *Cultural Geographies* 9: 286–312.

Metropolitan Planning Department. 1958. *Central Business District, Indianapolis*. Metropolitan Planning Department, Indianapolis, Indiana.

Moore, Leonard J. 1991. *Citizen Klansmen: The Ku Klux Klan in Indiana, 1921–1928*. Chapel Hill: University of North Carolina Press.

Murray, Freeman H. M. 1916. *Emancipation and the Freed in American Sculpture: A Study in Interpretation*. Published by the author, Washington, DC.

The Ohio Democrat. 1889. A Monument to Heroes. *The Ohio Democrat* 31 August, p. 3.

Pierce, Richard B. 2005. *Polite Protest: The Political Economy of Race in Indianapolis, 1920– 1970*. Bloomington: Indiana University Press.

Robinson, Leroy. 2010. Letter to the Editor: Sculpture is Appalling. *Indianapolis Recorder*, 16 September. Available at: <http://www.indianapolisrecorder.com/opinion/article_d304c6ff-47ee-5bb6-afce-b5531a03e18c.html> (accessed 9 August 2011).

Savage, Kirk. 1997. *Standing Soldiers, Kneeling Slaves: Race, War, and Monument in Nineteenth-Century America*. Princeton, NJ: Princeton University Press.

Weathers, Nelda A. 1924. How the Negro Lives in Indianapolis. Unpublished Master of Arts thesis, Social Service Department, Indiana University.

PHOTO ESSAY: INSTITUTIONAL SPACES

PETER METELERKAMP

BEGINNING with the orientalism of Le Gray, Beato, Fenton, and others, the use of the camera as an archaeological tool is almost as old as the medium itself. Indeed, the promise of the camera as a machine to arrest decay and preserve a record remains its primary appeal. But how to decide what to record? What matters? When it comes to the photography of contemporary structures and spaces, unsurprisingly the general tendency is to follow a search for the significant. This is, after all, a measure of intellectual seriousness, and is informed by a sense of the socio-historical moment. So (in notable contemporary practice) it may take forms such as the exoticism of Guy Tillim's evocative explorations of postcolonial cities in Africa in his *Avenue Patrice Lumumba* (2009), Lynne Cohen's enquiry into the banal horrors of the military-scientific establishment in *No Man's Land* (Thomas 2001) or Edward Burtynsky's portentous panoramas in *China* (2005). These are all replete with social and historical meaning, and their power is testimony to the camera as a tool for social and historical inquiry and as an agent in the preservation of material evidence. But what of the local, the innocuous, the relatively 'meaningless'? After all, structures and spaces speak equally of culture when they are most quotidian, 'ordinary', and unselfconscious, just as the lives of individuals and communities are made not only from 'significant' or exotic events, but from the small unconscious rituals of the everyday. How can the photography of place be used to engage with these small pulses in the flow of life? And, is it possible to create photographic correlatives that are both useful as denotative records, and responsive to what Bill Brandt famously called 'atmosphere'—that is to say the subjectively experienced qualities of our being in space?

This project, resisting the lure of the exotic, the monumental, or the picturesque (all tropes of framing that 'authorize' our visual knowledge of the world in different ways) is deliberately concerned with the inconsequential and the overlooked. In this it is a deliberate challenge to the hierarchies and categories of 'academic' and 'official' knowledge (just as the photograph is a challenge to the text), and shares some of the methodologies of feminist practice, making knowledge from 'below' and 'in-between', and finding relevance in the 'trivial'. Furthermore, unlike the consciously monumental work mentioned above, or work that might look at iconic sites such as Auschwitz (Norfolk 1998), or the Maze prison (Wyllie 2009), this is an attempt to turn the academic gaze self-referentially back on to the scrutinizing establishment and those who inhabit it. It is about the textures of our own lives as academics. What might these mute and oblique images of the vacant, the interstitial, and the 'taken-for-granted' tell us about our way of life?

More particularly the images in this project consider some of the interior spaces of my own university. This is a conscious inversion of the search for 'significance' somewhere 'out there' or 'then'—i.e. over geographical or temporal distance. It is a reminder that we are not less the stuff of history than the subjects we study. The places and structures I have photographed are in the first instance intrinsically performative: material agents in a factory for the production of social being, redolent with associative as well as direct functions. Behind these ways of thinking about spaces lie Foucault's inquiries into the architecture of power in *Discipline and Punish* (1975), and Bachelard's *Poetics of Space* (1969). Central, too, is Bourdieu's concept of habitus (1977), the deeply embedded habits by which groups perpetuate and reproduce themselves. For Bourdieu, the human body itself is both the 'embodiment' of social being and the site of its inscription. If we allow this, it follows that the spaces in which bodies move and have their being are as vital in 'embodying' and 'bodying forth' culture as the less material relationships which bind us into social connection.

As inhabited spaces, buildings and interior spaces are also a living map on which human relations and presences are inscribed. This means they serve as a complex indicator of the unacknowledged ways in which the character of a community and its internal contradictions and dialectics reveal themselves at a moment in time. While they show something of their explicit and conscious function, they also act as parchments for contrary and subversive forces in our communal life. Indifference and neglect, shabby compromise, unwitting irony, improvisation: all will be immediately recognized as features of the psychic landscape of a contemporary provincial Englishness.

Among the complex of meanings and relations I have considered and encountered in making the images for this project, a few pointers can be offered; not in an attempt to define or explain the images, but to invite reflection.

The images fall into several groups. First, there are images of spaces that construct and inscribe hierarchies; by scale, structuration of elevation, material finish or lack thereof. These are among the eternal signifiers of status that an archaeologist would bring to an excavation. The 'official' spaces of the institution can reveal some of the ways these planes of power slide over each other, intersect, and interact. But 'merely functional' transitional and managerial spaces also operate as vehicles for collective management. Such mundane structures as entrances, passages, and exits, perform functions of admittance and exclusion, and control the flow of human energy in the system. They are portals to social values which change over time, and they, too, can be studied as indicators of the assumptions about the channelling of energy and the forces that control or disrupt it.

On the other hand, atria and assemblies operate as zones of 'collection' inasmuch as they coagulate individual energies and needs to both produce and reflect assumptions about the nature of collective relations. In this project it is apparent that closely related to them are what in the world of commoditized consumption might be called 'comfort stations': points of retreat and recreation like those provided to troops in an ongoing campaign. The ways we cater for the needs of the body are gestures towards community; to 'relax' is to be safe in a collective embrace in which one's place is assured and secured. But by inviting the insertion of commoditized consumerism into the collective space, a simultaneous statement of capitulation and affiliation is being made. The collegial refectory that lay at the heart of the monastery has been displaced by capitalist techno-convenience. This tells us that we no longer have time for each other, and that consociation as an end in itself has become 'inefficient'.

Transactional spaces (lecture theatre, seminar room) produce relations in what might be called the 'mode of production' of the institution. Typically in the form of the lecture this is structured around a one-to-many relationship that privileges and underwrites oracular 'authority' while inviting an element of spectacle and performance, as in the 'brilliant lecture' (this structuring of relationships is part of what Ivan Illich (1973) meant by his famous phrase 'the hidden curriculum', as the social agency of education in reproducing hierarchies). In collegiate/democratic cultures this is mediated by the seminar as a structured spatial encounter of carefully managed intimacy and semi-equality designed to produce knowledge by the Socratic dialogic method. We should do well to remember that the original Academy was a factory for leadership; and the 'good degree' still enshrines modes of engagement that are thought necessary for the managerial class: Socratic discourse is not socially neutral. Laboratories, on the other hand, clearly offer a rather different idea of the way knowledge (as the primary official commodity of the institution) is produced and exchanged, with individual structured stations creating a form of parallel discovery through praxis. In this they embody belief in the efficacy of the empirical/Baconian scientific method, evolved in post-Renaissance Britain with its underbelly of sugar and slaves, and its dreaming spires promoting 'enlightenment'. None of these structures, and the relationships they construct, is inevitable; all depend on assumed epistemologies and ideas of how knowledge is produced, transmitted, and verified. These epistemologies are, of course also, not merely circumstantially but intrinsically, rooted in political assumptions.

Every institution is founded on lies it tells the public: it hides the means by which its products are contrived and presents them as 'complete'. But in a university this is not simply spectatorial; the 'public' includes its own members, who are simultaneously consumers of the institutional branding project and part of the 'back office'. Staff and students (who may also be staff) are both the employers/consumers and subjects/producers of institutional power. They need to be 'treated' but also 'disciplined'. Several photographs in this essay are concerned with spatial disconnection and incongruity, as concrete metaphors for this paradox.

More generally, both 'official' and 'unofficial' processes and forces are embodied at the institutional level—the former being what is noticed and acknowledged, what one may say enjoys a conscious social/aesthetic 'greeting'; the latter being what is simply 'there', and taken for granted. Several images are concerned with the 'unnoticed', and the incongruous relationship between the skin and the viscera of institutional life. This is, in institutional terms, not unlike a distinction between guests and servants, and a feature of the complexity of the traditional university is the way membership of these groups of 'stakeholders' shifts. But even the most 'insignificant' members of the institution leave their traces, if one cares not to overlook them.

A concomitant paradox of the way we inhabit institutions is that as individuals we simultaneously embrace and renounce our membership of them. I would suggest that this is not so much an incidence of Marxist 'alienation' or existential 'bad faith', as one of negotiated (albeit often not conscious) ambiguity. At one level contemporary white-collar identities are sustained and formed by bureaucracies and the hierarchies they convey and embed. The status they confer is jealously pursued and displayed; perhaps especially so in a university with its relative absence of direct material distinction. On the other hand members of the institution retain the necessary fiction of a 'personal' identity whose affiliations and affects do not map seamlessly onto that of our institutional personae. A subset of photographs in this project deals with the evidence of these interfaces between the 'public' and the 'personal', the former outward-facing and 'professional', the latter often curiously infantile and regressive, evidencing the persistence of childlike needs and patterns in a supposedly adult milieu. The psychic territories that subjects claim as 'individuals' are marked by memorabilia and other tokens of a 'private' self inscribing particularity and possession; meanwhile the public functionary simultaneously disowns the spaces (s)he occupies, and marks them with indifference. This, I would suggest, is not a matter of simple oppositions but a complex and highly charged conundrum, reaching to the heart of contemporary political and moral life.

Throughout our negotiation with space, both material and social, runs the trace of ritual. At its most basic this is the habituated pattern of the everyday that we recognize as routine. Then there are the small attentions we pay ourselves, and one another, as ways to ensure suture into our collective lives: the way we organize space for the comforts that reflect the rhythms of the body. And finally there are spaces arranged for those rituals we recognize as 'events' that have to do with the identity of the institution and those within it: in the case of the university, inductions, examinations, graduations, etc. In all of these the symbolic, the material and the social/discursive operate through sets of structures and signs, shaping and directing responses, readings, interactions; in short, 'putting us in our place'. Several photographs are concerned with these relentless and omnipresent discourses.

All of this is both photographic and archaeological. The paradox of the photograph, a medium bound to the immediate moment and by plenitude and presence, is that by the time the shutter closes what is offered is no longer the 'now' and the replete, but the absent and the 'no longer'. To read it depends on extrapolation and assumption. In photography and archaeology alike matter is made to stand for energy, the dead for the living, the absent for the present. We do not see 'what was there', but a narrative. The lens itself pretends; it takes the deployments of light and mass before it and flattens them into a simulacrum of an idea about the way that the world is ordered, derived from Renaissance assumptions about the nature of human perception, and entrenched and naturalized by the age of reason. But the lens also subverts its own mimetic tendency: flattening, juxtaposing, deranging. Susan Sontag claims that all photographs are in some sense surreal: 'Surrealism lies at the heart of the photographic enterprise: in the very creation of a duplicate world, of a reality in the second degree, narrower but more dramatic than the one perceived by natural vision' (1977: 52). So the camera both underwrites and challenges the 'real'. This is especially true of the monochrome image and its necessary abstractions.

Spatially, too, the photograph is a fiction, a postulate, an essay. But, after all, 'real' inhabited space itself is a factor of presence and absence, an articulation of obstacles and affordances for the body and the eye, not so much as a continuum as a set of permissions and prohibitions. So it is not too far-fetched to say that the projects of photography and archaeology alike are engaged in complex ascriptions of the meaningful and meaningless, significant and insignificant, and that in this they are like all other aspects of life. 'What begins as the main incident becomes the frame and vice versa in an infinite inversion of container into contents, margin into scene' (Armstrong 2005: 293).

In their reflexive concern with the utterly quotidian and mundane, the photographs made for this project take as their point of departure two ideas. The first is that that what is most 'ordinary' to those living in and with and through it may become revealing to the properly placed eye. The second is that because of its nature as a complex visual thing in its own right, ineluctably separated from the moment of exposure and reduced to smudges, the photograph may speak about the unspoken.

As soon as you go to places which people think are worth seeing, there is nothing left to see…because it is easier to listen. I am a firm believer in photography being able to decipher places, their stories, their history. If you listen enough. The camera has a good ear. But if it is noisy, it's hard to listen. (Wim Wenders, interview with Peter Aspden, *Financial Times*, 11 March 2011)

The dialectical relationship between presence and absence lies at the heart of human institutions, the epistemology of photography, and the archaeological project itself. The images that are the subject of this study invite meditation on some of these paradoxes.

Great Hall constructed in the 1920s from profits made in the tobacco trade

Vending machine in Victorian hallway

Improvised stairway in converted Georgian building

Security notice at porter's booth

Corridor under repair

Life sciences laboratory

Laboratory door

Resource Managers' office

Administrator's workstation

Reading packs for sale to students

Lost property in porter's booth

Corridor and Lecturer's office

Senior Lecturer's office

Admissions team office

Admissions team office

Rear hallway in Physics building

Dais with Chancellor's chair for use in degree ceremonies

Life Sciences corridor

Window in School of Arts

REFERENCES

Armstrong, Carol. 2005. Lee Friedlander: Museum of Modern Art, New York. *ArtForum*. September 2005: 293–4. Available at: <http://findarticles.com/p/articles/mi_m0268/is_1_44/ai_n27860626/> (accessed 1 June 2012).

Bachelard, Gaston. 1969. *The Poetics Of Space*, tr. Maria Jolas. Boston: Beacon Press.

Bourdieu, Pierre. 1977. *Outline of Theory of Practice*, tr. Richard Nice. Cambridge: Cambridge University Press.

Burtynsky, Edward. 2005. *China*. Gottingen: Steidl.

Foucault, Michel. 1975. *Discipline and Punish: The Birth of the Prison*. New York: Random House.

Illich, Ivan. 1973. *Deschooling Society*. London: Penguin.

Norfolk, Simon. 1998. *For Most Of It I Have No Words*. Stockport: Dewi Lewis.

Sontag, Susan. 1977. *On Photography*. London: Penguin.

Thomas, Ann. 2001. *No Man's Land: The Photography of Lynne Cohen*. London: Thames & Hudson.

Tillim, Guy. 2009. *Avenue Patrice Lumumba*. New York: Prestel.

Wyllie, Donovan. 2009. *The Maze*. Gottingen: Steidl.

PART IV

··

MEDIA AND MUTABILITIES

··

CHAPTER 37

....

BETWEEN THE LINES: DRAWING ARCHAEOLOGY

....

HELEN WICKSTEAD

37.1 INTRODUCTION

....

AT the height of the Second World War, as the European avant garde joined the displaced millions, *First Papers in Surrealism* opened in New York. The exhibition opening was dominated by a Marcel Duchamp installation, which later became known as *Sixteen Miles of String*. Drawn out between ceiling, walls, and floor, Duchamp's twine criss-crossed the gallery, weaving a lattice through which the rest of the exhibition (including works by Breton, Ernst, Masson, Matta, and Duchamp) could be seen. Because Duchamp's installation explores ways of relating line and surface (or, line and 'ground', as the surface of a picture is often called), art historians have discussed *Sixteen Miles of String* within the history of drawing (e.g. de Zegher 2010: 51–4). *Sixteen Miles of String* played a subtle game with vision, allowing the viewer to look through the string to the art objects, but also allowing them to transfer the focus of their vision, looking at the string, the artworks, or the installation in the gallery space (Vick 2008)—that is, looking at the lines or at the spaces between and around the lines. As a drawing that had left the ground, Duchamp's lines provided both a metaphor for flight and exile, and a deconstruction of perceptions of space and time based on the relations between lines and the spaces between. Duchamp's installation reveals how, during the twentieth century, the field of drawing began to expand in ways that redefined traditional notions of drawing, and showed how drawing might provide a way to think about relations between presence and absence, past and present.

In recent years, drawing has acquired a dramatically enhanced profile across a range of disciplines (Ingold 2007; Duff and Sawdon 2008; Garner 2008). It is increasingly 'drawn on' both as metaphor and means in the social sciences (Ingold 2011, 2012; Taussig 2011) and it has inspired philosophical explorations of presence and absence, means and ends, being and becoming (e.g. Derrida 1990; Agamben 2000; Badiou 2006). Drawing's attraction stems from the way it germinates and grows in spaces 'between': between being and becoming (Petherbridge 2010), between presence and absence (Derrida 1990), and between 'the "no longer" and the "not yet"' (McFadyen 2011).

In light of drawing's renewed salience, it seems timely to ask how the philosophy, history, and practice of drawing might contribute to archaeology. This chapter extends the boundaries of conventional understandings of drawing to apply concepts from recent drawing scholarship. It will explore some of the 'betweennesses' that circumscribe contemporary drawing as it intersects with archaeology. How might the gestural mark or trace of drawing be related to archaeological traces? And how might drawing's ability to 'write time' engage with archaeological concepts of time and image-making? I investigate drawings made by visual artists working alongside archaeologists as part of a programme of art residencies, using their drawings to explore contemporary philosophies and practices of drawing. Drawings are selected from the work of artists who took part in an eight-year research project called art+archaeology, which I directed with artist Leo Duff. Art+archaeology created 21 short-term funded residencies for visual artists on archaeological excavations, in museums and archaeological laboratories and office spaces. The huge variety of research outputs (including artworks, events, exhibitions, and art/archaeology public education programmes) cannot be summarized here. Instead, I use four specific drawing projects to lead the reader on a journey through the gestures, marks, traces, and absences of which drawing is composed, and to draw out the potential of drawing as a way of thinking through archaeology. From this, I suggest that drawing's ability to capture and hold on to 'betweens' is an important part of its value, and I discuss such 'betweens' in relation to art and archaeology.

While this chapter contributes to a growing body of archaeological literature drawing on contemporary art practice, art history and criticism (e.g. Edmonds and Evans 1991; Bender et al. 2000; Renfrew 2003; DeMarrias et al. 2004; Schofield 2006; Cochrane and Russell 2007; Dixon 2010; Bonaventura and Jones 2011), I do not focus on the relationships between archaeology and contemporary art in general terms (for this see Vilches 2007; Harrison and Schofield 2010: 105–19; Russell 2011; and, from a non-archaeological standpoint, Roelstraete 2009). In fact, this chapter explores a field that does not belong solely, or even primarily, to art—drawing.

I begin with a deceptively simple question: what is drawing? I then suggest how recent drawing scholarship has the potential to expand existing treatments of drawing within archaeology. The next four sections each explore a different aspect of drawing in relation to the work of a particular artist: 'Traces and marks' considers philosophies of the trace, and the 'betweenness' of presence and absence in drawing and archaeology. 'Gesture' considers how drawings convey meaning through gestural traces. 'Time, space, and becoming' examines how archaeological and artists' drawings inhabit time and space. Lastly, 'Line and ground' looks at the way drawing depends on relationality and the significance of this for recent theories of the political subject.

37.2 WHAT IS DRAWING?

In the last fifty years, drawing has become a radically 'expanded field' (de Zegher 2010; Dexter 2005; Garner 2008). In art, the twentieth century was the era in which the differences between drawing, painting, and sculpture became blurred, freeing line from its traditional relations to surface (de Zegher 2010: 68). Across disciplines, drawing embraced and was embraced by new technologies, playing an increasingly significant role in digital and virtual environments (Garner 2008; Petherbridge 2010). Contemporary drawing might include digital networks, sound, film and video, space and performance. As a result, definitions of drawing tend to be encompassing, looking to open up the field rather than shut it down.

One focus is on the making of marks and leaving of traces. Dexter, for example, defines drawing as 'a mark-making process used to produce a line-based composition' (2005: 5–6): 'Footprints in the snow, breath on the window, vapor trails of a plane across the sky, lines traced by a finger in the sand, all are drawing in and of the world' (2005: 5–6). Another focus is on drawing as movement, a 'kinaesthetic process of traction—attraction, extraction, pro-traction' (de Zegher 2010: 23): we might draw on, in, down, up, through, from and together and to. In an influential account of form-giving as 'movement, action…life', Paul Klee's *Pedagogical Sketchbook* (1960 [1925]) put the lines made by waterfalls, bird flight, and the bloodstream to work in drawing (Klee, cited in Fisher 2003: 218). Connecting the emphasis on mark-making with that on movement is a concern with gesture. Ingold links drawing to walking and talking: 'For whenever we walk or talk we gesture with our bodies, and insofar as these gestures leave traces or trails, on the ground or on some other surface, lines have been, or are being, drawn' (2011: 177). At its most elemental, these different treatments see drawing as concerning the unfolding relations among gestures, traces, and marks.

Definitions of drawing must acknowledge that, in English, drawing is both a verb ('draw-ing') and a noun ('a drawing'). This bivalence indicates one of drawing's most significant characteristics: drawing is both action and the traces of action, and this remains apparent when it is viewed (see Berger 2003: 105–18). Drawing 'forever describes its own making in its becoming' (Dexter 2005: 6) in lines which 'appear to write time' (Petherbridge 2010: 4). It contains the history of its own making as an 'internal, structural narrative, which enables reconstructive readings by viewers', and draws them into a 'potentially isomorphic inter-relationship with the effective processes of making' (Petherbridge 2010: 4). In other words, making sense of a drawing can involve re-enacting the gestures of its making. This writ-ing of time gives drawing an unfinished quality compared to other media (Newman 2003; Petherbridge 2010). Unlike painting and sculpture, drawing tends towards openness and incompletion. The drawing (noun) remains open to the possibilities of drawing (verb).

Attempts to define drawing risk shutting down its vitality, which stems from its continual 'becoming'. Petherbridge (2008, 2010) advances, not a definition, but an open-ended con-tinuum of 'betweenness' stretched between verb and noun, making and thinking, sketchy and finished. As a 'linear economy' of gesture, mark, and trace, drawing is 'performative act *and* idea;…sign, *and* symbol *and* signifier;…conceptual diagram as well as medium *and* process *and* technique' (Petherbridge 2010: 16, original emphasis). The 'betweenness' of drawing is perhaps its special strength, giving it the potential to undermine classic struc-tural divisions (see Newman 2003). Drawing is not just between verb and noun, but also between presence and absence, becoming and being, gesture and concept. Unfolding tem-porally, drawing lies in a state of perpetual becoming, between past and present.

37.3 DRAWING AND ARCHAEOLOGY: POTENTIAL FOR EXPANDING THE FIELD?

An expanded conception of drawing seems particularly appropriate to archaeology, which often deals with entities that blur the boundaries between conventional art categorizations (sculpture, painting, drawing, etc.) and so are already within the 'expanded field' (see Krauss 1979). The drawings archaeologists encounter in the field are rarely affairs of pencil and paper. They may be scratched, smeared, or impressed onto rock, earth, bone, or ceramic. They may be spray-painted, blown, applied, or ripped from a surface. They may, like Duchamp's *Sixteen Miles of String*, have left the surface completely, or may themselves create surfaces of woven, knotted, or drawn-out lines. The gestural marks and traces of plough-furrows, footprints, or fingers in the sand alluded to by drawing scholars (see Dexter 2005; Kovats 2007) are the meat and drink of archaeology. Yet, within archaeology, such phenomena are seldom considered *as drawing*. More often, drawing is discussed as a specific component of, say, rock art, ceramic analyses, or graffiti. This preference for a narrow, rather than expanded, conception of drawing makes it difficult for archaeologists both to see the relevance of much contemporary drawing practice and scholarship and engage productively with interdisciplinary drawing research (for a review of contemporary drawing research see Garner 2008).

Archaeology is also a discipline that draws within an 'expanded field'. The larger proportion of contemporary archaeological drawing involves the creation of mathematical vectors in digital environments, as in AutoCAD, GPS survey, and GIS. Seen from the viewpoint of drawing scholarship and history (e.g. Bermingham 2000), many of the gestures, traces, and marks created through activities such as excavation, surveying, and geophysics, would be understood as drawing. However, the assumption that drawing is only a matter of pencil (or Rotring), and paper (or drawing film), seems to cling. One consequence of this assumption is the belief that an increasing prominence of digital drawing spells the inevitable decline of 'drawing'. This denies the continuities between drawing on paper and other forms of drawing. In fact, drawing continues to thrive within archaeology, although much of it does not only take place on two-dimensional surfaces.

Within archaeology, concepts of drawing continue to be most prominently applied in those texts that chiefly concern 'pencil and paper' depictions. Archaeology's technical drawing traditions continue to develop, guided by successive pedagogical treatises and manuals (e.g. Piggott 1965; Hope Taylor 1966, 1967; Adkins and Adkins 1989; Hawker 2001). Alongside these texts are thought-provoking studies of specific types of drawing: for example, reconstruction drawing (e.g. Moser 1992; James 1997), finds illustration (e.g. Van Reybrouck 1998; Jones 2001), and field drawing (e.g. Bateman 2006; Carver 2010). This work focuses on how drawing constrains and enables the construction of disciplinary knowledge—on the performative role of drawing in creating archaeology as a discipline. With the influence of Science and Technology Studies (STS) (see Lynch and Woolgar 1988; Latour 1999) there has been a tendency to consider some drawing ('inscription') and drawings ('immutable mobiles') as steps within chains of scientific truth-making, rather than exploring their connections with artistic forms of making, despite the important role of art and art-history within STS literature (e.g. Latour and Weibel 2002). The expanded field of contemporary drawing suggests insights from drawing research and scholarship could be applied to a wider range of phenomena than is currently assumed.

37.4 TRACES AND MARKS

Drawing, like archaeology, is an art of traces. Brian Fay explores the absences of the drawn trace in relation to the absences of art historical and archaeological traces. Fay traces and re-presents the cracks, dust, and scratches that have accumulated over time on other works (such as Old Master paintings or silent film stock; see also Watkins, this volume; Noble, this volume). The traditional relationship between drawing and other media is reversed, so that drawing, usually understood as preceding a completed work, here follows the work's inevitable decline. Since parts of the paintings and film that Fay analyses gather the wear of history differently, the traces uncannily re-presence the original through the absences it has accumulated.

Philosophies of the trace recall drawing's mythological origins. Pliny reports an ancient story about the daughter of Butades the potter: on learning that her lover was going away she drew around his shadow, supplying drawing's creation myth. The myth emphasizes drawing's relation to absence, and thus its relation to the trace. The trace involves absence because it is indexical; that is, it carries with it something of the other of which it is a trace (on Peircian indexicality, see Ginzberg 1980; Pape 2008). However, drawing also shifts indexicality, allowing it to enter into relation with the sign. In the story of Butades's daughter, drawing emerges from two kinds of trace: the shadow and the daughter's tracing. The shadow is a trace that shows indexically the exact time and place of the lover's presence as an absence of light. However, when the daughter draws around the shadow she produces an index of another kind, functioning more like a sign or icon 'at once contextual and detachable' (Newman 2003: 94). Unlike the shadow that in its 'pure' indexicality draws attention to the space and time of its occurrence, the trace is capable of disturbing time and space: 'It has come from elsewhere, from a wholly other dimension, even an absolute exteriority' (Newman 2003: 94). The drawn trace is thus like the trace of archaeology. It is an index producing an absence that is also a presence, capable of disturbing the sphere of its manifestation.

What is the difference between a trace and a mark? Michael Newman suggests that it lies in the relation of each to presence and absence. With the trace, 'the other is required to be present...or...to have been present' (Newman 2003: 94). However, the mark emerges from the 'work of objectification' (Newman 2003: 94). It is marked, in short, by the absence of an absent other. What it bears witness to is the gesture and temporality of its own production. It is a trace, as it were of itself. Yet, both mark and trace speak of departure. Drawing's marks and traces re-enact desire and loss, producing both presence and absence simultaneously, a poignancy it shares with archaeology.

For his residency with art+archaeology Fay chose to work at Woodhenge, a place whose very name figures it as the 'absent other' to nearby Stonehenge. Woodhenge is marked, not by the presence of massive stones, but by the absences of long-disappeared prehistoric timber and stone settings whose locations are now marked by concrete posts, each colour-coded in institutional shades of gloss paint to signify their location on an archaeological plan. This concrete setting, built following archaeological excavation in the late 1920s, now seems itself like a monument to modernism, so that the site is both prehistoric remnant and ruin of a modernist archaeology. Figure 37.1 shows one of a series of drawings Fay made at Woodhenge, recording the gradual decay of paint encoding the concrete markers into the archaeological plan. In *Black Central Pillar* absence is dizzyingly multiplied (the absence of trace, crack, sign, code, marker, pit, and excavation site). Instead of a not-yet-present outside the work, absence constitutes the work.

Fay's art draws attention to the absences or 'blindnesses' of drawing; 'all the blind spots that, literally and figuratively, organize the scopic field and the scene of drawing' (Derrida 1990: 55). Drawing relates line and ground, producing an absence integral to itself. The

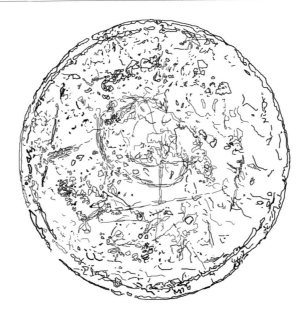

FIGURE 37.1 Brian Fay, *Black Central Pillar* (from the series *Pillar Drawings*, Woodhenge, 1927). Digital hand drawing on paper, 2007–10 (reproduced with permission from Brian Fay)

ground is contained as a kind of 'reserve' intrinsic to the line, 'perceptually present, but conceptually absent' (Bryson 2003: 151). When we look at a drawing, the individual traces and marks tend towards invisibility when the contours or outlines they compose are discerned. Likewise, the outline disappears at the point when the traces become visible (Derrida 1990: 53): 'At the instant when the point…moves forward upon making contact with the surface, the inscription of the inscribable is not seen' (Derrida 1990: 44).

Archaeology often figures the invisible as the 'not yet visible'; 'something whose spectacle of monumental ruins [calls] for reconstitution, regathering from memory, rememberment' (Derrida 1990: 52). However, following Merleau-Ponty, Derrida argues that the invisible is not simply another visible waiting to be discovered, but something intrinsic to consciousness itself: a place within the visible 'from which we cannot detach, ourselves and which we cannot objectify', which 'marks our attachment, or our adhesion, to the world' (Newman 2003: 98). Archaeology actively generates absences at the same time as it makes things present, partly through drawing—an art of traces constituted by, and proliferating, absence (see also Fowles and Heupel, this volume).

37.5 GESTURE

Historically, drawing and gesture have been interpreted together. In Renaissance Italy, drawing was understood as 'a means of giving concrete body to the repertoire of gesture envisaged in the mind' (Newman 2003: 103). By the eighteenth century the gestures of drawing were increasingly allied to a romantic view of the individual, expressing the 'inner being' of the artist (Newman 2003: 103). Modernity's break with this romantic ideal emerged from industrialization and psychoanalytic explorations of the unconscious, which rendered gesture compulsive and automatic. Neither gesture nor drawing can any longer be seen as communicating a unified inner subjectivity. In fact, much contemporary drawing is not best seen as communicating any exterior 'meaning'. If it refers to anything it is to 'its own exhibition as gesture' (Newman 2003: 104).

Gesture is sometimes seen as a pre-verbal form of communication, an elemental and inferior kind of speech. In the same way, drawing is sometimes seen as an evolutionary precursor to writing, an elemental and inferior form of visual writing. According to this view, gesture is to speech as drawing is to writing. Both are archaic and superannuated, made redundant by language, which supposedly communicates meaning more effectively. Behind this conception is the assumption that the primary function of gesture and drawing is to communicate as a language. This is an assumption with which archaeologists will be familiar, for we have long told ourselves that the primary function of archaeological drawing is efficient communication. One of the principal achievements of twentieth-century archaeology, according to Piggott, was the establishment of an 'agreed code of conventions' in drawing, a 'pictorial language' used to construct 'technical cryptograms' or 'ciphers' that must be made according to 'rules carefully observed by both transmitter and recipient' (1965: 165). Archaeological drawing created a supposedly universal scientific language without borders, with which all archaeologists should be conversant (Hope Taylor 1967). According to Hope Taylor (1966), drawing in archaeology was a matter of 'ends and means', the means for 'transmitting', as economically and elegantly as possible, a particular 'mental construct'.

Derrida (1990) raises the question of how drawing communicates when it tends towards invisibility. The individual marks that make up drawing become difficult to see once the subject is apparent. The mark becomes the line, the line becomes the contour, the contour becomes the image, and the image becomes the sign: a process of becoming that can always be reversed. The metaphor of code or language is not quite right here, since drawing is not always meaningful in this way. In Saussurean semiotics, the sign comprised an abstract relation between signifier and signified without continuity between the signifying and the non-signifying. However, in the drawn trace, there is the potential for occupying 'inbetweenness' between sign and non-sign. Traces and marks can occupy a status 'not yet sign, not yet writing' (Newman 2003: 100). There is a continuum, rather than an unbridgeable discontinuity between sign and non-sign (see Petherbridge 2010). Even the most conventional, technically produced, drawing offers something more than a code or language. This is not to say that drawing does not 'communicate', but that it does not only communicate like language.

If, as argued above, the marks of drawing can be seen as traces of gesture, then something of how drawing communicates might belong with gesture. Although gesture is commonly seen as pre-verbal communication, a language that failed, it is possible to see it otherwise. For Agamben, the gesture has 'precisely nothing to say' (2000: 58) because 'it is essentially always a gesture of not being able to figure something out in language' (2000: 56). What gesture communicates is communication itself along with its limits. Gesture is the 'exhibition of a mediality…the process of making a means visible as such' (2000: 57). The role of gesture is not to act as a means for the ends of transmitting a message, but simply to show up the '"being-in-a-medium" of human beings' (2000: 57). This is how we might interpret those contemporary drawings that seem to refer, principally, to their own exhibition as gesture. They are pure means, without any transcendence, pure gesturality: not drawing as the means to ends, but drawing without ends.

Rebecca Davies's series *An Exploration of Space and Time* (Figure 37.2) is a study of gesture connecting the means of drawing and the means of excavation. In *An Exploration*...Davies appropriates the conventions of archaeological planning to map the gestures of excavation. However, Figure 37.2 is not a straight excavation plan. It alludes to the metrics of archaeological recording with its intersecting grid lines and 'north arrow' but does not supply any actual means of attaching this drawing to the wider totality of site plans and excavation measurements. The drawing instead stages the gestures of excavation and drawing together, exhibiting them as gestures, connecting two kinds of means. When we follow the traces of a drawing with our eyes, we 're-enact' her gestures and the gestures of the excavators in the same movement. Davies encourages us to ask why the gestures of excavation are not, themselves, drawing. Excavation produces a prepared surface, or ground, on which the excavator draws, with trowel as much as pencil. The gestural traces of excavation are erasures, just as many other forms of drawing are made up of erasures. The stroke of drawing is paralleled by the stroke of the trowel.

The gestural trace of drawing creates a corporeal link between the drawer and the drawn. In this way, the drawer can speak of losing herself in the drawn, of *becoming* the drawn (Berger 2003: 119–46). We cannot only consider archaeological drawing as a process of distancing, as the exercise of an objectifying gaze. In the field, drawing follows the dynamics through which deposits came about—the way this ditch was dug, this fill accumulated. These dynamics, whether drawn with pencil, trowel, or any other apparatus, are dramatically re-enacted in the drawing (McFadyen 2011). There is a corporeal link between the processes which form materials and the actions of archaeologists who excavate them; between the actions of excavation and those of drawing; between those actions and viewing the drawing. The gestural trace is performed and re-performed across time.

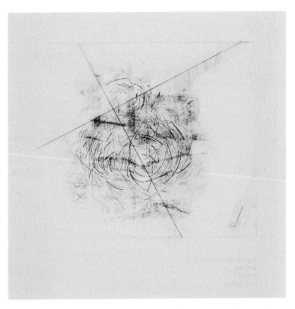

FIGURE 37.2 Rebecca Davies, *An Exploration of Time and Space No. 3* (detail). Etching on paper, 2008 (reproduced with permission from Rebecca Davies)

To see drawing as a visual language is to prioritize only the 'ends' of drawing, the 'message' it communicates. It is very often to ignore the 'means' of drawing itself. Even within the conventions of excavation plans and sections, drawn marks are routinely improvised as extemporary responses to particular situations (McFadyen 2011). Yet the marks and traces that compose archaeological drawings are rarely looked at in detail. Archaeological accounts of archaeological drawings still privilege the ends (disciplinary knowledge) over the means (drawing). The archaeology of archaeology's drawing has barely begun.

37.6 TIME, SPACE, AND BECOMING

Julia Midgley is an artist who works 'like an Official War Artist' (Midgley 2010) reporting events over specific time periods. During her residencies with art+archaeology, Midgley documented the movements of people, objects, and places on an excavation project, chronicling their unfolding as materials moved from excavation to laboratory and museum. Midgley's unique position meant that she was, in fact, the only person to witness this unfolding in many of its locations, since excavators would not, for example, follow samples to the radiocarbon laboratory, or artefacts to the illustrator's desk. Midgley's remarkable skill is to trace, in a moment, the motion of a scene. I have seen her capture exactly the outlines of surveyor and staff in the momentary pause they make while each reading is taken. In *Trench 22* (Figure 37.3), movements are superimposed, so that, for example, the Site Director appears numerous times as he moves about the site, pausing to chat with the excavators.

FIGURE 37.3 Julia Midgley, *Trench 22*. Pencil and watercolour, 2009 (reproduced with permission from Julia Midgley)

As archaeologists do, Midgley uses drawing to organize time-space. Drawing is both action and the traces of action, leaving lines that seem to write time: drawing presents the image 'together with the whole history of its becoming-image' (Bryson 2003: 150). The liquid lines of Midgley's drawings, the way her drawing pursues the unfolding moment, suggest that drawing is linked to 'becoming'. Drawing, Bryson argues, is different to painting, where the logic of composition relates the whole space to the frame. In drawing 'the law of the all-over—the set of pressures deriving from the four sides of the surface—may be observed, or not' (2003: 151, original emphasis). Line can draw its nature and shape with reference only to the local area (as when drawings coexist on the same surface). The 'ongoing present time of the drawn line can unfold in its own specific milieu, the precise area of space/time within which the lines are successively drawn' (Bryson 2003: 151). From the perpetual 'becoming' of drawing emerges drawing's logic of 'localized space and time'.

In Ingold's work (2007, 2011), the 'becoming' of drawing inspires critical perspectives on space and time. According to Ingold, the line of modernity, of maps and graphs, occupies space by drawing lines between survey points—by joining up the dots: 'What we see is no longer the trace of a gesture but an assembly of point-to-point connectors' (Ingold 2007: 75). To illustrate this process, Ingold (2007: 84–90) uses Goodwin's (1994) study of archaeological section-drawing, a form of drawing that is composed of measurements, transposed onto graph paper, which archaeologists join up in a process that allows localized space and time to be upwardly integrated into a totalizing, metrically ordered, space—a space 'of occupation, not habitation' (Ingold 2007: 89). In Ingold's more recent work this process appears like a re-institution of Bryson's 'law of the all-over' into both drawing and disciplinary ways of knowing (2011: 220–1).

Midgley's appropriation of the apparatus of archaeological field drawing—her use of hard pencils, drawing boards, and graph paper—creates a parallel between her practice and archaeological drawing. Midgley deliberately encourages the viewer to explore how her drawing works with space and time alongside archaeological drawing. From the outset it is apparent that, just as Midgley's practice involves measurement in some sense, so the gestural trace has not been completely erased from archaeological drawing. In fact, it is unusual for archaeological drawing to 'join the dots' between measurements (cf. Goodwin 1994). The experienced draughtsperson will, more often, sketch in a few measurements to 'get her eye in' and then extemporize around these, occasionally checking as she goes. This is not dissimilar from Midgley's practice, which involves careful observations that 'measure' the scene and guide the drawing. Drawing can be a discipline, 'a set of methods and procedures, an apparatus' (Bryson 2003: 152). It is rarely either pure gesturality, or pure measurement.

There is a further connection between Midgley's project and archaeology: the question of archive. The role of war artist is historically linked to that of archaeological draughtsperson (see Gough 1995; Bermingham 2000)—both deploy notions of witnessing and documentation. Excavation drawing both produces an archive, and is produced by the technical structure of archiving (see Derrida 1995: 17–18; McFadyen 2011). The temporal condensation of Midgley's drawings, the way they localize time-space within a particular scene, indexes each of the moments she draws to the excavation landscape at that point. Because the landscapes of excavation change, her 'archive' can be linked to the archive of each excavation she chronicles. Midgley's practice thus works with archive as an active concept, using the way archaeological archives are enacted to perform an alternative archiving within the interstices of the excavation. The excavation drawings and Midgley's drawings both inhabit 'the recursive time of re-reading' that Taussig attributes to drawings in fieldwork notebooks (Taussig 2011: 53). They flow with time, yet also arrest it.

37.7 LINE AND GROUND

Varvara Shavrova is a Russian-born landscape artist now based in China. In 2004 and 2005 she undertook two art+archaeology residencies on excavations at Shovel Down, Dartmoor. During this time she made numerous drawings of different kinds, from sketchbooks to huge graphite (2m × 0.75m) drawings based on archaeological field plans. She also worked with the site team to create participatory works, establishing a daily 'Drawing Hour' in which archaeologists and visitors produced uncensored freehand drawings. In 2005, Shavrova worked with archaeologist Lorraine Seymour and photographer Chris Chippendale to produce the *Interferences* series (Nos. 1–5). *Interferences* were created in the trenches using only materials available on site, such as string, nails, tape, and washing line (see Figure 37.4).

Figure 37.4 recalls Duchamp's *Sixteen Miles of String*; both are installation-drawings drawn out of twine. However, in *Interferences No. 3* the line has not left the ground, or, if it has, it has returned to it. Here, lines have colonized the ground, in ways that bring to mind Ingold's discussion of archaeological drawing as point-to-point connectors, as a mode of occupation (2007: 75). Whereas *Sixteen Miles of String* separates line from ground in a visual game involving looking at either line or background but not both at the same time, here line redefines the ground, stretching over it like a digital wire frame draped over the trench. The ground here is part of the drawing, so that line and ground cannot be appreciated apart from each other. We are returned again to the constitutive role of what I have earlier discussed

FIGURE 37.4 Varvara Shavrova, *Interferences No. 3*. String, nails, excavation trench, 2005 (reproduced with permission from Varvara Shavrova)

as 'absence', except that, in this case, part of what is absent and present in the line—the background—cannot be seen as blank space.

The background, as Benjamin observed, 'is indispensable for the meaning of the drawing, so that two lines can be related to each other only through the background' (1996 [1917]: 83). The graphic line confers an identity on the background, but the background also confers an identity on the line. In recent drawing, as de Zegher (2010) shows, the surface is not necessarily understood as the precondition of the drawing. Instead, line and ground are generative of each other so that the background is drawn as much as the line is: 'the ground has become as important as the line, to the point where there is a confluence, the line becoming ground and the ground becoming line' (de Zegher 2010: 119). Drawings like *Interferences No. 3* stress the interdependency of line and ground, the way each exist in reciprocal relation—in between the lines.

In drawing, 'the world is symbolized by the background, pages, screen or wall' (Badiou 2006: 42). It is the background, as much as the line, which might be seen as 'constitut[ing] our being and becoming, our relation to each other' (de Zegher 2010: 119). Drawing on, in, and from the background, the line redefines it as an open space, a space of possibility. For Badiou, the weakness of drawing—its relationality, its betweenness—offers a model for an alternative form of political subjectivity, one based on reciprocity and interdependency. The 'very essence of drawing', according to Badiou, is a 'movable reciprocity' between being and becoming, existence and inexistence:

> The question of drawing is very different from the question in Hamlet. It is not 'to be or not to be', it is 'to be *and* not to be'. And that is the reason for the fundamental fragility of drawing: not a clear alternative, to be or not to be, but an obscure and paradoxical conjunction, to be *and* not to be. (2006: 42)

Drawing's fragility offers a model for an alternative form of political subjectivity. Drawing institutes a new world 'not by the strength of means, like images, painting, colors, and so on, but by the minimalism of some marks and lines, very close to the inexistence of any place' (2006: 44). Likewise, in human relations, 'we have to find a form of action where the political existence of everybody is not separated from its being...Doing so we become a new subject. Not an individual, but part of a new subject' (2006: 44). According to this viewpoint, the key to a new world is the trick of drawing on the between.

37.8 CONCLUSION

Archaeology is like drawing. Both are arts of the trace, belonging simultaneously to past, present, and future. Drawing is made up of 'betweennesses'. It is both verb and noun, action and the traces of action, presence and absence. It is a reflexive medium that includes and bears witness to its own becoming in the way it writes time. Drawing is also a performative medium. The 'becoming' of drawing remains evident in the gestural traces it presents. Drawing can make the traces of its 'becoming' available through a process of re-enactment that can be performed in different ways through different viewings. Embracing reflexivity and performativity, drawing exhibits those qualities that are often central to archaeologies of the contemporary world (Harrison and Schofield 2010; Harrison 2011). It is these aspects that have inspired recent calls for a 'graphic anthropology' (Ingold 2011). However, archaeology is not only *like* drawing. The practice of archaeology, very often, *is* drawing. It seems anachronistic, and is certainly out of step with developments across disciplines, to assume that drawing is primarily a matter of pencil and paper. New technologies, and new uses, continue to transform drawing. Expanded understandings of what drawing *is* might allow archaeology to approach its own practices differently, and are appropriate to a discipline that, in the materials it studies, already encounters drawing within an 'expanded field'.

I have deliberately steered clear of making any prescriptions concerning the nature of the continually shifting encounter between archaeology and contemporary art. This is, I feel, a subject so broad as to be barely susceptible to generalization. However, among the most interesting recent archaeologies of the contemporary world are those that use archaeological approaches to investigate contemporary art (e.g. Dixon 2010; Oliver and Neal 2010 ; Bonaventura and Jones 2011). Many varieties of contemporary drawing would be highly amenable to a more systematic kind of analysis than I have applied here. What would it mean to 'excavate' the relations among gestures, traces, and marks? To analyse their 'stratigraphy'? Or to produce comparative studies of different drawings? Archaeology makes an exciting and distinctive contribution to interdisciplinary drawing research. In this way it helps explore one of the most elemental and pervasive phenomena of material life.

ACKNOWLEDGEMENTS

Art+archaeology was made possible by The Caroline Humby-Teck Trust. My co-director Leo Duff contributed enormously to its development and many successes. I would like to thank all the art+archaeology artists—Mark Anstee, Sian Bowen, Simon Callery, Chris Chippendale, Rebecca Davies, Leo Duff, Brian Fay, Janet Hodgson, Pil and Galia Kollectiv, Nadine Patterson, Julia Midgley, Simon Mills, Varvara Shavrova, and Gail Wight—for enriching my experience of archaeology and changing my life. Many thanks also to the Shovel Down Project and the Stonehenge Riverside Project for working alongside the artists and facilitating their research. Lesley McFadyen generously allowed me to read work that had not been published at the time this chapter was writen. Angela Piccini, Martyn Barber, Rebecca Davies, Brian Fay, and Julia Midgley read the text and offered encouragement. They are not to blame for its faults.

REFERENCES

Adkins, Lesley and Adkins, Roy. 1989. *Archaeological Illustration*. Cambridge Manuals in Archaeology. Cambridge: Cambridge University Press.

Agamben, Giorgio. 2000. *Means Without End: Notes on Politics*, tr. V. Binetti and C. Casarimo. Minneapolis: University of Minnesota Press.

Badiou, Alain. 2006. Drawing. *Lacanian Ink* 28: 42–8.

Bateman, Jon. 2006. Pictures, Ideas and Things: The Production and Currency of Archaeological images. In *Ethnographies of Archaeological Practice: Cultural Encounters, Material Transformations*, ed. Matt Edgeworth, pp. 68–81. Walnut Creek, CA: Altamira Press.

Bender, Barbara, Hamilton, Sue, and Tilley, Chris. 2000. Art and the Re-presentation of the Past. *Journal of the Royal Anthropological Institute* 6(1): 35–63.

Benjamin, Walter. 1996 [1917]. Painting and the Graphic Arts. In *Walter Benjamin: Selected Writings Volume 1, 1913–1926*, ed. Marcus Bullock and Michael Jennings, pp. 82–4. Cambridge, MA: Harvard University Press.

Berger, John. 2003. *Berger on Drawing*. Cork: Occasional Press.

Bermingham, Ann. 2000. *Learning to Draw: Studies in the Cultural History of a Polite and Useful Art*. New Haven and London: Yale University Press.

Bonaventura, Paul and Jones, Andrew (eds.). 2011. *Sculpture and Archaeology*. Farnham: Ashgate.

Bryson, Norman. 2003. A Walk for a Walk's Sake. In *The Stage of Drawing: Gesture and Act. Selected from the Tate Collection*, ed.Catherine de Zegher, pp. 149–58. New York: Tate Publishing and The Drawing Centre.

Carver, Geoff. 2010. Doku-porn: Visualizing Stratigraphy. In *Unquiet Pasts: Risk Society, Lived Cultural Heritage, Re-designing Reflexivity*, ed. Stephanie Koerner and Ian Russell, pp. 109–22. Farnham: Ashgate.

Cochrane, Andy and Russell, Ian. 2007. Visualizing Archaeology: A Manifesto. *Cambridge Archaeological Journal* 17(1): 3–19.

de Zegher, Catherine. 2010. A Century Under the Sign of Line: Drawing and its Extension (1910–2010). In *On Line: Drawing Through the Twentieth Century*, ed. Cornelia Butler and Catherine de Zegher, pp. 121–4. New York: Museum of Modern Art (MoMA.

Demarrias, Elizabeth, Gosden, Chris, and Renfrew, Colin (eds.). 2004. *Rethinking Materiality: The Engagement of Mind with the Material World*. Cambridge: McDonald Institute Monograph Series.

Derrida, Jacques. 1990. *Memoirs of the Blind: The Self-Portrait and Other Ruins*. Chicago and London: University of Chicago Press.

—— 1995. Archive Fever: A Freudian Impression. *Diacritics* 25(2): 9–63.

Dexter, Emma. 2005. *Vitamin D: New Perspectives in Drawing*. London and New York: Phaidon Press.

Dixon, James. 2010. Public Art and Contemporary Archaeology in the Context of Urban Regeneration: Ongoing Change in Central Bristol, 1940–2010. Ph.D. Thesis, University of Bristol, Bristol.

Duff, Leo and Sawdon, Phil. 2008. *Drawing: The Purpose*. Bristol: Intellect.

Edmonds, Mark and Evans, Chris (eds.). 1991. *Excavating the Present: An Art Exhibition of New Work by Twelve Artists*. Cambridge: Kettle's Yard Gallery.

Fisher, Joan. 2003. On Drawing. In *The Stage of Drawing: Gesture and Act. Selected from the Tate Collection*, ed. Catherine De Zegher, pp. 217–26. New York: Tate Publishing and The Drawing Centre.

Garner, Steve (ed.). 2008. *Writing on Drawing: Essays on Drawing Practice and Research*. Bristol: Intellect.

Ginzberg, Carlo. 1980. Morelli, Freud and Sherlock Holmes: Clues and Scientific Method. *History Workshop* 9: 5–36.

Goodwin, Charles. 1994. Professional Vision. *American Anthropologist* 96(3): 606–33.

Gough, Paul. 1995. 'Tales from the Bushy-Topped Tree': A Brief Survey of Military Sketching. *Imperial War Museum Review* 10: 62–73.

Harrison, Rodney. 2011. Surface Assemblages: Towards an Archaeology *in* and *of* the Present. *Archaeological Dialogues* 18(2): 141–61.

Harrison, Rodney and Schofield, John. 2010. *After Modernity: Archaeological Approaches to the Contemporary Past*. Oxford: Oxford University Press.

Hawker, Jacqueline. 2001. *A Manual of Archaeological Field Drawing*. Hertford: RESCUE.

Hope Taylor, Brian. 1966. Archaeological Draughtsmanship: Principles and Practice. Part II: Ends and Means. *Antiquity* 41(158): 107–13.

—— 1967. Archaeological Draughtsmanship: Principles and Practice. Part III: Lines of Communication. *Antiquity* 41(163): 181–9.

Ingold, Tim. 2007. *Lines: A Brief History*. London and New York: Routledge.

—— 2011. *Being Alive: Essays on Movement, Knowledge and Description*. London and New York: Routledge.

—— (ed.). 2012. *Redrawing Anthropology: Materials, Movements, Lines*. London: Ashgate.

James, Simon. 1997. Drawing Inferences: Visual Reconstructions in Theory and Practice. In *The Cultural Life of Images: Visual Representation in Archaeology*, ed. Brian Molyneaux, pp. 22–48. London: Routledge.

Jones, Andrew. 2001. Drawn from Memory: The Archaeology of Aesthetics and the Aesthetics of Archaeology in Earlier Bronze Age Britain and the Present. *World Archaeology* 33(2): 334–56.

Kovats, Tina (ed.). 2007. *The Drawing Book: A Survey of Drawing—The Primary Means of Expression*. London: Black Dog Publishing.

Krauss, Rosalind. 1979. Sculpture in the Expanded Field. *October* 8 (Spring): 30–44.

Latour, Bruno. 1999. *Pandora's Hope: Essays on the Reality of Science Studies*. Cambridge, MA: Harvard University Press.

—— and Weibel, Peter (eds.). 2002. *Iconoclash: Beyond the Image Wars in Science, Religion and Art*. Karlsruhe: Zentrum für Kunst und Medientecknologie.

Lynch, Michael and Woolgar, Steve (eds.). 1988. Representation in Scientific Practice. *Human Studies* 11(2/3): 99–364.

McFadyen, Lesley. 2011. Practice Drawing Writing Object. In *Redrawing Anthropology: Materials, Movements, Lines*, ed. Tim Ingold, pp. 33–44. Farnham: Ashgate.

Midgley, Julia. 2010. Drawing Lives: Reportage at Work. *Material Thinking* 4: 1–19.

Moser, Stephanie. 1992. The Visual Language of Archaeology: A Case Study of the Neanderthals. *Antiquity* 66(253): 831–44.

Newman, Michael. 2003. The Marks, Traces and Gestures of Drawing. In *The Stage of Drawing: Gesture and Act. Selected from the Tate Collection*, ed. Catherine de Zegher, pp. 93–111. New York: Tate Publishing and The Drawing Centre.

Oliver, Jeff and Neal, Tim. 2010. *Wild Signs: Graffiti in Archaeology and History*. Studies in Contemporary and Historical Archaeology 6. BAR International Series 2074. Oxford: Archaeopress.

Pape, Helmut. 2008. Searching for Traces: How to Connect the Sciences and Humanities by a Peircean Theory of Indexicality. *Transactions of the Charles S. Peirce Society* 44(1): 1–25.

Petherbridge, Deanna. 2008. Nailing the Liminal: The Difficulties of Defining Drawing. In *Writing on Drawing: Essays on Drawing Practice and Research*, ed. Steve Garner, pp. 27–42. Bristol: Intellect.

—— 2010. *The Primacy of Drawing: Histories and Theories of Practice*. New Haven and London: Yale University Press.

Piggott, Stuart. 1965. Archaeological Draughtsmanship: Principles and Practice. Part I: Principles and Retrospect. *Antiquity* 39(115): 165–76.

Renfrew, Colin. 2003. *Figuring it Out: What Are We? Where Do We Come From? The Parallel Visions of Artists and Archaeologists*. London: Thames and Hudson.

Roelstraete, Dieter. 2009. The Way of the Shovel: On the Archaeological Imaginary in Art. *E-flux* 4(3). Available at: <http://www.e-flux.com/journal/the-way-of-the-shovel-on-the-archeological-imaginary-in-art/> (accessed 8 January 2013).

Russell, Ian. 2011. Art and Archaeology: A Modern Allegory. *Archaeological Dialogues* 18(2): 172–6.

Schofield, John. 2006. *Constructing Place: When Artists and Archaeologists Meet*. London: Proboscis.

Taussig, Michael. 2011. *I Swear I Saw This: Drawings in Fieldwork Notebooks, Namely, My Own*. Chicago and London: University of Chicago Press.

Van Reybrouck, David. 1998. Imaging and Imagining the Neanderthal: The Role of Technical Drawings in Archaeology. *Antiquity* 72: 56–64.

Vick, John. 2008. A New Look: Marcel Duchamp, his Twine, and the 1942 First Papers in Surrealism Exhibition. *Toutfait.com: The Marcel Duchamp Studies Online Journal*. Available at: <http://www.toutfait.com> (accessed 1 June 2012).

Vilches, Flora. 2007. The Art of Archaeology: Mark Dion and his Dig Projects. *Journal of Social Archaeology* 7(2): 199–223.

....

CHAPTER 38

TWO RIOTS: THE IMPORTANCE OF CIVIL UNREST IN CONTEMPORARY ARCHAEOLOGY

....

JAMES R. DIXON

38.1 INTRODUCTION: RIOTS

....

THIS chapter is concerned with riots, that is to say with moments of unorganized violent disorder. Usually in archaeology we look to normative behaviours as the main indicators of what a society is like. Here, it is argued that more attention ought to be paid to those moments of rupture often reported as 'riot'. Much contemporary archaeology has concerned itself with 'othering' those things of the present and recent past with which we assume familiarity: graffiti, homelessness, personal effects, sexuality, abandonment, transport, leisure, mass production…(see Buchli and Lucas 2001: 9; Harrison and Schofield 2010: 1; Zimmerman, this volume). But, as contemporary archaeologists, we should not necessarily always be looking to create distance between ourselves as archaeologists and our own lives when proximity, intimacy, and individuality are among the things that contemporary archaeology might have unique access to among other, more traditional archaeologies (see Graves-Brown 2011). Here, I will address this potential by looking at riots as an existing act of both 'othering' and distancing and looking to what we can learn through familiarizing ourselves with the phenomenon (Jackson 1987b; Strathern 1987). Riots are (generally) short, unplanned episodes of violence into which all kinds of people can be drawn in relation to all sorts of situation. Rather than simply taking riots as 'sources' contributing to our understanding of the nature of whatever the rioters might have been for or against, we might look to the riot as a particular moment in which entire synchronic and diachronic slices of the world can be viewed at once, for a limited time (see Badcock and Johnson, this volume; Piccini, this volume; and White, this volume), and in a very particular way.

Of course we can also usefully look to understand riots as single events, unique actions, or even as durations, without recourse to the wider contexts that lead to and stem from them, as is the case with any event in the contemporary archaeological lens. However, I wish here to demonstrate the potential for contemporary archaeologists to consider the active revelation of the time and space external to an event through the course of the event itself. The way in which riots reveal in a moment a plethora of wider issues and processes is not dissimilar to the geological concept of the melange, a phenomenon whereby sheering forces mix rock in such a way that an entire history of geological formation may be visible in a single small area. The riot shows us most clearly the social melange, as it is only when violent disorder is brought into contact with seeming non-violent harmony that we are truly able to appreciate the total range of a social situation, through the actions themselves and the histories, futures, nears and fars enrolled in and implicated by them.

By their nature, riots could be considered part of the archaeology of protest (see e.g. Schofield 2009: 87–98; Badcock and Johnston, this volume) or even conflict or battlefield archaeology (see again Schofield 2009; Moshenska, this volume). I will, however, draw a distinction here. Whereas protests and wars tend to be lengthy and planned with stated aims, riots are short, largely unplanned on the part of participants and without structured aims. In particular, it is the short duration of riots which is of interest here, as we see a great deal of issues revealed by a very short period of violence, durations not usually included in archaeological analysis. We might also draw a distinction between riots and war (although not necessarily protest) where the former involves an element of choice, of conscious engagement, whereas a war waged by a state removes, to a point, the choice of the individual to engage and routinely subsumes non-combatant innocents into its horrors. Riots are, of course, all different and have different longer-term causes and implications in different places at different times (see Clement 2007; Jeffrey and Jackson 2012; Stenson 2012). Here, I wish to isolate and discuss simply the periods of violence within which wider contexts are revealed and acted upon.

Two riots in particular will be discussed here, one in Tallinn, Estonia, in April 2007 and another in Bristol, England, in April 2011. Through an archaeological perspective on these two riots, we can see the worth of bringing consideration of riots and civil unrest closer to the centre of contemporary urban archaeology to understand, in action, the mutual constitution of short durations of action and longer-term contexts. Alongside the general aim of contemporary archaeology to be multi-disciplinary in its work, consideration of these events will also look at how two artists have been involved with these riots. One, Kristina Norman, has produced a body of work looking to the afterlives of the reasons for civil unrest and how they can be elucidated through creating certain kinds of material engagement. The second, Laura Oldfield Ford, works to uncover the material conditions of daily life in the contemporary city, in particular producing work bringing observations, found texts and images together to represent the potential for future discord. My recent work in contemporary archaeology has developed entirely alongside engagements with artists. My position on the relationship between the two disciples is, broadly, that archaeology needs to develop more nuanced levels of art criticism than might be evident in current work in the area (see Renfrew 2003; Harrison and Schofield 2010: 105–19) if it is to engage with art beyond highlighting similarities between its practices and those of the archaeologist. However, here, I will use these two artists' work differently, as my more immediate subject is the artist's own perceptions of the material conditions of the riots I will discuss. In both cases I was aware of the works before I was knowledgeable about the riot events (in Bristol, the Oldfield Ford exhibition pre-dated the riot by some weeks) and this conditioned how I think about them.

38.2 PERSPECTIVE

The perspectives on both archaeology and on my subject matter that I will use here are derived from a lengthy period (2006–11) of studying the effects of a single shopping centre development on central Bristol. I undertook this work as an archaeologist, but I studied the effects of the development through the lens of public art, indeed I undertook the research in the Creative Arts department of the University of the West of England. This research looked in particular at the micro-political networks enacted through artistic and other interventions into the contemporary landscape, within the context of an understanding of that contemporary landscape developed through my own archaeological analysis of it. Thus, we might approach a public realm sculpture not simply as a finite object that signifies, for instance, a multi-national developer's disregard for existing communities, but as the fulcrum of a set of active processes, enrolments, and implications that spread far beyond the piece itself. Perhaps the most important belief I bring from this period of study is that archaeology has a particular role to play in understanding contemporary events as they are happening: history-being-made. It also has a particular unifying approach to multiple timescales, landscapes, and the relationship between people and things that can be used to help people understand, for better or worse, the places in which they live.

There are numerous methodologies that we might employ to elucidate the wider contexts revealed by a riot action. The analysis presented takes some inspiration from Bruno Latour's work on technical networks (e.g. Latour 1996). However, Latour's actor-network-theory (ANT) can be rather limited as an interpretive tool, so I recast it here as a practical methodology, particularly useful for uncovering and describing the links between seemingly disparate things, although of course we must 'do archaeology' at either end of any link we uncover. I also draw inspiration from Jacques Rancière's discussion of 'horizontal distribution' (Rancière 2004), the idea of placing more importance on combinations of possibilities (in ANT, 'emergent properties'), than on oppositions between objects and their meanings. Even when we introduce temporal dynamism into this analysis, for instance through the work on enrolment and implication in technical systems by Grint and Woolgar (1997) or Mark Hutchinson's 'four stages of public art' (2002), we avoid the epistemic fallacy inherent in thinking of things as predominantly produced through discourse, and the ontic fallacy of reducing myriad contexts to their physical manifestations (Hutchby 2001; Hutchinson 2002: 430).

Of course, it is desirable to add further degrees of complexity to such non-hierarchical network analyses. If we are to properly understand the nuances of the constant negotiation of different, sometimes disparate, enrolments and implications during the course of a riot, it is vital that we look to the concept of ecology as a framework within which to find and describe the things that matter to our analyses. Pertinently, for the Bristol example at least, some of the best work in this area has come from geographers Sarah Whatmore and Steve Hinchcliff. Whatmore did her early research work on the allotments and community gardens at St Werburghs, Bristol, close to Stokes Croft/Cheltenham Road (Whatmore and Hinchcliffe 2010). We can also look to the mutually constitutive nature of people and environments in times of civil unrest to further enlighten or complicate the relationship between people and things or people and other people (Clement 2007, 2012; Till 2012).

There are, of course, different kinds of politics at play in situations like the two riots described here, from an individual decision to protest, to unplanned group action, to international relations. As has been described above, these different scales and types of phenomenon all exist at the same time in the course of a riot and are of equal importance and influence. How then to approach the multiplicity of political perspectives and actions at play? Perhaps the best place to start is with Chantal Mouffe and her call for greater consideration of the nature of agonistic politics, the politics of active opposition. Mouffe sees the liberal notion of a 'middle-ground' of compromise between opposing positions as unsatisfactory, preferring an actively contested space between strongly held positions (Mouffe 2005). This perspective, as well as working as a good analogy for riot actions themselves, is important for the different role it affords objects and places, those subjects of archaeological analysis, as rather than representing compromises and being effectively shared, they can become actively contested and bear multiple meanings. The implications for things of a politics of this kind bears some resemblance to Sartrean notions of existential authenticity, wherein people and things are the entirety of how they are perceived, rather than being one thing or the other (Storm Heter 2006). Instead of feeling Rocquetin's nausea, a danger when allowing infinite possible meanings into the archaeological equation, we might instead embrace the freedom of analysis that comes from allowing objects multiple identities (Sartre 1965).

38.3 Two Riots

This section will focus on the two riots that form the central case studies of this chapter. A variety of sources have been used and the methods of gathering the information presented here are by no means consistent between the two events. I have learned about the riots in Tallinn retrospectively, through a combination of reading, interview, and site visits. The area in which the Bristol riot took place I know as a local resident and the information on the riot presented here is drawn from a combination of Twitter streams, news reports, and blog entries. I consider these reliable, at least insofar as they accurately demonstrate the complexity of the local politics of the area as I understand it. There is also increasing understanding of such new media outlets as a democratizing force, working directly against the inferential structures whereby mainstream news outlets reporting of events (even of the possibility of future events) is often conditioned by the nature of police briefings (Greer and McLaughlin 2010: 1041). It may need to be made clear that this chapter is concerned with the archaeological implications of studying riots, rather than with the politics of the events themselves. I was not aware of the riots in Tallinn until I came across Kristina Norman's work in the Kiasma contemporary art gallery in Helsinki in January 2011. I have a somewhat closer connection to the Bristol riot, having studied the area in which it took place on and off for five years beforehand and lived two streets away from the centre of the riot until just a few months before it took place (see Dixon 2009). However, I attempt, as far as is possible, to write here as a dispassionate archaeologist and this chapter is concerned only with the observable material conditions of both riots; for clarity of analysis, political positioning will be limited to those statements explicitly made by participants in the events.

38.3.1 The Bronze Night (Estonian: Pronksiöö)

The Bronze Night(s), also known as the 'April Unrest' occurred in Tallinn, Estonia, on 26–30 April 2007, following the relocation of a Soviet war memorial in the city and the exhumation of a number of Russian soldiers buried next to it. The removal itself took place at the end of a long political process connected to the establishment of an independent Estonia and an associated re-evaluation of the role of the nation in the Second World War. The then Prime Minister, Andrus Ansip, of the right-wing *Reformierakond* party, ruled that the part of the memorial that was a bronze effigy of a Russian soldier (known as 'Aljoša') should be removed and relocated, along with the soldiers buried at its feet (Norman 2009). The memorial had long been a gathering place for members of Tallinn's Russian-Estonian minority who would come together at the memorial at certain times to remember (not necessarily triumphantly, although this is implied in the justification for the removal of the statue) the war dead and the nation's Soviet past, with the laying of offerings, singing, and, more often than not, the drinking of vodka (Muhu 2008; Kurg 2009).

On 26 April, the exhumation of the bodies began (a sign on the fence around the site read 'Archaeological Excavation' although no further information is currently available on who the archaeologists were undertaking the work) and a crowd of protesters formed, swelling to around 1,000 over the course of the afternoon, as attempts were made to storm the enclosure. By midnight that evening, the centre of the city was in the midst of full-scale riot, with (mainly, but not exclusively) Russian-Estonian youths committing acts of vandalism and looting shops. This was followed by numerous arrests before violence died down in the early hours of the morning, by which time an emergency meeting of the Estonian government had decided to expedite the removal of the memorial and its relocation (then to an unknown 'holding' location).

The following night, rioting continued, this time with a better prepared police force combating the rioters with water-cannons and rubber bullets, and spread to some other predominantly Russian-Estonian towns. Violent rioting did not carry on past this night, although the next two days saw the creation of a strong volunteer police force and a call by Russian groups for all Russian-Estonian men to 'take up arms'. The 30th of April saw an organized 'slow-drive' through the city with much sounding of horns. By this time a Russian delegation had arrived in the city and, among other actions, called for the resignation of the Ansip government (Harding 2007; Norman 2009). On 1 May, they laid wreaths at the site of the relocated memorial and, although the debates surrounding the relocation were to continue, the riot can be said to have ended.

38.3.2 Tesco, Bristol

Rioting along Stokes Croft and Cheltenham Road in Bristol on the night of 23/24 April 2011 followed a not dissimilar pattern. During the day, it was announced that Avon and Somerset police would be arriving in the area to evict the occupants of a supposed squat, Telepathic Heights, on Cheltenham Road, with an associated charge that they were planning to attack the new Tesco store opposite the squat. Social media sites began reporting a growing police presence in the late morning. A small crowd gathered through the afternoon to witness and protest against the eviction, with a constant stream of events being reported on various social networking sites, notably Twitter, and even a live video stream of the eviction from the upstairs window of a local resident. The crowd grew as the eviction carried on into the evening, numbers swelling as local protesters were joined by others coming to the area from elsewhere in Bristol.

Over time, what had begun as a protest turned into a violent riot as protesters began to take their frustrations out on the police and the police likewise took their frustrations out on local people. Lines formed in the street (the Twitter stream describes a barricade of bicycles being eventually replaced by one of flaming bins) with protesters and police, the latter equipped with horses, alternately charging each other. In the early hours of the morning, the Tesco shop on Cheltenham Road became the focus of violence, having its windows smashed and graffiti sprayed on its frontage and the shop's entire stock of cigarettes stolen (Clement 2012). The Tesco supermarket had been at the centre of local political debate for some time, with a large, sustained movement of local people protesting against the company setting up another store in the area (there were already a number within walking distance), to the potential detriment of other local shops struggling to get by in a harsh financial climate. It would not be accurate to call the evening's events an organized anti-Tesco action, but it is certainly the case that what began as a protest against heavy-handed policing eventually turned its attention to the area's major symbol of corporate disregard for people and places.

This particular riot lasted only for one night, not slowing during daylight hours before recurring the following night as is often the case with larger occasions of civil unrest. However, the event is notable for the way in which news of the events was spread via social media, something which doubtless had an effect on events themselves. As well as the 'facts' of what was happening, by following the Twitter feeds of different people, including the MP for the neighbouring constituency Kerry McCarthy (McCarthy 2011a, 2011b), it was possible to pinpoint changes in the 'mood' of the protest and the moment when it became a riot. Tesco, certainly, seems to have become a focus for violence very late in the course of events and it is right to surmise that attention was driven towards it by the nature of the course of other events on the evening.

38.4 THE ART OF CIVIL UNREST

38.4.1 *After-War*

The case of the Bronze Nights was taken up by Estonian artist Kristina Norman in a series of works and interventions brought together as *After-War*, the Estonian exhibition at the 53rd Venice Biennial in 2009. As a Russian-Estonian herself, Norman was and is particularly sympathetic to the debates surrounding the relocating of the monument and the political situation surrounding it that led to the riots of April 2007.

Her work for *After-War* began with a film, *Monoliit* (2007), exploring the materiality of the soldier statue as if it had arrived in Tallinn from space (inspired by the monolith in Stanley Kubrick's *2001: A Space Odyssey*). Thereafter, in 2008, the work took a more interventionist turn, as Norman took miniature replicas of the soldier to the cemetery in which the memorial had been relocated and used them as a catalyst to conversation with people she encountered about the memorial, the events of April 2007, and the wider political situation. One of these miniature replicas of the bronze soldier was taken by someone and placed near to the pre-riot location of the war memorial of which it was a part, an act which resulted in people leaving offerings and candles alongside the miniature as they had done when the original had been *in situ*, a happening that was reported on the national news. Realizing the continued existence of the Russian-Estonian community's relationship with the space, as mediated through the image of the soldier, Norman developed these existing ideas of the importance of the physical presence of the image of the memorial (as distinct from the memorial itself) and developed another intervention which saw her construct (with Meelis Muhu) a full-size replica of the soldier coloured gold (Figure 38.1) and attempt to place it near to the original location of the memorial (it stood briefly before being removed by the police). Films of the making of the golden soldier and of the Estonian police's removal of it soon after installation form *After-War*, alongside the gold soldier effigy itself, a number of miniature replicas, and film of the Bronze Night riots.

What we see in Norman's durational artistic engagement with a particular political situation, especially taking account of the perspectives she focuses on of the materiality of the image of the memorial in question, is a complex relationship between a physical object, other objects representing that original object (see Schiffer, this volume), the expression of deeply held political and social beliefs (Astrov 2009; Laimre 2009), and the ways in which a community defines itself through the action of memorialization, erupting into riot when the central object of the memorial is removed. How Norman's work adds to our understanding of this relationship is that, by using the various replicas of the monument to revive the memorial acts that surrounded it in a particular location prior to removal, she demonstrates that any commemorative acts around the old statue in its new location are somehow of secondary importance to those acts of commemoration around new replicas in the original location. It is almost as if to say that the replicas, by occasioning such a revival, come to embody an emotional vitality that was always in existence, but which had been unsuccessfully transferred to the new location with the soldier itself. Thus, we begin to understand, through artistic intervention, the depth of the threat that was felt and which was the immediate cause of the civil unrest in question.

FIGURE 38.1 Still from *After War*, 2009 (reproduced with permission from Kristina Norman)

38.4.2 *Savage Messiah*

The ongoing project of artist Laura Oldfield Ford, *Savage Messiah*, consists of walks, urban drifts (making use of the Situationist technique of the dérive, a method of experiencing the essence of places by passing through them), during which Oldfield Ford engages with people and places, and collects images, either literally or by sketching. These come together in occasional exhibitions and the long-running zine *Savage Messiah*, in which she brings together many of the drift images with pieces of text, original and found, to describe and debate places, people and events (Sherwin 2011; Oldfield Ford 2012).

For the duration of February 2011, Oldfield Ford produced an exhibition in conjunction with the Arnolfini gallery, Bristol, in which she created eleven posters based on drifts around the city. Primarily these were left to be casually encountered by members of the public, although a map of the poster locations was produced by Arnolfini and Oldfield Ford led a walk around them to open the exhibition, as did the author on another occasion, specifically as an urban archaeologist. What becomes immediately clear is that by bringing together a number of found images of aspects of urban decay, the artist creates a clear visual distinction between the contents of the poster and its immediate surroundings. However, what one learns through the act of looking for each of the posters and perhaps 'straying off the beaten track' a little is that the urban decay depicted is never far away.

Although these works are not a response to the riots of April 2011, appearing sometime before that event, in them we see the material conditions that can be identified as a contributing factors in the events that led to the smashing of the Tesco frontage (Figure 38.2). It is significant that these material conditions are identified through the dérive process and

FIGURE 38.2 Cover of *Savage Messiah* zine accompanying Bristol exhibition (reproduced with permission from Laura Oldfield Ford)

juxtaposition of found images rather than being immediately apparent. We might suppose that Oldfield Ford's work exposes what is hidden by the veneer of respectability, imposed perhaps by lack of depth of engagement on the part of most who encounter central Bristol. Of course this veneer was also compromised by the riot itself. What Oldfield Ford's Bristol work, and the wider *Savage Messiah* project, show us is just how thin that veneer is, how beneath the fake harmony of consumerism and happy lives there is a 'truth' of hardship, decay, and violence that will, on occasion, reveal itself. It is to be found in discarded fast food wrappers and pictures torn from magazines and is observed not easily, but by durational engagement with places, both in the form of the drifts and 'off-site' in the forming of the juxtapositions of images and text that most accurately represent the potential of a place to experience civil unrest.

38.5 The Archaeology of Civil Unrest

38.5.1 Tallinn, Estonia, April 2007

From even this short summary of events, there are certain things we can infer from look-ing at the riots in Tallinn. Perhaps the most important of these is the way, not limited to situations such as this one, in which international politics can, however briefly, centre on individual objects, in this case a war memorial. This, of course, was a complex memorial, incorporating the bodies of a number of Russian soldiers and the animosity their excavation caused is not particularly surprising (see also Shepherd, this volume, and Fondebrider 2009, for more on the political contexts of exhumation). What is perhaps of more interest to us is the way in which the course of events ran. Beginning as a political debate (Blomfield 2007), events became the physical removal of the statue, which became a protest, which became a violent protest, which became widespread looting, all in the course of one afternoon and evening.

As this sequence of events takes place, different ideas and materials become involved and we can see how the relationship between people and objects changes or finds different expression over time. Of course, we begin only with the idea of the bronze soldier monu-ment and the history and community it represents. The soldier itself (and buried soldiers too) become enrolled in the events as soon as work begins to physically remove them from their location. Hidden behind fencing, this central object is invisible, both present and not present. This ambiguity reflects the ambiguity of the 'Estonianness' of Russian-Estonians, who are not considered full Estonian citizens, despite having been in the country for many generations in some cases (Triisberg 2009). The heightened uncertainty of events leads to physical violence against the police force, one of the more obvious physical manifestations of anti-authority action. As events escalate, more things, the shops of central Tallinn, become enrolled as symbols of a wider Estonian identity that is partially denied to those rioting, for whatever reason. The riot stops because it does not need to carry on.

Thus, over the course of a few hours, we see a fluid set of relationships between changing numbers of different people and different objects and ideas of objects. All of this is the Bronze Night, but it happens at multiple scales, from the individual Russian-Estonian protesting the loss of a memorial space to the speculative 'Army of Russian Resistance' calling for outright conflict, to members of the Russian government travelling to Tallinn for 1 May celebrations. It is connected to what the memorial is held to represent, to the physical memorial, to the uncertain future of the memorial, to the history of Estonian-Russian relations, the Second World War, and anti-capitalist sentiment at one and the same time. It takes the heightened emotions and actions of a riot to see all of these enrolments and implications together over the course of a few hours, a length of time largely absent from archaeological analyses

38.5.2 Bristol, England, April 2011

The Stokes Croft/Cheltenham Road area of Bristol had seen riots before, notably in April (again) 1980, when the riot in neighbouring St Pauls spilled over into it at times. Official accounts exist of the 1980 riot and these are of a different interest to the contemporary archaeologist, as they deal with the area almost as a battlefield, a militarized landscape of safe zones, rallying points, and forward and reserve lines (BTUC 1981; Dixon 2011).

But in 2011, the difference is that local events could be followed in real time by anybody with a laptop or smart-phone anywhere in the world. So, it is (or perhaps was) possible to appreciate how long the tension built up for after news of the police gathering for the raid on Telepathic Heights. Further, it was possible to realize the impact of the moment the police stormed the building, if only by the sheer speed at which the Twitter feed began to roll. Above all, following this event in real time made something of a nonsense of how the event was reported as a purely anti-Tesco riot (Allen 2011; Flintoff 2011; Taphouse 2011; Williams 2011). There were literally hours and hours of ebbing and flowing, moments of violence and moments of calm, before one person's attention turned to the windows of Tesco sometime around 2 a.m. with others following suit. The majority of those on the scene posting comments on Twitter described how quickly the hyper-violent phase of the riot happened.

As with events in Tallinn, witnessed 'in action' as opposed to seen with hindsight in the recent past, we can understand the changing relationships between people and things, and people and other people, with a much more nuanced understanding of how time and duration play their own roles in shaping events. The event has become associated with anti-Tesco feeling partly because of the vandalism itself, but also partly because of the suddenness with which the vandalism took place. People in the area had been leading a peaceful protest against the shop for some time before 23 April and although some kind of violence against it may have been foreseen, it was certainly not inevitable (Bakare 2011).

38.6 CONCLUSIONS

This chapter has suggested that riots are perhaps among the most important things that are under-considered in contemporary archaeology, for their power to uncover, for an observable duration, deep historical and wide geographical 'slices' through society. Archaeological approaches to duration will develop as we debate further the difference between contemporary archaeology and the archaeology of the contemporary past. Likewise, it may become possible, through extending small case studies like those presented here, to make the archaeology of a single riot useful for the study of all kinds of other discrete action. But riots ought to be studied in their own right and their potential to change the way we use archaeology to view both the present and past world is invaluable.

Riots are already an act of othering, an extreme statement of opposition between particular people and particular things, or other people. In the case of riots, rather than introducing a false distance between ourselves as archaeologists and events as data, we can approach them through proximity and, by following them as they unfold, with an emotional connection. Riots have huge implications that are felt far beyond their immediate locales and beyond their participants. As contemporary archaeologists we have a particular ability to demonstrate how these implications are made, in action, and the particular material conditions that contribute to their nature and effect. These integrated archaeological understandings of why riots happen and of what happens during them may, one day, have the potential to play an active role in better curating those conditions that make desperate people resort to violence in the first place.

ACKNOWLEDGEMENTS

The author would like to thank Laura Oldfield Ford, Kristina Norman, and Meelis Muhu for talks, walks, and other ongoing engagements.

REFERENCES

Allen, Sam. 2011. Bristol City council must support the community and reject Tesco. *Guardian*, 22 April. Available at: <http://www.guardian.co.uk/commentisfree/2011/apr/22/bristol-riot-tesco?INTCMP=SRCH> (accessed 5 February 2012).

Astrov, Alexander. 2009. The Work of Politics in the Age of Technological Responsibility. In *Kristina Norman—After War*, ed. Andreas Trossek, pp. 66–87. Tallinn, Estonia: Centre for Contemporary Arts.

Bakare, Lanre. 2011. The solidarity of Bristol's Stokes Croft community. *Guardian*, 25 April. Available at: <http://www.guardian.co.uk/commentisfree/2011/apr/25/stokes-croft-tesco-bristol?INTCMP=SRCH> (accessed 5 February 2012)..

Blomfield, Adrian. 2007. War of Words over Bronze Soldier. *The Telegraph*, 5 February. Available at: <http://www.telegraph.co.uk/news/worldnews/1541641/War-of-words-over-bronze-soldier.html> (accessed 5 February 2012).

BTUC. 1981. Slumbering Volcano? Report of an enquiry into the origins of the eruption in St Paul's Bristol on 2 April 1980. Bristol: Bristol TUC.

Buchli, Victor and Lucas, Gavin. 2001. *Archaeologies of the Contemporary Past*. London: Routledge.

Clement, Matt. 2007. Bristol: 'Civilising' the Inner City. *Race and Class* 48(4): 97–114.

—— 2012. Rage against the Market: Bristol's Tesco Riot. *Race and Class* 53(3) 81–90.

Dixon, James. 2009. Shopping and Digging. *British Archaeology* 105 (March/April): 32–7.

—— 2011. A True People's Archaeology. *British Archaeology* 119 (July/August): 48–9.

Flintoff, John-Paul. 2011. Banksy lobs a petrol bomb into the heart of the Tesco war. *Sunday Times*, 8 May. Available at: <http://www.thesundaytimes.co.uk/sto/newsreview/features/article620552.ece> (accessed 5 February 2012).

Fondebrider, Luis. 2009. Forensic Archaeology and Anthropology: A Balance Sheet. In *Memories from Darkness: Archaeology of Repression and Resistance in Latin America*, ed. Pedro Funari, Andrés Zarakin, and Melisa Salerno, pp. 47–54. New York: Springer.

Graves-Brown, Paul. 2011. Touching from a Distance: Alienation, Abjection, Estrangement and Archaeology. *Norwegian Archaeological Review* 44(2): 131–44.

Greer, Chris and McLaughlin, Eugene. 2010. We Predict a Riot? Public Order Policing, New Media Environments and the Rise of the Citizen Journalist. *British Journal of Criminology* 50: 1041–59.

Grint, Kevin and Woolgar, Steve. 1997. *The Machine at Work: Technology, Work and Organization*. Cambridge: Polity Press

Harding, Luke. 2007. Protest by Kremlin as Police Quell Riots in Tallinn. *The Observer*, 29 April. Available at: <http://www.guardian.co.uk/world/2007/apr/29/russia.lukeharding?INTCMP=SRCH> (accessed 5 February 2012).

Harrison, Rodney and Schofield, John. 2010. *After Modernity: Archaeological Approaches to the Contemporary Past*. Oxford: Oxford University Press.

Hutchby, Ian. 2001. Technologies, Texts and Affordances. *Sociology* 35(2): 441–56.

Hutchinson, Mark. 2002. Four Stages of Public Art. *Third Text* 16(4): 429–38.

Jackson, Anthony (ed.). 1987a. *Anthropology at Home*. ASA Monograph 25. London: Tavistock Publications.

—— 1987b. Reflections on Ethnography at Home and in the ASA. In *Anthropology at Home*. ASA Monograph 25, ed. Anthony Jackson, pp. 1–15. London: Tavistock Publications.

Jeffrey, Bob and Jackson, Will. 2012. The Pendleton Riot: A Political Sociology. *Criminal Justice Matters* 87(1): 18–20.

Kurg, Andres. 2009. The Bronze Soldier Monument and its Publics. In *Kristina Norman—After War*, ed. Andreas Trossek, pp. 49–65. Tallinn, Estonia: Centre for Contemporary Arts.

Laimre, Marco. 2009. Kristina Norman's After War. In *Kristina Norman—After War*, ed. Andreas Trossek, pp. 29–48. Tallinn, Estonia: Centre for Contemporary Arts.

Latour, Bruno. 1996. *Aramis, or the Love of Technology*. Cambridge, MA and London: Harvard University Press.

McCarthy, Kerry. 2011a. An Eye Witness Account of the Bristol Stokes Croft/Tesco Riot from Kerry McCarthy MP. Available at: <http://louderthanwar.com/blogs/an-eye-witness-account-of-the-bristol-stokes-crofttescos-riot-from-kerry-mccarthy-mp> (blog entry posted 24 April, accessed 5 February 2012).

—— 2011b. #stokescroft. Available at: <http://kerrymccarthy.wordpress.com/2011/04/24/stokescroft/> (blog entry posted 24 April, accessed 5 February 2012).

Mouffe, Chantal. 2005. *On The Political*. Abingdon: Routledge.

Muhu, Meelis (dir.) 2008. *Aljoša*. In-Ruum.

Norman, Kristina. 2009. Poetic Investigations. In *Kristina Norman—After War*, ed. Andreas Trossek, pp. 7–28. Tallinn, Estonia: Centre for Contemporary Arts.

Oldfield Ford, Laura. Bristol 1981//2011//2013 (posted 23 February 2011). Available at: <http://lauraoldfieldford.blogspot.com/2011_02_01_archive.html> (accessed 28 March 2012).

Rancière, Jacques. 2004. *The Politics of Aesthetics*. London: Continuum.

Renfrew, Colin. 2003. *Figuring it Out: The Parallel Visions of Artists and Archaeologists*. London: Thames and Hudson.

Sartre, Jean-Paul. 1965. *Nausea*. Harmondsworth: Penguin Books.

Schofield, John. 2009. *Aftermath: Readings in the Archaeology of Recent Conflict*. New York: Springer.

Sherwin, Skye. 2011. Artist of the Week 126: Laura Oldfield Ford. *Guardian*, 18 February. Available at: <http://www.guardian.co.uk/artanddesign/2011/feb/18/artist-week-laura-oldfield-ford> (accessed 5 February 2012).

Stenson, Kevin. 2012. 'Ealing Calling': Riot in the Queen of London's Suburbs. *Criminal Justice Matters* 87(1): 12–13.

Storm Heter, T. 2006. *Sartre's Ethics of Engagement: Authenticity and Civic Virtue*. London: Continuum.

Strathern, Marylin. 1987. The Limits of Auto-Anthropology. In *Anthropology at Home*. ASA Monograph 25, ed. Anthony Jackson, pp. 16–37. London: Tavistock Publications.

Taphouse, Jonathan. 2011. Bristol's Tesco Riot—In Pictures. *Guardian*, 22 April. Available at: <http://www.guardian.co.uk/business/gallery/2011/apr/22/tesco-police?INTCMP=SRCH #/?picture=373914746&index=2> (accessed 5 February 2012).

Till, Jeremy. 2012. The Broken Middle: The Space of the London Riots. *Cities* Available at: <http://www.sciencedirect.com/science/article/pii/S0264275112000315> (accessed 28 April 2013)..

Triisberg, Airi. 2009. Between Nation and People: On Concepts of (Un)Belonging. In *Kristina Norman—After War*, ed. Andreas Trossek, pp. 88–108. Tallinn, Estonia: Centre for Contemporary Arts.

Whatmore, Sarah and Hinchcliffe, Steve. 2010. Ecological Landscapes. In *The Oxford Handbook of Material Culture Studies*, ed. Dan Hicks and Mary Beaudry, pp. 440–58. Oxford: Oxford University Press.

Williams, Zoe. 2011. The Tesco riot is no surprise given people's powerlessness. *Guardian*, 28 April. Available at: <http://www.guardian.co.uk/commentisfree/2011/apr/28/tesco-riot-planning-law-bristol?INTCMP=SRCH> (accessed 5 February 2012).

CHAPTER 39

....

THE MATERIALITY OF FILM

....

LIZ WATKINS

39.1 INTRODUCTION

....

CELLULOID is material. The imaginary worlds that we see unfold at the cinema are an illusion; they are inscribed and projected by light, but rely on a cellulose nitrate or acetate base. The film stock, as substrate of the image, has tended to be suppressed rather than exploited by filmmakers. In addition to the information provided at the levels of image, content and narrative, each strip of film sustains layers of supplementary information in the marks and scratches of the pressures and static of the machines of production and replay. These marginalia, scrawled amidst the shadows of the photographic image, bear a direct relation to the circulation and storage of the film. These scratches offer an index of usage and so a trace of the life cycle of the film alongside the indexicality of the photographic image as the capturing of an instant. The photographic material of film is sensitive to light, heat, humidity, and touch. The image deteriorates and detritus accumulates registering the effects of its immediate environment. These anomalies form a register which betrays the duration of the film's existence and makes visible the substance that underpins the image. In this sense, what is legible of this contingent information is not bound to the image or narrative, but is evocative of 'the archival life of film' (Fossati 2009).

Studies of film frequently focus on predetermined questions surrounding representation and signification to account for the contemporary viewer's encounter with the image, overlooking the strata of information embedded in the substance that belies it. This material, prior to 1951, was made of cellulose nitrate, a thin, flexible, and transparent base coated with an adhesive layer of gelatine and a photosensitive emulsion of silver salts (Cherchi Usai 2000: 1–2). The ontology of this film material lies in the photographic index which for Bazin constitutes the authentic and the poetic of documentary film (Bazin 1967: 154). The veracity of the photographic as it appears to capture a moment, offering an image of time stilled, is refigured into the narrative of a documentary as it is assembled from fragments of film. The diverse pasts elicited by each section and frame are replayed in the illusion of a moving image that facilitates the imagination of presence. The historicity of the film operates between the frozen image as the capturing of an instant and its veiling by cinematic illusion of movement that elicits a play on temporality which is layered with the spectator's fascination with absence and presence in narrative. The indexicality of the photographic and the parameters of technology, frame, and image are an integral, but not determining dimension of meaning in documentary and narrative film. As Mary Ann Doane suggests, the historicity of the subject (2007) sustains a paradox of contingency and rationalization that is intrinsic to the emergence of narrative form and the affectivity of cinema as it engages a fascination and fear of disorder and uncertainty (Doane 2002). Within the machinations of the cinematographic document the film material, like image and narrative, can be read.

The film encountered 'in performance' (Elsaesser 1996: 20) offers a simulation of presence that is facilitated by the materials and processes it conceals. The residual marks of the film's histories indicate the mechanics of representation and press upon the 'forgetting' of the illusion on which spectatorship depends by making what is familiar of the image unfamiliar and 'distancing the observer from their own material world' (Harrison 2011: 141). An archaeological paradigm attentive to the provenance of the film also begins to discern its mutability. A comparative analysis of what is ostensibly the same film viewed on different media (35mm film stock, VHS video tape, DVD) discerns variations in image resolution and textual system (see Noble, this volume). This approach indicates the work of production and circulation as they can be traced across the surface of an ethereal image and the configuration of materials and technologies specific to each screening. By adopting a facet of the work of archivists in seeking to identify and date film fragments, a methodology that is responsive to the fragile substrate of the image can be developed. The practice of studying film materials on a flat-bed viewing table, of winding the film by hand and frame-by-frame, enables access to the edge of the film strip where date codes, different shapes and spacing of perforations, and the characteristics specific to different colour and sound processes are visible and betray the film's past.

Materials alter over time. The film strip is marked both by the effects of deterioration and design, from dust and fingerprints, to colours that fade under the heat of the projector lamp, and the edge marks or codes that denote the date of manufacture for the film stock. Colour processes such as tinting affect the breadth of the film strip, where the hues remain more intense toward its periphery away from repeated exposure of projection whereas more central to the image 'the colours have changed and are still changing' (Fossati 1996: 83). The visual characteristics of film stocks also vary (Gunning 1996: 57) so that the transposition of a dyed image to contemporary colour photographic emulsion offers only a 'simulation' of its source (Fossati 1996: 83). The process of producing simulacra has other effects. In instances where the full width of the film strip is printed on to a new material then a photographic image of perforations can be registered with each transfer, making visible an accumulation of layers that is indicative of how many generations intercalate between the film strip and its negative. Each configuration of details can facilitate the identification of film fragments otherwise dislocated into another historical and cultural context. Images, narratives, marks, and scratches, as the material traces of technologies and the imprint of the work and touch of the prior encounters of others are not explicative of the past, but are called into an archaeological conversation around the remains of the past in the present.

Film theory has tended to address the colour system of a film as a constant entity and yet the insidious effects of deterioration alter the fascia encountered by the viewer at each screening. In this sense, the positioning of the spectator in relation to the screen as fantasy object is uncertain. Materials and images, as the staging that mobilizes the spectator's desire, are as mutable as interpretations of the film text. A comparative analysis of a series of releases of what is seemingly the same film, but accessed using different media, indicates the significance of the provenance of materials, techniques, and technologies as social processes specific to each manifestation of the text. Within a community, cinema offers a commonality of narratives that are open to the imagined solitude of each spectator's interpretation. Cinema as an institution, however, is changing.

The continual emergence of different viewing technologies and capabilities affects the way we access the cinematic archive. For an archaeological approach that is concerned with the detritus of social production and interaction, of the interests signalled in the records kept, and in making sense of a mess of found fragments, the abandoned and relinquished materials and texts are accessed and shaped through a framework and epistemology specific to each viewing.

39.2 HERBERT G. PONTING'S DOCUMENTS AND NARRATIVES OF THE ANTARCTIC

The material and textual alterations that can be tracked across the different releases of 'the film' reveal a tension between its function as text and the instabilities of the substance from which it is made. For example, a study of the film footage of the British Antarctic Expedition (1910–13) encounters the effects of Herbert G. Ponting's re-editing of the material across an initial twenty-year period (Appendix 1) and suggests that his editorial decisions were caught within the possibilities of adaptation that are specific to the cultural and technological contexts particular to each release. A comparative analysis of different releases and prints indicates a paradox between the insistence of the film footage as scientific document and the development of a narrative to support its remobilization as a commercial enterprise in the film market. Each edit calls on the 'authentically poetic quality' that for Bazin can be found in the indexicality of the photographic (1967: 154). Ponting's work in reassembling still images and shots into new sequences takes the form of a historiographic practice. The instantaneity of the film as photo-sensitive register and the visual organization and temporality of narrative form distract from Bazin's insistence on the photographic as an unmediated record and draws it into a complicated staging of space and time around the irresolvable loss of the polar party (Galt 2006: 53–71).

The camera negatives were initially processed by Ponting in the Antarctic (Arnold 1967: 47) and returned to the UK in two consignments to be screened in two sections under the title *With Captain Scott R.N., to the South Pole* (1911 and 1912). Following his attempts to circulate the film in 1914 and 1919, Ponting began work editing *The Great White Silence* (1924). This edit is perhaps most notable for the fourteen different combinations of tinting, toning, and hand colouring, instructions for which were recorded by written instructions scratched into blank sections between fragments of exposed film (Figures 39.1 and 39.2).[1] These notes demarcate a colour design that is also significant to its themes and narrative.

[1] *The Times* (Saturday, 28 May 1910): 8. 'Captain Scott's Men. Science with the Camera. Terra Nova's Start Tommorrow', *Daily Mail* (31 May 1910) MS1453/39/1–2 Scott Polar Research Institute, Cambridge. 'To the South Pole', *The Bioscope*, 2 June 1910: 59. Each of these sources notes Ponting's intention to produce colour records of the Antarctic expedition. *The Bioscope* notes that the Lumière company supplied 'autochromatic plates, upon which Mr Ponting hopes to produce photographs in natural colours' (1910: 59). Ponting's written account of the expedition *The Great White South* (1921) was published shortly before the re-editing of his film footage began for *Silence* (1924) and is particularly attentive to colour (2000 [1921]: 30, 54). The inflection of chromatic schema across the black-and-white film footage of the polar expedition serves a narrative function, but can also be read as a gesture towards the reflection and refraction of light in the icescape. A point of reference for the specific effects of black-and-white orthochromatic film stock, which is less able to register the reds of the light spectrum, can be found in shots of the Union Jack in *Silence* as the *Terra Nova* leaves Cardiff Bay where the reds of the flag are omitted.

FIGURE 39.1 Ponting's colour instructions for a blue tone and yellow tint scratched into a section of film corresponding to the image from the BFI NFTVA 2010 digital restoration shown in Fig. 39.4 (reproduced with permission from BFI National Archive)

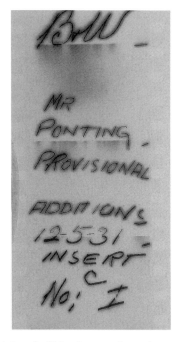

FIGURE 39.2 Ponting's provisional editing instructions circa 1931 scratched into a section of film (reproduced with permission from BFI National Archive)

Ponting's work 'perfecting [the] film record of the expedition' included the addition of inter-titles so that it could be circulated in regional theatres without further need to deputize lecturers (Ponting, 21 March 1924).

Ponting adapted the film footage again to produce *90° South* (1933). In keeping with technological developments, preparations involved transfer to a film stock with different perforations and an alteration from the speed of filming at a hand-cranked 16 frames per second (fps) to that of the 24fps of synchronized sound projection. The effects of such technical manipulations can be discerned in the instabilities of the image in relation to the frame (Ponting, 12 January 1933). The 1933 revisions also incorporated new maps, a 25ft landscape painting, a diorama, an amended animated line-and-map sequence, and incorporated samples of Ponting's still-photography. These edits were in line with his advocacy of the film's educational value, and sought to effectively convey the details of the expedition, its scientific work, and the fate of the polar party (Ponting, 15 August 1933). Each of Ponting's comments on the process of re-editing remarks his 'endeavours to resuscitate' and 'keep the story of the Expedition fresh in the public mind' (Ponting, 4 January 1926). In turn, the commissioning of new drawings and maps offered an interpretation of the landscape by rewriting the horizon and altering the orientation of geographical features to create an image of the Antarctic that was tailored to the retelling of the story of the expedition (Ponting, 30 October 1931):

> For the purposes of the film it has of course, been necessary to exaggerate the size of Mount Erebus; and naturally the distance from Ross Island to the Bay of Whales as compared with the height of the Great Ice Barrier cannot be shown in any great scale—but I think this map will serve the purpose very well. (Ponting, 30 October 1931)

Frank Debenham, a geographer on the expedition and later Director of the Scott Polar Research Institute notes from the drawings for *90° South* 'the unfortunate absence of the symmetrical dome of Mount Discovery—quite the nicest shape of any of the peaks we saw from Headquarters' whilst a good sense of 'the vast flatness of the Barrier' is retained (Debenham, 23 October 1931). The maps and models designed for the 1933 release were to offer the audience a more comprehensive sense of the journey and work undertaken, yet one that was attuned to the dramatic to sustain public interest. Cherry Garrard's comment that 'here in these pictures is beauty linked to tragedy—one of the greatest tragedies—and the beauty is inconceivable for it is endless and runs to eternity' (Cherry Garrard 1935: 391) finds Bazin's 'authentically poetic' in the unedited materials. Ponting's photographic work remained a significant component of the expedition's scientific exploration, to which the editing of the material into narrative form offered a supplementary text that elicited a scenario salient to the memory of the heroic age of polar exploration and the insinuation of the possibility of its forgetting. The commonality of the photographs and film, it seems, is that they could not 'themselves explain anything', but remain 'inexhaustible invitations to deduction, speculation and fantasy' (Sontag 1979 [1977]: 23). They remain open to a compassionate response from the viewer. They are fraught with the distancing effect of the mediations of technology, yet incite an investment in the (im)possibility of some detail as explicative of the loss of the Polar party.

The scientific work of the expedition extended beyond the moving image to Ponting's still-photography.[2] The handwritten notes on paper sleeves used to protect the

---

[2] 'A Chat with Mr Herbert G. Ponting, FGRS', *The Bioscope* 17(313) (1912): 121 and 123. Much of the 2,000 photographs and 25,000ft of film returned from the Antarctic 'was devoted to animal life and other scientific purposes [...] so that every phase of seal, gull and penguin life has been recorded' (121).

photographic plates signal that Ponting recorded different light conditions and natural phenomena such as the Australis Borealis. By detailing the geographical orientation, date, and time that the negatives were exposed the images offer coordinates of the expedition's colonization of the region and the extremities of empire. Archaeology of the expedition embodies a practice of detailing matter, from data recorded by image captions to the detritus embedded in the ice as an imprint of the inhabitation of the region (Pearson 2009). Materials are susceptible to the impact of the environment of filming and storage. Alongside the fleeting phenomena of light that registers an image as it effects a change in photosensitive emulsion, the film material records a physical trace such as the condensation of vapour and detritus that mark the proximity of the photographer and belie the seemingly objective record of the conditions in which it was produced. Exposure to liquids, the unintentional production of static and changes in temperature inflect the meanings that we interpret of the cinematographic document.

39.3 THE SUBSTANCE OF PHOTOGRAPHY

A focus on the image and narrative as the primary content of the film distracts from the contingent details that register in the photographic material itself. The vulnerability of photosensitive emulsion to liquids, heat, and light allows it to record information coincidental with environmental conditions. For instance, cinematography that employed nitrate film stock for work at low temperatures was susceptible to static which, as an electric charge, exposed the film and registered in fine threads like a lightning strike at the periphery of the frame.[3] Ponting's correspondence, now held at the Scott Polar Research Institute (SPRI) in Cambridge, comments on both the impaired function of camera oil and issues with the colour filters used for still-photography that dislodged as their metal frames contracted in response to changes in temperature between icescape and the enclosed space of his darkroom. Photographic equipment was affected as condensation formed, seeping into the emulsion and mottling the image (*British Journal of Photography*, 11 January 1924: 15–18). Such contingent marks infer the circumstances of the film's production and are submerged by the displacements of photographic duplication where studies increasingly focus on simulacra accessed through digital media without adequate attention to the provenance of the film.

Semiotic analyses encounter the desire to make mess take on meaning yet have tended to overlook the instabilities and other physical characteristics that enable the identification of film materials (Chare and Watkins 2012). Hypothetically, a strip of film bearing

---

[3] An example of the filigree marks of static can be found in the cinematography of *Nanook of the North* (Robert Flaherty, 1922). A study of the effects of static on photographic material can be found in 'Static Markings on Motion Picture Film', *British Journal of Photography* 72(3422) (4 December 1925), pp. 727–30. Ponting used both Lumière and Eastman kinematographic film stocks for the polar expedition (*British Journal of Photography*, 3 June 1910: 417–18). Other effects of filming in Antarctic conditions included 'the freezing on lenses of the vapour from the hand, and [...] the cracking of cementing balsam in lenses and filters' which have the potential to alter and reduce the clarity of image resolution (*British Journal of Photography*, 23 August 1912: 646).

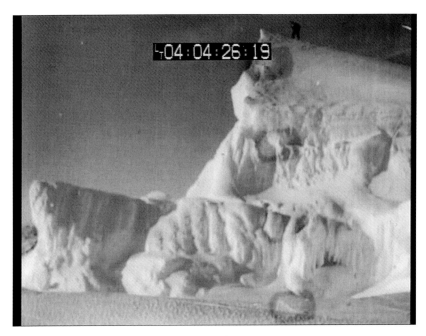

FIGURE 39.3 'The Matterhorn' iceberg from a digital file of the 1990s contact print produced from reel 6 of the Nitrate soft print (1923) that is held at the BFI NFTVA. The imprint of perforations can be seen across the image as a result of the film's storage (reproduced with permission from BFI National Archive)

the scratches left by a machine that is now obsolete is more significant as a record of the workings of that technology than for its image content. Within the historiographies of film genres and movements, film materials continue to rewrite themselves. The potential familiarity of an image or narrative is layered with information that can be interpreted of the material itself. Such details include the film gauge (8mm, 16mm, 35mm); differences in perforations which occur along the edge of the film strip (Figure 39.3); the edge mark or code that denotes the manufacturer and date the film stock was produced; the changeover dots that occur towards the periphery of the screen and that signal the timing of transfer between reels and are read by the projectionist in the cinema; and the various symbols that denote either a volatile nitrate base or acetate and later polyester Safety film.[4] The identification of a film and its provenance relies on an assemblage of details that can include the type of colour process and sound used (Brown 1990). Sound in the silent film era relied on the

---

[4] An image of perforations can be seen at a slight angle across a film-still from the 1990s contact print struck from the NFTVA 1923 nitrate soft print. This effect is caused by the film being poorly wound when in storage and has been removed from the 2010 digital restoration (Figure 39.4). Kubrick's 'Letter to Projectionists 8 December 1975' is reprinted in *FILM: Tacita Dean* (2011). This document signals the incorrect allocation of a changeover dot that occurs 1ft and 9 frames early in reel 3b. These denotations facilitate continuity of narrative between reels. This aberrant mark and the instructions to accommodate it are specific to the 1975 release prints of *Barry Lyndon* (Stanley Kubrick, 1975). Prints and copies of the film circulated at different times vary.

accompaniments of the piano, lecturers, and pre-recorded discs such as those manufactured by Vitagraph until the late 1920s when synchronized sound gradually became a more viable technology. Such developments meant that an auditory component could be registered and reproduced either from variable area or variable density optical sound tracks which were printed parallel to the image along the length of film. Technical amendments, such as those Ponting made for *90° South* as his 1933 edit of the expedition footage were in keeping with 'modern technique and [to] synchronize it throughout with a story and music' but proved 'an awfully difficult task' (Ponting, 12 January 1933) as 'the whole tempo of the film had to be changed, for it was taken at the silent speed of 16 [frames] to the second, and it all had to be changed to 24 to the second' (Ponting, 12 January 1933).[5] The shift in narrative is accompanied by the layering of sound over a composite image track of materials duplicated from the 1910–12 source elements with newly commissioned illustrations. The configuration of technical and physical characteristics of the film base becomes an increasingly complicated site that is both specific to the production of the film's most recent manifestation which has the potential to sustain simulacra of the earlier materials.

39.4 BEGINNING TO DECIPHER COLOUR TECHNOLOGIES AND PRACTICES

The historical context of a film includes a range of technical processes that constitute information to be deciphered in the identification of its found fragments. Such processes range from the effects of tinting and toning as processes which altered the chemical composition of the film image through to the ideology embodied in the colour balance and sensitivity of each film stock (Gunning 1996: 57). The colour technology used affects the chromatic resolution of the film as it is perceived during a screening. Tinting and toning, such as that found in Ponting's *Silence* (1924) colours an otherwise black-and-white image a single hue. Tinting coats the image in a transparent layer of dye and so is characterized by the coloration of the lighter areas of the composition and the retention of intense blacks. Toning, as a mordant that affects areas where the silver nitrate is most dense, sustains the integrity of the highlights and gives coloration to the shadows. The colour instructions scratched into sections of leader (Figure 39.1) indicate a chromatic design that underscores the narrative progression. However, the association of particular colours and meanings is specific to this edit of the film. Delpeut notes of the more general scope of his research into colour in the silent era at the Filmmuseum, there appeared to be 'no hidden theory, no codes that applied to all the colour film [...] every film is a new experience and any code you find

---

[5] '90° South—Review', *Sight and Sound* 2(7) (1933): 102–3 notes the technical competency of Ponting in the film's 'sense of smoothness and fluidity—a characteristic of fine cinematography' (102) in that it effaces the marks of production that might otherwise distract the viewer from the narrative. The review remarks on the 'artistic restraint' (103) of Ponting's revisions in 'preserving the continuity of the film [...] by means of the projection of a slowly moving panorama of arctic [Antarctic] scenery of remarkable beauty, accompanied by a commentary based on Scott's diary' (103). This section constructs material for the journey of Scott, Wilson, Oates, Bowers, and Evans to the Pole.

FIGURE 39.4 'The Matterhorn' iceberg from the BFI NFTVA 2010 digital colour grade of *The Great White Silence* (reproduced with permission from BFI National Archive)

in one film is broken in the next' (Delpeut quoted in Hertogs and de Klerk 1996: 23). The NFTVA's 2010 restoration of *Silence* diverges from the colouring and content and of the Dutch print (Figure 39.4). The colour score of a film can alter according to the national and geographical context of its distribution (Mazzanti 2009: 67–93). *Silence* was circulated in countries including Britain and Germany and, as *Expeditie naar de zuidpool 1910–1913* (1925/40) in the Netherlands. The comparison work undertaken by Angelo Lucatello for the BFI National Film and Television Archive's 2010 preservation and restoration of *Silence* details the differences in material and content of their 1923 soft print and the Netherlands Filmmuseum's *Expeditie naar de zuidpool 1910–1913* (1925/40) (Figure 39.5). The latter consists of various film stocks from Kodak (1925), to Agfa and Pathé (1929 onwards), additional frames detailing Dr Atkinson's frost-bitten hand and some sections are noted by Harold Brown ('Mr Brown') as missing. Lucatello notes that 'almost every scene in the Dutch copy is 5–20 frames shorter' than the BFI's 1923 print. As inter-titles are adjusted, new film stocks are utilized, fragments of film are added and frames omitted: the material and text are continually rewritten.[6] The mutability of film prevents us from addressing it as a single entity, but instead participates in configuring a scenario of loss that facilitates

---

[6] New inter-titles were produced using a photographic rather than digital process for the 2010 restoration of *Silence* to replicate a little of the instability and viable range of image resolution in keeping with previous releases. The variations that can be tracked across the re-edits and variants of *Silence* include a few frames of gulls feeding in the ocean at the side of the *Terra Nova* that are missing from the 2010 digital restoration. This anomaly manifests as an ellipsis in the movement of the ocean as the film is screened. The in-camera slippage that causes an unsteadiness of framing in a section detailing two expedition members boxing is retained in the restoration. These variations were kept as they as they trace the production and provenance of the film and yet cause relatively little distraction to the viewer. The restoration offers an image that appears both new (restored) and yet 'aged'.

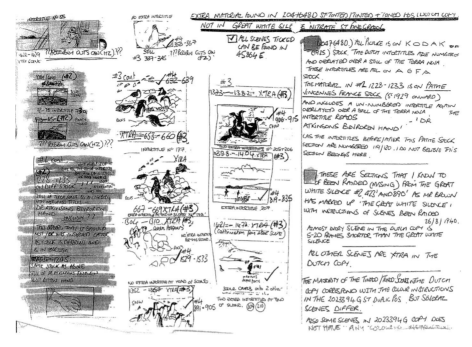

FIGURE 39.5 Angelo Lucatello's diagram and notes on comparison work for the BFI NFTVA's 2010 preservation and restoration of *The Great White Silence* (reproduced with permission from Angelo Lucatello)

Ponting's dramatic emphasis in narrative by imaging indexicality in its decomposition; the fantasy of the presence of the past replayed in the cinematic illusion of movement lies in tension with the imminence of loss made visible through the decomposition of the image. Ponting's photographic work elicits a historiographic process that adapts scientific exploration to narratives determined to sustain the memory of the expedition.[7] However, the effacement of the composition of the image offers poetic meaning to the fragility and affectivity of memory where the ascertainment and explanation of loss falter.

Cinema is changing. As an institution its structural concerns continue to shift in relation to the demands of new technologies. From the photographic to digital, from the theatre to home viewing, the moving image is produced by simulacra, of copies (of multiple prints, videos, discs) and as an illusion or image of reality. Studies that focus on the fascia of the image and formulations of the film text tend to overlook the historical specificity of the

---

[7] *Scott of the Antarctic* (Charles Frend 1948). In keeping with classic narrative cinema and filmed in three-strip Technicolor, Frend's film dramatizes the story of Scott's expedition and the push to the Pole. It includes a sequence detailing the photograph being taken of the five expedition members at the South Pole by Bowers, the negative of which was later found with Scott, Wilson, and Bowers by the search party. This restages one of the residing images of the expedition. The negatives of stills photography including those taken by other expedition members were under Ponting's control, whilst copyright for the film footage was held by Gaumont until 1914 when it was purchased by Ponting for £5,100. Mr Gent was Gaumont's signatory in Australia and New Zealand before travelling to the UK to work for Ponting for over 12 years in maintaining and preparing his photographs and films.

configuration of materials and technologies that support the production of each film and facilitate each screening. If, for example, each film stock already embodies a colour ideology as a result of its chemical formulation, a set of balances and limitations, then the aesthetic of materials in development and obsolescence offers a sense of the historical context that is embodied in the image (Gunning 1996: 57).

Colour invokes a diverse range of variously successful processes, from which three-strip Technicolor emerged as the technology used for *Becky Sharp* (Rouben Mamoulian, 1935), the first feature length film in 'natural colour'. In a statement suggestive of the Technicolor company's dye imbibition process (three-strip Technicolor), Wollen notes that between filming and public screening 'a whole technology of dyeing has intervened' (1985 [1980]: 24–5). Wollen indicates the work of the laboratories as he states that 'what you see is an image and that is the power of cinema, but it is also its power for you to not think about what you do not see, which is as much the sound track and the lab as anything else' (Wollen 1985 [1980]: 25). The Technicolor consultancy service advocated 'colour consciousness' (Kalmus 1935) producing a technology and aesthetic associated with three-strip Technicolor. Most prevalent between 1935 and the mid-1950s this schema of intensely coloured highlights to accentuate details against muted brown and grey base notes was intended to demonstrate their technology as integral to the production of narrative cinema. Film materials are integral to but not defining of the film as a historical and cultural construct.

In turn, innovations in the sensitivity of Eastmancolor film stock led to its increased use against the higher cost and perceived technical superiority of three-strip Technicolor. Eastmancolor has been associated with a grainier image (Haines 2003 [1993]: 132) and a tendency toward deterioration. As a consequence of a change in the chemicals used for developing the film, those printed during the 1970s were more susceptible to shifts in the colour balance; the cyan and yellow dyes tended to fade, leaving the film with a magenta or pinkish appearance (O'Connell 1979: 12; 'Colour Problem' 1980/1: 12–13; Jianhe and Xiangbei 1999: 40–3). The effects of fading can be seen in films such as *Jaws* (Steven Spielberg 1975). Commentators suggest that five years after the initial release of this film, the blue was 'leaving the waters while the blood spurting from Robert Shaw's mouth [was] getting redder and redder' ('Colour Problem' 1980/1: 12–32).

The duplication and exhibition of film affect the resolution of the image. Colour is susceptible to deterioration: colour fades and colour balances shift just as the chemical composition and material base of the film alter over time. As Paolo Cherchi Usai explains, the silver nitrate in the photographic emulsion of old films is composed of 'animal bones crushed and melted into a semi-transparent layer intermixed with crystals of silver salts' (2000: 113). Film materials decay gradually over time: 'emulsion shrinks, fades, peels off, exudes humidity; dirt, blotches and scratches become part of its identity' (Cherchi Usai 2011: 60). This process of decomposition becomes apparent in the accelerated dissolution of the image in films such as *Decasia* (Bill Morrison 2002) and *Lyrical Nitrate* (Peter Delpeut 1991). Each of these films was constructed from found footage from the early stages of cinema and incorporates fragments visibly affected by deterioration. The corruption of the image makes the materiality of the film perceptible in difference to the transient and ethereal image projected at the cinema. The accumulation of damage is specific to each print and registers an indexical trace of the life cycle of the film. Deterioration and decay diverge from the conceptualization of the photographic and 'structural status of a copy' as the splintering of 'the supposed unity of the original "itself" into nothing but a series of quotations' (Krauss 1999: 290; see also Lucas, this volume and DeSilvey, this volume). As a commodity the film is inherently paradoxical, lying between the promise of ownership that the dissemination of multiples facilitates and the reified object of the camera negative. These complex temporalities of materials and texts can be studied across a series of releases of what might otherwise be considered as the same film.

Analyses of shifts in the film substrate can require the detection of information that is not readily perceptible through the visual appraisal of the film, but can be discerned through analytic chemistry such as that undertaken at the Haghefilm Conservation B.V. (Amsterdam). João S. de Oliveira, Director of the PresTech Film Laboratory (London) notes the importance of this approach:

> if you're looking at all these black-and-white nitrate films that we handle, then they all have a certain degree of fading because of the nitrate decomposition [...] it is the first thing that happens to the film, so you tend to lose information where the silver deposits are finely divided in the highlights. If it is a negative, you lose detail in the shadows and if it is a print, then, in the highlights, but these elements, this changed stuff, is still in the film. (João S. de Oliveira [2010] 2013: 176).

Although a proportion of information may be lost, other details are retained yet imperceptible to unassisted visual analysis due to the chemical transformation of the film stock in decay. As a supplementary index of the film's use, the marks of deterioration evoke the process of exchange and sacrifice undertaken in each screening as the cause of a sometimes indiscernible, but gradual, decrease in the legibility of the image. The familiar aesthetic of silent cinema is in part a commonality and effect of deterioration. The indistinct areas are integral to the cognizance of each film still within the 'constraints and possibilities' of the medium (Doane 2007: 130). Such inconsistencies, as gaps and spaces, reside in image, text and archive acting as a reminder of erasure that is both familiar and haunting. For Rosen it is preservation that affirms the authenticity of the image, allowing the spectator to invest in the visible traces of damage that betray the age of the film's edifice (2001: 52). However, something that matters, something of the complexity and temporality of film materials sourced from diverse archives belies the synthesis of the scrawling threads of contact, the marginalia and decay particular to the history of each fragment as they are redrawn into a new narrative form. An attention to the materiality of film and archive seeks 'to make historical information, often lost or displaced, physically present' (Foster 2004: 4). In *Silence*, the 'very muteness of what is, hypothetically, comprehensible in photographs is what constitutes their attraction and provocativeness' (Sontag 1979 [1977]: 24).

39.5 PROVENANCE AND FASCIA OF IMAGE AND NARRATIVE

The complex edifice of the NFTVA's 2010 restoration of *Silence* as the 1924 version of Ponting's film footage of the British Antarctic Expedition (1910–13) is another step in a 'restoration trajectory' (Latour 2010). The image offers a point of access to the cinematic archive and a fascia that is itself susceptible to change. The production of a transfer or copy means that 'we never see an image, but one element in a cascade of transformations' (Latour 2010: 183) now encountered through digital media.[8] For Latour, without reuse the concept of the original would be diminished (Latour 2010: 183).

The impact of changing technologies on the ways in which we access and study the cinematic archive (Mulvey 2006) are situated amidst concerns over digital simulation of an analogue image. The digital restoration of *Silence* required the simulation of the aesthetics of applied colour processes that physically altered the composition of the photographic materials and of the effects of tinting and toning layered over same black-and-white image. Digital media make selected films more accessible, but also distract from the myriad details which trace the provenance of the film.

The image offered by the 2010 variant of *Silence* is a configuration of materials drawn from diverse pasts. The materials, marks, and scratches, like the image content recorded, constitute information to be interpreted. The restoration traces change, of the film *now* as it is encountered at a point of access specific to the configuration of technologies of each viewing. The mutability of the film image and narrative indicates the fragility of the material record and elicits a sense of uncertainty in the cinematic illusion of presence. In this sense the narrative operates across different tenses, of the provenance and imaginary worlds of the film, and so can appear reflexive in its relationship to the marks of production and decomposition in the staging of a scenario of loss. The solicitations of the material and image lie in the continual rewriting of the promised veracity and authenticity of the photographic index as it is rearticulated through the machinations of narrative cinema. The film studied signals an assemblage of artefacts, detritus and texts *now*, that is, a surface image of the material traces of others to be deciphered.

ACKNOWLEDGEMENTS

My thanks to Kieron Webb and Angelo Lucatello at the BFI National Film and Television Archive; Haghefilm Conservation B.V. and EYE Film Institute, Amsterdam; La Cinémathèque de Toulouse; the Scott Polar Research Institute, Cambridge; Deluxe Digital, London; the AHRC; and to Nicholas Chare for his insightful comments on materiality in the visual arts.

[8] *Scott's Last Expedition*, Natural History Museum, London 20 January–2 September 2012 <http://www.nhm.ac.uk/visit-us/whats-on/temporary-exhibitions/scott-last-expedition//index.html> (accessed 25 March 2012); *With Scott to the Pole*, Royal Geographic Society 16 January–30 March 2012. Each exhibition showed copies or new prints of Ponting's photographs magnified to illustrative purpose, rather than negatives or prints that were produced from them by Ponting or his assistant John Gent between 1912 and 1935. Notebooks, scientific findings (from drawings to preserved specimens), detritus (supplies), and other objects were included in the Natural History Museum exhibition; photographic materials, although fragile, are incorporated for image content for the purpose of display rather than the histories and technologies of materials.

Appendix 1

Film footage (1910–12) from Captain R. F. Scott's British Antarctic Expedition (1910–13)

- Ponting recorded approximately 25,000ft of film. The NFTVA hold 9811ft of original negative footage under the accession title *The British Antarctic Expedition 1910–1913.*
- In addition to its UK release, different versions of Ponting's film footage were circulated in countries including Germany (1924–5), France (1914 and 1922), Netherlands (1925) and Japan (1914).

1911 *With Captain Scott, R.N. to the South Pole* 3000ft film

- Handbills list 1911 for 1st and 2nd editions.[9] The 2nd edition consisted of material from the second consignment of film to reach Britain and was circulated prior to news of the fate of the polar party.
- This film footage is listed as black-and-white by the NFTVA, but other versions may deviate.

1912 *With Captain Scott, R.N. to the South Pole*

1912 *L'Expédition du Capitaine Scott au Pôle Sud*

1913 *The Undying Story of Captain Scott*

Released by Gaumont.

1914 *Vers le Pôle Sud avec le Capitaine Scott et Vie intime des animaux et des oiseaux dans les régions antarctiques*

- This version consisted of two sections of the 1912 edit of ***L'Expédition du Capitaine Scott au Pôle Sud*** and screened in June 1914 at Théâtre Réjane in Paris, sometimes under title *Vers le Pôle Sud avec le Capitaine Scott.*

1921 Ponting's written account of the expedition, *The Great White South*, was published by Duckworth.

1922 *L'Eternel silence. Nouvelle version cinématographique de l'Expédition Scott au Pôle Sud*

- A tinted and toned edit that was distributed by Film Triomphe in France.

---

[9] *Screenonline* gives 1911 and 1912 respectively.

1924 *The Great White Silence*

- Tinted and toned film with some black-and-white sections. *Silence* also included hand-coloured fragments and materials such as maps, models, and animated sequences that were commissioned on return to Britain.
- Inter-titles were added so the film could be screened without an accompanying lecture.
- A 1923 black-and-white Nitrate soft print of *Silence*, which includes instructions for colouring the film scratched into blank sections of leader between exposed film footage, is held at the NFTVA.

1925/40 *Expeditie naar de zuidpool* (1910–13)

- Tinted and toned version with Dutch inter-titles which is held at the Filmmuseum, Netherlands. This film was loaned to the NFTVA as part of the Lumière project to assist in the preservation and restoration (1990–2010) of *The Great White Silence* (1924).
- A preservation copy of this print was produced in 1959 as a 35mm black-and-white duplicate negative on an acetate base. In 1991 another preservation copy was made by Haghefilm Conservation B.V. for the Filmmuseum, Netherlands. The nitrate film was copied on to a colour inter-negative so that a new colour print could be made. This print was screened at the Filmmuseum cinema theatre in 1992 and 1995, then at Bologna in 1995. It was also circulated through Dutch repertoire theatres from 1995 to 1998 and then again in 2001.
- This version is substantially the same as *The Great White Silence*, but includes some shots that are not included in the 1923 soft print of *The Great White Silence* that is held at the NFTVA (e.g. still image of Dr Atkinson's frost-bitten hand). A digibeta video copy was also used as research material for the 2010 NFTVA restoration (see Figure 39.5).
- The found footage film *The Forbidden Quest* (Peter Delpeut 1993) includes tinted and toned sections derived from this print.

1929 *The Times* (27 February 1929) refers to a special screening of *The Epic of the South Pole* ('*The Epic of the South Pole, The Kinematographic Record of Captain Scott's Last Antarctic Expedition*' photographed and arranged by Herbert G. Ponting).

1933 *90° South*
A new script was formulated for this black-and-white, synchronized sound edit. New maps and models were also commissioned. The film includes voice-over by Ponting and an introduction by Rear Admiral Evans.

1990s *The Great White Silence* restoration begins at the British Film Institute

National Film and Television Archive. It is taken up again in 2009.

2009–10 NFTVA digital restoration of *The Great White Silence*
This preservation and restoration project was taken up from work that began in the 1990s. The Netherlands Filmmuseum loaned the 1991 restoration of their 1925 print of **Expeditie naar de zuidpool (1910–13)** to the NFTVA as part of the Lumière project. Comparison work of the Filmmuseum print and 1923 nitrate soft print was undertaken by Angelo Lucatello to identify camera negatives and best other material to reconstruct *Silence*.

The project produced a new master copy, colour prints for screening, and a HD master. The Archival Gala Screening was held on 20 October 2010 in Leicester Square, London.

2011 *The Great White Silence*

DVD and Blu-ray versions of the BFI NFTVA's digital restoration were released in the UK.

REFERENCES

90° South—Review. 1933. *Sight and Sound* 2(7): 102–3.

Arnold, H. J. P. 1967. Herbert Ponting as a Cinematographer. *Cinema Studies* 2(3): 47–53.

Bazin, André. 1967. Cinema and Exploration. In Bazin, *What is Cinema?* Volume 1, tr. Hugh Gray, pp. 154–63. Berkeley: University of California Press

Brown, Harold. 1990. *Physical Characteristics of Early Films as Aids to Identification.* Brussels: FIAF.

Chare, Nicholas and Liz Watkins. 2012. The Matter of Film: *Decasia* and *Lyrical Nitrate*. In *Carnal Knowledge: Towards a 'New Materialism' Through the Arts*, ed. Barbara Bolt and Estelle Morris, pp. 75–88. London: I. B. Tauris.

A Chat with Mr Herbert G. Ponting, FGRS. 1912. *The Bioscope* 17(313): 121 and 123.

Cherchi Usai, Paolo. 2000. *Silent Cinema: An Introduction*. London: BFI.

—— 2011. Untitled contribution. In *FILM: Tacita Dean*, ed. Tacita Dean and Nicholas Cullinan. London: Tate Publishing.

Cherry Garrard, Apsley. 1935. Mr H. G. Ponting—Obituary. *The Geographic Journal* 85: 391.

Colour Problem. 1980/81. *Sight and Sound* 50(1): 12–13.

Daily Mail. 1910. Captain Scott's Men. Science with the Camera. Terra Nova's Start Tomorrow. 31 May. MS1453/39/1-2 Scott Polar Research Institute, Cambridge.

Doane, Mary-Anne. 2002. *The Emergence of Cinematic Time: Modernity, Contingency, Archive.* Cambridge, MA: Harvard University Press.

—— 2007. The Indexical and the Concept of Medium Specificity. *Differences* 18(1): 128–53.

Elsaesser, Thomas. 1996. Panel Discussion. In *Disorderly Order, Colours in Silent Film*, ed. Nico de Klerk and Daan Hertogs, pp. 11–26. Amsterdam: Nederlands Filmmuseum Stichting.

Fossati, Giovanna. 1996. Colored Images Today: How to Live with Simulated Colours (and be happy). In *Disorderly Order, Colours in Silent Film*, ed. Nico de Klerk and Daan Hertogs, pp. 83–9. Amsterdam: Nederlands Filmmuseum Stichting.

—— 2009. *From Grain to Pixel: The Archival Life of Film in Transition*. Amsterdam: Amsterdam University Press.

Foster, Hal. 2004. An Archival Impulse. *October* 110: 3–22.

Galt, Rosalind. 2006. 'It's so cold in Alaska': Evoking Exploration between Bazin and *The Forbidden Quest*. *Discourse* 28(1): 53–71.

Haines, Richard W. 2003 [1993]. *Technicolor Movies: The History of Dye Transfer Printing.* Jefferson, NC and London: McFarland.

Harrison, Rodney. 2011. Surface Assemblages: Towards an Archaeology *in* and *of* the Present. *Archaeological Dialogues* 18(2): 141–61.

Jianhe, Xu and Xiangbei, Ge. 1999. The Color Restoration of Faded Colour Film Prints. *Journal of Film Preservation* 58/59: 40–3.

Krauss, Rosalind. 1999. Reinventing the Medium. *Critical Inquiry* 25(2): 289–305.

Latour, Bruno. 2010. Concluding Remarks: How to Inherit the Past at Best. In *Coping with the Past: Creative Perspectives on Conservation and Restoration*, ed. Pasquale Gagliardi, Bruno Latour, and Pedro Memelsdorff, pp. 181–201. Florence: Leo S. Olschiki, Civiltà Veneziana Studi 52.

Markings on Motion-Picture Film produced by Drops of Water Condensed Water Vapour and Abnormal Drying Conditions. 1924. *British Journal of Photography* 71(3323) (11 January): 15–18.

Mulvey, Laura. 2006. *Death 24 x a Second: Stillness and the Moving* Image. London: Reaktion.

O'Connell, Bill. 1979 Fade Out. *Film Comment* 15(5): 12.

Pearson, Mike. 2009. '*Professor Gregory's Villa*' and Piles of Pony Poop: Early Expeditionary Remains in Antarctica. In *Contemporary Archaeologies: Excavating Now*, ed. Cornelius Holtorf and Angela Piccini, pp. 83–94. Frankfurt: Peter Lang.

The Photographic Equipment of the British Antarctic Expedition. 1910. *British Journal of Photography* (3 June): 417–18.

Ponting, Herbert G. 2000 [1921]. *The Great White South*. New York: Cooper Square.

Rosen, Philip. 2001. *Change Mummified, Cinema, Historicity, Theory*. Minneapolis: University of Minnesota Press.

Scott Polar Research Institute:*British Antarctic Expedition 1910–1913*, Volume 7, MS280/28/7, Cambridge.(4 January 1926) H. G. Ponting, Letter to Frank Debenham.(23 October 1931) F. Debenham, Letter to H. G. Ponting.(30 October 1931) H. G. Ponting, Letter to Frank Debenham.(12 January 1933) H. G. Ponting, Letter to Frank Debenham.

Sontag, Susan. 1979 [1977]. *On Photography*. London: Penguin.

Static Markings on Motion Picture Film. 1925. *British Journal Photography* 72(3422) (4 December): 727–30.

The Times. 1910. Saturday 28 May. 8. MS1453/39/1-2 Scott Polar Research Institute. Cambridge.

To the South Pole: On the Cinematograph. 1912. *British Journal of Photography* (23 August): 645–6.

Watkins, Liz. 2013. Herbert G. Ponting's Materials and Texts. In *Color and the Moving Image: History, Theory, Aesthetics, Archive*, ed. Simon Brown, Sarah Street, and Liz Watkins. London and New York: Routledge.

Wollen, Peter. 1985 [1980]. Cinema and Technology: A Historical Overview. In *The Cinematic Apparatus*, ed. Teresa de Lauretis and Stephen Heath, pp. 24–5. London: Macmillan.

CHAPTER 40

....

THE BURNING MAN FESTIVAL AND THE ARCHAEOLOGY OF EPHEMERAL AND TEMPORARY GATHERINGS

....

CAROLYN L. WHITE

40.1 INTRODUCTION

....

DURING the Burning Man festival organizers and participants build and then remove all traces of a city that holds upwards of 50,000 participants (as of 2011). The city is built in August each year, fully occupied for one week, and then removed completely over the course of the following month (Figure 40.1). Using traditional archaeological methods along with ethnographic approaches and participant-observation, the project has explored the construction and inhabitation of the city before, during, and after its use. This project focuses on the materiality of Burning Man, aiming to examine the material dimensions of the festival and its significance for those who create, reside in, and deconstruct Black Rock City, a temporary and, ultimately, ephemeral site.

Ephemeral sites (by definition) leave little in the way of material remains and temporary sites are occupied for short periods of time. As, such they raise methodological and interpretive challenges for archaeologists of any time period. Despite the lack of physical evidence of these site types, ephemeral and temporary sites are created through distinctive circumstances and often represent important occasions in people's lives. Consequently, they merit special consideration.

The developmental trajectory of the discipline demonstrates that archaeologists were first attracted to the monumental, to the earliest, to the unusual, as subjects of study, but the daily, the commonplace, the typical have fallen under the scrutiny of the archaeologist (and anthropologist) in more recent times as part of a broader interest in the study of 'everyday life'. Nonetheless, ephemeral and temporary sites are underrepresented in archaeological inquiry, largely due to the challenges archaeologists face in assessing sites that leave so little physical trace. Archaeological study of the present, then, allows archaeological practices to

FIGURE 40.1 Aerial view of Black Rock City, 2011 (photograph: Jim Urquhart, reproduced with permission from Reuters)

be applied to temporary and ephemeral sites when they exist. Given the challenges of recovering past evidence of these sites, an archaeology of the present has an opportunity not only to reveal information about the specific event taking place, but also offers insights for scholars of more ancient sites of this type. In recording the event *as it occurs* and soon after it is over, contemporary archaeology can provide insight into the material culture, organization, and practices of participants in the events and in the sites that are created and destroyed by participants. Further, the ability to record the full life cycle of a site offers an opportunity to envisage the practice of site construction, inhabitation, and abandonment within a very short period of time. Of course, the ability to engage with participants at such an event offers insights that are never recoverable in more traditional (i.e., ancient) archaeological contexts. I will return to this important component of the project throughout the chapter.

As Harrison and Schofield discuss, one of the things that makes the practice of archaeology of the contemporary past distinctive, is that it examines both abandoned sites of the recent past and sites that are currently active (2010: 16). They note that methodological developments must be crafted in order to understand both 'living and extinct material practices'. One of the key contributions (and challenges) of the Burning Man project is to record the site as a place of both living and extinct practices and to examine the different sorts of data recovered from each entity. As such, the project has required me to utilize the traditional modes of archaeological analysis to address the materiality of what is left behind as I also develop new techniques and a more 'ethnographic' approach to record the site as a living place.

As a contemporary *event*, the Burning Man festival possesses a range of attributes that make it a place one can study *as it happens*, through participation, and as such it might be described as 'ethnographic archaeology'. Throughout the project I engage with the people who create and dismantle the site on every level, from the highest organizational levels to the smallest scale single-day participant. I also am able to see the ways that various governmental structures (both internal and external) impact the event. The ability to converse with participants and people who work to make the event happen, and to ask questions about the choices they make and the reasons behind those choices, sets the project apart from most archaeological projects (although the use of oral history is a common tool for archaeologists). As discussed in more detail below, the classification of this project as 'archaeology' brings out a number of questions about defining archaeological practice. It has forced a personal reconsideration of where the division lies between archaeology and ethnography, particularly in regard to the assessment of material culture.

40.2 A BRIEF HISTORY OF BURNING MAN

Burning Man began on the summer solstice of 1986 when Larry Harvey, Jerry James, and their children gathered on Baker Beach in San Francisco and burned an effigy of a man they had built. The 'meaning' of this first event was and remains ambiguous (Harvey 2011). A number of strangers joined the crowd around the bonfire, as described by Harvey, in 'acts of impulsive merger and collective union' (Dougherty 2006: 31). It was that feeling of inclusion, community, surprise, and spectacle that propelled them to repeat the event the following year.

In 1987, they burned the effigy again, building a taller (15 foot) man, and once again the feeling of participation and community resulted, as more strangers joined the party. They repeated the act the following year, and again, it attracted additional strangers to the scene. By 1988 Harvey and James began to publicize the event, and they built a man 40-feet tall, attracting members of the Cacophony Society (a San Francisco fringe group interested in adventurous mischief). In 1990 the event attracted between 500 and 800 people, and the police got involved in the event. Harvey agreed not to burn the man (in exchange for allowing the man to be raised on the beach; Dougherty 2006: 47–8).

The event had outgrown Baker Beach. Members of the Cacophony Society who participated in the Baker Beach event knew that the Black Rock desert playa provided a place where you could, according to one participant, 'Sit around and blow stuff up' (Dougherty 2006: 48). So they built a man and burned him on the Black Rock Desert on Labor Day weekend, 1990. The first playa event was celebrated by about 90 people, and many of the ideas of Burning Man were born: offering gifts, drinking, and bathing in nearby hot springs (Dougherty 2006: 54; Burningman.com 2012). The austere and unrelenting environment and the feeling of community somehow transformed this experience into a ritual to which people wanted to return year after year.

Attendance doubled annually to 1996 when 8,000 people attended (Burningman.com 2012). By 1996, increasing issues surrounding the scale and activity within the community necessitated changes. During the next several years, guns were outlawed, cars were restricted, the city streets were planned, and the Bureau of Land Management worked with the organizers to permit the event and plan for the removal of its traces after it was over (see Dougherty 2006 for the most complete history of the event).

Today the event is a highly organized 'managed chaos', with laid out streets, a sort of zoning with spaces assigned to theme camps, a large centre camp, and no commerce. In 2008, the first year of the project, the population peaked at 49,599 people, and in 2011 the festival sold out with over 53,000 participants. At the time of writing, the organization ran a ticket lottery in an attempt to accommodate more Burners and to create a more equitable distribution system. Over 80,000 people registered for the lottery, although the population cap remains at 53,000 participants.

40.3 MASSIVE SCALE

The scale of this project is intimidating and confronts a researcher directly with the inadequacy of traditional archaeological research methods to grapple with urban environments. Black Rock City occupies 4.54 square miles (Black Rock LLC 2011: 13) with a population of approximately 50,000 people. The city is permitted to occupy the space from 1 August to 5 October, to include all phases of set-up for the event and for the clean-up and removal of all evidence of the city from the playa surface. The event itself lasts a mere seven days.

I have been studying Black Rock City since 2006, and the trajectory of my research is itself a case study for how one might approach the examination of contemporary large-scale ephemeral and temporary sites archaeologically. I have also come to realize over the years that the standard archaeological approach to the event does not work entirely. I employ traditional archaeological techniques, which is to say that I approach the city as a large site, with individual camps viewed as features. I strive to sample consistently across the site, to obtain data from camps of various scales. I systematically record what I see, and collect artefactual materials during and after the festival.

Despite these baseline archaeological approaches, I have needed to modify my bag of archaeological tricks in order to adequately capture the dynamic environment. The most radically different of these is the capacity to speak with the city inhabitants directly. I ask participants to show me around their camp and we discuss the various components, often in extended interviews. Since these relationships have developed through the years, I am able to observe the participants and their camps beyond the interview, sometimes contradicting their own statements about the uses and meanings of places and objects.

In addition to the importance of ethnographic work and participant-observation, there are several changes in the way that I record information that warrant mentioning. Since the festival lasts only for a week, and the scale of the site is massive, time is of the essence. Rather than use a total station or other surveying and mapping equipment, I simply use digital photography to record as much information as possible. The goal of the time spent during the festival becomes one of revisiting camps from previous seasons while expanding the library of camps and meeting new informants. In the sections that follow I highlight some of the ways that the methods of recording have been different across the research themes addressed in this project.

40.4 FESTIVAL ARCHAEOLOGY

Festivals and other ephemeral events have received limited archaeological attention, and most of what has taken place has focused on events in the more distant past, with several notable exceptions. Andrew Petersen has studied ways that archaeologists might examine the pilgrimage of the Hajj, the sacred journey to Mecca that Muslims are supposed to complete once in their lives (1994). His work focuses on the routes pilgrims took on their way to Mecca. These routes (there have historically been three main ones) pass through arid desert landscapes, and the inhospitable nature of these landscapes necessitated the construction of facilities for the pilgrims along the route (Petersen 1994: 48). Petersen categorized the facilities along one of the pilgrim routes and notes the challenges of studying some of these elements, particularly since the Arabian Peninsula does not accommodate permanent settlement, and the form of subsistence is typically pastoral nomadism (1994: 54).

More recently, Claassen has looked at pilgrimage routes in Mexico, following on Victor Turner's work (1973). Claassen is interested in the transformation of 'spaces' into 'places' along such a route (2011: 493). Claassen documented the treatment of space along several pilgrimage routes, but what is most relevant here is the way that ephemeral events along these routes are made visible. In particular, Claassen focuses on two pilgrimage routes that people pass on their way to a rain-calling ceremony at the site of Ostotempan. Although Claassen's focus is on the way that individual pilgrims transform the landscape along the route, my interest in the study is the way that the shrines erected for pilgrims who have died along the route materialize the ephemerality of the passage. These shrines harden the event, the people, and the routine of the pilgrimage. They are sites to visit, to pass by, and to decorate with objects in order to make the event and its associated repercussions something real.

Helaine Silverman's work on the Nasca pilgrimage site of Cahuachi, located on the south coast of Peru, also resonates with the work I am conducting at Burning Man. Her work focuses on sacred settings and understanding the sorts of activities that take place in those sacred settings: 'Archaeologists must try to determine what kinds of activities occurred in these sacred settings: When, why, who participated (i.e., which individuals, social groups, other membership groups) in what way, and what this reveals about the structure and function of different institutions and interpersonal/intergroup relations within society' (Silverman 1994: 1). Although there is no question in this case about the location or function of Black Rock City, Silverman describes the site of Cahuachi as a '"now-you-see-it, now-you-don't" quasi-urban configuration' (Silverman 1994: 6). This description (aside from the use of the term 'quasi') suits Black Rock City perfectly. The city of Cahuachi was an early Nasca ceremonial centre, and 'depending on the day it could be bustling with activity or virtually depopulated' (Silverman 1994: 7). This city, like Black Rock City, came to life cyclically. Abandonment happened as quickly as construction, and over just a few days all that remained was a scattering of refuse left behind by pilgrims. These remains were then blown away by the wind, and three months later, very little was left on its surface.

John Schofield's work is most directly apposite to this project, as it shares an interest in the temporary and ephemeral and focuses on the cultural significance of the August 1970 music festival on the Isle of Wight (2000: 145–8). Schofield investigated the popular legacy of the festival as well as the material signatures of the purpose-built landscape that remain today. Schofield's work traces the history, controversy, and material remains of the festival; his analysis emphasizes the potential of such sites to understand discard patterns, but also emphasizes the importance of engaging these ephemeral sites as places with important cultural significance.

40.5 THE ARCHAEOLOGY AND ETHNOGRAPHY OF BURNING MAN

In August 2006, I visited Burning Man as the city was being constructed, during the 'early entry period'. I visited twice to assess the feasibility of a project at the event. Subsequently in 2008, I began to study the festival in earnest and established a collaborative project with Deborah Boehm, a cultural anthropologist. Since 2008, we have attended the festival together, each with specific priorities, but exploring together various components of the city that make it the compelling event that it is. In working together, we have not only been able to engage our own research priorities, but have also benefited from seeing the project through the lens of another anthropological subfield.

A critical part of this project is working with a cultural anthropologist. Although we have distinctive research interests, in working together we cast light on unrecognized aspects of the festival. The speed of social interaction at Burning Man is very slow, as temperatures are sweltering (over 38°C during the day on a regular basis), distances are vast, and there is a relaxed pace that governs the general tempo of life on the playa. Working with an anthropologist has allowed me to understand the way that human interaction contributes to a very nuanced understanding of the materiality of the city. Of course, talking with people and asking them about the aspects of the city that I am studying provides irreplaceable insight into the choices they make and the meaning they invest in their actions. We are currently preparing several collaborative publications that highlight the different angles from which we have approached each element within our own discipline and the fruitful results of bringing these views together, particularly as they relate to space and time (Boehm and White in prep.; White and Boehm in prep.).

We have spent the last five field seasons identifying key aspects of the festival: focusing on identifying major components of the infrastructure, attempting to understand the physical nature of the city itself, evaluating the relationship of people in individual camps to the broader community, and examining the experience of individuals in the city on a recurring basis. We have looked at many different aspects of the physicality of the city: the layout as represented by a clock with alphabetically named streets; the form and presence of institutional components and public spaces such as the Information Center, the Medical Tent, Media Mecca, the Arctic Zone (ice vendors), First Camp (the place where the members of the LLC and other staffers reside); and large theme camps providing food, art, erotic expression, religion, alternative energy, etc. We have looked at the range of art installations placed on the playa, including the man, of course, as well as The Temple. We have experienced the highs and lows of the weather, including several whiteout level dust storms, near freezing temperatures, and intense rainstorms that have turned the playa to mud. And of course, we have attended 'The Burn'.

40.6 BURNING MAN AS FESTIVAL SITE.

Black Rock City and the event of Burning Man offer an opportunity to examine almost any set of research questions, as any urban archaeological site might, but my focus has been on the physicality of the city. My primary interests in Black Rock City and the event of Burning Man have been to understand how the city is built each year. How do individual people live in this city? What are the material signatures of the lives of Burners while the festival is happening? What remains after the event is over? How can I examine the relationship between pubic and private spaces across the city?

One of the interesting, and unexpected, elements of this research is the chance to see the cyclical nature of an urban community. Archaeology usually offers insight into a snapshot of the life of a place—often following abandonment or at the very least a dénouement in the life of a residence/town/city/state. The live character of Burning Man means that one is able to obtain information about the processes of construction, of inhabitation, of abandonment, as each phase is unfolding. And although the event is characterized by change, events are repeated and structures are rebuilt, and people return year after year. This rapid cyclicality affords an opportunity to engage anew with the ideas developed the year before and to see those events *in action* as well as across their life cycle.

40.6.1 Building the City

In August, 'setup' begins. The Bureau of Land Management, a US federal agency, issues a special permit for the event, and thus there are special circumstances that allow the city to take control of the land. The setup phase of the city is launched with a ceremony that marks the placement of the man. This spot is selected during the permitting process by the Burning Man Staff and the Bureau of Land Management and placed with GPS. Following the placement of the city centre point, the rest of the city is laid out and an intensive period of construction begins.

Each phase of the project offers its own set of challenges as to how best to study it. Setup is a long-lasting event, but progress is fairly slow, and the scale of activity is massive, with large construction projects dominating the activities. Within that activity, however, is also a flurry of action on a much smaller scale.

A visit as it is being constructed reveals a different orientation within the city. Pockets of intensive activity mark the vast empty playa. The dominant mode of transport is the pickup truck. The people who populate the city at this time are a mix of volunteers and paid staff who build the infrastructure as well as some of the large temporary structures. The first thing built is First Camp, the large camp where Burning Man board members and other people who work directly with the board live before, during, and after the event. Other large structures that are prominent elements to anyone who attends are also constructed at this time: Center Camp, the man, the temple, and as the event approaches, individual theme camps and art projects are constructed before the event officially commences.

During the setup there are a number of features that fade into the city unobtrusively once the event begins. One of the first elements placed in the city is the 'DPW ghetto', where the people who build the city live. Their residences are typically trailers, affording more day-to-day comfort than a tent or other less robust accommodations. The DPW is provided with three meals a day, so the trailers do not have to provide cooking and eating spaces for the residents. The commissary is a large tented facility that provides meals for the DPW staff over the course of the event.

The setup phase of Burning Man also reveals the scale of construction that is undertaken. Heavy machinery almost dominates the landscape. The overall impression of the space during the construction of the city is the vastness of the open space against the presence of containers, construction materials, and isolated port-o-johns. The empty space gradually begins to fill as the official beginning of the event draws near. Finally, the day or two before, although the festival has not started, the city buzzes with activity.

40.7 LIVING IN THE CITY

For the past several years I have been studying two camps, and as a means of providing an overview of the sorts of components that this project engages with, I will present findings from those camps: Jungle Camp and Suntrakker Camp. I also want to offer several comments on the most ephemeral aspects of the event: the burning of the man and the temple.

40.7.1 Jungle Camp

Jungle Camp is a small theme camp, organized by 'Mojo' and 'Ahhrrr' who have been attending the event for the past eleven years. They work as greeters at the entrance to the event and this year brought a cadre of college students along with them, making for an interesting demographic. Mojo, like so many Burners I have met, is extraordinarily organized in her preparations, packing, and general camp organization. Jungle Camp has several readily recognized activity areas. It has overlapping spaces devoted to sleeping, eating, socializing, hygiene, and site maintenance. The main gathering space is the front shaded area of the camp where people socialize throughout the day, where meals are prepared and consumed, where entertaining takes place, and where most of the immediately needed food and other supplies are kept. The space is designed to accommodate far more people than live at the camp, which encourages and accommodates people who stop by and socialize with the residents (Figure 40.2).

The sleeping areas take up the most area of the camp. Mojo and Ahhrrr sleep in the RV (a 'recreational vehicle' or motorhome equipped with home amenities), and the other camp occupants live in hexayurts they have constructed from insulation panels. The different spaces speak to divisions along age lines of the inhabitants. A tour of one of the yurts shows that each occupant has a particular area for sleeping, for clothes storage, and for other materials. Bikes mark the entrance.

A secondary social space, located at the rear of the camp, was described by inhabitants as a place to hang out without attracting attention at the front of the camp. This is the place where people of Jungle Camp can go to escape the very public nature of the primary social space. The margins of the primary social space are key storage and staging areas for materials used throughout the day and for occasionally used items. Ubiquitous plastic bins store food, equipment, beverages, and other materials. Refuse is also highly organized.

Jungle Camp reflects environment-specific considerations and playa innovations. Since no water is permitted on the playa surface, the shower drains into a very large evaporating

FIGURE 40.2 View of public space in Jungle Camp (photograph: Carolyn L. White)

basin, a shallow plastic lined tank that holds grey water from showering and food prepara-tion. The camp is also sited specifically in relation to another important sanitation element: the port-o-johns. As Ahhrrr told me, they site their camp near the port-o-johns in the por-tion of the semicircle, but not too close! The orientation of the camp is located to face away from the prevailing winds and associated dust storms.

40.7.2 Suntrakker Camp

In 2008, in the midst of a massive duststorm, I was fortunate to stumble upon Suntrakker Camp, a small camp that is part of the large theme camp named Alternative Energy Zone. Suntrakker Camp is organized into several different activity areas. The camper provides the sleeping and eating areas, and the area marked 'Margarita Bar' shows the space for social-izing, and the scaffold view deck shows the space 'given' to the community to watch the sun-set. In practice, of course, there are some additional elements such as the staging area for the equipment used to transform the community space from 'front porch' to margarita bar. The practice of visiting the camp is largely reflective of its appearance on the two-dimensional page, but some of the three-dimensional boundaries and liminal spaces are far more visible than a two-dimensional plan can convey.

Each year I return to Suntrakker Camp, and with the cooperation of Bruce, the organizer of the camp, I am also given a plan of the camp as it changes from year to year. Like many Burners, Bruce is extremely meticulous about his preparation for Burning Man. Not only does he map the layout of the camp graphically, he also maintains a binder (each sheet of paper encased in a protective sleeve) of documentation to include multiple packing lists,

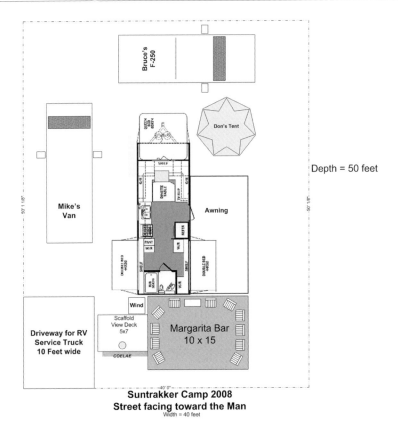

FIGURE 40.3 Plan of Suntrakker Camp, 2008 (reproduced with permission from Bruce Rogow)

construction diagrams for various camp components (Figure 40.3), photographs documenting the packing layout in his truck, budget sheets, maps of the route to the city, as well as a primer designed for present and future Suntrakker residents which communicates the basics of playa survival. Each element is documented with digital photography.

40.7.3 The Man and the Temple

The apex of the festival is the event of 'The Burn', the burning of the man. The man, as noted above, is constructed at the centre of the city—in fact, the city is built around the man. It is the focal point of the city. On Saturday night, festival participants gather around the structure and it is burned in a huge pyrotechnic bonanza. The platform changes year to year, but the form of the effigy itself does not change.

   The second major event of the festival is the Temple Burn. Each year a different artist or collective builds the temple. The form varies greatly, unlike the man. Over the course of the festival, participants make a sort of sub-pilgrimage to the temple It is located at 12:00, 2,400 feet away from the man towards the top of the clock.

FIGURE 40.4 Burning Man participant creating shrine with offerings at the temple, 2010 (photograph: Carolyn L. White)

The temple is a place of great spiritual importance to the participants. For many participants, the temple experience is a sort of culminating event of the year. Before Sunday night, participants journey to the temple. The atmosphere is quiet and serene. Despite the variability in design, the temple is constructed in such a way that there are alcoves and smaller spaces for people to sit quietly by themselves. People leave offerings in the temple to be consumed by the fire, as a way of saying goodbye to loved ones or marking a change in life (Figure 40.4).

The importance of each of the burns is highly variable from participant to participant, but the events punctuate the festival in critical ways. Following the burning of the man, Burners gather at the man base and collect material from the ashes. People gather bits of LED wire, glass, fireworks detritus, and other materials as mementoes and as raw material to refashion into gifts for the next year.

40.8 THE CITY DISAPPEARS

After the festival is over, people slowly disperse from the playa, lining the long road south to Reno in dust-covered vehicles driven by exhausted and elated Burners. But this is hardly the end of the event. It takes the Department of Public Works, under the direction of 'D.A.', two weeks to move the structures off the playa and then another week and a half to scrub the playa of all signatures of human presence. Clearly, this creates a challenge for future archaeological study.

Each city block is walked by a line of DPW staff to collect 'matter out of place' (MOOP). Problem areas (what archaeologists would consider 'features') are marked with a cone, and a 'Special Operations' crew drives around the playa to clean those areas. A third crew takes a more aggressive cleaning approach by dragging and sifting the soil for large-scale disturbances. The materials from this phase of the clean-up are deposited in large dumpsters, except for the objects scavenged by the DPW (or collected by visiting archaeologists). There is an interesting secondary trade in the artefacts collected by the DPW. Some people collect certain classes of artefacts such as safety pins, shell casings, and bobby pins, and the crew trades between them for more exotic items, often reworking them into clothing, jewellery, or other mementoes.

The process of removing the evidence of the man and temple is a major undertaking during the clean-up. When these structures are built, the playa is protected from the intense heat of the burns by a layer of degraded gravel. This material is excavated with heavy equipment and fresh material replaces it. The areas are regraded with the heavy equipment.

The clean-up process underscores the ephemeral nature of the event. By the time the inspection by the Bureau of Land Management occurs, there are very few small pieces of glow sticks, sequins, beads, dried limes and other food remains, string, tiny scraps of paper, rebar, tent stakes, zip ties, feathers, pine needles, wood fragments, bottle caps, nails, screws, cigarette butts, pipes, textile fragments, and other materials remaining on the playa.

The clean-up efforts undertaken by the DPW are finalized with the inspection by the Bureau of Land Management. The special use permit requires that the Black Rock LLC meet an inspection standard of presence of no more than one square foot of recovered trash per acre. The sites of collection are generated by random sample and the inspection is conducted in cooperation with the DPW. The efforts put forward by the DPW are, in essence, a full-scale archaeological survey of the site with a 100 per cent collection strategy. This means that very little remains to be collected during the inspection (I have been given the inspection artefacts for the last six years). Because so little remains, the standard collection techniques of the archaeologist are less relevant at this phase of the event. Rather, it highlights the importance of documentation before and during the festival.

40.9 PARTICIPATION AND EPHEMERALITY

The motto of Burning Man is 'No spectators'. This motto links with other elements of the festival, such as radical self-reliance, radical self-expression, gifting, and participation (there are ten guiding principles of Burning Man)[1] but it has proven to be a very useful model in my engagement with the project to understand the ways that contemporary archaeology forces a reconsideration of the data that archaeologists collect. Participant-observation, as cultural anthropologists have long known, offers the participant nuanced insight into the meanings and interpretations of a place. As a participant, you *create* data. In essence, all you

---

[1] The ten guiding principles are radical inclusion, gifting, decommodification, radical self-reliance, radical self-expression, communal effort, civic responsibility, leaving no trace, participation, and immediacy (<wwww.burningman.com>, retrieved 27 January 2012).

need to do is turn around and look behind you to take in the ways that you are making an imprint on the landscape and on other people in your interactions.

I would like to offer a few observations on the role of participation in an archaeological site that is active, on the role, in effect, of auto-archaeology (see Harrison and Schofield 2010: 92, 171–5; see also Lemonnier, this volume; May, this volume; and Rizvi, this volume). Two years ago, Camp Anthro (the camp I create with my UNR colleague) joined the Alternative Energy Zone, a large theme village that does not allow the use of generators within the camp. There are approximately 250 people in this village, which is one of the largest theme camps in the city. The relationship of Camp Anthro to the rest of the theme camp residents has varied each year, as neighbours have changed and the length of Camp Anthro's residence at Burning Man has varied. For example, in 2010, we were sited between two single member camps: Camp E-bike and Camp Berry. We were directly adjacent to Camp Starstruck, a camp with approximately 25 members. I recorded each of these camps and interviewed the participants as part of the larger project.

The following year, Camp Anthro returned to camp at the Alternative Energy Zone. We were sited once again beside Camp Starstruck but were adjacent to a new single-member camp, called Camp Gitmo-Sun. Once again, I recorded the camps. Mosey, the inhabitant of Camp Gitmo-Sun allowed me to photograph the complete setup of his camp. Camp Starstruck, once again, invited me to take photographs of their more elaborate camp setup, and were very amused by my interest in their food storage areas once again.

So, in a theme camp such as the Alternative Energy Zone, the interactions with individual camps do change year after year as different people live beside new people (and get along to varying degrees). But the experience is also very similar from year to year in that people bring many of the same materials with them. So Camp Anthro changes in some ways but is also remarkably similar as we expand and contract and reduce and expand the goods we bring with us to the desert. The material culture of Camp Starstruck changes in that the individual members have shifted to some degree, but each year they bring the same tents, stoves, sun shades, and other gear to set up the basic components of their camp. And, with Amanda and John at the helm of Camp Starstruck the general tone and approach of the camp is surprisingly consistent from year to year.

This consistency in the city is something that I would not recognize if I did not participate in the event. The same is true about the infrastructure at Burning Man. The people who build the city build things in a relatively consistent way each year. Center Camp, the information centre, and Media Mecca are built the same way each year unless there is a reason to redesign these spaces. So as temporary and ephemeral as the place of Black Rock City is, it is also as consistent in its form. It is only by returning to the event year after year that both change and consistency are visible.

40.10 CONCLUSION (AND ANTICIPATION)

This chapter has highlighted some of the ways the study of a large temporary and ephemeral site requires a reconsideration of what archaeology is and what it can be. As the world's largest 'leave no trace' event, the Burning Man festival is an archaeologist's worst nightmare. How do you study something that leaves nothing behind?

The archaeology of Black Rock City relies on an interpretive gaze derived from standard archaeological training and the implementation of standard archaeological methods. As is the case in all field projects, methods work best when they are flexible and remoulded to the field site at hand. The particular character of Black Rock City has forced revision of my own methods, most significantly: increased reliance on field photography, abandonment of a rigid daily schedule, and reprioritization of research threads as they unfold, particularly since one needs to talk to people when the moment arises.

The study of the Burning Man festival mandates a reconsideration of the ways that archaeology, as a mode of analysis, 'works'. Temporary sites are important components of people's lives and the challenges associated with understanding them do not diminish their significance, now or in the past. The centrality and resonance of the event in the lives of the participants underscores the importance of archaeological and ethnographical inquiry. Working with a cultural anthropologist has only highlighted the potential of such a collaborative approach that could be easily applied to contemporary projects and could be crafted to include ancient archaeological sites.

The cyclical nature of the creation, use, and destruction of Black Rock City exposes concurrent but contrasting elements of archaeology of the present. The Burning Man project considers a city in action, and my own use of the city contributes to its broader interpretation. At the same time, the event has already happened many times, and I work to understand what the site looked like in the past, year after year. Finally, the project is one of anticipation. It is an archaeological investigation of a city that is about to rise from the dust (quite literally) in north-western Nevada—an archaeology of the future.

REFERENCES

Black Rock LLC. 2011. Burning Man 2011 Operating Plan. <http://www.blm.gov/pgdata/etc/medialib/blm/nv/field_offices/winnemucca_field_office/nepa/recreation/0.Par.1113.File.dat/2011%20Operating%20Plan.pdf> (accessed 3 January 2012).

Boehm, Deborah, and White, Carolyn. In preparation. Archaeology of the Social, Ethnography of the Physical.

Burningman.com. 2012. <http://burningman.com/whatisburningman/about_burningman/bm_timeline.html> (accessed 23 February 2012 and 11 April 2012).

Burningmanproject.com. 2012. <http://www.burningmanproject.org/about> (accessed 13 February 2012).

Claassen, Cheryl. 2011. Waning Pilgrimage Paths and Modern Roadscapes: Moving Through Landscape in Northern Guerrero, Mexico. World Archaeology 43(3): 493–504.

Dougherty, Brian. 2006. This is Burning Man: The Rise of a New American Underground. Dallas, TX: BenBella Books.

Harrison, Rodney and Schofield, John. 2010. After Modernity: Archaeological Approaches to the Contemporary Past. Oxford: Oxford University Press.

Harvey, Larry. 2011. Media Myths. <http://www.burningman.com/press/myths.html> (accessed 13 February 2012).

Petersen, Andrew. 1994. The Archaeology of the Syrian and Iraqi Hajj Routes. World Archaeology 26(1): 47–56.

Schofield, John. 2000. Never Mind the Relevance: Popular Culture for Archaeologists. In Matter, Materiality and Modern Culture, ed. Paul Graves-Brown, pp. 131–54. London: Routledge.

Silverman, Helaine. 1994. The Archaeological Identification of an Ancient Peruvian Pilgrimage Center. *World Archaeology* 26(1): 1–18.

Turner, Victor. 1973. The Center Out There: Pilgrim's Goal. *History of Religions* 12(3): 191–230.

White, Carolyn and Boehm, Deborah. In preparation. Time, Interdisciplinarity, and the Burning Man Festival.

CHAPTER 41

OLYMPIC CITY SCREENS: MEDIA, MATTER, AND MAKING PLACE

ANGELA PICCINI

41.1 INTRODUCTION: A SITE

DURING the Vancouver 2010 Winter Olympic Games, thousands of people queued for up to two hours to enter a temporary structure at the corner of Cambie and Georgia Streets. I was one of 240,000 people who visited the 8000-square-foot pavilion (Four Host First Nations 2010). It was built outside the Queen Elizabeth Theatre (Arcop Group architects 1959), across the street from the brutally modernist CBC Vancouver headquarters (Paul Merrick architect 1975), a short walk away from BC Place Stadium, Canada Hockey Place, the central branch of Vancouver Public Library (Moshe Safdie architect 1996), the main Canada General Post Office (McCartner, Nairne, and Partners architects 1958), and Beatty Street Drill Hall (David Ewart architect 1901). For seventeen days, the Four Host First Nations (FHFN) Aboriginal Pavilion (Hotson Bakker Boniface Haden architects 2010) was located on a corner of Downtown Vancouver that performs place as civic, national, military, and international. Public service radio and television broadcasting, theatrical and dance performance, the national postal network, informational and archival holdings and circulation, sport (notably ice hockey), the most senior militia in the province, and popular music are all enacted *here* (see Mullins, this volume on race and monumentality in Indianapolis). The structures entangled with these practices gather in less than a square mile, in what Massey describes as the 'throwntogetherness' of the 'event of place' (2005: 149–62).

During the Games, the FHFN Aboriginal Pavilion intervened in the city block's narrative of West Coast architectural modernism and European cultural performance with a 65-foot-high inflated spherical screen and cedar, glass, and steel post-and-beam architecture. In addition to the performances of First Nations, Métis and Inuit elders, chiefs, singers, dancers, musicians, and filmmakers, the FHFN Aboriginal Pavilion enacted the 'local' through its architectural references to traditional Coast Salish houses. The structure sat among its more visibly concrete neighbours to remind people that the city of Vancouver occupies the unceded traditional and shared traditional territories of the Lil'wat, Musqueam, Squamish, and Tsleil-Waututh. Yet, even this sense of local is multiple, international, and modern:

> The Pavilion exterior is constructed using natural finishes of wood siding, glulam beams, glass, and cedar shingles. The clear fir slat ceiling complements the structure and is illuminated by recessed track lighting. Floors are showcased by intricately patterned engineered dark oak in the rotundra [sic] and textured stone tile in the gallery and lobby areas. The lobby uniquely features a 3Form wall panel that has a grass pattern similar to the long grass along the banks of the Fraser River where Musqueam is situated. (Syncra Construction n.d.)

As Sassen suggests, following Appadurai (1996), 'much of what we experience as the local because locally-sited, is actually a transformed condition in that it is imbricated with non-local dynamics or is a localization of global processes' (2006: 4; see also Byrne 2008 and Harrison 2010 on heritage as social action).

Inside the pavilion, the ten-minute film *We Are Here* ran several times daily. It was projected in 360° and was visible after dark to the crowds gathered outside. The story begins in the night sky. Digital animation and live action footage take the audience through the central hole in the roof of a Salish an house down to the hearth fire. An elder repeatedly strikes the floor with a talking stick. The scene changes and dancers fill the house. Another transition and the audience flies with an animated thunderbird past Black Tusk Mountain into the bright lights of Vancouver. A montage of British Columbia locations enacts a narrative of place and cultural heritage. Although I have a European settler background, I grew up in Vancouver learning First Nations histories filtered through colonial and neo-colonial museum displays, my family's enthusiastic appropriation of Canadian Aboriginal visual culture, and well-meaning teachers in the 1970s who helped us to build Coast Salish villages and taught us about adzes and oolichans. So, I 'know' that Black Tusk is the thunderbird's landing place, that Siwash Rock is a transformer stone, that when most of Vancouver burned down in 1886, the Squamish people rescued many of the Europeans who fled to the shores of the Burrard Inlet. The video ends with a montage of archival photographs and contemporary footage of the people who continue to live here, from proud early twentieth-century chiefs in regalia to mid-twentieth-century professional men to contemporary construction workers, teachers, and activists. Animated prehistoric petroglyphs combine with contemporary Métis jigging and traditional music performed in state-of-the-art recording studios. A female voice tells the audience 'we are here' in English and in different Aboriginal languages. There is a burst of fireworks and a final title sequence welcomes visitors to the Games in English and French. The statement 'we are here' alongside official English/French bilingualism provide what Appadurai describes as a 'circulating performative' that produces different local imaginaries about collective identity and democratic projects (2010: 10) and re-appropriates the Canadian nationalist project from an indigenous perspective.

I suggest that both the audio-visual narrative and the physical structure in which it was projected are such circulating performatives. This chapter therefore investigates the spaces, structures, and uses of Vancouver's Olympic screens in an attempt to produce an archaeology of the global Olympic brand as ephemeral (g)local event. Temporary pavilions and here-today-gone-tomorrow structures jostle with more permanent buildings (see White, this volume, on Silverman 1994). I suggest that screen structures are a significant monument type in the urban ceremonial Olympic landscape. Moreover, if the Olympics constitute collective ritual and if that ritual centres on the performance of place, then identifying

and analysing the structures of screen media as key monuments producing that performance may contribute to a broader understanding of the material practices of such rituals
and their role in enacting cultural change. I aim to provide an account of the simultaneity
of event rather than discuss excavation, ruination, or the abject (see Graves-Brown 2011).
Rather than approach archaeology as a practice of revealing what is hidden (Thomas 2004),
I am concerned with what is in plain view, what is obvious. This is what Law describes as
the 'ubiquitous performance of the anodyne' (2002: 139). Screens and screen media in the
twenty-first century city are certainly that. I suggest that ideological work is happening
through and with these physical structures and that they provide critical spaces for thinking
and acting otherwise.

41.2 AN OLYMPIC CONTEXT

Like World Expositions and FIFA World Cups, Olympic Games are mega-events (Roche
2000, 2003). They involve decades-long strategic initiatives that bend and channel global
capital through nation and city to produce the local from the global and vice versa—through
'bid books', political lobbying, business partnerships, stadia, temporary food stalls, sporting
events, public art, rerouted traffic, broadcasting rights, corporate branding, and property
development. The Games may be central to a hegemonic and totalizing discourse of neo-
liberal globalization masked as patriotism and masked further as progressive humanism
(see Lenskyj 2002). They reproduce problematic representations of race, class, and gender
(see MacAloon 1984; Billings and Angelini 2007; Daddario and Wigley 2007; Finlay and
Xin 2010; Liang 2010; Luo 2010). As a total advertising surface, the Games commodify
bodies and nations while aggressively transferring public assets into private hands through
property development (O'Bonsawin 2010), skewing public policy and funding towards
padding out the coffers of the International Olympic Committee, the local developer community, and the private security firm. Finally, despite Pierre de Coubertin's late nineteenth-
century rhetoric of marrying art, sport, and culture, the Olympic Games may be criticized
for promoting a 'bourgeois idea of competition, and a shackling of artistic freedom both
stylistically and substantively' (Inglis 2008: 465).

    Yet, the Olympic Games also provide opportunities to transform and regenerate cities
and communities, bringing millions of dollars of revenue to arts organizations and legacy
initiatives (Garcia 2004, 2008, 2009). The Vancouver 2010 Winter Olympic Games was
noted for its unique business and development partnerships with Aboriginal people, long
excluded from the 'national' stage. The Games generate and foster new forms of communication and democratic participation (Miah and Garcia 2012). In advance of the Vancouver
2010 Winter Olympic Games, social media activist-entrepreneurs Dave Olson, Kris Krug,
and Robert Scales wrote an open letter to the Vancouver Organizing Committee (VANOC)
to suggest they invite the city's social media community to design and run crowd-sourcing
projects alongside the official International Olympic Committee (IOC) media rights holders
(Rain City Studios 2009). VANOC chose instead (Krug, pers. comm. July 2009) to recruit
former CBC executive Rae Hull to develop Cultural Olympiad Digital Edition, which
included CanadaCODE, a bespoke website that invited visitors to upload images and videos to express what it means to be Canadian (Hull, pers. comm. July 2009; Hull 2010). Once

the Games began, the IOC realized it could do little to control the tide of image uploading from sporting events to Flickr and YouTube, so it launched an official Flickr group (Krug 2010). Elsewhere, W2 Community Media became 'the first ever independent social media center created to help non-accredited media journalists and bloggers to cover the Olympics' (McLaren 2010). Others have suggested that such public performances celebrating 'participation' were not unexpected or spontaneous but highly orchestrated (Klassen 2012). Either way, Vancouver 2010 was quickly branded the first fully social media games (Callari 2010; Miah 2010).

Yet, the Olympics do not take place against a homogeneous background of the city and the nation-state, a landscape that is 'given' rather than one that is emergent. As Moragas argues, 'the promotion and selection of values developed through a complex communication production process—signs, rituals, images, mise en scène, advertising, information—is the principal cultural—and political—responsibility of the Olympic Games staging process' (1992: 17, in Garcia 2008: 361; see O'Mahony 2012). In other words, the Olympic Games *perform* and are, therefore, not reducible to a closed representational narrative. Questions of the locally 'appropriate' or 'negative' (Garcia 2008: 363) take and make place as specific material-discursive formations. The very ubiquity of these formations (Law 2002: 139) presents an interesting challenge to understanding the Olympic Games, a challenge that is met by archaeology.

41.3 ARCHAEOLOGY AND THE OLYMPIC GAMES

How might an archaeological approach contribute new understandings of the Olympic Games? In what ways might archaeological methods offer the potential to think through ideological approaches to mega-events and 'event-scenarios' (see Elsaesser 2008: 90) in order to identify the workings of power as 'shifting, self-divided', as power that presents opportunities for successful opposition (Eagleton 1993: 216)? Might archaeology provide what Harrison (2011) frames as a 'surface' on which one might assemble heterogeneous materials that call into question the apparently seamless humanist and democratic message that the Olympic Games purvey?

Archaeology and the Olympic Games have, of course, been entangled from the beginning. Athens 1896 was in large part legitimized by the new archaeological practices of the late nineteenth century. In time for the 1936 Berlin Games, Emil Kunze and Hans Schleif were given responsibility for new excavations at Olympia (Kunze and Schleif 1937). More recently, archaeologists have contributed to Olympic Games scholarship, exploring the origins and expressions of the ancient Games, from the Bronze Age through to the Romans (see Raschke 1988; Young 2004; Spivey 2005). Archaeologists have also discussed photography in the context of constructions of 'antiquity' in late nineteenth-century Greece that were central to the production of the modern Games (Hamilakis 2001). Finally, with the return of the Games to Athens in 2004, attention turned to the relationship between archaeology and the contemporary Games (see Simandiraki 2005).

In my Olympics research, I hope to join recent calls for archaeologists interested in contemporary material formations to move beyond detailed catalogues of the abandoned in order to attend to the productively challenging task of surveying the 'spaces in which the past intervenes' (Harrison 2011: 153; see also Lucas, this volume; Olsen, this volume; and White, this volume). As Grosz writes:

> The past persists, and its virtual contents are rearranged, restructured, with each passing moment; it is because the past is contracted throughout the continuity of the present that history remains a political force, the site for the unravelling of the givenness of the present. (2004: 253)

This is not the antiquarian's 'reckless raking together of all that once has been' to envelop herself in 'an odour of decay' (Nietzsche 1980: 21). Voss (2010) and Harrison (2011) productively critique the (paradoxically) antiquarian tendencies of the contemporary archaeologist who simply catalogues archaeological traces and fails to understand that rather than push sweet wrappers and discarded fake blood tubes into 'the past' (see Piccini 2009) the potential of her practice is to acknowledge and actualize 'the past' as the object, in Benjamin's terms, of a construction whose place is formed not in homogeneous and empty time, but in the specificity of what is fulfilled by the here-and-now (Benjamin 1969a: 263). It is now that the past is both performed and located. Moreover, De Certeau suggests whatever that past

> holds to be irrelevant—shards created by the selection of materials, remainders left aside by an explication—comes back despite everything, on the edges of discourse or in its rifts and crannies: 'resistances', 'survivals', or delays discreetly perturb the pretty order of a line of 'progress' or a system of interpretation. (1988: 4)

While archaeologists have too literally associated such 'remainders' with the 'hidden, forgotten and abject' (Harrison and Schofield 2010: 1) their continual rearrangement suggests not a fixed past but an immanent now (Harrison 2011). Archaeological methods may enact multiple temporalities and spatialities although any human attempt to account fully for objects can result only in impoverished versions of what is, ultimately, the irreducibility of multiplicity (Latour, Harman, and Erdélyi 2011). Nonetheless, it remains important to open critical spaces for that multiplicity even in the face of its impossibility. Graves-Brown suggests that 'finding the other in the present is precisely what we need in order to counteract the hegemony of similitude' (2011: 140). I suggest that perhaps by attending to the multiplicity of the present we counteract that hegemony.

This is all very well, but where is the archaeology? Elsewhere I consider the use of archaeological imagery in moving image practices associated with the Olympics (Piccini 2012) while archaeologies of contemporary ephemeral and ritual sites successfully use conventional archaeological methods (Beck et al. 2009; Badcock and Johnston, this volume; White, this volume). In this work, I have not set out transects nor measured and drawn standing remains nor photographed features alongside ranging rods. Instead, I turn to a landscape survey approach: repeated field walking, photography, field notes, video, and collecting printed materials. I speak with people (see Fewster, this volume). These conversations may be described in terms of 'active interviewing' (Holstein and Gubrium 1995). That is, I acknowledge the interview as a dynamic process, a co-production that enacts research in the event of the meeting and its analysis. These structured conversations sit as one method within a traditional ethnographic practice of participant-observation, of living in and with the city of Vancouver—a city in which I was born and grew up, a city I left and a city to which I desire a return.

During the 2009 Cultural Olympiad and 2010 Olympic Games and Cultural Olympiad, I attended performances, screenings, and gallery shows. I talked with people involved in the Cultural Olympiad Digital Edition (CODE); CTV (the official Olympic broadcaster); at BC Tourism; the BC Film Commission; academics involved in monitoring and commenting on Olympic impacts in the city; artists concerned with the impact of Olympic funding on art in the city and the impact of the event on the city as civic, political space; and independent filmmakers struggling to find Olympics-related commissions. I went to anti-Olympic film screenings and I met a range of activists, including writers concerned about the Olympic neo-liberal tendency to privatize public space, architects critiquing the Games from a heritage perspective, and political activists who argued against the Olympics in terms of their role in generating poverty, producing homelessness, environmental degradation, and in ongoing colonization of Canada's first peoples: 'No Olympics on Stolen Native Land'.

Based on the historic link between the Olympics and archaeology, I wanted to hear what people in Vancouver considered the relationship in these Games to be. In most cases I was greeted with puzzlement. Why would archaeology have anything to do with the Olympics? Vancouver is a new city; it has no archaeology. Certainly, the Olympics had entered into business partnership with the Four Host First Nations and Coast Salish visual and material culture were branding the Games (Roth 2013: 192–217), but these are living cultures, they said, not archaeology. Sometimes people would tell me that they would love to see the archaeology and history of the city as part of the Olympic event (Kamala Todd, pers. comm. June 2009) but it was too problematic, too contested to be part of the official story. The public-facing message was that Vancouver was cosmopolitan, multicultural, future-facing.

The rejection of heritage by VANOC relates to the politics of archaeology in the city of Vancouver and the province of British Columbia, territories never legally ceded to the Crown by treaty (see also Oliver 2007 for his excellent discussion of land survey in British Columbia). In her discussion of the prehistoric Marpole Midden, Roy highlights the problem of what 'happens to land that does not become an Indian reserve but that is clearly marked with Indianness' (2007: 71). Although the Olympics constructed new sites to be marked with 'Indianness' and the opening ceremonies certainly relied on this (Piccini 2012), the fact that indigenous sites played no central role in the Olympic narrative supports Garcia's argument that Organizing committees only ever draw on uncontroversial images and materials with which both local and international audiences feel comfortable (2008). So, rather than continue to attempt to locate conventional archaeological narratives within the Olympic 'brand' (Holtorf 2007), I shifted to consider how the event itself might be considered archaeologically.

41.4 Vancouver 2010: Screen City

Samsung encouraged people to see the Games 'on all 3 screens': TV, computer, and phone. Added to personal screening devices were public art projections and installations, jumbo screens in public spaces, TVs and monitors, and touch screens in pavilions, shopping malls, buses, and boats. In short, the Olympic event was constituted by screen media and by the technologies and structures that project and transmit the moving image. Just as the relationship between archaeology and the Olympics is not new, neither is that between the city and the screen (see Clarke 1997; Bruno 2002; Brunsdon 2007; Connolly 2009; Robertson and Koeck 2010). Kracauer wrote that 'when history is made in the streets, the streets tend to move onto the screen' (1960: 98) while Eisenstein considered cinematic montage as architecture (1989). Benjamin also linked the moving image and urban architecture. He argued for the political potential of the distracted mass that absorbs the work of art and claimed that 'buildings are appropriated...by touch and sight' and this 'appropriation is accomplished not so much by attention as by habit.... Reception in a state of distraction...finds in the film its true means of exercise' (1969b: 240). With the 1970s and 1980s 'rediscovery' of such essays on 'modernity' (Elsaesser 2008: 88; see also Graves-Brown, this volume) increasing attention has since been paid to urban materialities and the moving image. Paul Virilio (1991a, 1991b) considers the screen as 'metaphoric register', a discourse that foregrounds 'dematerialization and disappearance' (Friedberg 2004: 183–5). However, Virilio's concern with loss and disappearance fails to register that whether a wall is made out of bricks or screens, it remains material. Screens have mass, chemical and mineral composition. Screens break when they fall. Screens get dirty. Screens need to be tethered to concrete structures or steel scaffolding to prevent them from flying away in the wind. As Sean Cubitt notes in his discussion of the history of cinema, 'we confront the double presence of the screen image as at once object and image' (2004: 92). The screen and screen image as object are both ubiquitous (Willis 2009) and specific (see Cubitt, this volume; Finn, this volume; Maxwell and Miller, this volume; and Noble, this volume). McCallum, Spencer, and Wyly ask *'What is the "City" that was constructed by Vancouver's bid to host the 2010 Games?'* (2005: 26, italics in original). The large-scale, publicly accessible screens of Vancouver 2010 begin to sketch an answer to this question.

Robson Square (Arthur Erikson architects 1978) was home to one of thirty-two VANOC-managed Celebration Sites set up throughout Vancouver to provide free space for residents and visitors to participate in activities, watch performances, purchase merchandise, and to watch sporting events and Cultural Olympiad Digital Edition (CODE) content. Celebration sites included the two large LiveCity sites: LiveCity Downtown (2,500 capacity) and LiveCity Yaletown (8,500 capacity) (Lupick 2010). Other Celebration Sites included Sochi House, city-sponsored open-air sites, and regional pavilions advertising business development opportunities. The Saskatchewan Pavilion encouraged visitors to imagine their futures in lentil farming while the Northwest Territories pavilion told visitors that the region enjoyed the highest weekly wages in all of Canada. In an international context, the State Development Corporation of Thüringia sponsored the popular German Haus and the Calabrian Tourism Board sponsored Casa Italia. As Berkaak notes with respect to the Lillehammer games:

> It became quite legitimate to evaluate cultural forms and performances in terms of their potential to attract customers and secure contract partners...and not to see them simply as expressions of inherent identity. (1999: 65)

Can these sites be resolved as simple marketing opportunities? A photograph of the Robson Square Celebration Site (Figure 41.1) shows a crowd of people looking at one of the films commissioned within the 'Bodies in Motion' strand of the Cultural Olympiad Digital Edition. Very few of the people in the photograph are watching the screen although they are gathered on the outdoor seating and bodily orientated towards it. The people are arranged by uniform: the free, yellow, plastic rain capes provided by BC Tourism, the red livery of

FIGURE 41.1 Robson Square Celebration Site (photograph: Angela Piccini)

Team Canada hockey, and the blue jackets of the armies of volunteers. The mise-en-scène on-screen mirrors that off-screen: in the video, two women in red dresses sit in a red rickshaw being pulled by a muscular man in a blue lycra exercise suit. The extension of screen space into the city takes shape via the steel scaffolding that supports the screen; the black borders of the screen that frame the city and image; the cables that tether the screen to the architecture of the Square with loops slung around concrete benches and fastened to features cloaked in tourist advertising; and the positioning of the screen against the urban skyline.

It is one of the few spaces in the complex where people may gather and sit. Since Robson Square's construction, this staircase has been a popular lunchtime spot for those who work in the Law Courts and in the office buildings, shops, and Vancouver Art Gallery that surround them. The existing uses of the site and the affordances of the standing architecture clearly shaped the location of the big screen, while also aligning the highly regulated spaces of the Olympics with the apparently *ad hoc*, informal use of the space at other times. However, the distribution of assembled bodies, their associated material culture, and the temporary screen stand in sharp contrast with the material-discursive practices in this site at other times, highlighting the regulatory aspect of the Games.

In parallel with the Games, Vancouver ran an ambitious Olympic and Paralympic Public Art Program: Bright Light, Mapping and Marking, Legacy Sites and Partner Projects. Rina Liddle's *We Are Watching* was produced within Bright Light. Based at the Jeffrey Boone Gallery, East Cordova Street, in Vancouver's Downtown Eastside (DTES), *We Are Watching* was a participatory work that implicated its audience in its production. There were two distinct components. A black-and-white video was projected in 4:3 ratio onto the back wall of the gallery, visible from the street through the gallery's window. The projection showed

CCTV footage of a street. As I watched, someone walked into the frame, stopped, looked up, and watched something for a while before continuing on his journey, eventually passing me outside of the gallery. I then walked east towards where I thought the man had been standing. I looked up and there, on the side of the building, was a projection of Olympic-related video footage. Liddle had invited people to send her material—everything from Olympic Resistance Network videos to mobile phone images of the torch relay. As I stood there looking up at this silent movie, a CCTV camera watched me and projected my image back into the gallery.

The outdoor projection was above fenced-off private parking space occupying ground that follows the line of the defunct CPR railway, which cut diagonally through Downtown Vancouver. Liddle's concerns with the relationship between private and public space and the spatializing practices of imaging technologies present a reflexive account of the forces enacted elsewhere in the urban Olympic landscape. Vancouver's DTES is repeatedly described as the 'poorest postcode in Canada' (e.g. Christoff and Kalache 2007; Bishop 2010) and the Olympic Games were widely criticized in the media and elsewhere (O'Bonsawin 2010) for appropriating this neighbourhood and driving out the homeless and working poor. Despite her critique of the privatization of space, Liddle's work sits in a complicated relationship to it. Bright Light artists participated in a remapping of the city instigated by the Olympics, a remapping that Jeff Derksen has written about in terms of the spatializing of social inequality (2010) and that Lois Klassen has called into question in her critique of the Games and participatory art practices (2010, 2012). Despite this scepticism, particularly with regard to the immediate recuperation of critical art practices by the economy of the Olympics (see also Cox et al. 2010), I suggest that Riddle's two screens intrude productively in the Olympic space, orientating spectators to the material structures through which the Olympics are produced.

Mapping and Marking commissioned eight works to 'celebrate, map and mark Vancouver during the 2010 Winter Games' (City of Vancouver 2010b). Three of these involved screen media practices: Fiona Bowie's *Surface*, Paul Wong's *5* and Project Rainbow's *Blue*. *Surface* sent a live camera feed from the bottom of a False Creek Aquabus (originally launched for Expo '86) to a video monitor on the ferry and a large LED screen mounted on the side of the Ocean Concrete factory at False Creek. Murky images of stickleback, seals, and Vancouver's submerged industrial archaeology contrast with the contemporary 'city of glass' (Coupland 2000) and focus the viewer's attention on the one remaining heavy industry in the centre of the city (Figure 41.2). For Zoooom, one of Wong's *5* events, participants were driven by coach through the city while watching *Snakes on a Plane* (dir. David R. Ellis 2006), which was filmed in Vancouver. *Blue* was an experimental film and dance documentary about the Canadian Women's Ski Jumping Team, who famously lost their appeal against the International Olympic Committee in the Supreme Court of Canada arguing that the IOC's refusal to allow women ski jumpers contravened the Canadian Charter of Rights. Project Rainbow was inspired by the ski jumpers' training process, responding to it through reference to Yves Klein's staged photograph *Leap into the Void* (1960) and Klein's 'International Klein Blue'. Project Rainbow's film combined specially choreographed work with the jumpers and documentary footage of the jumpers on the slopes. The film was hosted at Centre A, Strathcona Community Centre, the Chinese Cultural Centre and Soldier & Sons. It was also projected onto two LED screens on the Future Shop building at the corner of Granville and Robson Streets, Downtown Vancouver (Figure 41.3).

FIGURE 41.2 Still, *Surface*, Fiona Bowie (reproduced with permission from Inkblot Media, videographer Mike McKinlay)

FIGURE 41.3 Still, *Blue*, Project Rainbow (reproduced with permission from Inkblot Media, videographer Mike McKinlay)

The Project Rainbow booklet (2010) contextualized the project by observing that

> East Vancouver's downtown spaces, specifically Strathcona, Chinatown and The Downtown Eastside, currently occupy a critical zone of transition, and will continue to be greatly impacted by this year's events both in the short and long term. Thus, East Vancouver's landscape, much like the women ski jumpers, and much like a dancer in performance, occupies the precarious, liminal space of motion.

Both *Surface* and *Blue* used LED screens that have been at the centre of changes to Vancouver's planning by-laws. The screens are defined as 'automatic changeable copy signs'

FIGURE 41.4 *Walk In/Here You Are,* Christian Kliegel and Cate Rimmer (photograph: Angela Piccini)

and are regulated by Schedule G2 of Vancouver's Sign By-law 6510 (City of Vancouver 2006). The City requires that 10 per cent of video content on such screens, normally used for advertising, be cultural programming. With their City funding, *Blue* and *Surface* fulfilled that requirement.

Finally, Christian Kliegel and Cate Rimmer's Legacy project, *Walk In/Here You Are* returns me to the square mile in which I began. Kliegel designed an outdoor cinema in the entrance plaza of the Vancouver Public Library (Figure 41.4). Wooden decking and furniture encouraged new uses of the space. Unlike Robson Square, where the screen became part of the skyline, here the monumental wooden structure was framed against the façade of the Library. And where Robson Square showed films commissioned by CODE and sports, for *Walk In/ Here You Are* curator Cate Rimmer programmed film and video by artists including Stan Douglas, Jamie Hilder, Jeremy Shaw, Shannon Oksanen, and Weekend Leisure, who all play with notions of spectacle, promotion, and physicality. Kliegel repurposed furniture supplied by Vancouver Board of Parks and Recreation, including an iconic log from one of the city's public beaches. By fixing these directly on the decking surface such that they appear progressively to sink beneath the surface, Kliegel produces an assemblage that enacts an archaeology of Vancouver's parks to comment on the erasure of publicly accessible space in the city.

41.5 CONCLUSION

The FHFN Aboriginal Pavilion, Robson Square Celebration Site, and screenworks commissioned by the City of Vancouver Olympic and Paralympic Public Art Program mark out the space of the 2010 Games. These spaces were further territorialized in the form of the Games' security fencing and the hundreds of temporary security cameras installed for the event. These screen technologies concentrate the city in the eastern half of the Downtown core down to the north-eastern shores of False Creek and into the DTES and Strathcona. As spatializing practices, these screen structures continue work begun during Vancouver's first mega-event: Expo '86. For Expo '86, Vancouver began a regeneration process in a bid to become a world-class city, involving evictions of the poor, displacement of the homeless, and transferring of public space into private hands. After Expo '86, the land on which it was sited, and which much of Vancouver 2010 came to occupy, was sold at below-market rate by the province to property developer Li Ka-shing and his company Concord Pacific (see Surborg et al. 2008). That link between Expo '86 and Vancouver 2010 was highlighted in artist Jeremy Shaw's Cultural Olympiad work. While direct critique of the Olympics by artists was prohibited through their contractual relationship with VANOC (CBC 2010), Shaw intervened in the Olympics by reproducing Expo '86 posters that announced 'Something's Happening Here'.

Jeff Derksen suggests that the Olympics 'build up a marvellous catalogue of events prising possibility from sleepy hegemony' (2010: 60; see also González-Ruibal, this volume). The screen structures that populated Vancouver during the 2010 Winter Olympic Games might be dismissed in terms of their complicity in the capitalizing forces of VANOC. Certainly, the sheer mass of freely available spectacle during those seventeen days precipitated a dramatic cut to public-sector arts funding post-Games. However, this significant assemblage of screen structures produced multiple cities. Considering these structures as monuments within a ceremonial landscape identifies the shifting, self-divided aspects of Olympic power relations. With every effort to control discourse and control the movement of people, something always escapes. Resistance is found beyond direct action. Asking questions about the role of archaeology at the Vancouver 2010 Winter Olympic Games and approaching the city as an archaeological landscape in which pasts interrupt the space of now, troubles the rhetoric of Vancouver as 'new' and contributes to the 'unravelling [of] the givenness of the present' (Grosz 2004: 253). An archaeological approach to the Olympics productively manifests two entangled issues that all contemporary archaeologies face. In attempting to practise an archaeology of the ephemeral event by identifying materialities of shifting processes, I assemble traces at the surface in a manner that necessarily halts the process of event by producing a past in the present. However, this assembling is also an attempt to enact an archaeology of process. It is through this contingent practice, this consideration of the multiple performances of screen structures in the Olympic city, that archaeology can intervene in a city that continues to claim to be without a past, a city that frantically attempts to erase the material traces of anything not obviously here-now. Of course, in so doing, the city fails to grasp that it is attempting to erase the very here-nowness of the past, a presence now performed only through the present of the archaeological encounter.

ACKNOWLEDGEMENTS

This chapter would not have been possible without the generous support of University of Bristol and University of British Columbia, where I was a visiting scholar. Too many individuals, groups, and institutions to name here have participated in this research. I have benefited enormously from their generosity and, in many cases, friendship and from the challenging, stimulating, and energizing conversations and collaborations I have had with them and I therefore acknowledge their significant contributions to this work. I am especially grateful to Paul Graves-Brown, Rodney Harrison, Lois Klassen, Andrew Martindale, Jem Noble, and Rachel Walls for their helpful comments on versions of this chapter.

REFERENCES

Appadurai, Arjun. 1996. *Modernity at Large*. Minneapolis: University of Minnesota Press.
—— 2010. How Histories Make Geographies. *Transcultural Studies* 1: 4–13. Available at: <http://archiv.ub.uni-heidelberg.de/ojs/index.php/transcultural/issue/view/170> (accessed 31 August 2011).
Beck, Colleen, Schofield, John, and Drollinger, Harold. 2009. Archaeologists, Activists, and a Contemporary Peace Camp. In *Contemporary Archaeologies: Excavating Now*, ed. Cornelius Holtorf and Angela Piccini, pp. 95–122. Frankfurt: Peter Lang.
Benjamin, Walter. 1969a [1936]. Theses on the Philosophy of History. In *Illuminations*, ed. Hannah Arendt, tr. H. Zohn, pp. 255–66. New York: Schocken Books.
—— 1969b [1936]. The Work of Art in the Age of Mechanical Reproduction. In *Illuminations*, ed. Hannah Arendt, tr. H. Zohn, pp. 217–52. New York: Schocken Books.
Berkaak, Odd Are. 1999. In the Heart of the Volcano: The Olympic Games as Mega Drama. In *Olympic Games as Performance and Public Event: The Winter Olympic Games in Norway*, ed. Arne Martin Klausen, pp. 49–75. New York: Berghahn Books.
Billings, Andrew C. and Angelini, James R. 2007. Packaging the Games for Viewer Consumption: Nationality, Gender and Ethnicity in NBC's Coverage of the 2004 Summer Olympics. *Communication Quarterly* 55(1): 95–111.
Bishop, Greg. 2010. In the Shadow of the Olympics. *The New York Times*, 4 February. Available at: <http://www.nytimes.com/2010/02/05/sports/olympics/05eastside.html> (accessed 31 August 2011).
Bruno, Giuliana. 2002. *Atlas of Emotion: Journeys in Art, Architecture, and Film*. London: Verso.
Brunsdon, Charlotte. 2007. *London in Cinema*. London: BFI.
Byrne, Denis. 2008. Heritage as Social Action. In *The Heritage Reader*, ed. Graham Fairclough, Rodney Harrison, John H. Jameson Jr., and John Schofield, pp. 149–73. London, Abingdon, and New York: Routledge.
Callari, Ron. 2010. Vancouver 'Social Media' Olympics to Outpace Beijing. Available at: <http://inventorspot.com/articles/vancouver_social_media_olympics_outpace_beijing_37789> (accessed 19 February 2010).
CBC. 2010. Vancouver Poet Denounces VANOC 'Muzzle'. Available at:<http://www.cbc.ca/news/arts/books/story/2010/02/11/vancouver-poet-laureate-muzzle-clause.html> (accessed 10 April 2010).
Christoff, Stefan and Kalache, Sawan. 2007. The Poorest Postcode. *The Dominion*, 12 January. Available at: <http://www.dominionpaper.ca/articles/909> (accessed 31 August 2011).
City of Vancouver. 2006. Schedule G2, Sign By-law 6510. Available at: <http://vancouver.ca/commsvcs/bylaws/sign/sign.htm> (accessed 31 August 2011).
—— 2010. Bright Light. Unpublished leaflet, Olympic and Paralympic Public Art Program, City of Vancouver.
—— 2010. Mapping and Marking. Unpublished leaflet, Olympic and Paralympic Public Art Program, City of Vancouver.
Clarke, David. 1997. *The Cinematic City*. London: Routledge.

Connolly, Maeve. 2009. *The Place of Artist's Cinema*. Bristol: Intellect.

Coupland, Douglas. 2000. *City of Glass*. Vancouver and Toronto: Douglas & MacIntyre.

Cox, Geoff, Haq, Nav, and Trevor, Tom (eds.). 2010. Art, Activism and Recuperation issue. *Concept Store* 3, Arnolfini Gallery.

Cubitt, Sean. 2004. *The Cinema Effect*. Cambridge, MA: MIT Press.

Daddario, Gina and Wigley, Brian J. 2007. Gender Marking and Racial Stereotyping at the 2004 Athens Games. *Journal of Sports Media* 2(1): 29–52.

De Certeau, Michel. 1988. *The Writing of History*. New York: Columbia University Press.

Derksen, Jeff. 2010. Art and Cities During Mega-Events: On the Intersection of Culture, Everyday Life, and the Olympics in Vancouver and Beyond. Part III. *Camera Austria* 110: 60–1.

Eagleton, Terry. 1993. Ideology and its Vicissitudes in Western Marxism. In *Mapping Ideology*, ed. Slavoj Žižek, pp. 179–226. London: Verso.

Eisenstein, Sergei M. 1989 [1937]. Montage and Architecture. *Assemblage* 10: 111–31.

Elsaesser, Thomas. 2008. City of Light, Gardens of Delight. In *Cities in Transition: The Moving Image and the Modern Metropolis*, ed. Andrew Webber and Emma Wilson, pp. 88–101. London: Wallflower Press.

Finlay, Christopher J. and Xin, Xi. 2010. Public Diplomacy Games: A Comparative Study of American and Japanese Responses to the Interplay of Nationalism, Ideology and Chinese Soft Power Strategies around the 2008 Beijing Olympics. *Sport in Society* 13(5): 876–900.

Four Host First Nations. 2010. Cultural Sharing on a Global Scale. Available at: <http://www.fourhostfirstnations.com/march-1st-cultural-sharing-on-a-global-scale/> (accessed 1 September 2011).

Four Host First Nations and Vancouver Olympic Organizing Committee. 2010. Aboriginal Pavilion Fact Sheet. Available at: <http://www.fourhostfirstnations.com/ . . . /001FactSheet-PavilionFeb10EN.pdf> (accessed 1 September 2011).

Friedberg, Anne. 2004. Virilio's Screen: The Work of Metaphor in the Age of Technological Convergence. *Journal of Visual Culture* 3(2): 183–93.

Garcia, Beatriz. 2004. Urban Regeneration, Arts Programming and Major Events: Glasgow 1990, Sydney 2000 and Barcelona 2004. *International Journal of Cultural Policy* 10(1): 103–18.

—— 2008. One Hundred Years of Cultural Programming within the Olympic Games (1912–2012): Origins, Evolution and Projections. *International Journal of Cultural Policy* 14(4): 361–76.

—— 2009. The Cultural Dimension of the Olympic Games: Ceremonies and Cultural Olympiads as Platforms for Sustainable Cultural Policy. In *Barcelona 1992 and Olympic Studies: Twenty Years of Legacy*, ed. Miquel Moragas and Berta Cerezuela, pp. 153–64. Bellaterra: Centre d'Estudis Olímpics (CEO-UAB).

Graves-Brown, Paul. 2011. Touching from a Distance: Alienation, Abjection, Estrangement and Archaeology. *Norwegian Archaeological Review* 44(2): 131–44.

Grosz, Elizabeth. 2004. *Nick of Time: Politics, Evolution and the Untimely*. Durham, NC: Duke University Press.

Hamilakis, Yannis. 2001. Monumental Visions: Bonfils, Classical Antiquity, and Nineteenth-Century Athenian Society. *History of Photography* 25: 5–12.

Harrison, Rodney. 2010. Heritage as Social Action. In *Understanding Heritage in Practice*, ed. Susie West, pp. 240–76. Manchester and Milton Keynes: Manchester University Press and Open University.

—— 2011. Surface Assemblages: Towards an Archaeology *in* and *of* the Present. *Archaeological Dialogues* 18(2): 141–61.

Harrison, Rodney and Schofield, John. 2010. *After Modernity: Archaeological Approaches to the Contemporary Past*. Oxford: Oxford University Press.

Holstein, James A. and Gubrium, Jaber F. 1995. *The Active Interview*. London: Sage Publications.

Holtorf, Cornelius. 2007. *Archaeology is a Brand! The Meaning of Archaeology in Contemporary Popular Culture*. Oxford: Archaeopress.

Hull, Rae. 2010. *The CODE Book: How it Worked*. Cultural Olympiad Digital Edition.

Inglis, David. 2008. Culture Agonistes: Social Differentiation, Cultural Policy and Cultural Olympiads. *International Journal of Cultural Policy* 14(4): 463–77.

Klassen, Lois. 2010. Participating in Vancouver 2010. Paper delivered at Killer Texts: Graduate Studies Symposium, Emily Carr University, Vancouver.

—— 2012. Participatory Art at the Vancouver 2010 Cultural Olympiad. *Public* 45: 212–23.

Kracauer, Sigfried. 1960. *Theory of Film: The Redemption of Physical Reality*. Oxford: Oxford University Press.

Krug, Kris. 2010. IOC Loosens Citizen Photog Restrictions, Launches Flickr Group. *Mediashift*, 26 February. Available at: <http://www.pbs.org/mediashift/2010/02/ioc-loosens-citizen-photog-restrictions-launches-flickr-group057.html> (accessed 27 February 2010).

Kunze, Emil and Schleif, Hans. 1937. *Bericht über die Ausgrabungen in Olympia*. Berlin: Walter de Gruyter.

Latour, Bruno, Harman, Graham, and Erdélyi, Peter. 2011. *The Prince and the Wolf: Latour and Harman at the LSE*. Winchester: Zero Books.

Law, John. 2002. *Aircraft Stories: Decentring the Object in Technoscience*. Durham, NC: Duke University Press.

Lenskyj, Helen. 2002. *The Best Olympics Ever? Social Impacts of Sydney 2000*. Albany, NY: SUNY Press.

Liang, Limin. 2010. Framing China and the World through the Olympic Opening Ceremonies, 1984–2008. *Sport in Society* 13(5): 819–32.

Luo, Jialing. 2010. 'Betwixt and Between': Reflections on the Ritual Aspects of the Opening and Closing Ceremonies of the Beijing Olympics. *Sport in Society* 13(5): 771–83.

Lupick, Travis. 2010. Your Olympic Survival Guide for Music at LiveCity Vancouver. Straight.com. Available at: <http://www.straight.com/article-286302/vancouver/your-survival-guide-music-livecity-vancouver> (accessed 13 February 2010).

MacAloon, James L. 1984. Olympic Games and the Theory of Spectacle. In *Rite, Drama, Festival, Spectacle*, ed. James L. MacAloon, pp. 241–80. Philadelphia, PA: Institute for the Study of Human Issues.

McCallum, Katherine, Spencer, Amy, and Wyly, Elvin. 2005. The City as an Image-Creation Machine: A Critical Analysis of Vancouver's Olympic Bid. *Association of Pacific Coast Geographers Yearbook* 67: 24–46.

McLaren, Christine. 2010. W2's Winter Olympics Unaccredited Media Centre Opens its Doors. *The Tyee*, 10 February. Available at: <http://thetyee.ca/Blogs/TheHook/Media/2010/02/10/W2Opens/> (accessed 10 February 2010).

Massey, Doreen. 2005. *For Space*. London: Sage Publications.

Miah, Andy. 2010. The Vancouver 2010 Olympic Games: Predicting the First Major Controversy—New Media Activism. *The Huffington Post*. Available at: <http://www.huffingtonpost.com/andy-miah/the-vancouver-2010-olympi_b_453081.html> (accessed 14 February 2010).

Miah, Andy and Garcia, Beatriz. 2012. *The Olympics: The Basics*. London: Routledge.

Nietzsche, Friedrich. 1980. *On the Advantage and Disadvantage of History for Life*. Indianapolis: Hackett Publishing.

O'Bonsawin, Christine M. 2010. 'No Olympics on Stolen Native Land': Contesting Olympic Narratives and Asserting Indigenous Rights within the Discourse of the 2010 Vancouver Games. *Sport in Society* 13(1): 143–56.

Oliver, Jeff. 2007. The Paradox of Progress: Land Survey and the Making of Agrarian Society in Colonial British Columbia. In *Contemporary and Historical Archaeology in Theory*, ed. Laura McAtackney, Matthew Palus, and Angela Piccini, pp. 31–8. BAR International Series 1677. Oxford: Archaeopress.

O'Mahony, Mike. 2012. *Olympic Visions: Images of the Games through History*. Chicago: University of Chicago Press.

Piccini, Angela. 2009. Guttersnipe: A Micro Road Movie. In *Contemporary Archaeologies: Excavating Now*, ed. Cornelius Holtorf and Angela Piccini, pp. 183–200. Frankfurt: Peter Lang.

—— 2012. Materialities, Moving Images and the Vancouver 2010 Winter Olympic Games. *World Archaeology* 44(2): 291–305.

Project Rainbow. 2010. Blue. Unpublished leaflet, Olympic and Paralympic Public Art Program, City of Vancouver.

Rain City Studios. 2009. Open Letter to Vanoc. Available at: <http://raincitystudios.com/blogs-and-pods/daveo/open-letter-vanoc-media-relations-and-press-operations-social-media> (accessed 1 February 2009).

Raschke, Wendy J. (ed.). 1988. *The Archaeology of the Olympics*. Madison, WI: University of Wisconsin Press.

Robertson, Les and Koeck, Richard. 2010. *The City and the Moving Image: Urban Projections*. Basingstoke: Palgrave Macmillan.

Roche, Maurice. 2000. *Mega-Events and Modernity: Olympics and Expos in the Growth of Global Culture*. London: Routledge.

—— 2003. Mega-Events, Time and Modernity: On Time Structures in Global Society. *Time and Society* 12(1): 99–126.

Roth, Solen. 2013. *Culturally Modified Capitalism: The Native Northwest Coast Artware Industry*. Unpublished PhD dissertation. University of British Columbia.

Roy, Susan. 2007. 'Who Were These Mysterious People?' Ćəsna:m, the Marpole Midden, and the Dispossession of Aboriginal Lands in British Columbia. *BC Studies* 152: 67–95.

Sassen, Saskia. 2006. Making Public Interventions in Today's Massive Cities. *Static* 4. Available at: <http://static.londonconsortium.com/issue04/sassen_publicintervensions.php> (accessed 1 December 2011).

Silverman, Helaine. 1994. The Archaeological Identification of an Ancient Peruvian Pilgrimage Centre. *World Archaeology* 26(1): 1–18.

Simandiraki, Anna. 2005. Minoan Archaeology in the Athens 2004 Olympic Games. *European Journal of Archaeology* 8: 157–81.

Spivey, Nigel. 2005. *The Ancient Olympics*. Oxford: Oxford University Press.

Surborg, Bjorn, VanWynsberghe, Rob, and Wyly, Elvin. 2008. Mapping the Olympic Growth Machine: Transnational Urbanism and the Growth Machine Diaspora. *City* 12(3): 341–55.

Syncra Construction. n.d. The Musqueam Cultural Pavilion. Available at: <http://syncra-construction.com/project-appreciation/musqueam-pavilion_html.html> (accessed 1 December 2011).

Thomas, Julian. 2004. *Archaeology and Modernity*. London: Routledge.

Virilio, Paul. 1991a. *The Aesthetics of Disappearance*, tr. Philip Beitchman. New York: Semiotext(e).

Virilio, Paul. 1991b. *Lost Dimension*. Cambridge, MA: MIT Press.

Voss, Barbara. 2010. Matter Out of Time. The Paradox of the 'Contemporary Past'. *Archaeologies* 6(1): 181–92.

Willis, Holly. 2009. City as Screen/Body as Movie. *Afterimage* 37(2): 24–8.

Young, David C. 2004. *A Brief History of the Olympic Games*. Oxford: Blackwell.

CHAPTER 42

MATERIAL ANIMALS: AN ARCHAEOLOGY OF CONTEMPORARY ZOO EXPERIENCES

CORNELIUS HOLTORF

42.1 INTRODUCTION: AN ARCHAEOLOGICAL APPROACH TO UNDERSTANDING ZOOS IN THE EXPERIENCE ECONOMY

ACCORDING to sociologist Gerhard Schulze (1992), for the past few decades we have been living in a society in which experiences have become a central focus of life. This includes the preferences of individuals both as consumers and as social beings more generally. Subjectively believed properties of things matter more than their objective properties, and the consumers' satisfaction is dependent on what they believe themselves to have bought, not what they 'actually' bought (Schulze 1992: 442–3). Experience your life! is the categorical imperative of our age and we are thus all living in what Schulze called the Experience Society. Indeed, people increasingly appear to live their lives for the experiences they can have. Yet while each of us seeks a life (ful)filled by experiences, the respective social milieus we belong to influence what kind of experiences qualify in the pursuit of our respective life projects.

Joseph Pine and James Gilmore (2011) have taken the analysis of these trends in another direction. The two economists observed that businesses increasingly create experiences and memories of experiences rather than goods or services. They have therefore introduced the notion of the Experience Economy that, according to their analysis, has been replacing the previous economy of good and services. In this new economy, which still continues, customers pay money to spend time enjoying memorable, staged events that engage them in compelling and personal ways (see also Harrison, this volume).

Pine and Gilmore have made another, interesting distinction concerning the Experience Economy. On the one hand, they argue (2011: 22–32), there are the mechanics of what a produced good does or the character of what a service offered actually provides. On the other hand, there are the customers who experience using a good or a service. Pine and Gilmore argue that the customers' experience of using a good or a service needs to be foregrounded in order to succeed in the Experience Economy. This requires 'an experience-directed mind-set' which focuses on the design and orchestration of experiences using a given product.

Zoos are an important part of the Experience Society and, not surprisingly, they have a significant appeal to customers in the Experience Economy. There is a clear trend within zoos and animal parks towards providing ever more extraordinary experiences for visitors through memorable, staged events. Examples range from 'meet the keeper' to 'behind the scenes' tours and from 'spend a night at the zoo' to 'swim with dolphins'. Visitors are invited to enact animal-related fantasies thus escaping the routines of their everyday lives. Previously explicitly marked boundaries between animals and keepers on the one side and visitors on the other side are increasingly being eroded (Frost and Laing 2011). Historically, the link between a preference of contemporary zoo visitors for experiences and the match-ing attractions offered in present-day zoos is not entirely new. However, the scale and comprehensiveness in which visits to many of the major zoos have become thoroughly 'experientized' through both design and demand exceed previous patterns by far (for more comprehensive analyses of zoo history, see e.g. Montgomery 1995; Mullan and Marvin 1999; Baratay and Hardouin-Fugier 2002; Hancocks 2007).

Such is the appeal of becoming engaged in compelling and personal ways in zoos that they are doing extremely well in the Experience Economy. More than 700 million people visit the 1,300 zoos and aquariums worldwide linked to the World Association of Zoos and Aquariums (WAZA 2012). To compare, the total number of tickets for the 2012 Olympic Summer Games in London was 8.8 million; the grand total of attendees at all World Disney attractions around the globe in 2010 amounted to 120.6 million; and the most-viewed American TV broadcast of all times was the 2012 Super Bowl watched globally by nearly 167 million viewers (Figure 42.1). Annual zoo visits make all these mega events seem insig-nificant. Why is that the case?

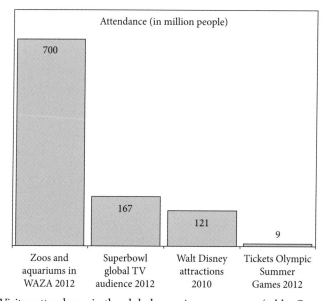

FIGURE 42.1 Visitor attendance in the global experience economy (table: Cornelius Holtorf)

At first glance, it seems rather obvious that one of the main appeals of zoos is to provide visitors with the opportunity of experiencing living animals. Observing wild animals in captivity is typically assumed to be the engaging experience zoos have to offer (e.g. Croke 1997). Indeed, according to the dictionary, zoos are 'a place where live animals are kept, studied, bred, and exhibited to the public' (Collins 2011). Similarly, the mission statement of, for example, Edinburgh Zoo (2012) is 'to inspire and excite our visitors with the wonder of living animals, and so to promote the conservation of threatened species and habitats'.

But how essential are live animals really for the zoo experience? To what extent can zoos succeed in providing visitors with sufficiently engaging experiences and a sense of wildlife *without* any living animals? These are some of the specific questions to be discussed in this chapter.

In what follows, I am offering an archaeological perspective on contemporary zoo experiences. Archaeologists are, among other things, used to studying material culture, not only regarding their patterns in space and time but also within larger theoretical frameworks. Here, I focus specifically on an analysis of material animals as part of the zoo experience, with implications for the role of living animals. Fittingly in the Experience Economy, I am adopting an experience-directed mindset (as defined by Pine and Gilmore 2011: 27), foregrounding how zoo experiences are designed and how visitors in turn experience what they find in zoos.

A study of contemporary material culture in the zoo turns out to be well suited to exploring previously neglected aspects of what visitors experience in a zoo. It emerges, among other things, that visiting a zoo is about something else than what it appears to be at face value as living animals are not as central to the zoo experience as is often assumed.

My argument will proceed by first making some theoretical distinctions on which the following analysis of animal representations and animal reifications will be based. I will conclude with a broader discussion of the developing character of zoo experiences on the one hand and of the potential of contemporary archaeologies on the other hand.

42.2 ANIMALS AND ANIMALNESS IN THE ZOO

Zoos do not only contain displays of living animals and facilities associated with them but also playgrounds, restaurants, cafeterias, educational centres, stages, shops, picnic areas, and other conveniences for visitors. Indeed, visitors probably spend as much time consuming food, watching other visitors or their children, and resting as they do studying animals.

This pattern is nicely represented in popular depictions of zoos such as IKEA's carpet for children's rooms (reproduced in Holtorf 2008b: fig. 1). On the image you see two zebras, two giraffes, two elephants plus a few ducklings, but most prominently there are a large entrance gate decorated with balloons, a stage, a boat ride on a lake, and a kiosk with outdoor eating area as well as several golf holes (!). This already suggests that living animals may be less central to the zoo experience than is commonly thought by those visiting zoos and possibly even those managing zoos. The Virtual Zoo provided by WAZA presents an idealized picture of a zoo that gives far more room to live animal displays than you will find in real world zoos (WAZA 2012). It does not contain a restaurant or cafeteria nor is there a playground, although practically every zoo has both.

In the following I wish to develop the idea that zoos are not so much about experiencing live animals as about experiencing animalness. Animalness is the quality of being an animal, providing a contrast to the visitors' humanness. Animalness can be witnessed and to some extent sensually experienced by visitors throughout the zoo, whether live animals are close or not. Ironically, live zoo animals are occasionally even trained in order to perform 'natural' behaviour that conforms to cultural expectations of what it means to be an animal in human eyes (Mullan and Marvin 1999: 129–30). This, incidentally, illustrates why a focus on animalness does not at all preclude anthropomorphism; it rather steers it in the direction of certain clichés rather than others (Mullan and Marvin 1999: ch. 1).

I will be suggesting that zoos can reach two of their main goals, education and entertainment, through visitors experiencing animalness. The other main goals of zoos, biological research and conservation, can be indirectly advanced by visitors experiencing animalness, too, for example when they are intended to learn about the need to conserve the rain forest or about particular zoological research results.

42.3 THINGS AND OTHER ANIMALS (MATERIAL ANIMALS I)

Zoos contain any number of things representing animals (Figure 42.2). These things evoke animalness in different ways and some of them even allow visitors to experience animalness physically, thus going far beyond the opportunities live animals can provide. Arguably, such material animals are more central to the zoo experience than most visitors tend to assume.

Common are animal sculptures that provide decoration and inspiration throughout the zoological garden. Many of these sculptures follow a naturalistic style and are made of durable materials like bronze or concrete so that they can be placed outdoors along the paths of the zoo. A special class of animal sculptures is, however, often displayed indoors. They are part of educational displays that may allow visitors to touch the sculpture, study what goes on inside the body of a particular animal species, or illustrate a particular behaviour. Other animal sculptures are linked to fund-raising initiatives for particular conservation projects, providing an extra stimulus for visitors to part with their money. Examples of three-dimensional representations of animals can also be found in some exhibits, in zoo shops and restaurants, contributing in each case to creating the right atmosphere, most commonly by suggesting stories about exploration in remote areas of the world.

Another subclass of animal sculptures can be found in playgrounds for children. Here children can sit, jump, or swing on animals made of plastic or wood. Such sculptural representations are more than the material manifestations of an animal theme for entertainment purposes. For children, they are often the preferred way of encountering animals in the zoo. Whereas adults have become educated about the special value of live animals, children are able to encounter, experience, and indeed enact animalness by physically exploring animal sculptures. Some particularly well-done examples can be found at Copenhagen Zoo. Here children can climb inside an enlarged turtle shell to get the physical sensations a turtle may have. They can also put their own head inside an enlarged empty rabbit head and look out through the opening of the eyes on either side, thus gaining literally insights in

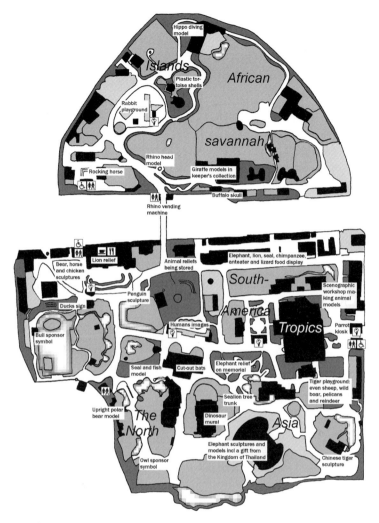

FIGURE 42.2 The ubiquity and variety of material animal representations at Copenhagen Zoo (map: Cornelius Holtorf based on fieldwork conducted in 2007/8)

their immense range of vision covering almost 360 degrees both horizontally and vertically (resembling a so-called fisheye view in photography). Whether or not humans can really get a sense of what it is like to be an animal, surely such displays are able to change the children's perspective and provide them with sensations that are based on other species' realities (for further examples and discussion see Holtorf 2000: 204). Such sensations and experiences are far more than what adults commonly learn from reading information boards containing trivial animal facts while gazing at some large carnivores basking in the sun.

However, there are some very notable exceptions of inspirational and educational animal sculptures that invite visitors of all ages to experience animalness. At Folsom City Zoo Sanctuary in California, USA, a wooden puma rests on the branch of a tree above the exhibit of its living mates. This sculpture outside the enclosure and well above the visitors' heads is able to give a much better impression of encountering a wild animal behaving naturally than a living puma sleeping, resting, or pacing behind bars ever will. Some animal sculptures are associated with a bench or other sitting opportunity so that the visitor gets the sensation of actually sharing that place with an animal and experiencing close bodily contact. Taking this idea further is Bart Walter's sculpture group *The Gathering* at the American National Zoo in Washington, DC. Seven life-size chimpanzee sculptures cast in bronze represent different social roles of chimpanzee individuals. They invite visitors to become part of the group and participate in its non-verbal communication with their own body language, thus enacting and performing animalness (Figure 42.3). As zoo director Lucy Spelman put it at the unveiling in 2002, the bronze sculptures are intended 'to inspire our visitors to develop stronger bonds with animals and motivate them to help protect nature', thus contributing to the very essence of what zoos intend to be about (Smithsonian's National Zoo 2002).

If I am right in arguing that things can take the role of animals in zoos and contribute to the heart of the zoo experience, I am effectively severing the direct link between living animals and the zoo experience. In order to experience animalness and thus nature in the zoo, you do not necessarily require living animals but in certain circumstances things can suffice. Zoos can reach their goals related to education and entertainment by providing visitors opportunities to encounter, experience, or even enact animalness. The necessary supply of animalness can be derived not only from living animals but also from suitable material animals.

Are zoos conceivable without any living animals at all? At least one animal park already exists that contains nothing alive except for the visitors themselves. The Swedish artist Eric Langert created in 1997 an exhibition entitled *My Animal Park* which has been travelling throughout Scandinavia since then. Langert's zoo consists of full-size animals constructed from materials that reflect the character of the species they portray. As he explains, 'I have made birds from Venetian blinds ribs whose technical properties represent for me the ultimate combination of weightlessness, pliability and strength...and furthermore associates to air and light' (Langert n.d.). This curious mixture of nature and technology allows visitors to experience part of the nature of animals, their bodies and their behaviour, without any living animals being near.

Something similar happens when visitors encounter artworks by Olly and Suzi. They have become known for their paintings and drawings which are made in close proximity to wild animals, often endangered predators, right inside their natural habitats. The idea is then to get the particular animal to interact with the work, ideally leaving some kind of mark. This interaction is also captured on camera. As Olly put it once, 'A tiger in a zoo moves in a very different way to one in the wild, and what we wanted to capture was the essence of the wild animal' (Mikhail 2001). It is indeed intriguing to what extent the battered paintings together with the accompanying photographs give visitors a sense of the presence—and indeed preciousness—of wild animals behaving naturally. The encounter with the wild is mediated by the artwork but somehow it nevertheless succeeds better than some zoo displays in evoking essential animalness. Although they have not exhibited in zoos, Ollie and Suzi did have a major exhibition 'Untamed' at the Natural History Museum in London in 2001/2.

Thus far I have argued that things, as material animals, can provide visitors with opportunities to encounter, experience, and enact animalness and thus help in fulfilling some of the ambitions of zoos that are related to entertainment and education about animals and

FIGURE 42.3 Visitors enact what it means to be part of a chimpanzee group when they enter Bart Walter's sculpture group *The Gathering*, unveiled in 2002 at the US National Zoo in Washington, DC (photograph: Cornelius Holtorf)

the natural world. Whereas this part of the argument can stand or fall by itself, there is the intriguing corollary that maybe there are some living animals in the zoo that in turn do not contribute to the experience of animalness and instead acquire thingliness, thus functioning as a variation of material culture. This is less a test of the validity of my first proposition and more a way of taking the argument one step further by offering a second proposition. Both sides of my argument do, however, put into question the seemingly inherent link between zoo experiences and living exhibits.

42.4 The Thing with Animals (Material Animals II)

Many living animals in zoos are humanized. Visitors do not only make sense of the animals in terms of the human nuclear family and human behaviour more generally but they are also increasingly anxious to know that the animals are being treated humanely. Whatever natural conditions may be like for their fellow species members in the wild, zoo animals need to receive nutritious food and proper medical care; their cages and enclosures ought to be spacious and clean; they must have opportunity to exercise their natural behaviour as far as possible; and they have the right to privacy outside the visitor's view. As a result of such humane treatment combined with appropriate zoological competence, zoo animals may live longer, suffer less disease and debilitation, and are often stronger than their counterparts in the wild (Montgomery 1995: 590–4). However, this amount of humanitarian care is not extended to all living animals in the zoo.

There are not only animals, such as rats, that are actively made unwelcome and even eradicated in zoos and other animals, such as mice and chicken, that are bred as food for carnivores but in the present context even more relevant are animals that acquire significance in zoos for their material associations and properties. In other words, there are some animals in the zoo that do not necessarily possess much animalness but instead are reified and acquire thingliness. By an animal's thingliness I mean the quality of the animal being a thing. One way in which animals are reified and acquire thingliness is through ambitious zoo architecture that determines much of the meaning of the animals it contains. In such enclosures the animals become little else than part of the built environment that communicates carefully designed messages to visitors. A good example is provided by the buildings constructed by the modernist architect Berthold Lubetkin (1901–90) for a number of English zoos. Among them is the famous Penguin Pool which opened in 1934 at London Zoo. Following the dictum of modernist architecture 'form follows function' the pool architecture was meant to express something that could be called penguinness and consists of penguin behaviour as imagined by the architect and manifested in his building (Figure 42.4). In effect, the enclosure became a machine in which concrete architecture and living animals together were meant to co-produce a sensual message to visitors about what it meant to be a penguin. The fact that the animals were actually living beings with particular needs too was not a main priority in the pool design; instead they were perceived as material entities that fulfilled the architectural design of their enclosure. As recently as 2004 the penguins were moved to another location in the zoo so that Lubetkin's penguin machine is now no longer functioning as it was originally intended (Shapland and Reybrouck 2008).

Living animals may also be rendered into things in zoos when they become commodities. It is easy to see how all zoo animals may be considered as commodities. They are trapped in enclosures, exchanged in captive-breeding programmes, and displayed to visitors who are paying a fee for the benefit of looking at them and subsequently spend more money on merchandise representing the animals as symbols of genuine and often vanishing nature (Mullan and Marvin 1999: ch. 7; Beardsworth and Bryman 2001: 96). Indeed, Ralph Acampora (1998) compared zoos with pornography insofar as both make the nature of their subjects disappear precisely by overexposing them to the visitors' gaze. According to such analyses zoos actually prevent visitors from experiencing animalness through their very display. However, these are rather abstract and general ways of commodification that might still be reconciled with a realization that the animals are living beings and appreciated as such.

A more concrete kind of reification and commodification is discernible when animals, or parts of them, are actually sold to visitors as things. Zoo animals are not commonly sold as food in zoo restaurants and zoo shops do not tend to sell much more of the animals than animal dung which promises benefits to the visitors' plants and gardens. There are, however, revealing exceptions. For example, peacock feathers cannot only be picked up along the paths of zoos in which they roam free but they are also on sale in zoo shops, as observed in Stuttgart's Wilhelma Zoo in southern Germany (Figure 42.5). For school children, such feathers are inexpensive souvenirs that effectively let them take home part

FIGURE 42.4 Berthold Lubetkin's 1934 Penguin Pool at London Zoo produced penguinness by letting the reified animals fulfil the intention of the concrete architecture surrounding them (photograph: Cornelius Holtorf)

of a zoo animal. It turns out that peacocks also provide one exception to the general rule that zoo animals are not offered as food in zoos. According to press reports from 2004, Nanning Zoo in China has been serving ostrich and peacock soup to visitors during the Chinese New Year celebrations. The meat was from animals previously held in the zoo. According to one report (Reuters 2004), a zoo spokesman declared that 'the main objective of the event was for visitors to understand that the zoo not only keeps animals for public viewing but also produces animals with "economic value" that can be eaten'. In other words, these animals were explicitly valued as commodities and effectively became very material animals.

Peacocks (peafowl) also provide a good example for a final way in which zoo animals can acquire thingliness. This is ironic insofar as they belong to the few species that often roam free through the zoo and are thus seemingly behaving most naturally. But although zoo visitors respect peacocks as living creatures and are excited when they get close to them, at the same time they do not necessarily possess a lot of animalness. Both children and adults tend to observe peacocks much longer and with much keener interest than they observe most other birds kept in zoos. Whereas children may enjoy chasing them as toys, the main attention peacocks receive from adults is often in relation to the chance of seeing them display their spectacular tails with the colourful train feathers—which is that part of the birds that has long been most reified. Originally, peacocks came from India where they have long had profound symbolic meanings and were considered sacred animals in Hinduism, among others closely associated with Lord Krishna who is wearing peacock feathers on his head. In Christianity they were associated with resurrection and

FIGURE 42.5 At Stuttgart's Wilhelma Zoo, visitors are welcome to acquire a token piece of the animal collection in the shop (photograph: Cornelius Holtorf)

renewal and became a symbol of eternal life partly due to the fact that the beautiful feathers are replaced annually (Reimbold 1983). Peacocks have thus long been surrounded by a very particular aura that is linked to the decorative qualities of their tails.

Although animals themselves, peacocks in the zoo frame the other animals and to some extent the overall zoo experience of human visitors. Adopting an experience-directed mindset, free-roaming peacocks in zoos to a considerable extent serve as mobile decoration and stimulus for visitors of all ages. They play a role that is more akin to the role of zoo playgrounds, architecture and ornamental flowerbeds than those of the other animals kept in their enclosures. In that sense, they are reified animals. If Bob Mullan and Garry Marvin (1999: 78) are right in stating that in zoos, generally, 'the animal is the actor on a decorated stage', peacocks belong in some ways to the side of the stage rather than that of the living animals. In fact, peacocks have been adorning gardens and parks for about 3,000 years, and they are mentioned in the Bible (1 Kings 10:22) as a precious ware imported by King Solomon. Indeed, insofar as peacocks make people halt, look, and enjoy themselves, they can be said to constitute sensual enrichment for zoo visitors while they move from one animal enclosure to the next. This suggestion is also supported by sculptures of peacocks that adorn park areas in several zoos in much the same way as living specimens, for example at Tierpark Berlin in Germany. At Antwerp Zoo, Belgium, and Parken Zoo in Eskilstuna, Sweden, there are even large peacock sculptures made from beautiful flowers!

42.5 DISCUSSION: UNDERSTANDING ZOO EXPERIENCES

Thus far I have been discussing different kinds of material animals, adopting an experience-directed mindset by foregrounding how visitors sensually experience different kinds of animals during their zoo visit. I have argued that live animals may be less essential for the visitors' zoo experience than is often assumed and that zoos can succeed in providing visitors with engaging experiences and a sense of wildlife without living animals being involved. This is because things can become material animals. They can possess, and allow, zoo visitors to experience the same quality that many live animals possess and that zoos to a great extent are all about: animalness. Mullan and Marvin (1999: 159–60) are right to argue that 'it is the oscillation between "like us" and "not like us" which accounts for much of the fascination' of zoos. However, they are wrong if they assume that the animals' otherness and thus the mentioned oscillation can only be perceived by observing the varied activities of living animals.

In the second part of my argument I questioned the link between zoo experiences and live animals by investigating a different kind of material animals: living animal in zoos that are being reified and therefore acquire thingliness. It turns out that not all living animals in zoos are in fact appreciated or experienced as living beings and that some are rather perceived as part of the built environment, part of decorative garden ornaments, or indeed commodities of various sorts.

Foregrounding experiences and studying the role of contemporary material culture in the zoo suggest that living animals are less central to the experience of visiting a zoo than is commonly assumed. Indeed, things and animals are not categorically separated in the zoo but are occasionally nearly interchangeable, with both contributing to zoo experiences that are widely appreciated by visitors. This implies a new understanding of the zoo as an institution—one that is in line with patterns of the Experience Economy. Zoos are usually understood as institutions that provide visitors with the service of allowing them to observe and learn about living wild animals in captivity. But the actual experience of visiting a zoo is not in fact mainly about observing and learning about living animals. This change of perspective from looking at the character of the service offered by a zoo to focusing on the experience of visiting a zoo has been captured well by Vicky Croke (1997: 99) who stated from an experience-directed mindset that 'the zoo is a noisy place, with a cacophony of roars, screeches, growls—not from the animals, but directed at them by visitors'. Zoo visits are, to a large extent, about humans spending time together as a couple or a family, relaxing in a pleasant cultural landscape of buildings and vegetation, engaging all the senses with memorable stimuli, enjoying the entertainment provided, learning something about animals and their habitats, contributing to the conservation of wildlife, and not the least they are about experiencing animalness. Given this characterization of the zoo, it does not matter much that few animals displayed in zoos have ever lived in the wild, or indeed would be fit to live in the wild. By the same token, material animals have an obvious potential in zoos.

Intriguingly, more and more zoos create so-called immersion exhibits in which living animals are no longer displayed in a way that makes them conveniently visible for the

FIGURE 42.6 The quasified wilderness in Burgers' Bush, Arnhem, celebrates authentic ani-malness by hiding the animals (photograph: Cornelius Holtorf)

visitor. Instead, visitors are getting the impression that they are entering the realm of the animals (Mullan and Marvin 1999: ch. 3; Hancocks 2007). Such exhibits invite visitors to engage in their own explorations in order to discover the animals. A prominent example of this trend is Burgers' Zoo in Arnhem in the Netherlands which has attempted to create actual natural conditions in huge, fully controlled halls containing entire biotopes (Hooff 2000). In Burgers' Zoo, in the Bush, Ocean, and Desert biotopes hundreds of animal species live free and only those that might become dangerous to visitors have their own enclosures. Although visitors may struggle to identify very many species, they appreciate emotionally the freedom of the invisible animals. What is more, based on my own experience, they will remember far longer those animals they actually do discover themselves (Figure 42.6). In the eyes of the visitors, Burgers' Zoo displays animalness under natural conditions rather than animals under cultural conditions, with resounding success. Arguably, in such exhib-its, by looking at fewer living animals than in traditional zoos, visitors experience more animalness.

As this example illustrates, the exhibition of living animals in the zoo has today become subordinate to what the sociologists Alan Beardsworth and Alan Bryman (2001) called the staging of elaborate quasifications of the 'wild'. Quasifications are not fakes that deceive visitors but evocative experiences which inspire and engage visitors through their skil-ful artificiality (see also Sanes 1998). Such experiences can be further enriched through active participation and increased levels of immersion of the visitors. Experiences are also enhanced by creating coherent themes that alter visitors' senses of the reality. Successfully themed environments captivate visitors by employing four techniques. They harmonize vis-itors' impressions with positive cues; they carefully eliminate negative cues; they stimulate all the senses; and they offer opportunities to purchase appropriately themed memorabilia (Pine and Gilmore 2011: chs. 2 and 3).

Zoo exhibits are commonly themed around notions of exploring particular habitats such as the South American rain forest or the African savannah. Here things do not only look the part in a very detailed way and with any distractions of the impression minimized, but they also sound, smell, and sometimes even taste and feel in correspondence with the relevant theme. Material animals play an important role in all this. As I discussed earlier, various kinds of animal representations contribute in different ways to harmonizing the visitors' impressions and providing additional visual and sometimes tactile stimulation by evoking animalness. By the same token, the visitor experience is enhanced through zoo design and architecture as well as through free-ranging but reified animals like peacocks that embellish the stage-set of the zoo. In addition, commodification processes allow visitors at appropriately located selling points to purchase topical mementoes of their visit in the form of a variety of themed representations of animals and occasionally even of parts of the animals themselves.

For the past few decades zoos have increasingly been setting themselves up along the theme of being conservation centres that care for species survival, thus replacing previously widespread perceptions of the zoo as repositories—or worse, prisons—of living animals. Most significant in the present context, however, is the way zoos develop the theme of encountering wild animals in nature. They are celebrating the signature division of modernity in which notions of wilderness, natural creatures, and primitive tribes are separated from those of cities, industry, and technology of Western civilization (Mullan and Marvin 1999; Beardsworth and Bryman 2001). It is therefore not surprising that rather than living animals being the primary attraction, animalness made accessible in exciting settings of wild nature provides the main appeal of zoos in the present. As Beardsworth and Bryman have it: 'Rather than the animals being the primary attraction, the settings themselves will become the main object of the visitor's entranced and admiring gaze' (2001: 100). As a result, the themed zoo becomes the location where modern, urban populations can enjoy a quasified form of wilderness close to home. Arguably this is why zoos are so popular today. This would also explain why zoos no longer compete with circuses featuring live animals and instead with enterprises like the Rainforest Café featuring quasifications of the wild (Beardsworth and Bryman 1999).

42.6 CONCLUSIONS: ON CONTEMPORARY ARCHAEOLOGIES

In this chapter I illustrated how an archaeological research approach can suggest a novel interpretation of the zoo experience. My archaeological approach consisted of combining an eye for the cultural significance of material phenomena with an experience-directed mindset, and bringing both to bear on contemporary zoos (see also Holtorf forthcoming). This perspective allowed me to contextualize recent changes in zoo design within larger economic trends of the contemporary world. Archaeology is thus not only a significant theme that crops up in various places linked to materializations of the Experience Society and Experience Economy but also a tool that can be used to understand more about the Experience Society and Experience Economy themselves (see also Holtorf 2009; Fewster, this volume; Harrison, this volume).

In my study, it turned out that zoo visitors may be mistaken when they describe their own experience of the zoo first and foremost in relation to the presence of live animals that inspire, excite, and educate them. It rather appears to be much more complicated in that zoos revolve around a range of experiences including, significantly, the experience of animalness. Through visitors experiencing or enacting animalness, zoos find that they can advance two of their main goals, education and entertainment. Yet animalness, as I have shown, emanates not only from living creatures but also from various things. Visitors do not appear to notice that experiencing animalness is the experience provided by the zoo as a whole, in a variety of ways, whereas experiencing living animals is nothing but one instance within that larger category. I also discussed how sometimes zoo visitors appreciate live zoo animals not at all as living creatures but rather as things, even though they may not always be aware of it. Schulze's dictum (1992: 442–3) that in the Experience Society the consumers' satisfaction is dependent on what they believe themselves to have bought, not what they 'actually' bought, thus needs to be modified in the light of insights gained from contemporary archaeology: the consumers' satisfaction is dependent on what they experienced in their minds and with their senses (animalness, reified animals), not what they believe or say they have experienced (living animals).

My discussion and the conclusions I arrived at hopefully suggest that even though the discipline of archaeology conventionally deals with 'dead' things of the past, occasionally it can contribute to improving our understanding of human experiences in the present. By studying material culture in an empirically open-minded and theoretically informed manner, we can expect contemporary archaeologies to produce many further important insights about the contemporary world.

ACKNOWLEDGEMENTS

The present chapter forms part of a larger research interest concerning the archaeology of zoos (e.g. Holtorf 2000, 2008a, forthcoming). Earlier versions of this chapter were presented at the International Council for Archaeozoology (ICAZ) Conference in Mexico City in 2006 and at the Nordic TAG Conference in Århus, Denmark, 2007. For helpful comments about a penultimate version of this chapter I am grateful to Laia Colomer and Angela Piccini.

REFERENCES

Acampora, Ralph A. 1998. Extinction by Exhibition: Looking at and in the Zoo. *Human Ecology Review* 5(1): 1–4.
Baratay, Eric and Hardouin-Fugier, Elisabeth. 2002. *Zoo: A History of Zoological Gardens in the West*. London: Reaktion.
Beardsworth, Alan and Bryman, Alan. 1999. Late Modernity and the Dynamics of Quasification: The Case of the Themed Restaurant. *The Sociological Review* 47: 228–57.
—— 2001. The Wild Animal in Late Modernity: The Case of the Disneyization of Zoos. *Tourist Studies* 1(1): 83–104.

Collins English Dictionary. 2011. <http://www.collinsdictionary.com> (accessed 12 March 2012).

Croke, Vicki. 1997. *The Modern Ark: The Story of Zoos—Past, Present and Future.* New York: Avon.

Edinburgh Zoo. 2012. About the Zoo. Available at: <http://www.edinburghzoo.org.uk/about/> (accessed 12 March 2012).

Frost, Warwick and Laing, Jennifer. 2011. Up Close and Personal: Rethinking Zoos and the Experience Economy. In *Zoos and Tourism: Conservation, Education, Entertainment?*, ed. W. Frost, pp. 133–42. Bristol: Channel View.

Hancocks, David. 2007. Zoo Animals as Entertainment Exhibitions. In *A Cultural History of Animals in the Modern Age*, ed. R. Malamud, pp. 95–118. Oxford and New York: Berg.

Holtorf, Cornelius. 2000. Sculptures in Captivity and Monkeys on Megaliths: Observations in Zoo Archaeology. *Public Archaeology* 1: 195–210.

—— 2008a. Zoos as Heritage. Special issue of *International Journal of Heritage Studies* 14(1): 1–90, ed. Cornelius Holtorf.

—— 2008b. Zoos as Heritage: An Archaeological Perspective. *International Journal of Heritage Studies* 14(1): 3–9.

—— 2009. Imagine This: Archaeology in the Experience Society. In *Contemporary Archaeologies: Excavating Now*, ed. Cornelius Holtorf and Angela Piccini, pp. 47–64. Frankfurt: Peter Lang.

—— Forthcoming 2013. The Zoo as a Realm of Memory. *Anthropological Journal of European Cultures* 22.

Hooff, Antoon J. M. van. 2000. Burgers' Zoo. In *Erlebnis- und Konsumwelten*, ed. A. Steinecke, pp. 279–88. Munich and Vienna: R. Oldenbourg.

Langert, Eric. n.d. My Animal Park. Available at: <http://www.langert.se> (accessed 17 March 2012).

Mikhail, Kate. 2001. Where the Wild Things Are. *The Observer*, 15 July. Available at: <http://www.guardian.co.uk/theobserver/2001/jul/15/features.magazine47> (accessed 20 March 2012).

Montgomery, Scott L. 1995. The Zoo: Theatre of the Animals. *Science as Culture* 4(21): 565–600.

Mullan, Bob and Marvin, Garry. 1999. *Zoo Culture: The Book about Watching People Watch Animals*, 2nd edn. Urbana and Chicago: University of Illinois Press.

Pine, B. Joseph II and Gilmore, James H. 2011. *The Experience Economy*, updated edn. Boston, MA: Harvard Business Review Press.

Reimbold, Ernst T. 1983. *Der Pfau. Mythologie und Symbolik.* Munich: Callwey.

Reuters. 2004. Zoo Visitors in a Flap over Peacock Soup. Available at: <http://forums.yellow-world.org/showthread.php?t=12991> (accessed 17 March 2012).

Sanes, Ken. 1998. Worlds in a Bottle: Zoos, Rain Forest Exhibits and the Lied Jungle. Available at: <http://www.transparencynow.com/zoos1.htm> (accessed 18 March 2012).

Schulze, Gerhard. 1992. *Die Erlebnis-Gesellschaft: Kultursoziologie der Gegenwart.* Frankfurt and New York: Campus.

Shapland, Andrew and Reybrouck, David van. 2008. Reconciling Natural and Historical Heritage Values: The Penguin Pool at London Zoo. *International Journal of Heritage Studies* 14(1): 10–29.

Smithsonian's National Zoo. 2002. Zoo Unveils New Chimpanzee Sculptures. Press release 18 June. Available at: <http://nationalzoo.si.edu/Publications/PressMaterials/PressReleases/NZP/GatheringStatues.cfm> (accessed 17 March 2012).

WAZA. 2012. Virtual Zoo. Available at: <http://www.waza.org/en/zoo/visit-the-zoo> (accessed 17 March 2012).

PHOTO ESSAY: ON SALVAGE PHOTOGRAPHY

CAITLIN DESILVEY,

WITH PHOTOGRAPHS BY STEVEN BOND

AND CAITLIN DESILVEY

THE disused cobbler's workshop occupied the back garden shed of a two-up, two-down terraced cottage in Carharrack, Cornwall. The shed was slated for demolition and the owner was looking for someone to rescue, or record, its contents. At the owner's invitation, I visited the site with two photographers several times during the winter of 2008–9. How I came to do so will be explained in the narrative to follow, but before I begin I'd like to pause to open up some of the questions to be explored in this essay.

The story I tell here can be understood, with a little bit of imagination, as linked to the legacy of what might be called 'salvage' photography. It began with an impulse to document a vanishing place in the interval before its disintegration, an impulse that contained elements of (as will become clear) both concern and compulsion. In this essay I explore this impulse and its implications; I find resources to understand it in the history of photography's engagement with (apparently) ephemeral places and peoples (Lippard 1992; Edwards 2006a). I also work through some of Walter Benjamin's ideas about images and their others: 'Every day the urge grows stronger to get hold of an object at very close range by way of its likeness, its representation' (Benjamin 1999a: 217). Benjamin never quite trusted this urge, and his writings work various strategies to undercut and illuminate it.

I hope the reflections in this photoessay might offer critical tools to other researchers who seek to engage with the material residues of the contemporary past through their photographic representation. Places like the abandoned cobbler's shop are not uncommon, though they are often only noticed when they are threatened with destruction. Usually the powers-that-be deem such places too marginal and mundane for formal preservation, though still worthy of some recognition of their passing: in comes the camera, a tool to 'record' these places (and in doing so partly discharge our guilt about their loss). The kind of recording that took place in the cobbler's shop did not follow the usual conventions for such work. If, as Michael Shanks claims, 'a multitude of photographs of a site are not so much a means of knowing it as a means of diverting its puzzles and uncertainties' (Shanks 1997: 81), this essay resists this diversion, and dwells for a while on the puzzles and uncertainties. I do so by working through four loosely defined stages in our photographic mediation of the cobbler's shop—invitation, intercession, intrusion, and invention.

1 INVITATION

William Speller established his boot and shoe repair business in 1930, and trained his two sons, Stephen and Frederick, to join him. The three of them worked together until Stephen eventually became the sole proprietor in the 1970s. People in the village kept bringing him their repairs through the 1980s, and Stephen oiled the machines faithfully once a week long after his jobs wound down. He died in February 2008, at the age of 92. Stephen's niece, who inherited the cottage, began to contact local museums, hoping to find someone to take on the contents of the workshop for display. By the time I was put in touch with her in December she had almost given up; her builder was eager to demolish the shed to begin work on the new water system, and time was running out. I offered to visit to see if I could help record the site. A friend had given me the names of two photographers who appreciated such places—Steven Bond and Charles Hall—and I invited them to come along.

Myrna Croome met us at the cottage and we walked through the half-gutted rooms to the narrow back yard. The four of us crowded into the two-room clapboard shed, the tiny rooms separated by a half-door. The immediate impression was one of extreme density—a space fully occupied by the accretions of several decades of labour. Shelves and drawers lined the walls, tools hung in ordered rows, shoes nestled against each other next to the raw materials of their repair, and the machinery gleamed in the dim light. The place seemed to be waiting for someone to return, to pick up the letters and bills scattered on the workbench, to sit on the swivel chair and finish tacking on a stray heel. I noted details—shoe

sole packets scribbled with notes, the dated advertisements on the walls, the 1975 job price list tacked inside the door. Two hanging balls of paper had the appearance of tattered grey wasps' nests. When I poked them I discovered the shop's financial archive, the innermost layers composed of 1950s invoices, the outermost layers including a 1999 electricity bill. I could see Steve and Charles also looking, taking it in. We asked Myrna if we could come back to take some photographs, and she said we were welcome to visit whenever we liked.

Here was an invitation, but to do what, exactly? The place seemed to be asking for some recognition, some attention to its physical presence and its compacted material history. In this first encounter all three of us were hooked—snagged by some thread we would have had a hard time naming. The invitation came, in this case, not only from Myrna but from something in the place itself. Our attraction was partly aesthetic—a response to textures and patterns, the quality of light on the worn objects—but it was heightened by the knowledge that what we were seeing was transitory, the objects poised in limbo before their eventual dispersal.

2 INTERCESSION

Over the next several weeks all three of us returned to the workshop, both together and alone, to take photographs. Charles volunteered to focus on straight documentation of the space, and his images present a restrained, middle-distance, meticulously executed record of the shop's form and contents. The images that Steve and I made were of a different order

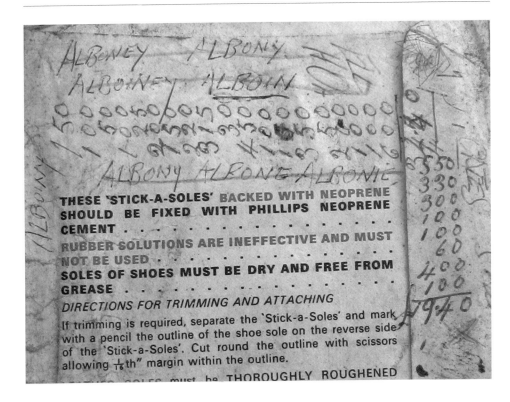

altogether, though similar to each other. They focused in 'close range' on details and textures—shrunken landscapes populated by tools and text, solitary shoes and scraps, accidental collages and telling fragments. Our optic was intimate and invasive, focusing down to the finest surface grain, as if we could push through to the other side and emerge in the moment when these things were still alive, still bound up with networks of exchange and encounter.

I can't speak for the others, but as I framed the contents of the shop with my camera I had the sense that I was acting as a witness, and that by taking the time to notice this place I was somehow giving something back to it. You could call it an intercession—in the sense of the term that implies intervention with the intention of bringing about a form of settlement or resolution. In the moment, the act of photographing seemed to work to smooth the gap between the shop's accreted past and its uncertain future.

Our photographs presented the shop's contents severed from context, fragments of place framed to curious effect. Inside the close-cropped images objects seemed to hum with significance—the woven speaker on the radio, the name scrawled on the bottom of the high-heeled shoe, the precise clusters of the hanging polish daubers, the advertising imagery populated with seductive maidens and knights in shining armour. Viewing the images on a computer screen afterward it seemed almost possible to reach through and touch the things, to smell the oily dust and creeping damp. The effect resembled Michael Taussig's description of 'tactile knowing', in which the visual opens onto other, unpredictable sensory engagements (1993: 25, 31). He

also writes (after Benjamin) about how 'the "magic" brought about by the "recently outdated" is a magic achieved by framing' (1993: 233). In our photographs this manifested as a distilled nostalgia, filtered through the production of indexical (digital) traces.

3 Intrusion

A month after our first visit the three of us met Myrna again to ask her some questions about the history of the shop. As we stood in the cramped, now familiar, space she suddenly commented, 'I feel it—they're gone. They were here and now they're gone' (personal interview, 12 January 2009). We felt it too. The space, that had been so dense, now felt strangely hollow. The objects and textures, which had been animated with a residual energy, now seemed inert and lifeless. And the materials in the shop seemed to have begun to disintegrate more rapidly—the mould bloom on the Phillips 'Stick-a-Soles' poster maiden seemed to have expanded, and a new layer of damp saturated the floor. It was as if before we arrived the place had been waiting for its occupants to return, but now it had given up.

After we left that day I tried to understand what was going on. I had a nagging feeling that our intervention was somehow partly responsible for the change that had come over the place. Except for the evidence of accelerated decay (which can perhaps be explained

by the disruption of the site's fragile equilibrium, the increased human traffic like oxygen rushing into a sealed box) it wasn't a physical change, but it felt real and somehow significant.

Searching for an explanation, I came back to Taussig's writing on sympathetic magic, 'this notion of the copy, in magical practice, affecting the original to such a degree that the representation shares in and acquires the properties of the represented' (Taussig 1993: 47; see also Harrison 2003). To borrow a term from photography's colonial history, you might say our cameras had become 'shadow-catchers', with our representations working somehow to diminish the power of the things we sought to reproduce (Lippard 1992: 31). There is a resonance here with Benjamin's ideas about the *aura*, and his argument that the act of representation alters our mode of perception, and our relationship to the represented. I recalled another comment that Myrna had made at our first meeting, while discussing her ambivalence about breaking up the shop to send it to become a museum display: 'As soon as you turn it into an exhibit its soul goes out of it' (personal interview, 12 December 2008).

Am I trying to say that our actions had a tangible effect on the things we documented? I'm not actually sure. It is one thing to assert that I percived the objects differently after documenting them; quite another to say that the things in themselves underwent some alteration through their representation. Taussig writes about the refusal to see the relationship between copy and contact as 'nonmysterious', insisting that there remains something 'powerful and obscure in the network of associations conjured by the notion of the mimetic' (Taussig 1993: 21). I can't shake the feeling that our compulsion to 'get hold' of these objects by way their representation extinguished some lingering spirit, even though we came to the

project with what we thought was concern and consideration. The photographs were agents in the transformation of this site; by framing the shop as an object worthy of our attention, we severed it from its past. And as soon as this transformation had been accomplished, I felt a desire to wind the clock back to 'first contact', the moment when we opened the door to the sealed space (Taussig 1993: 251).

4 INVENTION

This story only begins to touch on the 'puzzles and uncertainties' that characterized my brief engagement with this place. The feelings of intrusion and regret eventually gave way to an acceptance of the role our image-making played in the continued evolution of the site. 'In order for a part of the past to be touched by the present instant, there must be no continuity between them', Benjamin wrote (1999b: 470). In this instance, the act of reproduction introduced this break in continuity.

On the other side of this break it is possible to engage with the past in different ways—something is lost, but something is also gained. Carolyn Duttlinger's re-reading of Benjamin's concept of the aura suggests that the photograph can be understood as both 'the tool of the aura's destruction but also ... the site of its last appearance' (Duttlinger 2008: 83). She shows how Benjamin's writing contains an expansive (if ambivalent) understanding of the photographic aura as a quality 'which emerges from the encounter between viewer and image' (2008: 90). This concept resonates with other work on the relational and emergent properties of the photographic image (Edwards 2006b; Taussig 1993), in which analysis focuses on the power of images to prompt a connection with the viewer, through a reciprocal engagement in which the object seems to 'return the gaze' through the device of the photograph (Benjamin 1999c: 184). To the extent that our photographs of the cobbler's shop allow for this kind of connection, perhaps it is possible to partly forgive their trespasses.

Through this project I've also become more aware of the paradoxical nature of any salvage photographic project. In our encounter with the shop we all shared 'an appreciation of the transience of things, and the concern to redeem them for eternity'—but the appreciation and the concern were ultimately irreconcilable (Benjamin 1977: 223). As soon as the act of redemption was initiated, the quality of transience was threatened. Even the most delicate intervention alters the object irrevocably; every act of preservation is also an act of destruction. This fundamentally archaeological conundrum came to define my relationship to this place, but the story has a peculiar twist. The things weren't so transient after all. In the eleventh hour a local theme-park farm attraction came forward to offer to install the contents of the shop in their Cornish heritage display. The objects travelled to the site near Newquay, and found themselves reassembled in a convincing replica of the dusty shed (complete with fake cobwebs). If the photographs initiated the process of forcing the objects to represent their own past, the heritage exhibit completed it.

REFERENCES

Benjamin, Walter. 1977. *Origins of German Tragic Drama*, tr. John Osborne. London: New Left Books.
—— 1999a. The Work of Art in the Age of Mechanical Reproduction. In *Illuminations*, ed. Hannah Arendt, pp. 211–35. London: Pimlico.
—— 1999b. *The Arcades Project*, tr. Howard Eiland and Kevin McLaughlin. Cambridge, MA, and London: Harvard University Press.
—— 1999c. On some Motifs in Baudelaire. In *Illuminations*, ed. Hannah Arendt, pp. 152–90. London: Pimlico.
Duttlinger, Carolyn. 2008. Imaginary Encounters: Walter Benjamin and the Aura of Photography. *Poetics Today* 29: 79–101.
Edwards, Elizabeth. 2006a. Photography, 'Englishness', and Collective Memory. In *Locating Memory: Photographic Acts*, ed. Annette Kuhn and Kirsten McAllistar, pp. 53–79. New York: Berghahn.
—— 2006b. Photographs and the Sound of History. *Visual Anthropology Review* 21: 27–46.
Harrison, Rodney. 2003. 'The Magical Virtue of These Sharp Things': Colonialism, Mimesis, and Knapped Bottle Glass Artefacts in Australia. *Journal of Material Culture* 8: 311–36.
Lippard, Lucy. 1992. *Partial Recall: Photographs of Native North Americans*. New York: New Press.
Shanks, Michael. 1997. Photography and Archaeology. In *The Cultural Life of Images*, ed. Brian Leigh Molyneaux, pp. 73–107. London: Routledge.
Taussig, Michael. 1993. *Mimesis and Alterity*. London and New York: Routledge.

PART V

THINGS AND CONNECTIVITIES

CHAPTER 43

....

SILICON VALLEY

....

CHRISTINE FINN

43.1 INTRODUCTION

....

THE digital age has provided archaeology with a shot in the arm: the challenge of gathering, publishing, disseminating, theorizing, and reflecting upon the data generated by digital technologies is unique in its contingency. Intergenerational innovation means that an archaeologist today has witnessed technological evolution over years and decades, rather than centuries or millennia. This is contingent not just on the age of the archaeologist, but on the uptake of technologies at her institution or workplace; on the economics of updating hardware and software; and the means and ability to adapt to change. At the same time, archaeologists often teach students who have known no other environment than a digital one. For those who have not experienced the exponential leaps first-hand, the notion of computer and digital heritage will not be questionable: it is part of cultural history (see Cubitt, this volume; Miller and Maxwell, this volume). This is reinforced by the widening literature in the subject, a literature that overlaps with the history of technology culture (see Ceruzzi 1998) and specific histories of companies, machines, and individuals (see Bardin 2000; Isaacson 2011). Alongside these hardware histories are the stories of software (see Gates 1996; Lewis, 1999); popular books about social networking (Vise and Malseed 2005); and the cinematic adaptations of these histories in such films as *The Pirates of Silicon Valley* (dir. Martin Burke 1999) and *The Social Network* (dir. David Fincher 2010). Importantly, the stories of social networking and the Internet link hardware to software by focusing on the material culture of the present. These are the bones of contemporary archaeology. Paul Graves-Brown, in his study of the 'intangible artefacts' of the World Wide Web suggests that '... Web content is quite different from the traditional materials of the historian, but is equally not the traditional matter of archaeology' (2009: 17). So much of what we describe as contemporary archaeology engages with material that is uniquely ephemeral.

It is this working outside of traditional boundaries, which is also a factor of hardware and software innovation, that steers this chapter. I do not propose to write a history of computing, as that is well served already, but to argue that the artefacts of this material culture inhabit a category of their own. Even within the expanding parameters of contemporary archaeology, the material culture of digital technologies divides practitioners between those who have experienced the technological change first-hand and those who see it only historically—those who were 'born digital'. The artefacts that the older of us learned about as cutting-edge innovations, breathlessly reported in specialist media such as *Wired* magazine, or saw unveiled at consumer tech shows, are history—quite literally—to an increasing number of students, who directly experience only the rapid accumulation of upgrades, apps, and version releases laid down as different kinds of archaeological stratigraphies.

Innovations such as the Apple Classic, the Amstrad, and first-generation laptops have, in a short passage of time, become artefacts deemed appropriate for an archive collection. They can be observed in science and design museums as unsurprisingly as other artefacts described in the literature of contemporary heritage and elsewhere in this volume (see Cubitt; Miller and Maxwell). They appear in other contemporary material culture discussions that have helped to frame digital artefacts as items of academic interest, which are also the tools on which the works are written (Hicks and Beaudry 2006; Tilley et al. 2006; Harrison and Schofield 2011).

Given my vantage point, I propose to focus on the collections of Silicon Valley. To continue the archaeological analogy I first used in 2001, this is an area of lateral excavation, in which the practice is not archaeological 'digging', but journalistic. This area of research can be defined loosely as a 'find site'—the place where the data was found—but the gathering of data was not systematic, as in field survey, but driven by news instinct. As I wrote in 2001, 'my methodology was simple; I drove around, walked, talked, asked questions, and kept a journal with paper and pen' (xiii). This find site engages with the historical, the modern, the postmodern and also the yet-to-be-categorized—those future archaeologies which are contingent to accelerated innovation. This notion of contingent meaning, highly relevant to contemporary archaeology, is central to my argument: the artefacts of Silicon Valley's digital age have an added value currency which is directly linked to knowledge. How archaeologists classify them is linked to the experience of technology in flux. Alain Schnapp has argued (1996) that archaeology has always been deeply immersed in the specific cultural contexts within which it is practised. But my contention is that the parallel value systems of the digital age present a question of specificity: the material culture of Silicon Valley is linked to phenomena not yet in existence, but which, for example, are being incubated as ideas in top-secret research labs, or awaiting venture capital to become reality (see Fowles and Heupel, this volume, for a discussion of the absences of modernity on the flipside of these technological cultures).

In arguing for these artefacts' significance, I should give more personal context. I travelled to Silicon Valley in September 1999 by happenstance, with little knowledge of technology beyond a few classes in BBC Basic at night school in 1984. This is significant. If Silicon Valley is analogous to an archaeological fieldworking site, I was visiting without expectations, only curiosity. I had visited the Bay Area in 1984, with a computer programmer, so I saw Silicon Valley when it was still full of orchards and there was little élan for the non-specialist. On my return in 2000, I again travelled with the eye of a tourist, using travel guides to California to identify what others regarded as interesting or historical. In the middle of this, my stumbling upon of digital culture echoes Michael Shanks' identification (1992) of experience as integral to archaeology. I visited places of archaeological interest, mostly related to prehistory and Paleo-Indian settlement, and designated heritage sites, such as those along the Camino Real. I visited technology, art, and local history museums. I scanned news pages and classified ads, took coffee in the cafés of Palo Alto and Mountain

View, and drank beer with the networkers in San Francisco. I learned about projects about which I had to be silent and attended launches where the word went out as fast as Web 1.0 would allow. I was given access to adobes and Adobe, one of the major names, in which I found another archaeological analogy. I watched Julieanne Kost, Adobe evangelist at the company's San Jose headquarters, make artworks that were built up as layers and suggested they could be 'excavated' back to their Ur image (Finn 2001: 40).

I was reading the *San Jose Mercury News*, *Red Herring*, *Industry Standard*, *Wired*, and *Fast Company*, although I had no knowledge of the literature that, by 1999, was already substantial in America. These ranged from cultural studies, histories of technology, specialist business studies, and classics of cyber culture, written by futurologists and science fiction authors, many specific to the West Coast, and written by insiders who worked from a variety of disciplines (e.g. Coupland 1996; Winslow 1996; Bronson 1998; Cringley 1996; Friedberger and Swaine 2000). At the same time, San Jose University, in the heartland of my field site, was concluding a prescient ten-year-long study under anthropologists Chuck Darrah, Jan English-Lueck, and James Freeman. The Silicon Valley Cultures Project produced 'Living in the Eye of the Storm: Controlling the Maelstrom in Silicon Valley' (Darrah, English-Lueck, and Freeman 2000), which charted a decade of change-over-time in everyday experiences in a relatively small fieldwork area and later became an award-winning book for a wider audience (English-Lueck 2002). But my specialist reading began with the work of a cultural geographer, AnnaLee Saxenian, whose important work *Regional Advantage: Culture and Competition in Silicon Valley and Route 128* (1996) primed me on the essential similarities and differences between the suited and corporate East Coast landscape of IBM and the Digital Equipment Corporation (DEC), and that of the West, which had emerged out of counter-culture and sunshine.

Computer history was thus an emerging field when I began my research in 1999. Since then, the Computer History Museum in Mountain View has secured its position as an authority in collections of its kind, attracting increased interest to its real and virtual presence (computerhistory.org). Its artefacts are particularly dynamic, being a part of the area's living history, and the museum regularly sells out attendances at its ticketed speaker events. While there is a captive audience among the tech workers for talks on technology, this suggests a widening appreciation of the value of history in a place which is driven, as the tech chronicler Michael Lewis put it, by 'the new, new thing' which was both the title of his 1999 book and shorthand for the rate of change. The museum represents Silicon Valley history and is connected to the wider community through both its expanding online site and notable artefact donations. As a container of Silicon Valley memory, the museum collection also incubates retro tech as a commercial artefact.

Retro tech introduces the notion of nostalgia, the respect for discarded and defunct technologies, which goes beyond the traditional confines of 'collecting' (Figure 43.1). There is a vogue for retro computing as a means of accessing 'cool' artefacts, particularly those from the 1970s. These have an appeal quite different to that expressed by people who grew up with these technologies, who used and discarded them as out-of-date. The culture of collecting computer material is dynamic, both as a field of study and dissemination. It is contingent on the experience of the viewer. This might be argued for traditional field survey: someone used to picking out worked flint from stone chipped by tractor will have a higher hit rate because of knowledge accrued over time and experience. But here we are not dealing with the relative slow speed of prehistoric artefacts. Computer technology artefacts

FIGURE 43.1 Licence plate of the hearse used by a technology-recycling firm in Oakland, California, as a vehicle for its pick-ups of redundant computers (photograph: Christine Finn)

instead demonstrate an exponential rate of change-over-time, which means a tech museum would have to put boxed computers straight from launch into storage to bring them out as soon as they have gone through the cycle from cutting-edge production to mass-consumer to obsolete to discard to collection.

43.2 DATA GATHERING AND PUBLICATION

When I began my research, early attempts to work with Silicon Valley as a traditional fieldwork environment were frustrated by the accelerated rate of change. Disseminating technology research was problematic and contingent on access and uptake. I was excavating in some future world, my hoard carried back on the ten-hour flight to the UK often relating to just-out-of-date technology en route to the recyclers in Silicon Valley. In the early days of the Web, digital literacy was an important factor in putting a value on computer collectables, and therefore made a difference to what was discarded. This is not the same knowledge as that of the dealer making finds at a car boot sale in contemporary Britain; it is a knowledge specifically related to the artefact's production and use. Motherboards were often 'destroyed' to protect intellectual property, reminding me of the deliberate destruction of valuable weapons in the Iron Age and Pueblo pottery in American prehistoric sites (Finn 2001: 167).

Ten years on and vast amounts of intangible data—'deleted' tweets, emails, and petabytes of data on hard-drives and servers—are lost and found in a process perhaps analogous to the work of archaeological scientists. I have attempted to write with flux and the acceleration of technology (see Virilio 2000) in mind. As I have researched and surveyed the Silicon Valley scene—the material culture and its social mores—post-Web 2.0, I am aware that time continues to be marked differently in this terrain. Writing up research gathered between 2001 and 2011, for proofs to be prepared in 2012, and publication in 2013, means I am again presenting a snapshot, as much as a tomb and its contents can but give a sense of an ancient time.

43.3 HISTORY AND GEOGRAPHY

Silicon Valley is a place culturally and economically defined by the media, but it has no map coordinate beyond the branding of a cluster of Northern Californian cities on a peninsula 50 miles south of San Francisco. Marvin Cheek suggests that 'Officially, there is no such place as Silicon Valley...' and he notes that older inhabitants of the former fruit-growing landscape once known as 'The Valley of Heart's Delight' were sometimes unhappy at being labelled as now living in 'Silicon Valley' (2000: 3). Marc Augé's 'non-places' (1995), the transient spaces of super-modernity such as shopping malls and airports, can inform our understanding of Silicon Valley. Without an official, cartographic existence and relying on the commuting population of workers driving in from subdivisions Silicon Valley is non-place. Even the shopping malls seek to be of another place and time. Electronics chain Fry's was founded in Silicon Valley in 1985. Individual stores are archaeologically themed: Palo Alto is designed as a Wild West Saloon, San Jose is a temple from Chichén Itzá, and the Campbell store is modelled on Ancient Egypt, where, at time of visiting in 2000, fake sarcophagi and mummy cases dispensed computer hardware and software (2001: 15).

The branding of Silicon Valley therefore relies on linking traditional archaeological images to computing technology via computer museums in defunct companies, and electronics stores, such as Fry's, which sell potato chips alongside silicon chips. Although those who had seen the change from the orchards to Apples continued to trade stories at events such as the Vintage Computer Festival, and the fledgling Computer History Museum, the destruction of the old Valley was less seen as the loss of heritage as a move forward. Technological heritage was, however, central to the narrative and the archaeologies of great 'civilizations' were imported to tell that story.

The importance of Silicon Valley's heritage is marked in other ways, too. 'Woz Way' references Jobs's Apple co-founder, Steve Wozniak. Elsewhere the names of other innovators, such as Hewlett and Packard, live on buildings to their name. It is also a ritual space. When Steve Jobs died in 2011, shrines were made outside the company's Cupertino headquarters and at Apple stores worldwide. In this way, heritage is literally mapped on to the spaces of Silicon Valley, despite its non-existence as a formalized entity. Therefore, beyond civic and commercial references to an archaeologically informed past, Silicon Valley hosts other, more traditional, forms of heritage that seek to construct an archaeology of computing for the area.

43.4 THE INSTITUTIONALIZATION
OF COMPUTER HISTORY

My research into Silicon Valley came out of a chance encounter on a plane in 1999. I asked about the hand-held device—a Palm Pilot—clutched by the young man in the neighbouring seat. He told me: 'It comes out tomorrow. I designed the email for it.' That got me thinking about the place of new technology in the world of archaeology. Beyond geophysics technologies and other devices employed by archaeologists I wondered whether the artefacts of technology as such could provide a contemporary way of looking at change over time. What continues to fascinate me is the way that technological uptake varies and the impact this has on the material culture that remains as artefacts.

To address the idea of computer history I turn to discussing the institutionalization of these histories within museum and archival settings. It is important here to show how computer history has emerged as an academic field. The history of contemporary technology and ideas is well established in UK and US universities. However, the significance of studying computers as a specialist historical field was largely pioneered in America. At Stanford University, the proximity of technological corporations has meant that the relationship between innovation and archive has been well understood. Apple's donated archive is available online and has been a significant resource since the late 1990s under the curatorship of Henry Lowood.

The Intel Corporation HQ in Santa Clara was my own introduction to institutionalized computer collecting. I was surprised to learn, in 2000, that there was an in-house, curated museum dedicated to collecting the company's history. This suggested a potentially rich new area of conserving the materials of silicon chip manufacture and new approaches to the classification of contemporary technological objects. The Intel artefacts were numbered, catalogued, and kept in plastic bags as one might keep a Neolithic microlith. I traced one item, a cube of metal, which was a piece of microprocessor packaging, to the person who had donated it to Intel on his retirement. He had left hand-written notes about it, which were stored with the artefact. I went to interview George Chui, and so made a link between oral testimony and object, allying my research to contemporary archaeology. My interrogation of artefacts was complemented by less speculative analysis, and more constructive oral histories were reinforced by news events.

In 2000, the Computer History Museum was a series of temporary buildings at the NASA Ames site in Mountain View in Silicon Valley. The museum began from a number of artefacts, transferred from a science museum in Boston. When I first visited, it was possible to view objects by appointment thanks to a team of volunteer docents, many of whom had worked in the tech industry. Visitors and docents were experts, able to share first-hand stories and gather data, which helped illuminate the objects. With plans at the time for a purpose-built museum, the leading curator and academic historian, Dag Spicer, and his small team, decided to represent the complex and relative value history of these artefacts using a timeline approach. However, the dotcom crash made the museum unfeasible. Instead, the Computer History Museum took over a building left vacant by Silicon Graphics, adopting not just the impressive location off Highway 101 but also the traces of that relocated company, including chairs still bearing the name. This set of artefacts within an artefact helped to distinguish the unique perspective of the Computer History Museum.

The Computer History Museum evokes a mixture of curiosity and nostalgia, enhanced by narrative storytelling and traditionally curated exhibits. This is evidenced by the procedure devised for the collection posted on the website: 'The Computer History Museum is continually growing its collections of computing history materials. In particular, we seek items that engage our various audiences and can be used for interpretation, discussion or research' (<http://www.computerhistory.org/>). While it has an extensive 'Wish List' of collectables, the museum's curators must be selective: 'Collecting must be deliberate and sustainable, thus new artefacts are accepted into the collection after careful consideration by a team of curators' (<http://www.computerhistory.org/>).

In 2011, the museum was officially relaunched, with completion of its Revolution exhibit, charting the development of computer history. Visitor numbers suggest a growing interest which I would argue comes not simply from the objects becoming more valuable per se, but because the Valley of the Now has grown appreciative of its history especially since the dotcom crash. While there is perhaps no need to state what computer history stands for in Silicon Valley—even the new generation of Web 2.0 workers either remembers the golden days of the dotcom boom as tech workers, grew up with the crash, or is part of the booming social networking economy—the passing of Steve Jobs prompted global discussion about the Apple legacy, and suggested a greater understanding of how material culture impacts on the present and, potentially, offers lessons for the future. Until recently, the museum hosted the Vintage Computer Festival, so aligning the curatorial academic institution with the figure of the individual the computer collector hobbyist, a figure to which I will now turn.

43.5 COMPUTER COLLECTORS

Alongside the role of institutions in formalizing this computing heritage, individual collectors have been key to populating institutional collections. One of the distinct features of computer collectors or retro tech enthusiasts is that the majority are involved in the business of technology. These informed collectors offer a way in to a mode of interrogating the material culture of Silicon Valley. They often still work in the business at the time they donate artefacts to museums, and continue to work and socialize with others involved in computer history. The slower and broader perspective post dotcom bust gave more impetus to the idea of collecting Silicon Valley's past. Nostalgia became a driving force for collecting and revealed a fond mix of personal memory and personal computer.

In common with other hobbyist communities dedicated to the material culture of the twentieth and twenty-first centuries, most retro tech assemblages are hobbyist collections not attached to institutions. They exist in people's spare rooms, garages, workshops, and attics. Unlike the antiquarians inspired by the Classics, and divorced from their objects by centuries or millennia, these collectors are driven almost universally by first-hand experience. They have a tangible attachment to the personal stories contained in the objects. And if necessary, they have the code to access them. Their passion for salvaging history from dumpsters and thrift stores, as well as their commitment to explaining, engineering, and

FIGURE 43.2 Remains of 45th anniversary cake featuring edible archive photograph of the LINC, the Laboratory Instrument Computer, made for a Digibarn celebration at the Computer History Museum, during the Vintage Computer Festival, 2007. The LINC was the first 'personal' computer, in that it could be installed in a home (photograph: Christine Finn)

demonstrating the machines to the public is often neglected aside from their fellow enthusiasts. These networks grew out of early computer connectivity. Early mailing lists spawned collectives who specialized in a particular type of interest, computer, or company. Today these groups often overlap with academic interests, meet regularly for international conferences and publish proceedings (see <www.sigcis.org>).

Bruce Damer's Digibarn is an unorthodox and significantly personal Apple collection which is viewable online, and housed at a farm in the mountains overlooking the heartland of Silicon Valley (Figure 43.2). Damer's relationship with the artefacts goes beyond simply using Apple technology: his social group includes one of Apple's founders, Steve Wozniak, who donated artefacts for the collection. Damer is an avatar expert and author of a seminal volume on the subject (1998). He is both a technological innovator, working on projects for NASA, and an historian who has lectured on the history of avatars to employees at the headquarters of one of Web 2.0's early success stories, San Francisco-based Second Life. Damer is also a regular participant in the annual gathering of computer history enthusiasts, the Vintage Computer Festival.

The Vintage Computer Festival began as an annual event in the late 1990s and was devised by programmer and retro tech enthusiast Sellam Ismail, to bring together enthusiasts who had otherwise largely communicated only by digital means or telephone. This gave them the opportunity to set their old machines up and running and to share information and stories while also trading parts and gadgets. The Vintage Computer Festival is the direct descendant of the technological swap-meets organized by the Homebrew Club in a car park at the back of Stanford's linear accelerator lab in the 1970s and 1980s. These were significant meetings for computer pioneers who at that time were making computers from components and kits, inspired by the new magazines devoted to the idea of computers having potential as machines for home in addition to business. These dedicated engineers and programmers included Steve Wozniak and others who went on to found some of Silicon Valley's most distinctive companies. The annual West Coast event quickly extended to VCF East near Boston. The VCF Europa in Munich, a city which houses its own tech collection at the Nixdorf Science Museum, provided a vital hub for European collectors and enhanced the discrete similarities and differences between Silicon Valley and beyond. The differences are largely a product of the recurrent theme in this chapter: the impact of working within an innovation hub compared with the less direct relationships between artefact, innovator, and collector outside of the hub.

The Vintage Computer Festival continues the spirit of sharing information and resources to emphasize the importance and possibilities of specialist networking. The format includes a panel of speakers, a swap meet and competitions for the best display of exhibits. The focus is hardware and software and central to this is that the artefacts are working computers. One of the key reasons to show machines running is to demonstrate how the innovations of the recent past have impacted on technology which was developed within living memory. Those who used, designed, or were in some other way involved with machines from the 1970s and 1980s are able, in particular, to discuss in great detail the processes involved. Given that the Vintage Computer Festival is long established, in Silicon Valley terms, the history of the event alone provides an interesting intergenerational perspective of attendees: not just parents—mostly fathers—and children, but older brothers and younger siblings. Thus green screens and floppy discs, a game of Pac-Man or Breakout, evokes both nostalgia and interest in something 'new'. In addition, the machines bring with them a range of sensory elements. As one of the tech pioneers, Stan Mazor, reminded me of the time he walked into the Computer History Museum, 'the smell hit me in the head, and I remembered the old days in which I spent a lot of time around these old "computing engines"'(Finn 2001: 31).

Sellam Ismail started the Vintage Computer Festival while maintaining a day job as a programmer. He was driven by a passion for history and a sense of loss for his first computer, which he sold as a teenager. His retro tech collecting grew into a Vintage Computing site (<www.vintage.org>) during the dotcom boom, which connected collectors of specific machines with a generosity of knowledge. Ismail's 'fieldwork' involves crossing the country to pick up machines that are about to be dumped; he collects them in a former car factory in Oakland, north of Silicon Valley. These might include the contents of a garage, or a company's mainframes, often presented with other ephemera. There is little cherry-picking at this stage because speed is of the essence. The material is gathered on site, piled into a vehicle, and unpacked at a warehouse to be investigated later. This blanket consideration of the array is analogous to the collecting of finds during field survey and excavation: at the offset, little is discarded because everything is immediately relevant. However, the find process is also akin to rescue archaeology, contingent on people knowing about Ismail's mission, and him getting to the material before it is destroyed. However, unlike archaeologists excavating a known area of value or other collecting communities who can claim prescience—Dinky toys kept pristine with their boxes, for example—Ismail engages with a sense of history linked with memory and, significantly, his memory of using the artefacts he is trying to preserve. It was the seismic shift of the dotcom crash which, I would argue, gave a new focus and impetus to his work, as it was recognized that much of what he had preserved had been widely discarded by others.

Ismail's site transformed a hobby into a business rooted in this wider cultural interest in old tech. The several thousand distinctive models of computer, varying from DEC PDP11 mainframes to the early laptops the size of a briefcase, were transferred from his rented space in an old car factory, which was being developed as apartments, to a warehouse near Oakland close to a computer recyclers which made over old tech for reuse. Ismail also collected thousands of artefacts of ephemera, ranging from computer magazines, packaging, and advertisements, to T-shirts and other promotional giveaways. The many thousands of manuals in Ismail's collection, like the BBC Micro manuals at the Oxfam bookshop in Oxford, were most often discarded along with the machine. But with the machines saved and running again, the manuals prove invaluable to help access data otherwise 'lost' in an unused computer. The manuals act as a key to unlocking material trapped on a hard drive, or reading software encoded into obsolete discs—not simply on personal computers, but institutions including NASA. Ismail has helped a team of archaeologists access data, encoded in the 1970s, from a shipwreck off Florida, an apt example of this contemporary Rosetta Stone deciphering. The prescience of such techno-scavenging began to reach a wider public when Ismail began to be interviewed by national and international media (Finn 2003a, 2003b, 2008) and to present his research to the academic community (Ismail and Finn 2002).

A more controversial aspect of computer history is the reuse of old tech as souvenir artefacts. Aside from silicon chips made into jewellery or reworked as artworks (Figure 43.3; Finn 2007) computer collectors remain sensitive about redundant machines not being rebuilt but disassembled. Tony Cole, a VCF regular, drummed up enthusiasm for the notion of computers and heritage by acquiring an old Cray Supercomputer and taking it apart. Cole sold pieces as keepsakes or gifts to people involved in the technology industry, generating a 'value' of the machine perhaps linked to more traditional antiquarian pursuits. Notions of relative value are important to contemporary archaeology where objects can be spoken for, as well as spoken about. This is reinforced in the computer-collecting world by the idea of collecting for its own sake, not seeing a machine as an investment. However, in the last decade I have noted the distinctive widening between the modest dealing—or swapping— activities of collectors who have an interest in preserving heritage, and the eBay buyer who is prospecting for the next 'big thing' in collectables. In 2005, a collection of technological ephemera was offered for sale by a Christie's auction house, and thought to be so marketable it even went on tour to Stanford (Finn 2005).

However, computer hardware has been listed in antiques and collectables guides for over a decade. On eBay, one of the most active retro tech trade sites, the machines are often bought by investors, who are akin to wartime medal collectors with no personal connection to the artefacts. Online anonymity makes it difficult to differentiate those with a personal interest in 1970s PCs mix from generic collectors of 1970s memorabilia. The section on the UK eBay site called 'vintage computers' lists ephemera along with hardware and computer games, including mouse mats. At time of writing (April 2012) it included a 'Vintage Girl Guide Interest Badge' at the buy-now price of £3.49. A Commodore PET is also listed, in the week the machine's pioneer, Jack Tramiel, died. Priced at £249, it is considerably more than the €25 which I was offered one for at a Vintage Computer Fair in Munich in 2006.

FIGURE 43.3   Wire-d, a site-specific installation by the author, comprising old Silicon Valley technology gathered ad hoc from collectors and tech recyclers, made for the 2007 Vintage Computer Festival, Computer History Museum, Mountain View, California (photograph: Christine Finn)

These vintage tech collectors who are not connected with technology bring yet another new value system to the consideration of retro tech, selling for speculation, which is closer to the idea of the antiquarian dealer. As an anecdotal example, in 2010 I overheard a conversation about a BBC Micro for sale at a UK car boot sale stall: the seller and vendor exchanged nostalgic stories, but when the seller mentioned there were not many about, and so it would be collectable, it was swiftly bought.

In April 2000, I went to a small hall on the outskirts of Boston, to attend what was billed by the auctioneer, Skinner's, as one of America's first sales of collectable retro technology. The lots ranged from music-boxes and money-drumming automata, to signs advertising electricity and valve radios. The final lots included items owned by computer pioneer J. Presper-Eckert who, with his colleague John Mauchly, designed an important piece of computer kit: the Electronic Numerical Integrator and Computer, or ENIAC. I had a conversation with a close friend of Presper-Eckert's who was hoping to buy a piece of the memorabilia, a slide-rule, or tool kit he recalled him using. He was easily outbid in a sale which gave a very early indication of the growing value of such personally identifiable computer heritage. The star lot, a piece of the ENIAC itself, a vacuum-driven ring counter, went for a considerable sum to join Nathan Myhrvold's collection.

A decade later, in November, 2010, it was Christie's London sale room, rather than a rural hall, which hosted the sale of an early Apple 1, in essence the vital motherboard and associated letters of provenance. The buyer, paying just over £133,250, was Italian millionaire Marco Boglione. But this was not simply an investment piece. Boglione is a computer-history collector with heritage very much at heart. He only collected Apple artefacts, out of admiration for the company and its founders, and maintained an in-house engineer to maintain his artefacts. When he bought the Apple 1 he installed it in his keynote K-Way clothing store in one of Turin's smartest shopping streets, creating around it a small museum. This gave immediate context to his new acquisition and also provided an educational resource for his young customers. The addition of old adverts and footage was important, as was the name of his company: Basic. In their study of retro brands, Stephen Brown, Robert V. Kozinets, and John F. Sherry argue that 'there is considerable overlap among nostalgia, brand heritage and brand revival' (2003: 3). Through this experiential use of retro, Boglione provides a bridge between old and new generations of computer users, and a memorable marketing tool for his own business. Boglione, who was also planning a computer museum for Turin, was also touring the Apple 1 to academic institutions in Italy, showing the working model and initiating discussions about technological change. His interest, he stressed, was not as a result of nostalgia, but a respect for the old technology as a means to the new.

Apple's continual emphasis on the look of its objects, led by Jobs, creates an interesting subset of vintage computer collectors. In 2003, I travelled to Japan to interview Yumoto Hirohisa, who had bought an Apple 1 at a VCF auction in California in 2000 (Finn 2001: 184–7). Although not there in person to place the bid, he secured a significant piece of Apple history. He told me his interest was primarily in Apple because of respect for Steve Wozniak. In the lobby of a Tokyo apartment block, Hirohisa showed me his trophy, producing the motherboard from a briefcase with a similar flourish to an archaeologist revealing a find. He set it up on a table like a precious relic, the motherboard encased in transparent protective casing. His collection of retro technology was kept in its own apartment and he was not intending to share it with the public.

43.6 CONCLUSION

Silicon Valley's history is uniquely expressed in the material culture of its technology and its impact on the landscape and it provides a unique vantage point to consider observable change over time through the filter of the uniquely accelerating rate of change with which the area is associated. From the rapid advances of the 1970s and 1980s, which saw 'The Valley of Heart's Delight' transform into 'Silicon Valley', the origins of computer heritage come from an array of places: from the history of technology and ideas to the tech industry intertwined with the cultural landscape to the core global network of computer hobbyists, non-institutions, and those outside academia. Often unrecognized outside their peer groups, retro collectors have a direct connection with the technology they have chosen to help preserve. This gives them valuable insight into the objects and into the process of material acculturation. In saving the discards of this extraordinary era at a time when technology history was a specialist discipline, these part-time and unpaid curators were saving history. That these artefacts were defunct, outmoded, and most often unwieldy and unattractive, makes their efforts all the more laudable. The funding of tech history institutions, such as the Computer History Museum, is important to provide well-resourced centres of excellence, analogous with world-class archaeology museums. I know from my own experience that my learning as a non-techie foreigner 'excavating' Silicon Valley came from these collectors with their first-hand experience, commitment, and inside knowledge of unique industry.

Silicon Valley's dynamic provides a unique field site, in which the strata shift constantly, contingent on innovation and discard, fashion and nostalgia. The Valley affords lateral investigation. The Computer History Museum notes that its collection is 'constantly growing', which makes it something of a rarity to a generation of museum curators beset by storage problems. The distinction is that the collection has to keep growing to mark this technology's exponential change over time. The artefacts of the digital age can be viewed and reviewed within a year, rather than over decades, and the geographic and economic factors present a challenge to future collectors of the future who participate in the selection process through artefact use. This suggests an argument for the history of computer technologies becoming part of the archaeology curriculum as an extension of Thomsen's traditional Three-Age classification system: Stone, Bronze, and Iron. Technology mediates human and non-human practices and, as I have argued elsewhere: 'Without a sense of the past, there is a danger of raising a generation of change-junkies, weaned on the rush of accelerating technologies, for whom history has no relevance...In their world where nothing stands still, they are left with no space to evaluate why technological change happens and, crucially, its implications' (Finn 2004).

REFERENCES

Augé, Marc. 1995. *Non-Places: Introduction to an Anthropology of Supermodernity*. London: Verso.

Bardin, Thierry. 2000. *Bootstrapping: Douglas Englebart, Coevolution, and the Origins of Personal Computing*. Stanford, CA: Stanford University Press.

Bronson, Po. 1998. *The First $20 Million is Always the Hardest*. New York: Vintage.

Brown, Stephen, Kozinets, Robert V., and Sherry, John F. 2003. Teaching Old Brands New Tricks: Retro Branding and the Revival of Brand Meaning. *Journal of Marketing* 67: 19–53.

Ceruzzi, Paul. 1998. *A History of Modern Computing*. Cambridge, MA: MIT Press.

Cheek, Marvin. 2000. *Silicon Valley Handbook*. Emeryville, CA: Avalon.

Coupland, Douglas. 1996. *Microserfs*. New York: Regan Books/HarperCollins.

Cringley, Robert. 1996. *Accidental Empires: How the Boys of Silicon Valley Make Their Millions, Battle Competition, and Still Can't Get a Date*. New York: Addison-Wesley.

Damer, Bruce. 1998. *Avatars! Exploring and Building Virtual Worlds on the Internet*. Berkeley, CA: Peachpit Press.

Darrah, Chuck, English-Lueck, Jan, and Freeman, James. 2000. Living in the Eye of the Storm: Controlling the Maelstrom in Silicon Valley. Silicon Valley Cultures Project. Available at: <http://ww.svcp.org/pages/papers.html> (accessed 6 February 2013).

English-Lueck, Jan. 2002. *Cultures@Silicon Valley*. Stanford, CA: Stanford University Press.

Finn, Christine. 2001. *Artifacts: An Archaeologist's Year in Silicon Valley*. Cambridge, MA: MIT Press.

—— 2003a. Screensavers. *The Guardian*. Available at: <http://www.guardian.co.uk/technology/2003/mar/04/g2.onlinesupplement> (accessed 30 April 2012).

—— 2003b. Bits and Pieces: A Mini Study of Computer Collecting. *AIA Industrial Archaeology Review* 25(2): 119–28.

Finn, Christine. 2004. The Edge Annual Question. Available at: <http://www.edge.org/q2003/q03_finn.html> (accessed 30 April 2012).

—— 2005. 'Old Tech' and 'Old Tech Revisited': Diary in Rome culture blog, Humanities Lab, Stanford. Available at: <http://traumwerk.stanford.edu:3455/ChristineFinn/24> and <http://traumwerk.stanford.edu:3455/christinefinn/27> (accessed 30 April 2012).

—— 2007. Turning Old PCs into Art. The Guardian. Available at: <http://www.guardian.co.uk/artanddesign/artblog/2007/nov/06/turningoldpcsintoart200> (accessed 30 April 2012).

—— 2008. 'It's Big and It's Beautiful: The Rise of Retro Tech', The Essay, BBC Radio 3, 8–11 September.

Friedberger, Paul and Swaine, Michael. 2000. *Fire in the Valley: The Making of the Personal Computer*. New York: McGraw-Hill.

Gates, Bill. 1996. *The Road Ahead*. New York: Penguin Books.

Graves-Brown, Paul. 2009. 13 March 1993. The Library of Babel: Origins of the World Wide Web. In *Defining Moments: Dramatic Archaeologies of the Twentieth-Century*, ed. John Schofield, pp. 123–34. BAR International Series, Volume 5 of Studies in Contemporary and Historical Archaeology. Oxford: Archaeopress.

Harrison, Rodney and Schofield, John. 2011. *After Modernity: Archaeologies of the Contemporary Past*. Oxford: Oxford University Press.

Hicks, Dan and Beaudry, Mary (eds.). 2006. *The Cambridge Companion to Historical Archaeology*. Cambridge: Cambridge University Press.

Isaacson, Walter. 2011. *Steve Jobs*. New York: Simon & Schuster.

Ismail, Sellam and Finn, Christine. 2002. *Proceedings of the 6 Workshop, Archäologie und Computer* (Vienna, 5–6 November 2001)—CD-Rom edition. Forschungsgesellschaft Wiener Stadtarchäologie.

Lewis, Michael. 1999. *The New, New Thing: A Silicon Valley Story*. London: Penguin.

Saxenian, AnnaLee. 1996. *Regional Advantage: Culture and Competition in Silicon Valley and Route 128*. Cambridge, MA: Harvard University Press.

Schnapp, Alain. 1996. *The Discovery of the Past*. London: British Museum Press.

Shanks, Michael. 1992. *Experiencing the Past*. London: Routledge.

Tilley, Christopher, et al. (eds.). 2006. *Handbook of Material Culture*. London: Sage.

Virilio, Paul. 2000. *The Information Bomb*, tr. Chris Turner. London: Verso.

Vise, David A. and Malseed, Mark. 2005. *The Google Story*. New York: Bantam Dell.

Winslow, Ward (ed.). 1996. *The Making of Silicon Valley: A One Hundred Year Renaissance*. Santa Clara, CA: Santa Clara Valley Historical Association.

CHAPTER 44

....

BUILDING THOUGHT INTO THINGS

....

DAVID DE LÉON

44.1 INTRODUCTION

....

CAN thought be built into things? The question sounds like something a child might ask you, not because there is something inane about the query, but because we are asked to consider the merger of categories we have learned to keep separate. It is hard to imagine what it would mean for thought—perception, reasoning, and judgement—to be combined with, or built into, material objects of metal, wood, and clay. Perhaps it is the apparent incongruity of the idea that lies behind the allure of the many thinking objects we find in ancient and modern myth, be they mirrors with opinions on the things they reflect, or spaceships with dysfunctional personalities.

In this chapter I will be investigating *everyday objects*, rather than mythological. To this purpose I will retrace Bærentsen's (1989) analysis: that the actions and thought processes required to operate a rifle, at any one stage of its development, are 'built into' subsequent generations of the weapon.

The historical development of firearms is an ideal material for our purpose in many ways. First of all, Bærentsen has done a fine job of summarizing the developmental history of the rifle, and his thesis is both original and consistently pursued. Second, the artefacts and tasks examined can be understood without any specialized knowledge, and are sufficiently circumscribed to permit treatment in the present format.

In the process of retracing and critically evaluating Bærentsen's analysis, an alternative view gradually emerges in which greater emphasis is placed on the interplay between the physical properties of artefacts and the fine-detailed structure of the tasks performed.

The reanalysis is closely aligned with work in the field of situated cognition, which recognizes the importance of the physical and social environment for cognition. The surrounding world is no longer seen as something simply to be interpreted and acted on, but as something that can support, or even take part in the processes of cognition. It has been shown, for instance, that people can make use of the physical world to remember things (Beach 1988; Norman 1988; Hutchins 1995b), to simplify choice, perception, and internal computation (Clark 1997; Kirsh 1995), and to transform tasks in ways that make them less cognitively taxing (Hutchins 1990, 1995a; Norman 1991; de Léon 2002). The methodology is commonly ethnographical (e.g. Scribner 1986; Suchman 1987; Lave 1988; Hazlehurst 1994; Hutchins 1995a, 1995b; Hutchins and Klausen 1996) and more rarely experimental (Kirsh and Maglio 1994; Zhang and Norman 1994).

Although situated cognition acknowledges the significance of external physical and social structures to thought, the actual genesis, development, and appropriation of the material world figures to a negligible extent in the research. The present chapter thus serves the additional purpose of suitably extending the purview of situated cognition (also see de Léon 2002, 2006).

44.2 EARLY FIREARMS

The first documented hand-held firearms appear in the mid-fourteenth century. These consisted of little more than simple metal cylinders attached to wooden shafts, with the far end of the contraption supported by a stand. The guns were loaded with gunpowder and used to fire a bullet or a handful of stones. Discharging the gun was achieved by plunging a hot iron rod through a small hole in the top of the cylinder and into the gunpowder.

44.2.1 Firearm Design and Task Structure

In his analysis, Bærentsen draws attention to two crucial aspects of the task of firing the earliest guns. Using a hot iron rod as the means of igniting the gunpowder necessitated the close proximity of the gunman to a fire or a brazier in which to periodically heat the rod. The use of the hot iron thus greatly curtailed the movements of the gunman, and consequently, the positioning of the firearm.

The second aspect of the task, imposed by the design of the gun, pertains to the actual operation of the device. Putting the hot iron through the hole in the gun placed great attentional demands on the person using the weapon: attention being locked into finding the hole and into monitoring the motor actions required for fitting the hot iron into it. A consequence of this is that little attention is available for other, simultaneous aspects of the task, most importantly, the aiming of the gun at a chosen target. Due to attentional demands posed by the properties of the gun, aiming and firing become two incompatible actions which had to be carried out in succession.

44.2.2 The Gunman becomes Mobile

The next design innovation, appearing sometime during the fifteenth century, is the replacement of the hot iron—as the means of setting off the gunpowder—with a slow-burning fuse. With the fuse the gunman was no longer yoked to a source of heat, but able to carry the gun with him over greater distances as well as on horseback. The fuse, and the resulting portability of the gun, entailed further design changes in the gun itself, but it is the fuse which is predominantly responsible for the radical transformation of the structure of the task.

44.2.3 Changing the Timing of the Task

It seems unsatisfactory to suppose that the brazier has been 'built into' the fuse, as Bærentsen seems to suggest; even the fuse has to be lit at some point and at some source. In a way similar to the original hot iron, it too is an intermediary between a source of fire and the gunpowder which it is used to ignite. It cannot solely be the portability of the fuse that enables the greater movements of the gunman. The iron would likely be unwieldy and risky to carry on horseback, but the real problem is that the iron would cool off all too quickly, rendering it useless for the task at hand.

Here is, I think, the significant difference between the two artefactual complexes, accounting for the changes in the way that the task is performed. It is the fact that the fuse is able to retain a particular kind of state (i.e. combustion) necessary for subsequent operations, and that it is able to retain this state for a sufficient amount of time, that accounts for the acquired mobility of the gunman. The slow combustion of the fuse allows the gunman greater flexibility in choosing *when* to fire the gun. It is this change in the timing of the task which gives the gunman the greater freedom of movement. We have just seen the profound effect on task structure that may result from the substitution of just one artefact, or more correctly, one component of an artefactual complex. We have also seen how the nature of the change in the task was closely coupled to a particular property of the substitute artefact. This general view of the relation between the properties of artefacts and the tasks performed with them is one we derive from Cole and Griffin (1980), Hutchins (1990), and Norman (1991).

44.2.4 Aiming and Firing

In the following generation of guns, the fuse was mounted on the end of a mechanical arm running along the length of the barrel (see Figure 44.1). Firing the gun no longer required the kind of attentional resources previously needed as the arm could in principle be operated without looking. Attention could now instead be devoted to the different components of the task of aiming.

What has occurred here, Bærentsen tells us, is the objectification of the sensorimotor operations that previously made up the action of discharging the firearm. According to Bærentsen there are two aspects of the performance of the task which can both be said to have been 'built into' the material structure of the gun. One aspect is the sequence of motor actions itself—the physical movements of bringing the fuse to the aperture (the touch-hole) on the top of the gun. Bærentsen argues that these have been taken over and are now performed by the mechanical arm. The second aspect pertains to the perceptual and cognitive operations involved in finding the touch-hole, and in guiding and monitoring the motor actions of the task. The claim here is that these cognitive processes have been 'fixed', once and for all, in the physical structure of the artefact.

FIGURE 44.1 Firearm equipped with a mechanical arm. Drawing based on a manuscript dated 1411 (drawing by David de Léon)

How should we understand these claims? What might it mean to 'build in' or to 'materialize' motor operations, or to 'fix' perceptual and cognitive operations? Let's begin with the first idea, that the actual movements of the gunman are somehow captured by, or solidified in, the material structure of the mechanical arm.

44.2.5 Building Motor Operations into Things

There is a sense in which the mechanical arm does seem to have taken over the physical actions that were once performed by the operator of the gun. If we focus only on the movements made by the fuse, at least part of the trajectory of the fuse will be approximately the same, regardless of whether the fuse is mounted on a mechanical arm or gripped in a human hand.

At first sight it may indeed look as if the mechanical arm is mimicking the movements of the gunman's hand. However, without the gunman to pull on the arm, it would simply remain inert. Bærentsen is quite clearly not suggesting that the mechanical arm supplants the actions of the gunman; it is obvious that the agent has to initiate the action, as well as provide the necessary motive force. The separation of motor operations from the cognitive control of those operations is surely a distinction made for analytical convenience. But with the source of power extraneous to the arm, and the issue of control separated from that of execution, the question remains as to what it is that the arm has taken over: what is it that has been built in?

44.3 A SET OF FIVE INTERRELATED TRANSFORMATIONS

At this point I think it would be fruitful to present my own conceptualization of what the introduction of the mechanical arm will have entailed. I propose that we view the adoption of the new gun design as a set of five interrelated transformations.

1. *The Physical Structure of the Artefact Transformed*

The change in the design of the gun is a transformation of the physical structure of the artefact.

2. *The Structure of the Task Transformed*

In the case at hand, instead of having to locate the touch-hole on the top of the barrel of the gun and guide the fuse into it, the gunman has now only to pull on a mechanical arm.

3. *The Performance of the Task Transformed*

The physical constraints inherent in the artefact will both shape and guide the actions of the gunman while the arm is pulled. The agent operating the arm will not be impervious to the affordances offered, and will naturally respond and adjust to these, but the point here is that the arm will to some extent *forcibly* alter the direction of the manipulations of the person operating it.

4. *The Gunman's Movements Transformed*

As the movements of the gunman are transmitted by the arm, their direction and amplitude will be altered and transformed by the mechanical properties of the artefact. The upward movement of the gunman's hand will be transformed into a downward movement of the fuse. The extent of the transformation of the amplitude of the hand movement will depend on the placement of the pivot and the length of the various parts of the arm.

This fourth transformation is a transformation of the vector provided by the gunman. We can now note some ways in which the transformation of the structure of the task by the artefact is dependent on the artefact's ability to shape and transform the actions *within* the task. One thing the mechanical arm does is to greatly simplify the task facing the gunman. The arm has only one degree of freedom and this makes the attendant operation very simple. More important, almost all variation in the gunman's input will be absorbed by the arm, and channelled into an appropriate movement of the fuse at the other end. Since the task is also fairly insensitive to variations in timing, almost any tugging or pulling on the arm will be translated into an appropriate effect. The skill needed to operate the arm is therefore very slight.

The real elegance of the design is that the mechanical arm presents a simple task that requires little skill to perform, and the simplicity of this task is dependent on the properties of the mechanical arm. In addition, the properties of the arm ensure that the simple action required of the gunman will have the requisite effect.

5. *The Goal of the Task Transformed*

Finally, these changes to the task and artefact will have been accompanied by a concomitant transformation of the goal of the task. With attention released from the sub-task of discharging the gun, it could now be employed in other activities, such as improved aiming. Instead of hoping to just hit *someone*, the gunman could now select a specific target and aim to hit the chosen target. The introduction of the mechanical arm did not simply improve the gun, it also changed the kinds of task for which it was used. At a very general level of description the task has, of course, remained the same—wounding the enemy—but at a more specified level the task has become quite different.[1]

The co-evolution of tasks and artefacts has been called the task–artefact cycle (Carroll, Kellogg, and Rosson 1991). Tasks set requirements on the design of suitable artefacts. The resulting artefacts, in turn, suggest novel possibilities and impose new constraints, which taken together, often redefine the task for which the artefact was originally developed. The new task then sets new requirements and the cycle continues.

44.4 FIXING PERCEPTUAL AND COGNITIVE PROCESSES

We should now be in a better position to judge Bærentsen's claim that certain cognitive processes have been 'fixed' in the physical structure of the mechanical arm. The two things which have supposedly been fixed in the artefact are: the perceptual process of locating the hole on the top of the gun, and the cognitive process of guiding the fuse into the hole.

I am inclined to agree that there is at least a sense in which the process of finding the touch-hole has been set or fixed in the structure of the device. Whoever manufactured or calibrated the mechanical arm would have had to locate the hole in the top of the barrel—a process involving the perceptual mechanisms of the artisan responsible—and then set the arm appropriately. Thereafter, the mechanical arm will guarantee that the hole is 'found' every time the arm is pulled. To be able to operate the arm, it too must be found, of course, but its size and placement makes this an automatic consequence of handling the gun, and not chiefly a perceptual process.

Our intuition in this case seems to rest on the unspoken assumption that to qualify as having being 'fixed', a cognitive process has to be appropriately exercised during manufacture.

---

[1] The descriptions of the task are those of an outside observer and there is always some indeterminacy as to how the task is conceptualized by the agent himself (Draper 1993).

By this criterion, however, the cognitive process of guiding the fuse into the touch-hole will not qualify as having been fixed in the structure of the artefact. Making and placing the arm will involve numerous perceptual and cognitive judgements, but not the rehearsal of those performed by a gunman manipulating an unattached fuse.

Moving away from these criteria we might instead note the particular ways in which the mechanical arm replaces the cognitive processes of guiding and monitoring the movements of the unattached fuse. There is a part of the task, a certain task requirement, which remains constant through both generations of the gun. In both generations, the fuse has to pass through a certain trajectory. In one case the movements of the fuse are controlled by mainly cognitive processes, in the second case, most of the control is achieved through the physical constraints inherent in the artefact. Despite these differences, there is a sense in which the two are performing the same job.

44.5 Two Ways of Dividing One's Attention

The next change brought to the design of hand-held firearms is the introduction of the first spring-loaded locks. Instead of pulling on a large and cumbersome mechanical arm, the gun is now discharged by means of a delicate lever which releases a small spring-loaded arm. Bærentsen's take on this is that the last remaining vestiges of attention that were demanded by the mechanical arm have now been released. Complete attention could finally be devoted to aiming the gun. As a result, the stock of the gun changed shape, making it possible to rest it against the shoulder, thus further transforming the task of aiming. The introduction of lock and stock will also have made it easier to hold the weapon steady at the moment it was discharged, which would have greatly contributed to the weapon's accuracy.

We must be careful lest we think that the attentional demands placed on the agent have simply been blown away by the introduction of the spring-loaded lock. It is of course correct that attentional demands have been lessened. It so happens, however, that they turn up in a different place.

Like the mechanical arm, the spring-loaded lock is still dependent on the gunman for its motive power, but now in a more indirect and less immediate fashion. Motive power is supplied by the gunman when the gun is cocked, and stored in the mainspring until the time at which the trigger is pulled. Priming the gun requires the attentional resources of the gunman, but at a time when these are not being competed for. The ability of the spring to store energy (another instance of the ability to retain a change of state) solves the problem of limited attentional resources by redistributing the demand for these resources. The artefact permits part of the action of discharging the gun to be performed ahead of time, *storing* the action if you will. The action can then be deployed at a time when the gunman would not normally be able to perform the action in a satisfactory manner.

This is an interesting general strategy for handling limited attentional resources and can be compared with the slightly different strategy which lay behind the adoption of the mechanical arm. Whereas the spring-loaded lock is able to redistribute the demand for attentional resources over time, the mechanical arm of the prior generation of guns solved a similar problem by redistributing an attentionally demanding task over modalities.[2] With the first generation of guns, both aiming and firing made claims on visual attention. The mechanical arm was able to shift most of the attentional demand of firing the gun to a neighbouring channel.

44.6 Rationalizing Task Structure

Successive innovations in the design of the triggering mechanism—the wheel-lock, the snaphance lock, the flintlock, and the percussion lock—were all able to produce a triggering spark or explosion on demand, obviating the need for a burning fuse. This further simplified the use of the weapon; an entire step—that of lighting the fuse—being removed from the process of operating the gun.

According to Bærentsen the complex sensorimotor operations that were previously involved in servicing the fuse have partly been made redundant, and partly materialized, in the physical structure of the triggering mechanism. Again, I think that we can rather see this as a case of the artefact transforming task organization.

The kind of transformation that I believe has occurred here is a form of rationalization. Two actions which were previously separate—bringing the fuse in contact with a source of fire, and bringing the fuse in contact with the powder charge—have been brought together in a single action. Elements of the first action that are duplicated by the second action have been excised. That this is possible is due to the unique properties of the triggering mechanism—specifically the properties of the flint or pyrites—to convert a motive force into a spark.[3]

As with the previous transitions, the transition from mechanical arm to spring-loaded lock will have entailed changes to both structure and goals of the task. It will also have entailed changes to the structure and goals of related or even, what appear to be, unrelated tasks. The repercussions are vast and complex, and almost impossible to track. One interesting effect of the gradual move away from the use of a burning fuse is that the gunman was no longer as conspicuous during night or twilight hours, the momentary flare of a lock mechanisms being harder to track than a glowing row of smouldering fuses. This will have had clear tactical consequences.

44.7 Reorganizing Cognitive Task Structure

An aspect of the task of operating the earliest guns which has barely been touched upon, but which is by far the most time consuming and attentionally demanding of the processes

---

[2] The spring-loaded lock actually combines both of these strategies.

[3] I am simplifying the description and analysis of the process in order to bring the general idea across. In fact the locks which came to replace the matchlock did not ignite the powder charge directly, but via a small quantity of priming powder which first had to be deposited in the pan of the lock.

involved in servicing the gun, is the loading and reloading of the weapon. This was probably the most important single factor dictating the possible tactical uses of the gun. The
exact method used to load the earliest firearms varies, but generally involved the deposit
of a measured quantity of gunpowder and a shot down the muzzle of the barrel. After the
shot had been fired, and before a second shot could be discharged, the barrel of the gun had
to be cleaned out and the loading repeated. Here Bærentsen reminds us of the importance
of the soldiers' training. One thing soldiers are made to do is to practise ritualized sets
of movements, including those of loading, aiming, and firing guns. This programme of
training transforms the task of loading the gun in at least two ways. First of all, the movements learned have been carefully pared down to essentials. This is one way of reorganizing
the structure of a task without transforming the physical artefact. Secondly, the repeated
drilling of these sets of gestures eventually makes them automatic and almost effortless to
perform. We could see automatization as a kind of mental reorganization of the task (cf.
Hutchins 1997 [1986]). Outwardly, the gunman might seem to be performing the same
task, say loading a firearm, but the inner organization of the cognitive processes employed
may have changed.

44.8 COGNITIVE HOMEWORK

Fine tuning and automatization of the execution of the task minimizes the time the gunman
spends loading the gun and clearing out the bore of the barrel. But, regardless of how much
time is spent in training, there is still a limit to how quickly the gunman can perform the
task. There is one way, however, in which the gunman's time *off the battlefield* can be used to
speed up the loading of the firearm.

The procedure of loading the gun is made up of a number of separate activities. The
gunman has to deposit a measured quantity of gunpowder down the muzzle of the
firearm, followed by a shot wrapped in a small patch of cloth. The powder, shot, and
patch all have to be brought out from various containers and coordinated in the task
of loading.

Eventually an innovation was introduced that allowed part of this process to be
carried out in advance. The sixteenth century saw the introduction of pre-packaged
cartridges containing a shot and a measured quantity of powder. These paper packets
could be placed in the breech of a gun with altogether far less ado, and could be prepared by the gunman at his leisure, well ahead of the time when they were to be used.
Being able to divide up the performance of the task not only made it possible to distribute the task across time, but also across people (cf. Hutchins 1995a on the notion
of pre-computation).

For Bærentsen the paper cartridges are yet another case of 'fixing'. This time the claim
packs rather a lot of things into the paper cartridge, along with shot and powder. As
well as the motor operations of loading the gun, we find the deliberations, decisions,
and perceptual processes which used to form part of the activity. I will not reanalyse
these claims. Suffice it to say that loading the paper cartridges still requires certain motor
actions and cognitive processes. We do not get around these by wrapping them up in a
paper package.

44.9 PRE-COMPUTATION OR
FOSSILIZED PRACTICE?

Following these first few steps in the development of the rifle are countless innovations to every possible aspect of the gun's design. Improvements to the mechanism of the gun further simplified the process of loading and clearing and also increased the range of the weapon. Loading and clearing the gun became increasingly mechanized over time. Means were eventually found of exploiting the energy of the gun's recoil and using this for the automatization of loading and clearing the breech.

The range of the gun, and how fast it can be reloaded, is of little consequence if the target cannot be hit because the gunman's aim is too poor. Through the introduction of the shoulder-stock, the gunman could look down the length of the barrel—instead of seeing it from a slightly elevated angle—making it easier to judge the direction in which the gun was pointing. Lining up the muzzle of the gun with the chosen target is a predominantly perceptual task, whereas the previous task required a more complex set of judgements (cf. Clark 1997 on the generality of this type of transformation).

The perceptual task of aligning the gun with a target was eventually simplified by fixing a small projection near the muzzle of the gun. This innovation was later refined by the addition of a second, cleft projection, nearer the eye of the gunman, so that the first could be seen when the two were properly aligned.

Though these developments to the sight of the gun transformed the task of aligning the gun with a target, a mental correction still had to be made for the vertical deviation of the shot caused by gravity. To compensate for the effects of gravity on the shot, the gunman had to aim slightly above the intended target. How much above depended on the distance from the target and the velocity of the projectile. The standardization of the cartridge made the velocity of the projectile an invariant factor. With velocity held constant, estimating the vertical deviation of the shot was a matter of judging distance alone, and of being able to transform distance estimates into appropriate adjustments to the aim. I am assuming here that shooting practice engendered a *feel* for the relation between distance and displacement, and that the gunman did not consciously calculate the displacement.

In a later development of the sight, the displacement of the shot at various distances is *stored* in the structure of the artefact and does not need to be remembered or calculated by the gunman. The cleft was made part of an adjustable scale which could be moved up and down (see Figure 44.2). The markings on the scale were spaced to ensure an operative angle of the gun for every distance marked on the scale.

We can imagine several different ways in which the scale could have been calibrated. One way would be to take the gun out to the shooting range and calibrate the scale through a process of trial and error. Alternatively, the spacing of the markings could have been calculated with pen and paper. Whichever method was used will not be apparent from just looking at the weapon.

So what exactly, if anything, has been built into the scale? Is it a repository of practical experience, or is it an external memory for a set of computations? This depends partly on the history of the particular device we are looking at. There is a sense in which both can be considered repositories of practice, although in more or less direct ways. The hypothesized

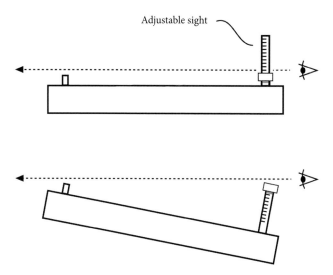

FIGURE 44.2 Schematic illustration of the adjustable sight compensating for bullet drop (drawing by David de Léon)

'mathematical' means of calibrating the scale is not untarnished by practice, but relies on procedures and tools that are themselves the products of accumulated practice and experience.

44.10 CULTURAL CHOICES

One of the things commending Bærentsen's analysis is his sensitivity to the interplay between practice, cognition, and artefact design. In this chapter I have tried to examine and scrutinize this interplay in greater detail: moving a little closer to the physical properties of the artefacts under consideration, and looking a little closer at the fine structure of the tasks in which we find them. There is, however, one corrective with which I would like to end.

The backbone to this chapter has been the historical development of the rifle. We have traced the evolution of this category of artefact for a part of its history. The analysis has been more inclusive than is usual in discussions of technology, involving lines of influence that weave together interactions between artefact design, cognition, task structure, and task goals. Although we have followed several causal chains, it is important to point out that we have not been describing a determined system.

With hindsight it may seem as if the evolution of an artefact has a direction, that design improvements accumulate over time, slowly shaping the artefact into its definitive form. Is it not an incontestable fact that modern firearms are superior to the simple guns with which we have been preoccupied? Perhaps. It may be tempting to imagine the task–artefact cycle as a kind of spiral which gradually approaches an optimum solution, winding its way towards an ideal form of the task and artefact.

It would be hard to deny that there is an accumulation of innovations in almost any artefact we choose to look at. The latest generation of an artefact category is often the direct response to the perceived shortcomings of the immediately preceding generation (Petroski 1992).

However, there are few tasks which ever reach a definitive and unalterable form. One reason is that surrounding activity rarely remains constant or unaffected by the evolution of the task. Take the rifle as an example. A plausible progression would seem to be towards deadlier and more accurate weapons—a scenario which is partly vindicated by the history of the modern rifle—but there are also limits to pure effectiveness. Weaponry that is too effective may be incompatible with other goals, for instance moral, political, economic, or even strategic goals.

Another limit to pure effectiveness is that rifle design, like all design, is by necessity a trade-off between the effectiveness at different types of tasks that might be performed with the weapon. What is essential to one task is sometimes an impediment to another. This is part of the reason for the great diversity of rifle designs, with special rifles for specialized tasks. The occasional branching of the developmental line of an artefact, with new cycles spinning off in different directions, is one thing which the task–artefact cycle fails to include.

There are plenty of instances when effectiveness is shunned for personal or cultural reasons. In the Upper Verdon valley in the south-east of France, for instance, the most experienced hunters are expected to hunt with a small-bored rifle—normally only used by women and youngsters—to demonstrate their superior proficiency (Govoroff 1993). This is only one of many examples of what Lemonnier (1992 and this volume) calls 'technological choice': cases of people choosing particular technologies, or parts of technologies, for other than purely instrumental reasons. Cultural influence on technology is more pervasive than we might at first think. An important influence on how any given piece of technology develops is how that technology is conceptualized in the culture which supports it (cf. Quilici-Pacaud 1993). The entrenched conception of what a gun is and does, for instance, is probably one of the most important determinants of the direction the development of the gun will take. There are design solutions which are perfectly valid on instrumental grounds, but which would never be pursued simply because the result would not look sufficiently gun-like.

ACKNOWLEDGEMENTS

This chapter is based on a conference paper from 1999. There I thanked my late and dear friend Henrik Gendenryd, as well as Peter Gärdenfors and Björn Nilsson. This time round I would also like to thank Alan Costall for occasionally spreading some of my old texts as I focus on *making* artefacts, instead of studying them.

REFERENCES

Bærentsen, Klaus B. 1989. Mennesker og maskiner. In *Et virksomt liv: Udforskning af virksomhedsteoriens praksis*, ed. M. Hedegaard, V. R. Hansen, and S. Thyssen, pp. 142–87. Aarhus: Aarhus Universitetsforlag.

Beach, King. 1988. The Role of External Mnemonic Symbols in Acquiring an Occupation. In *Practical Aspects of Memory: Current Research and Issues*, vol. 1, ed. M. M. Gruneberg, P. E. Morris, and R. N. Sykes, pp. 342–6. Chichester: Wiley.

Carroll, John M., Kellogg, W. A., and Rosson, M. B. 1991. The Task–Artifact Cycle. In *Designing Interaction: Psychology at the Human-Computer Interface*, ed. John M. Carroll, pp. 74–102. Cambridge: Cambridge University Press.

Clark, Andy. 1997. *Being There: Putting Brain, Body, and World Together Again*. Cambridge, MA: MIT Press.

Cole, Michael and Griffin, Peg. 1980. Cultural Amplifiers Reconsidered. In *The Social Foundations of Language and Thought*, ed. David R. Olson, pp. 343–64. New York: W. W. Norton.

de Léon, David. 2002. Cognitive Task Transformations. *Cognitive Systems Research* 3(3): 449–59.

—— 2006. The Cognitive Biographies of Things. In *Doing Things with Things*, ed. A. Costall and O. Drier, pp. 113–30. Aldershot: Ashgate.

Draper, Steve W. 1993. The Notion of Task in HCI. In *Bridges Between Worlds, INTERCHI'93 Conference Proceedings, Adjunct Proceedings*, ed. S. Ashlund, K. Mullet, A. Henderson, E. Hollnagel, and W. White, pp. 207–8. Reading, MA: Addison-Wesley.

Govoroff, Nicolas C. 1993. The Hunter and his Gun in Haute-Provence. In *Technological Choices*, ed. Pierre Lemonnier, pp. 227–37. London and New York: Routledge.

Hazlehurst, Brian. 1994. Fishing for Cognition: An Ethnography of Fishing Practice in a Community on the West Coast of Sweden. Unpublished Ph.D. dissertation, Department of Cognitive Science and Department of Anthropology, University of California, San Diego.

Hutchins, Edwin. 1990. The Technology of Team Navigation. In *Intellectual Teamwork: Social and Technical Bases of Collaborative Work*, ed. J. Galegher, R. Kraut, and C. Egido, pp. 191–220. Hillsdale, NJ: Lawrence Erlbaum Associates.

—— 1995a. *Cognition in the Wild*. Cambridge, MA: MIT Press.

—— 1995b. How a Cockpit Remembers its Speed. *Cognitive Science* 19: 265–88.

—— 1997 [1986]. Mediation and Automatization. In *Mind, Culture, and Activity: Seminal Papers from the Laboratory of Comparative Human Cognition*, ed. M. Cole, Y. Engeström, and O. Vasquez, pp. 338–53. Cambridge: Cambridge University Press.

Hutchins, Edwin and Klausen, Tove. 1996. Distributed Cognition in an Airline Cockpit. In *Cognition and Communication at Work*, ed. Y. Engeström and D. Middeleton, pp. 15–34. Cambridge: Cambridge University Press.

Kirsh, David. 1995. The Intelligent Use of Space. *Artificial Intelligence* 73: 31–68.

Kirsh, David and Maglio, Paul. 1994. On Distinguishing Epistemic from Pragmatic Action. *Cognitive Science* 18: 513–49.

Lave, Jean. 1988. *Cognition in Practice: Mind, Mathematics and Culture in Everyday Life*. Cambridge: Cambridge University Press.

Lemonnier, Pierre. 1992. *Elements for an Anthropology of Technology*. Anthropological Papers, 88. Ann Arbor, MI: Museum of Anthropology/University of Michigan.

Norman, Donald. 1988. *The Design of Everyday Things*. New York: Doubleday Currency.

—— 1991. Cognitive Artifacts. In *Designing Interaction: Psychology at the Human-Computer Interface*, ed. J. M. Carroll, pp. 17–38. Cambridge: Cambridge University Press.

Petroski, Henry. 1992. *The Evolution of Useful Things*. New York: Vintage Books.

Quilici-Pacaud, Jean-François. 1993. Dominant Representations and Technical Choices: A Method of Analysis with Examples from Aeronautics. In *Technological Choices*, ed. Pierre Lemonnier, pp. 399–412. London and New York: Routledge.

Scribner, Sylvia. 1986. Thinking in Action: Some Characteristics of Practical Thought. In *Practical Intelligence: Nature and Origins of Competence in the Everyday World*, ed. R. Sternberg and R. Wagner, pp. 13–30. Cambridge: Cambridge University Press.

Suchman, Lucy. 1987. *Plans and Situated Actions: The Problem of Human–Machine Communication*. Cambridge: Cambridge University Press.

Zhang, Jiajie and Norman, Donald. 1994. Representations in Distributed Cognitive Tasks. *Cognitive Science* 18: 87–122.

CHAPTER 45

....

ARCHAEOLOGIES OF THE POSTINDUSTRIAL BODY

....

SEFRYN PENROSE

45.1 INTRODUCTION

ARCHAEOLOGIES of the body are most familiar to us in terms of analyses of skeletal remains, through the forensic arm of the discipline, and through examination of the body's materials. These archaeologies contribute to our knowledge of the lives and deaths of long-dead and not-so-long-dead individuals and groups. However, archaeology's strength—perceived by some as a disciplinary weakness (e.g. Miller 1983; Hicks 2010: 60)—is in letting non-corporeal matter serve as a proxy for the body. While the imbalance of the strength of representations of the body may be clearly justified for bodies of the past, archaeologies of the contemporary are often defined by the lived or transitional nature of their subject matter. One of the most controversial (but also the most useful) defining characteristics of contemporary archaeology is the living resource: people, plants, and animals are still comprehensively involved in the sites of our studies, whether corporeally, materially, or mentally. As a result, the body itself may be seen as an archaeological site, and embodied selves as revealing as, and in pluripotential relationships with, non-corporeal matter.

This chapter focuses on *human* bodies as sites for archaeology in the contemporary setting, and particularly on human bodies at work and play (see Badcock and Johnson, this volume, on the body in protest/direct action). These bodies are predominantly British or North American, and are involved in the industrial/postindustrial transition in the capitalist system. The discussion herein focuses on the working 'well' or 'absent' body (Leder 1990). In doing so, this discussion does not examine in depth issues of difference, but suggests directions within the postindustrial transition in which the body may lead us. I outline three body 'events': the rise of scientific management and its creation of the assembly-line body; the subsequent emergence of the postindustrial managerial body; and the development of the gym-body, the body working-out. By unpacking these events, I track trajectories that clearly show how the body is in a reciprocal relationship with its economic framework which has shaped it, and which it shapes. In researching the postindustrial, it is clear that change has been written on bodies and by bodies in a manner that is still all pervasive in the sites in which we often work. Beyond the realms of ruin, the contemporary is a peopled, active, changing world. The following events and trajectories track the production of a materialist, economically constituted anatomy, which I propose as the beginnings of an archaeology of postindustrial change that is corporeal and incorporated, a bodily engagement. It is not my intention to avoid more nuanced engagements with bodies (cf. Haraway 1991; Butler 1993), rather to suggest a framework within which we might start to approach bodies within contemporary archaeology as admissible archaeological evidence.

45.2 BODY/BODIES

Behind every body is a complex set of circumstances that have brought it into being. I begin this exploration based on the acceptance of three overarching assertions. Firstly, the rejection of the division of mind/body (Gosden 2004; Thomas 2007). Secondly, that the body is a cultural construction that is in flux, with historical incarnations and interpretations. The body can be seen as a 'location' (Durkheim 1984; Shilling 2005: 11) for the material conditions of society (Marx and Engels 1978: 150), and for collective fabrication of society, constituting itself in relation to its conditions (Shilling 2005: 37). Further, bodies are assemblages of biological, sociological, and psychological circumstances, 'ensemble[s] of techniques of the body' that emerge in different cultures, what Mauss terms a 'psycho-sociological taxonomy' (Mauss 1973: 73). Thirdly, that the body is gendered. Feminism's engagement with the gendered form—as culturally determined—opened a discourse on the externally informed conditioning at work on the gendered body. The sexed body is gendered (Grosz 1994), and both sex and gender are products of the cultural hegemony (Butler 1993: 63). Accepting these understandings of the body and bodies as contextually contingent beings allows us to develop a view of the body in a reciprocal relationship with the world, mutually constituting and changing.

45.3 THE BODY AT WORK

The way that bodies have altered, and the way that working practices have altered to accommodate readings of the body, is illustrative of the lived transition from industrial to postindustrial. This section considers trends that have altered the working body in the last century and a half, and suggests ways in which, from a contemporary archaeological standpoint, we might track the transition to postindustrialism on the body itself. Work here is defined as those actions of the body engaged in production, but not necessarily limited to economic production. Conceptually, this section addresses moments in which particular sections of the workforce have been affected, bodily, by wider trends. We might consider the usefulness of Haraway's (1991) cyborg metaphor in this context. In terms of contemporary archaeology, it is my suggestion that an investigation of emergent capitalist bodies through the tracking of particular body work 'events' will enable a visibility in the record of changes to the lived body, the way it is lived, experienced, in Butler's terms, performed, that can enhance contemporary archaeologies of lived sites.

Capitalism is 'a world still very much engaged in making itself' as recent shifts in the economic cosmos have shown (Mrozowski 2006: 3). Capitalism has been engaged in a classificatory process, and continues to be so. In the first half of the twentieth century increased automation produced a semi-skilled or low-skilled urban populace and a new stratum of management worker. In the last half century, a postindustrial middle/worker class has emerged out of both these sectors, while the emergence of an urban non-worker class, or 'underclass', has altered the understanding of the term 'working class'. Although said to be a British preoccupation, class identifications associated with types of work have created confused and divided societies across the world, often, and perhaps always, written and differentiated on the body.

45.3.1 Taylorism

F. W. Taylor (1911) outlined how companies could operate more effectively by streamlining and ordering the work of the labouring body, and increasing the volume of management. The capacities of the body together with the mind were the route to increasing productivity, and hence to increasing profit. Capital was lost through the natural laziness of men (Taylor 1911: 3), and through simple, 'scientifically' determined steps, greater efficiency of the human body could be achieved for the betterment of all concerned (Taylor 1911: 4). The 'time and motion studies' that he proposed, based on work by Frank and Lillian Gilbreth (Gilbreth 1910), took the body as the base for capital achievement. The actions of the bodies—movements, forces, rest periods, lifting and carrying capacities—were examined, reduced to those that were purely necessary, and accompanied by a greater managerial role. The worker's body was effectively relieved of its autonomy. The studies did the same with machinery, fitting it to the men and women who worked it. The ultimate aim of Taylor's principles was to achieve a machine-like reliability that eliminated human and mechanical failing and ensured uniformity: of process, people, components, input, and output. Both Taylor and Gilbreth emphasized that only 'first-class men' (Taylor 1911: 18) or '100-per-cent quality' men (Gilbreth 1910: 23) should be employed for these studies, and that similar 'classes' of men should be sought for the same kinds of work. The highest achievable output therefore became the benchmark in their studies. It should be noted, however, that the Gilbreths applied their methods to women's typing pools. The presence of the 'first-class man' in the literature does not preclude women from this consideration of changes to workplace culture—in the home, factory, and office setting—despite elisions in the literature (Figure 45.1).

Taylor (1911) gave the example of workers shifting pig-iron from a stockpile to carts for transportation to the factory. Through time and motion studies, observers determined that the right sort of man could shift 47 imperial tons per day (1016kg/2240lb = ton) instead of the average of 12. By observing workers at close quarters and creating levels of hands-on management previously unknown, Taylorian bodies could be pushed to new limits.

Accompanying the reorganization of the physical labourer was the institution of a level of management that progressed from the lone foreman or gang-master to a category of middle management worker. For these men and women, work would be observational, ensuring that the work of others was done to time and with the correct motions. Both Taylor and Gilbreth acknowledged or claimed an understanding of anatomy that drove

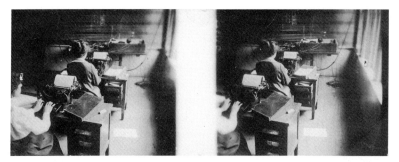

FIGURE 45.1 Stereoscopic motion study image of 'champion typists' by Frank B. Gilbreth, *c*.1915. (Kheel Center for Labor-Management Documentation and Archives, Cornell University)

their methods. Taylorism became influential in the structuring of the workplace, with the capacities of the body providing the central tenet behind the organization of factories, building sites, and offices, and effectively creating the categories of the blue- and white-collar worker. It ensured Taylor's canonization as the father of modern management and was instrumental in the rise of managerialism. The Taylorist separation of the conception and execution of labour fed Marx's category of 'alienated labour', when the *practical need* to labour was harnessed by exploitative forces (Marx 1978: 50, 75) in the new organized workplace.

45.3.2 Fordism

Assembly line manufacturing developed through the nineteenth century with the intention of speeding up manufacturing processes. At Ford's, the 'flywheel magneto moving assembly line' was honed according to scientific management methods, and automated. Each process of production was timed, and the moving assembly line meant that workers were ruled by its ever-increasing speeds, set according to time studies (Beynon 1984: 38). Workers performed one task, remaining stationary in most cases while the lines moved and converged through different sets of workers fulfilling different tasks (Figure 45.2). This kind of production allowed Ford to adopt economies of scale large enough that, although the work was difficult, high wages—the $5-day—ensured that workers were easily recruited, if not retained, and no other companies could come close to competing. It allowed Ford to build production to unprecedented levels, and to achieve his aim of creating a workforce that could consume what it made. In this way, machines took over the job of the foreman-timekeeper, removing the management to the 'planning room or department' specified by Taylor as a necessity for the effective corporation (Taylor 1911: 59).

At Ford's, Taylor's and Gilbreth's advice on the 'first-class' worker was extended to aspects of life beyond the workplace. Ford was an influential exponent of prohibition and forbade drinkers among his workforce, exclaiming to a reporter in 1930, '...do you think a man can work in this factory if he drinks? Well, he can't! We watch them as they come in. We smell their breaths' (quoted in *Time* 1930). Observation extended to the home, with Ford's 'Sociology Department' responsible for analysis of individuals, ostensibly to determine

FIGURE 45.2 Production line of the Austin A30 (Seven) in the Car Assembly Building at British Motor Corporation's Longbridge factory 1953 (reproduced with permission from British Motor Industry Heritage Trust)

whether workers were eligible for the profit-share system that made the company so attractive (Hooker 1997: 48). The Sociology Department's investigators, among them physicians, sought a template for 'good Ford men', based on a sound marital home, thriftiness, sobriety, and cultural aspects that determined that of the first 1,400 to be admitted, 1,381 were of British ancestry (Hooker 1997: 47). The pursuit of a puritanical figure was, according to Gramsci, necessary for the creation of a workforce prepared for the arduous and repetitive work that Ford's required. A man free from passion would be up to the task, but a man (women were initially barred from the $5-a-day scheme [Hooker 1997: 48]) distracted by sex or drink was not (Gramsci 1999: 601).

While Ford had many critics of his autocracy, the company's contributions to improvements in housing and care provision and commitment to 'Americanization' maintained its popularity. But the pressures on the body demanded by the assembly line led to significant physical or mental strain or illness in workers (Beynon 1984: 38), both long and short-term, with accidents and illnesses part and parcel of some jobs within Ford plants, and other, subtler strains, showing elsewhere. A letter from a worker's wife to Ford himself illustrates the difficulty of making the grade as a 'good Ford man':

> The chain system that you have is a *slavedriver*. My God!, Mr. Ford—My husband has come home & thrown himself down & won't eat his supper—so done out! Can't it be remedied? That $5 a day is a blessing—a bigger one than you know, but *oh* they earn it. (Volti 2008: 42)

The extreme mechanization and its toll contributed to strong trade unionism (representative perhaps of Marx's worker alienation as a driver for change [Marx and Engels

1978: 50]) within such industries since the monotony of the work contributed to the need to create other bonds and forms of mental satisfaction. The change in emphasis at Ford's from incentive to fear-driven production became explicit in the 1920s and 1930s 'as the paternalism of the Sociological Department [gave] way to the brutality of the Service Department' (Beynon 1984: 39). Workers were in the factory for their bodies to work as the machines. 'Fordization of the face' was enforced, with employees forbidden from smiling, laughing, even talking unnecessarily, a habit that for the long-term Ford employee, was taken home (Sward, in Beynon 1984: 44). Here, the machinized self (Mauss 1973: 50), embodied through the development of skills, defined and reiterated itself through practice: 'the body is not an "entity", but is experienced as a practical mode of coping with external situations and events… [f]acial expressions and other gestures provide the fundamental content of that contextuality or indexicality which is the condition of everyday communication' (Giddens 1991: 56). Fordization of the face at work and in the home was more than a habit. Ford's working practices were rolled out across the industrialized nations alongside scientific management studies.

45.3.3 The Line

The treatment of workers as machines perhaps inevitably led to the extension of the worker's bodily agency to the interruption of the machine. Workers at the Halewood Ford plant in Liverpool—the subject of a seminal sociological monograph by Huw Beynon—related how even the death of a worker could not stop the line:

> The line started. The foreman came across shouting 'get to work… get on the line'. And there we were sticking things on the cars and he was lying there. (Quoted in Beynon 1984: 86)

The timed unstoppable line was not so much the extension of the worker, a blurring of the boundaries of the body, but a driver. This was emphasized by the regular speed-ups that would occur, forcing workers to work faster, just as they had mastered the previous acceleration. Stopping the body, refusing to work the body, was a virtual impossibility. Breaking the line or sabotaging the line's cargo became a regular occurrence at many assembly-line factories, with materials or means in the workers' orbit performing detrimental tasks—spanners, glue, grinders—while the guilty operator could effectively remain removed from blame. These external mechanisms extended the worker's abilities (Malafouris and Renfrew 2010a) and while not necessarily extending the body itself, certainly acted as its proxies, its agents.

Assembly lines became standard practice across the world, leading to a global reshaping of industrial work. Where labour could be obtained cheaply, manufacturing often followed. The relocation of industry led to the growth of Asian economies, in great part because of the availability of female labour at low cost. Seguino examines many of the methods used to culture women into accepting poor working conditions and poor wages by reinforcement of 'gender norms and stereotypes that convince women to accept their low status [and] curb labour and political unrest' (Seguino 2000: 27). Female labour on manufacturing lines across Asia became the mainstay of technological export companies: women's bodies and their (sexed, gendered, and cultured) ability to withstand extreme tedium and discomfort over long hours enabled the boom in service employment in North America and much of Europe.

45.3.4 The Coming of the Postindustrial Society

Daniel Bell, whose *The Coming of Post-Industrial Society* (1999 [1973]) popularized the term that would come to define the technological shift in working patterns, forecast an era in which a computer-aided workforce would create a knowledge theocracy. Bell identified three technological revolutions: firstly the harnessing of steam; secondly the advent of electricity, and thus electrical power, and chemistry, and thus the invention of synthetics; and finally a third revolution based on four innovations. This third revolution was defined by the shift from mechanical, electromechanical, and electrical systems to electronics, miniaturization, digitalization, and software (Bell 1999 [1973]: xxxiii–xxxiv). These innovations reorganized older relationships. From the Second World War on, technological developments would revolutionize working relationships between the body and its things. For Bell, the 'new men' of the technological world would be the scientists, mathematicians, economists, and engineers who enabled the 'new intellectual technology', but this technocratic elite—fresh from Taylor's planning room—would be enabled in turn by a growing class of white-collar workers (Bell 1999 [1973]: 69, 344). The far-reaching effects of these innovations are evident; it is not just that machines—digital, electronic machines—have replaced some human labour, it is that they have enabled different jobs to be done. In Britain, following the Second World War, the number of people employed in manufacturing jobs decreased steadily, while the number of service positions rose. In 2010, around 5 million Britons worked in industrial jobs, half the equivalent figure of 1965. In that year, 12 million people (about half of all those employed) worked in services. By 2010, 23 million people worked in services, nearly 80 per cent of all those employed (OECD 2011). We might see the effects of these innovations as synergetic evidence of some truth to the cyborg myth. With those four innovations inserted between the human form and its material engagements, processes that could once have taken years now take minutes, even seconds. Tracking such changes on the body in some cases may just be a matter of looking at the development of the office chair: the cyborg-hybrid repository of the office-bound worker.

45.3.5 Ergonomics

The science of fitting tasks and objects to the body is not a new field: the first tool-using societies emerged from experiments in what might be considered ergonomics. But the Gilbreths' experiments in promoting the body at its most efficient might be seen as a milestone in the emergence of ergonomics as a major factor in the determination of how people function. By ensuring that the body did not have to exert effort over unnecessary tasks—such as bending down to retrieve bricks—the time and motion studies fitted bodies to more suitable working arrangements, for example, worktables were placed at a height that eliminated postures that, when repeated, could be harmful to the body. The increased awareness of the reduction of accidents and loss through better designed work environments, and of course the constant pursuit of increased productive output, led to more formalized foundations in the field. The embedding of the word 'ergonomics' permanently fixed the body's 'natural' capacities to its capacity for work (from Greek, *ergos* = work; *nomos* = natural law [Pheasant 1996: 4]). The development and impact of ergonomics offers explicitly archaeological data for explorations of the working body's mutability. Here, we can track the body's constituting of its working environment through the emergence of forms to enable it, and infer how bodies may have been altered by these forms.

Significant research during the Second World War into increasing the efficiency of the fighting man had been carried out by different nations' armed forces, particularly air forces. As the Cold War began to drive research and development, ergonomic progress was particularly relevant in the fields of atomic energy, defence, power production, and space programmes, where ergonomic factors could mean the difference between life and death. However, in industry, manufacturing, and in academic research, ergonomics also began to gather pace, with early use particularly in civil aviation and shoe manufacturing, and in Japan in domestic consumerism such as bicycle production and kitchen design (Singleton 1982: 5–7). Essentially a hybrid discipline, drawn from anatomy, physiology, psychology, architecture, engineering, and other sciences of the human form and human behaviour, ergonomics treated the human body as the subject, with the objective of 'fitting the job to the worker' (Singleton 1982: 5). This acknowledgement of the need to help, even ease, the working body might be considered part of a Foucauldian retreat and reorganization of the frameworks of power in its state-embodied sense. The understanding by industrial societies that power need not be so rigid, that accommodation was in all interests, led to an understanding that 'one needs to study what kind of body the current society needs' (Foucault 1980: 58). According to Hacking, 'categories of people come into existence at the same time as people come into being to fit those categories, and there is a two-way interaction between these processes' (Hacking 1995: 247; Meskell 1999: 23). In the science of accommodation of the human form, then, might be seen a taxonomy of synchronous adaptation: of management to workers, of workers to new environments, of new environments to new practices, and back again.

The impact on industrial and corporate settings was marked as organizations realized that using ergonomic principles in the workplace decreased both worker injuries (and hence lost profit) and worker unrest (likewise). In the office, the rise in computerization meant that the need for movement was eliminated by the desk-top computers that had exponentially occupied employees' desks (Olivares 2011: 25). Olivares' study of the evolution of the office chair identifies four phases in which the design of the chair altered significantly, from its emergence in the nineteenth century, through its mid-century improvement following advancements in materials production, to the need for comfortable and safe seating for long periods in the computer-driven workplace. The final phase identified by Olivares reflects the need to produce chairs sustainably (2011: 25). *A Taxonomy of Office Chairs* highlights how the body's changing needs have determined its environment. It also identifies subtler changes, such as the gradual collapse of hierarchical differentiation through design, suggesting that hierarchy is now determined in the office chair through materials rather than size (2011: 17). As an archaeological catalogue, the taxonomy is clear, but does it also represent a positive inversion (in photographic terms) of the changed body? Would Foucault's current body or Hacking's ready body reveal the forms that required these taxonomic shifts?

45.4 THE BODY WORKING OUT

45.4.1 The Rise of the Gym, the Fall of Fat

According to Mintel (2010), 5.6 million Britons have private gym membership. The average Briton lives within two miles of a private or public fitness centre, gym members are 60 per cent more likely to be single than non-members, they are 18 per cent more likely than the average adult to be heavy consumers of chocolate bars, while a third of them think of the calories in what they eat. They are twice as likely as non-members to use the Internet when they want to know something. Women gym members will spend on average 35 per cent more on shoes and 29 per cent more on handbags than the average woman (BMRB 2011). Gym chain Fitness First claims that 60 per cent of its members join to change their body shape, 26 per cent to improve health, and 2 per cent to get fitter.

Today's postindustrial gym-goers are products of an economic and societal process that has changed how we live and work. Gym-goers aim to tone the body, not improve health or fitness. The gym body is differentiated from the industrial body that received its fitness from physical work. The gym offers toning not usually gained through work: the industrial body does not have the washboard stomach or bulging biceps. The postindustrial body is materially different from the industrial body; it has been commodified as workers pay a monthly stipend to create it using machines. The after work work-out is industrially regimented, a Fordist use of time and space, but here workers set their own output and time constraint in which to achieve it. Like the office, the gym is open-plan, ergonomically designed, with solitary work-stations facing a TV screen. The evidence of place suggests a synchronicity of destinations, work and gym—often situated within the same complex, often on former industrial sites (Penrose 2010). We have seen a transition in which the body has become engaged in an amorphous cybernetic world that requires a different kind of forbearance than that required by the industrial body. It requires new kinds of machines to suit it.

In 1876—around the time that the young industrial apprentice Taylor was beginning to formulate his theories of scientific management—Swedish Gustav Zander took his vibrating fitness equipment to America. Developed for the purpose of strengthening and rehabilitating muscles, Zander's machines—among the first gym machines—found a constituency among the American business class, as 'a preventative against the evils engendered by a sedentary life and the seclusion of the office' (quoted in de la Peña 2005: 84; see Figure 45.3). The rise in popularity of machines like Zander's, in body-building and other physical cultures, was part of a general trend that subverted the image of the corpulent body as a successful body, against the thin body as unsuccessful (Stearns 2003: 12). In Paris, perennial setter of fashions, women's wear was promoting a slimmer figure, while northern European physicians had begun producing treatises on dieting. By 1900, it had become clear that there was a link between fatty diets and lifestyles and deterioration of organs (Stearns 2003: 35). Stearns puts this shift in fashions down to a growing association of fat with immorality, resulting in the final triumph of the athletic body. The parallel with the working body, made pure in Fordist regimes, is evident. Here, the machine again suggests a changing body. The trajectories of its alterations through material engagements, such as those with gym machines, constitute a 'location' for archaeology, a site of transition within an evolving world system.

Heilgymnastik.   (Medikomechanische Apparate von Zander).

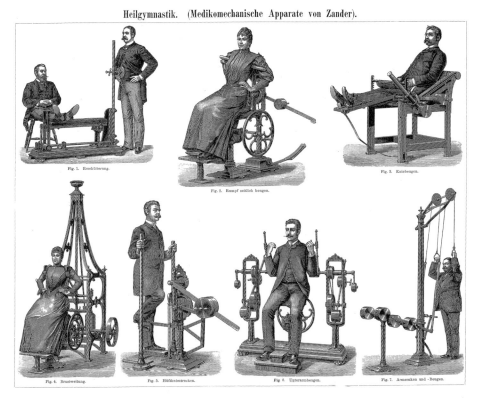

FIGURE 45.3   Zander's *Heilgymnastik* machines. *Medikomechanische Apparate von Zander* from *Meyer's Großem Konversations-Lexikon*, 1905 (author's private collection)

45.4.2 The State-Supported Body

In Britain, in the years leading up to and immediately after the Second World War, a drive to ensure a healthy workforce saw a trickle-down effect in health and fitness provision. Pre- and post-war Acts of Parliament established the provision of swimming pools, recreation grounds, and other leisure facilities, and the right to paid holiday leave (Physical Training and Recreation Act 1937; Holidays With Pay Act 1938); the National Health Service (National Health Act 1946); instigated a system of welfare benefits (National Assistance Act 1948); extended the teaching of compulsory physical education and the provision of sports facilities in schools—particularly swimming (Education Act 1936; 1944); distributed free milk to children (Free Milk Act 1946); and enshrined rights of access in the form of National Parks (National Parks and Access to the Countryside Act 1949). Gyms, lidos, pools, holiday camps, and campsites were instituted, explicit state-funded measures to support the body (Penrose 2007). Outside government, large organizations kept the working body fit in-house: many larger factories and corporations had their own sports complexes and clubs, with athletes as heroes on the payroll.

Exposure to the fit body—and to someone else's fit body in particular—in these ways legitimates Giddens's claim for the emergence of self-realization through the observation of others and self-differentiation. Whereas the working day's engagement with automation was to be endured, the display engendered in the public pool supports Foucault's notion of the desire for the self (Foucault 1980: 56), or at the least the desire for the self to become an object of desire. The lido and leisure time meant a nuanced collapse in class boundaries and a progressive exposure to different bodies. With heroes such as Johnny Weissmuller, Esther Williams, and Annette Kellerman, muscle beach platforms and glass-fronted public pools advocated the desired body to be attempted. The welfare state body, as seen by its neighbours and colleagues, was prepared for work, with an infrastructural layer that challenged the un-working body as unfit for work. Public health provisions such as slipper baths had, since the nineteenth century, been fixtures of swimming baths—placing cleanliness and healthiness in an indivisible relationship that was further cemented by mid-twentieth-century health reforms. A brief commitment to the 'outdoors' would later be nullified by the retreat behind glass, brick, and steel of sports provision, a further response and reorganization of the body's needs in its commitment to work.

45.4.3 Global Fitness

Today, the all-conquering gym is transforming bodies across the world, in varied cultural groups. Fat, until recently a badge of plutocracy in much of South-East Asia, is being busted by the rapidly growing white-collar classes. The Thai gym chain True Fitness has grown from one site in central Bangkok in 2005 to over 30,000 members across South-East Asia by 2010 (Limsamarnphun 2011). Fitness First now claims 50 per cent of its market share in the Asia-Pacific region, acknowledging 'phenomenal growth'. The regional manager dates the boom to 2002, when gyms became 'fashionable places for people to hang out' since 'Asian countries have become more addicted to fitness and weight loss, partly as a result of eating more fast foods' (Ebrahimi 2010). The manager of a Chinese fitness firm cites '[b]etter jobs and pay' as the reason why more Chinese are going to the gym: 'when you have money you care about how you look' (Enterprise China 2005). These societal changes are indicative of changing working practices. The office-based lifestyle enables pre- and post-work energy levels that are denied workers for whom work is physical, and engenders a desire to work-out. They are indicative of a degree of expendable income that allows gym membership. They also illustrate the spread of a more globalized, capitalist, body culture. But is this culture in itself then the new measure of success or a physical necessity born out of the new 'kind of body the current society needs' (Foucault 1980: 58)? Whereas the state used to ensure that its bodies were fit for work, the (generalized white-collar) individual has incorporated the message and exercises its own regime, allowing (in the UK) a state withdrawal from welfare provision that goes largely unchallenged. Hierarchy need not be so marked (as with the giant leather office chair) as workers have absorbed its messages and disciplined their own bodies.

45.5 Conclusion

The 'new' postindustrial worker is as self-disciplining as the industrial worker was disciplined. The boom of technology in the workplace has heralded a change of dynamic, essentially creating global offices with unlimited connections in time and space. Individuals with machines that, unlike the factory machine, are not possessive controllers of limbs, but cyborg enhancements of reach and capacity, allow a vast increase in productivity that has become part of the ethos of work fulfilment. The service economy has created a service class, a pioneering cross-cultural, male and female, diploma-educated, technocratic workforce increasingly based on 'theoretical knowledge and its codification into abstract systems' (Bell 1976: 343), the postindustrial society. But for all its connections, where the Fordist worker's iterations created trade unionism, the managerialized office worker is atomized. Does this worker fit Marx's profile of the alienated worker? Or, in a new iteration, perhaps one of Weber's 'last' capitalists, within the caged culture of disenchantment, 'specialists without spirit, sensualists without heart; this nullity imagines it has attained a level of humanity never before achieved' (Goethe, quoted in Weber 2001: 124). A century of managing the body, eliminating extraneous effort, and attaching worker to machine has created the chair-bound worker, augmented by the machine, who seeks further machines to exorcize the ghosts of sedentary work. It is expected, desired. But this is not a one-way relationship: the worker creates the governing norms; the 'nullity' has elbow room to act back on this environment.

What does this entail for archaeologies of the contemporary? We are left with the exographic images of bodies of the past—the imprint they have made on matter that survives—but in the present we are exposed to and engaged in this iterative process. I write from my open-plan office. More specifically, I write from an ergonomic chair, made for an apocryphal archetypal worker who is certainly bigger than me and, I suspect, male. The chair is no longer able to support my back, which is slightly damaged through a lifetime of stooping over desks. I know that I walk differently, hold my body differently, from my parents' and my grandparents' generations: those bodies were disciplined at school, prepared for work. Although I had typing lessons on an IBM Selectric typewriter at my primary school, and handwrote for much of my secondary schooling, I have conducted my entire adult working life in front of a computer, with my hands on a keyboard, in a succession of office chairs, and am now fazed by the idea of handwriting a complex document. Today, with my wrists resting on a gel pad to control against carpal tunnel syndrome, I have written a couple of thousand words in two dozen emails to friends and colleagues. I have spoken perhaps a tenth of that total in a handful of conversations with my co-workers around me. I have walked to the post tray once today. Beneath my office is a private gym with glass walls that allow the passerby to observe the bodies, but not the heads of those working out within. We have a corporate discount on membership. Harrison and Schofield (2009, 2010) have discussed the possibilities of autoarchaeologies, in which we examine the matter and remains of our own realms. Our bodily incorporation of these realms requires a braver engagement with the body itself. Of course this is not limited to our own engagement, a breakdown of the end of our working day, but this brief account illustrates the utterly intrinsic nature of the engagement of bodies in the world, that the worlds of work and leisure are related, and the values that we place on the well-being of bodies and their protection, moral and physical. The body in the world must be reconceptualized as an important part of our world, our means of experiencing the world (Gosden 2004), and the vehicle by which the world's means are transmitted, illustrative as it is of the lived experience, the essential object of any archaeology. By addressing the events of the body in contemporary archaeology and the body itself, we can provide insights and evidence for our inferences. We can distinguish differences and account for them, identify the spaces of workers' elbow room and the ways in which workers constitute their environment, and place individuality, difference, people, and things into our generalized theories. We can engage more fully with theories of embodiment and extended selves which are often only abstract. An archaeology which foregrounds the body is an archaeology which foregrounds the person, both individual and social, and places it in the historical context of the world that creates it and the worlds that it creates.

REFERENCES

Bell, Daniel. 1999 [1973]. *The Coming of Post-Industrial Society: A Venture in Social Forecasting*. New York: Basic Books.

Beynon, Huw. 1984. *Working for Ford*. Harmondsworth: Penguin.

BMRB (British Market Research Bureau). 2011. The Guide to Gym Members. Available at: <http://www.marketresearchworld.net/index.php?option=com_content&task=view&id=164> (accessed 11 June 2011).

Butler, Judith. 1993. *Bodies That Matter: On the Discursive Limits of 'Sex'*. London: Routledge.

de la Peña, Carolyn. 2005. *The Body Electric: How Strange Machines Built the Modern American*. New York: New York University Press.

Durkheim, Emile. 1984. *The Division of Labour in Society*. London: Macmillan.

Ebrahimi, Helia. 2010. Fitness First plans £1.2bn float in Asia. *The Telegraph*, 26 June.

Enterprise China. 2005. China gets fit. Available at: <http://enterprisechina.net/node/755> (accessed 11 June 2011).

Foucault, Michel. 1980. Body/Power. In *Power/Knowledge: Selected Interviews and Other Writings 1972–1977*, ed. Colin Gordon, pp. 52–62. New York: Pantheon.

—— 1988. *Technologies of the Self: A Seminar with Michel Foucault*, ed. Luther H. Martin, Huck Gutman, and Patrick H. Hutton. Amherst: University of Massachusetts Press.

Giddens, Anthony. 1991. *Modernity and Self-Identity: Self and Society in the Late Modern Age*. Stanford, CA: Stanford University Press.

Gilbreth, Frank B. 1910. *Motion Study: A Method for Increasing the Efficiency of the Workman*. New York: D. Van Nostrand.

Gosden, Chris. 2004. Aesthetics, Intelligence and Emotions: Implications for Archaeology. In *Rethinking Materiality: The Engagement of Mind with the Material World*, ed. Elizabeth C. DeMarrais, Chris Gosden, and Colin Renfrew, pp. 33–40. McDonald Monograph Series, Cambridge: Cambridge University Press.

Gramsci, Antonio. 1999. *Selections from the Prison Notebooks of Antonio Gramsci*, ed. Quintin Hoare and Geoffrey Nowell-Smith. London: Lawrence & Wishart.

Grosz, Elizabeth. 1994. *Volatile Bodies*. London: Allen & Unwin.

Hacking, Ian. 1995. *Rewriting the Soul: Multiple Personality and the Sciences of Memory*. Princeton: Princeton University Press.

Haraway, Donna J. 1991. A Cyborg Manifesto: Science, Technology, and Socialist-Feminism in the Late Twentieth Century. In *Simians, Cyborgs and Women: The Reinvention of Nature*, pp. 149–81. London: Free Association Books.

Harrison, Rodney and Schofield, John. 2009. Archaeo-Ethnography, Auto-Archaeology: Introducing Archaeologies of the Contemporary Past. *Archaeologies* 5(2): 185–209.

—— 2010. *After Modernity: Archaeological Approaches to the Contemporary Past*. Oxford: Oxford University Press.

Hicks, Dan. 2010. The Material-Culture Turn: Event and Effect. In *The Oxford Handbook of Material Culture Studies*, ed. Dan Hicks and Mary Beaudry, pp. 25–98. Oxford: Oxford University Press.

Hooker, Clarence. 1997. Ford's Sociology Department and the Americanization Campaign and the Manufacture of Popular Culture Among Assembly Line Workers *c.*1910–1917. *Journal of American Culture* 20(1): 47–53.

Leder, Drew. 1990. *The Absent Body*. Chicago: University of Chicago Press.

Limsamarnphun, Nophakhun. 2011. Working towards a Better Workout. *The Nation*. 8 October. Available at: <http://www.nationmultimedia.com/new/opinion/Working-towards-a-better-workout-30167098.html> (accessed 8 October 2011).

Malafouris, Lambrous and Renfrew, Colin. 2010a. The Cognitive Life of Things: Archaeology, Material Engagement and the Extended Mind. In *The Cognitive Life of Things: Recasting the Boundaries of the Mind*, eds. Lambrous Malafouris and Colin Renfrew, pp. 1–12. McDonald Institute Monographs. Cambridge: Cambridge University Press.

——(eds.). 2010b. *The Cognitive Life of Things: Recasting the Boundaries of the Mind*. McDonald Institute Monographs. Cambridge: Cambridge University Press.

Marx, Karl and Engels, Friedrich. 1978. *The Marx–Engels Reader*, ed. Robert C. Tucker. New York: W. W. Norton.

Mauss, Marcel. 1973. Techniques of the Body. *Economy and Society* 2(1): 70–88.

Meskell, Lynn. 1999. *Archaeologies of Social Life: Age, Sex, Class et cetera in Ancient Egypt*. Oxford: Blackwell.

Miller, Daniel. 1983. Things Ain't What They Used To Be. *Royal Anthropological News* 59: 5–7.

Mintel. 2010. Boomtime for budget exercise. Available at: <http://www.mintel.com/press-centre/press-releases/458/boom-time-for-budget-exercise> (accessed 12 June 2011).

Mrozowski, Stephen A. 2006. *The Archaeology of Class in Urban America*. Cambridge: Cambridge University Press.

Olivares, Jonathan. 2011. *A Taxonomy of Office Chairs*. London: Phaidon.

Organisation for Economic Co-operation and Development. 2011. OECD.StatExtracts. Available at: <http://stats.oecd.org/Index.aspx> (accessed 11 June 2011).

Penrose, Sefryn. 2007. *Images of Change: An Archaeology of England's Contemporary Landscape*. Swindon: English Heritage.

——2010. Recording Transition in Post-Industrial England: A Future Perfect View of Oxford's Motopolis. *Archaeologies* 6(1): 167–80.

Pheasant, Stephen. 1996. *Bodyspace: Anthropometry, Ergonomics, and the Design of Work*. London: Taylor & Francis.

Seguino, Stephanie. 2000. Accounting for Gender in Asian Economic Growth. *Feminist Economics* 6(3): 27–58.

Shilling, Chris. 2005. *The Body in Culture, Technology & Society*. London: Sage.

Singleton, W. T. (ed.). 1982. *The Body at Work: Biological Ergonomics*. Cambridge: Cambridge University Press.

Stearns, Peter N. 2003. *Fat History: Bodies and Beauty in the Modern West*. New York: New York University Press.

Taylor, Frederick Winslow. 1911. *The Principles of Scientific Management*. Project Gutenberg EBook #6435. Available at: <http://www.gutenberg.org/catalog/world/readfile?fk_files=1463318> (accessed 5 June 2011).

Thomas, Julian. 2007. Archaeology's Humanism and the Materiality of the Body. In *The Archaeology of Identities: A Reader*, ed. Tim Insoll, pp. 211–24. Abingdon: Routledge.

Time. 1930. National Affairs: Dirty Work at Dearborn. *Time Magazine*, 24 March.

Volti, Rudi. 2008. *An Introduction to the Sociology of Work and Occupations*. Los Angeles: Pine Forge Press.

Weber, Max. 2001. *The Protestant Ethic and the Spirit of Capitalism*. London: Routledge.

CHAPTER 46

··

THE MATERIAL CELLPHONE

··

RICHARD MAXWELL AND TOBY MILLER

Mobile phones have become affective technologies. That is, objects which mediate the expression, display, experience and communication of feelings and emotions.... They are an extension of the human body...building and maintaining...groups and communities. (Lasén 2004)

G[race] K[hunou]: A cell phone is the best accessory ever. Those without disposable income find ways of owning one and having airtime. A lot of the hip guys do not leave their cell phones in their cars or put them in their pockets. They hold them in their hands.... Another thing they have to be seen as having are the smallest cell phones. You lose points if you are seen with a heavy and big cell phone.... Cell phones are also very much a female accessory. For some women, having accessories such as these are a reason for having multiple boyfriends, whom they refer to as 'ministers'—that is, different boyfriends to provide for their different needs.

N[sizwa] D[lamini]: It is considered degrading to give someone a landline phone number, as it suggests that one does not have a cell phone. Even those who have one are not off the hook, as their phones have to be tiny, lighter, and look good.... Bigger ones are given names such as a 'brick'. (Mbembe et al. 2004: 504)

The increasingly faster and more versatile computers, appealing mobile phones, high-definition TVs, Internet, tiny music players, ingenious photo cameras, entertaining games consoles and even electronic pets give us the idea of a developed, pioneering and modern world. It is indeed a new era for many; but the dark side of this prosperous world reveals a very different reality, that far from taking us to the future, takes us back to a darker past. (Centro de Reflexión y Acción Laboral 2006)

[T]he woman came back carrying a small cardboard box. She went directly to Bosch and handed it to him, then bowed as she backed away. Harry opened it and found the remains of a melted and burnt cell phone.

While the woman gave Sun an explanation, Bosch pulled his own cell phone and compared it to the burned phone. Despite the damage, it was clear the phone the woman retrieved from her ash can was a match.

'She said Peng was burning that,' Sun said. 'It made a very foul smell that would be displeasing to the ghosts so she removed it'. (Connelly 2009: 243)

46.1 INTRODUCTION

WE are not archaeologists. Our backgrounds are in history, political science, philosophy, sociology, and communication studies. Our methods derive from the application of precepts from political economy and cultural studies, so we are concerned with the material relations of meaning and the interplay of subjectivity and power, emphasizing the materiality of discourse and the discursivity of materials. This cultural materialism refuses the notions that objects lack meaning or meanings exist independently of objects and the practices that bring them into the world. It is also profoundly connected to the fundamental question 'cui bono?' when discussing the allocation, utilization, and impact of resources. As such, the following examination of the cellphone[1] blends rather than juxtaposes political economy and cultural studies. In the past, our research has explored the relation of Hollywood's worldwide textual dominance to the international division of cultural labour upon which such textual power depends. Here we are also concerned with the workers who bring media into the world, emphasizing the material environmental impact of production and consumption of media technology as exemplified by the cellphone. Labour and environmental research takes us from the purely discursive life of the technology to the environmental and biophysical evidence it leaves in its wake. To get us there, we draw on an eclectic set of procedures: archival work, epidemiology, public policy, corporate accounts, science, and science studies.

The first two epigraph we quoted above are comforting. One speaks in universal terms about the phenomenology of the cellphone: everyone is embraced by and embracing what seems to be a natural extension of our very selves! The cellphone is soothing, helpful, special—an elemental force that has become part of us. The other quotation is more localized. It refers to life in Soweto after liberation from apartheid, where the cellphone's gift of commercial freedom has adapted to local gendered circumstances and *mores*. At the same time, this epigraph, too, is universal in claiming the phone's centrality to everyday life.

By contrast with the nurturing common sense of their predecessors, the second two epigraph are quite shocking. One comes from an account of the putrid, dangerous creation of cellphones in the electronics industry, which delivers the products that Sowetans and the rest of us own. The other references Hong Kong customs and the putrid, dangerous afterlife of cellphones once their cuddly qualities have become obsolete and they must be exterminated.

These differences should come as no surprise, given the provenance of the epigraph. The first derives from scholarship and publication funded by Vodafone, a major supplier of the objects that are so thoroughly humanized by its 'academic staff'. The second is written by humanities experts interpreting the life they see around them, but ignoring the fact that raw materials for cellphones are tearing huge swathes of their continent apart. By contrast, the third epigraph was generated by a non-governmental organization that seeks to protect and expand workers' rights in Mexican *maquiladoras*. And the source of the fourth is crime fiction, drawing on hard-boiled, code-driven detection to observe horror wherever it is found, almost without commentary.

---

[1] We wrote this chapter while living in the US and Mexico respectively, where the terms 'cellphone' and 'celular' respectively are the nomenclature. We'll therefore use 'cell' in our 'own' prose in this chapter, while recognizing that linguistic variations on 'mobile phone' or 'móvil' are common elsewhere and in much academic writing.

The key to bridging the gap between these quotations is a materialist one. A recent contribution from archaeology offers this contextualization:

> The phone has much in common with the portable artifacts of a more traditional archaeology, like flint hand-axes or pottery vessels....an object scaled to fit the human world....shaped to fit the hand and fingers, and has action capabilities...orientated towards other parts of the body. (Edgeworth 2010: 143)

Archaeology encourages us to track the life of this commodity as both a sign and a physical artefact. That means attending to dominant as well as latent meanings inscribed in the cellphone while acknowledging its discontinuity with the portable artefacts of antiquity because of its industrial provenance and environmental impact.

Cultural materialism holds in tension utopic and dystopic accounts of the cellphone, defining the key modes of conscious expression surrounding it. The former anchor the cellphone's historical time to a high capitalist consumerism that is said to deliver happiness, development, and revolution. They pay attention to personal and social rather than psychological and biological aspects. They love cellphones.

Dystopic accounts, by contrast, see the cellphone era as one of social fragmentation: managerial and administrative command and control demands lead workers and others on a frantic, alienated search for connectedness, leaving little time or inclination to ponder political-economic arrangements and alternatives. This dystopian perspective criticizes the quasi-religious nature of utopian discourse. It emphasizes protests (see Badcock and Johnston, this volume; Dixon, this volume) and studies that expose the harms that cellphones cause in the service of profit and bureaucracy—most significantly to workers and environment.

This chapter starts with a positive case for welcoming the cellphone as a transformative, even revolutionary, technology, then points towards crucial evidence that transcends the binary of utopian versus dystopian consciousness to chemico-mechanical materiality and environmental impact.

46.2 THE UTOPIAN RECORD: CELLPHONES MAKE YOU FREE

Ninety-four per cent of cell users aged 12–17 agree that cellphones give them more freedom because they can reach their parents no matter where they are....

Teens who have multipurpose phones are avid users of those extra features. The most popular are taking and sharing pictures and playing music:

83% use their phones to take pictures.
64% share pictures with others.
60% play music on their phones.
46% play games on their phones.
32% exchange videos on their phones.
31% exchange instant messages on their phones.

27% go online for general purposes on their phones.

23% access social network sites on their phones.

21% use email on their phones.

11% purchase things via their phones. (Lenhart et al. 2010: 5)

Cellphones are ubiquitous: they are utilized by half the world's population and technologically available to 90%, up from 145 million in 1996 to over five billion in 2010, including 85% of the US public. By the end of 2010, three-quarters of the world's cellphone accounts, about 4 billion, were held in the Global South. In Kenya, cellphone banking amounts to US$1 billion transactions a month. Of the 83% of US adults who own cellphones, three quarters use text messaging, 41.5 times on a typical day. In China, 73% of people aged 15–24 regularly access the Internet by phone, compared with under 50% in the US and the UK and less than 25% across Europe. The use of messaging is feminized, apart from Italy, Saudi Arabia, and China (International Telecommunication Union 2009; Smith 2010; NielsenWire 2011; Pew Research Center 2011; Voigt 2011).

The right adores such data. Manuel Castells, a renowned lapsed Marxist whose work has shifted from critical European urbanism to mainstream US communication studies, is one of the leading scholars forwarding utopian ideas about cellphones. In a 2007 study, he cited many positive features: cellphones broaden channels of communication, secure personal safety, integrate family life, improve peer groups, speed up rendezvous, and allow users to produce content, create their own language, and make personal statements in their choice of exterior design—i.e. they make users feel important (Castells et al. 2007: 246–58). He also claims that the device is politically transformative:

> The spread of instant political mobilizations by using mobile phones, supported by the Internet, is changing the landscape of politics. It becomes increasingly difficult for governments to hide or manipulate information. The manipulation plots are immediately picked up and challenged by a myriad of 'eye balls,' as debate and mobilization are called upon by thousands of people, without central coordination, but with a shared purpose, often focusing on asking or forcing the resignation of governments or government officials. (Castells 2007: 251)[2]

Using the same discourse, neo-classical economists and their *bourgeois* masters in business form a vanguard of institutional boosters. They promote cellphones as crucial to democracy, efficiency, pleasure, and development in the Global South (Jones 2008; Prahalad and Hart 2008; Sachs 2008; Houghton 2009; International Telecommunication Union 2008: 67–84, 2009: 2, 5; Hanna and Qiang 2010). Industry magazines such as *Advertising Age* positively salivate over the prediction that by 2013, there will be 4.5 billion users, well over half the world's population, as the absence of conventional telecommunications and financial

[2] In a similar vein, Ulrich Beck (2002), noted for his work on risk society, says that the cellphone has altered 'sociological categories of time, space, place, proximity and distance' as it 'makes those who are absent present, always and everywhere' (2002: 31). Such observations reinforce Castells's theories of 'timeless time' and 'space of flows'—imagine being in conversation with someone who abruptly takes an incoming cellphone call; they are no longer 'with you' but have entered into the network's timeless time and space of flows. For Castells, this is the fundamental materiality of communicating subjects in the network society.

infrastructure is overcome thanks to digital wallets and micro-payment systems (Shapiro 2010).

This happy state of affairs finds the world's leading media ratings company, Nielsen, publishing an unimaginably crass account that begins 'Africa is in the midst of a technological revolution, and nothing illustrates that fact [more] than the proliferation of mobile phones,' then notes casually that 'more Africans have access to mobile phones than to clean drinking water' (Hutton 2011).

It should not surprise us that private-sector idolatry and commercial targeting can claim that communications technology has priority over potable water in development policy. But this perspective is widespread. Credulous academics tell us that cellphones reduce poverty and corruption by empowering individuals and fostering the complete elimination of waste (Jensen 2007; Bailard 2009). Scholarly devotees to the utopian idea of the cellphone are captivated by a Schumpeterian wet dream in which cellphone consumers rise up and rebel against capital, even as they renew it in a bizarre alliance with entrepreneurs against corporate domination and closed markets:

> Our case studies range over several emergent industries based about consumer cocreation in digital media. Each has been made possible by new digital information and communication technologies centred about the Internet as a universal platform for social networks and business models, and about new digital consumer goods and services....the value-creation proposition about which business models are adopted and adapted is premised on the provision of content emanating from a distributed network of consumers or users operating in partnership with producers and, equally importantly, from the self-organization of the community protocols that coordinate such flows. This cultural and technological dynamic is both inducing new creative activities (e.g. MMOGs, video and photo-sharing) as well as displacing and disrupting extant industries (e.g. media journalism and music). (Potts et al. 2008: 465)

The New Right of cultural studies invests in such things with unparalleled zest. It's never seen a smart-phone application it didn't like, or a socialist idea it did. This is reminiscent of the Cold-warrior social scientist Ithiel de Sola Pool's account of land-lines' potential:

> The company president located himself at the place where most of his most critical communications took place. Before the telephone, he had to be near the production line to give his instructions about the quantities, pace, and process of production. Once the telephone network existed, however, he could convey those authoritative commands to his employees at the plant and could locate himself at the place where the much more uncertain bargaining with customers, bankers, and suppliers took place. (de Sola Pool 1980: 3)

But almost a century ago, Weber understood the role of the phone in fictive capital:

> The 'arbitrager' seeks a profit in that he simultaneously sells a good at a place where it is, at that moment, able to be sold at a higher price, while he buys it at a place where it is to be had more cheaply. His business is therefore a pure example of calculating the numbers. He sits at a telephone...and, as soon as he notices the possibility of, for example, making a profit from buying Russian notes or notes of exchange drawn on Russia available in London and then selling them in Paris, he places his orders. (2000: 344)

That encourages us to look to a less sanguine account of this technology.

46.3 THE DYSTOPIAN RECORD: CELLPHONES MAKE OTHERS UNFREE

[I]t is now necessary to impose silence in restaurants and places of worship or concert halls. One day, following the example of the campaign to combat nicotine addiction, it may well be necessary to put up signs of the 'Silence Hospital' variety at the entrance to museums and exhibition halls to get all those 'communication machines' to shut up and put an end to the all too numerous cultural exercises in SOUND and LIGHT. (Virilio 2004: 76)

More critical analyses point out that cellphones are surveillance tools of state control and corporate management. Jack Qiu offers telling examples from Malaysia, Britain, Australia, and China, where 'an industrial complex has emerged since 2000 to serve the control needs of the power elite' via cell monitoring (Qiu 2007; also see Baruh 2004; Turow 2005; Andrejevic 2006). The World Privacy Forum proposes that we are in a *One-Way Mirror Society*, where power accretes to corporations through the supposedly even-handed tool of interactivity (Dixon 2010).[3] This is a continuation of older dystopian assessments of communication, command, and control, famously fictionalized in Yevgeny Zamyatin's *We* (1924), Aldous Huxley's *Brave New World* (1932), and George Orwell's *Nineteen Eighty-Four* (1949).

Andrew Keen, a lapsarian prophet of the Internet, argues that the new landscape is abuzz with noise and ignorance rather than subtlety and knowledge (2007: 12). He sees a dreary world where constant clatter and frenzied imagery denature aesthetics in favour of uninterrupted stimulus. Media historian Dan Schiller challenges cellphone enthusiasts by demonstrating that social stresses fuel consumer needs, as people rush to buy inferior phone services at high cost. This is particularly the case in the US, where the decline in governmental oversight of telecommunication industries since the Second World War has diminished quality and regulation of competition (see Cubitt, this volume). Companies exploit social needs for connectedness in times of social fragmentation (Schiller 2007: chapter 8). Schiller describes the experience of displacement and deracination of modern life into a mode of sociality in which individuation (separateness and privacy) combines with mobility (transport and access). He argues that political-economic arrangements allow mobile telephony to emerge in a form befitting divided societies.[4] The cellphone is a very odd thing when seen in this light—built upon the stressful fragmentation of social life, corporate control, divisions between rich and poor, and the false promises of consumerism.

---

[3] Surveillance has long been a central strut of modernity, supposedly to make populations secure, content, and productive. With the expansion of state authority into the everyday, into all corners of life, the *quid pro quo* for the security afforded by governments became knowing everyone's identities and practices. The equivalent expansion of corporations into those everyday corners had as its *quid pro quo* for the provision of goods and services that they, too, know more and more about us.

[4] Perhaps the dystopian record should include Benjamin's Proustian lament for the loss of aura (1992: 184) thanks to a new technology that looks back at us and carries our images and statements into a reciprocal loop. How ironic that the supposed depersonalization of modern Parisian life was both exemplified and countered by the advent of the telephone as a commercial apparatus in the 1870s, simultaneously rendering the public private and the private public (Attali and Stourdze 1977: 97–8; Innis 1991: 60).

46.4 THE MATERIAL RECORD: CELLPHONES HARM THE EARTH AND ITS INHABITANTS

I work like a machine and my brain is rusted—19-year old female worker from Guangxi at the Compeq printed circuit board factory in Huizhou City, China. (quoted in Chan and Ho 2008: 22)

The spread of cellphones ahead of drinking water in Africa is only one environmental issue they pose. Cellphone design, production, and distribution have significantly augmented toxic elements in the biosphere: lead, mercury, chromium, nickel, beryllium, antimony, and arsenic as well as valuable metals, such as gold, silver, palladium, and platinum, tantalum (the mining of which has caused social and environmental harm in Africa) and flame retardants made of polybrominated diphenyl ethers. All cellphones need batteries, which contain poisonous components. As one environmental health scientist warned: 'In a phone that you hold in the palm of your hand, you now have more than 200 chemical compounds. To try to separate them out and study what health effects may be associated with burning or sinking it in water—that's a lifetime of work for a toxicologist' (quoted in Mooallem 2008: 42).

The companies whose names appear on cellphones subcontract their dirty work to miners, cottage assemblers, and manufacturers. The latter have grown in number since the 1990s and undertake approximately 60% of cellphone production (makeITfair and GoodElectronics 2009: 19–20). Both the environment and workers are vulnerable to harm throughout this supply chain. Investigations into Apple's Chinese suppliers, for example, found children assembling its gadgets, workers exposed to chemical poisoning, and searing workplace conditions that led to 17 suicides in the first eight months of 2010 at a Foxconn factory making iPhones. When the iPad was launched outside the US that year, protesters in Hong Kong responded to the deaths by ritually burning photographs of iPhones. Similar conditions exist in India, Mexico, and other offshore assembly sites (Barboza 2010; Maxwell and Miller 2012: ch. 4; Students and Scholars Against Corporate Misbehaviour 2010).

The semiconductor, the heart of all electronic equipment, is produced by hundreds of companies around the world for a market dominated by Intel, Samsung Electronics, Toshiba Electronics, Texas Instruments, Qualcomm, and ADM. A single semiconductor facility may require 832 million cubic feet of bulk gases, 5.72 million cubic feet of hazardous gases, 591 million gallons of deionized water, 5.2 million pounds of chemicals, including acids and solvents, and 8.8 million kilowatt hours of electrical power. Semiconductor workers are potentially exposed to skin irritants, acids that harm mucous and pulmonary tissue, and chemicals that can cause cancer, reproductive complications, and debilitating illnesses. The durable half-life of toxic waste emitted into the soil from semiconductor plants leaves groundwater and land unusable or highly dangerous for populations who live atop them long after culpable firms have departed. Entire communities like Endicott, New York—the original home of IBM—have seen their aquifer and soil cursed with such carcinogenic compounds as trichloroethylene (a solvent) that will remain active for decades (Grossman 2006: 109–11).

Raw material extraction and processing—the source of chemicals and minerals in cellphones—are responsible for lasting biophysical harm. Data from the Norwegian silicon-carbide industry's smelters indicate elevated risks of stomach and lung cancer by contrast with the wider population as a consequence of exposure to crystalline silica, dust fibres, and silicon carbide particles (Romundstad et al. 2001). In Democratic Republic of Congo, which has a third of the world's columbite-tantalite (coltan), over 90% of eastern mines are controlled by militias, who use threats, intimidation, murder, rape, and mutilation to enslave women and children and use their profits to buy weapons. Over five million people have perished in the civil war over the past decade. Congolese 'conflict' metals and minerals, such as coltan, are exported for smelting in China then mixed with the overall global supply and sold on the international commodities market as tantalum, a core component in capacitors that end up in phones and other electronic equipment (Montague 2002; Cox 2009; Global Witness 2009; Maxwell and Miller 2012).[5]

Together with their electronic cousins, cellphones amplify residential electricity consumption at unprecedented rates: they accounted for about 15% of global residential electricity consumption in 2009. At current levels, energy use by electronic cultural and communications equipment will amount to 30% of the global demand for power by 2022 and 45% by 2030, thanks to server farms (data centres with servers, storage machines, network gadgetry, power supplies, and cooling technology) and the increasing time people around the world spend staring at screens (Maxwell and Miller 2009: ch. 29).

By 2009, radiation from cellphones and other wireless electronic equipment became the focus of further documentation. Scientific studies have linked long-term exposure to cellphone radiation to two types of brain cancer (glioma and acoustic neuroma), salivary gland tumours, migraines, vertigo, and behavioural problems (Environmental Working Group 2009). This research has led European health agencies to issue warnings about cellphone radiation exposure and prompted lawmakers to consider legislation to reduce radiation from such devices. Regulators in several countries have recommended caution to adult users and extreme caution for children, pending ongoing research. The French Senate has proposed legislation to ban cellphone use by children under six and advertising directed to children under the age of twelve (Sénat français 2009). The European Parliament's resolution on health concerns associated with electromagnetic fields (INI/2008/2211) affirmed potential risks from a range of wireless electronic devices, including Wi-Fi/WiMAX, Bluetooth, and cordless landline phones and called for campaigns to educate citizens in the safe use of electronics and avoiding transmission towers and high-voltage power lines.

The International Commission on Non-Ionizing Radiation Protection has appealed for public policy to set limits on 'simultaneous exposure' to multiple electronic devices. The European Environment Agency followed up a major scientific review by the Bioinitiative Working Group of radiation from Wi-Fi, cellphones, and their masts by announcing in 2007 that immediate action was needed lest the latest fad end up as damned for its health

---

[5] Two remarkable documentaries illuminate these horrors: *Blood Coltan* (Patrick Forestier, 2008) <http://topdocumentaryfilms.com/blood-coltan> and *Blood in the Mobile* (Frank Piasecki Poulsen, 2010) <http://bloodinthemobile.org/categories/p/videos>, in addition to a more recent video report on cellphones and coltan <http://www.guardian.co.uk/world/video/2011/sep/02/congo-blood-gold-mobile-phones-video>.

Table 46.1 Global personal computer market by territory, second quarter 2011 and forecast 2011 and 2012

Territory	2011% Share	2011% Share	2012% Share
China	22.0	20.3	21.8
US	21.0	20.6	19.6
Others	57.1	59.1	58.5

Source: <http://www.idc.com/getdoc.jsp?containerId=prUS22997711&pageType=PRINTFRIENDLY>.

impact as lead and tobacco in the previous century. In the US, however, regulators all but ignored evidence that long-term cellphone use may be risky (Lean 2008; Organisation for Economic Co-operation and Development 2007; Environmental Working Group 2009: 18–22, 28, 3–4).

About 130 million cellphones are trashed each year in the US alone, where people purchase annual replacements. Once discarded, they generate further toxicity. As a growing part of the global electronic waste business (e-waste), cellphone salvage and recycling pose serious health and safety risks for workers: brain damage, headaches, vertigo, nausea, diseases of the bones, stomach, lungs, and other vital organs, and birth defects and disrupted biological development in children (Rydh 2003; Grossman 2006: 18–20, 44–45, and ch. 5 *passim*; Crosby 2007; Sadetzki et al. 2007; Hardell et al. 2009). These conditions result from exposure to heavy metals (lead, cadmium, and mercury, among others), dioxin emitted by burning wires insulated with polyvinylchloride, flame retardants in circuit boards and plastic casings containing polychlorinated biphenyls or newer brominated compounds, and poisonous fumes emitted while melting electronic parts for precious metals such as copper and gold. Cellphones can be found in this dangerous discarded state throughout the traditional sites selected by the wealthy to dispose of their detritus: Latin America, Africa, and Asia (Ray et al. 2004; Wong et al. 2007; Secretaría Federal de Asuntos Económicos 2008; Inform 2008; Leung et al. 2008; Ha et al. 2010).[6]

This North–South asymmetry is changing as India and China generate their own detritus. In terms of computer purchase, for example, the trends at mid-2011 are laid out in Table 46.1.

So-called emergent markets have startling e-waste implications in their mimesis and expansion of Yanqui excess: India, for instance, rings in its newfound wealth with eight to ten million new cellphone subscriptions a month, drawing on diesel-fuelled power sources to compensate for the absence of a functioning national grid (Greenpeace 2011: 13). We do not suggest that it is wrong for the Global South to participate in the same plenitude as the Global North. Rather, we wish to highlight the unsustainability of consumer practices pioneered by the latter and turbocharged by the former.

---

[6] These issues are graphically illustrated in *Panorama*'s programme on illegal e-waste recycling in West Africa, where 77% of British e-waste goes <http://news.bbc.co.uk/panorama/hi/front_page/newsid_9481000/9481923.stm> or *60 Minutes*'s harrowing account from China <http://www.cbsnews.com/stories/2008/11/06/60minutes/main4579229.shtml>.

Cellphones are also perilous to wildlife. Phone masts kill tens of millions of birds annually in the US, affecting over 200 species, and erode animals' natural defences, health, reproduction, and habitat. Between 1990 and 2000, the number of cell towers and antennae in the US grew to 130,000; 40,000 towers were 200 feet tall, and many reached a thousand feet (Center for Responsible Nanotechnology <crnano.org>; Ornithological Council 1999; United States Fish and Wildlife Service 1999; Wikle 2002: 46; Avatar Environmental 2004; Broad 2007; Schoenfeld 2007; Krasnow and Solomon 2008: 50, 62–3; Balmori 2009; Pourlis 2009). This may look like a domestic US matter, but birds are the most experienced and determined of globalizers, with boundaries set by geography rather than sovereignty.

46.5 CONCLUSION

> She hung up before he could say goodbye. Stood there with her arm cocked, phone at ear-level, suddenly aware of the iconic nature of her unconscious pose. Some very considerable part of the gestural language of public places, that had once belonged to cigarettes, now belonged to phones. Human figures, a block down the street, in postures utterly familiar, were no longer smoking. (Gibson 2010: 103)

The cellphone generates affect, money, detritus, and disease. It appears to consumers as a discrete object of material culture, but through its life causes harm to far-flung natural and biophysical environments as its by-products travel the Earth via an international division of labour comprised of miners, smelters, assembly and transport workers, consumers, salvage, and recycling. Human and non-human organisms endure similar burdens to those that were caused by older industrial products and processes—from smokestacks and chemico-mechanical methods dependent on abundant sources of electrical energy to the spreading sediment of poisonous waste.

This chapter has deployed cultural materialism via political economy and cultural studies to follow the life of the cellphone. Due to the heavy, heady environmental implications of this deadly yet playful apparatus, cultural-materialist method has been especially inflected with environmental studies. The record exposes contradictory interpretations of the cellphone's meaning and value. The utopian love affair with this latest wonder of communication technology evokes ancestral cries for community, progress, and freedom. Dystopian perspectives resonate with past techno-critical scepticism and research, focusing on the dangers of social fragmentation and intensified command and control functions created by machines that have become emblematic of twenty-first century modernity. Recognizing the multi-sided material paradoxes and contradictions posed by these newest of toys is a crucial task for our present and future.

REFERENCES

Andrejevic, Mark. 2006. Total Information Awareness: The Media Version. *Flow* 4(8). Available at: <http://flowtv.org/2006/07/total-information-awareness-the-media-version> (accessed 1 March 2012).

Attali, Jacques and Stourdze, Yves. 1977. The Birth of the Telephone and Economic Crisis: The Slow Death of Monologue in French Society. In *The Social Impact of the Telephone*, ed. Ithiel de Sola Pool, pp. 97–111. Cambridge, MA: MIT Press.

Avatar Environmental. 2004. Avian/Communication Tower Collisions. Prepared for Federal Communications Commission, 30 September. West Chester, PA: Avatar Environmental, LLC.

Bailard, Catie Snow. 2009. Mobile Phone Diffusion and Corruption in Africa. *Political Communication* 26(3): 333–53.

Balmori, Alfonso. 2009. Electromagnetic Pollution from Phone Masts: Effects on Wildlife. *Pathophysiology* 16(2–3): 191–9.

Barboza, David. 2010. Supply Chain for iPhone Highlights Costs in China. *New York Times*, 5 July. Available at: <http://www.nytimes.com/2010/07/06/technology/06iphone.html?pagewanted=all> (accessed 1 March 2012).

Baruh, Lemi. 2004. Anonymous Reading in Interactive Media. *Knowledge, Technology, & Policy* 17(1): 59–73.

Beck, Ulrich. 2002. The Cosmopolitan Society. *Theory, Culture & Society* 19(1–2): 17–44.

Benjamin, Walter. 1992. *Illuminations*, tr. Harry Zohn, ed. Hannah Arendt. London: Fontana.

Broad, William J. 2007. NASA Forced to Steer Clear of Junk in Cluttered Space. *New York Times*, 31 July: F4.

Castells, Manuel. 2007. Communication, Power and Counter-Power in the Network Society. *International Journal of Communication* 1: 238–66.

Castells, Manuel, Fernández-Ardèvol, Mireia, Linchuan Qiu, Jack, and Sey, Arab. 2007. *Mobile Communication and Society: A Global Perspective*. Cambridge, MA: MIT Press.

Centro de Reflexión y Acción Laboral. 2006. New Technology Workers: Report on Working Conditions in the Mexican Electronics Industry. Available at: <http://sjsocial.org/fomento/proyectos/plantilla.php?texto=cereal_m> (accessed 1 March 2012).

Chan, J. and Ho, C. 2008. *The Dark Side of Cyberspace*. Berlin: World Economy, Ecology & Development.

Connelly, Michael. 2009. *Nine Dragons: A Novel*. New York: Little, Brown and Company.

Cox, Stan. 2009. Cell Phones Generate Particularly Dangerous E-Waste. In *What is the Impact of E-Waste?*, ed. Cynthia A. Bily, pp. 18–26. Detroit: Greenhaven.

Crosby, Jackie. 2007. The Mania Over Apple's Latest Product Could Translate into an Avalanche of Electronic Waste. *Star Tribune*, 29 June: 1D.

de Sola Pool, Ithiel. 1980. Communications Technology and Land Use. *Annals of the American Academy of Political and Social Science* 451: 1–12.

Dixon, Pam. 2010. *The One-Way Mirror Society: Privacy Implications of the New Digital Signage Networks*. World Privacy Forum. Available at: <http://www.worldprivacyforum.org/pdf/onewaymirrorsocietyfs.pdf> (accessed 1 March 2012).

Edgeworth, Matt. 2010. Beyond Human Proportions: Archaeology of the Mega and the Nano. *Archaeologies: Journal of the World Archaeological Congress* 6(1): 138–49.

Environmental Working Group. 2009. *Cell Phone Radiation: Science Review on Cancer Risks and Children's Health*. Washington, DC: Environmental Working Group. Available at: <http://ewg.org/cellphoneradiation/fullreport> (accessed 1 March 2012).

Gibson, William. 2010. *Zero History*. New York: Putnam.

Global Witness. 2009. *Faced with a Gun, What Can You Do? War and the Militarization of Mining in Eastern Congo*. London: Global Witness.

Greenpeace. 2011. *How Dirty is Your Data? A Look at the Energy Choices that Power Cloud Computing*. Amsterdam: Greenpeace.

Grossman, Elizabeth. 2006. *High Tech Trash: Digital Devices, Hidden Toxics, and Human Health.* Washington, DC: Island Press.

Ha, Vinh Hung, Lee, Jae-Chun, Jeong, Jinki, Trung Hai, Huynh, and Jha, Manis K. 2010. Thiosulfate Leaching of Gold from Waste Mobile Phones. *Journal of Hazardous Materials* 178(2–3): 1115–19.

Hanna, Nagy K. and Qiang, Christine Zhen-Wei. 2010. China's Emerging Informatization Strategy. *Journal of the Knowledge Economy* 1(2): 128–64.

Hardell, Lennart, Carlberg, Michael, and Mild, Kjell Hansson. 2009. Epidemiological Evidence for an Association Between Use of Wireless Phones and Tumor Diseases. *Pathophysiology* 16(2–3): 113–22.

Houghton, John. 2009. ICT and the Environment in Developing Countries: Opportunities and Developments. Paper prepared for the Organisation for Economic Co-operation and Development. Available at: <http://www.oecd.org/dataoecd/40/25/43631894.pdf> (accessed 1 March 2012).

—— 2011. Mobile Phones Dominate in South Africa. *Nielsen Wire.* Available at: <http://blog.nielsen.com/nielsenwire/global/mobile-phones-dominate-in-south-africa> (accessed 1 March 2012).

Inform. 2008. *The Secret Life of Paper.* Video available at: <informinc.org/pages/media/the-secret-life-series/the-secret-life-of-paper.html> (accessed 1 March 2012).

Innis, Harold A. 1991. *The Bias of Communication.* Toronto: University of Toronto Press.

International Telecommunication Union 2008. *ICTs for Environment: Guidelines for Developing Countries, with a Focus on Climate Change.* Geneva: ICT Applications and Cybersecurity Division Policies and Strategies Department ITU Telecommunication Development Sector.

—— 2009. ITU Symposium on ICTs and Climate Change Hosted by CTIC, Quito, Ecuador, 8–10 July, ITU Background Report.

Jensen, Robert. 2007. The Digital Provide: Information Technology, Market Performance, and Welfare in the South Indian Fisheries Sector. *Quarterly Journal of Economics* 122(3): 879–924.

Jones, Van. 2008. *The Green-Collar Economy: How One Solution Can Fix Our Two Biggest Problems.* New York: HarperOne.

Keen, Andrew. 2007. *The Cult of the Amateur: How Today's Internet is Killing Our Culture and Assaulting Our Economy.* London: Nicholas Brealey Publishing.

Krasnow, Erwin G. and Solomon, Henry A. 2008. Communication Towers: Increased Demand Coupled with Increased Regulation. *Media Law & Policy* 18(1): 45–68. Available at: <http://www.nyls.edu/centers/projects/media_center/media_law_and_policy/archives> (accessed 1 March 2012).

Lasén, Amparo. 2004. Affective Technologies—Emotions and Mobile Phones. *Receiver* 11. Available at: <http://www.receiver.vodafone.com/11/articles/index03.html (no longer online), http://tinyurl.com/77vesy6> (accessed 1 March 2012).

Lean, Geoffrey. 2008. Mobile Phones 'More Dangerous Than Smoking'. *Independent*, 30 March. Available at: <http://independent.co.uk/life-style/health-and-wellbeing/health-news> (accessed 1 March 2012).

Lenhart, Amanda, Ling, Rich, Campbell, Scott, and Purcell, Kristen. 2010. *Teens and Mobile Phones.* Washington, DC: Pew Internet & American Life Project.

Leung, Anna, Nurdan, O. W., Duzgoren-Aydin, S., Cheung, K. C., and Wong, Ming H. 2008. Heavy Metals Concentrations of Surface Dust from E-Waste Recycling and its Human Health Implications in Southeast China. *Environmental Science and Technology* 42(7): 2674–80.

makeITfair and GoodElectronics. 2009. Improving Labour Standards in the Global Electronics Industry: Defining Strategies that Work. Round Table for the Electronics Industry and Civil Society Organisations, May, Amsterdam. Available at: <http://good-electronics.org/publications-en/Publication_3116> (accessed 1 March 2012).

Maxwell, Richard and Miller, Toby. 2009. The Environment and Global Media and Communication Policy. In *The Handbook of Global Media and Communication Policy*, ed. Robin Mansell and Marc Raboy, pp. 467–85. Oxford: Blackwell.

—— 2012. *Greening the Media*. Oxford: Oxford University Press.

Mbembe, Achille, Dlamini, Nsizwa, and Khunou, Grace. 2004. Soweto Now. *Public Culture* 16(3): 499–506.

Montague, Dena. 2002. Stolen Goods: Coltan and Conflict in the Democratic Republic of Congo. *SAIS Review* 22(1): 103–18.

Mooallem, Jon. 2008. The Afterlife of Cellphones. *New York Times*, 13 January: 38–43.

NielsenWire. 2011. Cellphones and Global Youth: Mobile Internet and Messaging Trends. Available at: <http://blog.nielsen.com/nielsenwire/online_mobile/cellphones-and-global-youth-mobile-internet-and-messaging-trends> (accessed 1 March 2012).

Organisation for Economic Co-operation and Development (OECD). 2007. *Extended Producer Responsibility*. Paris: OECD.

Ornithological Council. 1999. Deadly Spires in the Night: The Impact of Communications Towers on Migratory Birds. *Issue Brief from the Ornithological Council* 1(8). Available at: <http://nmnh.si.edu/BIRDNET/OC/issues/OCBv1n8.html> (accessed 1 March 2012).

Pew Research Center. 2011. Americans and Text Messaging. Available at: <http://pewresearch.org/databank/dailynumber/?NumberID=1324> (accessed 1 March 2012).

Potts, Jason, Hartley, John, Banks, John, Burgess, Jean, Cobcroft, Rachel, Cunningham, Stuart, and Montgomery, Lucy. 2008. Consumer Co-Creation and Situated Creativity. *Industry & Innovation* 15(5): 459–74.

Pourlis, Aris F. 2009. Reproductive and Developmental Effects of EMF in Vertebrate Animal Models. *Pathophysiology* 16(2–3): 179–89.

Prahalad, Coimbatore Krishnarao and Hart, Stuart L. 2008. The Fortune at the Bottom of the Pyramid. *Revista Electrônica de Estratégia & Negócios* 1(2). Available at: <http://portaldeperiodicos.unisul.br/index.php/EeN/article/viewArticle/39> (accessed 1 March 2012).

Qiu, Jack Linchuan. 2007. Mobile Messaging Service as a Means of Control. *International Journal of Communication* 1: 74–91.

Ray, Manas Ranjan, Mukherjee, Gopeshwar, Roychowdhury, Sanghita, and Lahiri, Twisha. 2004. Respiratory and General Health Impairments of Ragpickers in India: A Study in Delhi. *International Archives of Occupational and Environmental Health* 77(8): 595–8.

Romundstad, Pål, Andersen, Aage, and Haldorsen, Tor. 2001. Cancer Incidence among Workers in the Norwegian Silicon Carbide Industry. *American Journal of Epidemiology* 153(10): 978–86.

Rydh, Carl Johan. 2003. Environmental Assessment of Battery Systems: Critical Issues for Established and Emerging Technologies. Ph.D. dissertation, Department of Environmental Systems Analysis, Chalmers University of Technology, Göteborg.

Sachs, Jeffrey. 2008. The Digital War on Poverty. *Guardian*, 21 August. Available at: <http://guardian.co.uk/commentisfree/2008/aug/21/digitalmedia.mobilephones> (accessed 1 March 2012).

Sadetzki, Siegal, Chetrit, Angela, Jarus-Hakak, Avital, Cardis, Elisabeth, Deutch, Yonit, Duvdevani, Shay, Zultan, Ahuva, Freedman, Laurence, and Wolf, Michael. 2007. Cellular

Phone Use and Risk of Benign and Malignant Parotid Gland Tumors: A Nationwide Case-Control Study. *American Journal of Epidemiology* 167(4): 457–67.

Schiller, Dan. 2007. *How to Think About Information*. Urbana: University of Illinois Press.

Schoenfeld, Amy. 2007. Everyday Items, Complex Chemistry. *New York Times*, 22 December: C9.

Secretaría Federal de Asuntos Económicos. 2008. *Gestión de Residuos Electrónicos en Colombia Diagnóstico de Computadores y Teléfonos Celulares Informe Final*. Secretaría Federal de Asuntos Económicos, Cámara Colombiana de Informática y Telecomunicaciones, Ministerio de Ambiente, Vivienda y Desarrollo Territorial, Computadores para Educar, Universidad de los Andes, Bogotá.

Sénat français. 2009. *Projet de loi portant engagement national pour l'environnement*. Paris: Sénat français.

Shapiro, Judy. 2010. Why Mobile Technology is Still Going to Save the World. *Advertising Age*. Available at: <http://adage.com/article/digitalnext/mobile-technology-save-world/145084> (accessed 1 March 2012).

Smith, Aaron. 2010. *Gadget Ownership*. Washington, DC: Pew Research Center.

Students and Scholars Against Corporate Misbehaviour. 2010. Workers as Machines: Military Management in Foxconn. Available at:<http://sacom.hk/archives/740> (accessed 1 March 2012).

Turow, Joseph. 2005. Audience Construction and Culture Production: Marketing Surveillance in the Digital Age. *Annals of the American Academy of Political and Social Science* 597: 103–21.

United States Fish and Wildlife Service. 1999. *Bird Kills at Towers and Other Human-Made Structures: An Annotated Partial Bibliography (1960–1998)*. Washington, DC: Office of Migratory Bird Management.

Virilio, Paul. 2004. *Art and Fear*, tr. Julie Rose. New York: Continuum, New York.

Voigt, Kevin. 2011. Mobile Phone: Weapon Against Global Poverty. *CNN*, 9 October. Available at: <http://www.cnn.com/2011/10/09/tech/mobile/mobile-phone-poverty/index.html> (accessed 1 March 2012).

Weber, Max. 2000. Commerce on the Stock and Commodity Exchanges. *Theory and Society* 29(3): 339–71.

Wikle, Thomas A. 2002. Cellular Tower Proliferation in the United States. *Geographical Review* 92(1): 45–62.

Wong, Coby S. C., Wu, S. C., Duzgoren-Aydin, Nurdan S., Aydin, Adnan, and Wong, Ming H. 2007. Trace Metal Contamination of Sediments in an E-Waste Processing Village in China. *Environmental Pollution* 145(2): 434–42.

CHAPTER 47

THE CONTEMPORARY MATERIAL CULTURE OF THE CULT OF THE INFANT: CONSTRUCTING CHILDREN AS DESIRING SUBJECTS

SARAH MAY

47.1 INTRODUCTION

THERE is considerable anxiety in contemporary Britain, as in many other contemporary Anglophone countries, about children's material culture. This concern is usually expressed in relation to consumerism, commoditization, and materialism (Barber 2007; Hill 2011). Indeed a report released in 2011 by UNICEF UK identifies 'materialism' as a major theme in an exploration of how Britain could come so low in the European ranks of children's well-being (Nairn and Ipsos MORI 2011). However, most of these studies pay little attention to material culture itself.

In this chapter I examine the ways in which objects construct both parents and children as desiring subjects and how this construction is entangled with notions of the divine. I will begin by briefly summarizing the significant theoretical and research contexts for this study. I note two important themes—'consumerism' and 'the divine'—and use four vignettes drawn from my own experience to explore them further. This is framed as an 'autoarchaeological' investigation.

47.2 MY APPROACH: AN ARCHAEOLOGY
OF THE PERSONAL

I originally become interested in this topic when my son was three years old. I was reading Daniel Miller's book *A Theory of Shopping* (1998) at the time, and his minor point about the 'Cult of the Infant' struck a chord with me (1998: 123–4, discussed in greater detail below). My own questions about material culture and parenting linked to broader questions regarding the role of material culture in contemporary Britain. But how could I define the data set for something in which I was (and am) so completely immersed?

In attempting to address this question it became obvious that I would never be able to study all of the children's material culture available to me. I would either need to aggregate to produce generalized histories or examine only a small number of objects which could stand for the whole. My home, and the homes of my friends, are filled with and structured around children's material culture. Is it valid to base a discussion on such a personal observation? Do I need to consider other material, and if so why?

In many ways, these questions are familiar ones for archaeologists working on issues which are so close to them. Ulin and Finn grapple with similar questions in working with the remains of their family homes (Finn 2007, 2009; Ulin 2009). Finn's work employs archaeological methodology, including excavation. Archaeology performs the function of creating distance within the intimate. Ulin also uses excavation to explore the personal memory of her family past, but she 'is walking in the footsteps of the dead' (2009: 145).

Both of these are moving pieces of memory work, but I am engaged in something different. While I inevitably draw upon and augment my self-knowledge through the work, my primary interest is in the broader questions material culture, identity, and devotion outlined below. I haven't used archaeology's best known sampling method, excavation. But I do consider context and materiality in understanding the artefacts I discuss. It is archaeology *from* myself more than *of* myself.

The work I present here is perhaps closer to Schofield's work on his former office space (2009). Presented with an opportunity from his own life (the abandonment of the office in which he had worked for many years) to consider an issue of broader interest (the office as a contemporary work environment), he uses his material to draw out broader themes. But he waits for the moment of abandonment. The archaeological gaze rests on what remains with an interest in what is *absent*. Recently, Harrison has discussed the need to move on to an 'archaeology in and of the present' and links the focus on the abandoned and defunct to a fundamental discomfort with the functions of archaeology (Harrison 2011). In this work I am not interested in the uncanny, or the subaltern. I want to look at an issue which is alive in society and in my own life; so most of the material I'm interested in is still in use. It hasn't reached a pause in its life history. So is this an autoarchaeology or an autoethnography (Harrison and Schofield 2009; see also Lemonnier, this volume; Rizvi, this volume; and White, this volume)? I consider it to be archaeological because I begin with the things, their place and their trajectories (see also Harrison and Schofield 2010: 92).

Can my experience really shed light on these wider questions? My race, class, gender, age, and location all give me a highly specific view. In his recent book *Stuff*, Miller (2010) presents a deeply critical, if humorously written, view of middle-class mothers from North London and their use of material culture in constructing themselves as mothers. Describing and tacitly dismissing his informants' attempts to bring up children according to their own values, and focusing on the failings in gendering both for children and mothers, he states 'Parenting becomes a form of tragic practice, experienced as a series of inevitable defeats' (Miller 2010: 144). It was difficult for me to read this with an open mind, to see the useful and truthful in what felt like an attack.

His final statement, however, is deeply confusing 'While I have largely referred to mothers, this was my story as a parent too' (Miller 2010: 145). If it was his story, why not tell it that way? Since he begins his characterization with a (weak) consideration of the role of pain in childbirth, this isn't his experience. Reading this convinced me that, despite the drawbacks, it was better to be up front about the experience that drives my understanding than to hide behind an attempt to portray my experience as someone else's or vice versa.

Combining the need to reduce the superabundance of data to a manageable scale and the need to speak honestly about my place in the work (see also Edgeworth, this volume), this chapter is structured around four vignettes taken from my own daily life. Each is described and then discussed in relation to themes that have arisen from my reading. Although those themes reach further than my own experience, these are a twenty-first century middle-class English mother's observations. I have focused my observation on what I consider to be the less examined aspects of the biography of contemporary children's things. Finally I have tried to observe children with things and things with children and allowed these observations to lead my interpretations.

47.3 CHILDREN AND MATERIAL CULTURE

Much of the academic discussion about children and things has been led by psychologists (Litt 1986; Sutton Smith 1986, 1994, 2001). Understandably, they are more interested in the 'children' than the 'things' and it might be argued that they lack the disciplinary background to understand how the biographies of things might intertwine with those of children (but see Costall and Richards, this volume). There has also been some work on children's material culture by sociologists, scholars in cultural studies and design (Seiter 1996; Holmer Nadesan 2002; Moran 2002). The UNICEF report mentioned above was carried out by marketing experts (Nairn and Ipsos MORI 2011). The resulting understanding has focused heavily on the acquisition of things by children (Cook 2004), with a small amount of work on sharing (Bryan and London 1970; Staub and Noerenberg 1981; Hay et al. 1991). This focus represents a bias that also reflects current societal norms regarding what is considered to be the appropriate relationship between children and things.

There is a small but interesting body of work on children from an archaeological perspective (Moore and Scott 1997; Soafer Derevenski 2000; Baxter 2005; Wileman 2005). While children are sometimes present in archaeological accounts of the modern world (e.g. Buchli 2002), they are seen as adjuncts to adults rather than as agents in their own right. Even in my own work on zoos, an institution popularly associated with children, they are only barely visible (Axelsson and May 2008; May 2009). Where children's material culture is a topic of interest, it has largely been in relation to another topic such as gender (e.g. Buchli and Lucas 2000).

Baxter describes the role of material culture in socialization. 'This socialisation process transforms a newborn child into a social person capable of interacting with others' (2005: 29). But Baxter is mostly interested in toys for the socializing (largely gendering) messages they embody. Socialization is also how children learn to use material culture to convey their own messages, to be competent social actors. Appadurai describes the categories of commoditization, the ways in which an object moves in and out of the set of things it is appropriate to exchange (1988: 16). Understanding these social characteristics and manipulating them is key to becoming a competent member of a social group (Kopytoff 1988: 75).

47.4 Themes in Existing Research

47.4.1 Consumerism

The moral panic surrounding children and consumerism has been strong since at least the nineteenth century. Denisoff quotes a nineteenth-century text warning children of the dangers of toys and the child labour that makes them. What's more there's a strong tradition from the nineteenth century for representing children as essentially greedy therefore both easy prey for merchandisers and also drivers of consumerism. Indeed greed itself is characterized as 'child'-ish (Denisoff 2008).

Despite this long history, even in scholarly writing, there is a strong anxiety 'that the structure of childhood is eroding and children are suffering from serious physical, emotional and social deficits directly related to consumerism' (Hill 2011: 11). In most cases authors do recognize our sense of childhood as culturally constructed and many authors refer to Aries' famous assertion that 'the child' only came into existence in the seventeenth century (Sutton Smith 2001). Of course an anthropological perspective works from the premise that all social roles are culturally constructed and culturally specific (Soafaer Derevenski 2000) so this anxiety really translates to a sense that a key social role is shifting. It is interesting that the seventeenth century, the commonly referenced date for the origin of the Western notion of childhood, is also the date that Dawson gives for the emergence of the child as consumer (1998).

Many authors suggest that pollution of childhood represented by consumerism is an explicit goal of marketers:

> Today's moral missionaries, the marketing practitioners, try instead to generate in children a state of perpetual dissatisfaction by stimulating desire for the new and redefining what preceded it as useless junk—the ultimate purpose being to reproduce the cycle of perpetual desire in which consumer capitalist childhood is embedded. (Bauman 2006: 15)

This is linked to claims that 'play has become professionalized and tainted with adult cues, imagination and expectations; it no longer belongs to the creative mind of a child' (Hill 2011: 5). This is complicated by the fact that adults have always had a role in children's material culture. 'A toy is an object given to a child by an adult, yet children are told to take the toy and play with it by themselves or other members of their peer group' (Sutton Smith 1994: 135). Furthermore children's own agency undermines this control. 'The ability to transform toys into a variety of objects (and to transform a variety of objects into toys) gives these objects a different repertoire of meanings when children use them' (Baxter 2005: 43).

Some of the anxiety surrounding children and consumerism may be lessened if we look at the more complex biographies that surround the things themselves. As Joy points out;

> Processes such as procurement, manufacture, use, maintenance and discard, as well as storage, transport, re-cycling and re-use are all important in determining how artefacts eventually enter archaeological contexts (see Schiffer 1972: 157–60). (Joy 2009: 4)

Similarly, in her consideration of nineteenth-century childhood, Wilkie explores the ways in which children have chosen, used, altered, damaged, and discarded toys in ways that illuminate their lives far more than a simple history of acquisition would do (2000).

47.4.2 Material Culture and Devotion

It could be argued that the social anxiety surrounding the position of children in society stems from their reflection of aspects of divinity. Daniel Miller suggests that the contemporary 'cult of the infant' has taken over from 'patriarchy' as a dominant devotional form in recent decades (Miller 1998: 123–5). 'The Divine child' is a common image across many societies. Wileman considers the archaeological evidence for children and divinity in some detail (2005: 95–125) but most of her material concerns child sacrifice. This underlines the fact that devotion is not always gentle, and the sacralization of children may not be conducive to their happiness. But it also demonstrates the wide-ranging nature of children's divinity beyond the Christian image. She describes the god Krishna's mother discovering his divinity: 'One day Krishna takes some food he shouldn't and eats it, whereupon his mother demands that he opens his mouth so she can see what it is. He does so and, looking in, his mother sees the entire universe in all its glory, all within her young child' (Wileman 2005: 123).

The difference between these images of divinity and Miller's claim for the contemporary cult of the infant is that in Wileman's examples the child forms part of a larger system of belief and devotion. In Miller's argument, devotion to the child is the core of the spiritual practice (Miller 1998: 123–5). Pugh makes a similar suggestion:

> As mothers' work lives look more and more like fathers', who but the child is left to sacralize as the vessel of all that is dear about domesticity? As the percentage of single parent households maintains itself at historically high levels, who but the child is left to symbolize family devotion? As community bonds wither, who but the child is left to embody parents' emotional connections? (Pugh 2009: 35)

In his study of early to mid-twentieth-century Soviet homemaking, Buchli demonstrates the extent that children were sacralized in that society.

Byt reformers revived an old innovation from the 1920s, the *detskii ugolok* (the children's corner) or the *ugolok diadi Lenina* (Uncle Lenin's corner) that attempted to replace the pre-revolutionary Russian Orthodox *krasyi ugol* (icon corner). Here in the most visually prominent and well lit corner of the room a little microcosm was created. It was a separate world in miniature that reproduced the adult space in which it was embedded. (Buchli 2002: 220)

Miller's discussion of the sacralization of children in *A Theory of Shopping* obviously focuses on provisioning, but less attention has been paid to the life histories of the objects involved in this devotion. What would the devotional practice that Miller describes look like, beyond the acquisition practices that he describes? The use, curation, and disposal of these items is surely as charged as their acquisition. Some items, such as prams, have immense significance when purchased, but have little on disposal. Others, such as clothing, can increase in significance through curation. Marshall refers to this as the distinction between 'inscribed value' and 'lived value' (2008: 63–5).

Most of the work on desire and devotion in material culture centres on the gift (Strathern 1988; Rethmann 2000; Daniels 2009). But children do not always receive gifts in the ways that adults hope for. Burrell quotes a boy who demonstrates the complexity of gifting: 'I don't remember myself being so much excited because when I was born my father was in America, then he came back, then he went away, and I was receiving these Lego blocks all the time' (Burrell 2010: 20). The recent UNICEF report looks with horror on 'Boxes and boxes of toys, broken presents and unused electronics [which] were witness to this drive to acquire new possessions, which in reality were not really wanted or treasured' (Nairn and Ipsos MORI 2011, 4). But divine beings are rarely grateful for the gifts we give them.

One of the distinctive features of sacred material is that it is singularized and no longer available for commodity exchange (Kopytoff 1988). This is certainly a feature of contemporary children's material culture. While more and more is acquired and it is outgrown quickly, surprisingly little of it is re-commoditized, as will be discussed further in the vignettes below. This sacralization of children is often at odds with the developmental aspects of their dealings with material culture. In seeking to 'protect' children from the ravages of consumerism we create less competent adults who are more focused on acquisition and less aware of the rest of the life cycle.

47.5 Vignette #1: 'The Stick'

A. loves sticks. Since he has been able to walk he has picked up sticks and used them in his play. Sometimes they last only a little while, until he finds a 'better' one. Sometimes they become more precious and need to stay with him, to be brought home 'for the stick pile'. On a walk in the country the stick will have many uses. Sometimes it is for poking—things, friends. Sometimes it is a gun. Sometimes it is a walking stick, or a flying broomstick. The same stick plays all these roles. Sometimes he will name the stick. He chooses the stick for a range of qualities and comments on them, for example, if 'it has nice smooth bark'.

Sticks have value and currency for children his age. Friends out walking will squabble over sticks, trade them, ask parents to help look for similar sticks. In an urban park surrounded by bushes and trees A. had a stick (which was being a wand and instrument for tagging in a game of 'off ground tag'). Another boy he didn't know ran up and said 'When you're finished with that stick I need it!' and ran away again. When A. finished with the stick he left it where the boy spoke to him, but didn't give the stick to the boy.

Sticks that come home to the stick pile rarely get used again, but the stick pile itself is important. Recently, his parents had used his stick pile to store deadwood from the garden. When he noticed he went through and separated his sticks from 'garden sticks'.

English children in the twenty-first century are largely excluded from production. When they make things they are almost always gifts, and even where they make them for themselves they are encouraged to give them to their parents. In this case A. is producing material culture for himself by selecting and managing it as part of a collection. Collecting has long been recognized as an important component of play (Whitley 1929; Di Sanctis Ricciardone 2005). Moshenska describes the shrapnel collections made by children in London during the Second World War. Since they collected it themselves, they were free to trade it, and indeed to use it against adults who bothered them (2008). A. also has more control over the collection he has made. While we won't buy him guns, he can make them with sticks (see Costall and Richards, this volume). He is also under less obligation to share, a major element in adult moral lessons (Staub and Noerenberg 1981; Nairn and Ipsos MORI 2011).

He has greater freedom to trade with this collection than with most other things. Many schools in England have explicitly banned trading cards. One parent explains, 'the problem is that they start trading in Year 1 and the kids don't really understand the idea of trading. They just give the cards to their friends but the children might want them back a few days later. Sometimes the kids will say "I'll give you all these cards if you give me Wayne Rooney". It is an absolute nightmare' (Bristow 2011). This obviously varies. Kids' TV presenter Jamie Rickers says: 'It's all about swapability to become a playground craze—if you can't trade it, it'll not make it in the playground for very long' (Shropshire Star 2011). Rather than allowing children to learn trading in this way, the activity is restricted (see Eiser and Eiser 1976 for a view from 35 years ago). Because the only resources involved in the stick collection are his own, A. and his friends can practise this important aspect of the use of material culture unimpeded.

While not all children keep their sticks, the practice of childhood collecting is very widespread, and poorly studied. The last detailed study on children's collecting was in 1929 (Whitley 1929). Clearly for A., the collection has value beyond its individual elements. The stick pile is 'his', as well as the sticks that compose it. As with trading, the collection allows him to engage in activities, such as deciding what stays and what goes, that are otherwise restricted in relation to other forms of children's material culture which are managed by parents and carers.

47.6 VIGNETTE #2: 'THE WELLIE AND THE SANDAL'

Figures 47.1 and 47.2 show a pair of mismatched footwear found within metres of each other around the foreshore in Hampshire in summer 2011. The child's 'wellie' (Wellington boot) has been picked up and placed on a fencepost so that if someone comes looking for it they will find it. It won't get washed away, or too soggy with sand. The adult's sandal has been left

FIGURE 47.1 Child's lost boot rescued on a fence post. Strangers habitually care for the things which children lose (photograph: Sarah May)

where it is. It will soon be invisible or washed away. No one takes responsibility for it. The difference in how the objects are treated shows that object biographies are widely read. The wellie is read as a treasured possession of a child, its image of 'Lightning McQueen' marks it out as more than functional. It has been lost, perhaps as the child changed from wellies to other shoes while leaving the beach. Who picked it up? Another parent, aware of the joy of finding the lost item? It could be anyone. And the sandal? It's just a sandal, its owner should have been more careful. He or she can buy another pair.

This vignette brings the questions of desire, loss, and devotion together for me. The boot itself speaks of desire and the way that it is produced in, and experienced by, both children and adults. Obviously, both objects are lost, and may have become rubbish, so it raises questions regarding whether patterns of disposal are different for adult material culture and children's material culture. Finally it demonstrates the responsibility that strangers take for children's material culture, and the judgements of value which are embodied within such quotidian decisions.

The branding of children's clothing, toys, bedding, etc., with images from films and television is a particular site of anxiety for many people writing about children today (Hill 2011). It is seen as a particularly aggressive marketing technique because it exploits children's attachment to stories to create desires in other areas. It also ties in to the drive for the latest, the newest. This boot refers to the film *Cars 2* (dirs. Brad Lewis and John Lasseter 2011) and so, at the time of writing, is considered to be 'up to date'. We bought a second-hand 'laptop toy' branded with a Lightning McQueen image from the first *Cars* film (dirs. John Lasseter and Joe Ranft

FIGURE 47.2 A sandal is washed by the tide on a beach. We don't care for the things adults lose in the same way we do for children's things (photograph: Sarah May)

2006) in 2011 for the rather paltry sum of £2, because it was no longer considered up to date. This kind of branding shortens the commodity life cyle of an object, so that once it has been consumed by one child it loses most of its value. In Kopytoff's terminology, it has been singularized (Kopytoff 1988: 75, see also Graves-Brown, this volume). Although 'hand me downs' certainly still circulate within families, this kind of branding makes them more difficult to pass on to other children, particular those who are outside of the immediate family group. Children (and parents) are more aware of reduced status of a branding which is no longer current.

The sandal could have had a longer life than the wellie. The child will grow out of the wellie very quickly, and its branding ensures that it will have less value for another child. This should make the loss of the wellie less important than the sandal. But the reverse seems to have been interpreted as the case. Perhaps the ephemeral nature of the wellie's life makes it more precious to passing strangers. Perhaps it is because the branding marks it as beloved, whereas the sandal presents as simply functional. But the care taken with the wellie also betokens a care that the community takes with children's things more generally. I have seen children's items picked up, and particularly placed up high where they can be retrieved by parents of those who have lost them uncountable times across Britain since I began to watch for such phenomena.

Gavin Lucas has suggested that we need to consider disposal in a more positive light, as a significant practice in the construction of social selves (2002). If the child has become a significant subject of devotion in contemporary Britain, then we should expect to see their things handled with greater care. As discussed above, there is little in the literature on repair or the handling of sacred items, but we expect ritual items to be decommissioned with care. The wellie on the fencepost reflects a small act of devotion which is repeated daily by people who never think of why they do it.

47.7 Vignette #3: 'The Keyring'

M. is having difficulty starting the new school year. She's happy in class, but finds leaving her parents in the morning hard and has been tearful and 'clingy'. Her mother asks her what can be done to help. Would M. like to bring something in to help her feel safe? Yes. Penguin (her favourite soft toy). Her mother says that Penguin is too large to bring to school. Perhaps M. would like to bring something of Mummy's. Yes. Mummy's keyring with the pictures in it; perhaps the picture could be Mummy and Daddy. Overnight her mother prints a picture and puts it in the keyring. In the morning M. says she wanted a picture of Penguin in the keyring. But it is OK. There are no tears at drop off time. M. shows her friends the keyring during the day.

A. faced a similar sense of longing for home in the classroom but struggled to find the right object to hold him. Since he knew M.'s story, he suggested a keyring, but none was available. 'How about a fossil that you dug up on that day at the beach with Mummy and Daddy?' 'Good idea, let's try it'. A. chose the fossils carefully then tested them. He put the fossils in his pockets, walked away from Mummy and examined how he felt. The fossils didn't pass. In the end a fluorescent gecko toy passed the test and helped with the moments of anxiety. At pick up time A. says, 'I wasn't tearful today, even when gecko was away from me'.

The keyring and the gecko performed important roles for A. and M. They linked them to their parents and made them brave in the face of anxiety. In both cases the children showed other people, both children and adults, the keyring and the gecko, and that performance allowed them to share both their anxiety and their bravery with others. In both cases, once the anxiety was broken the object reverted back to its everyday role—left at home with no further special regard. Indeed A. recognized that gecko could be relegated to the school bag by lunch time.

Clearly, adults are deeply involved in these stories of how things support children in the challenges they face. Adults certainly use objects to support them in facing crises around pregnancy and birth (Layne 2000; Landzelius 2001). Cognitive psychologists use the concept of 'transitional objects' to describe the way in which a physical object can take the place of the mother–child bond at the point in development where the child begins to recognize the distinction between themselves and the rest of the world. The original formulator of the notion, Winnicott, saw it as a universal component in the development of a healthy child. Subsequent studies have shown the use of such objects to be culturally variable, and in no cases more common than amongst 47 per cent of children. Nonetheless, much research has been conducted to establish a link between the use of 'transitional objects' and later mental health (see Litt 1986 for a useful overview of this large area of research). The use of objects to reduce anxiety is a much broader practice than this, however, and an archaeological perspective may contribute something distinctive to questions surrounding this phenomenon.

47.8 Vignette #4: 'The Diggers'

When I began this work in 2009, 'the Diggers' (Figure 47.3) were A.'s favourite toys. They had come from a second-hand toy store in a plastic bag. They were a birthday gift, but their appeal didn't come from their status as gift. Their value lay in their size, their group value, and their suitability for the things A. did at the time.

Although they had distinct identities, they were always played with as a group and were kept in a particular shoebox. All of the people had names and the vehicles 'belonged' to particular people. Daddy had helped with the names, and receiving names had increased their play time considerably. Mostly they had pretty steady personalities, but they were sometimes joined by 'Bob the chimp', a 'trickster' character who would influence them. Sometimes A. told stories with the Diggers. Sometimes he and the Diggers (and Daddy) built things, especially in the sand pit. Sometimes the Diggers joined him when he did other things. For example, he was better at doing puzzles when the Diggers helped him.

Children's enlivening of dolls is such a pervasive phenomenon that it slips beneath our notice. The 'transitional object' does not include these companions of the older child (Litt 1986). Yet, many of us remember particular dolls with greater affection than the blanket of our babyhood. Much of the discussion of dolls has centred on gender (e.g. Baxter 2005: 44) but this should not blind us to the agency that they have in the lives of both boys and girls.

The dominant developmental perspective on children and material culture emphasizes that through socialization, children learn to adopt the contemporary Western ontological

FIGURE 47.3 'The Digger's' favourite toys and partners. In addition to starring in various stories, the Diggers helped A. do puzzles, solve problems, and face life's challenges (photograph: Sarah May)

separation of persons and things. Nairn and Ipsos MORI reflect this strong belief in the separate realms (and relative worth) of people and things when they say 'there was a distinct lack of material possessions in children's descriptions of a good day; it was people, *and not things* that made them happy' (2011: 26; my emphasis).

Young children don't necessarily make this distinction. They have no difficulty in accepting the idea that objects have agency. They regularly imbue things (everything from dolls, to cars, sticks and even Blu Tack) with liveliness, personality, and life. These things are partners in the imaginative worlds children create and they also provide support to children in the everyday worlds of home and school. The process of replacing this model with the inanimate view of objects held by most Western adults is complex and, like the rest of children's material culture, has not been explored in any substantial body of literature.

By 2010, A. had outgrown the Diggers. He was less interested in digging, and the Diggers didn't change. They were too small and too big at the same time. They didn't move as much as Playmobil. He didn't reject them, he just played with them less. They stayed in their shoebox more. In 2011 he identified them as 'baby toys' and I moved them, in their shoebox, to the shed.

The shed has many baby toys, and baby clothes and baby equipment, like prams. A. doesn't see them as 'his' baby things, just baby things. Sometimes he resists them being sent to the shed, and sometimes he 'rediscovers' something there with great joy, but he doesn't think of them as a store of his things. For some time we thought that another baby might use these things. With sadness we contemplate clearing the shed. Do we know anyone who would like these things? Should we give them to A.'s old nursery? Could we do a car boot sale? Should they be sent to a charity shop? Or the dump? One or two items have gone, but most are waiting for us to re-home them—including the Diggers.

For me, the Diggers have a longer object biography than many of the other objects discussed here. I know something of their manufacture, their acquisition, their use, management, and discard. The cycle that they have been through in our family has already been played out in another family. Made of plastic, with little in the way of fashionable branding these items have little inscribed value and are durable enough to survive many 'lifetimes' (Joy 2009: 545). But at this point, these dolls will be singularized because they were such active members of our family while they lived with us. Their lived value has increased to the point where we don't want to release them into commodity exchange again.

The discussion of the disposal or curation of these items is the most poignant part of the work that I have done for this chapter. Clearing the shed of these and other remains of A.'s babyhood is our task, not his. In doing so, we mourn the loss of that stage of his life, as well as acknowledging that we won't be having more children to play with them. Marcoux has discussed the 'caisser maison' ritual amongst the elderly population of Montreal as a process of constructing the self by emptying the house in preparation for death (Marcoux 2001). In considering the fate of the Diggers, I contemplate similar issues.

47.9 CONCLUSION

Children's material culture and the material culture of childhood are large topics (Lillehammer 2000; Brookshaw 2009), and while both are of great interest in contemporary society, there is still a relatively small body of literature which examines them critically. I have drawn on my own experience to create a small concrete data set with which to consider broader issues concerning this important topic. Although such an autoarchaeology is limited in what it can say about the diversity of experience, it avoids the pitfalls of purely anecdotal writing by its attention to concrete detail.

While children's material culture has complex use lives, there is a tendency for the analysis of the biographies of children's material to be cut short. All the interest is in the acquisition, which is conceived as equivalent to consumption. English children in the twenty-first century are largely excluded from production, exchange, management and repair, and disposal. This singularization partly reflects a more general truncated experience of material culture, but it is also a reflection of the sacralization of children. Nonetheless, children undermine these cultural expectations to create rich and lively biographies for and with their things. This chapter has suggested several lines of inquiry into these complex biographies and the role of material culture in the social and material worlds of contemporary children in Britain and elsewhere more broadly.

References

Appadurai, Arjun. 1988 [1986]. Introduction: Commodities and the Politics of Value. In *The Social Life of Things: Commodities in Cultural Perspective*, ed. A. Appadurai, pp. 3–63. Cambridge: Cambridge University Press.

Axelson Tony and May, Sarah. 2008. Constructed Landscapes in Zoos and Heritage. *International Journal of Heritage Studies* 14(1): 43–59.

Barber, Benjamin J. 2007. *Consumed: How Markets Corrupt Children, Infantilize Adults, and Swallow Citizens Whole*. London: W. W. Norton.

Bauman, Zygmunt. 2006. Children Make You Happier…and Poorer. *International Journal of Children's Spirituality* 11(1): 5–10.

Baxter, Jane E. 2005. *The Archaeology of Childhood: Children, Gender, and Material Culture*. Walnut Creek, CA: Altamira Press.

Bristow, Tom. 2011. Trading cards banned at Churchtown Primary School, *Southport Visitor*, 26 May. Available at: <http://www.southportvisiter.co.uk/southport-news/southport-sou thport-news/2011/05/26/trading-cards-banned-at-churchtown-primary-school-101022-28760316/> (accessed 9 September 2011).

Brookshaw, Sharon. 2009. The Material Culture of Children and Childhood: Understanding Childhood Objects in the Museum Context. *Journal of Material Culture* 14(3): 365–83.

Bryan, James H. and London, Perry. 1970. Altruistic Behaviour by Children. *Psychological Bulletin* 73(3): 200–11.

Buchli, Victor. 2002 [1997]. Khrushchev, Modernism and the Fight against *Petit-Bourgeois* Consciousness in the Soviet Home. Reprinted in *The Material Culture Reader*, ed. Victor Buchli, pp. 215–36. New York: Berg.

Buchli, Victor and Lucas, Gavin. 2000. Children, Gender and the Material Culture of Domestic Abandonment in the Late Twentieth Century. In *Children and Material Culture*, ed. J. Sofaer Derevenski, pp. 131–7. Abingdon and New York: Routledge.

Burrell, Kathy. 2010. The Enchantment of Western Things: Children's Material Encounters in Late Socialist Poland. *Transactions of the Institute of British Geographers* NS 36: 143–56.

Cook, Daniel, T. 2004. *The Commodification of Childhood: The Children's Clothing Industry and the Rise of the Child Consumer.* Durham, NC: Duke University Press.

Daniels, Inge. 2009. The 'Social Death' of Unused Gifts: Surplus and Value in Contemporary Japan. *Journal of Material Culture* 14(3): 385–408.

Dawson, Janis. 1998. Trade and Plumb-Cake in Lilliput: The Origins of Juvenile Consumerism and Early English Children's Periodicals. *Children's Literature in Education* 29(4): 175–98.

Denisoff, Dennis. 2008. *The Nineteenth-Century Child and Consumer Culture.* Aldershot: Ashgate.

Di Sanctis Ricciardone, Paola. 2005. Collecting as a Form of Play. In *Play: An Interdisciplinary Synthesis* (Play and Culture Studies: Volume 6), ed. Felicia F. McMahon, Donald E. Lytle, and Brian Sutton Smith, pp. 279–90. Lanham, MD: University Press of America.

Eiser, Christine and Eiser, J. Richard. 1976. Acquisition of Information in Children's Bargaining. *Journal of Personality and Social Psychology* 34(5): 796–804.

Finn, Christine. 2007–9. Leave Home Stay. Available at: <http://www.leavehomestay.com/> (accessed 10 September 2011).

Harrison, Rodney. 2011. Surface Assemblages: Towards an Archaeology *in* and *of* the Present. *Archaeological Dialogues* 18(2): 141–61.

Harrison, Rodney and Schofield, John. 2009. Archaeo-Ethnography, Auto-Archaeology: Introducing Archaeologies of the Contemporary Past. *Archaeologies* 5(2): 185–209.

————— 2010. *After Modernity: Archaeological Approaches to the Contemporary Past.* Oxford: Oxford University Press.

Hay, Dale F., Caplan, Marlene, Castle, Jennifer, and Stimson, Carol. 1991. Does Sharing Become Increasingly 'Rational' in the Second Year of Life? *Developmental Psychology* 27(6): 987–93.

Hill, Jennifer A. 2011. Endangered Childhoods: How Consumerism is Impacting Child and Youth Identity. *Media, Culture & Society* 33(3): 347–62.

Holmer, Nadesan M. 2002. Engineering the Entrepreneurial Infant: Brain Science, Infant Development Toys, and Governmentality. *Cultural Studies* 16(3): 401–32.

Joy, Jody. 2009. Reinvigorating Object Biography: Reproducing the Drama of Object Lives. *World Archaeology* 41(4): 540–56.

Kopytoff, Igor. 1988 [1986]. The Cultural Biography of Things: Commoditization as Process. In *The Social Life of Things: Commodities in Cultural Perspective*, ed. A. Appadurai, pp. 64–95. Cambridge: Cambridge University Press.

Landzelius, Kyra M. 2001. Charged Artifacts and the Detonation of Liminality: Teddy-Bear Diplomacy in the Newborn Incubator Machine. *Journal of Material Culture* 6(3): 323–44.

Layne, Linda L. 2000. He was a Real Baby with Baby Things: A Material Culture Analysis of Personhood, Parenthood and Pregnancy Loss. *Journal of Material Culture* 5(3): 321–45.

Lillehammer, Grete. 2000. The World of Children. In *Children and Material Culture*, ed. Joanna Sofaer Derevenski, pp. 17–26. Abingdon and New York: Routledge.

Litt, Carole J. 1986. Theories of Transitional Object Attachment: An Overview. *International Journal of Behavioral Development* 9: 383–99.

Lucas, Gavin. 2002. Disposability and Dispossession in the Twentieth Century. *Journal of Material Culture* 7(1): 5–22.

Marcoux, Jean-Sébastien. 2001. The 'Casser Maison' Ritual: Constructing the Self by Emptying the Home. *Journal of Material Culture* 6(2): 213–35.

Marshall, Yvonne. 2008. The Social Lives of Lived and Inscribed Objects: A Lapita Perspective. *Journal of the Polynesian Society* 117(1): 59–101.

May, Sarah. 2009. Then Tyger Fierce Took Life Away: The Contemporary Material Culture of Tigers. In *Contemporary Archaeologies: Excavating Now*, ed. C. Holtorf and A. Piccini, pp. 65–80. Frankfurt: Peter Lang.

Miller, Daniel. 1998. *A Theory of Shopping*. Cambridge: Polity Press.

—— 2010. *Stuff*. Cambridge: Polity Press.

Moore, Jenny and Scott, Eleanor. 1997. *Invisible People and Processes: Writing Gender and Childhood into European Archaeology*. London and New York: Leicester University Press.

Moran, Joe. 2002. Childhood and Nostalgia in Contemporary Culture. *European Journal of Contemporary Culture* 5(2): 155–73.

Moshenska, Gabriel. 2008. A Hard Rain: Children's Shrapnel Collections in the Second World War. *Journal of Material Culture* 13(1): 107–25.

Nairn, Agnes and Ipsos MORI. 2011. *Children's Well-being in UK, Sweden and Spain: The Role of Inequality and Materialism*. York: UNICEF.

Pugh, Allison. 2009. *Longing and Belonging: Parents, Children and Consumer Culture*. Berkeley, CA: University of California Press.

Rethmann, Petra. 2000. Skins of Desire: Poetry and Identity in Koriak Women's Gift Exchange. *American Ethnologist* 27(1): 52–71.

Schiffer, Michael B. 1972. Archaeological Context and Systemic Context. *American Antiquity* 37(2): 156–75.

Schofield, John. 2009. Office Cultures and Corporate Memory: Some Archaeological Perspectives. *Archaeologies* 5(2): 293–305.

Seiter, Ellen. 1996. Toys are Us: Marketing to Children and Parents. *Cultural Studies* 6(2): 232–47.

Shropshire Star. 2011. Six of the Best Pocket Money Playthings, *Shropshire Star*, 8 September. Available at: <http://www.shropshirestar.com/lifestyle/gadgets/2011/09/08/six-of-the-best-pocket-money-playthings/#ixzz1XSKOSIsM> (accessed 9 September 2011).

Sofaer Derevenski, Joanna. 2000. Material Culture Shock: Confronting Expectations in the Material Culture of Children. In *Children and Material Culture*, ed. Joanna Sofaer Derevenski, pp. 3–16. Abingdon and New York: Routledge.

Staub, Ervin and Noerenberg, Henry. 1981. Property Rights, Deservingness, Reciprocity, Friendship: The Transactional Character of Children's Sharing Behavior. *Journal of Personality and Social Psychology* 40(2): 271–89.

Strathern, Marilyn. 1988. *The Gender of the Gift: Problems with Women and Problems with Society in Melanesia*. Berkeley: University of California Press.

Sutton Smith, Brian. 1986. *Toys as Culture*. New York: Gardener Press.

—— 1994. Does Play Prepare the Future? In *Toys, Play and Child Development*, ed. J. H. Goldstein, pp. 130–46. Cambridge: Cambridge University Press.

—— 2001. *The Ambiguity of Play* Cambridge, MA: Harvard University Press.

Ulin, Jonna. 2009. Into the Space of the Past: A Family Archaeology. In *Contemporary Archaeologies: Excavating Now*, ed. Cornelius Holtorf and Angela Piccini, pp. 145–60. Frankfurt: Peter Lang.

Whitley, M. T. 1929. Children's Interest in Collecting. *Journal of Educational Psychology* 20(4): 249–61.

Wileman, Julie. 2005. *Hide and Seek: The Archaeology of Childhood*. Stroud: Tempus.

Wilkie, Laurie. 2000. Not Merely Child's Play: Creating a Historical Archaeology of Children and Childhood. In *Children and Material Culture*, ed. Joanna Sofaer Derevenski, pp. 100–114. Abingdon and New York: Routledge.

CHAPTER 48

··

VHS: A POSTHUMANIST AESTHETICS OF RECORDING AND DISTRIBUTION

··

JEM NOBLE

'O body swayed to music, O brightening glance,
How can we know the dancer from the dance?'
From *Among School Children* by William Butler Yeats (Finneran 1996)

IN 2009, the year after Japanese electronics manufacturer JVC (Japan Victor Company), creator of the VHS format (Video Home System), ceased production of the last line of stand-alone VHS video recorders (Broadcast Engineering 2008), I undertook an artist's residency at VIVO Media Arts in Vancouver, Canada—part of an eight-month stay, dwelling in the city with my partner and son—to consider the aesthetic qualities of VHS video as a dwindling feature of home-video practices. I was interested particularly in the qualities of degraded VHS image and sound with respect to the circularity of relations between the materiality of VHS technology, the engineered recordings it has potentiated, the practices these have both afforded, and the transformative effects of such practices on its materiality as they are evidenced in degrading picture and sound quality. My focus was drawn to the phenomenon of video rental as a spatial practice bound up with the material particularities of home-video technology and as a context of its intensive use associated with increased 'wear and tear'. With the generous assistance of VIVO and Limelight Video, my family's neighbourhood video library, my residency developed around a single rental VHS tape with respect to this idea.

The following chapter comprises a *katachrestic* presentation of differing registers from my research into the material-social circumstances through which the home-video phenomenon emerged, into specific aspects of the tape's history, and into the physicality of the medium, in order to provoke understandings of interconnectivity among these factors—part of their relational ontology—for aesthetic consideration. I draw on concepts of relational ontology and object ontology in philosophies of semiosis and performativity, rather than from the specific discourse of 'object oriented ontology', approaching objects as provisional, unfolding distributions of material and immaterial aspects and relations (physical, social, and conceptual)—existentially equal constituents of form (Bains 2006), and therefore pertinent to the realm of aesthetics, which I understand to be comprised of concerns with the experience of form and the form of experience. Of considerable importance in my approach to object ontology here are the notions 'distributed object' and 'distributed artwork' in the writings of anthropologist Alfred Gell (1998), and almost 80 years of art discourse from *Art as Experience* (Dewey 1934), through the conceptual aesthetics of the 1960s and 1970s and their legacy (Alberro and Stimson 1999), serving, in parallel with longer-standing currents in posthumanist and semiotic philosophy (Barad 2003; Bains 2006), to challenge distinctions between apparently discrete entities and the processes, systems, and relations in which their physical presence is inextricably embedded while situating those comprising the organizational capacities of human subjectivity within a broader matrix of agential forces.

> **Analog recording**: A recording in which continuous magnetic signals are written to the tape that are representations of the voltage signals coming from the recording microphone or the video camera. (Van Bogart 1995)

This chapter indicates rather than fills this theoretical outline and its relationship to archaeological discourse; it leaves the widespread global cultural impacts and legacies of VHS video technology (Ganley and Ganley 1987) largely untouched; it accounts for merely a few of the material-social and commercial contingencies potentiating the home-video phenomenon; it falls short of addressing the forensic specificities of materials in question and their geopolitical origins (see Maxwell and Miller, this volume); and sketches only some of the processes and outcomes of the artist's residency informing it, for such expansion has fallen beyond its scope. What follows instead is not an archaeological thesis but the extension of an artwork with archaeological undertones: an idiosyncratic inquiry illustrating some of the connectivities that write themselves into the material culture of place, shaping the place of material culture; a confluence of reference points, actions, and ideas offering a site-specific route through which to consider some of the complex material-social relations comprising a recording technology and its practices, and to question the determinacy of boundaries that such distinctions as material, social, technology and practice imply.

> **Backing**: See substrate. (Van Bogart 1995)

While the camera was the first production technology to record information synchronically in a detailed manner analogous to human sensory engagement, collapsing short durational exposures into still images, shifting certain optical qualities of visually static events through time and space, Edison's Phonograph (1877) was the first production machine for synchronic recording into a dynamic medium, enabling reproduction of durational phenomena and their circulation in materially encoded form. The idea of magnetic recording was conceived by American industrial print-maker Oberlin Smith in 1878 as a 'contact-free' method for making durational audio documentation, in response to sound quality limitations he recognized in Edison's phonographic system associated with the friction of its material surfaces (Daniel et al. 1999). Friction is one form of material transformation among many comprising traces that produce the archaeological record, speaking to both the social agency of objects in which they are inscribed (Gell 1998), and to the indifferent physical agency of human–non-human materialities with which this coincides (Latour 1993; Bennett 2010). In this sense, the development of recording technologies, bound up with the utilities and profitability of creating ever clearer recordings and ever more resilient, mobile means of

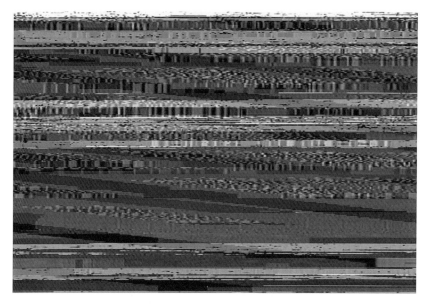

FIGURE 48.1 Copyright Notice. Digital image from colour VHS (*Harold and Maude*) (Jem Noble)

storing and distributing such traces while striving against those forged by unruly material tendencies, can be understood as a dialectic of remains—a conflict of purpose and accident in the capacities of matter as trace, speaking to the multiplicity of relations that objects perform in a world of immanent transformation, and to the fundamental indeterminacy of form in this respect (see Watkins, this volume).

> **Binder**: The polymer used to bind magnetic particles together and adhere them to the tape substrate. Generally, a polyester or polyether polyurethane based system. See polymer. (Van Bogart 1995)
>
> **Blocking**: The sticking together or adhesion of successive windings in a tape pack. Blocking can result from (1) deterioration of the binder, (2) storage of tape reels at high temperatures, and/or (3) excessive tape pack stresses. (Van Bogart 1995)

Home- or 'consumer' video technology emerged as a mass market proposition around twenty years after the first commercial video recorder was demonstrated by Ampex in the United States in 1956, only after technical innovations such as helical scanning, conceived in the late 1950s and developed throughout the 1960s, and the adsorption of cobalt into ferric oxide tape, achieved in the early 1970s, enabled the reduced tape lengths and increased recording bandwidth necessary for small, portable, durable enough cassettes capable of bearing sufficiently high quality recordings to warrant significant consumer interest (Daniel et al. 1999). With such interest amplified by increasing affordability driven by intense commercial competition, VHS video became the dominant format for home-video practices and determined the haptic and audiovisual aesthetics of home-video apparatuses and the recordings they facilitated from the late 1970s when it surpassed Sony's Betamax video system in the first media 'format wars' (Dobrow 1990), until the early 2000s, by which time alternative technical formations such as optical disc technologies and on-demand streaming services had begun to transform possibilities and expectations regarding the quality and availability of moving-image media.

> **Cinching**: The wrinkling, or folding over, of tape on itself in a loose tape pack. Normally occurs when a loose tape pack is stopped suddenly, causing outer tape layers to slip past inner layers, which in turn causes a buckling of tape in the region of slip. Results in large dropouts or high error rates. (Van Bogart 1995)
>
> **Curvature error**: A change in track shape that results in a bowed or S-shaped track. This becomes a problem if the playback head is not able to follow the track closely enough to capture the information. (Van Bogart 1995)

As a medium for making and relaying recordings, VHS video records in two markedly different ways: on the one hand it stores engineered signals in which optical and acoustical information is encoded, intended for precise decoding as durational phenomena; on the other it accrues the unintentional marks of its own material transformations. The first of these processes is engineered to facilitate experiences of moving pictures and sounds, shaped by structural conventions of production, perception, and interpretation that enable signification of differing temporalities and spaces within the closed duration of its intentional content, while the second is an accident of the technology's ongoing material configuration and performance, indifferent to these conventions and intervening in them through an indefinite process of alteration. Degradation—a relative term for alteration from an idealized condition—is a recording in its own right in as much as it is evidence of the processes and events that have caused it, but not in a way that relays anything analogous to an originary experience: in Peircean semiotic terms it is indexical to them, connected in a network of physical dynamics, as is an engineered recording in its own ways, but it is not iconical, in that it does not resemble them as the content of an engineered recording resembles what has been in front of a camera or near a microphone (Hartshorne et al. 1931–58: 8). This is the distinction to which Laura U. Marks refers when she says of film: 'The emulsion itself remembers the passage of time, when the image itself attempts to live in an eternal present' (Marks 2002: 96).

> **Dropout**: Brief signal loss caused by a tape head clog, defect in the tape, debris, or other feature that causes an increase in the head-to-tape spacing. A dropout can also be caused by missing magnetic material. A video dropout generally appears as a white spot or streak on the video monitor. When several video dropouts occur per frame, the TV monitor will appear snowy. The frequent appearance of dropouts on playback is an indication that the tape or recorder is contaminated with debris and/or that the tape binder is deteriorating. (Van Bogart 1995)

This 'remembrance', or evidence, is not an encoding and relaying of experiential phenomena, of optical and acoustical information conveying spatial and temporal relations, but a manifestation of material transformations, translated into abstract visible and audible phenomena by projection and amplification technologies. A scratch on the record registers a vibration through the stylus and is amplified as a sonic event with/in the music; a scratch in the film emulsion registers as a crack of light and appears as a large white line in the projected picture; the demagnetization of analogue video tape registers as a diffused wave displacing colour information across scan-lines comprising the image on a screen. In recording processes, such translation of material events marked across a recording surface re-maps their temporal relations according to the spatial logic of playback, creating a new durational event and experience of its own order, embedded in the experience of the recording over which it is written. This tension between semiotic registers of a recording, the overlaying of determinate and indeterminate marking processes, their different temporalities and capacities for conveying detail, is expressed differently by different recording media materialities—territories explored across a range of music, contemporary art, and materialist filmmaking practices often concerned with time, memory, and loss (DeNora 2000; Marks 2002; Katz 2004)—and can be understood as an unfolding production of historic relations by emergent material agency: a quality of all objects in their constitution as records of the past (Lucas 2005), but uniquely expressed in translation to picture and sound by those comprising recording and reproduction systems.

> **Flange pack**: A condition where the tape pack is wound up against one of the flanges of the tape reel. (Van Bogart 1995)

The resolution of picture and sound through the medium of video is no simple matter. It is partly conditioned by the composition of a television video signal, which is subject to variation in synchronization, chrominance, and luminance encoding specifications across differing national broadcasting standards (for example PAL, SECAM, NTSC) and partly by the origin of the signal's content, be it in film, video, live broadcast media, or a sequence of transpositions through these—a series of hidden indexical folds—all of which are mediated by configurations of machine components, lighting conditions, grading, developing, rendering, and duplication processes. Picture and sound resolution are also conditioned by the materials used in any given video-recorder and television/monitor configuration, implicating them in the complex geopolitics of industrial development that connect mundane domestic practices with global change: the flows and relays of capital investment, the mass extraction, processing, diffusion, and deposition of minerals, globalized labour-market ethics, distributions of economic and political power, ecological and environmental transformation. Additionally, and not least in the web of factors conditioning the qualities of video content, is the resolution of signals as audiovisual phenomena between screen, sound-system, and audience as objects of experience, mediated by an indeterminate complex of forces conditioning the phenomenological realm of a place-specific, perceiving, interpreting subject: autopoietic, psychical, libidinal, socio-linguistic, familial, material, economic, environmental, historic, and emergent to name a few.

> **Head clog**: Debris trapped in the playback head of a video recorder. Clogging of the playback head with debris causes dropouts. (Van Bogart 1995)
>
> **Helical scan recording**: The recording format in which a slow moving tape is helically wrapped 180° around a rapidly rotating drum with a small embedded record head. The tape is positioned at a slight angle to the equatorial plane of the drum. This results in a recording format in which recorded tracks run diagonally across the tape from one edge to the other. Recorded tracks are parallel to each other but are at an angle to the edge of the tape. (Van Bogart 1995)

Amid the complex of factors determining the resolution of video signals, each media format brings its own signature to picture and sound. VHS is one system for processing the electromagnetic waves of a video signal and encoding them into magnetic tape. Such a signal comprises complex synchronization, brightness, and colour information relating to a specified number of image frames every second, each comprising two interlaced fields of horizontal scan lines. Synchronization data determine the vertical position of these lines in a succession of rapid, downward scanning sequences through which each frame is resolved on a screen, by electrons fired from a cathode-ray tube in horizontal waves, or distributed across a field of gaseous or liquid cells. The ability to encode and reproduce such a signal accurately is partly a matter of how it is electronically mediated in order to be written into tape of a specific width and density. Videotape has a lower bandwidth than broadcast video signals and relies on the modulation and 'downconversion' of subcarrier waves to encode signals. For example, an NTSC video signal contains chrominance information in a subcarrier wave with a frequency of 3.58 MHz, which is downconverted to 629 KHz by standard VHS systems to fit on VHS tape. The NTSC signal has a resolution of 330 lines but VHS downconversion reduces this to 240 lines, so colour density, sharpness, and brightness are approximations of the original resolution (Capelo and Brenner 1998). The accurate reproduction of line positions in each scanning sequence comprising a video frame depends on the condition of tape, recording-head, and playback-head components and the dynamic stability of their interactions. These material factors are subject to compromise by a range of internal and external forces, which destabilize recorded signals and the capacity of tape transport mechanisms to align them accurately.

> **Hydrolysis**: The chemical process in which scission of a chemical bond occurs via reaction with water. The polyester chemical bonds in tape binder polymers are subject to hydrolysis, producing alcohol and acid end groups. Hydrolysis is a reversible reaction, meaning that the alcohol and acid groups can react with each other to produce a polyester bond and water as a by-product. In practice, however, a severely degraded tape binder layer will never fully reconstruct back to its original integrity when placed in a very low-humidity environment. (Van Bogart 1995)

> **Hygroscopic**: The tendency of a material to absorb water. An effect related to changes in moisture content or relative humidity. The hygroscopic expansion coefficient of a tape refers to its change in length as it takes up water upon an increase in the ambient relative humidity. (Van Bogart 1995)

The stability of signals recorded to video tape and the condition of mechanisms for their reproduction were factors affected significantly by the advent of video-rental culture. The rental phenomenon has provided an unparalleled context for the intensive circulation of recorded media, in which rental goods are afforded a strategic mobility uncommon to their non-rental counterparts, repeatedly exchanging contact with different hands, apparatuses, and domestic environments and associated with increased 'wear and tear'. This form of distribution can be characterized by the elastic movement particular to licensed lending practices, in which rented objects move outward from an originary point in a locale and then return, the duration of this process strictly controlled and, in commercial contexts, economized. This configuration of materials, people, finance, and the transformations they enact together, comprises an assemblage of relations in the wider field of relations that each phenomenon co-produces (Deleuze and Guattari 1988), and a social-material space of home-video practice that co-constitutes the broader relations of landscape (Lefebvre 1991). There are specifications for the environmental and technical conditions according to which video tape should be treated to prolong preservation, and while rental stores with tape collections may well adhere to these where possible, there is a significant aspect in which the care of a tape is beyond their control. This concerns its life in the landscape beyond their doors.

Lubricant: A component added to the magnetic layer of a tape to decrease the friction between the head and the tape. (Van Bogart 1995)

Each instance of taking a tape from a rental store on a journey to a place where it is played involves transitions in environmental factors: changing temperature, humidity, and air quality; proximity to surfaces bearing dust, grease, skin cells, traces of liquids; contact with machine parts prone to condensation and the transfer of matter from passing tape. Each instance of taking a tape from a video library on such a journey enacts new transformations across its various surfaces and these accumulate in the unfolding experiences of image and sound that the tape and its associated machinery permits, producing effects that become ever more tangible and affective (Marks 2002). These effects are complicit in producing a space of social-material relations, marking the dynamic entanglement of multiple agencies configured through video rental practice and other social-material practices that intersect it, constantly overwriting an unfinished record in the abstract hand of material instability that fosters molecular exchanges between forms, blurring their edges, enacting their diffusion through space and time, testifying to the relative and provisional nature of boundaries which material formations and practices perform (Barad 2003).

Magnetic particles: The magnetic particles incorporated in the binder to form the magnetic layer on a magnetic tape. Iron oxide, chromium dioxide, barium ferrite, and metal particulate are various examples of magnetic pigment used in commercial tapes. (Van Bogart 1995)

Video rental was not a planned aspect of home-video development (Secunda 1990). The potential of the medium for motion-picture distribution was only accidentally realized against the backdrop of widespread film-industry suspicion and fear over copyright infringement, although prerecorded video content was to become a larger grossing industry than theatrical film releases by the late 1980s (Secunda 1990), in spite of unlicensed,

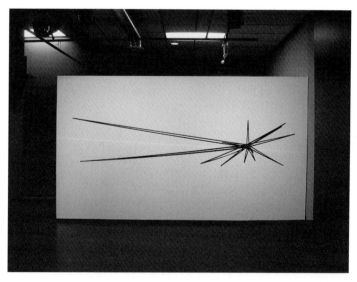

FIGURE 48.2 15 locations around Limelight Video; 6 m × 1 m wall-drawing with single VHS tape strip (Jem Noble)

'pirate-video' sales on an international scale. Seventy per cent of the $10 billion consumer video market at that time was generated by video rental practices (Secunda 1990), which had emerged through the coincidence of compact video cassette size, hyper-competitive market pricing of VCRs, high purchase-prices for prerecorded content, small-business innovation, and unanticipated consumer demand for seeing films outside of the cinema context, before being screened on television (Lardner 1987).

Licensed video rental services developed from the prerecorded video market, initiated in 1977 when Detroit entrepreneur Andre Blay acquired rights from Twentieth Century Fox Film Corporation to sell some of its titles on video tape. Blay established a mail-order distribution company called Video Club of America which generated widespread interest, soon after which other such operations proliferated across the continent, initially offering films for sale before realizing the potential for renting them to customers unwilling to pay high purchase prices ($70–$80) but happy to rent a tape for a night for $10 or under (Secunda 1990). Dominated by the VHS format from the late 1970s until the rise of DVD after its emergence in the late 1990s, economies of video rental practice were physically localized, partly owing to the size and weight of tapes— small enough to be easily carried, but too large and heavy for cheap postal distribution and retrieval—partly owing to the loss of chargeable time associated with postal transit, and partly owing to the ease of browsing and the spontaneity that a local space affords. These factors were eventually mediated by the spread of Internet communications and smaller, lighter, cheaper-to-produce DVD media, together enabling large-scale rent-by-post operations such as Netflix, launched in 1998, and by the development of on-demand streaming services tested since the early 1990s and proliferating as major commercial propositions after the turn of the millennium alongside free and subscription-based peer-to-peer file-sharing operations.

> **Mistracking**: The phenomenon that occurs when the path followed by the read head of the recorder does not correspond to the location of the recorded track on the magnetic tape. Mistracking can occur in both longitudinal and helical scan recording systems. The read head must capture a given percentage of the track in order to produce a playback signal. If the head is too far off the track, recorded information will not be played back. (Van Bogart 1995)

> *Limelight Video began life in 1983 as Video Stop with a small stock of eclectic movies, specializing in foreign and independent movies. About the same time, the store came to the attention of Don Newton, who was operating one of BC's first video stores on Robson Street in downtown Vancouver, who watched as the store acquired an impressive collection of movies. In 1992, Newton purchased Video Stop from Paul Norton, and shortly afterwards, changed the name of the store to Limelight Video. At that time, the video business had changed dramatically, with large chain stores driving out the small independent stores. It was recognized that in order to survive in the increasingly competitive business that we had to continue to specialize, to find a niche in the market, to create a video store that was unlike any of the chain stores. (http://www.limelightvideo.ca/about.html/ accessed 2 July 2009).*

> **PET**: Abbreviation for polyethylene terephthalate. The polymeric substrate material used for most magnetic tapes. (Van Bogart 1995)

> *We continue to purchase foreign and independent films, but over the years we have built up a diverse stock of documentaries, historical films, war films, musicals and music films, Academy Award winners, spiritual films, stand-up comedy, films about art and artists, travel films, science fiction and horror films, and many more. In addition, we have grouped together world-famous*

directors, such as Alfred Hitchcock, François Truffaut, Akira Kurosawa, Federico Fellini, Werner Herzog, and some lesser known directors from all over the globe. We have also acquired films from almost every film-producing country in the world, countries often represented at film festivals, but rarely seen in video stores—from South-East Asia, the Middle East, Australia and New Zealand, Russia, the British Isles, India, South Africa, India, and many other countries. And we have almost every Canadian film ever released on video (http://www.limelightvideo.ca/about.html/ accessed 2 July 2009).

Polymer: A long organic molecule made up of small, repeating units (literally, many mers). Analogous to a freight train, where each individual unit is represented by a freight car. At very high magnification, a chunk of polymer would resemble a bowl of cooked spaghetti. Plastic materials are polymers. The strength and toughness of plastics is due, in part, to the length of its polymer molecules. If the chains (links in the freight train) are broken by hydrolysis, the shorter chains will impart less strength to the plastic. If enough polymer chains are broken, the plastic will become weak, powdery, or gooey. See Binder. (Van Bogart 1995)

Print through: The condition where low frequency signals on one tape winding imprint themselves on the immediately adjacent tape windings. It is most noticeable on audio tapes where a ghost of the recording can be heard slightly before the playback of the actual recording. (Van Bogart 1995)

Limelight Video was a five-minute walk from where I was living with my family for the duration of our eight-month stay in Vancouver. We passed it frequently in our daily routines and often went in. We had arrived from the UK in December 2008 to an uncharacteristically heavy and lingering snowfall for the temperate West Coast climate and Limelight's cosy atmosphere of tightly packed shelf stacks, its friendly staff, and its vast video collection provided an instant, welcoming attraction that continued to feed our hunger for compelling films until our departure. Our familiarity with the store and with Adam O. Thomas, then manager, was the foundation of Adam's approach to Don Newton proposing Limelight's support for the artist's residency I was undertaking at VIVO, to assist my research into VHS video through the provision of access to its database of rental histories. Limelight has around 12,000 VHS tapes in its collection, at least 60 per cent of which are rare international titles unavailable in any other format.

Scission: The process in which a chemical bond in a molecule is broken either by reaction with another molecule, such as water, or by the absorption of a high energy photon. (Van Bogart 1995)

Stick slip: The process in which (1) the tape sticks to the recording head because of high friction; (2) the tape tension builds because the tape is not moving at the head; (3) the tape tension reaches a critical level, causing the tape to release from and briefly slip past the read head at high speed; (4) the tape slows to normal speed and once again sticks to the recording head; (5) this process is repeated indefinitely. Characterized by jittery movement of the tape in the transport and/or audible squealing of the tape. (Van Bogart 1995)

Sticky shed: The gummy deposits left on tape path guides and heads after a sticky tape has been played. The phenomenon whereby a tape binder has deteriorated to such a degree that it lacks sufficient cohesive strength so that the magnetic coating sheds on playback. The shedding of particles by the tape as a result of binder deterioration that causes dropouts on VHS tapes. (Van Bogart 1995)

The most-rented single VHS cassette in Limelight Video, to be distinguished from the most rented film on VHS (associated with more than one tape copy), was *Harold and Maude* (dir. Hal Ashby 1971; Paramount Home Video 1979), with 666 rental journeys along the trajectory of its existence at the time of my project and registered on the

Limelight database as having been acquired by Video Stop in 1987. I first saw this film with my partner many years before on VHS, courtesy of our local video library in Bristol, Twentieth Century Flicks, where we were allowed to see it free of charge in conjunction with renting another title, owing to the poor condition of the aged tape. My interest in VHS had been prompted by events marking the widespread commercial obsolescence of the format, and *Harold and Maude*—a black comedy and romantic drama dealing with issues of conformity and transgression—can be read as a pertinent dialectic where obsolescence is concerned. Harold is a dead-pan twenty-year-old, disillusioned with the social reality of his affluent family context in which he feels he has no place. As an expression of his malaise, he enacts the obsolescence he feels by realistically feigning acts of suicide before his disinterested, socialite mother. Harold takes comfort in habitually attending funerals, which is where he meets Maude, a 79-year-old with a similar ritual predilection motivated by different concerns. Maude is full of vigour, embracing life for all its possibility, overstepping boundaries, breaking rules, challenging the materialistic model of freedom that the conformist cultural backdrop of the story asserts. Thus begins a beautiful romance in which Harold's sense of futility is gradually worn away as participating in Maude's unbridled capers reveals his self-imposed confinement amid the contingent conventions of the dominant social order. Their romantic and physically intimate affair is cut short by Maude, who commits suicide on her eightieth birthday—a premeditated act born of her own sense of physical obsolescence determined by feelings of confinement amid the corporeal conventions of old age, offering a particularly individualistic take on freedom, arguably materialistic in its own way. This rupture finds uplifting resolution in the final scene as Harold abandons the last symbol of his existential malaise, a sports car he has converted into a hearse, over a cliff, walking into a positive future while the end credits roll, accompanied by the sound of Cat Stevens singing 'if you want to be free, be free'—anthemic in its support for the film's conclusion that a lesson in classical-liberal freedom and authenticity has been learned.

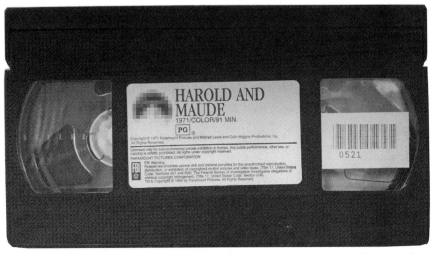

FIGURE 48.3 *Harold and Maude* cassette, Limelight copy (photograph: Adam O. Thomas)

Sticky tape: Tape characterized by a soft, gummy, or tacky tape surface. Tape that has experienced a significant level of hydrolysis so that the magnetic coating is softer than normal. Tape characterized by resinous or oily deposits on the surface of the magnetic tape. (Van Bogart 1995)

Stress: Force per unit area, such as pounds per square inch (psi). A tape wound on a reel with high tension results in a tape pack with a high interwinding stress. See tension. (Van Bogart 1995)

Substrate: Backing film layer that supports the magnetic layer in a magnetic tape. PET is currently the most commonly used tape substrate. (Van Bogart 1995)

I provided *Harold and Maude*'s 667th rental journey from Limelight Video, enfolding me into a temporally and spatially disparate community of people co-producing the same trajectory of material culture, sharing the same process of ritual exchange, swapping money for the same cassette and the promise of affective experience it embodies. I took the tape from the video library to my home, and to VIVO on Main Street to search for audiovisual traces of transformation associated with the effects of repeated use. Both cassette and tape were of surprisingly good quality, with few telltale marks of passage through hundreds of hands and machines around my neighbourhood. Its picture and sound had the same respectively diffuse and muted qualities that all VHS bears in comparison to today's video media, especially when filtering the textures of a 35mm print, with a subtle scattering of background snow or particulate 'dropout' throughout. The most intensive degradation was near the beginning (ironically affecting the copyright warning most severely) as Adam O. Thomas had told me to expect, given the increased strain on the tape at the end of the rewinding process: classic trapezoidal error, mistracking and decreased remanence, resulting in irregular chromatic displacement, down-scrolling static and audio distortion rendering original content indiscernible. Beautiful. Alongside this analysis of the tape, I examined its associated rental records, to which I had been granted access under strict terms of privacy, learning that detailed records only went back five years to retain space on the database. This recorded 29 journeys of the 667 the tape had shared, all associated with Limelight's current address. All locations except one were local. The sixteenth, moving in reverse sequence from my own rental, was to Revelstoke, a town in the provincial interior and a round trip of 1,130 km from the store. I decided to map the available information, assigning rental journey numbers to points corresponding with customer addresses, connecting each of these to the originary point of the video store with two lines, signifying an inward and outward journey. This was, of course, a highly approximate form of mapping. I had no idea whether the tape had been taken to the addresses of the people renting it, no inkling as to whether such components in the tape's trajectory were part of larger journeys involving different locations and purposes, or which routes may have been taken. While I had information relating to the number of days between the tape leaving the store and being returned, neither this temporal dimension, nor the overarching temporality of the documented history was represented in this way. The purpose of my map was to indicate a sequence of places implicated in the tape's history, and the kind of space they produced in relation to movement from a common point (see Penrose, this volume). Straight lines indicating this movement were lines 'as the crow flies', averages allowing for uncertain variations. The process was characterized by the inference of vectors from a set of discrete points, a process of tracking.

Tape transport: The mechanics used to guide and move the tape through the recording system and past the read and write heads of the recorder. The tape transport consists of the tape guide pins, capstan, rollers, tension controllers, etc. (Van Bogart 1995)

Tension: Force, or force per tape width. The force on a tape as it is transported through a recorder. A tape wound on a reel with high tension results in a tape pack with a high inter-winding stress. See stress. (Van Bogart 1995)

To elucidate the dynamic space of human–non-human entanglement represented by my partial and approximate map of the *Harold and Maude* cassette's rental trajectory, I wanted to re-familiarize it, re-figure its abstraction somehow, translate it back into the space, time, and experience of movement. I considered the possibility of enacting it, tracing an unbro-ken course in the landscape signifying the continuity and trajectory of the tape's unfolding being. The practice of artist Richard Long offered a distinct resource in this respect, partly comprising structurally and materially determined engagement in landscape: walking routes, performing actions, and leaving traces, proscribed by numerical systems, geograph-ical and material taxonomies, and idiosyncratic responses to found forms and features. Long's works are processes that speak to the dynamism and multiplicity of forces acting in and shaping the environment in which we participate, and the diverse temporalities and spatial scales enmeshed in their unfolding: astronomical, geological, meteorological, mate-rial, practical, and experiential. Although this practice is framed by an aesthetic distinction between natural and industrial worlds and a distanciation from the urban in the artist's preference for journeying (Long 1980), its formal signatures can serve just as well to address concerns with time, movement, and materiality in an expanded field of environmental forces including social, technological, and economic factors configuring the proliferation of materials in the built environment. Such forces are present in Richard Long's work, if not in his expressed concerns: for example, in the mass-production goods enfolded in his practice, such as a camera, clothing and camping gear, in petrochemically-assisted travel either side of each work's stated parentheses, in equipment and services facilitating production, exhibi-tion and trade of his images and installations, in the processes of hitchhiking and bicycling figured as materials in his early career.

Track angle: The angle that the track of a helical scan recording makes to the edge of the tape. This should correspond with the scan angle of the helical recorder—the angle that the tape makes to the equatorial plane of the rotating drum head. If the track angle and scan angle do not correspond, mistracking will occur. (Van Bogart 1995)

Richard Long often documents his landscape walks with photographs and text, maps, or purely textual works. His text works bear a sparse economy of words deliberately invoking the style of the wandering Japanese poets, resolved in an unmistakably distinct choice of fonts and colours. What is partly interesting about the sparsity of detail such works offer is the degree of abstraction by which they stand as records, making a complex, extended durational experience and pattern of material interactions almost immediately, if only approximately, intelligible, compressing temporal detail just as the conjunction of acciden-tal marks in a recording medium flattens the temporal order of their production. In Long's work walks are sculptural performances, or dynamic sculptures—aestheticized actions and entanglements producing spaces, forms, and patterns comprising landscape, leaving their own kinds of traces with different degrees of intention, manipulation, and indifference. The documents of such works extend their agency as associated material remains and as objects of contemplation, and Long even describes their intelligible rendering in the imagination of an observer as a kind of space, suggesting a sculptural reach over which he indicates

M   I   N   D
R   O   L   L

BEARING A VHS VIDEO TAPE IN MIND

A 54.2 KM BICYCLE RIDE IN WEST VANCOUVER

TRACKING IN REVERSE ORDER THE APPROXIMATE ELASTIC MOVEMENT
OF A RENTAL VHS VIDEO TAPE OF THE FILM HAROLD AND MAUDE
THROUGH THE CITY

BETWEEN LIMELIGHT VIDEO ALMA STREET AND CUSTOMER ADDRESSES
AS FAR AS ARCHIVAL RECORDS AND PHYSICAL CONDITIONS ALLOW
A CONTINUOUS JOURNEY

CANADA SUMMER 2009

FIGURE 48.4 *After Richard Long (2)*. Digital vector image (Jem Noble)

some productive claim (Long 1980). While such space may be metaphoric, describing the durational intensities of thought rather than dimensional magnitudes (Bergson 1950), how a process is imagined through engagement with its record can well be understood as an extension of its relational form, connected by indexical folds of actions and experiences (see Wickstead, this volume). In Long's documentary works, processes are aestheticized selectively through photographic, cartographic, and textual descriptions that offer outlines for imaginative engagement with what transpired. What such a document describes is a fraction of detail in the events with which it connects, detail of indeterminate complexity and reach which is nonetheless part of the relational matrix collapsed in its appearance—a selective configuration of unfolding relations diffused through space and time, of entitive distribution (Gell 1998; Bains 2006).

> **Trapezoidal error**: A change in the angle of a recorded helical scan track. Can result in mis-tracking. (Van Bogart 1995)

The complexity of relations that objects co-produce, including their capacities as traces in emergent historical trajectories, is the structure of material and immaterial entanglements comprising form, encompassing its sensibility and intelligibility, but always exceeding the scope of both of these boundary-making registers (Barad 2003), not least in the unfinished nature of distributedness—the dynamism of relations unfolding in time (Lucas 2005). In this way we might consider the aesthetic abstraction of formalized indeterminacy in a Richard Long work as the distribution of a named event throughout its performance, its intersecting processual components and its recording—constructed in the cultural framework through which partially schematized actions and their co-formation with materials and processes of boundless, inaccessible detail can be considered 'art objects'—as a parallel to the resolution of event as archaeology and of durational phenomena as data recording. That is, we might consider these as apparently discrete conjunctions of aspects and relations that are, in fact, continually extending, distributing and disturbing the integrity of agencies they index: as the tips of proverbial icebergs, their extent a provisional notion masking historic and emergent diffusions, infusions, transfusions, and confusions that deny the possibility of absolute boundaries—of persistent determinate form.

ACKNOWLEDGEMENTS

Thanks to: Kika Thorne, Asa Mori, Dinka Pignon, Sharon Bradley, Amy Kazymerchyck, and VIVO Media Arts; Adam O. Thomas, Don Newton, and Limelight Video; Fareed Armaly; A and M.

REFERENCES

Alberro, Alexander and Stimson, Blake (eds.). 1999. *Conceptual Art: A Critical Anthology.* Cambridge, MA: MIT Press.

Bains, Paul. 2006. *The Primacy of Semiosis.* Toronto: University of Toronto Press.

Barad, Karen. 2003. Posthumanist Performativity: Toward an Understanding of How Matter Comesto Matter. *Signs: Journal of Women in Culture and Society* 28(3): 801–31.

Bennett, Jane. 2010. *Vibrant Matter.* Durham, NC: Duke University Press.

Bergson, Henri. 1950. *Time and Free Will: An Essay on the Immediate Data of Consciousness.* London: George Allen & Unwin.

Broadcast Engineering. 2008. JVC Ends VCR Production after 32 Years. Available at: <http://broadcastengineering.com/products/jvc-ends-vcr-production-years-1103/> (accessed 12 June 2009).

Capelo, Gregory R. and Brenner, Robert C. 1998. *VCR Troubleshooting and Repair,* 3rd edn. Oxford: Butterworth-Heinemann.

Daniel, Eric D., Mee, Denis C., and Clark, Mark H. 1999. *Magnetic Recording: The First 100 Years.* Piscataway, NJ: IEEE Press.

Deleuze, Gilles and Guattari, Félix. 1988. *A Thousand Plateaus: Capitalism and Schizophrenia,* tr. Brian Massumi. Minneapolis: University of Minnesota Press.

DeNora, Tia. 2000. *Music In Everyday Life.* Cambridge: Cambridge University Press.

Dewey, John. 1980 [1934]. *Art As Experience.* New York: Perigee Books.

Dobrow, Julia R. (ed.). 1990. *Social and Cultural Aspects of VCR Use.* Hillsdale, NJ: Lawrence Erlbaum Associates.

Finneran, J. (ed.). 1996. *The Collected Poems of W. B. Yeats.* New York: Scribner.

Ganley, Gladys D. and Ganley, Oswald H. (eds.). 1987. *Global Political Fallout: The VCR's First Decade.* Norwood, NJ: Ablex Publishing.

Gell, Alfred. 1998. *Art and Agency.* Oxford: Clarendon Press.

Hartshorne, C., Weiss. P., and Burks, A. (eds.). 1931–58. *The Collected Papers of Charles Sanders Peirce.* Cambridge, MA: Harvard University Press.

Katz, Mark. 2004. *Capturing Sound: How Technology Has Changed Music.* Berkeley, CA: University of California Press.

Lardner, James. 1987 *Fast Forward: Hollywood, the Japanese and the Onslaught of the VCR.* New York: W. W. Norton.

Latour, Bruno. 1993. *We Have Never Been Modern.* Cambridge, MA: Harvard University Press.

Long, Richard. 1980. *Five, six, pick up sticks, seven, eight, make them straight.* Screen print on card. London: Curwen Press.

Lucas, Gavin. 2005. *The Archeology of Time*. London and New York: Routledge.

Lefebvre, Henri. 1991. *The Production of Space*, tr. Donald Nicholson-Smith. Oxford: Blackwell.

Marks, Laura U. 2002. *Touch: Sensuous Theory and Multisensory Media*. Kindle edition. Minneapolis: University of Minnesota Press.

Secunda, Eduardo. 1990. VCRs and Viewer Control Over Programming: An Historical Perspective. In *Social and Cultural Aspects of VCR Use*, ed.Julia R. Dobrow, pp. 9–24. Hillsdale, NJ: Lawrence Erlbaum Associates.

Van Bogart, John W. C. 1995. Magnetic Tape Storage and Handling: A Guide for Libraries and Archives. The Council on Library and Information Resources, Washington, DC. Available at: <http://www.clir.org/pubs/reports/pub54/> (accessed 10 June 2009).

CHAPTER 49

....

AUTOANTHROPOLOGY, MODERNITY, AND AUTOMOBILES

....

PIERRE LEMONNIER

49.1 INTRODUCTION

....

THE mere presence of a chapter about classic cars, written by an ethnographer of New Guinea in a volume dedicated to the archaeology of the contemporary world is a theoretical statement of sorts. It means that, notwithstanding the question Latour and I asked about the possible differences between 'traditional' and 'modern' technologies (Latour and Lemonnier 1994: 18), which several authors in this volume rightly address apropos 'modernity' or 'late modernity' (Harrison and Schofield 2010), I consider that some key features of the relationship that human beings build by making and using material things are common to humanity at large. By describing and analysing the interactions of a particular cohort of French (male) amateurs with old sports and racing cars, I aim at filling some poorly developed domains of the ethnography of car cultures, for, as Miller (2001a: 7) rightly put it, this particular strain of material culture studies lacks 'an empathetic account of car consumption in particular social contexts'. I do this in line with my previous approach, with respect to an anthropology of objects and techniques, that does not leave out material actions on the material world (Lemonnier 1992, 1993, 2012). A Maussian inspired paper, if you prefer, that raises an anthropological question having to do with what is at the core of the anthropology of objects, techniques, and material actions, namely: What do interactions with the material world do that words alone could not do? The answer I propose is that baby-boomers interested in old cars build, in a partially non-verbal way, a core of shared representations, emotions, practices, and strategies.

To get to this result, which parallels what I have theorized about particular artefacts of the Anga of New Guinea (Lemonnier 2012), I have had a retrospective glance at experiences in my own life, with no particular agenda regarding 'auto-anthropology' (Harrison and Schofield 2010: 92, 196; Muncey 2010). Beyond the poor pun, the 'auto-' category here refers to the particular object I focused on (my old car) and to the way I have enmeshed and put together historical sources, personal experiences, souvenirs, and observations. This interpretation of bits and remains of my own kid's or teenager's material culture is not a 'family archaeology' (Ulin 2009), for I have not excavated anything but boxes of model cars, piles of magazines, and other boxes full of photographs, museum catalogues, and race programmes. It is rather a sort of ethno-history, based on memories of the 1950s and 1960s that are only that, memories, but also on a participant-observation that goes back to the early 1970s (when I was seriously planning to undertake an ethno-psychiatry of motor racing [sic!]). I have no notebooks about it, but even though I was already an aficionado, I rapidly tried to have a sort of 'view from afar', if I dare quote Lévi-Strauss (1983).

Actually, once one agrees that the study of material culture is by definition multidisciplinary (e.g. Latour and Lemonnier 1994; Graves-Brown 2000; Buchli and Lucas 2001; Dobres 2005; Knappett 2005; Tilley et al. 2006; Harrison and Schofield 2010: 89–105), whether the ongoing interactions with particular cars of the mid-twentieth century belongs to archaeology, history, or anthropology does not matter much. After all, it is certain that the study of the remains of the contemporary world leads us 'beyond the traditional realms of archaeology' (Harrison and Schofield 2009: 198). However, if I follow Olivier (2011; see also Olivier, this volume), for whom archaeology, 'because it questions objects that have survived from the past, is not that much about what the past times looked like, but rather about what happened to those things made by men of the past', then the life-story of classic cars also belongs to archaeology (see also Merriman, this volume).

Moreover, bearing witness to a near past, classic cars *are* remarkable objects. First, unlike other cars, they never became 'ordinary objects' (Dant and Martin 2001) and remain an illustration of 'the rendering abstract of any practical goal in the interests of speed and prestige, formal connotation, technical connotation, forced differentiation, emotional cathesis, and projection in fantasy' (Baudrillard 2005 [1968]: 67). But, most of all, unlike the millions of destroyed or recycled cars, those sports cars considered as 'classic' (as early as the 1970s) constitute a small minority of vehicles that have survived and are still used. Indeed, many of them have begun a second racing career and have remained almost unchanged over forty or fifty years. They therefore illustrate what has to be done so that artefacts do *not* become archaeological items. As we shall see below, some of those classic cars are an illustration of the energy deployed year after year to freeze an object in time and protect it from decay. Not only they have not become 'hazardous waste' (Burström 2009: 133), but often the car you can see now on a circuit is supposedly the one that a given driver drove on a given circuit on a particular day, or even at a particular moment of a race: during the tests or as it was on the starting grid. They also counter the idea that new cars are always better (Sachs 1984: 136–49).

The anthropological contextualization of these artefacts nevertheless sheds light on the making of the European car culture in the 1950–60s, i.e. on a system of thoughts and material actions that pervade our everyday life and which we now take for granted. That was the period when racing cars were explicitly associated with the idea of progress, because the novelties tested on the track were supposed to be the makings of tomorrow's car. Then, as today, racing cars were 'impressive, active manifestations of human technical ability' (Shackleford 1999: 188). As for the amateurs—mostly men in their sixties—who can *now* afford to buy, drive, and collect these cars, their interest in racing cars of the 1950s and 1960s is a direct result of their having grown up in a particular cultural and historical ambience in which cars had a particular place and importance. They were raised in a car-related civilization in rapid development. Such was my case in the mid-1960s, when I first encountered a version of car culture that differed from mine. And this is where my case study starts.

49.2 INDIVIDUAL MEMORIES, SHARED PAST, AND COLLECTIVE PRACTICES

'Why do French people drive on the wrong side of the road?' I was too young then to fully appreciate this excellent example of British humour, but thanks to the father of my correspondent, a mere 30 minutes after I first set foot in England, fifty years ago, I already knew that car driving was something different in Britain. A few years later, I abruptly experienced this difference the moment I drove my own car out of the Southampton ferry terminal. A narrow, winding road at twilight in pouring rain and *on the wrong side* of the road turned my long-awaited encounter with British traffic into a nightmare, even though my car was a *right*-hand drive, namely a 1947 MG TC. That was also when I realized my enthusiasm for old racing and sports cars had long since turned into a kind of neurotic endeavour. Peering through the watery windscreen of a nearly brake-less car known for its unpredictable steering, what could have told me where the road might be?

Such an anecdote would be trifling if it were not commonplace among car collectors, each of whom has dozens of similar stories about both material encounters with their beloved object and the ins and outs of their general relationship to 'classic cars'—in this case those raced in the 1950s and 1960s, before the demands of aerodynamics radically modified the shape of sports cars. From an anthropological point of view, it is remarkable that this sort of *individual* relationship with an artefact is one of those physical and mental interactions with a piece of material culture that create, reproduce, and modify an ongoing network of *shared* practices, knowledge, and feelings among a series of individuals, in this case a *group* of amateurs. The mere mention of the desultory road-holding of a TC is enough to immediately unleash an almost infinite flurry of speech, images, and memories that *any* enthusiast (even someone you meet for the first time) would enjoy and fuel with his own piece of classic-car culture.

Indeed, whenever two or more classic-car aficionados come together, a single sentence may trigger a similar Wikipedia®-like deluge of references to particular models, racing feats, pilots, circuits, technical peculiarities, or comparisons with the 'old times'. Higgledy-piggledy they will allude to a renowned pilot's greatest feat ('Jim Clark's Lotus 23 at the 1962 Nürburgring'); to an outstanding racer of the 1950s–60s (there are dozens of those); to the particular sound of an engine (the screaming of a BRM V16); or to some technical breakthrough (disk breaks on the 1953 Jaguar C-Type). But most digressions about classic cars would make sense for several hundreds of thousands of former little boys of the 1950s. In Wittgenstein's words, these personal references to racing and sports cars of the past share a 'family resemblance' (Wittgenstein 1953; Needham 1978).

Besides memory-prompting phrases, many contemporary *practices*, ranging from model making to car maintenance in one's own workshop or attending specialized events, trigger similar evocations and cross-references of bits and pieces of classic-car culture. It is noteworthy that these are collective activities; you miss most of the fun if you go to a race or show alone. Also striking is the solidity and durability of this mixture of memories with past and *present* material collective practices.

49.3 BOYS, DINKY TOYS, AND CAR CULTURE: WHEN CLASSIC CARS WERE JUST CARS

To get a idea of what cars, racing cars, and the road-going *Gran Turismo* (GT) car were in the boy's world of the 1950s, one must think back to a time when the two main technologies that occupy kids' leisure time today—TV and the Internet—did not exist, and portable radios and record players were scarce or still to come (see Schiffer 1991 for the US situation). There were 350,000 TV sets in France in 1956 (Antoine and Oulif 1962: 132). Boys played at being Robin Hood, Tintin, or any hero of the typically French (and Belgian) comic books. The middle-class and wealthy kids had electric trains and Dinky white-metal aircraft. But, most of all, boys possessed several (or dozens of) 1/43rd model cars (I will use 'Dinky Toys' as shorthand for a general category). I write 'boys' because this is what my own experience as a kid is about, and because I have observed (and counted) that those attending today's historic racing or car shows are over 90 per cent male. Women are as rare in classic car racing as they are in other kinds of circuit races. The important question of what was the equivalent of cars and toy cars for girls in the 1950s is pending.

Daily games with 'petites autos' were part of being a boy in an industrial world in which cars were becoming a key aspect of almost everyone's material culture: there were only 2.7 million cars in France in 1954, but these figures were to be multiplied by ten over the next fifty years. Cars were everywhere and were used to go from one place to another, but they were present also in adult conversations and daily newspapers. News about speeding machines was sometimes overwhelming, as in 1955: alongside the Le Mans disaster,[1] this was the year of the Citroën DS, but also that of the 'Caravelle' aircraft and of the World Speed Record of the 'BB' and 'CC' electric locomotives (both reached 331 km/h).

The large place given to car-related news was proof of sorts that automobiles were important things in this world. The biggest popular weekly *Paris-Match* (1.8 million copies a week in 1958) devoted several pages to automobile-related events: the new models of the upcoming 'Salon de l'Auto' (often visited by the whole family) and the annual race at Le Mans, but also the construction of motorways, the opening of new assembly lines, sport or cinema stars with their glowing Cadillacs, and of course the details of every possible mechanical breakthrough. In the weekly 'newsreels' at the cinema, too, racing cars were presented as an example of the ongoing innovations that ordinary cars would soon adopt, while each team also advertised for various makes of accessories (brakes, headlights, batteries, tires, oil, etc.). The boys' magazines had a special section devoted to automobiles and their technical aspects (Figure 49.1).

The weekly issues of these journals also featured the achievements of drivers and kids would pretend they were Fangio, Ascari, Berha, Moss, Hawthorn, or Collins. Few boys got *The Racing Car Explained* (Pomeroy 1963) or *The Racing Car Pocketbook*, by D. Jenkinson (1962), who was Sir Stirling Moss's passenger in the Mercedes that won the 1955 Mille Miglia, one of the greatest car-racing feats ever, but books by or about Fangio (Merlin 1959; Fangio and Giambertone 1961), Moss (1964) or Trintignant (1957) were among boys' regular reading.

---

[1] More than 80 people were killed in the main stand by the debris of a Mercedes.

FIGURE 49.1 The 'Starter' pages in the boys' magazine *Spirou* are fixed in the mind of hundreds of thousand of those who were boys in the 1950s. The dedicated website <http://www.toutspirou.fr/Automobile/spirouet.htm> lists all the cars drawn by the artist Jidehem (J-D-M) between 1950 and 1987 (reproduced with permission from Editions Dupuis)

49.4 CLASSIC CARS BECOME HISTORIC OBJECTS (1960–70S)

In the mid-1960s, motorsport was developing in France, and most magazines (the weekly *L'Auto-journal* and the monthlies *L'Automobile* and *L'Action automobile et touristique*) comprised information on car racing; but several monthly publications also appeared that were dedicated solely to sports cars and car racing (track and rally): *Moteurs*, *Sport-Auto*,

Virage-Auto (a Belgian journal), and then *Echappement*. Specialized bookshops in Paris sold copies of British magazines, notably *Motor Sport* (since 1924) and, from 1965, *Cars and Car Conversion*, full of DIY information and largely devoted to maintaining sports cars and improving their performances. *Road and Track* (founded in 1947 in New York State) gave a glimpse of racing in the US.

Most magazines dealing with cars in general contained an historical section on 'legendary' cars; but as early as the mid-1960s, new publications began specializing in old cars only (*l'Album du Fanatique de l'automobile*). Again, French amateurs could get their hands on copies of *Thoroughbred & Classic Cars* (later known as *Classic Cars*, in the UK), launched in Britain in 1973.

The late 1960s also marked the appearance of specialized books. Those books in English written by renowned drivers and journalists (John Bolster, Dennis Jenkinson, Wilson McComb, Doug Nye, Paul Skilleter, or Timothy Nicholson, all considered as world experts) were the main source of information about classic cars. In particular, extremely well-documented and -illustrated booklets were published, notably by Profile Publications in the 1960s and 1970s, for the sake of model-making.

Simultaneously, famed racing-cars arrived in ad hoc museums. In England, the Montagu Motor Museum, founded in 1952, became the National Motor Museum in 1968. In France, a Musée de l'Automobile opened right on the Le Mans circuit in 1961. In Paris, the Retromobile motor show, devoted exclusively to 'vintage and classic cars', was held for the first time in 1975 (and every year since).

49.5 MODELS OR THE REAL THING? CLASSIC CARS AND THEIR SUBSTITUTES

The 1/43rd models were not yet the affordable little jewels they have become with the help of 'chemically milled' small pieces (wire wheels) and later on of the technique of 'photo-etching'; but in the late 1960s and early '70s, dozens and then hundreds of models of different sports and racing cars were produced after a British maker (John Day) had the idea of selling white-metal kits. Thanks to the growing number of sources of information about cars, it was now possible to produce an accurate model of almost any 'important' car, past or present. Choosing a model, making it or merely 'improving' it by adding a tiny fire extinguisher or roll-bar gave the amateurs an indirect but material contact with dream(ed) cars. A model became a sort of concentrate of the knowledge, material practices, memories, and feelings at the heart of a baby-boomer's complex relationship with the racing cars of their youth. Collecting a classic car was another.

In the late 1960s, sports cars were supposed to attract girls, but they also epitomized several of the ideas or myths then associated with cars: speed, freedom, (supposed) male technological ability (Shackleford 1999). For those—still quite rich young bourgeois—who could not buy a recent Porsche, Maserati, or Ferrari, and not even the revolutionary Jaguar E-Type revealed in 1961, the less expensive sports cars of the day (e.g. Austin-Healey 3000, Alfa-Romeo GT, Lancia Fulvia, MGB, Triumph TR4) were substitutes of the unaffordable GT cars.

FIGURE 49.2 Where it all started: the September 1965 issue of *Sport-Auto* in which this test was published (Rosinski 1965) also comprised a visit to the Shelby-Cobra factory in Los Angeles, and road tests comparing the MGB with the Triumph TR4. Another test of the TC was done in *Champion* in 1969 by the Formula 1 driver Jean-Pierre Beltoise (reproduced with permission from Mondadori France)

Without exception, all these 'ordinary' sports cars of the 1960s (and later 1970s) are now considered as 'classics', whatever their mechanical sophistication, rarity, or racing past.

Of course, a third- or fourth-hand road-going sports car produced in the tens of thousands differs from a racing car designed and assembled in order to maximize lightness, strength, endurance, durability, and speed. Yet, thanks to your classic-car knowledge, you knew that your particular model of ordinary sports car had effectively been raced at Le Mans. Or that it had had at least a famed racing career. Therefore, it *was* also a racing car and you had something in common with the great drivers. Anyway, a sound old Triumph TR, Porsche 356, or MGB cost at least double what I was given to buy a safe five-year-old Renault 8 (5,000 FF, i.e. £400 at the time) as my first car, but I had been dreaming of an MG TC since I first saw pictures of it as a teenager (Figure 49.2). I found one and I soon had the confirmation that driving a TC with the windshield folded flat on a small bumpy country road at 100 km/h is a sort of sport. At that speed, even a glance at the speedometer is hazardous because it is located in front of the passenger's seat, which means you have to take your eyes off the road for a long second, during which time the car may decide to jump somewhere you do not want to go.

49.6 A Non-Objective Account of a Mental and Physical Encounter with a Classic Car

My old-school seasoned mechanic tried to improve the braking and, indeed, for years the car only veered *slightly* to one (unfortunately randomly changing) side of the road whenever I pushed hard on the pedal. As for the steering, he proposed replacing the original steering box with a Fiat one. 'No way!', I said for the sake of authenticity, and until my last kilometre with that car, I had to foresee its reactions in a series of more or less predictable situations: emergency braking, sneaking between a highway guardrail and a (too) long lorry, driving on the M4 Severn Bridge on a windy day. After a while, I got used to gently turning the steering wheel until I felt a resistance that proved the existence of a real mechanical link between my actions and the position of the car on the road. For more than a year I waited either for spare parts or for Monsieur Fernand to find time to look at my unconventional car. Actually, waiting month after month for some good news from the garage is a major feature of classic-car ownership and part of those individual practices that finally create a shared culture about particular cars.

France is a country where DIY is quite limited when it comes to cars. A few people do basic car servicing such as changing break-pads, spark-plugs, or motor oil, but it is my feeling that, in the UK, more complex mechanical operations or body-repair are much more common. For lack of space (I lived in a flat) and patience (I am hopelessly awkward with any tool), I limited my mechanical interventions to things I thought I could do—cleaning the brake drums, valve adjustment, carburettor synchronizing, etc. In truth, my personal involvement in the process was mainly finding spare parts from the UK. I knew by heart the 'Workshop Manual' and the specialist catalogues, so that obtaining spare parts for the brakes, water-pump, rev-counter, or exhaust pipe took less than a month. The radiator-shell proved to be a nightmare, for I first decided that I could have it repaired (welded, reshaped, and re-chromed) and tried all sorts of craftsmen (from jewellers to dentists and sheet-metal workers), all of which progressively destroyed the shell.

In addition to what was needed to get a safe and well-running TC, I decided to improve its appearance and bought two famous accessories by 'Brooklands': a steering wheel with four sets of spokes, and one 'racing screen'. In order to make my car look even more like a vintage (of the 1930s) racer, I added leather straps to hold the bonnet closed. I tried to make a dashboard in brushed metal but something went wrong in my *chaîne opératoire* so that I ruined several metal sheets and gave up. The car looked right when I was confident enough to drive it across the Channel for a circuit to various mythical places.

49.7 Out of Southampton: a Visit to Classic-Car Culture Paradise

Choosing a *British* classic sports car is meaningful in itself. According to amateurs' shared representations, it meant that you like driving a convertible in the countryside with the top down whatever the weather. It meant not looking concerned by the puddle of oil under the gear-box or engine seal. In the late 1960s, driving a classic in Britain also gave you some taste of an ambience unknown anywhere else, for in the 1950s and '60s, Great Britain had more champions, more racing-car makers, more world-famous racing teams, legendary circuits, racing schools, race formulas, magazines, than any other country. Saturday after-noon black-and-white TV programmes on saloon-car competitions were also unique, as were the BBC radio commentators, who gave an unforgettably vivid image of a Grand Prix. Needless to say, as much as using the other side of the road, the different 'roadscape' and motorways were something to which I had to seriously adapt my driving (Edensor 2004: 103; Merriman, this volume).

The several MG specialist shops I visited were Ali Baba's caverns run by knowledgeable people who just recognized the exact bolt, screws, or tiny spring I was trying to describe in my approximate English. Historic racing had not yet developed into a business involving the annual organization of dozens of international competitions, but major classic racers of the 1950s already took part in competitions organized by the Historic Sports Car Club (since 1966). There were two Maserati 250F's, a Jaguar D-Type, ERA's, etc. (Figure 49.3) at the first race I saw (at Castle Comb, I think). Those cars I knew mainly as Dinky Toys were scream-ing for real around the tracks, and racing as fast as ever, thanks to more modern tires, brake pads, and oil. Access to the cars in the paddock was free and easy then and a mere notice 'Motor racing is dangerous' would keep you from getting too close to the track.

These memories of my first trip with the TC lack ethno-historic precision, but their very melange is precisely the point I want to make: the interest in classic cars is fed by inter-related *practices*—maintaining cars, going to races, shows, workshops, making models,

FIGURE 49.3 Castle Comb in July 1970. Except for my Dinky Toys, it was the first time I saw a Maserati 250F (two, actually, one red and one blue). Top left are a Frazer-Nash and two BMWs. For an amateur, there is no doubt that the wheel arch and the wheel that appear between the two men are those of a Jaguar XK120 (photograph: Pierre Lemonnier)

manipulating books and journals, etc.—that deal as much with material action as with abstract information (see Penrose, this volume). Shopping at Toulmin's (near London), for instance, meant a convergence of memories, information, emotions, and desires relating as much to comics, newsreels, model making, reading of dozens of booklets, books, and articles about MGs, as visits to circuits or looking at hundreds of pictures, drawings, and cutaways (Chapman 2009). Similarly, a pair of Maserati 250F's encountered on a circuit brings to the fan's mind anything from pouring molten lead inside a Solido model (to improve its road (carpet) holding), to reading (one more time) an account of Fangio's breaking the lap record ten times in one race at Nürburgring.

Also noteworthy is the involvement of four senses in the relations with classic cars. Sight, because there are so many details to look at and compare, notably with what one has previously seen in images or reproduced on a model. Hearing, in order to appreciate the squeal of the tyres or listen to the superb sound of a door or a bonnet closing. Touch is essential to appreciate the lightness of an aluminium panel. Smell has a lot to do with the fragrance of hot burnt castor oil and old leather seats. The fortunate amateur may even feel the infrasound emitted by big V8 engines at full throttle. Only taste is left out.

49.8 Knowledge, Practices, and Emotions: the Material Makings of Shared Representations

Today, enough boys of the 1950s have grown into wealthy adults, so that the interest in classic cars has evolved into a business. Historic racing has flourished, and there are over 900 classic-car shows a year in Great Britain alone. There are more and more classic-car sellers and numerous workshops maintain classics. Some fabricate 'replicas' of famed cars (also known as 'recreations' or 'continuations'). There also exist companies that transport classics and others that build timber garages; photographers who offer studios adapted to cars; high-security private car-park storage for classics, etc. Model cars are offered by the thousands and, even at the 1/43rd scale, some attain a level of detail that would have been unimaginable two decades ago (Figure 49.4). Hundreds of websites are devoted to every imaginable topic. Magazines flourish and now treat new topics such as controversies (why is a 1954 C-type replica made in 1983 more authentic than some other 'recreations'?) or the evolution of the classic-car market. 'We test the classics that you can buy' is a regular feature. Speculation is part of the game, and magazines carry magnificent advertisements for banks, auctions, or insurance companies. To paraphrase Miller (2000), classic-car magazines are 'traps' for the amateurs.

At the time of the trips to Britain I have described rather impressionistically, the amateur himself did most of the relational linking between different mutually reinforcing spheres of knowledge (including implicit knowledge) and practices, and magazines were the main physical means that gathered and potentially redistributed the various types of information fuelling a classic-car passion. Since the 1980s, the opportunities to share information and practices have increased considerably because, during any event related to classic cars

FIGURE 49.4 The high precision of some models that are the size of a Dinky Toy (1/43rd) simply leaves the amateur breathless. This model of Alberto Ascari's 1955 Lancia D 50 immediately evokes the Italian champion's plunge into the waters of Monaco harbour during the 1955 Grand Prix (model and photograph reproduced with permission from Steve Barnett)

(races, shows, auctions), the same clubs, models, 'automobilia', paintings, spare parts, books, etc., are present.

The network of practices related to classic cars has thrived, yet the relational aspect of the passion for cars is still that of the 1970s. The 'seamless web' (Hughes 1986) of ideas, objects, and material practices that make up an amateur's relationship with cars and pilots is composed of the convergence of three types of relations: (1) between a material object (a classic car) and its complex and changing historical and contemporary context; (2) between an individual and his own memories and ongoing interactions with classic cars year after year; and (3) between those people (mainly men in this chapter) who build and maintain social relations connected with classic cars. For each actor (amateur), the mixture of mutually interlocking engagements with dream cars is unique, but every amateur refers to a similar amalgam of memories, representations, and practices.

In other words, very private (Graves-Brown 2009), even sometimes intimate practices are at the core of intertwined thoughts and material actions that are enough to delineate a particular social grouping: in this case, that comprised of those French men in their fifties and sixties that have experienced, and enjoyed, in their own life, most of what I have described above as material aspect of a passion for old cars. By doing and making things in relation to these artefacts, that is, partly without words, men build a common 'classic car culture', made of a shared mixture of thoughts that is central to diverse ongoing social groupings and manifestations (car clubs, workshops, races, exhibitions, model-making, collection, etc.).

Now, what is striking is that, with regard to the complex question of the making of a shared world with things through material interactions, the technologies that characterize 'supermodernity' (Gonzáles-Ruibal 2008) modify neither the elements of classic car culture nor the series of relations I have just exposed. They merely offer an endless possibility to elaborate them, notably thanks to websites. Looking at a model or photo already ignited a Wikipedia®-like conversation decades before websites existed. Also, it appears that some objects—the models made from a kit lovingly assembled, the real old car you manage to restore, or the one you maintain—are more conducive than others to concentrating information and memories, and to generating an endless flood of images, emotions, and plans for the future.

These two remarks raise important theoretical issues, even though my chapter addresses only marginally questions in the sociology of 'automobilities' (Featherstone 2004), *technologie culturelle* of cars, and archaeology of the contemporary world. With respect to sociology, and regarding cars in general, my allusions to the labyrinth of relations between baby-boomers, cars, sellers, banks, insurance companies, sponsors of races and shows, magazines, and auction companies are in line with Baudrillard's description of the mechanism of the *Consumer Society* (1998 [1970]). And sure enough, I have explored the car's 'capacity to empower, and to have a positive impact on sociality' (Dant and Martin 2001: 149), but in a way that has not much to do with mobility.

In passing, nostalgia is only one ingredient of the shared mixture of contemporary practices, knowledge, and feelings converging to classic cars that I have described. What baby-boomers do while interacting with classic cars is much more than contemplating the passage of time (Burström 2009: 141), and more than a result of the 'inertia of continuity' (Graves-Brown 2009: 203). My point is not about how some thousands of men born in the late 1940s recall their boyhood. It is about the numerous manners in which they materially refer to a key artefact of that past—famous racing cars and their diverse substitutes—in a way that makes them engage immediately in particular kind of conversations and practices with whoever shares the same classic car culture.

Speaking of our exploration of the near past, the list of what this chapter does not deal with is long. I have not tried, for example, to link my ethno-history with automotive archaeology (e.g. Cotter 2005; Bailey et al. 2009; Burström 2009). However, although my main goal was not to answer the question 'what does archaeology add to our understanding that you can't get from the document?' (Holtorf and Piccini 2009: 10), my chapter nevertheless alludes to practices that have almost faded away (a particular way of driving and maintaining cars, of choosing them, of replacing them in a network of thoughts and actions, etc.) and tries to complement studies on car culture that straddle ethnography and archaeology (Pillsbury 1974; Sachs 1984; Moorhouse 1991; Post 1994; Graves-Brown 1997; O'Dell 1997; Shackleford 1999; Miller 2001b and the whole issue of *Theory, Culture & Society* devoted to 'automobilities' in 2004) by giving an idea of what a sports car was for a little boy, then teenager, when car production rocketed in Europe.

By contrast to studies on the archaeology of the recent past, my chapter is not about ruins, warfare, poverty, disasters, or reflection on modernity—e.g. the themes listed and illustrated in Harrison and Schofield apropos the archaeology of the contemporary past (2009: e.g. 189–90), but rather about fun and pieces of rather rich people's material culture— at least today, because classic car have become unaffordable. It is about marginal practices and people, yet not about 'subaltern identities and discourses' (Buchli and Lucas 2001). Moreover, looking as an anthropologist at historic noisy and polluting cars collected by wealthy enthusiasts is not *only* a way to grasp disappearing practices that once were anchored in artefacts now in the process of becoming archaeological. Nor is it only a way to glance at material interactions that paved the way to our contemporary usages of an artefact central to modernity. It is also, and first of all, a contribution to the anthropology of techniques and objects in general, highlighting the way people are prone to share a common world of ideas and practices in relation to material things.

Actually, the way in which my 'autoanthropology' complements other approaches to material culture of the recent past, including the archaeology of the contemporary, might reflect the kind of regularity—theoretical point, if I dare say—I want to stress. By mixing personal souvenirs, material *témoins*, and historical sources referring to various objects and practices relating to classic cars, I propose that, besides the exploration of 'The "System" of Automobility' (Urry 2004 quoted by Featherstone 2004: 2), that is itself embedded in a wider technical system (Lemonnier 1992: 4–11), we must also consider, on a reversed approach, how various domains of such a system of thoughts and material actions *converge* towards particular objects, particular cars, in a way that is at the core of the 'production of shared representations' (Godelier 2008).

As we have seen, the multiplicity, diversity, and time-depth of those physical actions related to the objects in question are crucial dimensions of their ability to bring people to act together. But if I now go back to the general question Latour and I asked about possible changes in the general relationship of human beings with artefacts in industrial societies, the case study of classic cars shows that objects and material actions may have a different status vis-à-vis non-verbal communication and the making of a shared world. In this respect, a 1954 Ferrari 375 Plus belonging to Ralph Lauren and admired at the Musée des Arts décoratifs in 2011 (exhibition 'L'art de l'automobile') has much in common with, say, a New Guinea garden fence or funerary drum (Lemonnier 2012). All these things—or rather, what people do and communicate because of them—put people together in a way words only could not achieve.

You may then observe a real piece of the True Cross, a mobile phone or iPod (Dant 2008) more or less do the same thing as an Anga sacred object or loved 1/43rd model, in the sharing of information, grouping people and making them do things together as social actors. Actually, this observation has fundamental theoretical consequences: it means that whatever we call 'the sacred' is based on relationships that do *not* differ from those of baby-boomers with iconic racing cars, and that we have to identify which artefacts have this role of 'resonators' (Lemonnier 2012). We need to understand in what respect the contemporary world modifies—or not—these relations that converge towards an object. One may think this brings us far from understanding late-modern material culture, but this is not the case: the Pentecostal pastor who baptized 21 of my New Guinea friends three months ago explained to the new believers that they 'now had the mobile phone of Jesus in their body'.

REFERENCES

Antoine, Serge and Oulif, Jean. 1962. La sociologie politique et la télévision. *Revue française de sciences politiques* 12(1): 129–44.

Bailey, Greg, Newland, Cassie, Nilsson, Anna, and Schofield, John. 2009. Transit, Transition: Excavating J641 VUJ. *Cambridge Archaeological Journal* 19: 1–27 (with contributions by Steve Davis and Adrian Myers).

Baudrillard, Jean. 1998 [1970]. *The Consumer Society: Myths and Structures*. London: Sage.

—— 2005 [1968]. *The System of Objects*. London: Verso.

Buchli, Victor and Lucas, Gavin. 2001. The Absent Present: Archaeologies of the Contemporary Past. In *Archaeologies of the Contemporary Past*, ed. Buchli and Lucas, pp. 3–18. London: Routledge.

Burström, Mats. 2009. Garbage or Heritage: The Existential Dimension of a Car Cemetery. In *Contemporary Archaeologies: Excavating Now*, ed. Cornelius Holtorf and Angela Piccini, pp. 131–43. Frankfurt: Peter Lang.

Chapman, Giles. 2009. *Haynes: The Classic Cutaways*. Sparkford: Haynes.

Cotter, Tom. 2005. *The Cobra in the Barn: Great Stories of Automotive Archaeology*. Minneapolis: Motorbooks.

Dant, Tim. 2008. iPod...iCon. *Studi Culturali* 5(3): 355–74.

Dant, Tim and Martin, Pete. 2001. By Car: Carrying Modern Society. In *Ordinary Consumption*, ed. Alan Warde and Jukka Gronow, pp. 143–57. London: Harwood.

Dobres, Marcia-Anne. 2005. *Technology and Social Agency*. Oxford and Malden, MA: Blackwell.

Edensor, Tim. 2004. Automobility and National Identity: Representation, Geography and Driving Practice. *Theory, Culture & Society* 21(4/5): 101–20.

Fangio Juan-Manuel and Giambertone, Marcello. 1961. *Ma vie à 300 à l'heure*. Paris: Plon.

Featherstone, Mike. 2004. Automobilities: An Introduction. *Theory, Culture & Society* 21(4/5): 1–24.

Godelier, Maurice. 2008. *In and Out of the West: Reconstructing Anthropology*. Charlottesville: University of Virginia Press.

Gonzáles-Ruibal, Alfredo. 2008. Time to Destroy: An Archaeology of Supermodernity. *Current Anthropology* 49(2): 247–79.

Graves-Brown, Paul. 1997. From Highway to Superhighway: The Sustainability, Symbolism and Situated Practices of Car Culture. *Social Analysis* 41(1): 64–75.

—— 2000. *Matter, Materiality and Modern Culture*. London: Routledge.

—— 2009. The Privatisation of Experience and the Archaeology of the Future. In *Contemporary Archaeologies: Excavating Now*, ed. Cornelius Holtorf and Angela Piccini, pp. 201–12. Frankfurt: Peter Lang.

Harrison, Rodney and Schofield, John. 2009. Archaeo-Ethnography, Auto-Archaeology: Introducing Archaeologies of the Contemporary Past. *Archaeologies* 5(2): 185–209.

—— 2010. *After Modernity: Archaeological Approaches to the Contemporary Past*. Oxford: Oxford University Press.

Holtorf, Cornelius and Piccini, Angela. 2009. Introduction: Fragments from a Conversation about Contemporary Archaeologies. In *Contemporary Archaeologies: Excavating Now*, ed. Holtorf and Piccini, pp. 9–29. Frankfurt: Peter Lang.

Hughes, Thomas Parke. 1986. The Seamless Web: Technology, Science, etcetera, etcetera. *Social Studies of Science* 16: 281–92.

Jenkinson, Dennis. 1962. *The Racing Car Pocketbook*. London: Batsford.

Knappett, Carl. 2005. *Thinking Through Material Culture: An Interdisciplinary Perspective*. Philadelphia: University of Pennsylvania Press.

Latour, Bruno and Lemonnier, Pierre. 1994. Introduction. Genèse sociale des techniques, genèse technique des humains. In *De la préhistoire aux missiles balistiques. L'intelligence sociale des techniques*, ed. Latour and Lemonnier, pp. 9–24. Paris: La Découverte.

Lemonnier, Pierre. 1992. *Elements for an Anthropology of Technology*. Ann Arbor: Museum of Anthropology, University of Michigan.

—— 1993. *Technological Choices: Transformation in Material Cultures since the Neolithic*. London: Routledge.

—— 2012. Technology. In *The Oxford Handbook of Linguistic Fieldwork*, ed. Nick Thieberger, pp. 298–316. Oxford: Oxford University Press.

Lévi-Strauss, Claude. 1983. *The View from Afar*. Chicago: University of Chicago Press.

Merlin, Olivier. 1959. *Fangio, pilote de course*. Paris: Desclée de Brouwer ('Belle humeur').

Miller, Daniel. 2000. The Fame of Trinitis: Websites as Traps. *Journal of Material Culture* 5(1): 5–23.

—— 2001a. Driven Societies. In *Car Cultures*, ed. Miller, pp. 1–33. Oxford: Berg.

—— (ed.). 2001b. *Car Cultures*. Oxford: Berg.

Moorhouse, Herbert F. 1991. *Driving Ambitions: A Social Analysis of the American Hot Rod Enthusiasm*. Manchester and New York: Manchester University Press.

Moss, Stirling. 1964. *Mes bolides et moi*. Paris: Flammarion ('L'aventure vécue').

Muncey, Tessa. 2010. *Creating Autoethnographies*. London: Sage.

Needham, Rodney. 1978. *Primordial Characters*. Charlottesville: University of Virginia Press.

O'Dell, Tom. 1997. *Culture Unbound: Americanization and Everyday Life in Sweden*. Lund: Nordic Academic Press.

Olivier, Laurent. 2011. *The Dark Abyss of Time: Memory and Archaeology*. New York: Altamira Press.

Pillsbury, Richard. 1974. Carolina Thunder: A Geography of Southern Stock Car Racing. *Journal of Geography* 73(1): 39–47.

Pomeroy, Laurence. 1963. *The Racing Cars Explained*. Weathersfield, CT: Mark Haber & Co.

Post, Robert C. 1994. *High Performance: The Culture and Technology of Drag Racing, 1950–1990*. Baltimore: Johns Hopkins University Press.

Rosinski, José. 1965. La MG TC. *SportAuto* 44: 56–9.

Sachs, Wolfgang. 1984. *For Love of the Automobile: Looking Back into the History of our Desires*. Berkeley, CA: University of California Press.

Schiffer, Michael B. 1991. *The Portable Radio in American Life*. Tucson and London: University of Arizona Press.

Shackleford, Ben A. 1999. Masculinity, Hierarchy, and the Auto Racing Fraternity: The Pit Stop as a Celebration of Social Roles. *Men and Masculinities* 2(2): 180–96.

Tilley, Chris, Keane, Webb, Küchler, Susanne, Rowlands, Michael, and Spyer, Patricia (eds.). 2006. *Handbook of Material Culture*. London: Sage.

Trintignant, Maurice. 1957. *Pilote de course*. Paris: Hachette ('Bibliothèque verte').

Ulin, Jonna. 2009. In the Space of the Past: A Family Archaeology. In *Contemporary Archaeologys: Excavating Now*, ed. Cornelius Holtorf and Angela Piccini, pp. 145–59. Frankfurt: Peter Lang.

Urry, John. 2004. The 'System' of Automobility. *Theory, Culture & Society* 21(4/5): 25–39.

Wittgenstein, Ludwig. 1953. *Philosophical Investigations*. Oxford: Basil Blackwell.

PHOTO ESSAY: THE OTHER ACROPOLISES: MULTI-TEMPORALITY AND THE PERSISTENCE OF THE PAST

YANNIS HAMILAKIS AND FOTIS IFANTIDIS

IN THE BEGINNING,
there is the ascend.

The uphill journey to get closer to it. To overcome its aura, to conquer '*the unique apparition of a distance*' (Benjamin 2008a: 23).

And along with it, the urge to capture it through your camera, to magically transform it into a picture.

But what is it that you will photograph?

The marble blocks and the columns, some still in place, some taken apart and now tightly arranged in rows (like well-behaved schoolchildren on a parade) ready for their reassembly, and some conserved, reconstituted and restored, more clean and more white and more ancient than before?

Or the national flag, reminding you that you are entering the most sacred national monument of the country?

Or would you rather go for the information panel, which neatly tells you '*the story*'?

And would you frame out the cranes and the other restoration machinery, which has been here for ever, now almost as much part of the Acropolis landscape as the Parthenon itself?

You may have come to look at antiquities, but we will make sure that it is modernity's sights (our modernity or yours?) that you will encounter in every step.

It is going to start raining in a minute.

WATCH YOUR STEP, or you will fall and break a limb.

And with the rain, this stony surface becomes even more slippery. It is not called '*The Sacred Rock*' for nothing.

Before the Parthenon, before even the Late Bronze Age citadel that stood here, before even its first Neolithic inhabitants, this was geology, this was just a rocky outcrop. Not that it was always so barren, devoid of any soil.

Take a look at any eighteenth-century engraving and you will see trees here. And then look at those mid-nineteenth-century photographs taken from the Philopappou Hill opposite, and you will understand: the huge spoil heaps, pilling up all the way from the bottom of the hill to its top, evidence of the extensive clearing of the site. We had to get to the bottom. We had to remove all post-classical layers, cleanse the sacred locale of all remnants of post-classical 'barbarity' (Hamilakis 2007).

I told you to wear better shoes. It would be better to take them off: a history of the Acropolis according to our bare feet (Ingold 2004).

WHERE ARE YOU GOING?

Our tourist guide does not say that we should take a diversion! Instead of continuing our ascend towards the centre of the hill and the Parthenon, you are taking a left turn; and now going down a few steps.

Why would you want to do this?

Just to admire the lushness of the Ancient Agora, complete with its palm trees?

Or the churches, and the nineteenth-century buildings that survive the immense archaeological cleansing of the site by the American School of Classical Studies in the 1930s (Hamilakis 2013)?

Whatever, you came here for, you did not expect to see amongst the rubble and the broken marble fragments, the headstones of Muslim graves, did you?

BUT THEN AGAIN, YOU DID NOT expect to see this either:

A bronze cannon, lying abandoned just inside the protective rope, not far from the foot of the Parthenon.

Stare into the dark tunnel of history and count the casualties.

Recall Benjamin, again (from memory): every document of civilization is at the same time a document of barbarity.

OR THIS:

nexttotheclassicalTemple of the Erechtheion, a classical architectural marble block but with an inscription in Arabic, struggling against gravel to remain visible, above ground.

It was in 1805 when the fragment was inscribed with a text praising the Ottoman governor of Athens, and then placed above a prominent entrance to the fortified citadel, overlooking the small town of Athens.

Photographs, Roland Barthes (1993 [1980]: 96 and passim) contends, embody two times simultaneously, the 'that-has-been' of when the photograph was taken, and the 'here-and-now' of its viewing. But what happens when a photographic object captures another material object which is itself multi-temporal? An object which embodies not only the time of its first creation, but also subsequent times, when the very same object, because of its temporal depth, its aesthetic-sensorial appeal, and its agency qualities, was invested with new meaning and mnemonic weight? The Acropolis is full of multi-temporal objects that defy the mono-chrony of the classical and resist its colonising effects. Their photographic materialisation adds further to their multi-temporal character, and their mnemonic impact.

'THE MOST 'CLASSIC' ANGLE of photographing the monument', says the archaeologist Yannis Stavridopoulos.

'That's me, in the mid-1980s; I am photographed wearing Kitt's jacket', he notes, referring to the 1980s American teenage TV hero, Knight Rider.

'I should mention that on the chest there were small red lights; unfortunately, at the photo you cannot see them blinking.'

WHY IS THERE SUCH AN impulse, such a burning desire to leave your trace here?

To carve your presence, to make your mark? Ignore the '*do not touch*' signs.

It is through your touch that you can read the scars upon the skin of the marble.

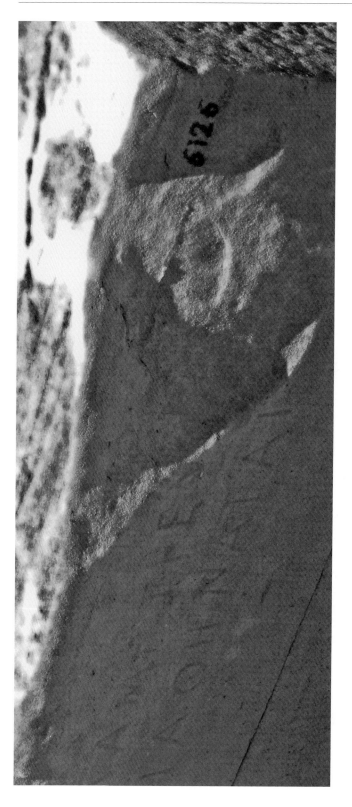

HUMAN EMOTIONS

and ancient civic and political statements, alongside the modern archaeological grid.

Desires of permanence and duration, and desires of classification, containment and control.

AND THE IMPULSE TO COMMEMORATE.

'In the night of the 30th of May 1941, the patriots Manolis Glezos and Apostolos Sandas removed the flag of the Nazi conquerors from the Sacred Rock of the Acropolis. (Installed by the "United National Resistance 1941–44" in 1982).'

Talking of sacredness,

why is this fountain here?

Should it not be at the entrance of the site?

And it looks too modern to have stood outside the small mosque which was once erected inside the Parthenon, when the Acropolis was an Ottoman citadel.

The 'unearthing' of the optical unconscious, Walter Benjamin claims (2008b: 276–88), is a key function of photography. By that he means the capturing of contingency, of the instant, which goes unnoticed in daily encounters, a moment which can then be revealed by the intense engagement with the photograph. In taking his insight further, it can be claimed that the photograph, as a technique for the management of attention (Crary 1992: 18), enables a sustained and in-depth engagement with the micro-locales of the world that go unnoticed in daily routines. Such reflection can also lead to unexpected connections and associations.

SACREDNESS COMES IN
VARIOUS GUISES.

The Christian Acropolis
(Kaldellis   2009)   is
another materiality that
refuses to be erased by the
forces of archaeology.

TIME TO GO.

This one we did not see on our way up. Shiny, new inscribed marble upon older, rusty and wrinkly ones.

This one, installed in 2011 by none other than than the Queen of Spain, is perhaps the most recent layer pilled on the top of this multi-layered land-scape: the government of Spain commemorating the medieval—fourteenth-century—Catalan and Aragonian presence on the Acropolis.

A landscape of commem-oration, a landscape con-tinually in the making.

WE HADN'T NOTICED THIS EITHER, it is not that prominently sign-posted, anyway.

Does the Acropolis need the seal of recognition from the UNESCO World Heritage scheme?

After all, is it not the Parthenon itself that adorns UNESCO's logo?

Yet its world is rather exclusive and limited, for it chooses to celebrate the classical alone, and mostly that second-half of the 5th century BC, as if the Acropolis ceased to be important after that.

I TOLD YOU there was not much to see here, but you still wanted to take a stroll around the hill.

Another small cement plinth, as inconspicuous as the one before. But this time, it sign-posts an absence. An empty space in front of it; three lines, in Greek, in Turkish, and a clandestine one, in Greek again.

Before it was demolished, the Little Mosque, now an evocative mnemonic void; but according to the ones who added the third line, here stood Aphrodite's Temple.

And someone else, or perhaps the same person, had tried to erase the Greek word for mosque. But if you look carefully, there is another, smaller graffito, next to the Turkish line, in Turkish again: 'Evet dogru!', 'That's right!', it says, this was indeed the location of a mosque.

The Acropolis landscape is nothing if not a landscape of contestation, a terrain of silent memories; and counter-memories.

AT LAST SOMETHING TO SEE DOWN HERE;

and to photograph.

A happy coexistence of the classical, the Ottoman, the Christian, the neo-classical, and the modern.

Or is it just the photographic framing of your multi-cultural fantasies?

Still, the area down here seems to have been spared of the cleansing frenzy at the Acropolis.

Yet everything is behind metal fences.

Pay for your entry or keep out: this is an archaeological site.

THE ACROPOLIS IS EVERYWHERE.
Even hanging from the neck of this woman, walking passed us on Areopagitou Street.

Dispersed and mobile corpo-reality, on the streets of Athens, in the galleries of London, in the global material and cyber-real ethno-scapes.

THE NEW ACROPOLIS MUSEUM.

A site of national pride, a new locale of global pilgrimage.

A place to see the Acropolis from, a space to be seen at. Bodies of stone, bodies of flesh. A play of reflections and shadows, a staged facade of mirrors, a liquid hyper-modernity.

Look carefully, and you will see the nineteenth century reflected on its glass surface. Along with your own face.

No photos allowed.

Cappuccinos are cheap though.

YOU ARE NOT SUPPOSED TO LOOK this way.

Nothing here to see, save for the 'ugly' modern apartment blocks.

You must have tried hard to take this picture, extending your lens high up above the screens which are here to guide your gaze towards the smiling archaic Kore, and towards the Acropolis hill opposite.

The history that this museum tells comes into a standstill sometime in the Roman period (if you search thoroughly enough, you may find one or two later objects). Here is another museum of oblivion (Hamilakis 2011), on par with the British Museum.

Forgetting colonialism in Bloomsbury, forgetting the rich, multi-temporal and multi-cultural life of the Acropolis in down town Athens.

TIME FOR OUR DESCEND UNDERGROUND, let's take the metro back.

No, these are just copies, the 'real' ones are in the British Museum; otherwise, would they let you sit so close to them?

THEY ARE FOLLOWING US.

And they are watching us.

Is this what panopticism means in the twenty-first century? Is it the moral authoritative gaze of the classical from the top of the tower of Western culture, or the cameras and the surveillance screens of the security company at the basement of the metro stations?

And where do the two meet?

ALAS POOR WALTER, despite your hopes, technologies of reproduction have anything but undermined bourgeois culture.

The mimetic machines of modernity keep enhancing that unique apparition of a distance. The power of the Acropolis, as auratic as ever.

I told you that they are following us everywhere, even at home. But at least here you can write back.

Further Reading

This essay is based on the photo-blog, The Other Acropolis (www.theotheracropolis. com), where more photographic material and other resources can be found; visitors are also encouraged to leave comments and feedback. On the relationship between the photographic and the archaeological, see Hamilakis 2001, 2008, 2009; Shanks 1997; Hamilakis et al. 2009; Bohrer 2011; amongst others. On the recent and contemporary lives of the Acropolis, in addition to the literature cited above, see Tournikiotis 1994; Hurwit 2000; Caft antzoglou 2001; Yalouri 2001. On multi-temporality, memory and duration, see Hamilakis and Labanyi 2008; Olivier, this volume; and of course, Bergson 1991.

Acknowledgements

The image on page 762 is based on a photograph by Yannis Stavridopoulos, reproduced here with his permission. The photo on page 771 was taken by Yannis Hamilakis. The rest of the images were produced by Fotis Ifantidis. In addition to the authors, Vasko Démou is also a member of The Other Acropolis Collective.

References

Barthes, Roland. 1993 [1980]. *Camera Lucida: Reflections on Photography*, tr. Richard Howard. London: Vintage.
Benjamin, Walter. 2008a [1935–6]. The Work of Art in the Age of its Technological Reproducibility (second version). In Walter Benjamin, *The Work of Art in the Age of its Technological Reproducibility and Other Writings on Media*, pp. 19–55. Cambridge, MA: Harvard University Press.
—— 2008b [1931]. Little History of Photography. In Walter Benjamin, *The Work of Art in the Age of its Technological Reproducibility and Other Writings on Media*, pp. 274–98. Cambridge, MA: Harvard University Press.
Bergson, Henri. 1991. *Matter and Memory*. New York: Zone Books.
Bohrer, Fredrick. 2011. *Photography and Archaeology*. London: Reaktion Books.
Caftantzoglou, Roxane. 2001. The Shadow of the Sacred Rock: Contrasting Discourses of Place under the Acropolis. In *Contested Landscapes: Movement, Exile and Place*, ed. Barbara Bender and Margot Winer, pp. 21–36. Oxford: Berg.
Crary, Jonathan. 1992. *Techniques of the Observer*. Cambridge, MA: MIT Press.
Hamilakis, Yannis. 2001. Monumental Visions: Bonfils, Classical Antiquity and 19th Century Athenian Society. *History of Photography* 25(1): 5–12 and 23–43.
—— 2007. *The Nation and its Ruins: Antiquity, Archaeology and National Imagination in Greece*. Oxford: Oxford University Press.
—— 2008. Monumentalising Place: Archaeologists, Photographers, and the Athenian Acropolis from the Eighteenth Century to the Present. In *Monuments in the Landscape: Papers in Honour of Andrew Fleming*, ed. Paul Rainbird, pp. 190–8. Stroud: Tempus.
—— 2009. Transformare in monumento: archeologi, fotografi e l'Acropoli di Atene dal Settecento a oggi. In *Relitti Riletti: Metamorfosi delle Rovine e Identità Culturale*, ed. Marcello Barbanera, pp. 179–94. Turin: Bollati Boringhieri.

—— 2011. Museums of Oblivion. *Antiquity* 85: 625–9.

—— 2013. Double Colonization: The Story of the Excavations at the Athenian Agora (1924–1931). *Hesperia* 82: 153–77.

Hamilakis, Yannis and Labanyi, J. 2008. Time, Materiality, and the Work of Memory. *History and Memory* 20(2): 5–17.

Hamilakis, Yannis, Anagnostopoulos, Aris and Ifantidis, Fotis. 2009. Postcards from the Edge of Time: Archaeology, Photography, Archaeological Ethnography (a photo-essay). In *Archeological Ethnographies*, eds. Yannis Hamilakis and Aris Anagnostopoulos, pp. 283–309. Leeds: Manney (special double issue of *Public Archaeology* 8: 2/3).

Hurwit, Jeffrey M. 2000. *The Athenian Acropolis: History, Mythology, and Archaeology from the Neolithic Era to the Present.* Cambridge: Cambridge University Press.

Ingold, Tim. 2004. Culture on the Ground: The World Perceived Through the Feet. *Journal of Material Culture* 9(3): 315–40.

Kaldellis, Anthony. 2009. *The Christian Parthenon: Classicism and Pilgrimage in Byzantine Athens.* Cambridge: Cambridge University Press.

Shanks, Michael. 1997. Photography and Archaeology. In *The Cultural Life of Images: Visual Representation in Archaeology*, ed. Brian L. Molyneaux, pp. 73–107. London: Routledge.

Tournikiotis, Panayotis (ed.). 1994. *The Parthenon and its Impact in Modern Times.* Athens: Melissa.

Yalouri, Eleana. 2001. *The Acropolis: Global Claim, Local Fame.* Oxford: Berg.

INDEX